D1449464

Preface

This book contains the papers and speeches of the 40th President of the United States that were issued by the Office of the Press Secretary during the period June 30–December 31, 1984. The material has been compiled and published by the Office of the Federal Register, National Archives and Records Administration.

The material is presented in chronological order, and the dates shown in the headings are the dates of the documents or events. In instances when the release date differs from the date of the document itself, that fact is shown in the textnote. Every effort has been made to ensure accuracy. Tape recordings of Presidential remarks are used to protect against errors in transcription, and signed documents are checked against the original to verify the correct printing. Textnotes, footnotes, and cross references have been provided by the editors for purposes of identification or clarity. Speeches were delivered in Washington, DC, unless indicated. The times noted are local times. All materials that are printed full-text in the book have been indexed in the subject and name indexes.

The Public Papers series was begun in 1957 in response to a recommendation of the National Historical Publications Commission. An extensive compilation of messages and papers of the Presidents covering the period 1789 to 1897 was assembled by James D. Richardson and published under congressional authority between 1896 and 1899. Since then, various private compilations have been issued, but there was no uniform publication comparable to the Congressional Record or the United States Supreme Court Reports. Many Presidential papers could be found only in the form of mimeographed White House releases or as reported in the press. The Commission therefore recommended the establishment of an official series in which Presidential writings, addresses, and remarks of a public nature could be made available.

The Commission's recommendation was incorporated in regulations of the Administrative Committee of the Federal Register, issued under section 6 of the Federal Register Act (44 U.S.C. 1506), which may be found in Title I, Part 10, of the Code of Federal Regulations.

A companion publication to the Public Papers series, the Weekly Compilation of Presidential Documents, was begun in 1965 to provide a broader range of Presidential materials on a more timely basis to meet the needs of the contemporary reader. Beginning with the administration of Jimmy Carter, the Public Papers series expanded its coverage to include all material as printed in the Weekly Compilation. That coverage provides a listing of the President's daily schedule and meetings, when announced, and other items of general interest issued by the Office of the Press Secretary. Also included are lists of the President's nominations submitted to the Senate, materials released by the Office of the Press Secretary that are not printed full-text in the book, and acts approved by the President. This information appears in the appendixes at the end of the book.

Volumes covering the administrations of Presidents Hoover, Truman, Eisenhower, Kennedy, Johnson, Nixon, Ford, and Carter are also available.

The Chief Editor of this book was William K. Banks.

White House liaison was provided by Larry M. Speakes, Assistant to the President and Principal Deputy Press Secretary. The frontispiece and photographs used in the portfolio were supplied by the White House Photo Office.

John E. Byrne
Director of the Federal Register

Frank G. Burke
Acting Archivist of the United States

PUBLIC PAPERS OF THE PRESIDENTS
OF THE
UNITED STATES

Ronald Reagan

1984

(IN TWO BOOKS)

BOOK II—JUNE 30 TO DECEMBER 31, 1984

UNITED STATES GOVERNMENT PRINTING OFFICE
WASHINGTON : 1987

Published by the
Office of the Federal Register
National Archives and Records Administration

For sale by the
Superintendent of Documents
U.S. Government Printing Office
Washington, DC 20402

Foreword

The end of 1984 was as exciting as the beginning.

In Dallas, at the Republican National Convention, we renewed our call to make America the "shining city on a hill" we have always envisioned. We took our campaign to the people, not as partisans, but as patriots proud of our record of peace and prosperity. We talked forthrightly about our record and about how much more needed to be done. In November, the American people honored George Bush and me again by allowing us to continue our service on behalf of the greatest people in the world. Our mandate was clear and would be a roadmap for the second term.

But all was not politics in 1984. Indeed, we were pleased and encouraged by the resumption of arms control negotiations with the Soviet Union. This was a welcome and important step in our effort to rid the world of the threat of nuclear war and was indicative of the wisdom of our policy for a strong national defense.

Our deep commitment to our fellow citizens of the world was activated on behalf of the people of Africa, as all segments of our society moved in to help the victims of famine. In a uniquely American way, our country came together on behalf of people who mattered to us simply because they were human beings. Nothing speaks better about Americans.

We ended 1984 deeply gratified and humbled by the support of the people and excited and eager to get on with the challenges of the second term.

Ronald Reagan

Contents

Administration of Ronald Reagan

1984

Radio Address to the Nation on Drug Abuse
June 30, 1984

The President. My fellow Americans, this week the Congress passed, and I will soon sign, a series of measures to reduce budget deficits by about $63 billion over the next 3 fiscal years. My approval of these measures should not by any means be considered the final action on deficits this year. The Congress still has much work to do to achieve spending restraint and help our economic expansion continue. I stand ready to use my veto to make sure it fulfills that responsibility.

Spending restraint and personal incentives for growth are the two greatest deficit reduction weapons we have. That's why the ultimate solution to budget deficits must be a mandatory restriction on the Congress' ability to spend and a simplification of the entire tax system, enabling us to broaden the tax base and lower personal income tax rates for all of you who work and earn. We're bound and determined to do this.

But today I don't intend to go on talking about the economy. I have a special guest. Nancy is here with me, and she'd like to speak to you about the problem of drugs and what, together, all of us can do about the problem.

Mrs. Reagan. Thank you, Ronnie.

During the past 2 years, I've traveled throughout our country, and what I've seen happening to our children is terribly frightening. In fact, sometimes it seems as if we could lose a whole next generation to drug abuse.

Cocaine, PCP, marijuana, alcohol, speed—these are the enemies of our children. They're cunning and treacherous and, oh, so very patient. As one former teenage alcoholic put it, "Alcohol will wait forever. It's always going to be there." And that child was right; which is why we must be there as well.

And this enemy shows no mercy. It still sends a chill through me to recall a visit I made sometime ago to an elementary school in Atlanta. I asked the class of third graders how many had been offered drugs, and almost every hand went up.

Many people still seem to think that substance abuse is something that happens to other families. There's a wall of denial that must be broken down. The truth is drugs and alcohol are everywhere available and everywhere abused. And now people are waking up to that fact.

A 16-year-old girl, who described herself as a recovering drug addict, wrote me to say that she was one of the lucky ones. "I'm doing fine now," she said, "but last Christmas I was in the hospital weighing 87 pounds and not caring whether I lived or died. I only took drugs for a year, but I'm sure I had a problem as soon as I started. I dropped a lot of my old friends because I only wanted to be friends with kids who could get drugs for me. When I collapsed in a public park from malnutrition and exhaustion due to cocaine, my new friends didn't lift a finger to help me. If it hadn't been for my parents, who came looking for me, I wouldn't be alive today."

Her letter isn't unusual. Other children have talked frankly to me about how young they were when they began to experiment with drugs and how school became little more than a place to buy dope and get high.

Most parents were completely in the dark. They just didn't believe it could happen to their kids. Again, the wall of denial. But there may be a light at the end of the tunnel—something that fills me with hope about our children's future and about our country's future. We're finally becoming aware of the terrible problem of drugs.

Three years ago there were only 1,000 volunteer parents groups organized to fight drug abuse. Today there are more than 4,000, and the number keeps growing. Yes, there is reason for hope. These are parents who have learned—some the hard way—that the most effective answer to the tragedy of drugs is involvement and knowledge. And, too, now they know that discipline is something you do for a child, not to him.

I'm asked so often what I think is the answer. And I always stress self-confidence, family communication, and active supervision. As a mother of a girl who was experimenting with LSD during the day and finishing a bottle of bourbon every night put it, "It's time for parents to take over and be parents again."

Ronnie, I know you join me in the belief that if we all work together, become more involved in our children's lives and more knowledgeable, we can help save a generation and help preserve its promise and hope.

The President. Well, I sure do know that, Nancy. And I can't imagine anything that could do more to brighten the skies of America's future.

Until next week, thanks for listening, and God bless you.

Note: The President spoke at 12:06 p.m. from Camp David, MD.

Remarks on Greeting Participants in the Cracker Jack Old Timers Baseball Classic
July 2, 1984

The President. Our guests today are some of the baseball players who will be in tonight's game. They call them the oldtimers. I don't see any oldtimers up here. All ready to go. But we're very pleased and proud to have them here.

Reporter. Mr. President, will you agree to negotiate with the Russians on space even if they won't talk about missiles?

The President. Sam [Sam Donaldson, ABC News], this isn't for that subject—but we stand by what we proposed yesterday, and we're in communication with them.

Q. Any progress with Dobrynin, sir?

Q. Did you make any progress with Dobrynin, sir?

The President. He was a guest at our barbecue last night. He——

Q. They say your position is totally unsatisfactory, sir.

The President. I can't go on talking about this. We are dealing with them and in communication with them.

Let me reiterate—tonight there's a much more important thing going on, which is the baseball game. [*Laughter*]

Harmon Killebrew. All right. Mr. President——

Q. Are you saying, Mr. President——

Mr. Killebrew. ——on behalf of the Old Timers Cracker Jack Game, I'd like to present this baseball to you. We hope that you'll be pulling for both teams tonight. Thank you very much.

The President. I'll just have to——

Q. Mr. President, are you setting up a condition to talk to the Russians?

The President. I'm not going to take that up now. There will be plenty of time for that.

Q. Are you saying that the TASS rejection is not a final rejection, sir?

The President. Isn't this a lovely baseball? [*Laughter*] All autographed by all these——

Q. All right, did you and Curly ever do any of these boys? [*Laughter*]

The President. What?

Q. You and Curly—did you ever do any of these boys?

The President. I'm afraid that I was probably ahead of all of you. I was broadcasting in the early and middle thirties.

Bill Rigney. Careful, you're starting to touch some nerves there. [*Laughter*]

The President. No, I don't think there's any of you——

Mr. Rigney. I started in '38.

The President. In '38? Well, I was through by then.

Mr. Rigney. Were you?

The President. Yes.

Ernie Banks. The Cubs won in '45.

The President. What's that?

Mr. Banks. 1945, the Cubs won the pennant.

The President. Yes. As a matter of fact, I was broadcasting the Chicago Cubs, his team, in those days when the only mathematical chance they had to win the pennant was to win the last 21 games of the season. And they did it, and it's still a record in the record books that's never been equaled. They won that last 21. And the last series, the last four games was with the Cardinals, the team that they had to beat.

Mr. Rigney. Is that the one Hartnett hit the home run?

The President. What?

Mr. Rigney. Gabby Hartnett hit the home run?

Mr. Killebrew. That was against Pittsburgh.

The President. My high spot in all of that was in the ninth inning of a game, the Cubs and Cards were tied up. I was broadcasting telegraphic report, and it was tied nothing to nothing, as I say. And the message that came through to me said the wire had gone dead. And I decided that I was just going to take a chance. So, I set a world record—Billy Jurges at the plate—for foul balls. [*Laughter*] I don't know how long he was up there, but it was a world record. And then when the wire was fixed, the first mes-

sage came in said he popped out on the first ball pitched. [*Laughter*]

Q. Mr. President, is baseball really more important than arms control? [*Laughter*]

The President. As of these particular moments, yes. I—courtesy to my visitors here.

Q. Mr. President, have you thrown the Soviets a curve ball or a sucker pitch? [*Laughter*]

The President. Well, I've been tempted sometimes to walk them. No—say, that's right, I did play Old Alex. [*Laughter*] I pitched him a fast ball. [*Laughter*]

Q. Is there anything else you'd like to talk about?

Q. Can you tell us anything about Dobrynin?

The President. All right. Let's go back.

Q. Can you tell us anything about Dobrynin, what happened last night? Anything at all?

The President. What?

Q. About Dobrynin, what you two talked about last night?

The President. We just discussed the situation there in a pleasant manner.

Q. Mr. President, did you give him a message to take back to Moscow this week?

The President. He'll have a message.

Q. Mr. President, who was doing the Cardinals games?

Note: The President spoke at 11:49 a.m. in the Rose Garden at the White House.

Appointment of Eight Members of the National Advisory Committee on Oceans and Atmosphere, and Designation of Chairman
July 2, 1984

The President today announced his intention to appoint the following individuals to be members of the National Advisory Committee on Oceans and Atmosphere. The President also intends to designate Anne Burford as Chairman.

Anne M. Burford, to serve for a term expiring July 1, 1987. She will succeed John A. Knauss. Mrs. Burford is an attorney and lecturer. She

was born April 21, 1942, in Casper, WY, and now resides in Alexandria, VA.

John E. Bennett, to serve for a term expiring July 1, 1986. He will succeed George G. Tapper. He retired as captain in the United States Navy after 25 years of service. He was born April 9, 1918, in Montpelier, OH, and now resides in Solana Beach, CA.

William Brewster, to serve for a term expiring July 1, 1985. He will succeed Jack R. Van

Lopik. He is vice president and director of the Atlantic Salmon Federation and chairman of the executive committee of the International Atlantic Salmon Foundation. He was born April 15, 1917, in Plymouth, MA, where he now resides.

Lee C. Gerhard, to serve for a term expiring July 1, 1986. He will succeed Warren Morton Washington. Dr. Gerhard is the Getty Professor of Geology at the Colorado School of Mines. He was born May 30, 1937, in Albion, NY, and now resides in Englewood, CO.

Judith Kildow, to serve for a term expiring July 1, 1986. She will succeed Sylvia Alice Earle. Dr. Kildow is associate professor of ocean policy, department of engineering, Massachusetts Institute of Technology. She was born February 16, 1942, in Chicago, IL, and now resides in Cambridge, MA.

Mary Ellen McCaffree, to serve for a term expir-

ing July 1, 1985. She will succeed James M. Waddell, Jr. Mrs. McCaffree was administrative assistant to U.S. Senator Slade Gorton in 1981–1983 and director of the department of budget and program development for King County in the State of Washington in 1978–1981. She was born February 25, 1918, in Eldorado, KS, and now resides in Hansville, WA.

Nathan Sonenshein, to serve for a term expiring July 1, 1986. He will succeed Jay Gordon Lanzillo. He is assistant to the president of Global Marine Development, Inc., in Newport Beach, CA. He was born August 2, 1915, in Lodi, NJ, and now resides in Monaga, CA.

Gordon Snow, to serve for a term expiring July 1, 1985. He will succeed Michael R. Naess. He is assistant secretary for resources of the California Resources Agency in Sacramento. He was born February 11, 1925, in Rush Springs, OK, and now resides in El Macero, CA.

Message to the Senate Transmitting the United States-Italy Convention on Taxation
July 3, 1984

To the Senate of the United States:

I transmit herewith, for Senate advice and consent to ratification, the Convention between the Government of the United States of America and the Government of the Republic of Italy for the Avoidance of Double Taxation with Respect to Taxes on Income and the Prevention of Fraud or Fiscal Evasion ("the Convention"), together with a supplementary Protocol and exchange of notes, signed at Rome on April 17, 1984. I also transmit the report of the Department of State on the Convention.

Important changes in United States and Italian tax laws and the development of a model tax treaty by the United States made it necessary to replace the existing income tax convention with Italy, which has been in force since 1956.

Among the principal features of the new Convention are the inclusion of the Italian local income tax among the taxes covered by the Convention and a reduction in the tax at source on most dividends. The Convention also introduces a limitation on the taxation at source of interest paid to residents of the other country. It provides a maximum rate of tax at source of 10 percent on royalties.

The protocol provides that the benefits of the Convention are limited to residents of the two countries, and otherwise clarifies and supplements the Convention. The exchange of notes sets out certain understandings between the two governments.

I recommend that the Senate give early and favorable consideration to the Convention, together with the supplementary Protocol and exchange of notes, and give advice and consent to ratification.

RONALD REAGAN

The White House,
July 3, 1984.

Remarks at a White House Ceremony Marking the Golden Anniversary Year of the Duck Stamp
July 3, 1984

The President. Secretary Clark and ladies and gentlemen, good morning, and welcome to the White House.

Today we join in honoring the 50th anniversary of one of the most successful and popular of all Federal wildlife conservation programs. Officially, the centerpiece of this program is called the Migratory Bird Hunting and Conservation Stamp, but to wildlife lovers across the country, it's known as the Duck Stamp.

The Duck Stamp was the brainchild of a famous Iowan and a great American, the award-winning editorial cartoonist and conservationist, J.N. Darling, known to all as "Ding." Ding was one of the foremost conservation figures of his day. And throughout his career as a cartoonist, that commitment to conservation came through loud and clear.

Sometimes Ding drew a bleak picture; but he did so for a purpose, to shake his fellow citizens out of their complacency about our resources. Too many still considered our resources inexhaustible, and Ding knew different. For millions of Americans, he made the concept of conservation come alive.

Ding saw the greed and the foibles that threatened to wreck our resources. But he also saw the abiding goodness of one very important species, his fellow man. Ding was convinced that Americans would respond to the call for help for our wildlife and that efforts could reverse the serious decline that was affecting our wildlife and waterfowl. And he was right on both counts. The people responded, and the waterfowl came back.

More than anything else, it was Ding's idea for a Duck Stamp that enabled the change to take place. The Duck Stamp quickly caught on with duck hunters, corporations, and conservation groups of all kinds. To date, nearly 89 million stamps have been sold for revenues totaling nearly $300 million. And those revenues have been used to purchase thousands of acres of wetlands. One hundred and eighty-six of our National Wildlife Refuges have been funded wholly, or in part, through the Duck Stamp program.

These refuges serve as a haven for waterfowl, protect fish and other wildlife, reduce flooding, and serve as natural water purifiers. For five decades, you, the sportsmen and conservationists, have been buying Duck Stamps and have been giving our nation a gift of beautiful wetlands and flourishing wildlife.

On behalf of all Americans, I thank you. And as Duck Stamps begin their second half-century, I believe we can expect to see more and more Americans join in your tradition of giving. So, thank you, God bless you, and now I'd like to sign the resolution proclaiming the week of July 1 through July 8, National Duck Stamp Week, and 1984 the Golden Anniversary Year of the Duck Stamp.

[At this point, the President signed S.J. Res. 270.]

Secretary Clark. Mr. President, I believe everyone here today shares your great appreciation for the Duck Stamp program, really America's finest and most successful conservation program, again bridging—as I know you've always desired to do—the private and public sectors.

And we're fortunate today to have the grandson of Mr. Darling, and Kip Koss, who is with us today to make a presentation. And Kip has followed the inspiration of his grandfather, dedicating his life to conservation. And at this time, Kip would like to make a little presentation.

Mr. Koss. Mr. President, 50 years ago, Ding Darling designed the first Federal Duck Stamp. It's been a marvelously successful program—3½ million acres of prime wetland habitat have been preserved forever.

I have here today an original Darling etching. It's titled "Design for the First Federal Duck Stamp, 1934." And with it is an RW–1, which is the first Federal Duck Stamp issued in 1934.

We conservationists here today—the Ding Darling Foundation, Izaak Walton League, Ducks Unlimited, National Wildlife Federation—we're all pleased to present this to you.

The President. Thank you very much. I think I should explain, I'm not crying. The tears are in my eyes because Bill Clark managed to aim this at the Sun, right in my eyes just as I turned around.

Thank you very much.

Reporter. Why did you name Anne Burford to that commission, Mr. President?

The President. I haven't any comment other than that, that I think she deserves some consideration. And we're very pleased

to give it and to have her back in the administration.

Q. Mr. President, Jay Hair, who organized this——

Q. The environmentalists say you should be ashamed of yourself, sir.

Q. ——didn't show up in protest because of the Burford appointment. What do you have to say to that?

The President. Haven't been to lunch yet. Maybe he'll be there.

Q. He's going to hold a press conference and denounce that appointment.

Note: The President spoke at 11:32 a.m. in the Rose Garden at the White House.

Secretary of the Interior William P. Clark also made remarks.

Proclamation 5216—National Duck Stamp Week and Golden Anniversary Year of the Duck Stamp, 1984
July 3, 1984

By the President of the United States of America

A Proclamation

Among our most cherished wildlife resources are migratory waterfowl. The ducks, geese, and swans of North America not only fascinate us with their beauty and spectacle, they remind us of the continuing values of a clean, safe, wholesome environment. The health of our waterfowl resources depends on the well-being of their environment. If the Nation's wetlands are lost, these birds and the many other fish and wildlife resources they support cannot thrive. In recognition of the vital link between wildlife and wetlands, the United States has created an extensive system of National Wildlife Refuges. This great array of wild lands and waters provides countless opportunities for our waterfowl to nest and feed. We have so many of these refuges to enjoy today because of the farsighted practices of successive generations of Americans.

This year marks the fiftieth anniversary of the passage of the Migratory Bird Hunting Stamp Act. To implement this law, the first

Duck Stamp was issued later that year. The Duck Stamp was the creation of Jay N. "Ding" Darling, an award-winning editorial cartoonist and pioneer conservationist. It was his idea that every waterfowl hunter in this country had a vital stake in wetland and waterfowl conservation and that each should share in the responsibility to maintain that wildlife tradition they held so dear.

In the 50 years that have passed since the introduction of the Duck Stamp, it has become one of the Nation's most successful conservation programs. Almost 90 million of the stamps have been sold, generating more than $285 million for waterfowl conservation. All or part of 186 National Wildlife Refuges—a total of 3.5 million acres—have been acquired through Duck Stamp revenues.

In the last 50 years, Americans have become increasingly aware that wetlands provide essential habitat for ducks and geese and contribute significantly to other wildlife resources including endangered species, open space recreation, commercial and sport fisheries, flood control, groundwater recharge and water purification. A recent study by the Department of the Interior concluded that the United States is losing wetlands at the pace of nearly one-half million acres every year, an area the size of the State of Rhode Island. Clearly, the Duck Stamp program is as important today as it was in 1934.

In recognition of the contributions of the Duck Stamp program, the Congress, by Senate Joint Resolution 270, has designated the week of July 1 through July 8, 1984, as "National Duck Stamp Week" and 1984 as "Golden Anniversary Year of the Duck Stamp" and authorized and requested the President to issue an appropriate proclamation.

Now, Therefore, I, Ronald Reagan, Presi-

dent of the United States of America, do hereby proclaim the week of July 1 through July 8, 1984, as National Duck Stamp Week and 1984 as the Golden Anniversary Year of the Duck Stamp. I urge all Americans to observe these occasions with appropriate ceremonies and events, including participating in this program.

In Witness Whereof, I have hereunto set my hand this third day of July, in the year of our Lord nineteen hundred and eighty-four, and of the Independence of the United States of America the two hundred and eighth.

RONALD REAGAN

[*Filed with the Office of the Federal Register, 4:51 p.m., July 3, 1984*]

Interviews With Representatives of Orlando, Florida, Television Stations
July 2, 1984

Legal Drinking Age

The President. Hello.

Scott Peelin [of WFTV–TV]. Mr. President, you changed your mind on raising the drinking age. Originally you had stood by the premise it was a State decision. Isn't this just another example of more interference by the Federal Government?

The President. Well, now, I'm having a little difficulty with this speaker here. I didn't catch the first part of your question.

Mr. Peelin. Well, from what we understand, sir, according to Transportation Secretary Dole, you changed your mind on raising the Federal drinking age. You originally had stood by the premise that it was a State decision. Isn't this just another example of the Federal Government getting involved in something that you had always said in the past was States rights?

The President. No, I don't think so. It's true that I am a strong advocate of States rights, and I don't like seeing the Federal Government cross the line and intervene, although it has done so once in this particular area with the 55-mile speed limit. That

was born of an emergency situation. It is true, also, that I would have preferred if all the States had come together on the drinking age being raised to 21, and without Federal interference.

But when I saw the figures—there are 23 States that have now adopted the 21 age limit. The others are a little behind or, in some instances, have refused to go along with this. But when I saw the figures, I realized that the cause was worth this risk of the Federal Government intervening. In Michigan, 43 percent was the drop in nighttime fatalities after this was passed; in Illinois it was 23 percent. In the first year after New Jersey adopted this, the fatalities among young people dropped by 39 percent in the first year. So, I think it is worth it.

But also there is some element here that could open the door to the Federal Government being involved, and that is the fact of the interstate situation, that States with the advanced drinking age now find that in adjoining States where they still have the age much younger, they cross the line and—

into the—or the other States, and then are faced with driving back with the result that we have seen.

I had that reversed. I should say the people—or the youngsters in the States where they have the 21 law cross the line into those that don't have it. And these percentage figures—and we're talking human lives of young people—I think warrant the action that we're suggesting. I would prefer that the other 27 States would do what the first 23 have done.

Jesse Jackson

Mr. Peelin. Sir, Jesse Jackson is now saying he would like to go to Russia to try and get dissident Andrei Sakharov freed as similar as to what he did recently in Cuba. You apparently don't think he should be traveling around the world exercising foreign policy. At least that's the impression the media is getting, because you have refused to meet with Mr. Jackson, and Mr. Shultz has refused to meet with Mr. Jackson. Do you think that Reverend Jackson should stop making these trips around the world, exercising U.S. policy?

The President. Well I have to say this: I'm delighted that the humanitarian gesture, for whatever reason—and I suspect very much the political reasons not on his side, but on the part of Castro in this most recent episode, had something other than humanitarianism behind it. But it isn't a case of what I think. It is a case that there is a law, the Logan Act, with regard to unauthorized personnel, civilians, simply going to—or citizens—to other countries and, in effect, negotiating with foreign governments. Now, that is the law of the land.

Mr. Peelin. Do you plan to take legal action against him, sir?

The President. No——

Mr. Peelin. Do you think our State Department should take action against Reverend Jackson?

The President. No, we're not going to take legal action. But I do feel that, while in this instance he was successful, there were things that make you pause and think. He went to Cuba with a list of some 25 Cuban political prisoners that he had been given of people that he felt warranted being freed. Only one of the prisoners that Castro re-

leased was on his original list. Now, I don't know why Castro chose to make others available and not this one, but I do believe that to intervene, for example, on this very delicate matter—on Sakharov—ignores things that might be going on in the quiet diplomatic channels that we have going forward.

Mr. Peelin. Sir, unfortunately we're out of time. Thank you so much for being with us today. We look forward to seeing you in the Daytona area on July 4th.

The President. I'm looking forward to it.

Legal Drinking Age

Mr. McDonough. Good afternoon, Mr. President. I'm Ed McDonough with WESH–TV in Orlando, Florida.

The President. Well, good to talk to you.

Mr. McDonough. My first question, Mr. President: You're expected to sign the bill that would order all States, including Florida, to raise their legal drinking ages to 21 within the next 2 years or lose their Federal highway funds. Our Governor Graham is in favor of the 21-year-old age limit, but he doesn't like the way the Federal Government went about imposing the limit on the States, calling it a violation of States rights. How do you respond to that, sir?

The President. Well, I can understand that, having been a Governor myself, and being a strong advocate of States rights and wanting to get more authority in the hands of the States. On the other hand, when the figures began to come in with regard to the 23 States that have already adopted the 21 age limit, those figures made it evident that so many lives were being saved because of this age limit. And with 27 of the States either refusing or just dragging their feet on doing something about it, I felt that we were justified in this.

We're talking about human lives, young lives. In Michigan, after adopting their 21 age drinking limit, the nighttime fatalities, particularly those related with alcohol, dropped by 43 percent. And in Illinois it was 23 percent; in New Jersey in the first year after they adopted such a law, the drop in alcohol-related accidents was 39 percent. Now, I think this many human lives indicate that the Federal Government was justified in taking this action.

In addition, there is some leeway here for believing that the Federal Government could get involved, in there is an interstate problem. A State can have a drinking age of 21; nearby State can have the younger age, and the youngsters that aren't 21, in that State, then are tempted to cross the State line to do what they want to do with regard to the drinking. And then they come back, driving again, and are now driving, having spent the day or the evening drinking. So, this does bring up a kind of an interstate—I'd almost say commerce—factor.

But I think the cause justifies this when you see the figures with regard to those States with the higher limit, and see the penalty that the others are paying for having a lower drinking age.

Space Program

Mr. McDonough. Mr. President, the budget for the Nation's space program, including the Kennedy Space Center here in Florida, has remained more or less the same over the past few years. Do you support an increase in that budget in the future, including a portion of the budget which would affect the space station project?

The President. Well, the budget, when we came here, 1981, was $5½ billion. For 1985 we have asked, and Congress has approved, $7½ billion. That is a 36-percent increase in the budget. And for the 4 years we've been here, the budget has increased more than the inflation rate. So, we're not just covering inflation.

But I believe in the space program, and now, as you know, we're looking forward to, and have asked for, research and study into a space station. And, naturally, the budget will reflect whatever the increased needs are for these worthwhile undertakings.

Immigration Legislation

Mr. McDonough. Mr. President, a final question. Some Florida farmers feel the new immigration law passed by Congress puts too much responsibility on them for enforcement of the law and not enough on the Federal Government. In the words of one Florida farmer, "The Government hasn't been able to control the borders for

the last 50 years; now it expects us to do it." How do you respond to that?

The President. Well, I know it's difficult, and I know that people are very concerned about this bill. On the other hand, our nation has lost control of its borders. Now, we're going to do everything else—we've asked for a thousand more on the Southwest border, a thousand more INS people—we want to resolve the problem of the illegal entrance.

At the same time we want some compassion for those people who have been living for a period of time in this country and have established families and roots here and have employment and all. But we have the problem of the undocumented worker coming into this country and then being victimized by some employers who know that he can't complain if he's paid less than the going wage or the minimum wage. We want to stop that.

So, the only way we can see is sanctions; but, at the same time, we want to make sure that there is a method whereby the individual can identify themselves as being a legitimate resident of this country. And all we ask is that the employer be subject to sanctions if they are trying to go around this bill and hire, knowingly, undocumented workers.

Mr. McDonough. Mr. President, thank you for being with us today. We look forward to your trip to Daytona Beach on Wednesday.

The President. Well, I'm looking forward to it.

Legal Drinking Age

Mr. Rinker. Hello, Mr. President. This is Glenn Rinker [of WCPX–TV] in Orlando.

The President. Well, hello there. Good to talk to you.

Mr. Rinker. Thank you, sir. Mr. President, Florida's drinking age is now 19. Do you have a message for our State's young people who argue, if they're old enough to vote, old enough to die for their country, they're old enough to drink?

The President. Well, the trouble is, some of them are dying, but not for their country. They're dying simply because of drinking and driving. And we have the evidence now—with 23 States that have adopted the 21 law, we have the evidence in the figures that show that that law saves lives.

In Michigan, after adopting it, the drop in this kind of fatalities was 43 percent. In Illinois it was 23 percent. In the first year after New Jersey adopted it, it was 39 percent. I think the numbers—the hundreds and even thousands of young people whose lives can be saved warrant us moving to this law.

The other thing is, that we haven't thought about, that at the younger drinking age—it is easier for people who have not yet reached that age to pass themselves off as being old enough to be sold liquor. When you raise the age somewhat it's a little more difficult for the 16- to the 17-year-old to pass themselves off as 21.

Offshore Oil Drilling

Mr. Rinker. Mr. President, how do you respond to critics who say that you're not concerned about the environment, particularly when it comes to offshore oil drilling in the Atlantic Ocean?

The President. Well, we are concerned about the environment. As a matter of fact, our regulations now to protect the environment are much greater than they have ever been before. The incident of oil spills is almost nonexistent; and we've had, for a whole generation, we've had offshore drilling.

But we also are requiring the, really, utmost in negotiations and discussions between the coastal States and the Federal Government. Now, most of the offshore drilling is under State jurisdiction. It is within the 3-mile limit, and these are State leases. We're talking about beyond the 3-mile limit, where there is probably the greatest available pool of oil, all around our shores, much more than what we have on land. And we think that necessity alone dictates that we explore this.

In many instances the Federal offshore wells will be far enough out that they won't even be visible from land. And, as I say, I think our regulations now are such that there is a safety factor that is actually greater than the safety factor of tankers that are

bringing imported oil to us from across the oceans.

Interest Rates

Mr. Rinker. Mr. President, with interest rates going up—and growth here in central Florida has been phenomenal—there's a lot of concern now by people who are being squeezed out by the variable rate home mortgages. What's your personal opinion about those mortgages, and should they have tighter controls than they do now?

The President. No, I would not like to see the Government moving into that field. But I have to tell you, we're distressed by the interest rates. Frankly, I see no justification for those rates remaining where they are.

Interest rates are determined by inflation. If you're going to lend money, you not only want a return in interest rate on your money, but you want to be sure that when the principal is paid back, it has the same purchasing power as it did before. And the only way to achieve that is by charging enough interest to offset inflation.

Now, we've reduced inflation so much that, as I say, there is no excuse for the interest rates staying where they are, and I believe the only reason for them staying there is pessimism. It's psychological. The people there in the money markets are not convinced yet that we have inflation under control.

Now, for the past month, or for this present—well, no, it's now the past month, June—the estimate a week or so ago was that inflation for that month was down to 2.6 percent. Now, that leaves a pretty high interest rate over and above that level. And we're just hoping that as we attack the deficit, as we continue to reduce the growth in government spending, that they will realize we do intend to keep inflation down.

Mr. Rinker. Are you going to exert any more personal pressure, sir, to bring down interest rates, say, against the Federal Reserve?

The President. Well, it isn't the Federal Reserve at this time. As a matter of fact, Paul Volcker uttered this same thing about this being psychology—that I have just uttered. The Federal Reserve has been increasing the money supply at the upper limits of its growth rate, commensurate with the growth rate in productivity and in the economy. Now, that's all we ask for—is that the money supply be increased so as to keep pace with the growth in the economy and not at a rate that would bring back inflation.

Mr. Rinker. Mr. President, thank you very much. We're looking forward to seeing you in Daytona on Wednesday.

The President. Well, I'm looking forward to it.

Note: The interviewers spoke by telephone with the President, who was in the Diplomatic Reception Room at the White House.

The interviews were released by the Office of the Press Secretary on July 4, the date of their broadcast in Orlando.

Address to the Nation on the Observance of Independence Day
July 4, 1984

My fellow Americans:

Happy Fourth of July! I've been thinking about the Fourth of July, 1976—8 years ago. Do you remember that great Bicentennial Day?

In New York, the tall ships came sailing up the Hudson, and in Boston, the rousing music of Arthur Fiedler and the Boston Pops had all of that city standing and cheering. In Baltimore, they had great parades, and in Philadelphia, they brought out the Liberty Bell and had a group of schoolchildren pat it with their hands so that it would make a sound without upsetting the crack in the bell.

A person who was there tells me that thousands of people surrounded the Liberty Bell, quietly and with respect. And then, a young fellow started to sing "God Bless America." And it spread through the crowd. And people were left quite hushed with happiness when it was over.

It was a wonderful day, and ever since, the Fourth of July has been as special as it was back in older times when it ranked with Christmas as an important day, a time for families to come together and for neighborhoods to explode with bright lights.

America still has so much to celebrate on this day—unity and affection, prosperity and freedom. Today, on July 4, 1984, there will be fireworks to commemorate that moment when Francis Scott Key saw through the glare of the rockets that our flag was still there. Somewhere a chorus will sing the old songs of love and affection for our country. Somewhere a family will

gather and salute the flag. Somewhere a veteran will be told, "Thanks for what you did." And in a courthouse somewhere, some of the newest Americans, the most recent immigrants to our country, will take the oath of citizenship.

Maybe today, someone will put his hand on the shoulder of one of those new citizens and say, "Welcome," and not just as a courtesy, but to say welcome to a great land, a place of unlimited possibilities. Welcome to the American family.

There are all kinds of people in that family, and they live in all kinds of conditions and circumstances. Perhaps you know an older person, a senior citizen who feels a little left out by all the younger people around him. Maybe you could take that person aside and ask, "What was the Fourth of July like in your earliest memories?" You might hear some pretty interesting stories. Perhaps there's someone who's lonely in your neighborhood, someone whose friends all left for the holidays, or a girl or boy who are pretty much on their own. Maybe today someone will invite one of them over to the barbecue.

Somewhere today I hope we will all pause for a brief moment and think of all we have to be thankful for and of the great future that lies before us.

The spirit of our nation is strong. The freedoms our forefathers won for us endure. We still stand for freedom throughout the world, which is why immigrants still come to us. No one emigrates to Cuba or jumps over the wall into East Berlin or seeks refuge in the Soviet Union. Those who look for freedom seek sanctuary here.

The United States is a leader in a world turning, day by day, toward freedom. In Central America and Africa and elsewhere, the tide of the future is a freedom tide. The impulse to create democratic government not only endures; it grows, and that, in spite of real resistance from those who believe in freedom not a bit.

Other countries see our entrepreneurial spirit and seek to emulate it. They see how a vigorous, free society allows man to move on and grow. They see how we're trying to make life better for man through scientific inquiry. They see us pushing into space. Other systems are locked on to the land, prisoners of a gravity of their own devising. America is a rocket, pushing upward and outward into space, into human history.

We have 208 years of history behind us. But somehow, these days, we know the whole world is before us. And we can feel as Teddy Roosevelt did when he surveyed the world at the turn of the century. He said, "We Americans see across the dangers the great future that lies beyond, and we rejoice as a giant refreshed, as a strong man ready for the race. The great victories are yet to be won; the greatest deeds yet to be done. There are yet in store for our people and for the causes we uphold, grander triumphs than have ever yet been scored."

Well, so it is, and it will be. Despite our differences and disagreements, this is a happy, decent, united country. The bells still ring for America. A philosopher said recently, "And for that, we must be truly grateful."

Happy Fourth of July! May God bless you, and may He continue to bless the Nation He showered with His love for more than two centuries.

Note: The President recorded the address on June 28 at the White House.

Remarks of the President and Ned Jarrett of the Motor Racing Network During a Radio Broadcast of the Pepsi Firecracker 400 in Daytona Beach, Florida
July 4, 1984

Mr. Jarrett. It's now a great pleasure and an honor to welcome President Ronald Reagan, who, as you know, was an athlete himself in college and has a keen interest in sports. So, on behalf of the people on Motor Racing Network, Daytona International Speedway, President Reagan, we welcome you.

The President. Well, Ned, I'm pleased to be here. This is a real kick for me. At the same time, however, having been a sports announcer myself, I'm kind of glad that I didn't have to broadcast this, because I'm having so much trouble trying to sort out who's on first.

Mr. Jarrett. Well, about the time the Air Force One was landing just behind the speedway here, we had a seven car draft for the lead that just made pitstops—what should be their last pitstops. That sometimes tends to break them up a little bit.

But Richard Petty, who is trying to win his 200th NASCAR Winston Cup victory here today, which would set an all-time record, is out front now in car number 43—and I believe you have some special ties to the owner of that car.

The President. Yes, and he's sitting right up here—Mike Curb, who is out there and—shouldn't mention this on a holiday like this, a partisanship—but we were kind of tied up in politics back in California. I won't mention which party. [*Laughter*]

Mr. Jarrett. Okay, we'll let that go by the wayside. I'm sure that you're amazed by the speeds that you're seeing these cars run here today and the control the drivers have over them.

The President. Yes, I am. And I've noticed one thing already. I've been here only a short time, but I've noticed that if you're trying to look at the number on the car, you better look when they're down the track a ways. You're not going to see it when they go by here.

Mr. Jarrett. They're running about 200 miles an hour when they go by our position right here.

The President. 200——

Mr. Jarrett. This is one of the fastest points on the racetrack.

The President. You know, there was a moment out there when the Air Force One was coming in, when I thought that we were over the track, and it was just one of the expressways in normal holiday traffic. [*Laughter*]

Mr. Jarrett. Sometimes it looks that way.

And I think that we should emphasize, even though these cars are going upwards of 200 miles an hour, they are specially built racecars. They're running, of course, on a specially built racetrack. And we—the folks who are listening in by radio in their cars—we wouldn't want them out there trying this on the highway.

The President. No, I hope not. Just——

Mr. Jarrett. Oh, excuse me.

The President. Well, I was just going to say—out there, let them stay bumper to bumper.

Mr. Jarrett. Well, they do run very closely, of course. Drafting—you perhaps have heard that term—and that is very normal and wins many races here on this racetrack. One car running, bursting the wind to open the other car, can run faster than he could normally run by himself by running directly behind the other car. That's why we see them running so close together.

Another thing that we have been pleased with, President Reagan, in this sport—back when I was driving a racecar, it made me feel good to know that I was providing the American public with something besides what I felt was top-notch entertainment, because it serves as a good proving ground for the automotive and after-market manufacturers to prove their products out here, which makes better and safer cars for our highway driving pleasure.

The President. Well, I know that that's always been one of the factors behind these great classic races, is what we learn about further improvements in automobiles. But

you've just proven something else about the sport here. This is the first time you've mentioned that about racing yourself, but here you are, hale and hearty and healthy.

Mr. Jarrett. Well, thank God for that. Well, I'll tell you, NASCAR has done a good job over the years, and the rules that go into the building of these racecars—sometimes they get in some pretty serious crashes, but because of the rules and the safety equipment that's built into the cars, the drivers most of the time are able to walk away. And thank God for that.

The President. Now, I just noticed one car that came into the pits, and I know that everyone was supposed to have had their regular pitstop. He looks as though he's got some problem. There isn't any rushing around, as there normally is.

Mr. Jarrett. That is true, and that is Kyle Petty. He's the son of Richard Petty, who is currently leading the race. Of course, Kyle has been racing on this circuit for about 4 years, and you are right that something is wrong with the car, because it's a longer than normal pitstop. Now they're pushing him down pit road, so maybe he'll get back out in the running, but certainly it's cost him any chance about ever winning this race.

The President. Yeah. Well, now, you have a son in a car out here, don't you?

Mr. Jarrett. Yes, I do. He's running his first super speedway event in NASCAR Winston Cup competition. And as we talk, Mr. President, it looked like Kyle Petty's car is being pushed off pit road and behind the wall, so that will be all for him today.

The President. Oh, well.

Mr. Jarrett. And it's a shame to run this near the end of the race with about 25 laps to go, and he was running very well in the event here today. So, he'll go back and see if he can see his dad win his 200th race here today.

Let's pick up the winner. You were an old sportscaster and see if we can—Richard Petty, of course, driving car number 43. Here he comes now off of turn four, the blue and red car. Why don't you pick him up and call him down through the front straightaway?

The President. Oh, wait a minute here.

Well—[*laughter*]—somebody just went past somebody right out here in front of us. I don't think that's informed anyone who's listening on the radio very much about the race, but I thought they changed positions just as they went by here.

Mr. Jarrett. They certainly did, and Cale Yarborough, who is running the car number 28, is gaining on Richard Petty right now, who is running out front. And you notice how high Petty runs through the wall—or through the turn up next to the wall and turns one and two, but that's his style of driving. You do see a lot of passing in this area right directly in front of us.

The President. Yes. I hadn't noticed that before. Just when they get past the finish line here, many of them make their move going into that upper turn.

Mr. Jarrett. Well, this is one of the fastest points on the racetrack, and the drafting takes such an effect right in this area of the racetrack. And that's one reason that they're able to make the moves and move around the cars in front of here. One car is sticking to the pavement a little bit better than another one. That helps him in this area where the—[*inaudible*]—is as we see.

Going into turn one, Cale Yarborough continues to gain on Richard Petty, so it looks like we'll have a shootout down near the end of this race between those two drivers. They pulled away from the balance of the field. Currently running in third place is Terry Labonte. Harry Gant is in fourth place and Bobby Allison in fifth place. And a fellow who has put on more good races with Richard Petty, David Pearson, is pulling into the pits now—the hood goes up on that car, and there's trouble on the racetrack, Mr. President. We need to give it to our turn announcer.

Mr. Jarrett. Well, President Reagan, that was Ken Ragan that scraped the wall. He spells his name, R–A–G–A–N. But he does have a sign on the back of that car: "Ragan's for Reagan." [*Laughter*] So, I know that you appreciate that.

The President. I didn't know I had a relative out here. [*Laughter*] Of course, I found out of the clan when I was in Ireland—and the clan Reagan over there, every family just sort of picked out the way they'd spell the name. [*Laughter*]

Mr. Jarrett. Well, yours has certainly become a popular one.

If you look directly across from us, Bobby Allison's pit, car number 22 where he's pitting there, and he has a special sign for you there on the wall. It's on the pit wall as you see the yellow stripe that goes across there. It says, "We love Ron."

The President. Well, I appreciate that very much.

Mr. Jarrett. Well, I know that a lot of these fellows are so pleased to have you here today and taking part in this big Independence Day celebration.

The President. I'm just marveling at you and your ability, as they come off that upper turn way over there, to pick out who they are and what position and all.

Mr. Jarrett. Well, see, I have——

The President. That's having lived down among them.

Mr. Jarrett. That's right. I have an advantage on you. I've been around this business for about 30 years and know the fellows and know the colors. And, really, when they get on the backstretch, the color is about the only way that you can pick out the car.

We'll watch Richard Petty now as he comes off of turn four, and you can see Cale Yarborough in the orange car is gradually picking up on him. They have some cars that they're coming up to put a lap on. Of course, they're running faster than those cars. That will help both of them as they pick up the draft of each of those cars as they come in front of them.

The President. In other words, Petty is in number one now.

Mr. Jarrett. Petty's in first place in the car number 43 and Yarborough in car number 28. Now, they are two of the biggest winners here. Yarborough has won 14 events on this speedway. Petty has won 10. He's won two of these Firecracker races. He's won seven of the Daytona 500 events.

And it'll be interesting to see, as they come up on this two cars that they're lapping now on the backstretch, Petty is able to move right up on the outside of them very carefully and get ahead of Yarborough going into that turn.

The President. You know, if I were faced with the responsibility of broadcasting this, Ned, and with Petty out in front, I would just keep watching Mike Curb down here to find out whether he was in front yet or fallen behind.

Mr. Jarrett. His reaction tells the story.

The President. Yes. [*Laughter*]

Mr. Jarrett. It certainly does. Well, he's—everyone here—I think Petty has such a tremendous following, and they've been waiting for him to win 200. The closest driver to him is David Pearson, who was in the pits there a moment ago. Pearson has 105 victories. But Petty has had such an illustrious career and has been so good for the sport. But he has his hands full now as Yarborough continues to, what we call in the sport, reel him in, because he's gaining on him.

The President. They're reversed right now as to their previous position when we first saw them out here in that one, two spot.

Mr. Jarrett. Yes.

The President. But holding at about the same distance but with the one who was second now first.

Mr. Jarrett. Yes. Yarborough made a little longer pitstop than Petty, and that gave him an advantage. But his car seems to be running a little bit faster run now, and he's close enough now that he can pick up the draft. And we'll keep you here for just a moment, and we'll let you call that pass, if he indeed does pass him.

The next time around, he should be right on his bumper as they go into turn one. He moves right in on the back bumper of Richard Petty. He's definitely in the draft as they go into that turn. So, we'll see if Yarborough can make the move.

See how high they go off the turn.

The President. Yes.

Mr. Jarrett. And Yarborough'll be trying to get a good running start down the backstretch. He might be a little too far behind this time to make the pass.

The President. He has crept up, though. He's only about half the distance he was on that last lap.

Mr. Jarrett. He's moved right in on his back bumper now.

The President. Yes. Yes.

Mr. Jarrett. Now, that's not the place to pass, as he comes off of that fourth turn. I don't think——

The President. It'll be down here to our right.

Mr. Jarrett. It'll be down here or going down the backstretch.

Here he is at the start-finish line, Yarborough.

The President. It looks like it's going to be——

Mr. Jarrett. Petty was still out front.

The President. Yeah.

Mr. Jarrett. Yarborough couldn't make the pass there. Let's see as he comes off of turn two what he can do with it there. He dips down to the low side. Petty will go high in the turn. Now Yarborough drifts up right behind him. And he is definitely in the full force of the draft now. With Petty opening up quite a space of wind in front of him, that lets Yarborough's car run a little bit freer. But he still can't make the pass as they go into turn three.

So, we're going to throw it back upstairs again, Mr. President. It's been a real pleasure having you here with us today for this Pepsi Firecracker 400.

The President. Well, it's a wonderful Fourth of July for me. And I wish everybody a very happy Fourth.

Mr. Jarrett. We know that you look forward to greeting the winner.

The President. All right.

Note: The President spoke at 12:02 p.m. from a viewing box in the grandstands of the Daytona International Speedway. Following the race, he greeted the winner, Richard Petty, in the viewing box.

Earlier in the day, the President started the race by telephone from Air Force One shortly after leaving Washington, DC.

Remarks at a Picnic Following the Pepsi Firecracker 400 in Daytona Beach, Florida
July 4, 1984

This has been a fantastic Fourth of July. And I've enjoyed certainly everything that I've seen since I've been here. And with the skill and the daring that we witnessed out there, and the pursuit of excellence that those drivers—and I mean all of them that are here—made stock car racing a major American sport. And I know that each of them probably is proud and has every right to be, and we're proud of them.

I want to take a special word to say—or say a special word about Bill France, Sr. Now, Bill France, Jr.—yes, I know what he's done. But I think that—I guess it was Bill, Sr., that got things really started. And then I've heard since I've been here that he's the grand old man of stock car racing. Where do they get this "old man" stuff? He's only 74. [*Laughter*] I tell you, the way I read old is, old is 15 years from where you are now. [*Laughter*] Seriously, to Bill, Sr., and Bill, Jr., they've accomplished so much, and they've added so much pepper to the American scene.

I think I can understand why stock car racing is so popular. Americans have always cherished mobility, and we greatly admire innovation. And by combining man and machine, stock car racing brings out the best of both of these American impulses.

I appreciate all the work that goes into those precision machines also, because it makes you realize that the race is won in the garage as well as on the track. So, congratulations to all of those workers out there that were keeping those competing cars out on the track.

Now, Richard Petty, congratulations, and to all the others, for a demonstration of skill and courage. This race puts the driver to the test. You've got to keep cool under great pressure. I was told that when I was up there watching it. Keeping cool, sitting so close to a hot engine, isn't easy, as I found out when Richard Petty came up and I met him. I thought he'd fallen in someplace on the way. [*Laughter*]

You need intense concentration and stamina, and it's amazing to see them out there, bumper to bumper at 200 miles an hour. We've all done a little bumper-to-bumper driving. I know—you have to, if you live in Los Angeles with the freeways, but you're not going quite that fast.

So, Richard Petty, your victory is something for which you and those who work with you can rightfully be proud. I know how you all feel, too, because I'm in a little race myself this year. [*Laughter*]

But to be a little serious, today we're celebrating our country's independence and freedom. Our Founding Fathers gave us a wonderful gift 208 years ago—a free country, a country where no one need live in fear and where everyone can speak and pray and live as he or she sees fit. As we commemorate our country's birth and its freedom, I hope we can take a little while today to breathe a little prayer of thanks for the great blessings that we enjoy in America.

I'm certain that if Jefferson and Adams and Washington were here with us today, they'd be sharing in the festivities. And if Patrick Henry were here, from what I've read about him, he'd have been out on the track with one of the cars. [*Laughter*] Our Founding Fathers were kind of gutsy, and we'd better not forget that. These patriots and all the others, rich and poor, of every race and religion, who worked and struggled and sometimes fought and died for our freedom, are with us in spirit today.

And, again, I just want to thank you all for letting me spend these few minutes with you. And God bless you, and God bless America. Thank you very much.

Note: The President spoke at 4 p.m. in the infield area of the Daytona International Speedway.

Statement by Principal Deputy Press Secretary Speakes on Elections in Guatemala
July 4, 1984

We have noted with pleasure the record turnout of Guatemalan voters in the July 1 Constituent Assembly elections. The bipartisan U.S. observer team and our Embassy in Guatemala report from visits throughout the country that the process was fair and open, well organized, and orderly. We applaud the Government of Guatemala for taking this important step in carrying out its commitment for a return to constitutional practices and the unprecedented response of the citizenry to the opportunity to participate in their political process. We wish the Guatemalans well as they prepare a constitution and proceed with elections for a new government next year.

Remarks at a Spirit of America Festival in Decatur, Alabama
July 4, 1984

Thank you, ladies and gentlemen. And thank all those wonderful young people that we've seen here in this parade. I don't know whether any of my remarks or what I'm going to say on this day can be as eloquent as seeing what really the future is all about in this great, free land of ours, and it is embodied in those young people that came by here.

What a wonderful festival this is. And one of the most impressive things about it is that you began this annual Fourth of July celebration 18 years ago when some people said that patriotism was out of style back in that period. Well, I guess here in Decatur it never was out of style.

When other people were burning our flag, you were waving it. And I don't know if a President has ever thanked you for that, but please accept my gratitude and admiration.

It's good to be here with Senator Denton, Congressmen Edwards and Flippo, and I was hoping and thought for a time, until some things intervened in the schedule—foul-ups here—that I was going to be able to greet my friend and your Governor, George Wallace.

We were Governors together when I was Governor of California. As a matter of fact, I was looking forward to telling a little thing about him, and now I'll just have to tell it to you and somebody relate to him, that once when I was attending a meeting as Governor of California in one of the hotels in Los Angeles, somebody told me as we were breaking up that your Governor, George Wallace, was in another part of the hotel. And I thought it would only be courtesy and friendly of me to drop over and pay my respects to him. And he was there, representing the best interests of Alabama, as he always does. And I walked into a meeting where he was telling a group of California business executives the advantages of leaving California and moving to Alabama. [*Laughter*]

But I want to congratulate Admiral Whitmire on receiving the Audie Murphy Patriotism Award. I knew Audie Murphy. He was a good man. He's buried, as you know, in Arlington Cemetery, and there's a simple stone at his grave that says: "Audie Murphy—Texas." But it could say Audie Murphy—American—because in one of our roughest hours his courage and plain decency cast a light on the entire Republic.

In World War II, a unit of ours that was routed by a superior enemy force—and Audie Murphy climbed into a World War II disabled tank, up on the turret, and turned the machine gun of that turret on the enemy, and all alone was trying to hold off the hundreds of advancing men of the enemy. At the same time, walkie-talkie radio—he tried to call for artillery support.

And when the artillery commander, wanting to know what his safe range was, asked how close the enemy was to him, Audie said, "Well, if you'll wait just a minute, I'll let you talk to them." [*Laughter*] Well, he was actually asking them to direct the artillery fire at his own position, because that offered the best opportunity of stopping the enemy.

But I'm so happy to be here tonight. I don't get to the South often enough to suit me. Come to think of it, I don't get to California as much as I'd like either. [*Laughter*] But I always feel a special affinity for this part of the country and the people in it.

And even now in these modern times when people who aren't from the South talk about it, they tend to dwell on the physical beauty of the Old South and wax poetic about moonlight on the magnolias. Well, of course the South is lovely, and that is true; but there are those—and I'm one—who feel a special affection for its people. I respect the values that took root here and the pride that's part of the southern character. I'm drawn to your good sense and decent traditions, your fidelity to God, and your faithfulness to your region. And I know that you love our country and are very protective toward it.

I mean no slight to the other parts of the country—to my heritage, which was up in the heartland there in the Middle West, or now my home in the West. But I have been struck when, now and then, on news for some reason or other—on the TV news—there will be an occasion where the commentator is talking to one of our men in uniform, and I've often been struck by how often the young man in uniform, when he replies, you hear the lilting cadence of Charleston or Memphis or Winston-Salem or Decatur. The South was the home of patriots in 1776, when a southerner drew up our Declaration of Independence. And it's the home of patriots today, 208 years later.

We're here tonight at a great celebration, a birthday party for the Nation. And we come together to honor those who invented this country and who saw to it that it would always be a place of high ideals. And we celebrate those who, in each generation, have protected those ideals and advanced the cause of democracy.

I'm trying to smile, but if I appear as if I'm frowning a little bit, it's those TV lights up there—[*laughter*]—so I'm not really frowning at all; I'm squinting.

But the cause of democracy, that's a subject of high seriousness when, on a night like this, it's hard to be somber and full of deep thoughts, it's hard not to be happy. We have so much to be thankful for.

When I was in China recently, I was privileged to speak to several hundred students at Fudan University in Shanghai. And I talked to them about our country. I'd had an opportunity to be questioned by a number of them, and I felt that they had a great interest in us and particularly in our young people, their peers here in this land. So, in talking to them, I wanted them to understand who we are as a people, and I told them that in many ways we're a nation that loves to contend with itself. We love to argue. And we're free to argue, and that's as it should be.

But I told them that we always managed to stay united around certain things: our central belief that all men are created equal and our belief that democracy is the fairest and most honorable political system yet devised by man. And they seemed to understand. I sensed a very favorable reaction from them and was very pleased by that. And, of course, what I said was true. We are great arguers. But in spite of all our differences, we're still a united country, and we celebrate that unity today. We celebrate, too, the miracle of 208 years of freedom.

I want to talk to you about something, if I could, that I've been thinking about a great deal lately. You know, when you work in the Oval Office, a lot of problems cross your desk. We're repeatedly reminded that there's a lot to do, so many causes to carry about—or care about, and carry forward in our country and in the world. But I think what's impressed me most and what's given me a very deep feeling over the last 3½ years is how very lucky we are. We are truly blessed to live in this time and this place.

Now, I say that because there are so many people that get more attention than they deserve. They run around and survey the modern landscape and see the problems of mankind, and they say, "Oh, it's such a troubled world." We hear people say that this is a terrible century and that we live in an increasingly totalitarian age, that freedom is dead or an illusion to begin with, and man is just a powerless victim of historical forces and that history is something beyond our control, something we can't affect. Well, the counsel of these sour souls would seem to be that mankind has had it and we might as well just give up. Well, let me tell you, they aren't talking about the American people I know.

This is a wonderful time to be alive. And we're so lucky because as a people, we still have the opportunity to be patriots, and as a nation, we still stand for something.

Look at the challenges of our time. God has granted us the challenge to change our own country and to make it better by moving it closer to the intentions of the men who invented it.

We have the challenge to make America even more free than she is; to ensure greater freedom in the marketplace, where our boldness and our power and our genius can bloom. We must work for greater freedom for you so that you can benefit from your labors and so that your earnings will remain where they belong—in your pockets and purses for your families and in your neighborhoods.

We have the power and the challenge to expand freedom in all areas of life; freedom of inquiry and thought, freedom for the practice of religion, freedom in commerce. Ours is the challenge to advance the interests of the family, the challenge to protect the interests of the smallest unit of government, the hometowns of America, where the expression of the public will is most directly felt.

You know, I've often had a feeling sometimes there in the National Government—I even had it sometimes at the State level—never in my hometown—the feeling that sometimes if we just slipped out, we in government, and closed the doors, turned the key, and disappeared for a while, it'd take you a long time to miss us.

We stand for freedom in the world. We see the gulags and the prisons, those places

where man is not free to do work of his choosing and profit from his labor, places where the freedom to worship God has been extinguished and where souls have withered. But we're blessed by God with the right to say of our country: This is where freedom is. This is the land of limitless possibilities.

And you don't have to travel too far in the world to realize that we stand as a beacon, that America is today what it was two centuries ago, a place that dreamers dream of, that it is what Winthrop said standing on the deck of the tiny *Arabella* off the Massachusetts coast, with a little group of Pilgrims gathered around him, and he said, "We shall be as a shining city for all the world upon the hill."

It isn't so of other places and other systems. Can you think of a time when you heard of a West Berliner jumping over the wall to get into East Berlin? Can you think of a time when someone took a homemade balloon—hot-air balloon and tried to float from free Western Europe into Czechoslovakia? Or when someone took a leaky fishing trawler on a death-defying journey so they could enjoy the freedom of Havana, Cuba? Can you think of a time when any family, thirsting for opportunity, left a democracy to live in a country that was not free?

The truth is that the totalitarian world is a tired place held down by the gravity of its own devising. And America is a rocket pushing upward to the stars. Other countries see our entrepreneurial spirit and seek to emulate it. More and more, the world is reawakening to the fact that freedom is better than tyranny, that democracy is better than the iron fist of dictators, that freedom is the one condition in which man can flourish. And man was meant to flourish, was meant to be free. And that is why we were created. That's why it's been said that democracy is just a political reading of the Bible.

The world has flirted with systems other than democracy, and for a while, some of them were in vogue. There were those who said our problems are intractable, and we need huge government to tell us what to do. For a while, the doctrine of Marx and

Lenin seemed something new and revolutionary. And some among us said, "Well, that's an idea. We should look at it." Well, all for a while. Times have changed. Man has moved on, and more and more we can see that the tide of the future is a freedom tide.

Man still thirsts for freedom. And wherever the persecuted fight for freedom, our souls and our spirits are with them. We're with the trade unionist in Krakow, Poland, marching behind a crucifix. We're with the Afghan rebel fighting the tanks with an undying ancestral will. We're with the people of Central America, who struggle each day for liberty.

And in spite of decades of troubles and sometimes self-doubt, look across the world for the persecuted and punished, for those who yearn to be free, for those who fight for the right to worship, to speak freely, to write what they want, to enjoy the freedom God meant us to have. For all those people, America's not just a word; it is a hope, a torch shedding light to all the hopeless of the world.

You know, throughout the world the persecuted hear the word "America," and in that sound they can hear the sunrise, hear the rivers push, hear the cold, swift air at the top of the peak. Yes, you can hear freedom. It was so 208 years ago, and it's so today.

My friends, we're so lucky. We've been granted the right to stand for something. So much of our greatness is behind us, but so much of our greatness is still before us, out there waiting for us to take advantage of it. It is, in truth, a wonderful time to be alive. And those young people that I mentioned first, with those present in our country who have been trying to frighten them into believing that maybe there isn't a future for them, don't any of us who are grown up let them believe that for one moment. They're going to see things we've never seen, they're going to have advantages we've never had.

I thank you. God bless you, and may He continue to bless the Nation that has showered this land with love for more than two centuries. Thank you all. God bless you all.

Note: The President spoke at 6:53 p.m. at Point Mallard Park.

Following his remarks, the President went to the Huntsville Hilton Hotel in Huntsville, AL, where he remained overnight. The following morning, he attended a reception for Reagan-Bush workers at the hotel.

Proclamation 5217—Veterans' Preference Month, 1984
July 5, 1984

By the President of the United States of America

A Proclamation

Forty years ago—on June 27, 1944—President Franklin D. Roosevelt signed into law the Veterans' Preference Act. This statute brought together, for the first time, laws, Executive orders, and regulations extending back to the Civil War which granted preference in Federal employment to veterans.

The primary purpose and philosophy of the Veterans' Preference Acts are to assist veterans in obtaining and retaining Federal jobs for which they qualify. They constitute not only a means of rewarding veterans for their service in the Armed Forces, but also a means of preventing them from being penalized, in the search for employment, by the fact that the months or years they spent in the service of their country isolated them from the civilian world. In recognition of the economic disadvantage suffered by this service, these Acts seek to give these veterans a favorable position in competing for Federal employment. At the same time, the veterans' preference laws have been drafted so that they are compatible with the merit principle of public employment.

Veterans' preference is but a partial recognition of the great debt of gratitude that the country owes to those who have served in the Armed Forces. Its success is evidenced by the fact that 40 years after World War II, 30 years after Korea and 10 years after Vietnam, veterans comprise 39 percent of the non-Postal Federal work force and 52 percent of the Postal work force.

In recognition of the fortieth anniversary of the Veterans' Preference Act, and to honor the men and women who have served their country in the Armed Forces, the Congress of the United States, by Senate Joint Resolution 297, has designated June 1984 as "Veterans' Preference Month," and has authorized and requested the President to issue a proclamation in observance of that month.

Now, Therefore, I, Ronald Reagan, President of the United States of America, do hereby proclaim June 1984 as Veterans' Preference Month.

In Witness Whereof, I have hereunto set my hand this fifth day of July, in the year of our Lord nineteen hundred and eighty-four, and of the Independence of the United States of America the two hundred and ninth.

RONALD REAGAN

[*Filed with the Office of the Federal Register, 4:37 p.m., July 5, 1984*]

Remarks at the General Motors Technical Center in Warren, Michigan
July 5, 1984

I had a few notes here for some remarks based on very little information, but some in anticipation of what I was going to see. I thank you and Roger and Howard and all of you who have been giving this demonstration and this look into the future. All I can say is, I like what I see.

You know, Mark Twain, we all know, was one time reported dead. And he replied with a statement that his death had been exaggerated. [*Laughter*] And I couldn't help but recall that with regard to some of the people who have been counting this industry out and announcing its demise. And they're going to be proven, I'm sure, as wrong as the doomcriers who were going to bury Mark Twain.

I know there are some very distinguished—I see some very distinguished faces around this table. You represent an enormous productive power, and your industry is vital to the health, the vitality of our country. And it isn't taken for granted by anyone in this administration. Unlike some socialist countries, the future is not in the hands of government; it's in your hands.

And I was going to come here and suggest or urge you to be bold. You have been bolder than I was even going to suggest. Your vision and confidence are crucial if America is to meet the great challenges that face us in the—and remain prosperous—in the eighties. And many of us here remember, I'm sure, when American business was untouched by war and was the undisputed leader of the world. But that era is over. Government, industry, and labor are operating under different rules in a much more competitive world. And all of us will have to do better if we're to remain an industrial and economic force such as we have been.

But I have seen enough to know I don't have to tell you that. You're already doing it. And you're already working together, which I was going to say would be admirable if it was done.

Something we've tried to end, which I never could understand when it was prevalent, was the adversarial relationship between government and business in our country. And those in government should want business to succeed, should want new workers to be hired and want you to make a profit. We're trying to create an economic climate of success by bringing inflation

1003

under control at our end and holding down taxes and unnecessary regulation. But, as I say, it isn't just up to government. Ingenuity, courage, and hard work were the essential ingredients of the American success story, and I think what is happening here is in keeping with that great entrepreneurial spirit.

With the Saturn concept, as I've seen, General Motors is heading into the future not just with an idea of survival, but with an idea of triumph, and that's the attitude that all American business should have. And I think we're seeing more than that—more of that spirit that's cropping up all over our country.

I've always had a faith that American business, working in cooperation with American labor, can meet and beat the combination [competition]. [1] And I say that I also speak from your standpoint; I think I'm the only one that's ever held this job who is a lifetime union member—[laugh-ter]—and six times president of my own union.

And I have seen such miracles so far, and I feel like I've just been to the Pentagon—with the Chiefs of Staff over there, I can't talk about that, either—[laughter]—so I can't talk about all that I've seen.

But as inspiring as all of this and this great technological advancement that I've seen was that great advance that's on that planning board over there. And I just—well, what I've seen has reaffirmed my faith in American business and American industry. And, my goodness, I can't wait for the next summit meeting. [Laughter]

Note: The President spoke at 1:35 p.m. in Design Studio 3 at the center, after several briefings on the company's Saturn project. Following his remarks, he was given the opportunity to test drive a prototype of the experimental automobile on the grounds of the center.

Remarks at the General Motors Assembly Plant in Orion Township, Michigan
July 5, 1984

Thank you, Roger. Governor Blanchard, Senators Levin and Riegle, Congressman Bill Broomfield, the State and local officials, Jim McDonald, Les Richards, [2] ladies and gentlemen:

I have seen so much that I told Roger just a little while ago, I can't wait for the next summit conference, I've got so much to tell some of our friends from around the world.

But, also, I had the privilege of driving a prototype car just a little while ago. And Roger was brave enough to get in the other seat. And I reminded him that for 3½ years I've been sitting in the back seat. [Laughter] But fortunately, I have to tell you, it literally drove itself.

---

[1] *White House correction.*

[2] *President of General Motors Corp. and manager of the assembly plant, respectively.*

Well, yesterday we celebrated Independence Day, when all Americans come together and with good cheer and revelry commemorate our freedom. Today, we herald another step forward that will ensure that America remains the free and prosperous land that God intended it to be. I've always believed that with freedom, hard work, and the profit motive, there's nothing that Americans can't do. Well, this plant represents the "can do" spirit for which your industry and America have always been known.

It took great courage for all of you to make this kind of an investment. In a time of great uncertainty, General Motors proved that they had faith in our country and faith in our country's economy. Since 1979 more than $50 billion has been spent by your industry—scrapping old plants, building new ones, developing technology, and retraining employees—and over $23 billion of that $50 was spent by General Motors right here in America.

President Dwight Eisenhower, who dedicated the GM High Tech Center, which I just visited, once said, "The future will belong, not to the faint-hearted, but to those who believe in it and prepare for it." Well, you're preparing for our future, for a better future. So, let our competitors take note today: The American automobile industry is back—back with pride, back with teamwork, and back with performance that can and will make us number one.

This plant is a result of the bold leadership of your industry and an admirable commitment to the future of America. And I think your plant symbolizes a new spirit of cooperation between management and labor. That cooperation reflects the determination of this industry not just to survive but to triumph. And we know that the UAW put its full support behind this endeavor.

Keeping faith with that good will, I understand that General Motors chose this site over three less costly locations, permitting them to put laid-off General Motors employees back to work. You're showing just how much can be accomplished when management and labor speak with each other, instead of at each other; when management and labor work together, instead of against each other.

I'd like to take this opportunity to congratulate the UAW and the entire American labor movement. During these last few years of severe economic stress, organized labor has played a responsible and constructive role in rebuilding American industry.

You've demonstrated, when the chips are down, what people can do working together freely, rather than at the dictates of some central planner or bureaucratic mandate of government. I happen to believe the last thing your industry needs is the Federal Government bringing in outsiders to tell you how to run your business and how much to pay your workers.

And let me just share with you a conviction that I feel deep in my bones. If we Americans keep working together to improve quality, keep investing in America's technology to become more productive and

hold down costs, then, yes, we can outcompete, outperform, and outsell the pants off anybody, anywhere in the world.

Earlier today, I was at the Tech Center taking a look at your Saturn project. The energy and creativity out there confirmed my belief that mankind is on the edge of a new era of opportunity and progress. Putting technology to work for us, which is what your Saturn project is all about, will ensure that when the future gets here, Americans will be leading the way. Space-age technology is being put to use to make certain America remains on the cutting edge of progress, new products, and new jobs. The confidence and positive outlook experienced here today—or evidenced here today is the kind of optimism and pride in our way of life cropping up in cities and towns in every part of our country.

It's a far cry from the gloom and doom of just 4 years ago. Sometimes it's hard to remember that only a short time ago people were counting America out. They were claiming that we were a nation in decline, that our best days were behind us. Inflation was running in double digits, robbing working people and the elderly of the value of their savings. Economic stagnation was throwing more and more people out of work and destroying any chance for the poor to better their lot.

The auto industry, like the rest of the country, was on the edge of catastrophe. In 1980 alone, the Big Three [3] lost $4 billion. And then came the recession, the culmination of years of too much taxing, spending, and regulating by those who claimed they could spend your earnings better than you could.

Well, we've been determined to chart a new beginning for America. And I know that it hasn't been easy. That recession was deeper and longer than predicted. But these problems had been building up for 20 years.

We were determined to find a real economic cure, not just resort, as they had so often in the past, to another political quick fix. There've been eight recessions since

---

[3] *Chrysler Corp., Ford Motor Corp., and General Motors Corp.*

World War II, and seven of those were treated with quick fixes. There's no compassion in snake oil cures. We weathered that storm together, and now the Sun is shining on a strong economy and on an American automobile industry that is moving forward again.

We went to work to get control of Federal spending that had been increasing 17 percent a year. We've cut that in half.

Taxes had more than doubled just between 1975 and 1981, leaving working people paying taxes at a rate that only a short time before had been reserved for the extremely well-to-do. This ever-increasing tax load was driving money away from the private sector that could have been spent buying new cars or investing in new plants and equipment. With a 25-percent across-the-board tax cut, we've prevented the people from being mauled by tax increases, and we've indexed the rates so that ordinary people won't be pushed by inflation into higher and higher tax brackets.

We immediately moved to reduce the regulatory burden which bound the hands of our most productive citizens with Federal redtape. And I'm proud to say, we made a special effort on behalf of the auto industry, saving you hundreds of millions of dollars at a time when every dollar counted.

It took time to put our program in place and time to take effect. And the same was true for all the auto industry. And I salute all of you who kept your faith when things were especially tough. And I know they were tough. But by working together, by believing in each other, we've turned the situation around.

In the last 19 months, we've enjoyed economic expansion even beyond our own expectations. In the first quarter of this year, the economy grew at the astonishing rate of 9.7 percent. Second quarter growth appears to have been solid—not quite 9.7, but still higher than anyone had expected. And inflation ran at only 3.6 percent in the first 3 months of the year. For the first time in over a decade, we're enjoying a strong economy, falling unemployment, and low inflation all at the same time. And we're determined to keep it that way.

You know, those selling the old no-win notion that you can't have growth without high inflation have been proven wrong. Having a degree in economics myself, I feel free to talk about too many economists have a watchchain with a Phi Beta Kappa key at one end of the chain and no watch on the other end. [*Laughter*] They were wrong when they said that inflation and interest rates couldn't come down. They were wrong when they said recovery wouldn't come, wrong when they said expansion couldn't last. And I think if they keep running down America, they're going to be wrong again.

What we're seeing is that things are getting better. Across America, businesses are showing a profit, laid-off workers are being rehired, and new employees are being brought on board. Over 6 million new jobs have been created in the last 18 months. Now, Europe calls this—in fact, to my face at the last summit meeting—the American miracle.

Well, last year the auto industry had a good year. General Motors has been reopening plants and putting on second shifts all over the country. And I'm told that in the last 18 months you've brought 90,000 men and women back onto the payroll.

And this expansion isn't just confined to big business. Over 600,000 new businesses were incorporated last year. And most of these were small businesses—the Mom and Pop store, the entrepreneur kind of business. John Naisbitt, futurist and author of "Megatrends," said earlier this year that: "1984 has arrived just in time to witness an explosion of bottom-up entrepreneurialism and the dawn of an era that may offer our best hope yet. . . ."

Well, we have every reason to be confident. Our country has recaptured the pride and community spirit that was for so long an essential part of our national character. You folks here at GM have much of which to be proud in this account. You not only build cars; you're making this country the decent place that we want it to be.

Orion employees alone donated almost $86,000 to the United Way last year. You also gave your wholehearted support these last 2 years to the GM/UAW Christmas Care and Share Program, feeding the needy through donations of canned foodstuffs and cash. Orion employees serve on the boards of many community organizations, including the YMCA, the Pontiac Urban League, and the United Way.

I especially want to congratulate Michelle Roberts, production technician in taillight assembly. She works tirelessly for the United Way and also recruits volunteers from your ranks for worthy community projects. Mr. Roberts'—or Miss Roberts', I should say, citizenship is an example to all of us. And Herman LaFayette—he's helped over a thousand young adults in the Junior Achievement program. He's also worked as a counselor at a local halfway house for former prisoners.

Your company deserves some recognition on this count. General Motors' annual award for excellence in community activities is the kind of program of which any corporation should be proud. It highlights the public service of employees like Kenneth Mehl, who's a city councilman of Westland, and Wallace Holland, a former GM employee who is now the mayor of Pontiac.

I think Americans—all of us—have come to a better appreciation of the values that bind us together. We're seeing a new respect for family and neighborhood. Remember when it was fashionable to claim that God is dead? Well, today I think we're seeing that He's alive and well in the hearts of our people. And we're grateful to Him for the many blessings that He's showered upon us.

We're rededicating ourselves to the values that define our character, that make us a good and worthy people, and that can and will keep America strong and secure and free. Our forefathers left us a wondrous land of liberty. And now it's up to us. This dedication today, the cooperation and the hard work behind it, the community spirit and the heartfelt patriotism of everyone who works here, are part of a rebirth of freedom. This generation of Americans is meeting the test. We intend to pass on a country as prosperous and free as the one that was given to us.

And I can't tell you how much I appreciate your letting me join you here today. Thank you. Good luck, God bless you, and God bless America.

Note: The President spoke at 3:10 p.m. at the dedication ceremonies inside the plant. He was introduced by Roger B. Smith, chairman of General Motors Corp.

Prior to his remarks, the President met with members of the executive committee of General Motors and Orion workers at the assembly plant.

Following his visit to the plant, the President traveled to San Antonio, TX, and the San Antonio Marriott Riverwalk Hotel, where he remained overnight.

Interviews With Representatives of San Antonio, Texas, Television Stations
July 2, 1984

Immigration Legislation

Mr. Marrou. Hello, Mr. President. This is Chris Marrou [of KENS–TV] in San Antonio.

The President. Chris, glad to talk to you.

Mr. Marrou. Of course, there's a lot of interest here in south Texas in the Simpson-Mazzoli bill, and it has now gone through the House, surprised a number of people here. What are your personal feelings about that version of the bill?

The President. Well, I'm a little constrained as yet, because it's still in conference and there are two versions now. And the conference committee, when they come back from recess, will then take up the matter of resolving their differences. Actually, the differences are not very great. And it is reasonably close to what we asked the Congress for. So, I'm hopeful that they'll come together on something that I can sign.

Mr. Marrou. You don't see any circumstances under which you might veto it?

The President. Well, I never like to talk about that. It would have to have some elements in it that I don't think are there right now. But I never really discuss veto or no veto until I see what's on my desk. But I believe that it is a legitimate effort to regain control of our borders. We know that in that about 120 miles of the 2,000-mile border—that 120 miles in the Southwest—is our greatest problem. And we have approved a thousand more INS personnel.

Mr. Marrou. There's a lot of fear among Hispanics in this area that perhaps they'd have to carry some sort of ID card or something like that to prove they're citizens even though their families have been for decades. What would you say to them?

The President. Well, we want to take every precaution we can to see that there won't be what so many fear—just an automatic ruling of them out as employees. That would be unconscionable. And we want to be very careful that while we have safeguards to prevent employers from hiring the undocumented workers, that at the same time there is no discrimination against those who will be legalized under this bill, those who may still be undocumented but who've lived for a long period of time, put down roots in our society. We want to give them the right to legally live here and those who, as you say, are citizens.

Now, it may require some evidence, but I don't think it would be anything onerous or heavy for anyone to bear.

Interest Rates

Mr. Marrou. Interest rates are starting to go up again somewhat. And I believe you said before you don't think they have anything to do with the deficit. What do you think's causing them?

The President. I think simply the pessimism on the part of so many out in the money market, their unwillingness or inability to believe that we do have inflation under control. Now, inflation has been at 3.6 percent for the first quarter of this year. The month of June it was estimated that it would probably come in at 2.6 percent, so we're still going in the right direction. It is their fear of lending money and then having inflation go up as it has seven times

before this in recessions since World War II. But this is a different kind of recovery. It isn't based on artificial stimulants of the economy, the quick fix, so-called, that we've had before. This is a legitimate recovery and expansion with the creation of some 6 million new jobs in the last 18 months alone, things of that kind.

So, I think maybe if we can persuade the Congress to even more cuts in the spending growth, they'll begin to see that we're serious about fighting inflation.

Mr. Marrou. You think you can convince them to cut spending growth a little more?

The President. Yes, I do.

Views on the Presidency

Mr. Marrou. Sort of a personal question here around the July 4th holiday: A lot of people—everyone, I suppose—still believes in America that just about anybody can grow up to be President. Patriotism is increasing. Could you tell us what is the first time you remember ever thinking, "I'd like to be President someday"?

The President. Will you believe I never had such a thought? I always believed that you pay your way. So, when I was in show business and, therefore, had some ability to attract an audience, I used to campaign for people I believed in and causes I believed in. As a matter of fact, for much of my life I was a member of the other party—the Democrat Party—and campaigned for them. And, then, when I found I could no longer follow the course that the party had taken, I became a Republican.

But when they first appealed to me—a group—to run for Governor of California on the basis that I had the best chance of defeating the incumbent after all the work I'd done in politics, I fought as hard as I could against it and said, no, for them to find a candidate, and I would campaign for the candidate.

I have to say, however, after those years in public service, when I gave in finally and did that reluctantly, I found it the most rewarding and fulfilling experience of my entire life.

Mr. Marrou. Thank you, Mr. President.

The President. Thank you.

___

Immigration Legislation

Mr. Scott. Mr. President, David Scott [of KMOL–TV] here. Thanks for being with us.

The President. Well, it's a great pleasure.

Mr. Scott. The Simpson-Mazzoli immigration bill—a lot of folks down here in Texas don't like it for a lot of different reasons. Some people say it handles illegals in an arbitrary fashion, that it will produce discrimination against legal Hispanics here, that it's going to hurt businessmen, that it's going to be costly, that it won't be effective. Do you think it's fair? Do you think it's balanced? Do you think it's cost-effective?

The President. Yes, I think the bill as introduced is cost-effective and is fair. And it's also necessary, because the simple truth is we've lost control of our borders. And no country can afford that.

Now, all of the things that people are fearing—these are very solid and real considerations of ours. And I'm convinced that we can protect our Hispanic American citizens from discrimination just on the basis that an employer might be afraid to hire them. We're going to protect their rights. At the same time, we're also going to have compassion and legalize those who came here some time ago and have legitimately put roots down and are living as legal residents of our country, even though illegal. We're going to make them legal.

We also, I think, in this bill, are taking action against those employers who literally entice illegal entry into the country with the promise of jobs, but then take advantage of those individuals, knowing they can't complain, and pay them less than scale, deny them things that they should have in their employment simply because they're in a sense being blackmailed by the employer because of their illegal status. And we want to put an end to that.

But I think all these other objections can be met because we simply intend to meet them.

Mr. Scott. Why, then, sir, have your most ardent supporters down here in Texas fought you on this bill? And might not it cost you in this State come fall?

The President. Well, I hope that they would give us the benefit of the doubt and recognize how much we mean to protect their interests.

Social Security

Mr. Scott. Let's talk about Social Security a moment. A lot of people in this country—Democrat and Republican, economists—tend to feel that we can't get a handle on the Government deficits and we can't get a handle on straightening out Social Security unless some fundamental change is made in it next year. Now, why aren't any of the Presidential candidates talking about this, or can you guarantee us that come 1985 you won't have to go at Social Security with an ax?

The President. Well, there's one thing we will not do: We will not pull the rug out from under those people who are presently getting Social Security and are dependent on it. Nor has that ever been our intention, in spite of a lot of political demagoguery that flowed out of Washington and was multiplied as it went out through the country and—that somehow we were out to destroy this program. Since we've been here, we have increased the Social Security payments for the average married couple by $170 a month. More people are getting it and getting more than ever have before.

If there is anything needed to be done to that program—and these are things that we'll be looking at in the coming years—it will have to do with—people are presently paying in and whether they're being fairly treated because, if you will remember, the biggest single tax increase in our nation's history was passed in 1977 before we got here. And it is in the Social Security payroll tax. And there is a possibility—well, probability, that many people, young people now paying in will never be able to receive as much as they're paying. But no plan will be allowed to reduce the payments to the present recipients of Social Security. This has been my pledge from the very beginning.

Mortgage Interest Deduction

Mr. Scott. As a lameduck next year, should you be elected, sir, you'd be in a unique position to be able to do some courageous political things without having to worry about reelection. If there is a major tax reform bill, for example, do you antici-pate that you might support, for example, removing tax deductions on home mort-gages?

The President. No. This came out of a discussion I had with a panel recently on a trip out in the country, and I was talking generally about all the areas that are being explored, whether flat tax or whatever it might be, in reforming the income tax. The income tax—the base must be broadened, because there are a hundred billion dollars in tax not being paid by people who legiti-mately owe it today.

This is one thing we want to do. But we also mean to simplify it. It is absolutely too complex. When the taxpayer has to hire professional help to find out how much he or she owes the Government, that's not fair.

But, no, I believe that the mortgage in-terest deduction is legitimate and is proper. And I stand for it.

Mr. Scott. Mr. President, thank you, good health, and good luck to you, sir.

The President. Thank you.

Immigration Legislation

Ms. Daniels. Hello, Mr. President. This is Deborah Daniels at KSAT in San Antonio.

The President. How do you do.

Ms. Daniels. I'd like to ask you about the Simpson-Mazzoli bill. It's created a lot of controversy here in south Texas—we're so close to Mexico. A lot of people don't like it. How do you feel about it, and do you think it's going to solve our immigration prob-lem?

The President. Yes, I think it is, as well as they can be solved. We've lost control of our borders, there's no question about that. And it is necessary and would be necessary for any country in that situation to do some-thing about it.

Now, we recognize the great problem is in the 120 miles of our border, about that much, down in the Southwest. But we think that the program is going to provide for documented workers crossing the border to fill needs, particularly in agriculture. We think that we, with compassion, are going to recognize the problem of those undocu-mented immigrants to our country who

have been here for a number of years, who've established a base and a home and put down roots, and we're going to legalize them.

And I think we're also, in this bill, going to stop the exploiting of the undocumented worker by some employers who hire them much more cheaply than the law should allow and do so because it's a form of black-mail. They know that the individual can't complain because of their undocumented status.

So, all of these things we're trying to solve in this problem. Now, there may be some glitches here or there, but, believe me, we don't want any penalty imposed on people simply because someone is reluctant to take a chance on hiring them because of their Hispanic heritage. And we're going to do everything we can to protect against that.

I think that the bill can be worked out to the point that it will resolve some of our worst problems and will benefit a great many people presently living in this coun-try.

Hispanic Americans

Ms. Daniels. Mr. President, the Hispanics are a growing political force. I'd like to know how important you feel the Hispanic vote will be in the upcoming election, and what are the Republicans and your adminis-tration offering Hispanics?

The President. Well, let me say that they are very important, as they were in 1980. And you bet I want their vote. Well, I'd like to have everybody's vote. But I'm going to try very hard for them.

I think, at the same time, that we have more to offer them than they've been of-fered over the last few decades by the phi-losophy of the other party. The other party has believed in handouts, grants, welfare—the making of people dependent. And in my view, the Americans of Hispanic origin, their values are based on family and reli-gion, on all the basic good values of ethics and work ethic, and they want to be inde-pendent. And that's what we offer—is op-portunity.

Our program is one aimed at offering them not the dependency of having to hold out their hand for government to give them a handout, forever in bondage to the Government. Our offer: jobs, opportunities, a chance to be self-sustaining, to provide for themselves and their families. And I think this is what the average Hispanic American wants more than anything else. And we're offering it.

Women

Ms. Daniels. I'd like to put the same question to you about women. We're hearing a lot about the gender gap as the election closes in. What is the Republican Party doing to attract women?

The President. I am glad you asked me that. I don't believe that any administration in this country has ever done as much as this administration is doing with regard to discrimination against women in the marketplace or wherever it might be—employment in government and all.

First of all, we have, out of the 4,000 appointments that I can make in government, almost half of those are women. There has never been anything like that. Secondly, there's never been three women on the Cabinet before, as there are now. And I have appointed the first woman to be a Justice of the Supreme Court.

But that is only scratching the surface. No other administration has gone through, as we're going through, all the statutes, all the Federal laws and regulations, to find and eliminate those that contain language that is discriminatory against women. We have already implemented this in hundreds of those regulations. We have people in 50 States that are working toward doing the same thing, because I had done that as Governor in California, in the State statutes and laws.

Our tax policies that we put into effect has reduced the marriage penalty tax. We have almost doubled the tax credit for working mothers for child-care credit that they must have. We have removed the so-called widow's tax from inheritances—no tax due on the inheritance.

All of these things have added up to more advantages for women than, as I say, have ever been provided by any administration. And maybe it's beginning to get around, because just last week, some national polls revealed that the gender gap has turned the other way by a slight margin—a majority of women have announced themselves as supportive of our administration.

Ms. Daniels. All right. Thank you very much, Mr. President.

The President. Thank you.

Note: The interviewers spoke by telephone with the President, who was in the Diplomatic Reception Room at the White House.

The interviews were released by the Office of the Press Secretary on July 6, the date of their broadcast in San Antonio.

Remarks at the Annual Convention of the Texas State Bar Association in San Antonio
July 6, 1984

Reverend clergy, Blake Tartt, Mayor Cisneros, secretary of state, the gentlemen here on the dais, and you ladies and gentlemen:

I'm going to, before I start, just take a second to return to my past and give you kind of a news commentary. Just in case that you haven't caught the news early this morning, the Labor Department has announced the unemployment figures for June. And from 7.4, if you counted the people in uniform—and they certainly are employed—7.5, if you just count the civilians, and as of the end of June that had gone down to flat 7 for the total unemployment and 7.1 for the Nation as a whole. And 6,700,000 people have gone into new jobs in the last 19 months in our country.

Incidentally, it is the first single administration since—well, more than 20 years ago, that has reduced both unemployment and inflation in the same period of time.

But now I'll get on with the business of the day, and it begins with saying it is great to be back in Texas. You know, all Americans like to think that they're a little bit of Texas, because Texas is such a big and great part of America. You're so much a part of our national past, and because you stand for growth and energy, you stand for the best in our future as well.

Now, I guess it's just instinctive for Texans to think big. I mentioned to Jim Baker a few months ago that with the election coming up, I probably should get out and meet some people. [*Laughter*] And the next thing I knew, I was in China, where there's a billion of them. [*Laughter*]

And I know everybody expects me to be political this morning, but this is an official stop, so I'll resist the temptation to comment on all the odd causes and special interest groups the other party seems to be embracing these days. [*Laughter*] And I don't know what the secretary of state meant when he said that I might come back before November. [*Laughter*] I don't know why that was.

But, you know, I've discovered that much of the Texas legend is true. For example, never try to top a Texan. I made that mistake a few years ago. I was talking to a Texan, a friend of mine, about our ranch up in the mountains near Santa Barbara. And he just kind of got around to asking how many acres. And I said, "Six hundred and eighty-eight." Then he asked me if I'd bought it at a toy store. [*Laughter*]

There is, of course, more to Texas than even the legend. One journalist noted a few years ago in Atlantic magazine how ludicrous the attitude of some of his fellow northeasterners seemed after he had experienced firsthand the friendliness, the genuineness, and the opportunity of Texas. Well, I know how he feels, because I've felt that way myself a good many times. Believe me, I can remember a couple of primary days, not to mention the last general election, when my affection for all things Texan was completely unbounded. [*Laughter*]

Now, I'm sure you're all aware, too, of the contributions that Texans have made to this administration: the Vice President, George Bush; chairman of the Senate Armed Services Committee, John Tower;

and, as you've been told, Chief of Staff at the White House, Jim Baker. Anne Armstrong is Chairman of my Foreign Intelligence Advisory Board, and now Deputy Attorney General Carol Dinkins.

So, Texas continues to be very much a part of the American story. And what a story! During the past few years, Americans and Texans have been riding together. It wasn't long ago, after all, when our national economy was in its worst mess in years, when our national security was badly endangered, endangered not only by Soviet expansionism and a massive Soviet arms buildup but even by threats and aggressions from tiny nations run by bullying despots and dictators.

From Washington we heard only an elaborate and disheartening series of excuses about our national and international problems. We were told these problems were basically insoluble and that we had to accommodate ourselves to stagflation, to limitations on growth, to living with less. And some said our political institutions and constitutional system weren't up to functioning in the modern world. And, worse, some said all of this was the fault of the American people, who, we were told, suffered from a crisis of confidence.

Well, there was a breakdown in America, but it had precious little to do with our political system or the American people. It had everything to do with 63 square miles of riverfront real estate called the District of Columbia and some of the politicians and bureaucrats who've been bivouacked there too long.

Now, ladies and gentlemen, this administration wasn't in office but a few minutes before we went to work on some of those same national problems that some said had no solution. And we aimed our fire at the high spending and taxes and unnecessary Federal regulations that were thwarting the spirit of enterprise and faith in hard work in America. And today, as we look at an expanding economy and a low inflation rate, we can see how far we've come from the days when inflation was running at 12.4 percent, the prime interest rate was 21½, unemployment was climbing, and we were entering our fourth straight year of stagnant or declining productivity.

On the international front, too, there have been dramatic changes. This administration spoke candidly about the wrongs and dangers of totalitarianism; we checked its advance; we rebuilt our defenses; we revitalized our alliances. And yet, at the same time, we launched the most comprehensive series of arms reduction proposals in our nation's history.

Now, I know it's a political year. Some may expect me to stand here and claim this was a victory for one administration or one political persuasion. But as I've said many times before, this victory went far beyond any one person or any party. It was a victory that belonged to the people, because they were the ones who, time after time, forced the grasping politicians and indifferent bureaucrats in Washington to do what all the smart sayers and seers said was impossible: cut Federal spending, cut individual tax rates, end the unfairness of bracket creep by indexing tax rates to inflation, thin out the thicket of Federal regulations, fight waste and fraud, rebuild our defenses, and resist totalitarian expansionism in Central America. And I think if this administration deserves credit, it's only for having the kind of trust in the people that made us willing to take our case to them and seek their support.

We dared to do it then, and we dare to do it now for one simple reason: We believe we were speaking for a new political consensus in America, a consensus that objected to government intrusions into areas where government was neither competent nor needed, but a consensus that was also critical of government's failure to perform its legitimate and constitutional duties like providing for the common defense and preserving domestic tranquillity; a consensus, in short, that wanted to get government off our backs, out of our pockets, and back to the standards of restraint and excellence our forefathers envisioned.

Now, it's true that the focus of much of our effort in Washington during the past few years has been on those twin crises we inherited on entering office—the crisis of our economy and our national security. But now that our economic expansion is well underway, and now that America's international prestige and security are being enhanced and restored, I've had the chance to report on another crisis that we've been working on quietly but, I think, effectively, and one that I know concerns all of you— the crisis of crime in America.

Two weeks ago in Hartford, I reported to the National Sheriff's Association on the steps we've been taking since our first few days in office to fight the menace of crime in America. You know how dangerous that menace had grown. Violent crime had risen 50 percent in a decade. It was costing more than $10 billion in financial losses, touching 30 percent of America's homes, and taking the lives of more than 23,000 Americans a year.

I noted then something basic and something obvious: The American people are fed up with leniency toward career criminals, and they're fed up with those wrongdoers who are openly contemptuous of our way of justice and who do not believe they can be caught and, if they are caught, are confident that once the cases against them enter our legal system, the charges will be dropped, postponed, plea-bargained, or lost in a maze of legal technicalities that make a mockery of our society's longstanding and commendable respect for civil liberties.

I also noted the American people have lost patience with liberal leniency and pseudointellectual apologies for crime. They're demanding that our criminal justice system return to realism; that our courts affirm values that teach us right and wrong matters, and that individuals are responsible for their actions, and retribution should be swift and sure for those who prey on the innocent.

And the will of the people is at last being felt again. Reported crime dropped 4.3 percent in 1982, and that was the first decline since 1977. And reported crimes for last year showed an even more remarkable 7-percent decrease. This is the sharpest decrease in the history of the crime statistics and the first time the serious crime index has shown a decline for 2 years in a row.

Now, a few people want to attribute the encouraging downward trend in crime to the fact that there are fewer members of the population now in the crime-prone age group. Well, I challenge this view. Coincidence isn't necessarily cause. The truth is that crime has sometimes risen with population growth and sometimes not. There's nothing historically inevitable about it. Between 1970 and 1982, for example, the numbers in the crime-prone age group did drop slightly by about 1 percent, but serious crime went up 40 percent.

No, the real explanation for the drop in crime lies in the nationwide crackdown on career criminals in America. The growth of Neighborhood Watch associations, the new statutes in many States toughening criminal penalties, and the sweeping steps we've taken at the Federal level are all indications of this new consensus, of a return to traditional values and an insistence that criminal predators who make a mockery of those values be brought to justice.

And that's why, from our first few days in office, the Attorney General and I gave the closest attention to the kind of candidates picked for Federal judgeships. Yes, we wanted candidates who were sensitive to the rights of the accused, but we also wanted candidates who understood that society and the innocent victims of crime had rights that needed protection, too.

We moved to crack down on the growing menace of illegal drug trafficking. We increased our law enforcement budget by more than 50 percent and added over 1,900 new investigators and prosecutors. Most of them went to work in the 12 new regional drug task forces that we established around the country. And these task forces are already cracking major drug rings. They've initiated 620 cases; they've indicted more than 2,600 individuals. And 143 of these indictments have been under the "Drug Kingpin" law, which carries maximum penalty of life imprisonment without the possibility of parole.

We've also declared war on organized crime in America. I'm proud to tell you that organized crime convictions are up from 515 in fiscal 1981 to 1,331 in 1983. And we're getting longer prison sentences and, for the first time, making a serious effort to confiscate the financial assets of the mobsters. And our new organized crime commission has begun hearings on the structure of the mob today in America and its money-laundering techniques, and its work will now be greatly broadened, because just last week it received subpoena powers from the Congress.

Believe me, we have it within our power to shatter the regional and national syndicates that make up organized crime in America. And this administration seeks no negotiated settlement, no détente with the mob. Our goal is to cripple their organization, dry up their profits, and put their members behind bars, where they belong.

Now, the list goes on about the offensive that we've been carrying on against crime during the past 3½ years. Our local law enforcement councils under our U.S. attorneys have helped improve cooperation with State and local law enforcement agencies. We've implemented most of the recommendations of our task force on violent crime. We appointed a task force on the victims of crime that has come up with legislation that will compensate crime victims, and not from tax dollars, but from the penalties paid by criminal wrongdoers. We've won some important legislative victories, making it easier for the IRS to work on organized crime investigations and revising the posse comitatus law to permit the use of military resources against the international drug traffickers.

But I have to tell you today that the major part of our legislative initiative against crime remains right where it has remained for the last 3 years—dead in the water in the House of Representatives.

Now, our crime package includes bills calling for bail reform, tougher sentencing, justice assistance to States and localities, improvement in the exclusionary rule and the insanity defense, and major reforms affecting drug trafficking, prison crowding, capital punishment, and forfeiture—all of these reforms are badly needed and constitutionally sound. In fact, yesterday the Supreme Court agreed with one of our proposals concerning the exclusionary rule. But the Congress—[*applause*]. Now, I'm happy to hear that applause for that particular court decision. But the Congress still needs to enact our proposals so that the Supreme Court's rationale will be applied to the full range of appropriate searches.

Our core crime package has already passed the Senate once by a vote of 91 to 1. But in the House of Representatives, the leadership keeps it bottled up in committee.

Now, this isn't at all surprising. This is the same liberal leadership that has done nothing but stand in the way of initiatives the American people want and need—initiatives like tuition tax credit to help hardworking families; enterprise zones to provide jobs to those who yearn for progress; a constitutional amendment mandating a balanced Federal budget; and, yes, an initiative to return the freedom of voluntary prayer to children in every school across our land.

We're not about to quit—not on those initiatives and not on our crime bill. We're going to do what we've done in the past. We're going to do what we've done in the past. We're going out to the heartland; we're taking our case to the people. That's why we're here today. The liberals in the House can stand again in the way if they want to, just as they did when they opposed spending cuts and tax cuts, rebuilding our military strength, or helping El Salvador and other nations resist totalitarian rule. But they didn't win then—and here's a flash from the Gipper—they're not going to win now. [*Laughter*]

So, I do have some advice this morning for the House leadership: Stop kowtowing to the pundits and the special interests, and start listening to the American people. The American people want this anticrime legislation; they want it now; and with your help, they can get it. Please tell your elected representatives you expect full and fair representation, and that means getting this bill out on the floor of the House for a vote.

But I believe the issue goes beyond this urgently needed crime legislation. This new consensus that I've been talking about goes deeper than just an interest in a limited, but effective rule of law. It understands that law is not just a way of preventing one citizen from taking advantage of another. It's also the collective moral voice of society. And so, it understands that laws and government, the power of the state and politics itself, can never really account for the moral or material progress of a society. At root, these things are reflections of much

deeper currents, the wisdom, the energy, and the decency of the people themselves.

"You may think that the Constitution is your security." Justice Charles Evans Hughes once said that. Well, he said, "It is nothing but a bit of paper. You may think that the statutes are your security—they are nothing but words in a book. You may think that elaborate mechanism of Government is your security—it is nothing at all unless you have sound and uncorrupted public opinion to give life to your Constitution, to give vitality to your statutes, and to make efficient your Government machinery."

Over a decade ago, it was Supreme Court Justice Lewis Powell who noted that, as our society grew more developed, we saw a weakening of the "most personal" focus—or forms, I should say, of authority: "the home, the church, the school and community," which once gave direction to our lives. He wondered how we could survive without the "humanizing authority" of these institutions that in the past "shaped the character of our people."

Well, other writers and thinkers in our time have made similar observations. Dr. Charles Malik, the former President of the U.N. General Assembly, wondered how it was that in so many universities what he called the wonderful living values of the great tradition were all but forgotten in the curriculum.

And a few years ago, social critic and theologian Michael Novak wrote about the weakening of family values. "The family nourishes 'basic trust.' And from this springs creativity, psychic energy, social dynamism. . . . Familial arts that took generations to acquire can be lost in a single generation, can disappear for centuries. If the quality of family life deteriorates," and then he said, "there is no 'quality of life' " if it does.

And that's why it's so important to make our government leaders respond to the demands of the people, to make them reduce the role of government and restore government's legitimate functions. It is also why restoring common sense and decency to our criminal justice system is equally vital.

For too long, our criminal justice system has ignored reality and moral values. As former New York Police Commissioner

Robert McGuire said: "In the criminal courts, cases are being trivialized in ways independent of the evidence, instead the system being geared to treat each individual case as a manifestation of antisocial behavior. The main impetus is to dispose of it. No one is talking about the morality of crime."

Well, our goal then is not to pass laws that will make the people good. Our goal is to have our laws and legal institutions reflect the goodness of our people and to reflect the things they most deeply believe in. We need to make our criminal justice system reflect once again the innate decency and sound values of the American people.

I began by speaking today about the Texas legend. Its hold even today on the American people is easy to understand. Not far from here, 187 men gave a display of personal valor and commitment to ideals the world will never forget. And sometimes it's forgotten that only a few miles from here, a young colonel named Robert E. Lee held his first real command.

"Who are you, my boys?", he once shouted to some regiments arriving just in time to fill a gap and prevent disaster at the Battle of the Wilderness. "Texas boys," came back the reply. And Lee shouted, "Hurrah for Texas!" And he waved his hat and tried to lead them into battle. And it was then that they grabbed the bridle and the stirrups of his mount, and the cry went up, "Lee to the rear!" And they refused to budge until he removed himself from danger, and then they turned and fought and saved the day.

Robert E. Lee, this southerner who criticized secession and called slavery a great moral wrong, would become himself an American legend; yet a man who thought—though he rode off into myth and glory, would suffer cruelly in his own time. After the dissolution of his cause, he would work to bind up the Nation's wounds. And to those pessimistic about the Nation's future, he once said, "The truth is this: The march of Providence is so slow and our desires so impatient; the work of progress so immense and our means of aiding it so feeble; the life

of humanity is so long and that of the individual so brief, that we often see only the ebb of the advancing wave and are thus discouraged. It is history," he said, "that teaches us to hope."

Well, if we look to history, if we examine closely the last few years and see how far we've come, we can say that these have been hopeful years and be grateful for them. And let us move forward now together to bring about a new age of reform, to complete our national renewal, and to bring about a new birth of freedom.

I'm going to say something right now that—I know I run a risk because there are so many people that want to portray me as trigger happy. I want to tell you something—I never see these young men and women in our Armed Forces in uniform without having a swell of pride that puts a lump in my throat. And how anyone could think that any man would want to send them out to lose their lives—it's just impossible.

And I just have to tell you at the risk, however, as I say, of endangering myself in this, I received a letter not too long ago from the Ambassador to Luxembourg. And he had been up on the East German frontier visiting our armored cavalry regiment there. And as he went back to his helicopter, a young 19-year-old trooper followed him, and he asked the Ambassador if he thought he could get a message to me. Well, being an Ambassador, he figured he could. And then the young fellow stood there at attention and said, "Mr. Ambassador, will you tell the President we're proud to be here, and we ain't scared of nothing."

And you know something? You know, that's all we have to remember. How can anyone in the United States of America, in the world today, be scared of anything? We are truly a shining city on a hill.

God bless you all.

Note: The President spoke at 10:09 a.m. at the San Antonio Convention Center. He was introduced by Blake Tartt, president of the Texas State Bar Association.

Following his remarks, the President returned to Washington, DC.

Radio Address to the Nation on Law Enforcement and Crime
July 7, 1984

My fellow Americans:

I'd like to talk with you today about a subject that's been a priority since this administration's first day in office—fighting crime in America.

When we came to office, crime was taking the lives of over 23,000 Americans a year. It touched a third of American homes and resulted in about $10 billion a year in financial losses. Yet, just as America has regained her economic strength and international prestige in the last few years, so, too, the crime problem in America has shown improvement for the first time in many years.

In recent speeches in Hartford, Connecticut, and San Antonio, Texas, I've pointed out that the 7-percent decrease in crime reported for last year is the sharpest decrease in the history of the crime statistics, and it marks the first time the serious crime index has shown a decline 2 years in a row. Of course we still have a long way to go; but this statistic does demonstrate that our efforts and those of State and local governments are finally having an impact on crime.

At the State level, for example, numerous legislatures have passed tough new sentencing laws. And here at the Federal level, we've taken several critically important steps.

First, from our first day in office, the Attorney General and I have emphasized the importance of appointing to the Federal bench, including the Supreme Court, judges determined to uphold the rights of society and the innocent victims as well as the rights of the accused.

Second, we've launched an all-out assault on the illicit drug trade—that fever swamp of career criminals in America. Taking our cue from the success of our South Florida Task Force, we've brought aboard more than 1,200 new investigators and prosecutors and established 12 regional task forces throughout the United States to crack down on the big money drug traffickers.

The results of that effort have been encouraging. The drug task forces have initiated 620 cases; they've indicted more than 2,600 individuals; and 143 of these indictments have been under the "Drug Kingpin" law, which carries a maximum penalty of life imprisonment without the possibility of parole.

Third, we've launched a full-scale offensive on the home ground of career criminals—organized crime itself. Organized crime arrests have nearly tripled, and confiscation of their assets is also sharply up. Our new commission on organized crime has brought much needed public attention to this problem, and as soon as it receives subpoena power, it will do even more.

Believe me, we in the administration have been trying to speak up for you, the millions of Americans who are fed up with crime, fed up with fear in our streets and neighborhoods, fed up with lenient judges, fed up with a criminal justice system that too often treats criminals better than it does their victims.

Too many Americans have had to suffer the effects of crime while too many of our leaders have stuck to the old, discredited, liberal illusions about crime—illusions that refuse to hold criminals responsible for their actions.

For example, I wonder how many of you know that the major part of our legislative initiative against crime remains right where it's remained for the last 3 years, dead in the water in the House of Representatives. Now, our crime package includes bills calling for bail reform, tougher sentencing, justice assistance to States and localities, improvement in the exclusionary rule and the insanity defense, and major reforms affecting drug trafficking, prison crowding, capital punishment, and forfeiture. All of these reforms are badly needed and constitutionally sound. In fact, our core crime package has already passed the Senate once by a vote of 91 to 1. But in the House of Representatives, the liberal leadership keeps it bottled up in committee.

I told a group of Texas lawyers yesterday,

we're not about to quit on our crime bill. We're going to do what we've done in the past. We're going out to the heartland, and we're taking our case to you, the people. And so, I'm asking for your help today. Please send a message to the House leadership. Tell them to stop kowtowing to the special interests and start listening to you, the American people.

Americans want this anticrime legislation, and they want it now. And if those of you listening will lend a hand, we can get it now. Please tell your elected representatives you expect full and fair representation, and that means getting this bill out of committee and onto the floor of the House for a vote.

We've made real progress against crime in the last few years. Together, we can keep up the good work.

Until next week, thanks for listening, and God bless you.

Note: The President spoke at 12:06 p.m. from Camp David, MD.

Remarks and a Question-and-Answer Session With Regional Editors on Foreign and Domestic Issues
July 9, 1984

The President. Good afternoon, and welcome to the White House. It's a pleasure to have you all here. And I know you want to get to the question-and-answer period, so I'll keep these opening remarks brief.

I often recall the difference between President Washington and President Harrison. George Washington gave an inaugural address of less than 150 words, and he was a great leader, as we all know. William Henry Harrison gave an inaugural address that lasted nearly 2 hours on a cold, wintry day, and a month later he died of pneumonia. [*Laughter*] So, with your permission I'd like to touch just briefly on two of our administration's main efforts, and with my luck probably they were covered in some of your briefings already.

But, anyway, first, the economy. When we took office, I think we inherited a mess: raging inflation, declining real wages, soaring interest rates. Indeed, the month of the inauguration the prime interest rates soared to over 21 percent, the highest level since the Civil War. Our administration moved quickly to turn that around.

We cut the growth of Federal spending. We pruned needless regulations, passed an across-the-board personal income tax cut, and enacted an historic measure called tax indexing. Indexing means that government will never again profit from inflation at the people's expense. And today we have one big program that we think is helping every man and woman in America. It's called economic expansion.

Since we took office, inflation has plummeted; productivity, investment, and real wages have risen; and for the past year, the gross national product has been growing at a rate that's astounded the professors and pessimists. I don't know why I separate them. [*Laughter*]

The best news of all since the expansion began is that some 6.7 million Americans have found jobs. The unemployment rate has taken the steepest nosedive in more than 30 years. And our country has produced new jobs faster than any other industrialized nation on Earth.

But these are all statistics. I think there's a better way that you can tell our program is working—and I understand that a reference was made to it already this morning, and, Don, you stole my thunder—it's true the critics don't call it Reaganomics anymore.

But, second, foreign affairs. We're working hard to give American policy new strength, new firmness, and new purpose. In Europe, we're helping to hold the Atlantic alliance together under intense pressure from the Soviet Union. In Central America, we're strengthening the forces of democracy and economic progress. And in Grenada, we joined the Caribbean democracies in setting a nation free.

In our dealings with the Soviets, we've shown again and again that we remain unshakably determined to support freedom and the struggle for freedom in the world. But we're also eager and willing to negotiate genuine and verifiable arms reductions. And we continue to hope that the Soviets will sit down with us this fall, as they themselves first suggested, to discuss the control of weapons in space and, we hope, on Earth as well.

Recently, Morton Kondracke, the executive editor of the New Republic, summed up our foreign policy very well. He wrote that our administration "has altered the correlation of forces in the world in America's direction." Well, I believe America is stronger, prouder, and more joyful than she was just a few years ago. We still have a long way to go, but we've made a good beginning.

And now, I know you must have some questions.

Yes, ma'am?

Republican Party Platform

Q. Mr. President, I'm Sue Kopen from WCBM-Radio in Baltimore. I just wanted to know if we could look a couple of weeks, a few weeks down the pike to the convention, and what we might expect to emerge as the party's platform—forthcoming?

The President. Well, that's going to be up, pretty much, to those that are framing the platform, because I'm not going to give any orders to them. I think that from what I have heard, from some people that are involved, that they're—it's probably going to be pretty much of a broad statement of principles, of what it is we try to do without trying to get down too much into specifically how it must be done.

Now, there was another young lady, and then I'll——

Black Voters

Q. Mr. President, I'm Jane Saxton, Indianapolis Visions magazine. I wonder what you and your administration and your party would like to do this fall to attract black voters—if anything—or if the Republican Party is merely going to write black voters off?

The President. Certainly we are not counting them out or simply ignoring them. Not at all. As a matter of fact, I think one of the great frustrations I have is that this— what we have done with regard to minorities, with regard to people who still have a way to go to have some of the advantages that they've been denied in the past—that that is one of the better kept secrets of our success and what we've done.

We've had a program to aid the black colleges and universities; because when I came here, I said I think they're such a part of history—they fulfilled a need for so long when there was discrimination that made the advantage of education hard to get for many of our minorities—that they must, that institution must be preserved. And we've been working on that.

I think the very recovery program—the fact that the greatest decrease in unemployment was in the minority community, and particularly among blacks. We have two programs before the Congress that are buried now, or stopped in the House of Representatives without coming to the floor for a vote, that both would be of, especially, advantage to—and particularly young blacks—would be the two-step minimum wage to allow employers to hire young people who have no job experience, who are starting out to get their first job at a lower rate than the present minimum because that minimum ·today has priced a great many jobs young people used to have, priced the jobs out of existence. People are just not having things done that they would have done.

The other one is the enterprise zones. We started that almost 3 years ago. It is still buried and has never come to the floor for a vote. Some States have already moved out on their own and they can't as effectively, because the tax incentives aren't as great just at the State level. But in that regard, in those States where they've done it, some of the stories are just miraculous of what the advantages have been.

And so, I think that we've—it has to do with our own administration here. And this isn't a new thing with me or born of politics. When I was Governor of California, I appointed more members of the black community to executive and policymaking positions than all the previous Governors of California put together. And, as I say, this is a rather well-kept secret.

And if we can find a way for those people to know what we've done, I think that they would choose our policies rather than the policies of the past, and that would be of the future if the Democrats were in control, because those policies sentence too many people to the bondage of welfare-ism rather than opening up jobs and opportunity for them.

Yes?

Jesse Jackson

Q. Mr. President, Jerry Fogel, KCMO-Radio at Kansas City. Do you feel that the recent travels and negotiations by Reverend Jackson might send a signal to future Presidential candidates and these candidates for nomination that such activities are okay and will not be prosecuted under the Logan Act or any other legislation?

The President. Well, the prosecution under the Logan Act—and I think in an answer I gave to a question recently on that sort of led me—or suggested I was astray on that. The Logan Act is very specific, and I was only calling attention to the fact that there is such a thing and that private citizens cannot go and literally try to negotiate terms and arrangements with foreign governments.

I don't think there's been any evidence of that being broken by Reverend Jackson. I think that it would be very dangerous if this became a political ploy for candidates in the future. Anyone that wants to go simply as a citizen, a private citizen, and try to do a humanitarian thing as he successfully did in Syria—and I'm grateful to him for it because I know it's something I couldn't have done officially. I'm grateful that those people were released that were in the Cuban prisons. I could have done without some of the criticisms of American policy that were made while he was in those foreign countries.

But it is a thin line that has to be walked. And I would hope that it would not become a general practice.

Now, I promised you.

Sanctions Against Poland

Q. Chester Grabowski from New Jersey's Post-Eagle, editor. Speaking of foreign policy, I'm wondering when our President will lift the restrictions and sanctions against the Polish people, specifically to lift Polish airlines, which does not allow the people to go back and forth to Poland. It's quite a job to get to Poland today with the sanctions that have been imposed by your government.

The President. I can tell you that this is very much on our minds. And we are seeking to find a way to remove the restrictions that are penalizing the people of Poland more than they are the so-called Government of Poland. And we would like to do that. At the same time, we don't want to send a signal that might be interpreted as that we no longer feel as we do about the Polish Government. So, we're trying to find a way.

Chesapeake Bay

Q. President Reagan, I'm Gary Tuchman from WBOC–TV in Salisbury, Maryland. In your State of the Union Address, you mentioned the cleanup of the Chesapeake Bay. Now, I'm wondering what made you decide to mention that in your State of the Union Address and how committed are you to the cleanup?

The President. I am very much committed to it, just as I'm very much committed to the entire problem of the environment. And that's one of the other best-kept secrets about our administration.

No, this—you couldn't be here in this proximity to that—and it is the largest such body of water on our—the entire thousands of miles of coast of the United States. And its decline in quality—what has been done to it—just is unconscionable. And we are pledged to reverse that, just as we're pledged to—and have added millions of acres to the wilderness territory, have made the most extensive cleanup of the national parks that's ever been made, to restore their safety and health features, and now are going to add additional parkland to those parks.

But, no, it was done for that reason. It is a great and a very unique ecosystem.

Yes?

Abortion

Q. We're grateful for the invitation, since we're not part of the Washington press corps. Thank you for looking to the rest of the country as well.

We hear of human rights, of citizens' rights, minority rights, and women's rights. And I'm wondering, Mr. President, when and how are the rights of the unborn human children going to again be protected in this nation?

The President. Well, we're striving very hard to do that. I know what you're talking about. First of all, with regard to those who some would deny life to after they're born because they are born less than perfect, I wish everyone could have been where I was a few Sundays ago, at the opening of the disabled games—international games that take place every 4 years, this year for the first time in the United States up in New York, and seen those people and their happiness and their enthusiasm, and to think that someone might have decided at their birth that they should not be allowed to live.

I ran the 440 in high school, and it was quite a shock to me to see that a man today is running the 400 meter in under 50 seconds with one artificial leg. And I never got under 50 seconds. [*Laughter*] I didn't get within about 9 seconds of that.

Yes?

Grenada

Q. Mr. President, Paul Jeffers, WCBS, New York. There's this new, big airport—landing strip in Grenada the Russians and the Cubans were building that I understand was almost near conclusion. And I'm wondering, sir, if you're planning to inaugurate it with Air Force One, say, sometime in October? [*Laughter*]

The President. Oh, don't you think that'd look a little obvious? [*Laughter*]

No, but I'll tell you, the job that our people did down there was magnificent. And anyone who thinks that that was a mistake should simply talk to some of the people from Grenada, not just our medical students, our American students there. The people of Grenada believe they were rescued from a Communist domination that had already affected their lives. So, I'm very proud of our military. They only had 48 hours to plan that, too. And they did it.

Abortion

Incidentally—could I just take a second—I left off a part of the answer to your question, too. I know the other part must have had to do with abortion. And I still have to feel that the Constitution already protects the unborn, unless and until someone can prove that the unborn child is not a living human being. And after months of hearings before committees in the Congress, no one could prove that.

Now, if any one of us came upon a body and we couldn't determine whether it was living or dead, we certainly wouldn't bury it until someone proved to us that it should have been buried. And I feel that one of the great moral sins that is violating our very constitutional guarantee of right to life is now prevalent in abortion on demand.

Q. Mr. President, Cameron Harper from WTHR, Indianapolis.

Ms. Mathis.[1] This will be the last question, Mr. President.

The President. Ah. That always happens. [*Laughter*]

Interest Rates

Q. All morning long, your advisers have been telling us—and you mentioned it at the beginning of your remarks—about the economy improving. But as the economy is improving, as inflation is maintaining at a much lower level and, in fact, going down, the prime interest rate in this country is going up. Who's to blame for the prime interest rate going up, and at what point do you think it will continue—will it turn around and go back down?

The President. Well, I had made a prediction in the fall, and I know there are a lot in the press corps that—here in Washington—that are just wringing their hands waiting to see whether I'll have to say I was

---

[1] *Susan K. Mathis, Acting Deputy Director of Media Relations.*

wrong or not. Maybe I was—guessed too soon. I'll still stick with it, because I'm an optimist and I think that most economic prognosticators are pessimists.

I think the interest rates are where they are—and it is psychological. It is because after seven previous recessions since World War II, the money market out there is just not convinced that we have inflation under control or that, politically, we will not yield to the previous practice of artificially stimulating the economy to get an artificial fix, a quick fix, to bring us faster out of the recession.

And every time they did that in those seven previous times, they came out of the recession, but with an inflation rate that was higher than it was before. Now, the man who's going to lend money, or the woman who's going to lend money, has to know that they can get an interest rate that is going to cover the depreciated value of their money during the period of time that money is lent. And I think it is—they just look at every sign. We got a good, sound recovery going, and then they say, "Oh, well, maybe it's heating up too fast."

Well, we had about 50 years or so back there and—a little—around and before the turn of the centuries in which this country had an economy that was at a boom rate, and it didn't bring on inflation, and it didn't bring on any of the evil things that they say.

There's nothing wrong with economic growth. And so, I hope we'll continue it. But I think it is just the psychology that they are fearful. It's been done to them before. It's an election year. They believe that if anything should start to happen, there will be an attempt at a quick fix. Well, there won't be; we don't believe in it. There's going to be sound recovery.

Q. If I could follow up, sir. You are known for some fairly persuasive power when it comes to dealing with individuals. And I'm thinking, in particular, of the banks that are responsible, in your opinion at least, for the prime rate being up. Why can't you persuade them to—why can't you persuade them to your way of thinking?

The President. Well, we think that maybe the persuasion should be based on a few deeds. For example, I think as it moves through the Congress—and it looks favorable—our downpayment on the deficit is going to have, I think, a salubrious effect out there when that's passed, when they find out that the deficits are very probably not going to be as great as they've been projected, and when they find out, also, after the election, that is—if we're still here—that we're not through fighting the deficits, because I've been out on the mashed-potato circuit for 30 years preaching against deficit spending, and I'm determined that we're going to eliminate it.

And to that end, I would appreciate your editorial help——

Q. Amen.

The President. ——in getting passed the balanced budget amendment. And then, please give me a line-item veto. Don't let me face those porkbarrel bills in which I've got to sign the good and take the bad with it. As a Governor, I line-item vetoed in 8 years, 943 budget items, without ever having the veto overthrown.

So, we'll take those two, and you can——

Ms. Mathis. Thank you very much, Mr. President.

The President. And you thought I was the boss. I'm sorry we can't get to the rest. If you have further briefings, remember those questions for those who brief you.

Note: The President spoke at 1:10 p.m. at a luncheon in the State Dining Room at the White House.

Letter to the Speaker of the House and the Chairman of the Senate Foreign Relations Committee Reporting on the Cyprus Conflict
July 9, 1984

Dear Mr. Speaker: (Dear Mr. Chairman:)

In accordance with Public Law 95–384, I am submitting herewith a bimonthly report on progress toward a negotiated settlement of the Cyprus question.

Since my last report to you there have been several developments in the Cyprus question worthy of note. On April 17 the self-declared Turkish Cypriot "state" announced the formal exchange of ambassadors with the Government of Turkey. We strongly opposed this development and declared publicly our concern that it could set back the U.N. Secretary General's efforts in the search for progress. We also repeated our opposition to any diplomatic recognition of the self-declared entity.

On May 8 I informed the Congress that the Administration intended to request authorization for a "Cyprus Peace and Reconstruction Fund" of up to $250 million to be utilized on Cyprus at such time as a fair and equitable solution acceptable to both Cypriot communities is reached, or when substantial progress is made toward that goal. I intend this commitment to be a symbol of the shared concern of the Administration and the Congress for promoting genuine progress on Cyprus. I was pleased that a committee of the House of Representatives has included this fund in an authorization bill it is considering.

On May 11 the United Nations Security Council passed Resolution 550 which condemned the Turkish Cypriot community for several actions it had taken. We found it necessary to abstain on the resolution, believing its language unlikely to contribute to the goal of a negotiated settlement. We reiterated to the Council our continuing opposition to the Turkish Cypriot community's declaration of statehood and our determination to see progress made under the aegis of the Secretary General. Following passage of that resolution Secretary Shultz's Special Cyprus Coordinator, Richard Haass, and other Administration officials undertook intensive consultations with both Cypriot parties, with U.N. officials and others on the potential for progress on the question.

On June 15 the Security Council met again on Cyprus, this time to renew, unanimously, its mandate for U.N. peacekeeping forces in Cyprus (UNFICYP). The resolution approved on that date is identical in text to the previous renewal in December, 1983. Following the vote the Turkish Cypriot representative told the Council his community could not accept the resolution but would continue its cooperation with the U.N. forces on the same basis as that announced by the Turkish Cypriots in December, 1983. We view this continuation of the vital U.N. peacekeeping mandate as a positive sign that the parties to the Cyprus question do intend to continue the search for a solution. I am enclosing a copy of the Secretary General's report to the Council on UNFICYP activities.

At the time of the June Security Council vote the Turkish Cypriot side pledged to maintain the unoccupied status of the city of Varosha and presented to the Secretary General its latest ideas on possible next steps toward a solution. We welcomed the Varosha announcement and hope the ideas presented, as well as the comprehensive framework presented previously by the Government of Cyprus, can assist the Secretary General as he resumes efforts under his good offices mandate.

Sincerely,

RONALD REAGAN

Note: This is the text of identical letters addressed to Thomas P. O'Neill, Jr., Speaker of the House of Representatives, and Charles H. Percy, chairman of the Senate Foreign Relations Committee.

Proclamation 5218—African Refugees Relief Day, 1984
July 9, 1984

*By the President of the United States
of America*

A Proclamation

The United States and the American people have a long and proud tradition of helping those who are in need. In Africa, the needs of refugees cry out for continued attention. So, too, do the needs of the host countries who, despite their own limited resources, have accepted the refugees in the best tradition of humanitarian concern. Their generosity has led them to make great sacrifices.

We in the United States are mindful of the burdens that are borne by the refugees and their host countries. We are dedicated to the cause of meeting their needs now and in the future. We fervently hope that the Second International Conference on Assistance to Refugees in Africa, which begins July 9, 1984, will lead to a sustained effort by the international community to help African countries effectively cope with the refugee burden. Our own efforts have been and will continue to be in support of the African refugees and their host countries.

In order to heighten awareness in the United States of the needs of Africa's refugees and the needs of their host countries, the Congress, by H.J. Res. 604, has designated July 9, 1984, as "African Refugees Relief Day" and has requested the President to issue a proclamation in observance of that day.

As we reflect on the situation of refugees and their host countries, I hope Americans will be generous in their support of voluntary agencies that provide relief and development assistance to Africa. Further, I wish special consideration be given to the extraordinary hardships borne by women refugees, their children, and other vulnerable groups. The innocent victims of civil strife and war deserve our special concern.

Now, Therefore, I, Ronald Reagan, President of the United States of America, do hereby proclaim July 9, 1984, as African Refugees Relief Day.

In Witness Whereof, I have hereunto set my hand this 9th day of July, in the year of our Lord nineteen hundred and eighty-four, and of the Independence of the United States of America the two hundred and ninth.

RONALD REAGAN

[Filed with the Office of the Federal Register, 10:31 a.m., July 10, 1984]

Proclamation 5219—National Ice Cream Month and National Ice Cream Day, 1984
July 9, 1984

*By the President of the United States
of America*

A Proclamation

Ice cream is a nutritious and wholesome food, enjoyed by over ninety percent of the people in the United States. It enjoys a reputation as the perfect dessert and snack food. Over eight hundred and eighty-seven million gallons of ice cream were consumed in the United States in 1983.

The ice cream industry generates approximately $3.5 billion in annual sales and provides jobs for thousands of citizens. Indeed, nearly ten percent of all the milk produced by the United States dairy farmers is used to produce ice cream, thereby contributing substantially to the economic well-being of the Nation's dairy industry.

The Congress, by Senate Joint Resolution 298, has designated July 1984 as "National Ice Cream Month," and July 15, 1984, as

"National Ice Cream Day," and authorized and requested the President to issue a proclamation in observance of these events.

Now, Therefore, I, Ronald Reagan, President of the United States of America, do hereby proclaim July 1984 as National Ice Cream Month and July 15, 1984, as National Ice Cream Day, and I call upon the people of the United States to observe these events with appropriate ceremonies and activities.

In Witness Whereof, I have hereunto set my hand this ninth day of July, in the year of our Lord nineteen hundred and eighty-four, and of the Independence of the United States of America the two hundred and ninth.

RONALD REAGAN

[*Filed with the Office of the Federal Register, 10:32 a.m., July 10, 1984*]

Remarks to State and Local Officials in Tilghman Island, Maryland
July 10, 1984

The President. Thank you all very much, and it really is a pleasure to be here. And I think all of us owe a special thanks to the ladies of the auxiliary for the fine meal that they've prepared for us today.

Well, this has been a most informative visit, and I've appreciated meeting with you and having this opportunity to learn about how you earn your livelihood and about this unique area. You already know how I earn mine. [*Laughter*]

And I've enjoyed very much breaking bread with you in this particular building. My father was a member of a volunteer fire department in my hometown when I was a lad. And the thousands of volunteer fire departments across America symbolize, I think, the strong sense of community, which is such an admirable part of our American character. By getting involved and working together, we Americans have always been confident that we can do whatever has to be done. And that confidence is kind of an American trait.

I remember many years ago, when I was that high and Americans first began kind of touring and going back to the old country to see where they or their ancestors had come from. At first we weren't too welcome in those countries, because we seemed kind of brash and maybe a little overconfident to the people there. And I remember one story of a farm couple from the Midwest who went back and were in Italy and the guide was telling them about

the volcano there and how much power was generated and the tremendous heat and so forth when this erupted and all the things it did. And this old boy listened just about as long as he could. And then he said, "We got a volunteer fire department at home, put that thing out in 15 minutes." [*Laughter*]

But, as I was saying about cooperation, that spirit of cooperation is certainly manifesting itself in the efforts to save one of the country's most precious national treasures, the Chesapeake Bay.

I know that Mac Mathias and John Warner, Marjorie Holt, Herb Bateman, worked closely with the White House and along with Roy Dyson successfully secured congressional support for the bay. And on the executive side, Bill Ruckelshaus, over at EPA, has made this a priority project.

I also want to extend a hearty word of congratulations and thanks to Governors Hughes, Robb, and Thornburgh for their magnificent cooperation. Having been a Governor myself, I know how difficult it is to do this sort of thing without getting bogged down in bureaucratic back and forth. But with their leadership, these three Governors have put their States in the forefront of a very worthy and productive endeavor.

And this same good will can be found among all concerned, whether in Federal, State, or local government, or in the private sector. Saving the bay has united a coalition of diverse interests and activated a broad range of individuals. I know, for example, the Chesapeake Bay Foundation has over 1,300 volunteer bay watchers in the region. And there's also been much more done by groups like Ducks Unlimited and the National Wildlife Federation. All of us working together not only can save the bay; we're going to save the bay and restore it.

Now, H.L. Mencken, that spirited newspaperman from Baltimore, once labeled the bay "a great big protein factory." Well, Mencken is known to have enjoyed oysters on the halfshell and steamed crabs. There are tales about the invigorating powers of the oyster known even back as far as the days of Thomas Jefferson—not that he told me personally. [*Laughter*] But many of you may be related to the people who provided Mencken with those shellfish. This is more than an income for you, it's a way of life. And believe me, we aren't going to let anything destroy it.

Clearly the time for action is now. The oyster crop and the crab harvest are down. Other statistics like those concerning the decline of the striped bass are also cause for concern. This is not a question of environmental concerns versus economic development. We can and will preserve the bay without hurting the economy or stopping growth. In fact, much of the economic vitality of this region depends on conserving the bay and its many resources.

I made a commitment to do this in my State of the Union Message, and the Fish and Wildlife Service and the Department of the Interior are fully behind our effort. I can promise you today the Federal Government will do its utmost to cooperate with all concerned in a balanced and effective program to protect the bay. Conservation like this is not partisan politics; it's common sense.

Of course, we're talking about more than a bay. We're talking about a body of water that nurtured those hardy souls in the first permanent English settlement in Jamestown. We're speaking of a body of water that served as a vehicle for commerce for the middle colonies, enabling our young country to grow and prosper. This body of water means a livelihood to many of you and is a source of recreation and enjoyment

for millions of Americans. It's our responsibility to pass on to our children in America, as free and strong as what was passed to us, and also to pass on to the next generation in America as beautiful and productive an America as the one that we were handed. We mean to do just that. And with your strong support, I know we will.

And I've enjoyed this chance to get acquainted with you. God bless you all.

And I would like to present two flags that have flown over the White House. One is for the volunteer fire department—here. And the other is for a park that I understand is just across the way.

William Blades. Thank you very much, Mr. President.

And, Mr. President, there's supposed to be a bushel of crabs in here now, but it's— [*laughter*]. Anyway, we regret that Mrs. Reagan couldn't come with you. And we're sending back to the White House with you a bushel of hard crabs and two dozen soft crabs. And we thank you for coming, sir.

The President. Well, I certainly appreciate that. And I want you to know if they're not here right now, it's because—if I know those fellows of mine—somebody's intercepted them and said, "Let's get them on the helicopter!" [*Laughter*]

Mr. Blades. Here they come.

The President. Oh, here they come.

Mr. Blades. They bite you. Watch it, they bite.

The President. Oh, yeah. I'm not going after them barehanded. [*Laughter*]

Mr. Blades. That's the soft crabs.

The President. I can touch those. Well, thank you all.

Note: The President spoke at 12:43 p.m. following a luncheon in the Tilghman Volunteer Fire Department building. Among the guests at the luncheon were Governors Harry R. Hughes of Maryland, Charles S. Robb of Virginia, and Richard L. Thornburgh of Pennsylvania. Mr. Blades is president of the Tilghman Volunteer Fire Department.

Prior to the luncheon, the President visited the town's Dogwood Harbor Wharf, where he talked with local watermen.

Earlier in the day, the President began

his visit to Maryland's Eastern Shore with a stop at the Blackwater National Wildlife Refuge. While there he received briefings from Under Secretary of the Interior Ann Dore McLaughlin and refuge manager Don

Perkuchin on endangered species and new acquisitions. He then viewed the refuge from an observation tower.

Following the luncheon, the President returned to Washington, DC.

Remarks on Signing the Food for Peace Day Proclamation
July 10, 1984

Well, 30 years ago today—and you've probably been told this several times—President Dwight D. Eisenhower signed into law Public Law 480, the Food for Peace Program. And 10 years before the signing ceremony which took place here at the White House, President Eisenhower launched the Normandy invasion. And only the year before the signing ceremony he was first sworn in as President. It's possible that on July 10th, 1954, Ike thought most of his great moments were behind him. But that was not so, as this program proves, for in time it grew to become one of the greatest humanitarian acts ever performed by one nation for the needy of other nations.

I'm delighted to welcome here today Ike's Secretary of Agriculture, Ezra Taft Benson, who was present when the Food for Peace bill was signed. Welcome. Glad to have you here.

Food for Peace is still the largest food aid program in the world. Over the last 30 years, it's delivered almost 653 billion pounds of food to people in over 100 countries. It's helped bring hope and new economic opportunity to more than 1.8 billion people. Statistics are, by their nature, dry, but bear with me for a moment as I give you just a few more—with the hope that they haven't been given to you already.

Food for Peace has delivered 27,000 tons of food a day to recipient countries for three decades now. And the value of those U.S. farm products exceeds $33 billion—more than $3 million a day over the history of the program.

All of those numbers give us a sense of the scope and the magnitude of this program. But its great contribution is that it's an instrument of American compassion.

And it also reflects America's practicality. We recognized 30 years ago that people who are hungry are weak allies for freedom. And we recognized, too, that except in emergencies, handouts don't help. From the beginning, recipient countries paid for a significant part of the food they received.

The businesslike approach is one of the strengths of this program. We've never attempted to make countries who receive our food become dependent on our aid. In fact, we've used our aid to foster economic development around the world. And that is an important reason why, over the years, many of the nations that have received our aid have eventually become major commercial partners.

In the early days of Food for Peace, the major recipient nations were the war-devastated economies of Europe: Italy and Spain, West Germany and Japan. And with time and with the help of Food for Peace, those economies regained their strength. They began to pay cash for American farm commodities. Many of these countries have become our top commercial partners. Eight of our top 10 agricultural markets are former recipients of Food for Peace aid. And Japan is now our number one agricultural market on a cash basis. And that has not only been good for the American farmer and the American economy; it's been good for our international relations.

Food for Peace has been very important in spreading good will and generosity throughout the world. When droughts and flooding from the *El Niño* weather disturbances destroyed food crops in Peru, Bolivia, and other Latin American countries last year, Food for Peace took the lead in providing emergency relief. During the 1966 famine in India, roughly 60 million people are estimated to have been sustained for 2 years by Food for Peace shipments.

Today we face a severe and widespread famine in Africa, which is threatening the lives of millions. And, once again, Food for Peace is saving lives. We've already agreed to provide over $400 million for food assistance to Africa in this year alone. And I want to announce today a major initiative to help the starving people of America—or of Africa, I should say, and the world. It's a new program to help us deliver food more quickly and smoothly to those who suffer the most from the ravages of famine.

I will shortly propose legislation to create a $50 million Presidential fund allowing us to set aside existing foreign aid resources to meet emergency food aid needs. By prepositioning food stocks overseas where the requirements are the greatest, we can respond to emergency situations more rapidly and effectively. I will also propose authority to allow the Food for Peace Program to reduce the burden of transportation costs on the most needy countries. And all this is aimed at reducing the loss of life to acute hunger in the Third World.

Food for Peace has come to embody the spirit of American voluntarism. The Federal Government has developed a strong partnership with the private sector to help feed malnourished infants and children, to help mothers and the aged and the disabled. This cooperative effort with private and voluntary organizations includes such agencies as CARE and Catholic Relief Services, and many other groups are helping, also.

In short, the Food for Peace Program has become a wonderful means by which a nation of abundance has helped those in need. It's helped us expand agricultural markets, get needy allies back on their feet, and help potential allies become strong allies for freedom. Food for Peace has helped to coordinate the charitable impulses of the private sector. It's helped feed the weakest people in the world.

And this record of progress is the result of what happened 30 years ago today, when Dwight Eisenhower picked up a pen and signed a piece of paper that quietly—and, with no great attention from the wise, he changed the world. I think Dwight D. Eisenhower would be very proud of what the Food for Peace Program has accomplished. I certainly am, and I'm proud to be able to mark with you its anniversary today.

May Food for Peace continue its great work; may it continue to be administered wisely; and may we continue to combat hunger and malnutrition throughout the world.

Now, I thank you all again for being here, and God bless you.

And now I'll sign this proclamation which designates today, July 10, 1984, as Food for Peace Day.

Note: The President spoke at 1:50 p.m. in the East Room at the White House.

Proclamation 5220—Food for Peace Day, 1984
July 10, 1984

By the President of the United States of America

A Proclamation

July 10, 1984, is the thirtieth anniversary of the signing of the Agricultural Trade Development and Assistance Act of 1954 (Public Law 480). This legislation, signed by President Eisenhower, began the largest food assistance program ever undertaken by one country on behalf of needy people throughout the world, the Food for Peace program.

The productivity and abundance of U.S. agriculture have made this generosity possible. During the thirty years of this program, more than 300 million tons of agricultural commodities and products valued at approximately $34 billion have been distributed to over 150 countries. This food has helped reduce world hunger and improve nutritional standards.

The Food for Peace program has served as an example for other countries which have joined the United States in the effort to provide food aid to needy people. It has served as a model for others to follow and continues to meet changing needs and situations.

The Food for Peace program has accomplished multiple objectives: to combat hunger and malnutrition abroad, to expand export markets for U.S. agriculture, to encourage economic advancement in developing countries, and to promote in other ways the foreign policy of the United States.

In recognition of the accomplishments of this program, the Congress, by Senate Joint Resolution 306, has designated July 10, 1984 as "Food for Peace Day" and has author-ized and requested the President to issue a proclamation in observance of that day.

Now, Therefore, I, Ronald Reagan, President of the United States of America, do hereby proclaim July 10, 1984, as Food for Peace Day, and I call upon the people of the United States to commemorate this occasion with appropriate ceremonies and activities.

In Witness Whereof, I have hereunto set my hand this 10th day of July, in the year of our Lord nineteen hundred and eighty-four, and of the Independence of the United States of America the two hundred and ninth.

RONALD REAGAN

[*Filed with the Office of the Federal Register, 10:24 a.m., July 11, 1984*]

Statement on Signing the Bankruptcy Amendments and Federal Judgeship Act of 1984
July 10, 1984

I am pleased to sign today H.R. 5174, the Bankruptcy Amendments and Federal Judgeship Act of 1984. This legislation carries out a number of critically needed reforms. The bill is the product of long and arduous negotiations among many interested parties. It represents a compromise that may not be satisfactory to all concerned in each of its respects. I am satisfied, however, that the bill adequately addresses the major problems that resulted from enactment of the Bankruptcy Reform Act in 1978.

The bill restructures the bankruptcy courts system in order to comply with a 1982 decision of the Supreme Court regarding the authority of bankruptcy court judges under the 1978 act. It also remedies abuses by both debtors and creditors in consumer bankruptcy proceedings and protects farmers and commercial fisheries from unfair losses that are sometimes incurred when grain elevator operators and fish processors go bankrupt.

I note with special pleasure a provision of H.R. 5174 that would prohibit a debt incurred as a result of drunk driving—where a drunk driver is successfully sued for causing an automobile accident, for example—from being discharged in bankruptcy. This proposal is one of many made last year by the Presidential Commission on Drunk Driving and complements a number of other initiatives that my administration has undertaken in this important area. I am hopeful that it will act as an additional incentive in keeping drunk drivers off our nation's roads.

H.R. 5174 also resolves a troublesome problem concerning the status of labor contracts in bankruptcy proceedings. In my view, an unfettered collective bargaining system is essential to cooperative and effective relations between labor and management. The way in which collective bargaining agreements are treated in bankruptcy is critical. This legislation meets the interests of labor by prohibiting unilateral rejection of labor agreements without court review of whether rejection is necessary. The bill also meets the interests of both labor and business by providing debtors with the flexibility they need to reorganize successfully and preserve jobs for workers. In these cases, bankruptcy courts are required to recognize the great importance that matters of this nature hold for workers and management alike by resolving questions related to collective bargaining agreements in a timely manner.

There are two provisions of H.R. 5174 that I find particularly objectionable.

First, the provisions of the bill that authorize the creation of 85 new Federal judgeships present a potential constitutional problem. Section 201 of the bill creates 24 new court of appeals judgeships but states that I may not appoint more than 11 judges before January 21, 1985. Similarly, section 202 creates 61 new district court judgeships, but prohibits me from appointing more than 29 judges before January 21, 1985. I believe that these provisions clearly violate my constitutional authority under the appointments clause of the Constitution to submit nominations to the Senate and to make appointments after receiving the Senate's advice and consent. As a practical matter, I do not consider it likely that I will appoint more than 40 new judges before the date set forth in H.R. 5174. Consequently, although my actions will be consistent with these provisions, the purported restrictions of my appointments authority will have no actual effect. My acquiescence in these provisions should in no way be considered as a precedent for future congressional limitations on the constitutional appointments authority of the President.

Second, section 382 of the bill places limitations on the fees that a handful of bankrupt estates currently owe the referees salary and expense fund. As I emphasized in 1981 when I withheld my approval of H.R. 4353, a similar proposal that was presented to me as a separate bill, I strongly object to attempts of this nature to confer private relief on a few to the direct detriment of others who are similarly situated and who have met their legal obligations. This is especially true in this case, which I understand involves a giveaway in excess of $20 million. I would have vetoed this section of H.R. 5174 had it passed the Congress as "stand alone" legislation.

I sign this bill with the following additional reservations. I have been informed by the Department of Justice that the provisions in the bill seeking to continue in office all existing bankruptcy judges are inconsistent with the appointments clause of the Constitution. I am also advised that the Administrative Office of the U.S. Courts has reached the same conclusion. Therefore, I sign this bill after having received assurances from the Administrative Office that bankruptcy cases may be handled in the courts without reliance on those invalid provisions. At the same time, however, I urge Congress immediately to repeal the unconstitutional provisions in order to eliminate any confusion that might remain with respect to the operation of the new bankruptcy system.

Note: As enacted, H.R. 5174 is Public Law 98–353, approved July 10.

Remarks on Signing the Annual Report of the Council on Environmental Quality
July 11, 1984

Thank you all. We did pick a warm day for this, didn't we? Alan Hill and William Mills and Jacqueline Schafer, and friends of America's natural heritage, thank you for coming here today.

It's most fitting that we sign the 14th annual report of the Council on Environ-

mental Quality on Theodore Roosevelt Island.

One of ours—[*referring to the noise made by an airplane taking off from Washington National Airport*]? [*Laughter*]

This 88-acre preserve is a living memorial to a unique leader of this nation, a man with great personal strengths of vision and energy and conviction, who rallied the American people to the protection and preservation of its natural resources.

When Teddy Roosevelt became President, our land, forests, and wildlife had been exploited for more than a hundred years. Some four-fifths of our prime forests had been leveled. Untold acres of rich farmland had been washed away and lost in river mudflats. Wilderness areas were unprotected; wildlife had been destroyed in appalling numbers; and some native wildlife species had been totally destroyed. But the consequences of these lost resources had not yet dawned on the public conscience. Well, President Teddy Roosevelt fired the imagination of the American people, shook our nation from its lethargy, and began to rescue the public domain.

The U.S. Forest Service was created; more than 243 million acres were reserved for conservation; 55 bird and game refuges and 5 national parks were established. The Inland Waterways Commission was created to redeem water power for public use. The Antiquities Act authorized preservation of cultural and historical landmarks for the benefit of future generations.

President Roosevelt reached the American conscience, and conservation and environmental protection became an inseparable part of the American creed. He told us, "The nation behaves well if it treats the natural resources as assets which it must turn over to the next generation increased and not impaired in value."

Well, these words must remain an inspiration to all of us, an obligation to everyone charged with the stewardship of our natural resources. The challenges we face today are both numerous and complex.

As you know, during the sixties and seventies many beneficial advances in science, technology, and economic development produced new and unwelcome threats to our environment and the quality of life. And once again, America's conscience was deeply touched. A new and vigorous environmental movement burst forth across our country. The American people joined together in a great national effort to protect the promise of our future by conserving the rich beauty and bounty of our heritage. As

a result, our air and water quality is far better today than it's been in many years. We've reclaimed rivers and wilderness areas that were gravely threatened.

We can all be proud of the advances that have been made during this rebirth of the environmental movement. As the 14th annual report on the Council on Environmental Quality makes clear, we're making solid progress protecting and improving the quality of America's air, land, and water resources.

Now, some are ignoring the progress that we've made in just the last few years in this. But it has continued, and it has been made. By almost any measure, the air is cleaner now than it was when the Clean Air Act was passed 14 years ago. And we achieved this success despite a 60-percent increase in coal-fired electric generating capacity and a 40-percent increase in the number of miles traveled by cars and trucks.

We've also seen improvement in the quality of surface water all across the country. And sometimes it still gets noisy out here—[*referring to the noise from another airplane taking off from the airport*].

The number of people that are served by wastewater treatment systems has nearly doubled just since 1970. And salmon, trout, and other species of fish are returning to rivers where they hadn't been seen for generations. Just down the river from here, around Haines Point, there used to be signs that warned potential swimmers and boaters of the dangers of the polluted waters of the Potomac. Well, today pollution warning signs are gone, and the fish have returned. And this grand old river is making a long overdue comeback.

But we have much work yet to do. Even as many environmental problems have been brought under control, new ones have been detected. And all the while the growth and shifts of population, economic expansion, and the development of new industries will intensify the competing demands on our national resources.

If we've learned any lessons during the past few decades, perhaps the most important is that preservation of our environment is not a partisan challenge; it's common sense. Our physical health, our social happiness, and our economic well-being will be sustained only by all of us working in partnership as thoughtful, effective stewards of our natural resources.

We must and will be sensitive to the delicate balance of our ecosystems, the preservation of endangered species, and the protection of our wilderness lands. We must and will be aware of the need for conservation, conscious of the irreversible harm we can do to our natural heritage, and determined to avoid the waste of our resources and the destruction of the ecological systems on which these precious resources are based.

We must and will be responsible to future generations, but at the same time let us remember that quality of life means more than protection and preservation. As Teddy Roosevelt put it, "Conservation means development as much as it does protection." Quality of life also means a good job, a decent place to live, accommodation for a growing population, and the continued economic and technological development essential to our standard of living, which is the envy of the whole world.

We can best serve the interests of the American people and generations yet to come by seeking to harmonize competing interests and to reconcile legitimate social goals. And in doing these things, we'll be a trusted friend to both the environment and to the people.

And now I'm going to move over to that table and sign the 14th annual environmental report. But before I do, I want to thank Alan Hill, the Chairman of the Council on Environmental Quality, and all the other people who took part in preparing this environmental report. Your good efforts, together with a national spirit of cooperation, will help us move forward toward the goals that we all want—the preservation of America's natural beauty, the protection and conservation of her natural resources, and a future that is economically prosperous, environmentally safe, and scenically beautiful.

So, thank you, and God bless you all.

Note: The President spoke at 1:40 p.m. on Theodore Roosevelt Island.

In his opening remarks, the President referred to the Chairman and members of the Council on Environmental Quality.

Message to the Congress Transmitting the Annual Report of the Council on Environmental Quality
July 11, 1984

To the Congress of the United States:

I am pleased to transmit to the Congress the Fourteenth Annual Report of the Council on Environmental Quality.

I have long believed that our Nation has a God-given responsibility to preserve and protect our natural resource heritage. Our physical health, our social happiness, and our economic well-being will be sustained only to the extent that we act as thoughtful stewards of our abundant natural resources.

As this report describes in detail, we are continuing to make demonstrable progress protecting and improving the quality of the Nation's air, land, and water resources. By almost any measure the air is cleaner now

than it was when the Clean Air Act was passed in 1970. Since the passage of the Clean Water Act in 1972, the volume of industrial pollutants released into lakes, rivers, and estuaries has declined sharply. In spite of economic and population growth over the past decade, water quality has remained the same or improved in virtually all United States rivers.

Our Nation is justifiably proud of this record. Since 1970, we have passed comprehensive environmental legislation that is a model for the rest of the world. We have shown people everywhere that we have the environmental awareness, the political will, and the technical understanding necessary to resolve the resource use conflicts that arise inevitably in a populous, highly industrialized nation.

But our past success should not blind us to the fact that in the future we will face even more complex questions regarding the use of our natural resources. Chemicals, both old and new, will continue to be invaluable aids in our economic development, but the benefits they bestow on all of us will have to be balanced against any possible adverse health effects caused by exposure to such chemicals. Population growth, economic expansion, and the development of new kinds of industries will intensify the competing demands on our natural resources.

In the future, we will improve our stewardship of the Nation's wealth of natural resources if we apply well the lessons of the past. We have learned that scientific understanding is essential to any successful regulatory program, but that when scientists are unsure, politicians should act with caution. We have learned that regulatory actions can be effective when they are clearly defined and strongly enforced, but that without careful attention to relative benefits and costs, they can waste one resource while preserving another. Most important of all, we have learned that the Federal government has played an important role in protecting and preserving natural resources, but that it has not acted and should not act alone. In the past, State and local governments, businesses, and private citizens all have made important contributions to environmental research, land preservation, habitat protection, and enhancement of environmental quality. If we are to continue the progress we have seen in the past, the partnership between government, businesses, and private citizens must be expanded in the future.

RONALD REAGAN

The White House,
July 11, 1984.

Note: The 341-page report is entitled "Environmental Quality 1983—14th Annual Report of the Council on Environmental Quality."

Proclamation 5221—Year of the St. Lawrence Seaway and St. Lawrence Seaway Day, 1984
July 11, 1984

By the President of the United States of America

A Proclamation

Since the French explorers of the Sixteenth Century, people have searched for a reliable way to sail into the heart of our continent. The opening of the St. Lawrence Seaway in 1959 made this dream a reality and opened North America's agricultural and industrial heartland to deep draft ocean vessels. The Seaway forged the final link in a waterway extending over 2,000 miles from Duluth, Minnesota to the Atlantic Ocean.

The building and operation of the St. Lawrence Seaway, considered one of man's most outstanding engineering feats, was a joint project of the United States and Canada and stands as a symbol of the valued and constructive cooperation which long has existed between the two countries. On the 25th Anniversary of the completion of the Seaway, it is appropriate that we recognize its role in promoting our economic prosperity.

In the quarter century since Queen Elizabeth and President Eisenhower joined in its dedication, more than one billion metric tons of cargo, valued at more than $200 billion, have moved along this trade and transportation route. As grain has moved from the farmlands of the United States and Canada to help feed the hungry around the world, Great Lakes cities have grown into international seaports. The second largest cargo shipped on the Seaway is iron ore, important to the industries of both countries.

I urge all Americans to join with our good neighbors in Canada in observing this Anniversary. Let us celebrate together a quarter century of partnership in the spirit of friendship and cooperation that has long marked United States-Canadian relations, and pledge our continued support of the international Seaway which links our two countries.

In recognition of the valuable contributions of the St. Lawrence Seaway to the Nation, the Congress, by House Joint Resolution 567, has designated 1984 as the "Year of the St. Lawrence Seaway" and June 27, 1984, as "St. Lawrence Seaway Day," and authorized and requested the President to issue an appropriate proclamation.

Now, Therefore, I, Ronald Reagan, President of the United States of America, do hereby proclaim 1984 as the Year of the St. Lawrence Seaway and June 27, 1984, as St. Lawrence Seaway Day, and I urge all Americans to join in appropriate observances.

In Witness Whereof, I have hereunto set my hand this eleventh day of July, in the year of our Lord nineteen hundred and eighty-four, and of the Independence of the United States of America the two hundred and ninth.

RONALD REAGAN

[*Filed with the Office of the Federal Register, 10:10 a.m., July 12, 1984*]

Memorandum on the Delegation of Authority for Reports and Determinations Concerning El Salvador
July 11, 1984

Memorandum for the Secretary of State

Subject: Delegation of Authority for Reports and Determinations Concerning El Salvador

By the authority vested in me as President by the Constitution and statutes of the United States of America, including Section 621 of the Foreign Assistance Act of 1961, as amended, and Section 301 of Title 3 of the United States Code, I hereby delegate to you the functions conferred upon me by the Joint Resolution "Making an urgent supplemental appropriation for the fiscal year

ending September 30, 1984, for the Department of Agriculture" (Public Law 98–332), insofar as they relate to El Salvador in an unnumbered paragraph entitled "Military Assistance" and to Section 108.

This memorandum shall be published in the *Federal Register.*

RONALD REAGAN

[*Filed with the Office of the Federal Register, 1:52 p.m., July 13, 1984*]

Note: The memorandum is printed in the Federal Register *of July 17.*

Remarks to the National Campers and Hikers Association in Bowling Green, Kentucky
July 12, 1984

The President. Thank you, Porky. Thank you, and Secretary Clark, Congressman Natcher, it's a great pleasure to be back in Kentucky. And I'm delighted to join all of

you, members of the National Campers and Hikers Association, here in this beautiful setting.

Audience member. We love you!

The President. Thank you. I know you've come from all over this land, and I've just come from Mammoth Cave National Park. [*Laughter*] And I want to give special thanks to those who make it possible for us to enjoy Mammoth Cave and all our national parks, our National Park Service.

Many of you have used camping facilities maintained by the Park Service or hiked on trails the Park Service has blazed, so I'm sure that you join with me in a feeling of great gratitude for the men and women of our National Park Service.

Now, I'm told that there are more than 20,000 of you here today, from retired couples to young families with infant children—an all-American gathering of people from every walk of life firmly united in enjoyment of the great outdoors. For more than 20 years, your National Campers and Hikers Association has been helping to enjoy the land, but in addition, in many cases, helping to preserve the beauty of the land itself.

Ever since taking office, we've urged Americans to become active in voluntarism programs, and your conservation work provides an inspiring example. You maintain wildlife refuges; you plant trees, clean up streams, parks, and highways. You've raised funds to protect endangered species like our nation's symbol, the bald eagle, and you've worked with the Department of Agriculture to control the spread of the gypsy moth, which is a blight on our woodlands.

There's another aspect of your association that I want to applaud, your support for the family. The American family is the foundation of our country's goodness and strength. Take away the sense of purpose that raising a family gives to men and women, take away the love, support, and training that children get from their parents, and all that we hold dear in this land will be in jeopardy. But by promoting activities that everyone from grandparents to toddlers can enjoy, you're keeping families together, and you're keeping them strong.

Today I want to speak about a matter that concerns us all: our efforts to protect our country's national heritage. It was near the turn of the century that concerned citizens, naturalists, and explorers first brought to the Nation's attention a series of grave threats to our environment. They pointed at dwindling resources, unprotected wilderness areas, imperiled wildlife, and a public that was uninformed.

One of the central figures in that movement, I know, has been mentioned already here today—Theodore Roosevelt, a great President, who for the first time outlined the legitimate role of the Federal Government in protecting our environment. He also, I think, was the fellow that was responsible for adding the West Wing to the White House, where the offices are, because his wife told him one day, when the White House was also all the Presidential offices, she said, "If I'm going to raise a half a dozen kids, you're going to get your people out of here." [*Laughter*]

But he said, "of all the questions which can come before this nation, short of the actual preservation of its existence . . . there is none which compares in importance with the great central task of leaving this land even a better land for our descendants than it is for us. . . ." Well, I know that all of us take pride in the measures that were set in motion by President Theodore Roosevelt and the environmental movement of his day.

In 1916 our National Park Service was created, and today it cares for 335 sites, with a total area that is bigger than Tennessee, West Virginia, and Kentucky put together. Our parks include wonders like the desert majesty of the Grand Canyon, the icy beauty of Mount McKinley; and last year alone, they were enjoyed by some 254 million visitors.

In the years since the founding of our National Park Service, other landmark environmental legislation has been passed. 1964 Wilderness Act called for areas to be set aside in wholly natural environments, lacking even roads. In 1973 the Congress passed the Endangered Species Act, one of the most far-reaching laws anywhere—anywhere in the world—to prevent the extinction of plants and animals.

During the sixties and seventies, we became aware of the growing threat of pollution, and in 1970 we created the Environmental Protection Agency. At the time some claimed that, despite the EPA, economic progress would bring in its wake more and more pollution. But advances in science and technology, born out of our system of free enterprise, combined with the work of the EPA to prove just the opposite.

There has been a 60-percent increase in coal-fired electric generation capacity during the last 14 years. Yet powerplant sulfur emissions today are lower than they were in 1970. During the decade of '70 to 1980, the number of miles traveled by cars and trucks on our highways increased by nearly 40 percent. Yet, at the same time, total pollution from those cars and trucks actually dropped by almost 20 percent. Over the same period, we've seen dramatic improvement in the quality of surface water throughout the country. Today salmon and trout are returning to rivers and streams where they haven't been seen for generations.

America has built a proud record of achievement in protecting her natural heritage over the past three-quarters of a century. At the same time that our population was growing by leaps and bounds and we were building the most productive economy on Earth, we were protecting our lands and wildlife and working successfully to keep our air and water clean.

Sadly, though, in recent years our environmental efforts began to lose some of their energy and direction. Indeed, by the time our administration came into office, the Federal Government had become somewhat negligent in its care of our natural heritage. Our parks have suffered funding declines for maintenance and were in disrepair. At Yellowstone National Park alone there were health and safety hazards that would require millions of dollars to correct.

America's wetlands were in grave danger of disappearing. State plans to combat pollution had been allowed to pile up in an enormous backlog. And the vital task of preserving endangered species had been neglected, because the Government had failed to complete the necessary recovery plans—even though those plans had long ago been mandated by the Congress.

Well, a few years ago we were faced with the worst economic crisis since the Great Depression and a weak and vacillating foreign policy that had lost the respect of friend and foe alike. Yet, even while we moved to address these twin crises, we were determined to move quickly and effectively to deal with the Federal Government's lagging efforts to protect our environment.

One of our most important efforts has involved hazardous wastes. Where wastes were mismanaged in the past, we've moved aggressively under the Superfund program. By the end of this year, the Environmental Protection Agency expects to have undertaken more than 400 actions to address contamination threats. At hundreds of other national priority sites, long-term work is underway to remove wastes and eliminate contamination of valuable land and groundwater. And as I told the Congress in that State of the Union Address, I'm committed to seeking an extension of that Superfund law. Negligent handling of toxic wastes threatens the health of thousands of Americans. And I pledge to you that your government will take all the necessary steps to protect the American people against the menace of hazardous wastes.

To combat water pollution, our administration has established more stringent standards for 19 critical industries. To deal with the threat of lead poisoning, we've issued regulations that sharply reduce the amount of lead in gasoline. In controlling pesticides, we're handling more reviews of new chemicals, and we've moved against the dangerous pesticide EDB, ethylene dibromide.

And as a first practical step to deal with acid rain, our administration is conducting extensive research. Now, some have suggested that, oh, this is just government studying something to death. No, it isn't. The more we've learned, the more we've realized how little we know about the problem that is causing some of our lakes to die and some of our forests to be affected. And so, during the coming year, we plan to spend $127 million on further research, so that before we turn loose recommendations as to what must be done about it, we'll know really what we're talking about; and we won't be wasting your tax money or that of business and industry which would increase the prices for things that you buy. As this research produces answers, we're going to put that information to work. And we'll keep working until we provide reliable protection for all our natural resources.

Each of us knows the thrill we get when we see an eagle in the mountains or a deer in the forest, and I'd like to tell you how we're trying to preserve the rich beauty and bounty of our lands and wildlife. We've added many miles to our National Trails System. And we've put scores of historic sites on the National Registries of Historical and Natural Landmarks. And to expand our National Wild and Scenic River System, we proposed adding 245 river miles along 8 different rivers.

We have a proposal that, if enacted by the Congress, will be the first comprehensive effort in our history to protect our nation's wetlands. And our Coastal Barriers Resources Act is already protecting large sections of our Gulf and Atlantic coasts, including more than 700 miles of dunes, beaches, and marshland.

To preserve our wildlife, we're working with the State of California to create a wildlife sanctuary that will protect thousands of seals and sea birds. In Texas, we're helping the State government at Aransas National Wildlife Refuge to protect the whooping crane. And we've completed recovery plans for more than 80 endangered species. Today the California condor, the Atlantic salmon, the peregrine falcon, and many other magnificent creatures have a new chance to multiply and flourish and to be here to greet our great-grandchildren.

And this brings me to a measure that I know is close to your hearts particularly: our work to refurbish and beautify our national parks. Like everyone who's ever seen them, we view our national parks as the crown jewels of the American land. And when we took office, we reversed a decline in funding that had been going on for their upkeep and inaugurated a 5-year, billion-dollar effort to give our parks the improvements they so badly needed. And I'm delighted to announce that this vital program has proceeded so well that it will be finished in 1985, a full year ahead of schedule. From Independence Hall in Philadelphia

to the Redwood Forest in California, our great national parks are getting the treatment they deserve. At Mammoth Cave National Park, our park restoration and improvement program has funded a universe of repairs and improvements. And I was just shown some of them a little while ago. Throughout the park, for example, cave trails and footpaths have been reworked to keep the caves accessible to their millions of visitors.

No treasure, I don't believe, means more to the American people than the Statue of Liberty. And right now, that grand lady in New York Harbor is getting special attention. With help from Lee Iacocca, the chairman of Chrysler, and his advisory commission, we've begun an effort to raise $230 million to give the statue and Ellis Island some sorely needed repairs. Already the American people have contributed a sizable amount.

And schoolchildren across this country have sent dimes and nickels that total more than a million dollars for this refurbishing job. The repairs will be completed in time for Miss Liberty's 100th birthday celebration on the Fourth of July, 1986. It's going to be quite a party, and you're all invited. Maybe we can announce that it's the greatest facelift that's ever been given. [*Laughter*]

But just as we believe in preserving our natural heritage, we're committed to putting it to the best possible use for the American people. Today some 175 million Americans over the age of 12 regularly participate in outdoor recreation. That's a substantial increase over past decades. And as members of the NCHA, you won't be surprised to hear that some 46 million Americans are campers. But perhaps you didn't know that more than 50 million are boaters, and some 64 million are fishermen, and about a hundred million are swimmers.

Now, make no mistake, the American land belongs to the American people, and we intend to keep it open for the American people. You may remember that under past—well, over the years past, there's been—well, there were some efforts to deal with energy shortages by attempting to ration gas and trying to keep you from using your recreational vehicles, your RV's. At one point, the Department of Energy even proposed a Sunday ban on motorboating. Now, officials admitted that the ban would have very little effect on gas supplies. But they claimed that it would have symbolic value. Well, they were right about that. The proposal did symbolize a government that had grown a little arrogant and intrusive, a government that seemed to believe that the American people should be kept away from their own lakes, rivers, and parks.

Well, forgive me, but we take a different view. We believe the environment includes people and that they, now and always, have a right to enjoy the American land. But I'm happy also to say that under our energy policy, I don't think we should ever again face a severe shortage of gasoline. Indeed, when we decontrolled, oil prices—or oil supplies increased, and today the price of gas at the pump is actually lower than it was in 1981. But if we do face a gas shortage, this administration will never respond by trying to keep the American people from enjoying the great outdoors.

In short, we believe that you can be a friend to the people at the same time that you're a friend to the land. And we're convinced that working through the wonders of science and technology, the human mind can enable our economy to grow, providing new jobs for millions, while at the same time enhancing our precious natural resources. And on these principles we have proceeded and we shall continue to act as long as we hold office.

Three thousand years ago the psalmist wrote, "I will lift up mine eyes unto the hills, from whence cometh my help." The American writer and naturalist Henry David Thoreau, whose 167th birthday we celebrate today, expressed a similar belief. "In wildness," he wrote, "is the preservation of the world." Well, today in this great open field, we know that those two writers, though separated by the centuries—what they both thought and felt.

Here in the open, close to the land, we feel refreshed and free. Here we see clearly what is important in life—the liberty our country offers, the love of our families and friends. And here it is that we're given a strong sense of the majesty of our Creator. I just have to believe that with love for our natural heritage and a firm resolve to preserve it with wisdom and care, we can and will give the American land to our children, not impaired, but enhanced. And in doing this, we'll honor the great and loving God who gave us this land in the first place.

I thank all of you for what you're doing. And God bless you all. And God bless America.

Mr. DeCabooter. Mr. President, the National Campers and Hikers Association, since it is a family camping organization, would like to present to you, President Ronald Reagan, and Mrs. Reagan—membership into the National Campers and Hikers Association.

The President. Thank you very much.

Mr. DeCabooter. And along with that, a little memento welcoming you to the National Campers and Hikers Campvention, 1984, Bowling Green, Kentucky.

The President. Thank you very much. I appreciate these and am honored by them.

I want you to know also I'm not a stranger to what it is that you love so much out there. As a matter of fact, I haven't had as many chances to do that now as I would like. But the last time I remember taking a pack trip into the High Sierras. And we had our small son along with us at the time, Nancy and I, and when we picked a place to stretch out our sleeping bags on the ground, he decided he was going over there between a couple of pine trees. And he went over there, and then we settled in.

And all of a sudden here he came—with his sleeping bag—*[laughter]*—and he put it down right by me. And then I heard the most wonderful words in the world. He says, "Well, here we are—all huddled around old dad." *[Laughter]*

Thank you all very much.

Note: The President spoke at 12:12 p.m. at the Beech Bend Campground. In his opening remarks, he referred to Richard (Porky) DeCabooter, president of the National Campers and Hikers Association, who introduced the President and Secretary of the Interior William P. Clark.

Earlier in the day, the President was briefed on the park restoration and improvement program by Robert L. Deskins,

Superintendent of Mammoth Cave National Park, and then was given a tour of a portion of Mammoth Cave.

Following his appearance at the gathering, the President returned to Washington, DC.

Message to the Congress Transmitting a United States-Denmark Fishery Agreement
July 13, 1984

To the Congress of the United States:

In accordance with the Magnuson Fishery Conservation and Management Act of 1976 (Public Law 94–265; 16 U.S.C. 1801 *et seq.*), I transmit herewith a governing international fishery agreement between the United States of the one part and Denmark and the Faroe Islands of the other part signed at Washington on June 11, 1984.

This agreement is one of a series to be renegotiated in accordance with that legislation to replace existing bilateral fishery agreements. I hereby commend this agreement to the Congress.

RONALD REAGAN

The White House,
July 13, 1984.

Remarks at a White House Luncheon for Elected Republican Women Officials and Candidates
July 13, 1984

Good afternoon, and welcome to all of you. I'm delighted to see you. And before I get into my remarks, I have to share some news with you.

You probably got this news in the briefings that have taken place already. But just in case you didn't—and if you did, it's worth repeating—our goal for the American people is a strong, growth economy with stable prices. And this morning it looks like we hit the jackpot, made a triple play. Industrial production in June was up. Retail sales in June were up. And producer prices were unchanged for the third month in a row, 0.0.

So, now I can go on that it's good to see so many old friends and also to meet some new ones, and to be joined by two of the favorite women in my life, Nancy and Maureen. I want to begin by giving each of you my heartfelt thanks for all that you've done for the Republican cause.

Politics is often fun and sometimes glam-

orous, but in the end it's the hard work of people like you that makes it possible for us to put our beliefs into practice. Your role is especially important because you demonstrate a Republican commitment to American women. And that's a commitment that runs deep.

It is kind of appropriate today I should be saying this—[*laughter*]—because, you know, some people have tried to keep this very fact I've just mentioned a secret. Well, first it was the Grand Old Party that gave its backing to women's suffrage. And then it became the first to elect a woman to the United States Congress and the first to elect women to the United States Senate who are not just filling out unexpired terms.

Today the two women in the Senate, my friends Nancy Kassebaum and Paula Hawkins, are Republicans, the only two women in the Senate. And we have nine outstanding Republican women in the House of Representatives. And I really bring this up because I think it's time that they have more company there.

Now, all of us are aware of the events that transpired yesterday among the Democrats. They have their ticket, and I'm looking forward to campaigning against it on the issues. As I said yesterday, their choice of a Vice-Presidential nominee [Geraldine A. Ferraro] is historic. And so was appointing Sandra Day O'Connor to the United States Supreme Court. And I have to tell you that the day I appointed her was one of the happier days of my life.

But what about that foolishness that it's the other major party that represents the interests of women? The truth is the Republican Party represents those interests best and in a serious and a long-term manner. We Republicans think women should change America. And that's why we have Ambassador Jeane Kirkpatrick as an eloquent and courageous voice at the United Nations. And she is changing America, as are Elizabeth Dole at Transportation and Margaret Heckler at the Department of Health and Human Services, and as are Katherine Ortega, the Treasurer of the United States, and Martha Seger at the Federal Reserve Board.

Then there's Carol Dinkins at the Justice Department and Ann Dore McLaughlin at the Department of Labor—who briefed me for my trip to Chesapeake Bay on Tuesday—Patricia Goldman at the National Transportation Safety Board, Faith Ryan Whittlesey and Margaret Tutwiler here at the White House, and so many others, like Lenora Cole-Alexander at the Department of Labor, Mary Jarratt at Agriculture, Donna Tuttle at the Commerce Department, Barbara McConnell at the CAB, and Nancy Harvey Steorts at the Consumer Product Safety Commission. And I could go on, but we'd run out of time. All are changing America, and they're changing it for the better.

Now, I know that he who lives by the crystal ball sometimes winds up eating glass. [*Laughter*] But I've said this before, and I'll say it again: There is going to be a woman President of the United States one of these days soon, and she's going to be a Republican. Why? Because we have the great talent. The women who have advanced in

our party and who are coming up through the ranks today are doing it by merit. And the American people, recognizing this, will support such a woman when she runs.

The Conservative Party of Great Britain chose Margaret Thatcher as their leader not because she was a woman, but because she was the best person for the job. There was no tokenism or cynical symbolism in what they did. She became leader of her party and Prime Minister of Great Britain because she was judged by her peers to be a superior leader. And that's how the first Republican woman President will do it.

I have to tell this—I probably shouldn't—but there was a little argument and someone, I thought, got out of line at the summit meeting in England. And I was, because it was a male, I sought her out afterwards—she was presiding—and said, "Margaret, I think that was out of line, and he shouldn't have said this." And Margaret very quietly said, "We women understand when men are being childish." [*Laughter*]

But look around you at the great talent that is in this room. The advancement of women in this party is more evidence of the growing fact that increasingly the Republican Party is the party of ideas. We're the new thing in politics these days. We are taking creative steps to free up the economy. We have the new and vital economic ideas. We're taking a new look at the family and its pivotal place in society. And we're the ones with fresh new insights on tax structure. And we're the one with the courage, conviction, and the compassion to increase personal incentives for every working American. Our party fairly crackles with ideas and dynamism, with the bustle of pioneers looking into the future and trying to make it better than the present or the past.

The past 3½ years—if you noticed—we have, all of us together, changed our country. We've led the way in helping the public understand that the great contention between the free world and the totalitarians is the preeminent struggle of our times. We've led the way in helping our country appreciate anew the fact that economic justice comes from economic freedom and that big government does not liberate men and women; it holds them down. What we've accomplished is the most exciting domestic political development since the New Deal.

And all of you in this room are an integral part of that new revolution. You're the incredible talent that's lighting our party with tremendous energy. The Republican Party is the party of the future, and it is up to all of us to reach out to all of the people in this country, to go to the union halls and the fire stations and the street corners and get the word out and let people know that the party with a vision wants their support, needs their support, and deserves their support.

It all comes down to you. Scores of gifted Republican women like you are serving in public office outside Washington. In the 23 State primaries that have been held this year to select candidates for State and Federal offices, in addition to incumbents, our party fielded over 200 women, and more than 150 of you came out of your primaries victorious.

Now, I know you're having briefings all day, but if you'd allow me, I'd like to take a moment to give you an overview of some of the other things we've been trying to do—and I'll be brief, because maybe you've already heard them. I may be plowing some ground that's already been plowed, but there are some specific proposals that we're making, working on, that directly affect women in America.

On the legislative front, we've made proposals to really toughen child support enforcement: to improve State collection of child support payments and require the adoption of proven and effective enforcement techniques. Bills containing these measures have passed both the House and the Senate, and we hope they'll emerge from a conference committee ironing out the differences between them within the next few weeks.

In pension reform, we have proposed legislation to increase protection for widowed and divorced spouses and to help women earn their own pension credits. That bill is also well on its way to enactment.

Tax equity for women is another vital field. Many of our tax equity proposals are contained in the deficit reduction act—the thing we call a downpayment—which I expect to sign very soon. The Congress, for example, adopted our proposal to permit contributions to nonprofit dependent care organizations, such as daycare centers, to be treated as tax exempt. We are more than disappointed that the Congress dropped our proposal to raise the spousal IRA limit from $2,250 to $4,000, but we're going to keep on pushing for that one, and we'll get it.

These, as well as other measures that have been passed, represent a significant advance for American women. But there's one achievement that's done more to give American women opportunity and independence than all the others combined, and it's called economic expansion.

When I took the oath of office, inflation was in double digits, the prime interest rate had hit its highest peak since the Civil War, and economic growth had just about disappeared.

The economic crisis struck women especially hard. Most elderly Americans living on fixed incomes are women, and their purchasing power was eaten up by inflation. Women saw jobs become more and more scarce, and a 12.4-percent inflation rate made buying groceries and paying bills a nightmare. The thousands of women who wanted to start their own businesses saw a 21½-percent prime interest rate slam the doors of opportunity.

Well, last year there were some 600,000 new businesses that started up, and the greater proportion of them were started by women. But the interest rates weren't 21½ percent anymore.

Now, we made the economy priority number one. We reduced the growth of Federal spending. We eliminated needless regulation, reduced personal income tax rates. And we passed an historic reform called tax indexing, that means the Government can never again use inflation as a tax increase to profit at the people's expense. We reduced the marriage tax penalty, almost doubled the maximum child-care credit, increased the limits for IRA and Keogh contributions, and eliminated estate taxes on family farms and businesses for surviving spouses.

And our greatest triumph is in the area of

employment. Right now more people are employed in the United States than at any other time in our history. And we've beaten back unemployment to 7 percent. But if you just take women's unemployment, it's less than 7 percent.

Today, from Maine to California, there's a powerful economic expansion that is taking place. As a matter of fact, I had an angry, scholarly economist write me to tell me to stop calling it economic recovery. He said, "We're past that—it is now economic expansion." [*Laughter*] And I believed him. But inflation has plummeted by more than two-thirds since we took office. It's been running at 3.6 percent for the last 3-month period.

And, as I mentioned, the Producer Price Index in June was announced this morning as unchanged—that's the third month in a row. And if we want to take it for 12 months, that's the one that precedes and predicts what the inflation rate is going to be—the Producer Price Index—it's been 2.2 percent for the last 12 months.

Retail sales, as I said, are up. The American worker's real wage is rising. Investment by U.S. business and new plants and equip-ment has risen at its fastest rate for any recovery in the last 30 years.

We Republicans have more than a good record. Together we've changed and will continue to change our country. For the last 30-odd years or more, the political debate in Washington was all having to do with how much they were going to spend and the new spending proposals. And nobody's stopped to notice that for the last few years, the debate in Washington has been all entirely on how much are we going to cut. And we've never cut as much as I think we should, but we're going to keep on doing that, too.

We know that our nation's best days are still ahead of us. We can build a country where all women and men have the chance to go forward just as far as their dreams and talents will take them—an open society led by new ideas. It's all very exciting, and we're doing it, all of us together. And if we succeed in getting the word about—out about who we are and what we're accomplishing—then I feel sure the Nation will follow us.

So, thank you, God bless you, and let's have dessert. [*Laughter*]

Note: The President spoke at 12:51 p.m. in the State Dining Room at the White House.

Executive Order 12484—Amendments to the Manual for Courts-Martial, United States, 1984
July 13, 1984

By virtue of the authority vested in me as President by the Constitution of the United States and by Chapter 47 of Title 10 of the United States Code (the Uniform Code of Military Justice), in order to prescribe amendments to the Manual for Courts-Martial, United States, 1984, prescribed by Executive Order No. 12473, it is hereby ordered as follows:

Section 1. The third paragraph of Executive Order No. 12473 is amended by inserting "12315," after "12306,".

Sec. 2. The fourth paragraph of Executive Order No. 12473 is amended by striking out "revised" and inserting in lieu thereof "reviewed".

Sec. 3. Part II of the Manual for Courts-Martial, United States, 1984, is amended as follows:

a. The Rules for Courts-Martial are amended so that the first letter of the first word of each subparagraph that is preceded by a colon or a dash is capitalized.

b. The subsection designation of R.C.M. 305(*1*) is amended by striking out "(*1*)" and inserting in lieu thereof "(1)".

c. R.C.M. 502(b)(2)(B) is amended by striking out the comma at the end thereof.

d. R.C.M. 506(a) is amended by inserting a comma after "selection".

e. R.C.M. 703(f)(3) is amended by inserting "of" after "determination".

f. R.C.M. 901(d)(4)(B) is amended by striking out "convening authority" and inserting in lieu thereof "authority who detailed the counsel".

g. R.C.M. 1003(b) is amended by italicizing the headings of the paragraphs and subparagraphs thereof.

h. The third sentence of R.C.M. 1107(e)(1)(C)(ii) is amended by striking out "lesser offense" and inserting in lieu thereof "lesser included offense".

i. The second sentence of R.C.M. 1107(h) is amended by striking out "provides" and inserting in lieu thereof "provide".

j. The fourth sentence of R.C.M. 1108(b) is amended by inserting "of" after "regardless".

k. R.C.M. 1110(b)(2)(B) is amended by striking out the comma between "accused" and "upon".

l. R.C.M. 1112(f)(2) is amended by inserting a comma between "rehearing" and "but".

m. R.C.M. 1113(c)(2) is amended by striking out "Undersecretary" and inserting in lieu thereof "Under Secretary".

n. The first sentence of R.C.M. 1113(d)(2)(C) is amended by inserting a comma between "concerned" and "unless".

o. The introductory clause of R.C.M. 1201(a)(2) is amended by inserting a dash after "which".

p. R.C.M. 1201(b)(3)(C) is amended by striking "authority or unless" and inserting in lieu thereof "authority, unless".

q. R.C.M. 1209(a)(2)(A) is amended by striking out the third comma and inserting in lieu thereof a semicolon.

Sec. 4. Part III of the Manual for Courts-Martial, United States, 1984, is amended as follows:

a. Mil. R. Evid. 315(e) is amended by striking out "guard of police" and inserting in lieu thereof "guard or police".

b. Mil. R. Evid. 321(a)(2) is amended—

(1) by inserting a colon after "if" in the introductory clause; and

(2) by capitalizing the first letter of the first word in subparagraphs (A) and (B).

c. Mil. R. Evid. 601 is amended by striking out "this" and inserting in lieu thereof "these".

Sec. 5. Part IV of the Manual for Courts-Martial, United States, 1984, is amended as follows:

a. The rules governing the punitive articles are amended so that—

(1) the subparagraph headings are italicized; and

(2) The first letter of the first word after the semicolon in each Note is capitalized.

b. The sample finding of the specification accompanying paragraph 2b(3) (concerning Article 79) is amended by inserting a semicolon after the phrase "willfully and unlawfully kill".

c. paragraph 10b(3)(d) (concerning Article 86) is amended by striking out "that" and inserting in lieu thereof "That".

d. Paragraph 42b(3) (concerning Article 117) is amended by striking out the semicolon and inserting in lieu thereof a period.

e. Paragraph 51b (concerning Article 125) is amended by redesignating subparagraphs (a), (b), and (c) as subparagraphs (1), (2), and (3) respectively.

f. The subparagraph designation for the sample specification in paragraph 68 (concerning worthless check offenses under Article 134) is amended by striking out the "d" and inserting in lieu thereof "f".

g. The sample specification in paragraph 95 (concerning misprision of a serious offense under Article 134) is amended by striking out the comma after "to about _____ ".

h. The sample specification in paragraph 96 (concerning the offense of obstructing justice under Article 134) is amended by striking out "[(recommend dismissal of the charges against said _____)" and inserting in lieu thereof "[recommend dismissal of the charges against said _____]".

Sec. 6. Part V of the Manual for Courts-Martial, United States, 1984, is amended as follows:

a. The third sentence of paragraph 2a is amended by striking out "paragraph" and inserting "subparagraph" in lieu thereof.

b. Subparagraph 4b(2) is amended by striking out "subparagraph" each time it appears and inserting "paragraph" in lieu thereof.

c. Paragraph 5b is amended by striking

out "subparagraph 5d" and inserting in lieu thereof "paragraph 5d".

d. Subparagraphs 5b(1)(A), 5b(1)(B), 5b(2)(A), and 5b(2)(B) are amended so that the first letter of the first word thereof is capitalized.

e. The introductory clause of subparagraph 5b(2) is amended by inserting a dash after "command".

f. Subparagraph 5b(2)(B)(vi) is amended by striking out the semicolon and inserting a period in lieu thereof.

g. The third sentence of subparagraph 5c(1) and the first sentence of subparagraph 7f(1) are amended by striking out "part" and inserting in lieu thereof "Part".

Sec. 7. The Secretary of Defense, on behalf of the President, shall transmit a copy of this Order to the Congress of the United States in accord with Section 836 of Title 10 of the United States Code.

RONALD REAGAN

The White House,
July 13, 1984.

[*Filed with the Office of the Federal Register, 10:11 a.m., July 16, 1984*]

Executive Order 12485—Central Intelligence Agency Retirement and Disability System
July 13, 1984

By the authority vested in me as President of the United States of America by Section 292 of the Central Intelligence Agency Retirement Act of 1964 for Certain Employees, as amended (50 U.S.C. 403 note), and in order to conform further the Central Intelligence Agency Retirement and Disability System to certain amendments of the Civil Service Retirement and Disability System pursuant to Public Law 98–94, it is hereby ordered as follows:

Section 252(h)(2)(A) of the Central Intelligence Agency Retirement Act of 1964 for Certain Employees, as amended, shall be deemed to be amended by striking out "October 1, 1982" and inserting in lieu thereof "October 1, 1983.".

RONALD REAGAN

The White House,
July 13, 1984.

[*Filed with the Office of the Federal Register, 10:12 a.m., July 16, 1984*]

Proclamation 5222—Year of the Ocean
July 13, 1984

By the President of the United States of America

A Proclamation

The United States has long depended upon the ocean for food, transportation, national security, and recreation. Today, the ocean has become even more important to the people of our Nation—as a source of petroleum and minerals and an avenue for foreign trade. In addition, the ocean is a constant source of employment for hundreds of thousands of Americans each year.

This Nation is the steward of the resources of the ocean. Americans have long cherished the freedom of the coastal regions which border our shores. The ocean is the link between the many countries with which we have shared the discoveries of modern technology in the development of oceanography.

Our increased use of the ocean requires

that we work to protect this resource effectively and efficiently. In order to do so, we must educate Americans concerning the role of the ocean in our lives and our responsibility to match increased uses of marine resources with vigilant efforts to preserve the ocean environment for the benefit of future generations.

In recognition of the importance of expanding public awareness and knowledge of the importance of the ocean and its resources, the Congress, by Senate Joint Resolution 257, has designated July 1, 1984, to July 1, 1985, as the "Year of the Ocean" and has authorized and requested the President to issue a proclamation in observance of this event.

Now, Therefore, I, Ronald Reagan, President of the United States of America, do hereby proclaim the year July 1, 1984, to July 1, 1985, as the Year of the Ocean. I call upon the people of the United States to observe such celebration with appropriate activities.

In Witness Whereof, I have hereunto set my hand this thirteenth day of July, in the year of our Lord nineteen hundred and eighty-four, and of the Independence of the United States of America the two hundred and ninth.

RONALD REAGAN

[*Filed with the Office of the Federal Register, 10:10 a.m., July 16, 1984*]

Note: The proclamation was released by the Office of the Press Secretary on July 14.

Radio Address to the Nation on Environmental Issues
July 14, 1984

My fellow Americans:

I'd like to talk to you today about our environment. But as I mentioned earlier this week, in doing so I might be letting you in on a little secret—as a matter of fact, one of the best-kept secrets in Washington.

More than 15 years ago, the State of California decided that we needed to take action to combat the smog that was choking the beautiful cities of my home State. Out of that concern was born the first serious program to require manufacturers to build cleaner cars and help control air pollution. The auto industry had to build two kinds of cars—one that would be for sale in the other 49 States and one that would meet the stiff antipollution standards required in California.

We had other concerns in California, such as protecting our magnificent and unique coastline. And we took the lead in that area as well. It took the rest of the Nation a few years to catch on, but in 1970 the Congress followed California's lead and enacted the Clean Air Act. Other laws to protect and clean up the Nation's lakes and rivers were passed, and America got on with the job of protecting the environment.

Part of the secret I mentioned is that I happened to have been Governor of California back when much of this was being done. Now, obviously, neither the problems in California nor those nationally have been solved, but I'm proud of having been one of the first to recognize that States and the Federal Government have a duty to protect our natural resources from the damaging effects of pollution that can accompany industrial development.

The other part of the well-kept secret has to do with the environmental record of our administration, which is one of achievement in parks, wilderness land, and wildlife refuges. According to studies by the Environmental Protection Agency, the quality of our air and water has continued to improve during our administration. In many big cities, the number of days on which pollution alerts are declared has gone down. And if you live near a river, you may have noticed that the signs have been coming down that used to warn people not to fish or swim.

We came to Washington committed to respect the great bounty and beauty of God's creation. We believe very strongly in the concept of stewardship, caring for the resources we have so they can be shared and used productively for generations to come. And we've put that philosophy to work, correcting deficiencies of past policies and advancing long-overdue initiatives.

Let me give you some facts that our critics never seem to remember. When we took office in 1980, we faced a dusty shelf of reports which pointed out our predecessors had been so busy spending money on new lands for parks that they seriously neglected basic upkeep of the magnificent parks we had. So, we temporarily put off acquiring new parkland and started a new billion-dollar, 5-year program to repair and modernize facilities at our national parks and wildlife refuges. If you've been to just about any national park lately, you've probably seen the results.

We've nearly finished repairing the damage from years of neglect, and I've asked the Congress for almost $160 million to resume buying lands to round out our national park and refuge systems.

We also took the lead in developing a new approach to protecting some 700 miles of undeveloped coastal areas—the dunes, beaches, and barrier islands that are some of our most beautiful and productive natural resources.

Now, there are some who want you to believe that commitment to protecting the environment can be measured by comparing the budgets of EPA under the previous administration with those proposed and approved by the Congress under my administration. But they deliberately ignore that the major Federal environmental laws are designed to be carried out by the States in partnership with EPA.

By the time the clean air, clean water, and other big programs put in place in the early 1970's moved into their second decade, the States had largely taken over the job formerly performed by the Federal Government. With the successful delegation to the States, EPA, under the leadership of Bill Ruckelshaus, has been freed to move on to the challenges of the 1980's—such as cleaning up abandoned toxic waste dumps.

Under our administration, funding for the Superfund cleanup program will have increased from just over a hundred million dollars in 1981 to $620 million in 1985. By the end of this year, EPA expects to have undertaken more than 400 emergency actions to remove and contain public health hazards. And because we recognize that we need to do more cleanup work than the current law provides, I'm committed to seeking an extension of the Superfund program.

As I said, our progress on protecting the environment is one of the best-kept secrets in Washington. But it's not, by far, the only secret. And I'll have more on that in the months ahead.

Until next week, thanks for listening, and God bless you.

Note: The President spoke at 12:06 p.m. from Camp David, MD.

Remarks on Signing the Captive Nations Week Proclamation
July 16, 1984

I know I speak for Vice President Bush when I say that we're delighted to have you all here and delighted to welcome you. But I'm very much aware that in your case that word "delight" does not nearly suffice.

I look at you, and I know I'm looking at people who have seen and suffered the full gamut of totalitarian terror. Some of you lost friends and loved ones in your struggles. And some of you risked your lives and all your earthly belongings, and you'll bear scars for the rest of your life. You're men and women of courage, heroes who have devoted a lifetime to struggle for God's greatest gift—for freedom. And for that, I can only say I'm honored to be here with you today, and I'll be proud to stand by you always.

You understand that the struggle for freedom is the preeminent struggle of our time. One of the great tragedies of our age is that ugly, sinister walls continue to deny for the millions trapped behind them the most basic yearnings of the human spirit. And let us make it plain that we must and will condemn all tyrants who deny their citizens human rights, whether they be dictators of the left or the right.

I've often thought to myself—in fact, I've mentioned a few times—I don't think there is a left or right, because if you follow that far enough either way, you suddenly find they've come together, and they all have the same characteristics. I think we ought to start talking about an up or down—up to the ultimate in individual freedom, consistent with an orderly society, or down through statism until you arrive at totalitarianism.

But for the sake of our security and for the sake of our freedom, let us understand the nature of the single greatest challenge to human rights in the world today: It's the challenge of one system that puts itself above God, that demands control over people's lives, and that defines its very existence by the relentless drive to conquer more and more lands. And that system is, today, Communist totalitarianism.

Look at the lesson of history. Many nations today have been conquered by force—not by moral force, not by persuasion, and certainly not by the tides of history. No, they were seized by forces of violence—by tanks and guns in Poland, Hungary, and Czechoslovakia; by bombs, chemical poisons, and forced starvation in Afghanistan, Vietnam, and Kampuchea; and everywhere by the forces of persecution against innocent people—people whose only crime might have been a simple faith, a love of their God, a longing to worship as Moslems, Buddhists, Jews, or followers of Jesus Christ. They were taken captives by force, and they remain captives by force.

The citizens of Nicaragua are the latest to join this unhappy lot, victims of the campaign of persecution against liberty and faith that follows every Communist takeover. The Archbishop of Managua, Miguel Obando y Bravo, and the members of his flock have recently been singled out as enemies by the Sandinista regime. Last week the Archbishop said, "We're in the presence of a Marxist-Leninist government that cannot accept an independent Church. The government's goal," he said, "is to eliminate the Church, to eliminate priests who are loyal to the Pope and to the Church hierarchy." And Pope John Paul II said, "I express my firm disapproval in my intimate participation in the suffering of the Church in Nicaragua." And I know I speak for millions of Americans who join the Pope in saying we, too, disapprove, and yes, people of Nicaragua, we, too, suffer with you.

Democracy is far from perfect. But democracy does not wage war on its neighbors; it doesn't build walls to keep its people in; and it doesn't organize armies of secret police to spy on them and keep them quiet. Democracy reflects all the mistakes, all the frailties, but also all the deepest hopes and dreams of the human spirit. And democracy rests upon a noble principle that has and always will make tyrants tremble: Government derives its legitimacy from the consent of the governed.

And that is why people with their innate good sense have never chosen of their own free will to live as slaves. But millions have risked their lives to escape the darkness of oppression and to live in the sunlight of freedom. And that's why we can say here today with certain knowledge that our path is the right and good path and that, yes, democracy is the way of the future.

To all those trapped in tyranny, wherever they may be, let us speak with one voice—not as Republicans or Democrats, but as Americans—saying you are not alone; your dreams are not in vain. Hold onto your dreams, because the tide of the future is a freedom tide, and totalitarianism cannot hold it back.

We're peaceful people. We occupy no countries. We seek no confrontation with any nation. As I've said repeatedly, there's nothing we want more, nothing we're trying harder to achieve than to bring about a more peaceful world. Peace is our highest aspiration. We're prepared for peace and prepared to persist for peace.

James Russell Lowell wrote, "Endurance is the crowning quality in patience, all the passion of great hearts. One day, with life and heart, is more than enough to find a world."

We will always summon our freedom to work another day to make this world a safer place. But as we go forward in this worthy endeavor, let us also remember who we are and what we stand for. We're a nation under God, and His divine spirit of truth and love must guide and always remain central to our existence. Yes, we stand for peace, but we stand for peace with freedom and for peace with dignity.

And when we speak of the dignity of the individual, nothing could be more tragic than the fate of the Nobel Prize winner, Doctor Andrei Sakharov, and his wife, Yelena Bonner, who are currently suffering severe persecution and are cut off from the rest of humanity. The world demands to know the fate of these two good and courageous people. So, to those who believe our policy must always be willful ignorance of ugly truths, must be silence in the face of persecution, and appeasement or surrender to aggression, I say, no, that price is far too steep, and we dare not and will never pay it.

If our observance of Captive Nations Week is to have meaning, then it must be observed in word and in deed. Today I'm calling on people everywhere who enjoy the blessings of liberty to join with us in helping the freedom fighters in Afghanistan, because they need our support, they want our support, and they deserve our support. The cause of peace is not served by a conquering force of more than a hundred thousand Soviet troops. The cause of peace will only be served when those troops are out and Afghanistan belongs again to the Afghan people.

And today I'm appealing to those who refuse to help the freedom fighters in Nicaragua, refuse to assist their courageous struggle for democracy, for freedom of the press, and for freedom of assembly and worship in their homeland. I urge you to ponder long and hard, to reflect on the fatal consequences of complacency and isolationism, and, above all, to understand that freedom is never more than one generation away from extinction.

It's vital for the sake of our own future that the Congress and the American people respond to the democratic aspirations of the Nicaraguan people. Freedom's greatest shield is a shield of truth, and our shield is stonger today than ever before.

I'm proud to tell you that we've begun an initiative that will bring words of truth and a message of hope to millions of imprisoned people throughout the world. The construction budget of the Voice of America was only $2.6 million in 1981. So, our administration has developed a 6-year, $1 billion program to modernize the Voice of America. And I'm pleased to report that the Congress has voted to provide nearly a hundred million dollars for 1985.

We're also committed to expanding significantly the ability of Radio Free Europe and Radio Liberty to communicate with the peoples of Eastern Europe and the Soviet Union. And we're pleased that the Congress has authorized the establishment of Radio Marti, which will broadcast the truth to the people of Cuba.

There is cause for hope and promise. And so, I thank you for your faith, for your courage. And I thank you for standing together, because, with you by our side, we'll keep our sights on the farthest stars; we'll climb higher; we will be a shining city on a hill. Our time is now.

And now I'm going to sign the Captive Nations Week proclamation. And thank you very much, and God bless you all.

Note: The President spoke at 11:30 a.m. in the East Room at the White House.

Proclamation 5223—Captive Nations Week, 1984
July 16, 1984

By the President of the United States of America

A Proclamation

Once each year, all Americans are asked to pause and to remember that their liberties and freedoms, often taken for granted, are forbidden to many nations around the world. America continues to be dedicated to the proposition that all men are created equal. If we are to sustain our commitment to this principle, we must recognize that the peoples of the Captive Nations are endowed by the Creator with the same rights to give their consent as to who shall govern them as those of us who are privileged to live in freedom. For those captive and oppressed peoples, the United States of America stands as a symbol of hope and inspiration. This leadership requires faithfulness towards our own democratic principles as well as a commitment to speak out in defense of mankind's natural rights.

Though twenty-five years have passed since the original designation of Captive Nations Week, its significance has not diminished. Rather, it has undeniably increased—especially as other nations have fallen under Communist domination. During Captive Nations Week we must take time to remember both the countless victims and the lonely heroes; both the targets of carpet bombing in Afghanistan, and individuals such as imprisoned Ukrainian patriot Yuriy Shukhevych. We must draw strength from the actions of the millions of freedom fighters in Communist-occupied countries, such as the signers of petitions for religious rights in Lithuania, or the members of Solidarity, whose public protests require personal risk and sacrifice that is almost incomprehensible to the average citizen in the Free World. It is in their struggle for freedom that we can find the true path to genuine and lasting peace.

For those denied the benefits of liberty we shall continue to speak out for their freedom. On behalf of the unjustly persecuted and falsely imprisoned, we shall continue to call for their speedy release and offer our prayers during their suffering. On behalf of the brave men and women who suffer persecution because of national origin, religious beliefs, and their desire for liberty, it is the duty and the privilege of the United States of America to demand that the signatories of the United Nations Charter and the Helsinki Accords live up to their pledges and obligations and respect the principles and spirit of those international agreements and understandings.

During Captive Nations Week, we renew our efforts to encourage freedom, independence, and national self-determination for those countries struggling to free themselves from Communist ideology and totalitarian oppression, and to support those countries which today are standing face-to-face against Soviet expansionism. One cannot call for freedom and human rights for the people of Asia and Eastern Europe while ignoring the struggles of our own neighbors in this hemisphere. There is no difference between the weapons used to oppress the people of Laos and Czechoslovakia, and those sent to Nicaragua to terrorize its own people and threaten the peace and prosperity of its neighbors.

The Congress, by joint resolution approved July 17, 1959 (73 Stat. 212), has authorized and requested the President to designate the third week in July as "Captive Nations Week."

Now, Therefore, I, Ronald Reagan, President of the United States of America, do hereby proclaim the week beginning July 15, 1984, as Captive Nations Week. I invite the people of the United States to observe this week with appropriate ceremonies and activities to reaffirm their dedication to the international principles of justice and freedom, which unite us and inspire others.

In Witness Whereof, I have hereunto set my hand this 16th day of July, in the year of our Lord nineteen hundred and eighty-four, and of the Independence of the United

States of America the two hundred and ninth.

RONALD REAGAN

[*Filed with the Office of the Federal Register, 10:41 a.m., July 17, 1984*]

Statement on the Conference on Confidence and Security Building Measures and Disarmament in Europe
July 17, 1984

Today I met with Ambassador James E. Goodby, the chief of the U.S. delegation to the Conference on Confidence and Security Building Measures and Disarmament in Europe. This Conference, commonly known as the CDE or the Stockholm Conference, involves the U.S., Canada, and 33 European nations and is part of the East-West dialog which originated in the Helsinki accords of 1975.

Ambassador Goodby briefed me on the second round of the Conference, which has just concluded, and on the prospects for progress when the talks resume in September. He noted the continuing efforts of the U.S. and our NATO allies to achieve an outcome which will genuinely increase mutual confidence and reduce the risk of war in Europe. Earlier, in the first round of the Conference, the West put forward a package of concrete proposals designed to achieve these goals.

In an effort to achieve progress in Stockholm, I announced in June in my address to the Irish Parliament that the United States is prepared to consider the Soviet proposal for a declaration on the non-use of force if the Soviet Union is willing to discuss concrete measures to put that principle into action. We are disappointed, however, that the Soviet Union has so far failed to join the great majority of the 35 participating nations at Stockholm, who have demonstrated a desire to begin such concrete negotiations.

I assured Ambassador Goodby that he has my continuing strong support in our efforts to get on with the practical negotiations for which this Conference was intended. We will continue to do our best to achieve progress at Stockholm, just as we and our allies are working hard together in other multilateral areas of arms control—such as the East-West conventional force talks in Vienna and the 40-nation Conference on Disarmament in Geneva.

We are equally ready to seek resolutions to bilateral U.S.-Soviet arms control issues on a flexible basis, but there must of course be a willingness on both sides to engage in practical discussions. We, for our part, will not be found wanting.

Nomination of Leon Jerome Weil To Be United States Ambassador to Nepal
July 17, 1984

The President today announced his intention to nominate Leon Jerome Weil to be Ambassador to the Kingdom of Nepal. He would succeed Carleton S. Coon, Jr.

Mr. Weil was with Steiner Rouse and Co. in New York, NY, in 1950–1974, serving successively as registered representative, branch office manager, partner, executive vice president, and chairman of the executive committee. Since 1974 he has been with Herzfeld and Stern in New York, NY, as general partner and is currently senior vice president. He has been a member of the President's Council on Physical Fitness and Sports since 1981. He is also a member of the board of trustees of Outward Bound,

Inc., the Robert A. Taft Institute of Government, and the Berkshire School (Sheffield, MA).

Mr. Weil graduated from Princeton University (B.A., 1949). He is married to the former Mabel Selig and has three children. He was born June 15, 1927, in New York, NY.

Statement on an Agreement To Improve the Direct Communications Link Between the United States and the Soviet Union
July 17, 1984

I am happy to be able to announce today that we and the Soviet Union have reached agreement to expand and improve the operation of the direct communications link, or the hotline.

This agreement is a modest but positive step toward enhancing international stability and reducing the risk that accident, miscalculation, or misinterpretation could lead to confrontation or conflict between the U.S. and the Soviet Union.

With the addition of a facsimile capability, we will not only be able to exchange messages faster; but for the first time we will be able to send graphic material such as maps or pictures which would play a crucial role in helping to resolve certain types of crises or misunderstandings.

The negotiations which led to this agreement began about 1 year ago, August 1983, based upon a series of proposals that we first made in May 1983.

In developing this and other initiatives designed to reduce the risk of war due to accident, misunderstanding, or miscalculation, we had the benefit of excellent advice from a number of key congressional leaders, including Senators Warner and Nunn and the late Senator Jackson.

I see this agreement as both an appropriate technical improvement to the hotline, which has served both our governments well for over 20 years, and as a good example of how we can, working together, find approaches which can move us towards a reduction in the risks of war.

Remarks on Signing a National Minimum Drinking Age Bill
July 17, 1984

That's not emotion—that's that light right there in front of me. [*Laughter*] Well, thank you all, and please be seated. Vice President Bush and—did I see my friend Governor Kean here? There. How are you? Governor Kean, Members of the Congress, and Secretary Dole, Candy Lightner, all of you who've been fighting this good fight: Good afternoon, and welcome to the White House.

When I accepted my party's nomination for the Presidency—that was 4 years ago today—I shared a vision of the future. I said that we needed a rebirth of an American

tradition of leadership at every level of government and private life as well.

I said that we needed a rebirth of an American tradition of leadership of that kind, because the United States of America is unique in world history. It has a genius for leaders at many—of many leaders on many levels. And since then we've seen the rise of a great national movement, a movement that's led by men and women in all walks of life. It began in the community; it spread to State governments; and now it's won wide support here in our Nation's Capital—the movement against drunk driving.

The bill we're gathered to sign today reflects the will of the American people. It takes the battle to stop drunk driving one crucial step further. And permit me to tell you why I believe that this bill is so important.

We know that drinking plus driving spell death and disaster. We know that people in the 18-to-20 age group are more likely to be in alcohol-related accidents than those in any other age group. We know that America has a clear stake in making certain that her sons and daughters, so full of vitality and promise, will not be crippled or killed. And I know there's one—we all know that there is one simple measure that will save thousands of young lives that are in the drinking age—if we, or if we raise the drinking age, I should say, to 21.

Now, raising that drinking age is not a fad or an experiment. It's a proven success. Nearly every State that has raised the drinking age to 21 has produced a significant drop in the teenage driving fatalities. In the State of New Jersey, whose Governor made it a very personal crusade for himself, the rate dropped by 26 percent; Illinois, it has fallen 23 percent; in Michigan, 31 percent. And when the Commission on Drunk Driving submitted its report, it forcefully recommended that all 50 States should make 21 the legal drinking age.

And yet, today, less than half that number have the age-21 law. And that leaves us with a crazy quilt of different States' drinking laws and far too many blood borders, borders where teens drive across to reach States with lower drinking ages. And these teenagers drink and then careen home and all too often cause crippling or fatal accidents.

This problem is bigger than the individual States. It's a grave national problem, and it touches all our lives. With the problem so clear-cut and the proven solution at hand, we have no misgiving about this judicious use of Federal power. I'm convinced that it will help persuade State legislators to act in the national interest to save our children's lives, by raising the drinking age to 21 across the country.

Now, many have toiled hard to make this bill possible—Members of Congress, Secretary Dole, thousands of concerned Americans like Mothers Against Drunk Driving, the Students Against Drunk Driving—by supporting legislation, they've done this nation a service. And each of them certainly have my heartfelt thanks and, I think, the thanks of all the people in our country.

So, God bless you. And I am now going to write instead of talk, I'll sign.

Note: The President spoke at 1:29 p.m. in the Rose Garden at the White House. In his opening remarks, he referred to Candy Lightner, president and founder of Mothers Against Drunk Drivers, and Secretary of Transportation Elizabeth H. Dole.

As enacted, H.R. 4616 is Public Law 98–363, approved July 17.

Statement on Signing the Land Remote-Sensing Commercialization Act of 1984
July 17, 1984

I am pleased to sign H.R. 5155, a bill that facilitates the commercialization of the Federal Government's civilian land remote-sensing satellite system, known as Landsat. This legislation, which recognizes that competitive private sector involvement in land remote sensing is in the national interest, is a good example of cooperation between the administration and Congress.

One of the administration's primary goals in implementing this legislation will be to develop a program that requires minimum government involvement. The administration's policies of limiting burdensome governmental regulation and encouraging competition in the marketplace will guide the Secretary of Commerce's implementation of this legislation, and we will make every effort to minimize the duration and amount of any Federal subsidy.

Two provisions of the bill deserve special comment since the Attorney General has advised that they establish a procedure which is unconstitutional. Sections 202(c) and 303(c) require the Secretary of Commerce to transmit to the appropriate congressional committees any decision to enter into a contract under titles II and III of the bill and to wait for 30 days before implementing that decision. These sections also provide that the committees may, in effect, waive the prescribed waiting periods. Under the Supreme Court's decision in *Immigration and Naturalization Service* v. *Chadha*, 103 S. Ct. 2761 (1983), Congress, including committees of Congress, may not be given power which has "the purpose and effect of altering the legal rights, duties and relations of persons, including . . . Executive Branch officials . . .," through procedures which bypass the constitutional requirements for valid legislative action. Thus, the provisions in this bill purporting to empower the relevant committees to "waive" the 30-day waiting period are, under that Supreme Court decision, unconstitutional.

I extend my appreciation to the Congress for the careful and timely consideration given this legislation, and I look forward to the successful commercialization of the Landsat system. This commercialization represents one of the administration's major efforts to return to the private sector those activities which it can best perform.

Note: As enacted, H.R. 5155 is Public Law 98–365, approved July 17.

Statement on Signing the Deficit Reduction Act of 1984
July 18, 1984

I am today signing H.R. 4170. In signing this important legislation, I must vigorously object to certain provisions that would unconstitutionally attempt to delegate to the Comptroller General of the United States, an officer of Congress, the power to perform duties and responsibilities that in our constitutional system may be performed only by officials of the executive branch. This administration's position on the unconstitutionality of these provisions was clearly articulated to Congress by the Department of Justice on April 20, 1984. I am instructing the Attorney General to inform all executive branch agencies as soon as possible with respect to how they may comply with the provisions of this bill in a manner consistent with the Constitution.

Note: As enacted, H.R. 4170 is Public Law 98–369, approved July 18.

Nomination of Larry C. Williamson To Be United States Ambassador to Gabon and Sao Tome and Principe
July 18, 1984

The President today announced his intention to nominate Larry C. Williamson, of California, a career member of the Senior Foreign Service, class of Counselor, as Ambassador to the Gabonese Republic and to serve concurrently and without additional compensation as Ambassador to the Democratic Republic of Sao Tome and Principe. He would succeed Francis Terry McNamara.

Mr. Williamson served in the United States Marine Corps in 1951–1953 as first lieutenant. He entered the Foreign Service in 1958 and was staff assistant and deputy to the United Nations adviser in the Bureau of European and Canadian Affairs in the Department in 1959–1961. He was economic affairs officer in Freetown (1961–1963) and deputy principal officer and economic officer in Lusaka (1963–1966). In the Department he was international relations officer in the Executive Secretariat (1966–1968) and career management officer in the Bureau of Personnel (1968–1969). He was on detail to the Office of Economic Opportunity as executive secretary in 1969–1970. He was economic and commercial officer in Dar es Salaam (1970–1973), commercial attaché in London (1973–1977), and counselor for economic and commercial affairs in Nairobi (1977–1980). In 1980–1981, he was in the Department as Deputy Director of the Office of East African Affairs, and Director of the Office of African Inter-Regional Affairs in 1981–1983. Since 1983 he has been Chief of the Aviation Negotiations Division in the Bureau of Economic and Business Affairs.

Mr. Williamson graduated from the University of Louisville (B.A., 1951) and the University of California at Berkeley (M.A., 1957). His foreign languages are French and Kiswahili. He was born May 16, 1930, in Fort Smith, AR.

Remarks by Telephone to the Annual Convention of American Ex-Prisoners of War
July 18, 1984

The President. I just want to say that this is a great honor for me—all of you by your examples have set a pattern of dedication to country and duty—and to address you now on this your 37th annual convention.

I know that you represent POW's from every major war—World War I, II, and Korea and Vietnam. And all four of those wars have taken place in my lifetime. There were 121,000 Americans in the war that I participated in, World War II. And you deserve the Nation's respect and gratitude for the sacrifices.

Those service men and women who were placed in circumstances, including all of you—they called for special sacrifice and extraordinary bravery. Only those who have been POW's can realize the trauma of being captured and the indignities and hardships that you had to endure. And your families suffered with them. I know that's one of the reasons why you're out in front of all of us in continuing to show compassion for the over 2,000 Americans that are unaccounted for in Southeast Asia and their families and what they're going through. So, I just welcome this opportunity to thank all of you.

You know, in a previous life of mine, I played in a picture called "Prisoner of War" that had to do with Korea, and—the Korean war—and I thought that, well, that was the closest example that I had then in that make-believe, and in the close contact with a true prisoner who guided us in many of the things that we were doing on the screen—a former prisoner—and I thought that that would probably be the only experience that I had that was at all in keeping with what you have gone through. Then, of course, I began thinking about my present job. [*Laughter*]

No, seriously, I think we all do know and just—I welcome this opportunity to wish you well in this 37th annual convention and at the same time then to thank you on behalf of all Americans for the sacrifice that you made.

Mr. Ferruci. The over 1,000 former POW's and their wives here in the room appreciate the time that you've taken to speak with us this morning.

The President. Well, God bless you all.

Mr. Darrington. Mr. President, as you can see and—hear, rather, this is a very appreciative group for you and for our love of our country. And we want you to know again that we appreciate you calling, speaking to the American Ex-prisoners of War in our 37th annual convention.

The President. My heartfelt thanks to you. Good luck.

Mr. Ferruci. Thank you.

Mr. Darrington. Thank you.

Note: The President spoke at 1:26 p.m. from *the Oval Office at the White House to the convention in Seattle, WA. Tony Ferruci was the convention's program director and Earl Darrington is national commander of the American Ex-Prisoners of War.*

Remarks to an Outreach Working Group on United States Policy in Central America
July 18, 1984

I'm very pleased to be here with you. And I want to take this opportunity to thank Faith Whittlesey for her continuing efforts to keep all of you informed about developments in Central America and about United States policy for that region.

Over the last year, these Central American outreach group meetings have been held. You've heard from dozens of witnesses telling you what has happened to them, to their country, and to their hopes for freedom, democracy, and peace.

Tomorrow will be an especially poignant anniversary for our democratic Nicaraguan friends. They'll recall the joy that they felt 5 years ago. A dictatorship was defeated, and a democracy was promised for their future by the Sandinistas, who had led the revolution. But the Sandinista revolution is a revolution betrayed, a revolution that has left in its wake a trail of broken promises, broken hearts, and broken dreams.

Tragically, there is far less personal freedom, far more repression in Nicaragua today than there was 5 years ago. And I'm told there are several among you here who have seen firsthand the truth of these words.

The Nicaraguan people are trapped in a totalitarian dungeon, trapped by a military dictatorship that impoverishes them while its rulers live in privileged and protected luxury and openly boast their revolution will spread to Nicaragua's neighbors as well. It's a dictatorship made all the more insulting, all the more dangerous by the unwanted presence of thousands of Cuban, Soviet-bloc, and radical Arab helpers.

I know you've heard how the Catholic Church has been persecuted and treated as an enemy by the Sandinista regime. When the priests who were expelled from Nicaragua reached Costa Rica last Monday they celebrated a mass in San José with Archbishop Roman Arrieta of San José. The Archbishop said in his homily, "There were still in the world men and women of good will who did not believe a totalitarian regime had enthroned itself in Nicaragua." Then he said, "Now those people know the truth."

Well, unfortunately, all of them don't know the truth. I have just read in today's press where September 14 to 16 in Cleveland, Ohio, there will be a meeting brought about by several organizations in our country, and it will be—or is billed as a nationwide conference against U.S. military intervention in Central America. Well, if 55 trainers in a country like El Salvador is military intervention, I think they're exaggerating a little bit.

The Pope, who was so outrageously insulted during his mass in Managua in March of 1983, asked for prayers for the church in Nicaragua. He expressed his disapproval and his intimate suffering with those who live under the boot of Sandinista oppression. And as I said on Monday at the marking of Captive Nations Week, I know I speak for millions of Americans who join the Pope in saying: We, too, disapprove. And, yes, people of Nicaragua, we, too, suffer with you.

If the Sandinistas want cooperation and friendship from the civilized world, then they can start by treating their own citizens in a civilized manner. They can start honoring their promises of freedom—freedom of speech, freedom of assembly, freedom of worship. And they can agree to abide by the most basic and honorable principle of a democracy: that government must derive its legitimacy from the consent of the governed.

All of us who cherish democratic values should insist the Sandinistas permit genuinely open and fair and free democratic elections. We must insist that the Sandinistas, like their Guatemalan, Honduran, and El Salvadoran neighbors, open their doors to representatives from democratic organizations to observe their upcoming elections, especially the Organization of American States, OAS, because it was to the OAS that they promised democracy. And the OAS recognized the Sandinista regime based on these promises.

Tomorrow, I will be meeting in South Carolina with Caribbean leaders who know from firsthand experience how a hostile country in their midst can threaten their stability and security. As our Congress returns next week, I urge them once again to understand our responsibility as a trustee of freedom and to vote for the resources that I have requested to support democracy in Central America. And I hope all of you will continue attending these Central American outreach meetings.

Aleksandr Solzhenitsyn once asked: "Can one part of humanity learn from the bitter experience of another? Is it possible to warn someone of danger? How many witnesses have been sent to the West in the last 60 years? How many waves of emigrants? How many millions of persons? They're all here. You meet them every day. You know who they are: if not by their spiritual disorientation, their grief, their melancholy, then you can distinguish them by their accents or their external appearance. Coming from different countries, without consulting with one another, they have brought you exactly the same experience; they tell you exactly the same thing—they warn you of what is now taking place and of what has taken place in the past."

Well, I do believe that it's possible to warn of danger, to learn from the millions of witnesses who have come to the West fleeing totalitarianism. But we must not turn a blind eye and a deaf ear to the truth. We must have the wisdom to understand, and we must have the courage to act.

This you are helping us do. And I can only say, thank you all, and God bless you.

Note: The President spoke at 2:31 p.m. in Room 450 of the Old Executive Office Building.

In his opening remarks, the President referred to Assistant to the President for Public Liaison Faith R. Whittlesey.

Statement on Signing the Department of Housing and Urban Development—Independent Agencies Appropriation Act, 1985
July 18, 1984

In signing H.R. 5713 into law, I note that seven of its provisions purport to limit my authority, and the authority of the affected department or agency heads, to use funds otherwise appropriated by this bill, unless the Committees on Appropriations of both the House of Representatives and the Senate approve of those expenditures. Three of these provisions would purport to permit those committees to authorize the Administrator of NASA or the Administrator of the VA to exceed certain secondary limits on the amounts that may be spent on several specified activities, by using otherwise appropriated funds; a fourth would purport to allow those committees to authorize the Administrator of NASA to enter into certain leases or construction contracts that otherwise must be specified in an appropriations act. The appropriations made for the Environmental Protection Agency and the Federal Emergency Management Agency, and section 409 of the general provisions applicable to all appropriations made by this bill, contain similar provisions.

The Attorney General has advised me that, under the Supreme Court's decision in *INS* v. *Chadha*, 103 S. Ct. 2764 (1983), Congress, including committees of Congress, may not be given power that has "the purpose and effect of altering the legal rights, duties and relations of persons, including . . . Executive Branch officials . . . ," through procedures that bypass the constitutional requirements for valid legislative action. Thus, the provisions in this bill purporting to empower the Appropriations Committees to approve certain expenditures of funds absent participation by both Houses of Congress and the President are unconstitutional.

I fully recognize the interest of Congress and its committees in preserving oversight and accountability over the discretion Congress grants to the executive in such important areas as the obligation of appropriations. I do believe, however, that the time has come, with more than a year having passed since the Supreme Court's decision in *Chadha*, to make clear that legislation containing legislative veto devices that comes to me for my approval or disapproval will be implemented in a manner consistent with the *Chadha* decision. I strongly urge Congress to discontinue the inclusion of such devices in legislation, because doing so serves no constructive purpose after *Chadha* beyond introducing confusion and ambiguity into the process by which the executive's obligations are discharged.

Note: As enacted, H.R. 5713 is Public Law 98–371, approved July 18.

Remarks to the Executive Committee of the President's Private Sector Survey on Cost Control in the Federal Government
July 18, 1984

Well, I want to welcome you all here today. And I'm sorry about the change in plans, but it did look, earlier, as if it was going to rain. And then I must tell you, we lucked out completely. The last time we moved something hastily inside, because of the fear of rain, the Sun came out, it was beautiful outside, and we were already inside. Well, it's just been raining cats and dogs; started just as we left the White House. So, we made the right decision. [*Laughter*] And, besides, I've never played the Kennedy Center. [*Laughter*]

We do hope to see all of you at some future time at your White House, and I do mean your White House. Nancy and I have always thought it was awfully important to remember that we're just temporary tenants there. Of course, it's no secret that we're hoping for a renewal of the lease— [*laughter*]—but we haven't forgotten that this home belongs, first, to the American people and to no one else. And it's in that spirit I wanted to speak to you today.

As I said recently in Texas, the changes that have been brought to government signify far more than a victory for any one person or any administration or political philosophy. When these changes were first proposed, the seers of Potomac land said it couldn't be done, that our problems were too vast and complicated, that our political institutions couldn't function anymore. They said that we couldn't simultaneously cut the growth of government, reduce tax rates, spark an economic expansion, launch a war on crime, rebuild our defenses, stop the expansion of totalitarianism, and put forward the most extensive series of arms reduction proposals in our nation's history.

Well, they were wrong. All those things are being accomplished, and they're too vast and sweeping to be the work of any one person or one administration. The impetus for those changes has come from what has always been the real source of America's success and greatness, the American people, themselves.

Now, I'm talking about all the average citizens who time and again have made their voices heard here in Washington, who said they'd had enough excuses from politicians and indifferent bureaucrats, the heartland people who took back their government from a Washington-oriented leadership that stood for pessimism, defeatism, and ineptitude.

And one example of the people's newfound influence here in Washington has been a cost-cutting revolution that this administration began the day it took office. Unheralded, almost unreported, it's a quiet revolution that's reaching into every part of the Government, pruning, shearing, cutting, cutting back bureaucracy, making it more efficient and less wasteful, and making it more responsive to the people.

Three years ago I called waste, fraud, and mismanagement in the Federal Government an unrelenting national scandal. Well, today, although we're still a long way from home, that scandal is starting to relent. And let me tell you why: From discovering benefit checks still being sent to the deceased to finding a hammer the Pentagon was paying $400 for, our Inspectors General, auditors, and administrators are putting the squeeze on billions in waste and mismanagement.

Through the President's Council on Integrity and Efficiency, we've used the Inspectors General as a strike force to cut out billions in waste, fraud, and mismanagement. All our Inspectors General are doing a remarkable job. Take a look at what's being done in just one department, Health and Human Services. In 1981 the Inspectors General program there accounted for 517 convictions in fraud-against-the-government cases and $165 million in savings. Only 2 years later, that office under Richard Kusserow, a former FBI supervisor that we brought in from Chicago, was responsible for more than 800 fraud-against-the-government convictions and $1.4 billion in savings.

Now, many of you will also know that the maze we call the Federal bureaucracy includes some 350 different accounting systems; 150 civilian payroll personnel systems; 1,100 payment centers, most of them poorly coordinated and many of them incompatible, with no effective cash or debt management. Under a carefully designed program called Reform '88 we are now bringing about some of the management reforms and cost reductions that will clear out this jungle and make some sense of Federal procedures and organization.

Accomplishments so far include the collection of billions of dollars in delinquent debt, reduction of paperwork by 32 percent, and suspending publication of an estimated 155 million copies of marginally useful Federal publications.

To ensure that reforms occur and that savings are made, we examined progress made during formal management reviews with each Federal agency as part of the budget process. But ultimately, I believe history will record the American people's biggest victory over bureaucracy and big government began with the work of you who are here today.

I think all of you remember the skepticism, the cynicism, and even the scorn with which the permanent Washington establishment greeted the announcement of the Grace commission. You know, I remember during the last campaign, anytime you brought up the problem of waste, fraud, and mismanagement in government, many people who'd gotten used to the ways of Washington said it was just campaign rhetoric. They said such problems were so engrained, and, as they like to say in this city, "structural," that nothing could be done about them.

Well, something was done about them, and in large part, we have all of you to thank for that. The end product of your 18 months of hard work was 2,478 recommendations on how to cut the deficit, conveyed in 36 task force reports, 11 special reports, and a two-volume final report to the President. Your 21,000 pages of the 48 reports are supported by 1½ million pages of documentation, and your survey was conducted at no cost to the Government, with $75 million donated by the private sector in personnel, materials, supplies, equipment, and travel costs.

Now, I think you all know that I pledged to you last January not just talk but aggressive action on your recommendations. Well, I received a very thick memorandum the other day. It noted that our special task forces set up to review and implement your proposals have currently completed their reviews of 44 percent of the issues, and more than 80 percent of those issues have been forwarded for implementation.

You know, the review process involves very complex and detailed computerized data, all of which was summarized recently in that very thick memorandum that was sent my way. Kind of reminds me of the time that a government official said he was so disturbed by duplication in government that he was appointing not one, but two commissions, to study the problem. [*Laughter*]

But, you know, this is one time that I'm glad government is producing paperwork, because all of this paperwork is being produced to keep a careful tab on how work is progressing on your recommendations. It's kind of fun, isn't it? Just think—you, as private citizens, now have the bureaucrats making out forms, instead of the other way around. [*Laughter*]

I've just signed a major part of our deficit downpayment package which is intended to reduce the deficit by $62 billion. Now, we're determined to get the full downpayment of nearly 140 billion over these next 3 years, so I'll be ready with a veto pen to make sure the spending restraint that we need is fully reflected in the remaining appropriation bills to complete that downpayment.

But for the future, what we need most are long-term reforms to ensure sustained reductions in spending growth. And that's why we'll press on for constitutional amendments to mandate a balanced Federal budget and to permit a line-item veto. And we'll continue to press for reduced spend-

ing growth by adopting the kind of commonsense, long-overdue measures that you have proposed.

So, I wanted to take this opportunity to give you a progress report on our waste and fraud campaign and to thank each of you for all that you did during the course of your work on the Grace commission. I know it meant many hours away from your jobs and families. Each of you here today, whether you personally worked on the Grace commission or stood by and supported your friend or spouse, symbolize the best in America—a willingness to set aside individual preferences for the common good of the country.

Our critics said it couldn't be done. Well, it was done because of a remarkable man named Peter Grace and because of remarkable people like yourselves. I'm grateful, and your country's grateful. You've given something back to America. You should be very proud of that. Your work was courageous and daring; you didn't seek the approval of the Washington establishment, but produced a report that shook the foundations of the establishment.

Napoleon once said to one of his commanders, "If you start to take Vienna, take Vienna." Well, there's a lot of work left to be done on your recommendations, but believe me, this administration has learned from your example. And I can promise you, again, not just talk but aggressive action. And believe me, together we're going to take Vienna.

Thank you. God bless you all. Thank you very much.

Note: The President spoke at 4:30 p.m. in the Concert Hall at the John F. Kennedy Center for the Performing Arts.

Remarks at a Summit Conference of Caribbean Heads of State at the University of South Carolina in Columbia
July 19, 1984

Fellow heads of state, our host, the president of this university: I must say, when you mentioned honorary degrees, you

reawakened a sense of guilt. I'm quite cognizant of the honor and the pleasure, but I recall also that when my own alma mater gave me an honorary degree 25 years after my graduation, I told them at the time I had thought the first one they gave me was honorary. [*Laughter*]

It's a special honor and a pleasure for me to participate in this gathering of leaders from the Caribbean. You're among our nearest neighbors and our closest friends. Our societies, economies, and histories have been intertwined from the earliest days of the Americas.

As we face the future together, I think we have good reason to be confident. For, years ago—4 years ago, I should say, economic prospects were bleak, and the forces of tyranny were on the move, emboldened by what seemed to be a paralysis among the democratic peoples of the hemisphere. But by joining together with courage and determination, we've turned that situation around.

Now, the tide of the future is a freedom tide. The free people of this hemisphere are united and share a common sense of purpose. Nowhere is that more apparent than with the United States and the Caribbean democracies as has been so evident in our meeting today.

Over these past 4 years, we've strived to encourage democracy, enhance the economic vitality of the region, and cooperate in the defense of freedom. Now, these are not separate goals. They are mutually reinforcing. President Jorge Blanco pointed that out earlier this year when he observed, "Bread, health, education, liberty, democracy, and peace are indivisible and irreplaceable values."

I firmly believe that democratic government is the birthright of every American. And when I say "American," I'm talking about all of us in this Western Hemisphere, which together is called the Americas—all of us from the North Slope of Alaska to the tip of Tierra del Fuego. And much progress has been made. Today 26 of 33 independent countries in the hemisphere, countries with 90 percent of the hemisphere's population, are democratic or in transition to democracy. You realize when I refer to "democratic," I do so with a small "d." [*Laughter*]

Your own democracies are an example to developing countries everywhere. That's not to say that you don't face great challenges. The worldwide recession has profoundly affected the Caribbean with market prices for key commodities you produce dropping even as the costs of your imports were rising. The United States has been hard pressed economically. But we've done our best to help and provide hope, and we'll continue to do so. The United States has a deep and abiding interest in the well-being of its neighbors.

In the last 3 years, we've begun to put our own economic house in order by cutting down the growth of government spending and regulations. We're enjoying high growth, declining unemployment, and low inflation. And we've become, once again, an engine for worldwide economic progress. We believe the secret of that success is lower tax rates. And that's a secret everyone can share and benefit from.

At the same time, we've increased our aid to the region and helped strengthen the International Monetary Fund's ability to assist countries with debt problems. But let's be realistic; stopgap measures with the IMF are merely that—temporary solutions. The ultimate solution is strong and steady growth in every Caribbean country.

Our Caribbean Basin Initiative, now getting underway, gives your people new access to the world's largest and most dynamic government—market, I meant to say—too much television. [*Laughter*] It encourages job-creating business investment for growth and prosperity and is being put into place at a time when a strong dollar and an expanding American economy can translate into greater demand for your products. The Caribbean Basin Initiative is part of our broader, overall economic strategy to improve economic vitality and raise living standards throughout the Caribbean.

We can and must work together to improve the well-being of our people and to ensure our safety, as well. I'd like to take this opportunity to congratulate many of you for your courage and leadership in turning back the Communist power grab in Grenada last fall. We can be proud that thanks to the unity and determination of our democracies, we saved the people of that troubled island; we restored their freedom; we revived their hope in the future; and we prevented danger and turmoil from spreading beyond Grenada's shores. Let us always remember the crucial distinction between the legitimate use of force for liberation versus totalitarian aggression for conquest.

But what was happening in Grenada was not an isolated incident. The Soviet bloc and Cuba have been committing enormous resources to undermining our liberty and independence. Nowhere is this threat more pressing than in Nicaragua, a country which today marks the fifth year of Sandinista dictatorship.

The Sandinista revolution, like Castro's revolution, is a revolution betrayed. And now faced with mounting internal pressures and disillusionment abroad, the Sandinistas have announced an election for November of this year. We would wholeheartedly welcome a genuine democratic election in Nicaragua. But no person committed to democracy will be taken in by a Soviet-style sham election.

The situation in Nicaragua is not promising; but if the Sandinistas would keep their original commitment, permit free elections, respect human rights and establish an independent nation, conflict in the region would subside.

In the meantime, we have a moral responsibility to support anyone who aspires to live in a true democracy, free from Communist interference. If the democratic peoples do not stand together, we certainly will be unable to stand alone.

Just a few years ago, totalitarianism was on the rise. But there's a new spirit among democratic peoples. Prime Minister Adams described it when he said, "There is a com-munity of interest among democratic countries which can transcend ethnici—ethnicis—city"—I'm sorry—twisting that word up—"and differences in economic development." This spirit is a powerful new force for freedom in the world today.

What we do together, as a family of free men and women, will determine what the future will be like for our children. If we're strong enough to live up to our shared values, the promise of freedom and opportunity for the New World will at long last be realized. By working together, the free people of this hemisphere can make certain that the next century will indeed be our century, a democratic century.

I've thoroughly enjoyed being with you here today. And I hope that after my attempt to pronounce a word that I stumbled over, that you won't take that honorary degree away from me, Mr. President. But, again, it's been a great pleasure. I know that I must return to Washington now. I think meetings of this kind should be a regular feature in the years ahead, and we shall look forward to that.

Thank you, and God bless you all.

Note: The President spoke at 2:07 p.m. in the ballroom at the Russell House Student Center. The 3-day conference was hosted by the university.

In his opening remarks, the President referred to James B. Holderman, president of the University of South Carolina, who had awarded the President the honorary degree of doctor of laws during his visit to the university on September 20, 1983, to address a convocation.

Following his remarks, the President returned to Washington, DC.

Nomination of Robert W. Helm To Be an Assistant Secretary of Defense
July 19, 1984

The President today announced his intention to nominate Robert W. Helm to be an Assistant Secretary of Defense (Comptroller). He would succeed Vincent Puritano.

Since June 1982 Mr. Helm has been serving as Director of Defense Programs and National Security Telecommunications Policy for the National Security Council.

Mr. Helm was a professional staff member at the Los Alamos Scientific Laboratory, Los Alamos, NM, in 1975–1978. In 1978 he was a member of the U.S. comprehensive test ban negotiating delegation in Geneva, Switzerland, representing the Defense Nuclear Agency and supporting the Joint Chiefs of Staff representative. In 1979 he joined the minority staff of the Senate Budget Committee as the senior analyst for defense and international affairs. From 1980 until joining the National Security Council staff, he served as senior defense analyst on the majority staff of the Senate Budget Committee.

He graduated from the University of Wisconsin (B.S., 1973) and the Fletcher School of Law and Diplomacy at Tufts University (M.A., 1975). He is married and resides in Arlington, VA. He was born August 19, 1951, in La Crosse, WI.

Nomination of Andrew John Strenio, Jr., To Be a Member of the Interstate Commerce Commission
July 19, 1984

The President today announced his intention to nominate Andrew John Strenio, Jr., to be a member of the Interstate Commerce Commission for a term expiring December 31, 1985. He would succeed Reginald E. Gilliam, Jr.

Since July 1982 he has been Assistant Director for Regulatory Evaluation, Bureau of Consumer Protection, Federal Trade Commission. Prior to joining the Bureau of Consumer Protection in January 1982, Mr. Strenio was staff economist for the Council of Economic Advisers in 1980–1981; attorney with the law firm of Wald, Harkrader & Ross, in Washington, DC (1980); and research associate with the Huron Institute of Cambridge, MA (1978–1979). In 1977–1978 Mr. Strenio researched and wrote "The Testing Trap," a book about the educational testing industry.

Mr. Strenio graduated from Princeton University (A.B., 1974) and Harvard Law School (J.D., 1978). He is married, has one child, and resides in Bethesda, MD. He was born April 3, 1952, in Erie, PA.

Nomination of Walter C. Wallace To Be a Member of the National Mediation Board
July 19, 1984

The President today announced his intention to nominate Walter C. Wallace to be a member of the National Mediation Board for a term expiring July 1, 1987. This is a reappointment.

Since 1983 he has been a member of the National Mediation Board. Previously, he was corporate counsel and director of industrial relations for Multi-plant, national manufacturer of metal products, in 1980–1982; partner in the law firm of Ables & Wallace, Washington, DC, in 1975–1980; president of the Bituminous Coal Operators Association in Washington, DC, in 1973–1975; vice president for administration of Hudson Pulp & Paper Corp., New York City, in 1962–1973; General Counsel for the Presidential Railroad Commission in 1961; and Assistant Secretary of Labor (Manpower), chief staff assistant to the Secretary of Labor, and United States Representative, International Labor Conference, Geneva, Switzerland, in 1955–1961.

He graduated from St. John's University (B.A., 1948) and Cornell Law School (LL.B., 1951). He is married, has one child, and resides in New York, NY. He was born March 25, 1924, in New York City.

Message to the Congress Reporting Budget Deferrals
July 20, 1984

To the Congress of the United States:

In accordance with the Impoundment Control Act of 1974, I herewith report one new deferral of budget authority for $8,006,000 and six revised deferrals of budget authority which now total $68,528,548. The deferrals affect the Departments of Energy, and Health and Human Services.

The details of the deferrals are contained in the attached reports.

RONALD REAGAN

The White House,
July 20, 1984.

Note: The attachments detailing the deferrals are printed in the Federal Register *of July 26.*

Remarks at a White House Ceremony Marking the Observance of National P.O.W./M.I.A. Recognition Day
July 20, 1984

Ladies and gentlemen, distinguished guests, welcome. We are here today to recognize and honor a small, but very special group of Americans: our former prisoners of war and those who are still missing.

Four times in this century we have been forced, painfully and reluctantly, to send our men and women to fight in wars on foreign shores. Some of them made the supreme sacrifice of their lives. Some others made sacrifices in many ways equally grave—they were imprisoned by the enemy.

Their incarceration often included beatings and torture, starvation, and all forms of emotional and psychological abuse. It also entailed the terrible loneliness of living through lost years, of seeing the days tick away without friends, without loved ones, without family and community.

What has sustained such men and women in their isolation is a question I think all of us have asked ourselves many times. What kept them going when faith waned, as it must have, and questions began to haunt and doubts began to accumulate. We hear the stories of the returned prisoners of World War II and Korea and Vietnam, and we marvel at how they kept going.

I recall that when many of our prisoners returned from Vietnam 11 years ago, a number of them said there were three things that helped them survive captivity and return with honor: faith in God, faith in their fellow prisoners, and faith in their country. By faith; they didn't mean only love—though they demonstrated that in abundance. They meant a heartfelt belief that they would not be abandoned, that we at home would move mountains to return them safely to us after the war.

Our prisoners of war have been and are the bravest of the brave. They kept a trusting heart, they retained their spirit and their will, and they kept the faith. They trusted us, and that trust did us great honor.

Among us here today are some American prisoners of war. May I say that you are, as the great always are, more than the sum total of yourselves. You're a testament to the strength and the character of the American people. You are a symbol of our spirit.

You're an expression of American trust. Your heroism is as old as war itself, as old as names like Andersonville and Los Baños and Camp 5 and the Hanoi Hilton.

Most of those places are gone now or empty, but the silence left in their place surely echoes with the quiet, unheard valor of those who suffered there and clung to the belief that their government and their loved ones would be *semper fi*—"always faithful." We honor you, and that honor is unending.

There are others to whom we must be *semper fi*: those who are still missing—the men who went across the sea, who never returned and whose fate is unknown.

Along with us today are some of the relatives and friends of those still missing—from Korea and Vietnam. They, too, have shown more than their share of heroism, holding the standard for those who went away and are not yet returned to us, insisting that the world remember and respond, asking all of us to help them in their great effort, never giving up or abandoning hope.

Our administration inherited the challenge of accounting for the missing in January of 1981, two decades after the first man was placed on the missing list in Vietnam and almost three decades after the armistice in Korea. There'd been many obstacles and excuses in that time as to why progress could not be made. We found 3 years ago that the greatest obstacle that we could face and would continue to face was the passage of time.

Despite the daunting specter of 31 years since the end of the Korean war, we have pressed the Government of North Korea for an accounting. We will continue to do so. But I want you to know that we've received some valuable information from some dedicated veterans of that war on possible grave locations of some of their fellow soldiers, and we're acting on this information. If it is confirmed, we will return their remains to their homes and to their loved ones.

We're in regular dialog with the Government of Laos. And through reciprocal actions, that government seems to have gained a greater understanding of the importance to us of the POW–MIA issue. We in return have gained a greater understanding of their feelings and problems. This process has led us to discussions of joint crash site searches.

And in this regard, I want to pass on some good news to you. Late last night, we were informed by the Government of Laos of official agreement in principle to excavation of a U.S. crashsite. We're working out the details now. We welcome this cooperative gesture.

In Vietnam, the Government turned over the remains of several more U.S. servicemen 3 days ago. The Vietnamese also offered to resume technical-level meetings in August, and we appreciate these actions. We look forward to an acceleration of the process, an acceleration that was pledged to our delegation that traveled to Hanoi in February.

Ann Griffiths [1] helped to arrange those negotiations. And, Ann, we appreciate your help and all that you've given to this process.

It's important to note that 30 years ago today, July 20th, 1954, the Geneva accords were signed. It was hoped that the truce agreement would bring peace to the Vietnamese people. Instead, they have been at war ever since. And those wars have caused untold human suffering. Today, Vietnam continues to fight in Kampuchea and on its northern border. Nearly 10 years after the end of hostilities, the United States and the Government of Vietnam still have major differences.

But we're encouraged that Vietnam has agreed in principle that our two countries should cooperate on the POW–MIA issue as a separate humanitarian effort. Peaceful cooperation, negotiations with its neighbors in Kampuchea, and resolution of the POW–MIA issue provide the key for ending Vietnam's isolation. Normal relations with the international community can bring an end to the long suffering of the people of Vietnam. And I believe it to be in Vietnam's own interest to choose this path. It's a decision that we would truly welcome.

I'm mindful that I stand here before the families of many of the missing. I'm mindful

---

[1] *Executive director of the National League of Families of American Prisoners and Missing in Southeast Asia.*

that you gave your sons and husbands and fathers into the care of our government when they left to fight for our nation. You knew they might die in battle. But you had, and will always have, every right to expect that your government will not abandon those who failed to return.

In this, you, too, showed trust, and I tell you again, your trust will not be in vain. For many years, you stood alone in your quest for answers. Well, today you're not alone. And I tell you from my heart, you will never be alone again.

Across the Nation this week, hundreds of ceremonies are taking place in an outpouring of concern and understanding and solidarity. Balloons are being released across the country; a prayer ministry is ongoing; and the small black and white flag you see over this house flies proudly. All of this is good and fitting.

In January of last year, I said to you that we must fulfill our obligations as a matter of highest national priority. Much has happened since then to give us some hope of progress. It's agonizingly slow for you and for us. But we must not lose faith in each other because of lack of action from the other side.

Two months ago I received the remains of the unknown serviceman of Vietnam. And I said to all the Nation—and most especially to all of you—that we write no last chapters; we close no books; we put away no final memories until your questions are answered. Your husbands, fathers, and sons and brothers did their duty by this Nation, and this Nation will do its duty by them. Today we stand together.

And soon we will look up and see, as a symbol of our longing, a missing-man flyover. And today I pledge—and we will not rest until that formation is complete.

May God bless you always.

Note: The President spoke at 10:01 a.m. on the South Lawn of the White House.

In his closing comments, the President referred to the upcoming overflight of the Navy's Blue Angels.

Appointment of Dorothy Maney Tella as United States Representative on the Statistical Commission of the United Nations Economic and Social Council
July 20, 1984

The President today announced his intention to appoint Dorothy Maney Tella to be Representative of the United States on the Statistical Commission of the Economic and Social Council of the United Nations. She will succeed Joseph W. Duncan.

Since 1983 she has served as Chief of the Statistical Policy Office and Chief Statistican in the Office of Information and Regulatory Affairs at the Office of Management and Budget. Previously, she was proprietor of Dorothy M. Tella & Associates in 1981–1983; director of the Trends and Perspective Center at the Chamber of Commerce of the United States in 1973–1981; senior research economist of the Georgetown University Income Maintenance Project in 1970–1973; senior associate of the Planning Research Corp. in 1968–1970; economist, Office of Research and Statistics, Social Security Administration, in 1967–1968; and economist, Office of Economic Research, Central Intelligence Agency, in 1961–1967.

She graduated from Mount Holyoke College (A.B., 1958) and Harvard University (A.M., 1961). She also attended the Institut d'Etudes Politiques, University of Paris, France. She is married and resides in McLean, VA. She was born October 23, 1936, in Madison, TN.

Remarks at a White House Ceremony Marking the 15th Anniversary of the Apollo 11 Lunar Landing
July 20, 1984

The President. That announcement left a little something out.[1] It should have been at least "and company." [*Laughter*]

Well, Neil Armstrong and Buzz Aldrin, Mike Collins, Jim Beggs, and all our Apollo astronauts, the men and women of NASA here and those watching from NASA locations around the country, our friends out at the Space Pavilion at the World's Fair in New Orleans, and ladies and gentlemen:

It's a great pleasure to welcome you here to the White House. And as I look around, I can't help thinking that I haven't seen so many stars in one place since I was on a backlot of Warner Brothers. [*Laughter*]

We celebrate today a unique moment in the history of mankind—*Eagle's* touchdown near the southwestern shore of the Sea of Tranquility. It's hard to believe that 15 years have passed since we first heard Neil Armstrong's words. I know it's been that long, but why don't any of you look any older? [*Laughter*]

Today's celebration also brings back a very fond memory. In August 1969, after a long quarantine, the White House honored the Apollo 11 crew with a dinner in California. As Governor, I had the opportunity to introduce the President, and I remember looking out at our dinner guests—Ambassadors and other representatives from 83 countries, 44 State Governors, 50 Members of the Congress, 14 members of the Cabinet, and the leadership of NASA—and thinking that the men and women of NASA changed forever our concept of the universe and our relation to it. No longer could there be any mistake about the common heritage and common destiny of all people.

The Apollo program was a noble achievement of the mind, the heart, and spirit—and the most ambitious and complex program ever undertaken in peacetime. The lunar landings were a dazzling triumph of exploration. The *Mayflower* did sail on. Gus

---

[1] *Customarily, the President is announced to an audience as he enters the room.*

Grissom, Ed White, Roger Chaffee opened the trail, and we'll always remember their tragic sacrifice. But the program went on, and 12 Americans landed on the Moon.

By the end of the Apollo program, the *Columbia*, the *Endeavor*, the *America*, and the other command modules had returned 27 Apollo astronauts safely from the Moon and its vicinity. And, oh, how our astronauts, with their quiet confidence, superb professionalism, and inner strength, lifted our feelings, our spirits, and our feeling of good will.

Apollo enriched our intellectual and economic life and awakened us to mankind's boundless horizon. We carried a new sense of pride and became more confident that we've only seen the beginning of what a free and a courageous people can do. And, of course, the Apollo program was a supreme test of technology, always at and often beyond the cutting edge.

Never before had the requirements of reliability, accuracy, and efficiency been as demanding. Never before had the quality assurance testing for each of the thousands and thousands of components been as relentless, and our developers and inventors responded with unprecedented creativity. Our finest minds in government, industry, and universities all pulled together, and one sparkling technical innovation followed another. Which one of you, or was it someone else, however, that sat there at takeoff and said that your mind was on the fact that this had been built by the lowest bidder? [*Laughter*]

But all the while, our space research and engineering served the down-to-earth needs of our own people and people everywhere.

The Apollo project spawned communications, weather, navigation, and Earth resource satellites, and many new industries like solid-state electronics, medical electronics, and computer sciences. It opened the door to exciting scientific and commercial opportunities, opportunities like the programmable heart pacemaker which uses technology first developed to send coded instructions to orbiting satellites. Cordless home appliances and surgical instruments grew out of requirements of Apollo's lunar experiments. Even the fabric roof of Pontiac, Michigan's Silver Dome, home of the Detroit Lions, was made from the product developed for NASA's spacesuit.

The era of Apollo helped us build a technological base that was second to none, but we've only touched the edge of possibilities in space. The Apollo experience was only a beginning for America. From Apollo came the shuttle, the world's first true space transportation system, and another victory for the American spirit. The space shuttle opened a new era to pursue the many scientific, educational, industrial, and commercial opportunities of space, and as long as we challenge our imagination and aim high, there's no end to the potential of space.

There's never a time when we can stop moving forward, when we can stop dreaming. And so, this past January, in my State of the Union Address, I challenged our nation to develop a permanently manned space station and to do so within a decade. And I'm very pleased that the Congress has authorized funds enabling NASA to take the first steps in the design of America's space station.

The footprints on the Moon showed us that America's future can be determined by our dreams and our visions. The shuttle and our space station will help make those dreams come true. Our freedom and well-being are tied to new achievements and pushing back new frontiers. We'll push back those frontiers and open new doors to discovery, opportunity, and progress.

I also said in that State of the Union Address that we would soon develop initiatives to help promote private sector investment in space, and we're now embarking on that course. We'll do all we can to ensure that industry has a routine access to space and a suitable, reliable place to work there. And we'll do this without needless regulatory constraints. Eleven successful shuttle flights mean that we're on the verge of a space transportation system that can dependably support space industries.

And the benefits our people can receive from the commercial use of space literally dazzle the imagination. Together we can produce rare medicines with the potential of saving thousands of lives and hundreds of millions of dollars. We can manufacture superchips that improve our competitive position in the world computer market. We can build space observatories enabling scientists to see out to the edge of the universe. And we can produce special alloys and biological materials that benefit greatly from a zero-gravity environment. By accepting the challenge of space we'll carry forward the same courage and indomitable spirit that made us a great nation and that carried our Apollo astronauts to the Moon.

As you know, Dr. George Low, the guiding light behind the Apollo program, passed away earlier this week. Dr. Low began his career as a research scientist and progressed to key leadership positions in the manned space flight program, including manager of the Apollo spacecraft program. He played a leading role in all the Apollo missions and directed the Apollo 11 flight.

Dr. Low also served as Deputy Administrator and Acting Administrator of NASA and was instrumental in the planning of the shuttle program. For the past 8 years, he continued his lifelong efforts to build a better tomorrow while serving as president of Rensselaer Polytechnic Institute.

We're grateful for what George Low has done and the ideals he stood for, and we'll miss him very much. I know you join Nancy and me in extending heartfelt condolences to the Low family.

But I'm sure George Low would be pleased that we're honoring our achievements and the promise of space with a proclamation designating today as "Space Exploration Day." Let us use this occasion as a commitment to our future, to the best of America. And let it be a reminder of America's spirit of exploration, our desire to cross new horizons and to learn more about ourselves and the world around us.

And now I will sign the proclamation. I thank you, and God bless you all. And I can't help but think—all the things I've been saying here about the progress that's been made—I, a one-time second lieutenant of horse cavalry, will now sign the space proclamation.

[*At this point, the President signed the proclamation.*]

Mr. Armstrong. May I respond?

The President. You may. [*Laughter*] Please do.

Mr. Armstrong. Mr. President, what a wonderful occasion this is. We have here today a very large fraction of the people who, over the first quarter-century of the space age, conceived, executed, managed, and flew those flights that made their mark on the last quarter of this century.

May I also speak on behalf of these people and say how much we share your belief that the progress made during that first faltering two decades plus of the space age has been important to our country and citizens around the world and how much we appreciate your commitment to continued progress in these areas, as expressed in your State of the Union Address and confirmed here today.

And on behalf of all of us at NASA, my crew here on the stage, may we leave you with a small memento representing the 15th anniversary of this flight, where we carried this American flag to the Moon and returned it.

The President. Well, thank you very much.

Thank you all again. You're still beyond—all of you—my capacity to imagine. I remember my first time out there at Edwards for the landing of the shuttle, and they hurried us up on the platform and said, "It's coming in." And, so, I hurried up there and started watching the sky. And I said, "Where is it?" And they said, "It's over Honolulu." [*Laughter*] And we *were* just in time. [*Laughter*]

Note: The President spoke at 2:09 p.m. in the East Room at the White House.

Proclamation 5224—Space Exploration Day, 1984
July 20, 1984

By the President of the United States of America

A Proclamation

Space exploration is a quest for knowledge—knowledge about what lies outside the confines of the Earth's atmosphere and knowledge about the Earth itself. The information obtained adds greatly to the accumulated wisdom of mankind necessary for an understanding of the fundamental processes and origins of life, providing insight into perplexing mysteries of the universe. Because space has no boundaries, the information and benefits from space exploration accrue to mankind's advantage in many different spheres.

For 25 years, since the first primitive spacecraft heralded the dawn of the Space Age, the United States has expanded the frontier of space research; and the fruits of this research have been shared with scientists of other countries, reflecting the peaceful nature of our exploration. For example, the National Aeronautics and Space Administration has sent remotely controlled satellites on missions to measure the winds of Mars, count the rings of Saturn, and record volcanic activity on a moon of Jupiter; weather satellites have intensely studied the Earth's weather patterns; and communications satellites have profoundly changed modern life as events and impacts are known instantly and felt worldwide. Near-Earth satellites inventory our agricultural resources, search for mineral deposits, and measure the ecological impact of forest fires and volcanic eruptions. New products for industry, home, and medical use also have moved into the private sector.

As we have employed unmanned satellites to conduct research in space, we have also utilized the presence of man. Fifteen years ago, on July 20, 1969, people around the world witnessed the wonder of a human voice being transmitted from Tranquility Base:

"That's one small step for Man . . . One giant leap for Mankind."

as an American astronaut became the first human to set foot on truly foreign soil—the Moon. The Apollo project evinced our technological leadership and preeminence in space.

The success of America's Space Shuttle, the most sophisticated space research vehicle yet developed, reaffirms the spirit of confidence, courage, pride, ingenuity, and determination which has characterized the history of America's space program. As the Shuttle continues to demonstrate and expand its capabilities, and as we progress towards a permanently manned space station, the spirit of July 20, 1969, burns brilliantly, leading our journey into the future.

Space exploration is part of the human adventure. Through it, we challenge ourselves to strive and to achieve. By exploring, we are not just finding out more about our physical environment, we are finding out more about the human condition.

It is said there are two fundamental differences between human beings and other species: we have souls and we have curiosity. The exploration of space is a testament to each of these differences. It is our curiosity which drives our explorations, and it is our soul which gives these explorations meaning.

In recognition of the achievements and promise of our space exploration program, the Congress, by House Joint Resolution 555, has designated July 20, 1984, as "Space Exploration Day" and authorized and requested the President to issue a Proclamation to commemorate this event.

Now, Therefore, I, Ronald Reagan, President of the United States of America, do hereby proclaim July 20, 1984, as Space Exploration Day. I call upon the people of the United States to observe the occasion with appropriate ceremonies and activities.

In Witness Whereof, I have hereunto set my hand this 20th day of July, in the year of our Lord nineteen hundred and eighty-four, and of the Independence of the United States of America the two hundred and ninth.

Ronald Reagan

[*Filed with the Office of the Federal Register, 10:44 a.m., July 23, 1984*]

Nomination of Crete B. Harvey To Be a Member of the Federal Farm Credit Board
July 20, 1984

The President today announced his intention to nominate Crete B. Harvey to be a member of the Federal Farm Credit Board, Farm Credit Administration, for a term expiring March 31, 1990. She would succeed John D. Naill, Jr.

Ms. Harvey is the owner of Harvey Arabian Farms in Sterling, Ill. Since obtaining the farm in 1961, she has expanded the total grain and livestock production in addition to breeding and showing Arabian horses. She serves as a member of the Farm Bureau Association of Illinois, the American Horse Council, the Top Farmers of America Association, and the International Arabian Horse Association.

She is married, has three children, and resides in Sterling, IL. She was born July 10, 1929, in Butte, MT.

Appointment of Bruce Nestande as a Member of the Advisory Council on Historic Preservation
July 20, 1984

The President today announced his intention to appoint Bruce Nestande to be a member of the Advisory Council on Historic Preservation for a term expiring June 10, 1988. He will succeed Gerald Wallette.

Since 1981 Mr. Nestande has been a member of the Orange County Board of Supervisors. He was a member of the California State Assembly in 1974–1980. During this time he served on the following committees: Human Resources (chairman); Select Committee on Veterans Affairs (chairman); Criminal Justice, Housing and Community Development; Ways and Means; and Resources, Land Use and Energy. He was a special assistant to Gov. Ronald Reagan (1971–1972, 1974) and executive director of the California Republican Party in 1972–1973.

He graduated from the University of Minnesota (B.S., 1960) and Lincoln University (J.D.). He is married and resides in Orange, CA. He was born January 28, 1938, in Minneapolis, MN.

Appointment of Enrico Mihich as a Member of the National Cancer Advisory Board
July 20, 1984

The President today announced his intention to appoint Enrico Mihich to be a member of the National Cancer Advisory Board for a term expiring March 9, 1990. He would succeed Irving J. Selikoff.

Dr. Mihich is director of the Grace Cancer Drug Center at Roswell Park Memorial Institute in Buffalo, NY. He is also director of the Department of Experimental Therapeutics and institute coordinator for therapeutics. He has been with the institute since 1957 and his duties also include serving as head of the drug development and formulation unit. He is on the staff of the State University of New York as adjunct professor of biochemical pharmacology, School of Pharmacy, and research professor of pharmacology, Department of Pharmacology, School of Medicine.

He graduated from Italian Liceo Scientifico (B.S., 1944) and the Faculty of Medicine at the University of Milan, Italy (M.D., 1951). He is married, has one child, and resides in Buffalo, NY. He was born January 4, 1928, in Fiume, Yugoslavia.

Statement by Chief of Staff James A. Baker III on the Presidential Campaign Debates
July 20, 1984

The President looks forward to debating the Democratic nominee—on reasonable terms at a reasonable time.

Today's request for six debates cannot be taken seriously, however. It is obviously a partisan tactic intended to focus attention on words not actions—on promises uttered in debates, rather than on proven records.

Both President Reagan and former Vice President Mondale have well-established records. The former Vice President served with President Carter for 4 years. President

Reagan has served the Nation for the succeeding 3½ years. These records provide a telling comparison, a uniquely valuable basis on which the American people can render judgment.

Radio Address to the Nation on Commercial Space Initiatives
July 21, 1984

My fellow Americans:

Yesterday we marked the 15th anniversary of the first manned landing on the Moon. We all remember that great moment when Neil Armstrong said, "Tranquility Base here. The Eagle has landed." But that wasn't our last great moment in space. In fact, it's become increasingly clear that most of our great moments are ahead of us.

For 25 years, we approached space with a certain amount of derring-do. It was the last frontier, and we would be its first pioneers. Space seemed like a vast, black desert, but now we're ready to make the desert bloom.

I'm talking about opening space up to business, to private enterprise; opening space up to commerce and experimentation and development. Why? To improve the quality of life on Earth. We've learned in the past few years that in the zero gravity of space it's possible to manufacture drugs and pharmaceuticals of a purity much greater than is possible on Earth—and in much greater quantities.

The zero gravity of space is allowing us in the space shuttle and soon in a manned space station to experiment with new drugs and new cures for diseases. Do you have a friend or relative with diabetes? Some scientists believe that in space it's possible they may be able to produce a cure for diabetes within the next decade.

In space we also find new opportunities for important breakthroughs in cancer research. Now, cancer research is one of those phrases that to some people means we're still thinking and getting nowhere. But a number of scientists now believe that a cure for some types of cancer might be produced in space sometime in the not-too-distant future.

That's not all. In space we can manufacture crystals that have many times the yield and purity of those made on Earth. These will help maintain America's leadership in the computer industry. We can also develop new metals that are lighter and stronger than any we've ever known.

So, the promise and the potential are there. And private industry, private research groups, medical groups, and all sorts of businesses want to get up into space and invest. But it's very costly. It'll involve long-term investment, commitment, and imagination.

For the past year now, our administration has been studying ways to encourage private investment and development. And we've come up with a number of new initiatives to achieve that goal. These initiatives don't involve a special interest treatment of any sort. What they come down to is a policy designed to do away with laws that inadvertantly discriminate against companies that do business in space rather than on the ground.

We also want to make sure these companies are not stymied by needless regulation. For example, the way the law is written now, products made in space might be subject to import tariffs because they weren't made in America. Well, we're going to change that. Another example: Businesses which operate at home receive various kinds of tax incentives. But, again, as the laws are written now, space products companies would not receive those incentives. We'll be looking at that, too.

Also, to encourage research and development, we've been working in partnership with industry and academia to expand basic research opportunities, achieve new breakthroughs, and give U.S. companies making space-age products a boost on the way to the marketplace.

As our country moves into high-tech industries, space will be a big part of the future. As space-related businesses take off, the economy will benefit. Ultimately, it could well mean tens of thousands of jobs, billions of dollars in new foreign trade, and tens of billions of dollars added to the gross national product.

Some of our new initiatives will be accomplished through Executive order. Others will require congressional action. We're confident that these measures will win considerable support.

I'm proud of our work in this area, of our ability to recognize what private companies have recognized: that we have cultivated space for the past 25 years, and now is the harvest time. Now is the time to reap the practical fruits of all that daring.

You know, we've been hearing a lot lately from politicians who keep talking about how dark the future is. Well, I think the narrowness of their vision stems from a kind of blindness to the adventure that technology continues to offer us. Those folks have such a strangled sense of possibilities. But in space, the possibilities are endless. It's good news for all mankind and for our country.

Until next week, thanks for listening, and God bless you.

Note: The President spoke at 12:06 p.m. from Camp David, MD.

Statement by Principal Deputy Press Secretary Speakes on President Reagan's Meeting With President José Napoleón Duarte of El Salvador
July 23, 1984

During his brief visit to Washington today, El Salvador's President José Napoleón Duarte met with President Reagan this morning at 11 a.m. for half an hour, with the Vice President present. From the State Department, the meeting included Secretary Shultz and U.S. Ambassador to El Salvador Thomas Pickering.

Following his meeting with President Reagan, President Duarte went to the Hill to meet with House Majority Leader James Wright. We believe he was also seeing Jamie Whitten, chairman of the Appropriations Committee, and Clarence Long, chairman of the Foreign Operations Subcommittee of the Appropriations Committee, and possibly others.

Following his meeting on the Hill, President Duarte was to return to New York City. He's there for meetings with U.N. officials, the Americas Society, and others.

President Duarte gave a full readout of the meeting, discussing his assessment of developments in El Salvador, his very successful trip to Europe, and the administration's efforts during the current 3-week congressional session to secure pending FY 84 supplemental funds and complete con-

gressional action on the Central American Democracy, Peace, and Development Initiative. We have nothing to add to what he said.

As you know, we still hope to secure that portion of the FY 84 supplemental request which has not been acted on (for El Salvador this includes $134 million in economic assistance and $117 million in military assistance) and the Central America Democracy, Peace, and Development Initiative plan request for all of Central America, which includes for FY 85 $1.376 billion ($1.12 billion in economic and $256 million in military assistance for the region). Of the $1.376 billion requested, $473.6 million would be for El Salvador—$341.1 million would be for economic assistance and $132.5 million would be for military assistance.

The administration in February requested a supplemental appropriation of $659 million to begin meeting the most urgent needs identified by the National Bipartisan Commission on Central America. $312.7 million in the FY 84 supplemental ($134 million in economic and $178.7 million in military assistance) is for El Salvador.

As you know, some $61.7 million in urgently needed military assistance for El Salvador was passed by the Congress. The remaining $117 million in military assistance and $134 million in economic assistance have not been acted upon and, at this point, are both urgently needed by the Government of El Salvador, as are the $266 million in economic assistance and $142 million in military assistance requested in February for other countries in Central America.

We will be striving for House action on our requests for the Henry Jackson plan and the supplemental funds for El Salvador.

Nomination of John B. Waters To Be a Member of the Board of Directors of the Tennessee Valley Authority
July 23, 1984

The President today announced his intention to nominate John B. Waters to be a member of the Board of Directors of the Tennessee Valley Authority for a term expiring May 18, 1993. He would succeed Simon David Freeman.

Since 1961 Mr. Waters has been a general partner in the law firm Hailey, Waters, Sykes, and Sharp in Sevierville, TN. He is also president of the Tennessee Bar Association. In 1969–1971 he was Federal Cochairman of the Appalachian Regional Commission. Since 1978 he has been a member of the Tennessee-Tombigbee Waterway Authority. He has served as a member of the Governor's Committee on Economic Development (1971), the State of Tennessee Industrial and Agricultural Commission (1971), and was representative for the State of Tennessee to the Southern Growth Policy Board (1971–1975).

He graduated from the University of Tennessee (B.S., 1952; J.D., 1961). He is married, has two children, and resides in Sevierville, TN. He was born July 15, 1929, in Sevierville.

Appointment of Margaret DeBardeleben Tutwiler as Deputy Assistant to the President for Political Affairs
July 23, 1984

The President today announced the appointment of Margaret DeBardeleben Tutwiler to be Deputy Assistant to the President for Political Affairs.

Miss Tutwiler has been serving most recently as Special Assistant to the President and Executive Assistant to the Chief of Staff. She has been responsible for liaison with the Republican National Committee and the Reagan-Bush '84 committee.

Prior to joining the White House staff, Miss Tutwiler was director of scheduling for George Bush in both the primary and general election campaigns of 1979–1980. In 1977–1978 she was a public affairs representative for the National Association of Manufacturers. She participated in the 1976 Presidential campaign as executive director of the President Ford committee of Alabama.

Miss Tutwiler was born and raised in Birmingham, AL, and received her bachelor of arts degree in political science from the University of Alabama in 1973.

Remarks to National and State Officers of the Future Farmers of America
July 24, 1984

It was too hot to keep you waiting out here. I'm sorry that I'm a few minutes late.

I thank you for that warm farm welcome, and I'm delighted to be with those of you who represent America's bedrock industry. Agriculture is a driving force in our nation's economy, and the Future Farmers of America are working hard to keep it that way.

I know that you'll be meeting with our Secretary of Agriculture, Jack Block—or have you done that already and am I way behind? He'll probably spin a few of his stories. And Jack was a Greenhand of the Knoxville, Illinois, chapter of FFA. But we both like to put on a blue denim jacket whenever we get the chance, and I remember some—once, years ago, having an experience.

Now, I'm a rancher—I've got a ranch. But I had an experience that taught me how little a great many people know about farming. You know, most people just think that you put something in the ground, stand back, and wait for it to grow up—it's that easy. And I guess maybe I was guilty of some of that, even with a ranch, because with all that space and everything, I got the idea that why shouldn't we have our own eggs for breakfast. So, I put in a battery of chickens and everything, and it was just great. We did have our own eggs. And they only cost me $1.65 apiece. [*Laughter*]

But all of us, I think, know that God has blessed America with a vast and a fertile land. But it's ingenuity and muscle and sweat that have made our farms the envy of the world. And the last thing our farmers need is government getting in the way and making the job even tougher.

You know, there's a story about a young fellow who was—well, he was a city fellow, but he hired out to work on a farm during the harvest season. And the first morning, everyone was up before dawn, and the new hired hand and the farmer made their way out toward the—in the dark—toward the oat field. Neither one of them said a word on the way out, and finally the city fellow

asked what kind of oats they were going to cut, wild oats or tame oats. And the farmer was a little surprised, and he said, "Well, tame oats, of course." And the kid said, "Well, why are we sneaking up on them in the dark?" [*Laughter*]

Well, that's about as much, as I say, as some people know about what past policy mistakes and economic difficulties meant to our farm community.

Our record of agricultural productivity is unmatched anywhere in the world. And it didn't come about thanks to double-digit inflation. In the 3 years before 1981, farm costs jumped an outrageous 45 percent, and that was nearly $40 billion, the largest 3-year increase in our history. And today we've knocked the wind out of inflation. For the last 3 months, it's been running at 3.3 percent.

Our farmers and our ranchers don't produce the most wholesome and varied foodstuffs known anywhere as a result of 21½-percent interest rates. When we took office, that's where the prime rate stood. I know that some of our critics have very short memories, but you and I know that a 21½-percent interest rate is a devastating blow to an industry that spends a fifth of its cash outlays on interest expenses. Well, we've cut them by 40 percent. But don't get me wrong, they're still too high, and we're not going to stop until we get them lower. And one of these days—and I hope it's very soon—some people will wake up and realize that not only is inflation firmly under control, but we intend to keep it that way.

And with signs of future price trends pointing to low rates of inflation as far as we can see, I can't help believing that there's no excuse for interest rates being where they are. We can all understand why, if there is inflation, you have to get back in interest if you've loaned money, you have to get back the loss of the value of that money over the period of the loan due to inflation, plus your earnings on it. But the interest rates today are outrageously high, and they cannot have any excuse in inflation for their being at that level.

In 1982 nearly one-fifth of the world's agricultural products was shipped from American ports. That didn't happen— thanks to grain embargoes and protectionism. The grain embargo was a cruel, painful blow, and it was terribly unfair. And that's why one of my first actions on this job was to lift that embargo. And as long as I'm here, our farmers will never again be made the scapegoats for a foreign policy of weakness and indecision.

What we're doing and will continue to do is move in a positive direction, pursuing new export markets and working to remove export barriers. Our trade teams have been continuously on the go in search of new markets. Jack Block has been knocking on doors all over the world, and he's going to keep on knocking.

His efforts are paying off. We've negotiated new import quotas with Japan that will lead to near doubling of beef exports and a 54-percent increase in citrus exports over the next 4 years.

On another front, we've demonstrated our determination to aggressively maintain exports, including a strong American challenge to the European Community's subsidy program. As a result, the European Community has joined us in serious discussions in an effort to solve some of the problems caused by their subsidized exports.

Now that we've regained our reputation as a reliable supplier, we mean to maintain that reliability and that image. And today, at home, we're hard at work on the 1985 farm bill. The Department of Agriculture will continue to solicit farmers' views on this important bill. So far, they've accepted hundreds of pages of written recommendations and held listening sessions around the country. The latest session was held just last week in Dallas.

Now, you know, I don't get a chance to talk enough to the farm community to suit me. You represent the best in America. Our farmers and ranchers have always honored and lived by the values and traditions that make America great: faith, family, neighbors helping neighbors, hard work, free enterprise, and independence. We can touch the spirit of America in our farm communities. And, again, much is owed to the Future Farmers of America.

FFA is giving more than a fine start to young people like yourselves. By cultivating traditional values, leadership skills, and patriotism, the Future Farmers of America ensure the strength and vitality of our country.

Before I close, I want to say a few words about the thousands of volunteers and private industry sponsors who are reaching out to America's future. FFA has some 14,000 adult teachers and State advisers—good, caring Americans who are offering a gift that'll last a lifetime: the gift of opportunity. That's all made possible because of the generosity of the private sector. This year business and industry are expected to give over $2 million to provide incentive awards to FFA members. In fact, your State Presidents Conference in Washington wouldn't have been possible without the support of the Chevrolet Motor Division of General Motors. And I'm sure that Bob Burger, general manager of Chevrolet, who is with us today, is very proud of what his organization is doing.

You all deserve to be very proud. With your help, our young people will be ready to meet the challenges before them and turn them into opportunities for their families, their community, and for America.

I have to tell you just one more farm story before I quit. [*Laughter*] Maybe you know this one about the old boy that had taken over some creek bottom land. And it was rocky and covered with brush. Cleaned the brush; he got rid of all the rocks and hauled them away, and then he planted. And he really had a beautiful garden there. And one day at church he asked the minister to come back with him after the sermon and take a look at what he'd accomplished.

Well, the reverend arrived, and he looked, and he said, "Those melons, oh my, God has certainly blessed this land. I've never seen anything so wonderful. And look at the corn. I've never seen anything as tall as that. God certainly has been good to this place." And he went on that way, until finally the old man, who was beginning to shuffle a little bit, said, "Reverend, I wish you could have seen it when the Lord was doing it by Himself." [*Laughter*]

Well, I know you won't be caught in that

kind of a spot. But thank you all very much for being here. God bless you.

Note: The President spoke at 1:31 p.m. in the Rose Garden at the White House.

The President's News Conference
July 24, 1984

Legislative Priorities

The President. I have a brief statement here.

The Congress is back this week for a session that's lasting only until August 10th, but that's enough time for the House of Representatives to approve legislation that would benefit all Americans.

Among the many important issues now facing the Congress is legislation that will help reduce deficits, reward work and thrift, make our cities and neighborhoods safer, and increase personal liberties throughout our land. Legislation that could do these things is already before the Congress. It's been bottled up in the House for months, and in some instances, even years. But something can be done.

I have talked with the House Republican leadership. They have pledged to try again to bring six key measures to the floor for a vote.

First, a constitutional amendment requiring a balanced budget. And we must balance it, not by raising the tax rates of hardworking Americans, but by insisting that government spend no more than it takes in.

Second, a proposal granting spouses working in the home the same individual retirement rights, IRA's, as spouses working outside the home. Each spouse could save and deduct from taxation up to $2,000 a year. The House had a chance to enact this initiative in a bill I signed just days ago, but they dropped it.

Third, a proposal offering incentives for investment in 75 enterprise zones to create jobs, independence, and hope for people in inner cities and other economically distressed areas.

Fourth, a bill allowing tuition tax credits for low- and middle-income parents who

pay to send their children to parochial or independent schools while also paying their full share of taxes to support public schools.

Fifth, a comprehensive anticrime package to crack down on criminals through restrictions on bail, tougher sentencing, and stricter enforcement of drug trafficking laws.

And sixth, an equal-access bill permitting religious student groups the same freedom to meet in public high schools during nonschool hours as right now other student groups are allowed to do.

These reforms are long overdue, and they would benefit all the people. It's time to test the new realism and to see if the Democratic leadership will move from words to action.

Now, Maureen [Maureen Santini, Associated Press].

Federal Tax Increase

Q. Mr. President, your advisers have publicly disagreed with Walter Mondale's assertion that a tax increase will be necessary next year in order to help cut the enormous Federal deficit. While your advisers say you don't want a tax increase next year, they have refused to flatly rule out the possibility. Will you now flatly rule out the possibility of seeking a tax increase next year if you're reelected?

The President. Yes. I have no plans for a tax increase. I believe it would be counterproductive with regard to the present recovery, or expansion. Indeed, I believe that the tax cut that we had is largely responsible for the recovery that we're having.

Maybe they left that for me to say. I know that for Mr. Mondale, he has repeatedly and over the years supported tax increases on any number of occasions. He was opposed to our indexing, which is a provision that would benefit the lower- and middle-income people almost exclusively, because they would be the ones that could—without indexing—could be moved up into higher tax brackets by inflation. Those who are already in the high tax brackets can't be moved up. They're already there.

But I have one thing to say about a tax increase with regard to our problems. The only way that I could see is that—government is taking a percentage of the gross national product that is higher than the revenues—the percentage that is being taken in revenues now from that same gross national product. Now, if, after all of our best efforts, if we have gotten government costs down to the point at which we say they cannot go any lower and government still meet its responsibilities and provide the services that are required of it, and that is still then above the percentage taken by taxes, then you would have to look at the tax structure in order to bring that up, to meet that minimum level of government expenditures.

But I think we're a long way from that point with regard to bringing government down to where it could be brought down. We're looking right now—and we have a task force working on 2,478 recommendations made by the Grace commission of ways in which government can be made more economical and more efficient by simply turning to modern business practices in all of these different ways instead of sticking with some oldtime government practices that are way behind the times.

And I believe that to raise taxes without waiting for what I had just said, I think that to do that would simply open the door to more spending. That's been the pattern of the past, and it is a pattern that—as a matter of fact, Vice President Mondale has stated that his own belief in it. In '76 he publicly stated on a television show that he had voted time after time to raise taxes on his own constituents. So, he believes in tax increases, and I believe that our goal must be to, wherever possible, reduce the tax burden for our people.

We are—let me just say, we are—I've ordered, or asked the Treasury Department to come in before the end of the year with options on tax simplification and ways in which we can broaden the base and thus lead to the ability to further reduce the individuals' rates by broadening the base. And the fairness of all of this goes without saying. But, also, the simplification—I think it's practically immoral, the complexity of the tax laws and what we impose on the people with regard to their tax obligation, and I think it can be simplified. And I believe that there will be some options brought to me in December, as I had requested.

Q. Sir, if I may follow up. Do you think that there's room in the Federal budget to cut spending so deeply that you can balance the budget that way? And, if you believe that, is it possible, do you think, to do that without going into entitlements and Social Security, and are you willing to go that deep?

The President. No, what we're looking forward to is the fact that as the recovery takes place, you are going to see some contributing factors to further reducing the deficit. A large part of the deficit, when it went up so far, was because of the depth of the recession. But today there are 7 million more people working than were working in 1980. Now, that's 7 million people that are not a burden on the Government or being taken care of; that's 7 million more people paying taxes.

And so far, we have found repeatedly, and still are finding, that we have overestimated the deficits, and much of the overestimation is our underestimating the revenues that we're going to get. So, I think that there is still a large area in which we can go.

Now, you mentioned Social Security, and that brings to mind something I want to get off my chest right now about Social Security. As you know, in the regulations of Social Security, if the inflation rate falls below 3 percent, there are no more COLA's—cost-of-living adjustments, or additions—for people getting Social Security. We, now, in the last 3 months, have been down around 3.2 or .3 with regard to inflation—the inflation rate. If, when we come to the period, which is the third quarter of the year, and inflation is below 3 percent, we have asked the Social Security recipients to take a 6-month delay in getting their cost-of-living adjustment. And if it is below 3 percent, I am going to ask the Congress to permit the payment of a cost-of-living adjustment to the Social Security recipients.

Helen [Helen Thomas, United Press International]?

Geraldine Ferraro

Q. Mr. President, Geraldine Ferraro says you're not a good Christian on grounds that your budget cuts have hurt the poor and the disadvantaged. Do you think you're a good Christian, and why? And I'd like to follow up.

The President. Well, Helen, the minute I heard she'd made that statement, I turned the other cheek. [*Laughter*]

As for her qualifiers, that our budget practices had victimized the poor and the needy, there is not one single fact or figure to substantiate that charge. I know that's been the talk. I know there's been a lot of demagoguery about that. But all of the programs for the needy that are means-tested programs, they were $47 billion in cost when we came here. They're now around $64 billion.

Everyone that, for food stamps, for example, that has an income or earnings of up to 150 percent of the poverty level is eligible for food stamps. Out at the State—where the States administer them, programs like AFDC, there the requirement is based on what is the needs level in that particular State. And, therefore, they set the basic benefit according to 130 percent of that.

But we are aiding more people and spending more money on those programs than has ever been spent in history. So, there's no basis for this demagoguery that somehow we have punished and are picking on or trying to get our recovery on the backs of the needy.

Now, Andrea, the other—oh, you had a——

Q. I know that Congress doesn't agree with you—the Congressional Budget Office. But I'd like to ask you—Ed Rollins said today that the Ferraro nomination to the number two spot could be one of the biggest busts in history. And do you think so, and do you think you'll be hurt?

The President. Helen, I wouldn't touch that question with a 10-foot pole. I understand he's retracted it already.

Andrea [Andrea Mitchell, NBC News], I told you the other day that you could ask a question Tuesday night.

Q. Thank you very much. Mr. President, you just said that you were turning the other cheek as to Mrs. Ferraro's suggestion about whether or not you're a good Christian. Some of your own strategists have said that there's a double standard in the way that she is being covered because she is a woman—that a male candidate could not get away with that particular suggestion about the President. Do you think that that's fair, that she should be able to suggest that you're not a good Christian and not be criticized for it?

The President. Well, I think that's a decision that all of those who—of you who do the criticizing has to make. I have never been one to campaign against opponents. I prefer to campaign on our record, what we've done and what we intend to do. And that's the way I'm going to conduct myself in this campaign.

Q. Could I just ask you how—what kind of strategy are you going to use against the first woman Vice Presidential candidate? And if you are not willing to debate Walter Mondale, let's say, a half a dozen times, as Mr. Baker has suggested you're not, would you let George Bush debate Geraldine Ferraro six times?

The President. Well, I think this is a decision for those who are working on the strategy of the campaign to deal with, and I'm going to let them do that. And, again, I know that George feels the same way that—as George, himself, has said, that his campaigning is going to be to try and get the top of the ticket elected, which seems to make some sense.

But let me—I'd better switch over here for some more. And may I—of course, and I don't mean to offend with regard to the followups—and I understand why you had them—but we've been reduced in the number of questions we get to ask when everybody has a followup. So, ask them both at once.

Sam [Sam Donaldson, ABC News], do you want to——

Central America

Q. Sir, Mr. Mondale said in his acceptance speech that 100 days into his Presidency he would stop the secret war against Nicaragua. I assume that you're going to continue your policy down there in that respect. And he also implied, of course, once again, that you, as President, will be trigger-happy and will get us into war. How will you answer both of those?

The President. Well, I'm not trigger-happy, and having known four wars in my lifetime, I'm going to do everything I can. I think the greatest requirement is to strive for peace, and I'm going to do that.

And, again, I think there was some demagoguery in this. But it's my understanding that all of you have been given a report—has a kind of a green cover—on the Nicaraguan situation, and it has also been delivered to every Member of the Congress. And I think if—believe me, I wouldn't "round file" those. I'd look at them, because the information is in there that reveals that everything we've said about the Sandinista government is a proven fact. They are trying to destroy El Salvador by providing the rebels there with the wherewithal to do it. They are a totalitarian government.

But you'll also find in there a statement by Ogarkov of the Soviet military. This was prior to our rescue mission in Grenada. But he openly stated that after all the years of only having a base in the Western Hemisphere in Cuba, that now they had bases here in Nicaragua and in Grenada. Well, they don't have one in Grenada anymore. And I think that it is the responsibility of this government to assist the people of Nicaragua in seeing that they don't have one in Nicaragua.

Q. Mr. President, on the same subject, Vice President Bush has asserted that Mondale and the Democrats don't understand the Communist threat in Central America. Do you agree?

The President. That they don't understand the Communist threat? Well, either that or they're ignoring it.

Q. Do you think they're ignoring it?

The President. What?

Q. Do you think they're ignoring it?

The President. Well, they seem to be opposing everything that we've tried to do, including the aid to El Salvador. As a matter of fact, I've been very worried that their niggardly treatment of El Salvador is such that we might see—it's comparable to letting El Salvador slowly bleed to death. And then they would be able to point a finger and say, "Well, see, your program didn't work."

Bill [Bill Plante, CBS News]?

Federal Budget Reductions

Q. Mr. President, you say that you won't raise taxes. Yet people in your administration have said, including Mr. Stockman, [1] that if the huge budget deficit is to be reduced at all, that there will probably have to be cuts in some of the major entitlement programs, such as medicare, veterans benefits, farm price supports. Now, you said in an interview earlier this year that you weren't going to discuss things like that in an election year. And I'd like to ask if you don't think that you owe an explanation of what you might cut to the people in an election year?

The President. Well, I've told you about those 2,478 recommendations that have been made. We are going to look at every area where we can cut, but at the same time we're going to do what I said from the very beginning: We are not going to destroy the safety net for those people who, through no fault of their own, must depend on government.

Q. Sir, that wouldn't rule out looking at those programs—veterans benefits, medicare, farm price supports, for example.

The President. A number of those that I'm sure will be looked at.

Sanctions Against Poland

Q. Mr. President, the Polish Government is releasing hundreds of political prisoners in a move that appears to meet one of your conditions for normalizing relations. You have removed some of the sanctions you imposed a couple of years ago. Will you

---

[1] *David A. Stockman, Director of the Office of Management and Budget.*

remove others, and if so, when do you think you'll be acting?

The President. Ralph [Ralph Harris, Reuters], we're studying what they've done in their legislation on amnesty very carefully right now. Our purpose from the beginning has been, with regard to the sanctions, that we know that in some instances those sanctions are penalizing not only the Government of Poland, with which we're not in very much sympathy, but the people themselves. We don't want to impose hardships on the people.

And if their legislation on amnesty and things of that kind have met the conditions that we laid down—yes, we will meet with regard to lifting the sanctions.

Yes?

1984 Presidential Campaign

Q. Mr. President, you've just said now that you don't conduct negative campaigns, and yet your surrogates have been doing so. George Bush said today that Geraldine Ferraro was too liberal; Helen told you about Ed Rollins' remark. Are you saying that these people don't speak for you?

The President. Well, I don't think that in a campaign you can ignore the things that other people or opponents have said and pretend that they'd never said them. I have responded here myself to some charges that—already this evening—I have said had no basis in fact or figure, whatsoever.

Now, that I think that we can do. But to ask questions that I thought indicated that how are you going to plan to campaign against someone—basically the campaign is going to be on behalf of what our own programs are and what we intend for the people.

Q. In other words, sir, they are speaking for you.

The President. What?

Q. They are speaking for you?

The President. Yes. If someone says something that I have to disagree with, I'll be the first to let them know.

Yes?

Interest Rates

Q. Mr. President, a few hours ago in the Rose Garden you said that with inflation so low, it's outrageous that interest rates should be so high. Who's doing this? Is it the moneylenders, and is it the bankers? Do you think that they're gouging the American public, and, if so, what are you going to do about it?

The President. No, I've said many times that I think there's a psychology at work. We've had so many recessions since World War II—seven or eight. I've been saying seven, but someone has indicated that I was wrong by one, that it might be eight, so seven or eight before this one. All of those were cured by the quick fix; all of them used the artificial stimulant of money that raised inflation. And all of them only lasted for a couple of years, maybe three or four, at the most, and then there was another recession following. And this one is different. I believe the basis for this recovery is sound and solid.

And so, I just think that what we're seeing is an unwillingness out there, an inability to believe that we have control of inflation, that it's not going to go back up. And anyone who's in the business of lending money must know, particularly if it's going to be long-term money, that he must get an interest rate—he or she—that is going to return the original purchasing power that was loaned, making up for that loss of inflation, then plus the earning power or the earning capacity, the interest that they want as profit on that loan.

Well, right now, if there's still that unwillingness to accept that we have a recovery and that it is one with a declining inflation rate, then the financial market is very jittery. And frankly, I do not see any real reason other than just this kind of lack of trust or confidence that is responsible for the present interest rates.

Voter Registration

Q. Mr. President, how do you feel about the fact that throughout the South your political workers are striving to register as new voters affluent people and white people while shunning poor people and black people?

The President. They're not doing that. I want everybody registered that can. I think that democracy, if it's to work, then everybody that's eligible to be a voter should be registered, and they should vote. And I think sometimes the declining number of people voting is because we have satiated them with campaigning over such long periods of time that they finally come to a ho-hum attitude and go their way. But, no, this whole idea that we don't want the votes of certain people in this country is absolutely ridiculous. We do want them.

And if it comes to the affluent, I did think that it was kind of interesting to see some of the people that were onstage at the convention in San Francisco that were talking about their love for the poor and our affinity for the rich, when they themselves were not only rich, but they were selling seats on the floor for $5,000. And you could meet and eat with the candidate or have your picture taken with him for a hundred thousand dollars. And they had some other alternatives in there at ten, twenty, and fifty thousand dollars.

The simple truth of the fact is that for more than a quarter of a century, the Democratic Party has raised the bulk of its contributions from contributions of a hundred dollars and up. And the Republican Party, the so-called country club party, has raised the bulk of its donations from a hundred dollar contributions and down.

Q. Would you say then that that's an instruction to the Republican Party, that all the black voters that can join the rolls should be joined as an effort on your part?

The President. We've got a voter registration drive. I think it goes with every campaign. But we're doing it. Now, we're not drawing the line, and we don't have any—we're not going to shove aside anyone else. We're going to ask everybody that will to register.

Yeah?

Richard M. Nixon

Q. Mr. President, there was some talk about whether President Carter would appear at the Democratic convention, because he might hurt Mr. Mondale politically. But he was there. I'm wondering, it's been 10 years since Mr. Nixon was in the Presidency, and you've sought his advice and appear to think highly of him. I wonder whether you think it might hurt you politically if he were to be at your convention and if he were to campaign with you.

The President. Well, it's a question that I don't have to answer, because he himself has ruled out coming to the convention and has, I believe, publicly stated that he has no intention of participating in a campaign.

The young lady right——

U.S.-New Zealand Relations

Q. Thank you. Mr. President, could the United States continue its defense commitments to New Zealand if it's denied port access for nuclear ships? And, if this happens, would it affect American trade with New Zealand? And I have a followup, please.

The President. I don't think that it would affect trade. But I do know—and I would rather not get in too deeply to anything, because that is something that will be worked out and negotiated with the new Government of New Zealand. And I have every reason to be optimistic that there won't be any denial to our ships.

Q. To follow up, though, if the port access is denied, as the Labor Party says it will do, would the United States conclude a separate peace treaty with Australia?

The President. Well, as I say, I don't want to get into things or anything that might sound as if I'm pressuring or threatening or anything of the kind. So, let me just say that we're going to do our best to persuade them that it is in their best interests as well as ours for us to continue with our alliance with ANZUS, those countries as we have been.

Edwin Meese III

Q. Mr. President, I'd like to ask you about the leadership situation at the Justice Department, both in terms of reality and symbolism. You have an Attorney General in Mr. Smith who wants to get out; and you have a nominee, Mr. Meese, who wants to get in, but the Republican Senate won't let him in. Is that the most effective and efficient way to run the Department of Justice? Does there come a time when you want Mr. Meese to withdraw his nomination?

The President. Right now there is an investigation going on at Mr. Meese's request, and until we know the results of that investigation, I don't think that there's any answer I could give to that. He asked for that in response to the furor that was raised about him.

I have every confidence in him, and I'm appreciative of the fact that Attorney General Smith wanted very much to return to private life but has agreed that he will stay as long as this situation prevails and until it is resolved. And I'm confident that, myself, that we're going to find out that Mr. Meese is guilty of no wrongdoing.

Q. Mr. President, in—oh——

The President. No——

Anne M. Burford

Q. In regard to another one of your nominations, the Senate late this afternoon voted 73 to 19 to request that you withdraw the nomination of Anne Burford to serve on an environmental advisory committee. That includes more than 30 Republicans. Will you take that direction?

The President. No, I won't. Ms. Burford was called before a House committee when she was head of the EPA, and she obeyed the instructions that we gave her. The House committee was trying to obtain documents, and we exercised executive privilege on the ruling of the Justice Department that those documents were part of investigation reports and that if there was any evidence brought up that would lead to legal action against anyone they could be compromised by opening them up to the Congress.

So, she obeyed her instructions, and there was not one single allegation that was proved in any way that stood up under all the shouting and the furor that went on. And therefore, I am standing by the appointment that I have made. And I am pleased that the resolution that was passed was nonbinding.

Q. In regard to that, your critics have come out very strongly recently in criticism of your environmental policies. Do you see the Anne Burford appointment as a liability to you during this election year?

The President. And in that regard, once again, I ask all of you of an investigative nature to take a look at what our record is with regard to environmentalism. There is not one fact substantiating many of the charges that had been made.

We have continued doing what we came here to do—clean air and clean water, and both are cleaner than they've been for a long, long time. We have refurbished and reestablished the health and safety factors of the parks and are now going to return to adding territory or land to the park areas. We have vastly increased the wilderness lands.

There isn't anything that can be proven that we have not been meeting fully our responsibilities with regard to—in the protecting of the environment.

Geraldine Ferraro

Q. Mr. President, the "good Christian" issue aside, your plans to make a campaign stop at an Italian dinner at a Catholic church named for the patron saint of women in a New York City suburb on Thursday would indicate that you're at least a bit concerned about the impact of Geraldine Ferraro on the election. Could you assess for us your views on what the impact of a woman on the Democratic ticket will be?

The President. Well, no, I think this is just another step forward in the recognition of the new place of women that has been long overdue. I think it is significant. I think it was significant when a woman took her place—Sandra Day O'Connor—on the Supreme Court; when we had three women on our Cabinet; and when we have some 1,600 in very responsible positions, Presidential appointees, in our administration.

But, no, that's a logical step and one that possibly is overdue. So, I have no criticism on that base at all.

Q. But, sir, I think you suggested it was a token gesture. I know you didn't say that outright, but your remarks indicated to some you felt that way.

The President. Glad you asked that. [*Laughter*] I was speaking to a room full—the dining room, as a matter of fact—of Republican women, all of whom were—some were candidates, but the bulk of them were elected government officials at various levels of government—Republican women elected officials from all over the United States. And in talking about a subject that I thought would be of interest to them, I was delivering a talk that had been put down on paper many days before Ms. Ferraro was spoken of as a nominee or chosen.

And I was talking about my own personal experience with meeting Margaret Thatcher when I was a Governor and she was the newly chosen head of the Conservative Party in England, which is when we first met there. And I was talking about how she had been chosen by the Conservative Party to be their leader; obviously on the basis that she was the best qualified person in the party to have that job. And I used the phrase, I said there was no tokenism or symbolism connected with it. I was talking about Margaret Thatcher and the Conservative Party of England; I didn't have Ms. Ferraro in mind and certainly not when I put that down on paper.

Ms. Thomas. Thank you, Mr. President.

The President. Well, Helen, we've got to get rid of these second questions.

Note: The President's 26th news conference began at 8 p.m. in the East Room at the White House. It was broadcast live on nationwide radio and television.

Remarks at a Reagan-Bush Rally in Austin, Texas
July 25, 1984

The President. I want to thank you for always reminding me that if you want to see where America's dreams reach toward wide open sky, where her spirit of progress is as strong as her heart is big, then come to the Southwest and come to the great State of Texas.

I'll take up where the Vice President left off on one point: At their convention, the leadership of the Democratic Party gave Texas the back of their hand. Well, we've come to give you a message from our heart: We care about Texas. We care about your citizens and the values that you all live for. But rather than saying "your," maybe I should be saying "our," for you've made me feel at least like an adopted son.

And you've also given me and the country one of your finest. Believe me, Texas has no more loyal son than my partner, George Bush. And I use that term, "partner," advisedly. With all due respect to those who have served in that office before, I don't believe there has ever been a Vice President that has been so involved at the very top level in all that is going on in our country and in the decisions that are being made. He is untiring, totally faithful, and I am so grateful for what he brings on the basis of his experience as a Congressman, his experience as the Director of the CIA, as our Ambassador to the United Nations, and as our representative to the Republic of China. I just happen to think he's the best Vice President we've ever had.

Now, I'm also thankful for the friendship and the support of great Texans like John Connally, Bill Clements, John Tower, and Phil Gramm. They've worked with courage and common sense for growth, for stable prices, and for a strong America.

But, you know, when Phil Gramm tried to help us control government spending and taxing, he infuriated the national Democratic leadership. So, he did the honorable thing—he left his party. He joined ours. But then, where he didn't need to do this, having just been returned to office, he went back to the voters of his district to give them a chance to register approval or disapproval on the action he'd taken. And thank heaven—they registered approval.

They stuck with him then, and I'm confident that Texas will stick with him now. I'm confident that Republicans, Democrats, and Independents will join together to elect Phil Gramm your next United States Senator.

Now, with this talk about switching parties, I remember when I cast my first vote. I was a Democrat. And I cast it for Franklin Delano Roosevelt in 1932. He ran on a platform to reduce the Federal budget by 25 percent, to eliminate useless boards, commissions, agencies, and bureaus, and restore the autonomy of State and local governments that he said had been unjustly seized by the Federal Government. Ask yourselves which party could run on that platform today?

Audience. Republicans! Republicans! Republicans!

The President. Certainly not those we heard and saw in San Francisco. But then, with all respect to millions of fine, patriotic citizens who are Democrats in this country today, let us ask, were those people in San Francisco truly representative of those millions of rank-and-file Democrats across this land?

Audience. No!

The President. To those of you who are still Democrats—and I know there must be many here—and who might share my belief that government should not plunder more of our earnings, should not seize greater power over our lives, but should work to ensure the ultimate in individual freedom consistent with an orderly society, then I extend an invitation to you, and to millions of others: Come where you will be welcome and appreciated. Join George Bush and Phil Gramm and me, and together we'll make history on November 6th, 1984.

You know, when I heard some of the things that were being said last week in San Francisco—and I didn't watch all the convention—[*laughter*]—there's some punishment you just don't deserve. [*Laughter*] But from what I did hear, and then maybe the next day read about, I couldn't help but think that maybe the fog is so thick out there that it was getting inside their heads. [*Laughter*] But maybe there's another explanation. The national Democratic leadership is going so far left, they've left America.

I'm sorry they seem to see only misery and feel only fear and never stop pining for the days of tax and tax and spend and spend. They offer a three-point program: Fear the future, ignore the present, and forget the past.

And one promise that was made at that convention by one of them made me think of a suggestion I got for the income tax. It was a plan we will not adopt. It was a sample form. On one line, you put down how much you'd earned, and on the other line it said, "Send it." [*Laughter*]

But they offer a three-point program—as I said—forget the future, ignore the present, and forget the past. I've found a way to put their pessimism to constructive use. It's a sure-fire diet that you can use to lose weight. And there's only one rule: You only eat on the days the pessimists say something good about America.

Well, permit me to make three small points of my own.

Point one: Those responsible for punishing America with record inflation, record interest rates, record tax increases, credit controls, farm embargoes, gas lines, no growth at home, weakness abroad, and phony excuses about malaise are the last people who should give sermonettes about misery, unfairness, and compassion.

Point two: Today they offer new realism. Well, forgive me, but their new realism seems to begin right where their old ideas left off: billions in new spending; higher taxes on small business, family farms, and every other working family. And we must answer with a firm unequivocal no.

Audience. No!

The President. Point three: A little barometer of discomfort that Jimmy Carter and his Vice President used in 1976. They created the misery index by adding the inflation and unemployment rates. In '76 that came to 12½ percent. And they said our candidate had no right to seek reelection with a misery rate as big as 12½. Well, since the Democratic leadership devoted hours in San Francisco to talk of misery, I hope I'll be pardoned for taking 10 seconds to say we cut their misery index almost in half from the 19½ it was in 1980 to 10.3 today. And we'll bring it down even more if they'll just get out of the way.

We'll campaign on our record—and, yes, on theirs as well—and for ideas we believe will bring new hope to all Americans. We intend to represent only one special interest group—you, the people.

Let me pose the question they never got around to in San Francisco. Which major industrial nation today has the strongest currency; the strongest economic growth— 7½ percent for the last quarter—inflation of only 3—well, it's only been 3.3 percent for the last 3 months; labor force participation at an all-time high; fastest rate of job creation, as you've just been told. There are 7 million more people employed in the United States today than were working in 1980.

Last year there were a record 600,000 business incorporations, its fastest growth in business investment in 30 years; the largest increase in real after-tax personal income since 1973; and leadership in developing jobs and markets for the future in science and high technology, both on Earth and in outer space.

Well, I think you know which nation fits all of those, and the initials are U.S.A.!

I'm sorry the other side still doesn't know any of this, but then they never have understood the economy. They still think that GNP stands for gross national promises. [*Laughter*] They've never understood that incentives are the driving force of growth and human progress, that if we work or save more than before, our reward will be greater than it was, and we'll be challenged to lead more productive, worthy lives. They don't understand, but America does; and I believe that challenge will be the choice of a new generation.

Incentives, initiative, and innovation are sparking a revolution in America. We see it here in Austin with your great commitment to technological leadership. But we mustn't stop until we simplify the entire tax system, until we make taxes more fair, easier to understand, and most important, until we bring your personal tax rates further down; because if we bring them down enough, the underground economy will shrink, the world will beat a path to our door, and no one will be able to hold America back. So, please, don't let them bury the American dream in their graveyard of gloom and envy.

Endless tax increases, deeper dependency, planned protectionism, certain sacrifices, and veiled quotas—we don't need that kind of progress, do we?

Audience. No!

The President. I've always been told that if you want to make a Texan's neck swell, you tell him where to line up and what to think. Well, this election offers the sharpest,

most important choice in modern times—greater freedom or coercion.

Last night I asked the leadership of the Democratic Party to support six key measures for our future—legislation that will benefit all Americans, legislation that's been bottled up by a do-nothing House leadership. For example, they seek to reduce deficits, but the futile way—by raising taxes on America's families.

Audience. No!

The President. Right. I'm asking—why not do it the right way, the fair way, the effective way? Why not insist that government spend no more than government takes in? Why not insist that Speaker O'Neill permit a vote on——

Audience. Boo-o-o!

The President. I hope they're listening in Washington. [*Laughter*]

But why shouldn't he permit a vote on the constitutional amendment mandating a balanced Federal budget?

Fairness for families means a spouse working in the home would enjoy the same individual retirement rights, IRA's, as a spouse working outside the home. Each should be able to save and exclude from taxation up to $2,000 a year. We'd like that bill passed now.

Tuition tax credits would help low- and middle-income parents paying to send their children to parochial or independent schools while also paying their full share of taxes to support public schools.

You know, it's fine to get way out there in the nether regions—out in the abstract someplace—and talk about our great national family. But how about a little help for the real families who sustain our neighborhoods, our churches, and our schools? The forgotten Americans in all those years of their domination have been those parents who sit around a table at night deciding how to pay their bills and put their kids through school. How about a little compassion for them, too?

Then there's our bill offering incentives for investment in 75 enterprise zones that would bring jobs and growth and hope for people in inner cities and in other distressed regions. But here's the rub again. Enterprise zones have been blocked for 2 years by the same people who gave those fine speeches about opportunity and fairness. Well, do they want to end the welfare bondage or they just want to filibuster forever about the nice things they'll do someday, somewhere, somehow, for somebody?

We think it's not asking too much that Americans be able to take a walk after dark without having to cringe in fear. We have a strong anticrime proposal that would provide new restrictions on bail, tougher sentencing, and stricter enforcement of drug trafficking laws. Lives are at stake. So, if we still can't get a vote on that, maybe it's time to move some politicians out of office to get the criminals off the streets.

And finally, last night I asked the House to pass the equal-access bill. It would permit religious student groups the same freedom that other student groups now have to meet in public high schools in their vacant rooms during off-hours. This is—let me repeat—this is in nonschool hours. I believe the God who blessed this land of ours never deserved to be expelled from our schools in the first place.

Well, I'm pleased to give you some good news, and just received—take out your pens, members of the press—[*laughter*]—today I have just been informed the House of Representatives finally passed, despite stubborn resistance by its liberal leaders, the equal-access bill, 337 to 77. But let's make one thing plain: While this long-overdue action is welcome, it's certainly not sufficient. They should put their new realism to work and take action on each of those other five requests that they've bottled up for so long; and together we will make America great.

And let me just suggest to you the steps that we've taken, the steps we've taken to reverse years of neglecting our military security—shameful neglect—have not made America less secure; the steps we've taken have made us more secure. If the sons and daughters of this nation can risk their lives to protect our freedom in a dangerous world, then we have a moral obligation to give them, in the way of protection, the finest we can in weaponry, in machinery.

I want to tell you something. When you see one of those young men or women out on the street in uniform, if you haven't done it already, give them a smile and maybe ask them where they're from and tell them, maybe, you're a little grateful for what they're doing. I have to tell you that nothing in this job has made me more proud than the young men and women who are representing our country in uniform. They have the highest level of intelligence and education of any who have ever represented our country in the past in uniform. They are the best trained. They have an esprit de corps that just won't stop.

And I know—I was an officer once, and I know that in civilian clothes you're not supposed to salute. But I also know that if I'm Commander in Chief and when they started throwing those highballs at me, I'm going to salute 'em back.

Thank you for your wonderful Texas welcome today and for being with us here and sharing your joy and spirit.

And before I go, I do want to ask you a question that you may have heard before. Tell me, are you better off today than you were 4 years ago?

Audience. Yes!

The President. Well, all right. Let me ask another: Is America better off than she was 4 years ago? [*Applause*]

Audience. Reagan! Reagan! Reagan!

The President. Then I'm going to assume—I won't even ask this one—I'm just going to assume that you don't want to go back to the days of America being second best.

Audience. No!

The President. Let's keep going forward together.

Thank you, and God bless you all. Thank you very much.

Note: The President spoke at 12:45 p.m. at Auditorium Shores. He was introduced by the Vice President.

Following his remarks, the President went to the Hyatt Regency Austin Hotel, where he met with leaders of Texans for Reagan-Bush. He then traveled to Atlanta, GA, and the Waverly Hotel, where he met with Southern Republican leaders. He remained at the hotel overnight.

Nomination of Anthony Cecil Eden Quainton To Be United States Ambassador to Kuwait
July 25, 1984

The President today announced his intention to nominate Anthony Cecil Eden Quainton, of Washington, a career member of the Senior Foreign Service, Class of Minister-Counselor, as Ambassador to the State of Kuwait. He would succeed Francois M. Dickman.

Mr. Quainton was a research fellow at Oxford University (England) from 1958 to 1959. He entered the Foreign Service in 1960 as commercial officer in Sydney. From 1962 to 1963, he attended Hindi-Urdu language training at the Foreign Service Institute. He was economic officer in Karachi (1963–1964), in Islamabad (1964–1966), and political and economic officer in New Delhi (1966–1969). In the Department he was

senior political officer for India from 1969 to 1972. From 1972 to 1973, he was political officer in Paris and deputy chief of mission in Kathmandu from 1973 to 1976. He was Ambassador to the Central African Republic from 1976 to 1978. In the Department he was Director of the Office for Combatting Terrorism with the rank of Ambassador from 1978 to 1981. From 1981 to 1984, he was Ambassador to the Republic of Nicaragua.

Mr. Quainton received his A.B. (1955) from Princeton University and B.Litt (1958) from Oxford University. His foreign languages are Spanish, French, Urdu, Hindi, and Russian. He was born April 4, 1934, in Seattle, WA.

Nomination of Robert E. Barbour To Be United States Ambassador to Suriname
July 25, 1984

The President today announced his intention to nominate Robert E. Barbour, of Tennessee, a career member of the Senior Foreign Service, Class of Minister-Counselor, as Ambassador to the Republic of Suriname. He would succeed Robert W. Duemling.

Mr. Barbour entered the Foreign Service in 1949 as a clerk in Basra, Iraq. From 1950 to 1951, he was an intern in the Department. He was an administrative assistant in Tokyo from 1952 to 1954 and attended Vietnamese language training at Georgetown University from 1954 to 1955. He was political officer in Saigon (1955–1957), principal officer in Hué, Vietnam (1957–1958), political officer in Paris (1958–1961) and in Saigon (1961–1963). From 1963 to 1967, he was desk officer for Western European affairs in the Department. From 1967 to 1972, he was political officer in Rome and

attended the Royal College of Defence Studies in London from 1972 to 1973. In the Department he was special assistant to the Under Secretary of State for Political Affairs (1973–1974), Chief of the Performance Evaluation Division (1974–1975), Director of the Office of Western European Affairs (1975–1976), and Deputy Assistant Secretary of State for European Affairs (1976–1978). He was deputy chief of mission in Madrid from 1978 to 1984. Since 1984 he has been Deputy Examiner of the Board of Examiners for the Foreign Service in the Department.

Mr. Barbour received his B.A. in 1949 from the University of Tennessee. His foreign languages are Spanish, French, and Italian. He was born December 23, 1927, in Cleveland, OH.

Nomination of Brandon Hambright Grove, Jr., To Be United States Ambassador to Zaire
July 25, 1984

The President today announced his intention to nominate Brandon Hambright Grove, Jr., of the District of Columbia, a career member of the Senior Foreign Service, Class of Minister-Counselor, as Ambassador to the Republic of Zaire. He would succeed Peter D. Constable.

Mr. Grove served in the United States Navy from 1954 to 1958 as lieutenant. In 1959 he entered the Foreign Service as vice consul in Abidjan. In the Department he was staff assistant to the Under Secretary of State (1961–1962), and special assistant to the Deputy Under Secretary of State for Management (1962–1963). He was special assistant to the Ambassador in New Delhi (1963–1965) and political officer in Berlin, United States Mission (1965–1969). In the Department he was Director of the Office of Panamanian Affairs (1969–1971), member of the Senior Seminar in Foreign Policy (1971–1972), and Deputy Director of the Policy Planning Staff (1972–1974). From 1974 to 1976, he was deputy chief of mission in Berlin, German Democratic Republic. In the Department he was Senior Foreign Service Inspector (1976–1978) and Deputy Assistant Secretary of State for Inter-American Affairs (1978–1980). From 1980 to 1983, he was consul general in Jerusalem.

Mr. Grove received his A.B. (1950) from Bard College and his M.P.A. (1952) from Princeton University. His foreign languages are French and German. He was born April 8, 1929, in Chicago, IL.

Nomination of William Lee Hanley, Jr., To Be a Member of the Board of Directors of the Corporation for Public Broadcasting
July 25, 1984

The President today announced his intention to nominate William Lee Hanley, Jr., to be a member of the Board of Directors of the Corporation for Public Broadcasting for the remainder of the term expiring March 26, 1987. He would succeed Karl Eller, who has resigned.

Mr. Hanley is presently serving as president, chairman of the board, and chief executive officer of Hanley Co., Inc., in New York, NY. He is a trustee of the International Center for the Disabled and the Greenwich (CT) Hospital, serving as chairman of its planning committee, a director of the Boys Club of Greenwich, and education chairman for the metropolitan New York chapter of the Young Presidents Organization. Mr. Hanley previously served as a member of the Board of Directors of the Corporation for Public Broadcasting for a term which expired March 1, 1984. He graduated from Yale University (B.A., 1964).

He is married to the former Alice Hoffman and has five children and resides in Greenwich, CT. He was born January 27, 1940, in New York, NY.

Nomination of Helen J. Valerio To Be a Member of the National Advisory Council on Women's Educational Programs
July 25, 1984

The President today announced his intention to nominate Helen J. Valerio to be a member of the National Advisory Council on Women's Educational Programs for a term expiring May 8, 1987. This is a reappointment.

Mrs. Valerio is senior vice president and treasurer of Papa Gino's of America, Inc., in Dedham, MA, a family restaurant chain of 110 restaurants located throughout New England and New York. She cofounded the company with her husband in 1957.

Mrs. Valerio is married, has three children, and resides in Framingham, MA. She was born November 23, 1938, in Chelsea, MA.

Nomination of Clifford J. Murino To Be a Member of the National Science Board
July 25, 1984

The President today announced his intention to nominate Clifford J. Murino to be a member of the National Science Board, National Science Foundation, for a term expiring May 10, 1990. He would succeed Edwin Ernest Salpeter.

Mr. Murino is currently president of University Corporation for Atmospheric Research in Boulder, CO. Previously, he was president and research professor, Desert Research Institute, University of Nevada system (1980–1983); director, atmospheric technology division, National Center for Atmospheric Research (1975–1980); vice president for finance and research, St. Louis University (1971–1975); and vice president for research, St. Louis University (1969–1971).

Mr. Murino graduated from St. Louis University (B.S., 1950; M.S., 1954; Ph.D., 1957). He is married, has three children, and resides in Boulder, CO. He was born February 10, 1929, in Yonkers, NY.

Appointment of James Curtis Mack II as a Member of the President's Commission on White House Fellowships
July 25, 1984

The President today announced his intention to appoint James Curtis Mack II to be a member of the President's Commission on White House Fellowships. This is a new position.

Mr. Mack is currently executive director of Citizens for the Republic in Santa Monica, CA. Previously he was assistant to the Regional Director and assistant veterans services officer, Veterans Administration regional office, Los Angeles (1973–1979). He has served in the United States Air Force and the Air Force Reserve since 1969 and currently holds the rank of major.

Mr. Mack was listed in America's Outstanding Young Men in 1973 and was nominated by the 5th U.S. Air Force for the 10 Outstanding Young Men of America in 1971.

Mr. Mack graduated from the University of Southern California (B.A., 1967; M.P.A., 1969; M.A., 1976). He resides in Los Angeles, CA, and was born December 22, 1944, in Los Angeles.

Remarks at a Reagan-Bush Rally in Atlanta, Georgia
July 26, 1984

The President. Senator Denton and Carroll Campbell and Paula Hawkins, thank you all very much—and for those kind words.

You know, a few weeks ago I was down in Alabama at a rally, and I told the people there that I'm always happy when I'm in the South. I guess I feel kind of at home here. The South has always given more than its share to this country, more than its share of greatness and courage. Here are the traditions, in this special place, that shaped our country, and they endure. There's a steadiness of purpose, a fidelity to ideals, the type of thing that made someone say, just a few years ago, that "the South is where this country will be saved."

Now, this is an interesting time in our national life. Last week the Democrats picked their nominees. The election year has begun now that both sides have their tickets. I've been in Georgia and in the South a number of times since I was elected President; I'll be back a number of times.

But I want you to know something. The other party apparently thinks the South just isn't important this year; it just doesn't deserve much attention. Well, I'll tell you how George Bush and I feel about the South. We won't write it off; we won't kiss it off, or try to buy it off. The South is worth fighting for; the South is worth listening to.

The South is America at its best. You know those folks who are writing off the South out there in the fog in San Francisco, they were busy talking and filling the air with eloquent-sounding words; as a matter of fact, big clouds of words. But a lot of those words contained what Winston Churchill called "terminological inexactitude." [*Laughter*] That's a nice way of saying they said a few things that weren't true.

The future, according to them, is dark and getting darker, and Americans are very unhappy. According to the other party, there's nothing to hope for but despair, and we have nothing in store but fear itself. In fact, I thought it sounded a little bit like one of those disaster or horror movies in which they picked me to play the monster. [*Laughter*] Do you get the feeling—I don't know whether you did or not, but do you get the feeling that they don't like me very much? [*Laughter*]

Well, it was great dramatic rhetoric, but the fog has cleared, and this is a good time to look at the record, to look at the facts. Now, the plain truth is that 4 years ago our economy was in a shambles. Inflation, their disease, has come like a thief in the night to rob our savings, rob our earnings, and take the bread off our tables.

Four years ago a tyrant held our diplomats hostage. Four years ago our defense had deteriorated to the point where many of our ships couldn't leave port. Many of our aircraft were so old that they'd been flown by the fathers of the pilots who are now flying them. And 4 years ago the Soviets took the free nation of Afghanistan for their own.

American prestige seemed like a memory. Our standing in the world had fallen. Our government was talking about a malaise. You remember that talk, and you were the ones that were supposed to be having the malaise.

Well, 4 years later America is a very different place. And the Democrats are saying that it's my fault. They keep insisting that I take responsibility for it. Well, they've talked me into it. [*Laughter*] But I'll only take the blame if you'll join me, because we couldn't have done anything we've done without your help.

So, if you'll join me, I'll take the blame for inflation falling by almost two-thirds, as you've been told. And I guess that makes us responsible for the economy expanding and the country growing and building again. And it's our fault that the prime interest rate fell from that 21½ percent, our defenses are stronger, that we cut taxes for every American so that everyone can keep more of the money they earn and spend it on their children and their families and their neighborhoods.

Now, you'll have to be patient with me here, because I've got a lot of admitting to do. [*Laughter*] 106 million Americans now have jobs. That's more than at any time in our history, and it's 7 million more jobs than were held in 1980. That's right—it's our fault. [*Laughter*] We've created 6.7 million new jobs in the last 18 months. That's our fault again, too.

Their misery index, as you've been told, was almost 20, and now it's barely half that. And I apologize. That's our fault. [*Laughter*] You remember the misery index. Our opponents invented it for the 1976 campaign by adding the unemployment rate and the rate of inflation. And it was 12½ in '76. And they said that was disgraceful. So, in 4 years they ran it up to about 20. As a matter of fact, as of 4 years ago right now, it was 21.8. And in 3½ years we've brought it down, as you've been told. It's now 10.3. And that was one thing they didn't mention—was having a misery index this year. [*Laughter*]

You know, when you start to talk about the facts, the fog really lifts. And when the fog lifts you can see the country the way it really is.

Now, I'm not talking about big statistics that exist way off in the air someplace. Things are better right here in Atlanta, too. Between 1980 and 1983, total employment increased in Atlanta by almost 11 percent. By the end of the year, it is expected to have increased by 14 percent. Housing starts in your city have gone up 93 percent since 1980.

And our progress isn't only economic. Nationally, violent crime fell last year for the first time in a decade. And here in Atlanta, violent crime is down almost 16 percent since 1980.

The plain truth, the economy—or the recovery is real. It's based on commonsense fact: that if you allow the people to keep the fruits of their labor, then they'll work hard and make money and save money and invest money. They have an incentive. But kill that incentive, and you kill economic expansion. And that's precisely what the opponents would do.

They talk about the budget deficits. But they don't tell you that the budget problem is a spending problem. They don't tell you that all spending originates in the Congress, which has been controlled by the Democratic Party for 46 of the past 50 years.

They don't want to control their spending. They want to keep spending and raise your taxes so they can keep on spending. And that's what they say they'll do. And believe me, of all the promises they made, that's the one they'll deliver on if you give them a chance.

When they talk about austerity, they don't mean tightening Tip O'Neill's belt. [*Laughter*] They mean tightening yours, around your neck.

I want to interject something here. The other night in the press conference, I made a statement with regard to the pledge at the convention about their candidate would promise he would raise taxes. And he means it. He's never missed a vote on raising taxes. But then I gave my own position, which is that, no, we have no plans and will not raise taxes. But I added one qualifier, and it seems to be presently being distorted. And let me make it plain what I said.

They have suggested that I put an "if" in there and said, "Well, *if*, you know, we get all the spending cuts that we can and still we haven't gotten the balance between taxes and spending together, why then we'll have to look at the tax." That isn't what I said. What I said was, if and when we bring government spending down to where we have a government that can fulfill its responsibilities and do those things the people require of government, and then, at that bottom level, that still is above what our tax system is bringing in in revenues, yes, then we would have to look and make those two balance so that we would be spending within our means. But we're a long way from getting down to that bottom line of what is absolutely necessary for government's expenses.

It's kind of interesting to note that in a half dozen years before this administration came here, taxes in the United States were tripled and the deficits totaled $650 billion. Raising taxes just gives them a license to keep on with their deficit spending.

The plain truth is, our administration is on the right track. We've turned away from failed ideas about a huge government taking your money and redistributing it.

We've moved on to ideas that work. The plain truth is that we're finally making our defense system stronger, and for only one reason, because weakness invites trouble and strength deters it. And yet, in spite of all of their rhetoric about our gigantic deficit-causing defense spending, our defense budget is lower than the one that their President in 1980 had projected for this particular time—because Presidents must project about 5 years ahead under the law as to what they think's going to happen. We're spending less than they said they were going to spend on defense and doing a better job of it.

The plain truth is there's a mood in this country, a general feeling that, indeed, America is a decent and a just place, and it deserves our love and fidelity.

There's a mood, a general feeling that patriotism isn't something to be embarrassed about, but something to be proud of. There's a mood in the country, a general feeling that once again, there's a lot to be hopeful about. Our optimism has once again been turned loose. And all of us recognize that these people who keep talking about the age of limits, are really talking about their own limitations, not America's.

The plain truth is, things are better. Facts are facts, and the other side is hoping that you won't look at the record. Well, we're hoping you will.

I couldn't be addressing a crowd in this place, and of this number, without realizing that I must be speaking to a great many Democrats who are here. But your Democrat Party has been a great party. I was a Democrat, too. And I supported and campaigned for Franklin Roosevelt and Harry Truman, because I felt they were for a strong America, a fair and decent America that wouldn't shrink from its responsibilities in the world and wouldn't retreat or run from the challenges of the times.

I was a Democrat longer than I have presently been a Republican. But I think that the current leadership of the Democratic Party, the leadership that we saw last week in San Francisco—I think their instructions for getting to the convention were: Go west to San Francisco, and then turn left.

They've gone so far left that they've left the mainstream. And I know that those of you who still are Democrats, or who have been, I know that you've been thinking about these things, and you're aware of them, also. So, I want to put out my hand, and let you know that if you're starting to feel that your party has abandoned you, then we're holding out a hand and asking for your continuing help. We can't do it without you.

From my own experience——

Audience. 4 more years! 4 more years! 4 more years!

The President. Thank you. I give in. [*Laughter*]

My friends, we want the support of every group, of every individual in this country, and we're going to fight for it from one end of this country to the other. We're going to ask you to help us build a new America, a freer nation. We're going to barnstorm this country. We're going to get out on the stump out there, and from stump to stump, we're going to tell the plain truth. We believe in freedom. We believe in America.

The 1984 election will determine the course this country takes for the rest of the country [century]—as Senator Hawkins told us. This election offers the clearest choice in many years—the clearest philosophical choice, the clearest choice between principles and visions.

This election is about leadership. It's about what we want for our children—a free nation, or more bondage of the tax-and-tax and spend-and-spend variety, a strong nation that is deeply proud of the ideals that it presents to the world, or a nation that begs on its knees for kindness from tyrants?

Audience. No!

The President. Right, no.

We want a free nation where our children can grow and become anything they want to be, or, on the other hand, those who want a tired place where a big government far away will take everything they work hard for.

Audience. No!

The President. No. I think like you.

We all want a great nation to be greater, a nation of free and equal Americans who stand together in the glow of fellowship and in the light of God. That's the country I'm working for, and that's the road that we want to walk down. And I say to you: Come on and walk down the road with me.

Thank you for coming out here today, thank you for listening to me, and God bless all of you.

Note: The President spoke at 12:07 p.m. at the Cumberland Shopping Mall.

Following his remarks, the President traveled to Elizabeth, NJ.

Remarks at a Reagan-Bush Rally in Elizabeth, New Jersey
July 26, 1984

The President. Matt Rinaldo, thank you for your very kind and generous words. And I could say that for the others who've spoken here.

This is a special day for us, and already you've given us many gifts. As we flew into Newark, we saw the lovely steeples of Elizabeth. It almost seemed that they were reaching up to say, "Come over to see us." And you do make us feel that welcome.

Along with Congressmen Rinaldo and Courter; and our outstanding candidate for the Senate, Mary Mochary; our Secretary of Labor, Ray Donovan; and reverend clergy—I have the—our great Governor, Tom Kean—and of meeting and being able to give my heartfelt thanks to your fine mayor, Tom Dunn, of being able to listen to one of the best bands in New Jersey, and maybe even in America, the Elizabeth High School Band—and, of course, meeting all of you.

Your devotion to your city makes me understand why you say, "Elizabeth is a proud lady." You know, so often when people talk of America's heartland, they speak of the Middle West or the Great Plains, and certainly those regions are deserving of that description. But there's another heartland in America—a heartland of the streets; a kind of place that welcomes tremendous numbers of people—Italians, Cubans, Puerto Ricans, Portuguese, blacks, Irish, Polish-Americans, and all the others here that the mayor mentioned; the kind of a place where more than 30 languages are spoken in an excellent school system, and they're proud of it. It's the kind of place that doesn't subtract from America's strength, but adds to it by bringing us new dreams, filling us with new strength, and enriching the values, traditions, and patriotism that we share. It's a place like Elizabeth, New Jersey, and you be proud of what you give America.

You know, somewhere in the history of every American family is a person or persons who became American not by birth, but by choice. I've always believed that ours is a chosen land, that it was placed here by some divine providence, placed here between the two oceans to be sought out and found by people from every corner of the Earth, people who had a special love for freedom and the courage to uproot themselves and leave their homelands and friends and to come here to create something new in all the history of mankind, a country where man is not beholden to government; government is beholden to man.

These people came with their faith and their families to work and to build. They didn't come seeking streets paved with gold. They didn't come asking for welfare or some special treatment. They came for freedom and opportunity. And they seized both with such a vengeance that no matter how often they fell down, they kept picking themselves up until they could leave a better life for their loved ones. And their examples of courage, multiplied millions of times over, created the greatest success story the world has ever known.

But 4 years ago we knew that dream was being stolen from us. Interest rates were rising to record thresholds of pain. Inflation had come like a thief in the night—as you've already been told here today—to rob us of our earnings, our savings, and to take the bread off our tables. And all this was done, mind you, under the guise of compassion and fairness. Well, it's true that those policies were fair in one sense; they didn't discriminate. They made everybody miserable.

But did they have the courage to rein in a government that was growing by 17 percent a year in cost? No. In fact, they said it was your fault. Do you remember when they told you that you suffered from a malaise? They said the problem wasn't government spending too much; the problem was that you weren't being taxed enough. Well, that was nonsense then, and it's nonsense today.

Do you mind if I just interject something here and explain something to you? The other night on the press conference, I replied to a question that had to do with someone who has said there will be a tax if he is elected—and then said that there would be a tax even if he wasn't because, while I won't admit it, I will have to do it. Well, I responded, and I said flatly, "I will not raise taxes." And then I went on to explain that there could be one situation that would defeat anyone in that regard. And since then, that has been distorted, and several voices have been raised, the latest one in Washington, to say that I was really waffling and holding the door open, saying, "Well, I won't raise taxes—well, I will." No.

What I said was—and I think you'd all have to agree with the common sense of this—if, when we have gotten government spending in Washington down to the point that it is the lowest that it can be reduced to and still allow the government to provide the services that government is responsible for to the people of this country, and then it should turn out that the percentage to maintain that minimum level is more of the gross national product than the percentage presently being taken in taxes, obviously, you would have to readjust. But that is only if you have gotten government down to where it cannot be reduced one more penny and perform those services.

It was not saying that, "Well, if I get some deductions but can't get all I want—" No, if you raise taxes before you've gotten government down to that point, you will never get rid of government deficits and government spending.

Four years ago, a tyrant held our diplomats hostage. Our defenses had deteriorated to where many of our ships couldn't leave port. Many of our aircraft were so old that they'd been flown by the fathers of the current flyers, pilots of those machines.

Four years ago, the Soviets invaded the free nation of Afghanistan, the latest in the series of countries to fall to communism in that decade. The former Vice President said, "I cannot understand; it just baffles me, why the Soviets these last few years have behaved as they have." He didn't understand. But the American people did.

And four years ago, the American people said, "We want a new beginning." You reminded Washington—there must be an echo in here.[1] [*Laughter*]

You reminded Washington that we're a government of, by, and for the people; not the other way around. And you said it's time to put earnings back in the hands of the people, time to put trust back in the hands of the people, and time to put America back in the hands of the people.

Well, now, 4 years later, America's quite a different place. And our friends out in San Francisco kept saying that it's all my fault. [*Laughter*] They kept demanding that we take responsibility. Well, all right, I'm ready, if you are, because we couldn't have done any of the things we did without your help.

Inflation has fallen from 12.6 percent in June of 1980 to under 4 percent; as a matter of fact, 3.3 percent for the last 3 months. And in that same period of time the Producers' Price Index, which indicates what the inflation rate's going to be down the road, has been zero for that period of time. But if that's what they want, okay, we'll take the responsibility for that.

Now America's leading the world with the most powerful economic expansion in peacetime history. Nearly 7 million jobs have been created in the last 18 or 19 months. Investment is rising at the fastest rate in 30 years. And after-tax personal income is up by the sharpest amount since 1973. It's all our fault, and we'll take the blame.

---

[1] *The President was referring to a heckler in the audience.*

The misery index and the inflation rate to the—you know, you add the inflation rate to the unemployment rate. You'll remember that the previous administration, they did that in 1976. They said that Jerry Ford's misery rate, unemployment plus inflation, was 12½, and that was disgraceful and that no man had a right to seek reelection with a misery rate of that size. Well, it was 20 percent the day I walked into the Oval Office, and now it's only 10.3 percent, and that's our fault, again.

And, yes——

Audience. We want Reagan! We want Reagan! We want Reagan!

The President. Thank you very much. You've talked me into it. You can have me. But let me go on, again, if I can.

We take the blame for cutting taxes so that you can keep more of what you earn to spend on your children and in your neighborhoods, which is your right.

And please be patient, I have to take the responsibility for something else. Today, the young men and women who protect our freedom are better educated, have a higher percentage of high school graduates than any military force in our nation's history. They are better paid. They are better equipped. They are better trained than 4 years ago. They're keeping the peace and our freedoms more secure.

Look around the world, in the past 4 years, not a single country has fallen to communism, and that in itself makes it a safer world. But none have fallen to communism, but one nation has been set free from the clutches of Fidel Castro. I'm talking about Grenada. And we'll take the responsibility for that one, too.

Audience. Reagan! Reagan! Reagan!

The President. When American soldiers——

Audience. Reagan! Reagan! Reagan!

The President. I have a terrible feeling that I'm enjoying what you're saying more than you're enjoying what I'm saying. [*Laughter*]

Well, listen, when American soldiers and sailors and marines arrived in Grenada, thousands of people lined the streets to cheer and shower them with gratitude. Yet our critics in San Francisco were upset, angry, and ashamed. Well, I don't believe that our medical students who were getting an education there in the medical school in Grenada were upset to see those Army Rangers coming. And I don't believe their parents were upset to see them home safe again.

We had a little gathering on the South Lawn of the White House after some of our forces came back—about 400 or 500 of those students and then 40, representing the branches of the service, 40 in uniform, who had returned from Grenada, and it was so wonderful. They were all about the same age, those in uniform and the students. And to have the students—they couldn't keep their hands off those young people in uniform. And they came back to us and they said, "We, once upon a time, we didn't feel like this, but now, they saved our lives."

And they told me, one group, of how they were lying under the beds in their dormitory with the bullets coming through the building and the gunfight. And then they heard an American voice, identified himself as a sergeant in the Rangers. And he told them, "Come on out." And they took them to the helicopters to get them out of there. And they—these students told me the Rangers put themselves between them and where the firing was coming from, in order to get them to the helicopters. I don't believe the people of New Jersey are the least bit ashamed of America standing up for human freedom.

You know, sometimes our friends seem so upset by what we do that it makes them talk funny. One speaker in San Francisco called the economic expansion an illusion. That's right. They think prosperity is an illusion. And they think peace through strength is destabilizing. Well, let me tell you what I think: Only if you read the record of their administration backward does it have a happy ending. [*Laughter*]

Well, this is 1984, and we might remember George Orwell's warning about '84, that ". . . if thought corrupts language, language can also corrupt thought." Others may try to fool the public; our campaign will be one of clear thinking and honest talk with the American people. We will never accuse you of greed when you work to earn extra income to spend it the way you want to. And we will never thank them for compassion when they try to take your money to spend it the way they want to spend it.

And while it's fine to talk in abstract concerns—or about their concern for our great national family, how about a little help for the real families who support our churches, our neighborhoods, and our schools? The parents who sit around the table at night deciding how to pay their bills and put the kids through school—how about a little compassion for them, too?

So, how about a vote on tuition tax credits—a vote to help low- and middle-income parents paying to send their children to parochial or independent schools while they also pay their full share of taxes to support the public schools?

And fairness for families means a spouse working in the home should enjoy the same individual retirement right, IRA's, as a spouse working outside the home. Each spouse should be able to save and deduct from taxation up to $2,000 a year, and we'd like that bill passed now.

You know, when I see those who helped create a national crisis systematically resisting the good we're now trying to do, I'm reminded of a comment by a great leader. He said, "Those . . . who are frightened by boldness and cowed by the necessity for making decisions, complain that all we have done is unnecessary and subject to great risks. Now that these people are coming out of their storm cellars, they forget there ever was a storm." Well, those words were spoken about the Great Depression of the thirties; they were spoken by President Franklin Delano Roosevelt in the fall of 1934.

I know there are many among you who are old enough to remember it firsthand, as I do, what we struggled through together in that Great Depression. And that's why I want to ask you something important—a question you may have heard before. Tell me, are you better off than you were 4 years ago?

Audience. Yes!

The President. I think you've already told me the answer to the next one. Is America better off?

Audience. Yes!

The President. Then I won't even ask the third one, because I know the answer already. No, you don't want to go back to the days of America being second best.

Audience. No!

The President. Well, with you by our side, I know that America's best days are ahead. Our best days are ahead if we remember growth and opportunity are what the American dream is all about.

Now, the other side has a plan for your future. They call it new realism. But it would seem to begin right where their old ideas left off—higher and higher taxes on your families. Now, is that what your idea of the American dream is all about?

Audience. No!

The President. Not mine. Is that what your idea of fairness is all about?

Audience. No!

The President. Well, we have a different vision. We must not stop until we simplify the entire tax system; until we make your taxes more fair, easier to understand; and most important, until we have a reform that brings your personal tax rates further down. And those incentives—with those incentives must come a long overdue reform still bottled up by the House leadership—a constitutional amendment mandating a balanced Federal budget, government spending no more than it takes in.

To those who think that tax rates are the answer to all the problems—here in your city, Mayor Dunn has reduced tax rates in 3 of the last 6 years. Growth has increased; jobs have increased; revenues have increased. And you've always had a balanced budget, because by law you can spend no more than 5 percent above the previous year's budget. It makes sense.

Andrew Jackson described this. He said, "One man with courage makes a majority." I happen to believe the Democratic mayor of Elizabeth, New Jersey, has more courage than all the members of the House Democratic leadership in Washington, DC.

Now, we've proposed—as has been hinted up here once today—we've proposed an innovative idea called enterprise zones to stimulate investment in areas of high unemployment. Areas in this region would be helped by enterprise zones. So, wouldn't you think that they would embrace this initiative to create jobs, independence, and hope for people trapped in welfare bondage——

Audience. Reagan! Reagan! Reagan!

The President. No. Thank you very much. I'll have an answer in a minute for that, but I just wanted to tell you that despite more than 2 years of waiting, despite support from a majority of Democrats and Republicans, led by your own fighting Matt Rinaldo, the House leadership has blocked enterprise zones from coming to a vote, even though their own membership would vote for it if they would allow them to.

Forgive me, but I must ask them: In the name of growth, stop talking billions for dependency, and start creating enterprise zones for opportunity.

And now I think they deserve an answer over there. We *are* trying to rebuild the United States Navy back up to 600 ships, and the only thing that is slowing us down is the Democrat leadership of the Congress that keeps cutting the budget for building those ships.

In the name of America, stop spreading bondage, and let's start spreading freedom. We can preserve the dream of America, but we must not waste the genius of one mind, the strength of one body, or the spirit of one soul. We need all our people, men and women, young and old, individuals of every race, to be happy, healthy, and whole. And that's what our job is all about.

And if you stick by us, as you have before, then we'll keep proving all those so-called experts wrong, and we'll show them that 1985 will be even better than 1984.

So, thank you. Thank God for Elizabeth. God bless Elizabeth, and God bless all of you. Thank you.

Note: The President spoke at 4:22 p.m. outside the Elizabeth City Hall.

Following his remarks, the President traveled to Hoboken, NJ.

Remarks at the St. Ann's Festival in Hoboken, New Jersey
July 26, 1984

Thank you, Archbishop Gerety, thank you so much. Thank all of you, our host, Governor Kean—we have a young lady here, I shouldn't talk politics, so I won't say a candidate, but a mayor of a nearby city who's here. Mary, [1] pleased to have you here. And I'm pleased to be with all of you.

I didn't know that I was going to learn a little more family history; I thought I'd picked up most of it in Ballyporeen, Ireland, a short time ago. [*Laughter*] But I don't know if you—any of you or all of you know how this came about. A few weeks ago I got a letter from a Mr. Santo A. Milici, and even the letterhead was appetizing. It said, "St. Ann's Festival, A Feast for the Senses." Nancy saw it, and she said, "Honey, I think you ought to go to Hoboken." [*Laughter*]

---

[1] *Mary Mochary, mayor of Montclair, NJ, and Republican Senatorial candidate.*

We kept reading, and the letter told about what a great American city Hoboken is—of course, Frank Sinatra had already told me about that—and how you're the most dynamic town in the Tri-State area. We read about the outdoor continental cafe and the midway with rides and games and special entertainment. And my staff saw it, and they said, "Let's go to Hoboken."

But I'll tell you what did it. I'll tell you about your secret weapon. I heard about your zeppoles. And so, here I am in Hoboken.

I'm very happy to be here at your 74th festival in honor of St. Ann. There's something so special about that 74. [*Laughter*] Oh, if you're thinking what I think you're thinking, no, that's one yet to come. [*Laughter*] As a matter of fact, it's the next one.

A few days ago a member of my staff was here, and she asked a local woman, "Why's this church and this parish so important to you?" And the woman said, "I was baptized here, I made my first communion here, I made my confirmation here, I was married here, and my children were baptized here." Now, I know that remark says a lot about continuity, not only the continuity of a neighborhood but the continuity of tradition and faith and family.

At this festival and at other festivals, such as the one last week over at Our Lady of Mount Carmel, you show a lot of caring and involvement and allegiance. And these are the things by which our nation lives. God makes the world turn on its axis and keeps the Sun and the stars in place, but you are the people who keep America going, who make America happen every day.

I'm only the head of a civil government, a secular authority. It's probably true that politics is the prose of a culture, but religion is its poetry. Governments are passing things in the long history of the world, but faith and belief endure forever.

You know these things, of course. You show them in your actions as you honor your God, as you work in your parish, and as you carry the image of a saint through the streets. In doing these things, in adding to the religious and cultural life of our nation, you replenish our country. You reflect the values that help our nation flourish. And so, I think it's appropriate for me, as the head of a civil government, to simply say, thank you for being what you are—the backbone and the best.

Now, this, as you may have heard someplace, is an election year. [*Laughter*] And I am a candidate for reelection. It's traditional for candidates to talk about their accomplishments and their triumphs and to brag a bit if they can. But I hate to brag. I'm the President, after all, and I wouldn't do that. [*Laughter*]

I won't—I'm not going to talk about the extraordinary economic expansion that's taking place—[*laughter*]—about how all of us have more income to spend. Business is good, and taxes are down, and retail sales are up, and working people are enjoying a big increase in personal income, and more Americans are working now than ever before—7 million more than were working

in 1980—but I won't. I wouldn't do that—I won't talk about those things. [*Laughter*]

I could talk about how last year, for the first time in 10 years, violent crime went down—and how America's at peace in the world, in a more stable world, and now we're building up our defenses to a reasonable level again, but I won't. I wouldn't do that. [*Laughter*]

And I could talk about how there's a resurgence of pride in our country, a reemergence of the knowledge that we live in a good and decent place, and we represent good and decent things in the world. And once again our young people know that, and respond to it, and are proud of it. But, no, I wouldn't say that. I'm not going to talk about that.

Now, it's true that when you're out on the campaign trail and you start to get very eloquent about all the wonderful things you've accomplished, you can get yourself in trouble. I don't know if you ever heard the story about Teddy Roosevelt. And no matter what you may have heard, he did not tell me this story himself. [*Laughter*] About how once in a campaign he was giving a terrific old stemwinder of a speech and a heckler interrupted him very rudely.

And this fellow in the audience kept yelling, "I'm a Democrat." Teddy finally just stopped cold and said, "All right, sir, why are you a Democrat?" And the fellow said, "Because my father was a Democrat, and my grandfather was a Democrat, and my great-grandfather was a Democrat." And Teddy went in for the kill. He said, "Well, sir, what if your father were a jackass, and your grandfather were a jackass"—[*laughter*]—"and your great-grandfather were a jackass; what would you be then?" And the fellow says, "A Republican!" [*Laughter*] Now, you see, bragging can get you in trouble.

Now, this is a fine and a happy evening, but just for a moment I want to be serious here. There are great issues at stake in this election, deeply serious issues. They have to do with how we live and how we care for each other.

There are four questions I've been thinking about a great deal since the convention in San Francisco. There are four questions that I feel may be of special concern to you.

And I hope they are, because they concern me.

Here's the first question: Why do some who claim to represent the party of compassion feel no compassion whatsoever for the most helpless among us—the unborn? How can they parade down the street wearing compassion as if it were a cloak made of neon and they have no compassion for the most helpless of God's creatures?

Question two: Why did those who claim to represent the middle class take such high moral offense at the idea of giving the middle class a break by giving them tuition tax credits to help them bear the cost of sending their children to a parochial or independent school and then those children— or those parents who pay for that pay taxes, their full amount of taxes to support the public schools? They ask no help in bearing the extra cost they incur, and isn't it fair, just bottom-line fair to help them with a tax credit? Now, why is the other side so opposed to giving the middle class that simple and compassionate help?

And question three: How can the leadership on the other side, as they did last week, open each session of their great convention with an injunction to the Lord and end each session with a prayer to God and still insist on denying that right to a child in a public school who might want to do that?

The leadership of the House of Representatives has repeatedly resisted voluntary prayer in school—and I do mean voluntary. This was distorted in the debate to think that somehow we were asking for organized prayers in these public schools in which you had to wonder, well, who was going to be responsible for those and so forth. That wasn't the issue at all.

The issue was something that was illustrated in one of our States recently when some children, doing what they did at home, in the school cafeteria wanted to bow their heads and give thanks, say grace before they ate. And they were told they could not do it, and a court upheld the school authorities in saying that they couldn't do that. This was just simply the voluntary right of any individual who felt the urge and the need to be able to pray and shouldn't be denied because he was in a so-called public building.

Thankfully, a majority of Republicans and Democrats finally rose up in defiance yesterday and passed the equal-access bill. Now, by what logic do they resist? If they're so opposed to children witnessing prayer, why did they condone such a big show of it last week? I grant you they need prayer, but what do you suppose they were trying to prove or hide?

Question four: Why do those who claim to represent the most enlightened thought on Central America refuse to listen to the testimony of one of the greatest moral leaders of our time, His Holiness Pope John Paul II? Last year John Paul went to Nicaragua on a mission of peace. He went armed only with love and a message of goodness. This is what happened to the Pope when he went into the land of the Sandinista regime.

He was forced to stand in the brutal sun, this man who'd languished so long in a hospital bed after being shot. He was forced to stand in the brutal sun as Daniel Ortega, the leader of the Sandinista government, delivered a long and hate-filled diatribe against the West. Then he was booed and jeered by the Sandinistas when he tried to speak. The Sandinistas tried to humiliate His Holiness. They didn't know that it's not possible to humiliate that kind of greatness. When they booed him and jeered him, he said, *"Silencio"*—silence—and they were silenced by the sheer force of his majesty.

Two weeks ago Pope John Paul II stood on the balcony overlooking St. Peter's Square, and he said that the Sandinista government is oppressing the Catholic Church of Nicaragua. He deplored the arrest and deportation of priests. He spoke out to protect the Catholic Archbishop of Managua against repeated pressure from the Sandinistas who, the Archbishop has charged, are trying to abolish the Church of Rome and replace it with a so-called popular church.

Why can't those who claim to represent the most enlightened opinion on Central America come to grips with what is happening there? Why can't they admit that the Sandinistas are only totalitarian thugs who are squelching freedom in their country, including the freedom of religion?

Those are just four questions. I ask you to ponder about them, think about them this evening or tomorrow, and to give them long thought. Three questions—these questions, these four questions help define the differences between my administration and the other side. They help define what the issues this year are about. You can come to some hard truths as you answer these questions.

And if you have any doubt—and I don't think you do—about where we stand: We are for life and against abortion. We are for prayer in the schools. We are for tuition tax credits. And in Central America, we're rather more inclined to listen to the testimony of His Holiness the Pope than the claims of Communist Sandinistas.

But I don't wish to leave you on a somber and serious note. There's much to be happy about this evening, much to be joyous about in our country.

And I'll let you in on something else I've been thinking about. I want to serve another 4 years as your President. I make no bones about it. And there's some very serious reasons for it, but there's one I haven't talked about. I've been thinking about it now and then at night, or in a spare moment, when I'm summing up a day or thinking about the next one.

I've been thinking that I feel something in common with Franklin Delano Roosevelt, the much-admired President of my youth—I cast my first vote for President in 1932 for him—and John Kennedy, that bright spirit, and Teddy Roosevelt and Harry Truman. They all loved the Presidency, loved the bully pulpit of the office, loved looking out for the interests of our country. So do I, and so would I for the next 4½ years. And I have no reservations about throwing my candidacy on the mercies of the good people of St. Ann's Church in Hoboken, New Jersey, and asking them to give the kid a chance. [*Laughter*]

And I do want to say if they'd have played one more chorus of "The Spirit of Notre Dame," I was going to do a broken-field run through the tables there. [*Laughter*] Do some table-hopping. I told the Archbishop and was surprised he didn't know. Maybe you'd be interested to know: I was extremely proud when I found out recently that every year they run that picture at Notre Dame for the incoming freshman class, as that's student indoctrination. [*Laughter*]

Well, anyway, thank you all. God bless you. And now I have to work for my supper. I have to pull, I understand it, the winning raffle ticket.

Note: The President spoke at 6:55 p.m. at St. Ann's Catholic Church. He was introduced by Archbishop Peter Gerety.

Following his remarks, the President returned to Washington, DC.

Proclamation 5225—Coast Guard Day, 1984
July 27, 1984

By the President of the United States of America

A Proclamation

On August 4, 1790, the oldest continuous seagoing service of this Nation was formed. The United States Coast Guard was originally organized as "a fleet of cutters" to stop illegal smuggling from the sea and collect revenue due on goods coming to the young Nation. Later called the Revenue Cutter Service, this small organization combined with the Life Saving Service in 1915 and assumed its now famous name—the United States Coast Guard.

Today, Coast Guard contributions to our Nation in the areas of national defense, maritime law enforcement, search and rescue, aids to navigation, merchant marine safety, environmental protection, ports and waterway safety, and boating safety have become a benchmark by which professional maritime excellence is judged.

This Nation relies heavily on the readiness of the Coast Guard's active duty, reserve, and civilian employees and the voluntary contribution of the 40,000 members of the Coast Guard Auxiliary to rescue victims, protect our environment, and defend this Nation, as the Coast Guard has done in every major conflict in which the United States has been involved.

The Congress, by Senate Joint Resolution 150, has authorized and requested the President to issue a proclamation designating August 4, 1984, as "Coast Guard Day."

Now, Therefore, I, Ronald Reagan, President of the United States of America, do hereby proclaim August 4, 1984, as Coast Guard Day in recognition of the profound importance of the missions and responsibilities entrusted to the Coast Guard. I invite all the Armed Forces—the Army, Navy, Marine Corps, Air Force, and Coast Guard—the Departments of Defense and Transportation, other Federal departments and agencies, the Governors of the States, the chief officials of local governments, and the people of the United States to observe this day in an appropriate manner.

In Witness Whereof, I have hereunto set my hand this twenty-seventh day of July, in the year of our Lord nineteen hundred and eighty-four, and of the Independence of the United States of America the two hundred and ninth.

RONALD REAGAN

[Filed with the Office of the Federal Register, 11:44 a.m., July 27, 1984]

Proclamation 5226—National Volunteer Firefighters Recognition Day, 1984
July 27, 1984

By the President of the United States of America

A Proclamation

Throughout our history, the American spirit has been distinguished by the ready willingness of neighbors to join together and help one another. The tradition of voluntary community service is as important today as it was in the founding years of our country.

Our Nation's volunteer firefighters carry on this truly American tradition of citizen response for the common good. Like the Minutemen of our early years, these volunteers are ready to respond on short notice to help fellow citizens in need. Volunteer firefighters protect our lives, our families, and the economic life of our communities from the threat of destructive fire, often at great personal sacrifice. But these volunteers are more than firefighters. In many communities, they respond to a wide range of natural and technological emergencies.

These trained and organized volunteers, our neighbors, are a valuable national resource. It is fitting and proper that a grateful Nation should recognize the vital contributions of the one million men and women who serve in our Nation's volunteer fire and rescue companies and departments.

The Congress, by Senate Joint Resolution 136, has designated August 18, 1984, as "National Volunteer Firefighters Recognition Day" and has authorized and requested the President to issue an appropriate proclamation.

Now, Therefore, I, Ronald Reagan, President of the United States of America, do hereby proclaim Saturday, August 18, 1984, as National Volunteer Firefighters Recognition Day, and I call upon all Americans to join in appropriate programs, ceremonies, and activities to recognize the valuable contributions of these public-spirited volunteers.

In Witness Whereof, I have hereunto set my hand this twenty-seventh day of July, in the year of our Lord nineteen hundred and eighty-four, and of the Independence of the United States of America the two hundred and ninth.

RONALD REAGAN

[Filed with the Office of the Federal Register, 11:45 a.m., July 27, 1984]

Nomination of Charles D. Baker To Be Under Secretary of the Department of Health and Human Services
July 27, 1984

The President today announced his intention to nominate Charles D. Baker to be Under Secretary of Health and Human Services. He would succeed John A. Svahn.

Since 1974 Mr. Baker has been president, chairman, and chief executive officer of Harbridge House, Inc., in Boston, MA. Previously, he was Deputy Under Secretary of the Department of Transportation in 1969; Assistant Secretary for Policy and International Affairs, Department of Transportation, in 1970–1971; vice president of Harbridge House, Inc., in 1965–1969; and with Westinghouse Electric Corp. in 1955–1961.

He graduated from Harvard College (B.A., 1951) and the Harvard Graduate School of Business Administration (M.B.A., 1955). He is married, has three children, and resides in Rockport, MA. He was born June 21, 1928, in Newburyport, MA.

Statement by Principal Deputy Press Secretary Speakes on Arms Control Talks With the Soviet Union
July 27, 1984

This morning's TASS statement misrepresents our position, which is that we have accepted the Soviet proposal for discussions in Vienna in September without preconditions. Our preparations are continuing vigorously, and we expect to be in Vienna. We do not believe that such discussions are impossible, and we are continuing to deal with this subject in private diplomatic channels.

The United States finds it very disturbing that the Soviets portray the United States as responsible for the breakdown of the nuclear negotiations in Geneva when the world knows the Soviets walked out of those discussions. Already existing nuclear systems deserve our most urgent attention. If the Soviets do not choose to listen to our views on this subject, they need not, but for us and for mankind, this subject is too important to ignore. This U.S. approach does not represent a precondition. We will take whatever the Soviets say on antisatellite weapons seriously and respond constructively. We simply point out that we wish to restore exchanges on the subject of offensive nuclear arms. The world has a right to expect the U.S.S.R. and the United States to maintain such discussions.

Message to the Senate Transmitting a Patent Cooperation Treaty
July 27, 1984

To the Senate of the United States:

With a view toward receiving the advice and consent of the Senate to withdraw a reservation made by the United States when depositing its instrument of ratification of the Patent Cooperation Treaty on November 26, 1975, I transmit herewith a copy of the Patent Cooperation Treaty, 28 UST 7645, TIAS 8733, signed at Washington on June 19, 1970. I transmit also, for the information of the Senate, the report from the Department of State with respect to this matter.

When depositing its instrument of ratification with the World Intellectual Property Organization in 1975, the United States made three declarations, one of which was a reservation under Article 64(1)(a) of the Treaty to the effect that the United States would not be bound by the provisions of chapter II. Of the present 36 parties to the Treaty, only five others are not bound by chapter II. Patent applicants from States bound by chapter II are accorded extended time limits before having to initiate foreign patent processing, which permits a more thorough patent protection and commercial evaluation of the products involved.

The Treaty consists of two substantive chapters. Chapter I affords applicants a period of 20 months from the priority date of the international application to undertake national patent processing. During this period, applicants obtain an international search report to help them decide whether to proceed with patent prosecution.

Chapter II is optional and gives applicants additional time and an international preliminary examination report, thereby allowing them to become even more selective of the countries in which they ultimately decide to proceed.

The United States made a reservation concerning chapter II in 1975, primarily because of then-prevailing opinion that divergent patent examining methods and systems of other potential member countries made adherence impracticable. This concern has been alleviated. To carry out the provisions of chapter II, implementing legislation will be necessary. This legislation has been drafted and will be forwarded shortly. Article 64(6)(b) of the Treaty provides that the withdrawal of a reservation to chapter II shall take effect three months after the Director General of the World Intellectual Property Organization has received notification of such a withdrawal. To ensure that our domestic laws conform with our expanded international obligations, I do not plan to notify the Director General of the withdrawal of our reservation to chapter II until after the Senate has informed me of its advice and consent to the withdrawal and Congress has enacted all legislation necessary to implement that withdrawal domestically.

Adherence to chapter II of the Patent Cooperation Treaty is in the best interest of the United States. I recommend, therefore, that the Senate give early and favorable consideration to this matter and give its advice and consent to withdrawing the U.S. reservation previously made under Article 64(1)(a) of the Treaty.

RONALD REAGAN

The White House,
July 27, 1984.

Appointment of Three Members of the Commission on Presidential Scholars
July 27, 1984

The President today announced his intention to appoint the following individuals to be members of the Commission on Presidential Scholars:

Sherleen Sue Sisney, to serve as a member during her tenure as National Teacher of the Year. She will succeed Leroy E. Hay. Mrs. Sisney has been a teacher of history and economics at Ballard High School in Louisville, KY, since 1971. She is married, has one child, and resides in Prospect, KY. She was born October 19, 1946, in Stillwater, OK.

Sammie Lynn Scandlyn Puett has been serving as a commissioner of the department of human services for the State of Tennessee since 1980. Previously she was commissioner of the department of general services for the State of Tennessee. She is married and resides in Nashville, TN. She was born September 7, 1936, in Knox County, TN. This is a new position.

Donna F. Scott is a member of the Idaho State Legislature. She is married, has six children, and resides in Twin Falls, ID. She was born September 28, 1934, in Filer, ID. This is a new position.

Appointment of Two Members of the Committee for Purchase from the Blind and Other Severely Handicapped
July 27, 1984

The President today announced his intention to appoint the following individuals to be members of the Committee for Purchase from the Blind and Other Severely Handicapped:

Hugh Leonard Brennan, to be the Department of Commerce member. He will succeed Richard Miller Hadsell. He is Director of the Office of Procurement and Federal Assistance at the Department of Commerce. He is married, has four children, and resides in Potomac, MD. He was born May 31, 1936, in East Orange, NJ.

Rear Adm. Edward Keith Walker, to be the Department of the Navy member. He will succeed Andrew A. Giordano. Rear Admiral Walker is Commander of the Naval Supply Systems Command in Washington, DC. He is married, has two children, and resides in Arlington, VA. He was born January 23, 1933, in Annapolis, MD.

Radio Address to the Nation on the Summer Olympic Games
July 28, 1984

My fellow Americans:

There are many serious things that will occupy our attention in the coming weeks and in the fall, but today I find my thoughts turning away from politics to something equally important, but happy, too.

Eleven weeks ago, I greeted the Olympic torch when it was carried to the White House by a young man, a fine young athlete who had carried it high for almost a mile. Today the torch arrives in Los Angeles, and I'm thinking of what a journey it knew, and what a country it traveled through.

The journey started in the East, in Manhattan, in front of the United Nations. From there it arced South and West, and passed from person to person in a marvelous relay. It was carried by former Olympians and handicapped kids, by elderly women and young athletes bright with the speed of youth.

They held the torch high and passed the flame on to one another. They took it up hills and through lonely towns in the darkness, along gray highways at twilight and through bright towns at noon. They carried it past the malls and the airports, through the suburbs and cities, up the hills of steel towns, and along the flat routes of America's heartland. They carried it through the gathering heat of the West in early summer, and they took it to Los Angeles, where today the torch lights the Olympic flame and the games begin.

Everywhere the torch went people came out of their homes and poured into the streets to cheer and wave the flag and urge the runners on. This outpouring reflected, I think, the new patriotism that has swept our land.

So much of that new spirit involves our young people. It's seemed to me for some time now that there's a spirit of renewal among the young. It's as if they understand the future is great and huge and waiting for them. They seem to know once again that America is worth loving, worth caring about. They seem to take a quiet pride in all this nation was and is; they show a happiness with our country that's wonderful to see.

I think we can hear and discern in their music these days, certainly more than in the past, an optimism and a feeling of affection for our nation.

And there are the young people who will represent America in the games themselves. They, too, show a marvelous spirit. They represent our country not in some kind of narrow, nationalist sense, but in a wider sense: They reflect the things we taught them about human conduct and human effort—all the good things they learned on the playing fields and at the gym, on the city streets and in the playgrounds of America. In those places they learned that the pursuit of excellence is a fine thing in and of itself, and the elusive pursuit of perfection is one of the things that makes man human. They learned that you play by the rules, with a sense of fairness and generosity, that you don't cheat, and that you take both victory and defeat with the same kind of grace and dignity.

Our young athletes deserve great credit. They were born with great gifts—God blessed them with the physical talent that made it possible for them to compete in sports. But after that—after the original gift—after that it was all effort.

To become champions they had to work hard, with discipline and desire and no small amount of tenacity. What they are and what they've done gives us a lift. It's always inspiring when we see young men and women try to resist gravity, to fight fatigue, to, in the words of the first astronauts, push out the edge of the envelope—push out of the things that hold us down and push on to new possibilities, new records.

Today it begins, and our athletes are ready. They will stand there, over the next few days; they'll poise themselves on the blocks, stand at the edge of the diving board, or stand with their toes on the line and wait for the shot to go—and they'll know they're not alone. They'll hear the roar of the crowds, the great substantial cheer of the crowds, and—who knows?—if they listen close, maybe they'll hear the sound of Jesse Owens cheering, Babe Didrikson and Jim Thorpe, maybe they'll hear the cheers of all the young American athletes who once stood on the blocks waiting for the race to begin. Our young people are running for their country, running for greatness, for achievement, for that moving thing in man that makes him push on to the impossible.

The torch is passed; the games begin; the 23d Olympiad of the modern era commences. And as it does, just for a moment, we think of the words of the psalms: "This is the day which the Lord has made; Let us rejoice and be glad. . . ."

Until next week, thanks for listening, and God bless you.

Note: The President recorded his remarks in the Map Room at the White House for broadcast at 12:06 p.m.

Remarks to United States Athletes at the Summer Olympic Games in Los Angeles, California
July 28, 1984

Thank you, Bill Simon. This is a genuine pleasure for me and for Nancy. We've been avid sports fans, and I have been all my life. And to be with you here, the men and women who will be wearing our colors in the 23d Olympiad of the modern games is a memory I know we're going to cherish.

I'm certain that you'll remember these games as the highlight of your life as well— and not just the games. You've been preparing for this competition for many years. You know better than most it isn't just the will to win that counts; it's the will to prepare to win. And from what I see here, we're ready.

I see some familiar faces. I've enjoyed following your progress. When I visited you at the Olympic Training Center in Colorado Springs a while back, you all gave me an official warmup suit. I've been using it just before meeting certain Members of the Congress. [*Laughter*] I also received a little gift from our ice hockey team—a hockey puck inscribed, "The puck stops here." [*Laughter*] Believe me, I've put that one to good use, too.

I want you to know just how proud all of us are to have you representing us. And when you see us out on the stands waving

1105

Old Glory, you know that we're waving it for you.

The same spirit is evident all across this land. Back in the middle of May, I met the official Olympic torch carrier at the White House. As that flame has made its way across America, it's been greeted with cheers, accolades, and flags, by young and old, Americans of every race and religion.

Journalists have described and analyzed this outpouring of unity and positive feeling. They also noted that this year's Fourth of July celebrations were extraordinarily joyous occasions. There is a new patriotism spreading across our country. It's an affection for our way of life, expressed by people who represent the width and breadth of our culturally diverse society. And the new patriotism is not a negative force that excludes, but a positive force, an attitude toward those things that are fundamental to America, that draws together our freedom, our decency, our sense of fairplay as a people.

In so many ways, you represent this new spirit. I know I speak for all your fellow citizens—no matter what political persuasion, no matter what race or religion, no matter if poor, middle class, or affluent—when I tell you that you are our team. And each and every one of you, well, we're with you a hundred percent.

During these games, you'll be competing against athletes from many nations, but most important, you're competing against yourself. All we expect is for you to do your best, to push yourself for one more fraction of a second or one notch higher or one inch further. Each time you do that, you've created a magic moment of beauty and excellence in which all of us will share.

The American ideal is not just winning; it's going as far as you can go. If by pushing yourself to the limit you set a record or win a medal, you'll hear us. We'll probably look a little silly expressing our pride in your accomplishment, but our affection and pride is something that you can count on. We'll be cheering—win, lose, or draw.

These games are the culmination of the work and dedication of thousands of people. I think Peter Ueberroth has done an exceptional job. United States Olympic Committee President Bill Simon has assured me

you're the best team ever. And Bill, himself, deserves our special thanks for all that he's done. And of course, I'd like to mention your executive director, Don Miller, and all the coaches and managers who've made this possible, and these captains who are here on these steps with us.

This has been a team effort all the way. Corporations have done their part. Individual contributions have played a major role. Those who couldn't give money, volunteered—I understand 50,000 volunteers here, backstage—to get these games underway. They've been donating their time and energy to the success of the games.

Special recognition should go to Rafer Johnson and Donna de Varona and their Olympic Spirit Team. These Olympians have put out an enormous effort on your behalf and on behalf of the Olympics. And today you are joining this special fraternity of individuals who have competed in previous Olympics. It's an honor no one can take away from you.

Many years ago, believe it or not, I competed in sports, and coaches were known for spurring us on with some pretty punchy phrases and dialog—or monolog. And looking back now, I realize those coaches were just as excited at the time as we were. And the same is true right now, you can be certain of that. We're all in this together. And we know that we can count on you to push yourselves to the limit.

So, set your sights high, and then go for it. For yourselves, for your families, for your country—and will you forgive me if I just be a little presumptuous—"do it for the Gipper." [*Laughter*]

God bless you all. We'll be watching. Thank you all.

Note: The President spoke at 1:52 p.m. at Heritage Hall on the campus of the University of Southern California, site of one of two Olympic villages for participating athletes. Following his remarks, he went to the Los Angeles Memorial Coliseum to participate in the opening ceremonies of the games.

Following the ceremonies, the President left Los Angeles and traveled to Rancho del Cielo, his ranch near Santa Barbara, CA, to begin a 3-week vacation.

Nomination of Edward J. Streator To Be the United States Representative to the Organization for Economic Cooperation and Development
July 28, 1984

The President today announced his intention to nominate Edward J. Streator, of New York, a career member of the Senior Foreign Service, Class of Career Minister, as the Representative of the United States of America to the Organization for Economic Cooperation and Development, with the rank of Ambassador. He would succeed Abraham Katz.

Mr. Streator served in the United States Navy from 1952 to 1956 as lieutenant. He entered the Foreign Service in 1956 and was on detail to the International Cooperation Administration as junior management assistant. He was economic officer in Addis Ababa (1958–1960) and political officer in Lomé (1960–1962). In the Department he was intelligence research analyst in the Bureau of Intelligence and Research (1962–1964), and staff assistant to the Secretary of State (1964–1966). He was deputy political/military adviser to the North Atlantic Treaty Organization (NATO) in Paris (1966–1968) and deputy political counselor at NATO in Brussels (1968–1969). From 1969 to 1975, he was Deputy Director of the Office of NATO Affairs in the Department. From 1975 to 1977, he was deputy chief of mission, then Deputy United States Permanent Representative to NATO in Brussels. Since 1977 he has been deputy chief of mission in London.

Mr. Streator received his A.B. in 1952 from Princeton University. His foreign language is French. He was born December 12, 1930, in New York, NY.

Nomination of Robert R. Davis To Be a Commissioner of the Commodity Futures Trading Commission
July 30, 1984

The President today announced his intention to nominate Robert R. Davis to be a Commissioner of the Commodity Futures Trading Commission for a term expiring April 13, 1989. He would succeed Philip M. Johnson.

He is presently serving as senior economist for the Joint Economic Committee of the United States Congress. Previously, he was international economist, vice president and economist, economic research office, Harris Trust and Savings Bank in Chicago, IL (1979–1984); financial economist in the Division of Research of the Federal Deposit Insurance Corporation in 1977–1979; economic consultant for National Management Consultants, Inc., in 1976; and visiting assistant professor, department of economics, Vanderbilt University, in 1975–1976.

He graduated from Virginia Polytechnic Institute and State University (B.A., 1972; M.A., 1974; Ph.D., 1977). He is married and resides in Alexandria, VA. He was born April 3, 1949, in Atlanta, GA.

Appointment of Paul B. Simmons as Special Assistant to the President and Director of the Office of Policy Information
July 30, 1984

The President has appointed Paul B. Simmons as Special Assistant to the President and Director of the Office of Policy Information.

Mr. Simmons has served as acting executive secretary of the Cabinet Council on Human Resources since September 12, 1983. Previously he was Deputy U.S. Commissioner of Social Security in 1981–1983. He served 4 years, beginning in February 1977, on the senior staff of Gov. James R. Thompson of Illinois, first as director of the State of Illinois Washington office and later as executive assistant to the Governor. He was also director of the Governor's Cost Control Task Force.

Mr. Simmons was a special assistant in the office of the Assistant HEW Secretary for Legislation in 1975–1976; associate commissioner of the New York State Department of Social Services in 1972–1974; executive assistant to the New York State Commissioner of Health in 1969–1972; and with the Capital Newspapers Group of the Hearst Corp. in 1964–1969.

He graduated from St. Michael's College (B.A., 1964) and the State University of New York Graduate School of Public Affairs (M.A., 1965). He is married, has one child, and resides in Washington, DC. He was born February 6, 1942, in Portland, ME.

Appointment of Michael A. Driggs as Special Assistant to the President for Policy Development and Assistant Director for Commerce and Trade
July 30, 1984

The President today announced his appointment of Michael A. Driggs to be Special Assistant to the President for Policy Development and Assistant Director for Commerce and Trade.

Since March 1982 Mr. Driggs has been Deputy Assistant Secretary for Automotive Industry Affairs at the Department of Commerce. Previously, Mr. Driggs served as Executive Director of the Chrysler Corporation Loan Guarantee Board at the Department of the Treasury; as a budget examiner

at the Office of Management and Budget; and as an intelligence officer in the U.S. Army.

Mr. Driggs received his master of public administration degree with an emphasis in public finance and economics from West Virginia University in 1973 and his B.A. from West Virginia University in 1969.

Mr. Driggs was born on October 12, 1947, in South Charleston, WV. He resides in the District of Columbia.

Message to the Annual Conference of the National Urban League in Cleveland, Ohio
July 30, 1984

It is a great pleasure for me to send greetings to all the members of the National Urban League as you gather for your annual conference.

The prospect for urban America is bright today because of the strength of the ongoing economic expansion. The rapid decline in unemployment, coupled with a very low level of inflation, has brought a renewal of prosperity and economic opportunity throughout most parts of our Nation. But there are still some areas and groups which have not fully shared in the general recovery. These areas and groups need an extra boost to join the rest of the Nation, and that is why I have proposed legislation to permit the designation of Enterprise Zones in selected cities across America. On July 24, I called upon the House of Representatives to bring this key measure to the floor for a vote. This proposal has the best potential to build on the progress we have made and to create jobs, independence and hope for people in inner cities and other economically distressed areas. It is time for Congress to complete action on this vital legislation.

We will not be satisfied with our economic progress until it has spread to every town and neighborhood in our Nation. For many years, the National Urban League has led the way in directing the Nation's attention to the still unresolved problems of our inner cities. I congratulate you on your many decades of distinguished service to America, and I stand ready to work closely with you on ways we can achieve further progress.

Please accept my best wishes for a most successful conference.

RONALD REAGAN

Remarks by Telephone to a Meeting of the National Governors' Association in Nashville, Tennessee
July 31, 1984

Governor Thompson. Mr. President, this is Jim Thompson. We have the Governors of the Nation assembled here, and we appreciate very much your calling this morning.

The President. Well, Jim, thank you very much, and thank all of you for letting me participate in this way.

In our meeting last February at the White House and other subsequent meetings with Governors, we've discussed the importance of keeping the economy on sound footing, and we've discussed the importance, also, of getting the Federal deficit under control and of reducing unemployment. I'm pleased to report we are making progress on both of these fronts.

Regarding the deficit, I understand your concerns, especially about high interest rates and how they affect the States' own economic recovery. I'm pleased to report that we now estimate the deficit to be well below that which was projected last February. My recent signing of the deficit reduction downpayment package is clearly a first step. And I pledge that I'll continue to work to bring down deficits. We'll have to work together with Congress to get spending under control, as well as to pass a constitutional amendment requiring a balanced budget.

On the employment side, more Americans are working today than ever before in our history. And I'd like to congratulate all of you on the work that you've done in your States to implement the Joint [Job] Partnership Training Act. It's working well, and 70 percent of those undergoing training have been able to find permanent jobs. That's a dramatic improvement over the old CETA approach. The increased numbers of Americans working because of the economic expansion means more revenue for the States, as well as the Federal Government. And I know this is good news for all of us.

This kind of success justifies the faith we've had in returning power and responsibility to the States. Our invaluable dialog has made our partnership in federalism possible, and our fine working relationship and communication must continue.

Jim, I wanted to congratulate you on the great job that you've done as the National

Governors' Association chairman. And to John Carlin I want to offer my congratulations on your election as the new chairman of NGA. I look forward to working with you and all of the members of NGA during your chairmanship.

Governor Thompson. Thank you, Mr. President. We do appreciate your taking the initiative to speak to us today.

And on a personal note, I think we all had a special feeling on Saturday evening as we watched you and our American athletes join together with other nations of the world with the common goal of excellence. And we were proud for you and proud for our country's athletes.

I'd like to thank you for the access that your administration has granted to the Governors. We have met with Cabinet Secretaries, with your staff, and with you to express our concerns about issues ranging from health care cost containment to highway funding. Those are issues that are near and dear to Governors' hearts, and we appreciate your accessibility, even if we do not always agree.

Your comments indicating your commitment to work with us on the pressing issues of the future are welcome, especially on the issue of deficit reduction. The downpayment just approved is welcome, but, obviously, as you say, only a first step. And we are committed to continue our efforts to work with you and the Congress.

"Flexibility" is a key word to Governors.

If JTPA has been a success, as you indicate, it has been a success largely because of the capability that the States have to tailor the program to our needs.

In the Medicaid program, the waivers that have been granted by HHS will allow States to implement badly needed cost containment measures. However, we still need greater flexibility in this area, Mr. President, if we are to achieve our common goal: holding down health costs.

We are full partners in the Federal system, and we sincerely appreciate you calling in recognition of that partnership. We look forward to a continuing dialog with you and your administration on these and other issues.

Thank you very much.

The President. Jim, thank you. Governor Carlin, look forward to working with you. And, believe me, I am committed to what I have long held, the belief that our nation, as a federation of sovereign States, that is the very basis of our freedom. And so, I'll continue to work with all of you. And, again, thank you for letting me participate in this way.

Goodbye.

Governor Thompson. Goodbye, Mr. President, and thank you.

Note: The President spoke at 9:45 a.m. from Rancho del Cielo, his ranch near Santa Barbara, CA.

As printed above, the remarks follow the White House press release.

Appointment of James S. Stockdale as a Member of the National Voluntary Service Advisory Council
July 31, 1984

The President today announced his intention to appoint James S. Stockdale to be a member of the National Voluntary Service Advisory Council. He will succeed Roy Pfautch.

Since 1983 Mr. Stockdale has been deputy secretary of the California Health & Welfare Agency in Sacramento, CA. Previously he was Deputy Under Secretary for

Intergovernmental Affairs at the Department of Health and Human Services. He was executive director of the California Reagan-Bush campaign in 1980; political director of Citizens for the Republic in 1978–1979; and manager, State and local government affairs, Phillip Morris, Inc., in New York City (1977).

He graduated from Gustavus Adolphus

College (B.A.) in St. Peter, MN, and the University of South Dakota School of Law (J.D., 1972). He is married, has three children, and resides in Carmichael, CA. He was born December 16, 1937, in Pierre, SD.

Telephone Interview With Mort Crim of WDIV-TV in Detroit, Michigan
July 27, 1984

Automobile Labor-Management Negotiations

Mr. Crim. Thank you, Mr. President, for joining us today here on News 4.

The President. Well, pleased to.

Mr. Crim. There are several issues that are of unique interest to the people of Michigan and the people of Detroit. Right now the auto companies are negotiating with the UAW. Many of the workers are saying that Reaganomics has not worked for them, that the auto companies are registering record profits, that they have been forced to give concessions. What do you say to these workers?

The President. Well, I think Reaganomics has moved—or worked for everyone, in that we do have a recovery. And we have 7 million more people at work today than were working in 1980. Now, I hope that in the coming negotiations—certainly, government should not interfere. As a former union president, myself, I believe that these problems are between management and labor to work out.

But I do think that we have to keep in mind—yes, workers did make some concessions. On the other hand, while the automobile companies now are back in a profit position, there were several years there in which they were running tremendous losses. And I hope that there will be not only fairness, as there should be, but some restraint also in the negotiations, that we don't do anything right now at this point to turn off the recovery, the expansion that we're having. It is one of the best recoveries in all the seven or eight recessions that have occurred since World War II.

And other than that, I'm not going to inject myself into the middle of that battle. But I don't think it's fair for anyone to suggest that they have not benefited from this recovery. We were in a very precarious state—our entire industrial capacity as a nation.

Federal Deficits

Mr. Crim. Mr. President, you promised during your campaign a balanced budget by the end of your first term. Instead of a balanced budget, we have record deficits. Chairman Lee Iacocca of Chrysler Corporation calls that "the largest threat to a healthy auto industry that exists." How do you answer him?

The President. Well, I answer it by saying that we have had continuous deficits for 50 years. I've been one of the loudest voices, I guess, back over the years in saying that this was a false policy for this country to follow. It followed a policy that believed that a little inflation was good for us. And I, 20 years ago, said that a little inflation one day becomes runaway inflation. And it did in this present time.

Now, when I promised an economic program that, before the end of my term—first term—would eliminate deficits, before the election even took place the economy had so worsened that I said that promise no longer could be kept, that the situation had changed from the time that I, with the help of some fine leaders in this country and business executives, had put together an economic plan to try and bring us down from inflation and deficits and everything else.

We are going to continue to try. The size of the deficits now were in large part brought about by the recession that we were in. They were cyclical, as it's called, because they were the product of that recession. As we recover, we're finding that our own projections of deficits are too high. We're also finding that our projections of the government revenues after our tax cut—our projections were too low, that we are receiving more money than we had anticipated in tax revenues.

So, all of this is helping to bring down the deficits below the projected point. But more than that, we have to continue reducing government costs. The Federal Government simply costs too much and is taking too high a percentage of the gross national product. To continue doing that would run the risk of going back into the repeated cycles of recessions that we've had.

But I think now that, with this economy, which is on a sound basis, with continued trimming of government spending, I think that we will get a handle on the recession and on the deficits.

Detroit Tigers

Mr. Crim. Mr. President, let's talk about

something real pleasant now: an organization that has been going up faster than the gross national product, and I'm talking about our own Detroit Tigers. Have you been following their exploits?

The President. Yes, I have, as a matter of fact. I know that they're in first place of the Eastern Division of the American League and the—I think their win-loss run is about 695 percent or so. [*Laughter*] And all I can say is, "Bless you, boys."

Mr. Crim. And all we can say is, "Thank you, Mr. President." And the Detroit Tiger fans are grateful.

The President. Okay.

Mr. Crim. Thank you very much.

Note: The interview began at 2:47 p.m. in the Diplomatic Reception Room at the White House. It was recorded for later broadcast.

The interview was released by the Office of the Press Secretary on August 1.

Telephone Interview With Don Cannon of WTAE-TV in Pittsburgh, Pennsylvania
July 27, 1984

Social Security

Mr. Cannon. Mr. President, my name is Don Cannon. I'm with WTAE television in Pittsburgh, and my first question deals with Social Security. You have proposed, and Congress is about to dispose of, an increase in payments to recipients. Now today, Mr. Pickle, chairman of the House Social Security Committee, is saying that the tax, FICA, will have to be raised next year, or the taxable base will have to be raised to cover this increase. How do you respond to that, sir?

The President. No, I don't think it will, but I'll tell you why we felt it was fair to do what I announced the other night.

It is true that the regulations for governing Social Security COLA's, as they're called—cost-of-living increases—prescribes that there is no cost-of-living increase if inflation is below 3 percent. Now, there is a possibility that it may fall just below 3 per-

cent in the third quarter of this year, which is the measuring point as to whether or not—or what the COLA will be.

And we have asked, as a part of our program that put Social Security on a sound financial footing, when it was due to go bankrupt along about July of 1983—and the bipartisan commission that came up with a proposal to fix this—part of it called for a 6-month delay in a cost-of-living adjustment for the people on Social Security. And because of that, because of their taking that 6-month delay, we just felt that it was only fair that even if inflation went below the 3 point mark—and it may very well do that, because for the last 3 months it's been running at 3.3 percent—that it would only be fair for us for one more time to give this cost-of-living increase. Then, if we continue on down with inflation, why, this would be the end. This would be a one-time thing. We think that's only fair.

Tax Increases

Mr. Cannon. Mr. President, Mr. Mondale, in his acceptance speech last Thursday in San Francisco, said you had a secret tax plan; that regardless of who was elected President next year, or this year, taxes would have to be raised; that he was leveling with the American people, and you would not. What's your response to that, sir?

The President. Well, my response is that he was half right. He was right about the fact that he would give us a tax increase, because if you look at his record when he was a Senator, he's voted for every tax increase ever proposed—and, I think, sometimes has proposed them himself. So, I'm quite sure that he would raise taxes.

I'm quite sure that I would not, because to me a tax increase is a last resort, when there is no other thing to do. A tax increase, I think, could very well upset the recovery that we have.

I believe the biggest single factor in the recovery that we have right now which has resulted in a restoration of profits to the automobile industry, to the housing industry—we're building twice as many homes as we were building in 1980, now. I mention those two industries because either one of them can start a recession all by itself. Well, to have a tax increase could very well upset this recovery. The tax cut that we've had is the biggest factor, as I say, in that recovery. And so, I have no secret plan.

What we do have—I have asked the Treasury Department to study and bring to me by December some proposals for tax reform—number one, to simplify it. The tax code has become so complicated that the average citizen just cannot compute what they owe the Government. And we want to have a more simple and a more fair tax system, and we want to see if we can't have

one that will broaden the base so that we can actually reduce the rates on the individuals paying.

When you stop and think that because of the complexity of the tax law right now, there is probably a hundred billion dollars of tax that is legitimately owed and not being paid. And those who are freeloading on their fellow taxpayers, I think, should be brought into the payment of tax.

Steel Imports

Mr. Cannon. Mr. President, will you accept the recommendations of the U.S. International Trade Commission that the domestic steel industry needs relief in the form of tariffs and quotas over the next few years to bail out the industry?

The President. Well, we have their finding that the steel industry has been harmed by imports, but they, then, will be coming back with recommendations as to what the answer should be, sometime in September. And my comment can only be that I am waiting to see what their recommendations are going to be.

Pittsburgh Pirates

Mr. Cannon. Finally, sir, you had a benediction for the Tigers. Do you have one for the Pirates? We're in last place, as you know. [*Laughter*]

The President. Well, you know, in the job that I'm in, I know that I can't really take sides with anyone. So, having been a sports announcer broadcasting major baseball myself, I can just wish them well.

Mr. Cannon. Thank you, Mr. President.

Note: The interview began at 2:54 p.m. in the Diplomatic Reception Room at the White House. It was recorded for later broadcast.

The interview was released by the Office of the Press Secretary on August 1.

Telephone Interview With Mike Schneider of WPLG-TV in Miami, Florida
July 27, 1984

U.S.-Cuba Relations

Mr. Schneider. Hello, Mr. President, this is Mike Schneider in Miami. It's good to be able to talk to you again, sir.

The President. Good to talk to you, Mike.

Mr. Schneider. The first question is, Mr. Castro just celebrated yet another anniversary in power in Cuba. Lots of questions there: He reportedly wants to talk to the United States, and there are rumors in Miami right now that the United States is negotiating in some secret capacity with the Cubans, possibly about the return of the Mariel criminals. Is that true? What can you tell us about that?

The President. Yes, there's been an indication that they're willing to talk about this, and we have been in communication with them and certainly are ready to talk. No plans have been set, as yet, for that, but to talk about the so-called Marielitos.

Mr. Schneider. Is there a good possibility that those people can be returned in the near future?

The President. I believe so, unless they go back on things that they have already said to us. And we see no indication of that. Yes, I think it's a matter of numbers and deciding how many, but they've expressed a willingness to take back.

Mr. Schneider. How soon could that be, sir? Possibly this year?

The President. I would hope so.

Immigration Legislation

Mr. Schneider. The Simpson-Mazzoli bill, sir—a lot of people down here have very strong emotions on that. Especially in the Cuban-American community there's been strong support for it. Those people thought that you supported that bill. Now we hear that if the House version of it is accepted and goes to your desk, you, in fact, will not sign it. That's what we've heard. Is that true, and if so, why this apparent flip-flop?

The President. Well now, Mike, it's no flip-flop with me. And I never comment on whether I'll veto something until I see it finally on my desk, because sometimes what's been an apple up on Capitol Hill, turns into an orange before it gets here, or vice versa. But it is true that I support the Senate version of that bill.

The House has injected some things in the bill that I find it very difficult to support. It would give us very great problems. Now, it hasn't gone into conference yet, but someplace in conference they usually come down between the two versions. And I will have to wait and see what is there.

But, yes, I've had to say that the House version would be unacceptable to me, because——

Mr. Schneider. What is——

The President. ——of the things that had been added.

Mr. Schneider. If I may, sir, what is it in the House version that you find objectionable?

The President. Well, for one—and there are a number of things, but for one, alone, is a tremendous cost factor that didn't exist in the other bill.

Entitlement Programs

Mr. Schneider. The question now refers back to Mr. Mondale's charges that—he of course says that he will raise taxes, and he claims that you will, too. You say that you won't, that you'll try to cut spending. And there are many people in our area concerned that the spending cuts could come, of course, in Social Security or in Medicare packages, or in packages that aid the elderly. What can you say to reassure those people?

The President. Well, first of all, with regard to Social Security, we have absolutely no plans whatsoever to change that. As you'll remember, Social Security was made the object of a great deal of demagoguery in the 1982 election. And there were a great many falsehoods spread which had the terrible effect of frightening many people dependent on that program, in spite of the fact that we tried in every way we could to tell them we were not going to pull the rug out from under them. But we were faced with Social Security bellying up bankrupt in July of '83. In fact, to get some checks out, we had to borrow money.

Then, after the election, we had a bipartisan commission put together, and we worked out a plan which has put Social Security on a sound footing for—well, as far as we can see, to the year 2025. So, we're not making any changes in that.

Now, Medicare is a problem that we have to meet, because Medicare has something of the same problem that Social Security previously had, and it is faced—not as immediate in danger, as was Social Security—but it is faced with problems of fiscal insecurity in the next few years; before 1990. So, we are going to have to follow the same procedure and come up with a plan that ensures the fiscal soundness, because there are 28 million people in this country depending on Medicare for their health services.

Social Issues

Mr. Schneider. Mr. President, there are those who claim that a second Reagan administration would be a much more dogmatic, conservative administration, that you'd be pushing harder on your so-called social agenda—pushing for a constitutional ban on abortion, for a ban on school busing. Would that happen under a second Reagan administration?

The President. Well, I have been strongly in favor of a number of measures—the tuition tax credits, for one. And now we've made some progress in the last few days on prayer in schools. But I certainly wasn't seeking to impose prayers; I simply wanted to give them permission to pray if they wanted to, and it'd be up to them.

And, with regard to abortions, I feel that unless and until someone can establish that the unborn child is not a living human being, then that unborn child is protected by the constitutional protection of life, liberty, and the pursuit of happiness. And if you found a body and you didn't know whether it was dead or alive, you wouldn't bury it until you found out for sure that it was not living. And I feel the same way about the unborn child.

In fact, all of the medical evidence, so far, proves definitely that the unborn child is a living human being. And we have no right to take its life unless it would be taking that life in protection of the mother's life.

Mr. Schneider. Mr. President, thank you very much for letting the people of south Florida know how you feel. We appreciate it.

The President. Thank you.

Note: The interview began at 3 p.m. in the Diplomatic Reception Room at the White House. It was recorded for later broadcast.

The interview was released by the Office of the Press Secretary on August 1.

Telephone Interview With Forrest Sawyer of WAGA-TV in Atlanta, Georgia
July 27, 1984

Presidential Campaign Debates

Mr. Sawyer. Mr. President this is Forrest Sawyer in Atlanta. It's a pleasure to talk with you.

The President. Forrest, hello.

Mr. Sawyer. Let's start with some good old-fashioned politics. Geraldine Ferraro has said that if this is a campaign without national debate, then it will dwindle to name-calling. Jimmy Carter has said he's con-

vinced that you're going to try to avoid a debate. And you've said you're going to leave it up to your campaign manager. It's a critical issue. Why not decide yourself and declare whether or not you want to debate?

The President. I've said all the way, I support the idea of debate; debated in the last election and would do so in this next one. I did not accept that statement of Vice President Mondale that we should have a half a dozen or more debates. As a matter of fact, I think we could bore the pants off the viewers if we did something of that kind. But I believe that there is something that we can agree upon in the nature of debating, and I look forward to doing that.

Mr. Sawyer. How many would you like, sir?

The President. Frankly, I think two would be as many as the public should stand for. But, again, as I did say that I think that those who work on the planning of strategy and the schedules, and so forth, have to be considered in this, and I am looking forward to listening to their counsel and advice.

Mr. Sawyer. Would you like Vice President Bush to debate Ms. Ferraro?

The President. That is another issue that I think has to be decided involving them and involving strategy. Remember, the election really is between the two candidates for President. You can't get elected Vice President unless the head of the ticket wins.

Anne M. Burford

Mr. Sawyer. Sir, let's talk about the environment. Anne Burford left the Environmental Protection Agency under a cloud. You have reappointed her to an advisory committee on oceans and atmospheres, and that has upset environmental groups. Since she left the EPA in such a shambles, why reappoint her?

The President. Well, I don't think she did leave it in a shambles. And I just believe that when someone has been the victim of an attempted lynching, then someone ought to come to the rescue.

Anne Burford was called up to appear before a House committee. And the House committee was demanding documents from her, and we ruled, with the advice of the Justice Department, that we were going to stand for executive privilege and not make them available, because those documents were part—well, they were investigatory reports. And if it developed that in the continuing investigation there was reason for legal action against other individuals, that could be compromised by opening up those records. So, she was simply carrying out our orders in refusing to make those records available and certainly didn't deserve the treatment that she received.

And I said from the very first that while they made it impossible for her to do anything but resign, that I was going to find a place for her, because I wanted her as a part of our administration.

Recreation Area in Georgia

Mr. Sawyer. Mr. President, an environmental issue of critical concern to Georgians: the Chattahoochee River National Recreation Area. Originally, 6,500 acres were intended to be purchased. Under your administration, that has been cut to something less than half, and whether more critical lands will be purchased is up in the air. Will you free more money for purchase?

The President. Well, my understanding is that in the review of that land and the study of that land, 3,600 acres has been approved for addition to that park. At the same time, more land—I don't know whether it's limited to the 6,500 or the balance of it that you mentioned or whether more land has been or is being studied, and we are talking about trying to get together with counties, local communities, and the State in efforts for a joint purchase of additional land. And I can't tell you what the situation is with regard to that right now, or what the balance is that's being considered.

Nicaragua

Mr. Sawyer. Mr. President, Nicaragua. You are giving money for what some people call a not-so-secret war there. You are supporting anti-Sandinista guerrillas, whose open aim is to overthrow the government. Yet your administration has been saying you don't support the overthrow. How do you square those two?

The President. No, actually, what those people are, those so-called guerrillas, or *contras,* as they're called in Nicaragua, are actually—and for the most part, people who were participants in the original revolution and then had that revolution stolen from them by the Communist Sandinistas. And some of them were ousted from the country, some of them were jailed; they were denied any part in the government.

What we're trying to support down there is the honest desire of the people of Nicaragua to have the revolution that was promised them. The Sandinistas and the others had promised the Organization of American States that the revolution's goals were freedom of the press, freedom to have labor unions, human rights, freedom of speech and assembly, freedom of religion—all the things that we believe are democratic.

Once in, the Sandinistas ousted the others and have a totalitarian, Marxist-Leninist—a Communist government, totalitarian and with a denial of the rights of the citizens, and the people down there are being oppressed by that government. And we believe that we have an obligation to support the legitimate demands of the Nicaraguan people.

Mr. Sawyer. Mr. President, from Atlanta, thank you for the conversation.

The President. Thank you.

Note: The interview began at 3:06 p.m. in the Diplomatic Reception Room at the White House. It was recorded for later broadcast.

The interview was released by the Office of the Press Secretary on August 1.

Telephone Interview With Rose Stanley of KAKE-TV in Wichita, Kansas
July 27, 1984

Farm Policy

Ms. Stanley. Mr. President, this is Rose Stanley from KAKE–TV in Wichita, Kansas. For our first question—comes from the Breadbasket. Since the Department of Agriculture was formed in 1862, one of the perceived objectives was to preserve the family farm. The number of family farms has dwindled because their economic viability has declined. Realistically, is it still a realistic goal of government to preserve the family farm?

The President. Yes. As a matter of fact, I can understand what the problems have been, because agriculture was probably hurt worse in the cost-price squeeze of the recent recession and the inflation than probably any other segment of our society. The land values went up. The interest rates also went up.

They borrowed excessive amounts of money based on the artificial land value that had been created by inflation. And then, when we managed to bring inflation back down, and, hopefully, that we're going to eliminate it entirely, they were left with the depressed land values. But the cost of production rose 45 percent for the American farmer in just the brief period of a couple of years. And at the same time, the production was such, and the booming crops, that the prices were depressed.

Now, we know that they're going through hardships. We have done a number of things to be of help and are trying to help all that we can. The PIK Program was part of that, that I think did save a number of farmers. But we are—Secretary Block, our Secretary of Agriculture, is out on a listening expedition throughout the country, hearing the problems of the farmers and their recommendations so that we can come up with a new farm bill in 1985.

Women's Issues

Ms. Stanley. On the subject of women, inasmuch as Geraldine Ferraro is on the Democratic ticket, do you think that a GOP victory in November would set back the women's movement?

The President. Not at all. I think this was just a natural thing that could have happened to either party and should have happened. And I am one who has said for some time that I think we are in the near future going to see a woman President in this country. Now, I happen to hope she'll be a Republican woman.

And I think that our record would indicate that's very possible. After all, we took the lead in appointing a woman to the United States Supreme Court for the first time. It is the first time there have been three women as members of our Cabinet. And we have some 1,600 women in very top positions throughout our government here. Those of the—some 4,000 that a President can appoint—in our administration 1,600 of those are women already and doing fantastic and wonderful jobs.

So, I don't think a setback of this kind—it—in fact, the other day a Democratic Senator said the contest now is not whether a woman should be a candidate; it's whether is this the right woman for that particular job?

Ms. Stanley. You have appointed Elizabeth Dole, Margaret Heckler, Sandra Day O'Connor, Jeane Kirkpatrick. Yet there is still a charge of perception by some that you are antiwomen. How——

The President. I know——

Ms. Stanley. How do you respond to that?

The President. ——and it is very frustrating, because as Governor of California, I was the first one among the 50 Governors to start a survey and a search of State statutes and regulations to eliminate any that in their language discriminated against women. And we were most successful with that. When I came here to Washington, I instituted the same kind of search at the Federal level and then set out to encourage the rest of the Governors to do this at a State level. And about half of them right now are changing laws—or State statutes and regulations to eliminate this.

We have changed a number of them here at the Federal level and have more to go. Many of them require legislation to change. We've changed what we can by Executive order. And so, I don't understand why there should be this attitude, except that sometimes I suspect that maybe some of the organized groups out there have a political bias also and are partial to one party over the other.

U.S. Supreme Court

Ms. Stanley. Finally, during the next 4 years it's anticipated that the next President will have to fill up to five vacancies on the U.S. Supreme Court. What philosophical criteria will you be basing your decisions on?

The President. I want judges who will interpret the law and not legislate and think that their job is to make the law. And I think in recent years we've had some examples of the Court actually taking the job of the Legislature and legislating rather than interpreting.

Ms. Stanley. Thank you very much, Mr. President.

The President. Well, thank you.

Note: The interview began at 3:12 p.m. in the Diplomatic Reception Room at the White House. It was recorded for later broadcast.

The interview was released by the Office of the Press Secretary on August 1.

Telephone Interview With Dorothy Fuldheim of WEWS-TV in Cleveland, Ohio
July 27, 1984

Views on the Presidency

Ms. Fuldheim. Mr. President, thank you very much for this opportunity. I wanted to ask you this question: Through the years you've been in office, why do you want to be President, with all of the burdens and responsibilities?

The President. Well, the funny thing is, I kind of greet that question with mixed emotions, because for all of my life, while I was

active in supporting candidates and causes that I believed in, simply because I believe that you have to pay your way, and life had been very good to me, and the business that I was in gave me some recognition, and I could attract an audience and help at fundraisers and things—I did that. But I never wanted or thought that I would seek public office. Then I was persuaded to, for the Governor's job in California.

And, you know, someone has once said that life begins when you begin to serve. And I found there that life did begin. I thought that I would regret leaving the occupation and profession that I had practiced for so long. But I found it so fulfilling. And now, at this stage of my life, I want to continue to serve.

Tax Increases

Ms. Fuldheim. Well, I hope you do continue.

I'd like to ask you something else. Is there any truth to the rumor that you're waiting until after the election to increase the taxes? This bothers me a great deal.

The President. Let me tell you, there's been a distortion of something I said. Maybe I answered too much of an answer in the press conference sometime ago when I spoke about that.

No. No plans, nor do I believe that we need a tax increase. We're going to reduce the deficits by the way they should be reduced, which is reducing the cost of government. To me, a tax increase is a last resort. My opponent has made it plain that to him it's a first resort. And his record indicates he really feels that way.

Now, what I said that was misinterpreted—I tried to explain that if, when we have gotten government costs down to the point at which they could not be reduced any farther and government still be able to perform the services it's responsible for, then, if the tax policy did not match the outgo, you would have to look and adjust the situation then. But we're nowhere near that. And I am still going to go after what I think is fat in government and get it out of there.

And believe me, I have no plans, other than this last resort thing that I mentioned—if that should turn out to be true someday down the road, years from now—I have no intention of asking for a tax increase.

Blacks and Voter Registration

Ms. Fuldheim. Mr. President, I also have the same attitude to fat that you do, only mine has to do with my body, not with taxes. [*Laughter*] Do you think that Jesse Jackson has increased the importance of the black vote in the United States?

The President. Oh, I think he has. I think he's been responsible for one thing—something that maybe the rest of us couldn't have done—and that is to get a great many people who hadn't bothered to participate in the political arena, who hadn't registered to vote, to get them to register and now to participate as voters.

I would like to see everybody that is eligible to vote—see them registered and see them voting. That would really be our democracy at work. Over recent years we've seen declining numbers going to the polls to vote in elections, and I think part of it is because we've just satiated them with political campaigns that run too long—until they seem like they're always hearing about a political campaign, whether at the local or State level, or at the national level. And, no, I'm glad to see more people registering and getting ready to participate.

Nuclear Weapons

Ms. Fuldheim. One final question, and this really is a serious one. All nations are beginning to construct more nuclear weapons. Our Defense Department said the other day that our nuclear armament is inadequate, and that we will have to increase it more to be competitive. I don't understand it. We spend billions of dollars.

The President. They are right about that—unless we can persuade the Soviet Union, and until we can persuade them to come back to the so-called START and INF talks, which are negotiations to reduce the number of weapons on both sides.

But we have less nuclear power today than we had 20 years ago. We've withdrawn a thousand nuclear weapons from Europe, and we plan to withdraw another 1,400. In the last 10 years, the Soviet Union has added 800 ballistic missiles, intercontinental ballistic missiles of the MX type that we're seeking to build. We're trying to get permission from Congress to build 100 of those. But they have built 800 in these last 10 years; we have built none—zero.

And we are so far behind that we run the risk of having lost a deterrent capability; in other words, having a capability that says to them, you better not fire—just as they're saying to us, we better not fire. And so, what we're trying to do is update and modernize with these hundred weapons.

Our weapons that we have on hand right now are of such an early generation that the Soviets have produced and deployed about four new generations of weapons while we have produced none. And their weapons have greater accuracy, greater power, than our old-fashioned ones. So, we're seeking just a hundred MX missiles.

Ms. Fuldheim. Mr. President, thank you very much. I hope you come and visit soon again.

The President. I would like that. And thank you very much.

Note: The interview began at 3:18 p.m. in the Diplomatic Reception Room at the White House. It was recorded for later broadcast.

The interview was released by the Office of the Press Secretary on August 1.

Statement by Assistant to the President for National Security Affairs Robert C. McFarlane on Arms Control Talks With the Soviet Union
August 1, 1984

The United States has made clear to the Soviet Government in a series of high-level messages that it accepts the Soviet Union's June 29 proposal and is prepared for serious talks in Vienna on outer space, including antisatellite weapons. We have expressed our view that the problem of weapons in space cannot be considered in isolation from the overall strategic relationship, but that we have no preconditions for the Vienna agenda.

Despite this clearly stated, positive stand on our part, the Soviet Union has alleged that the United States has rejected the Soviet proposal. The latest Moscow press briefing repeated these charges, despite the clear statement of the United States position in a series of high-level messages conveyed to the Soviet Government in diplomatic channels.

In our communications with the Soviets, we have stated our view that their proposal for a conference on the militarization of outer space is an excellent idea and that we are prepared to have a U.S. delegation in Vienna on September 18 to engage in such negotiations.

We recently presented a proposal for a possible joint Soviet-American announcement on the content and objective of the Vienna talks. This proposal states explicitly that the aim of the talks should be to work out and conclude agreements concerning the militarization of outer space, including antisatellite systems and other aspects of this issue.

In response to the Soviet proposal of a mutual moratorium on antisatellite tests from the outset of the talks, the United States expressed a readiness to have our negotiators consider what mutual restraints would be appropriate during the course of negotiations. The latest Soviet statements have converted this proposal into a precondition, a transformation which suggests a disingenuous Soviet approach. We continue to believe that possible mutual restraints are an appropriate subject for the negotiations; the joint statement, however, should not prejudge the outcome of these negotiations.

The Soviet Union has repeatedly misrepresented the U.S. position regarding the opening of arms control talks between our two countries in Vienna. From this latest Soviet statement, it appears that the Soviets were not serious about their proposal. We regret this. As noted above, we have consistently accepted their proposal to meet in Vienna. We prefer that this matter be dealt with in diplomatic channels.

Informal Exchange With Reporters Prior to a Meeting With Archbishop Pio Laghi, Apostolic Delegate to the United States
August 1, 1984

The President. You, of course, know who our guest is. I don't have to tell you. And we're very pleased and proud to have him here.

Q. Mr. President, do you think Poland went far enough in its amnesty so that you can lift some of the sanctions?

The President. These are the things that we're going to discuss today.

Q. Mr. President, the Soviets say that your position has made it impossible to meet in Vienna next September.

The President. Well, you've had a press conference on that and have heard what my statement was.

Q. What do you have to say about it? What do you tell them?

The President. No, I'm not going to take any questions on that at a photo opportunity.

Q. Is there anything you can do to get them there?

The President. What?

Q. Is there anything you can do to get them to Vienna?

The President. We're doing everything we can.

Q. Thank you, sir.

Q. Are you disappointed by Mrs. Burford's letter?

The President. I'm not going to comment on those things here. We're here to talk with our visitor about another situation. All right?

Q. Thank you.

Note: The exchange began at noon, following the arrival of the Archbishop at Rancho del Cielo, the President's ranch near Santa Barbara, CA.

Following a working lunch, the White House announced that the President and the Archbishop exchanged views on a number of issues, including East-West relations, the situation in Central America, and recent events in Poland.

As printed above, the exchange follows the White House press release.

Statement by Principal Deputy Press Secretary Speakes on United States Sanctions Against Poland
August 3, 1984

The President has taken note of the release of political prisoners announced by the Polish Government on July 21. He believes that it represents a significant move in the direction of national reconciliation in Poland. Therefore, in accordance with his step-by-step approach for dealing with the Polish situation, he has decided to take two steps.

First, the President has authorized the lifting of the ban on landing rights for regularly scheduled flights by the Polish state airline, LOT, subject to the regularization of our civil aviation relationship, and the full reestablishment of scientific exchanges between the United States and Poland.

Second, the President has indicated that complete and reasonable implementation of the amnesty decision will create a positive atmosphere that would allow the reactivation of Poland's application for membership in the International Monetary Fund. The United States would, of course, consider any final application on its merits, including Poland's willingness to fulfill the obligations of IMF membership.

The purpose of our sanctions has from the very beginning been to encourage movement away from confrontation toward reconciliation in Poland. While the United States remains concerned with the situation in Poland, we view the Polish Government's amnesty declaration as a potentially positive development.

The United States is prepared to take further positive steps in response to further significant movement toward national reconciliation in Poland. In the meantime, we will be consulting with our NATO allies and others on the situation in Poland and a Western response to it.

Radio Address to the Nation on Deficit Reduction and Taxation
August 4, 1984

My fellow Americans:

Lately, you may have heard a lot of talk about a so-called secret plan to raise your taxes. Well, I've made it clear that we have no such plan. But apparently, such a plan exists, nonetheless. It's not our plan; it's not yours. It's the plan of the Democratic nominee for President.

When he accepted the Democratic nomination, he declared that he will increase your taxes. He said it several times since. But he still hasn't said exactly how. He has, however, come close to saying how much he would raise your taxes.

It takes a little calculation, but here's how it all adds up. The Democratic nominee has said he accepts deficit projections of over $200 billion a year, as far as the eye can see. Now, I don't accept them. And if we can keep our economy growing strongly, no one will have to. But he says he accepts them.

On top of those deficit projections, the Democratic nominee says he would add new government spending. How much? Well, he says his increases would total about $30 billion per year.

Senator John Glenn, on the other hand, said the cost of the Democratic nominee's promises would really come to somewhere between $90 and $170 billion. The Wall Street Journal reported estimates of experts that the amount of increased spending would come closer to $90 billion. So, let's use that for working purposes.

The Democratic nominee says he will make some budget cuts. He says he'll cut defense, health care, and agriculture programs by a total of $55 billion to $65 billion. And although his plan isn't likely to produce them, he says he expects interest savings of $15 billion to $20 billion. Now, that would bring his total savings to less than $90 billion. So, when you add it all up, the Democratic nominee's savings, assuming he would achieve them, still don't quite add up to enough to pay for the likely cost of his promises. And the deficits would be even higher than he assumes, except for one thing—there's another element to all this, another promise.

The Democratic nominee says he'll cut those deficits by two-thirds. How? By raising taxes. He says he estimates increased taxes of "at least $60 billion." He says he would get these by doing such things as deferring indexation, capping the third year of your tax cut, and adding a tax surcharge—all supposedly targeted at higher income taxpayers. Well, the truth is he'd need an increase of more than twice his $60 billion, an increase of $135 billion to square with his promises. That averages $1,500 in increased taxes for every American household, and one way or another, that means you. It's the same tired old formula—tax and tax to spend and spend.

I think the Democratic nominee owes the American people not a partial explanation, but a full explanation of how and where he expects to get that $1,500 more per household, over $135 billion in increased taxes. That's the secret that should be brought to light.

My approach to deficit reduction is entirely different, and it's no secret. We should reduce deficits first and foremost by continuing our economic growth and by reducing wasteful government spending.

Through the Grace commission, for example, we've developed 2,478 recommendations of possible ways to reduce spending without hurting the needy. These recommendations are no secret. We've made them public. We've already begun to implement almost 20 percent of them. We're still completing our review of the rest, but they're there for all to see, and every one that is worth implementing will be implemented.

As for taxes, my approach there is also well-known and no secret. We have already reduced personal income tax rates for all Americans by 25 percent. That has not only lightened your burden, it's helped give us the strong economic growth, without inflation, that we now enjoy.

Our tax cuts have meant more money for you to spend and invest and for you to save and use as you wish; more money to create jobs and expand the economy. I mean to keep that growth going and not stifle it with a new burden of taxes. And I mean to simplify the tax system and broaden its base so that we can bring income tax rates further down, not up. That, too, is no secret. I announced it in this year's State of the Union Address to the Congress.

Finally, let me tell you one more thing that should be no secret in case the Democrats talk of so-called secret plans has you worried. I will propose no increase in personal income taxes, and I will veto any tax bill that would raise personal tax rates for working Americans or that would fail to make our tax system simpler or more fair.

Until next week, thanks for listening. God bless you.

Note: The President spoke at 9:06 a.m. from Rancho del Cielo, his ranch near Santa Barbara, CA.

As printed above, the address follows the White House press release.

Informal Exchange With Reporters on Tax Reform
August 6, 1984

Q. Mr. President, Walter Mondale says you're not telling the truth when you say you won't raise taxes next year. He says you're going to have to do it, sir.

The President. Walter Mondale is not telling the truth. I've said it before, and I will say it again. And no matter how many of you try to put in a hedging line, we have no plans for, nor will I allow any plans for, a tax increase.

Q. Sir, the Congressional Budget Office is releasing figures today which says they think you're going to have bigger deficits than your own projections.

The President. They haven't told me yet.

Q. Mr. Vice President, you've been here before, haven't you, sir?

The Vice President. Second trip.

Q. Second? You missed the ride this morning.

The Vice President. Thanks.

Note: The exchange began at noon, prior to a luncheon meeting with the Vice President at Rancho del Cielo, the President's ranch near Santa Barbara, CA.

As printed above, the exchange follows the White House press release.

Nomination of Robert D. Stuart To Be United States Ambassador to Norway
August 7, 1984

The President today announced his intention to nominate Robert D. Stuart to be Ambassador to Norway. He would succeed Mark Evans Austad.

Mr. Stuart served in the United States Army from 1942 to 1945. In 1947 he began a career with the Quaker Oats Co. in Chicago, IL, and following some minor positions was assistant to the vice president (1954–1955), vice president for pet foods (1955–1959) and for grocery (1959–1962), and president (1962–1966). From 1966 to 1976, he was president and chief executive officer, and chairman of the board and chief executive officer from 1976 to 1981. From 1981 to 1983, he was chairman of the board and since 1983 has been chairman of the finance committee.

Mr. Stuart graduated from Princeton University (B.A., 1937) and Yale Law School (J.D., 1946). His foreign language is French. He was born April 26, 1916, in Hubbard Woods, IL.

Nomination of Mario F. Aguero To Be a Commissioner of the Copyright Royalty Tribunal
August 7, 1984

The President today announced his intention to nominate Mario F. Aguero to be a Commissioner of the Copyright Royalty Tribunal for the term of 7 years from September 27, 1984. This is a reappointment.

Mr. Aguero is currently a member of the Copyright Royalty Tribunal. Previously, he was owner-president of Havana East Restaurant in New York (1972–1982); a producer and sponsor of various events in the entertainment field (1961–1976); vice president and owner of Enterprises Latinos Corp. (1960–1963); and president and owner of Caribe Artists Corp. (1950–1961).

He is founder and president of the organization ARTE (Artists Radio Television Espectaculos) and is a New York member of the First Hispanic Council.

He is married, has one child, and resides in New York, NY. He was born May 1, 1924, in Camaguey, Cuba.

Appointment of Charles B. Wilkinson as a Member of the Board of Visitors of the United States Air Force Academy
August 8, 1984

The President today announced his intention to appoint Charles B. Wilkinson to be a member of the Board of Visitors to the United States Air Force Academy for a term expiring December 30, 1986. He would succeed Edmund G. Brown, Jr.

Mr. Wilkinson is currently the chairman of the board of the Public Employees Benefit Services Corp. in Oklahoma City, OK. Additionally he is director of the Coach of the Year Football Clinics and is a sports announcer for the Entertainment Sports Program Network. For the last 3 years he has been president of the Gymnastics Federation. Previously, Mr. Wilkinson served as coach of the St. Louis Cardinals football team (1979–1980); chairman of the board of Planned Marketing Associates (1971–1975); consultant to President Nixon and member of the White House staff (1969–1972); and was a special consultant to President Kennedy on physical fitness (1961–1964). Mr. Wilkinson served as assistant coach (1946) and then head coach and athletic director at the University of Oklahoma (1947–1963).

He retired to run for the United States Senate in 1964.

Mr. Wilkinson graduated from the University of Minnesota (B.A., 1937) and from Syracuse University (M.A., 1940). He is married, has two children, and resides in St. Louis, MO. He was born April 23, 1916, in Minneapolis, MN.

Message to the Congress Transmitting the Annual Report on United States Nuclear Nonproliferation Initiatives
August 8, 1984

To the Congress of the United States:

I have reviewed the activities of United States Government departments and agencies during the calendar year 1983 related to preventing nuclear proliferation, and I am pleased to submit my annual report on this subject pursuant to Section 601(a) of the Nuclear Non-Proliferation Act of 1978 (Public Law 95–242).

The report concludes that U.S. non-proliferation initiatives during 1983 continued to contribute positively to the important goal of preventing the further spread of nuclear explosives.

As I have stated on a number of occasions, nuclear proliferation would pose a severe threat to international peace, regional and global stability, and the security interests of the United States and other countries. I continue to regard the prevention of the spread of nuclear explosives as a fundamental national security and foreign policy objective, and I remain firmly committed to the pursuit of policies designed to advance our non-proliferation goals.

RONALD REAGAN

The White House,
August 8, 1984.

Nomination of Lloyd Kaiser To Be a Member of the Board of Directors of the Corporation for Public Broadcasting
August 9, 1984

The President today announced his intention to nominate Lloyd Kaiser to be a member of the Board of Directors of the Corporation for Public Broadcasting for a term expiring March 1, 1989. He would succeed James T. Hackett, term expired.

Since 1970 Mr. Kaiser has served as president and general manager of Metropolitan Pittsburgh Public Broadcasting, Inc. Over the last 10 years, MPPB, Inc., which began as WQED/13 and WQEX/16, has grown to include WQED–FM, Pittsburgh Magazine, and the newly formed QED Enterprises.

Mr. Kaiser has produced many programs, including "The Chemical People," a community outreach program attacking teenage drug and alcohol abuse. WQED has won 6 Emmys among the more than 100 awards received since Mr. Kaiser became president.

Prior to his position at WQED, Mr. Kaiser served as founding general manager of public television station WITF in Hershey, PA, for 6 years. Prior to that post, he initiated public television in Rochester, NY.

Mr. Kaiser was founding vice chairman of

the board of directors of the Public Broadcasting Service (PBS) from 1969 to 1971; vice president of the Eastern Educational Network from 1970 to 1972; and chairman of the operating committee of PPTN, the Pennsylvania Public Television Network, from 1973 to 1975.

Mr. Kaiser graduated from the University of Michigan (B.A., M.A.). He served as an assistant professor of speech and broadcasting at the State University of New York and was director of radio and television at Lehigh University.

Mr. Kaiser is married, has two children, and resides in Oakmont, PA. He was born August 1, 1927, in Alpena, MI.

Nomination of Rosalie Gaull Silberman To Be a Member of the Equal Employment Opportunity Commission
August 9, 1984

The President today announced his intention to nominate Rosalie Gaull Silberman to be a member of the Equal Employment Opportunity Commission for the remainder of the term expiring July 1, 1985. She would succeed Cathie A. Shattuck, resigned.

Since 1983 Mrs. Silberman has served as Special Assistant to Commissioner Mimi Weyforth Dawson at the Federal Communications Commission. Previously, she was director of public relations, San Francisco Conservatory of Music, in 1982–1983; executive director and secretary-treasurer, New Coalition for Economic and Social Change, in 1981–1983; and was director of communications and press secretary to Senator Robert Packwood (R-OR) in 1977–1979.

Mrs. Silberman has served as a member of the National Advisory Council on the Education of Disadvantaged Children and chaired the legislative subcommittee. She also served on the board of Widening Horizons, a volunteer organization which emphasized the importance of career development and planning for inner-city youth. She was a teacher in Montgomery County, MD, where she developed a program for disadvantaged students, promoting language development and skills with creative arts as a teaching tool.

Mrs. Silberman graduated from Smith College (A.B., 1958). She is married, has three children, and resides in Washington, DC, and San Francisco, CA. She was born March 31, 1937, in Jackson, MI.

Statement by Principal Deputy Press Secretary Speakes on Proposed Economic and Military Aid for Central America
August 9, 1984

The President has been following congressional action on the armaments supplemental bill with regard to funding for Central America. He was quite pleased with the strong support yesterday in the Senate for this funding, evidenced by overwhelming votes against proposed amendments to delete or reduce funds for Central America.

He also noted a favorable action by the House Appropriations Foreign Operations Subcommittee in approving most of the military aid for El Salvador requested for fiscal year '85 and a significant portion of the economic aid requested for El Salvador for fiscal year '85.

The President continues to call on Congress as a matter of national urgency to provide fiscal year '84 and fiscal year '85 funding for Central America. These funds were requested by the administration in accordance with the recommendations of the National Bipartisan Commission on Central

America. They are clearly needed in the region, and it is in our country's interest to provide them.

The President hopes that the fiscal year '84 supplemental will go through the House-Senate conference today and be approved by both Houses, before recessing, with full funding for Central America.

We will work with the bipartisan leadership of the conference committee toward this outcome.

The supplemental bill complements the fiscal year '85 Central American appropriations request and begins funding for the Henry M. Jackson plan, which we forwarded to Congress in February. Together, the fiscal year '84 supplemental and fiscal year '85 bills provide over a 2-year period the economic assistance to stabilize and stimulate recovery in Central American economies, lay the foundation for long-term development, and permit military assistance necessary to provide security essential to protect that economic growth. These vitally urgent programs should not be delayed.

Note: Larry M. Speakes read the statement to reporters at his daily press briefing, which began at 10:07 a.m. in the Vista Mar Monte Room at the Santa Barbara Sheraton in Santa Barbara, CA.

Message to the Senate Transmitting a United States-China Agreement on Taxation
August 10, 1984

To the Senate of the United States:

I transmit herewith for Senate advice and consent to ratification the Agreement between the Government of the United States of America and the Government of the People's Republic of China for the Avoidance of Double Taxation and the Prevention of Tax Evasion with Respect to Taxes on Income, together with a supplementary protocol and exchange of notes, signed at Beijing on April 30, 1984. I also transmit the report of the Department of State on the Agreement.

The Agreement is the first complete income tax treaty between the two countries. A limited treaty concerning the taxation of income from international shipping and air transportation, signed at Beijing on March 5, 1982, was approved by the Senate on July 27, 1983 and is now in force.

The Agreement is based on model income tax treaties developed by the Department of the Treasury, the Organization for Economic Cooperation and Development, and the United Nations. The provisions of the Agreement are reciprocal and, like other tax treaties, represent a balanced package of benefits and concessions.

The Agreement will contribute to a long-run expansion of economic relations between the two countries by providing clear rules as to the tax consequences of investing or working in the other country. It reduces the tax which residents of one country must pay to the other on certain types of income, such as dividends, interest, and royalties and provides limited exemptions for visiting teachers, researchers and students. The Agreement also assures nondiscriminatory taxation in the host country, and provides a mechanism for cooperation between the tax authorities to try to resolve any potential problems of double taxation.

I recommend that the Senate give early and favorable consideration to the Agreement and give its advice and consent to ratification.

RONALD REAGAN

The White House,
August 10, 1984.

Radio Address to the Nation on Congressional Inaction on Proposed Legislation
August 11, 1984

My fellow Americans:

I'm pleased to tell you that today I signed legislation that will allow student religious groups to begin enjoying a right they've too long been denied—the freedom to meet in public high schools during nonschool hours, just as other student groups are allowed to do. This has been given the shorthand label "equal-access legislation."

You might remember that I recently asked the House Democratic leadership to permit a vote on equal access and to permit votes on five other legislative measures important to you and your families that they, the Democratic leadership, had bottled up. Well, the Congress recessed yesterday, and the House Democratic leaders are returning to their districts. Some of these leaders and other Democrats have been campaigning on what they call their "new realism." But before they give too many speeches about all the wise things they promise to do for America, I want to give you a little report card on what they in fact did do—or, rather, did not do—as their new realism was put to the test.

Of those six important pieces of legislation we requested, specific measures to help reduce deficits, reward hard work and thrift, make your neighborhoods and cities safer, and increase personal liberties, only one was voted on—the equal-access bill. Equal access was only voted on after a majority of the House, led by the late Carl D. Perkins, defied the Democratic leadership, which continued to resist right up to the bitter end.

Of the remaining five proposals to test the new realism, not one was brought to a vote. So much for the test of the new realism. If the Democrats were given a report card, one out of six right would have meant a failing grade, a red letter "F."

When the Democratic leadership keeps saying no to America, they show how far they are from new realism and how far they've drifted from mainstream thinking. We asked for a vote on a constitutional amendment mandating a balanced Federal budget. We will insist that the Congress move toward a balanced budget, not by imposing new taxes on your families, but by spending within its means and allowing economic growth to continue.

The overwhelming majority of Americans agree with this position, but the House Democratic leaders don't. They don't want spending restraint, because their party has made so many campaign promises, promises they intend to fund by raising your taxes more than $1,500 per household.

We asked for a vote on our enterprise zones bill to provide incentives for people to invest, work, hire, and start up new businesses in economically distressed areas. This measure has been passed twice by the Republican Senate. It's supported by a majority of Members in the House, including many Democrats, and by a broad coalition of community leaders. We're ready to designate 75 zones to create opportunity, independence, and hope for our neediest citizens. But the Democratic leadership said no.

We asked for a vote on our proposal granting spouses working in the home the same individual retirement right, IRA's, as spouses working outside the home. Each could save and exclude from taxation up to $2,000 a year. The House Democratic leadership said no.

We asked for a vote allowing tuition tax credits for low- and middle-income parents who pay to send their children to parochial or independent schools, while also paying their full share of taxes to support public schools. The House Democratic leadership said no.

And we asked for action on our comprehensive anticrime package to crack down on criminals through new restrictions on bail, tougher sentencing, and stricter enforcement of drug trafficking laws. This bill passed the Senate 91 to 1, but the House Democratic leadership said no.

You might be interested to know what

House Speaker Tip O'Neill has called these proposals for a balanced budget, expanded IRA's, enterprise zones, tuition tax credits, tougher law enforcement, and equal access for students. He says they're "a right-wing agenda." Does the Democratic leadership truly believe that common sense in budgeting and greater opportunity and security for people is a right-wing agenda?

The Presidential nominee of the Democratic Party and his running mate could have asked the Speaker to give democracy a chance—could have, but didn't. They, too, said no.

All this has gotten me to thinking about a great Democrat. Just 36 years ago, Harry Truman called the 80th Congress the "do-nothing Congress." One thing is sure: Harry Truman wasn't afraid of the American people. He wasn't afraid of democracy, of putting issues to the test of a vote. Were he with us now, I think he would relish the chance to run against those who proclaim a new realism and then do nothing.

Until next week, thanks for listening, and God bless you.

Note: The President spoke at 9:06 a.m. from Rancho del Cielo, his ranch near Santa Barbara, CA.

Statement on Signing the Insider Trading Sanctions Act of 1984
August 11, 1984

I have signed H.R. 559, the Insider Trading Sanctions Act of 1984. This legislation makes several important changes to the Federal law governing insider trading in securities. Most important, it strengthens the penalties for violating Federal securities fraud law, which reflects my commitment to enforcing all our country's laws—both on Main Street and Wall Street.

The U.S. securities markets are the fairest in the world. Insider trading is the exception, not the rule. Nevertheless, abuses by insiders and those who receive their tips erode investor confidence in the securities markets. Public investors may be less willing to place their money at risk in securities if they believe that other traders, unlawfully utilizing material nonpublic information, have unfair advantages.

The legislation authorizes the Securities and Exchange Commission to seek a new civil penalty against persons who violate existing provisions of law in connection with certain purchases or sales of securities. This bill also increases the maximum criminal penalty for any violation of the Securities Exchange Act of 1934 to $100,000, adds commodities law violations as the basis for statutory disqualification under that act, and authorizes the Commission to remedy proxy and tender offer violations administratively.

Note: As enacted, H.R. 559 is Public Law 98–376, approved August 10.

Statement on Signing the Education for Economic Security Act
August 11, 1984

I have signed H.R. 1310, a bill entitled the Education for Economic Security Act.

This bill responds to two deeply felt concerns of this administration: first, the need to improve the quality of science and mathematics education in our country and, second, the need to restore freedom of religious speech for students attending public schools.

Science, mathematics, and technology have special importance in this country. Our economic and military strength, as well as our health and well-being, depend to a great extent on continuing developments in these areas. If we are to maintain our strength and independence, we cannot afford to allow our skills in these fields to diminish. Yet the disturbing fact is that the quality of science and mathematics education in our nation is declining, due in large part to a growing shortage of qualified science and mathematics teachers.

This administration proposed legislation in January 1983 that focused upon the shortage of teachers by authorizing scholarships for science and mathematics teachers in grades 9 through 12. The administration has also already established a program of Presidential Awards for Excellence in Science and Mathematics Teaching, similar to the one in H.R. 1310. I am very pleased to see that this bill emphasizes the critical importance of teacher training in improving the quality of science and mathematics education in activities authorized for the Department of Education and in endorsing the excellent ongoing science, mathematics, and engineering programs of the National Science Foundation.

I am also very pleased to approve the equal-access provisions of the bill. It has been the consistent policy of this administration to support the right of students in public secondary schools to meet voluntarily for religious purposes in school facilities during noninstructional periods, a right which this bill recognizes. I believe the equal-access provisions of this bill represent an appropriate balance among the free speech rights of students in public second-

ary schools, the prohibition against government establishment of religion, and the need to maintain in our public schools an orderly environment which is conducive to learning. These provisions honor, in a public school setting, this country's heritage of freedom of thought and speech, and I am delighted that they now become the law of the land.

H.R. 1310 is far from a perfect bill. It has a number of serious weaknesses: It is too expensive; it authorizes too many complex and administratively burdensome programs; it duplicates some existing activities; it authorizes unnecessary or inappropriate programs that are unrelated to improving science and mathematics instruction in our country; and it denies State and local governments the broad flexibility and decision-making authority they need to address local educational needs in the most effective manner.

I want to make clear that my approval of H.R. 1310 does not indicate endorsement of the objectionable provisions of the bill. Nor will I feel compelled to request funding at the excessive levels authorized by H.R. 1310. I believe, however, that the need to enhance the quality of science and mathematics instruction and to protect the rights of public school students to free speech, including religious speech, tips the balance in favor of approval.

Note: As enacted, H.R. 1310 is Public Law 98–377, approved August 11.

Nomination of Richard E. Carver To Be an Assistant Secretary of the Air Force
August 11, 1984

The President has nominated Richard E. Carver to be an Assistant Secretary of the Air Force (Financial Management), Department of Defense. He replaces Russell D. Hale, who has resigned.

Mr. Carver has been mayor of Peoria, IL, since 1973. Previously he was president of the Carver Lumber Co. He is a lieutenant colonel in the Air Force Reserve and is co-

ordinator of admission counseling, downstate Illinois, for the United States Air Force Academy. He is immediate past president of the U.S. Conference of Mayors.

Mr. Carver graduated with a B.S. degree in business administration from Bradley University in Peoria. He was born September 28, 1937, in Des Moines, IA. He is married, has four children, and resides in Peoria, IL.

Statement Expressing Opposition to a Federal Tax Increase
August 12, 1984

I have reduced the tax burden on the American people, and I want to reduce it even further. I have no plan to raise taxes, nor will I allow any plan for a tax increase. My opponent has spent his political life supporting more taxes and more spending. For him, raising taxes is a first resort. For me, it is a last resort.

Therefore, I will use the power and authority of the Office of the President to: (1) continue strong economic growth, (2) eliminate wasteful government spending, and (3) reduce the size of government, as the means to reduce the deficit. As I said at my last press conference, after—and only after—wasteful government spending has been reduced to its absolute minimum would I consider raising taxes to eliminate any gap between revenues and expenditures. Even then, I would not consider raising the personal income taxes of working Americans.

This election will offer the American people a sharp contrast between my opponent, who promises to raise taxes, and me, who will do everything I can to avoid having to. And if the Congress would give the President of the United States line-item veto authority—which 43 State Governors now have—and pass a constitutional amendment mandating a balanced budget, the deficit could satisfactorily be reduced by reducing wasteful Federal spending instead of raising the taxes of the American people.

My opponent has said that he will reduce the deficit by two-thirds in 4 years. To do this, and fulfill his campaign promises to various interest groups for additional spending, will require that taxes be increased by over $135 billion. My opponent owes the American people an explanation of exactly how and why he would impose this enormous and stifling burden of additional taxes on the American people—over $1,500 in additional taxes for every American household.

Statement by Principal Deputy Press Secretary Speakes on the President's Opposition to a Federal Tax Increase
August 12, 1984

Over the past several days I have been asked a number of questions concerning the President's position on taxes. Those questions have been submitted to the President, and his answers are as follows:

Q. Mr. President, you say you have no plans to raise taxes, but do you absolutely rule out the possibility of any tax increase to reduce the deficit?

A. A President of the United States should never say never, but a tax increase has always been for me a last resort. I will first want to do everything I can to reduce the deficit by keeping our economy growing and reducing wasteful Federal spending.

Q. So, raising taxes remains an option or a possibility?

A. I have no plans to raise taxes. I have throughout my political life been opposed to raising taxes. I do not want to see this wonderful economic expansion of ours jeopardized by tax increases. I would first want to know that government had been reduced to its barest minimum.

Q. Mr. President, are you ruling out other tax increases in addition to personal income tax increases?

A. I will do everything I can to avoid raising taxes on the American people. I will try to reduce the deficit by continuing strong economic growth and reducing wasteful Federal spending.

Q. Mr. President, will you rule out any tax increase in 1985?

A. I have no plans for a tax increase in 1985 or beyond. And as I said in my press conference, the only time I would consider a tax increase in order to reduce the deficit would be if I felt we had reduced wasteful government spending to the absolute minimum.

Q. Mr. President, on August 6 the Vice President was asked if you were keeping your options open on taxes except for an increase in the personal income tax. He said, "Any President would keep his options open. Conditions can dramatically change one way or the other." Do you agree with that statement?

A. Yes, but that does not in any way lessen my strong opposition to increasing taxes. I would seek to reduce the deficit by continuing strong economic growth and reducing wasteful spending and doing everything I could to avoid raising taxes.

Remarks to United States Olympic Medal Winners in Los Angeles, California
August 13, 1984

Thank you, Bill Simon, and thank you all very much. As the newest member of the team, I'm trying to figure out how I qualify. [*Laughter*] In high school, there was the 880 relay. But we only finished second in the State finals in that. And then there was swimming, but in my day we didn't do a flip turn. So, I'd have to learn that if I am going to qualify in that.

But anyway, ladies and gentlemen of America's team at the 23d Olympiad—and Bill Simon has said it all—you did us proud. You're heroes, every one of you living proof of what happens when America sets its sights high and says, "Let's create a little excellence."

And you gave us moments that we'll never forget. There was Blatnick dropping to his knees in thanks. And Mary Lou Retton getting that perfect 10. There was Steinseifer and Hogshead hitting that wall at the exact same hundredth of a second. And Carl Lewis' smile when he tied Jesse Owens' record.

There was something very special about the Olympics; there was a special spirit to it. You gave us all such a lift. You gave us something to be unified around and cheer for together. And I think maybe you possibly heard down on the field that cheer. It went something like, U.S.A.! U.S.A.! Well, it

doesn't matter whether you won the gold or the silver or the bronze; the cheer was for you, and for all of you.

The specialness of this Olympics was apparent from the beginning. You walked into the opening ceremonies with a special kind of pride, a vibrant and a very human delight that was transmitted to the crowds and that was picked up by the people who were watching on TV. Throughout the games, I couldn't help but think that if the people of the world judged Americans by what they saw of you, then they think, "Americans? Well, they're generous and full of serious effort; they're full of high spirits; they're motivated by all the best things. They're truly a nation of champions."

And I want to take a moment here to single out and say thank you to the uncelebrated story and the people—your coaches and trainers, your parents and friends—all the quiet people who stood behind you when the shot rang out and the race began. And, yes, those you may have defeated, but whose own efforts helped push you to do your best. Every hero knows that no hero does it alone. The people who stood behind you deserve our thanks. And the way I see it, there ought to be an Olympic event in moral support, and they'd get a perfect 10.

I want to say, too, that the city of Los

Angeles did a marvelous job, and there are a lot of terrific people in this town. Just about everyone in this city had to put him- or herself out some way, one way or another, while the games were on. They not only did it; they did it with a smile. They won the admiration and the thanks of the entire country.

This is a good time also to thank the generous corporations that decided a few years back to contribute money and personnel and time to help our athletes. They proved that the profits reaped from a free economy can be used to help our young people compete on an even footing with the state-subsidized athletes of other countries. Those corporations did us proud. And so did Bill Simon, who led this great citizens effort. So did the Los Angeles Olympic Organizing Committee and the U.S. Olympic Committee.

The 23d Olympiad of the modern era is over, but it will never be forgotten. It was attended by more countries than ever before. There was more competition than ever before. There was more brilliant talent than ever before. And, as you know, a lot of records were broken.

The games were a triumph, a triumph of friendly and generous competition, a triumph of fellowship, and a triumph of the spirit. And it turned out that nothing could mar those games, nothing could detract. The only losers of the 23d Olympiad were those who didn't or couldn't come.

As for those who did, what greatness they and you all showed us. I know you're impressed by the athletes the other countries sent—the South Korean boxers, the Chinese gymnasts, the Romanian athletes, the Jamaicans, the Japanese. For a lot of us, one of the really indelible images of the games was of Gabriela Andersen-Schiess of Switzerland walking dazed and dehydrated to the finish line, refusing to give up, pushing on even when all her strength was gone, summoning up just that last bit of reserve and crossing that line. She truly was heroic.

And I have just a final point here. One of the things I noted and liked so much as I watched the games on TV was that often in many of the events, you could sort out or figure out who represented what country, except with the American athletes. With the American athletes, we almost always had to see the U.S.A. on your uniforms, because our team came in all shapes and sizes, all colors and nationalities and races and ethnic groups. And I was thinking, you can talk on and read forever books about the melting pot; but the past 2 weeks, there it was winning medals for us, representing us every day—140 countries represented here in the only place in the world where those who are competing for this nation had the bloodlines and the background of more than those 140 countries.

And so, I say to you, the great melting pot team of 1984, the members of America's team at the 23d Olympics, thanks for the memories and thanks for the great moments and thanks for being what you are, genuine heroes.

And you know what, 1984 has a kind of special significance for me. [*Laughter*] I'm finding it to be a very interesting year. But after what I saw of you and what you did at those Olympics, I can't wait till '88. [*Laughter*] Just can't wait.

Thank you all very much, and God bless you.

And now, you remember that right before the games you gave me a gift of all your Olympic teams pins. And today I want to return the favor. I have a gift for the future U.S. Olympics Hall of Fame. It is the American eagle and is given to honor the members of America's team at the '84 games, because you've soared to greatness.

Note: The President spoke at 10:31 a.m. in the Los Angeles Ballroom at the Century Plaza Hotel. He was introduced by William E. Simon, president of the U.S. Olympic Committee.

Prior to his remarks, the President was made an honorary member of the U.S. Olympic team with the presentation of an Olympic blazer by medalists Steve Lundquist and Mary Lou Retton.

Nomination of Harvey J. Feldman To Be United States Alternate Representative for Special Political Affairs at the United Nations
August 14, 1984

The President today announced his intention to nominate Harvey J. Feldman to be the Alternate Representative of the United States of America for Special Political Affairs in the United Nations, with rank of Ambassador. He would succeed Charles M. Lichenstein.

Mr. Feldman entered the Foreign Service in 1954 as consular officer in Hong Kong. He was consular officer in Tokyo (1957–1958) and in Nagoya, Japan (1958–1960). In the Department of State he was international relations officer from 1960 to 1962. He attended Chinese language training in Taichung in 1962–1963 and was political-military officer in Taipei from 1963 to 1965. He was on detail to the United States Information Agency in 1965–1970 as cultural officer in Hong Kong. In 1970–1972 he was political officer in the Bureau of International Organization Affairs and a member of the Policy Planning Staff in 1972–1973. He was counselor for political affairs in Taipei (1973–1975) and deputy chief of mission in Sofia (1975–1977). In 1977–1979 Mr. Feldman was country director for Republic of China affairs in the Department. He served as Ambassador to Papua New Guinea and to Solomon Islands in 1979–1981. Since 1981 he has been the Washington Representative of the United States Permanent Representative to the United Nations at the Department of State.

Mr. Feldman graduated from the University of Chicago (A.B., 1951; M.A., 1954). He was born June 25, 1931, in Brooklyn, NY. He is married, has two children, and resides in Washington, DC, and Dade County, FL.

Nomination of Melvyn Levitsky To Be United States Ambassador to Bulgaria
August 14, 1984

The President today announced his intention to nominate Melvyn Levitsky to be Ambassador to the People's Republic of Bulgaria. He would succeed Robert L. Barry, resigned.

In 1963 Mr. Levitsky entered the Foreign Service and attended German language training at the Foreign Service Insititute. He was Foreign Service officer general in Frankfurt (1963–1965), consular and political officer in Belém, Brazil (1965–1967), and political officer in Brasilia (1967–1968). In the Department of State he was political officer for Brazil (1968–1969) and staff officer in the Executive Secretariat (1969–1971). In 1971–1972 Mr. Levitsky attended Russian language training at the Foreign Service Institute. He was publication procurement officer (1972–1973) and political officer (1973–1975) in Moscow. In the Department he was officer in charge of U.S.-Soviet bilateral relations (1975–1978), Deputy Director (1978–1980), and Director (1980–1982) of the Office of United Nations Political Affairs. He was Deputy Assistant Secretary of the Bureau of Human Rights and Humanitarian Affairs in 1982–1983. Since 1983 he has been on detail to the United States Information Agency as Deputy Director of the Voice of America.

Mr. Levitsky graduated from the University of Michigan (B.A., 1960) and the State University of Iowa (M.A., 1963). He attended the University of Chicago Law School in 1960–1961. He was born March 19, 1938, in Sioux City, IA. Mr. Levitsky is married, has three children, and resides in Bethesda, MD.

Statement by Principal Deputy Press Secretary Speakes on the President's Meeting With Jewish Women Leaders
August 16, 1984

The President met this morning with a group of distinguished women leaders representing a cross section of the American Jewish community. Their discussion focused on foreign policy issues and concerns, including U.S.-Israeli relations. The President expressed his commitment to the security of Israel and his belief that the United States can play an important role in assisting the dialog between Israel and her neighbors.

The President stressed his administration does not condone anti-Semitism in any form. The President discussed the third International Women's Conference which will take place next year in Nairobi, marking the end of the United Nations Decade for Women, noting that while the original goals of the previous two United Nations Women's Conferences (in Mexico City in 1975 and Copenhagen in 1980) were noble, both conferences became dominated by po-litical issues extraneous to these goals. Specifically, these conferences became fora for attacks on the State of Israel and an infamous association of Zionism with racism.

The President made clear today that the United States will actively oppose any conference agenda item which deviates from important women's issues and calls for the discussion of nongermane political issues, including any agenda item that could be used as a vehicle to defame Israel. The United States has consistently opposed such efforts, most recently at the United Nations Population Conference in Mexico City earlier this week.

In particular, the President noted that the United States will oppose any agenda item at the Nairobi Conference which associates Zionism with racism. If, despite our efforts, such an agenda item is adopted, the United States will have no choice but to consider seriously canceling its participation in the conference.

Remarks on Signing the Child Support Enforcement Amendments of 1984
August 16, 1984

Thank you, and thank you for letting me join you.

This symposium is an example of the commitment with which Margaret Heckler—Secretary Heckler—and this administration are approaching the very important problem of child support enforcement. And with your help we hope to put the new authority for child support enforcement, provided by House Resolution 4325, into practice quickly and efficiently. The advice from this symposium should help us get things off to a running start.

Of course, advice from "on high" isn't always as pleasant as the guidance that we're getting here. Perhaps you heard about that fellow that fell off a cliff, and about halfway down managed to grab a shrub or a limb sticking out from the side of the cliff. He was dangling about 500 feet above the rocks, down below. And he looked up and yelled, "Is anyone up there?" And no one answered. He yelled, "Lord, if you're up there, tell me what to do!" And a voice came from the heavens and said, "If you believe, let go." [*Laughter*] And he took another look at the rocks down below and said, "Is there anyone else up there?" [*Laughter*]

Well, we've had some children in this country, and they've been dangling above the rocks waiting for help. And today, we sign into law legislation that will give them the helping hand they need.

It's an unfortunate fact of our times and one in four American children live in single-parent homes, and millions of these children endure needless deprivation and hardship due to lack of support by their absent parent. The failure of some parents to support their children is a blemish on America. As a decent and caring people, it behooves us to come to grips with the devil-may-care attitude of some of our citizens that has left too many children in dire straits.

Understanding the situation, we've already moved forward to do what we can. In this administration, the Department of Health and Human Services has put a special emphasis on the Federal-State child support enforcement program. In 1983 this program collected some $2 billion in support for the children. Yet this is still only a portion of what is owed. And with billions of dollars still unpaid each year, our child support enforcement system needs new tools, new muscle, and new commitment throughout the Nation. And that's what this legislation is all about.

Last year, I proposed that we bolster our Federal-State child support system by mandating effective and proven collection practices. I believe that we should emphasize service to all children, welfare and nonwelfare alike, and improve incentives for State government to get the job done. The Child Support Enforcement Amendments bill contains all these features.

This legislation represents a significant break from the tradition of simply throwing tax money at a problem. Instead of creating more dependency on government, we're requiring responsible behavior by our citizens. And this is the kind of innovative and principled approach to problemsolving that will make a difference. It will not only make a difference in the lives of our children but for so many women who have been forced through no fault of their own on to welfare rolls due to abandonment. Left with the full load to bear, they often find themselves trapped in a cycle of unhappiness and destitution.

The goal of our efforts is not just the transfer of funds. We also hope to discourage abandonment and, if families do split up, to encourage the absent parents to invest time and love in their children. Permitting individuals to ignore parental obligations and giving the bill to the taxpayers in the form of higher welfare costs have been tantamount to a stamp of approval. And this is not the kind of message public policy should be sending out.

There's been much talk of late about the importance of family and traditional values in our society. Well, that's a traditional—or a welcome change, I should say, from the days when the simple virtues of goodness and decency were often laughed at, even ridiculed. But one thing is certain: It's deeds, not words, that count. Many policies of the past were anything but supportive of the family. Programs like this, on the other hand, are not only aimed at justice for the children but also at encouraging ethical behavior and bolstering vital social institutions like the family.

We hope that by placing the responsibility where it should be, on the parent, people will be encouraged to make moral decisions. Our administration is trying to bring this kind of spirit to all its endeavors.

I want to congratulate everyone concerned with this effort. By passing this legislation, the Congress has acted honorably, in the best bipartisan manner, for the benefit of children who really need the help. Many people deserve thanks on this occasion for what they've done to make this possible. Those of you here on the platform have earned a special word of appreciation.

Since the Congress is in recess, many other Members who worked long and hard on this bill can't be with us. And I want to express my special appreciation to Senate Finance Committee Chairman Dole, Senators Bill Armstrong and Russell Long, under whose able management the legislation passed in the Senate. In the House, Dan Rostenkowski, Carroll Campbell, Barbara Kennelly, and Barber Conable were instrumental in steering the bill through the legislative process.

State and local governments have also been a positive force, and I believe this legislation underscores a change that's taken place in the way we do things. As demonstrated by this symposium, we've developed new working partnerships with

State and local government. And in the months ahead, that working relationship will be put to use to carry out this new law with maximum effectiveness.

And you've already heard a little bit of history about my home State of California and all, and it was a part of a key welfare overhaul reform at that time. And our success was what moved me to testify before the Senate Finance Committee in support of a nationwide child support enforcement system. So, as you can tell, I have a very special reason myself to celebrate today.

And with that said, I shall go sign House Resolution 4325, the Child Support Enforcement Amendments of 1984.

Note: The President spoke at 3:28 p.m. at the Symposium on Child Support Enforcement at the Sheraton Washington Hotel. The symposium was organized and convened by Secretary of Health and Human Services Margaret M. Heckler.

As enacted, H.R. 4325 is Public Law 98–378, approved August 16.

Message to the Senate Transmitting a Convention Relating to the Distribution of Programme-Carrying Signals Transmitted by Satellite
August 16, 1984

To the Senate of the United States:

With a view to receiving the advice and consent of the Senate to ratification, I transmit herewith the Convention Relating to the Distribution of Programme-Carrying Signals Transmitted by Satellite, signed by the United States on May 21, 1974. I also transmit, for the information of the Senate, the report of the Department of State with respect to the Convention.

The Convention obligates States party to the Convention to prevent interception and distribution on or from their territory of program-carrying signals transmitted by satellite. The purpose of the Convention is to clarify the status of satellite signals, in view of the uncertain nature of the commitment with respect to satellite signals which States have undertaken by adhering to other conventions which bear on radio communications and copyright. The Convention does not impose obligations on States party to it with respect to signals emitted from a satellite and intended for direct reception by the general public (direct broadcast satellite signals) or with respect to purely private

reception and viewing of program-carrying signals provided there is no further distribution of such signals.

Ratification of the Convention will constitute an important policy statement by the United States concerning the unauthorized interception and distribution of television programs transmitted by satellite and will benefit United States television program producers, distributors and broadcasters by extending to them protection in other countries party to the Convention from unauthorized distribution of their works transmitted by satellite. In view of these benefits, there is strong support for early ratification of the Convention by the U.S. industries concerned with the creation and dissemination of television and radio programs.

I recommend, therefore, that the Senate give early and favorable consideration to the Convention and give its advice and consent to ratification.

RONALD REAGAN

The White House,
August 16, 1984.

Letter to the Speaker of the House and the President of the Senate Transmitting Proposed Emergency Food Assistance Legislation
August 16, 1984

Dear Mr. Speaker: *(Dear Mr. President:)*

I am transmitting today proposed legislation, the "President's Emergency Food Assistance Act of 1984," together with a section-by-section analysis and supporting justification.

On July 10, 1984, the thirtieth anniversary of the P.L. 480 Food for Peace Program, I announced a major five-point emergency food aid initiative designed to reduce the suffering and loss of life brought about by acute hunger situations overseas. The proposal I am transmitting today carries out, in part, that initiative by authorizing:

—the creation of a special $50 million Presidential fund designed to provide emergency food and related assistance more quickly and effectively; and

—the payment of inland freight and distribution costs under Title II of P.L. 480 in special emergency cases.

I consider enactment of this legislation of great importance and would appreciate your efforts in seeing that it is enacted.

Sincerely,

RONALD REAGAN

Note: This is the text of identical letters addressed to Thomas P. O'Neill, Jr., Speaker of the House of Representatives, and George Bush, President of the Senate.

Nomination of J. Stapleton Roy To Be United States Ambassador to Singapore
August 16, 1984

The President today announced his intention to nominate J. Stapleton Roy, of Pennsylvania, a career member of the Senior Foreign Service, Class of Minister-Counselor, as Ambassador to the Republic of Singapore. He would succeed Harry E.T. Thayer.

In 1956 Mr. Roy entered the Foreign Service and was intelligence analyst in the Bureau of Intelligence and Research Department. He attended Chinese language training in Taichung (1958–1959) and was political officer in Bangkok (1959–1961), consular officer in Hong Kong (1962), and political officer in Taipei (1962–1964). From 1964 to 1965, he attended Mongolian language studies at the University of Washington in Seattle, WA, and was international relations officer in the Bureau of European Affairs in the Department from 1965 to 1968. He attended Russian language studies in Garmisch, Federal Republic of Germany, from 1968 to 1969. He was administrative officer (1969–1970) and political officer (1970–1972) in Moscow. From 1972 to 1974, he was Deputy Director of the Office of Soviet Union Affairs in the Department. He attended National War College from 1974 to 1975. In the Department he was Deputy Director of the Office of People's Republic of China and Mongolian Affairs from 1975 to 1978. He was deputy chief of the United States liaison office (1978–1979) and deputy chief of mission (1979–1981) in Beijing. Since 1981 he has been deputy chief of mission in Bangkok.

Mr. Roy graduated from Princeton University (B.A., 1956). His foreign languages are Chinese-Mandarin, Russian, and Thai. He was born June 15, 1935, in Nanking, China, of American parents.

Nomination of William Arthur Rugh To Be United States Ambassador to the Yemen Arab Republic
August 16, 1984

The President today announced his intention to nominate William Arthur Rugh, of Maryland, a career member of the Senior Foreign Service, Class of Minister-Counselor, as Ambassador to the Yemen Arab Republic. He would succeed David Eugene Zweifel.

Mr. Rugh entered the Foreign Service with the United States Information Agency in 1964 and was assigned to language and area training in Beirut. He was assistant cultural officer in Cairo (1965–1966), assistant public affairs officer in Jidda (1966–1967), branch public affairs officer in Riyadh, Saudi Arabia (1967–1969), and country public affairs officer in Jidda (1969–1971). He was senior policy officer of the Office of Assistant Director for Near East and South Asia in the Agency from 1971 to 1972. He was on a leave of absence as a fellow at the Council on Foreign Relations in New York City from 1972 to 1973. From 1973 to 1976, he was Deputy Assistant Director for Near East in the Agency. He was country public affairs officer in Cairo from 1976 to 1981, and since 1981 he has been deputy chief of mission in Damascus.

Mr. Rugh graduated from Oberlin College (B.A., 1958), Johns Hopkins University School of Advanced International Studies (M.A., 1961), and Columbia University (Ph.D., 1964). From 1958 to 1959, he attended Hamburg University in Germany. His foreign languages are Arabic and German. He was born May 10, 1936, in New York, NY.

Proclamation 5227—Women's Equality Day, 1984
August 16, 1984

By the President of the United States of America

A Proclamation

On August 26, 1920, the 19th Amendment, which guarantees women the right to vote, became part of the Constitution, the supreme law of our land. By that measure, women became equal partners with men in the responsibilities of citizenship.

The contributions of American women to free government in the United States date back to the Colonial Era. The importance of those contributions has been recognized by writers such as the French historian Alexis de Tocqueville, who attributed the success of the American experiment in self-government largely to the extraordinary qualities of our Nation's women.

In democracies, government is founded on popular consent, expressed through the process of free elections. Indeed, the absence of free and fair elections is a crucial element by which we define regimes that are not democratic. By exercising the right to vote, American women and citizens of other free countries continue to affirm their faith in self-government.

The 19th Amendment gives women the same political means as men have to participate in the process of self-government. On this 64th anniversary of its ratification, we honor the pioneer suffragettes, and we applaud today's women who are pioneering in fields new to women and men alike. Most importantly, we reaffirm our national commitment to the goal of equal opportunity for each individual to pursue and to achieve her or his goals.

Now, Therefore, I, Ronald Reagan, President of the United States of America, do hereby proclaim August 26, 1984, as Women's Equality Day. I call upon all Americans and friends of popular government around the world to mark this occasion with appropriate observances.

In Witness Whereof, I have hereunto set my hand this 16th day of August, in the year of our Lord nineteen hundred and eighty-four, and of the Independence of the United States of America the two hundred and ninth.

RONALD REAGAN

[Filed with the Office of the Federal Register, 4:32 p.m., August 17, 1984]

Note: The proclamation was released by the Office of the Press Secretary on August 17.

Proclamation 5228—Fortieth Anniversary of the Warsaw Uprising
August 17, 1984

By the President of the United States of America

A Proclamation

Forty years ago, one of the most heroic battles of World War II, the Warsaw Uprising, occurred. Polish resistance to aggression throughout World War II had been courageous and uncompromising. As the Nazi forces retreated before advancing Soviet armies, the Polish Home Army that led the resistance seized its chance to throw off the Nazi yoke. For sixty-three days, the people of Warsaw fought against insurmountable odds, endured unimaginable suffering, and made countless sacrifices to regain their independence. Nevertheless, the lightly-armed resistance fighters were overwhelmed by the full weight of Hitler's war machine. The Nazis mercilessly crushed the uprising while Soviet forces passively looked on from across the Vistula River. Warsaw lay in rubble. Two hundred-fifty thousand Poles were killed, wounded, or missing. Yet the victims of the Warsaw Uprising did not die in vain.

The example of those who fought for freedom during the Warsaw Uprising is a stirring chapter in history, as vivid today as it was then. The ongoing struggle of the faithful, the shipyard workers of Gdansk, the miners of Silesia, and farmers throughout the countryside is but a continuation of the proud history of the Polish quest for freedom.

It is right that we pay tribute to those who sacrificed all for independence and freedom. All of us who share their passion for freedom owe the heroic people of Warsaw and all of the valiant people of Poland a profound debt.

The Congress, by Senate Joint Resolution 272, has resolved that the United States should join in recognizing the Anniversary of the Warsaw Uprising.

Now, Therefore, I, Ronald Reagan, President of the United States of America, do hereby proclaim August 1, 1984, as the Fortieth Anniversary of the Warsaw Uprising.

In Witness Whereof, I have hereunto set my hand this seventeenth day of August, in the year of our Lord nineteen hundred and eighty-four, and of the Independence of the United States of America the two hundred and ninth.

RONALD REAGAN

[Filed with the Office of the Federal Register, 4:33 p.m., August 17, 1984]

Proclamation 5229—Polish American Heritage Month, 1984
August 17, 1984

By the President of the United States of America

A Proclamation

The United States is a country in which people of many different heritages are bound together by a common dedication to democratic principles. The mosaic of ethnic diversity invigorates our culture and strengthens our society. For this reason, the Polish American Congress and other Polish American clubs and organizations across the country are celebrating August 1984 as Polish American Heritage Month.

The millions of Americans who trace their ancestry to Poland have made vast contributions to our Nation. Tadeusz Kosciuszko and Kazimierz Pulaski crossed the ocean to help the American colonies win their independence. Throughout the last two centuries, thousands of Polish Americans have fought bravely to help preserve that independence. Polish Americans have also made outstanding contributions in the arts, the sciences, and in industry and agriculture. Through these efforts they have helped in innumerable ways to establish a strong and free United States.

Americans of Polish descent take great pride in and honor two great world leaders who have their roots in Poland. Both Pope John Paul II and Lech Walesa, the Nobel Peace Laureate and founder of the Solidarity Labor Federation, have gained the world's respect and admiration. Solidarity has been continuing the Polish people's struggle for freedom since its founding in August 1980.

The Congress, by House Joint Resolution 577, has designated August 1984 as "Polish American Heritage Month" and authorized and requested the President to issue a proclamation in observance of this occasion.

Now, Therefore, I, Ronald Reagan, President of the United States of America, do hereby proclaim August 1984 as Polish American Heritage Month, and I urge all Americans to celebrate this month with appropriate observances.

In Witness Whereof, I have hereunto set my hand this 17th day of August, in the year of our Lord nineteen hundred and eighty-four, and of the Independence of the United States of America the two hundred and ninth.

RONALD REAGAN

[*Filed with the Office of the Federal Register, 4:34 p.m., August 17, 1984*]

Remarks at a White House Luncheon Marking the 40th Anniversary of the Warsaw Uprising
August 17, 1984

The President. Your Eminence and members of the Polish Home Army, and members of the Polish American Congress, distinguished guests, *dzien dobry* [good day].

I'll say welcome to the White House, but before I go further with my remarks, there is something—a little news note here that I think you might be interested in. This happens to be Ken Tomlinson's last day as Director of the Voice of America. He's done a terrific job and is with us today. And, Ken, thank you very much for a job well done.

Well, now I'd like to offer our apologies for having to postpone our program last month. I know that many of you'd made travel arrangements and that the changes in my schedule caused you some difficulties. I am, however, delighted that we're all here today and together for this important commemoration.

It's always an honor for me to be with individuals like yourselves who understand the value of freedom. I'm reminded of a story about a conversation between one of our citizens and a Soviet citizen. The American described the freedom of speech that we have here in the United States, and the citizen of the Soviet Union said, "Well, we're free to speak in the Soviet Union just like you are in the United States." He said, "The only difference is you're free after you speak." [*Laughter*]

But today we pay tribute to a nation which for two centuries has struggled for freedom and independence. From the uprisings in 1794, the November uprising in 1830, and then again in 1863, the people of Poland demonstrated courage and a commitment to human liberty that inspired free men and women everywhere.

And this 200-year record of perseverance and bravery coincided with the development of our own precious liberty here in the United States, and that is no mere coincidence. Our two peoples drank from the same well of freedom, held dear the same Judeo-Christian values, respected the simple virtues of honesty and hard work. And even today, it's often noted that unlike many others, our two peoples take their religious convictions seriously. These heartfelt convictions have kept the spirit of freedom burning in our hearts, especially during times of great adversity.

Pope John Paul II has said, "Freedom is given to man by God as a measure of his dignity. . . ." And "as children of God," he said, "we cannot be slaves." Well, I know that you feel as I do; we're truly blessed in this time of great need, to have a spiritual leader like Pope John Paul II.

The continuing suppression of the Polish national identity brought wave after wave of Polish immigrants to the United States. And for that, we can be grateful. We all know the list of contributions and the names of those who rose to great prominence. But just as important are the millions who came here and, with their hard work and with their moral strength, helped shape the American character.

During this century, Americans and Poles have stood side by side in those two conflagrations that swept the world. The First World War, unfortunately, did not end all wars, but it did result in the reestablishment of the Polish state.

This month, we commemorate a desperate battle of the Second World War, an heroic attempt by free Poles to liberate their country from the heel of Nazi occupation, and to protect it from postwar, foreign domination. For years they covertly resisted the occupation forces. And then in 1944, for 63 brutal and agonizing days, ill-equipped and overwhelmingly outnumbered, they—and I could say, many of you—held off the Nazi war machine. And it's fitting that we and all free people take special care to remember this occasion.

Of those who fought for freedom, and those who put their lives on the line for human liberty, I can think of none who should be prouder than those who can say, "I fought in the Polish Home Army."

And today we honor three individuals, heroes of the Polish Home Army, never given their due after the allied victory. And it's my great honor to now present the Legion of Merit to the families or representatives of these men.

So, let us salute Stefan Rowecki, who led the Resistance until he was captured and executed by the Gestapo.

[*At this point, the President presented the award to Jan Morelewski, president of the Polish Home Army Veterans Association.*]

Next, his son will arise, the son of Bor-Komorowski, leader of the Warsaw uprising, who later died in near poverty in exile in London.

[*The President presented the award to Adam Komorowski.*]

And finally, General Leopold Okulicki, who was lured into a trap and died under suspicious circumstances in Moscow.

[*The President presented the award to Zdzislaw Dziekonski, chairman of the Warsaw Uprising Commemorative Executive Committee and director of the Polish American Congress.*]

These brave men and the courageous individuals who fought under their command represent the best of the human spirit. They risked all for their ideals, for their God and country, at a time when the odds were so much against them. They're now part of the inspiring legacy of the Polish people.

If there's a lesson to be learned from the history books, it is that Poland may be beaten down, but it is never defeated. It may be forced into submission, but it will never give up. It may be pressured to acquiesce, but it will never accept foreign domination and the suppression of God-given freedom. After two decades of brutal foreign domination, we witnessed, just a short time ago, a resurrection of the indomitable spirit of the Polish people. And I assure you we have not forgotten and will never forget Solidarity and the freedom of the Polish people.

There are some, of course, who seem all too willing to turn a blind eye to Soviet transgressions, ostensibly to improve the dialog between East and West. But those who condemn firm support for freedom and democracy—who, in order to prove their sincerity, would project weakness—are no friends of peace, human liberty, or meaningful dialog.

Our policies toward Poland and other captive nations are based upon a set of well-established principles.

First, let me state emphatically that we reject any interpretation of the Yalta agreement that suggests American consent for the division of Europe into spheres of influence. On the contrary, we see that agreement as a pledge by the three great powers to restore full independence and to allow free and democratic elections in all countries liberated from the Nazis after World War II, and there is no reason to absolve the Soviet Union or ourselves from this commitment. We shall continue to press for full compliance with it and with the Charter of the United Nations, the Helsinki Final Act, and other international agreements guaranteeing fundamental human rights.

Passively accepting the permanent subjugation of the people of Eastern Europe is not an acceptable alternative. In 1981, when it appeared that Poland would suffer a similar fate to that of Hungary in 1956 or Czechoslovakia in 1968, we raised our voices in support of the Polish people. And we did not remain passive when, under intense Soviet pressure, martial law was imposed on them.

Many credit, trade, and fishing privileges extended to Poland, due to its somewhat broader degree of freedom than other Eastern European countries, were suspended. At the same time, we have assisted voluntary organizations to provide humanitarian aid through the Polish church to avoid hurting the very people we want to help.

I would especially like to commend the work of Al Mazewski and the Polish American Congress. In cooperation with the church, they've provided over $40 million worth of food, clothing, and medical supplies to the people of Poland. And I know that I speak for Nancy—my wife is thrilled to have been selected honorary chairman for the Polish American Congress' Infant Charity Drive. We both wish you the best on this worthwhile project.

I've pledged that our sanctions can be lifted, one by one, in response to meaningful improvement of the human rights situation in Poland. For example, a complete and reasonable implementation of the Polish Government's amnesty decree would create a positive atmosphere that would allow reactivation of Poland's application for membership in the International Monetary Fund.

In the meantime, we've agreed, along with our allies and private organizations, to help fund a Polish church program to assist individual farmers. I am pleased to announce today that I am seeking support for a $10 million American contribution to the pilot phase of the church's program. And we will follow the progress of this program carefully to determine whether additional support should be forthcoming.

Perhaps the most significant thing that we can do is let the Polish people and all the people of Eastern Europe know that they're not forgotten. And that's why we're modernizing Radio Free Europe, Radio Liberty, and the Voice of America. Our radio programming is becoming the mighty force for good that it was intended to be. As the Scriptures say, "Know the truth and the truth will make you free." Well, our broadcast will carry the truth to captive people throughout the world.

The free peoples of the world are in ideological competition with the followers of a doctrine that rejects the basic tenets of freedom and declares the worship of God to be a social evil. As important as this competition is, until recently the democracies, including the United States, seemed paralyzed by uncertainty and lacking the will to compete.

In the last 3½ years, we've quit apologizing, and at long last we're standing up and being counted. As our United Nations Ambassador, Jeane Kirkpatrick, said, we've taken off our "Kick Me" sign. We're proud of our way of life; we're confident that freedom will prevail, because it works and because it is right. We believe the free peoples of the world should support all those who share our democratic values.

The National Endowment for Democracy, which I first proposed in a speech before the Parliament in London 2 years ago, has been established to encourage the democratic forces and the development of free institutions throughout the world. Its concerns include nonviolent, democratic movements like that of Solidarity in Poland.

And the rise of Solidarity is a matter of historic significance. It continues to be an inspiration of all free people that the Marxist-Leninist myth of inevitability is crumbling. Communism has brought with it only deprivation and tyranny. What happened in Poland is one sign that the tide is turning. The Polish people, with their courage and perseverance, will lead the way to freedom and independence, not only for themselves but for all those who yearn to breathe free.

The battle cry of the Polish Home Army still rings true: "Poland is fighting. Poland will live. Poland will overcome."

Thank you all for being here today, and God bless you.

Mr. Korbonski. Mr. President, on behalf of former underground Home Army soldiers, who celebrate this month the 40th anniversary of the Warsaw uprising, in my native Poland and throughout the world, and who are presently here, I thank you very much for what you said about our history, about Warsaw uprising, about your understanding of the Yalta agreement, and about Solidarity, which, in my opinion, is also underground, but which fights for freedom and independence of Poland by other means than arms.

Your words broadcast to Poland by Voice of America and Radio Free Europe will bring a new inspiration, new hope, to our people in Poland. To what you said about the Warsaw uprising, I want only to add a few words.

First of all, that you, our American allies, contributed to this heroic struggle. On the 18th of September, American Air Force armada welcomed enthusiastically by the embattled population of Warsaw, parachuted very badly needed supplies.

Mr. President, 1984 is not a year for mourning. It is true that we have suffered tremendous human and material losses during the uprising. But they were well balanced by the immaterial, spiritual, moral gains. In these defeats, they were seeds of victory. Warsaw uprising demonstrated to the whole world the indomitable Polish spirit—our unshakable will to live free and independent.

From then, 36 years later, Solidarity was born. There would be no Solidarity in 1980 if there were no Warsaw uprising in 1944. Mr. President, such spirit, such will are not alien to you. You practice them daily in the pursuit of your foreign policy.

Mr. President, I, as the last chief of the Polish wartime underground State, thank you very much for bestowing these high American military decorations on our dead national heroes—General Rowecki, Komorowski, and Okulicki, who were my close friends. And in order to express our gratitude for your unshakable support for the Polish cause, I have the great honor to decorate you with the Home Army Cross.

The President. Thank you very much.

Note: The President spoke at 1:09 p.m. in the State Dining Room at the White House.

In his opening remarks, the President referred to His Eminence John Cardinal Krol, Archbishop of Philadelphia.

Stefan Korbonski is honorary chairman of the Warsaw Uprising Commemorative Executive Committee and president of the Polish Council of Unity in the United States.

Radio Address to the Nation on Administration Policies
August 18, 1984

My fellow Americans:

Something very bright and happy and hopeful has been happening across our country in recent days. We've watched a grateful nation shower its affection on those who showered us with glory—our Olympic athletes.

Theirs was a triumph of faith and hope. In honoring them, ours has been a celebration of the new patriotism. Nancy and I saw our athletes in Los Angeles the day after the Olympics ended. You could just feel their joy and energy. And when our famous gymnast, Mary Lou Retton, stood on her toes to give me a hug, I couldn't help thinking, "How can anyone not believe in the dream of America?"

Now, I've been accused of being an optimist, and it's true. All my life I've seen that when people like Mary Lou have a dream, when they have the courage and opportunity to work hard, when they believe in the power of faith and hope, they not only perform great feats, they help pull all of us forward as well.

Somehow, the idea that American progress begins with spirit and a willingness of the heart was ignored during the 1970's. The intellectual establishment was so busy demanding more power for government, more bureaucracy, regulation, spending and—oh, yes—more and more taxes, they forgot all about the secret of America's success—opportunity for people, for all the people.

When the economy reached the point of collapse by the end of the seventies, they began talking about our crisis of spirit, about our malaise. But we hadn't given up hope; we just hadn't been allowed to hope.

So, when we came to Washington in 1981, we said, "Let us renew our faith and our hope. We have every right to dream heroic dreams." We put together an economic recovery program that made a radical break with past policies. For the first time since the administration of John Kennedy, we cut tax rates significantly for every working American. We told the

people, "America's destiny is back in your hands. If you work harder and earn more than before, your reward will be greater than it was."

But from the beginning, the old-guard establishment—people who still make policy from abstract statistics, theories, and models rather than looking at the reality of human behavior—have filled the airwaves with gloom, predicting our program couldn't meet our goals. And from the beginning, they've been wrong: When they said inflation and interest rates wouldn't come down, when they said recovery wouldn't come, when they said the expansion wouldn't last, and when they said the deficit wouldn't come down.

Recently, many liberal analysts have been reviewing our record and our prospects. Their message remains: "hasn't worked; can't be done." So, when the Urban Institute came out with a study a few days ago, it was only natural that some of the press would look for the same old doom and gloom. For example, they didn't report that the study also said elderly Americans have clearly done better under our policies with real gains in disposable incomes, nor that the social safety net is still largely intact for the nonworking poor. Even the Urban Institute said there is no evidence that working welfare mothers who have been eliminated from the rolls are quitting their jobs to requalify for benefits, and that despite all the furor, it finds surprisingly few changes from 1980 with respect to the environmental, public lands, and water resources activities of the Federal Government.

And no one seems to mention that the centerpiece of our policy, the tax cut, was not fully in place until 1983. Our program has just begun. But let's look at the record since it has: over 6 million jobs created; a surge in investment and productivity; a record 600,000 business incorporations; the biggest increase in real after-tax personal income since 1973; and perhaps most important, a new spirit of optimism and confidence about America's future. It's clear that once people get a chance to show what they can do—well, America got well and got strong.

What isn't clear is why those pessimists, with so little faith in people, so little understanding of incentives, and so many bad predictions, are not more humble and not treated a little more skeptically by the media.

In 1984 we face an historic choice. Will we heed the pessimists' agenda of higher taxes, more bureaucracy, and a bigger welfare state leading us right back to runaway inflation and economic decay, or will we continue on our new road toward a true opportunity society of economic growth, more jobs, lower tax rates, and rising take-home pay?

I believe the spirit we've seen during and after these Olympics reveals something very important about America. We believe in ourselves, we're hungry for real opportunity, and we're up to any challenge.

Until next week, thanks for listening, and God bless you.

Note: The President spoke at 12:06 p.m. from the Oval Office at the White House.

Remarks at a Meeting With Members of the Agricultural Community in Sedalia, Missouri
August 19, 1984

Thank you, Governor Bond. Before we get started, I want you to know how pleased I am to get a chance to meet with all of you here in Missouri. I know the Vice President, as Kit told us, has met some of you on the Governor's Advisory Council on Agriculture in Columbia last April. And I won't get to see the university on this trip, but I'm delighted to be here at the State fair.

Being a farmer has been anything but easy in these last several years. From our first day in office, we've been trying to help the farm community recover from past policy mistakes, economic difficulties, and I think we have turned a corner. With the task of writing up a new farm bill for 1985 before us, we're looking to get American farmers and agribusiness leaders' thoughts and ideas on the issues that we'll be addressing.

Jack Block has already been holding listening sessions in Chicago, Riverside, Atlanta, Syracuse, Dallas, and plans to hold another on September 6th in Davenport, Iowa. He would have been with me here today, except there's something going on in Dallas, and—[*laughter*]—and he's gone down there.

But he's heard from over 200 farmers, ranchers, and agribusiness representatives from all over the country, and he's received over 1,000 pages of written testimony. We think this input from those who know the farm business inside-out and whose lives are most affected by farm legislation will make our new farm bill the best that we've ever had.

And now, I'm going to turn the program over to your director of agriculture, Jim Boillot. And I'll listen.

[*At this point, several participants in the meeting made brief statements. The President then resumed speaking.*]

Thank you.

Well, let me just say I'm sorry that we've run out of time in hearing these. And as you've seen, I've been making a few notes up here.

We intend to have, and are going to have, a very comprehensive approach to this whole thing now that we're coming to the time for a new farm program.

And I told you of what Jack Block has been doing, the other information that he's been gathering, and I can assure you that all of these matters are going to be very much on our minds as we try to find an answer to this.

The one question there with regard to the deficit—believe me, I've been making speeches out on the mashed-potato circuit for years about deficit spending. It was a regular part of government policy over the last 50 years. Now, all of a sudden, it isn't a part of government policy—it's mine. [*Laughter*] And I'm responsible. But we recognize the threat in those, and we are embarked on a program. We believe that as this economic recovery continues, I am optimistic about what we're going to see in that regard, and the increased position in government revenues, and so forth.

I want you to know in spite of all the things that you've heard, where someone has said that a tax increase is the first resort, tax increases in my book will always be a last resort. We have no plans for a tax increase. We are going to continue along the lines that we have in trying to get further government reductions in spending. We don't think that we have begun to get eliminated all the fat that is in government.

Now, I know that some people on the other side say, "Well, what would you eliminate in the line of spending?" Well, I think that's an argument they've been using for, again, about 50 years, to justify their spending. My approach to it is, "How do we get government programs administered more efficiently and more economically and with less overhead, and still fill government's responsibility?"

And right now, we have before us 2,478 specific recommendations by the Grace commission. Peter Grace headed up a group to do something that we did in California, and we had 2,000 leaders from every activity volunteer to help in that. And that is the result, these recommendations. We have a task force working virtually around the clock on this—we've already been able to implement some that we can just simply do administratively; many will take legislation—but to see what of these—we don't say that all of them are going to turn out to be things that are practical—but to see how much we can implement these. And as I say, the goal is to get rid of the inefficiencies and the uneconomic things that government is doing.

You've spoken on a number of things that I've had some familiarity with myself—soil erosion, and so forth. All of these, as I say, are going to get our best thinking on how

we approach the new farm program. And there aren't any of us that are not aware of the basic importance of agriculture. It is the very basis of an economy any place. And the remarks about subsidized competition, believe me, we have been leaning on our friends from abroad quite heavily on this very matter and even have taken advantage of some opportunities, like one with regard to flour in Egypt recently, to show them that we weren't going to stand back and let this go on. We believe in free trade, but we believe in fair trade, and we're going to keep on.

We have a friend in Japan that is doing everything he can to meet some of our problems there with regard to a farm market—marketing in Japan. Like the President, he can't just issue an order, he's got a legislature, too. [*Laughter*]

But I think we are making some headway here. And I do know of the seriousness of your problems, not only from nature in the last few years but the seriousness of the economic problems.

One of the problems—we're all very proud of the fact, and I think it's a great advantage that we've been able to reduce inflation. But on the other hand, when you had runaway inflation over the long period of time that you had, you had an economy that became geared to a continuing inflation. And the comedown from that has difficulties as well, just as you have spoken here with regard to depreciating land values once inflation has gone on to the downward trend. But we're going to keep on staying ahead of that.

And as to interest rates, I think there's been some indication just recently that the long-term notes, there has begun to be a certain slide. I have said before and I'll say again, I think the only justification for the high interest rates right now is the inability out in the money markets and the business community to believe that we really have gotten a handle on inflation. They're looking over their shoulder, and they're charging interest rates accordingly. And maybe the market recently is an indication that they're beginning to become true believers.

But we're not going to resort to a quick fix and try to get back to the old-fashioned way that we've had over the seven or eight recessions since World War II of an artificial stimulant to try and end the so-called recessions, and all they did was bring on another inflation—or another recession a few years later that was worse than the one before. This time, I think we're on the way to a real recovery and a solid expansion. And you've got to be able to share in that, too. And we're going to do our utmost to see that you do.

Now, I know that I'm holding you up from that sale of champions that's already underway over there in the Coliseum. And

believe me, all these things that I've heard here will be acted upon.

Thank you very much.

Note: The President spoke at 2:27 p.m. in the Youth Building Cafeteria on the Missouri State fairgrounds. He was introduced by Gov. Christopher (Kit) S. Bond.

Following the meeting, the President went to the shorthorn barn to view a livestock display and then proceeded to the coliseum, where he watched the Junior Champion Auction and addressed the fairgoers.

Remarks at the Missouri State Fair in Sedalia
August 19, 1984

Thank you very much. And, Kit, Governor Bond, I appreciate your warm words and your gift, and I'm delighted that in view of my previous occupation you didn't say, "Sweets to the sweet." [*Laughter*] "Ham to the ham" wouldn't—[*laughter*]——

Well, you know, I've been to quite a few so-called cattle shows in my time, so I just want you to know it's great to be here with you and with your champions and tomorrow's leaders to see the real thing. We only wish we could have brought you—although I understand you did get a little yesterday—some rain. Anymore, in saying anything of that kind out in farm country in America, I have to ask first, "Did you have too much or too little?" But I understand that you—like us in California—you've been having too little. So, I hope that the clouds that were here when we came in will do their duty for some more.

As we drove in, I couldn't help thinking what a tonic to come here to your State, where corn and milo grow, to be with people who work with the soil, the sweat of their brow, and the ache in their back, people who share an abiding love for God and family, people for whom words like "personal initiative," "self-reliance," and, yes, "generosity" are everyday facts of life. You are the heart of our country. [*Applause*] And if this is "Show Me" spirit, just show me more. [*Applause*]

But there is another fact of life right now in this heartland: a powerful economic expansion which has given birth to millions of new jobs and a spirit of hope, but has not still spread thoroughly and throughout this farmbelt. And I've come today to see you, to meet with you, to listen to Missouri farmers and Governor Bond's Advisory Council on Agriculture, and to give you three important messages of my own.

First, after years of drift and decline and deepening despair, America is moving forward again. But our progress won't be complete, it won't be good enough, and we won't rest for 1 minute until all our people are moving forward together.

And the second thing I want to tell you is that we will make this progress together. We'll make it because our history tells us so. Those who've been proven right in the last 4 years are not the do-nothing pessimists who only see America wringing her hands; it's been the millions of hard-working achievers who see America raising her hands.

You know, we have so many strengths in this country, but I think the greatest are often ignored by those so-called Washington experts. Because I'm talking about a different kind of strength—strength born of a dream, strength of motivation and confidence that ours truly is the freest land in the world. Ours is a society that rewards honest toil, risk-taking, and achievement, for the factory worker, the small businessman and, yes, the family farmer, because the promise for America is for everybody, no matter who you are, who your parents are, or what lonely corner of the world you may have come from.

We're strong because we still believe in a bedrock principle: We are a government of, by, and for the people, not the other way around. And we're strong because we know that true greatness begins with the deepest treasures of the human spirit, with faith and courage, with loyalty and love, with a quiet, unselfish devotion to our families, our neighbors, and our nation.

I couldn't help but think of these things as I watched our Olympic athletes. Didn't you get the feeling that the Soviets must have been relieved when the closing ceremonies for the Olympics were over? [*Applause*] But the one thing they'll never see is closing ceremonies for America.

These values reach deep into our national character. They're rooted in the lives of our parents and grandparents, of all those who settled these hills and tilled this good earth. And they live on each day in people like you in Sedalia, in Knob Noster, La Monte, Smithton, Pilot Grove, and in Sweet Springs.

The heritage of our past will bring forth the harvest of our future. And that's why there's a third message I want to give you: We must all move forward together. We will move forward together, and we'll do it by strengthening one of our most cherished, vital institutions—the American family farm.

We know the problems that still haven't gone away. The threat of crippling droughts and floods is still with us and always will be. Credit burdens are still too heavy, largely because of high interest loans during the late seventies while the value of land that farmers use as collateral for their loans was dropped as inflation has come down, and that's keeping financing difficult.

But some other things have gone away. And I believe that getting rid of them makes the future for family farmers much brighter and more hopeful than before.

The first, most important thing is that we got rid of a cynical, wrong-headed, totally unfair grain embargo. I seem to remember someone who now says he opposed the embargo in private, speaking a little differently in 1980. He said then, "What we've done will really sting." Well, someone got stung, all right, but it wasn't the Soviets. They're still in Afghanistan. It was thousands like you who deserved better from your own government. And for the life of me, how do you show you're strong by punching yourself in the breadbasket?

Now, forgive me, and I'm going to hate myself for saying this, but their foreign policy went against the grain. [*Laughter*] That embargo——

[*At this point, the President was briefly interrupted by two men in the audience who began shouting. The men intermittently shouted protests throughout the remainder of the President's speech.*]

That embargo cost farmers 17 million tons of grain sales to the Soviet Union in 1 year.

Is there an echo in here? [*Laughter and applause*]

But the worst loss was the long-term loss of American credibility as a reliable supplier and billions in long-term sales.

But we're doing things a little differently. I believe our foreign policy reflects priorities that are based on common sense. One of my first actions as President was to remove the embargo, and we're doing our best to help you work your way back, strengthen your prices, increase your exports, and regain your reputation as reliable suppliers.

We've begun rebuilding—[*interruption*]—we've begun rebuilding America's defenses. And after all those years of shameful neglect, I can tell you that today America is more secure, and the men and women representing us in uniform are the brightest and the best that we've ever had.

Our efforts are beginning to pay off. In 1980 we had weak defenses, a weak economy, and a grain embargo that filled your bins and emptied your wallets. [*Interruption*] In 1984 we have stronger defenses, a stronger economy, and grain sales to the Soviet Union, the country our critics say won't deal with us. Well, over 20 million metric tons they bought since last October. And if they want to buy more, we'll sell more. [*Interruption*]

We're also—[*interruption*]—we're also moving aggressively to expand markets—[*interruption*]. If I could do that, I wouldn't have to use the mike. [*Laughter and applause*]

But what we're trying hardest to do is to move aggressively to expand markets and open other markets that have been closed. [*Interruption*] Last November I met with Prime Minister Nakasone of Japan, and this spring our two countries reached an agreement that should virtually double American beef exports over the next 4 years.

So, we got rid of the grain embargo. We're going after the other barriers to American exports around the world. We took action and eliminated the huge crop surpluses that had piled up after the embargo. And we expect the value of agricultural exports this year will be up almost 10 percent over last year.

Inflation, that cruel and dangerous enemy, has been beaten down to about 4 percent. And we intend to keep it down. In 1979 and 1980 the prices farmers had to pay shot up by one of the biggest 2-year increases in history. In 1982 and '83 farm cost levels increased by the smallest 2-year rise in 15 years.

The killer prime rate of 21½ percent in 1980 has dropped to 13 percent, which is still too high. But remember, we've broken with tradition, we've resisted the quick fix, and that's making all the difference. With inflation low and confidence building that it will stay low, then I just have to believe that interest rates can come down more and will come down more.

In the meantime, the Farmers Home Administration will continue reaching out to help tens of thousands of farm borrowers hold on to their farms and stay in business. [*Interruption*]

Now, there's one other change we've made, and it hasn't been too popular back in Washington. We came to Washington with a radical idea: America's economic problems weren't caused by you living too

well, they were caused by government living too well. So, we struggled to reduce personal tax rates by 25 percent, to provide help and hope to individuals, to small farms, and to family farmers who pay taxes by the personal rates. Next year, your taxes will be indexed so that government can never again profit from inflation at your expense by shoving you up into a higher tax bracket just because you got a cost-of-living pay raise.

Also, we believe it's not right for widows and children to lose what generations of love and toil have created. So, the estate tax exemption will increase to $600,000 by 1987, and of even greater help, there will be no estate tax for a surviving spouse.

Now, everything that we're trying to do is directed toward one—[*interruption*]——

I'll raise *his* taxes. [*Laughter and applause*]

Everything that we're trying to do is directed toward one challenge: to rekindle opportunity so everyone has a chance to pursue the American dream. America can only grow if you grow, can only prosper if you prosper; and America can only be strong if you are strong. And that's why I'll fight any attempt to destroy these reforms or to impose new taxes on your families. If the born-again budget balancers have discovered the meaning of frugality, let them start by imposing some frugality in Washington, DC, and not in Sedalia, Missouri.

For some people, tax increases are a first resort; for me, they'll be a last resort. Forgive me, but those who have forgotten about the grain embargo, forgotten about killer interest rates, forgotten about runaway inflation, forgotten about soaring fuel costs, and who now intend to increase taxes $1,500 per household if they're going to keep their promises—Missouri is the Show Me State, not the Snow Me State.

We have no plans to raise taxes by any amount on anybody at any time—period. Our plan is to make the tax system more simple, more fair, and, most important, to bring your tax rates further down. That's our idea of compassion.

And that's our idea of progress, too. For if we restrain spending, reduce tax rates further, and keep our economy growing by over 5 percent a year, we can sharply reduce the deficit through growth. Yes, it's a difficult but by no means impossible challenge.

So, I'd like to leave you with this thought: Let's take our cue from our Olympic athletes. Rather than punish success, rather than raise taxes, let us challenge America to raise her sights and reach for greatness. Let's go for the gold, let's go for growth.

You who struggle so hard and devote so much and give of yourselves to feed the hungry are a true light of hope for all the world. And through you, America can be the source of all the hopes and dreams that she was placed on this good Earth to provide. I thank you for what you do every day. I thank you for giving me this chance to be with you to share your joy and spirit.

Thank you, and God bless you all.

Note: The President spoke at 3:26 p.m. at the coliseum on the State fairgrounds. He was introduced by Governor Bond, who gave the President a country ham.

Following his visit to the State fair, the President returned to Washington, DC.

Remarks at a Reagan-Bush Rally in Cincinnati, Ohio
August 20, 1984

The President. I have a feeling that I ought to quit right now while I'm way ahead. But it's great to be in the city of the Bengals and the Cincinnati Reds. It's great to know that Pete Rose has come back home. I talked to him on Air Force One coming out here.

And it's an honor to stand up here with two of your great sports heroes, Johnny Bench and Bob Trumpy. And I'm heartbroken, because I have an invitation in my pocket that just came and that my schedule won't allow me to accept. And that was that Bob Howsam invited me to the ballgame tonight and said that I could broadcast a couple of innings, which I used to do for a living. But I'm afraid the schedule will have me a long way from here.

Let me add that we have five of America's newest heroes up here, all of them members of America's team at the Olympics.

Have they been introduced? They have?

Oh, they tell me you've already met them, because I was going to ask them to stand up so you could say hello to Darell Pace and Betsy Mitchell and David Wilson and Kim Rhodenbaugh and Julie Isphording. The day after the Olympics closed, they gave me one of those jackets and made Nancy and me members—honorary members of the team.

It's great also to be in a city that has become a symbol of the economic renaissance that's been sweeping our country. I'm happy to be here, because Cincinnati has always been very kind to visitors, who are almost always impressed by what Cincinnati has to offer.

The writer Stephen Birmingham came here just a few years ago. He suggested that your city is smooth, understated, efficient, and conservative. I like that last part best.

Now, John Gunther, in his book "Inside USA," he said Cincinnati is "packed with charm" and has a certain "stately" quality. And even Charles Dickens once came here in 1842 and said, "Cincinnati is . . . cheerful, thriving and animated."

Audience member. No more Reagan! No more Reagan!

The President. But——

Audience. Boo-o-o!

The President. You know, as I say, Charles Dickens said that "Cincinnati is . . . cheerful, thriving and animated,"—and I was just going to say, but there are always dissenters. [*Laughter*]

Now, one writer said in 1981 that "Cincinnati is so disciplined, so straight," is how he put it, "that you used to have to cross the river into Kentucky to have a good time." [*Laughter*] Now, that isn't true, is it?

Audience. No!

The President. I didn't think so. I have a

feeling it was slander, and I just wanted to make sure. [*Laughter*]

I'm very proud to stand up here with members of the Taft family of Ohio. William Howard Taft was a great Republican President. His son, Robert A. Taft, was "Mr. Republican" in the Senate. His son, Robert Taft, was another great Republican Senator, and his son, Robert Taft, is a Hamilton County commissioner. Now, I don't know if there are any other Tafts waiting in the wings, but I wouldn't want to run against them. [*Laughter*]

And let me say that I don't have to visit Ohio to benefit from the good judgment and support of the Taft family. Back in Washington I have the help of William Howard Taft IV. He is an appointee in our Department of Defense.

I'm also proud to stand up here with two of your great Congressmen, Bill Gradison and Bob McEwen. They've given us such staunch support in Washington. And make sure they continue to be there to give that support.

Now, it's typical of candidates out on the stump that they list all the statistics that back up their assertion that indeed they deserve another term. And I could stand here and outline the economic facts of our national life. I could tell you about how the gross national product is soaring, how inflation has plummeted. I could tell you that 600,000 new businesses were incorporated in this country last year and how 6½ million new jobs were created in the past 19 months. In fact, we created more jobs in the month of June alone than all the Common Market countries in Europe created in the last 10 years. Now, I could tell you all those things, but I won't. [*Laughter*]

What's more pertinent and more to the point is simply to talk about what's happening here in the Blue Chip City.

Cincinnati's thriving. You're not in economic recovery; you're in economic expansion. Just look around, look around at all this construction, at the gleaming office towers and the shops and the restaurants below. I understand that 67 new businesses have been created here in the central business district since 1980. The building trades are booming. In the last 4 years, 16,000 new jobs have been created here, and it's estimated that over the next 4 years another 7,000 new jobs will be added. You put that all together, and you realize Cincinnati's a modern boomtown. And she's not alone.

Now, none of this happened by accident. None of it happened by chance. It took hard, concerted effort by the leaders, the builders, business and working people of your city. Men like Tom Nies, who started out 15 years ago with $600 and what he called "an impossible dream." He was a worker at IBM. His field was computers; but he loved Cincinnati, and he wanted to stay here. So, he started his own company, Cincom Systems, and it has grown by leaps and bounds.

In 1980 it had 637 employees; it now has 1,350. Four years ago, it had sales of $36 million a year; now its sales are $95 million a year. Four years ago, its return on investment was 6 percent, and today it's 30 percent. Now, Tom Nies says something very interesting. He says, "Only in a healthy America can this happen."

Well, a healthy America is one in which individuals can choose the work they want, start a business if they want—and those businesses can create jobs. And the jobs create a demand for housing and services, and that in turn creates more jobs as the healthy spiral continues.

Let me tell you more about that healthy spiral. It's based on the simple proposition that growth is good. And it starts with a foundation of faith—faith in the spirit of a people under God and faith that the Government will continue policies that will reward effort. And as for continuing policies that will reward effort, believe me, we will.

We've tried to create an environment in which business can bloom and people can blossom. We've failed to create the kind of America that we seemed to be sliding into a few years ago. What we've done is simply a people's program. You can call it populism or some other high-sounding phrase; but what it comes down to is creating an environment that will help the people help themselves.

Now, there are those—and they will go unnamed here—who sit back and see our success, and they try to peddle the tired old cliche that helping the economy means helping the rich. They encourage envy and division and resentment. They deal mostly in falsehood and fiction. But I don't think the American people will buy what they're selling.

The truth is, what we've done has been done to help all the people. And we couldn't have done it without you, the people. Somehow, that truth, that message, always seems to get lost. But when inflation was lowered, it helped all the people. When interest rates were lowered, it helped all the people.

When tax rates were cut for every living American in this country, everyone—not just the rich, not just the middle class, not just the poor—when income tax rates were cut across the board, it helped all the people. And today the average family is giving Uncle Sam $900 less than if our tax cut had not been passed. And when tax indexing goes into effect next year, it will help all the people, because never again will the Government be able to benefit from your efforts to keep up with inflation by moving you up into higher tax brackets.

And we ask for no great credit, because in the truest sense, no credit is due to us. We didn't do anything but get government out of the way of the American people. It's your recovery. All we did was remove some of the obstacles so you could make the race. And let me tell you about what else we're going to do to get out of your way. We're going to simplify the tax system, actually make it understandable and clear and fair. And when we do that, your tax rates are going to come down, not go up.

Now, that's what we've done; this is what we've achieved; and this is what we mean to do.

And the central question of 1984 is, do we want to go back to the old days?

Audience. No!

The President. Do we want to listen to the falsehood and fiction of the other side? Do we want to retreat?

Audience. No!

The President. I don't think we do. In 1980 the American people were in a mood to win, and they did. In 1984, again, they're in a mood to win, and they will.

I've been talking about what we did to help the people with the help of the people. But let me tell you what the other side will do to the people. They will—and they've declared it—raise your taxes.

Audience. Boo-o-o!

The President. They'll put the roadblocks up again. They'll provide the kind of leadership that will make sure we all put on our hair shirts and feel properly despairing and itchy again—[*laughter*]—the kind of leadership that will stop growth and start talking about the age of limits. Do you remember 4 years ago when they were talking, we had to get used to an age of limits? Things couldn't be as good as they were. Well——

Audience member. They're better!

The President. Thank you. [*Laughter*]

The only thing that's limited is their optimism and imagination. Calling for a tax increase was their typical knee-jerk reaction, and believe me, when their knee jerks, you get kicked. [*Laughter*]

You know, months back, when Senator John Glenn of Ohio was running for President, he got a bad rap. The leaders of his party wouldn't listen to him. His opponents ignored him and his policies. But he told the truth. He said the policies of the current Democratic nominee would cause a huge increase in spending and taxing. He said those policies revealed a fundamental lack of support for an adequate national defense.

Well, I think the Senator with the Right Stuff was right when he criticized the candidate with the Left Stuff. John Glenn is an authentic American hero. And it's too bad the leaders of his party stopped listening.

He knows, as you know, that we do not live by material things alone, that the hunger for spiritual values has transcendent importance in the life of man on Earth. We all need to believe in things that are bigger than us: to believe in the importance of religion and the central importance of the family; to believe there is a God to be worshiped and ideals to be honored; to believe in the principles upon which this nation was founded, and have pride, honest pride, in the success of those principles. These are things which, in the past few years have been renewed and reborn—taken out and looked at again, considered again as a new thing, a helpful thing, by which we live.

The past few weeks, the whole Nation watched the Olympics, and we were moved by what we saw. We saw all the pride and love of America unabashedly on display. We saw all that America can do when she sets her sights high, all that individuals can achieve when they dedicate themselves to achievement. We saw our young people, in many ways the trendsetters of society, show that it's in style again to put your hand over your heart when the flag goes by, and it's in style again to sing the words of the national anthem.

Did you see the people in the stands and our athletes on those winning blocks? Did you see how they held those hard high notes when they came to that part about "the land of the free, and the home of the brave"? They held those notes. They were proud. And we were proud of them, too.

It happens that—you might have suspected—I'm involved these days in a race. [*Laughter*] And I have no hesitation about setting my candidacy before you, the working men and women of America. That's why I'm here, and that's why I came here—

to put my case before you as I make my way to the convention of our party in Dallas. You are the judges in this contest, and that makes me glad. Our whole impulse, in all our policies, in all of our administration comes down to this: Trust the people. And we do. And I'm happy to put my faith in your hands.

I thank you. I thank you for coming here to see us and thank you for listening to this speech. And the day is beginning to get warm. I thought maybe I wasn't going to be able to say that, but it is kind of warm out here in the sun, so I better let you go so we can get back to the air conditioning. [*Laughter*]

Audience. No! No!

The President. No? But anyway——

Audience members. We love you, Ron! We love you, Ron! We love you!

The President. Thank you. And I love you, and God bless all of you. Thank you very much.

Note: The President spoke at 12:35 p.m. in Fountain Square. Prior to his remarks, he toured the atrium area of the Procter & Gamble world headquarters building.

Following his remarks, the President traveled to Decatur, IL.

Remarks at a Reagan-Bush Rally in Decatur, Illinois
August 20, 1984

The President. This is a very special treat. Having been a Governor myself, I decided that the uniform for up here on the platform had already been determined by Jim Thompson, so I joined him. And I'm happy he made it that way, too.

Well, this is a very special treat. When I was growing up—and it wasn't too far from here—I never dreamed that I'd be flying into Decatur on Air Force One. As a matter of fact, when I was growing up, there wasn't an Air Force One. [*Laughter*] But I am proud of my Illinois roots. This is where I learned about the values of faith and family and work.

A century and a half ago, a young Frenchman named Alexis de Tocqueville

toured our fledgling democracy, and he claimed that he was in search of the secret of our greatness, even that—150 years ago. And then he finally declared that he had found it. He said, "America is great because she is good. When America ceases to be good, America will cease to be great."

Well, I firmly believe in the goodness of our country and our people. And I think we're witnessing a transformation in America, a return to those values that we all learned here in this heartland. The roots of the new patriotism are right here, and it is the heartland of America.

There's been much talk about the work ethic, of late. The first job I ever had was working on a construction crew, and it was here in Illinois. I was 14 years old. And I want you to know I haven't forgotten something. I was swinging a pickax on that job; and I wasn't swinging it to help somebody in Washington live better, I was working so our family could live a little better.

In the last 3½ years, we've kept taxes down so that people will be able to keep more of what they earn. And that's the way to develop a work ethic. There are some people around right now that you're hearing from that—they've made it evident that a tax increase is their first resort. Well, believe me, it's our last resort. In these last 3½ years, we've kept taxes down so that people will be able to keep more of what they earn. And that's the way it's going to be.

For the last 3½ years, we've been trying to restore the economy so there would be jobs for those who wanted them. It took time to put our program in place, and it took time for it to take hold. The debate now, however, isn't whether the program is working. People are arguing about how long the expansion will last. Well, don't worry about the gloom-mongers. They're the same ones who said the program wouldn't work in the first place.

We've ignited, for the first time in decades, high growth, decline in unemployment, and inflation going down all at the same time. Now, this is creating so many jobs that our European allies are calling it the American miracle—6½ million new jobs just since the recovery began. More people in our country are working right now than ever before at any time in our history. We're not tied to the failed policies of the past, policies that relied on more taxing, more spending, and more government.

Right here in Decatur, as the Governor told you, you're trying out an idea that I'd like to see put to use nationally. Thanks to Governor Thompson and your Mayor Anderson, Decatur is one of eight areas designated by the State of Illinois as an enterprise zone, and I understand the list is growing. Your community and your State are in the forefront of this novel approach to development.

All over America, entrepreneurs are investing in new ideas. All we needed to do was to get government out of the way. This is no time to go back. America is moving forward again, and together we can keep her moving forward.

I would like to point out to you—this idea of the enterprise zones, and being done here at the State and local level—it is an idea that we have been trying for almost 3 years to get done at the national level—nationwide. And in the Democratic-dominated House of Representatives, they have kept that program buried and will not even allow it to come out to the floor for a vote. Remember that when you start voting for Congressmen this year.

But I know the schedule calls, and we have to move on to some other errands here in this community. I want to thank you, Governor Jim Thompson and Senator Chuck Percy and each of you, for coming out here to welcome me back to my home State.

But before I go, I just want to add one thing. I want to congratulate your new world champion fast-pitch softball team.

Dais guest. There they are, Mr. President.

The President. Where?

Dais guest. Right up there——

The President. Ah!

Dais guest. ——on the top row.

The President. There they are, waving their caps. Congratulations.

And a special greeting to Dr. George and Mary Waller, whose son, David, raised right here in Decatur, is most helpful on my staff in Washington, DC.

So, thank you again for coming out here. Oh, boy, nostalgia's beginning to move in. I could stay and visit, but I know we haven't time, and we've got to move on. But God bless you all. This is just wonderful to see you and be here again.

Thank you. Thanks very much.

Note: The President spoke at 2:02 p.m. at the Decatur Municipal Airport.

Remarks at an Agricultural Forum in Decatur, Illinois
August 20, 1984

Thank you very much, Roger Miller. And I want to thank Dwayne Andreas for his hospitality at ADA [ADM], where I've been able to see American agribusiness at work.

And my greetings to Governor Thompson and Senator Percy, who've been with me here on the visit so far today. I hope that I'll be able to continue for some time extending greetings in Illinois to Governor Thompson. I hope that I will be able to extend those greetings on a daily basis in Washington for some time to Senator Percy. That means both of us have to live in Washington. [*Laughter*]

But I was thinking of the importance of Senator Percy's returning there, because when I think of the position we would be in if we did not have what we have had in the Senate—well, I don't think we would be having the expansion you spoke of at such a level.

I have to tell you how impressed I was— and once again, nostalgia started flowing when, coming in on Air Force One, I was seeing those rows of corn, those cornfields and the soybeans stretching out there as far as I could see from the plane. I was going to say something about the importance of—I know anytime that I head toward a rural area anymore, I have to find out in advance, now, do I go there and commiserate about the floods or the drought? [*Laughter*] But I find neither here, that you've had some pretty good rainfall and that, while all of the State couldn't say this, you were doing pretty well in this area.

I do understand something about farmers' problems. I remember some years ago when Ezra Taft Benson was the Secretary of Agriculture, and he was out in a time of hardship meeting with some farmers and hearing some of their problems. And one particular place, there was one man that was really giving him a bad time. His complaints were numerous, and he was going on about them. And, finally, Ezra turned to a staff member and looked at some notes that were shown him, and then turned back and said, "Well, now, wait a minute. You

didn't have things all too bad here. Last year you had 29 inches of rain." And the man said, "Yes, I remember the night it happened." [*Laughter*]

But I do thank you for making us all feel so welcome here, quite a bit more welcome than the first time I visited this distinguished university. It was back in 1929. I was playing right guard on Eureka College football team. Night football was quite a rarity. As a matter of fact, I think we might have been one of—possibly the first of the games of night ball. The lights were not up to the same standard that they are today. Millikin's colors being blue and white, they appeared on the field with blue and white jerseys with circular white patches here. And the ball was white—[*laughter*]—because of the dimness of the lights. We were there in our dark maroon jerseys. And I just want you to know that—I'm a little embarrassed to say this—the score was 45 to 6. The 6 was Eureka's. [*Laughter*]

I found that I was playing, also, opposite in the line of someone that is a citizen of your area of some prominence, George Musso, now in the Football Hall of Fame, after 8 years all-pro tackle. You played both offense and defense in those days, and George outweighed me 100 pounds. [*Laughter*] And I decided that I wasn't going to go over him. [*Laughter*] I wasn't going to go through him. And I remember once I was going around him, and I ran into our tackle on the other side coming around him on the other side. [*Laughter*]

Well, anyway, I still remember back, also, when the Chicago Bears used to be the Staley football team here in Decatur. And it seems to me they had a better record before they moved than they've had recently. [*Laughter*] There must be something catching about the winning spirit in Decatur. I hope it's very catching.

You've always been innovators. In fact, I remember when John Beall invented the cornsheller back in 1875. I was just a small boy at the time. [*Laughter*] And you've never given up when the going got tough.

I'm convinced that what you're doing will be a victory for all America. If people want to see the country at her best, if they want to see the bright light of adventure and innovation and hope bringing economic growth, security, and human progress to people throughout the world, let them come here to the heartland and to Decatur, Illinois. They'll see miracles being created from America's abundant renewable resources by the men and women of Archer Daniels Midland and A.E. Staley.

It wasn't long ago that we were being told that our best days were behind us. The crippling inflation, the record interest rates, and the energy crisis were so severe they would destroy the greatest heritage of our past—our faith and hope that have always brought us the harvest of a better future. Well, here in the land of Lincoln, I'm afraid you didn't listen very well to those cries of gloom. The progress—and I've heard described on my visit to those plants here today—I've just heard described, would inspire your countrymen and fill their hearts with pride.

From corn and soybean processing that produce food products to feed a hungry world, to exciting research and production in hydroponics, to your pioneer work in ethanol that increases demand for farm products, creates new jobs, and leads to greater energy security for our country—it's all happening here, because here in America's heartland, you are on the cutting edge of progress.

When we took office in 1981 only 75 million gallons of ethanol fuel were being produced. This year more than 450 million gallons will be produced, requiring more than 180 million bushels of corn. It just goes to show, there's no limit to what free people can do when the gloom-and-doomers stand aside and get out of the way.

In our Food for Peace efforts, the United States has delivered over 27,000 tons of food a day to recipient countries for three decades. The value of these U.S. farm products exceeds $33 billion—more than $3 million each and every day. And who could put a pricetag on the good and simple virtues of decency and generosity that are the heart of Food for Peace and of the people who support it?

Sometimes I wish more attention were paid to facts like these. They underline one of the most compelling lessons of the 20th century: Capitalism, not socialism, is the most progressive, revolutionary, and powerful economic force for good in the world today. For only where freedom lives is economic growth strong, does opportunity thrive, and are the forces of human betterment always at work. Socialist countries are held down by a gravity of their own making. In America—something like a rocket shooting to the stars.

Agriculture is a driving force in our economy, and leaders like you can be proud that you have a record of productivity unmatched anywhere in the world. From our first day in office, we have been trying to help the farm community recover from past policy mistakes and economic difficulties.

We know that the Federal Government has an important role to play as a partner to the farm community—and not a senior partner. I think the gist of that role is to help farmers do what they can't always do on their own: seek out new markets—as you indicated—counter unfair trading practices for our trading partners, promote research, provide a measure of protection from erratic weather and natural disasters, and create a proper environment for supply-and-demand forces to allocate resources efficiently.

We began by insisting that the Department of Agriculture represent farmers first, which wasn't always true in the past. And representing those interests has led to several changes that I believe give us hope for a brighter future.

The first was ending a cynical, wrong-headed, totally unfair grain embargo. I remember someone who now says he was opposed to that embargo privately, but he was speaking a little differently in 1980. He said the grain embargo was a strong, absolutely crucial action that would force the Soviets to pay a heavy price for their aggression in Afghanistan.

I guess it's difficult to see the world clearly when you're scrooched down behind the American farmers. [*Laughter*] We, of course, know that it was they—or, I should say, you who paid the heavy price, not the Soviets. They're still in Afghanistan.

Farm prices declined, and our entire agricultural marketing system—elevators, barge lines, railways, millers, and exporters—was disrupted. The embargo cost farmers 17 million tons of grain sales to the Soviet Union. But the greatest loss was the loss of American credibility around the world as a reliable, long-term supplier.

Now, I know it hasn't been easy, trying to make a comeback from that situation. But, make no mistake, we are coming back. In 1980 we had weak defenses, a weak economy, and that grain embargo that filled your bins and emptied your wallets. In 1984 we have stronger defenses, a stronger economy, and grain sales to the Soviet Union— the country our critics say won't deal with us—of over 20 million metric tons since last October. And if they want to buy more, we'll sell more.

We've reached an agreement with Japan that will open up their markets to American beef. We expect that our beef exports to Japan will virtually double over the next 4 years. We eliminated huge crop surpluses, and we expect the value of farm exports to be up nearly 10 percent over last year.

As we've moved to revive these markets overseas, we're strengthening the greatest market of all, the American market, with a powerful, noninflationary expansion, as you've been told.

In the 2-year period of 1979 and 1980, prices that farmers had to pay shot up nearly 30 percent—one of the worst 2-year increases in history. And the purchasing power of farmers' net income plummeted 42 percent in 1980. But in a period of 1982 and 1983, farm cost levels increased only 7.3 percent, the smallest 2-year increase in 15 years. And we believe net farm income in 1984 will be the highest since 1973.

Interest rates are down, although I couldn't agree with you more—certainly not down enough. And credit burdens are still too heavy, largely because of high interest loans during the late seventies. The value of land that the farmers use as collateral for their loans has dropped. But we're hopeful on interest rates, because we haven't succumbed to the quick fix. So, inflation has dropped to about 4 percent or less, even as our economy has expanded

with terrific power. If we can keep inflation down—and confidence is building that, indeed, we can—then I'm convinced interest rates will come down more.

I want to reaffirm my absolute determination to protect the tax reforms we've made—accelerated cost recovery to stimulate business investment; personal tax rate reductions, which have benefited many family farms; indexing to prevent inflation from pushing taxpayers into higher tax brackets; and estate tax changes, increasing the exemption to $600,000 by 1987 and, of even greater help, abolishing the estate tax for a surviving spouse.

We will resist any and all tax increases. Our plan is to simplify the tax system— make it more fair, easier to understand— and to bring your personal rates further down. Our agenda is an agenda for growth and opportunity for all Americans.

Now let me discuss briefly today another issue of enormous importance to the farm community. As you know, my opponent made a big promise to the leadership of the AFL–CIO. He pledged his support for protectionist legislation called domestic content. This would force foreign and domestic manufacturers of automobiles sold in the United States to build their cars with an escalating percentage of U.S. parts and domestic labor.

He couldn't have been thinking of American workers when he made his promise, because, as the Congressional Budget Office itself pointed out, domestic content would destroy far more jobs than it would save. It would add substantially to the cost of a new car. And the cost of protectionism for one group of workers would be passed on to another group down the line.

And if domestic content passed, every other industry would become a target for foreign retaliation. Dick Gallagher, president of the Iowa Soybean Association, said: "We cannot afford a major surge in world trade protectionism that could be triggered by the domestic content bill." He's right. A true friend of farmers would renounce immediately his or her support for such misguided legislation. Our administration is determined to create jobs the right way, with economic growth, technological innovation—and we've created 6.4 million new jobs in the last 19 months.

You know, Albert Einstein once said that "Everything that is really great and inspiring is created by individuals who labor in freedom." And freedom is what we're trying hardest to preserve and strengthen— for you, your children, and your children's children. And without freedom, we will surely fail. And, again, I can only tell you that all of the discussion that is going on today—increasing taxes is not in anything in our mind. We have no plans to do such a thing. Others may have taxes as a first resort. For us, they are only a last resort, a last, desperate resort. Now, with this freedom, we can remain an inspiration to all the world and unlock the golden door of progress for years and generations to come.

Now, gentlemen, I'm going to take back all that I've heard here today, because we are having a comprehensive study made. Jack Block has been out all over the country, as you know, listening to farm leaders. He has over a thousand pages of written testimony on these problems, and we now, for the first time, as you know, in a great many years, are faced with redrawing the government farm program. And we will be doing that on the basis of all of the input and the information that we have been receiving from around the country. So, I assure you that all of the concerns that you mentioned will be getting our deepest consideration.

And I want you to know that I feel just as closeminded about protectionism as I sounded a moment ago about taxes. I am not in support of protectionism, and I know that it is a two-way street. It can be used against us. And we have been working with our friends and allies in the other industrial States. And I think we are making some sizable progress, as I mentioned, with regard to the one incident of Japan.

Yes, we believe in free trade, but only if it's fair trade. And that will be our policy.

I thank you all for welcoming us to your city and to this university. I thank you for your kindness, and I thank you more than anything, because whether you realize it or not, you are the ones that brought about this return to the America that I think we all know and remember so well, not the America of the doomcriers. Without you, without the people, none of the gains that we've made could ever have been accomplished. And so, I thank you for making America the great and good Nation that it is.

Thank you. God bless you.

Note: The President spoke at 3:46 p.m. in the Richard Treat University Center at Milliken University. He was introduced by Roger Miller, president of the university.

Prior to the forum, the President was given a tour of the Archer Daniels Midland processing plant by company chairman Dwayne Andreas and other executives.

Following his remarks, the President returned to Washington, DC.

Proclamation 5230—Hawaii Statehood Silver Jubilee Day
August 21, 1984

By the President of the United States of America

A Proclamation

On August 21, 1959, President Dwight D. Eisenhower proclaimed Hawaii the fiftieth State. The admission of Hawaii to the Union has proved to be of immense benefit both to the United States and to the State of Hawaii. On the twenty-fifth anniversary of Hawaii's Statehood, we recognize the many contributions the people of Hawaii have made to our country.

Hawaii is blessed with clean waters, pure air and extraordinary natural beauty. These attributes have made it an outstanding center of tourism, attracting people from many different countries. Moreover, Hawaii's ethnically diverse people have shown a warm spirit of friendship toward all the peoples of the world.

Hawaii is one of our major agricultural

States. It is the Nation's largest producer of sugar cane and pineapple, and the only major domestic source of coffee, macadamia nuts and certain kinds of flowers. Always on the frontiers of technological progress, the State is an outstanding leader in commercial aquaculture, astronomy, ocean science and energy research and development. It is also essential to our national security as the site of some of the country's most renowned defense facilities. Finally, it is an important international commercial center and base for cultural and technical exchange with the Pacific nations.

In honor of the twenty-fifth anniversary of Hawaii's admission to the Union, the Congress, by Senate Joint Resolution 248, has resolved that August 21, 1984, shall be known throughout the Nation as "Hawaii Statehood Silver Jubilee Day" and authorized and requested the President to issue an appropriate proclamation in observance of this anniversary.

Now, Therefore, I, Ronald Reagan, President of the United States of America, do hereby proclaim August 21, 1984, as Hawaii Statehood Silver Jubilee Day, and I call upon the people of the United States to observe this day with appropriate activities.

In Witness Whereof, I have hereunto set my hand this twenty-first day of August, in the year of our Lord nineteen hundred and eighty-four, and of the Independence of the United States of America the two hundred and ninth.

RONALD REAGAN

[*Filed with the Office of the Federal Register, 11:08 a.m., August 21, 1984*]

Nomination of William L. Eagleton, Jr., To Be United States Ambassador to Syria
August 21, 1984

The President today announced his intention to nominate William L. Eagleton, Jr., of Washington, a career member of the Senior Foreign Service, Class of Minister-Counselor, as Ambassador to the Syrian Arab Republic. He would succeed Robert P. Paganelli.

Mr. Eagleton served in the United States Navy from 1944 to 1946. In 1949 he entered the Foreign Service as political officer in Madrid and was political officer in Damascus from 1951 to 1953. From 1953 to 1954, he attended language and area studies in Beirut. In the Department, he was country officer for Syria and Lebanon from 1955 to 1959. He was consul in Tabriz, Iran (1959 to 1961), and attended language and area studies in Tangier (1962). He was Chargé d'Affaires in Nouakchott (1962–1964) and political officer in London (1964–1966). From 1966 to 1967, he was a Woodrow Wilson fellow at Princeton University and chief of the United States Interests Section in Algiers from 1967 to 1974. From 1974 to 1976, he was Director of the Office for Southern Europe in the Department, and diplomat in residence at Colorado State University from 1976 to 1977. He attended language and area studies in Tunis from 1977 to 1978 and was Chargé d'Affaires in Tripoli from 1978 to 1980. Since 1980 he has been chief of the United States Interests Section in Baghdad, Iraq.

Mr. Eagleton graduated from Yale University (B.A., 1948). His foreign languages are French, Spanish, and Arabic. He was born August 17, 1926, in Peoria, IL.

Nomination of Nam Pyo Suh To Be an Assistant Director of the National Science Foundation
August 21, 1984

The President today announced his intention to nominate Nam Pyo Suh to be an Assistant Director of the National Science Foundation (Engineering). He would succeed Francis S. Johnson.

Mr. Suh is currently professor of mechanical engineering at the Massachusetts Institute of Technology. He is also director of the Laboratory for Manufacturing and Productivity at MIT and has been director of the MIT-Industry Polymer Processing Program since its founding in 1973. Mr. Suh is serving as director of Surtech Corporation of New Hampshire, director of Intelitec Corp., and chairman of the board of Axiomatics Corp. and Mixalloy Corp. Previously he was associate professor of mechanical engineering at MIT (1970–1975).

Mr. Suh graduated from MIT (S.B., 1959; S.M., 1961) and Carnegie-Mellon University (Ph.D., 1964). He is married, has four children, and resides in Sudbury, MA. He was born April 22, 1936, in Korea, immigrated to the United States in 1954, and became a U.S. citizen on May 1, 1963.

Message to the Senate Transmitting a United States-Cyprus Convention on Taxation
August 21, 1984

To the Senate of the United States:

I transmit herewith for Senate advice and consent to ratification the Convention between the Government of the United States of America and the Government of the Republic of Cyprus for the Avoidance of Double Taxation and the Prevention of Fiscal Evasion with Respect to Taxes on Income, together with an exchange of notes, signed at Nicosia on March 19, 1984. I also transmit the report of the Department of State on the Convention.

The Convention replaces an earlier convention signed at Nicosia on March 26, 1980, but returned by the Senate for renegotiation in December 1981. The new Convention incorporates the provisions of the 1980 treaty and includes revisions designed to eliminate the potential for abuse by third-country residents.

I recommend that the Senate give early and favorable consideration to this Convention, with the related exchange of notes, and give its advice and consent to ratification.

RONALD REAGAN

The White House,
August 21, 1984.

Appointment of Caroline Leonetti Ahmanson as a Member of the President's Committee on the Arts and the Humanities
August 21, 1984

The President today announcd his intention to appoint Caroline Leonetti Ahmanson to be a member of the President's Committee on the Arts and the Humanities. This is a new position.

Mrs. Ahmanson has been involved in

business, cultural, civic, national, and world affairs and has traveled worldwide to encourage cultural exchanges and for people-to-people programs as well as to promote trade for the United States and the Los Angeles area. Mrs. Ahmanson is currently Chairman of the Board of the Federal Reserve Bank of Chicago and chairman of the board of Caroline Leonetti, Ltd. (a self-improvement center she founded in 1945). She is vice president of the board of directors of the National Committee on United States-China Relations and vice president of the board of directors of the Los Angeles World Affairs Council. Additionally, she serves on the City of Los Angeles Economic Advisory Council and has served as senior vice chairman of the Los Angeles Area Chamber of Commerce.

Mrs. Ahmanson has two children and resides in Beverly Hills, CA. She was born April 12, 1918, in San Francisco, CA.

Appointment of Charles M. Bloch as a Member of the National Voluntary Service Advisory Council
August 21, 1984

The President today announced his intention to appoint Charles M. Bloch to be a member of the National Voluntary Service Advisory Council. He would succeed Leslie Lenkowsky.

Mr. Bloch is currently president of Land Factors, Inc., a real estate firm. Previously, he was president of Crown Construction Co. (1962–1976); an insurance underwriter with Mutual of New York (1960–1962); and production coordinator, Aircraft Engineering & Maintenance Co. (1958–1960).

Mr. Bloch attended the College of San Mateo. He is married, has two children, and resides in Danville, CA. He was born October 22, 1933, in Oakland, CA.

Appointment of Linda Chavez as a Member of the Council of the Administrative Conference of the United States
August 22, 1984

The President today announced his intention to appoint Linda Chavez to be a member of the Council of the Administrative Conference of the United States for a term of 3 years. She would succeed Edward C. Schmults.

Ms. Chavez is currently Staff Director for the Commission on Civil Rights. She also serves as assistant to the president, American Federation of Teachers (AFT), AFL–CIO, and as editor of American Educator. Previously, she was a consultant for the President's Reorganization Project, Civil Rights Section, Office of Management and Budget (July-September 1977); and was on the professional staff, Committee on the Judiciary, Subcommittee on Civil Rights and Constitutional Rights, U.S. House of Representatives (1972–1974).

Ms. Chavez graduated from the University of Colorado (B.A., 1970) and attended the University of California at Los Angeles (1970–1972) and the University of Maryland (1974–1975). She is married, has three children, and resides in Bethesda, MD. She was born June 17, 1947, in Albuquerque, NM.

Appointment of Four Members of the President's Committee on Mental Retardation
August 22, 1984

The President today announced his intention to appoint the following individuals to be members of the President's Committee on Mental Retardation for terms expiring May 11, 1987:

Albert L. Anderson would succeed Raymond M. Peterson. He is currently a pedodontics specialist in San Diego, CA. He is married, has three children, and resides in San Diego. He was born January 17, 1923, in Sanger, CA.

Lee A. Christoferson is currently chairman of the department of neurology science at the University of North Dakota. He is married, has six children, and resides in Fargo, ND. He was born June 9, 1921, in Bemidji, MN. This is a reappointment.

Jerry P. Larson would succeed Kathleen M. Barrett. He is currently director of the student and volunteer program at Tinley Park Mental Health Center. He was born December 9, 1946, in Chicago, IL, and resides in Berwyn, IL.

Ruth Warson is currently a clinical nursing instructor in Studio City, CA. She is married, has three children, and resides in Studio City. She was born April 11, 1928, in Seligman, AZ. This is a reappointment.

Remarks at a Reagan-Bush Welcoming Rally at the Republican National Convention in Dallas, Texas
August 22, 1984

Audience. 4 more years! 4 more years! 4 more years!

The President. Thank you all very much. Well, I have to tell you, I like that sound. Maybe I shouldn't say anything. I should take Billy Joel's advice—you know that fine young singer from New York. He said, "Leave a tender moment alone."

Well, I will say one thing. You may represent 50 States——

Audience member. You're right, Ron!

The President. That's Iowa. [*Laughter*]

You may just be visitors, but did you ever catch the Texas spirit. You sure have.

Now, I wouldn't want to brag—certainly not in Texas—but, you see, I've always felt—I'm a born optimist, and I like to feel I carry some of that Texas spirit with me 365 days a year.

And it's been a lot easier to do that, and it doesn't hurt a bit, having a loyal son of Texas, George Bush, as my partner. His intelligence, his integrity, his experience, and his faithful service do make him—what has already been said here once—the best Vice President this country's ever had.

But the people of this Lone Star State have always been very good to me. And I guess I arrive feeling a little like that husband who sent a telegram to his wife on their 25th anniversary. And it read: "Can't live without you. Request you renew contract indefinitely." Well, in our case, we'll settle for just 4 more years.

Audience. 4 more years! 4 more years! 4 more years!

The President. All right.

Audience. 4 more years! 4 more years! 4 more years!

The President. Thank you.

I've just come from a delightful visit with a man who's given a great deal to our party and much to our country—President Ford. And I'm pleased to report to you that Jerry is ready to go all out for our ticket—top to bottom, from here to election day.

But we are honored to be here where the spirit of progress and patriotism is as strong as the heart of Texas is big. Texans play hard, and Texans play to win. There's—you have an expression down this way that I like. You don't just score victories; you romp 'em.

Your great Dallas Cowboys did much to establish that tradition. Maybe that's why Coach Landry, Roger Staubach, Danny White, all the players gained a reputation— much to the chagrin of many in Washington, I might add—of being larger than life.

The Dallas Cowboys have come to be known as America's team. And may I suggest that by the time this convention ends, the Republican Party will be on its way to being America's party.

There are many reasons for this—many reasons. We'll be America's party because it is the interest of all the people—that party that we represent.

When we asked for the people's help to bring down inflation, to bring down interest rates, to cut tax rates for every working American, and to index taxes so that never again could government profit from inflation at the people's expense—when we accomplished each of these important victories, we only did it with the people's help. And all of the people, as a result, have been helped.

Now, our opponents haven't had an easy time with our success. They've come up with an antidote: Bring back the Carter-Mondale administration.

Audience. No!

The President. Well, I was going to ask if you wanted that—but I just wanted to check. [*Laughter*]

We Republicans want to keep going forward, and we want to bring America's heritage with us. We say without embarrassment that we seek to honor our traditions, that we believe our fellow citizens are good and decent people. And their values and aspirations deserve to be respected—not patronized. For us, words like faith, family, work, and neighborhood are not slogans to be dragged out of the closet every 4 years. They are values to respect and to live by every day.

We will be America's party because the American dream begins with opportunity, and our goal is to build an opportunity society for every man, woman, and child. We'll do it because GOP doesn't just stand for Grand Old Party; it also stands for Great Opportunity Party. Now, you'll forgive me, lately it looks like that letter "D" in their name is going to stand for defeatism, de-

cline, dependency, doom, and despair. You can take your pick of any one or all of those.

Standing for opportunity means that we're determined, despite the do-nothing Democratic leadership, to push forward for enterprise zones, to push forward for a youth opportunity wage, so that people can get off unemployment, get off welfare, and get the chance for decent jobs that they deserve. And I happen to believe that helping people climb higher and make it on their own is a darned sight more progressive and compassionate than keeping them down and dependent on government for the rest of their lives.

Now, standing for opportunity means that we will push for spousal IRA's; that is, for wives who may not be working and earning, but housewives, that they too will be able to deposit in IRA accounts with the same advantages that those who are working have. We're going to push for tuition tax credits, for the protection that will come from passage of our comprehensive crime package, and for a constitutional amendment mandating the Federal Government spend no more than the Federal Government takes in.

And, yes, we want to enact an historic reform of our tax system. We need a tax reform that makes the system simple enough to understand, fair to all, and that can bring everyone's tax rates further down, and not up.

You know, this thing of making it simpler, an amendment that I think, if I remember correctly, is about 16 words is now 37 feet of wall space taken up by books on the regulations that go to make up the income tax law alone. And the Government has the nerve to tell the people of this country: "You figure out how much you owe us, and we can't help you, because our people don't understand it, either. And if you make a mistake, we'll make you pay a penalty for making the mistake." We think we ought to be able to send you a bill and tell you what you owe, not the other way around.

And that leads me to something else that I believe with all my heart, because we represent all the people, because we represent an agenda of opportunity to benefit all the people—from excellence in education to developing new frontiers in space and high technology: The Republican Party is America's party of the future.

Now, we know what the other side wants. And for heaven's sakes, don't argue with them. Don't argue for 1 second. Just let them be the party of tax and tax and spend and spend. And the Republican Party will continue to be the party of growth and growth and jobs and jobs. That's our idea of progress and compassion. For if we restrain spending, reduce tax rates further, and keep our economy growing, we can sharply reduce the deficit through that growth.

Now, what I'm suggesting is let's take our cue from our Olympic athletes. Rather than punish success, rather than raise taxes, let's challenge America in the next 76 days to raise her sights and reach for greatness. Let's go for growth, and let's go for the gold.

Audience. We want Reagan! We want Reagan! We want Reagan!

The President. You know—I thank you—and I've spoken before about our fine leaders in the House and Senate. But I just take this moment to salute all of you. And there are so many bright stars who are reaching out to all Americans and charting the path to a brighter future. So, let me say to the members of the news media who are present, those new ideas that you're always looking for, the vision for the future, leadership for the Nation, you've finally come to the right place. It's all right here at this convention in Dallas, Texas.

Dallas is a winning town, and we'll leave Dallas united. We'll leave here strong, and we'll take our case to the people. I want to remind you, in 1980 the American people were in a mood to win, and they did win. And in 1984 they're in a mood to win again, and they will.

My friends, it's good to be here, all of us together. I've just never seen anything like this. And I keep wondering, are those sheets? Going to be a lot of sleeping on the mattress tonight. [*Laughter*]

But our nation is more than 200 years old. But somehow, America has never been newer, never been younger, and never been more full of hope. We've been truly blessed. And for this we must be truly thankful.

May God bless you, and may He continue to bless our beloved country. Thank you very much.

Note: The President spoke at 4:22 p.m. in Atrium I at the Loew's Anatole Hotel. He was introduced by Vice President George Bush. Prior to the rally, the President met at the hotel with former President Gerald R. Ford.

Later in the evening, the President and the Vice President watched the television coverage of the 1984 Republican National Convention, including the convention's tribute to the First Lady and the nominating speeches. They were joined in the hotel suite by Mrs. Reagan and Mrs. Bush for the roll call of the States.

The President remained overnight at the hotel, where he stayed during his visit to Dallas.

Remarks at an Ecumenical Prayer Breakfast in Dallas, Texas
August 23, 1984

Thank you, ladies and gentlemen, very much. And, Martha Weisend, thank you very much. And I could say that if the morning ended with the music we have just heard from that magnificent choir, it would indeed be a holy day for all of us.

It's wonderful to be here this morning. The past few days have been pretty busy for all of us, but I've wanted to be with you today to share some of my own thoughts.

These past few weeks it seems that we've all been hearing a lot of talk about religion and its role in politics, religion and its place in the political life of the Nation. And I think it's appropriate today, at a prayer breakfast for 17,000 citizens in the State of

Texas during a great political convention, that this issue be addressed.

I don't speak as a theologian or a scholar, only as one who's lived a little more than his threescore ten—which has been a source of annoyance to some—[*laughter*]—and as one who has been active in the political life of the Nation for roughly four decades and now who's served the past 3½ years in our highest office. I speak, I think I can say, as one who has seen much, who has loved his country, and who's seen it change in many ways.

I believe that faith and religion play a critical role in the political life of our nation—and always has—and that the church—and by that I mean all churches, all denominations—has had a strong influence on the state. And this has worked to our benefit as a nation.

Those who created our country—the Founding Fathers and Mothers—understood that there is a divine order which transcends the human order. They saw the state, in fact, as a form of moral order and felt that the bedrock of moral order is religion.

The Mayflower Compact began with the words, "In the name of God, amen." The Declaration of Independence appeals to "Nature's God" and the "Creator" and "the Supreme Judge of the world." Congress was given a chaplain, and the oaths of office are oaths before God.

James Madison in the Federalist Papers admitted that in the creation of our Republic he perceived the hand of the Almighty. John Jay, the first Chief Justice of the Supreme Court, warned that we must never forget the God from whom our blessings flowed.

George Washington referred to religion's profound and unsurpassed place in the heart of our nation quite directly in his Farewell Address in 1796. Seven years earlier, France had erected a government that was intended to be purely secular. This new government would be grounded on reason rather than the law of God. By 1796 the French Revolution had known the Reign of Terror.

And Washington voiced reservations about the idea that there could be a wise policy without a firm moral and religious foundation. He said, "Of all the dispositions and habits which lead to political prosperity, Religion and morality are indispensable supports. In vain would that man (call himself a patriot) who (would) labour to subvert these . . . finest [firmest] [1] props of the duties of men and citizens. The mere Politician . . . (and) the pious man ought to respect and to cherish (religion and morality)." And he added, ". . . let us with caution indulge the supposition, that morality can be maintained without religion."

I believe that George Washington knew the City of Man cannot survive without the City of God, that the Visible City will perish without the Invisible City.

Religion played not only a strong role in our national life; it played a positive role. The abolitionist movement was at heart a moral and religious movement; so was the modern civil rights struggle. And throughout this time, the state was tolerant of religious belief, expression, and practice. Society, too, was tolerant.

But in the 1960's this began to change. We began to make great steps toward secularizing our nation and removing religion from its honored place.

In 1962 the Supreme Court in the New York prayer case banned the compulsory saying of prayers. In 1963 the Court banned the reading of the Bible in our public schools. From that point on, the courts pushed the meaning of the ruling ever outward, so that now our children are not allowed voluntary prayer. We even had to pass a law—we passed a special law in the Congress just a few weeks ago to allow student prayer groups the same access to schoolrooms after classes that a young Marxist society, for example, would already enjoy with no opposition.

The 1962 decision opened the way to a flood of similar suits. Once religion had been made vulnerable, a series of assaults were made in one court after another, on one issue after another. Cases were started to argue against tax-exempt status for churches. Suits were brought to abolish the words "under God" from the Pledge of Allegiance and to remove "In God We Trust"

---

[1] *White House correction.*

from public documents and from our currency.

Today there are those who are fighting to make sure voluntary prayer is not returned to the classrooms. And the frustrating thing for the great majority of Americans who support and understand the special importance of religion in the national life—the frustrating thing is that those who are attacking religion claim they are doing it in the name of tolerance, freedom, and open-mindedness. Question: Isn't the real truth that they are intolerant of religion? [*Applause*] They refuse to tolerate its importance in our lives.

If all the children of our country studied together all of the many religions in our country, wouldn't they learn greater tolerance of each other's beliefs? If children prayed together, would they not understand what they have in common, and would this not, indeed, bring them closer, and is this not to be desired? So, I submit to you that those who claim to be fighting for tolerance on this issue may not be tolerant at all.

When John Kennedy was running for President in 1960, he said that his church would not dictate his Presidency any more than he would speak for his church. Just so, and proper. But John Kennedy was speaking in an America in which the role of religion—and by that I mean the role of all churches—was secure. Abortion was not a political issue. Prayer was not a political issue. The right of church schools to operate was not a political issue. And it was broadly acknowledged that religious leaders had a right and a duty to speak out on the issues of the day. They held a place of respect, and a politician who spoke to or of them with a lack of respect would not long survive in the political arena.

It was acknowledged then that religion held a special place, occupied a special territory in the hearts of the citizenry. The climate has changed greatly since then. And since it has, it logically follows that religion needs defenders against those who care only for the interests of the state.

There are, these days, many questions on which religious leaders are obliged to offer their moral and theological guidance, and such guidance is a good and necessary

thing. To know how a church and its members feel on a public issue expands the parameters of debate. It does not narrow the debate; it expands it.

The truth is, politics and morality are inseparable. And as morality's foundation is religion, religion and politics are necessarily related. We need religion as a guide. We need it because we are imperfect, and our government needs the church, because only those humble enough to admit they're sinners can bring to democracy the tolerance it requires in order to survive.

A state is nothing more than a reflection of its citizens; the more decent the citizens, the more decent the state. If you practice a religion, whether you're Catholic, Protestant, Jewish, or guided by some other faith, then your private life will be influenced by a sense of moral obligation, and so, too, will your public life. One affects the other. The churches of America do not exist by the grace of the state; the churches of America are not mere citizens of the state. The churches of America exist apart; they have their own vantage point, their own authority. Religion is its own realm; it makes its own claims.

We establish no religion in this country, nor will we ever. We command no worship. We mandate no belief. But we poison our society when we remove its theological underpinnings. We court corruption when we leave it bereft of belief. All are free to believe or not believe; all are free to practice a faith or not. But those who believe must be free to speak of and act on their belief, to apply moral teaching to public questions.

I submit to you that the tolerant society is open to and encouraging of all religions. And this does not weaken us; it strengthens us, it makes us strong. You know, if we look back through history to all those great civilizations, those great nations that rose up to even world dominance and then deteriorated, declined, and fell, we find they all had one thing in common. One of the significant forerunners of their fall was their turning away from their God or gods.

Without God, there is no virtue, because there's no prompting of the conscience. Without God, we're mired in the material, that flat world that tells us only what the senses perceive. Without God, there is a coarsening of the society. And without God, democracy will not and cannot long endure. If we ever forget that we're one nation under God, then we will be a nation gone under.

If I could just make a personal statement of my own—in these 3½ years I have understood and known better than ever before the words of Lincoln, when he said that he would be the greatest fool on this footstool called Earth if he ever thought that for one moment he could perform the duties of that office without help from One who is stronger than all.

I thank you, thank you for inviting us here today. Thank you for your kindness and your patience. May God keep you, and may we, all of us, keep God.

Thank you.

Note: The President spoke at 9:26 a.m. at Reunion Arena. He was introduced by Martha Weisend, cochair of the Texas Reagan-Bush campaign.

Statement on Signing the Retirement Equity Act of 1984
August 23, 1984

I am pleased to sign into law H.R. 4280, the Retirement Equity Act of 1984. This important legislation is the first private pension bill in our history to recognize explicitly the importance of women both to the American family and to the Nation's labor force. It contains significant measures to enhance women's ability to earn pensions in their own right. It improves and protects the vital role of pensions as retirement income to widows.

An end to inequities in the provision of pension benefits to women has been a top priority of my administration. In September 1983 I sent to Congress our own pension equity bill. I am pleased that most of that bill has been incorporated into this legislation I have now approved.

Existing pension rules, when originally enacted, did not fully anticipate the dual roles many women have come to play as both members of the paid labor force and as wives and mothers during periods of full-time work in the home. Provisions in many pension plans now operate in ways that fail to recognize paid work performed by women at certain periods in their lives and penalize them for time spent in childrearing. To address this inequity, the Retirement Equity Act lowers the age limits on participation and vesting, permitting more pension credits to be earned during the early working years when women are most likely to be employed. The legislation also eases break-in-service rules so that parents who bear children and stay home to care for them in the early years will no longer lose the pension credits they previously earned while working.

The Retirement Equity Act also clarifies that each person in a marriage has a right to benefit from the other's pension. No longer will one member of a married couple be able to sign away survivor benefits for the other. A spouse's written consent now will be required on any decision not to provide survivors' protection. The legislation also helps assure that when a vested employee dies before retirement, the employee's surviving spouse will benefit from the pension credits the employee has earned, and it restricts considerably the latitude now allowed pension plans to impose additional conditions on survivors' benefits. Survivors' benefits will be paid automatically in more instances than now. In addition, the bill makes it clear that State courts can allocate pension rights in divorce cases and other domestic relations settlements.

The enactment of this legislation has been a bipartisan effort, and I wish to thank the many Members of both the House and Senate for their hard work. This law is a most significant addition to our continuing efforts to remove economic discrimination against women in our nation.

Note: As enacted, H.R. 4280 is Public Law 98–397, approved August 23.

Nomination of Rita R. Colwell To Be a Member of the National Science Board
August 23, 1984

The President today announced his intention to nominate Rita R. Colwell to be a member of the National Science Board, National Science Foundation, for a term expiring May 10, 1990. She would succeed Ernestine Friedl.

Mrs. Colwell is currently vice president of academic affairs and professor of marine microbiology at the University of Maryland. She has served as a consultant to the Environmental Protection Agency and as a consultant to the Advisory Committee on Science Education and Biology and Oceanography, National Science Foundation (1970–1975).

Mrs. Colwell graduated from Purdue University (B.S., 1956; M.S., 1958) and the University of Washington (Ph.D., 1961). She is married, has two children, and resides in Bethesda, MD. She was born November 23, 1934, in Beverly, MA.

Nomination of Pauline Crowe Naftzger To Be a Member of the National Museum Services Board
August 23, 1984

The President today announced his intention to nominate Pauline Crowe Naftzger to be a member of the National Museum Services Board for a term expiring December 6, 1988. She would succeed Neil Harris.

Mrs. Naftzger is a Smithsonian national associate, a member of the National Geographic Society, and a fellow of the L.S.B. Leakey Foundation. She is a life member of the Museum of National History, Los Angeles, and a member of the President's Circle, Los Angeles County Museum of Art. A 22-year member of the Los Angeles County Museum of Art's Docent Council, she has served on its board as well as being a lecturer and guide.

Mrs. Naftzger holds a bachelor of arts degree from the University of California at Los Angeles and a master of liberal arts degree from the University of Southern California. She is married, has three children, and resides in Beverly Hills, CA. She was born December 19, 1927, in Beverly Hills.

Appointment of Four Members of the National Advisory Council on Adult Education
August 23, 1984

The President today announced his intention to appoint the following individuals to be members of the National Advisory Council on Adult Education for terms expiring July 10, 1987:

Lily Ring Balian is currently administrator for civic action at Northrop Corp. in Los Angeles, CA. She is married, has three children, and resides in Los Angeles. She was born July 17, 1925, in Chicago, IL.

B.L. Chain would succeed Ruth Thone. He is currently the mayor of Hattiesburg, MS. He is married, has four children, and resides in Hattiesburg. He was born September 19, 1929, in Hattiesburg.

Mae M. Duggan would succeed Louis Stevens Ridgeway. She is currently executive director of the Thomas J. White Foundation. She is mar-

ried, has five children, and resides in St. Louis, MO. She was born May 20, 1919, in St. Louis.

Julia G. Fernald would succeed Daniel E. Brennan, Sr. She is currently chairman of the board of directors of the William Paterson College of New Jersey Foundation. She is married, has three children, and resides in Upper Montclair, NJ. She was born November 25, 1927, in Washington, DC.

Remarks to the Republican National Hispanic Assembly in Dallas, Texas
August 23, 1984

Buenos tardes. Mis buenos amigos, gracias, gracias. This has truly been a convention to remember. I see so many old friends here, and we've shared many memories together. It's great to be here with Tirso and Sally del Junco, with Katherine Ortega, Congressman Manuel Lujan, and Governor Ferré.

Having come from California, I wouldn't feel at home unless there was a strong Hispanic flavor to these festivities. Hispanic Republicans are an increasingly important part of a Republican coalition, and the fact is pretty hard to miss with Katherine Ortega giving the keynote at this convention. I'm mightily grateful to have her on our Republican team and proud to have her serving as Treasurer of the United States. She's one of a multitude, more than 225, of our appointments of Americans of Hispanic descent throughout our administration.

Now, there's a record number of Hispanic delegates at this convention. The other party considers Americans of Hispanic descent a separate interest group, but we Republicans see you as representative of the mainstream of our party and of our country.

We're not a party of special interests that divides America into camps. We're a party of people who share the same love of country and God, who have the same respect for family and hard work. We're people who appreciate our freedom and are not ashamed to admit that we still feel a stirring inside every time we see the flag waving in the wind. And knowing the strong values

that we share, I predict that in the years to come it is the Republican Party that Americans of Hispanic descent will flock to in ever-increasing numbers.

We're a party that will build not bigger bureaucracy in Washington, but an expanding economy throughout our land. We aren't for dependency, but for independence and upward mobility. We're not for handouts and welfare; we're for jobs and opportunity.

There's been a lot of talk lately about family. Well, I'm glad to see that some on the other side have finally discovered traditional values. [Laughter] But we don't wait for election years to proclaim our allegiance to those things that are fundamental to our way of life. Furthermore, we're not just using slogans and empty words; we've got tangible policies to back up our words.

We favor a tuition tax credit, for example, to give parents more say in their children's education. Now, education is an issue that underscores the choice the American people will be making in November. We Republicans call for increasing standards; the liberals are for increasing taxes and spending. We're for restoring discipline to the classroom; the liberals are for increasing taxing and spending. We're for more local control and community cooperation with teachers and schools; liberals are for more taxes and spending. [Laughter] You tell me who has the better plan for your children's education.

The voters, if we help them see beyond the rhetoric, have a real choice in November on this issue and on the issue of crime, as well. We Republicans are not just mouthing tough slogans against crime; we've proposed tough legislation to deal with crime, and the liberal leadership of the House has it bottled up in committee. The people deserve to hear from those now touting the commitment to fight crime. How do they feel about the anticrime package that liberals have held up in the House of Representatives? Republicans say let's get that bill through the process and start getting more criminals off the streets.

The liberals talk about jobs, yet it was their taxing, spending, regulating, and inflating policies that knocked the wind out of the private sector that provides those jobs. When we Republicans talk about jobs, we don't mean make-work, do-nothing jobs.

It took us time to overcome the mess that we inherited, but our program is working and so are millions more Americans. In the past 19 months, 6½ million people have found jobs, and our recovery is benefiting a cross section of America. Since it began, for example, more than 575,000 Hispanics have found work. But we have an enterprise zones proposal to help people in regions that still haven't benefited from the expansion.

Enterprise zones would provide a real opportunity and break the bonds of dependency, and if we could elect a few more Republicans to the Congress, maybe we could force the liberal Democratic leadership to permit a vote on that bill.

You know, the people vote nationwide and elect a Republican President. They vote statewide and they elect a majority of Senators. But then, when it's broken down into the congressional districts, somehow we seem to keep having a majority in the House of Representatives of the other party. I think it's time we took a good look at who has been in charge over the years, every 10 years, of laying out those districts.

Americans of Hispanic descent, like the rest of us, believe in the dignity of work. There is an empty ring when the liberals talk about the work ethic. You can't be the party of high taxes and the champion of the work ethic at the same time. Republicans

offer incentives to work, save, and invest. We want people to keep more of their paychecks, to do as they see fit with their money and the money that they've earned.

The liberal big spenders act like everything belongs to the government and we should be grateful for what they let us keep. As a matter of fact, it was only a few years ago that they coined an expression they were using over and over again called "tax expenditures." And when you interpreted what they were talking about, they were talking about the legitimate deductions that we take in computing our income tax, and they were saying that that was an expenditure of tax money, to let you keep your own money for those purposes. [*Laughter*] Well, we're going to get rid of that term.

What we who are Republicans want is a strong America. We've been rebuilding our economy, rebuilding our defenses, and, yes, rebuilding the American spirit. And that's a job that takes all of us working together. Our most important job now is getting the word out to the people. Each of us, young and old, men and women, Americans who love our country and who come from every religious, ethnic, and cultural background, we have a job to do. And I know that you're already doing so much, and especially the young people. Isn't it grand to see so many wonderful young people at this convention?

Now, that was a cue for what I'm going to say next, because one of those young men, Pedro Vargas, from Houston, Texas, was the youngest Hispanic election judge in this State on primary election day last May. He is just 18 years old. And he's a member of the Republican National Hispanic Assembly and is doing his part for the cause.

Pedro and all the other fine young people in this country are what this election is all about. Very simply, we want to leave them—our generation must leave them—an America as strong, as free, and filled with opportunity as the America that we were given when we were young. Together, we can do just that, and I know that I can count on you.

I don't feel self-conscious or like I'm bragging at all when I talk about what's been accomplished in these last 3½ years, because none of us did it by ourselves. If we hadn't been able to turn to you, the people, and if you had not made some people in Washington not necessarily see the light, but made them feel the heat—[*laughter*]—we wouldn't have accomplished what we've accomplished so far. So, *muchas gracias* and *vaya con Dios.*

Note: The President spoke at 12:35 p.m. in the Khmer Pavilion at the Loew's Anatole Hotel. He was introduced by Tirso del Junco, chairman of the Republican National Hispanic Assembly.

Remarks at a Republican National Committee Fundraising Luncheon in Dallas, Texas
August 23, 1984

Thank you all for inviting me here today. [*Laughter*] I wanted to be here to thank all of you for your generosity to our party and your dedication to our cause. And in the midst of the hoopla of this convention, I also wanted a chance to share a few quiet words with you about where we're going in the next few weeks and months.

You know, the events of this week have shown me once again how much is at stake this year, how much depends on the efforts of people like yourselves. Over these few weeks, all America has seen the choice that we'll face in November. On the one hand, they've seen our party, the party of new ideas and fresh initiatives, the party of energy and excitement, the party of the future. And on the other hand, they've seen the other party with its worn out, discredited, far-left ideology that caters to special interests, and that's the party they saw in July.

So, while that other party is trying to return us to the days of malaise and defeatism, we'll bring a message of hope about America's future to the people. We're leading America to economic expansion and progress, to opportunity for all our citizens and, we hope, someday, freedom and self-government for all the people of the world. I think the election returns this year and for many years to come will show that our party is truly the party of the eighties and beyond. I really think that that's why the American people voted the way they did in 1980 and that's why they supported us when we needed their help in getting those

tax cuts and spending cuts through the Congress.

But you know, despite all the defeats they've suffered, the Democrats still aren't listening to the people. What we must do now is go to the American people with that long list of legislative initiatives favored by the American people but held up in the Congress by liberal Democrats. I mean the balanced budget amendment, the tuition tax credits, and enterprise zones—not to mention an anticrime bill that passed the Senate on a 91-to-1 vote, but which the liberal Democrats have kept bottled up in committee. They won't even let it come out to the floor for a vote.

Now, we have to use these as instances of the ideological stubbornness and intransigence of the liberal Democrats. This year we must speak to the American people about what distinguishes the two major political parties of this country. The other day I said the GOP has a new meaning: It is now the Great Opportunity Party.

We're the party of the future, and they're the party of the past. We're the party of new ideas, and they're the party of tired old cliches. We're the party of growth; they're the party of stagnation. We're the party—and we've proved it this past week—of open and freewheeling debate. They're the party that says, "See it our way or else."

Well, the truth is we are, in this year, 1984, a new thing in history—a new Republican Party, a giant reemerging on the scene. And we will be content to be the minority party no more.

The leadership of the Democratic Party—and by that I mean the eccentric clique that was calling the shots in San Francisco and not the rank-and-file members—the leadership of the party has abandoned the principles that formed their party. They're no longer the party of Jefferson and Jackson, and they speak no more for the working people of this country.

But there is one party that does—our party; one party that speaks for working people and entrepreneurs and risk-takers and dreamers and great souls and heroes—the kind of people who made this country and who keep it going every day. There is one party that sees the future not as a big dark cloud waiting to rain on us, but as a great and happy challenge waiting to be seized.

I don't mean in any way that it shouldn't rain around Dallas, here where you need it so much. [*Laughter*] You just don't need *their* kind of rain. [*Laughter*]

It's the Republican Party, the party of the new majority, founded 130 years ago and lifted to greatness by the candidacy of an awkward and obscure lawyer who had some new ideas himself. And when he had won the Presidency, he said some words that reflect what all of us think when we look at the policies of the other party. He said: We must disenthrall ourselves with the past, and then we will save our country.

Well, Abe Lincoln was one great dreamer, one great risk-taker, one great soul, and one great hero. And I think he would be proud of his party today.

So, this year there's a lot more at stake than just a national ticket. We need to remind the people of the liberal Democrats' record in the Congress, especially in the House of Representatives, and especially on the issue of taxes and deficits. We need a Congress that won't thwart and won't obstruct the people's visions of domestic legislation. We need a Congress that won't try to gut the defense budget or lead America down the garden path of naivete in our dealings with those who do not wish us well.

We have to send a message to the American people: Only by electing a Republican House of Representatives and a Senate can we get on with the Nation's business. Only by electing a Republican House and Senate can we get the Democratic Party to return to the mainstream of American politics.

You know, you have to go back—well, in 20 of the last 32 years, the people have chosen to have Republican Presidents. But for 14 of those 20 years, the Democrats have held both Houses of the Congress and one House, the House of Representatives, for an additional 4 years, these last 4. In only one 2-year period of all those 20 did a Republican President have the help of a Republican Congress. That was the first 2 years of Dwight Eisenhower. I believe we should appeal to the inherent fairness of the American people and ask them to elect a Congress that would help a President fulfill his promises, the promises that the people must have approved when they elected him.

That's the task before us this year. And together, I think we can do it. We can move forward with all the important legislation I mentioned. We can give the American people that era of national renewal that we promised them. And I thank you all for all that you've done, but more than that, I ask you to take one message to the people. Yes, we're proud of our record in office. But most of all, we have to talk about the future and how bright it can be with a Republican President and Vice President, a Republican majority leader, and a Republican Speaker of the House.

Just a few minutes ago, George and I were meeting with a group of Republicans, our Hispanic Republican Assembly, and I was talking to them about this congressional thing. And, you know, it's time for the American people to really look at how government runs. You know, I hear about "the President's budget." There isn't a line in the Constitution that lets the President spend a nickel. Everything, all the spending that's done starts over there in that House of Representatives. But I told them, isn't it funny that when the people of this country, voting as a nation, choose so often a Republican President, and then when voting statewide they choose a majority of Republican Senators, shouldn't we be asking ourselves why it is that for all but 4 of the last 50 years, the Democrats have controlled the House of Representatives, which is elected in congressional districts? And I think it has to do with who's been in charge in these 50 years, every 10th year, when they laid out those districts. And maybe if we do that, the people of this country will begin to see not that there has been pure government of and by the people, but that there has been a deliberate thwarting of what the people, as a whole, have made evident they want. And then maybe the people will go to the polls with a little idea of redressing a grievance in mind.

Well, that's enough of that. I thank you all very much for letting us be here.

You know, I've been an after-luncheon speaker for a long time, many years, but this is the first time that I've been a luncheon speaker and no lunch, because I have to go on—[*laughing*]—some more is scheduled before the evening takes place.

Thank you all. God bless you all.

Note: The President spoke at 1:09 p.m. in the Chantilly Ballroom at the Loew's Anatole Hotel.

In his remarks, the President referred to the Vice President.

Remarks Accepting the Presidential Nomination at the Republican National Convention in Dallas, Texas
August 23, 1984

The President. Mr. Chairman, Mr. Vice President, delegates to this convention, and fellow citizens: In 75 days, I hope we enjoy a victory that is the size of the heart of Texas. Nancy and I extend our deep thanks to the Lone Star State and the "Big D"—the city of Dallas—for all their warmth and hospitality.

Four years ago I didn't know precisely every duty of this office, and not too long ago, I learned about some new ones from the first graders of Corpus Christi School in Chambersburg, Pennsylvania. Little Leah Kline was asked by her teacher to describe my duties. She said: "The President goes to meetings. He helps the animals. The President gets frustrated. He talks to other Presidents." How does wisdom begin at such an early age?

Tonight, with a full heart and deep gratitude for your trust, I accept your nomination for the Presidency of the United States. I will campaign on behalf of the principles of our party which lift America confidently into the future.

America is presented with the clearest political choice of half a century. The distinction between our two parties and the different philosophy of our political opponents are at the heart of this campaign and America's future.

I've been campaigning long enough to know that a political party and its leadership can't change their colors in 4 days. We won't, and no matter how hard they tried, our opponents didn't in San Francisco. We didn't discover our values in a poll taken a week before the convention. And we didn't set a weathervane on top of the Golden Gate Bridge before we started talking about the American family.

The choices this year are not just between two different personalities or between two political parties. They're between two different visions of the future, two fundamentally different ways of governing—their government of pessimism, fear, and limits, or ours of hope, confidence, and growth.

Their government sees people only as members of groups; ours serves all the people of America as individuals. Theirs lives in the past, seeking to apply the old and failed policies to an era that has passed them by. Ours learns from the past and strives to change by boldly charting a new course for the future. Theirs lives by promises, the bigger, the better. We offer proven, workable answers.

Our opponents began this campaign hoping that America has a poor memory. Well, let's take them on a little stroll down memory lane. Let's remind them of how a 4.8-percent inflation rate in 1976 became back-to-back years of double-digit infla-tion—the worst since World War I—punish-ing the poor and the elderly, young couples striving to start their new lives, and work-ing people struggling to make ends meet.

Inflation was not some plague borne on the wind; it was a deliberate part of their official economic policy, needed, they said, to maintain prosperity. They didn't tell us that with it would come the highest interest rates since the Civil War. As average monthly mortgage payments more than doubled, home building nearly ground to a halt; tens of thousands of carpenters and others were thrown out of work. And who controlled both Houses of the Congress and the executive branch at that time? Not us, not us.

Campaigning across America in 1980, we saw evidence everywhere of industrial de-cline. And in rural America, farmers' costs were driven up by inflation. They were devastated by a wrongheaded grain embar-go and were forced to borrow money at exorbitant interest rates just to get by. And many of them didn't get by. Farmers have to fight insects, weather, and the market-place; they shouldn't have to fight their own government.

The high interest rates of 1980 were not talked about in San Francisco. But how about taxes? They were talked about in San Francisco. Will Rogers once said he never met a man he didn't like. Well, if I could paraphrase Will, our friends in the other party have never met a tax they didn't like or hike.

Under their policies, tax rates have gone up three times as much for families with children as they have for everyone else over these past three decades. In just the 5 years before we came into office, taxes roughly doubled.

Some who spoke so loudly in San Francis-co of fairness were among those who brought about the biggest single, individual tax increase in our history in 1977, calling for a series of increases in the Social Securi-ty payroll tax and in the amount of pay subject to that tax. The bill they passed called for two additional increases between now and 1990, increases that bear down hardest on those at the lower income levels.

The Census Bureau confirms that, be-cause of the tax laws we inherited, the number of households at or below the pov-erty level paying Federal income tax more than doubled between 1980 and 1982. Well, they received some relief in 1983, when our across-the-board tax cut was fully in place. And they'll get more help when in-dexing goes into effect this January.

Our opponents have repeatedly advocat-ed eliminating indexing. Would that really hurt the rich? No, because the rich are al-ready in the top brackets. But those work-ing men and women who depend on a cost-of-living adjustment just to keep abreast of inflation would find themselves pushed into higher tax brackets and wouldn't even be able to keep even with inflation because they'd be paying a higher income tax. That's bracket creep; and our opponents are for it, and we're against it.

It's up to us to see that all our fellow citizens understand that confiscatory taxes, costly social experiments, and economic tin-kering were not just the policies of a single administration. For the 26 years prior to January of 1981, the opposition party con-trolled both Houses of Congress. Every spending bill and every tax for more than a quarter of a century has been of their doing.

About a decade ago, they said Federal spending was out of control, so they passed a budget control act and, in the next 5 years, ran up deficits of $260 billion. Some control.

In 1981 we gained control of the Senate and the executive branch. With the help of some concerned Democrats in the House we started a policy of tightening the Feder-al budget instead of the family budget.

A task force chaired by Vice President George Bush—the finest Vice President this country has ever had—it eliminated unnec-essary regulations that had been strangling business and industry.

And while we have our friends down memory lane, maybe they'd like to recall a gimmick they designed for their 1976 cam-paign. As President Ford told us the night before last, adding the unemployment and inflation rates, they got what they called a misery index. In '76 it came to 12½ per-cent. They declared the incumbent had no right to seek reelection with that kind of a misery index. Well, 4 years ago, in the 1980 election, they didn't mention the misery index, possibly because it was then over 20 percent. And do you know something? They won't mention it in this election either. It's down to 11.6 and dropping.

By nearly every measure, the position of poor Americans worsened under the leadership of our opponents. Teenage drug use, out-of-wedlock births, and crime increased dramatically. Urban neighborhoods and schools deteriorated. Those whom government intended to help discovered a cycle of dependency that could not be broken. Government became a drug, providing temporary relief, but addiction as well.

And let's get some facts on the table that our opponents don't want to hear. The biggest annual increase in poverty took place between 1978 and 1981—over 9 percent each year, in the first 2 years of our administration. Well, I should—pardon me—I didn't put a period in there. In the first 2 years of our administration, that annual increase fell to 5.3 percent. And 1983 was the first year since 1978 that there was no appreciable increase in poverty at all.

Pouring hundreds of billions of dollars into programs in order to make people worse off was irrational and unfair. It was time we ended this reliance on the government process and renewed our faith in the human process.

In 1980 the people decided with us that the economic crisis was not caused by the fact that they lived too well. Government lived too well. It was time for tax increases to be an act of last resort, not of first resort.

The people told the liberal leadership in Washington, "Try shrinking the size of government before you shrink the size of our paychecks."

Our government was also in serious trouble abroad. We had aircraft that couldn't fly and ships that couldn't leave port. Many of our military were on food stamps because of meager earnings, and reenlistments were down. Ammunition was low, and spare parts were in short supply.

Many of our allies mistrusted us. In the 4 years before we took office, country after country fell under the Soviet yoke. Since January 20th, 1981, not 1 inch of soil has fallen to the Communists.

Audience. 4 more years! 4 more years! 4 more years!

The President. All right.

Audience. 4 more years! 4 more years! 4 more years!

The President. But worst of all, Americans were losing the confidence and optimism about the future that has made us unique in the world. Parents were beginning to doubt that their children would have the better life that has been the dream of every American generation.

We can all be proud that pessimism is ended. America is coming back and is more confident than ever about the future. Tonight, we thank the citizens of the United States whose faith and unwillingness to give up on themselves or this country saved us all.

Together, we began the task of controlling the size and activities of the government by reducing the growth of its spending while passing a tax program to provide incentives to increase productivity for both workers and industry. Today, a working family earning $25,000 has about $2,900 more in purchasing power than if tax and inflation rates were still at the 1980 level.

Today, of all the major industrial nations of the world, America has the strongest economic growth; one of the lowest inflation rates; the fastest rate of job creation—6½ million jobs in the last year and a half—a record 600,000 business incorporations in 1983; and the largest increase in real, after-tax personal income since World War II. We're enjoying the highest level of business investment in history, and America has renewed its leadership in developing the vast new opportunities in science and high technology. America is on the move again and expanding toward new eras of opportunity for everyone.

Now, we're accused of having a secret. Well, if we have, it is that we're going to keep the mighty engine of this nation revved up. And that means a future of sustained economic growth without inflation that's going to create for our children and grandchildren a prosperity that finally will last.

Today our troops have newer and better

equipment; their morale is higher. The better armed they are, the less likely it is they will have to use that equipment. But if, heaven forbid, they're ever called upon to defend this nation, nothing would be more immoral than asking them to do so with weapons inferior to those of any possible opponent.

We have also begun to repair our valuable alliances, especially our historic NATO alliance. Extensive discussions in Asia have enabled us to start a new round of diplomatic progress there.

In the Middle East, it remains difficult to bring an end to historic conflicts, but we're not discouraged. And we shall always maintain our pledge never to sell out one of our closest friends, the State of Israel.

Closer to home, there remains a struggle for survival for free Latin American States, allies of ours. They valiantly struggle to prevent Communist takeovers fueled massively by the Soviet Union and Cuba. Our policy is simple: We are not going to betray our friends, reward the enemies of freedom, or permit fear and retreat to become American policies—especially in this hemisphere.

None of the four wars in my lifetime came about because we were too strong. It's weakness that invites adventurous adversaries to make mistaken judgments. America is the most peaceful, least warlike nation in modern history. We are not the cause of all the ills of the world. We're a patient and generous people. But for the sake of our freedom and that of others, we cannot permit our reserve to be confused with a lack of resolve.

Ten months ago, we displayed this resolve in a mission to rescue American students on the imprisoned island of Grenada. Democratic candidates have suggested that this could be likened to the Soviet invasion of Afghanistan——

Audience. Boo-o-o!

The President. ——the crushing of human rights in Poland or the genocide in Cambodia.

Audience. Boo-o-o!

The President. Could you imagine Harry Truman, John Kennedy, Hubert Humphrey, or Scoop Jackson making such a shocking comparison?

Audience. No!

The President. Nineteen of our fine young men lost their lives on Grenada, and to even remotely compare their sacrifice to the murderous actions taking place in Afghanistan is unconscionable.

There are some obvious and important differences. First, we were invited in by six East Caribbean States. Does anyone seriously believe the people of Eastern Europe or Afghanistan invited the Russians?

Audience. No!

The President. Second, there are hundreds of thousands of Soviets occupying captive nations across the world. Today, our combat troops have come home. Our students are safe, and freedom is what we left behind in Grenada.

There are some who've forgotten why we have a military. It's not to promote war; it's to be prepared for peace. There's a sign over the entrance to Fairchild Air Force Base in Washington State, and that sign says it all: "Peace is our profession."

Our next administration——

Audience. 4 more years! 4 more years! 4 more years!

The President. All right.

Audience. 4 more years! 4 more years! 4 more years!

The President. I heard you. And that administration will be committed to completing the unfinished agenda that we've placed before the Congress and the Nation. It is an agenda which calls upon the national Democratic leadership to cease its obstructionist ways.

We've heard a lot about deficits this year from those on the other side of the aisle. Well, they should be experts on budget deficits. They've spent most of their political careers creating deficits. For 42 of the last 50 years, they have controlled both Houses of the Congress.

Audience. Boo-o-o!

The President. And for almost all of those 50 years, deficit spending has been their deliberate policy. Now, however, they call for an end to deficits. They call them ours. Yet, at the same time, the leadership of their party resists our every effort to bring Federal spending under control. For 3 years straight, they have prevented us from adopting a balanced budget amendment to the Constitution. We will continue to fight for that amendment, mandating that government spend no more than government takes in.

And we will fight, as the Vice President told you, for the right of a President to veto items in appropriations bills without having to veto the entire bill. There is no better way than the line-item veto, now used by Governors in 43 States to cut out waste in government. I know. As Governor of California, I successfully made such vetos over 900 times.

Now, their candidate, it would appear, has only recently found deficits alarming. Nearly 10 years ago he insisted that a $52 billion deficit should be allowed to get much bigger in order to lower unemployment, and he said that sometimes "we need a deficit in order to stimulate the economy."

Audience. Boo-o-o!

The President. As a Senator, he voted to override President Ford's veto of billions of dollars in spending bills and then voted no on a proposal to cut the 1976 deficit in half.

Audience. Boo-o-o!

The President. Was anyone surprised by his pledge to raise your taxes next year if given the chance?

Audience. No!

The President. In the Senate, he voted time and again for new taxes, including a 10-percent income tax surcharge, higher taxes on certain consumer items. He also voted against cutting the excise tax on automobiles. And he was part and parcel of that biggest single, individual tax increase in history—the Social Security payroll tax of 1977. It tripled the maximum tax and still didn't make the system solvent.

Audience. Boo-o-o!

The President. If our opponents were as vigorous in supporting our voluntary prayer amendment as they are in raising taxes, maybe we could get the Lord back in the schoolrooms and drugs and violence out.

Something else illustrates the nature of the choice Americans must make. While we've been hearing a lot of tough talk on crime from our opponents, the House Democratic leadership continues to block a critical anticrime bill that passed the Republican Senate by a 91-to-1 vote. Their burial of this bill means that you and your families will have to wait for even safer homes and streets.

There's no longer any good reason to hold back passage of tuition tax credit legislation. Millions of average parents pay their full share of taxes to support public schools while choosing to send their children to parochial or other independent schools. Doesn't fairness dictate that they should have some help in carrying a double burden?

When we talk of the plight of our cities, what would help more than our enterprise zones bill, which provides tax incentives for private industry to help rebuild and restore decayed areas in 75 sites all across America? If they really wanted a future of boundless new opportunities for our citizens, why have they buried enterprise zones over the years in committee?

Our opponents are openly committed to increasing our tax burden.

Audience. Boo-o-o!

The President. We are committed to stopping them, and we will.

They call their policy the new realism, but their new realism is just the old liberalism. They will place higher and higher taxes on small businesses, on family farms, and on other working families so that government may once again grow at the people's expense. You know, we could say they spend money like drunken sailors, but that would be unfair to drunken sailors—*[laughter]*——

Audience. 4 more years! 4 more years! 4 more years!

The President. All right. I agree.

Audience. 4 more years! 4 more years! 4 more years!

The President. I was going to say, it would be unfair, because the sailors are spending their own money. *[Laughter]*

Our tax policies are and will remain prowork, progrowth, and profamily. We intend to simplify the entire tax system—to make taxes more fair, easier to understand, and, most important, to bring the tax rates of every American further down, not up. Now, if we bring them down far enough, growth will continue strong; the underground economy will shrink; the world will beat a path to our door; and no one will be able to hold America back; and the future will be ours.

Audience. U.S.A.! U.S.A.! U.S.A.!

The President. All right. Another part of our future, the greatest challenge of all, is to reduce the risk of nuclear war by reducing the levels of nuclear arms. I have addressed parliaments, have spoken to parliaments in Europe and Asia during these last 3½ years, declaring that a nuclear war cannot be won and must never be fought. And those words, in those assemblies, were greeted with spontaneous applause.

There are only two nations who by their agreement can rid the world of those doomsday weapons—the United States of America and the Soviet Union. For the sake of our children and the safety of this Earth, we ask the Soviets—who have walked out of our negotiations—to join us in reducing and, yes, ridding the Earth of this awful threat.

When we leave this hall tonight, we begin to place those clear choices before our fellow citizens. We must not let them be confused by those who still think that GNP stands for gross national promises. [*Laughter*] But after the debates, the position papers, the speeches, the conventions, the television commercials, primaries, caucuses, and slogans—after all this, is there really any doubt at all about what will happen if we let them win this November?

Audience. No!

The President. Is there any doubt that they will raise our taxes?

Audience. No!

The President. That they will send inflation into orbit again?

Audience. No!

The President. That they will make government bigger then ever?

Audience. No!

The President. And deficits even worse?

Audience. No!

The President. Raise unemployment?

Audience. No!

The President. Cut back our defense preparedness?

Audience. No!

The President. Raise interest rates?

Audience. No!

The President. Make unilaterial and unwise concessions to the Soviet Union?

Audience. No!

The President. And they'll do all that in the name of compassion.

Audience. Boo-o-o!

The President. It's what they've done to America in the past. But if we do our job right, they won't be able to do it again.

Audience. Reagan! Reagan! Reagan!

The President. It's getting late.

Audience. Reagan! Reagan! Reagan!

The President. All right. In 1980 we asked the people of America, "Are you better off than you were 4 years ago?" Well, the people answered then by choosing us to bring about a change. We have every reason now, 4 years later, to ask that same question again, for we have made a change.

The American people joined us and helped us. Let us ask for their help again to renew the mandate of 1980, to move us further forward on the road we presently travel, the road of common sense, of people in control of their own destiny; the road leading to prosperity and economic expansion in a world at peace.

As we ask for their help, we should also answer the central question of public service: Why are we here? What do we believe in? Well for one thing, we're here to see that government continues to serve the people and not the other way around. Yes, government should do all that is necessary, but only that which is necessary.

We don't lump people by groups or special interests. And let me add, in the party of Lincoln, there is no room for intolerance and not even a small corner for anti-Semitism or bigotry of any kind. Many people are welcome in our house, but not the bigots.

We believe in the uniqueness of each individual. We believe in the sacredness of human life. For some time now we've all fallen into a pattern of describing our choice as left or right. It's become standard rhetoric in discussions of political philosophy. But is that really an accurate description of the choice before us?

Go back a few years to the origin of the terms and see where left or right would take us if we continued far enough in either direction. Stalin. Hitler. One would take us to Communist totalitarianism; the other to the totalitarianism of Hitler.

Isn't our choice really not one of left or right, but of up or down? Down through the welfare state to statism, to more and more government largesse accompanied always by more government authority, less individual liberty and, ultimately, totalitarianism, always advanced as for our own good. The alternative is the dream conceived by our Founding Fathers, up to the ultimate in individual freedom consistent with an orderly society.

We don't celebrate dependence day on the Fourth of July. We celebrate Independence Day.

Audience. U.S.A.! U.S.A.! U.S.A.!

The President. We celebrate the right of each individual to be recognized as unique, possessed of dignity and the sacred right to life, liberty, and the pursuit of happiness. At the same time, with our independence goes a generosity of spirit more evident here than in almost any other part of the world. Recognizing the equality of all men and women, we're willing and able to lift the weak, cradle those who hurt, and nurture the bonds that tie us together as one nation under God.

Finally, we're here to shield our liberties, not just for now or for a few years but forever.

Could I share a personal thought with you tonight, because tonight's kind of special to me. It's the last time, of course, that I will address you under these same circumstances. I hope you'll invite me back to future conventions. Nancy and I will be forever grateful for the honor you've done us, for the opportunity to serve, and for your friendship and trust.

I began political life as a Democrat, casting my first vote in 1932 for Franklin Delano Roosevelt. That year, the Democrats called for a 25-percent reduction in the cost of government by abolishing useless commissions and offices and consolidating departments and bureaus, and giving more authority to State governments. As the years went by and those promises were forgotten, did I leave the Democratic Party, or did the leadership of that party leave not just me but millions of patriotic Democrats

who believed in the principles and philosophy of that platform?

One of the first to declare this was a former Democratic nominee for President—Al Smith, the Happy Warrior, who went before the Nation in 1936 to say, on television—or on radio that he could no longer follow his party's leadership and that he was "taking a walk." As Democratic leaders have taken their party further and further away from its first principles, it's no surprise that so many responsible Democrats feel that our platform is closer to their views, and we welcome them to our side.

Four years ago we raised a banner of bold colors—no pale pastels. We proclaimed a dream of an America that would be "a shining city on a hill."

We promised that we'd reduce the growth of the Federal Government, and we have. We said we intended to reduce interest rates and inflation, and we have. We said we would reduce taxes to provide incentives for individuals and business to get our economy moving again, and we have. We said there must be jobs with a future for our people, not government make-work programs, and, in the last 19 months, as I've said, 6½ million new jobs in the private sector have been created. We said we would once again be respected throughout the world, and we are. We said we would restore our ability to protect our freedom on land, sea, and in the air, and we have.

We bring to the American citizens in this election year a record of accomplishment and the promise of continuation.

We came together in a national crusade to make America great again, and to make a new beginning. Well, now it's all coming together. With our beloved nation at peace, we're in the midst of a springtime of hope for America. Greatness lies ahead of us.

Holding the Olympic games here in the United States began defining the promise of this season.

Audience. U.S.A.! U.S.A.! U.S.A.!

The President. All through the spring and summer, we marveled at the journey of the Olympic torch as it made its passage east to west. Over 9,000 miles, by some 4,000 runners, that flame crossed a portrait of our nation.

From our Gotham City, New York, to the

Cradle of Liberty, Boston, across the Appalachian springtime, to the City of the Big Shoulders, Chicago. Moving south toward Atlanta, over to St. Louis, past its Gateway Arch, across wheatfields into the stark beauty of the Southwest and then up into the still, snowcapped Rockies. And, after circling the greening Northwest, it came down to California, across the Golden Gate and finally into Los Angeles. And all along the way, that torch became a celebration of America. And we all became participants in the celebration.

Each new story was typical of this land of ours. There was Ansel Stubbs, a youngster of 99, who passed the torch in Kansas to 4-year-old Katie Johnson. In Pineville, Kentucky, it came at 1 a.m., so hundreds of people lined the streets with candles. At Tupelo, Mississippi, at 7 a.m. on a Sunday morning, a robed church choir sang "God Bless America" as the torch went by.

That torch went through the Cumberland Gap, past the Martin Luther King, Jr., Memorial, down the Santa Fe Trail, and alongside Billy the Kid's grave.

In Richardson, Texas, it was carried by a 14-year-old boy in a special wheelchair. In West Virginia the runner came across a line of deaf children and let each one pass the torch for a few feet, and at the end these youngsters' hands talked excitedly in their sign language. Crowds spontaneously began singing "America the Beautiful" or "The Battle Hymn of the Republic."

And then, in San Francisco a Vietnamese immigrant, his little son held on his shoulders, dodged photographers and policemen to cheer a 19-year-old black man pushing an 88-year-old white woman in a wheelchair as she carried the torch.

My friends, that's America.

Audience. U.S.A.! U.S.A.! U.S.A.!

The President. We cheered in Los Angeles as the flame was carried in and the giant Olympic torch burst into a billowing fire in front of the teams, the youth of 140 nations assembled on the floor of the Coliseum. And in that moment, maybe you were struck as I was with the uniqueness of what was taking place before a hundred thousand people in the stadium, most of them citizens of our country, and over a billion worldwide watching on television. There were athletes representing 140 countries here to compete in the one country in all the world whose people carry the bloodlines of all those 140 countries and more. Only in the United States is there such a rich mixture of races, creeds, and nationalities—only in our melting pot.

And that brings to mind another torch, the one that greeted so many of our parents and grandparents. Just this past Fourth of July, the torch atop the Statue of Liberty was hoisted down for replacement. We can be forgiven for thinking that maybe it was just worn out from lighting the way to freedom for 17 million new Americans. So, now we'll put up a new one.

The poet called Miss Liberty's torch the "lamp beside the golden door." Well, that was the entrance to America, and it still is. And now you really know why we're here tonight.

The glistening hope of that lamp is still ours. Every promise, every opportunity is still golden in this land. And through that golden door our children can walk into tomorrow with the knowledge that no one can be denied the promise that is America.

Her heart is full; her door is still golden, her future bright. She has arms big enough to comfort and strong enough to support, for the strength in her arms is the strength of her people. She will carry on in the eighties unafraid, unashamed, and unsurpassed.

In this springtime of hope, some lights seem eternal; America's is.

Thank you, God bless you, and God bless America.

Note: The President spoke at 9:11 p.m. at the Dallas Convention Center. Prior to the President's speech, the delegates watched a film which concluded with the introduction of the President.

Following the convention proceedings, the President and Mrs. Reagan attended a reception at the convention center for officials and guests of the Republican National Convention.

Remarks to Members of the Republican National Committee and the Reagan-Bush Campaign Staff in Dallas, Texas
August 24, 1984

Thank you very much. You know, Paul, if you really have all morning been talking about all those things you said, then I haven't got anything left to say. [*Laughter*] That's what I was going to talk about.

No, I want to thank you. It's a privilege to be with so many hard-working and dedicated Republicans. And with regard to the interruptions last night, afterwards I said to George, I said, "I thought there for awhile I was going to have to do the speech one word at a time." [*Laughter*]

But it's a special honor to greet the women and men who've just become the new Republican National Committee. And incidentally, if we are the reason for all of this, we wouldn't have been in a position to be responsible for all of this if it hadn't been for people like you putting us here, and we're most grateful.

Each of you has dedicated years of effort to the cause that unites us. And today, you take up positions of the highest responsibility in one of the oldest, proudest political parties on Earth—a party that's always stood for human freedom, a party that's given the world leaders like Theodore Roosevelt and Dwight David Eisenhower and, yes, Abraham Lincoln.

Your positions give you an opportunity to serve our country in an historical manner. And on behalf of all Republicans, I give you a heartfelt congratulations.

During your time in office you'll face many challenges, but none will be greater than the challenge you face in the next 74 days. And I just know that with the people by our side, we will—and by "we" I mean Republicans—we'll lead not only our party but our country. And we'll fight this campaign with every ounce of strength we have, and the people will win.

Our strategy is simply stated: We'll go to the people—to *all* the people—we'll speak of our beliefs; we'll stand on the record; we'll deal in the facts.

The opposition has already begun to try to pit one group of Americans against another. But the election of '84 will be a battle not of groups, but of ideas. And we'll wage it with joy and vigor.

We know that our constituency is everyone in this country. Our special interest group is the American people. And our intent is to keep promoting policies that will help all of the people and help the people of this country to help themselves.

This year offers us an historic opportunity to get across an historic truth: that we are the party of new ideas; we are the party of the future; and we are the party whose philosophy is vigorous and dynamic. The old stereotype of a kind of pudgy, stolid, unimaginative Republican—there may be a few cartoonists around that still want to portray us as that, but they're lying in their teeth if they do.

This isn't going to be a cakewalk. I know that all of you know that. And it's no time to sit on our laurels. 1984 is the year when we can get out there in the union halls and the VFW, the church meetings, and get out the word. As a matter of fact, we'll be walking away from here in a few minutes, because Nancy and I are due in Chicago to speak to the VFW this afternoon at their national convention.

But we want to get out the word on how, through cutting tax rates, we're making the GOP stand for "Great Opportunity Party," and get out the word on how our policies have enhanced America's strength and this has made the peace that we enjoy more solid and durable; get out the word on how inflation has plummeted and unemployment has fallen and the value of the dollar is higher and the economy is expanding. And we didn't do this to help some of the people; we did it to help all of the people.

Things are going so well that the opposition has had to reverse the meaning of a few words and concepts. Indeed, at their meeting in San Francisco, one of their speakers called the economic expansion—

and I quote—an "illusion." Well, it's pretty hard to cash an illusion. [*Laughter*] People are cashing bigger checks.

But according to the opposition, prosperity is an illusion. Strong defenses—and this again is quoting them—are "destabilizing." And if you read the record of the last administration backward, it has a happy ending. [*Laughter*]

Well, this expansion has already lasted 20 months without fueling inflation. It's given nearly 6½ million more Americans, as I said last night, jobs. There's nothing dangerous about an expansion that is based on hard work and innovation, and the American people know it.

Looking to the future, it's clear that the opposition has only one innovation to offer—strange for them, too—a huge tax increase. But that's their usual knee-jerk reaction, and as I said the other day, when their knee jerks, we get kicked. [*Laughter*]

But let's get the word out on that one, too. Our people don't believe, or our party doesn't believe, that the people are undertaxed. We believe the Federal Government is overfed. To bring the budget under control, we need more Republicans elected who will support the line-item veto and the balanced budget amendment. You've heard me say that before, but we're going to keep on saying it, because every poll indicates that the American people support those measures overwhelmingly, once again showing that the leadership of the other party totally is ignoring what their own people are telling them they want.

And to spur new investment, to enable the people to keep a greater share of their earnings, we need that historic simplification of the tax code. And if we can broaden that base, if we can begin to get the unpaid tax that is now out there from those who are freeloading on their neighbors, we can reduce the rates for everyone.

Our vision is and must be an America of greater incentives, more growth, and new opportunities. But let me leave you just one last thought from my heart: Holding this office has allowed me to see as never before how richly our nation has been blessed. Around the world, totalitarians tread ideals underfoot and oppress millions. But in America, it's still our privilege to stand for liberty.

This election is for more than our party and more than the White House; it's for the future of our beloved country, the place Mr. Lincoln called the "last, best hope of man." For the sake of our children and the millions on Earth who look to America for hope, I know that we'll fight the good fight, we'll keep the faith.

There was one thing—I know that many of the things I've said here were repeated many times in the convention, because they had to do with the actual record of what we've been doing in the management of the Government, but I think you might be pleased to know—you'll remember back a couple of years ago when we were talking about a private sector initiative, encouraging that. And thousands of volunteers came forth with every kind of idea, and we had a commission, temporarily put together, that collected, and then in the White House we had computerized the literally thousands of programs throughout the country that citizens and community groups have themselves put in place to solve some problems that heretofore our opponents always would think was only for government to do.

Well, we still maintain a headquarters in that private initiatives, and there's hardly a week goes by that we don't have something that we pick up the phone to them and say, "Hey. . ." And sometimes it's a problem only involving one individual that we've heard about, or that we've read in the press about, with a situation that government isn't equipped to solve, and we call them. And you know, a couple of days later a call comes back: All taken care of. And the same thing is true with programs.

In Washington one day I turned on the television, and I saw a bunch of fellows out there, and they were painting houses and they were doing all sorts of things and carrying things in and out, and then the TV cameraman was stopping them, and they were being questioned. Well, some were lawyers and some were doctors and some were business people and even some judges, and yet they were painting houses and so forth.

And I thought, my gosh, they're doing that—this must be Texas, this must be that "Christmas in April" program in a town here in Texas where all year long they collect the information about the elderly, the disabled, the people who can't afford to fix up their houses, to restore the plumbing, to do the things that need doing. And when they've got all this list complete, then the merchants contribute the paint and the things of that kind, and then the people go out, and "Christmas in April" is refurbishing all those houses for those people in need.

And, by golly, it was Washington, DC, that was doing it, because our private sector initiative had carried the word throughout the country of "Christmas in April," and every community, literally, that heard about it said, "Hey, that's a good idea," and took it up. And we haven't talked much about that; it isn't the easiest thing to talk about, I guess. But it is showing that the America that used to have a barn-building bee when a farmer's barn burned, when they used to help the fellow that got injured to harvest his crop and all, that America has always been here. The Government just tried to take some of your fun away from you. And we're stopping that.

Thank you all, and God bless you all. And we're now going to go and talk to the VFW. Thank you.

Note: The President spoke at 10:34 a.m. in the Chantilly Ballroom at the Loew's Anatole Hotel.

In his opening remarks, the President referred to Senator Paul Laxalt of Nevada, general chairman of the Republican Party and chairman of the Reagan-Bush Reelection Committee.

Following his remarks, the President traveled to Chicago, IL.

Remarks at the National Convention of the Veterans of Foreign Wars in Chicago, Illinois
August 24, 1984

Commander and Commander, Governor Thompson, Senator Percy, our Representatives Hyde and Martin, you ladies and gentlemen, I thank you very much for your warm welcome.

I'm delighted to have another chance to speak to the Veterans of Foreign Wars. Last year, I told you that I would fly halfway around the world for the honor of meeting with the VFW. Well, it's not quite that far from Dallas to Chicago—[*laughter*]—but it sure is a great way to wind up a terrific week.

Now, before I say anything else, I want to congratulate all of you for reaching an important milestone—your 2-million membership goal. You can be proud. For 85 years, the VFW has stood united in support of the values which have made our Republic great, and today you're doing it better than ever.

Four years ago, right here in Chicago, I stood before your convention, and when you think back to 1980, it's hard to forget the mess America was in, hard to forget the

foolish talk of a malaise, the unfairness of runaway price increases, 21½-percent interest rates, weakened defenses, Americans held hostage, and the loss of respect for our nation abroad. It seemed that we woke up every morning wondering what new humiliation our country had suffered overseas, what disappointing economic news lay waiting for us on the front page.

We knew we couldn't continue on that road. We knew we had to change course and get America back on her feet. And we knew that peace and freedom could not be protected without cost and commitment, without perseverance and courage.

One cannot sit in the Oval Office without realizing the awesome responsibility of protecting peace and freedom and preserving human life. The responsibility cannot be met with halfway wishes. It can be met only by a determined effort to pursue and protect peace with all the strength that we can bring to bear.

My deepest commitment is to achieve a stable, enduring peace, not just by being prepared to deter aggression but also by bringing steadiness to American foreign policy, by being prepared to pursue all possible avenues for arms reduction, by ensuring that our economic strength leads the way to greater stability through growth and human progress, and by having the spiritual strength and self-confidence that enables us to reach out to our adversaries.

Well, I think we've come a long way together. In fact, I believe we've closed the books on that dismal chapter of failed policies and self-doubt. May it never return. And our progress wouldn't have been possible without you of the VFW and millions of other concerned Americans.

Gone are the days when we abandoned principle and common sense. Gone are the days when we meekly tolerated obvious threats to our peace and security. Gone are the days when we either sought to achieve overnight grandiose arms control agreements that were bound to fail, or when we set our sights so low that the agreements permitted the numbers and categories of weapons to soar.

We have made a new beginning, a dramatic, far-reaching step toward a much better, safer, and more secure future.

To all of you who have served your country with such courage and distinction, and to all the young men and women who look to their future, I can tell you today from my heart: The United States of America is prepared for peace.

And because we're stronger than before, we can be confident that we're in a position to secure a future of peace, not peace at any price, but a true, meaningful, lasting peace supported by freedom and human dignity.

As I said last night in Dallas, our military serves to protect our freedom and keep the peace. None of the four wars in my lifetime and none of the wars that you have seen came about because we were too strong. History shows that weakness invites tyrants to believe that the price of aggression will be cheap. And while military strength alone is not enough to ensure a more secure world, without military strength, there can be no effective diplomacy, no meaningful negotiations, no real security, no lasting peace.

Our military forces are back on their feet, substantially stronger and better able to protect the peace today than they were 4 years ago. We're still not where we need to be, but we're getting there.

And the payoff is in performance. In Grenada, with less than 72 hours notice, our forces successfully rescued 600 American students, disarmed Cuban and peoples revolutionary armed forces, and restored the chance for democracy to that troubled island.

As one company commander of the Army's 1st Ranger Battalion explained—now quote: "The lead assault elements had less than 24 hours between the time we were issued our final combat orders and our departure for Grenada. We fought with the equipment on which we were trained. The equipment worked throughout the operation. New laser rangefinders gave accurate distance to targets, and the night vision devices operated up to standards. And of the 150 Rangers in my company, only 2 had ever seen combat before, yet they all performed like seasoned veterans. What it all adds up to is that our highly motivated soldiers, together with excellent training and reliable weapons, gave us the combat edge."

Well, come to think of it, I seem to remember that it took critics weeks to decide whether it was a good idea to rescue our students. They should have asked the students, for those students were already home. Incidentally, Nancy and I were pleased to have about 400 of them on the South Lawn at the White House and about 40 of the men who had returned from Grenada, representing all four branches of the service that had been there. And it was wonderful to hear these young people—and they were all the same age, the students and the military—but it was wonderful to hear these young students tell us that, yes, they had been prone to kind of look down on the uniform and all, but not anymore.

And we heard stories about how, when they were escorted to the helicopters after they'd lain overnight and for hours under their beds in the dormitories because of the bullets coming through the buildings, and then our Rangers arrived, and when it came time to go to the helicopters, those young fellows in uniform put themselves between the students and where the firing was coming from.

They couldn't keep their hands off of them. They'd throw their arms around, and then they'd come back to us and tell us how wonderful they were. It was a great sight.

Well, that young Army officer said—and what he said about his own Ranger battalion, about being able to take on combat operations on short notice, get the job done and get it done right, was just as true for our other units. The 22d Marine Amphibious Unit had just embarked at Morehead City, North Carolina, for a normal rotation to the eastern Mediterranean when their orders were changed to Grenada. With no advance warning, with very little time, they put together their operational plans, went ashore, professionally accomplished their mission, and then continued on their way.

Because we were willing to take decisive action, our students today are safe, Grenada is free, and that region of the Caribbean is more peaceful and secure than before. But let no one confuse that situation with an inescapable reality of the modern age. When it comes to our nuclear forces—I've said it before, and I'll say it again—a nuclear war cannot be won and must never be fought. And that's why we've put forward and will continue to pursue one of the most extensive arms control programs in history.

During the months that the START and INF talks were underway, we proposed seven different initiatives, and none of these were offered to the Soviets on a take-it-or-leave-it basis. Indeed, we made a number of adjustments to respond to the stated concerns of the Soviet side, and that's why we've put forward new proposals on reducing the levels of conventional forces in Europe, on a worldwide ban on chemical weapons, on ways to help reduce the possibility of conflict in Europe, and why we're working to prevent the spread of nuclear weapons.

Ours is the pursuit of a stable and enduring peace, but at the same time, it would have been indefensible and immoral to allow the deterrent posture we need to protect the peace to continue deteriorating as it was. Now, some may insist they're just as

committed to a strong deterrent even as they would cancel the B-1 bomber and the Peacekeeper missile. They may deny that a nuclear freeze would preserve today's high, unequal, and unstable levels of nuclear weapons, and they may deny a freeze would reduce any incentive for the Soviets to return to the negotiating table and resume the search for equitable and fair reductions. But that way of thinking only reminds me of what Sam Rayburn, a very wise Democratic Speaker of the House, once said: Any jackass can kick a barn down, but it takes a carpenter to build one. [*Laughter*]

When I took office, our newest long-range strategic bomber was 19 years old. Early next month, the first B-1 bomber will roll off the production line. In 1981 our newest strategic submarine was 14 years old. Today three new Trident submarines are at sea; a fourth was delivered in January, 6 weeks ahead of schedule; and seven more are under construction, on schedule and within budget.

When I took office, the debate on modernizing our aging, land-based missiles had gone on for more than a decade. Today we've completed five successful tests of the Peacekeeper, and deployment plans are on schedule. And let me take this opportunity to thank all of you for your much-needed support in our battle for the Peacekeeper. We must make sure that no adversary ever has reason to misjudge our deterrent posture or question our resolve to protect the peace, and we couldn't have gotten this far without your help. I've said before many times; I'll say it again, where you've been of help is, there are many in Washington that you do not need to make them see the light, just make them feel the heat. [*Laughter*]

Now let me say a word about one of our most important safeguards of peace and freedom, and I'm not talking about bullets or guns, but about heart and spirit. Once again, young Americans wear their uniforms and serve their flag with honor and pride. From the NATO lines to the Demilitarized Zone of Korea and at bases and ports all across America and all over the world, young Americans are carrying on in your footsteps, in the courageous footsteps of those who stood in harm's way so that others might have a chance to find freedom, peace, and happiness. In fact, no improvement in our military readiness has been more dramatic or more important than the improvement in the quality and retention of our service men and women.

You know, the critics kept telling us that the all-volunteer military would never work and, as soon as the economy turned around, we'd be faced with severe enlistment and retention problems. Well, forgive me, but those are the same people who were wrong on inflation. They were wrong on unemployment. They were wrong on interest rates. They were wrong on the recovery. And there they go again. We're now in the 21st month of the best economic recovery since 1949, and last year was the best we've ever had for reenlistment in both the Navy and Air Force and one of the Army's best years for recruiting. And those trends are continuing.

You know, every time I see a young service man or woman I get a lump in my throat thinking of how lucky we are to have them serving our country and protecting our freedom with real honor, courage, and competence.

I believe that we've come too far, struggled too hard, and accomplished too much to turn back now. Once again the world knows that America will stand up for freedom, democracy, and peace with human dignity. And once again America is prepared for peace.

I don't know whether you're aware of this, but in every year from 1975 to 1980, armies, largely supplied by Moscow, or Soviet forces themselves, invaded or seized control of a different country. First, Vietnam, then Angola, followed by Ethiopia and Cambodia—finally, Afghanistan. Well, since 1981, that pattern has stopped. And in 1983 Grenada was saved. And every once in awhile, it's important to remember that success can also be measured by the disasters which do not happen.

Talking about those people in uniform, as I said last night at the convention—I quoted what General Marshall had said in World War II when he was asked what was our secret weapon, and he said, "The best

damned kids in the world." Well, you aren't kids anymore, but there's another generation who are, and you can say the same thing about them.

I have to tell a little story—I promised all my people I wouldn't tell this anymore, I've told it so often, but I have to tell it to you. It has to do with Grenada. Not too long ago, the Armed Forces Journal over in the Pentagon came over and delivered me a little plaque, and they had engraved on that plaque some paragraphs from a letter received from a marine lieutenant, flyer of a Cobra, who had been at Grenada and then had gone on to Lebanon. And he wrote back to the Armed Forces Journal, and he said when he was at Grenada, he noticed that every news story contained someplace the line, "Grenada produces more nutmeg than any other spot on Earth." And he decided that appeared so often, that it was a code—and he had broken the code.

And he said, number one, Grenada produces more nutmeg than any other spot on Earth. Number two, the Soviets and the Cubans are trying to take Grenada. Number three, you can't have eggnog without nutmeg. And number four, you can't have Christmas without eggnog. And he said, number five, the Soviets and the Cubans are trying to steal Christmas. [*Laughter*] And he said, number six, we stopped them. [*Laughter*]

We can be confident that history is moving in the direction of self-government and human dignity. To paraphrase Jefferson, men and women are not born with saddles on their backs. Political systems based on a dreadful denial of the human spirit will, in the end, fail.

In our own hemisphere, 26 of 33 Latin American countries today are democracies or are striving to become democracies. Now, this represents 90 percent of the region's population—up from 50 percent only a decade ago.

We see this yearning for freedom and democracy among the brave people of Eastern Europe, in Afghanistan, in Africa, and elsewhere. The spirit of men and women to breathe free is a mighty force that cannot and will not be denied. Our country is the leader of the free world, and today we're providing that leadership. In my meetings with foreign leaders, they've often told me how good it is to know what the United States stands for once again.

Now, before I close, I want to thank your outgoing commander in chief, Cliff Olson, for all that he's done, and I want to congratulate your incoming commander in chief, Billy Ray Cameron. I will always remember your strong support. It stayed rock solid even when the going was rough, but then you've always been a tower of strength. The VFW has always set high standards, lived up to them, and looked out for America, just as you've always looked out for the veteran.

The VFW and the Ladies Auxiliary didn't become great organizations by accident. You've done it through hard work and outstanding leadership. You've done it by serving our nation's veterans in your communities, volunteering your services to our veterans, fighting the good fight for a strong, safe, and secure America, supporting our POW–MIA efforts, sponsoring youth activities, directing your highly acclaimed drug abuse and safety projects, your Voice of Democracy Scholarship program, and so many other worthwhile projects.

I think of your patriotism, and I just have to wonder: How can anyone not believe that the heart of America is good, that the spirit of America is strong, and that the future of America is great?

I wish all Americans could have stood with me this past June on the windswept cliffs of Pointe du Hoc. I wish all Americans could have felt the faith and belief, the loyalty and love of those brave men of Normandy. You know what I mean—you're the veterans of foreign wars. You've been there.

But one of the Rangers of 40 years ago, now 63 years old, the day before we arrived, scaled the 100-foot cliff that he had climbed on D-day and did in just 7 minutes, still one of the best damn kids in the world. [*Laughter*]

You understand that we are what we are because of Normandy and a thousand other lonely battlefields. Words could never express what the patriotism of generation after generation of American heroes means

for the very soul of our nation. But you and I do know that we're free because of those who went to Omaha Beach and Guadalcanal, Mig Alley and Pork Chop Hill, Khe Sanh and the Iron Triangle.

I'll never stop working as hard as I can to make sure that our nation keeps its special commitment to those who served, to those who have kept the torch of liberty burning brightly. Because of you, America's best days are still to come, and with faith, freedom, and courage, there's no limit to what America can and will accomplish.

Forgive me, but before I leave, I must share something with you, because you've evoked memories too moving, too important to ignore. When we visited the Normandy beaches this past spring, we were told that the French citizens came up to those veterans of ours who had returned, took them by the hand, and said, with tears in their eyes, "We were only young at the time, but we will always remember what you did and what it has meant to us."

When I look at you, when I think of all you've lived and known and learned from your lifetime of service, a lifetime of honor, I can't help wondering, who, more than you, could better understand how precious are the gifts of life and freedom and faith? Who more than you has the courage and the wisdom to help us protect these gifts for our children and for our children's children?

You are wise men of history whose burdens have become our blessings. Your struggles preserved democracy, and today all of us are lifting America into a new springtime of hope. Yes, in my heart I know it is true: America's future must be a future of peace, and together, we'll see to it that it's done.

I know that your convention ended and that you remained here to receive me, and I'm most grateful to you for that. Thank you, and God bless you all.

Note: The President spoke at 1:57 p.m. in the International Ballroom at the Conrad Hilton Hotel. He was introduced by Billy Ray Cameron, incoming VFW commander in chief.

Remarks on Signing a Bill To Commemorate the Illinois and Michigan Canal
August 24, 1984

Thank you all for coming. I'm delighted to be here with Governor Thompson and cosponsors Senator Chuck Percy and Congressman Tom Corcoran and Representatives Henry Hyde and Lynn Martin to sign Senate bill 746.

We're pleased that this legislation enjoyed strong bipartisan support, including cosponsorship by Senator Dixon and the longtime support of Congressman Mel Price.

The legislation commemorates the Illinois and Michigan Canal, which was a main artery of commerce in the 19th century, by designating a National Heritage Corridor from Chicago to LaSalle-Peru, Illinois. The legislation also establishes a National Heritage Corridor Commission to assist local and State entities in any appropriate preservation treatment or renovation of the old structures of the canal. We believe such activity will stimulate tourism, jobs, and economic growth, as well as greater cooperation between local, State, and Federal Governments.

So, with that said, I am pleased to sign the bill.

Note: The President spoke at 2:45 p.m. in the Grand Ballroom at the Conrad Hilton Hotel in Chicago, IL. Following the ceremony, the President went to Camp David, MD, for the weekend.

As enacted, S. 746 is Public Law 98–398, approved August 24.

Executive Order 12486—Establishment of Emergency Board No. 204 To Investigate a Railroad Labor Dispute
August 24, 1984

Establishing an Emergency Board To Investigate a Dispute Between Port Authority Trans-Hudson Corporation and the Brotherhood of Railroad Signalmen

A dispute exists between the Port Authority Trans-Hudson Corporation and the Brotherhood of Railroad Signalmen representing employees of the Port Authority Trans-Hudson Corporation.

The dispute has not heretofore been adjusted under the provisions of the Railway Labor Act, as amended ("the Act").

A party empowered by the Act has requested that the President establish an emergency board pursuant to Section 9A of the Act.

Section 9A(c) of the Act provides that the President, upon such a request, shall appoint an emergency board to investigate and report on the dispute.

Now, Therefore, by the authority vested in me by Section 9A of the Act, as amended (45 U.S.C. section 159a), it is hereby ordered as follows:

Section 1. Establishment of Board. There is established, effective August 25, 1984, a board of three members to be appointed by the President to investigate this dispute. No member shall be pecuniarily or otherwise interested in any organization of railroad employees or any carrier. The board shall perform its functions subject to the availability of funds.

Sec. 2. Report. The board shall report its findings to the President with respect to the dispute within 30 days after the date of its creation.

Sec. 3. Maintaining Conditions. As provided by Section 9A(c) of the Act, as amended, from the date of the creation of the board, and for 120 days thereafter, no change, except by agreement of the parties, shall be made by the carrier or the employees, in the conditions out of which the dispute arose.

Sec. 4. Expiration. The board shall terminate upon the submission of the report provided for in Section 2 of this Order.

RONALD REAGAN

The White House,
August 24, 1984.

[Filed with the Office of the Federal Register, 10:46 a.m., August 27, 1984]

Note: The Executive order was released by the Office of the Press Secretary on August 25.

Announcement of the Establishment of Emergency Board No. 204 To Investigate a Railroad Labor Dispute
August 25, 1984

The President announced the creation of Presidential Emergency Board No. 204 to investigate and make recommendations for settlement of a current dispute between Port Authority Trans-Hudson Corporation and employees represented by the Brotherhood of Railroad Signalmen. The President, by Executive order, created the emergency board pursuant to an appropriate request as mandated by the Railway Labor Act.

The emergency board procedures of the Railway Labor Act applicable to commuter railroads provide that the board will report its findings and recommendations for settlement to the President within 30 days. The parties must then consider the recommedations of the emergency board and endeavor to resolve their differences without engaging in self-help during a subsequent 90-day period.

Radio Address to the Nation on Administration Policies
August 25, 1984

My fellow Americans:

The campaign of 1984 is underway. This campaign is about what it was like 4 years ago and what it's like today. But even more important, it's about the future. I believe our Republican Party is the true party of the future because our vision, ideas, and proposals seek to bring out the best in America by challenging the best in our people. The Great Opportunity Party believes in challenging people to do better. The Democratic leadership still insists on challenging government to grow bigger.

Our vision of a strong, secure future rests on our confidence that Americans can continue making progress toward four specific goals: strong, steady economic growth; developing the frontiers of science, high technology, and space; strengthing our community of shared values; and building an enduring peace.

As a nation, we've already begun meeting the challenges we set forth 4 years ago. I won't rehash all the problems we faced, but from a collapsing economy to weakening defenses, to rising rates of crime and poor educational performance, it was clear that America was in deep trouble. We were being led by a group of pessimists whose ideas had been threadbare for years and they hadn't even noticed. The realities of a changing world had long since passed them by.

We said if Amerca is to be a successful leader in the world again, we must face up to the problems that have dragged us down. And we must begin doing that by trusting the people again. We said that together, we must meet the challenges of reducing the growth of government, bringing down inflation and interest rates, and cutting tax rates to create jobs and get our economy moving again—and America has. We said we must restore America's ability to defend itself and fulfill its responsibilities as a trustee of freedom and peace in the world—and America has.

We met our challenges before, and we can meet them again.

As for our first goal—economic growth—our position is clear. We've seen from the mistakes of the past and from the recent recovery that our economy grows best when earnings flow not to government, but stay with the people and in the economy. That's why we must meet the challenge of simplifying our tax system, making it more fair, easier to understand, so we can bring personal tax rates further down, not up.

With strong economic growth, we'll continue bringing down deficits. We must also control spending, and one tool is a constitutional amendment mandating that government spend no more than government takes in. Another is a line-item veto, so that a President can veto specific spending requests without vetoing an entire appropriations bill. Until the leadership of the Democratic party supports these two long-overdue reforms, they should close their mouths forever about budget deficits.

Our second goal—developing America's next frontiers in science and high technology and into the far reaches of space—will enable us to surge forward on the crest of progress and peaceful change.

We have it within our power to make astonishing advances in technology and medicine, and that will make us a more competitive, successful, and healthy people. Our greatest resources and hope for the future are the minds and hearts of our people.

That's why our third great goal is to help revive America's traditional values: faith, family, neighborhood, work, and freedom. Government has no business enforcing these values, but neither must it seek, as it did in the recent past, to suppress or replace them. That only robbed us of our tiller and sent us adrift.

Helping restore these values will bring new strength, direction, and dignity to our lives and to the life of our nation. It's on these values that we'll best build a future.

Finally, we must continue meeting the challenge of working for a more peaceful world in which individual liberty can flourish. Today we're at peace, and this is good. I've seen four wars in my lifetime. I remember Pope Paul VI saying to the United Nations: "No more war. War never again."

To continue the peace we enjoy, we must show clear support for our allies and exhibit strength and steadiness to those who wish us ill. Setting goals, meeting challenges, striving for excellence are key to the endless possibilities the future holds in store for America. It's not for the Federal Government to set those goals, but we can help challenge Americans to challenge themselves in all areas of their lives and, like our Olympic athletes, to reach for greatness.

I'll be speaking more to you about this in the days ahead. Until next week, thanks for listening, and God bless you.

Note: The President spoke at 12:06 p.m. from Camp David, MD.

Remarks to Women Administration Appointees on Women's Equality Day
August 26, 1984

Welcome to the White House. I want to thank each one of you for joining us here today, and I want all of you to know how grateful I am—as George expressed it so well—me, too—for all that you've meant and all your contributions to our administration.

Now, I know it's a little warm, and I

know it's August, and here we are, and that reminds me of a sweltering, hot day in my boyhood on a Sunday morning going to church. And the preacher handled the situation very well. He said, "I'm going to preach, because of the heat, the shortest sermon you've ever heard." And he said just seven words: "If you think it's hot now—wait." [Laughter]

So, I'll follow his example. I'll do a little more than seven words—[laughter]—but I'll try to keep it short.

Today, on this Women's Equality Day, we remember the history of women in America. We celebrate all the gains that women have made. During our early years, women cooked, cleared fields, harvested crops, raised the children who would go on to make this the greatest Nation on Earth.

Yet while in those early, difficult days women were partners in hard work, in many other respects their value and dignity was ignored. In many States it was difficult for women to get a public education. In the working world, women were prevented from holding most jobs. Worst of all, women were denied our most fundamental right, the democratic right to vote.

As America became a more mature and thoughtful nation, all this began to change. The suffrage movement at the turn of the century had a profound effect. World War II broke down many of the barriers that women used to confront in the workplace. And the 1960's gave rise to a women's movement that has made all of us aware of the rightful role of women in our society, a role that includes full access to the professions and complete equality before the law.

We still have a long way to go, but already American women are finding opportunities that their forebears never dreamed of. Today two-thirds of women between 25 and 44 work in paid positions. Half our college students are women, and growing numbers of women are doctors, lawyers, police, and military officers.

You know, I can't help thinking that women like you—women who have accepted the burdens of government service and worked so successfully to give our country a new birth of freedom and vitality—show clearly just how much American women can accomplish.

For example, take a certain woman—I think her name is Maureen. [Laughter] Maureen has worked in radio and television, she's promoted overseas trade, has run for political office, and today she's helping her old man communicate to women all that our administration is trying to accomplish. [Laughter]

Now, not related but very close, is our Ambassador to the United Nations, Jeane Kirkpatrick. Ambassador Kirkpatrick has raised three sons, written five books, and holds a professorship at Georgetown University. And in her own words, let me quote: "My experience demonstrates to my satisfaction that it is both possible and feasible for women in our times to successfully combine traditional and professional roles. All that is required is a little luck and a lot of work."

Well, one of my proudest days in office came when I appointed Sandra Day O'Connor to be the first woman on the United States Supreme Court. And she, too, illustrates all that the modern American woman can achieve. Justice O'Connor has brought up three sons, pursued a brilliant legal career that has ranged from private practice to service as the assistant attorney general of Arizona. Today she's setting an example for all our daughters as one of the highest ranking women in American history.

Because of the sweeping and exciting social changes our country has undergone, it no longer makes sense to talk about a great divide between women and men. There are no longer any men's issues or women's issues, just issues that concern each of us as Americans. That's why it's our policy to benefit all Americans, and to do so not by raising taxes, or multiplying regulations, or fattening the Federal bureaucracy, but by promoting economic growth. Growth is good for everybody.

And tomorrow morning—I can't tell you the details, it isn't fair—tomorrow morning there will be some information that will be released with regard to growth in our economy. And believe me, it will be continued good news.

The economic expansion that our policies produced has already distinguished itself as the strongest sustained economic expansion in America since 1949. And not even during the boom years of the fifties, when our nation was providing millions of new jobs and achieving unparalleled industrial strength—not even then was our economy so vital, or our progress so rapid. And as this expansion provides new opportunities for all Americans, it's giving American women a powerful lift.

Last year, women filled almost three-quarters of all the new jobs in managerial, professional, and technical fields. Today the number of women-owned businesses is growing three times faster than the number of those owned by men. And over the next 4 years, we'll work to promote still more economic growth and still more opportunities for women.

I just have to believe that, together, we can make America a place where women are free to pursue careers, raise families, or both—a place where women not only succeed, but do it with style.

You're probably wondering why I didn't stop at seven words, but I couldn't get in all I wanted to say if I had. [*Laughter*] But now, thank you for being here again, and God bless all of you. And I guess it's time to picnic now—after we have our picture taken.

Note: The President spoke at 5:53 p.m. on the South Grounds of the White House following remarks by Maureen Reagan, Vice President George Bush, and the First Lady.

Proclamation 5227 of August 16 proclaimed August 26 as Women's Equality Day.

Remarks During a Visit to Jefferson Junior High School
August 27, 1984

The President. Thank you all very much. And, Secretary Bell and Principal Vera White, ladies and gentlemen, and most of all, you the students who are in and will be entering this fine school: It's a genuine honor to be with you today to help celebrate the vitality of young minds and the superb education that Jefferson Junior High School provides.

Last year, Secretary Bell and the Department of Education awarded Jefferson a Secondary School Recognition Program award, and today in just the brief time I've been here, I've seen why. Jefferson is truly one of the outstanding schools in America.

I've just come from an excellent math-count seminar with your teachers, Mrs. Sue White and Mr. John Coleman, and I'd been thinking, would you mind if I borrowed Mrs. White and Mr. Coleman to help the Congress with the budget? [*Laughter*]

And I'm delighted to be with you today, because Jefferson Junior High is setting an example of academic excellence for schools all across our country. Students at Jefferson Junior High receive just the training they need to go on to successful careers in high school and from there to good jobs and college. This school, I've already sensed, hums with excitement. It's sort of like being with a football team the week before the opening game. At Jefferson Junior High the game is life itself, and the goal is education. And I can tell, you already know you're going to win. It's that sense of teamwork at this school that's impressed me most this morning.

The teachers and staff play their part with enthusiasm and skill. To keep themselves at the top of their form, they constantly evaluate themselves and each other, and they participate often in teacher workshops. And in the classroom, Jefferson Junior High teachers and high school teachers and staff never stop giving. I understand, for example, that the teachers participating in today's orientation session are volunteering their time.

Parents of Jefferson Junior High students also play a critical role. And, again, they play it—I've seen already—with enthusiasm. Parents have organized themselves to get in touch with other parents if their children fail to appear in school. They help with activities. And parents who are members of the Home-School Association help to give Jefferson teachers the honors that they deserve.

I have been in schools, back several years ago when I was Governor, State of California, and I have seen such a difference here and in some of the schools that I was in. Here, I'm sure there's no mother that's going to say to me, as one did in California, that she found out almost by accident that her son, leaving home every morning for 10 weeks, had never shown up in school. And no one in school ever contacted or told her that he wasn't present. That's just an impossibility here, I know.

But, believe me, it's the kind of parent support that you're getting that can make the difference between a mediocre school and a true temple of learning. You Jefferson mothers and fathers are showing parents throughout the district and throughout America that it can be done, and you certainly, for one, have my heartfelt gratitude.

The stars of the Jefferson team are you, the students—and when I say stars, I mean stars. I've been watching and listening this morning—they haven't given me very much time—but I don't think I've ever seen a brighter or more attentive group of young Americans. When I think back to my own school days, I've just seen Shakespeare being portrayed here, I didn't run into that until I was well into high school. I understand that foreign languages—I didn't run into those until I was well into high school.

Now, this school will expect a great deal of you. And you'll be asked to arrive on time and work hard all day and develop your talents through activities like music and sports. And if it's any consolation, I'll tell you that I have a lot of homework to do, too, because at the end of your day, I know that's when you just come to the moment when you then have to face homework.

Jefferson Junior High will hold you to high standards, but that's not a prescription for gloom. Far from it. It's a recipe for happiness and success. This school holds a firm belief in the dignity and the worth of every one of you and is going to hold each of you—or help each of you to live up to your

very best. Yeah, there'll be low moments—there are in any great enterprise. But most of the time you'll be caught up in the excitement of learning. And at the end of your time here, you'll be standing tall, facing the future with confidence and courage.

You students are the stars of the team, but let me say a few words about your coach—your principal, Mrs. Vera White. Now, I've spent some time with Mrs. White, and I can only describe her as a genuine torrent of energy and ideas. Her devotion to this school shines through in all that she says and does. She's proud of the teachers, proud of the facilities, and proud of each one of you. If Jefferson Junior High really were a football team, I think Mrs. White could take you to the Superbowl.

I know some of the things that she's said—some from hearing them myself and some from hearing them from others. She's said, "I let every child know I care enough to make them learn in school. I have high expectations of everyone including myself. I tell the kids, 'Just go for it,' and that's what I do, too. Every student in my school knows that I expect them to succeed." And you do.

That's the way Jefferson Junior High is—a team where teachers, staff, parents, students, and principal work together to achieve excellence. You're winners, every one of you. And you're showing schools throughout America that they can be winners, too.

I want to thank you for inviting me to share in the Trojan spirit. And if I can leave you with just one thought, it's this: Always remember that the key to America's future lies in your hearts and minds, and that you'll get only as much out of your education as you put in. So, to borrow a few words from your principal—Go for it!

Thank you. Thank you, and God bless you all.

I know there's a microphone there, and I had hoped—anytime my people know that I get around young people, I hope that I will have time to take any questions. I'm afraid that our time's about exhausted, but could I cheat and ask this—could I take one question?

Yes.

Q. Good morning, Mr. President. I'm Arminta Thompson, associate editor of the Jefferson Trojan Times. And my question to you is: What do you think is the most important issue facing today's education?

The President. I think the most important issue—and it's very obvious that it has taken place here—is this drive for excellence.

About a year ago, we got our first report from a commission that I'd appointed on excellence in education, because of the problems facing schools throughout this country. There was a nationwide problem. Ten percent, fully, of the 17-year-olds in our country were functionally illiterate. And to get by, many schools had reduced the requirements in math and science, foreign languages, had gone to extended freedom—choosing courses that the students wanted to take. And the result has been a grave decline over the last 20 years in the SAT scores, the college—university entrance scores.

And in just this year, since that commission's report was made public and transmitted to all the schools, there has been just a revolution. It shows that education, that teachers, staff, administrators of schools, and, I think, parents and teachers were waiting and begging for this drive for excellence that we now see. And here, your requirements for math, for science, for the things that you're doing are evident that that is the most essential thing.

It's too late once we get behind to try and catch up with those who have gone before. But you here are now the beneficiaries of that. And I have a feeling that this school didn't wait for that excellence in education report. I have a hunch that you've been practicing it. And you were probably one of the examples they used.

Q. Thank you.

The President. Well, you're more than welcome.

And let me just close and say this, because I'm sure that if I had time for more, somebody would ask—I'm going to tattle on your principal now. She let me know that sometimes the age of the facilities here concerns you, and you wonder about that. Don't. I attended six elementary schools myself, and one high school. And in none of them was there a library. I think the facilities aren't nearly as important as the humanity in the facilities.

But I find this quite sufficient in view of what I learned in myself. I could even stand here in the gymnasium and tell you that in our high school gymnasium in my day, there were a few places on the floor that you couldn't try for a basket because the beams holding the ceiling up interfered. So, I think you can be proud of your facilities, of your teachers, of your whole school here. And I know that you are.

God bless you all.

Note: The President spoke at 11:24 a.m. in the school's gymnasium. Earlier, he toured the school and attended several classroom demonstrations.

Remarks at a Ceremony Honoring the 1983–1984 Winners in the Secondary School Recognition Program
August 27, 1984

Secretary Bell and ladies and gentlemen, I'm delighted to be here today to join you in honoring some of the finest secondary schools in America. And I want to extend a special greeting to the students in the audience. May I also extend a warm welcome to the principals who are here today, including Mrs. Vera White, who was kind enough to show me through Jefferson Junior High School this morning.

You know, the jobs of principal and President are somewhat alike: both of us have to keep a lot of people happy. You have the PTA; I have the voters. [*Laughter*] And you have unruly children, and I have—well—[*laughter*]—I'd better not name names, but let me put it this way: When a Congress leaves town, it's no accident we call it a recess. [*Laughter*]

But I am pleased to help honor the 262 middle, junior, and senior high schools that are receiving awards today for outstanding educational performance. Today we honor you for doing a superb job of educating students and for setting an example that all our schools can follow.

We must remember, though, that American schools have not always performed as well as those represented here today. From the early sixties to 1980, combined SAT scores declined steadily, dropping by 90 points. Science achievement scores of 17-year-olds showed a steady drop. And, most shocking, our National Commission on Excellence in Education reported that in 1980 more than one-tenth of America's 17-year-olds could be considered functionally illiterate. The dropout rate increased so much that by 1982, 27 percent of our students failed to complete high school, and dropout rates among minority students were higher than 40 percent.

Now, this erosion in academic achievement took place during the very period, overall, when spending was up by over 600 percent. The crisis in our schools was symptomatic of a much larger crisis in our country. We were living under a tired philosophy of government knows best. It was out of touch with the reality of a changing world. And while spending was going up, that tired philosophy was dragging America down.

Big taxing and spending had led to soaring interest rates and inflation, and all over the world our once-proud nation was no longer known for strength and resolve but for vacillation and self-doubt. The future seemed clouded. And since the whole aim of our schools is to prepare our children for the future, it was only natural that when leaders lost faith in our future, many of our principals, teachers, and students felt robbed of their sense of purpose and self-esteem.

Well, the American people decided to put a stop to that long decline, and in the past few years our country has seen a rebirth of vitality and freedom—a great national renewal. We've knocked inflation down, and all across our land a powerful economic expansion is providing new products and new work for millions. Once again, the United States is respected throughout the world as a force for peace and freedom. This is a springtime of hope for America.

When we came to Washington, we knew that the problems in education hadn't developed overnight and couldn't be cured overnight. We knew the key to educational improvement was not proposing still more Federal involvement and control, but helping to chart a new course that challenges State and local governments, teachers, administrators, students, and parents to meet the goals of an agenda for excellence.

That's why one of our first actions was to appoint a National Commission on Excellence in Education. And today—from Maine to California—parents, teachers, school administrators, and principals have begun the crucial work to carry out the Commission's recommendations by improving fundamentals of basic teaching and learning. Since the Commission's report, we've been witnessing a great reawakening of learning, reflecting a culmination of concern over the quality of American education at all levels.

On the State level, progress has been significant. When our administration took office only a handful of States had task forces on education. Today they all do, and many have begun to work on pay incentives for teachers. They know that to promote good teaching we must reward good teachers.

On the local level, parents, teachers, and administrators are making dramatic strides. The PTA reported last year that after a 20-year decline in its membership, 100,000 new members joined the organization. As with so many challenges throughout our history, the American people are showing again that it can be done.

Although we're doing much to make our schools more like the temples of learning we all want them to be, I don't believe there's an educator in this room, or in America, who wouldn't agree that we've barely begun. Our challenge is to sustain and build on the progress that we're now making.

As we strive to move forward, let's remember one essential precondition for success: We cannot reach for the future without a firm grasp of basic educational tools and the importance of traditional values.

Learning cannot take place without discipline. Today, in schools across our land, many teachers can't teach because they lack the authority to make students take tests and turn in homework. School disorder destroys the learning atmosphere, drives good teachers out of teaching, and hurts minority and low-income students who are concentrated in urban schools where the problem is most severe.

To keep learning in our schools, we must get crime, drugs, and violence out. We cannot expect to raise a new generation of responsible leaders in a lawless environment. We cannot expect young Americans to master the complexities of computers if they're high on drugs and alcohol. We must teach our sons and daughters a proper respect for academic standards, for codes of civilized behavior, and for knowledge itself.

As the National Commission forcefully argued, we must also get our students back to the proper study of basic subjects. Today too many students are allowed to abandon vocational and college prep courses, so when they graduate, they're prepared for neither higher education, nor work, nor the training they may later need to keep up with technological advances. In 1980, 35 States required only 1 year of math for a high school diploma; 36 required only 1 year of science. This, too, must stop. We must insist that all our students master math, science, history, reading, and writing, the fundamentals of our civilization.

Earlier this month, I signed into law the Education for Economic Security Act. It authorizes more scholarships for science and math teachers to help raise the level of instruction in those crucial basics. But it isn't just basic subjects that need to be taught; it's also basic values. If we fail to instruct our children in justice, religion, and liberty, we will be condemning them to a world without virtue, a life in the twilight of a civilization where the great truths have been forgotten.

In many schools, students are being taught the dangers of nuclear weapons and the burdens of national defense. Well, let's make certain they understand not only the price of defending America but the price of failing to. The students from St. George's University School of Medicine learned in Grenada that freedom is worth sticking up for.

And while it makes sense that our children learn of our nation's problems, I hope they're also learning that Americans are good and decent people who face up to those problems with courage and conviction.

Yes, we're human, we have our faults. But by any objective measure, we live in the freest, most prosperous nation in the history of the world, and our children need to know that. Jeane Kirkpatrick, Ambassador to the United Nations, said, ". . . we must learn to bear the truth about our society, no matter how pleasant it may be." [*Laughter*]

So, we've identified long-neglected problems. We're beginning to turn them around. We're remembering the all-important foundation of basic educational tools, values, and discipline—all good and important steps of progress, but still not good enough. If the world of learning is to meet the needs of America's future, then we must clearly see where America is headed.

You know, during my own lifetime I've seen this country change so much. When I was a boy, dirt roads were still the rule. Cars had been invented, but very few people had one. In the winter, people got around by horse and sleigh. A huge number of Americans were farmers, and the one-room schoolhouse was common.

Those dirt roads gave way to sleek interstate highways. The commercial development of the airplane, then the creation of the jet engine, revolutionized our transportation. In agriculture, innovations in farm equipment and techniques made it possible for more and more workers to leave the fields to pursue other jobs. As they did so, our great industries grew—became the mainstay of our economy.

Today we're well into a new revolution driven by technologies that offer virtually unlimited opportunities for satisfying jobs and personal fulfillment. This revolution is based in large part on an American breakthrough—development of the microchip. A current author has noted: "Through a vast burst of creativity in the use of microchips, the human race has projected its computational technology beyond all time and size into new galaxies of inner space, where distances are measured in billionths of a meter, time is measured in trillionths of a second, and costs drop to thousandths of a penny."

I, just a few years ago, received a great shock when I was told about a satellite of ours and a communications thing—in which the entire Encyclopaedia Britannica could be transmitted in a matter of something like 3 or 4 seconds.

Today our children learn to tell time on digital watches. They mix traditional games like baseball with the latest video craze. And they grow up with constant exposure to the mass media, watching television some 25 hours a week. Today's children can expect to live longer, have more leisure, enjoy better health, change jobs more often, and move to more new locations then ever before.

We've heard it said that our nation's most important recess [resource] [1] is the mind of a child, and that's truer than ever. Not long ago we were asking how America could bring the world of learning into better harmony with the world of work. Well, those worlds must not only come together, but also strengthen and enrich each other.

Our vision of education must be as forward-looking as our vision of the rest of American life. This will mean a school system that teaches our children how to enrich their lives by using telecommunications as educational tools, that shows them how to educate themselves so they'll be able to keep their skills current in an ever-changing job market, and that gives them an appreciation of the arts and humanities so that they may broaden their vision and deepen their understanding of the values that give life meaning.

One way of helping American schools better serve and shape our future is to keep bringing technology into more classrooms. Now, when I was a boy, an apple was some-

---

[1] *White House correction.*

thing you brought the teacher. [*Laughter*] Today you learn on an Apple or a Mac-Intosh or an IBM.

Already our schools and universities have begun to make extensive use of the technological revolution. Young children can use computers to teach themselves colors and basic concepts like "up" and "down" or "fast" and "slow." Others, older students, can use computers to sharpen their grasp of virtually any subject from math to history. Computers can tie in with vast libraries and, in effect, put those libraries in every classroom. One dramatic advantage of the new technology is that, as we put it to use in our schools, it can ease the burden on our teachers. In any given classroom, some students are able to work quietly with computers while their teacher spends time with others—perhaps with students who require more personal attention.

At the same time, technology can produce new opportunities for learning in the workplace and the home. Audiovisual courses can teach workers how to use new techniques and equipment, and computers can help them prepare for new fields. In the home, personal computers can put all the world's great art, literature, and drama at a family's fingertips. Two-way cable television stations can bring classroom instruction into the living room, and new techniques of viewer participation can enable people in the home to take tests and practice skills. If we apply technology to education with thoughtful skill, good education will be available to all. Education and technology will enable all to participate fully in the wonders and benefits of American life.

One area where those wonders and benefits is most apparent is space. It's long been a goal of our space shuttle, the program, to some day carry citizen passengers into space. Until now, we hadn't decided who the first citizen passenger would be. But today I'm directing NASA to begin a search in all of our elementary and secondary schools and to choose as the first citizen passenger in the history of our space program one of America's finest—a teacher.

Now, I promise you there will be a little bit of voluntarism in that, also. [*Laughter*] But when that shuttle lifts off, all of America will be reminded of the crucial role that teachers and education play in the life of our nation. I can't think of a better lesson for our children and our country.

So, now we know that there's reason for hope. We can see an exciting future, but we also know what the current problems are. We've defined them, studied them, quantified them. We've made some progress in combating them, but not enough. Now is the time to set ourselves some additional challenges.

We've slowed the downward trend in SAT scores in the past few years. We may even have ended that trend. But that isn't enough. We have to do better. We have to challenge ourselves further, and we must challenge ourselves as individuals. The state can't do it for us. This town and the Federal Government can't do it for us. We have to challenge ourselves to get moving again.

I propose that, like an Olympic athlete, we set ourselves some goals—four specific challenges—and go for it.

Before this decade is out, scholastic aptitude test scores should regain at least half the losses of the last 20 years—a big challenge. And we know what hurdles lie ahead, but it's doable if we try.

Another challenge before this decade is out: States should reduce their high school dropout rates to less than 10 percent. A big task? You bet. But from the teachers and principals and administrators that I've met over the past 3½ years, believe me, they've—or should I say, you?—are up to the challenge.

Challenge number three: Violence in the schools is, in some ways, the toughest of our problems. But, again, I know we're up to it. Already school and community concern has begun to pay off. A Gallup Poll now shows that the number of parents with children in public schools who cite violence as their major concern is down from 29 percent last year to 23 percent this year. And that's reason to cheer. But, again, it's not enough. We have to do better.

So, here's our goal: Before this decade is out, every school in the Nation should have adopted clear discipline codes, and the percentage of parents who cite school safety as a major concern should be half of what it is now.

You know, our country is perfectly poised to meet these challenges and reach these heights. So many things have begun righting themselves the past few years, or, I should say, you have helped right them. It's a time of good feeling about the future. It's a time of progress. And we're showing ourselves again that effort and dedication and tenacity really make a difference.

As a young fellow said recently, "America's on top again." And we can reach the top in education again, if only we try.

And that brings me to a fourth and last challenge. We can judge our success in turning the schools around by measuring public confidence in the schools. In 1980 only 35 percent of Americans gave the schools an "A" or even a "B" when they were asked to grade them in a poll. Well, the latest Gallop Poll shows 42 percent now give the schools an "A" or a "B." That's a solid increase, but it's not enough. We have to do better. We've got to challenge ourselves further. And so, before the decade is out, this general level of confidence in our schools should grow at least another 20 percent so that a solid majority of our people give our schools an "A" or a "B"—no, make that an "A+" or a "B+."

Less than 2 years ago, one of our great Olympic heroes, Jeff Blatnick, was lying in a operating room being operated on for cancer. He vowed he'd come back, reach his potential, and meet his destiny. And a few weeks ago, we saw him drop to his knees in joy and thanks when he won an Olympic gold medal in wrestling.

My friends, there's nothing we can't do if we set our minds to it. There's nothing we can't achieve. And like those shining young men and women that we sent to the Olympics, we'll stick to these goals; we'll meet them; and this will change our country. We will continue to be what we've already started to be: America reemergent on the scene, full of dynamism and vision; America renewed in a golden age of learning.

I thank you for inviting me here today. It's an honor to meet these scholastic heroes, our Olympians of the classroom. And as school doors open this week and you and 45 million of your fellow students return to your classrooms, I wish you success in your studies, success in helping America meet these great challenges for excellence in education in the 1980's and beyond.

Thank you. God bless you all.

Note: The President spoke at 2:34 p.m. in the Grand Ballroom at the J.W. Marriott Hotel. In his opening remarks, he referred to Secretary of Education T.H. Bell, whose Department sponsors the program.

Appointment of Five Members of the Intergovernmental Advisory Council on Education
August 27, 1984

The President today announced his intention to appoint the following individuals to be members of the Intergovernmental Advisory Council on Education for terms expiring July 27, 1988:

Glenn Stratton Carew will succeed Roberta T. Anderson. He is an accountant in private practice. Previously he served as a professor of accounting at the University of Georgia and Clemson University. He graduated from Piedmont College (B.S., 1968) and the University of Georgia (M.A., 1970). He also completed his Ph.D. course work at the University of Georgia. He has one child and resides in Athens, GA. He was born August 21, 1942, in New Bedford, MA.

Selma S. Morrell will succeed Joseph L. Knutson. She is a former elementary schoolteacher with over 14 years of experience in public and private schools. She has served as a member of the National Education Association. She has five children and resides in Albuquerque, NM. She graduated from Brigham Young University (B.A.). She was born February 8, 1931, in Malta, ID.

George N. Smith is a reappointment. Since 1967

Mr. Smith has been serving as superintendent of Mesa Unified Schools in Mesa, AZ. He also serves as president of the Arizona State Board of Education and is past president of the Arizona School Administrators' Association. He graduated from the University of Utah (B.S.) and Arizona State University (M.A., Ed.D.). He is married, has four children, and resides in Mesa, AZ. He was born February 11, 1927, in Safford, AZ.

James B. Tatum is a reappointment. Mr. Tatum is president of the Crowder College board of trustees and a member of the board of directors of the Association of Community College Trustees. He is also president of Tatum Motor Co. in Anderson, MO. He graduated from the United States Military Academy (B.S., 1947). He is married, has four children, and resides in Anderson, MO. He was born July 24, 1925, in Carthage, MO.

Gonzalo A. Velez is a reappointment. He is vice principal of the Newark Eastside High board of education in Newark, NJ. He graduated from the University of Santo Tomas in Manila, Philippines (A.B, B.S.E., Ph.B., M.A.). He is married, has two children, and resides in West Orange, NJ. He was born October 26, 1941, in the Philippines.

Statement on Signing a Bill Establishing the Martin Luther King, Jr. Federal Holiday Commission
August 27, 1984

I have today signed H.R. 5890, which establishes a temporary commission to encourage and advise on appropriate observances of the first legal holiday commemorating the birth of Martin Luther King, Jr., which will occur on January 20, 1986.

The Commission can make a significant contribution by assisting governmental and private organizations in arranging for appropriate ceremonies to honor this great and distinguished man.

I have been advised by the Attorney

General that, in view of the requirements of the appointments and the incompatibility clauses of the Constitution, a majority of the members of the Commission, and therefore the Commission itself, may perform only ceremonial and advisory functions.

Note: As enacted, H.R. 5890 is Public Law 98–399, approved August 27.

Message to the Congress Transmitting a United States-European Economic Community International Fishery Agreement
August 27, 1984

To the Congress of the United States:

In accordance with the Magnuson Fishery Conservation and Management Act of 1976 (Public Law 94–265; 16 U.S.C. 1801 *et seq.*) (the Act), I transmit herewith the text of a governing international fishery agreement between the United States and the European Economic Community (EEC), which was initialed at Washington on June 27, 1984.

This agreement will replace the existing governing international fishery agreement with the EEC, which entered into force on June 9, 1977, and is now due to expire no later than September 30, 1984. This agreement may be signed by the European Economic Community only following the completion of EEC internal procedures, which are now underway. I am transmitting this final text to you prior to its signature. While it is the usual practice to transmit to the Congress only signed agreements, it is my intention in this case that this transmittal initiate the period for Congressional review under Section 203(a) of the Act (16 U.S.C. 1823(a)) to further the objectives of that Act. Like other such agreements, it will enter into force only after the completion of the requirements of Section 203 of the Act, signature of the Agreement by both Parties, and written confirmation that the internal procedures of the EEC have been completed.

RONALD REAGAN

The White House,
August 27, 1984.

Remarks at a Presentation Ceremony for the 1983 Young American Medals for Bravery
August 28, 1984

The Young American Medal for Bravery is so special that the law mandates that it be given to the recipients only by the President of the United States and is to be given to no more than two young people a year. And two points are made by these directives. One is that the recipients are so important to us that the Chief Executive of the Nation must personally honor them. And the other is that the winners are the very bravest of the brave.

Now, it's been said that of all the virtues, courage is the most important, because without it we would never have the strength to practice the others. Now, that's a comment about moral courage. But what about physical courage? The stories of these two young men tell us something about that.

Both these young people made a conscious decision under pressure to ignore personal safety, to ignore personal—or potential pain and the possibility of death, and do an incredibly heroic thing—save another human being from death.

On the evening of February 3d, 1983, the home of then 11-year-old Brian Gill was the scene of a terrible fire. Brian escaped without harm and was standing near a tree when he realized that his 3-year-old sister had become separated from his father and was still inside. Brian ran back into the house, which was now engulfed by flames. He felt his way along a wall, followed the sound of this sister's coughs, made his way to her side, and pulled her outside to safety. His little sister survived, and so did three other sisters. His 2-year-old brother, however, perished.

Almost 2 weeks after the fire in Brian Gill's house, 17-year-old, then, Jim Morris, was driving along an overpass near Grants Pass, Oregon. It was late and he was returning from work. Driving along, he and a companion looked down to see a car in flames on Interstate 5. A station wagon had been struck by a truck and was in flames, its gas tank ruptured. Morris raced for the car; and when he got there, he saw the driver, Thomas Bishop, trying desperately to get out. But Bishop was disoriented and shaking badly, and Jim tried to open the door of the burning car, but it stuck. So, he thrust himself through the driver's window, grabbed Bishop under the arms, and single-handedly pulled him to safety through the window. Less than a minute later, there was an explosion, and the entire inside of the car was engulfed in flames.

Later, Thomas Bishop wrote to Morris: "It required much courage for you to come through those flames." If it had not been for what Jim Morris did, Thomas Bishop might not be alive. If it had not been for what Brian Gill did, his sister would not be alive.

As I look at these two young heroes, all I can think is how proud we are of you. And we're thankful for you.

I want to say to our audience, these are America's children. And look at what kind of people they are. The actions of these young men reflect great strength of character. We can only wonder how, at such a tender age, they managed to develop it.

I happen to think that it's always hard to be young. The young are so vulnerable and often feel misunderstood. But the children and teenagers and young adults our society has produced the last 20 years or so seem in some ways to have had it harder than many of us older folks did. We grew up in a different America—an America of small towns and big families; an America where generations lived together and lines of authority, both within the home and outside it, were clear. We did not, for whatever reasons, question the premises of life so much. It seemed a more secure age.

But the world is changing. And the facts of our life have changed. Throughout our history we've relied on the family as the principal institution for transmitting values. But these days the American family is very different from what it was. Many families are headed by a single parent. Families are smaller, not only with fewer children but with fewer generations living together. The extended family is increasingly a thing of the past, and so is the old tradition of generation after generation living in the same town and the same house.

We're a country on the move. We're wed to mobility, and the ties that bind us seem looser. We watch a lot of television, seeking continuity and reassurance in the regular and predictable appearance of our favorite TV stars and programs. They visit us—as if they were a friend or relative coming by for the evening. TV is increasingly becoming the American neighbor. And the fact that it serves that function reflects what it is that we're missing.

The point I'm making is that we're an America of changing institutions and changing traditions. And change can be difficult, especially for young people.

In the sixties, the first generation to completely feel the assault of modern life almost came apart. Our youth seemed disoriented. But now in the eighties, when some would have thought that things would be worse, they seem better. The young people of today are so solid, so alive to the good things in life, the deepest pleasure. They seem to care about the things worth caring about.

The polls show they're intensely patriotic. And they're very interested in home, career, and family—all of the things that go into creating what we call society.

You saw the Olympic athletes a few weeks ago—teenagers, many of them. You saw that they had faith in themselves; faith that great effort will be rewarded, that trying to improve your talents is worth it. You saw the love of country that they displayed with a shining lack of self-consciousness.

Somehow amidst all this change, all this movement, our young people have held on. What we're seeing, I think, is a reappreciation of our sense of national roots; a reappreciation of the traditions and values our country lived by; a reappreciation of the things that give us a sense of continuity, a sense that there is a purpose to life. And many of our young people seem to be doing it on their own, as if they're personally rediscovering these things and making them new again.

I'm not talking about nostalgia for the past, but refinding what worked about the past and bringing it into the present and the future. Refinding our bearings, forging a sense of continuity where it doesn't exist outwardly in the facts of our lives, we have to recreate connections—connections with our family, between the family and the community. We need guideposts to help us find the way. And all this will evolve as we bring the best along with us.

People wonder why there's such a feeling of hope these days, and they come up with reasons—oh, the stock market's up, inflation is down. That's only a part of it. I think we're feeling hope again, because we're taking old values and making them new again. And by giving them new life, they're giving us new life.

These two young heroes that we see here today reflect the achievements and heroism of a shining new generation. But as we honor them it's good for us to think of the quiet heroes of that generation—the children who are starting out with some of the odds against them, the quiet heroes who haven't had a chance to develop their potential and show us their greatness.

Think of a child who's in a foster home. Many of them have special needs, and too many have a difficult time finding stable and loving permanent homes. Many have been abused in some way. Think of a child with drug problems—a child who, because of bad judgments or peer pressures, becomes a slave to a terrible addiction. Think of a young person with a drinking problem enslaved in the same way and needing our concern. Think of a young person in high school who, for a whole combination of reasons, decides to drop out and end his or her education forever. Usually we say that child failed to continue. Sometimes I wonder if it isn't also true that we failed and our schools failed that child.

So many of these young people with things going against them early on are quiet heroes trying to do their best. I believe we must challenge ourselves, personally, to help them personally; to show them our support and affection; and to show them we care—asking today that all of us commit ourselves to those silent heroes; that together we accept a national challenge and see to it that children in foster care are given our special affection, that we make sure they're in loving homes.

We must make a greater effort to make our educational system so exciting and rewarding that young people don't want to drop out.

We must help those addicted to drugs and to alcohol by recognizing their problem.

Just today, however, it is Brian Gill and Jim Morris, who deserve our applause. Gentlemen, you represent the extraordinary courage of an extraordinary new generation. You're brave. You're decent. And we're proud of you. It's good to know that the future of our land will be in the hands of people like you.

I would now like to present to Brian Gill and Jim Morris the Young American Medal for Bravery.

[*At this point, the President awarded the medals.*]

Thank all of you very much, and God bless you. And I know you'd better get in the shade. [*Laughter*] Thank you very much.

Note: The President spoke at 1:31 p.m. in the Rose Garden at the White House.

Proclamation 5231—Ostomy Awareness Month, 1984
August 28, 1984

*By the President of the United States
of America*

A Proclamation

Ostomy is a type of surgery which allows for drainage when a person has lost the normal function of digestive or urinary systems due to birth defects, disease, injury or other disorders. Nearly 1.5 million Americans have had ostomy surgery, and approximately 125,000 new ostomates join their ranks each year.

Ostomy was formerly referred to as "the secret surgery" because ostomates did not want others to know. Today, largely through the efforts of the United Ostomy Association, Americans needing this treatment are becoming more aware of the opportunities for education, mutual aid, and support that are of such great benefit to them and to their families. Increased public understanding of ostomy will eventually help dispel the fear of those about to undergo this surgery as well as the fear that confronts their families. Both the Federal government and the private sector are deeply committed to the proper care and advance-

ment of knowledge about gastrointestinal diseases and public education about ostomy.

To increase public acceptance of ostomy surgery and to emphasize the need for continued educational efforts, the Congress, by House Joint Resolution 587, has designated the month of August 1984 as "Ostomy Awareness Month" and authorized and requested the President to issue a proclamation in observance of this month.

Now, Therefore, I, Ronald Reagan, President of the United States of America, do hereby proclaim August 1984 as Ostomy Awareness Month, and I call upon all Americans to observe this month with appropriate ceremonies.

In Witness Whereof, I have hereunto set my hand this twenty-eighth day of August, in the year of our Lord nineteen hundred and eighty-four, and of the Independence of the United States of America the two hundred and ninth.

RONALD REAGAN

[*Filed with the Office of the Federal Register, 4:05 p.m., August 28, 1984*]

Statement on Signing a Bill Establishing a State Mining and Mineral Resources Research Institute Program
August 29, 1984

I have today signed H.R. 4214, a bill to establish a State Mining and Mineral Resources Research Institute Program, and for other purposes.

As its title suggests, the bill would reauthorize the Department of the Interior's program for funding State mining and mineral resources research institutes. In order to assist in the operation of this program, the bill also continues the Committee on Mining and Mineral Resources Research, which was originally established in 1977 under the Surface Mining Control and Reclamation Act to advise the Secretary of the

Interior on matters relating to mining and mineral resources research. H.R. 4214 would require the Committee to assist in the determination of organizations eligible for funding under this act.

I am concerned that since two of the current Committee's members were appointed by private organizations, the requirement to assist in determining eligibility for Federal funds could raise fundamental constitutional questions. The Attorney General has advised me that this vesting of authority to assist in the determination of eligibility for Federal funds in a committee that includes members appointed by private organizations could constitute a violation of the appointments clause, article II, sec. 2, cl. 2, unless the responsibilities of the Committee are given a careful narrowing construction. The Supreme Court has decided that all persons "exercising significant authority pursuant to the laws of the United States," must be appointed by the President. *Buckley* v. *Valeo*, 424 U.S. 1, 126 (1976). For this reason, I am signing the bill based on my understanding that this committee, which includes members appointed by private organizations, would only perform advisory functions.

The research goals which this bill seeks to further must be carried out consistent with the Constitution. Accordingly, I have direct-

ed the Secretary of the Interior to seek the advice of the Attorney General in implementing this act to ensure that it does not transgress constitutional limitations.

Finally, I must reiterate my concerns that the mineral institute program is no longer an appropriate use of Federal funds, given changes in the mineral industry since the program's inception in 1977 that have reduced the demand for technical personnel. My administration will continue to propose reductions in Federal funds for the program, in the belief that it should be funded primarily by State and private sources.

Note: As enacted, H.R. 4214 is Public Law 98–409, approved August 29.

Message to the Senate Returning Without Approval a Public Broadcasting Funding Bill
August 29, 1984

To the Senate of the United States:

Since the adjournment of the Congress has prevented my return of S. 2436 within the meaning of Article I, section 7, clause 2 of the Constitution, my withholding of approval from the bill precludes its becoming a law. Notwithstanding what I believe to be my constitutional power regarding the use of the "pocket veto" during an adjournment of Congress, however, I am sending S. 2436 to the Senate with my objections, consistent with the Court of Appeals decision in *Kennedy* v. *Sampson*, 511 F.2d 430 (D.C. Cir. 1974).

Public broadcasting constitutes an important national resource and contributes to the diversity of news, information, and entertainment choices available to the American public. Under S. 2436, however, Federal funding for public broadcasting would be increased by too much too fast. The Fiscal Year 1987 authorization of $238 million for the Corporation for Public Broadcasting represents a 49 percent increase over the already enacted funding level for 1986. Likewise, next year's spending on new public broadcasting facilities grants would

be authorized at $50 million or four times this year's appropriation.

When all of the demands on the Federal budget are taken into account, increases in spending on public broadcasting of the magnitude contemplated by this legislation cannot be justified. They are incompatible with the clear and urgent need to reduce Federal spending. Moreover, this view is clearly shared by a large portion of the House of Representatives as indicated by the 176 votes in favor of the Oxley amendment to reduce the three-year authorizations by 25 percent.

In disapproving this bill, therefore, I urge the Congress to consider a revised bill providing more reasonable and moderate increases for the Board for Public Broadcasting along the lines of the Oxley amendment. I also reiterate my strong opposition to the huge increases for public facilities grants contained in S. 2436 and the unjustified expansion of this program to include repair and replacement of existing equipment.

I must also stress that my firm insistence on scaling this bill back to more fiscally responsible levels in no way jeopardizes the continued operations of public broadcasting stations across the Nation. Under the established funding mechanism, ample appropriations have already been enacted into law for all of Fiscal Years 1985 and 1986. Funding for another 25 months is already guaranteed.

Thus, the issue regarding S. 2436 is really one of long-range fiscal prudence. Given the magnitude of the deficit cuts that will be needed in the years ahead, I do not believe we can justify locking-in public broadcasting funding levels for 1987–1989 that are so obviously excessive. To do so would be wholly inconsistent with our pledge to slow the growth of spending and reduce the size of the deficit.

Accordingly, I am disapproving S. 2436.

RONALD REAGAN

The White House,
August 29, 1984.

Remarks During a Visit to the Goddard Space Flight Center in Greenbelt, Maryland
August 30, 1984

The President. Thank you, Jim Beggs. I'm a little self-conscious right now about arriving in kind of an old-fashioned way—in a helicopter. And after what I've seen here, I'm even more self-conscious about the fact that I'm a captain of the horse cavalry. [*Laughter*]

But I'm delighted to be with you today and to have this chance to say congratulations on this morning's lift-off of the *Discovery* mission. I'm honored to meet all of you who are making this great adventure happen. You've sparked the dreams and imagination of the Nation—from the youngest boys and girls in classrooms across our country to individuals like myself who are approaching the outer limits of their middle-age years. [*Laughter*]

You go quietly about your work, far removed from the glare and the gloss and the glitter of public spotlights. But what you do is important. You're expanding our wealth of knowledge, and with that knowledge, you're fueling a mighty tide of progress, carrying the hope of an optimistic future for people here and everywhere.

Yours is the work of a true revolution; not a revolution poisoned by hatred and violence and the will to conquer, but one that's rising from the deepest yearnings of the human spirit that challenge the limits of knowledge and to put the power of discovery at the service of our most noble and generous impulses for decency, progress, and, yes, for peace.

Today, on behalf of a grateful nation, I salute you and your colleagues in private enterprise and the academic world. You're the heroes of high-tech; the pulse of America's technological power; the champions of a confident people whose faith and courage are pushing America up and out to a world of wonders for us, our children, and our children's children.

The space age is barely a quarter of a century old, but already we have taken giant steps for all mankind. And our progress is a tribute to American teamwork and excellence. We can be proud that we're first, we're the best; and we are so because we're free.

There's nothing that the United States of America cannot accomplish, if the doubting Thomases would just stand aside and get out of our way. In a single generation, we've freed ourselves from the bounds of Earth; we've set our footprints on the surface of the Moon; we've used our instruments to explore space, the Sun, and our sister planets; and our space shuttle provides the first reusable space transportation system for research, commercialization of space, and scientific exploration.

Meeting these great challenges has given us benefits far more valuable than our original investments. It has proven wrong those dreary souls who lacked the vision to support your efforts. With their pessimism, America could never have gotten off the ground. And with your space shuttle, we have again and again. And I'm convinced your success confirms a vision that we share: An America unafraid, reaching into space with courage and leadership, will be an America unsurpassed. We have it within our power to create a bounty of new jobs, technologies, and medical breakthroughs surpassing anything we've ever dreamed before or imagined.

We already benefit daily from a modern revolution in worldwide communications. We can communicate with each other at a moment's notice, virtually anywhere on the globe. We can anticipate tomorrow's weather and prepare for it. Our space shuttle system provides access to space for science, technology, communications, and national security.

Only a few weeks ago, we watched the Olympics on television, sharing excitement with people all over the world. I can remember—and believe me it doesn't seem long ago—when we lived in the horse-and-buggy days of television. We couldn't see a breaking event on the other side of the world until the film was shipped here. But, today, thanks to your research and development work, we have modern communications satellites beaming crystal-clear telecasts worldwide.

Another quiet revolution in technology has also been driven, in part, by the rigors of our space program. New materials from plentiful natural resources like carbon and silicon are taking the place of expensive metals in virtually all manufactured products. Our automobile engineers in Detroit are using lightweight, super-strong, plastic-like materials to reduce the weight of modern cars—and consumers are getting the benefits in the form of more miles to the gallon.

Computers using microchips are constantly redefining our world as they become smaller, more powerful, and less expensive. Those chips are the heart of inexpensive electronic calculators now commonplace in the workplace, community, and classroom.

Sometimes these technological changes take place so gracefully over time that we hardly notice them. Today our children have access to more computer power than most professional scientists and engineers had in their laboratories at the beginning of the space age.

Dr. Robert Jastrow, chairman of the first NASA lunar exploration committee, predicted nearly 2 years ago that the computer industry would double in size by 1986, becoming America's biggest business. Already, tens of thousands of practical applications of space and aeronautical technology are touching our lives. I've just seen an exhibit here with a vast array of new products from lifesaving vests for firemen to sophisticated aerial-scanning techniques to locate and identify everything from schools of fish to mineral deposits to healthy timberland.

In medicine we're seeing the vision of technology with a human face with one miraculous breakthrough after another. The procedure called CAT scanning uses a computer to compile a clear picture from x rays taken at different angles, often permitting patients to avoid the risks and discomforts of surgery. CAT scanning has come a lifesaver in detecting diseases of the brain and other vital organs.

The pioneer field of computer-controlled walking has given hope to thousands of paralyzed Americans that, someday, they may walk again.

The widespread use of sound waves allows doctors to avoid potentially harmful use of x rays. Using sound waves to monitor the progress of babies inside the womb permits earlier diagnosis of problems, a safer pregnancy and delivery for the mother, and better health for the baby.

HTS, for Human Tissue Stimulator, sends electrical impulses through wire leads to targeted nerve centers or particular areas of the brain, providing relief from pain and stopping unwanted involuntary motion. I'm happy to point out that HTS was sponsored by the Goddard Space Center.

I've also been shown a hand-held x-ray machine and the Programmable Implantable Medication System, called PIMS, that administers medication automatically within the body.

It would be difficult to put a pricetag on the value of these human benefits. Even more dazzling opportunities lie ahead, if only we have the faith and courage to keep pushing on. Each technological breakthrough enables us to work from a new and higher plateau. It opens the door to great leaps in productivity which would have been considered unthinkable only a few decades ago.

Permit me to suggest that the fraternity of pessimists, who today insist strong growth will ignite high inflation, are looking at abstract statistics, theories, and models, not the reality of a changing world. They do not see that as we acquire more and more knowledge from new technologies, we no longer move forward in inches or feet; we begin to leap forward.

Working the zero-gravity environment of space, we can manufacture in just 1 month's time lifesaving medicines that it would take 30 years to manufacture on Earth. And we can manufacture crystals of exceptional purity that may enable us to produce super computers and make even greater breakthroughs in productivity.

Our vision is not an impossible dream; it's a waking dream. As Americans, let us cultivate the art of seeing things invisible. Only by challenging the limits of growth will we have the strength and knowledge to make America a rocket of hope shooting to the stars.

High technology is born from capital, and more capital will require continued incentives for risktaking and investment, not tax increases, which would stifle growth. We support high-tech, not high taxes. The Federal Government must constantly endeavor to strengthen the private economy, while supporting research and development, particularly in universities, to train tomorrow's industrial and academic scientists and engineers.

Our agenda for excellence in education at the elementary and secondary school level is also crucial, so students, like those I met at Jefferson Junior High School on Monday, can acquire the knowledge to enter universities and, one day, step into these vital positions of leadership and responsibility.

Between 1981 and 1985, Federal investment in basic research will have increased by almost 30 percent in real terms. And we will carry forward that strong commitment

into the future. We will also continue our support of tax credits for industrial R&D expenses, and we'll strive to lessen concerns that cooperative R&D between companies may violate antitrust statutes.

With the power of economic growth and the courage and determination of a free people, we can keep our number one challenge in space—to develop a permanently manned space station, and do it within a decade. From that space station, we can carry out the kind of work in medicines and crystals I mentioned a moment ago; we can conduct new research, explore the distant planets, and, at the same time, unlock the vast potential for commerce in space by easing tax laws and regulations which discriminate against commercial ventures. And we'll be doing all these things for the sake of a more peaceful and prosperous world.

America has always been greatest when we dared to be great. We will be leaders in space, because the American people would rather reach for the stars than reach for excuses why we shouldn't. And as American technology transforms the great black night of space into a bright new world of opportunities, we can use that knowledge to create a new American opportunity society here at home. We can ensure every person has not only an equal chance but a much greater chance to pursue the American dream.

To do this, we must maintain and increase our older industries ability to compete in the world, stimulate creation of sunrise industries, and meet the challenge of ensuring American leadership and prosperity into the 21st century. Call me an optimist, but I'm convinced that if we do accept this challenge, if we maximize incentives, invest fully in the new technologies, and strive for the great breakthroughs in productivity, then, yes, we can outproduce, outcompete, and outsell the pants off anybody, anywhere in the world.

We can build an America that offers productive, secure job opportunities for all our fellow citizens, from assemblyline workers to research scientists in new industries such as biotechnology, robotics, and information processing.

We can meet our goal of assuring adequate supplies of affordable energy so that never again will the American people be held hostage by a foreign cartel.

We can apply new agricultural technologies to preserve our soil and environment, and dramatically enhance productivity through improvements in crop yields and resistance to disease and harsh environments. We can enhance our world leadership in agricultural production and in nutritional assistance to millions who look to America for hope and for help.

If we're to keep our economy healthy and strong, we need to stay healthy and strong ourselves. Our success will depend on each person's willingness to adopt healthy habits, our collective ability to improve an already effective health care system, and our continued research and pioneer work in the kinds of medical technologies you're developing right here. Before this decade is out, our administration is committed to reducing significantly the death rate for all age groups and to ensuring older Americans can live healthier, longer, and more productive lives. We can, and we must.

The dream of America is much more than who we are or what we do. It is, above all, what we will be. We must always be the New World—the world of discovery, the world that reveres the great truths of its past, but that looks forward with unending faith to the promise of the future. In my heart, I know we have that faith. The dream lives on. America will remain future's child, the golden hope for all mankind.

Thank you for welcoming me today. And thank you for all you do, and thank you for your courage to dream great dreams. God bless you all.

Mr. Beggs. Mr. President, if we may offer and present to you a small token of our appreciation for your coming here today. As you know, on the last shuttle mission, we went up and repaired a satellite. And that satellite, the Solar Maximum Mission Satellite, was developed here at Goddard; and indeed, the repairs were designed and developed here at Goddard. And they were installed with cooperation with the Houston Mission Control and the Houston astronauts, of course. It was a very successful mission, and we now have another very valuable scientific satellite working again for several years.

This model is a glass-blown model of that, showing the astronaut on his way out. And we hope that it will remind you many times, both of the visit to Goddard, as well as the strong support that you have given to this program and which we very much appreciate. And the encouragement which you continue to offer—we thank you for that very much.

Since the model is fragile, we'll deliver it to the Oval Office.

The President. Thank you very much. Thank you. Thank you very much.

Mr. Beggs. What do you do up there without a horse? [*Laughter*]

The President. Thank you all very much. And now, as a little girl told me in a letter a few years ago—I'll get back to the office and go to work. [*Laughter*]

Thank you.

Note: The President spoke at 11:31 a.m. in Building 10 at the Center. Prior to his remarks, the President was given a tour of displays of space program activities by James M. Beggs, Administrator of the National Aeronautics and Space Administration, and Noel Hinners, Director of the Goddard Space Flight Center.

Message to the Congress Transmitting an Alternative Plan on Federal Civilian Pay Increases
August 30, 1984

To the Congress of the United States:

Under the Federal Pay Comparability Act of 1970, the President is required to make a decision each year on what, if any, pay adjustment should be provided for Federal employees under the General Schedule and the related statutory pay systems.

My pay advisors have reported to me that an increase in pay rates averaging 18.3 percent, to be effective in October 1984, would be required under existing procedures to raise Federal pay rates to comparability with private sector pay rates for the same levels of work. However, the law also empowers me to prepare and transmit to Congress an alternative plan for the pay adjustment if I consider such an alternative plan appropriate because of "national emergency or economic conditions affecting the general welfare."

Accordingly, after reviewing the reports of my Pay Agent and the Advisory Committee on Federal Pay, and after considering the adverse effect that an 18.3 percent increase in Federal pay rates might have on our continuing national economic recovery, I have determined that economic conditions affecting the general welfare require the following alternative plan for this pay adjustment:

In accordance with section 5305(c)(1) of title 5, United States Code, the pay rates of the General Schedule and the related statutory pay schedules shall be increased by an overall percentage of 3.5 percent for each schedule, with such increase to become effective on the first day of the first applicable pay period beginning on or after January 1, 1985.

Accompanying this report and made a part hereof are the pay schedules that will result from this alternative plan, including, as required by section 5382(c) of title 5, United States Code, the rates of basic pay for the Senior Executive Service.

RONALD REAGAN

The White House,
August 30, 1984.

Statement on Signing the Departments of Commerce, Justice, and State, the Judiciary, and Related Agencies Appropriation Act, 1985
August 30, 1984

Today I am signing into law H.R. 5712, a bill to provide appropriations in 1985 for the Departments of Commerce, Justice, and State, the Judiciary, and related agencies.

I am grateful for the successful efforts of the Senate and the House of Representatives in keeping the total level of spending in this bill at an acceptable level.

I am, however, concerned about section 510 of the bill, which is intended to prohibit the Federal Trade Commission from spending appropriated funds to enforce certain provisions of the substantive antitrust laws. First, this provision raises questions pertaining to the separation of powers among the branches of government, because it seeks to permit unwarranted intrusion by Congress into pending law enforcement proceedings brought by an administrative agency. Second, by including a rider on an appropriations bill rather than by amending substantive law, Congress has attempted to prevent the Federal Trade Commission from carrying out the constitutional duty of executing the substantive antitrust laws. I am hopeful that, at the earliest possible date, appropriate legislative action will be taken to amend existing substantive law so as to specify the intention of Congress regarding the Federal Trade

Commission's authority under the antitrust laws.

I am also concerned about the bill's provision relating to the Legal Services Corporation, which purports to mandate continued funding for current grantees of the Corporation at essentially the same level of funding as in fiscal year 1984, unless action is taken prior to January 1, 1985, by Directors of the Corporation who have been confirmed by the Senate. To the extent that this provision may be intended to disable persons appointed under the Constitution's provision governing Presidential appointments during congressional recesses from performing functions that directors confirmed by the Senate are authorized to per-

form, it raises troubling constitutional issues with respect to my recess appointments power. At my request, the Attorney General is looking into the question whether this provision can, consistent with the Constitution, effect this intent.

In this regard, I urge the Senate to avoid any constitutional issues by acting promptly on the confirmation of the Board members I have nominated, who have been the subject of extensive hearings and action by the Senate Labor and Human Resources Committee.

Note: As enacted, H.R. 5712 is Public Law 98–411, approved August 30.

Statement on Signing a Bill Establishing a National Commission on Agricultural Trade and Export Policy
August 30, 1984

I have today signed H.J. Res. 600, the agricultural trade and export policy commission act.

H.J. Res. 600 would establish a National Commission on Agricultural Trade and Export Policy to conduct studies of agricultural trade and export policies, programs, and practices of the United States, and to make recommendations to the President and Congress.

The congressional sponsors of this legislation see the Commission's work as providing recommendations for the agriculture community, the administration, and the Congress to consider as they work together in developing the 1985 farm bill. I expect the 1985 farm bill to be an historic watershed in laying the groundwork for assuring the continuation of a prosperous and productive agricultural economy. While I am not convinced that we need yet another commission to study agricultural policy, I hope the Commission will constructively join the debate on the future direction of American agriculture, including that of agricultural trade and exports.

Numerous other groups, including the President's Export Council, official industry

advisory groups, and the President's Working Group on Future Food and Agriculture Policy, are also examining the many issues that can affect the future course of American agriculture. We hope that the free exchange and critical review of all such views will lead to the development of farm legislation that sets a sound course for agricultural policy.

In signing H.J. Res. 600, however, I must express my concern about the membership of the Commission. Under this resolution the Commission is to be composed of 3 officers from the executive branch, who serve in a nonvoting capacity, and 32 members who are either selected by, or are Members of, Congress. Although the Commission would appear to serve primarily legislative functions, this bill would place the Commission partly within the executive branch. I believe that creation of such a commission, which is neither clearly within the executive branch, nor clearly within the legislative branch, tends to blur the functional distinction between the governmental branches that is fundamental to the concept of separation of powers. It would be more appropriate for the Commission to be composed either entirely of members selected by the legislative branch, if it is to serve primarily legislative functions, or entirely of members appointed by the President, if it is to serve the executive branch.

Moreover, I do not consider it advisable to have the Secretary of Agriculture or any other executive branch official receive private donations to assist the Commission.

The Department of Agriculture will provide such staff resources as are needed from existing resources and make use of Commodity Credit Corporation funds as authorized to cover travel expenses, per diem, and other expenses as needed.

Note: As enacted, H.J. Res. 600 is Public Law 98–412, approved August 30.

Remarks to Chapter Presidents of the Catholic Golden Age Association
August 31, 1984

The President. Thank you very much, and it's a joy to have all of you here. It's very kind of you to understand the scheduling demands of a few weeks ago and to come back again and give me the chance to meet with you.

I was thinking of how I was going to begin my remarks here. I started thinking about my feelings on age, and they can be summed up by this greeting: "Hi, kids." [*Laughter*]

Age is a state of mind; it's an attitude. The distinguished philosopher, Dr. Satchel Paige, who also played a little baseball, once summed this up with a question. He said, "How old would you be if you didn't know how old you was?" [*Laughter*] Well, now, you think about that. I've already made my decision. I've been 39 for the last 34 years. [*Laughter*]

But I want to personally say hello to some remarkable people here on your board of directors. There's Margaret Mealey, whose work I've known of for some time. She's been honored by five former Presidents for her work with many organizations, including the USO and the National Council of Catholic Women. She is president of the Catholic Golden Age Association. She is a marvel, and we're proud to have her here today.

And Bishop Thomas Dolinay, of my home State of California, and we're very happy to have him here. He tends a small and humble flock in a wee little parish that extends from southern California to Alaska—

[*laughter*]—so he thought coming all the way to Washington was just a little Sunday outing. [*Laughter*]

And I want to recognize, also, Tom Hinton, whose marvelous work through the years has made him known to and respected by every bishop and just about every priest in the United States.

And I want to mention, even though she couldn't be here, Sister Bernadette de Lourdes. All of you know her work. She's one of the reasons that some writers who muse on humanity conclude that there are saints among us.

Now, there are a number of things I want to talk about today, and I'm going to get to it. But since we'll be talking about Federal programs that have had some problems, I want to tell you a story that I heard about how such problems can happen anywhere.

Please don't think me irreligious, but the story goes that one day Saint Peter was happily walking around near the Pearly Gates, and he heard a funny little sound and saw a lot of little things scurrying about and realized that heaven had a new delegation of mice. And he leaned down and talked to them, and he said, "How do you like it up here?" And they said, "Well, the accommodations are superb." But they had a complaint. They said heaven is so large, their legs were so short, that it was hard for them to get around and see everything. So, Saint Peter ordered that they all be given roller skates. And they put them on, and the next day they were darting all over, having a heck of a time there. And a week later, St. Peter went for his stroll—and no mice. He looked around, and he couldn't find them. And all of a sudden he came upon a fat and happy old cat that was sleeping in the corner. And he said, "Well, cat, how are you doing? How do you like heaven?" And the cat said, "It's paradise. It's clean, it's quiet, the weather's nice, and those meals on wheels—delicious." [*Laughter*]

But, seriously, I think I have a sense of what concerns you and what your concerns are and what the realities are for older people in America. Those 85 and older are almost the fastest growing segment of our population. Back in 1920, the percentage of our population aged 65 or older was less than 5 percent. Now it's more than twice that, and growing. So things are getting better. And as the baby boom generation gets older—and some of them are entering their forties—the senior citizens of our country will be a huge group, and their interests will continue to be a matter of great concern to our society.

There are some problems I'm going to talk about that touch on your concerns. They're important public programs, but they've had their share of problems.

First, there is Social Security. No American need fear for the integrity and future of the Social Security system. As a result of the recommendations of our bipartisan commission which were enacted by the Congress, we rescued Social Security from imminent bankruptcy and assured its good health well into the next century.

We've also proposed something that will benefit the millions of people who depend so much on Social Security now. Under present law, as you know, Social Security beneficiaries would receive no cost of living increase next January if the cost of living adjustment is below 3 percent. Well, given the progress that we've made in fighting inflation, that could be a real possibility. But we should and we can give Social Security recipients the full cost of living increase in a timely manner, because there has been a delay in their receiving a Social Security increase that was due and that was a part of our settlement to make Social Security fiscally responsible. So, I have asked the Congress, to amend the law to assure that this is

done, and that in January, 3 percent or no 3 percent, there will be such a cost of living adjustment.

Second is Medicare. All our actions have been aimed at making it stronger and assuring its continuation. Millions of Americans depend on the Medicare program to help meet their health care costs, and while it's not in the same immediate trouble that Social Security was, we must ensure the long term solvency of the Medicare program. And I'm confident that we can find the right solutions in a bipartisan manner, just as we did with Social Security.

We've already taken the first step by establishing a new method of paying hospitals under the Medicare program. Ever since Medicare was established in the mid-1960's, hospitals were paid pretty much whatever they spent. Giving hospitals a blank check resulted in costs that were rising out of control. Now, under a new program, hospitals are paid set rates, and if the hospital can provide care for less, they get to keep the savings. Now, this has successfully reduced cost increases while ensuring that the quality of the hospital care stays high. We're monitoring this new prospective pay system closely to continue to assure that quality is preserved while health cost inflation continues to go down.

Third—doctors and the high cost of medical care. It's terribly tough when you're tight on funds and get sick. It's tough when you're not tight on funds, but you have an ongoing ailment and you're hit with a lot of bills.

Now, this past July, we established a 15-month freeze on doctors' charges to Medicare patients. And believe me, we're trying both to control costs for older Americans and the Government. And we're doing everything we can to try to ensure that medical care will be both available and affordable for all the senior citizens in our country.

There's a whole host of other related issues that have to do with the quality of life for older Americans—crime for one. Our administration is making extra efforts to help local law enforcement help those agencies combat street crime as a great national menace. In the past 2 years, we have actually seen a drop in the overall national crime rate. In fact, for 3 years in a row, there has been a drop, and that's the first time this has ever happened in our history. And I assure you that we intend to continue our efforts in a second administration.

We believe, as you do, that decent people have the right to walk the streets at night or take a stroll through a park. We're a little tired of the fact that, with all the locks on our doors and such, it's the law-abiding part of our society that is really locked up. We're tired of it, as you are, and we're trying to do something about it.

We live in a time of great challenges. That doesn't worry me, because all of us have seen again and again that America is very good at meeting challenges. One of the great challenges of our time is to improve the quality of life for all Americans, and especially our older citizens. The folks who've paid their dues, who kept the world going during the tough years of the thirties and the Depression, and the forties and the war, and the fifties and sixties and seventies and beyond—all of you have earned the right to sit back and take it easy and let the world take care of itself. But you don't. You're in there swinging. You're contributing to things that no one else could. You're our most valuable asset, and I'm proud to be one of you. I'm proud we're still in there slugging together.

We have every right to be proud of our generation. You know, there are only a few generations in all of history that have ever had to preside over a great transition period, and ours was one of those. We've lived through four wars and a Great Depression that toppled governments and brought misery such as younger generations have never seen.

We're one of those rare generations, as I say, that saw in a lifetime—in our lifetime— a great transition. Our young people today are going to see astounding things, but they'll never see quite the great change that we saw. We literally went from the horse and buggy to walking on the Moon.

Back in those riotous days of the sixties, when I was a Governor out in California, a group of students from our University of California campuses demanded a meeting with me. And they kind of had a chip on

their shoulder, but I was pleased to meet with them, because in those days if I went near a campus I could start a riot. And their spokesman—when they came in, they slouched in, in the usual uniform of that day—and their spokesman, resplendent in T-shirt and barefoot, he opened by telling me it was impossible for me to understand them. He said, "Your generation doesn't understand its own sons and daughters."

I tried to pass it off, I said, "Well, we know more about being young than we do about being old." [*Laughter*] And he said, "No, I'm serious." He said, "You didn't grow up in a world of instant electronics, of computers figuring out problems that once took months and even years. You didn't have nuclear power and jet travel and journeys out into space"—and so forth.

Well, you know, usually in a thing of that kind, you don't think of the answer until the whole meeting is over and you're home. But he talked just long enough for the Lord to bless me with the answer, and when he paused for breath, I said, "You're right. Our generation didn't have those things when we were your age. We invented them." It sure did change the tone of the discussion. [*Laughter*]

Well, all of us care about older Americans and their financial security—and I could say "ours" instead of theirs. We see the younger people growing up these days, and they'll be living in a world we can't even envision. And we care about those young people, and we care about our country and its future.

And that's why I'm asking that we go forward to meet a challenge together. To build a future—or a world in which the future generations of America can be free from fears about economic security, free from fears that when they're old they'll be superfluous people, free from fears that they won't have a place in the work force if they want one, that they'll be lonely or that they'll be forgotten. We have to ensure that the aged get the respect they deserve, that they have opportunities to express their creativity, that there are challenges for all of us.

And I ask all of you, particularly, to bring your wisdom and your experience and your creativity to those questions, so that together we can help those young ones on their way up. Remember, Cicero said, "If it wasn't for the elderly correcting the mistakes of the young, there would be no state."

And now, thank you. It's an honor to meet with you here today, and God bless you all.

Miss Mealey. Mr. President, on August 15th of this year we met at the Shrine of the Immaculate Conception on the feast of Our Lady of the Assumption, to whom Catholic Golden Age is dedicated, to participate with thousands of our members in a eucharistic celebration to light symbolic candles and to pray for peace. This ceremony was duplicated throughout the country by thousands of members and their friends, from Alaska to Florida, from New York to California.

We know, Mr. President, it was not possible for you to be with us on that occasion. But we did want you to have a copy of the prayer which was led by Archbishop Pio Laghi and said by all those present. We know your dedication to peace is our dedication to peace. So, we take great pride in presenting this to you.

And, Mr. Reagan, we pray that God will continue to bless you and Mrs. Reagan, and we thank you sincerely for receiving us today.

The President. Thank you all very much. Now I'll get back to the office and go to work. [*Laughter*] Well, thank you all very much.

Note: The President spoke at 2 p.m. in the East Room at the White House. The association is a national nonprofit organization representing the interests of Catholic and non-Catholic senior citizens.

Radio Address to the Nation on the Observance of Labor Day
September 1, 1984

My fellow Americans:

This weekend marks the 90th observance of Labor Day, a well-deserved tribute to the working men and women whose dreams and hard work helped build America into the greatest Nation in the world. We know that what is good for the American worker is good for America. And as we prepare for a new season of work, I believe there's good reason for giving a hopeful thumbs up.

The outlook on Labor Day weekend 1984 is for a continuation of strong, steady economic growth, more jobs, and low inflation. We still have great challenges to meet, which I'll speak about in a moment. But we should also recognize the progress we've made together. It's an important source of confidence and inspiration for our future.

In the last 19 months, the jobless rate has fallen farther and faster then any recovery in the last 30 years. We've seen the creation of 6½ million new jobs. The United States has created, on average, more jobs each month than all the Common Market countries combined in the last 10 years. The

Europeans are calling our success the American miracle.

A case in point is the automobile industry. Unemployment peaked at 28 percent in 1980. By this July, auto industry unemployment was down to 6.1 percent, and there were 153,000 more people at work in auto industry jobs than 4 years ago.

A key reason the job growth has been so strong is our success in keeping inflation down. We haven't seen unemployment and inflation drop during any term since the Kennedy administration. And we're determined to bring inflation further down, just as we're determined to simplify our tax system so we can bring your tax rates further down, not up, as my opponent would do, harming the growth and progress we've made.

With inflation and tax rates down, the American miracle can continue: interest rates can come down further; peoples' earnings can continue to buy more; investment and productivity can keep on growing; new businesses can develop new products and markets; more jobs can be created; and all Americans can share in a dynamic, exciting future.

Our future can be one of boundless opportunity if we challenge the limits of growth through reforms like tax simplification and fight inflation by passing two long-overdue reforms: the balanced budget spending limitation amendment and the line-item veto.

We must also meet the challenge of pushing back our newest frontiers of science, high technology, and space. It's been estimated that high technology industries create jobs eight times as fast as low technology industries. Just as important, the knowledge we gain from the technological revolution enables our older industries to modernize their plants and equipment, increase their ability to compete in the world, and maintain and expand their work force.

Our citizens need training to step into these jobs, and that's why we initiated the Job Training Partnership Act. That act will train more than 1 million people a year to become productive, self-supporting citizens in the private economy.

One sure way to spur jobs through new technology is by promoting more research. On Thursday morning I visited the employees of Goddard Space Flight Center and assured them our administration will continue its strong support for research and development, particularly in our universities. Between 1981 and '85, Federal investment in basic research will have increased by almost 30 percent in real terms. The importance of research work in universities reminds us that we must go forward with our agenda for excellence in education so today's students at the elementary and secondary school level can go on to college and acquire the knowledge to work in our rapidly changing world.

At the same time, we must stimulate economic development in inner city areas that have not benefited from technological innovation or the economic expansion. We've proposed enterprise zones, offering strong incentives for people to start up new businesses in up to 75 areas of high unemployment, and a youth employment opportunity wage to open up job opportunities and reduce the high levels of teenage unemployment, especially among black youth.

Both enterprise zones and the youth employment opportunity wage would reduce dependency—providing new hope for millions—and they're supported by a broad coalition of minorities. But both have been blocked by the Democratic House leadership, the very people who profess compassion. Americans aspiring to lift themselves up should never be held down by partisan politics. We will keep our economy strong, and we will not rest until it can bring a job to the home of every American.

Until next week, thanks for listening. God bless you.

Note: The President spoke at 12:06 p.m. from the Oval Office at the White House.

Remarks by Telephone to Crewmembers on Board the Space Shuttle *Discovery*
September 1, 1984

The President. Well, hello to Hank and both Mikes and Steve and Judy and Charlie. Sounds like a little community or town you've got going up there.

Listen, we're following your exploits, and you're doing a great job. How's it going? Any surprises so far?

Astronaut. Mr. President, it's going real great. It's very nice of you to call us. We think we've got a good boat here, a tremendous addition to our national transportation fleet.

The President. Well, any surprises so far?

Astronaut. Well, I guess for the five rookies here, it's a big surprise for them. This is just a really tremendous ride. You ought to try it some time.

The President. [*Laughing*] Well, you don't

mind if I think that over?

Listen, I want you to know that the men and women in the Navy and at Hughes Aircraft were thrilled by your perfect deployment of SYNCOM. That communications satellite is going to help all of us in this country, and believe me, we're grateful for your great part in getting it up there and getting it launched. And now, as of this morning, just a little while ago, you're three for three with the launch of the AT&T communications satellite.

Astronaut. Well, thank you, Mr. President. As a member of the Air Force, we're glad to help out the Navy any way we can.

The President. [*Laughing*] All right.

Listen, you know, I know the previous astronauts have now and then been able to pinpoint various things down here that they can see from the vantage point of space. And how do we look from up there? Have you seen anything unusual or things that you're going to be reporting on?

Astronaut. Well, Mr. President, I guess the biggest thing to us is that the world is covered with an awful lot of water, which is important to those of us in the Navy, anyway.

The President. Yes. [*Laughing*] Of course, it has been a season in which some of the Earth that shouldn't be covered with water has been covered with water, too.

Listen, your work up there is helping to make it easier for the people of the Earth to communicate with each other, so on top of being spacemen and a spacewoman, you're doing some very good work for your fellow citizens of Earth. And we're very thankful, and we're also very proud.

May I ask, is Dr. Judy Resnick near by?

Astronaut Resnick. Yes, sir, Mr. President.

The President. Well, Judy, how is it—your first flight? How is it going? Is it all that you hoped it would be?

Astronaut Resnick. It certainly is, and I couldn't have picked a better crew to be flying with, even if they are all Air Force and Navy and Army guys fighting about who's best.

The President. Well—[*laughing*]—as for that, what does an electrical engineer do in space?

Astronaut Resnick. Whatever they tell me to.

The President. [*Laughing*] Well, listen, I also want to wish a happy 36th birthday to Charlie Walker. Now I know the birthday isn't until Wednesday, but I have the feeling that you'll all be so busy, and he'll be busy, as you'll all be finding a parking place at Edwards, so I just thought I'd send the greetings now.

Astronaut Walker. Thank you very much, Mr. President.

The President. Well, happy day.

Listen, what you're doing is so exciting that—you mentioned about myself being up there. As I say, I'll have to think about that for a while and then see whether I can appoint myself as passenger. But our thoughts and our prayers are with you, believe me, and I say that for myself and Nancy and, I know, for all America.

But there is one thing: I'm hesitant about making any suggestions to all of you up there who know so well what you are doing, but if you will remember to just now and then build some "down" time so you can just sit back and watch the world go by. You know, there was a wonderful flier once—his name was Magee—he wrote a poem about the freedom that he felt flying above the Earth. And he'd fly with as much altitude as he could get, and as he put it, "lose the bonds of gravity and hurtle through the clouds," and as he put it in one line of his poem, "touch the face of God."

I hope that with all that you're doing up there, I hope that you will have time for a moment like that. We're all very proud of you. God bless you all.

Astronaut. Thank you, Mr. President. As you're well aware, we're only part of a very large team that makes this happen, and we'd like to accept your kind words on behalf of everybody that helped get the *Discovery* airborne and helped us do this mission.

The President. I'll go along with that. And now, I'll say goodbye and let you continue with what you're doing. And we'll all be watching you on TV. Goodbye.

Astronaut. Goodbye, sir. Thank you very much.

Note: The President spoke to the astronauts at 12:15 p.m. from the Oval Office at the White House. *Discovery's maiden voyage was manned by Henry W. Hartsfield, Jr., Michael L. Coats, Charles D. Walker, Steven A. Hawley, Judith A. Resnick, and Richard M. Mullane.*

Appointment of James Bopp, Jr., as a Member of the President's Committee on Mental Retardation
September 1, 1984

The President today announced his intention to appoint James Bopp, Jr., to be a member of the President's Committee on Mental Retardation for a term expiring May 11, 1987. He will succeed Vicki Marie Click.

Mr. Bopp is an attorney with the firm of Brames, Bopp & Haynes in Terre Haute, IN. He served as special deputy prosecutor for the Marion County Prosecutor's Office 1977–1979; instructor of commercial law at Indiana University School of Business 1977–1978; and deputy attorney general for the State of Indiana, 1973–1975.

He graduated from Indiana University (B.A., 1970) and the University of Florida College of Law in 1973. He is married and resides in Terre Haute, IN. He was born February 8, 1948, in Terre Haute.

Appointment of Four Members of the Advisory Commission on Intergovernmental Relations, and Designation of Vice Chairman
September 1, 1984

The President today announced his intention to appoint the following individuals to be members of the Advisory Commission on Intergovernmental Relations for terms of 2 years:

John Henry Sununu, Governor of the State of New Hampshire, will succeed Lamar Alexander;

William H. Hudnut III, mayor of Indianapolis, IN, will succeed Margaret Hance;

Robert Martinez, mayor of Tampa, FL, will succeed James Inhofe; and

Miles Yeoman Ferry, president of the senate, Salt Lake City, UT, will succeed Ross O. Doyen.

The President also intends to designate John Henry Sununu as Vice Chairman.

Appointment of Three Members of the Department of Defense Retirement Board of Actuaries
September 1, 1984

The President today announced his intention to appoint the following individuals to be members of the Department of Defense Retirement Board of Actuaries. These are new positions.

Thomas P. Bowles, Jr., to serve for a term of 5 years. He is a principal and advisory director of Tillinghast, Nelson & Warren, Inc., in Atlanta, GA. He is a fellow and past president of the Society of Actuaries. He is married, has three children, and resides in Atlanta, GA. He was born October 12, 1916, in Birmingham, AL.

John H. Grady, to serve for a term of 15 years. He is a partner of the Actuarial, Benefits and Compensation Consulting Division of Coopers & Lybrand in New York City. He is a fellow of the Society of Actuaries. He is married, has two children, and resides in New Canaan, CT. He was born December 26, 1946, in Waco, TX.

A. *Haeworth Robertson,* to serve for a term of 10 years. He is managing director of William M. Mercer-Meidinger, Inc., an international firm of employee benefit and compensation consultants, in Washington, DC. He is a fellow of the Society of Actuaries. He has three children and resides in Washington, DC. He was born May 10, 1930, in Oklahoma City, OK.

Appointment of John F.W. Rogers as a Member of the Advisory Council on Historic Preservation
September 1, 1984

The President today announced his intention to appoint John F.W. Rogers to be a member of the Advisory Council on Historic Preservation. He will succeed Gerald P. Carmen.

Mr. Rogers is currently Assistant to the President for Management and Administration and Director of the Office of Administration. He joined the White House staff in January 1981 and has responsibility for the administrative operations of the White House and the Executive Office of the President.

Before joining the White House staff, Mr. Rogers was special assistant for administration at the American Enterprise Institute of Public Policy Research (AEI) and prior to that worked at the U.S. Senate and the White House during the Ford administration.

Mr. Rogers is a graduate of the George Washington University and recipient of the Trautman Scholarship. He represents the President on the board of trustees of the U.S. Capitol Historic Society and is a member of the board of the National Building Museum. He was born in Seneca Falls, NY, on April 15, 1956.

Informal Exchange with Reporters on the Presidential Campaign
September 2, 1984

Q. The polls show that you don't have a chance of losing. Can you lose it?

The President. The only poll I'm going to believe in is the one they take on November 6th.

Q. What about this religious issue that's come up? Are you all overplaying it?

The President. No, but I think some people in your profession here are.

Q. Jesse Jackson said this morning that this attempt to exploit religion is going to blow up in your face.

The President. Well, he'll have to speak for himself. What I was commenting on was the great movement that has been going on, more and more, to attack religion by some who pretend that they're acting within the Constitution—those people who would deny such things as chaplains in the military, and "In God We Trust" on our coins, and so forth. That's what I was commenting about. I'm not seeking to install a state religion in any way.

Q. Do you feel good about the campaign as you start this trip?

The President. Yes. I always enjoy campaigning.

Q. Are you going for a 50-State sweep?

The President. I'm going to run 1 point behind.

Q. Thank you, sir.

Note: The exchange began at 2:43 p.m. on the South Lawn of the White House as the President was preparing to depart for a trip to California, Utah, and Illinois.

Upon his arrival in Irvine, CA, the President went to the Irvine Marriott Hotel, where he remained overnight.

Message on the Observance of Labor Day
September 3, 1984

Today, we pay tribute to America's working men and women, and I join with all Americans in celebrating the dignity and productivity of our working people. Labor Day brings a fitting opportunity to salute those who built our great nation and whose spirit, hard work and courage are now building a new era of lasting economic expansion filled with greater opportunities for all our people.

America is on the move again. We're witnessing the fastest rate of job creation in the world—7 million jobs in the last year and a half—and today, more Americans are working than ever before. The erosive effect of inflation on workers' paychecks has ended, and the increase in after-tax personal income is the largest in our history.

A rising economy and greater opportunity give us confidence, but our work is far from finished. Too many of our fellow Americans are still out of work or down on their luck. We must not and will not rest until everyone who wants a job has found one, until all Americans can reach as high as their vision and talents take them. We must and we will make certain that the American dream remains a springtime of hope for all our people. Meaningful work, not welfare, is every American's hope, and we have a continuing responsibility to make those hopes a lasting reality.

Labor Day, 1984, also finds American workers facing many new and different challenges and opportunities. The nature of our labor is changing rapidly. Occupations unheard of just ten years ago are opening up opportunities. America's future growth and prosperity depend on how well we take advantage of these opportunities.

We must also compete effectively in foreign markets. Exports account for 25 percent of the total value of all goods produced in our country. Exports mean jobs for our people and growth for our economy. We're committed to keeping markets open to free trade, and to make them grow.

As America's workers enjoy this holiday, let us all be thankful for the prosperity we have achieved and let us work together to meet the challenges ahead and turn them into opportunities for all Americans.

RONALD REAGAN

Remarks at a Reagan-Bush Rally in Fountain Valley, California
September 3, 1984

The President. Governor Deukmejian, Senator Wilson, the distinguished Members of the Congress, and one who, if you do what's right, and I know you will, is going to again be a Member of the Congress, Bob Dornan, and believe me, I say with pleasure—fellow Californians:

I knew I was at a Republican rally before I came up here when I heard the voice of Johnny Grant. I think he's pretty traditional with all of us.

All these people here on the dais who are helping so hard, and all of you, you'll forgive me a little home State pride, but I can't help but thank you for giving me an opportunity to get away from those puzzle palaces on the Potomac—[*laughter*]—to return home and kick off our campaign.

I have just been given the latest figures. There are 50,000 of you here in this gathering, and there are 15,000 of you—I hope who can still hear at least—but who could not get in, and we're grateful to all of you for your coming out here, too.

Being here among friends, seeing familiar faces, getting just a hint of that breeze from the Pacific Ocean renews our strength and purpose as we start our march to victory this November. And let me add, when people need a little sunshine in their lives and a feel for the optimism that fills the soul of this beautiful country, then I can assure them they'll find it in Orange County.

I told you how many individuals there are, but there's an Orange County, California, to an Orange County in Vermont, to Orange County, Florida, to Orange County, Indiana, to Orange County, Texas. My friends, we're going to use this national campaign to build a fire of hope that links all America together.

In 1980 we said, "The time is now to build a new beginning for this beloved nation of ours." And in 1984 we're saying that the great crusade we began really never ended; we are just beginning.

We don't seek a victory for any partisan purpose. Today we set out to achieve a victory for the future over the past, for opportunity over retreat, for hope over despair, and to move up to all that is possible and not down to that which we fear.

Eleven days ago in Dallas, we said what is still true today. This election campaign is about the clear choices that will be before the American people. The choice goes to the very heart of our purpose. It's about the vision we see for America, the kind of world we'll leave for our children.

We said that we would welcome to our side Democrats who believed in our cause. And I'm very pleased to have learned since I've been here and to report that right here in Orange County five locally elected officials have changed parties. And this morning I met one of your supervisors who said that he did so as a result of our invitation in the acceptance speech there in Dallas.

Well, this year we present to the people of America a sparkling vision of tomorrow, a belief that greatness lies ahead, only waiting for us to reach out for it. We present to the people four great goals to build our tomorrow. We present a chance, this time a real chance, finally to maintain sustained economic growth without inflation. We offer a challenge to ensure that the United States of America remains today and forever prepared for peace. We put forward a philosophy that proudly proclaims the rich traditional values that fill our lives and have permitted our nation to endure. And we will continue to insist that there is no such thing as a life without uncharted frontiers, and that is our mission—to seek them, not cringe from them.

Now, we've heard what others have offered to American people today, in this year. They have said that America is nothing if it isn't promises. Well, America isn't about promises; it never has been. America is about promise. It's about possibility. We grew and prospered. We protected our liberties and those of others. We built energetic cities and fed the world. And we did all these things not because of promises, but because we Americans decided that we must see things brightly through the expanding visions of opportunity and vision, and not darkly through the prism of the past.

For too many years, we lived with the idea that there had to be inflation, that we must be satisfied with higher taxes, that high interest rates just might be acceptable, and that government just had to keep growing.

Well, we challenged all those assumptions, because they were false. Together, we began the task of controlling the size and activities of the government by reducing the growth of its spending, while passing a tax program to provide incentives to increase productivity for both workers and industry.

Today, of all the major industrial nations of the world, America has the strongest economic growth, one of the lowest inflation rates—only one-third of what it was 4 years ago—the fastest rate of job creation—6½ million jobs in the last 19 months; a record 600,000 business incorporations in 1983—and the largest increase in real, after-tax personal income since 1973. We're enjoying the fastest rate of business investment in 40 years. And America has renewed its leadership in developing the vast new opportunities in science and high technology.

The American people deserve all the credit for the way they pulled us from the depths of the economic mess that we were left with. And frankly, I think they have trouble understanding why some people persist in distorting the facts.

Just night before last, a high-ranking official of the AFL–CIO was interviewed on national television. It's hard for me to understand how someone in his position could be as unknowing as he seemed to be about the national employment situation. He charged that our tax policy was beneficial to the rich only, and yet, there had been, as he said, little of that money invested in production facilities to provide new jobs, so unemployment was getting worse.

Well, he might like to know that there are more people employed today in the United States than ever in our history. And as I just noted, more than 6 million new jobs have been created in less than 2 years. In the auto industry alone, there are nearly 150,000 more people employed than were working in 1980 in that industry. As for business and industrial development, I just pointed out, it's increased at the fastest rate in any recovery since World War II.

I wonder if he knows that a short time ago the AFL–CIO was supportive of those who wanted to cancel the third year of our tax cut and indexing. Now, that cancellation would have dumped almost three-quarters of the resulting tax increase, 74 percent, on those who are earning less than $50,000 a year. And then he accused me of plotting to destroy the unions. Well, does he know that I'm the only one who ever held this office who is a lifetime member of an AFL–CIO union? I——

Audience. Ronnie! Ronnie! Ronnie!

The President. I was six times president of my union, and I led it in the first strike that it ever called. Now, with distortions like these, our detractors would like you to think that we hadn't made any progress.

You know, sometimes they remind me of a baseball story—I know that my friend, Gene Autry, here, probably knows this story. It's about a baseball rookie and his kind of know-it-all manager. It was a crucial game in the pennant race, tied up in the bottom of the ninth. And this rookie was called on as a pinch-hitter, and he went in

and won the ball game with a booming homerun that went right over the right center field bleachers. And he crossed third—or came in around third and crossed homeplate with a big grin on his face, and the manager was waiting for him. And the manager ripped into him. He said, "Your stance was all wrong. Your swing was awkward. You held your arms too high." And when he paused for a breath, the kid said, "Yeah, but how about the distance?" [*Laughter*]

Well——

Audience. 4 more years! 4 more years! 4 more years!

The President. [*Laughing*] All right.

Audience. 4 more years! 4 more years! 4 more years!

The President. Okay.

Audience. 4 more years! 4 more years! 4 more years!

The President. Okay. Okay, you talked me into it. [*Laughter*]

As you see, our job is not done, and that's why we're here. But we've made a pretty good start. And now we can see a future where inflation doesn't consume us, where people can find new and challenging jobs, and where they can finally have some hope that this economy is back on track and America is on top.

Now, rebuilding the economy has also allowed us to restore our ability to keep the peace. The future of America relies completely on the state of our preparedness. We're not out for any territorial gain or to impose ourselves on anyone but, believe me, America must never again let its guard down.

We must always be strong so that we're prepared for peace. Ours is the most peaceful, least warlike nation in modern history. The reason we have a military is symbolized by a sign over the entrance to Fairchild Air Force Base in Washington State. It says, "Peace is our Profession."

Now, for the sake of our children, for the sake of our children and the safety of our Earth, we'll continue to invite all nations, including the Soviet Union, to join us in keeping the peace and in reducing and, yes, ridding the Earth of the awful threat of destructive nuclear weapons.

Building prosperity and maintaining our strength also permit us to keep our strong values—faith, work, family, neighborhood, freedom, and peace. And those are not just words, they're expressions of what America means, definitions of what makes us a good and loving people.

We must do more than talk about these values; we must restore them and protect them against challenge. And we must use our resources in and out of government to allow our historic values to enrich the lives of all who follow us—allowing our faith to be heard and to be felt, infusing our schools with the finest of quality, giving law enforcement all the tools they need to fight crime and drugs, and never limiting the opportunities for any American—all those belong to the future that we will build. And we didn't come all this way as a nation without such values, and we can't step into tomorrow without the continued strength and moral stamina they give us.

Nothing in our future is more technically challenging than our exciting new frontiers. The space shuttle *Discovery* circles the Earth this very moment. It reminds us that America has always been greatest when it does not shrink from greatness. We must always follow our dreams to distant places and prepare to live in space for peaceful, economic, and scientific gain. That's why I directed NASA to develop a permanently manned space station, and to do it within a decade.

Expanding those frontiers of technology requires boldness of spirit and confidence about what lies ahead. It requires restoring a system of education that demands excellence, that rewards merit, and that can instill in our children the highest level of intellectual achievement. And believe me, on this day, in this year, you and I can say we're not afraid of tomorrow.

You know, President Eisenhower once shared a story that tells us much about ourselves. A government worker had just arrived in Washington in 1953, and he was passing the National Archives building in a taxi and saw this motto carved on one of its pedestals: "What is Past is Prologue." Well, he'd heard that Washington cabdrivers were noted for knowing all the Washington answers, so he asked the driver about that motto. "Oh, that," said the driver, "well that's just bureaucrat talk. What it really means is, 'You ain't seen nothin' yet.'" [*Laughter*]

Well, as far as we're concerned, that's America's message to the world. We've got everything before us. We're going to build an economy that you can give to your children and say that it will ensure and fulfill the lives of our next generation. We're going to go to work to break the cycles of dependency on government so that free men and women have the surging spirit of boundless opportunity. We're going to build a peace that won't fail if we don't fail. And we're going to be unafraid of exploring all that's beyond this Earth. We're going to leave—and proudly leave—sturdy and indestructible values so that in the 21st century our shield will be their shield.

And on this day which celebrates the productive work of men and women everywhere, let us pledge again to revere the past and to learn from it. But let us be determined it is the future we will celebrate. That's our message this year. We'll carry it across America: You ain't seen nothin' yet.

Thank you all, and God bless you. Thank you.

Note: The President spoke at 11:19 a.m. at Mile Square Regional Park. He was introduced by Gov. George Deukmejian.

Earlier in the morning, the President and Mrs. Reagan attended a reception for local Republican leaders and Reagan-Bush campaign leaders at the Irvine Marriott Hotel in Irvine.

Remarks at a Reagan-Bush Rally in Cupertino, California
September 3, 1984

The President. Well, thank you very much.

Audience. 4 more years! 4 more years! 4 more years!

The President. All right.

Well, Governor Deukmejian, Senator Wilson, Congressman Zschau, ladies and gentlemen, thank you all very much. And a great, big thank you to the De Anza Dons for allowing us to use your field.

Well, happy Labor Day. I just want you to know how happy Nancy and I feel being with you today. You know, it started yesterday when I got on Air Force One. I couldn't help but thinking: California, here I come. But I've come to ask a simple question: Will you take freedom's next step with me so we can continue the new beginning we made 4 years ago? [*Applause*]

You know, I've been traveling around the country quite a bit recently, and I've been noticing something—and please correct me if I'm wrong—but it does seem that Americans look happier than they looked 4 years ago when we were campaigning. You seem like people who even believe in your future again. As a matter of fact, you seem like you're better off than you were 4 years ago.

Now, I know that you don't want to hear about interest rates that reached their worst peak since the Civil War, back in 1980, and about double-digit inflation, or about huge, unfair tax increases on working families, growth that ground to a halt, or about the loss of freedom and steady decline of U.S. leadership abroad. So, I won't talk about those things. And believe me, our opponents don't want to talk about them either. But we want to talk about the present and the future, about what Americans are doing together, and what we must continue to do to make America great again and let the eagle soar.

What we've done for 21 straight months, and what we must continue to do, is create powerful economic growth while keeping the inflation monster locked in his cage. And that's how we've created what our European friends are calling the American miracle.

What we've done, and must continue to do, is help restore an environment in which traditional values can flourish—family, work, neighborhood, freedom, and faith in God.

In those values lies the heart of a good and decent people and the golden hopes of a nation as generous and peaceful as the world has ever known. We're seeing a rebirth of these values, not to return to some mythical past, but to build on strengths for a creative future as we renew the quest for excellence at all levels of our society.

What we've done, what we must continue to do, is keep America prepared for peace with freedom and human dignity by being prepared to deter aggression, by bringing steadiness to American foreign policy, by being prepared to pursue all possible avenues for arms reductions, by ensuring that our economic strength leads the way to greater stability through growth and human progress, and by having the spiritual strength and self-confidence to reach out to our adversaries.

And what we've done and must continue to do is to help push back our newest frontiers in education, high technology, and space. America has always been greatest when she dared to be great. I'm convinced we will be leaders in developing these frontiers, because the American people would rather reach for the stars than reach for excuses why we shouldn't.

We can forget that pack of pessimists that are roaming our land. If we strengthen incentives, invest fully in new technologies, and strive for new breakthroughs in productivity, then we can outproduce, outcompete, and outsell anybody, anytime, anywhere in the world. And as we use our knowledge to help older industries modernize and help develop new sunrise industries, we can create a bounty of new opportunities, jobs, and improvements in the quality of life surpassing anything that we've ever before dreamed or imagined.

My friends, this we can do if you'll give us your support. The truth is, we've already got a good start, so I hope I'll be forgiven for pointing out one difference between ourselves and our opponents. We believe in high tech, not high taxes. The Silicon Valley produces some of the most advanced technology in the world. I'm told that you actually have a computer that was able to add up all the promises that have been made by the other side. But when that computer tried to add up all the tax increases it would take to pay for them, it blew a fuse.

They intend to fund their campaign promises by raising taxes more than $1,500, on the average, per household.

Audience. Boo-o-o!

The President. Now, I knew that that wasn't what you thought your future should be. The future we're building is not one of special interest groups, one or another, but for all the people. And let me offer a little proof in the form of a question. Which major industrial nation today has the strongest economic growth, 7.6 percent for the last quarter?

Audience. U.S.A.!

The President. Inflation of only 4.1 percent?

Audience. U.S.A.!

The President. Labor force participation at an all-time high, the fastest rate of job creation, 6½ million more people working the last 19 months alone? A record 600,000 business incorporations last year? The fastest rate of business investment in 40 years? Handsome productivity gains, the largest increase in real, after-tax personal income since 1973? And, yes, leadership in developing jobs and markets for the future in science and high technology, both on Earth and in outer space?

I figure you know which nation fits all of those, and its initials are U.S.A.!

Audience. U.S.A.! U.S.A.! U.S.A.!

The President. Thank you. The American people deserve all the credit for the way that you've pulled us from the depths of the economic mess that we were left with. I think the American people have trouble understanding why some people persist in distorting the facts.

Just night before last, a high-ranking official at the AFL–CIO was interviewed on national television. Now, it's hard for me to understand why someone in his position could be as unknowing as he seemed to be about the national employment situation. He charged that our tax program was beneficial to the rich only, and yet, even after they got all that money, there had been very little investment in production facilities to provide new jobs, so, he said, unemployment was getting worse.

Well, he might like to know that there are more people today than ever in our nation's history who are employed. And, as I just noted, more than 6 million new jobs have been created in less than 2 years. In the auto industry, there are nearly 150,000 more people employed than were working in that industry in 1980. As far as business and industrial investment, I just pointed out, it is at the fastest rate of any recovery since World War II.

Now, I wonder if he knows that a short time ago, his AFL–CIO was supportive of those who wanted to cancel the third year of our tax cut and cancel indexing. That cancellation——

Audience. Boo-o-o!

The President. ——that would have dumped about three-quarters, 74 percent of the tax increase, on all those earning below $50,000 a year. And when he accused me of plotting to destroy the unions, does he know that I'm the only fellow that ever held this job who is a lifetime member of an AFL–CIO union? I was six times president of my union, and I led it in the first strike that it ever had to call.

Now, with distortions like these, our detractors would like to have you think we've made no progress.

You know, they remind me of a baseball rookie. He had a kind of a know-it-all manager. And it was a crucial game in the pennant race and tied up in the bottom of the ninth. And they put him in as a pinch-hitter. And he boomed one way out over right center field and clear over the bleachers into the street. And, of course, by the time he rounded third and headed for the plate, he had a broad grin on his face. Got to the dugout and that manager, that know-it-all manager, was waiting for him. And the first thing he said was, "Your stance was all wrong. You were awkward up there. You held your arms too high." And when he paused for a breath in his criticism, the kid says, "Yeah, but how was it for distance?" [*Laughter*]

Today, America is moving in a new direction. For the first time since the administration of John Kennedy, the flow of earnings and power from the people to the Government is not increasing, it's going the other way—flowing from the Government back to the people. And we intend to keep on going in this new direction for a brighter future.

We want to enact an historic reform of tax simplification that makes the system easier to understand, fair to all, and that can bring everyone's tax rates further down, not up. Might we consider taking our cue from our Olympic athletes? Rather than discourage risktaking and punish success, rather than raise taxes, let's go for growth, and let's go for the gold.

We want to handcuff the big spenders by enacting a line-item veto and a constitutional amendment mandating that government spend no more than government takes in. Now, you know there are some that say you can't do that. Well, right here in California we have both of those here in our constitution. I used that veto more than 900 times when I was Governor here, and our budget stayed balanced. And your Governor now stands ready and is armed with that, and that's why you have surpluses and balanced budgets.

Audience. Duke! Duke! Duke!

The President. We're pushing for something called enterprise zones so people can get off unemployment and welfare and get the chance for decent jobs that they deserve. Our dream is to help every American climb as high as he or she can go. Now, isn't that more compassionate than keeping people down in dependency for the rest of their lives? That enterprise zones legislation is bottled up by the majority leadership in the House.

Audience. Boo-o-o!

The President. We think that it's time for every American to have the protection, also, of our anticrime package; time for spouses working in the home to receive the same rights for IRA's as spouses working outside the home; and time for working

families who pay to send their children to parochial and independent schools—and pay their full share at the same time of taxes to support the public schools—that they should receive the simple justice of tuition tax credits.

Now, the trouble is our opponents treat each new idea the old-fashioned way—they spurn it, they turn it down. You know, I hate to say this, but the age factor may play a part in this election. No, not mine. It's their ideas are too old.

Now, the party whose nomination that I hold may be the minority party for now, but we have the majority of good and new ideas. We believe in opportunity and opportunity for all. GOP doesn't stand just for Grand Old Party, it also stands for great opportunity party. We believe that everyone deserves an even place at the starting line. And the more we encourage economic development, the more jobs that are created—jobs for young people just getting out of school, jobs for people denied opportunity in the past—the more all Americans can share in a dynamic, exciting future.

And let me make one thing plain today: We will not be satisfied until all Americans understand that they're welcome with us and belong with us. The Republican Party won't be complete again until more black Americans feel that it is their home again. The Republican Party won't be complete until Hispanic Americans and every individual in this country understands that we are the party of opportunity, the party of growth, the party of the future—and that party is America's party.

We take no one for granted. We don't think we "own" any group. We consider nobody "ours." We do not appeal to envy, and we don't seek to divide and conquer. What Abe Lincoln said once must be said again: A house divided cannot stand.

To all those Democrats who were loyal to the party of F.D.R., Harry Truman, and J.F.K., but who see that its current leaders have changed it, that they no longer stand firmly for America's responsibilities in the world, that they no longer protect the working people of this country, we say to them: Our arms are open. Join us.

I believe in my heart that by changing

our country these past 3½ years we're making it a better country—a country of greater freedom, opportunity, confidence, and hope. And that's the America I'm working for this year. That's the America I intend to work for in the next 4 years.

Audience. 4 more years! 4 more years! 4 more years!

The President. Well, my dream for America—and I know it's one you share—is to be the kind of success story that this valley has—see that story multiply a million times. And with you by our side, we'll make history again, and our victory will be America's victory.

And now, I just want to thank all of you for sharing this afternoon with us. God bless you all. Thank you.

Audience. Reagan! Reagan! Reagan!

The President. And you send this Congressman Zschau back to Washington. We need him.

All right. Thank you very much.

Note: The President spoke at 3:32 p.m. in the track and field area of the De Anza Community College. He was introduced by Gov. George Deukmejian.

Following his remarks, the President traveled to Salt Lake City, UT, and went to the Little America Hotel, where he remained overnight.

Remarks at the Annual Convention of the American Legion in Salt Lake City, Utah
September 4, 1984

It's wonderful to be back with you today. All of you in the American Legion have served your country honorably in time of war, but you've also served her nobly in time of peace by making the American Legion one of the most important and effective civic organizations in our country's history. I salute you today, as do all Americans.

You know, one of the great things about the American Legion is the broadness of your agenda. While you pay special attention to matters of military readiness and foreign policy, any issue of the American Legion magazine shows how well informed all of you try to be about a broad range of domestic issues. And it's on the broad range of issues that I want to talk with you today. So, for a few moments, let's talk about the unfinished business that awaits us as a nation and as a people.

I think we can all be proud of the economic progress America's made in the past few years. I won't bother to recite here all the statistics about how the inflation, interest rates, and unemployment have come down, or the many indicators that demonstrate America's current economic expansion, because the real question you and I must now ask ourselves is how can we solidify the gains we've made and ensure that the prosperity we're now enjoying will endure not just for the rest of this decade, but on into the next century.

To do this, we have to make sure the Federal Government never goes on a spending spree like the one it was on when we came into office. Just in case you've—[*applause*]—well, I was going to say just in case you've forgotten, but evidently you haven't forgotten—[*laughter*]—Federal spending nearly tripled in the decade of the seventies. Taxes doubled in the 5 years before we took office.

The liberals in Washington who were so sure that we could spend ourselves rich and drink ourselves sober were surprised to see the economic mess they'd created. They didn't understand the real problem in Washington and the real reason for our recent economic woes was really very simple—in fact, if this sounds familiar, maybe it's because I've been saying it for so long: Government is too big, and it spends too much money.

Now, no one feared government's tendency to spend and tax and become the oppressor of the people more than those who built this nation. They had lived with the anxiety of a collapsing currency and runaway inflation, and that's why the Founding Fathers gave us that remarkable Constitution that placed so many checks and balances on government. But they also wisely provided for an amendment process through which later generations could perfect the constitutional system. Well, the performance of government in the last few decades shows the Constitution needs a little perfecting, and the people need a lot more protection from the fiscal transgressions of government.

I think that all of you know that the balanced budget amendment would put sharp restrictions on Federal spending, that it would force the Federal Government to do what so many States and municipalities and all average Americans are forced to do—to live within its means and stop mortgaging our children's future. So, today I'm asking for your support and help. We need the balanced budget amendment. We need it for America's future. Is that contrary to the ideas of the Founding Fathers? No, it isn't. When the Constitution was adopted, Thomas Jefferson said there was an oversight—it should have contained a clause forbidding the Government from borrowing.

Second, we need to give the office of the Presidency the powerful tool it needs to cut out the porkbarreling and special interest expenditures buried in those catch-all appropriation bills the liberals in the Congress are so fond of. Today I'm asking for your support and help. We need the line-item veto. We need it for America's future. Now, is that a wild experiment? [*Applause*] I asked, is that a wild experiment, as some have suggested? No. Forty-three Governors have that right. I had it when I was Governor, and it works.

Finally, our current tax system burdens some too heavily, while permitting others to avoid their fair—or to avoid paying their fair share. It makes honest people feel like cheats, and it lets cheats pose as honest citizens. It encourages the underground economy and wastes millions of manhours on forms and regulation. It drives money needed for growth and investment and jobs into unproductive tax shelters. It is an obstacle to entrepreneurial spirit and economic expansion. To put it simply: Our tax system is unfair, inequitable, counterproductive, and all but incomprehensible. Even Albert Einstein had difficulty with his Form 1040. [*Laughter*] And he said: "This is too difficult for a mathematician. It takes a philosopher." [*Laughter*]

So, let's end the trauma of April 15th. Let's stop the nightmare of tangled regulations and twisted requirements that every American faces at income tax time. Let's make it possible to bring everybody's tax rates further down, not up. And today I'm asking for your support and help. We need a simplified tax code. We need it for America's future.

Now, as we get America on the road again economically, we also need to return her to respect for the sound values and traditional beliefs that account for her greatness. And to accomplish this, we must rectify two of the greatest wrongs of the past few decades.

First, we must rid ourselves once and for all of the old liberal superstition that crime is somehow the fault of society and not the wrongdoer who preys on innocent people. Now, we've already appointed some very fair but tough-minded judges. And I just wish there was time to report to you in detail on the efforts of the tough new steps this administration has taken against drug trafficking and organized crime. What it all means is that we're putting more career criminals in prison than ever before. So, it should be no surprise that for the first time in many years, the crime statistics are coming down and staying down, and have been coming down for 2 years in succession.

Yet critical legislative initiatives against crime remain right where they've remained for the last 3 years—dead in the water in the House of Representatives. Our Comprehensive Crime Control Act includes bills calling for bail reform; tougher sentencing; justice assistance to States and localities; improvement in the insanity defense; and major reforms affecting drug trafficking, prison crowding, and forfeiture. All of these reforms, and others we've forwarded, are badly needed and constitutionally sound. In fact, our initiatives—the core crime bill—

passed the Senate by a vote of 91 to 1. But in the House of Representatives, the liberal leadership keeps them bottled up in committee.

So, today I'm asking your support and help. We need this tough, new anticrime legislation. We need it for America's future.

And when I keep saying we need your support and help, what I mean is that there are people in Washington that need to hear from you. You know, it is not necessary to make some of them see the light, as long as you make them feel the heat. [*Laughter*]

Now, there's another major wrong done to traditional American values that needs to be corrected. Our forefathers were religious people, and they were also enlightened enough to realize the follies of religious intolerance. What they did, on one hand, was to erect a wall in the Constitution separating church and state and, on the other hand, they provided in the same document for the free exercise of religion. They knew that morality derives chiefly from religious faith and that no government—or that government no more should handle religious expression than it should show preference for one religious group over another.

Now, I can't think of anyone who favors the Government establishing a religion in this country. I know I don't. But what some would do is to twist the concept of religion, freedom of religion, to mean freedom against religion. So, let me repeat what I've always believed: Religion is one of the traditional values which deserves to be preserved and strengthened. We are and must remain a pluralistic society. When we speak of church and religion, we speak of them with a small "c" and a small "r," so as to include within the constitutional protection all churches and all religions. The unique thing about America is that every single American is free to choose and practice his or her own religion, or to choose no religion at all, and that right must not and shall not be questioned or violated by the state.

We must protect the rights of all our citizens to their beliefs, including the rights of those who choose no religion. That is why our administration opposes any required prayers in schools. At the same time, we call for the right of children once again to pray voluntarily in our public schools, and that stand is in the spirit of the Constitution as our Forefathers wrote it and as we have lived it for most of our history. Let us restore that balance.

So, today again, I'm asking your support and help. We need the prayer amendment. We need it for America's future.

But in addition to strengthening our economy and reasserting traditional American values, our agenda for the future must promote economic growth by extending new opportunities to all our citizens. Right now, this administration has before the Congress a series of measures that would give us a great start in this direction. But, once again, these are measures that have been held up by the liberal leadership in the Congress and, once again, we're going to need your help to get them moving: first, tuition tax credits for the parents of parochial or independent school children; second, the Federal enterprise zones bill that will provide jobs and opportunity for those in our inner cities; and third, a youth employment opportunity wage so that young people, especially minority youngsters, can get that first job they need to begin their climb up the economic ladder.

So, today I'm asking again your support and help. We need tuition tax credits, enterprise zones, and a youth employment opportunity wage. We need them for America's future.

And finally, let me turn to a matter I know is of special interest to all of you—America's national security, the safety of her people, the right to a future of peace and freedom. We've come a long way in the past few years in restoring our "margin of safety." I mentioned at this convention in 1980 that we needed this. Today every major commander in the field agrees that America's military forces have better people, who are better armed, better equipped, better trained, with better support behind them.

Now, besides moving to restore the strategic balance, we've added tanks, fighting vehicles, combat aircraft, and we've also added some 70 ships to the U.S. Navy. We will have 600 ships 4 years from now if the Congress honors our budgetary requests. In the past 3 years, we have added to our sealift capability more than in all the years since World War II. And our 1983–85 budgets reflect a 100-percent increase in sustainability funding, which will significantly increase staying power for all our armed services.

Now, just take Europe alone. We can now deliver 25 percent more tonnage there in case of crisis, and we've improved our air sortie rate by 60 percent. And both on land and in the air, we have more accurate weapons, newer equipment than ever before. Now, these are the kind of things which will make sure we never have to cross the nuclear threshold.

Yes, our defenses are being restored. And so, too, are our alliances. We have completely reoriented American foreign policy, imbuing it with a new energy and moral purpose. And in the process, we have rallied our friends throughout the world. Even as we've successfully resisted Soviet expansionism, we've opened a wide series of diplomatic initiatives that will eventually bear fruit not just in arms control treaties, but in arms reduction treaties.

And most of all, we've been candid about the differences between our way of our life and that of totalitarian systems. We've carried on the struggle of ideas. We have spoken up for freedom. We're determined to keep America a beacon of hope to the rest of the world and to return her to her rightful place as a champion of peace and freedom among the nations of the Earth.

But now, there are four important things we must do to move forward with the gains we've made in foreign policy.

First, we must complete the task of military modernization and improved readiness. This is directly related to the prospect for arms reductions. In the past, we've succeeded best when we've bargained from strength. We have a moral obligation to pursue technological breakthroughs that could permit us to move away from exclusive reliance on the threat of retaliation and mutual nuclear terror. We must pursue vigorously research on defensive technologies that can permit us to intercept strategic ballistic missiles—fired deliberately or accidentally—before they reach our own soil or that of our allies. Now, some are calling this "Star Wars." Well, I call it prudent policy and common sense.

Second, we must maintain our traditional alliances. Our interests and NATO's are complementary. Their strength helps us, and vice versa.

Third, we must continue to work hard toward balanced and verifiable arms reduction treaties with the Soviets, treaties that will be made all the more feasible by maintaining our resolve to keep our defenses strong.

And fourth, we must continue our forward strategy for freedom and speak up for human dignity whenever it's threatened. I preach no manifest destiny, but I do say we Americans cannot turn our backs on what history has asked of us. Keeping alive the hope of human freedom is America's mission, and we cannot shrink from the task or falter in the call to duty. In the past 4 years, we've offered renewed hope to millions of people in developing lands, and we're beginning to see them turn away from the East and toward political and economic systems based on personal freedom. So we must not be apologetic about our nation's commitment to freedom. We must present to the world an America that is not just militarily strong, but an America that is morally powerful—an America that has a creed, a cause, a vision of a future time when all people of the world will have the right to self-government and personal freedom.

So, today, again, I ask your support and help. We need to continue to restore our strength, to pursue emerging technologies, to consolidate our alliances, to move forward energetically with strategic arms negotiations and, most of all, to continue proclaiming the American dream of human freedom to the entire world. We need these things, and we need them for the sake of America's future.

Another subject of great interest to Legionnaires is the POW–MIA issue, and your responsible support of our efforts and the National League of Families is greatly appreciated. We've made some recent progress with both Laos and Vietnam, and we'll continue our highest priority efforts until we achieve the fullest possible accounting of these brave men.

And, by the way, I want to add something that also needs to be said here. The men and women veterans who've proudly served their country in the military have earned more than simply the respect of their countrymen, they have earned the benefits to which they're entitled, including veterans preference in government employment. As long as I'm President, those will be the policies of the United States Government. And I want you to know that as long as I'm President, the door of the Oval Office is open to you, to your leaders, and to your concerns.

You know, I can't leave this discussion without thanking all of you in the American Legion for the enormous help that you've given us on the Central American issue. It's been a long struggle and, thanks to your efforts, we're finally making progress. But the struggle isn't over yet. There are still those in the Congress who want to hinder our attempts to help El Salvador, and there is also a move underway to desert the freedom fighters in Nicaragua. So, on this issue and many others, I hope you'll think about sending a reminder to the Capital this year. I hope you'll think about ending that stalemate in Washington by voting this year for responsible candidates at the congressional level, so that this administration can have a Congress it can work with and our agenda for the future can become reality.

I think you join me in my belief in this agenda for America's future. It's one that will create growth, opportunity, and progress at home and pursue peace and freedom abroad. From reducing the growth of government to supporting prayer in our classrooms, we aim to strengthen families, local communities, private institutions, and voluntary organizations. Our goal is to reaffirm traditional American values while we get government out of the way of our people and their boundless capacity for change, innovation, and progress. Our hope is to keep alive America as a beacon of hope, a shining city in a world grown weary of war and oppression.

You know, I wanted to speak to all of you today about the future, because I believe the things so many of you struggled for so valiantly have not just endured, they have grown and prospered and turned brighter with the years. What a change from only a few years ago when patriotism seemed so out of style! I'm not sure anyone really knows how the "new patriotism" came so quickly, or when and how it actually began.

Was its seed first planted that day our POW's, who had braved a horrendous captivity in North Vietnam, came home, said, "God bless America," and then actually thanked us for what they said we had done? Or was it at the 1980 winter Olympics and the miracle of Lake Placid—you remember the chants of "U.S.A.!" and the hockey team that didn't know it couldn't do the impossible? Or maybe it was that unforgettable moment when after 444 days of captivity our Iranian hostages came home to parades and freedom.

Well, wherever the new patriotism came from, there can be no gainsaying its arrival. Maybe you've seen the television show "Call to Glory" that celebrates Air Force officers serving in "the twilight struggle" of the cold war. Or maybe you've heard country singer Lee Greenwood's new song, "God Bless the U.S.A.," whose first verse says it so well:

> "If tomorrow all the things were gone I'd
> worked for all my life
> And I had to start again with just my
> children and my wife
> I'd thank my lucky stars to be living here
> today
> 'Cause the flag still stands for freedom,
> and they can't take that away."

And I wonder if anyone can forget that scene on the White House lawn last November shortly after the Grenada rescue operation. What a change it was to see young students praising and thanking our military. And as my friend Paul Laxalt recently noted, what a change to see graffiti on foreign walls that doesn't say "Yankee Go Home," but says, "God bless America."

Or how about those young men and women on our Olympic team this summer? Who's ever said more about this country than those young Americans? Can we forget those young American sprinters who swept the 200-meter race, and then, led by Carl Lewis, went around the track with a flag, embraced their families, and then knelt to pray?

And what about the moment when they introduced George Foreman, the former Olympic champion who was brave enough to wave a tiny American flag at the 1968 Olympics when he had won his fight, after there had been a demonstration previous to that in which there was no flag-waving? The news accounts described how the fans in Los Angeles rose and cheered, filling the old arena with an emotional ovation that brought tears to many. "All I've ever tried to tell anyone," George Foreman said, "is that I'm not a black man or a white man or anything else. All I've ever been was an American."

And for me there was that visit to Normandy earlier this year, where I read the letter of a loving daughter who had promised her father, a Normandy veteran who had died of cancer 8 years earlier, that someday she would go back to Normandy for him. She would see the beaches and visit the monuments and plant the flowers at the graves of his fallen comrades. "I'll never forget what you went through," she had told her father, "and, Dad, I'll always be proud." Well, reading her letter was one of the hardest speeches that I ever gave. But I'm sure you, of all people, understand. For many of you, even though your days of military service are receding, there are still reminders like that, poignant and piercing.

It's always been so for old soldiers. There's a story told about General Grant during the final weeks of his life. He had begun his last journey by train to upstate New York, and the newspapers were already filled with headlines, "Grant is dying." He was in a race against time, hoping to finish his memoirs and give his family back the financial security lost by those he had trusted too well.

And outside of Albany, coming around a bend, his train halted briefly. It was near a flagman's shanty. The flagman came out and looked up through the train window into the General's eyes. The flagman waved his arm. There was no hand. "General, I lost that with you in the Wilderness," the flagman said, "and I'd give the other one to see you well." Well, as Grant's wife and the doctor wept, the old General's lips tightened and his hand went up quickly as he took his hat off in a final salute to an old comrade.

Nimitz and Halsey, MacArthur, Bradley, Patton, Ike—they're all gone now. And boys who stormed the beaches for them at Normandy or Iwo are grandfathers now. Korea, too, fades into memory. And even Vietnam now belongs less to journalists or politicians than to scholars and historians.

In the book by Gene Smith, in which that story about General Grant is recounted, there's another story about an old soldier. His name was R.J. Burdette. And he returned years later to an old battlefield, one he had told his wife he could find stone-blind. But when he got there, there was grass and violets. It was May, and children were playing on what he recalled as a shell crater. And although in his memory, he wrote, there was still the day of "might and strength and terror, it was gone."

Well, I know you join me in a prayer today that for America such days and places are gone forever; that as much as we honor those who died to make us free, we also fervently hope that such sacrifice will never again have to be asked for, and that the day is not far off when there will be no new battlefields to visit and no old soldiers stories to hear.

Some will say that such hope is in vain, that the weight of history or human experience is against us. Well, I don't believe it's too much to hope that the years ahead will bring peace and freedom not just for the people of this kindly, pleasant, greening land called America, but for all mankind.

Thank you, and God bless you all.

Note: The President spoke at 11:12 a.m. at the Salt Palace. He was introduced by Keith Kruel, national commander of the American Legion.

Earlier in the day, the President met with local Republican leaders at the Little America Hotel. He then went to the Church of Jesus Christ of Latter-Day Saints, where he was greeted by Gordon B. Hinckley, the second counsellor in the first presidency of the church. The President then met with church officials in the First Presidency

Board Room in the Administration Building at the church.

Following his remarks at the convention, the President traveled to Chicago, IL.

Informal Exchange With Reporters on the Presidential Campaign
September 4, 1984

Q. Mr. President, what did you mean by that new spirit enveloping America? What did you mean by that?

The President. I think it's evident every place you go. Everyone is optimistic and everyone is gung-ho to go forward with the kind of expansion we're having. We've got 6 million new jobs in the country. We've got the fastest business expansion that we've had—600,000 new incorporations. Everybody's ready to go.

Q. Mr. President, have you laid the religious issue to rest? Some of your aides have said that with your statement today you are finished talking about religion on the campaign trail.

The President. Well, I was only talking about it because I was speaking at a prayer breakfast, and then what I said was greatly distorted. My concern was not with government invading religion, it's with all those people that are trying to make government turn around and interfere with people's right to practice religion.

Q. Who distorted that, Mr. President, and how was it distorted?

The President. I guess it lost something in the translation.

Q. You've had a campaign kickoff, and you haven't even mentioned Walter Mondale by name. Why not?

The President. Why should I? [*Laughter*]

Q. Thank you; you're wonderful.

Note: The exchange began at 4:40 p.m. upon the President's arrival at O'Hare International Airport in Chicago, IL. The President then went to the Hyatt Regency Hotel, where he remained overnight.

Remarks and a Question-and-Answer Session at the "Choosing a Future" Conference in Chicago, Illinois
September 5, 1984

The President. I'm honored to be here this morning with all of you very distinguished ladies and gentlemen. It was kind of good to fly in yesterday on Air Force One and see the city of the big shoulders again.

All my life, I've believed in miracles. I believe that if you truly have faith, your dream will come true. And now after 39 years of waiting, the miracle is happening. The Chicago Cubs are on their way to a National League pennant. [*Laughter*]

I have to tell you what that means to me personally. I was broadcasting the Cubs in 1935 when the only mathematical chance they had to win the pennant was to win the last 21 games of the season—[*laughter*]—and they did! [*Laughter*] And it still stands today as an unequaled record. When I'm in the presence of such greatness, how can I feel intimidated by a little challenge like running for President? [*Laughter*]

And if you share my belief that all things come together for good, then how can we not believe the success of the Cubs bodes well for our nation's heartland?

Permit me to commend AmeriTrust Corporation and its fine chairman, Jerry Jarrett, for your leadership in sponsoring "Choosing a Future" for mid-America. Your survey identifying the significant economic difficulties we know your region faces, as well as strategies for overcoming them, represents a far-reaching and impressive private sector economic development initiative.

"Choosing a Future" reflects the spirit of

partnership between government and industry essential to lasting industrial or economic growth in human progress. And it portrays a people with the realism to see clearly and the courage and confidence to go far.

When we talk about the great changes in America in recent years we often describe them in statistical ways, and I'll be guilty of that before I finish. But I think the most significant change, a good and hopeful one, has been the change in America's attitude—our renewed confidence and the higher value that we place on the truly important things in our lives.

Ben Franklin once said that, "When the well's dry, we know the worth of water." Well, 1980 marked such a moment for America. It was, in a sense, a great moment of truth; a time in our history when it seemed to many that America's well finally had run dry from a philosophy of bigger and bigger government. It was time to begin putting back what we had lost.

For half a century, we'd been giving government greater power over our lives. We did this with the best and most honorable of intentions. But by 1980 the full impact of distorting our economy, of draining spirit from the heart of our people, and of permitting our traditional values of faith, family, and work, neighborhood, and freedom to be undermined—all of this had come home to roost.

The worst trauma was not the breakdown in our economy or the humiliating setbacks that we suffered abroad. Being sick was bad, but the worst thing was when they told us we couldn't get well; that the problems were just too big, and government wasn't to blame, we were to blame.

Can you imagine what the fate of England would have been if before the Battle of Britain in World War II, the English had not heard those words: "We shall fight them on the beaches, we shall fight them in the streets," but, instead, had been told: It's no use, you suffer from a malaise?

Well, Americans didn't give up hope; we just hadn't been allowed to hope. And that's why in 1981 we said let's renew our faith and hope. We have every right to dream heroic dreams. Let us make a new begin-

ning with one revolutionary idea—freedom.

From day one, the driving force behind everything we've done in economic policy from reducing the growth of Federal spending, which soared over 17 percent in 1980 alone, to lowering tax rates and providing new incentives for business investment, to cutting back the jungle of regulations, to supporting stable monetary policies has been to put our future back in the people's hands, so working Americans could make America great again.

And somebody out there must be doing something right—21 straight months of economic growth, with the monster of inflation still locked in his cage. Today one industrial nation in the world has the strongest economic growth, 7.6 percent for the last quarter; inflation of only 4.1 percent for the last year; labor force participation at an all-time high; the fastest rate of job creation, 6½ million more people working in the last 19 months alone; a record 600,000 business incorporations last year; the fastest rate of business investment in 40 years; robust productivity gains; the largest increase in real, after-tax personal income since 1973; and leadership in developing jobs and markets for the future in science and high technology, both on Earth and in outer space. Well, I think you know the one nation I'm describing: Its initials are U.S.A.!

America is on the move again. But I repeat today what I said in 1981: Our challenge is to move America forward and to make sure that nobody gets left behind. One continuing challenge for the future must be to clear away the remaining roadblocks to economic growth without inflation, and do it for all Americans.

We do not believe, as some propose, that higher taxes on income, capital, and labor is the way to reduce budget deficits. That idea was bad policy before, and it's bad policy today. Entrepreneurs must not be discouraged; they must be encouraged.

So, we must move forward into the future with an historic simplification of the tax system, a tax system more fair and easier to understand, so we can bring everybody's income tax rates further down, not up. Strong economic growth will keep deficits coming down and, make no mistake, the deficit is coming down, and it would come down even faster if the Congress would give us a constitutional amendment mandating government spend no more than government takes in, and a line-item veto, so that a President could veto specific spending requests without vetoing an entire appropriations bill. [*Applause*] Well, bless you for that. I had it for 8 years as Governor of California, and I miss it. [*Laughter*]

Another reform could bring hope and opportunity to depressed neighborhoods in Chicago and pockets of despair throughout the Midwest. Imagine an abandoned ghetto with people working again in shops and firms and restaurants. Imagine their families living in more secure neighborhoods with less crime. Well, we can and will have this rebirth in America if the House of Representatives would just give us a vote on our enterprise zones proposal.

Less than a year ago, Spiegel, Inc., dropped the idea of moving to the Sun Belt and announced a $20 million renovation project on Chicago's South Side that preserves thousands of jobs and can lead to many more. They stayed because of a State-sponsored enterprise zone plan. With enactment of our enterprise zone legislation, there could be more and more such stories.

We understand, too, the challenges your agricultural and industrial regions face. We've tried to help you meet those challenges in a number of ways—by ending a totally unfair, wrongheaded grain embargo; by restoring grain sales to the Soviet Union—over 22 million metric tons since August of 1983; by reaching an agreement with Japan that will virtually double our beef exports over the next 4 years; by accepting an understanding with Japan permitting our auto industry to get back on its feet after the killer interest rates in 1980; by working aggressively for more open markets and by opposing protectionist legislation like "domestic content," which would revive inflation, provoke retaliation, and destroy American jobs and farm exports.

May I suggest that the most productive food growers in the world—the kind of leaders who once invented the assembly line, who manufacture our cars, and who have given us the hard-hat spirit and the expertise that made American business second to none—can outproduce, outcompete, outsell anybody, anytime, anywhere in the world.

We can and we must go forward, all of us together, building an economy that spurs the initiative and ingenuity to create sunrise industries and make older ones more competitive. To do this, we must meet the challenge of developing our next frontiers in science, technology, space, and education.

In my travels across this land, I've seen a vision of America's future too often ignored in Washington, an America unafraid, pushing back those frontiers with courage and leadership, becoming once again America unsurpassed. A new revolution is rising from the deepest yearnings of our nation's spirit to challenge the limits of knowledge and to put the power of discovery at the service of our most noble and generous impulses for decency, for progress and, yes, for peace.

I saw that in Decatur, Illinois—men and women not only processing corn and soybeans to produce food products that feed a hungry world but putting into practice breakthroughs in the field of hydroponics and pioneering work in ethanol to increase demand for farm products, create new jobs, and give greater energy security to our country. America's heartland is on the cutting edge of progress.

I saw us meeting that challenge on the assembly lines in Kansas City and Detroit, where investments to modernize and the introduction of robotics are helping the American automobile industry come back stronger than ever, and where engineers are using lightweight, super strong, plastic-like materials to reduce the weight of modern cars, and consumers are getting the benefits from more miles to the gallon.

I saw us meeting that challenge when the people at Goddard Space Flight Center showed us how practical applications of space and aeronautical technology are transforming our lives—from life-saving vests for firemen to sophisticated aerial scanning techniques to locate and identify everything from schools of fish to mineral deposits to agricultural resources.

I saw the vision of technology with a human face. Miraculous medical wonders like PIMS, the programmable implantable medication system, can administer medication automatically within the body. HTS, the human tissue simulator, can send electric impulses through wire leads to targeted nerve centers or areas of the brain, giving relief from pain.

Who could put a price tag on the value of these human benefits? Even more dazzling opportunities lie ahead, if only we have the faith and courage to keep pushing on. Each technological breakthrough enables us to work from a newer, higher plateau of knowledge, and each breakthrough opens the door to a new leap in productivity considered impossible only a few decades ago.

The great untold story of the technological revolution is the awesome potential for productivity power. If we meet the challenge of building a manned space station, for example, we can manufacture in 1 month's time life-saving medicines that would take 30 years to manufacture on Earth. We can manufacture crystals of exceptional purity that could enable us to produce larger, faster computers, the super computers, and achieve even greater productivity gains throughout our economy.

My friends, we can create a bounty of new opportunities, technologies, and improvements in the quality of life surpassing anything we've ever before dreamed or imagined. Our vision is not an impossible dream; it's a waking dream. If we cultivate the art of seeing things impossible, if we challenge the limits of growth, we'll have the strength and knowledge to make America a rocket of hope shooting to the stars.

I believe we will be the leaders in space because the American people would rather reach for the stars than reach for excuses why we shouldn't. And as our technology transforms the great, black night of space into a bright new world of opportunities, we can use that knowledge to create an American opportunity society here at home. We can ensure that every person has not only an equal chance, but a much greater chance to pursue the American dream.

I promise you we'll do our part. We'll support high tech, not high taxes. We'll constantly endeavor to strengthen the private economy, to support tax credits for incremental research and development, strive to lessen concerns that cooperative R&D ventures between companies may violate antitrust statutes, and continue our strong commitment to support basic research and development, particularly in universities, to train tomorrow's industrial scientists and academic scientists and engineers, and build our nation's intellectual capital.

You know, the more we look at our changing world, the more we see that the problems and challenges we face are interrelated. The American opportunity society will blossom from the progress of a growth economy. That progress will hinge on our ability to push back the frontiers of science, technology, and space. Meeting those challenges depends on education. And our success in education will depend on what kind of people we have in our schools, what values we absorb and bring forward into the future with us. The world of learning and the world of work must not only come into better harmony, they must strengthen and enrich each other.

So, our vision of education must be as forward-looking as our vision of the rest of American life: a school system that teaches our children how to enrich their lives using telecommunications as educational tools; that shows them how to educate themselves so they will be able to keep their skills current in an ever-changing job market; and that gives them an appreciation of the arts and humanities that give life meaning.

The sense of our boundless potential and the spirit of excellence are rising again in America. In every State in the Union in the past 3 years, there has been a resurgence of interest in our schools and a resurgence of commitment to excellence. SAT scores are turning up again, and the back-to-basics movement has proved itself not old-fashioned, but indispensable to progress. We've come far in just a few years, but it isn't enough. We've got to do more and we will.

In the past few decades, many of us turned away from the enduring values, from faith, the work ethic, and the central importance of the family. We had something of a hedonistic heyday. But it's passing. We've righted ourselves, and across the country there's a rebirth of the traditional values that guided our fathers and mothers and guided our nation. We affirm this trend, not to return to some mythical past, but to build on proven strengths for a creative future.

There's another challenge for us to think about. In the history of our nation we've had problems with ill-spirited divisiveness— one race thinking it was better than another, one generation thinking it was superior to another. We've had religious divisions. We've had our share of bigotry. We've had tensions between this class or this group and that. And one of the good changes of recent years is that we've outgrown a lot of that nonsense. But we must commit ourselves to doing better. We are and must remain a pluralistic society, but we're also one nation together. We're brothers and sisters equal in the eyes of God and equal under the law.

No one group in this country is better than another. No one race or religion or sex or color is better than another. And no region is better or worse than another. It's time we erased the last vestiges of intolerance, bigotry, and unkindness from our hearts. Decency demands this and so does our history.

There's a final challenge. It may seem remote from issues of regional economic development, but it's a most fundamental challenge, for if we ever failed to meet it, the value of our economic progress and our spiritual progress, too, would be lost. It's the challenge to maintain peace in the world, peace with our neighbors and our allies and our adversaries. I think you well know my feelings on this; they've been shared by most American Presidents down through our history. Simply stated: If we're strong, we will discourage those who would disrupt peace. If we maintain our strength, we will maintain peace, and there is no threat to the world in this.

America has always been a peaceable country. We've never loved war. We're the least warlike powerful nation in the history of the world. We can be trusted with the military power that is our responsibility to hold. We maintain it only for the good, never for territorial gain or imperialist desires. We work for peace by staying strong, so that we may be a nation at peace with ourselves and at peace with the world.

If we keep these things in mind, if we retain our economic strength, help our children, strengthen the bonds that keep us together, and work for peace, then the well will not run dry again. We will have replenished it—and more. We'll move forward. The future will be bright and shining; our nation will continue to be what it's always been—a place of refuge for those who come from places that are not free and not fair, a place of great hope and endless possibilities.

Winston Churchill surveyed the Western World, and he said, "We have not journeyed all this way across the centuries, across the oceans, across the mountains, across the prairies, because we're made of sugar candy." Well, like many of you, I share his spirit. We can do anything when we set our minds to it.

The dream of America is much more than who we are or what we do; the dream is what we will be. We must always be the New World, the world of discovery, the world that reveres the great truths of its past but that pushes on with unending faith toward the promise of the future. In my heart, I know we have that faith. The dream lives on. America will remain future's child, the golden hope of all mankind.

Thank you for welcoming us here today. And thank you for all that you give us. And thank you for your courage to dream great dreams. God bless you all.

Mr. Thomas. As I indicated earlier, President Reagan has indicated that he'd be willing to take a few questions from our audience. We have collected your cards. Our committee has reviewed them and tried to distill the essence of them into a few succinct questions which I have. So, I'll ask the President to come back to the podium at this time, and I'll address those questions to him.

Mr. President, looking over the questions, this audience is very concerned about four things, I would say in this order—the federal deficit, interest rates, our international competitive position, and the Chicago Cubs. Now, you've already dealt with the last one—[*laughter*]—so we'll get on with the others.

And the first one deals with our Midwest economy. We had an excellent panel discussion this morning, and I think we all would agree we have challenges and opportunities here. But one of our very significant problems in the Midwest is the very substantial net outflow of tax dollars to other, faster-growing regions of this country. Now, what might you suggest that we do to reverse this trend, if you have any thoughts on that particular subject?

The President. Federal tax dollars going——

Mr. Thomas. Federal tax dollars going from the Midwest to other parts of this country. Substantial net deficit—or net outflow.

The President. Well, we have been trying a thing that we call federalism, and we've run into some of the same kind of opposition we've written on some of the—or we've run into on some of the other things we tried. One of the things that we would like to see more of is block grants, where that's all that we can resort to, instead of the Federal Government dictating and spending the money.

It's true that there are, oh, probably someplace between a dozen and 20 States that are considered to be the rich ones, and they must help support the others. What we would like to do, even rather than block grants, and what we have not done as much of as we would like, and that is to wherever possible turn back to the States and local communities tax sources that presently are held by the Federal Government, and turn back with them the responsibility for functions that properly should be administered at State and local level that the Federal Government is not as well equipped to perform as they are.

And I think in this way there would be some help with what you're saying. I know it has to seem unfair when you're in one of those States. Recently, some years ago, when New York was having its great problems with bankruptcy, I thought at the time that it was pretty ironic that New York was considered way up at the top of the list as one of the States that could afford to help out the other States.

Mr. Thomas. Thank you. Next question: Given your position on personal income taxes, what do you propose to do to tackle the deficit?

The President. Well, I know that I'm accused of not being very specific on this. I think we've been more specific than almost any administration that I can remember, if you will look at the program that we started to implement when we first came here.

Now, what we're going to continue to do are two things in attacking the deficits. One of them is look at the deficit as being partly structural and partly the result of the economic slump. Now, as you bring back the economy and it expands, even at the lower tax rates that we put in as an incentive to help bring back the economy, your revenues grow. They don't shrink. So, we are reducing the deficit right now. The one for this year will probably be some 20-odd billion dollars less than we had estimated ourselves that it was going to be, simply because of the economic recovery. That is one thing.

The other thing is reducing government spending. I still think that a federal government has a higher overhead than is necessary. We haven't made all the gains that we wanted. As a matter of fact, had we gotten all that we asked for in our first submission of our program, the deficit would be between $40 billion and $50 billion less right now.

But we see the deficit as one in which, as the economy improves—and that brings up revenues without increasing the actual rates on the individual—and if, at the same time, we can continue—we have 2,478 specific recommendations by the Grace commission, where they came in and looked at all of government and made recommendations, as businessmen and women, as to where government could be run more like a productive business—we have a team looking at those. We have already implemented by administrative decree some 17 percent of those.

Now, as we bring government costs down, the share that government is taking from the private sector, and as the recovery brings income up, there must be a point out here at which those two will meet. Now, if they don't—and this is what I mean by those today who are saying that the first resort is increased taxes. We say it is the last resort. If you come to a point where you've done all you can do with regard to economic recovery, and the revenues fall short of that line, and you've done all you can do to bring government down to be as efficient and economical as it should be and still perform the services that we can expect of government and those two are apart, then you have to look at your tax system to bridge that difference.

But today, to suggest a tax increase simply for the cure of the deficit—we've had any number of tax increases over the last 50 years, and we have had regularly deficits every year for 50 years, every year since World War II. Well, we had them during the war, but that's the kind of deficit we could expect, and then you'd pay off in the years following the war. But in the 5 years before we came here to office, the taxes doubled in those 5 years and the deficits increased.

The deficit we have to face is an effect, not a cause. The cause is when government takes too big a percentage from the private sector, you're going to have economic troubles. Government is going to become a drag on the economy. And this is what we're trying to cure.

Mr. Thomas. Thank you, Mr. President. Next question: What changes do you foresee in the administration's stance with respect to protectionism if reelected? Specifically, do you favor import restrictions to help our steel industry, keeping in mind on the one hand that imports account for about 25 or 30 percent of total usage in this country while, on the other hand, our midwestern manufacturers must be able to buy steel at world prices in order to be competitive. It's an easy question, sir. [*Laughter*]

The President. Well, it isn't easy. We do know that sometimes—and our law provides for this—that sometimes there are emergency situations in which an industry has suffered unfairly, and temporarily you can give that industry some help to get it back on its feet.

Basically, however, I think we have to be opposed in principle to protectionism because it's a two-way street. Having looked for my first job in the depths of the Great Depression—graduating in 1932—I, looking back, have some idea of what the Smoot-Hawley tariff bill did to the Depression worldwide. And I think that free trade is the best answer. But free trade must also be fair trade. And what you have recited there is that many times the protectionism can help heal a particular segment, but no one pays any attention to the disaster or the depression that is created over here in other areas.

And this is true in some places where fabricators find themselves at odds with the mineral producers. Now we're studying this very carefully, because it is true, free trade must be fair trade. And it is true that in some instances the competition is unfair, that things like steel had been sent into this country that are subsidized by a foreign government and are selling below their cost of production, which our people can't do. And there we have rules and have invoked them in these 3½ years at times to prevent that. And we'll continue to do that.

Mr. Thomas. Next question: Is there a real possibility that the line-item veto that you mentioned in your address will be approved in your next term?

The President. Oh, we're going to fight hard for that, and we need all your help and support.

I said yesterday out in Salt Lake City, we need, in Washington, your input to some of the people there who balk at some of these progressive measures. It isn't necessary to make them see the light, you must make them feel the heat. [*Laughter*]

I'm going to look down here at the end where Jim is.

Jim, do you have line-item veto?

Governor Thompson. Yes, sir.

The President. See? Forty-three States. I had it as Governor of California, and I inherited a situation out there where, in spite of a constitutional provision that we could not have a deficit, I walked into office in the middle of the fiscal year and we already had a deficit.

The line-item veto—I invoked it more than 900 times in those 8 years, and we didn't have an unbalanced budget very long. We solved that problem. It's absolutely necessary; it's the most vital tool.

Now, the Congress has the right to overcome that veto, to override it, if they feel strongly enough to do it. You know, in all of my more than 900 vetoes, the legislature that had passed the bills to begin with never once overrode one of those vetoes. They never once dared stand up and publicly vote for that single item that they had agreed to put into another bill.

So, please write letters, send wires, twist arms. We need the line-item veto, and we're going to try for it, all out.

Mr. Thomas. We have one last question. This is a little different thrust, but very important, nevertheless. Affirmative action and job training have been of great assistance to minorities. Since your administration has reduced the impact of these programs, what do you propose to do to replace them?

The President. What we are opposed to is not affirmative action so much as a quota system. And having grown up, as I did, in a time when there were prejudices of all kinds, you find that the quota can be used, actually, as an instrument of discrimination, not to cure it. We have in place today throughout the country a job training program that we believe encompasses the proper ideas, and that is that as a team between the Federal Government, local authorities, and local businesses to train people in those areas for the jobs that are available in those areas.

The Federal Government in the past, with many of its job training programs, they really were just make-work programs. They didn't train anyone, really, for a specific job, and there was no relationship between the area where the training was taking place and the residence of the people and whether there were jobs once they were trained, that there would be jobs in those areas. Now, this program of ours—incidentally, the CETA program, only about 18 cents out of each dollar actually went into job training in that program. That's why we don't have it anymore. In this program, over 70 cents of every dollar is being spent on actual job training, and already we're seeing

tens of thousands of people going through that program and almost immediately out into productive jobs.

Now, I know that there's been a lot of criticism that somehow I am opposed to civil rights. My mother and father would come back and jump on my back if I ever did. I was raised to believe that there's no sin greater than prejudice or bigotry. And I grew up that way. In fact, back in those days, broadcasting the Cubs and all, I was one of the handful of sports commentators throughout the country that was even then campaigning for an elimination of the rules that had kept minorities out of organized baseball, and, finally, there was triumph in that.

I was fighting for civil rights before they called it civil rights. And so any translation of this criticism of the management of some of the affirmative action programs in an attempt to make that look as if I'm not supportive of the elimination—the goal in this country must be, and we haven't completely reached it yet, but it must be the day will come when whatever is done to someone, or for someone, is neither because of nor in spite of any difference in race or religion.

Mr. Thomas. I was given the signal that that was the last one.

The President. Thank you all very much. They tell me that I have to leave now; I'm due back in Washington. There's a Senator down there that knows that's because today the Congress is coming back, and I can't leave them there by themselves. [*Laughter*]

So, thank you all. This has been a great pleasure.

Note: The President spoke at 9:39 a.m. in the Grand Ballroom of the Hyatt Regency Hotel. He was introduced by Richard Thomas, president of the Economic Club of Chicago, the sponsor of the conference.

Earlier in the day, the President met at the hotel with local Republican leaders. Following his remarks, the President returned to Washington, DC.

Nomination of Linda M. Combs To Be a Deputy Under Secretary of Education
September 5, 1984

The President today announced his intention to nominate Linda M. Combs to be Deputy Under Secretary for Management, Department of Education. She would succeed Charles L. Heatherly.

Mrs. Combs is currently Executive Secretary at the Department of Education. Previously, she was Deputy Executive Secretary, Department of Education (1982); manager for national director, student loan operations, Wachovia Educational Services, Inc. (1980–1982); and was a schoolteacher in Winston-Salem County, NC (1968–1979).

Mrs. Combs graduated from Appalachian State University (B.S., 1968; M.A., 1978). She is married and resides in Arlington, VA. She was born June 29, 1946, in Lenoir, NC.

Nomination of Vilma Rosso Taracido To Be Assayer of the New York Assay Office
September 5, 1984

The President today announced his intention to nominate Vilma Rosso Taracido to be Assayer of the United States Assay Office at New York, NY. She would succeed Saul Silverman.

Mrs. Taracido served as a senior research assistant at the Sloan Kettering Institute for Cancer Research in 1972–1983. Previously, she was a quality control supervisor, Travenol Laboratories (1967); research technician, National Institutes of Health Laboratory of Perinatal Physiology (1965); and quality control technician, Western Fehr (1964).

Mrs. Taracido graduated with a bachelor of science degree from Catholic University of Puerto Rico. She is married, has three children, and resides in New Rochelle, NY. She was born August 26, 1941, in Ponce, PR.

Nomination of Mary L. Azcuenaga To Be a Commissioner of the Federal Trade Commission
September 5, 1984

The President today announced his intention to nominate Mary L. Azcuenaga to be a Federal Trade Commissioner for the term of 7 years from September 26, 1984. She would succeed Michael Pertschuk.

Mrs. Azcuenaga is currently Assistant General Counsel for Legal Counsel in the Office of the General Counsel at the Federal Trade Commission. Previously, she was a litigation attorney, Office of General Counsel, FTC (1982); assistant to the Executive Director, FTC (1981–1982); Assistant Regional Director, San Francisco regional office, FTC (1977–1980); and assistant to the General Counsel, FTC (1975–1976).

Mrs. Azcuenaga graduated from Stanford University (A.B., 1967) and the University of Chicago Law School (J.D., 1973). She is married and resides in Washington, DC. She was born July 25, 1945, in Council, ID.

Remarks at the International Convention of B'nai B'rith
September 6, 1984

Thank you. Max Fisher, if I'd be really smart, I'd just sit down and leave your introduction do it, and I wouldn't speak. I thank you very much. He's a longtime friend.

And I thank all of you. It's a deep honor for me to speak to you, the members of one of the oldest and largest Jewish organizations in America. For more than 140 years, B'nai B'rith has sponsored religious, cultural, and civic programs, conducted studies of vital issues, combated bigotry, and worked tirelessly to advance the cause of tolerance and humanity. And because of your efforts, today our country has a bigger heart, a deeper sense of the generosity of spirit that must always define America. And on behalf of all Americans, I thank you.

Four years ago, as a private citizen, I argued that the strength and well-being of the United States and Israel are bound inextricably together. "No policy," I asserted, "no matter how heartfelt, no matter how deeply rooted in the humanitarian vision we share, can succeed if the United States of America continues its descent into economic impotence and despair."

Well, today, as President, I come before you to report on the progress that we've made together during these past 4 years. Once again, I want to talk about American policy toward Israel—today's new policy of deepened friendship and strengthened support. But first, permit me to share with you my view of how working together the American people have replaced our own nation's descent into impotence and despair with the rebirth of freedom, prosperity, and hope.

Four years ago, we saw the first years of back-to-back, double-digit inflation since World War I. The prime interest rate was rising sharply, and in December 1980 it reached a point not seen since the Civil War. In just 4 years, taxes roughly doubled, and average monthly mortgage payments more than doubled, and the real after-tax income of the average American actually began to decline. It all added up to the worst economic crisis our country had faced since the Great Depression.

In foreign affairs we had lost the respect of friend and foe alike, and our willpower had grown weak and soft, undermining commitments to allies like Israel. Our leaders seemed to have lost faith in the American people and in America's future. They spoke of a national malaise. On television, we saw the Stars and Stripes being burned in foreign capitals. And from Afghanistan to Grenada, the Soviets were on the march. Seldom in all its proud history had the United States of America reached such a pathetic state of apparent impotence.

Well, today, just 4 years later, we're seeing not humiliation but well-justified pride—pride in our country, our accomplishments, and ourselves. On the economic front, from New York Harbor to San Diego Bay, a vast and vigorous economic expansion is taking place. Inflation has plummeted to just 4 percent, and the prime interest rate has fallen by almost 9 points.

Productivity is up, consumer spending is up, housing starts are up, and take-home pay is up. Our tax rate reductions have restored incentives to the American people, and when tax indexing goes into effect this January, they'll get more help in the form of long overdue protection against the unfairness of bracket creep.

The best news of all: During the past 19 months, 6½ million men and women have found jobs that we've created—on an average, each month, more jobs than all the Common Market countries combined created in the last 10 years. Europe is calling our success the American miracle.

Well, as we've worked to promote economic growth we've made certain that the safety net for the truly needy has remained in place. Indeed, after correcting for inflation, under our administration average food stamp payments, medicare payments, medicaid payments, have all risen. We can and are promoting economic vitality, while showing the disadvantaged genuine compassion.

On civil rights, we have enforced the law with new determination. The Justice Department, since we took office, has filed more criminal charges on civil rights violations, brought more violators to trial, and achieved more civil rights convictions than ever before. So, let no one doubt our commitment. As President, I will enforce civil rights to the fullest extent of the law.

Yet, at the same time, we remain unalterably opposed to an idea that would undermine the very concept of equality itself—discriminatory quotas. Ours is a nation based on the sacredness of the individual, a nation where all women and men must be judged on their own merit, imagination, and effort; not on what they are, but on what they do. Now, you know, I can remember a time—I'm old enough to remember a time—when America did have quotas, and they were used in an attempt to make discrimination legitimate and permanent, keeping Jews and other targets of bigotry out of colleges, medical schools, and jobs. And I can't state it too forcefully: This type of thing must never happen again.

To combat crime, our administration has increased the law enforcement budget by more than 20 percent, established 12 regional drug task forces around the country, and hired more than 1,900 new investigators and prosecutors. We've also reasserted some very basic values—values that say there *is* such a thing as right and wrong, that the innocent victim is entitled to as much protection under the law as the accused, that individual actions do matter, and that, yes, for hardened criminals preying on our society, punishment must be certain and swift.

And now that we're getting back to these fundamentals of our Judeo-Christian tradition, the will of the people is at last being done. In 1982 reported crime dropped 3 percent—the first decline since 1977. And last year reported crime dropped 7 percent, and this is the first time the serious crime index has ever shown a drop for the second year in a row, and the sharpest decline in crime statistics since 1960.

In the Armed Forces, our troops have newer and better equipment, and their morale has soared as we've begun to give them the pay, the training, and the respect they've always deserved. And in foreign affairs, our country is being respected again throughout the world as a leader for peace and freedom. We've strengthened our relations with Asian allies like Korea and Japan, deepened our friendship with China. In Europe, we and our NATO allies went through months of Soviet attempts to divide us and emerged more firmly united than ever. And in Central America, we're supporting the free nations of the region against the threat posed to them by the Sandinista regime in Nicaragua.

In July of 1983 it was my privilege to meet a brave refugee from Nicaragua, Isaac Stavisky. He told me about the 50 Jewish families who had emigrated to Nicaragua from Eastern Europe since the 1920's, and about the tragedy that befell them. But let me read you Isaac's own words:

"Nicaraguan Jews never encountered anti-Semitism until the Sandinistas started their revolution . . . Graffiti by Sandinistas was widespread, with attacks on Jews and their religion. One was, 'Death to the Jewish pigs.' In 1978 the Sandinistas sent a strong message to the entire community when the synagogue was attacked by five Sandinistas wearing face handkerchiefs. They set the building on fire by throwing gasoline in the main entrance doors, shouting PLO victory slogans and anti-Jewish defamatory language . . . Once the Sandinistas came to power . . . they moved swiftly against Jews. Jewish-owned properties were among the first to be confiscated and Jews were forced into exile."

Permit me to add that on the first anniversary of the Sandinista revolution, Yasser Arafat visited Nicaragua and spoke these words: "What the Nicaraguan people did in Nicaragua will be done by the Palestinians."

Well, today some in our national life would have America take a position of weakness in Central America or, through callous indifference, withdraw from that region altogether. These politicians would give free reign to Marxist-Leninists who would persecute Central American Catholics and Jews, leaving them defenseless against Sandinista intolerance.

We stand foursquare on the side of human liberty. And I pledge to you that we will maintain that stand as long as I am in this office.

Anyone who has contemplated the horror inflicted on Jews during World War II, the deaths of millions in Cambodia, or the travail of the Mesquito Indians in Nicaragua must understand that if free men and women remain silent in the face of oppression we risk the destruction of entire peoples. I know that B'nai B'rith has been among the most concerned of the groups advocating American support for the Genocide Convention. With a cautious view, in part due to the human rights abuses performed by some nations that have already ratified the documents, our administration has conducted a long and exhaustive study of the convention. And yesterday, as a result of that review, we announced that we will vigorously support, consistent with the United States Constitution, the ratification of the Genocide Convention. And I want you to know that we intend to use the convention in our efforts to expand human freedom and fight human rights abuses around the world. Like you, I say in a forthright voice, "Never again!"

Now, there's one final aspect of our national renewal that I must mention: the return that millions of Americans are making to faith—faith as a source of strength, comfort, and meaning.

This new spiritual awareness extends to people of all religions and all beliefs. Irving Kristol has written, "the quest for a religious identity is, in the postwar world, a general phenomenon, experienced by Jews, Christians, and Muslims alike. It does not seem, moreover, to be a passing phenomenon, but rather derives from an authentic crisis—a moral and spiritual crisis as well as a crisis in Western, liberal-secular thought."

In our country, Kristol asserts, "Ever since the Holocaust and the emergence of the state of Israel, American Jews have been reaching toward a more explicit and meaningful Jewish identity." And according to Rabbi Seymour Siegel of the Jewish Theological Seminary, this trend among American Jews is illustrated by a growing interest in Jewish history and the Hebrew language, and by the rise of—and I hope I get this right—Baal Teshuva movement—a powerful movement of Jews, young and old,

Orthodox, Conservative, and Reformed, returning to the ancient ways of the faith.

As Americans of different religions find new meaningfulness in their beliefs, we do so together, returning together to the bedrock values of family, hard work, and faith in the same loving and almighty God. And as we welcome this rebirth of faith, we must even more fervently attack ugly intolerance. We have no place for haters in America.

Well, let me speak plainly: The United States of America is and must remain a nation of openness to people of all beliefs. Our very unity has been strengthened by this pluralism. That's how we began; this is how we must always be. The ideals of our country leave no room whatsoever for intolerance, anti-Semitism, or bigotry of any kind—none. The unique thing about America is a wall in our Constitution separating church and state. It guarantees there will never be a state religion in this land, but at the same time it makes sure that every single American is free to choose and practice his or her religious beliefs or to choose no religion at all. Their rights shall not be questioned or violated by the state.

During the dark days of World War II, legend has it, an event took place that I believe is a timeless symbol of regard for our fellow men that true tolerance and brotherhood demand. Soon after the Nazis invaded Denmark in 1940, they published an edict that all Jews identify themselves by wearing an armband showing the Star of David. Well, the next day the Christian King of Denmark appeared in public. He was wearing a Star of David. I was told on my one visit to Denmark there, that after he had done that every citizen of Denmark, from then on, appeared in the streets wearing the Star of David.

We in America have learned the lesson of the Holocaust; we shall never allow it to be forgotten. Oppression will never extinguish the instinct of good people to do the right thing.

In America, Jew, Christian, Muslim, believers of all kinds, and nonbelievers, too— as George Washington wrote to a Jewish congregation in Rhode Island—each "shall sit in safety under his own vine and fig-tree, and there shall be none to make him afraid."

A renewal of faith and confidence, a resurgent economy, a rebirth of strength and purposefulness in our foreign relations—yes, we Americans *have* made a new beginning, just as 4 years ago I said that we must. And this new beginning is good not only for us but for our allies. And now, it is to our relations with Israel that I would like to turn.

The first step in understanding American-Israeli relations is to recognize our common values, aspirations, and interests. This has fundamental consequences for our diplomacy in an environment of widespread hostility to Israel. Nowhere does this hostility appear more clearly than in that international institution that should be a citadel of good will, but that all too often becomes a platform for propaganda—the United Nations. From the 1970's on, the United Nations has too often allowed itself to become a forum for the defamation of Israel.

In 1975, for example, the United Nations Third Committee proposed an anti-Semitic resolution that condemned Israel as racist. The American delegate, Leonard Garment, objected forceably, arguing that the resolution used the word racist not as a term for "a very real and concrete set of injustices, but merely an epithet to be flung at whoever happens to be one's adversary." Those were his words.

Nevertheless, the resolution passed by 70 votes to 29, with 27 abstentions. The resolution then went to the United Nations General Assembly which ratified it by a vote of 72 to 35. The words that our Ambassador to the United Nations, Daniel Patrick Moynihan, spoke at that moment of shame were forthright and courageous. "The United States rises to declare before the world that it does not acknowledge, it will not abide by, and it will never acquiesce in this infamous act."

Well, sadly, in the years thereafter the United States did not always give Israel such steadfast support. American policy toward Israel was often weak and muddled. It reached a low point on March 1, 1980. That day the American delegate to the United Nations actually voted in favor of a resolution that repeatedly condemned

Israel. Some 48 hours later, President Carter disavowed the vote and announced to the press that it had all been a mistake— a bad mistake. And it certainly had.

Well, since taking office our administration has used every effort to reaffirm before the world our unwavering support for the State of Israel. And in the United Nations, our stand has been made unmistakable by our Ambassador and your good friend, Jeane Kirkpatrick. Just 3 weeks ago at the United Nations Population Conference in Mexico City, we joined Israel in opposing and voting against a resolution that attacked the State of Israel. And let me make it plain to the friends and enemies of Israel alike that what Max Fisher just told you is absolutely true and still the policy of this Government, and that if ever expelled, yes, Max, and all of you, we walk out together with Israel.

In concrete terms, our administration has strengthened the American-Israeli alliance in three crucial ways. First, we have upgraded and formalized our strategic cooperation. For the first time in history, under our administration, the United States and Israel have agreed on a formal strategic relationship. The American-Israeli Joint Political-Military Group has already begun regular meetings. Together, we're developing plans for joint efforts to counter the Soviet threat to our mutual interests in the Middle East.

Recently, we renewed an American-Israeli memorandum of agreement that provides for cooperation in military research and development, procurement, and logistics. Under the terms of the agreement, the United States has already purchased Israeli-manufactured radios, remotely piloted vehicles, antitank weapons, and components for sophisticated aircraft. We, in turn, are making available the latest technology for the development of the Israeli-designed LAVI fighter aircraft and for a new class of missile attack boat, the SAAR 5.

Second, we've markedly increased our economic assistance to Israel. From 1981 to 1984, we provided Israel with aid amounting to nearly $9½ billion, more than has been provided by any previous administration over a comparable time. Just as important, we have restructured the form of our assistance. Indeed, in 1985 our entire $2.6 billion in aid to Israel will take the form not of loans, but of grants.

And third, we have begun formal negotiations with Israel for a free trade area agreement. When signed and ratified, this agreement will allow the duty-free entry of Israeli products into the United States and will at the same time completely open the Israeli market to American goods. Over the past 5 years, our trade with Israel has been growing at an average annual rate of some 10 percent. This free trade agreement will enable that vital economic partnership to grow even more quickly in years to come.

These measures have made our relations with Israel closer and our friendship stronger than at any time in the history of our two nations. Indeed, Prime Minister Shamir recently described American-Israeli relations as having never been better. And that warm relationship is crucial as we strive together for peace in the Middle East. So, let me outline our work in this regard.

America's peace efforts still stand on the foundation of the Camp David accords. Those accords, which established peaceful relations between Israel and Egypt, led to the return of the Sinai to Egypt by Israel in April of 1982, and the United States was proud to play a central role in achieving this step of the Camp David process. Then on September 1st of 1982, I set forth a set of fair and balanced positions on the key issues—issues which the negotiating parties must deal with to achieve a lasting peace. The positions I outlined included our firm opposition to the formation of any independent Palestinian state. Today those positions remain fully valid, and they represent the foundation of our continuing labors.

And let me assure you, we will never attempt to impose a solution on Israel, nor will we ever weaken in our opposition to terrorism by the PLO or by anybody else. As I said when I addressed you in 1980, terrorists are not guerillas or commandos or freedom fighters or anything else. They're

terrorists, and should be identified as such. We will go on working with all our hearts to help the people of the Middle East achieve a just and lasting settlement—a settlement that agrees, in the words of my statement of September 1982, that Israel "has a right to exist in peace behind secure and defensible borders, and it has a right to expect its neighbors to recognize this."

When I spoke to you 4 years ago, peace was eluding the Middle East. It still does. But now we and the State of Israel have far greater cause for hope.

Today the United States is rebuilding its defenses, and that is restoring confidence in our leadership and making the parties more willing to take risks for peace. Today the United States has re-energized its vast and productive economy, and that will help to make Israel more prosperous. And today the United States has stopped wringing its hands apologetically and once again begun to play its rightful role in the world with faith, confidence, and courage. And that means Israel can depend on us.

We who are friends of Israel may differ over tactics, but our goal remains always unchanged—permanent security for the people of that brave State. In this great enterprise, the United States and Israel stand forever united. And as we approach the Jewish holiday of Rosh Hashanah, let us pray that the new year will be a *Shanah Tovah Umetukah*—a good and sweet year for both America and Israel.

For make no mistake: In a world where so many are hostile to freedom, where millions live in poverty and oppression, those few nations who share the light of liberty must stand together. If we do not, we take the awful chance that the darkness will overwhelm us one by one. But standing together, we can pierce the darkness and shed our light over all the Earth.

Thank you. God bless you all.

Note: The President spoke at 11:33 a.m. in the Sheraton Ballroom at the Sheraton Washington Hotel.

Message to the Congress Transmitting a Report on Exclusions From the Merit Pay System
September 6, 1984

To the Congress of the United States:

Supervisors and management officials in GS–13, 14, and 15 positions throughout the Federal Government are covered by the Merit Pay System as required by Chapter 54, Title 5, U.S. Code, unless otherwise excluded by law.

Upon proper application from the heads of affected agencies and upon the recommendation of the Director of the Office of Personnel Management, I have, pursuant to 5 U.S.C. 5401(b)(2)(B), excluded two agencies from coverage under the Merit Pay System. In addition, one agency previously excluded because of emergency conditions will no longer be excluded.

Attached is my report describing the agencies to be excluded and the reasons therefor.

RONALD REAGAN

The White House,
September 6, 1984.

Note: The exclusions affect employees of the Office of Administration, Executive Office of the President, and the Office of the Federal Inspector for the Alaska Natural Gas Transportation System. The Federal Aviation Administration in the Department of Transportation is no longer excluded from coverage.

Message to the Congress Reporting a Budget Deferral
September 6, 1984

To the Congress of the United States:

In accordance with the Impoundment Control Act of 1974, I herewith report one revised deferral of budget authority which now totals $331,964,058. The deferral affects the Department of Energy.

The details of the deferral are contained in the attached report.

RONALD REAGAN

The White House,
September 6, 1984.

Note: The attachment detailing the deferral is printed in the Federal Register *of September 13.*

Appointment of Three Members of Emergency Board No. 204 To Investigate a Railroad Labor Dispute
September 6, 1984

The President today appointed the members of Emergency Board No. 204, created by Executive Order No. 12486 of August 24, 1984, effective August 25, 1984. This Emergency Board will investigate a dispute between the Port Authority Trans-Hudson

Corporation and the Brotherhood of Railroad Signalmen representing employees of the Port Authority Trans-Hudson Corporation.

Robert E. Peterson, of Briarcliff Manor, NY, will serve as Chairman. He is an arbitrator who has served as chairman and neutral member of over 70 boards of adjustment. He has held various positions in personnel and labor relations for the Long Island, New York, and Pennsylvania railroad systems. He was born December 5, 1929, in Bronxville, NY.

Daniel G. Collins, of Amagansett, NY, has been a professor of law at the New York University School of Law since 1961. He is also an impartial member of the New York Office of Collec-

tive Bargaining. He was born March 29, 1930, in Brooklyn, NY.

Herbert L. Marx, Jr., of New York, NY, serves as a permanent arbitrator to the United States Postal Service and postal unions for the northeast region. He is also a member of the Office of Collective Bargaining for the city of New York. He was born February 1, 1922, in New York City.

Memorandum on the Delegation of Authority for Reports to Congress on El Salvador
September 6, 1984

Memorandum for the Secretary of State

Subject: Delegation of Authority for Report Containing a Determination Concerning El Salvador

By authority vested in me as President by the Constitution and statutes of the United States of America, including Section 621 of the Foreign Assistance Act of 1961, as amended, and Section 301 of Title 3 of the United States Code, I hereby delegate to you the functions conferred upon me by Public Law 98–396 (Second Supplemental

Appropriations Act, 1984) in the "General Provisions" of Chapter XII, insofar as they relate to El Salvador.

This memorandum shall be published in the *Federal Register.*

RONALD REAGAN

[Filed with the Office of the Federal Register, 4:01 p.m., September 18, 1984]
Note: The memorandum is printed in the Federal Register *of September 18.*

Memorandum on the Denial of Import Relief for the Copper Industry
September 6, 1984

Memorandum for the United States Trade Representative

Subject: Copper Import Relief Determination

Pursuant to Section 202(b)(1) of the Trade Act of 1974 (P.L. 93–618), I have determined the action I will take with respect to the report of the United States International Trade Commission (USITC), transmitted to me on July 16 concerning the results of its investigation, on the merits of providing import relief to the copper industry.

In view of all relevant aspects of this case, I have determined that granting import

relief is not consistent with our national economic interest. The imposition of import restrictions—either in the form of quotas, tariffs, or orderly marketing agreements—would create a differential between U.S. and world copper prices. Consequently, it would seriously disadvantage the copper-fabricating industry in the United States, which employed an estimated 106,000 workers in 1983, vis-a-vis foreign competitors. Such a result would, over time, shrink domestic demand for copper and add to the serioius problems faced by U.S. copper producers.

Import relief would also adversely affect the export earnings of the foreign copper-producing countries, many of which are heavily indebted and highly dependent on copper exports. It would, therefore, complicate our efforts to maintain the stability of the international financial system and lessen the ability of foreign countries to import goods from the United States. Finally, there are encouraging signs that the economic recovery is beginning to have a favorable effect on world copper prices; stocks have fallen considerably this year and a significant price increase is expected in the near future. The denial of import relief on copper should act as a signal and as encouragement to our partners around the world to resist protectionist acts and, thus, will foster that recovery.

In order to help ease the difficult problems now faced by many workers in the U.S. copper industry, I have directed the Secretary of Labor to work with State and local officials to develop a plan of job retraining and relocation assistance for workers in affected industries. In addition, I have directed the Secretary of Commerce to actively monitor the domestic copper industry including inventories and the levels of copper imports.

RONALD REAGAN

[*Filed with the Office of the Federal Register, 2:45 p.m., September 7, 1984*]

Note: The memorandum is printed in the Federal Register *of September 11.*

Letter to the Speaker of the House and the President of the Senate on the Denial of Import Relief for the Copper Industry
September 6, 1984

Dear Mr. Speaker: (Dear Mr. President:)

In accordance with Section 203(b)(2) of the Trade Act of 1974, I am writing to inform you of my decision today not to grant import relief to the copper industry.

In view of all relevent aspects of this case, I have determined that granting import relief is not consistent with our national economic interest. The imposition of import restrictions—either in the form of quotas, tariffs, or orderly marketing agreements—would create a differential between U.S. and world copper prices. Consequently, it would seriously disadvantage the copper-fabricating industry in the United States, which employed an estimated 106,000 workers in 1983, vis-a-vis foreign competitors. Such a result would, over time, shrink domestic demand for copper and add to the serious problems faced by U.S. copper producers.

Import relief would also adversely affect the export earnings of the foreign copper-producing countries, many of which are heavily indebted and highly dependent on copper exports. It would, therefore, complicate our efforts to maintain the stability of the international financial system and lessen the ability of foreign countries to import goods from the United States. Finally, there are encouraging signs that the economic recovery is beginning to have a favorable effect on world copper prices; stocks have fallen considerably this year and a significant price increase is expected in the near future. The denial of import relief on copper should act as a signal and as encouragement to our partners around the world to resist protectionist acts and, thus, will foster that recovery.

In order to help ease the difficult problems now faced by many workers in the U.S. cooper industry, I have directed the Secretary of Labor to work with State and local officials to develop a plan of job retraining and relocation assistance for workers in affected industries. In addition, I have directed the Secretary of Commerce to actively monitor the domestic copper industry including inventories and the levels of copper imports.

Sincerely,

RONALD REAGAN

Note: This is the text of identical letters addressed to Thomas P. O'Neill, Jr., Speaker of the House of Representatives, and George Bush, President of the Senate.

Nomination of Jon R. Thomas To Be an Assistant Secretary of State
September 7, 1984

The President today announced his intention to nominate Jon R. Thomas to be Assistant Secretary of State for International Narcotics Matters. He would succeed Dominick L. DiCarlo.

Since 1982 Mr. Thomas has been serving as Deputy Assistant Secretary of State for International Narcotic Matters. Previously, he was senior staff member of the policy planning staff at the Department of State 1980–1982; president and chief executive officer of a mid-south distributor for a five-State area for Toro lawn, golf course, and irrigation products, 1977–1980; and operations officer at the Central Intelligence Agency, 1971–1977. He was a member of the U.S. Special Forces (Green Berets), 1966–1969, and received several decorations, including the Silver Star, Bronze Star, and Purple Heart.

Mr. Thomas graduated from the University of Minnesota (B.A., 1970). He is married, has two children, and resides in McLean, VA. He was born January 7, 1946, in Minneapolis, MN.

Nomination of Carl Edward Dillery To Be United States Ambassador to Fiji, Tonga, Tuvalu, and Kiribati
September 7, 1984

The President today announced his intention to nominate Carl Edward Dillery, of Washington, a career member of the Senior Foreign Service, Class of Counselor, as Ambassador to Fiji, to the Kingdom of Tonga, to Tuvalu, and to the Republic of Kiribati. He would succeed Fred J. Eckert.

Mr. Dillery was an insurance examiner at the Washington Insurance Examining Bureau in Seattle, WA, 1953–1955. In 1955 he entered the Foreign Service as foreign affairs officer in the Bureau of Far Eastern Affairs in the Department. He was foreign affairs officer in Tokyo (1957–1958) and in Kobe-Osaka (1958–1961). In 1961–1965 he was international relations officer in the Bureau of Scientific and Technological Affairs in the Department. He attended the University of California at Berkeley in 1965–1966. He was chief of the economic section in Brussels (1966–1967) and province senior adviser, CORDS, Vietnam (1968–1969). In 1970–1971 he was on detail to the Department of Defense in the Office of the Chief of Naval Operations, and in 1971–1972 he was political officer in the Bureau of Political-Military Affairs in the Department. He attended the Industrial College of Armed Forces in 1972–1973. He was deputy political counselor in London (1973–1976), and deputy chief of mission in Nicosia (1976–1978). In the Department, he was Deputy Director (1978–1979) and Director (1979–1982) of the Office of Southern European Affairs. Since 1982 he has been Director of the Office of United Nations Political Affairs.

Mr. Dillery graduated from Seattle Pacific College (B.A., 1953) and George Washington University (M.S.A., 1973). His foreign languages are French and Japanese. He was born December 17, 1930, in Seattle, WA.

Nomination of Joe O'Neal Rogers To Be United States Executive Director of the Asian Development Bank
September 7, 1984

The President today announced his intention to nominate Joe O'Neal Rogers to be United States Executive Director of the Asian Development Bank with the rank of Ambassador. He would succeed John Augustus Bohn, Jr.

Since 1981 Mr. Rogers has been executive director of the House Republican Conference. Previously, he was economic counsel to Senator William L. Armstrong, 1980–1981; director of the Task Force on Economic Policy, House Republican Research Committee, 1979–1980; economist for the Experimental Technology Incentives Program at the National Bureau of Standards, 1978–1979; assistant professor at Wake Forest University, 1977–1978; and lecturer at the University of Western Australia, 1974–1976.

Mr. Rogers graduated from the University of Oklahoma (B.A., 1971) and Duke University (M.A., 1973; Ph.D., 1978). He is married, has three children, and resides in Arlington, VA. He was born December 4, 1948, in Oklahoma City, OK.

Nomination of Howard D. Gutin To Be a Member of the Board of Directors of the Corporation for Public Broadcasting
September 7, 1984

The President today announced his intention to nominate Howard D. Gutin to be a member of the Board of Directors of the Corporation for Public Broadcasting for a term expiring March 1, 1989. He would succeed William Lee Hanley.

Since 1981 Mr. Gutin has been serving as president and general manager of the Southwest Texas Public Broadcasting Council, KLRN–TV in San Antonio and KLRU–TV in Austin. Previously, he was with KLRN–TV as vice president, acting general manager, and station manager (1980–1981); vice president for production of the Southwest Texas Public Broadcasting Council (1979–1980); lieutenant colonel in the United States Army as Director of Media at the Academy of Health Sciences, Fort Sam Houston, TX (1971–1978); audiovisual consultant to the Surgeon General, U.S. Army, and the Army Medical Department worldwide (1971–1979); and administrative assistant and senior aide to the Surgeon General, U.S. Army, 1969–1971.

Mr. Gutin graduated from the University of Nebraska (B.A.) and the U.S. Army Command and General Staff College. He is married, has three children, and resides in San Antonio, TX. He was born August 17, 1930, in Patterson, NJ.

Informal Exchange With Reporters on Domestic Issues
September 7, 1984

Q. Mr. President, come on over.

Q. What about Mr. Meese?

Q. Are you going to reappoint Mr. Meese?

Q. Meese.

Q. Oh, hurrah!

Q. I win! I win!

Q. What about Meese?

Q. Are you going to reappoint Mr. Meese if you're reelected?

The President. Well, I have not seen the report yet, as no one has. But barring anything unforeseen, and I don't expect anything of that kind, I haven't changed my mind about him.

Q. Sir, Senator Thurmond has said in that report that he's not going to hold hearings in this session. That means that you'd have to resubmit if you're reelected. Would you do that?

The President. Yes.

Q. What do you think about Thurmond not holding hearings this fall?

The President. Well, I can understand the crowded agenda that they have with regard to the election and the necessity to adjourn for campaigning and so forth. So, no, I don't think there's anything unusual about that at all.

Q. Do you think that God is a Republican? Do you think that God is a Republican, as Mondale charges?

Q. Let him answer it.

The President. No. I have no answer to any of those things that what's-his-name said.

Q. Are religion and politics necessarily intertwined, as you said in Dallas?

The President. In the sense that I said it in Dallas, which none of you have correctly reported.

Q. Wait——

The President. The correct words to use is there is a wall of separation. And some anti-religionists are trying to break down that wall. And what I was saying was in the context of, yes, definitely, there is a connection between morality and politics, and should be, and too many neglect it.

Q. Will you meet with Gromyko?

Q. Sir, what's Mondale——

Q. Will you meet with Gromyko? Are you going to try to meet with Gromyko?

Q. I said that you'd come over, and I win.

Note: The exchange began at 3:28 p.m. on the South Lawn of the White House as the President was preparing to depart for a weekend stay at Camp David, MD.

Radio Address to the Nation on Education
September 8, 1984

My fellow Americans:

Young people across the country returned to school this week. The approach of autumn marks the end of the year, but somehow it always seems to be a time of new beginnings in the home and the workplace and in the classroom.

We've seen a great resurgence of interest in how our public schools run the past few years. We've seen a new seriousness about the importance of education in our lives. You may remember when a commission we appointed almost 3 years ago to study the state of our schools concluded that if another country had done to our schools what we ourselves did to them, we would be justified in calling it an act of war.

But already things are beginning to turn around. It's been one of those great American stories, a little like how neighbors used to band together to raise a house out of the wilderness. Teachers and school principals and school boards have joined with parents and local community leaders to turn things around. Scholastic aptitude test scores are turning up. Academic performance is up, and more parents are showing confidence in the schools.

Forty-two percent of Americans now grade their local schools with an "A" or "B," and that's up 11 percent since last year. A number of schools are leading this academic renewal. Katahdin High School up at Sherman Station, Maine, was named by the Department of Education as an exemplary school. At Katahdin, they encourage students and teachers to work together and understand each other's problems. They have firm disciplinary rules. Teachers feel they have a say in how the school is run. They can get the supplies they need. And they're looking to the future. This little school of 260 students has seven computers.

Then there's Jefferson High School in Los Angeles, a big city school with 2,000 students, most of them Hispanic or black. Principal Francis Nakano came to Jefferson 2 years ago and found walls full of graffiti and halls full of unruly youngsters. But Nakano turned it around. He started with discipline—fast, firm, and fair. He overhauled the buildings to create a climate for learning. He encouraged learning, recognizing and giving honors to the school's best scholars and helping slow learners with a special program that has them sign a personal contract accepting responsibility for their own progress in return for special, individual instruction.

These are just two schools that are a part of our national renewal in education. But what we're doing isn't enough; we've got to do better. I propose that this week the young people starting school and their parents and future employers accept some challenges, and they'll be tough challenges, the type you have to meet by yourself.

First challenge: Before this decade is out, we should regain at least half of what we lost in the sixties and seventies on scholastic aptitude test scores. As I said before, those scores are inching their way up, but not fast enough. Now, if you think that "I can't do anything to help," you're wrong. If you're a student who will take the scholastic aptitude test this year, study hard and do your very best. You can help lift our national average.

Second, violence and disorder have no place in our schools. Parents worry about it, and so do many children. Before this decade is out, we should reduce crime in the schools so much that it becomes a mere anecdote in studies about our schools.

Third, there's the problem of dropouts. Our high school dropout rate is now 27½ percent. I propose that before this decade is out the public schools of this country reduce the dropout rate to 10 percent or less. You know, when a girl or boy drops out of school, we tend to think the child failed the system. But I wonder sometimes if it isn't also true that the system failed the child. Sometimes they just need that extra little bit of care and motivation.

There's one other great challenge I want to speak to you about: watching too much TV. Now, I don't want to sound like a scolding parent, but time given to a television show that ought to be given to a school book is time badly used. TV is entertaining and sometimes educational. It's part of the fabric of our lives. But watching TV is passive, it's not living life.

Life involves effort and growth. You won't grow by watching a situation comedy, though you can grow by reading a book. I hope we aren't becoming a nation of watchers, because what made us great is that we've always been a nation of doers.

A dynamic and secure American future requires keeping today's economic expansion strong for tomorrow. And to meet that challenge, we must begin meeting these crucial educational challenges today.

Until next week, thanks for listening, and God bless you.

Note: The President spoke at 12:06 p.m. from Camp David, MD.

Message on the Observance of Grandparents Day
September 8, 1984

Americans are showing a renewed attention today to the importance of strong families for raising the next generation of Americans. Families are the chief repository of our nation's values but, more than that, they are centers of love and affection, where each individual is accepted as a unique person, created in the image of God.

Grandparents play a crucial but often unrecognized role in the strength of America's families. They provide their grandchildren with a living sense of continuity with our past and so with the confidence to face an uncertain future. Grandparents provide love, instruction and adult authority to their grandchildren just as they once provided them to their own children. Sometimes grandparents live in the same home as their grandchildren and sometimes they live many miles away, but in either case they can and often do play a very important role in their grandchildren's development.

Some grandparents are retired and have the time and energy to devote themselves to the many volunteer efforts which distin-guish our nation and contribute so greatly to the general welfare. In this way, they share their experience in life not only with their own families, but with many others as well. Those grandparents deserve a special word of thanks from all of us.

In recognition of the creative participation of grandparents in the lives of their families and of our nation, Congress has designated the first Sunday after Labor Day as National Grandparents Day. Nancy and I urge all Americans to set aside time to honor their grandparents on September 9.

RONALD REAGAN

Interview With Andrew Neil and Jon Connell of the Sunday Times of London
September 6, 1984

Q. Are you all geared up for the campaign, Mr. President?

The President. Yes, although I know what it's going to be like, because I've had one experience as Governor of California running for reelection, and you have to be Governor at the same time.

Q. Yes.

The President. You have to do the job, too, in campaigns. So, it won't exactly be the kind where you go out on extended tours as it was 4 years ago.

Q. May I proceed with that?

The President. Yes.

Q. You are so far ahead. Are we seeing a sea change in American politics? [*Laughter*]

The President. I'm not going to be tempted by those. I'm worried, as a matter of fact, that maybe too many people are going to get complacent and think their votes aren't needed.

Q. And not turn out.

The President. I keep remembering a Republican candidate named Dewey. [*Laughter*]

Q. So, you think there's a danger of getting too overconfident, perhaps, with such a lead in the polls?

The President. Not for me. I never was that way when I was in sports and athletics. I always figure—[*inaudible*]—I'm going to run one vote behind.

Q. Why do you think Mrs. Thatcher could be elected last year on policies not too different from yours? You see the election in Canada. You're way ahead in the polls. What's happening?

The President. Well, I won't speak for another country, I'll speak for my own. I think there has been a growing awareness on the part of people in both parties here that the increase in government and in government intervention in what had traditionally been the private sector, and so forth, is finally catching up with us. The people have found that the cost of government has skyrocketed and that there are things that government cannot do as well as the private sector. And I think this is what we're seeing.

I think here in our own country that we came to a point in which government's relationship with its own business and industrial community was adversarial rather than——

Q. Working together.

The President. ——cooperative. Yes. And there seems to have been quite a reaction to that once we started to turn it around.

And the debate for these last 3½ years that—for about 50 years, had been one of, well, how much are we going to spend on this program and that program, and what new programs? Suddenly, the debate for these last 4 years, it turns out, has been how much can we cut the spending?

Q. So, the debate's on your terms now?

The President. Yes.

Q. And you changed to that extent. It's you setting the agenda.

The President. Yes. But I think in a way the people determine that, also.

Q. When you— if you get reelected—not when, *if—[laughter]*—what's going to be your major priority on the international scene? I think that's what people in Europe——

The President. On the international scene? Well, it has to be peace, and it has to be reduced arms, particularly in the strategic field. I have to believe that if we can persuade the Soviet Union to join in reducing those weapons, that perhaps we can all see the wisdom of not only reducing but eliminating. I don't think the world should have to live with this threat hanging over it. And it really doesn't make any sense. Every weapon that's ever been introduced until this one has had defensive measures that followed. And you could look at war as winnable or losable in the normal sense. But we've come to a point now that a previous President of ours, Dwight Eisenhower, said might happen. We've come to a point where a war with the weapons now at hand—there is no foreseeing a victory or defeat in the traditional terms. The weapons are capable of destroying mankind and civilization. When that time comes, as he himself said, then it's time for the nations to sit down and find another way of settling disputes.

Q. I hope, Mr. President, in getting—*[inaudible]*—administration, the kind of fissures that seem to be growing between Western Europe and the United States do not get deeper. There sometimes seems to be trends in the 1980's that are pulling us a bit apart.

The President. Well, my feeling is that, yes, that I came in and inherited such a situation. But I believe that these summit meetings that we've been having—I believe that that has been changed. I don't think we've ever been closer to our NATO partners than we are now. And Margaret

Thatcher has had a great deal to do with that.

I've got to take a second to tell you one thing. When we had the summit at Williamsburg, and the first dinner the first night, the heads of state, we all met and dined at what had been the British colonial Governor's mansion. So, I was all set for it. And I was waiting until we were all settled, and then my line was going to be, "Margaret, if one of your predecessors had been a little more clever, you would be hosting this gathering." *[Laughter]*

So it all worked out that way, and I started, I said, "Margaret, if one of your predecessors had been a little more clever." She said, "I know. I would have been hosting this gathering." *[Laughter]* She said the line.

Q. She's quite clever.

The President. She really is.

Q. Mr. President, thank you very much for seeing us.

The President. Well, it's good to see you.

Q. Thank you very much. It's good to see you looking so well.

The President. Well, I feel good.

Written Responses to Questions

Q. You have always argued that America must only negotiate with the Soviet Union from strength. The Reagan years have seen a rebuilding of America's military might, yet the Soviets stubbornly refuse to talk. What would a second Reagan administration do to bring Moscow to the negotiating table?

The President. We are determined to reduce arms and the danger of nuclear war by negotiating balanced, fair, and verifiable agreements. And it's important to remember that we are talking and negotiating with the Soviets—at the CDE Conference in Stockholm and at the MBFR talks in Vienna. We are not just sitting back and waiting. In fact, at our suggestion, we successfully negotiated a new and better hotline agreement that further reduces the possibility of misunderstandings and accidents.

With regard to the START and INF talks, we cannot, of course, compel the Soviet

Union to return to the negotiating table. But I think these negotiations will be resumed eventually, because they are as much in Soviet interests as in ours. And I would point out that the world community of nations wants the Soviet Union to resume negotiations. But the Soviet political structure has had three leaders in as many years, and this has undoubtedly complicated and slowed Soviet decisionmaking. An example of this was the Soviet refusal to meet with us in Vienna after we accepted their suggestion to initiate discussions on space weaponry. We were accommodating, but Moscow continually backtracked and invented excuses not to go. As Foreign Minister Howe so aptly phrased it, "They wouldn't take 'yes' for an answer." We, nonetheless, will continue to be patient and hold to a steady policy.

Q. Many in your administration are privately concerned that Europe is not pulling its weight in the Atlantic alliance. Do you share their concern and, if the Europeans continue to lag behind America in rebuilding their defenses, would a second Reagan administration consider pulling out at least some U.S. troops from Western Europe?

The President. Let me begin by saying that for us, the Atlantic alliance is an anchor, an enduring affirmation of the vitality of Western civilization and an unshakable commitment to the defense of democracy and individual liberty. The defense of Europe and America is indivisible. We are dedicated to peace. That means NATO must be strong enough to make certain that conflict does not begin.

But we cannot be content with the accomplishments of the past. We cannot rest easy with the knowledge that NATO has made possible the longest period of European peace and prosperity in modern history.

As we look to the future, there are compelling reasons to strengthen even further our unity and our capability to sustain the peace. That is why the United States has made major improvements in our defenses, both by modernization and by increasing the readiness and sustainability of those forces. And that is why our NATO allies should also improve their defenses. We understand the cost and sacrifices, but we are confident that all members of the alliance

understand that our collective security will continue to be an indispensable bulwark against aggression and tyranny. We particularly applaud British efforts to augment the strength of its frontline ships and aircraft.

My administration opposes any move to reduce the U.S. commitment to Western Europe, and we will continue to do so. It is my intent to maintain the force in Europe necessary to sustain the peace and to perform their assigned mission in support of NATO's strategy. And as I have said repeatedly, we have absolutely no plans of any kind to reduce the number of U.S. troops assigned to Western Europe's defense.

Q. Why do you think that the Reagan image is perceived very differently abroad than it is at home—that whereas it seems popular with a majority of Americans, even many conservative British and Europeans are prone to see you as a potentially trigger-happy cowboy? Will a reelected Ronald Reagan be concerned to correct that image?

The President. I hope there is a better understanding of what we and our allies are trying to do than your question suggests. Our basic belief is that a nuclear war cannot be won and must never be fought. In an effort to build an enduring peace and to reduce the level of arms, we have presented the most comprehensive set of arms control and weapons reduction proposals in history.

As I noted in my State of the Union speech this past January, we must and will engage the Soviet Union in a dialog as serious and constructive as Soviet leaders permit. We all recognize that there is no more important consideration than the development of a better working relationship with the Soviet Union—one marked by greater cooperation and understanding and leading to stable, secure, and peaceful relations.

This has been and will continue to be a primary goal of my administration. We and the Soviets need to find ways to eliminate the threat and use of force in solving international disputes, to lower arms levels, and to establish a better working relationship with each other. We remain ready to negotiate fairly and flexibly and without preconditions. When the Soviet leadership decides to return to the START and INF negotiating table, we'll meet them halfway. And our allies fully share these aims and objectives, as the NATO declaration this past May pointed out. And at the London summit this past June, the industrialized nations agreed on a common approach that demonstrates the fundamental consensus that exists among our governments on our approach to relations with the U.S.S.R.

I hope more people will come to understand that I have no higher priority than strengthening peace. Our perseverance and patience will, in time, move us toward a safer and more peaceful world. And if the American people return me for a second term, I will continue to pursue these goals.

Q. Rightly or wrongly, many Europeans blame record U.S. deficits for stymying their economic recovery. You won in 1980 promising to balance the budget. Why should policies to cut the deficit in a second term be believed?

The President. We are determined to reduce the deficit, and I firmly believe it can and will be done. We need to attack the fundamental problem, which is excessive Federal spending. We are trying to deal with the deficit problem not by taxing America into a recession, as some would do, but by making government live within its means and building an economy that generates jobs and tax revenue. Our economic recovery has already brought down the deficit from the dire predictions of 2 years ago.

I might also point out that the economic recovery in America is helping to stimulate growth in the economies of the West European countries. Indeed, we have witnessed a revival in world trade with a marked rise in exports from Europe to the U.S., which has helped to spread the benefits of our recovery.

Our attack on the deficit has commenced. I recently signed legislation which enacted a "downpayment" package that makes a start at deficit reduction over the next 3 years. A commission I appointed to look for ways to improve the efficiency of the Federal Government has come up with about 2,500 specific recommendations on how government can be made more economical by implementing modern-day business

practices. We've just begun to implement them.

I have been trying to get a balanced budget amendment to our Constitution. I am also working to get the line-item veto adopted, by which a President can veto individual items in an appropriations bill without vetoing the entire bill. Forty-three State Governors have that tool. I had it in California, and it works.

We won't even consider raising taxes until after we have cut Federal spending to that minimum level which is necessary to finance truly necessary activities. The best way to bring down the deficit is through prudent government spending levels and strong economic growth and expansion. That's our program in a nutshell, and it will benefit Europe as well as America.

Q. What will a reelected Ronald Reagan do to disprove the common criticism that he has been content to see spending cuts fall disproportionately on the weakest members of society and that he cares only for the "achievers" in America?

The President. That kind of charge is just not true. The fact is we've been working to better focus the spending of tax dollars on programs that meet people's needs.

Our reforms are reducing fraud, waste, and abuse and targeting welfare programs to better serve the truly needy, rather than those who ought to work and be self-supporting. The money saved by these reforms has already helped make it possible for three-fourths of the States to raise either their payment standards or payment levels under a program that aids truly needy families.

I understand how politically rewarding it is for critics to pretend we've been unfair, but the facts just don't bear them out. And remember, those critics are the same people whose ruinous inflation fell so heavily on the poor, especially in 1979 and 1980. This government is spending more money on social programs than ever in U.S. history, but at last somebody's trying to make those programs work better.

Q. Isn't there a danger that Ronald Reagan is more popular than the Republican Party, and the much-heralded new Republican majority will vanish with the retirement of Ronald Reagan?

The President. Well, I'd like to see this new Republican majority you're talking about. In fact, the Republican Party is still a minority party, and that means we're still outnumbered nationwide in terms of party registration. But I think you have to look beyond that to see the real strength and vitality of the Republican Party.

There was a time when the opposite party was able to portray Republicans as rather stodgy types, resistant to progress. But in recent years that's changed dramatically. Today it's the Republican Party that has new, forward-looking ideas, that stands for a revitalized economy and jobs. It's the leaders of the Democratic Party who are tied to the failed policies of the past.

You can see this in the fact that one of the Republican Party's great strengths in 1984 is its appeal to the youngest generation of voters. What I'm saying is that the new vibrancy and confidence of the Republican Party goes far beyond the political fortunes of any one candidate, including myself. This party is on the move, and I sense it will continue to carry the momentum for a long time.

Note: The interview began at 4:40 p.m. in the Oval Office at the White House.

As printed above, the interview follows the White House press release, which was released by the Office of the Press Secretary on September 9.

Remarks at a Polish Festival in Doylestown, Pennsylvania
September 9, 1984

The President. Cardinal Krol, thank you very much. Governor Thornburgh, Senator Arlen Specter, Congressman Larry Coughlin, two candidates for Congress, Elise du Pont and Dave—I can't read my own writing here, Dave. [*Laughter*]

Audience member. Dave Christian.

The President. That's right. You know. Okay. All right.

And to all of you, *dzien dobry* [good day].

Well, since my childhood I was always told about the luck of the Irish. And after the Illinois lottery, that phrase is bound to be changed a bit—[*laughter*]—the luck of the Polish. Now, that has a nice ring to it, doesn't it?

I think we're all winners because we have the great good fortune to be living in the United States of America. And I think we're all winners because we have the great fortune to be living in the United States of America. And I have the delight of being back in the great State of Pennsylvania.

I realize that I repeated myself when I said something there, but if I had to say something twice, I don't know of anything more important to say than about the pleasure of living in the United States of America.

When Pennsylvania was one of the original 13 States, little did I realize at the time that someday there would be 50. [*Laughter*]

This has been a most inspiring day. This shrine with its magnificent stained glass stands out not only as a monument to the heart and soul of Polish America but as a tribute to the cause of human freedom itself. And those who chose the location for this shrine did their job well.

Not far from here, our Declaration of Independence was penned and our liberty proclaimed. Not far from here, General George Washington and his ragtag army, many of the soldiers without shoes, endured a winter of despair. And it was in that time of darkness for America when giants in the cause of human liberty stepped forward and helped turn the tide.

Etched in the stained-glass windows of this shrine are the images of Casimir Pulaski and Tadeusz Kosciuszko. These heroes from faraway Poland helped spark a flame of liberty that still burns white hot in the soul of all who cherish freedom. And from what I'm seeing today, that is especially true of the Americans of Polish descent.

I just had the opportunity of visiting the

memorial to that great Polish statesman, composer, and pianist Ignace Jan Paderewski. He saw in the eyes of Polish immigrants a great love of freedom. ". . . wherever peoples gather," he said, ". . . to crown a hero with the laurels of liberty, there you can boldly take the leading place because you are Poles."

Well, I was honored to welcome such people to lunch at the White House just a few weeks ago, the veterans of the Polish Home Army. Their valor in the struggle against Nazi oppression has never been surpassed in the annals of human conflict. I was more than a little in awe of them. And I'm proud that after 40 years, the proper tribute has finally been paid to the commanders of the Polish Home Army.

Those who believe that they have crushed the Polish spirit with guns and brute force are wrong. They should remember the Polish Home Army and remember that lesson of history: Poland may be temporarily subdued, but the Polish people will never be defeated.

It wasn't that long ago when a new force for freedom emerged in Poland, the Solidarity union movement. And 4 years ago, when I kicked off my campaign, I was joined on the platform in the shadow of the Statue of Liberty by the stepfather of Lech Walesa, a working man with strong arms who emigrated to this country and could speak to us only through an interpreter. He's passed away, I'm sad to say, since that day. But his son lives on, and no matter how they try to suppress it, so does the spirit of Solidarity.

We Americans have a natural sympathy for those who suffer under the oppressor's boot in Poland. We see in the Polish people a mirror image of our own commitment to the simple virtues of honesty and hard work. The millions of Polish immigrants who came to America—many were your own fathers and mothers—these brave and sturdy people helped shape the American character. Their energy, sweat, and muscle built our factories; their moral strength is part of our national backbone.

We Americans who are not related to Poland by blood are related to her by spirit. Just as Polish immigrants decades ago bolstered America's resolve to live up to its

ideals, so, too, a brave son of Poland now inspires all of mankind. The world is truly blessed that in this time of peril and confusion a spiritual leader of great historical significance is with us. We've sought his advice and guidance on numerous occasions, and I can only say, thank God for Pope John Paul II.

You know, when I was in the chapel earlier I could sense the love and pride that went into the re-creation of the Black Madonna. And I'm told that as a symbol of the brave Polish peoples' religious faith and freedom, Our Lady has been a special inspiration to the Holy Father.

During our modern times when tyranny darkens much of the world, it is fitting that the Pope should find strength and solace from the Lady enshrined on the Hill of Light. Pope John Paul has said, "Freedom is given to man by God as a measure of his dignity." And "as children of God," he said, "we cannot be slaves."

I have to interject something here. I have seen held up several times back there a banner with regard to Yalta. There is one thing about that that I have to say. Let us not be tempted into giving Yalta as coverage to those who have violated that agreement; that the agreement never gave them the power to dominate the countries of Eastern Europe and Poland as they have.

Audience. 4 more years! 4 more years! 4 more years!

The President. All right. All right. [*Laughter*]

Our country's days of apologizing are over. America is standing tall again, and don't let anyone tell you we're any less dedicated to peace because we want a strong America.

I've known four wars—four wars—in my lifetime, and not one of them came about because we were too strong. Weakness is the greatest enemy of peace. We're trying to build a future for our children that is free, prosperous, and secure—a future of boundless hope and opportunity. And we're not doing this by wishful thinking in foreign affairs or by going back to economic policies that failed.

Our new beginning is a far cry from the defeatism, decline, and despair of only 4 years ago. We were then on the edge of an economic disaster. Today we're in one of the most powerful economic expansions in 40 years. More than 6 million people have found work in the last 20 months. Our European allies are calling this the American miracle. Small business incorporations are at a record high. Productivity is robust again, with research and development paving the way for an even brighter tomorrow. And, my friends, I said this the other day, and it's worth keeping on saying: You ain't seen nothin' yet.

Audience. 4 more years! 4 more years! 4 more years!

The President. All right. All right.

While all this is happening, inflation has been knocked down from 12.4 to 4.1 percent. And, you know, when I hear some people talking about fairness, I'm reminded of the misery index they devised by adding the inflation and unemployment rates. But when they were in charge, the misery index was over 20. Today it's 11.6, and we'll bring it down more if they'll just stand aside and get out of the way.

Now, I know that some would never give us any credit and, frankly, the credit doesn't belong to us. It belongs to you, the people. Our victory against inflation, the wonderful resurgence of growth—these are your victories; they're America's victories. If I could just offer a little friendly advice for our critics: next time, rather than say things that seem to run down America, how about giving the American people a pat on the back?

You in the Keystone State certainly deserve a pat on the back. You're aiming high, striving to make Pennsylvania's economy strong and competitive for the future. And I happen to believe you're blessed with one of the best Governors in our nation today— Dick Thornburgh. Dick has a great gift of being able to pull together the many strengths and resources of your people.

Your Governor's Ben Franklin Partnership Program is a model for America. You can be proud that your State government, the business community, and many of your fine universities—like the University City Science Center, Pennsylvania, Penn State, Lehigh, Bucknell, Lafayette, Carnegie Mellon, University of Pittsburgh, and

others—are working in harmony to spark technological growth and create secure jobs for the future. You can be proud that Pennsylvania is leading the way and showing it can be done.

And what you're seeing in America is a fundamental change in the direction of our country. No longer is an ever increasing share of your earnings being drained off into the Federal coffers. Today more of your earnings are staying with your families in your neighborhoods in your State, right where they belong.

Now, we've got challenges to overcome, but we won't overcome our problems by going back to the days when the Federal Government was taking more and more, knocking the economy right off its feet in the process. Raising taxes is an old answer. Some say it's the only answer. I say it's the wrong answer.

You know, I hate to say this, but I'm afraid the age factor may play a part in this election: Our opponents ideas are too old.

Audience. 4 more years! 4 more years! 4 more years!

The President. All right. I won't fight it. [*Laughter*]

But you know, I hate to say this, but they also seem to treat each new idea the old-fashioned way—they reject it.

We're breaking new ground. And we must have the courage to keep moving forward with an historic simplification of the tax system. We intend to make the tax system more fair, easier to understand, so we can bring yours and everybody's income tax rates further down, not up.

Now, a certain candidate for national office said the other day that the biggest difference between us is our policies toward people of average means. And he's right. With our tax program, a family of average means today is paying $900 a year less in income taxes than if that candidate's last tax program were still in place.

And what about the future? Just to pay for the spending promises he made will require a tax increase of almost $2,000 for every household. Now, somehow I think that working families will see more fairness in our plan—lower tax rates for all—so that we can have more jobs, more growth, and more opportunity for all the people of Pennsylvania.

We want to build a fire of hope that links all America together, because with all of us going forward together we can build an American opportunity society that gives every person an equal chance and a much greater chance to pursue the American dream.

I think we should take our cue from our Olympic athletes. Let's go for growth and go for the gold. There's a world of opportunity ahead if we can only break away from the logjam of the past. Enterprise zone legislation is a good example. It's been blocked by the old-line leadership of the House for almost 2 years. Yet this innovative idea would channel the vitality of the private sector to the depressed areas of our country where people need it the most.

Now, I know this is not an exclusively partisan event, but after nearly 30 years of control, isn't it time for some fresh leadership in the House of Representatives? [*Applause*] And we can start by electing Dave Christian to the Congress.

Audience. Run, Christian, run!

Mr. Christian. Thank you.

The President. All right. [*Laughter*] Okay. Thank you. And, Elise, we won't leave you out either. We need new voices there, so you have a candidate to send down there. And let's just return Larry Coughlin, who's doing a fine job.

A spirit of renewal and hope is alive again, and it will not be deterred by appeals to envy that would turn us against ourselves and take us back to the days of defeat and self-doubt. I do not believe in an America divided by envy, each of us challenging the other's success. I believe in an America inspired by opportunity, each of us challenging the best in ourselves.

The new patriotism is a positive force that unites us and draws us together—all of us—from every race, religion, and ethnic background. It gives us confidence because it's based on enduring values which we hold so dear—the dignity of work, respect for family, faith in a loving God, a belief in peace through strength, and a commitment to protect the freedom which is our legacy as Americans.

Now, I believe that by changing our

country these past 3½ years we've been making it a better country—a country of greater freedom, opportunity, confidence, and hope. And that's the America I'm working for this year, and that's the America I mean to work for in the next 4 years.

Audience. 4 more years! 4 more years! 4 more years!

The President. Well, to all those Democrats who have been loyal to the party of F.D.R., Harry Truman, and J.F.K., but who believe that its current leaders have changed it—that they no longer stand firmly for America's responsibilities in the world; that they no longer protect the working people of this country—we say to them, "You are not abandoned, our arms are open, join us. Come walk with us down the new path of hope and opportunity."

Just over 300 years ago, William Penn and a hearty band of settlers came here to establish a land of tolerance and liberty, a place where everyone, no matter what faith, could come to pray, to work, to achieve, and to build a great country. And we still believe in those things.

Sometimes on television at the White House I see ads encouraging people to vacation here saying, "You've got a friend in Pennsylvania." Well, after meeting you today, I feel I have a friend in Pennsylvania. And I want you to know that Pennsylvania has a friend in the White House.

Thank you all, and God bless you. But now I have a little surprise. Father Lucius?

Almost all the turmoil in Poland—amidst all of that, a brave woman made her way to the American Embassy under the watchful eye of martial law to deliver a special gift. And the care and love taken in making this tapestry reflects, I think, the depth of affection between our two peoples. It's the kind of treasure one places in a prominent place in the security of a home. There's a message to all of us in every stitch, and that message is, "Please don't forget us, because we're part of the same family."

Now, for those of you who can't see it, the tapestry has the image of the Black Madonna with Child, flanked on one side by the seal of Poland and on the other by the seal of the United States. And underneath the American eagle, she was careful to stitch very carefully, so the words, "In God We Trust" are very recognizable. And I think she was telling us that the people of Poland share that trust.

And she sent this as a gift to the people of the United States. And I can think of no more fitting place for it to reside than in this shrine, which is such an important symbol of the ties between our countries, and I am proud to present it to you at this time.

Thank you all again. God bless you.

Audience. 4 more years! 4 more years! 4 more years!

Father Lucius. Mr. President, I would like to present to you from the Pauline Fathers and the Shrine of our Lady of Częstochowa three medals.

One medal is 600th anniversary of our Lady of Częstochowa, which we celebrated in 1982. The Pauline Fathers are custodian of this beautiful shrine in Poland for 600 years, so that the commemorative medal.

Second one is the medal, commemoration of 300th anniversary of Vienna—defense of Vienna, Polish nation, and our King Sobieski. He defended Christianity because Pope asked him, and Pope said that Poland is always felt faithful—*Polona semper fidelis.*

And another is 40th anniversary of uprising in Warsaw. Beautiful medals, and we will be very honored if you keep in the White House. Thank you, Mr. President.

The President. Oh, I will, and I'll be honored to have them. Thank you very much. I'm very honored to have those. Thank you.

Note: The President spoke at 3:47 p.m. near the National Shrine of Our Lady of Częstochowa.

The festival is an annual event sponsored by the Society of Shrine Volunteers. While at the festival, the President visited the chapel and placed a wreath at the Paderewski Monument.

Following his remarks, the President returned to Washington, DC.

Letter to the Chairman of the United States International Trade Commission on Tobacco Price Supports
September 7, 1984

Dear Madam Chairwoman:

Pursuant to Section 22 of the Agricultural Adjustment Act of 1933, as amended, I have been advised by the Secretary of Agriculture, and I agree with him, that there is reason to believe that flue-, fire-, and dark air-cured tobacco and burley tobacco, in unmanufactured form, wherever classified in the Tariff Schedules of the United States, are practically certain to be imported under such conditions and in such quantities as to materially interfere with the price support and production adjustment programs for tobacco conducted by the Department of Agriculture.

The United States International Trade Commission is therefore directed to make an immediate investigation under Section 22 of the Agricultural Adjustment Act of 1933, as amended, to have precedence over other investigations the Commission may be conducting, to determine whether the above-described articles are practically certain to be imported under such conditions and in such quantities as to materially interfere with the tobacco price support and production adjustment programs now conducted by the Department of Agriculture, and to report its findings and recommendations at the earliest practicable date.

Sincerely,

RONALD REAGAN

[The Honorable Paula Stern, Chairwoman, United States International Trade Commission, Washington, D.C. 20436]

Note: The letter was released by the Office of the Press Secretary on September 10.

Appointment of John D. Gordley as Special Assistant to the President for Policy Development and Assistant Director for Food and Agriculture
September 10, 1984

The President today announced his appointment of John D. Gordley to be Special Assistant to the President for Policy Development and Assistant Director for Food and Agriculture.

Since February 1981 Mr. Gordley has been a legislative assistant to Senator Robert J. Dole, responsible for developing legislative and policy initiatives on domestic and international agricultural and trade issues. From 1976 to 1980, he was a market analyst and regional director for Africa with U.S. Wheat Associates, Inc.

Mr. Gordley received a master of international management degree from the American Graduate School of International Management in 1976, a M.A. in history from Boston College in 1973, and a B.A. in history from Grinnell College in 1971. He has also taught international affairs at the Schultz American School in Alexandria, Egypt.

Mr. Gordley was born on October 20, 1949, in Yonkers, NY. He is married and resides in Alexandria, VA.

Nomination of United States Representatives and Alternate Representatives to the 39th Session of the United Nations General Assembly
September 10, 1984

The President today announced his intention to nominate the following individuals to be Representatives and Alternate Representatives of the United States of America to the 39th Session of the General Assembly of the United Nations:

Representatives

Jeane J. Kirkpatrick, Representative of the United States to the United Nations;

Jose S. Sorzano, Deputy Representative of the United States to the United Nations;

Charles McC. Mathias, Jr., U.S. Senator from Maryland;

John H. Glenn, Jr., U.S. Senator from Ohio; and

Robert D. Ray, former Governor of Iowa, and currently president of Life Investors, Inc.

Alternate Representatives

Richard Schifter, Deputy Representative of the United States in the Security Council of the United Nations;

Alan Lee Keyes, Representative of the United States on the Economic and Social Council of the United Nations;

Harvey J. Feldman, Special Assistant to the Representative of the United States to the United Nations, Bureau of International Organization Affairs, Department of State;

Preston H. Long, retired, vice president of Trainer Wortham, Inc.; and

Guadalupe Quintanilla, assistant provost of the University of Houston.

Nomination of Two Members of the Boards of Trustees of Federal Insurance Trust Funds
September 10, 1984

The President today announced his intention to nominate the following individuals to be members of the following three boards:

—the Board of Trustees of the Federal Hospital Insurance Trust Fund, for terms of 4 years, new positions;

—the Board of Trustees of the Federal Old-Age and Survivors Insurance Trust Fund and the Federal Disability Insurance Trust Fund, for terms of 4 years, new positions; and

—the Board of Trustees of the Federal Supplementary Medical Insurance Trust Fund, for terms of 4 years, new positions.

Mary Falvey Fuller, of San Francisco, CA, is an independent management consultant specializing in business planning, finance, and product/market strategy and in technology-based and financial services industries. She was vice president of finance for the Shaklee Corp. in 1981–1982. She graduated from Cornell University (B.A., 1963) and Harvard Business School (M.B.A., 1967). She was born October 28, 1941, in Detroit, MI.

Suzanne Denbo Jaffe, of New York, NY, is deputy comptroller of New York State, Division of Investments and Cash Management. Previously, she was executive vice president of Lehman Management Co., Inc., in 1982–1983; and with Century Capital Associates in 1971–1981. She graduated from the University of Pennsylvania (B.A., 1965) and New York University (M.A., 1967). She was born April 17, 1943, in Washington, DC.

Remarks on Signing the National Hispanic Heritage Week Proclamation
September 10, 1984

Thank you all very much, and *buenas tardes*. See, I'm showing off. [*Laughter*] But welcome to the White House. You know, it's always a pleasure for me to greet people here. We should all be proud that this is one of the few executive residences in the world that's open to the people. So, when I say to you, "*Mi casa es su casa,*" it's literally true.

And just as true, and something none of us should ever forget, is that this country belongs to all of us. Today we celebrate this with the proclamation of National Hispanic Heritage Week, 1984.

Our country often has been described as a nation of immigrants. Well, there is much truth in that description. And yet, today we recognize that the forebears of many Americans of Hispanic descent—well, it was the United States that came to them, not the other way around.

That's true in Puerto Rico, throughout the Southwest. We Californians fully appreciate the highly developed Hispanic culture that existed in our State prior to its becoming part of the United States. As in the other States of the Southwest, there were thriving Hispanic cities, governments, ranches, and businesses. There was also a mission system built by a remarkable Franciscan priest named Father Junipero Serra, who's now under consideration for sainthood. I might add that all Californians are very proud of these missions.

Out there, when you start thinking of the historic pueblo of Los Angeles or the wonderful restored missions not as just part of the State's heritage but part of your heritage, then you know you've become a true Californian. And most of us Californians came there from someplace else ourselves. [*Laughter*]

Today, with this proclamation, we're reminding our fellow citizens that our Hispanic heritage is something of which all

Americans can be proud. We're also celebrating the contemporary contributions of Americans of Hispanic descent. Having been in the profession I was in for most of my adult life, I knew many Americans of Hispanic descent in the performing arts. Anthony Quinn is showing off some of that talent right now at the Kennedy Center here in Washington.

There are, of course, many more—the beautiful Delores del Rio, Desi Arnaz, José Feliciano, José Ferrer, Cesar Romero, Ricardo Montalban, and many more.

In other professions, the list is equally impressive, from ophthalmologist Dr. Castro Viejo to fashion designer Oscar de la Renta. And today we honor them, but more importantly, we honor all those many millions of our citizens who so exemplify the values of family, work, and respect for God and love of country.

And when it comes to these basic building blocks of character, no group of citizens should be prouder than Americans of Hispanic descent. Over the years the contributions made by these people just by being good Americans have had an enormous impact on our way of life. With hard work they've built large corporations and accomplished great things. And when we look for exemplary individuals who have overcome great odds and endured much personal hardship, we know we'll find many in the Hispanic community. We only need to look there to see living proof that the American dream is alive and well. Whether their roots are from Cuba, Puerto Rico, Central America, or Mexico, they're here building a better America.

And yet success is not only measured in commercial and business accomplishment. Let us acknowledge the millions of heroic parents throughout the Hispanic community who, even though struggling to make ends meet, manage to raise their children with dignity and pride, see that they receive a good education, and teach them the values that are so important to Hispanic Americans—the same values that help bind this nation together.

This is the character of the people which we applaud with Hispanic Heritage Week. We also recognize a love of country underlined throughout our history by so many acts of courage and valor. Within the Hispanic community are a host of heroes to whom this country owes a debt we can never repay.

I think of one, Allen Clark, whose mother is Hispanic. He lost both legs while serving his country in Vietnam. when he came home, his body was broken, but his spirit never faltered. He went back to school. He earned his master's degree in business administration. He served his State in a high government post and is now a successful businessman. He's an inspiration to all who know him. And what gave him the confidence to overcome such a life-shattering experience? Well, he credits those values to his mother—the values that his mother taught him early in life—as the source of his strength.

Let's be grateful to heroes and to the mothers of heroes, as well. And as we sign this proclamation, let us particularly note the strength and dignity of Hispanic women.

And today it gives me great pleasure to sign this proclamation and to honor the wonderful people with whom we share that most precious title—American.

God bless you all.

Note: The President spoke at 1:48 p.m. in the East Room at the White House.

Proclamation 5232—National Hispanic Heritage Week, 1984
September 10, 1984

By the President of the United States of America

A Proclamation

One of the greatest strengths of our Nation is the rich mixture of people from various cultural backgrounds, and few groups have contributed more to our Nation than Americans of Hispanic heritage. In many communities across the land, Hispanics are a vital element in fostering America's achievements in the arts and industry, in agriculture and education, in religion and business, in science and politics, and in every other aspect of American life.

Hispanic Americans were among the first settlers in the New World, some arriving in America long before the United States became an independent Nation. They came in search of a better life for themselves and their children, and they have helped to create a richer life for all of us.

In our international relations, Hispanic Americans also contribute to our Nation's identity—our own perception of who we are and our role in the world, as well as others' perception of us. The strong family and cultural ties which bind Hispanics in the United States with our nearest neighbors are an important element of the strength of the Western Hemisphere. The freedom of our neighbors is our freedom. Their security is our security. We Americans seek economic progress and justice for mutual benefit throughout the hemisphere, and we look to Americans of Hispanic heritage for leadership as we work together toward these goals.

In recognition of the many achievements of the Hispanic American Community, the Congress, by Joint Resolution approved September 17, 1968 (Public Law 90–498), authorized and requested the President to issue annually a proclamation designating the week which includes September 15 and 16 as National Hispanic Heritage Week.

Now, Therefore, I, Ronald Reagan, President of the United States of America, do hereby proclaim the week beginning September 10, 1984, as National Hispanic Heritage Week, in recognition of the Hispanic individuals, families, and communities that enrich our national life. I call upon the people of the United States, especially the educational community, to observe this week with appropriate ceremonies and activities.

In Witness Whereof, I have hereunto set my hand this tenth day of September, in the year of our Lord nineteen hundred and eighty-four, and of the Independence of the United States of America the two hundred and ninth.

RONALD REAGAN

[*Filed with the Office of the Federal Register, 10:31 a.m., September 11, 1984*]

Remarks at the Presentation Ceremony of the Congressional Gold Medal Honoring Hubert H. Humphrey
September 11, 1984

The President. Ladies and gentlemen, honored guests, and most especially, Muriel Humphrey Brown, we're here to honor one of American political history's great happy warriors.

Hubert Horatio Humphrey was the mayor of a great midwestern city. He was a United States Senator for 23 years. He was majority whip for his party in the Senate. He was Vice President of the United States. He ran for President three times and won the nomination of his party in 1968, when he came within a few hundred thousand votes of the Presidency.

Now, these are the facts of his career, but somehow they don't quite capture him. To get a surer sense of his real dimensions one must speak of his nature, his character, his personality.

There was in Hubert Humphrey a great joy of life and a truly buoyant civility. He was robust and energetic. He loved the battle. He was warm and affectionate. He was hearty and spirited. And he was nothing if not effusive. When he spoke, the words poured out of him. Some said he was deeply, endlessly articulate, and then there were others that said he was downright garrulous. [*Laughter*] But either way, he'd laugh when someone said he'd never had an unuttered thought. [*Laughter*]

He was a masterful politician. Issues were everything to him, mere strategy a bore. He was no bully; his art was persuasion. He asked that he be remembered as "an effective man of government," and he was certainly that. He lived in clamorous times, but he was ever optimistic. He was involved in all the great struggles of his time, and he tried to affect them, always for the better.

In 1948 he touched the conscience of his party when he took the floor of the Democratic Convention to make a passionate appeal for civil rights. In the sixties, he was deeply involved in the struggle that followed the U.S. commitment to Vietnam.

He was a liberal who was an internationalist, a liberal who understood that America was great and has serious responsibilities in the world, a liberal who was strongly anti-Communist. He loved justice. He believed our Constitution is a living document that is reborn every day. He was a passionate democrat—small "d" and big "D"—who tried to make the world better according to his lights. And no one was better than he at infusing his followers with a fighting spirit.

Hubert Humphrey was generous. After John Kennedy beat him in the Democratic primaries of 1960, he dropped out of the race and went to work to elect Kennedy President. It wasn't pro forma, the campaigning that he did for Kennedy, it was real. And when J.F.K. won the White House, Majority Whip Humphrey mobilized his constituencies, mustered his majorities, and helped J.F.K. get the Congress to pass such legislation as the Peace Corps.

He may have been generous to a fault. He was famously patient with human frailty, and it was said that you could hurt him with impunity. Once, an old friend betrayed him and it damaged Humphrey politically. Another friend, a fellow Senator, took him aside and said, "Hubert, I know you're not going to be rough with so-and-so after he did what he did to you, but couldn't you at least be mad at him for 2 weeks?" [*Laughter*] Humphrey probably laughed and shook his head and refused. It isn't possible to exaggerate the number of people who considered him their friend.

Thirty years after his great career began, 30 years after he was elected the youngest mayor ever of Minneapolis, Hubert Humphrey was told that he was dying. He fought his sickness with the same spirit with which he'd lived his life. A week after his last operation, Humphrey showed up at an AFL–CIO convention to give a long-promised speech. He was thin and wan and his hair had gone white. He began his speech, "I may start out a little wobbly, but I'm going to end up damn strong." He spoke for almost an hour, and he pounded the lectern so hard it jumped.

In the last few weeks of his life, as he lay dying, an amazing healing process began. He got a WATS line, and he called his old friends and his old adversaries and one after one he told them, "I wish you well." And the calls came in, too, from all across the country. Old opponents called in, and young people just entering politics. Powerful political figures called, and obscure farmers. It was as if all of them were trying to reconnect with a part of an unchanging political past, trying to touch for the last time a special spirit and a special style that would go with Hubert Humphrey's passing. It's said that a lot of love passed along the lines those last few days. There was a lot of forgiving and a lot of encouraging and a lot of sharing of wisdom.

His passing left Washington a lesser place. He left a big silence behind him. He was a fine man, a patriot. And he understood that though good men and women can disagree on this issue or that, we must always stay bound by a common love of country.

Hubert Humphrey was a robust and

active player in the dramas of our time for more than 30 years. He was a vivid presence on the scene. And looking back over his career, it's fair to say that his greatest contribution to his country was his life, a life that affirmed the vitality of democracy, affirmed the fact that the democratic process is alive and full of movement and action and great plans and decent dreams.

I'm very proud today and very honored to present to Mrs. Muriel Humphrey Brown the Congressional Gold Medal for distinguished service to the Federal Government and the American people in honor of the great, happy warrior: Hubert Horatio Humphrey.

Mrs. Brown. Thank you, Mr. President, so very, very much, not only for presenting the medal but that most beautiful message and summation of Hubert's goals and life.

When we—children and wife and friends—planned Hubert's funeral, it was not a funeral ceremony that we planned. It was a celebration of his life. And I find that today, with this great tribute, this is a continuation of that celebration of that man's life. He was one man who made a great change in the life of our country. Thank you again, so very much.

Now I'm to introduce the continuation of the Humphrey family in my son, Hubert Humphrey, Jr. "Skip" Humphrey.

Mr. Humphrey. Mr. President, ladies and gentlemen, honored guests: On behalf of my mother, my sister, and my brothers, and all of the members of our family, we grate-fully accept the medal honoring Hubert Humphrey.

I know if he were here today, he would suggest that all this fuss over his public life is just too much and not necessary. But privately, he would have thoroughly enjoyed the limelight and attention being given to him today. [*Laughter*]

I remember well the notes and letters I received from Dad telling me of the visits with the President and with other dignitaries. He wanted to share with his family the infatuation, the love he had for his country, its political institutions and its people.

We accept this medal for the people that Hubert Humphrey represented—the people who live in Minnesota, the people from all walks of life, in all circumstances of need. And we accept this medal as a challenge to keep Hubert Humphrey's faith with the people and the land of America.

Thank you for honoring the courage, hard work, faith, and integrity of a man we deeply love.

As always, I would say it's the words of Hubert Humphrey that best express how he felt about life and politics in America. So, let me just close with a quote. He said: "I have enjoyed my life, its disappointments outweighed by its pleasures. I have loved my country in a way that some people consider sentimental and out of style. I still do. And I remain an optimist with joy, without apology about this country and about the American experiment in democracy."

Note: The President spoke at 10:46 a.m. in the Rose Garden at the White House.

Remarks and a Question-and-Answer Session With Reporters on a Meeting With Soviet Foreign Minister Andrei Gromyko
September 11, 1984

The President. Didn't have anything else to do.

Q. Good for you.

The President. [*Laughing*] Well, good afternoon, and I'd like to make a short statement, and then I'll be pleased to take some questions.

I've invited Soviet Deputy Premier and Foreign Minister Andrei Gromyko to meet with me at the White House on September 28th, and Mr. Gromyko has accepted.

I believe it's important to use the opportunity provided by Mr. Gromyko's presence in the United States to confer on a range of issues of international importance.

One of my highest priorities is finding

ways to reduce the level of arms and to improve our working relationship with the Soviet Union. I hope that my meeting with him will contribute to this goal, as our administration continues to work for a safer world.

End of statement.

Q. Mr. President, sir, after 3½ years of very little progress in U.S.-Soviet relations, some people might consider this a political ploy on your part to answer Mr. Mondale's charges that you've been lax in this area. How would you respond to that?

The President. Well, I would answer that the facts would belie any such supposition. The fact is we have proposed meetings with the Soviet Union on a number of occasions and for a number of reasons. We have not retreated from any meetings with them. And this is the time of the opening of the U.N. General Assembly, and he has announced his intention to come here. And so, I extended an invitation that while he's here, to come down to Washington.

Q. Do you think that they now believe that you're certain to be reelected and want a meeting now because of that?

The President. You'll have to ask them what their reasons are for accepting.

No, I was going to Maureen [Maureen Santini, Associated Press].

Q. Thank you, Mr. President. You said yourself, in the past, that you think some people think you're trigger happy, and from polls we can see this is one of the main concerns of people in this election campaign. Do you think this meeting will help people come to your way of thinking; that you're not the trigger-happy cowboy you say people like to portray you as? *[Laughter]*

The President. Well, the most important thing is what understanding I can reach with Foreign Minister Gromyko to maybe convince him that the United States means no harm.

Q. You have always said that a summit meeting should be well prepared and have a reasonable chance of success. This isn't a summit meeting, but——

The President. No.

Q. ——do you feel that this meeting with Mr. Gromyko meets that standard, and how

much can you really accomplish in a brief meeting at the White House?

The President. I don't know. The meeting will be confidential, but we're here. And as I say, I think that maybe with all the specifics that are before us in the various treaty negotiations—some of which are continuing, but some of which they have walked away from—I think maybe the time has come that anything that can perhaps get a better understanding between our two governments maybe should precede any resumption of dealings on specifics, if there can be an easing of any suspicion or hostility.

Q. Do you have any concerns at all that the Soviets might use this meeting to try to embarrass you during the political campaign?

The President. Well, again, you'll have to ask them what their intentions are.

Q. But do you have any concerns about that, sir?

The President. What?

Q. Do you have any concerns?

The President. No.

Q. Mr. President, there are reports that you're about to release a study showing Soviet violations of past arms control treaties. Are you going to release it, and are you afraid that might sour the atmosphere for this meeting with Mr. Gromyko?

The President. No, this is a matter that is required of the Congress, that we are to provide the Congress with a report. This report is being readied. I haven't had a chance to study it as yet. And, so, this is not some action by us or aimed at the Soviet Union. It's supposed to be a factual report that the Congress requires.

Q. Well, but are you concerned that it might sour the atmosphere for this meeting that's coming up?

The President. I have no way of knowing.

Q. Well, if you release a report listing their violations of past treaties, isn't that kind of a statement on what you think of how they've conducted themselves?

The President. But this isn't some choice of mine. This is something required by the Congress.

Q. Mr. President, do you have any

sense—you and your advisers—as to who is really in charge in the Kremlin and whether Mr. Gromyko is now sharing a much larger role of that collective leadership and what the health situation is with Mr. Chernenko?

The President. Andrea [Andrea Mitchell, NBC News], I'm not going to comment on what my opinion might be there. We know that the Government of the Soviet Union has traditionally been a kind of a collective government by the Politburo, and some leaders have over the years shown themselves as more dominant than others in that kind of collective. But I'm not going to hazard any guesses here because I've been facing a problem that no other President has faced, and that is the great turnover that in 3 years of my term in office we've had three leaders there. And I'm just not going to hazard a guess. I'm going to deal with the Government as it's presented to me.

Q. Is it your sense that with that kind of collective leadership that you might still be able to get a resumption of arms talks? And what is your relative priority between the strategic negotiations resuming and initiating talks on space weapons? Which would be the most critical as far as you're concerned?

The President. Well, we've never put any preconditions on any talks, contrary to what had been claimed against us. And I think that all of these tie together.

You can't talk about militarization of outer space without recognizing that all the strategic ballistic missiles come by way of outer space. So, I think the most important thing to begin with is to see if we cannot lessen this threat hanging over the world— and for which the Soviet Union and the United States are mainly responsible—of these powerful weapons that could affect nations, all nations, whether they were involved in a controversy or not. That would have an effect on all of civilization, and I just want to see if we can't do something that will rid the world of this threat.

Sam [Sam Donaldson, ABC News]?

Q. Mr. President, Walter Mondale has now tabled a fairly specific budget reduction plan and says it's only fair that you do the same before the election. Will you, sir, and if not, why not?

The President. Well, I don't think he's really submitted a budget—or a deficit reduction plan. I think he's submitted a tax plan, a tax increase plan. In fact, the only real specifics—three specifics there—have to do with taxes.

As for any specifics on our part, they're voluminous, and they go back to 1981. I submitted four budgets and will be submitting a fifth before this term is out. And in all of those, they have thousands of words of substantiation, and had we been granted what I had asked in those budgets the deficit today would be $40 to $50 billion less.

So, we believe that the deficit will be reduced by continued growth of the economy and by getting control of spending to where it does not increase faster than the increase in revenues from the growth in economy.

Now, this year, already, the budget is $20 billion less than what we ourselves had estimated at the beginning of the year, and that's largely due to faster economic growth.

Let me point out, if growth could continue at 4 percent, the revenues for government, without raising anyone's taxes, would be $400 billion bigger by 1989. If we could keep the growth rate at 5½ percent, the deficit would just about disappear from that alone.

Now, to keep the spending increase down we have already reduced the rate of increase in spending by almost two-thirds. So, we're going to continue along that line. We have 2,478 specific recommendations for improving the management of government for further economies that have been submitted by the Grace commission, which I asked to serve and to come in with recommendations for us. And we've got other facts that go along with this, specifics before the Congress: the enterprise zones, which are tied into increasing the economy, the enterprise zones legislation. We have the balanced budget amendment, the line-item veto. I think that I've put more specifics on the table in this term than probably any administration I know.

Q. But, sir, if I may, growth alone won't do it, because you yourself have said previously that spending cuts are the way you want to achieve your goal. Isn't it fair to spell out to the American people precisely what cuts you have in mind?

The President. Yes, but what I'm saying, Sam, they're there. Take a look at the budgets I've already submitted and look at the cuts that I've asked for and was not given.

Now, what specifically has he proposed, other than some additional spending and his tax cuts and whacking away at the defense budget? But, as I say, the specifics are there and attested to by thousands of words of documentation.

Q. So, if we take your last budget, sir, and look at them, look at the specifics, we'll have your next plan?

The President. You will have a continuation of what we've been on.

It's as simple as this: If that rate of increase in spending can be brought down, as we've brought it down already, if at the same time, through economic growth, the rate of revenues begins to climb at a steeper rate, those two lines have to meet, and where they meet is a balanced budget. And this is what our plan is. [*Laughter*] If I had a blackboard—but I would have looked like a teacher.

Q. Thank you, sir.

The President. What?

Q. Thank you, Mr. President.

Q. Could I——

The President. I was hoping to get beyond the second row.

Q. Mr. President?

The President. I can't. Maureen said no.

Q. Yes, but you pointed your finger. [*Laughter*]

The President. No, but let me tell you——

Q. The moving finger points, and having pointed——

The President. No, let me just say we'll be back, and we'll be having more of these. So——

Q. Oh, when?

The President. What?

Q. Before the election?

Q. We'd like to make a date.

Q. What about debates?

The President. I'm just going to wait and surprise you again.

Q. Are we going to have a full-scale half-hour news conference, sir, before the election?

The President. I don't know, but I've been talking about that myself.

Q. When's the first debate, Mr. President?

The President. What?

Q. When's the first debate?

The President. Can't take any more questions.

Q. How's the campaign going so far?

The President. Save them for the next time. Save it for the next time.

Q. But we're not certain there's going to be a next time, sir. [*Laughter*]

Note: The President spoke at noon in the Briefing Room at the White House.

Statement on the Conference on Confidence and Security Building Measures and Disarmament in Europe
September 11, 1984

The third round of the Conference on Confidence and Security Building Measures and Disarmament in Europe (CDE) opens today in Stockholm. The U.S. delegation, headed by Ambassador James Goodby, will be returning to the negotiating table with the delegations of Canada, our European allies, the European neutral States and the countries of the Warsaw Pact.

The Stockholm Conference arises out of the Conference on Security and Cooperation in Europe (CSCE), which produced the Helsinki accords of 1975. In the various followup negotiations that form part of the Helsinki process, we and our allies continue to seek balanced progress in both the security and human rights areas. The CDE negotiations, which began last January, are a potentially productive new part of the broad East-West dialog.

The U.S. and other Western Nations have proposed at the Stockholm conference a series of concrete measures for information, observation, and verification, designed to reduce the possibility of war by miscalculation or surprise attack. These measures would apply to the whole of Europe from the Atlantic Ocean to the Ural Mountains.

The Soviet Union, on the other hand, has taken a more rhetorical approach to the Conference, seeking the adoption of declarations which are embodied in other international agreements. In an effort to bridge this difference in our approaches, I made it clear in my address to the Irish Parliament in June that the U.S. will consider the Soviet proposal for a declaration on the nonuse of force as long as the Soviet Union will discuss the concrete measures needed to put that principle into action.

This new move on our part has not yet been met with a positive response from the Soviet Union. With the summer break behind us, we hope the Soviets will now be ready for the flexible give-and-take negotiating process which is necessary to move forward.

To prepare for the third round, Ambassador Goodby has consulted closely with our allies and conducted useful talks here in Washington with the head of the Soviet del-

egation to the Conference. The Ambassador and his delegation continue to enjoy my strong support in their efforts to achieve concrete results at Stockholm.

Our work in the Stockholm Conference complements our many other efforts to reach agreement on confidence-building measures. We and our allies have put forward similar proposals in the Vienna talks on East-West conventional force reductions (MBFR). Further, the United States has advanced confidence-building measures bilaterally with the Soviet Union in our successful effort to upgrade the "hotline" communications link and in our proposals for additional direct communications ties between our two countries. We have also made such proposals in the negotiations on strategic arms (START) and on intermediate nuclear forces (INF).

Unfortunately, the Soviet Union still not returned to the START and INF talks since walking out of these two vital negotiations late last year and also has been unwilling or unable to follow through on its own proposal for talks on space arms control issues. I am convinced that the U.S. and the Soviet Union share a deep obligation to all humanity to get on with the urgent business of reducing nuclear arms. The United States is ready to do its part. I sincerely hope that the Soviet leadership will soon find its way to return to these negotiating tables.

Remarks Announcing Modifications in a Grain Agreement With the Soviet Union
September 11, 1984

Well, listen, I'm very happy to welcome all of you back, and I'm looking forward to discussing some important farm issues with you. But first, let me share some news with you for America's farm community.

Consistent with the long-term agreement on grain sales, we've decided—and the Department of Agriculture is notifying the Soviet Union—that the Soviets can increase by 10 million metric tons their purchase of

wheat and or corn for shipment during the second year of the agreement. And the ceiling for the second year of agreement is being raised to 22 million metric tons. And I've said many times, our philosophy is against the unfair and the wrong-headed policies of grain embargoes, and we're going to continue to do everything we can to strengthen markets for America's farmers. They're the most productive people, I think, on the face of the Earth.

So, I just thought that you'd like to have that news.

Note: The President spoke at 3:05 p.m. in the Cabinet Room at the White House, where he was meeting with a group of Members of Congress to discuss farm issues.

Nomination of Edward J. Philbin To Be a Commissioner of the Federal Maritime Commission
September 11, 1984

The President today announced his intention to nominate Edward J. Philbin to be a Federal Maritime Commissioner for the term expiring June 30, 1989. He would succeed James V. Day.

Since June 1984 he has been a consultant to the Chairman of the Federal Maritime Commission. Previously, he was Acting Assistant Secretary for Reserve Affairs at the Department of Defense in 1983–1984; Deputy Assistant Secretary for Reserve Affairs at the Department of Defense in 1981–1983; Commander AFIS/RE Detached Training Site 10, March Air Force Base, CA, in 1979–1981; and visiting professor of international law at the Air War College in 1978–1979. He served in the United States Naval Air Reserve in 1949–1954. He served on active duty in the United States Air Force in 1957–1959 and subsequently as a reservist.

He graduated from California State University (B.S., 1957), the University of San Diego School of Law (J.D., 1965), and the Air War College. He was born September 7, 1932, in New York, NY, and now resides in Burke, VA.

Nomination of John N. Griesemer To Be a Governor of the United States Postal Service
September 11, 1984

The President today announced his intention to nominate John N. Griesemer to be a Governor of the United States Postal Service for the remainder of the term expiring December 8, 1986. He would succeed John R. McKean.

Since 1956 Mr. Griesemer has served as superintendent, vice president, and president of Griesemer Stone Co. He is also presently serving as president of General Warehouse Corp., Springfield Ready Mix, and Joplin Stone Co., a company he started in 1963.

Mr. Griesemer graduated from the University of Missouri (B.S., 1953). He is married, has five children, and resides in Springfield, MO. He was born November 30, 1930, in Mt. Vernon, MO.

Appointment of Edmund S. Hawley as Deputy Assistant to the President for Intergovernmental Affairs
September 11, 1984

The President has announced his intention to appoint Edmund S. "Kip" Hawley as Deputy Assistant to the President for Intergovernmental Affairs.

Mr. Hawley has served as Special Assistant to the President for Intergovernmental Affairs since July 10, 1983.

Previously Mr. Hawley was Deputy Assistant Secretary for Governmental Affairs at the Department of Transportation under Secretaries Drew Lewis and Elizabeth Dole. The Office of Governmental Affairs was responsible for the Department's legislative programs before Congress as well as its relations with State and local officials and public interest groups.

Prior to serving in the Department of Transportation, Mr. Hawley was an attorney with the firm of Gaston, Snow, Ely, and Barlett in Boston, MA.

Mr. Hawley has received a bachelor of arts degree from Brown University in Providence, RI, and a law degree from the University of Virginia. He is married and resides in Silver Spring, MD.

Appointment of Theresa Ann Elmore as Special Assistant to the President for Intergovernmental Affairs
September 11, 1984

The President has announced his intention to appoint Theresa Ann Elmore as Special Assistant to the President for Intergovernmental Affairs. Ms. Elmore is currently the Director of White House Administration and the White House liaison for the arts and humanities.

Prior to joining the White House, Ms. Elmore was active in Republican politics serving as a member of the Reagan-Bush Inaugural Committee, national deputy finance director for the 1980 George Bush for President campaign, also served as adviser and finance director to several U.S. senatorial campaigns, and was on the Ford finance committee as well as inaugural and campaign staff of President Nixon.

Currently a member of the advisory board for the Center for the Study of the Presidency, Ms. Elmore is also a member of Outstanding Young Women of America, Charter 100, and Executive Women in Government.

Ms. Elmore graduated from Georgetown University School of Business Administration in 1973. She was born on October 10, 1949, in Bethesda, MD.

Appointment of D. Edward Wilson, Jr., as Special Assistant to the President for Administration and Deputy Director of the Office of Administration
September 11, 1984

The President today announced his intention to appoint D. Edward Wilson, Jr., to be Special Assistant to the President for Administration and Deputy Director, Office of Administration.

Mr. Wilson is currently General Counsel, Office of Administration. From May 1982 to January 1984, he was Associate Counsel to the President, and served as Associate Counsel, Office of the Counsel to the President, from April 1981 to May 1982. In his new position he will continue to report to John F.W. Rogers, Assistant to the President for Management and Administration and Director, Office of Administration.

Prior to joining the White House staff, Mr. Wilson was an associate with the law firm of Morgan, Lewis, and Bockius in Washington, DC. He graduated from the University of Virginia (B.A., 1973) and

Georgetown University Law School (J.D., 1976). He is married, resides in Arlington, VA, and was born in New Orleans, LA, on December 23, 1951.

Letter to the Speaker of the House and the President of the Senate on NATO Conventional Defense Capabilities
September 12, 1984

Dear Mr. Speaker: (Dear Mr. President:)

Pursuant to section 1104(b) of the FY 1984 Defense Authorization Act (P.L. 98–94), this report contains my views and recommendations on improving NATO conventional defense capabilities. These views and recommendations take into consideration the findings in Secretary Weinberger's report on "Improving NATO's Conventional Capabilities." I have reviewed that report and endorse its recommendations. It is the product of thorough research and contains a candid assessment of NATO's achievements to date and additional needs for the future.

Few disagree with the pressing need to improve NATO's conventional forces in order to enhance deterrence and defense. The quality of NATO's equipment and the readiness and skill of the forces manning that equipment have improved significantly over the last several years. The absolute defense capabilities of NATO forces are substantially greater today than three or four years ago. However, the measure of adequacy in deterrence and defense is not any static or absolute ability, but a dynamic relationship to the threat opposing that defense. The Warsaw Pact threat has increased by an even greater qualitative and quantitative increment, creating the necessity that NATO be ever more efficient and effective.

In analyzing the requirements for conventional force improvements, we must remember that NATO's principal objective is not to fight and win a war, but to ensure that a war in Europe does not occur. Further improvements in conventional capability would augment a vital element of overall deterrence and lessen pressure for early escalation to nuclear confrontation. At the same time, as the DoD report concludes, conventional forces cannot totally supplant the nuclear dimension of deterrence. NATO must also continue to maintain a credible nuclear deterrent, as outlined in Secretary Weinberger's report on NATO's Nuclear Posture.

NATO's strategy must be based on the geographic and political realities of NATO, and the fact that NATO, as a defensive alliance, concedes the initiative at the outset of conflict. In this context, flexible response and forward defense provide the only viable deterrent and defense strategy for the Alliance. NATO's task is to do a better job of providing the forces and the doctrine to support the strategy.

The United States can be proud of our leadership by example over the last several years. We must continue to pursue those programs we have already begun, while seeking even more effective ways to enhance conventional defense. The support of Congress, in providing the funding for operations and maintenance costs, readiness, sustainment improvements, new equipment, force structure, research and development, and other defense programs, is essential to our efforts. However, the United States cannot fill the gap alone. Every member of the Alliance must participate in improving conventional forces. The Allies recognize the need, and now must make the additional sacrifices needed to improve further NATO's military capabilities. The recent debate in the U.S. Senate will provide reinforcement to those Allies trying to assume their proportional burden. We will continue to prod all Allies to make better contributions to NATO defense.

Secretary Weinberger's report and the Supreme Allied Commander-Europe's (SACEUR's) independent assessment spell out the most important areas that need improvement. I agree with their recommendations. We must carefully balance our efforts, both by program area (such as readiness) and by task (such as defense against a first echelon). We must ensure that defense efforts and resources provide the most effective product for defense. We must critique the application of resources until we are satisfied that they are producing the optimum defense capability possible. No one can afford wastefully duplicative development programs, nor pursue programs that have only a limited military need. In sum, we must have a military strategy and an investment strategy. And these strategies should encompass our own programs and those of Allies—in closer integration and cooperation than ever before.

The fundamental and inescapable reason for American cooperation and leadership is that a strong NATO defense is in our basic national self-interest, and we simply cannot succeed by ourselves. The plans and programs in the current United States defense budget and five-year defense plan support these objectives. While we will continue to review plans and modify requests to fit new opportunities and requirements, enduring Congressional willingness to support required defense programs is essential if we are to improve NATO's conventional defense. No plan, no matter how well conceived, can succeed if the resources to achieve it are insufficient or inconsistent. We and our Allies have recognized NATO's conventional defense problems, and have taken the first steps toward recovery. Now, we must accelerate our efforts.

Making the changes necessary to supplement existing plans or to replace those which become obsolete requires bold thinking and leadership. We will continue to consult closely and frequently with our NATO Allies and with the U.S. Congress on new and better ways to use defense resources. There is no "instant" solution to any of the existing problems. Solutions will be achieved only by a long-term commitment. Nonetheless, we must start down the right paths, which are presented in Secretary Weinberger's report.

United States programs emphasize the need to provide the strategic lift to rapidly supplement in-place forces and to augment the thin strategic reserves available to SACEUR. We are working with Allies to ensure that Europe is prepared to receive these reinforcements and get them to where they can be most effective. We have stressed the need to increase the funding levels in the unglamorous but tremendously cost-effective Infrastructure Program. For example, by providing shelters and other supporting capabilities for aircraft, we can substantially improve the survivability and hence the capabilities of our Air Force.

Improving NATO's deterrent and defense posture will also require the Alliance to move in entirely new directions and to modify existing projects. "Exploitation of Emerging Technologies" is a fine example of new directions. This initiative, proposed by the United States in mid-1982, has already stimulated identification of projects for accelerated development. Although it will still be several years before this initiative contributes directly to NATO's defense capabilities, this effort marks an important first step in using the West's major advantage: its technological base.

In the short term, we must improve the deterrent capability of the conventional leg of NATO's deterrent Triad by increasing readiness and sustainability. Over the longer term, we must devote the necessary resources to provide all of the elements of an effective defense. This will require a clear understanding by the publics in all NATO countries of the nature and magnitude of the threat we all face.

I ask the Congress to join in the important endeavor of strengthening NATO's conventional defense.

Sincerely,

RONALD REAGAN

Note: This is the text of identical letters addressed to Thomas P. O'Neill, Jr., Speaker of the House of Representatives, and George Bush, President of the Senate.

Letter to the Speaker of the House and the President of the Senate on the NATO Tactical Nuclear Posture
September 12, 1984

Dear Mr. Speaker: *(Dear Mr. President:)*

Pursuant to section 1105(b) of the FY 1984 Defense Authorization Act (P.L. 98–94), this report contains my views on the DoD report on the tactical nuclear posture of the North Atlantic Treaty Organization (NATO). This is the first of four reports required by the FY 1984 Defense Authorization Act. It analyzes some of the most crucial problems facing U.S.-NATO defense policy, both because of the weapons involved and the essential role of nuclear weapons in NATO's deterrent posture.

I have reviewed Secretary Weinberger's very comprehensive report on the nuclear posture of NATO, and I strongly endorse the report's recommendations. I therefore urge the Congress to provide the necessary support so that the agreements reached within the Alliance for improving NATO's nonstrategic nuclear forces (NSNF) can be sustained.

The military threat to the Alliance has not lessened since the last report in 1975. There have been significant improvements by both the U.S. and the Europeans in conventional and nonstrategic nuclear forces over the last several years. Nonetheless, the quantitative military balance has, in fact, worsened. Our goal remains not to match the Warsaw Pact system-for-system or warhead-for-warhead, but to maintain forces adequate for credible deterrence and defense. NATO can accomplish this objective by continuing force improvement, including both nuclear and conventional modernizations, and by developing more effective use of our defense resources. Meanwhile, we will continue to work to achieve equitable and verifiable arms reductions which would assist NATO to obtain greater stability and security at lower levels of defense effort.

In October 1983, the NATO Nuclear Planning Group (NPG), as part of a theaterwide improvement of NATO's nuclear posture, decided to withdraw an additional 1,400 warheads over the next five to six years, in addition to the 1,000 warheads withdrawn in 1980. The basis for these decisions was a broadly supported Alliance study. This study was used as the cornerstone for the DoD report. Thus, the recommendations and intermediate steps outlined in the DoD report to improve NATO's nuclear posture are fully consistent with the views of our Allies.

I am fully aware of the views in the Congress that we should do more to improve our conventional forces. I intend to take a balanced approach to improving our capabilities in both areas. You have received a report from DoD which looks at conventional plans and requirements in detail. I shall be providing my views on how to pursue some of those recommendations soon. It is true that we need to continue to improve our conventional forces. However, it is essential that, in the process of examining conventional problems, we not lose sight of the very essential, significant contributions that credible, survivable, and stable NATO nuclear forces make to enhancing conventional defense or of the fact that such nuclear forces are presently our most credible deterrent to chemical attack.

I especially endorse those recommendations that improve the survivability of NATO's nuclear forces. Closely associated security improvements will also do much to improve the safety of our weapons in peacetime. I have placed significant emphasis on carrying out such improvements. I intend to encourage our Allies to take an equally serious view of the problem. We are working through several NATO organizations to obtain Allied assistance in and agreement to making needed improvements.

At Montebello, Defense Ministers agreed to make further stockpile reductions which leave the stockpile at its lowest level in the last twenty years. At the same time, the Allies agreed that NATO must pursue appropriate modernization programs so that this reduced stockpile will continue to constitute an adequate and credible deterrent. I will support both the stockpile level decision and the modernization programs which will ensure a credible deterrent. Present U.S. defense programs and budgets provide the means to implement these decisions. I ask for your support to ensure that they can be carried out in an orderly and timely fashion. The DoD report accurately documents the need, and outlines the remedial measures which we will be pursuing. The associated requirement to improve our target acquisition and communications capabilities is also well documented in the report.

As I mentioned earlier, NATO's nuclear posture correctly constitutes NATO's most effective deterrent against Soviet use of chemical weapons. We must do better than that, which is why the U.S. should develop a limited but modern chemical capability to serve as a direct deterrent against Soviet chemical use. U.S. defense budgets and programs include the necessary steps to sustain this deterrent.

NATO Allies are aware of the requirements for nuclear modernization and improvements in survivability and security. The U.S. will continue to provide the leadership and encouragement to stimulate the Allies to participate in their portions of future programs. As a result of the 1979 dual-track decision on LRINF, NATO is proceeding with deployments in the absence of a satisfactory negotiated arms reduction agreement which would make such deployments unnecessary. I stand fully committed to seek an equitable and verifiable arms reduction solution, and, as I have said many times, the U.S. is ready to recommend negotiations without preconditions at any time. Until such a negotiated solution is reached, however, the U.S. must provide the means to ensure that the nuclear posture of NATO does not deteriorate to such a degree that deterrence is threatened.

NATO's conventional, chemical, and nuclear forces are inextricably linked in achieving the Alliance's objective of deterrence and defense. If we are to maintain deterrence and live in peace and freedom, we must continue to improve each capability. Secretary Weinberger's report on NATO's nuclear posture has outlined the current situation and a practical way to proceed towards an enduring nuclear posture in NATO. I fully endorse his recommendations.

Sincerely,

RONALD REAGAN

Note: This is the text of identical letters addressed to Thomas P. O'Neill, Jr., Speaker of the House of Representatives, and George Bush, President of the Senate.

Message to the Congress Transmitting the Annual Report of the Railroad Retirement Board
September 12, 1984

To the Congress of the United States:

I hereby submit to the Congress the Annual Report of the Railroad Retirement Board for fiscal year 1983, pursuant to the provisions of Section 7(b)6 of the Railroad Retirement Act, enacted October 16, 1974, and Section 12(1) of the Railroad Unemployment Insurance Act, enacted June 25, 1938.

The Railroad Retirement Board informs me that, despite recent legislation, Railroad Sickness and Unemployment Insurance benefit payments continued to greatly exceed tax revenues in FY83 thereby requiring additional loans from the Railroad Retirement Account. The Railroad Sickness and Unemployment Insurance debt to the Railroad Retirement Account more than doubled in FY83 to a total debt of $575 million by the end of the year. Legislation will be needed before September 1985— when borrowing authority expires—to ensure the restoration of the Railroad Sickness and Unemployment Insurance Account to financial balance and ensure the repayment of its debt to the rail pension fund. I urge the Congress to enact promptly my legislative proposal which would restore the solvency of the RSUI fund without imposing an undue burden on any party involved—

the general taxpayer, rail management, rail labor or the rail pension fund.

RONALD REAGAN

The White House,
September 12, 1984.

Remarks at Dedication Ceremonies for Santa Maria Towers in Buffalo, New York
September 12, 1984

Thank you all, and Bishop Head, thank you. Senator D'Amato, Mayor Jim Griffin, Congressman Jack Kemp, Ned Regan, Ed Rutkowski, ladies and gentlemen:

It's a wonderful tonic to be in Buffalo and to be with so many of America's finest. I know that I'm looking today at citizens who don't consider themselves Democrats or Republicans, so much as deeply patriotic Americans who are concerned about your country and determined to do all you can to make tomorrow better.

From our first day in office this has been our objective, as you've been told, was to reduce the growth of spending, to lower tax rates, provide incentives for investment, rebuild our defenses, and fight crime, so we can get our economy moving again, build a stronger America, and make your future more secure.

Well, America is moving forward again, but we won't be satisfied until the economic expansion reaches into every community of our nation. The America we're fighting for is one in which no one gets left behind, from Buffalo to the Bronx, from the Great Lakes to the Great Salt Lake.

I want to talk about our challenge, but let me just say how honored I am to help you celebrate the dedication of the Santa Maria Towers. It's people like you, and inspiring projects like this, who show us that the heart of America is good, the spirit of America is strong, and the future of America is great.

No single sector of our nation—government, business, labor, or nonprofit organization—can solve our problems alone. But by working together, pooling our resources,

and building on our strengths, we can accomplish great things. And the Santa Maria Towers, this wonderful project for senior citizens and the handicapped, is truly a great thing.

I have had an opportunity, briefly, to see what is inside the Towers here, and you all have every reason to be proud. We peeked out the window a little while ago. [*Laughter*]

But older Americans want and deserve to be full participants in the economic and social life of America. As Longfellow said, "age is opportunity no less than youth itself."

Santa Maria Towers, under the sponsorship of the Catholic Diocese of Buffalo and Catholic Charities, and with the support of the Federation of Italian American Societies and our Department of Housing and Urban Development, will be doing its part. I'm also encouraged by the efforts of the Saint Stanislaus Community Organization to establish the Monsignor Adamski Village just a short distance from here. Buffalo is telling America that your neighborhoods and communities are caring for your senior citizens and handicapped.

The handicapped may face limitations, but they have no limitations on their courage to do what others say cannot be done. Our disabled citizens want what all of us want—the opportunity to contribute to our communities, to use our creativity, and to go as far as our God-given talents will take us. They deserve no less, and I believe that we can make their dream come true.

We've seen remarkable achievements in medicine and technology, education and rehabilitation, in equal access and greater economic independence. Voluntary efforts by the private sector and the many worthwhile Federal programs help in a thousand ways, but we've only made a beginning.

His Holiness Pope John Paul II recently remarked we must meet the challenge to build a society "where to live is to work for the good of others, where to govern is to serve, where no one is used as a tool, no one left out, no one downtrodden, where all can live in real brotherhood."

We live in a time of great challenges. Well, do you know something? Americans are very good at meeting challenges. Ask the senior citizens in Santa Maria Towers. They kept the world going during the tough years of the thirties and the Great Depression, through the forties and the war and beyond.

But our senior citizens also know that when you lose faith in the people, you can go wrong in a hurry. I think they remember what it was like only 4 years ago having to live on a fixed income with back-to-back years of cruel, double-digit inflation. In fact, all of us remember what it was like to have a broken economy, with the highest prime interest rates since the Civil War, taxes roughly doubling in 4 short years, and real after-tax income of the average family actually declining.

Well, that's behind us now. And it's behind us because there's no limit to what proud and free people can do if they're given a chance. The people of Buffalo understand that. Americans everywhere have always understood that. It was you that told us it was time to put earnings back into the hands of the people, time to put government back into the hands of the people, and time to put America back into the hands of the people.

And that's exactly what we've been trying to do with the strongest economic expansion in 40 years and inflation all the way down from 12.4 percent to 4.1 percent. But we must remove the remaining roadblocks to growth and jobs, without inflation, so a city like Buffalo will finally enjoy all the warmth from the sunlight of prosperity. And with your support, and with strong leaders like Jack Kemp back in Washington and Jill Emery of New York's 34th District,

who we need in Washington, that's exactly what we're going to do.

Now, together we'll move forward into a brighter future with an historic simplification of the tax system. We must make that system more fair and easier to understand so we can bring everybody's income tax rates further down, not up.

Now, I don't believe, as my opponent most assuredly does, that government's greatest challenge is to convince us higher taxes will be good for America. I believe that F.D.R., Franklin Delano Roosevelt's words remain true today: "The only way to keep the Government out of the red is to keep the people out of the red." And that means more jobs through opportunity and economic growth, not fewer jobs through unfair tax increases that destroy growth.

The Democratic candidate contends that working Americans wouldn't be hurt by his tax increases. That's a fairy tale. [*Laughter*] His plan would hurt working Americans by raising their taxes and by stifling economic growth. With your support, we'll make sure that no one puts that ball and chain around America's neck.

We will move forward into a brighter future by insisting that government spend no more than government takes in. And we could make that happen if the Congress would give us a balanced budget constitutional amendment and a line-item veto, giving a President power to veto specific spending requests without vetoing an entire bill. I'm so homesick for that. [*Laughter*] As a Governor I had that right, and in 8 years I vetoed line-item things more than 900 times without ever having a veto overturned by the Legislature.

We can move forward into a brighter future with enterprise zone legislation, which Congressman Kemp and I support, and which could bring opportunity to so many distressed areas if the Democratic leadership in the House of Representatives would stop stonewalling and give us a vote on our enterprise zones proposal.

We can move forward into a brighter future by strengthening incentives to create sunrise industries and make our older firms more competitive. If we enhance our leadership in the marketplace of tomorrow—

high technology, science, education, and space—we'll create more opportunities, more jobs for all our people.

We'll move forward into a brighter future by making it possible for you to walk your neighborhood streets without being afraid. For too many years, crime has sapped the strength and vitality of our people. Well, common sense is finally beginning to pay off. In 1982 reported crime dropped 3 percent. Last year there was a 7-percent drop, the sharpest decline since 1960. Right here in Buffalo, reported crime last year dropped a remarkable 9 percent.

But we need to do even more, and we can. The Senate has passed our core crime proposal, an historic and tough anticrime bill. They passed it by a vote of 91 to 1. But the liberal Democratic leadership in the House of Representatives has kept it bottled up in committee ever since. Isn't it time for your voices to be heard in Washington, DC? You know, you don't have to make those people see the light, just make them feel the heat. [*Laughter*]

Finally, the future of America relies completely on our ability to keep the peace and protect our freedom. We're not out for any territorial gain or to impose ourselves on anyone. Ours is the most peaceful, least warlike nation in modern history. But believe me, America must never again let its guard down. The reason we have a military is symbolized by a sign over the entrance to the Fairchild Air Force Base in Washington State. That sign says, "Peace is our profession." Well, as far as we're concerned, that's America's message to the world.

Now, to all those who have been loyal to the party of F.D.R., Harry Truman, and J.F.K., but who believe that its current leaders have changed the party, that they no longer stand firmly for America's responsibilities in the world, that they no longer protect the working people of this country, we say to them, "Join us. Come walk with us down that new path of hope and opportunity."

Together, we're going to build an economy that you can give to your children and that will ensure and fulfill the lives of the next generations.

[*At this point, the President was briefly interrupted by shouts from someone in the audience.*]

There's an echo in here. [*Laughter*]

We're going to go to work to break the cycles of dependency on government so that free men and women have the surging spirit of boundless opportunity. We're going to build a peace that won't fail if we don't fail. And we're going to be unafraid of exploring all that's beyond this Earth. We're going to leave—and proudly leave—sturdy and indestructible values so that in the 21st century, our shield will be their shield.

That's our message this year. We'll carry it across America. I've said, and I'm going to keep on saying, Al Jolson was right: You ain't seen nothin' yet.

I want to thank all of you of Santa Maria Towers for my needlepoint flag, and I got your other gift inside there. And I thank you all very much. And to all of you, thank you all, and God bless you.

Note: The President spoke at 11:55 a.m. at Santa Maria Towers, a nonprofit, low-income housing project for the elderly and handicapped.

Prior to the dedication ceremony, the President visited Mrs. Anna Grasso, a 74-year-old widow, and toured her apartment in the project.

Remarks at a Luncheon With Community Leaders in Buffalo, New York
September 12, 1984

The President. Thank you all very much. Bishop Head and Mr. Mayor, I thank you for a most gracious introduction, and all who have spoken here. I have to say a nerve was touched when our master of ceremonies referred to the Gipper and his first ball carrying at Notre Dame as a freshman. You know, that was all true. That was a part of his life story. You didn't finish and tell them that I ran through the varsity all the way—80 yards—for a touchdown. [*Laughter*]

And then Gip, as he came back from crossing the goal line, tossed the ball to Rockne and said, "I guess the boys are just tired." [*Laughter*]

But the real thrill was—8 years in the line in high school and college, and I wound up carrying the ball for 80 yards on a touchdown. And to have two quarterbacks here saying so many nice things about a right guard—[*laughter*]——

Q. You were a right guard?

The President. Right guard. Oh, I wouldn't have played the other one. [*Laughter*]

It's wonderful to be here at D'Youville College and be able to break bread with members of the Federation of Italian American Societies and the Saint Stanislaus Community Organization.

It's good to be in your city. You know, when friends from foreign countries come to the United States—and I do see a lot of them lately—and ask where they should go to see America, I always say, well, don't go to the obvious places, the biggest cities or the resorts that are well known and such. Go to a small town in South Carolina, or spend some time in a suburb outside Phoenix, or go to upstate New York and head west and spend awhile in a town like Buffalo.

Now, Buffalo, I'm told, has a great motto. It's "The City of Good Neighbors." And that's instructive, I think. Buffalo was settled by waves and waves of immigrants from Germany and Ireland and Italy and Poland and—name it—virtually every other country. And there was great migration here from within the United States. New Englanders and people from eastern New York came to work on the Erie Canal. And after that, black citizens came from the South. Buffalo is a real melting-pot town, and it's been very easygoing about it, very open and embracing of everyone. That's a great triumph, and something for all of you to be proud of—just another reason why you should be talking proud.

I was just over at Santa—I'd been saying Santa—the Santa Maria Towers, and that place is a splendid example of what individual people and groups can do to better their society. I would also like to applaud your efforts to establish the Monsignor Adamski Village. Together, the Saint Stanislaus Community Organization, the Diocese of Buffalo, Catholic Charities, and your Italian-American associations have a lot to be proud of.

You know, a few years back when I told the Congress and the reporters and the journalists of Washington that the people of America are a great and vigorous people who are awfully good at ordering their own lives and running their own towns and cities, well, there were a few snickers here and there. But I think all of you prove that in America, where there is private need there is private response. And the response of the citizens of this country is worth a million times what government intrusion is worth.

Now, this is a political year, which I have a feeling you've noticed. [*Laughter*] And I speak here today as President, of course, but also as a candidate for reelection. And I don't want to stand at the stump and tell you all the reasons our administration deserves a second term. I'd just like to talk to you a bit about how we see the world and what we've done in Washington and all that we mean to do to make this a freer country.

We want to take a free country and make it freer. Part of human freedom is economic freedom, and our policies respect that. We believe that when you tax something you put a kind of artificial limit on its production. When you put heavy income taxes on a working man or woman, you make it less worth their while to work hard and get ahead. But let them keep more of the fruits of their labor, and you encourage greater work and greater productivity. You encourage investment, and the economy grows. Jobs are created and more people work and pay their modest taxes, and the healthy spiral continues.

And we tried to achieve prosperity while lowering inflation, because inflation is a terrible thief and another discourager from saving your money and investing in the future. After 3½ years of our stewardship, I don't think it unfair to report that what we've created so far is the first real cycle of peace and prosperity without inflation since the 1960's.

We've got the economy growing again, and it's created 6 million jobs in the past 20 months in this country. Last year 600,000 new businesses were incorporated, and that was a record. The prime interest rate, which 4 years ago had reached the highest point since the Civil War, has fallen. Retail sales are up. Consumer confidence is up. So much is up that I almost hate to give you the downer: Inflation is down to just about 4 percent. [*Laughter*] And I don't need to remind you that 4 years ago, it was up more than three times that high.

There's still a lot that remains to be done; our work isn't finished. But the point I'm making is that for the first time in years our economy is on the right track again; not only on the right track, but chugging along like a big, powerful locomotive. And I don't think we want to go back. And I just want to highlight here that some of our opponents would go back. They've already told us that as soon as they're in, they'll start raising your taxes. And they'll do it again and again and again.

How do I know that? Because they've been running Congress for 42 of the last 50 years, and that's what they did for 42 of the last 50 years. Well, I think the only bills that we want to see go higher are your Buffalo Bills, not your tax bills. [*Laughter*]

Opportunity creates growth, and together they give everybody a better chance to take part in the good life that America promises. And one way to help the economy keep growing and keep expanding is through some prudent and helpful legislative initiatives.

We think it's time for America to move into the future with an historic simplification of the tax system—a tax system more fair, easier to understand, so we can bring everybody's income tax rates further down, not up. And with regard to making it simpler, you know, one of our truly great mathematicians, worldwide, actually had to confess he had trouble with his 1040. [*Laughter*]

You know, you have a great Congressman here, Jack Kemp. Jack is one of that great breed of creative new Republicans bursting with new ideas. And I think that all of us converge around one principal idea—opportunity. We don't believe in an America divided by envy, each of us challenging the other's success. We believe in an America inspired by opportunity, each of us challenging the best in ourselves.

Now, sometime back Jack put forth an idea called enterprise zones, which we strongly support. This bill is a shining example of a legislative initiative that will encourage economic freedom and get cities that are in trouble back on their feet again.

The enterprise zones bill would declare the older, distressed parts of a city to be special zones where special economic opportunity is encouraged. Businesses that go into those zones would be taxed at a much lower rate than if they were up on Main Street. Imagine adding to enterprise zones a bill that offers, during the summer months, a youth employment opportunity wage for teenagers, so that shopkeepers and others would be encouraged to hire those who are often disadvantaged and members of minority groups. It would be another—but lower—minimum wage for young people who are trying out for that first, or that summer, or that part-time job.

Now, you take these ideas, and you apply them to the distressed parts of Buffalo. Imagine those parts of your city blooming again, with kids coming home from school and having jobs to go to, with parents having a reason to care about the neighborhood, and with new local businesses adding to your tax base.

These are the things we need, and if you give us your support, these are the things we'll fight for in that second "4 more years!"

The liberal leadership in the House of Representatives, people who speak on and on about their compassion for the needy, have not only failed to pass enterprise zones, they've refused to even allow the Members of the Congress to vote on it. That's why we need new leadership in the House. We need people who recognize when opportunity knocks; we don't need people who knock opportunity.

Now, people, of course, don't live by economic matters alone. What's in their soul is more important than what's in their bank account. And that's why I'm so heartened and moved by the return to values that we've witnessed in the past few years. Young people love their country again and are trying to make it a better, kinder place. And once again, the family is being recognized as the center of society.

I think our government should help make it easier for those who believe in traditional values. And that's why I've supported, and will continue to support, tuition tax credits for those who pay into the tax system to support public schools, but who also take their savings to send their children to a parochial or independent school. And I support, and will continue to support, the right of voluntary prayer in the schools. And I don't mind telling you that we need the help of people like Al D'Amato and Jack Kemp and Jill Emery in the Congress if we're to prevail.

I'm running for reelection because I believe in the future, and I want to help make it a better and freer place for our children and our children's children. Together, we can build an American opportunity society that will give every person an equal chance and a much greater chance to pursue the American dream. Our work has just begun, and I'd feel like a quitter if I just packed up and went back to the ranch and forgot about the great challenges of our time.

This is an important election. It offers people of this nation the clearest, sharpest choice in half a century. And that's just fine, because the issues are really so big. Your vote is important; your decision is critical.

I want to say just one last thing here. Of all the things that I've been proud of in these going on 4 years since I've been in Washington, one of them is the quality of the young men and women who today wear the uniform of our country. They're at the highest level by actual statistics of any that have ever served our country. And I remember back—I know there was a time in recent years when we worried and we wondered—but I remember back when General Marshall was asked in World War II what was our secret weapon. And Bishop and reverend clergy and Sister, if you'll forgive me, the General said, "The best damn kids in the world."

Well, I guess an awful lot of the kids today are the grandsons of those best kids in the world. And believe me, they're carrying on the tradition, those young men and women in uniform. When you see them now and then on the street, maybe smile and tell them you're proud of them. I know I am.

Thank you all. Thank you for having me here. God bless you.

Note: The President spoke at 1:23 p.m. in the dining hall at the student center of D'Youville College. The luncheon was sponsored by the Federation of Italian American Societies and the Saint Stanislaus Community Organization.

Following the luncheon, the President met at the college with Erie County Republican leaders and Reagan-Bush campaign leaders. He then traveled to Endicott, NY.

Remarks at a Reagan-Bush Rally in Endicott, New York
September 12, 1984

The President. Thank you.

Audience. 4 more years! 4 more years! 4 more years!

The President. All right. Thank you. Thank you, Senator, and Madame Mayor, and the others here on the dais, and all of you ladies and gentlemen. Thank you for a most heart-warming reception.

By the way, during our flight into Link Field, Air Force One might have gotten off a little, a little off course, and the pilot came back to say he had just a little trouble finding Broome County. And I told him just to radio down and ask a simple question: "Which way E.J.?"

It's good to be here in Endicott at the very center of your beautiful "Valley of Opportunity." Warm greetings to your outstanding Senator, Alfonse D'Amato, your county executive, Carl Young, and your mayor, Marion Corino, and to a superb candidate for the Congress, Connie Cook. Connie, America needs more Republicans in the House of Representatives, and I can't tell you what a pleasure it'll be to have you there on our team.

And of course, as I said already, a special greeting to the majority leader and president pro tem of the New York State Senate, Warren Anderson. Andy, for more than three decades you've served in the New York State Senate with skill and devotion. You've dedicated yourself to justice, liberty, and economic growth. And because of your efforts, people in this valley and throughout New York State lead fuller, freer lives. On behalf of all Americans, I thank you.

Traveling today, we've flown over a good part of the Empire State. New York is lovely this time of year. And I thought, looking down from that altitude, that I detected just a touch of color beginning to appear in the trees. And there were great rivers like the Susquehanna threading their way across the land. And I couldn't help thinking of those majestic towers of Manhattan, the hard-working, patriotic neighborhoods of the boroughs, and the thriving cities and towns that dot your upstate—

places like Rochester, Buffalo, Syracuse and, yes, Binghamton, Vestal, Johnson City, and Endicott.

You know, it occurred to me that maybe the other side thinks that we'll just concede this great State of New York. Well, they're in for a little surprise. We're not conceding anything to anybody; we're in New York to win.

I know that this valley holds a special story—one of hardship overcome, of determination, hard work, family, and faith. And in many ways, your story is America's story.

It began almost a century ago, when one of the men legendary in the history of this valley, George F. Johnson, came here and established a shoe factory, the Endicott-Johnson Corporation. Soon the factory prospered, word spread all the way to Europe, and when immigrants from Poland, Russia, Czechoslovakia, Italy, and a dozen other countries reached America's shores, thousands of them are said to have asked the way to this valley of opportunity in the only English they knew—"Which way E.J.?"

They came here with few possessions, many with nothing but the clothes on their backs. And they asked only the chance to work, and work they did—long, hard hours tanning hides, cutting leather, stitching together the finished shoes. And as family helped family and neighbor helped neighbor, schools were built, houses were constructed, churches and synagogues were established. And this valley became home to some of the proudest communities in our nation, towns that had seen firsthand all that free men and women can accomplish.

In time, however, the shoe business changed. The factories in town began to offer fewer jobs, and some feared that prosperity would leave this good valley forever. Yet one group of men and women had a great vision, a vision to bring this valley prosperity it had never before dreamed possible, a vision to launch a revolution that would change the world.

Their leader was Thomas Watson, Sr. He had grown up in a small town called Painted Post, down the road from here, where he learned how to stick with a job until it's finished. Watson started with a company whose mainstays were punchcard machines and time clocks. And in 1953—a long time ago for some of you, but just the other day for some of us—[*laughter*]—the company that Watson had renamed IBM began making the first mass-produced commercial computer in history—the 650—less than a half a mile from this spot.

Scores of the IBM workers were sons and daughters of immigrants who had worked in the shoe factories. When they began, the best market researcher predicted that fewer than 1,000 computers would be sold in the entire 20th century. Well, IBM's first model sold almost twice that number in just 5 years, and now there are IBM plants in Endicott and around the world. And the computer revolution that so many of you helped to start promises to change life on Earth more profoundly than the Industrial Revolution of a century ago.

Already, computers have made possible dazzling medical breakthroughs that will enable us all to live longer, healthier, and fuller lives. Computers are helping to make our basic industries, like steel and autos, more efficient and better able to compete in the world market. And computers manufactured at IBM Owego—where some of you work—guide our space shuttles on their historic missions. You are the people who are making America a rocket of hope, shooting to the stars.

Today, firms in this valley make not only computers but flight simulators, aircraft parts, and a host of other sophisticated products. The shoe business has adjusted to the economic conditions and is working again. Your schools are better than ever. Your neighborhoods are strong. You still have a vigorous sense of ethnic pride. You can't talk to Mayor Corino for long without feeling how proud she is to be an Italian American. And here, you carry a sense of civic loyalty that shows up in organizations like the Tri-Cities Opera and the Roberson Center. I know how proud you all must be to live here. You've shown me that. And I just have to believe that the lesson of this valley is a lesson for our entire nation: With

opportunity, there's no limit to what Americans can achieve.

Opportunity, the chance to work hard and make our dreams come true—this is just what our administration is laboring to provide.

You know, in 5 years, taxes doubled, average monthly mortgage payments more than doubled, and the real after-tax income of the average American actually began to decline. Our opponents preach a great deal about fairness. Well, it's true, their policies were fair in one respect: They didn't discriminate; they made everybody miserable.

Now, we could go on, but we don't want to talk about their failures, do we? I can assure you, they don't. Well, then, let's talk about how, by working together, we're achieving great successes today, and we'll go on to build an even greater nation tomorrow.

On the economic front, we've knocked inflation down from 12.4 to 4.1 percent. And today, from Maine to New York to California, a vast economic expansion is surging ahead.

And now, I think I see at least one or two students in the audience. It's test time.

Audience. Boo-o-o!

The President. [*Laughing*] I'd like to ask you some questions about a certain country. Now, I don't want to give away the answer by naming the country. I'll give you just a little hint. It has three initials, and it's first two are U.S.

Now, of all the great industrialized nations in the world, which has shown by far the strongest, most widespread, and most sustained economic growth?

Audience. U.S.A.! U.S.A.! U.S.A.!

The President. All right. All right.

Audience. U.S.A.! U.S.A.! U.S.A.!

The President. All right, I've got more questions. What country had a record 600,000 new business incorporations last year alone?

Audience. U.S.A.!

The President. U.S.A.!

Audience. U.S.A.!

The President. What nation is showing the fastest rate of business investment in four decades?

Audience. U.S.A.!

The President. And what country can say that its productivity is up, its consumer spending is up, and its take-home pay is up?

Audience. U.S.A.!

The President. And during the past 20 months, what country created 6 million new jobs?

Audience. U.S.A.!

The President. And what nation created, on the average, more new jobs each month during the last 12 months than all the countries of Western Europe put together created over the past 10 years?

Audience. U.S.A.!

The President. You scored 100. That's right, U.S.A.!

And, my friends, you ain't seen nothin' yet. For the first time since the administration of President Kennedy, the share of earnings flowing to the government is not increasing. Today more of your earnings are staying with your families, in your neighborhoods, in your State, right where they belong.

To all those Democrats who have been loyal to the party of F.D.R., Harry Truman, and J.F.K., but who believe that its current leaders have changed that party, that they no longer stand firmly for America's responsibilities in the world, that they no longer protect the working people of this country, we say to them, "Join us. Come walk with us down the new path of hope and opportunity."

I can speak to that because I did that already. I was a Democrat, and I changed when I found I could no longer follow the course of the leadership of that party.

With your support, during the next 4 years, we'll keep going forward. We'll start by keeping government under control, by enacting a line-item veto and a constitutional amendment mandating that government stop spending more than it takes in. We'll fight for enterprise zones to help Americans in disadvantaged areas get off unemployment and welfare and start climbing the economic ladder.

Others would raise your taxes and the taxes of working families all across America. Well, we're not going to let them enact their tax plan, not on your life. Our pledge is for tax simplification, to make the system more fair and easier to understand, so we can bring yours and everybody's income tax rates further down, not up.

The American people aren't undertaxed; the Government in Washington is overfed. You know, I sometimes think that the main difference between ourselves and the other side is we see an America where every day is the Fourth of July, and they see an America where every day is April 15th. [*Laughter*]

Now, as our economy grows we'll need to go forward with the values of faith, family, neighborhood, and good, hard work. And together, we're already making an impressive start.

In the past 4 years, we've helped lead a grassroots revolution to recommit our schools to an agenda for excellence that will reach every child in this land. Teachers, school principals, and school boards are joining with parents to bring back discipline and higher standards. And what do you know? After 20 years of decline, achievement, by all the records, is up.

And today, schools like Union-Endicott have begun using computers to give our sons and daughters better education and to prepare them for an exciting world where the great challenges will lie not just here at home, but in the limitless frontiers of science, technology, and space.

We're cracking down on crime. We say with no hesitation, yes, there are such things as right and wrong and, yes, for hardened criminals preying on our society, punishment must be sure and swift. Last year reported crime dropped 7 percent, the steepest decline since 1960.

We're rebuilding America's defenses, and our nation is at peace. In New York's beautiful north country, 165 miles due north, lies the Army's Fort Drum, one of the finest all-weather land training installations anywhere in the United States. As the Secretary of the Army announced yesterday, we have chosen Fort Drum to be the home base for one of the Army's new light infantry divisions. Troops stationed at Fort Drum will be able to reach quickly any of the world's potential troublespots. And they'll have the benefit of some of the finest year-round training available.

And let me make one thing plain: We're not out for any territorial gain or to impose

1287

ourselves on anyone. But believe me, America must never again let its guard down. And since 1980, not a single nation has fallen to Communist aggression. And the people of one nation, Grenada, have been set free.

Now, you may remember that some on the other side compared the American mission in Grenada with the Soviet invasion of Afghanistan.

Audience. Boo-o-o!

The President. When I first heard that, it sort of touched my temperature control. The people of Afghanistan risked their lives to combat the Russian troops. Our men, by contrast, entered Grenada at the request of six Caribbean democracies and received from the Grenadian people themselves an emotional demonstration of gratitude. And today, less than a year after that mission, when the job was done, every American combat soldier has come home—every one.

We'll let our opponents ponder Soviet motives in world affairs all they want. We intend to concentrate on America's goal, which is human liberty.

When those immigrants came to our shores and said, "Which way E.J.?," they were asking which way opportunity, which way peace, which way freedom.

My dream for America, and I know it's one you share, is to see the kind of success stories in this valley multiply a million times over. And with you by our side, I just know we're going to make history again. Our victory will be a victory for America's future and the land that President Lincoln called, "the last, best hope of Earth." And that nation will rise to meet her greatest days.

I can't tell you how grateful I am and how you've warmed my heart, but I thank you. And God bless you all.

Note: The President spoke at 4:34 p.m. at Ty Cobb Field at Union-Endicott High School.

Earlier, the President went to the IBM Systems Technology Division facility, where he toured the plant and was briefed on computer production and the final product assembly. He then went to Union-Endicott High School, where he met with Tri-Cities Republican leaders.

Following his remarks, the President returned to Washington, DC.

Remarks at a Dinner Honoring Howard H. Baker, Jr.
September 12, 1984

Thank you very much. And thank you, Bill. I think it's a great pleasure for all of you to have a distinguished humorist like Bill Buckley here to chair this event. He isn't a Carl Reiner, but—[*laughter*]—Karl Malden, maybe. [*Laughter*] But this is quite an assembly. I know there are dozens of Senators and Representatives, and I believe that virtually the entire Cabinet is here, which explains why Mike Deaver has gone to sleep already. [*Laughter*]

We're all here to pay our respects to Howard Baker, and the occasion is billed as a "roast." Now, to the uninitiated, that has nothing to do with the entree—[*laughter*]—as the guest of honor will find out. I must confess I'm not much of a roaster. I believe that if you can't say something nice about a person, you shouldn't say anything at all. So, in conclusion—[*laughter*]——

No, I've been a long admirer of the cool, calm, collected way that Howard approaches things. Just Monday, we had a leadership meeting there in the Cabinet Room, and Howard took over almost immediately—[*laughter*]—in his calm way. And he said, "Here it is Monday, and tomorrow's Tuesday, and the next thing it's Wednesday. Half the week's gone, and we haven't done a damn thing." [*Laughter*]

But he's won a place in history. He made the world safe for snail darters. [*Laughter*] And he told me on the steps of the Capitol, at the time of the Inaugural 4 years ago, he said, "Mr. President, I want you to know I will be with you through thick." [*Laughter*] And I said, "What about thin?" He said, "Welcome to Washington." [*Laughter*]

But he's done everything he can to help me. I asked for a 30-percent tax cut, and he gave me 25. Some people might say you came up a little short, Howard. [*Laughter*] Now, I'm not going to go into that kind of joke. [*Laughter*] But here's a man with a distinguished career that he's had in the Senate. He is a lawyer of distinction and will be returning to Tennessee, and the thought has come to me—the United States Supreme Court. We could use a "little" justice. [*Laughter*]

All I can say is that whoever succeeds you in the Senate leadership, Howard, is going to have a mighty big camera bag to fill. [*Laughter*] Howard has done what I think most of us would agree is the impossible.

He has made Lowell Weicker and Jesse Helms work together like a team—"The Bad News Bears." [*Laughter*] So, Howard, if I may just say one serious word tonight, it is "goodbye." [*Laughter*]

But then I must add, and this time in real seriousness, Howard Baker has been a true friend. He's been a lion in support of the cause which unites us. And you will be missed more than you know, and I'm not going to let myself think about it, because it hurts too much. But thank you, Howard. God bless you.

Note: The President spoke at 7:58 p.m. in the International Ballroom at the Washington Hilton Hotel.

Memorandum on the Combined Federal Campaign
September 12, 1984

Memorandum for the Heads of Executive Departments and Agencies

Our Administration is committed to improving the lives of all people. We can be proud of our record of encouraging a broad spectrum of private sector initiatives. We know that it takes a great effort by individuals, groups, voluntary organizations, and corporations to accomplish this most important mission. We are key members of the team, and must do our part through our leadership of the Combined Federal Campaign in our respective agencies and our direct personal involvement. It takes a team effort to get the job done right.

I am pleased to announce that Secretary of Agriculture John R. Block has agreed to serve as the Chairman of the fall 1984 Combined Federal Campaign for the National Capital Area. I ask that you personally serve as Chairman of the campaign in your organization and appoint a top official as your Vice-Chairman. Please advise Secretary Block of the person you designate.

I urge you to take a personal interest in this year's campaign by working with your employees to achieve new levels of support for the programs of the Combined Federal Campaign. The private voluntary agencies and our neighbors in need are depending on us. Together, let's make this the best campaign ever.

RONALD REAGAN

Note: The memorandum was released by the Office of the Press Secretary on September 13.

Memorandum on the Combined Federal Campaign
September 12, 1984

Memorandum for All Federal Employees and Military Personnel

In each of the past 23 years, Federal employees and members of the Armed Forces have had the opportunity to show their concern for those in need through participation in the Combined Federal Campaign. I ask each of you now to continue that tradition of voluntary sharing.

Through the Combined Federal Campaign, we can help relieve pain and health problems now and support research to help eliminate them in the future. We can help our neighbors without making them dependent on government. We can assist the less fortunate in other countries, extending a nurturing hand to friends around the world.

Americans have a record of generosity and concern for others unmatched by any other country in the world. I am confident that our proud record will continue in the fall 1984 Combined Federal Campaign. While the decision to give is personal and voluntary, I encourage each of you to join me in wholeheartedly supporting this year's CFC.

RONALD REAGAN

Note: The memorandum was released by the Office of the Press Secretary on September 13.

Informal Exchange With Reporters on Foreign and Domestic Issues
September 13, 1984

Q. Why is Dobrynin coming to see you, sir?

The President. Why what?

Q. Why is Dobrynin coming to see you?

Q. Gromyko.

The President. We did agree. We're going to have a meeting. We invited him, knowing that he was coming to the United Nations.

Q. Mr. President, what about Walter Mondale's—[*inaudible*].

The President. Well, again, as I say, my specifics have been there for almost 4 years. We have submitted four budgets—three—and one to go. And they contain all the things that we're trying to do to reduce government spending and to increase the growth of the economy, which will increase revenue. They're all there for anyone to see, including some legislation still before the Congress that Tip O'Neill has refused to allow the Congress to vote on.

Q. Tip O'Neill says that 43 billion of those cuts is in Social Security from 1981. Are you still planning to go for that?

The President. That song they sing—he was a part of the bipartisan commission that came forth with the plan to put Social Security on a sound fiscal basis. It's been adopted. Social Security is secure as far as we can see into the next century, and we're not going to touch the benefits of the people on social security.

Q. He said in March you're going to have to take another look at Social Security, that it still needs some attention.

The President. Not that I know of. There are still two future tax increases in the Social Security payroll tax between now and 1990, which they passed in 1977—the biggest single tax increase in our nation's history.

Q. Will you rule out future reductions? Will you rule out future reductions for feeding programs for women, infants, and children?

The President. Right now we are spending more on those programs, on food programs, than ever before in history. Spending for food for the needy of all kinds is up 37 percent since 1980.

Q. But will you rule out a future reduction?

The President. We're looking at thousands of suggestions, most of which have to do with improving management. I still insist that government overhead for providing benefits is still much too high. You can make further budget cuts without affecting how much actually goes to help the needy.

Q. Mr. President, in your talk you're criticizing the Doubting Thomases in your speech who are putting down America. Who specifically are you talking about?

The President. Some of you might not like it if I answered that question specifically. But I've noticed that there's never a "good news" economic story on the evening news that was not accompanied by, or buried by, finding some individuals who have not yet benefited by the economic recovery.

Q. What's wrong with fair criticism?

The President. It isn't criticism at all. It's ignoring the fact that—we know there are still individuals who have not been helped. The whole aim of the program is finally to get to everyone, but we also know that there are millions of people that have gone back to work, the economy is booming—all of the figures that I've been giving in speeches. So, it would be fair to present this in a balanced way.

How come none of you've mentioned the polls?

Q. Well, what do you think of the polls?

The President. Goody. I just wanted to say, President Dewey told me to run scared and not be overconfident. So, the only poll I'm going to listen to is the one that takes place November 6th.

Q. You said that before.

The President. What?

Q. Are you going to win in a landslide this time?

The President. I'm going to run scared. Yes, I know I've said it to you before, I'm waiting for you to repeat it in your news accounts.

Q. [*Inaudible*]—specific budget deficit reduction plan between now and the election?

The President. As I say, our whole economic program is aimed at this, and it's there and has been there in every budget. The deficit today would be $50 billion less if the Congress, the House of Representatives, had agreed to the cuts we asked for, beginning in 1981.

Q. Then this is all the Hill's fault?

The President. What?

Q. The deficit is all the Hill's fault at this point?

The President. Well, since they have been approving deficit spending for—with just a few exceptions—virtually throughout 50 years, in 42 of which they have dominated the Congress, I would have to say that they can't remove themselves from the blame. Our deficit this year is over $20 billion less than we ourselves projected that it would at the beginning of the year. And this has been brought about by the gains in the economy. And that is still the best way of approaching added revenues for government, is through improving the economic base.

Q. On a scale of 1 to 10, how much are you enjoying the campaign?

The President. What?

Q. One to 10, how much are you enjoying the campaign? With 10 being the highest?

The President. Well, I had a good time all day yesterday. I think I'll have a good time today.

Okay, let's go.

Note: The exchange began at 9:55 a.m. on the South Lawn of the White House as the President was departing for a trip to Nashville, TN.

Remarks to Members of the High Technological Corridor Board in Nashville, Tennessee
September 13, 1984

Thank you all very much. And thank you, Governor Alexander, and Senator Baker. Thank you all.

I must say that I stand here with mixed emotions. I'm filled with admiration and respect for the things that you were telling me about your State. But, at the same time, when you opened with all of those words about the prevalence of Ph.D.'s here, that always touches a nerve with me, because when I got my bachelor's degree in college, some 25 years later my alma mater awarded me an honorary degree and compounded a sense of guilt I had nursed for 25 years, because I always figured the first one was honorary. [*Laughter*]

But it is wonderful to be back in Nashville, world capital of bluegrass and country music and the proud home of a man that we'll soon honor with a giant happy birthday, Mr. Roy Acuff.

Whenever I visit your Volunteer State, I get a real tug knowing that I'm standing on this hallowed ground of heroes. The spirit of Tennessee was Davy Crockett daring to push back frontiers and open up the West— they were a different kind of frontier then—Andrew Jackson, knowing one man with courage makes a majority, blazing a revolution that put power back in the hands of the people. And today that spirit is alive in an economic expansion that's creating hope and bringing Tennessee's unemployment down. So, I salute you and I salute your fine Governor.

For people seeking the newest frontiers, my advice is come to the Oak Ridge-Knoxville high-tech corridor, and you'll see America at its best. Believe me, when it comes to encouraging growth, expanding opportunities, and charting a course for excellence in education, Lamar Alexander and the people of Tennessee are giving a lesson in leadership to all America. You are creating the greatest wealth we could wish for— wealth of knowledge. It fuels a mighty tide of progress and carries hope for an optimistic future to people here and everywhere.

From the days of Bunker Hill to the Conestoga wagon, the cotton gin, smokestack industries, the Manhattan Project, and now the world of advanced and high technology, the American Revolution has been carried forward in the brave dream of pioneers— people with the faith, courage, and vision to invent the future and the marketplace of tomorrow.

Ours has never been a revolution poisoned by hatred and the will to conquer, but one rising from the deepest yearnings of the human spirit to challenge the limits of knowledge and to use the power of discovery for our most noble and generous impulses for decency, progress and, yes, for peace.

We see it in that high-tech corridor where your industries have become America's new trailblazers—new energy-related systems to make energy more affordable; radiation detectors to monitor radiation and pollutants; disease-free plant varieties that can greatly expand our nursery stock and woodlands; vital research against cancer; and medical innovations, like CAT scanners, to detect diseases of the brain and other vital organs.

You know, I can't help but wonder if a lot of the problems that are plaguing this nation wouldn't disappear if we could just borrow the people and companies in this corridor and put them inside the beltway in Washington, DC. There's nothing the United States of America can't do, if those Doubting Thomases would just stand out of the way and get out of our way.

Together, your small and large businesses throughout Tennessee are taking us another step into the future—new markets, new jobs, and valuable knowledge to help us compete for leadership in the world area of technological development.

I don't think you need convincing that America has no mission of mediocrity. We haven't come all this way just to wind up a second-best nation. Leave that tired vision for the fainthearted souls. We're not in this historic competition just to survive or just to do well, America is in this to win. The crown we're striving for is not a crown of pride or glory; ours is a battle for human progress, for excellence at every level of society.

Sons and daughters of Tennessee can meet this challenge. Together, we can blaze this trail and win this battle. And if we're to honor the tradition of Crockett and Jackson, America must win it, and I believe we will win it.

I know in Europe—when you told me about your experience there, Lamar—at the recent summit conference that I attended, I know that I had been advertised in the media as going to face a real grilling and all kinds of criticism from my fellow leaders of the industrial nations that I'd be meeting with. It didn't happen. I had the same experience you did. They were all waiting there to find out, "How'd we do it?" Well, the word, again, is a single word, really—freedom.

Look how far we've already come. In a single generation, we have freed ourselves from the bonds of Earth. We've set our footprints on the surface of the Moon, used our instruments to explore space, the Sun, and our sister planets.

Satellites enable us to communicate with each other at a moment's notice virtually anywhere on the globe. We can anticipate tomorrow's weather and prepare for it. And thousands of practical applications of space and aeronautical technology are touching our lives, from lifesaving vests for firemen to aerial scanning techniques to locate and identify everything from schools of fish to mineral deposits to healthy timberland.

New materials from natural resources like carbon and silicon are replacing expensive manufactured products. And engineers are using them to reduce the weight of modern cars, with consumers getting the benefits of more miles per gallon.

Computers using microchips are redefining our world as they become common in the workplace, community, also, and in the classroom. Many children have access to more computer power than most professional scientists and engineers had in their laboratories at the beginning of the space age.

In medicine, we're seeing the vision of technology with a human face. The pioneer field of computer-controlled walking has given hope to thousands of paralyzed Americans that someday they may walk again.

Doctors can now use sound waves to monitor babies inside the womb, ensuring safer pregnancy and delivery for the mother and better health for the newborn. We've learned how to send electrical impulses to targeted nerve centers or particular areas of the brain to provide relief from pain. And we've developed a system that can administer medication automatically within the body.

We could put a price tag on the value of these human benefits, but who would want to do that? Who can even imagine the wonders that lie ahead if we just have the faith and the courage to push on. While I was growing up, the Model A was just replacing the Model T. And now, a child may grow up to see space travel become commonplace.

The secret weapon of the technological revolution is productivity, power—awesome power. Each breakthrough in knowledge lifts us to a new, higher plateau, paving the way for great gains in productivity. Agricultural economies barely advance; industrial economies move forward in inches and feet; and an advanced technological economy can leap forward.

Working in the zero-gravity of space, we can manufacture in 1 month's time lifesaving medicines that it would take 30 years to manufacture on Earth. And we can manufacture crystals of exceptional purity that may enable us to produce super computers and make even greater breakthroughs in productivity.

But some economists and politicians are afraid of growth, afraid it will reignite inflation. Well, I'm afraid they may suffer from time warp. They seem to be stuck in one period, while all of us are entering another. They seem to see our economy only as an old and quivering thing in the industrial age, rather than a strapping young adolescent beginning to flex its muscles in the technological age.

We don't need economic doctors telling us we must ration our strength. We need

1293

economic doctors who will help America build her strength. And we don't need more politicians insisting we have deficits because you're not taxed enough. Those deficits ballooned from an economy that didn't grow enough and from 50 years of a government that's been spending too much.

Some people have labored so long at making government bigger, they've developed a knee-jerk addiction to tax increases. And every time their knee jerks, we get kicked—[*laughter*]—and that's when growth suffers most.

I'm asking for your strongest support for two long-overdue reforms, supported by the American people, but resisted by the Democratic leadership—a constitutional amendment mandating that government spend no more than government takes in and a line-item veto giving a President the power to veto individual items in appropriation bills. Your Governor has it. I had it when I was the Governor of California. And I remember with great joy the kick I got out of vetoing—[*laughter*]—more than 900 times in those 8 years, and never having one of those vetoes overridden. So remember, you don't need, with regard to some in Washington, to make them see the light, just make them feel the heat. [*Laughter*]

We came to Washington determined to spark new growth in the economy and slow the growth of government. Well, with your support and Senator Baker's, we've had 21 straight months of economic growth. That is the best expansion since World War II. Government spending growth has been cut by more than half; inflation at 4.1 percent is down by two-thirds; interest rates are down; the deficit is coming down and, yes, continued growth will keep it coming down. So, pardon me, but somebody back there must be doing something right.

But these aren't my victories, they're your victories, America's victories. And that's why I want to offer a little friendly advice to our critics: Rather than saying things that always seem to run America down, how about giving the American people a pat on the back?

Government must encourage technological growth by supporting research and development, particularly in our universities, to train tomorrow's leaders. Between 1981 and 1985, Federal investment in basic research will have increased almost 30 percent in real terms. We'll carry forward that strong commitment, continue to support tax credits for industrial research and development expenses, and strive to lessen concerns that cooperative research and development between companies may violate antitrust statutes.

Let's remember that technology is born from capital, and capital requires incentives for risk-taking and investment. We've seen dramatic proof of this relationship. The 1978 capital gains reduction, followed by our 25-percent reduction in tax rates and the shortening of depreciation schedules for business investment, have given an enormous shot in the arm to risk-taking and entrepreneurship in America.

In 1977 the venture capital industry was almost dead, with commitments of only $39 million. By 1983 the new incentives had increased those commitments to $4½ billion—more than 115 times as much. New business incorporations set a record last year, will probably do so again this year. The rate of business investment is the strongest in 40 years; productivity is rising; America's created 6 million new jobs in the last 20 months—and I know I stole it from Al Jolson, but you ain't seen nothin' yet.

If the Democratic candidate had had his way, the top rate on capital gains would not have been cut from 49 to 20 percent, it would have been spiked up to 70 percent. His adminstration fought the historic reduction in capital gains and demanded the higher rate, which they said would bring in more revenue. Well, we're getting more revenue today at the new lower rate than we were getting before. And that's the secret of good tax policy.

The choice today is just as crucial. Will we heed their call to raise tax rates, penalizing risk-taking, investment, and increasing the taxing burden on working families, farmers, and small businesses and corporations—the same antigrowth, proinflation policy that brought our economy to its knees by 1980? Or will America go forward and challenge the limits of growth with an historic simplification of the tax system, making it fairer, simpler, and lowering everybody's income tax rates so we can have more jobs, growth, and opportunity for all the people of America?

You know, Roy Acuff composed a song called "We Live in Two Different Worlds." And the choice in 1984 is between two very different worlds. They see America wringing her hands; we see America raising her hands. They see America divided by envy, each of us challenging our neighbors' success; we see an America inspired by opportunity, each of us challenging the best in ourselves. We believe in knowing when opportunity knocks; they seem determined to knock opportunity.

Well, I believe the American people are saying, "Don't hold us back. Give us a chance and watch what we do." America has always been greatest when we dared to be great. And you can feel a new spirit in this land to excel again. The new patriotism is a mighty force for good, drawing us together—all of us, from every race, religion, and ethnic background—giving us courage and confidence to surge toward great new challenges in the future.

I believe America can and will meet our number one challenge in space: to develop a permanently manned space station and to do it within a decade. We can conduct new research, explore distant planets, unlock the vast potential for commercial ventures, and do it all for the sake of a more peaceful, prosperous world.

As American technology transforms the great black night of space into a bright new world of opportunities, we can use our knowledge to create a new American opportunity society here at home. We can ensure that every person has not only an equal chance but a much greater chance to pursue the American dream.

We can build an America that offers productive, secure job opportunities for all our fellow citizens, from assembly line workers in our older industries to research scientists in new industries such as biotechnology, robotics, and information processing.

If we strengthen incentives, invest fully in the new technologies, and reach for great breakthroughs in productivity then, yes, we can and will outproduce, outcompete, and outsell anybody, anywhere in the world. We can ensure adequate supplies of affordable energy, because America must never again be held hostage by a foreign cartel. We can apply new agricultural technologies to preserve our soil and environment, and dramatically enhance crop yields for the benefit of millions who look to us for help and hope.

Our nation is more than 200 years old, but somehow America has never been younger, never been more filled with hope. Everything is before us. And if we keep America free, everything will be possible. The land that President Lincoln called "the last, best hope of man on Earth," will rise to meet her greatest days, and the eagle will soar.

Well, I thank you today for your warm welcome, and thank you for what you did for Tennessee and for America, and what you're doing for America and your State every day of the year.

Thank you again, and God bless you all.

Note: The President spoke at 11:19 a.m. in the Memphis Room at the Opryland Hotel.

Following his remarks, the President met at the hotel with local Republican leaders and Reagan-Bush campaign leaders.

Remarks at a Birthday Celebration for Roy Acuff in Nashville, Tennessee
September 13, 1984

Thank you, Roy. And thank you all, ladies and gentlemen. Thank all of you up here on the stage, the great artists of the first of all American art forms, country music. I guess now that I've appeared at the Opry, I've really arrived.

I'm going to interject something here, just a little note that was not part of my prepared remarks, except I might also say, Roy, that the whole thing of being here a couple of days early, no problem at all for me.[1] But if the 13th had fallen on tomorrow, I'd have really had problems then. [Laughter] Friday the 13th.

But I just want to say here that I talked this morning to the husband of Barbara Mandrell,[2] and he asked me if I would say thanks to so many of you who have contacted them and who have called and who've expressed concern. And I know that she's a member of the family and should be here, too. And you all know she was in an accident. And I told him that I was sure that everyone was doing what we were doing, and that was praying that everything was all right, and praying, also, for the tragedy of the White family, and a prayer that she'll be well soon. But he said she's doing very well; so is their son. And the children are all right, also. So, I thought you'd be glad to hear that.

And now, I'll get on with it's wonderful to be here in Nashville. And it's wonderful to be here in Tennessee. This is one of those special States. It's more than just a place; it's a state of mind. The secret of Tennessee, the way I see it, is its people and the music they make. And, you know, the man who founded the Opry explained a little about both when he said, "The Grand Ole Opry is as simple as sunshine. It has a universal appeal because it's built upon good will, it expresses the heartbeat of a large percentage of Americans who labor for a living." Well, I agree.

And now, we're here today to celebrate the 81st birthday of the King of Country Music. And, Roy, the other day I met with some senior citizens in the White House, and I told them the only way I could sum up my feelings about older folks is to greet them by saying, "Hi, kids." [Laughter] So, now I want to share my thoughts about a kid named Roy Acuff who, in a couple of days, will be celebrating the 42d anniversary of his 39th birthday. [Laughter]

---

[1] Mr. Acuff had earlier referred to the fact that his birthday was September 15.
[2] The President had telephoned Ken Dudley earlier in the day.

You know, he was born the son of a Baptist minister up in Maynardsville in 1903. He showed a certain talent for music when he was a boy, and he was so good at sports that he walked out of high school with 13 letters. The New York Yankees wanted him to come up north, but I guess Roy didn't want to leave home. He stayed in Tennessee, worked as a callboy on the L&N Railroad, and hung around the house learning to play the fiddle.

In the 1930's he joined a traveling medicine show, and he put together a group, and soon he had his own radio shows over in Knoxville. Roy started making records, and that was in the 1930's when labor practices were not what they could have been. In one session, it was so hot in the studio that the band recorded in their underwear. [Laughter] You may have heard of a few of the songs that they were working on. One was the "The Great Speckled Bird," and the other was "Wabash Cannonball." In an earlier appearance of mine—not here—Roy and his band played that, as he said, for about 45 minutes from—[laughter]—my entrance and greeting of a lot of people.

But he first played at the Opry in 1938. And soon he and the Smokey Mountain Boys were regulars, and they were so popular that they beat out Frank Sinatra in some of the national music polls. It's no exaggeration to say that Roy Acuff brought country music into the mainstream of American life. And he and his music were so much a part of our lives, it's said that during World War II when the Japanese would storm a beach they would yell, "To hell with Roosevelt, to hell with Babe Ruth, and to hell with Roy Acuff!" [Laughter]

A few years later a Governor of Tennessee was invited to appear at the Opry, and he turned it down with the statement that he thought country music was "disgracing the State." Roy Acuff didn't like that a lot. [Laughter] So, he ran for Governor in the next primary. [Laughter] He didn't win, but he made his point. I don't think a lot of politicians criticize country music anymore.

In 1962 Roy Acuff became the first living musician to be honored as a member of the Country Music Hall of Fame. A few years after that he was in a bad car accident, but within months he was up and out of his sick bed to entertain the troops in Vietnam. And he was there to sing at the White House when the POWs returned in 1974.

Roy Acuff isn't just a great artist, he's a fine man and a patriot. He loves America, and he's stuck by her through thick and thin. I'm personally honored by the opportunity to come and to honor him. And, Roy, I know I'm speaking for everyone here when I say you will always be the King of Country Music and, therefore, the only appropriate thing to say on your 81st birthday is, "Long Live the King!"

There's one thing I want to add, something I was thinking about on my way down here on the plane. All of you are aware, I think, that there's a great resurgence of patriotic feeling sweeping the country. And it's heartening, and I've been moved by it. You could see it during the Olympics, how the crowds out in Los Angeles would wave the flag and sing along to "The Star Spangled Banner." And you can hear it in the popular music these days, and you'll hear it when Lee Greenwood sings "God Bless the U.S.A."

Now, there are a lot of reasons, I guess, why this good spirit has returned to our land. But it got a lot of encouragement from Nashville. It's the people of this city who never forgot to love their country, who never thought patriotism was out of style. And I know you were just expressing how you felt; you didn't know that you were doing your country a great service by keeping affection for it alive in your songs. But you were doing it a service, and I don't know if anyone has ever thanked you. But if not, thank you. People like you make me proud to be an American.

Now, this is such a fine day, and I look at all of you and somehow I don't see why the other side keeps saying things are so terrible in this country. According to them, we're in desperate straits. So, I hope you don't mind my asking, do you feel better off than you did 4 years ago? [*Applause*]

Could it be because the economy is expanding again, and we have real prosperity without inflation, and because there are 6 million new jobs in the country in the past 20 months, and that you have a friend in the White House who doesn't believe that you're undertaxed? [*Applause*]

Well, then, let me ask you one more question: Is America better off than it was 4 years ago? [*Applause*]

Now, the other side keeps saying the answer to all this success is to start another old round of tax and tax and spend and spend. I think we all better remember that the other side's promises are a little like Minnie Pearl's hat—they both have big price tags hanging from them. [*Laughter*] But the price tag on those promises comes to over $1,800 for every American household.

And I don't know about our opponents, but there's an old country and western song called "Home on the Range," where seldom is heard a discouraging word. I guess they haven't campaigned there yet. [*Laughter*] You could invite them here. If you don't, that's just as well. [*Laughter*] But they couldn't perform here anyway, because all they do is sing the blues. [*Laughter*]

The truth is there are things to be happy about and proud of in this country these days. The misery index is just about half what it was, and the forces of international communism have not, in these past few years, been gaining ground. And here at home the decent, homely virtues, the wholesome habits, are in style again.

There's so much before us, so much of the future to be seized and shaped by us. We can simplify the tax system so that people aren't sick with worry and confusion every April 15th. And if we do, we can continue to lower tax rates, which will further encourage the working men and women of this country and further encourage economic expansion.

We can continue the fairness of our foreign policy so that our friends will know that we're their friends, and our adversaries will know we're not a doormat.

And we can continue together to encourage respect for traditional values. We're greatly blessed in this country. We've been allowed to stand for something. So much of our greatness is behind us, but so much of our greatness is still before us.

dreams. And no matter what your party, I hope you can join with us this year and walk with us toward a better future. You're wanted and welcome. And no one should feel left out. Our party is open to you and waiting for you.

And I thank you so much. I thank you, Roy, and Lee, and all of you. God bless you all.

And now, Roy, we have a little something special for you here. I was going to bring it in, but my pocket was full.

Note: The President spoke at 1:15 p.m. in the Grand Ole Opry Theater at Opryland, U.S.A. Following his remarks, a cake was brought out on stage and everyone sang "Happy Birthday." Prior to his appearance at the celebration, the President met with Mr. Acuff at his residence.

Following his remarks, the President returned to Washington, DC.

Remarks at a Ceremony Honoring Hispanic Excellence in Education
September 14, 1984

The President. Well, thank you all very much, and welcome to the White House. *Buenas tardes.*

This is National Hispanic Heritage Week, and I know you've been told already, and I can think of no better way of topping off the week's activities than with a ceremony that highlights the invaluable role of education.

With a median age of 23, compared to 31 for non-Hispanics, as a group, Americans of Hispanic descent are younger than their fellow countrymen. And this enormously increases the importance of education to the Hispanic community.

It's encouraging to observe, in recent years, the marked improvement in the level of schooling of young Hispanics. Since 1970 the percentage of college graduates has doubled, and the number of Hispanics finishing high school has increased dramatically. What we see is a picture of a group of our citizens on the move.

Americans of Hispanic descent are moving into the business and professional community as never before. They—and that includes some of you with us today—are playing a major role throughout this administration. This generation of young Americans of Hispanic descent, due to an expanding economy and increasing opportunity, will have it within its grasp to achieve more and advance further than any generation of Hispanics at any time, in any country of the world.

And this is especially true for the young people who are here today. I know you've been selected because you've demonstrated superior academic skills, outstanding leadership, or exemplary service to your community.

I want to congratulate all of you for your personal standards and for what you've already accomplished. I know your families are proud of you, and so am I. We want you to soar like eagles in the coming years as you finish your education. We want you to shine in whatever endeavor you choose when you get out of school.

We also hope you'll help others along— others who may be having a difficult time. The dropout rate among Hispanic students is still far from acceptable. I'm asking Secretary Bell to look into this, but let's not kid ourselves: There are no easy answers. We need your support in letting your peers, other young Hispanics, know just how vital it is to stay in school and get an education. You can help them understand what a bright future beckons if they'll just take advantage of their educational opportunities.

Perhaps some of you in the not too distant future may be teachers yourselves. And I can think of no other profession which offers as much of a chance to help others in such a meaningful way, doing things that will change people's lives.

And today, thanks to the efforts of responsible people all over the United States, there is a new commitment to excellence in education. In the past 4 years, more than half of our country's 16,000 school districts have increased the number of credits required in subjects fundamental to a good education. And by 1985 almost 40 percent more will have raised their standards.

All 50 States have now convened task forces on education. Forty-one have upped their graduation requirements in just the past 3 years; 34 of them did so since April of last year. Forty-two States have begun initiatives to improve teacher preparation or certification, and 20 have enacted or endorsed master teacher, career ladder, or merit pay programs to attract top students—perhaps like some of you here—attract them into the teaching profession and to reward our best teachers.

There's new emphasis on discipline and evidence of increased parental involvement—irreplaceable assets that money can't buy.

And as for money, the overall resources committed to education in this country in the last 4 years have increased by 32.4 percent. And that's not money being taxed away by the Federal Government and sent back to local areas with Federal guidelines and bureaucratic mandates and a kind of a Federal carrying charge. This increase represents a local investment by concerned citizens and parents. It represents more local authority, more community control, and more responsibility in the hands of those directly involved.

Perhaps one of the most heartening trends has been the emergence of a new spirit and direct support of education by the business community, professional associations, and fraternal associations. Today we're especially proud of the part the U.S. Hispanic Chamber of Commerce is taking in helping Hispanic students. This event today wouldn't have been possible without them. The scholarship program that they're starting will be helping some of you get through college.

I want to personally thank Hector Barreto and his big-hearted amigos for what they're doing. Hector, and men and women like him, struggled long and hard, overcame great obstacles to get where they are. Today he's a successful businessman; yet he started out picking potatoes. He's someone young Hispanics can look up to.

Today we honor some giants in the field of education—individuals to whom all Americans owe a debt of gratitude. And it's my pleasure to present to them these outstanding leadership awards of the Department of Education. Their contributions are improving the well-being of their fellow Americans of Hispanic descent and of the country as a whole.

And I'm especially happy that we're able to honor the late Dr. Rivera. I had the pleasure of meeting him at a private session here at the White House last year. I found him to be a thoughtful man, and he will be missed.

We're grateful for him and for the invaluable contributions all of our honorees here have made. These recipients are heroes of a better life, heroes of increased opportunity, heroes who use their time, energy, and creative talents to help the young.

Now, Secretary Bell, I believe you have the list of recipients.

Secretary Bell. Mr. President, our first awardee—and I think it's appropriate that we start with him—is the famous Jaime Escalante. The Los Angeles teacher received nationwide publicity for his outstanding work in teaching mathematics, bringing students clear up through calculus. It's attracted so much attention, he's been written up in national magazines. So, it's a pleasure to present him to you as the first award receiver.

And secondly, Mr. President, we honor Dr. Thomas Rivera. Sadly, as you just indicated, Dr. Rivera died almost a year ago. And as the chancellor of the University of California at Riverside and as professor of Spanish literature, he attained many distinctions in the field of education. And it's a real pleasure to present to you his widow, Concepcion, who will accept the award on his behalf.

The second awardee, Mr. President—you may not have heard this is his birthday today—is Dr. Edward Aguirre. He's chairman of the board of trustees of the National Hispanic University, and he's a former U.S. Commissioner of Education. In fact, he followed me as Commissioner of Education.

So, I'm pleased to present Dr. Aguirre to you.

Next, Mr. President, Dr. Pilar Barbosa de Rosario—began teaching while still a teenager, a very outstanding author, a very distinguished professor and highly respected educator, accomplished wonders in Puerto Rico, and is dean of the Puerto Rican historians and an educator that we've been too long in honoring. And I'm pleased to present Dr. de Rosario to you now.

Next, Mr. President, is the president of one of our outstanding universities that's serving Hispanic youth. Dr. Miguel Nevarez—president of Pan American University, a long-time educator, even an activist for attaining more education for Hispanics, a very distinguished executive. It was my privilege to give the commencement address at his campus last year. And he's highly regarded in the Rio Grande Valley as an outstanding educator, and I'm proud to present him to you.

And, now, Mr. President, Francisco Sanchez. We call him "Frank" Sanchez, superintendent of schools from Albuquerque, New Mexico. Mr. President, he was a member and a leader in our National Commission on Excellence in Education. He's a trustee on the college board that gives these SAT tests. And we hope we're soon going to be able to announce that they're going up a little bit. So, it's a pleasure to present to you an outstanding school leader, widely known nationally, Frank Sanchez.

And, now, Mr. President, another distinguished university president, Dr. Lauro Ca-vazos, president of Texas Tech University and Texas Tech University of Health Sciences Center. He presides as president over two institutions. He's also an author, an instructor in medical sciences, a very distinguished academic leader in higher education, and I'm honored to present him to you, Mr. President.

And then, Mr. President, Olympia Rosado—a teacher, a very outstanding author, and today, a newspaper columnist, Mr. President, widely acclaimed for her professional and personal accomplishments. She's a great champion for education for youth. And we couldn't make these awards without including Olympia in this group, and it's a pleasure to present her to you.

Then lastly, Mr. President, Esther Buckley, who is a member of the U.S. Civil Rights Commission and a math and science teacher of great distinction from Laredo, Texas. And Esther wasn't able to be here because there's a Commission meeting today. And so we will present her award to you, but I wanted to mention her as also an award recipient.

Thank you very much, Mr. President, for honoring these educators.

The President. Thank you.

Note: The President spoke at 1:19 p.m. at the ceremony in the Rose Garden at the White House. In addition to the educators, 80 Hispanic youth, designated by the U.S. Hispanic Chamber of Commerce for their achievements, were represented at the ceremony.

Executive Order 12487—Adjustments of Certain Rates of Pay
September 14, 1984

By the authority vested in me as President by the Constitution and laws of the United States of America, and in accordance with section 2207 of the Deficit Reduction Act of 1984 (Public Law 98–369), it is hereby ordered as follows:

Section 1. Executive Order No. 12456 of December 30, 1983, as amended, is further amended by replacing Schedule 8 attached thereto with the corresponding new Schedule 8 attached hereto.

Sec. 2. The adjustments of rates of pay made by section 1 of this Order are effective on the first day of the first applicable pay period beginning on or after January 1, 1984.

RONALD REAGAN

The White House,
September 14, 1984.

[*Filed with the Office of the Federal Register, 4:24 p.m., September 14, 1984*]

Note: *The schedule is printed in the* Federal Register *of September 18.*

Nomination of John C. Lawn To Be Deputy Administrator of Drug Enforcement
September 14, 1984

The President today announced his intention to nominate John C. Lawn to be Deputy Administrator of Drug Enforcement, Department of Justice. He would succeed Frederick A. Rody, Jr.

Since 1982 Mr. Lawn has been serving as Acting Deputy Administrator, Drug Enforcement Administration, Department of Justice. Previously, he was Special Agent in Charge of the FBI Office in San Antonio, TX, in 1980–1982; Section Chief of FBI Headquarters in 1979–1980; Assistant Special Agent in Charge of the FBI Office in Kansas City, MO (1977–1979); and Supervisor of FBI Headquarters in 1973–1977.

He graduated from St. Francis College (B.A., 1957) and St. John's University (M.A. 1964). He is married, has four children, and resides in Fairfax Station, VA. He was born June 2, 1935, in Brooklyn, NY.

Nomination of Charles H. Dallara To Be United States Executive Director of the International Monetary Fund
September 14, 1984

The President today announced his intention to nominate Charles H. Dallara to be United States Executive Director of the International Monetary Fund for a term of 2 years. He would succeed Richard D. Erb.

Since 1983 Mr. Dallara has been serving as Deputy Assistant Secretary of the Treasury for International Monetary Affairs. Previously, he was U.S. Alternate Executive Director to the International Monetary Fund in 1982–1983; special assistant to the Assistant Secretary of the Treasury for International Affairs in 1981–1982; special assistant to the Under Secretary of the Treasury for Monetary Affairs in 1979–1980; and international economist in the Office of International Monetary Affairs in 1976–1979.

He graduated from the University of South Carolina (B.S., 1970) and the Fletcher School of Law and Diplomacy (M.A., 1975; M.A.L.D., 1976). He is married, has one child, and resides in Annandale, VA. He was born August 25, 1948, in Spartanburg, SC.

Nomination of Jasper R. Clay, Jr., To Be a Commissioner of the United States Parole Commission
September 14, 1984

The President today announced his intention to nominate Jasper R. Clay, Jr., to be a Commissioner of the United States Parole Commission, Department of Justice, for a term of 6 years. He would succeed Oliver James Keller, Jr.

Since 1976 Mr. Clay has been commissioner of the Maryland Parole Commission. Previously, he was associate member of the State of Maryland Board of Parole in 1969–1976; district supervisor, Baltimore City District Office, Division of Parole and Pro-bation in 1968; and staff specialist in training and development in the Maryland Division of Parole and Probation in 1966–1968.

He graduated from Morgan State University (B.S., 1954). He is married, has two children, and resides in Columbia, MD. He was born November 26, 1933, in Fairmont, WV.

Statement on the Death of Josyf Cardinal Slipyj
September 14, 1984

It is with deep sense of loss that I acknowledge the death of Josyf Cardinal Slipyj, Major Archbishop of the Ukrainian Catholic Church, and extend my condolences to Ukrainians throughout the world.

When we remember Cardinal Slipyj's 18 years in Soviet prison camps, when we reflect that he was condemned to the gulag because he refused to betray his church, we see the power and strength of the human spirit brought clearly into focus.

Even after release from that long imprisonment, Cardinal Slipyj's spirit and energy were not lessened. Between his release in 1963 and his death at the age of 92, he traveled the world to visit Ukrainian Catholics and visited President Ford here in the White House. He established a Ukrainian Catholic seminary, built the impressive St. Sophia Ukrainian Catholic Church and the Ukrainian Catholic University. Recently, he was deeply involved in the planning of a worldwide celebration for the millenium of Christianity in Ukraine to take place in 1988.

Cardinal Slipyj's commitment to God and the freedom of men was unshakable, despite punishment and exile for his beliefs. Because of his inspired life, he has long been a symbol of the strength of God and human spirit. He will remain such, cherished not only by Ukrainians, but by men and women of good will in all nations.

Radio Address to the Nation on the Presidential Campaign
September 15, 1984

My fellow Americans:

When I set out on this campaign, I said this election would offer one of the clearest choices in 50 years. One major element in that choice is simply this: whether America will continue to champion the great, driving idea for your future—economic growth through individual opportunity—or whether our nation will return to the past and stifle that growth.

We're determined to keep the mighty engine of this nation revved up to build a future of lasting economic growth without inflation that reaches every American from the Bronx to Birmingham to San Francisco Bay. All that we've done and all that we mean to do is to make our free country freer still, to bring to each of you greater opportunities to build that stronger future.

We believe opportunity is the true engine of progress, the captain of great endeavors. And that's why we asked you in 1981 to give America a new beginning—why we fought for and won a 25-percent tax rate reduction for everyone; tax indexing to keep inflation from pushing you into higher tax brackets; estate tax reductions for family farms and small businesses; a reduction in the marriage penalty tax; an increase in the child care tax credit; deregulation of banking, allowing a higher rate of return for small savers and new incentives for IRA's and Keogh contributions.

These incentives are sweeping fresh winds of progress across America. Along with restraints on government spending and regulating, they're bringing America the strongest surge of economic growth, jobs, business investment, and spendable income since the 1950's.

We're no longer talking about promises, but about progress. But while that progress is a welcome change from the past, it won't be good enough until everyone can share it. So, when people ask, "Where do we go from here?", my answer is, "Forward, with more opportunity for more growth for all Americans."

We're seeing proof that rewarding people who work and invest and save to get ahead is creating stronger growth and, in turn, helping still more people to find jobs and build a better life. So, we want to take this idea of incentives a big step further. We want to enact an historic simplification of our tax system, make the system more fair, easier to understand, so we can bring everybody's income tax rates further down, not up.

Next, we want to put the power of incentives to work in distressed areas of our cities and countryside. We want to establish enterprise zones where taxes and regulations would be cut for anyone starting up or expanding a business. Imagine ghettos across America with people off welfare working to support their families. Imagine their families living in more secure neighborhoods with less crime, feeling hopeful again about their future. Enterprise zones can do this for America.

To make a free country freer still, we want to ensure that those who produce our food and fiber have markets for their prod-

ucts. We've made a good start. Already, we've ended the last administration's disastrous grain embargo, restored grain sales to the Soviets with over 23 million metric tons sold in the last year, given them the go-ahead this week to buy up to 10 million tons more, and reached an agreement with Japan to virtually double our beef exports over the next 4 years.

So, you have a clear choice in 1984. To every American we offer new opportunity, lower tax rates, more jobs, rising take-home pay, and a brighter future for everyone. My opponent offers the biggest single tax increase in our history, $85 billion per year, he says, but really much more if his promises are fully funded. All told, his tax increase could amount to an additional tax of $1,800 per household, a giant stop sign that would bring America's economic growth and your opportunities for the future screeching to a halt. His plan would take us back to the worst misery index of the past. Ours would enable all of us to go forward together and build new opportunity for the future.

We're really talking about two different worlds. They see America wringing her hands; we see America raising her hands. They see America divided by envy, each of us challenging our neighbor's success; we see America inspired by opportunity, each of us challenging the best in ourselves. We believe in knowing when opportunity knocks; they seem determined only to knock opportunity.

I think Americans are saying: Don't hold us back. Give us a chance and watch how high we fly. And that's just what we want to help you do.

Till next week, thanks for listening, and God bless you.

Note: The President spoke at 12:06 p.m. from the Oval Office at the White House.

Remarks at the Annual Dinner of the National Italian American Foundation
September 15, 1984

The President. Thank you very much. Thank you.

Audience. 4 more years! 4 more years! 4 more years!

The President. Thank you, Frank. Thank you very much. Mr. Toastmaster, reverend clergy, and all of you, I'm very happy to be here with all of you. In fact, let me try this—*[laughter]—sono molto contento di essere qui.* [I'm very happy to be here.]

And I, too, would like to extend an official welcome to our honored guests from Italy who are with us here this evening.

As I look out at all of you here this evening, I can't help but think that you're a living affirmation of the sometimes desperate dreams of those world changers who came here and invented America. I say desperate dreams because those who traveled here, by wind-driven ship or by steamer, wouldn't have been making that terrible journey unless they were in search of something that had eluded them at home—economic opportunity, or personal freedom, or a chance to make one's mark.

The Italian-American experience was never an easy one, but it was one of great triumph. Italians, of course, made their mark on this country early on. An Italian found it, it was named for an Italian, and it was explored by Italians. But after that came the immigrants, and it wasn't easy for them. The Jews of the roiling ghettos, the Irish living 10 to a room in Boston, and the Italians looking for work in Philadephia—all shared some rough beginnings. But what distinguished these groups of immigrants is that they yielded more than their share of genius. In fact, you might say that Ellis Island was one big incubator for American greatness. All of the immigrants, and certainly the Italians, changed our country by adding to the sum total of what we are. They did not take from, they added to.

The Italians did it by hard work. They went to New Orleans and became longshoremen and fishermen. In Washington and Oregon and in my home State of California, they started out as hired hands and eventually built up their own farms. In Pennsylvania, they took the heavy lifting jobs, the manual labor. In New York, Chicago, and Boston, they opened barber shops, fruit stands, restaurants and eventually, small banks.

These immigrants were guided by habits, principles, and traditions that they took from the old country and transplanted here. They believed in the central importance of the family, the dignity of hard work, and faith in a just God who would reward effort and encourage virtue. They stayed in America and worked hard, and little by little, secured the things that eluded them. They became the backbone of the American middle class.

Many of them went on to great achievements and to fulfill the desperate dreams of their fathers and grandfathers, their mothers and grandmothers. I was told the other day about one family that had done especially well, by the way. It was a few years ago, and they moved out of their apartment in the city into a big house out on Long Island. And a friend said to the 12-year-old son, "How do you like your new house?" And he said: "Oh, we love it. I have my own room, my brother has his own room, my sisters have their own rooms. Poor Mom, she's still in with Dad." [*Laughter*]

I want to add that the thing I like about Italian-American families is that no matter how many rooms they have, they're always together. The family bond is strong and loving. There are numerous examples, of course, of Italian-American triumphs. Many of them are sitting here on this dais. One of them was recently chosen to be the Vice Presidential candidate of her party, and I understand the pride that all of you feel. And, Congresswoman Ferraro, all I can say is—and here I go again—*[laughter]—"Congratulazoni."*

Monsignor Geno Baroni used to say, "There are only two lasting things we can leave our children. One is roots, the other is wings." And what can we do these days to make sure that our children are given both? And what can we do to ensure that all of the immigrant sons and daughters of our country have the same chance to prosper as the sons and daughters of Italy have?

My views on these things, I think, are well known. We believe that the Italian traditions of faith and family, the dignity of work, and the importance of effort should be encouraged. And that's why we tried to gear so many of our efforts toward the family, the prime generator of life and human virtues. We believe that protecting economic freedom means fighting inflation with unrelenting determination, for inflation is the deadliest tax of all.

Because we believe in justice, we've tried to make society a safer place. We believe that families have the right to take a walk together in a park, in the dark, in the city, without having to fear for their lives. They pay taxes for that right, but violent crime has deprived them of it. We're tough on crime, and we think we must be. Defendants have their rights and always will and always must. But victims and potential victims, too, have their rights, and we've tried very hard to make sure those rights are respected.

Let me add here that in the area of organized crime and drug trafficking, our Government and the Government of Italy have formed an extraordinary joint working group. Representatives of Italy's Interior Ministry will be in Washington soon for intensive high-level meetings with the Justice Department. The Italian Government's co-operation on this matter has been complete, and I believe the working group is another reflection of the excellent relations that exist between our two countries.

Italy, by the way, deserves a lot of credit and the thanks of the world for its heroic efforts to fight crime and domestic political terrorism. All of us remember that day in 1982 when Italy liberated General James Dozier from the hands of the Red Brigades. The courage of the Italian forces took our breath away. And I had the pleasure in Rome of meeting the young men that finally broke through that last door in the face of the enemy guns and effected the rescue. And I want to tell you, I'd feel you could

send them to do some very tough jobs without arms. They were the most capable young men I've seen in a long time. Italy's been very effective in this fight, and they're setting an example for the world.

We believe in the neighborhood. We believe that the closer political power is to the people it affects, the better it will be wielded. We believe that human experience has taught us that local control is an integral part of political freedom. And we believe, finally, that the first and last key to making sure America will always be a haven for the immigrants who've enriched it is to ensure the peace.

And to ensure the peace, we must remain militarily strong. Down through our history most American Presidents have understood this. Our friends know well something that we know and something that our adversaries know: America can be trusted with military might. We don't like war; we never have. We're not an expansionist country or an imperialist country. We seek only to protect, never to act as the aggressor.

Our nation must always remain what God, in His wisdom, intended it to be—a refuge, a place of safe haven for those looking for the human rights that have eluded them in the place of their birth. And it must always be a place of limitless opportunity for the children and grandchildren of the dreamers who journeyed here. If we keep these things in mind, then, truly, the children of the future will have both roots and wings, and the dream will endure.

Before I leave you tonight, I want to add just one more thing. Decades and decades back, there was an Italian immigrant who came to America. And he started a family and worked hard and raised his children as best he could. One of his sons became a milkman. He, too, worked hard and married and had a family. And then the mailman—or the milkman, I should say, raised his children as he had been raised. They were taught to respect honesty, decency, and hard work. They struggled to make ends meet. All of the money went to the education of their children. They put one son through college, and when he said he wanted to be a doctor, they put him through medical school. Because of their diligence, the son became a prominent surgeon in a great hospital. And one day that surgeon, that son of a milkman, saved the life of a President of the United States who'd been shot. I know this story, because I was the patient.

Dr. Joseph Giordano is the surgeon. The hero of this story is Joseph Giordano, Sr.—retired milkman and inheritor of the Italian-American tradition.

I have thanked the Giordanos, but I've not had a chance to personally thank a group like this for all that you've done to keep the tradition alive. And so, *grazie.* Thank you all very much. God bless you.

Note: The President spoke at 10:56 p.m. in the International Ballroom at the Washington Hilton Hotel. He was introduced by Frank Stella. Other speakers at the dinner included the Vice President and the Democratic Presidential and Vice-Presidential candidates, Walter F. Mondale and Representative Geraldine A. Ferraro, respectively.

Remarks on Receiving the Report of the United States-Japan Advisory Commission
September 17, 1984

The President. Well, I'm going to turn the meeting over to you, except to say that I'm delighted here and to have the report that I know you are going to present. I think we're all agreed on the improvement that has been made and the things that really remain to be done in our relationship with Japan. I think that's one of the most important partnerships we have. So, David.

Mr. Packard. Well, thank you very much, Mr. President, for taking time from your busy schedule to be with us, and I want to present this report to you from the Commission.

Now, I would like to quickly point out that this is a joint effort. The Japanese and Americans continue to work very closely together, and the report is really an agreement between both members. As you can expect, there might have been some things that would have been said if we'd had complete freedom to say them, but I was very encouraged by the fact that the Japanese have been very forthcoming and very much interested.

I think we all came out of this study with the conclusion that this is an extremely important relationship not only in the short term but in the long term. In addition to the work that we did in discussing these issues among the Commission members, we had a number of studies done on various aspects of this relationship—a very good study on agricultural policy, a good study on industrial policy. And we also had a study made to try and get some idea about what the options would be in the long term—what would happen if we continued a close partnership with the Japanese over the next 10 or 15 [years] or even into the next century, and if we didn't.

And I think the conclusion we've come to is that this relationship is so important that we have no option but for both of our countries to work very hard to maintain this close cooperation. And I think that out of that, and really in part out of some of the things that you and your associates have done here, our recommendation is that this relationship will benefit from better management. And I think the exercise that we went through when you presented the yen-dollar issue to the Prime Minister this last fall, the fact that Secretary Regan followed up on that, and George Bush went over—it was an example, I think, of the way some of these issues can be managed in a more effective way than simply the reactive process that has come about.

Now, the Japanese are presenting their report to the Prime Minister at about this time, and I have a wire here from the Japanese Cochairman. I thought I might just read an excerpt from this because he especially wanted to have you realize that the Japanese have concurred in the programs.

And he is going to approach a meeting with the Prime Minister:

"And our plan is to strongly underscore a major point in the report; that is the importance of the U.S.-Japan relationship and the fact that the two leaders should pay priority attention to this relationship. We will obviously stress the growing importance and opportunities for cooperation of our two nations in global affairs, and we'll certainly point out some of the problems, particularly in the management of the relationship. But we will discuss them in the context of a need for greater bilateral cooperation.

"Some of the problems, if left unresolved, will undermine our capabilities to make joint contributions to the global economic and political health and advancement. We hope to encourage our Prime Minister to instruct the government officials, as well as the leaders in the private sector, to study the report carefully and to implement some of the recommendations. And it is our belief that a deep, mutual confidence and a strong commitment to the shared goals between your President and our Prime Minister are providing us with a golden opportunity to maximize our cooperative relationship.

"Public officials as well as the private sector in both countries should seek to find ways to further promote such cooperative relationships and also improve management of some of the frictions inevitable in an interdependent and close bilateral relationship. We are very pleased that the President, Secretary Shultz and other members of the Cabinet [will be present when you present the report], and that in itself demonstrates the importance your government leaders are attaching to our bilateral relationship. We hope that you will convey to your President the deep respect from the members of the Japanese Commission. It was our privilege to serve your President as well as our Prime Minister in this meaningful joint project."

The President. Well, that's fine.

Mr. Packard. So, we hope that this will provide some guidance to move ahead with what you've already started here, and we think you've made very good progress so far. But we also think there's a lot of opportunity to continue the work that's being done. And it's been a great pleasure for us to participate in this program.

Let me just conclude by saying that unless you feel otherwise, we consider the work of this Commission to be finished. But if any of us, individually, can be helpful in implementing some of the recommendations that you may wish to adopt, we stand ready to do so.

The President. Well, Dave—and all of you—I just want to give you a heartfelt thanks. I think it's magnificent what you have done. And I'm glad to hear the last few words that you said, because it's very possible that—[*laughter*]—that I might follow my thank you with occasionally saying, "By the way, would you . . . ?" [*Laughter*]

Mr. Packard. Well, we're ready to help, because we think it's an important issue. And we're just delighted with the progress you've already started in this area.

The President. Well, God bless you all. Thank you very much. All right.

Reporter. Mr. President, what do you think of Mr. Mondale meeting with Gromyko?

The President. I have no problem with that at all.

Q. Do you think he's trying to one-up you by seeing Gromyko first? [*Laughter*]

The President. I have no problem with that at all. [*Laughter*]

Note: The President spoke at 9:45 a.m. in the Roosevelt Room at the White House. David Packard, chairman of the board of Hewlett-Packard, Inc., is the U.S. Chairman of the Commission.

The Commission's report is entitled "Challenges and Opportunities in United States—Japan Relations—September 1984" (Office of Public Communication, Department of State, 109 pages).

Statement by Principal Deputy Press Secretary Speakes on the United States National Committee for Pacific Economic Cooperation
September 18, 1984

In his meeting today with the Committee, President Reagan will point to the growing importance of the Pacific to the United States and reiterate his personal commitment to strengthening and expanding America's cooperative ties with nations of that region. The President will make his remarks during a reception given for a group of prominent Americans active in U.S. relations with the nations of the Pacific Basin.

The White House reception precedes the founding meeting of the group, the United States National Committee for Pacific Economic Cooperation. The bipartisan committee includes approximately 50 leaders from the country's business, government, and academic communities, and is an outgrowth of regional economic discussions held over the past 4 years. Its formation is an impor-

tant step in the continuing progress toward improved communications and cooperation among the countries of the Pacific.

The Committee, a private nonprofit body, corresponds to similar bodies being formed elsewhere in the Pacific region. Among its roles will be coordination of the United States contribution to the region-wide economic dialog carried out under the auspices of the Pacific Economic Cooperation Conference. It is also expected to serve as a focal point of U.S. economic policy and strategy toward the Pacific. Serving on the Committee are Members of Congress, leading corporate executives involved in Asia-Pacific trade, representatives from several executive branch departments and agencies, numerous Asia-Pacific scholars, and representatives of such organizations as the Asia Foundation and the Asia Society.

Remarks to the United States National Committee for Pacific Economic Cooperation
September 18, 1984

Good morning. Thank you very much for being here and for a warm welcome.

As a Californian, I've long recognized the importance of the Pacific region. And I am pleased that during this administration we've been able to expand and deepen our ties with the countries of the Pacific Basin. And I look forward to hearing your views on the issues that we face.

The market-oriented economies of the Pacific have achieved a sustained and impressive economic growth. We in the administration value highly our relationship with the countries of the Pacific. We look forward to working with them to develop policies which will sustain the impressive

record of economic growth for the benefit of our citizens, of our Pacific partners, and our global, free-market system.

President Theodore Roosevelt said almost at the turn of the 20th century, years ago, that the Atlantic was the ocean of the present and the Pacific is the ocean of the future. Well, I think his vision was a clear one. And today I think we've seen proof of that.

I congratulate all of you on your foresight and commitment to recognizing the importance of the Pacific to our nation's future and acting upon it. Your advice and counsel will be important to our continued effort.

Your group includes four Senators, four Members of the House, seven members of the executive, in their unofficial capacity, and I think this demonstrates a bipartisan commitment of both branches. And all of us are in your debt for what you're doing and wish you well. Thank you very much.

Note: The President spoke at 9:44 a.m. in the Rose Garden at the White House.

Nomination of William J. McGinnis, Jr., To Be a Member of the Federal Labor Relations Authority
September 18, 1984

The President today announced his intention to nominate William J. McGinnis, Jr., to be a member of the Federal Labor Relations Authority for a term of 5 years expiring July 1, 1989. He would succeed Ronald W. Haughton.

Since 1965 he has been president of McGinnis Associates, consultants to management. He is also serving as a part-time member of the National Advisory Council on Vocational Education. Previously he was a staff consultant to Industrial Relations Counselors, Inc., in Philadelphia, PA, in 1963–1965. In 1980 he was elected municipal commissioner in the township of Long Beach, NJ.

Mr. McGinnis received his master of science degree from Rutgers University. He is married, has three children, and resides in Brant Beach, NJ. He was born January 11, 1946, in Philadelphia, PA.

Nomination of Two Members of the National Museum Services Board
September 18, 1984

The President today announced his intention to nominate the following individuals to be members of the National Museum Services Board, Institute of Museum Services, National Foundation on the Arts and the Humanities:

Richard J. Herczog, to serve for a term expiring December 6, 1988. He would succeed Emily Rauh Pulitzer. Since 1978 Mr. Herczog has been serving as vice president and chief operating officer of the Greater Los Angeles Zoo Association. Previously he was director of employee auxiliary service for McDonnell Douglas Corp. in 1968–1978. He is a member of the American Association of Museums. He graduated from UCLA (A.B., 1946; B.S., 1948). He is married, has three children, and resides in Los Angeles, CA. He was born February 16, 1923, in Cleveland, OH.

Fay S. Howell, to serve for the remainder of the term expiring December 6, 1986. She would succeed Dorothy J. Tyson. Since 1950 Mrs. Howell has been a member of the High Museum in Atlanta, GA, and is currently serving there as administrative vice president and as a member of the executive committee. She has been a member of the arts alliance board since 1979 and is now serving as secretary. She is married, has five children, and resides in Atlanta, GA. She was born February 26, 1929, in Atlanta.

Remarks Announcing a Farm Credit Initiative Program
September 18, 1984

The President. I'd like to make a statement now on the announcement of our farm credit initiative.

Our approach to the farm economy and the problem of farm credit is based on the belief that the future will be better than the past, and that the right program is a transitional program that helps farmers get from the high inflation, high interest, and economic disasters of the previous administration to the stable growth, low inflation, and lower interest rates that all of us are bringing about.

And I'm pleased to announce today a four-part program that will permit many troubled farmers to put together financial plans that will give them more secure hope for the future. Secretary Block will provide a more detailed discussion, but let me give you the highlights.

First, I've directed the Farmers Home Administration to agree to defer for 5 years up to 25 percent of the principal and interest payments owed by farmers who need breathing room to return to a sound financial footing. And these deferrals will be made available on a case-by-case basis as part of comprehensive transition plans to get farmers back on their feet.

Second, in order to assist those who do not participate in the FmHA programs, we'll be making available $630 million in loan guarantees that will be used to facilitate additional lending by private banks as part of financial recovery plans.

Third, we'll be enlisting the aid of experts from the community to help farmers develop financial plans.

And fourth, Farmers Home will expand its ability to serve the public by contracting with local banks and other financial institutions to handle routine paperwork processing in areas that have experienced delays and backlogs.

This, we believe, is a balanced approach that treats farmers as individuals and that recognizes our basic objective must be to help people through temporary difficulties, not create a massive new Federal program that will destroy the private credit system that serves the majority of farmers' needs.

End of statement.

Secretary Block. Once again, if I might add one point, I think it's important that we all appreciate that this package is a debt-restructuring, debt-management package, which is really what farmers need today. I think more than they need large sums of new money, they need to have a package to help restructure the existing debt.

Reporter. Mr. President, is this a bailout of farmers like the Chrysler Corporation?

The President. No, I don't think there's any comparison here between that and what we're proposing.

Senator Percy. We're hoping to pay back 7 years early, also, though.

The President. Yes. [*Laughing*] Yes, Chrysler turned out to be a good deal.

Q. Will this help you win the vote in the farm belt?

The President. What?

Q. Will this help you win the vote in the farm belt?

The President. Now, I know that none of you standing over there on that side of the table are going to believe this: It wasn't done with that mind. It was done because there are people out there that need help.

Q. Mr. President, Walter Mondale says U.S. policy for Nicaragua is unclear. How do you respond to that?

The President. Well, that doesn't have much to do with farming, but—[*laughter*]——

Secretary Block. Is that agricultural? [*Laughter*]

The President. No, I'm just making it a point—I'm not going to respond to my opponent on these matters that he brings up. I'll be discussing them on my own and not in answer to his questions.

Q. Thank you.

Note: The President spoke at 1:23 p.m. in the Cabinet Room at the White House following a meeting with Senators from key farming States, members of the executive committee of the American Farm Bureau Federation, and representatives of agricultural organizations, including groups involved in farm production, banking, and trade interests.

Secretary of Agriculture John R. Block and Senator Charles H. Percy of Illinois also made remarks.

Appointment of Mimi Rodden as a Member of the Advisory Council on Historic Preservation
September 18, 1984

The President today announced his intention to appoint Mimi Rodden to be a member of the Advisory Council on Historic Preservation for a term expiring June 10, 1988. She would succeed Steven F. Arvizu.

Mrs. Rodden served 4 years as the State historic preservation officer for Nevada. She was a member of the docent council for the Nevada State Museum and was responsible for the first Western States Conference of Museums and the Arts.

She is married, has two children, and resides in Carson City, NV. She was born June 7, 1935, in Elko, NV.

Nomination of Michael Huffington To Be an Assistant Secretary of Commerce
September 18, 1984

The President today announced his intention to nominate Michael Huffington to be an Assistant Secretary of Commerce (Trade Administration). He would succeed Lawrence J. Brady.

Since 1976 he has served as director, executive vice president, and chief financial officer of Roy M. Huffington, Inc., in Houston, TX. Previously he was cofounder and director of Simmons and Company International in Houston, TX (1974–1976). He was with the First National Bank of Chicago in 1972–1974.

Mr. Huffington graduated from Stanford University (A.B., B.S., 1970) and Harvard Business School (M.B.A., 1972). He was born September 3, 1947, in Dallas, TX, and now resides in Houston, TX.

Memorandum on the Denial of Import Relief for the Steel Industry
September 18, 1984

Memorandum for the United States Trade Representative

Subject: Steel Import Relief Determination

Pursuant to Section 202(b)(1) of the Trade Act of 1974, (P.L. 93–618, 88 Stat. 1978), I have determined the actions I will take with respect to the report of the United States International Trade Commission (USITC) dated July 24, 1984 concerning carbon and alloy steel.

I have determined today under Section 203 of the Trade Act that import relief is not in the national economic interest for the following reasons:

1. In responding to this pressing import problem, we must do all we can to avoid protectionism, to keep our market open to

free and fair competition, and to provide certainty of access for our trading partners. This Administration has repeatedly, and most recently at the London Economic Summit, committed itself to "resist continuing protectionist pressures, to reduce barriers to trade, and to make renewed efforts to liberalize and expand trade in manufactures, commodities and services."

2. It is not in the national economic interest to take actions which put at risk thousands of jobs in steel fabricating and other consuming industries or in the other sectors of the U.S. economy that might be affected by compensation or retaliation measures to which our trading partners would be entitled.

3. This Administration has already taken many steps to deal with the steel import problem. In 1982, a comprehensive arrangement restraining steel imports from the European Community was negotiated. This Administration has also conducted an unprecedented number of antidumping and countervailing duty investigations of steel imports, in most cases resulting in the imposition of duties or a negotiated settlement. In addition, the governments of Mexico and South Africa have unilaterally imposed voluntary restraint on exports, leading to the termination of unfair trade complaints.

However, I have decided to establish a government policy for the steel industry. I believe that this new policy is the best way to respond to the legitimate concerns of the domestic industry while maintaining access to our market for those who trade fairly.

I am directing you to coordinate and direct the implementation of this policy for the U.S. steel industry which includes the following elements:

1. The United States Trade Representative (USTR) will negotiate "surge control" arrangements or understandings and, where appropriate, suspension agreements with countries whose exports to the United States have increased significantly in recent years due to an unfair surge in imports—unfair because of dumping subsidization, or diversion from other importing countries who have restricted access to their markets. The USTR will negotiate additional such arrangements and understandings, if necessary, to control new surges of imports that

result from subsidizing, dumping or other unfair or restrictive trade practices during the next five years. If agreements cannot be reached to control new surges from countries that are guilty of unfair practices, the President will use his authority under the unfair trade laws including Section 301 of the Trade Act of 1974 to assure that these countries do not maintain unrestricted access to the United States market.

2. The United States Trade Representative will reaffirm existing measures with countries that have voluntarily restrained their exports to our market, and will take necessary steps to ensure the effectiveness of these measures. Specifically the Administration will support legislation in the Congress to make enforceable at our borders all voluntary agreements and "surge control" arrangements.

3. The United States Trade Representative will consult with our trading partners to seek the elimination of trade distortive and trade restraining practices in other markets to lead to the liberalization of steel trade around the world.

4. The Department of Commerce will continue to rigorously enforce our unfair trade laws. Further, the Department of Commerce and the United States Trade Representative will self-initiate unfair trade cases including antidumping, countervailing duty and Section 301 actions when appropriate.

5. The United States International Trade Commission will be asked to monitor the efforts of the steel industry to adjust and modernize, and to prepare an annual report for the President on those efforts.

6. The Secretary of Commerce will establish an interagency group to analyze all U.S. government domestic tax, regulatory and antitrust laws and policies which could hinder the ability of the steel industry to modernize.

7. The Secretary of Defense and the Federal Emergency Management Agency will analyze domestic steel plate rolling capacity in relationship to emergency needs, and to recommend to the President appropriate actions if deficiencies are found to exist.

8. The Secretary of Labor will work with state and local governments to develop a

program to assist workers in communities adversely affected by steel imports.

9. The United States Trade Representative will closely monitor the trade elements of this program and the resultant import trends and report them to the President on a quarterly basis.

The Administration's hope is that this combination of actions, taken without protectionist intention or effect would enable one of the United States' most basic and vital industries to return to a level playing field, one in which steel is traded on the basis of market forces, not government intervention, and one in which the market

would seek a return to a more normal level of steel imports, or approximately 18.5 percent, excluding semi-finished steel.

This determination is to be published in the *Federal Register*.

RONALD REAGAN

[Filed with the Office of the Federal Register, 4:40 p.m., September 18, 1984]

Note: The memorandum is printed in the Federal Register *of September 20.*

The memorandum was not issued as a White House press release.

Letter to the Speaker of the House and the President of the Senate on the Denial of Import Relief for the Steel Industry
September 18, 1984

Dear Mr. Speaker: *(Dear Mr. President:)*

In accordance with Section 203(b)(1) of the Trade Act of 1974, I am transmitting this report to Congress setting forth the action I am taking pursuant to that section with respect to import relief for the U.S. industry producing carbon and alloy steel products, and the reasons for my decision.

Sincerely,

RONALD REAGAN

IMPORT RELIEF—CARBON AND CERTAIN ALLOY STEEL

As required under Section 203(b)(1) of the Trade Act of 1974, I am transmitting this report to Congress setting forth the actions I will take with respect to carbon and certain alloy steel following the affirmative finding of the United States International Trade Commission (USITC) under Section 201(d) of the Trade Act. Since my action differs from that recommended by the USITC, I have included the reasons for my decision:

I have determined today, under Section 203 of the Trade Act, that import relief is not in the national economic interest for the following reasons:

1. In responding to this pressing import

problem, we must do all we can to avoid protectionism, to keep our market open to free and fair competition, and to provide certainty of access for our trading partners. This Administration has repeatedly, and most recently at the London Economic Summit, committed itself to "resist continuing protectionist pressures, to reduce barriers to trade, and to make renewed efforts to liberalize and expand trade in manufacturers, commodities and services."

2. It is not in the national economic interest to take actions which put at risk thousands of jobs in steel fabricating and other consuming industries or in the other sectors of the U.S. economy that might be affected by compensation or retaliation measures to which our trading partners would be entitled.

3. This Administration has already taken many steps to deal with the steel import problem. In 1982, a comprehensive arrangement restraining steel imports from the European Community was negotiated. This Administration has also conducted an unprecedented number of antidumping and countervailing duty investigations of steel imports, in most cases resulting in the imposition of duties or a negotiated settlement. In addition, the governments of Mexico and

South Africa have unilaterally imposed voluntary restraint on exports, leading to the termination of unfair trade complaints.

However, I have decided to establish a government policy for the steel industry. I believe that this new policy is the best way to respond to the legitimate concerns of the domestic industry while maintaining access to our market for those who trade fairly.

The implementation of this new policy for the U.S. steel industry will be coordinated and directed by the United States Trade Representative and includes the following elements:

1. The United States Trade Representative will negotiate "surge control" arrangements or understandings and, where appropriate, suspension agreements with countries whose exports to the United States have increased significantly in recent years to the detriment of our national economy. He will negotiate additional such arrangements and understandings, if necessary, to control new surges of imports that result from subsidizing, dumping or other unfair or restrictive trade practices during the next five years. If agreements cannot be reached to control new surges from countries that are guilty of unfair practices, the President will use his authority under the unfair trade laws including Section 301 of the Trade Act of 1974 to assure that these countries do not maintain unrestricted access to the United States market.

2. The United States Trade Representative will reaffirm existing measures with countries that have voluntarily restrained their exports to our market, and will take necessary steps to ensure the effectiveness of these measures. Specifically the Administration will support legislation in the Congress to make enforceable at our borders all voluntary agreements and "surge control" arrangements.

3. The United States Trade Representative will consult with our trading partners to seek the elimination of trade distortive and trade restraining practices in other markets to lead to the liberalization of steel trade around the world.

4. The Department of Commerce will continue to rigorously enforce our unfair trade laws. Further, the Department of Commerce and the United States Trade Representative will self-initiate unfair trade cases including antidumping, countervailing duty and Section 301 actions when appropriate.

5. The United States International Trade Commission will be asked to monitor the efforts of the steel industry to adjust and modernize, and to prepare an annual report for the President on those efforts.

6. The Secretary of Commerce will establish an interagency group to analyze all U.S. government domestic tax, regulatory and antitrust laws and policies which could hinder the ability of the steel industry to modernize.

7. The Secretary of Defense and the Federal Emergency Management Agency will analyze domestic steel plate rolling capacity in relationship to emergency needs, and to recommend to the President appropriate actions if deficiencies are found to exist.

8. The Secretary of Labor will work with state and local governments to develop a program to assist workers in communities adversely affected by steel imports.

9. The United States Trade Representative will closely monitor the trade elements of this policy and the resultant import trends and report them to the President on a quarterly basis.

The Administration's hope is that this combination of actions, taken without protectionist intention or effect would enable one of the United States' most basic and vital industries to return to a level playing field, one in which steel is traded on the basis of market forces, not government intervention, and one in which the market would seek a return to a more normal level of steel imports, or approximately 18.5 percent, excluding semi-finished steel.

Note: This is the text of identical letters addressed to Thomas P. O'Neill, Jr., Speaker of the House of Representatives, and George Bush, President of the Senate.

Appointment of Brigadier General Edward Honor as a Member of the Committee for Purchase from the Blind and Other Severely Handicapped
September 19, 1984

The President today announced his intention to appoint Brig. Gen. Edward Honor to be a member of the President's Committee on the Purchase from the Blind and Other Severely Handicapped. He would succeed Jimmy Ross.

General Honor is currently Director of Transportation, Energy and Troop Support, Office of the Deputy Chief of Staff for Logistics, Department of the Army. Previously he was Director of Resources and Management, Office of the Deputy Chief of Staff for Logistics, United States Army (1981–1983); Deputy Director for Planning and Resources, Logistics Directorate, J–4, Organization of the Joint Chiefs of Staff (1979–1981); Director for Plans, Doctrine, and Systems, United States Army Materiel Development and Readiness Command (1978–1979); and Commander, Military Traffic Management Command, Transportation Terminal Group-Europe, Rotterdam, Netherlands (1976–1978).

General Honor received a B.A. degree from Southern University A&M College. He is married and resides in Fairfax, VA. He was born March 17, 1933, in Melville, LA.

Nomination of Arthur W. Schultz To Be a Member of the President's Committee on the Arts and the Humanities
September 19, 1984

The President today announced his intention to nominate Arthur W. Schultz to be a member of the President's Committee on the Arts and the Humanities. This is a new position.

Mr. Schultz is chairman of the board of trustees of the Art Institute of Chicago, having served as a trustee since 1975. He retired as chief executive officer of Foote, Cone & Belding Communications after 34 years of service in 1982.

Mr. Schultz is a trustee of the University of Chicago, chairman of the visiting committee to the division of the humanities of the University of Chicago, and vice chairman of the Chicago Council on Foreign Relations.

He graduated from the University of Chicago. He is married, has two children, and resides in Chicago, IL. He was born January 13, 1922, in New York, NY.

Nomination of P.A. Mack, Jr., To Be a Member of the Board of the National Credit Union Administration
September 19, 1984

The President today announced his intention to nominate P.A. Mack, Jr., to be a member of the Board of the National Credit Union Administration for the term expiring August 2, 1989. This is a reappointment.

Since 1979 Mr. Mack has been serving as a member of the National Credit Union Administration. Previously he was administrative assistant to Senator Birch Bayh (1970–1979) and an officer at the Harris Trust and Savings Bank and the Continental Illinois National Bank in 1957–1970. In addition he has been owner and manager of Mack Farms in Delavan, IL, since 1955.

He graduated from Purdue University (B.S., 1952) and Indiana University (M.B.A., 1955). He is married, has two children, and resides in Washington, DC. He was born September 8, 1930, in Chicago, IL.

Remarks at a Reagan-Bush Rally in Waterbury, Connecticut
September 19, 1984

The President. Thank you all very much. Reverend clergy, Mayor Mike Bergin, Secretary Baldrige, and the other guests here on the dais, and all of you people:

It's wonderful to be in Waterbury. I've been here before, you know, and I always had a good time. I've been by Immaculate Conception and Apothecary Hall and the train station, and I've kept myself abreast of the recent doings here. So, I think I can say with real knowledge and pride, "I'm up on Waterbury," too.

I know that your door has always been open to all those Americans who came here as Italians, and the Irish, the French, the Poles, the Hispanics, the blacks. They made this a place where hard work is the rule, not the exception; a place where bedrock values took root—faith in a loving God, belief in family, and love of a country that gave them, and you, opportunity, peace, and freedom.

Yes, we're up on Waterbury, and Waterbury is up on America.

I remember campaigning here when I was running for the Republican nomination in the winter of 1980. It was awfully cold then, but your warmth made up for it. And I remember that day that I talked about the problems of the time—inflation, the energy crisis, and high taxes.

Well, that was 4 years ago, and since then, all of us together have managed to do something about those problems, haven't we? [*Applause*] Four years ago, unemployment in Waterbury was over 9 percent, and now it's way below 6. In the last 4 years, Waterbury has created almost 5,000 new jobs.

Across the country, take-home pay is up, and families have more to spend. And retail sales are up, and industrial production is up. So much is up that I hate to give you the downers: The tax rates are down; inflation is down; so is the prime interest rate, which by 1980 had reached the highest level since the Civil War. I guess that's what the other side means when they say there's a down side to the Reagan recovery. [*Laughter*] But let me correct something that has been misnamed, misnamed the Reagan recovery. It's the American recovery, because you did it. All we did was get government out of your way, and now it's the American expansion.

So, it seems to me things are a little bit better than they were 4 years ago. I don't want to take that for granted. Are you better off?

Audience. Yes!

The President. Do you think America is better off?

Audience. Yes!

The President. Well, it's nice to know we agree. [*Laughter*]

But I don't think the American recovery is confined to economic matters. There's a new mood in the country these days. Uncle Sam is seeming mighty jaunty. Our brilliant and optimistic young students and scholars and workers are all the leaders in this, and our young people, particularly. Your older brothers and sisters are showing renewed interest in the values and traditions by which this country flourished for more than two centuries. And it seems to me the older folks, the senior citizens of our country, are feeling pretty bouncy, too. Believe me, I hope I'm like that when I get old. [*Laughter*]

But our work isn't done; there's so much ahead of us. The future is out there. It's waiting to be seized and shaped; great frontiers in science, technology, and space waiting to be discovered and pushed back. And we can do it. We can do it because we saw with our Olympic athletes that when our people pull out all the steps—the stops, I should say—to meet a challenge, nothing can hold America back.

And I think that one challenge we're ready to meet as a nation, because it's so crucial to our future, is to make America's educational system a great center of leadership for excellence. And we've already begun. This morning we received word that the average scholastic aptitude test score, the thing we call the SAT's, has gone up a full 4 points. Now, 4 points doesn't sound like very much. It is just, however, the biggest increase in those scores in the last 21 years, and it's the second increase in 3 years. But it's not enough; we've got to do better.

So, I propose a challenge to all of us: It's time for America to lift her sights, time for us to resolve that before this decade is out we'll raise scholastic aptitude test scores nationwide. We'll make up half of all the ground that was lost over the last 20 years, which was more than 100 points. We must also reduce the dropout rate in our schools from 27 percent to 10 percent or less. And this will require a great national commitment by students, teachers, administrators and, most certainly, by American parents.

The challenge isn't easy but, my friends, we can meet it, just as we can continue to champion strong economic growth with greater individual opportunity.

We can simplify our tax system. We can make it more fair, easier to understand, so everyone in the country won't be sick with worry and confusion every April 15th when you face that complicated tax form. You know, it's good to remember that Albert Einstein said, *he* didn't understand it. [*Laughter*] But if we do that, if we simplify the taxes, we'll be able to push yours and everybody's income tax rates further down, not up. And with that money they're saving, Americans could spend and save and invest, and that would further boost the economy, and more jobs would be created.

We can pass an enterprise zones bill that would declare the older, distressed parts of cities to be special zones where business life

would be encouraged through tax incentives to start up, train, and hire workers. The House Democratic leadership has bottled up that bill in committee. For 2 years, they've refused to allow the Congress to vote on it.

And we could add to enterprise zones a youth employment opportunity wage for teenagers, so that employers would be encouraged to hire those who are disadvantaged and, particularly, members of minority groups.

As Secretary Baldrige told you, we've created 6 million jobs in the last 20 months. It's a good record, better, in fact, than any other nation, but still not good enough. And I pledge to you that I won't rest until every American who wants a job can find a job.

So, I propose that we lift our sights toward a second challenge for America: By this time next year we must have passed enterprise zones, passed the youth opportunity wage, found ways to simplify the tax system, and all of us must go forward to make this expansion so strong that millions of jobs will be created in distressed areas where our fellow citizens need help the most. This, America can and must do.

There's more to be done, but we're on the right track—not only on the right track, but I think we're chugging along like a pretty big, strong locomotive.

But do you know what the other side would do? The other side has put up a giant stop sign to stop the economy dead in its tracks. They've come up with an idea so old, so tired, that it could very well be called a cliche. Their wonderful idea is— can you bear the suspense? Their wonderful idea is to raise your taxes again and again and again.

Audience. No!

The President. Now, I know I'm mixing metaphors here, but it seems to me the other side is so upset at the good health of the economy that they've decided to give us a dose of the medicine that made us sick. [*Laughter*] You know, even Waterbury never had that much brass. [*Laughter*] Maybe the other side just made a miscalculation. They heard the American people have a lot more moneys to spend, so they thought that we would buy anything.

Do we want to go back to the old days of misery, misfortune, and malaise?

Audience. No!

The President. Do we want to return to that time of taxes and timidity—that reign of error?

Audience. No!

The President. Well, I want to tell you something I've been thinking of since this morning. Over there on the balcony of the Elton one night in 1960, just as the mayor told you, young John Kennedy stood there in the darkness. It was almost 3 o'clock in the morning. His campaign was near ending, and he was exhausted. But the night was bright with lights, and they lit the faces of the tens of thousands of people below who had showed up to cheer John Kennedy on.

And he stood down—looked down at them. He smiled in the glow, and even though it was the fall, it seemed like springtime, those days. I see our country today, and I think it is springtime for America once again—so many new beginnings. And I think John Kennedy would be proud of you and the things you believe in, proud of the stoutness of your hearts and the vision in your soul.

I hope there are some members of his party here today. I don't believe it would be possible to have this big a crowd in Waterbury without having a lot of Democrats here. Well, I was a Democrat once, for a large portion of my life. And it's a funny thing about party affiliation. Whether you inherited it for generations back in your family, maybe you embraced it on your own when you were young, but it can be a very wrenching thing, I found, to change parties. You feel as if you're abandoning your past. But I tell you truly, the only abandoning I see is that the Democratic leadership has abandoned the good and decent Democrats of the J.F.K., F.D.R., and Harry Truman tradition—people who believe in the interests of working people, who are not ashamed or afraid of America standing up for freedom in the world.

And if you see it as I do, I have to tell you, join us. And by us, I hope you'll join John Rowland and Larry Denardis and Hershel Klein, Roberta Coontz, Stewart McKinney, and Nancy Johnson. Don't think, any

of you, that you don't have a political home. You will listen to the arguments and issues in this campaign, and I think by the end you may decide your home is with us. And I hope you do. And believe me, you will be welcomed. I hope you'll walk with us down the new path of hope and opportunity.

And now I'm supposed to end my speech, but I don't want to go. Can I stay just long enough to add one more thing? [*Applause*] It's something I've been thinking about a great deal lately. I have to tell you that nothing, and I mean nothing, has made me prouder the past, almost-4 years than the young people who are serving our country in uniform. By any measure, they're just the best. You know, someone back in World War II asked General George Marshall what was the secret of America's success, what was our secret weapon in that war. And General Marshall said, "The best damn kids in the world."

Well, those young men and women who are serving today are the grandsons and granddaughters of those heroes of World War II. And I'll tell you, they're still the best damn kids in the world. Maybe when you, now and then, see one of them walking along the street, you might just go out of your way to nod or smile or say hello, and let them know how all of us feel about them.

And now, I do have to go, but it was, believe me, wonderful to be here. Can I come back again?

Audience. Yes! 4 more years! 4 more years! 4 more years!

The President. Thank you.

Audience. 4 more years! 4 more years! 4 more years!

The President. Thank you very much. I do have to go, but it's wonderful to be here. I'd love to see you all again. Waterbury's made a real difference in my campaign, just as it did in John Kennedy's, and I will always remember.

Thank you. God bless you.

Note: The President spoke at 12:21 p.m. at the Waterbury Town Green. Following his remarks, the President went to the Red Bull Inn, where he met with local Republican leaders and Reagan-Bush campaign leaders. He then traveled to Hammonton, NJ.

Remarks at a Reagan-Bush Rally in Hammonton, New Jersey
September 19, 1984

The President. Thank you very much. You know, it's been almost 8 weeks. I was even starting to get a little lonely, but now I feel glad again. I'm glad I'm back in your great State of New Jersey. And I'm glad to be back with a leader that I know you respect as much as I do, your fine Governor, Tom Kean.

Tom understands that we build a better future with economic growth and that we build economic growth from opportunity and that we create opportunities by ensuring excellence in education. Well, your Governor has helped you create economic growth. He's helped you bring unemployment down and is helping you create one of the best educational systems in the country. And in my book, that makes Tom Kean one of America's best.

You know, today my treat is seeing for the first time the Blueberry Capital of the world. It's the home of the fighting Blue Devils and the St. Joe Wildcats and your fighting State Senator, Bill Gormley; a town whose schools offer 4 years of three different foreign languages—your town, Hammonton, New Jersey.

You know, when I was in Elizabeth, I told them their band was very good. And now I know I was right, their band is up there with Hammonton's Blue Devil band.

But I'm honored to be with you. We've come to Hammonton, just as we went to Elizabeth and Hoboken and Doylestown and Buffalo and Endicott and Waterbury, because you're what America is all about. You are America's future.

Americans like you—and your mothers and fathers and their parents—here in Hammonton I know that means many proud Italians and hard-working farmers who want to keep those farms in your family. All of you have given the ideas, the muscle, the moral courage and, yes, the spiritual strength that built the greatest, freest nation the world has ever known.

You didn't come here seeking streets paved with gold. You didn't come asking for welfare or special treatment. You came for freedom and opportunity. And we see that spirit in the faces of Hammonton: two people who recently you honored on their 50th wedding anniversary, Mr. and Mrs. Frank Mazza, and a woman who's still a picture of youthful vitality named Mrs. Mamie De Marco, who recently celebrated her 89th birthday.

And we see that spirit, also, when tragedies bring forth the nobility and kindness of our people, pulling us together, giving us strength to go on, to keep living for tomorrow. These moments show us that America's great because—as a French philosopher said many years ago—America is good.

I think there's a new feeling of patriotism in our land, a recognition that by any standard America is a decent and generous place, a force for good in the world. And I don't know about you, but I'm a little tired of hearing people run her down.

We've come through some tough times, but we've come through them together—all of us, from every race, every religion, and ethnic background. And we're going forward with values that have never failed us when we lived up to them—dignity of work, love for family and neighborhood, faith in God, belief in peace through strength, and a commitment to protect the freedom which is our legacy as Americans.

All that we've done and all that we mean to do is to make this country freer still. America's future rests in a thousand dreams inside your hearts. It rests in the message of hope in songs of a man so many young Americans admire—New Jersey's own, Bruce Springsteen. And helping you make those dreams come true is what this job of mine is all about.

We hear shrill words from some who were in charge 4 years ago. But may I suggest that those who gave us double-digit inflation, record interest rates, tax increases, credit controls, farm embargoes, long lines at the gas stations, no growth at home, weakness abroad, and told us that it was our fault, that we suffered from a malaise—they're not exactly experts on the future of growth and fairness in America.

I will say, however, their policies were fair. They didn't discriminate; they made everybody miserable. But I didn't come to dwell on their failures, I came to talk about how together we're going to make this great nation even greater.

With your help, we've knocked down inflation from 12.4 to 4.1 percent. And today, from the Jersey shore to San Francisco Bay, economic expansion is carrying America forward. I'd like to ask you some questions, if I could—I know there are some young people present—some questions about a certain country. Now, I won't give away the answer by naming the country, but I will give you a little hint. It has three initials, and its first two are U.S.

Now, of all the great industrialized nations in the world, which has shown by far the strongest, most sustained economic growth?

Audience. U.S.A.!

The President. All right, what country can say its investment is up, its productivity is up, its take-home pay is up, and its consumer spending is up?

Audience. U.S.A.!

The President. And what country during the past 20 months created 6 million new jobs?

Audience. U.S.A.!

The President. And what country created, on an average, more new jobs each month during the past 12 than all the countries of Western Europe created over the past 10 years, all put together?

Audience. U.S.A.!

The President. Now, you get a hundred. You got it right. And, my friends, you ain't seen nothin' yet.

Today, more of your earnings are staying with your families, in your neighborhoods, in your State, where they belong. And we have the rare opportunity to give our children the gift of peace and prosperity without inflation. America has worked too hard for this progress to let anybody destroy it with a massive tax and spending scheme. That would be the equivalent of about $1,800 more in taxes per household, and it would ruin the growth and your opportunities for the future.

For them to introduce that blueprint for bondage in Philadelphia, the very birthplace of our liberty, was a betrayal of the American people. Now, they could have introduced their tax increase in Atlantic City, but then that would have been unfair. The people who go to Atlantic City gamble with their own money, not yours.

Well, we won't let them put that ball and chain around America's neck. I don't think that you in south Jersey believe your families were put on this Earth just to help them make government bigger. They want to enact a massive tax increase to put in their new so-called trust fund. Well, we don't want their new government trust fund; we want a government that trusts you.

You know, I have to tell you, I'm afraid that the age issue may be a factor in this election after all: My opponent's ideas are just too old.

We're talking about two different worlds. They see America wringing her hands; we see America raising her hands. They see America divided by envy, each of us challenging our neighbor's success; we see America inspired by opportunity, all of us challenging the best in ourselves. We believe in knowing when opportunity knocks; they go out of their way to knock opportunity. They see an America where every day is April 15th, tax day; we see an America where every day is the Fourth of July.

Aren't you saying we want to think big and aim high? And aren't you saying don't hold us back, give us a chance and see how high we fly? Well, that's what we want to help you do. So, I have some bad news for our opponents: Our economy will still be healthy come the November election. But I have some worse news for them: Our economy will still be that way in November of 1988.

Our work isn't done. The future is waiting to be seized; great frontiers in science, in technology, in space—waiting to be discovered and pushed back. And we can do it. We can do it because, as we saw with our great Olympic athletes, when America goes for the gold, nothing is going to hold her back.

And I think one challenge we're ready to meet as a nation, because it's so crucial to our future, is to make America's educational system a great center of leadership for excellence. And we've begun already. This morning we received word that the average scholastic aptitude test score, that thing we call SAT, the college entrance exams, has gone up a full four points. And that's after nearly 20 years of steady decline of more than a hundred points. And this is the second increase in 3 years, and it's the biggest increase—it doesn't sound like much, four points—but it's the biggest increase in 21 years. But it's not enough; we've got to do better.

It's time for America to lift her sights, time for us to resolve that before this decade is out we'll raise scholastic aptitude test scores nationwide. We'll make up half of all the ground that was lost over the last 20 years, and reduce the dropout rate from 27 percent to 10 percent or less. And this will require a great national commitment by students, teachers, administrators, and most certainly, by America's parents.

The challenge isn't easy, but, my friends, we can meet it, just as we can continue to champion strong economic growth with greater individual opportunity. We can simplify our tax system, make it more fair, easier to understand, so that we can bring yours and everybody's income tax rates further down, not up. You know, when I say make it easier to understand, did you know that Albert Einstein once said that he found the 1040 tax return form too difficult for him to understand? [*Laughter*]

We can pass an enterprise zones bill that would encourage people, through lower tax rates, to start up businesses and to train and hire workers in distressed areas. The House Democratic leadership has bottled up that bill for 2 years in committee.

And we could add to enterprise zones a youth unemployment [employment] [1] opportunity wage for teenagers, so that employers would be encouraged to hire those who are disadvantaged and members of minority groups and young people who are just starting out with no job experience, to get their first job.

We have, as I said, created 6 million jobs

_____
[1] *White House correction.*

in the last 20 months. That's a good record, better than any other nation, but it's not good enough. I pledge to you, I won't rest until every American who wants a job can find a job.

Now, I propose also that we lift our sights toward a second challenge: By this time next year we must have found ways to simplify that tax system, passed the enterprise zones, passed a youth opportunity wage, and all of us must make this expansion so strong that millions of jobs will be created in distressed areas where our fellow citizens need help the most. This America can and must do.

Our goal is an American opportunity society giving everyone not only an equal chance but a greater chance to pursue that American dream. And we can build that future together if you elect people to the Congress who will not vote for tax increases but vote for growth and economic progress. I'm talking about electing Mary Mochary— wife, mother, and attorney—to the United States Senate. Stand up there. There.

We couldn't have done any of the things that we've done if we didn't have that bare majority that we have in the United States Senate. They need more help. You send her up there.

Ms. Mochary. Thank you.

The President. All right.

Ray Massie, businessman and educator of great experience, and other progrowth candidates like Jim Saxton and Fred Busch, to help Jim Courter there in the House of Representatives and to give Tip O'Neill fits. [*Laughter*]

To all those Democrats—and I hope there are many here—who have been loyal to the party of F.D.R. and Harry Truman and J.F.K., people who believe in protecting the interests of working people, who are not ashamed or afraid of America's standing for freedom in the world, we say to you, "Join us. Come walk with us down that new path of hope and opportunity."

I was a Democrat most of my adult life. I didn't leave my party, and we're not suggesting you leave yours. I am telling you that what I felt was that the leadership of the Democratic Party had left me and millions of patriotic Democrats in this country who believed in freedom.

Walk with us down that path of hope and opportunity, and together we can and we will lift America up to meet our greatest days.

Thank you all. Thank you for your wonderful New Jersey welcome, and thank you for sharing with us your joy and spirit. And God bless you all. Thank you.

Note: The President spoke at 4:40 p.m. at Bellevue and Central Avenues. Following his remarks, the President met with local Republican leaders and then returned to Washington, DC.

Remarks and a Question-and-Answer Session With Reporters on the Bombing Near the United States Embassy Annex in Beirut, Lebanon
September 20, 1984

The President. I know that you're all aware of the tragic event in Beirut with regard to our Embassy. We've been in touch with Reg Bartholomew, our Ambassador there. He has been slightly injured, but we do know that he walked to the hospital for treatment of his wounds on his own.

We know there are several deaths. So far, the only ones we know of are among the Lebanese employees. We know that the suicide vehicle crashed through barricades at the end of the street. It did not enter the compound, but exploded in the street in front of it, with damage to the building. There are a number that are wounded. We have word that a few are critically wounded among the employees. We're still trying to get full information on all of that.

I'd like to express my sympathy to those who have suffered wounds, to the families of those who might be killed. And the State Department will be keeping you informed as we get additional information.

Q. Sir, do you approve of the hounding of Ferraro and Mondale by the antiabortion——

The President. [*Inaudible*]

Q. Do you approve of the hounding of Ferraro and Mondale by antiabortion supporters? They've been docking their heels at every turn.

The President. I don't know anything about that. I'm just going to comment on this particular incident here before we get underway.

Now, Andrea [Andrea Mitchell, NBC News], you had——

Q. [*Inaudible*]—the condition of Ambassador Bartholomew, Mr. President?

The President. Yes, we have, directly from him. He has been in contact with us. And he claims that he has some cuts, but he is not seriously wounded at all and, as I say, he walked on his own to the treatment center.

Q. Do you think the Embassy annex was adequately protected? What is your judgment of that?

The President. Yes, as I say, they have barriers—similar to what we have here for a vehicle that has to get through—at the ends of the street. It negotiated these, was under fire, and exploded in the street. It did not penetrate the barriers leading into the Embassy building. And the force of the explosion was such that it, of course, damaged the building and wounded and killed some people. Now, we don't know, we still do not know how many of those are actually Embassy personnel and how many might simply be people on the street.

Q. What do you think this says about your policy in the Middle East? Some people have said that since the marines were withdrawn we've neglected the Middle East.

The President. Andrea, we know that the worldwide terrorist movement has targeted a great many people, not only our own but of other countries, too, worldwide. And this is a part of that. We've been aware of this. You have to live, and you have to do your best to protect yourself, but you have to know that these terrorist groups are threatening all over the world.

Q. Mr. President, are you going to do anything more at the Embassy in Beirut to support the personnel there?

The President. Are we going to what?

Q. [*Inaudible*]

The President. Well, these are things that are going to be a part of our planning, whatever we can do. But we can't, on the other hand, crawl in a hole someplace and stop performing.

Q. Mr. President, isn't this latest bombing a reminder that your policy in Lebanon has failed?

The President. No. We're aware that this threatens our people wherever they are in the world, because these terrorist groups in many instances—or most instances are opposed to everything that we stand for.

Now, I'm going to have to get on the 'copter and leave, but I know the State Department will be keeping you informed as we get more information.

Note: The President spoke at 8:32 a.m. on the South Lawn of the White House, prior to his departure for visits to Iowa and Michigan.

Earlier in the morning, the President was informed of the bombing by Assistant to the President for National Security Affairs Robert C. McFarlane. The President discussed the incident by telephone with Assistant to the President James A. Baker III and met with Mr. McFarlane and Secretary of State George P. Shultz prior to speaking with the reporters.

Aboard Air Force One en route to Iowa, the President spoke by telephone with U.S. Ambassador to Lebanon Reginald Bartholomew, who was in a Beirut hospital for treatment.

Remarks at a Reagan-Bush Rally in Cedar Rapids, Iowa
September 20, 1984

The President. Thank you very much. Thank you.

Audience. 4 more years! 4 more years! 4 more years!

The President. All right. Thank you. As long as you feel that way, well, it's okay, it's all right with me.

Well, thank you, Governor Branstad. And thank all of you for a very warm welcome.

Before I begin the remarks today, let me say a few words about the cowardly act of terrorism that we learned of early this morning. The suicide attack against our Embassy annex in East Beirut has saddened us all, of course. It's another painful reminder of the persistent threat of terrorism in the world. I have talked with our Ambassador, Reg Bartholomew, on the way out here, who, although injured himself, expressed pride on behalf of the dedicated Americans who are serving with him.

In this moment of anger and sorrow, our prayers are with those who are bereaved,

while our commitment to the cause of peace remains firm. I'm proud, as all Americans should be proud, of the brave Americans who are serving our nation throughout the world in the cause of peace for people everywhere, and even more proud after talking to our Ambassador there, who emphasized that we must continue, we can't just withdraw in the face of this kind of terrorism.

But now, it's good to be back in Iowa, in the very heart of our nation. And it's good to be in the proud and thriving town of Cedar Rapids. And I was most pleased to be accompanied on the way out here with the fine Members of the Congress from your State, Tom Tauke and Cooper Evans and Jim Leach and, too, our superb Senators, Chuck Grassley and Roger Jepsen. Believe me, we couldn't have accomplished what we have without our majority in the Senate, and Chuck and Roger are in the front rank of that Senate majority.

And I had another greeting that really touched my heart here today, and that was a special greeting from 6-year-old Katie Beckett. Three years ago, Katie was trapped in a hospital. Her doctors agreed that Katie, who had trouble breathing, could safely go home but it seemed there were regulations that forced her to stay, even though home care for Katie would have cost only a fifth of the cost of her hospital bills.

Well, Congressman Tauke told Vice President Bush about Katie, and the Vice President told me. And I engaged in what is one of my favorite hobbies—cutting a little red-tape. And today, Katie is living where she should—at home with her parents.

But like all America, Cedar Rapids has a story to tell. Not so many decades ago, this land around here was open prairie—rugged and unproductive. And while I mention prairie, I have to say you've got a school named Prairie. And many years ago, the students of that school, when President Eisenhower was coming here, formed out on the athletic field a greeting to him. And a young lady who's a member of our staff, Jan Duvall—now her married name—was a part of the "I" in that greeting. [Laughter] And I think she must have had something to do with it, because just a few minutes ago coming past that school, out there the full length of the athletic field was a greeting to me by all the students, forming the letters—[applause]——

Well, as I say, this was open prairie. And then the pioneers began to settle here: Yankees, Germans, Swedes, Norwegians, and immigrants from many other nations—men and women as hardy as the land. They plowed the sod, they planted crops, they dotted the land with farmhouses and built lovely towns like Cedar Rapids. And soon, Iowa contained some of the richest farmland in history, feeding tens of millions in America and around the world.

Cedar Rapids itself became a dynamic city, making breakthroughs in agricultural marketing and management, and helping develop the radio and electronics industries, and establishing fine high schools like Washington, Jefferson, and Kennedy, and Prairie, and great colleges like Coe, Mount Mercy, Kirkwood Community College. And you've shown the world that with opportunity there's no limit to what Americans can accomplish.

Yet in recent years, we must remember, the light of opportunity in our country almost went out. In just 5 years, taxes nearly doubled, average monthly mortgage payments more than doubled, and the real, after-tax income of the average American began to decline. In foreign policy we saw strength replaced with weakness, and America lost the respect of friend and foe alike. They imposed a grain embargo that made you farmers pay for their mistakes. How do you show that you're strong by punching yourself in the breadbasket? You'll forgive me for this one, but their foreign policy went against the grain. [Laughter]

Our opponents preach a great deal about fairness. Well, it's true that they were fair in one respect: Their policies didn't discriminate; they made everybody miserable. [Laughter]

We could go on and on, but we don't want to talk about the failures of the past. Believe me, neither do our opponents. So let's talk about something that Americans are good at, and that's success.

After years of drift and decline, this great nation is moving forward again. And during the past 4 years, we've knocked inflation down from 12.4 to 4.1 percent. And since then, in the most recent months—that's for the whole previous years—it's down as low, on a monthly basis, now, as 2.9 percent. During the past 20 months, we've created 6 million jobs and brought unemployment down at the fastest rate in the last 30 years. Our progress won't be complete until every State and every American can feel all the warm sunshine of America's economic expansion.

There's one way that we could bring this economic expansion to a halt, a sudden halt. And, yes, our opponents have found that one way—raise taxes. Now, I know it's hard to believe, but after decades of a rising tax burden they've actually proposed a massive, new tax increase. That's to pay for the promises they've made in this campaign. All told, their tax increase would be the equivalent of more than $1,800 increased tax per household. Their tax increase is a giant stop sign that would bring our entire economy and your opportunities for the future screeching to a halt. Are you prepared to sit back and let them do that to America?

Audience. No!

The President. You know, we all watched the Olympics this summer, and we cheered to see American athletes go for the gold. Well, making our economy bear the burden of their tax hike would be like having a coach tell an Olympic swimmer to do the laps carrying an anvil or a runner to sprint with a ball and chain. Come November, the American people are going to get to vote on our coaches. And come November, the American people are going to tell Coach Tax Hike to go find another team someplace else.

Our pledge is for tax simplification, to make the system more fair and easier to understand, so that we can bring yours and everybody's income tax rates further down, not up. Tax simplification can provide powerful new incentives for economic growth. We'll fight for enterprise zones to help Americans in disadvantaged areas get off unemployment and welfare and start climbing the economic ladder. And if we can keep government under control, we can do it by enacting a line-item veto and a constitutional amendment mandating that the Government stop spending more than the Government takes in.

You might have noticed that our opponents are trying to appeal to traditional Democrats by comparing themselves to Harry Truman. Well, President Truman kept a sign on his desk that said, "The Buck Stops Here." If our opponents are elected, their sign will say, "Your Bucks Stop Here." [*Laughter*] And forgive me, but Harry Truman believed—with F.D.R. before him and John Kennedy after him—in strength abroad and self-reliance at home. To all those Democrats—and I hope there are many here—who feel that under its present leadership the Democratic Party no longer stands behind America's responsibilities in the world, that it no longer represents working men and women, we say to you: "Join us."

Before this decade is out we must raise scholastic aptitude tests—but I'm getting ahead of myself here in shuffling my notes. What I intend to say before I get to apti-

tude tests is, to those that I have termed—or probably are still Democrats, as I once was for most of my life, come walk with us down the new path of hope and opportunity that we have. As our economy grows, we'll need to go forward with the bedrock values that sustained the first Iowa settlers and that nourish us today. And they're the simple values of faith, family, neighborhood, and good, hard work. And we're already making a good start.

In the past 4 years we've helped lead a grassroots revolution to recommit our schools to an agenda for excellence that will reach every land—or schoolchild in this land. And yesterday, we learned that the average scholastic aptitude test scores have gone up a full four points. That doesn't sound like very much, but that's after a nearly 20-year decline that's totaled around 100 points or more. It is the second increase in 3 years, and it's the biggest increase in 21 years.

But I believe we can do better. So, I'm asking you to help America lift her sights. Before this decade is out, we must raise the scholastic aptitude test scores nationwide, make up half of all the ground that was lost over the last 20 years, and reduce the dropout rate from almost 28 percent to 10 percent or less.

We must continue cracking down on crime. We say with no hesitation, yes, there are such things as right and wrong. And yes, for hardened criminals preying on our society, punishment must be swift and sure. In 1980 the crime rate was rising. Last year reported crime dropped 7 percent. That's the steepest decline since 1960. And I'm pleased to learn that Iowans have made a particular effort to seize the initiative in combating crime. You've established a crime prevention Citizen's Watch program in every one of your counties. That's an accomplishment that few States can match.

May I just interject something on that subject here? There've been two tragedies in Iowa that have saddened us all. In 1982, young Johnny Gosch disappeared while delivering newspapers on his morning route in Des Moines. Then, just 6 weeks ago, another newspaper boy, Eugene Martin, also disappeared.

Well, I want you to know that I've spoken with Jim Gannon, the editor of the Des Moines Register. We've pledged our full support in the search for these two boys. And this past June, we established the National Center for Missing and Exploited Children in Washington to help locate missing children across America. So far, the Center has received thousands of telephone calls and helped hundreds of parents. Nancy and I join all of you, I'm sure, in praying for the safe return of Johnny and Eugene. And I pledge to you that none of us will rest until the streets in Iowa and throughout this nation are once again safe, particularly for our children.

Now, let me just conclude by saying that we're rebuilding America's defenses, our nation is stronger, America is at peace. And since 1980, not a single nation has fallen to Communist aggression. And the people of one nation, Grenada, have been set free. As I will tell Soviet Foreign Minister Gromyko when I meet with him in a few days, we seek no territorial expansion and are making no effort to impose our will on anyone. But we will never again allow the United States of America to let down its guard.

And if I could leave you with one last thought from my heart, it's that the American dream is a living thing—it's always growing, always presenting new challenges, new vistas, and new dreams. And throughout Cedar Rapids and throughout Iowa, there are young couples today saving to buy homes of their own, mothers and fathers who want to give their children a better education, men and women with dreams of making the good earth of Iowa still more fruitful, the good town of Cedar Rapids still healthier and more prosperous, and America herself stronger and better still. My vision of America, and I know it's one you share, is of a land where all have the opportunity to work hard and to make these dreams come true.

And if you don't mind, I have to tell you a little personal experience that came to my mind as I was looking down at those green fields in those last few minutes before we arrived. Back in 1948, in that other life of mine—[*laughter*]—I was sent to England to be in a movie called "The Hasty Heart."

And on the weekends, never having been there before, I would rent a car and driver and have him take me out to see the countryside. And particularly, I happened to have mentioned that I'd heard about pubs out there in the countryside that were 700 years old. Well, one day he pulled up in front of one and apologized because it was only 400 years old. [*Laughter*]

Well, we went in, and we sat there. And we were being served by a nice, matronly woman. And there was an elderly man down at the other end of the room serving other people. And pretty soon—she probably heard us talking—and she said, "You're Americans, aren't you?" And we said, "Yes, we are." "Oh," she says, "during the war, there were a bunch of your lads, a great bunch of them, stationed just down the road." And she said, "They would come in here in the evenin', and we'd have a song-fest." And she said, "They began calling me 'Mom' and called the old man 'Pop.'"

"And then," she said, "one Christmas Eve we were in here all alone, and the door burst open and there they was." She said, "They came in, and they had presents for us." And by this time she's looking beyond us, and there's a tear on her cheek. And she's really looking back into memory in telling this. And then she looked down and she said, "Big strapping lads they was, from a place called Iowa." [*Laughter*] When she said this, I could just picture those big strapping lads, and then I had a tear on my cheek. [*Laughter*]

My friends, together we can make America that shining land of opportunity and hope. And with you by our side, I know we will. Thank you all for coming out here, and God bless you.

Audience. 4 more years! 4 more years! 4 more years!

The President. All right. I have to move on. But just one promise before I go: that you will send these Congressmen back there, and you'll send Roger Jepsen back to do what he's been doing.

Okay. Thank you.

Note: The President spoke at 10:03 a.m. at the Cedar Rapids Municipal Airport. He then traveled to Norway, IA.

Informal Exchange With Reporters in Norway, Iowa
September 20, 1984

Q. Mr. President, how could that bombing have happened? I thought there were all kinds of precautions that were taken after the last one?

The President. I'm not going to say more about that till we get more details, except, Bill [Bill Plante, CBS News], I will say this: It did not get into the compound. Apparently, according to the Ambassador—I've spoken to him—it simply was exploded in the street; that it crashed through some barriers in the street further up the road and was exploded.

Q. Well, are we going to——

Q. Are you satisfied with the security, sir?

Q. ——going to take any retaliatory action, sir? Is there anyone we can retaliate against?

The President. I can't discuss anything of that kind.

Q. Are you satisfied with the security, sir?

The President. Yes.

Q. Pardon?

The President. What?

Q. Are you, sir?

The President. Well, as much as I know about it, yes. It seems to have—I think if someone is determined to do what they did, it's pretty difficult to prevent it.

Q. Mr. President, do you have any intelligence as to why this would have happened now?

The President. We've just known for a long time that not only ourselves but people of other countries—officials throughout the world—are under a threat of terrorist activity right now.

[*At this point, the President discussed the soybean crop production with farm owner John Brockschink and his son-in-law Don Wiebold. After several minutes, the exchange resumed.*]

Q. Mr. President, Walter Mondale and Geraldine Ferraro have criticized you for your failed policy in Lebanon and the deaths of marines there. Do you think today's attack in Beirut will reopen that criticism of your policies there?

The President. I don't know what they're going to say, and I'm not going to comment on their charges and accusations in any way. I'm not going to reply to them.

Q. Well, did you think you have any responsibility for what happened today, Mr. President? Your policy?

The President. No. I don't see how anyone in this country—we have a program in which, in cooperation with our allies, we're trying our best to find an answer to the international terrorist problem. And as I say, we're—all of us—targets of that, probably because of what we believe and what our principles are, and they disagree with them.

Q. When you welcomed the hostages back from Iran, you said on the South Lawn that terrorism—and everyone thought you meant something like this—would be dealt with swiftly. Are you going to deal with this swiftly?

The President. As swiftly as you can. Speaking of hostages, that's a different subject. Actually, the only defense you have against terrorist activities is if you can infiltrate and intercept and know in advance where they're going to strike.

Q. Will you retaliate for this act, sir?

The President. I can't discuss that.

Q. Is it hard to campaign after a tragedy like this, sir?

The President. It doesn't add joy to the event.

Q. Did you consider canceling today's trip at any point?

The President. We talked about that, but realized that what's the difference whether I'm there or here? You're President wherever you are, and I have as fast a communication on these matters wherever I am, so——

Q. From the soybean field or the White House you can do the same thing?

The President. Yup. [*Laughter*]

Note: The exchange began at 10:50 a.m. while the President was touring a soybean field at the farm of John and Louise Brockschink.

Remarks and a Question-and-Answer Session With Farmers in Norway, Iowa
September 20, 1984

The President. Thank you all very much. I thank you. I thank Jack Block, also. He's been, I think, a very fine Secretary of Agriculture, and I know his heart is really in what he's doing.

Governor Branstad, and the Members of the Congress that are here with us, our Senators:

Before I begin the remarks that I intended to make today, I'd like to repeat something that I said at the airport when I came in—that's a few words about the cowardly act of terrorism that we learned of early this morning.

The suicide attack against our Embassy annex in East Beirut has saddened us all, of course, and it's another painful reminder of the persistent threat of terrorism in the world. I've talked with our Ambassador, Reg Bartholomew. He was in the hospital, and I was in the plane on the way here when we talked. He's injured, himself, but he said it was not serious and, actually, he walked out of the Embassy after the explosion and walked to the hospital on his own. He's quite a guy. And he expressed pride on behalf of all the people that are serving there with him.

But in this moment of anger and sorrow, our prayers are with those who are bereaved, while our commitment to the cause of peace remains firm. And I'm proud, as all Americans should be proud, I think, of the brave Americans who are serving us in the Foreign Service all over the world in the cause of peace for people everywhere.

But now, I want to thank the Brockschink family for being so kind to invite us here today in the midst of this busy time for all of you. I have a few things I'd like to say, and then I'd be very pleased to take your questions for a period of time.

First, with the hard work and great courage of our people, the farmers' number one market is coming back. America in September of 1984 is moving forward with an economic expansion that's given birth to 6 million jobs—new jobs—and new hope. We're a stronger nation today than we were 4 years ago.

And second, while we welcome that progress, we know it's incomplete. Too many of you have yet to benefit from it, and we won't be satisfied until you do.

My third point is, even though your road to prosperity's been longer and the grade is steep, we're moving in the right direction again, and we're closer to our goal than we were.

[The President was briefly interrupted by the noise of a plane flying overhead.]

I hope it's one of ours. *[Laughter]*

In January 1981, we were left the legacy of record inflation, record interest rates, the highest peacetime tax burden in history, and a farm embargo that had inflicted terrible damage not just on short-term sales, but on our long-term reliability and credibility as a supplier. Well, all the initiatives that we've taken since our first days in office—and that we'll continue to pursue—have been aimed at getting to the root of your problems to help family farmers and ranchers turn things around for good.

How have we tried to help the family farmers who, day-in, day-out, probably face greater difficulties than any other group in our country? Well, by bringing down inflation, which had destroyed the profitability of farming in 1980. We went from one of the largest 2-year increases ever in prices that farmers paid in '79 and '80 to the smallest 2-year rise in 15 years in 1982 and '83. And the most recent inflation rate has been at 2.9 percent. If we had to go back and take the whole year getting to that point, why, it's down around 4.0 percent.

But we won a long-overdue change in our tax laws that will protect thousands of widows and children from losing what generations of love and toil have created. The estate tax exemption will increase to $600,000 by 1987 and, of even greater help, there will be no estate tax for a surviving spouse.

We ended the unfair, unwise grain embargo. And my opponent now says he opposed the embargo privately, but the record shows that he supported it publicly and enthusiastically.

Well, we ended the embargo, and we've reestablished our sales to the point where, since last October, the Soviets have bought 23 million metric tons of grain. And, as you may know, I approved raising the ceiling so that they may buy an additional 10 million tons in the next year. And we'll raise the ceiling again if they use those up.

We're aggressively moving to open up other markets that had been restricted. We reached agreement with Japan to double its purchase of Amercian beef exports over the next 4 years. And I think we have a friend there in the Prime Minister, Nakasone. He's got his political problems with his legislature, as I do with mine, but—[*laughter*]—he really is working in tandem with us.

The effects of the grain embargo, combined with the bumper crops in '81 and '82, left us with huge carryover supplies. So, when action was stymied in Congress, we moved to develop the PIK program. And farmers set aside nearly 80 million acres and got paid in kind with reserve stocks. Now, that program and last year's drought cut the U.S. feed grain stocks by 73 percent.

And we're trying to help tens of thousands of farm borrowers hold onto their farms and stay in farming. The Agriculture Department is lending money to 270,000 beginning farmers and farm borrowers who can't get credit elsewhere. And in the last 3 years, the USDA Farmers Home Administration has doubled its regular operating loans for farmers.

And this week, we announced another major initiative to assist farmers trying to cope with debt burdens. The Farmers Home Administration will permit a deferral for 5 years of up to 25 percent of the principal and interest payments owed by farmers who need breathing room to return to a sound financial footing. And the deferrals will be made available on a case-by-case basis.

And we want to assist those who do not participate in the FmHA programs, so Farmers Home will make available $630 million in guarantees of loans by private banks as part of rescheduling plans for troubled farmers.

Our road is hard because the difficulties that built up were so great. But we've righted ourselves. We're moving forward again.

And it puzzles me how some could already forget that only 4 years ago, they left the farmer stuck in the swamp. And I'm troubled that those who gave us the grain embargo, and the nightmare of double-digit inflation, and 21-percent interest rates don't seem to have learned their lesson. They're proposing what would amount to a new one-two punch against American farmers— a massive protectionist program that would provoke foreign retaliation, particularly against our farm exports, and a massive tax increase that would hit nearly a million people who earn income from farming. And if all of their promises are fully funded, it would be the equivalent of more than $1,800 in taxes per household.

Now, those are not my idea of friendship for farmers or fairness for farmers or a better future for farmers. They would reap a harvest of hardship and take us back to the past, to what has already failed. We firmly believe that the initiatives we're taking with you will make you stronger for the future.

And now, rather than me going on with a monolog here, let me hear from you. I know that you may have some questions. I know that our time is very limited, but fire away.

Q. Mr. President, I have a two-part question. Mr. Grimes, an economist from Missouri, has figures that say U.S. pork producers' market is being depressed by $6 per market animal. Canada's Federal and Provincial assistance program seems to be giving Canadian pork producers an unfair advantage over U.S. pork producers. A number of U.S. Congressmen have signed a letter encouraging you to call an agriculture and forestry trade summit with Canada following the current elections. Mr. President, what is the progress of these talks.

The second part of the question, if I may go on, Mr. President: The current Economic Report of the President reports, "the growth in world cereals imports in the last decade has been fueled mainly by growth in per capita income, with growth in population being a significant but less important factor." Is the President's office being used in any way to urge other countries to increase their per capita income?

The President. Yes. We have a Secretary of Agriculture who's a world traveler by now. And we have made substantial gains with some of our trading partners in this field. And right now, he has been meeting with the Trade Minister of Canada on this very subject of the import of Canadian hogs. And we believe in free trade, but we believe it's got to be fair trade. And I don't know what progress they're making or how much progress.

Would you like to comment, Jack?

Secretary Block. Well, Mr. President, I talked with the new Minister of Agriculture yesterday in Canada. You know, he's only been aboard just this week. We needed to wait till he was there. And I asked him—I told him of our problems with them and our trade questions and asked if I could have a meeting with him and we could work to resolve the differences. He agreed to a meeting, and we will be setting one up and moving on that subject as fast as we can. So, we're right on top of it.

The President. All right. And as to the answer to the other problem, as I say, we have been working on that. In fact, we recently—several months ago, if I remember correctly, was the timing of it—we did a certain thing with regard to some shipments of grain products to Egypt, which sort of was like hitting a mule with a club to get his attention. And it was to get the attention of our trading partners in the European Community. And I think we did get their attention on that. So, we're making progress there, too.

Q. Thank you, Mr. President, for your answer.

Q. Mr. President, you have stated your opposition to any grain embargo. Is it not true that the domestic content legislation is, in reality, an embargo? What is your position on this?

The President. We're opposed.

Q. Good.

The President. Strongly opposed. [*Applause*] Yes, wait, if I could just say this one

thing about protectionism. In so many areas, so many times, we're able to prove that protectionism for one particular segment that might be construed as saving jobs in that one—you can turn and prove that it'll lose three or four times as many jobs in other areas of our economy. And it's just a two-way street, and we're not going to go down that street.

Q. Mr. President, I would like to look at this problem in just a little bit different vein. I believe that a good business deal will make even stranger bedfellows than politics. I believe that mutually beneficial, reciprocal trade would probably do more for our national interests—and can serve the cause of world peace—than any other single thing that I can think of. I'm just wondering if you—[*inaudible*]——

The President. Yes, we believe in that. As I say, we've got to play on a level field. We can't keep on playing this game where we're downhill and trying to go uphill to score, and they're up there rolling down. And I think we have made progress, and we're going to continue. In fact, at the summit meeting in London, that was the gist of my messages to our trading partners over there in that meeting. And I met with a great deal of agreement with them on the fact that we've got to oppose protectionism.

Now, all of us recognize you can come to some situation where there is some particular segment or something that has been unfairly hurt, or that simply needs some breathing room to get back on its feet, and you can temporarily give them a hand. But you must be very careful that that, also, does not penalize others in our economy. But believe me, we're dedicated to free but fair trade.

Q. Mr. President, we thank you very much for the contributions you've made this past week to agriculture with the $660 million, and I——

The President. Six hundred and thirty. [*Laughter*] See, I'm always cutting. [*Laughter*]

Q. We have to have some concern, that the very large national deficit that is causing our high interest rates that we currently have. What can you, what can Congress, and what can we do to bring the national debt into line, so that we may all make a comfortable living?

The President. Let me just say with regard to the whole subject of the deficit: Actually, the only connection that anyone could make with our deficit and high interest rates would be if there was such a demand for lending capital that the Government shut out the private sector. That hasn't been true. Because of our tax cut across the board, because of the tax depreciation things that we put in for industry, and so forth, they have been investing at a faster rate—business and industry in America—than has been true for years and years, and without shutting off the supply.

For one reason—because there's been a pretty healthy rate of savings by individual Americans, now, since the tax cut. The deficit is a result, not a cause. And the deficit is the result of the Government spending too great a share of the private sector's money. And what we've got to get is government down. Because what difference would it make in the deficit if you taxed and eliminated the deficit, simply by increasing the taxes, and the Government is still taking that same amount of money out of the private sector?

The problem with our economy is that reducing of the gross national product by government. So we do have plans, in spite of what you may have heard from some other sectors here. And we are specific. We think we've been very specific. Our economic program that we advocated in 1981, and are still going forward with, calls for sizable reductions. We never got all we wanted.

If we had gotten what we asked for from the Congress, the deficit would be $50 billion less than it is right now. But the two things that we have to do—we've cut the rate of increase in government spending more than in half, bringing that line down. Now, as we do things, such as the tax cut—and they may point to that and say, "Well, that's what did away with government's revenues and increased the deficit." No, it increased the growth in the economy and brought about the recovery to the point that the revenue line is now coming up more steeply, not because your taxes have been raised, but because as a result of the

incentive from that tax program, there is recovery.

And so, what we're working toward, continuing to try and get—we've got 2,478 specific recommendations for better management of government that was brought to us by the Grace commission. Now, this was a private sector group—leaders from all over the country—that, under Peter Grace, at my request, formed themselves into a group to go and take a look at all of government and find out where it was doing things that business gave up doing a long time ago and to modernize and so forth. And we have a team studying those recommendations. Now, we don't know how many of those we'll find practical to—and some will take legislation. We've already implemented 17 percent of them that we could do administratively to further decrease government costs.

But when we can get those two lines—the increase in government spending and the increase in revenues by way of the recovery—to come to a point together, we've eliminated the deficit. And we, in addition to that, have what we call the downpayment, where we got a compromise thing of some tax reforms, plus some further savings that we got bipartisan agreement on, to put into effect, that will further do it.

And we do have the deficits now in a declining line. This year's deficit at $174 billion is $21 billion less than we ourselves projected that it would be this year. And that's a mistake we like to make. So, we're determined.

Secretary Block. Mr. President, your time is short.

And the President can only take one more question. Remember, the President has asked for a constitutional amendment requiring a balanced budget. And that'll get us this. And your President asked for it. The Senate Republicans and the Senate have supported it. But Tip O'Neill and the Democrats in the House have blocked it.

The President. They had it buried in committee for 2 years. And there's one other—thank you for reminding me. That's what I should have added. I rambled on and forgot that. The other thing that I want is something that I had as Governor and that 43 Governors have—line-item veto. This thing of sneaking an extravagant, not-worth-it measure into a bill that you have to sign when it comes to your desk because you need the rest of the bill—but if you had, as I had then, that you could pick out that one part and say, "I sign the bill with the exception of clause such-and-such."

As Governor, I vetoed more than 900 such things in the 8 years that I was there, and never had a veto overridden on one of those things. So, it's a tool that I think will help us.

I was going to call on him if that's the last question. I'm sorry about the rest.

Yes?

Q. Mr. President, it's rather evident that much of the future welfare of our industry depends on exports. And many of the developing countries have been former recipients of our Food for Peace Program. And I was wondering—and they have become viable trading partners with us now—is there anything being done under Public Law 480 that can be done?

The President. I think so. And with regard to exports, that is also a priority of ours. And that's why he's a traveling salesman and has been going around the world so much on this, to develop and encourage more exports, because we know that—good Lord, you have progressed. They talk about high-tech revolutions, the American farmer is high tech himself. You can not only feed all of America, you can feed an awful lot of a hungry world. And we're going to do ev-

erything we can to see that those markets are open to you.

Now, I know I've got to go. Did you want to add something?

Secretary Block. Just to say that between now and the first of October, there will be $2 billion of GSM 102 credits announced for countries that need our grain and need our agricultural crops. And we're going to start moving them. We're going to move them fast during the harvest period.

The President. I made a general statement, and he made it specific.

Well, I know I have to go and move on here, but I just want to tell you one thing. I can't resist. When Jack introduced me as knowing something about farming, and I think I do, I do have to tell you how I learned some of those lessons. Maybe it'll ring true with some of you.

I had a ranch—well, I have a ranch—but I was running grazer cattle at the time. And then it just dawned on me, with all that space out there and everything, why didn't I put in a battery of chickens and raise our own eggs and have eggs at home. And I did. And it worked just fine. It was wonderful to sit down, our own eggs there at the breakfast in the morning, until I found out that they were costing me $1.65 an egg. [Laughter] So, I gave up poultry. [Laughter]

Well, thank you all very much. Thank you.

Note: The President spoke at 11:03 a.m. in the barnyard area of the farm of John and Louise Brockschink. He then traveled to Fairfax, IA.

Remarks at a Community Picnic in Fairfax, Iowa
September 20, 1984

Thank all you so very much. It's great to be in Iowa again.

And before I begin the remarks I'd intended to make today—I know that some of you were at the airport and won't mind having to hear it again—I feel that I should say a few words about the cowardly terrorist act that occurred this morning early in Beirut. The suicide attack against our Em-

bassy annex in East Beirut, I think has saddened all Americans, of course. And it's another painful reminder of the persistent threat of terrorism in the world.

I had an opportunity on the way here—on the plane—to talk to Ambassador Reg Bartholomew, who, although injured himself, expressed to me his pride on behalf of the dedicated Americans serving with him.

And then, he was in the hospital and he said to me, "We mustn't let things like this push us out of doing what we must do throughout the world."

So, I know in this moment of anger and sorrow, our prayers are with those who are bereaved, and our commitment to peace remains firm. And I'm proud that our Americans in the Foreign Service, who are serving all over the world, are of the caliber and the quality that they are.

Now, I know this morning at the airport I mentioned some schools, and it had nothing to do with some of the charges that have been made against me, it was just an oversight that I didn't, in naming some of the fine schools there, name the two parochial schools of La Salle and Regis, I believe. Do I have it right? Well, all right. I apologize for the oversight. And I know also that I'm only a few miles away from someplace and just want you to know that I know that, in addition to all the great agricultural products and everything of Iowa, this button says, to those of you who are too far away, that I'm a Number 1 Bodicar fan. I guess I don't have to tell any of you who that is—[*laughter*]—and what it is.

But I stopped counting a number of years ago the number of times that I've been in your good State, including a tenure of some 5 years that were very happy years in my life. But I can tell you, however, instead of all those times, about the time I didn't come. In fact, I'll never forget it. [*Laughter*] It was the caucuses in 1980—[*laughter*]—and I was feeling pretty bouncy, I guess, and pretty sure of the outcome. And I didn't realize so many people had grown up that didn't know Dutch Reagan—[*laughter*]—and you handed me something of a surprise for which I'm ever grateful. You reminded me that no matter what the polls and the pundits say, run hard. And that's what I mean to do this year.

I also want to congratulate you on being a most discerning State, because the Republican you did support in 1980 is George Bush. And he's the best Vice President this country has ever had.

Now, I've been following how things are going here and what your triumphs and travails have been. And I want you to know that I'll always agree with the journalist,

Harrison Salisbury, who said: "Iowa, the land and the people—I would match it against the world!" And I stand with another writer who said, "There are few more beautiful sights in America than Iowa's farmlands in early autumn . . . ." The most pertinent thing that I've read about Iowa is a report from a journalist who said just a few years ago: "Iowa is graced by absolutely marvelous people . . . They are clean, brave, thrifty, reverent, loyal, and honest. . . ."

So, I've decided something. Air Force One is pretty big. And maybe if we all squeeze and everything, I'd like to take all of you back to Washington, because we need more of your kind. Be sure when you see me running out of here—which I'll have to do because we're due in Michigan pretty quick—that you'll fall in line. [*Laughter*]

But seriously, I'd like to talk to you about how things are going nationally and about some local problems that I'm aware of and which I want very much to address.

Nationally, I think it's fair to report that the country's economy is recovering and economic expansion has begun. The fight against inflation continues, and now inflation is less than one-third of what it was in 1980. And if it continues at the rate of just the last couple of months or so—it's under 3 percent. Interest rates have gone down, though not enough, by any means. And the employment picture is very good. We've created 6 million new jobs in this country in the past 20 months; 600,000 businesses were incorporated last year, and that's a record in our entire history.

And none of this happened overnight, and none of it happened by accident. Our economic success is a direct outgrowth of the practical application of a practical philosophy: We believe that the way out of the economic morass of the 1970's was to let all the American people keep more of their hard-earned money, instead of sending an ever-larger amount to support Federal spending programs that were out of control.

We cut tax rates for individuals, and we cut taxes for business. And what we said would happen happened: The economy recovered and then expanded. Now, all of this is good news, but it's not enough—not by a long shot. We've got to do better.

Here in Iowa, farmers are still feeling the effects of years and years of bad government policy and neglect. When the Federal Government wanted to make a foreign relations point, when they wanted to make a point with the Soviet Union, they cut off the grain sales and left you holding the bag. When interest rates hit the highest point since the Civil War, they made it impossible for you to operate. When inflation gouged you, they didn't hear your cries. And on top of all that, as if that weren't enough, estate taxes on your farms were so high that you couldn't even keep the family farm in the family anymore.

Well, I know about your problems. And as I see it, there is no America without the American farm. You not only feed the country, you feed the world. We owe you a lot, and you're the last people in this country who deserve to be taken for granted or taken for a ride.

So, first, we ended the grain embargo. You know, as we do, that if we refuse to sell the Soviets grain they simply go to other suppliers, and that's what they did. And the only ones who suffered from that kind of lightswitch diplomacy were America's farmers. So, we ended the embargo and negotiated a new and expanded grain agreement with the Soviets. Since last October, they have bought 23 million metric tons of grain. And as you may know, I approved raising the ceiling so they can buy an additional 10 million metric tons in the next year.

By bringing down inflation, we went from one of the largest 2-year increases ever in prices farmers paid in '79 and '80 to the smallest 2-year rise in 15 years in '82 and '83. As for interest rates, we've cut the prime from a high of 21½ percent in 1980 to 13 percent today.

I know that operating loans are a point or two higher, and that's still too high, but it's an improvement. As for estate taxes, we fought hard and finally succeeded, thanks to the help of your Republican Congressmen in the House and your two Senators. Now the estate tax exemption is to increase to $600,000 by 1987, and we've seen to it that there will be no estate tax for a surviving spouse.

So, once again, families have a chance to keep the family farm. And I want to add here that I see this estate tax business as crucial to the interests of the farm belt. All of those taxes taking a farm right from under a family—when I think about it, it's like a scene from the "Grapes of Wrath," with the fellow in the bulldozer being the tax man knocking down the farm that a family had lived on for generations. Well, we've tried to stop that bulldozer dead in its tracks and keep the farm intact.

We've been working for some time on the problem of farm debts and land values. So many farmers have been struggling with debt burdens. In the last 3 years, the Farmers Home Administration has doubled its regular operating loans for farmers. And to provide further assistance, Farmers Home will now permit a deferral of up to 25 percent, for up to 5 years, of the principal and interest payments owed by farmers who need breathing room to return to a sound financial footing. And this will be done on a case-by-case basis. And for those who do not participate in the FmHA programs, Farmers Home will make available up to $630 million in guarantees of loans by private banks as part of rescheduling plans for troubled farmers.

But let me be very clear about one thing. A partial recovery and a partial expansion isn't enough. We won't be happy until the American recovery stretches across this country like a blanket, with the Midwest safe and warm inside. Until the farmers recover, then our recovery is not complete. In the past few years you've known droughts and other natural disasters, and we've tried to make sure that our programs provide a helping hand.

You know, speaking of disasters of that kind, I remember when a previous Secretary of Agriculture—some years ago—went out on kind of a tour of the farm belt. And there'd been some problems at that time. And one fellow was giving him a really bad time, and he turned to an aide, and he looked at some notes that he had there, and then turned back and said, "Well, now wait a minute. Things weren't all that bad." He said, "You had 29 inches of rain last year." And the farmer said, "Yeah, I remember the night it happened." [*Laughter*]

So, we've introduced some soil conservation initiatives that will help ensure that our breadbasket will feed the world not only today, but tomorrow. And we've targeted a larger portion of our Federal funds to States such as Iowa, where the soil erosion is a major concern.

And let me add that no one has helped us more in our efforts than Roger Jepsen, your terrific Senator, and Chuck Grassley, another hero of the cause. And in the House we have the help of Tom Tauke and Cooper Evans. Iowa has sent some very fine people to Washington, and they're fighting for Iowa every day.

And there's probably no group in this country for which I feel a more natural affinity than America's farmers, and not the least because the very qualities it takes to work and run a farm are the very qualities it takes for a citizenry to run the country. I'm talking about the decent and enduring values of hard work and thrift and planning for the future and investing in the future.

You know, it can be said that investing in the future is the most faithful act a man or woman can make. And when you invest your hard work and your money and your effort and your time, you show an extraordinary faith in our system, our culture, and our country. This is the faith of the heartland, and it's what our future is built on.

Just a few years ago, in 1979, Pope John Paul II came here to Iowa. And he surveyed the rolling fields of autumn, and he spoke of the future. At the farm museum near Des Moines, he was greeted by 350,000 people who opened their arms to that man of peace and hope. And he told them of the importance of agriculture and how with agricultural abundance comes special responsibilities to human needs. He said, "Conserve the land well, so that your children's children . . . will inherit an even richer land than was entrusted to you . . . ."

And after he spoke, there was a moment that was described as a "hushed unison," as the vast crowd began the final hymn of the day, whose opening lines were "Oh beautiful for spacious skies, for amber waves of grain." And a person who was there said at that moment "the visit achieved a union of spirit . . . beyond sentimentality." It was a special moment, but such moments aren't uncommon in America. Despite our differences, we are—all of us—in America, in 1984, part of a great hushed unison, a great unspoken unity. And, as I travel the country in my quest for reelection, I think: May it ever flow unbroken.

How many of you weren't at the airport rally today? Then, I'm going to tell you. Those who were there are going to have to hear something again. I hadn't told it, I just thought about it for the first time in many, many years, a little personal experience I had in 1948. I'd gone to England to make a picture called "The Hasty Heart." And on the weekends, never having been there before, I'd hire a driver and a car and have him show me the countryside outside of London. And——

[At this point, the President was briefly interrupted by a train whistle.]

Quiet! *[Laughter]*

Is that his campaign train? *[Laughter]*

But he stopped one evening, as the Sun was going down on one of those weekends, a pub that he said was 400 years old. And we went in, and a matronly woman, a very nice lady, was serving us. And down, some tables down, was an elderly gentleman, and he was—they were the only two, evidently, running this place.

And when she heard us talk for awhile, she said, "You're Americans, aren't you?" And I said, "Yes, we are." And then she said, "Oh, there were a great number of your chaps stationed just down the road from here during the war." And she said, "They used to come in every evening, and they'd have a songfest." And she said, "They called me 'Mom' and they called the old man 'Pop'."

And by this time, she's not looking at me anymore. She's looking kind of out into the distance with memory, and there's a tear on her cheek. She said, "It was a Christmas Eve. We were here all alone." And she said, "The door burst open and in they come, and they had presents for us." And then she said—and this is why I'm telling you the story—she said, "Big strapping lads they was, from a place called Iowa." *[Laughter]*

And then I had a tear on my cheek.

Well, I thank you so much for your very wonderful hospitality and for the warmth and kindness that comes so naturally to Iowans. And I want you to know that I enjoyed both the beef and the pork for lunch. [*Laughter*] No argument about that.

Thank you all, and God bless you.

Note: The President spoke at 12:15 p.m. on the lawn of St. Patrick's Catholic Church. Following his remarks, the President traveled to Grand Rapids, MI.

Statement on the Report of the Independent Counsel Investigating Edwin Meese III
September 20, 1984

It's always gratifying when the honor of a just man is vindicated, and that's exactly what has happened with the report of the Independent Counsel on Ed Meese. It's a particularly happy moment for me because I've known and worked with Ed Meese for many years, and I know how much he's given of himself in service to his country and community. He is one of the most decent and honorable men I've ever known, so I'm not surprised by the outcome, but congratulate him in any case on his vindication.

I intend, if I am reelected, to resubmit his nomination as soon as Congress reconvenes in January. I'm confident that the Senate will confirm him, and I know he'll be a truly distinguished Attorney General.

Remarks to Employees of Westinghouse Furniture Systems in Grand Rapids, Michigan
September 20, 1984

Thank you all very much. And before I begin the remarks I'd intended to make today, let me, if I can, just say a few words about the cowardly act of terrorism that we learned of early this morning. The suicide attack against our Embassy annex in East Beirut has saddened us all, of course. It's another painful reminder of the persistent threat of terrorism in the world.

I talked with our Ambassador, Reg Bartholomew, who, although injured himself, expressed pride on behalf of the dedicated Americans that were serving with him. I called him on the flight out here. He was in the hospital there. But he's quite a guy, as are a lot of those Foreign Service people of ours. He had walked out of that explosion to the hospital under his own power. And he was telling that all he had were some cuts and things, and he says, "I'm going to get out of here tomorrow." And he will.

But in this moment of anger and sorrow,

I think our prayers are with those, the bereaved who have lost someone there, and our commitment to the cause of peace remains firm. And, of course, we have sympathy for those who are injured. I'm proud, as all Americans should be proud, of the brave Americans that are serving, as I said, throughout the world in that service.

But I now come to this part of the day, and I have enjoyed this visit so much. Actually, it's been a bit nostalgic for me. Back in an earlier life, part of my job at that time was visiting manufacturing plants in connection with the TV show that I was doing and speaking to employees under very similar circumstances to these. I don't want to give away my age—[*laughter*]—but I can tell you that the plants I was visiting then looked like log cabins compared to what I've seen here today.

Now, I look at you, and I know I'm looking at America's future, and it looks great. If our country is to remain prosperous, the standard of living of our people is to be maintained. If America is to remain a leader in world affairs, we must have policies that encourage this kind of investment in the future. We aren't going to have it if politicians tax away our take-home pay, tax away the resources needed for investment, and tax the vitality out of our economy.

Now, I wouldn't want to strike a partisan note, but I happen to think that America needs high tech a lot more than she needs high taxes.

I know you folks here in Michigan have had your fill of politicians insisting that what you need is another tax increase. We need to focus our efforts on economic growth and expanding opportunities for people. We've already tried the old ideas that rely on bigger government and more taxes as a solution to our problems. The old solutions more than doubled our taxes just between 1976 and 1981. They gave us murderous double-digit inflation, sky-high interest rates, unemployment, economic stagnation, and national insecurity.

Now, there are those who would divide us, appealing to envy and promising something for nothing. Well, I think the American people are too decent and too smart to be taken in by such divisiveness. What we want to do is work and build and produce for growth and expansion, so that all of us and our families will be better off.

And I have to say something to you in just the short time that I've been here also. Family, yes, it's the center of our whole system and our whole civilization and policy in this country. But within this plant, in just this last short time, I've seen a larger family relationship that bodes well for increased productivity in our country, and it's the relationship that you all have.

Three and a half years ago we started America on a totally new course, a new beginning. We cut the tax rates by 25 percent across the board. We cut the growth in Federal spending in half and trimmed away needless and counterproductive regulations. It took time to reverse trends that had been building for the few years previous to that, but we've proven the gloom and doomers are wrong.

We're in the midst of the most vibrant and vital economic expansion in 40 years. Six million new jobs have been created. The pessimists said it couldn't be done. But we stayed the course, and now our country is reaping the rewards of high growth and low inflation. We know here in Michigan progress is far from complete, but that only makes us more determined than ever not to rest until every single person who wants to work can find work.

And I don't think we need to waste any more time listening to those who keep telling us what we can't do. Leave them be to harp on about no growth and limits and lowering our expectations. We say America should shoot for the stars, strive for the best and, like our Olympic athletes, go for it. And if you look close, you see it beginning to happen all over the country, and that's why things are improving.

I can think of no finer example than your facility, which we're dedicating here today, and you men and women who are earning a living here by manufacturing high-quality products of which you can be proud.

The courageous decision to modernize this plant, to invest in the future, was made at a time when this division of Westinghouse was not showing a profit. It was a vote of confidence in America. This plant also represents a new level of cooperation and good will, as I said, between management and labor. And I've been told that most all of you—management and labor— were part of the planning process, helping to rearrange the workplace in a way to maximize efficiency, laying out the space to facilitate the work flow and improve production quality.

I understand that many of you who work in production were sent to customers, getting some direct feedback on your work. You—all of you—are doing a fantastic job. I think the last thing you need here is bureaucrats or Federal officials coming here to tell you how to run your business.

Today, thanks to a gutsy investment and a commitment to succeed on the part of all concerned, you're putting out products that are competitive with any in the world. Now, this is part of America's new confidence, part of the new patriotism. And I think the world is about to learn that once we Americans put our mind to it and are provided the proper tools and equipment, we can outproduce, outsell, and outcompete anybody in the world.

Success creates success. Momentum creates momentum. What you're producing, for example, will help make other companies more efficient. By doing your job professionally and the very best you can, benefits can accrue all the way through the system and eventually be enjoyed in one way or another by everyone. And that's what made ours the great country that it is.

I think it's also impressive that while working hard, you've taken the time and effort to get involved in community service. I know you were part of a fundraising effort, a charity golf classic, that raised $90,000 to buy equipment for the training of paramedics. I'm told that with the equipment you helped provide, the lives of many people in your local area will be saved. And that's quite a gift.

I know that a couple of years ago, Lee Raterink, former president of your local union, made a special gift to charity. Lee, they tell me that you sported rather long hair in those days. [*Laughter*] You pledged 1 inch of hair for every $100 donated by your fellow workers to the Muscular Dystrophy campaign. They also tell me you almost ended up with a crew cut. [*Laughter*] Well, that's the Michigan spirit.

And finally, I'd like to add my special congratulations to Albrie Love, Jr., who received the Westinghouse award for excellence for involvement in minority activities. [*Applause*] Your service to your fellow man in the Salvation Army, the Urban League, and, yes, in counseling your fellow employees is deeply appreciated. Now, you've just heard that it was. [*Laughter*]

And let's not forget that all of you can be proud that your company was an official sponsor of the Olympics. What you're doing is showing the world what America is all about. A few years ago, some people were counting us out. Now the whole country's telling the world, "You ain't seen nothin' yet."

Greg Meyer, who comes from this area, won the Boston Marathon last year. Well, all of us are in the race for the long haul. We're part of the same team, the American team, and we ain't coming in second. We're going to keep working together, building and producing to keep this country number one and the best country on the face of this planet. And thank you for doing more than your part. It'll be my honor to help you dedicate this facility to the American spirit, which is what you're all about.

And let me just extend a word of personal gratitude also, that my talking about the few years before we came here, I wasn't in any way talking about the days when a gentleman on this platform was the President of the United States. It was going uphill then. It started to go downhill, and we've just tried to put it back on that uphill course.

He didn't know I'm going to say this, but I have to tell you this. I'm going to tell it to another group here today, also. He and I in a way go back about 50 years. Oh, we didn't know each other for 50 years. But we did, 50 years ago, share a kind of a unique experience. He was in the center of the line, down in Michigan Stadium—[*laughter*]—in a football game against the University of Iowa, and I was up in the press box broadcasting that game. [*Laughter*]

Thank you very much. Thank you all.

Note: The President spoke at 4:12 p.m. in the welding-fabric department of the Westinghouse Furniture Systems facility. He was introduced by former President Gerald R. Ford, who greeted the President upon his arrival in Michigan.

Prior to his remarks, the President attended a briefing in the Learning Center and toured the electrical department of the facility.

Remarks at a Reagan-Bush Rally in Grand Rapids, Michigan
September 20, 1984

The President. Thank you all very much. And before I begin the remarks that I intend to make today, let me say a few words, if I could, about the cowardly act of terrorism that we learned of early this morning. The suicide attack against our Embassy annex in East Beirut has saddened all of us, of course. It's another painful reminder of the persistent threat of terrorism in the world.

I've talked with our Ambassador, Reg Bartholomew, who, although injured himself, expressed pride on behalf of the dedicated Americans who were serving with him. In this moment of anger and sorrow, our prayers are with those who are bereaved, while our commitment to the cause of peace remains firm. And I'm proud, as all Americans should be proud, of the brave Americans serving our nation throughout the world in the cause of peace for people everywhere.

But now, we've just been visiting with your good friends in Iowa. And now, what a wonderful way to cap our day to be back with you in the Wolverine State. I can't imagine a better place to begin our Michigan campaign than right here in your all-American city—the center of the 5th District, the home of our 38th President of the United States. And you don't have to be in Grand Rapids long to understand how this town gave us someone as good—no, forgive me—as great as Jerry Ford.

Your spirit of hard work, your belief in each other, and your faith in the future are making Grand Rapids one of the best success stories in the Middle West. Now, I've just been out to the Westinghouse plant and seen an unbeatable combination for our future—men and women from labor and management joining together to pool their resources, and not only saving their company but developing advanced technologies to make it stronger, bigger, and better than ever before.

Now, some people seem to spend their time traveling back and forth across America wringing their hands in despair. Well, thank heavens for people like you—you, who rolled up your sleeves, went to work, and together have created almost 13,000 jobs for the Grand Rapids area in the last 3 years.

This is the brand of leadership that Jerry Ford gave America. He helped heal the Nation's spirit, he brought back our economy, he began rebuilding our defenses. And when Jerry Ford left, America was better off than before.

I have to tell you a little personal thing here about Jerry Ford and myself. I can begin it by saying we go back 50 years, except that we didn't know it 50 years ago. It was just that we happened then—without realizing or knowing each other—we happened to share an experience. Jerry Ford was down on the floor of the Michigan Stadium, in the center of the line down there, playing for Michigan against the University of Iowa. And I was up in the press box broadcasting that game on radio.

One of the greatest tragedies of our time was seeing the America that Jerry Ford made well and strong again brought to its knees by people who didn't know then—and who don't know today—what common sense and strong leadership are all about. My friends, we——

Audience. 4 more years! 4 more years! 4 more years!

The President. All right.

Audience. 4 more years! 4 more years! 4 more years!

The President. All right. All right. I'll give in, you talked me into it.

Well, America made one mistake, and we paid dearly for it. Let's make sure this November 6th we don't make the same mistake all over again.

Four years ago, we had to cope with, as Jerry told you, the double-digit inflation nightmare and the interest rates of 21 percent and the highest peacetime tax burden in our history, zero growth, rising crime rate, scholastic aptitude test scores that had been falling for two decades, a foreign policy as feeble as it was fearful, and to top it off, the people in Washington whose only answer was, "All of you suffer from a malaise." Well, the American people didn't suffer from any malaise; they suffered from leaders who denied them opportunity, and opportunity is what we're putting back in the hands of you, the people.

You know, with this being football season and Michigan being a powerhouse football State, maybe you've noticed in our Nation's Capital the same thing I have: When all the last team ever did was punt, isn't it great to see America scoring touchdowns again?

Unlike 4 years ago when crime rates were going up but scholastic aptitude test scores were going down, today the crime rate is going down and scholastic aptitude test scores are going up.

Our economy is not falling apart. Our defenses are not being neglected. America's being looked up to again as a leader for peace and freedom. And not 1 square inch of additional territory has fallen to Communist aggressors since 1981.

Now, Jerry Ford told you about inflation and what it's down to. We won't be satisfied until inflation is 0.0. And while here in Michigan things are looking up after a long period of hard times, we cannot and we will not be satisfied until every person in your State who wants a job can find a job.

But let's recognize the progress we have made. I can see there are many students in our audience here today. I heard somebody a little while ago, when I was offstage, asking you some questions. I want to ask some questions, too. I won't give the answer away by naming the country I'd like to ask about, but a little hint: It has three initials, and its first two are U.S.

Of all the great industrialized nations in the world, which has shown by far the strongest, most sustained economic growth?

Audience. U.S.A.!

The President. What country can say its investment is up, its productivity is up, its take-home pay is up, and its consumer spending is up?

Audience. U.S.A.!

The President. And what country, during the past 20 months created 6 million new jobs?

Audience. U.S.A.!

The President. And what country created,

on the average, more new jobs each month during the past 12 months than all the countries of Western Europe created over the last 10 years?

Audience. U.S.A.!

The President. All right. You get 100. You passed.

Audience. U.S.A.! U.S.A.! U.S.A.!

The President. All right.

Audience. U.S.A.! U.S.A.! U.S.A.!

The President. All right. Yes. And you ain't seen nothin' yet.

Believe me, there's nothing we can't do if we could get some long-overdue reforms passed by the Congress. Now, I'm talking about a constitutional amendment mandating that government stop spending more than government takes in and a line-item veto, giving the President power to veto individual items in appropriation bills to get rid of some of the useless extravagance.

There's another change that we must have: an historic simplification of the tax system. Do you know that Albert Einstein said that he couldn't understand the form 1040? [*Laughter*] We want to make that entire system more fair, easier to understand, so we can bring yours and everybody else's tax rates further down, not up.

You know, I've said that this election offers the American people the clearest choice in 50 years. Nothing illustrates better the nature of that choice than their obsession with raising your taxes and our determination to stop them. You see, they have the same problem today that they've always had: They promise too much and they spend too much. Just to pay for their promises in this campaign would result in the equivalent of an $1,800 tax increase for every household. Now——

Audience. Boo-o-o!

The President. I know—[*laughter*]—you've had a taxpayer's revolt here in Michigan. But considering the magnitude of what's at stake today, would you agree that nothing could be quite so revolting as what they do to you and to all the taxpayers of America?

Well, I've been traveling our nation, and I've heard what our people feel. And believe me, there's no doubt about where they stand on this question. Come November 6th, America will rise up and answer my opponent's issue number one—his tax increase—with an emphatic, unequivocal no.

You know, each day——

Audience. 4 more years!

The President. ——each day, our people do what they've always done best, and that is create not only prosperity but also the very ability of the United States to perfect and enjoy a wider array of freedoms than any other nation in history. That's America. People paying a fairer share, but always keeping a fair share. And that's where we and the other side part company. Their first loyalty is to government; our first loyalty is to the people—all the people.

Audience. 4 more years!

The President. And that's why we have such dramatically different visions of the future. They want a new so-called trust fund for their tax increases. Well, we don't want their tax increases or their new trust fund; we want a government that trusts you. Their legacy to our people would be— or to our children, I should say—would be built-in tax increases that could only be described in one way—from here to eternity. [*Laughter*] Our legacy can be——

Audience. 4 more years!

The President. ——our legacy can be an American opportunity society with lower tax rates for all. Now, they see an America where every day is April 15th tax day; we see an America where every day is the Fourth of July.

The tax increases they propose are recovery killers; they're destined to crush the initiative and spirit of the people, designed to destroy jobs and economic growth, and, yes, make no mistake, destined to make the deficit much higher, not lower.

My friends, the choice for 1984 is clear and crucial: Will we let them take us back to their failed past, whose memory remains still so fresh and painful?

Audience. No!

The President. Will we let them erect their giant stop sign and bring America's economy and your families' opportunities for the future screeching to a halt?

Audience. No!

The President. Or will we continue on the high road of hope?

Audience. Yes!

The President. Will America continue to champion the great, driving idea for your future: Economic growth through lower tax rates, more jobs, rising take-home pay, and greater opportunities for every American?

Audience. Yes!

The President. That's our vision for tomorrow, and it's a far better vision.

To all those Democrats who've been loyal to the party of F.D.R. and Harry Truman and J.F.K.—and I hope there are many present; I was one for most of my adult life—people who believe in protecting the interests of the working people and who are not ashamed or afraid of Americans standing for freedom in the world, for those Democrats who are here, I say, "Join us." And by "us," I also mean Guy Vander Jagt and Hal Sawyer and Mark Siljander and your fine Senatorial candidates, your candidate Jack Lousma, your other candidates for the Congress—Paul Henry and Jackie MacGregor for the House of Representatives. Come and walk with us down the new path of hope and opportunity, and together we can lift America up to meet our greatest days.

No army is as powerful as an idea whose time has come. In 1980, millions of Americans from all walks of life came together for the common cause of freedom. We united under a new banner for opportunity, for growth, and progress. We fought to make a new beginning. We struggled to rescue our nation. And all during those momentous days, our ranks have continued to swell.

Today the power of that idea has become a mighty tide for progress. And with Democrats and independents joining us in larger and larger numbers, the power of that idea can become a tidal wave for progress. Those politicians who remain stuck in the past—well, they cannot and will not hold us back. It's time for them to stand aside and get out of our way.

We're not going back to weakness; we're going forward to make America stronger than today. And together, we'll make sure that America is back up on top.

When I spoke of these candidates and these incumbent Congressmen here and how we need them, the last time that a

Republican administration had a Congress of its own persuasion to help it to do the things it had told the people it wanted to do was in the first 2 years of the Eisenhower administration. And since then, until 1980—or till 1981, they have controlled both Houses of the Congress. And now, since '81, we at last have controlled one, the Senate. And we couldn't have accomplished what we have without that one. But, oh, how far we can march if we have both Houses of the Congress subscribing to our philosophy of more freedom and opportunity for the people.

So, I thank all of you. Jerry Ford, I thank you. I thank all these wonderful candidates here. And I thank all of you wonderful people for this grand Michigan welcome. Believe me, I go back to Washington from here very much inspired. Thank you.

Note: The President spoke at 5:17 p.m. in the Ah-Nab-Awen Bicentennial Park, which is adjacent to the Gerald R. Ford Museum. He was introduced by former President Gerald R. Ford.

Following his remarks, the President returned to Washington, DC.

Message to the Congress Transmitting the Aeronautics and Space Report of the President
September 21, 1984

To the Congress of the United States:

I am pleased to transmit the report of the Nation's progress in space and aeronautics during calendar 1983, *Aeronautics and Space Report of the President, 1983 Activities*. It is provided in accordance with Section 206 of the National Aeronautics and Space Act of 1958, as amended (42 U.S.C. 2476).

The quest for knowledge about and beyond the earth, as well as profitable use of that knowledge, advanced in 1983. In the 25th anniversary year of the formal founding of the Nation's space program, four operational flights of the Space Shuttle expanded service to the government for civil use and for national security. They also served the private sector for commercial advantage and for university research. The first Shuttle flight of the reusable laboratory Spacelab was, in addition, a triumph of international cooperation. Built by the European Space Agency and flown by NASA, Spacelab carried both U.S. and European scientific experiments and crew; the largest crew yet launched into space included among its six members the first European to orbit in a U.S. spacecraft. On an earlier mission, the first American woman astronaut in space helped launch two satellites from the Shuttle.

Twenty-seven satellites launched during 1983, five of them from the Shuttle, went to work in communications, navigation, weather forecasting, and space science. One of these made numerous discoveries about the universe as it surveyed the entire sky.

Aeronautical research continued to develop technology to maintain the preeminence of civil and military aviation and the predominance of U.S.-built aircraft in the world's commercial fleet.

The Nation can be proud of 25 years of achievements, as well as these and others reported for 1983.

RONALD REAGAN

The White House,
September 21, 1984.

Statement on the Mutual and Balanced Force Reduction Negotiations
September 21, 1984

Today I met with Ambassador Maynard W. Glitman, the new U.S. Representative to the Mutual and Balanced Force Reduction (MBFR) talks in Vienna. This negotiation, which involves members of both the North Atlantic Treaty Organization (NATO) and the Warsaw Pact, aims at enhancing stability and security in Central Europe through the reduction of conventional forces to equal, lower levels of manpower on both sides. Such reductions would reduce the risks of war in Europe and promote mutual confidence.

Ambassador Glitman and I discussed the current status of the negotiations and the prospects for progress when the talks resume at the end of this month. We reviewed recent efforts by the U.S. and our NATO allies to give renewed momentum to the negotiations and to produce an equitable and verifiable agreement. Specifically, on April 19, 1984, the West put forward a major new initiative which addresses in a flexible manner the basic issues which stand in the way of an MBFR agreement. These issues include the "data problem"—i.e., the dispute over the size of Warsaw Pact forces in Central Europe—and the question of verification.

The Eastern response to this latest Western initiative to move toward an effective agreement has been disappointing. The Soviet Union and its allies have refused to engage in a detailed discussion of the proposal. If our proposal is examined on its merits, substantial progress could be achieved in these negotiations. Now that the Eastern negotiators have had several weeks during the summer recess to address the Western proposal in their capitals, we hope they will return to Vienna with a constructive response.

Ambassador Glitman and his Western colleagues have my full support in their efforts to move these negotiations forward. We in the West will do our part to achieve concrete results, and I have urged Ambassador Glitman to take every opportunity to probe for possible areas of movement.

Our efforts in MBFR are part of our broader commitment to achieving progress in arms reduction and other security negotiations. About 2 weeks ago, the Stockholm Conference on Disarmament in Europe resumed its efforts to negotiate confidence-building measures designed to reduce the risk of surprise attack. The United States and other NATO participants have put forward major, concrete proposals in Stockholm that would significantly enhance security in Europe. Similarly, in the 40-nation Committee on Disarmament in Geneva, the United States has put forward a proposal for a complete, verifiable ban on chemical weapons.

In the Geneva negotiations on both strategic and intermediate-range nuclear forces, the START and INF talks, the United States has put forward major proposals that would radically reduce or—in the case of INF—totally eliminate an entire class of nuclear missiles in U.S. and Soviet arsenals. Unfortunately, the Soviet Union walked out of these talks late last year and still has not agreed to return.

In June the United States agreed without preconditions to the Soviet offer to hold talks on space arms control issues. However, the Soviet Union has thus far been unwilling to follow up their own proposal by beginning such negotiations.

It is my firm belief that the U.S. and the Soviet Union share a special responsibility to take the lead in bringing about real reductions in the levels of forces. We will continue to keep this issue at the top of our agenda in discussions with the Soviet Union.

Proclamation 5233—National Sewing Month, 1984
September 21, 1984

By the President of the United States of America

A Proclamation

The home sewing industry is important to our Nation's economy and is an activity shared by many Americans. Approximately fifty million Americans sew at home, and nearly forty million sew at least part of their wardrobe. Their initiative, creativity and self-reliance are characteristic of the people of our Nation.

Sewing at home helps keep down the cost of clothing, and the sewing industry generates over $3,500,000,000 annually for the economy of the United States. Home sewing also enhances the career opportunities of many Americans in fields such as fashion, interior design, patternmaking, retail merchandising and textile design.

In recognition of the importance of home sewing to our Nation, the Congress, by Senate Joint Resolution 302, has designated the month of September 1984 as "National Sewing Month" and has authorized and requested the President to issue a proclamation in observance of this month.

Now, Therefore, I, Ronald Reagan, President of the United States of America, do hereby proclaim September 1984 as National Sewing Month, and I call upon the people of the United States to observe September with appropriate ceremonies and activities.

In Witness Whereof, I have hereunto set my hand this twenty-first day of September, in the year of our Lord nineteen hundred and eighty-four, and of the Independence of the United States of America the two hundred and ninth.

RONALD REAGAN

[*Filed with the Office of the Federal Register, 4:15 p.m., September 21, 1984*]

Proclamation 5234—Youth of America Week, 1984
September 21, 1984

By the President of the United States of America

A Proclamation

More than fifty million young Americans contribute to the vitality of our Nation. In their values, aspirations and accomplishments we see reflected not only a rich heritage but a vision of America in the future. It will be a society generous in spirit, strong in character and sincere in purpose—one in which freedom and opportunity give rise to responsibility and excellence.

Just as young Americans can be proud of their contribution to our Nation, they also share a vital part of the life of the smaller community of the family. In this first school where the values of self-reliance, compassion and initiative are taught, the younger members make special contributions to foster the unique identity and sharing of each family. And they prepare for the time when they too will pass on to a new generation the values of our heritage.

For those young Americans in special need we continue to offer support in a variety of activities within the public and private sectors. These support programs are an investment in our national future, and many of the best of them rely not on large sums of money but on the unpaid service of volunteers who contribute their time and experience to the task of forming the next generation. Just as importantly, young people themselves are one of our best sources of volunteers because their energy and idealism give them a natural motivation to devote themselves to helping others.

To assure the Nation's youth of our commitment to share our knowledge, experience and wisdom as they mature towards a full appreciation of democratic principles, the Congress of the United States, by Senate Joint Resolution 597, has designated the week of September 2 through September 8, 1984, as "Youth of America Week" and has authorized and requested the President to issue a proclamation in observance of that week.

Now, Therefore, I, Ronald Reagan, President of the United States of America, do hereby proclaim the week of September 2 through 8, 1984, as Youth of America Week.

In Witness Whereof, I have hereunto set my hand this twenty-first day of September, in the year of our Lord nineteen hundred and eighty-four, and of the Independence of the United States of America the two hundred and ninth.

RONALD REAGAN

[*Filed with the Office of the Federal Register, 4:16 p.m., September 21, 1984*]

Note: The proclamation was not issued as a White House press release.

Proclamation 5235—National School-Age Child Care Awareness Week, 1984
September 21, 1984

By the President of the United States of America

A Proclamation

The care and education of children has always been society's most important task, since a nation's children are its future. The love and instruction young people receive during their formative years help to set their characters for the rest of their lives and so determine the kind of society we all live in.

Patterns of child care are changing rapidly as a majority of women spend part or all of their adult lives as members of the labor force. Yet the need of young people for love and guidance remains as important as ever, and we all have a responsibility to make sure that they continue to receive it.

The Federal government has been actively involved in working with State and local governments, voluntary and nonprofit agencies, and businesses to encourage the creation of appropriate programs for school-age children. The White House Office of Private Sector Initiatives has launched a series of forums for chief executive officers of major corporations to promote increased private sector involvement in child care.

The Department of Health and Human Services is also sponsoring a number of initiatives to help American families meet their child care needs. These projects are increasing knowledge through research, demonstrating new program models, making valuable information available to parents and providers, and helping to develop local child care systems.

But today, as in the past, the most important environment forming the characters of our young people is the family. Families face new challenges, but the American family has proved to be a most resilient institution. It remains the primary vehicle by which parents seek to develop their children into healthy and confident adults. The task before us is to strengthen the family and help it when necessary so that it will continue to perform its unique civilizing function.

The Congress of the United States, by House Joint Resolution 544, has designated the week of September 2 through 8, 1984, as "National School-Age Child Care Awareness Week" and has authorized and requested the President to issue a proclamation in observance of that week.

Now, Therefore, I, Ronald Reagan, President of the United States of America, do hereby proclaim the week of September 2 through 8, 1984, as National School-Age Child Care Awareness Week.

In Witness Whereof, I have hereunto set my hand this twenty-first day of September, in the year of our Lord nineteen hundred and eighty-four, and of the Independence of the United States of America the two hundred and ninth.

RONALD REAGAN

[Filed with the Office of the Federal Register, 4:17 p.m., September 21, 1984]

Note: The proclamation was not issued as a White House press release.

Remarks on Signing the National Drug Abuse Education and Prevention Week Proclamation
September 21, 1984

The President. Thank you very much. And now that we have Nancy properly placed, she and I welcome you all here to the White House. Senator Chiles and Congressman Bennett, our distinguished guests, and ladies and gentlemen:

Good morning, and again, welcome.

We're here to thank the—to mark the progress, I should say, of the fight against drug abuse and to commit ourselves to an even greater national effort in the months ahead. Within the last several years, I think America has come to its senses about drug abuse. We raised a battle flag and declared war on one of the gravest problems that I think is facing our nation. Action replaced debate. We knew the fight wouldn't be easy, but we also knew we couldn't afford to lose. We're fighting for the health of our children and the future of America.

Well, we've made a lot of progress during these past 3 years. Permissive attitudes are giving way to a new sense of responsibility. Hopelessness and helplessness are being replaced with optimism and a willingness to join together in the fight. Concerned parents are banding together, and hundreds of community and business organizations have joined the ranks. Education programs are erasing 20 years of wrong-headed attitudes about drug use. And we're taking aim where it counts the most: teaching the drug users and potential drug users to say no to drugs.

At the Federal level, we've taken strong measures to crack down on big-money drug traffickers and to catch drug smugglers in the act. Yet we all know that we have a long way to go. About one-fourth of our nation's young people continue to abuse drugs or alcohol, and too many children are still getting into drugs every day. And thousands of teenagers are killed every year in auto accidents due to drunk and drugged driving.

As you know, Nancy has traveled across America visiting schools and treatment facilities, seeking every opportunity to promote an antidrug, proachievement generation. In her travels, she's come home to me with stories of heartbreak that she's seen, and broken dreams and families and lost lives. But she's convinced, and she's convinced me, that all of us—if we work together, become more involved, more knowledgeable, and step up the fight—can save a generation and help preserve its promise and hope.

And doing just that is the heart of our 1984 national strategy for prevention of drug abuse and drug trafficking. The 1984 strategy will be released next week during National Drug Abuse, Education, and Prevention Week. But let me tell you that we'll be striving to reinforce the program that is now in place. We're on the right track, we don't need to change direction, but we do need to step up the pace.

The Federal Government will redouble its efforts to stop drug trafficking, punishing drug traffickers, and increase international cooperation to control narcotics. But ultimately, victory can only come from the dedication and commitment of private industry, public organizations, local government, and citizen volunteers. We need to get more people involved, particularly in prevention programs. And we'll be calling on the American people to help us.

To win this fight, we're going to need the kind of help that those of you here have given to your communities and to all of us. And I know that for each of you here today there are thousands of other caring Americans who are also giving of themselves. None of you ever expected any reward for what you did. That's the way it's always been in America. But believe me, I'm delighted that we have the opportunity to recognize you today.

As chairman of the Texans' War on Drug committees, Mr. Ross Perot is helping to make Texas one of the worst places in the world for drug users, pushers, dealers, and traffickers. And his committee is now a model for many other States.

Mrs. Marsha Menatt Schuchard and Mrs. Loretta "Sis" Wenger have contributed unsparingly of their time, energy, and talents to make lasting contributions to the National Drug Abuse Prevention Program. Mrs. Schuchard was the inspiration behind an acclaimed TV documentary and is the author of two important books on the dangers of marijuana. Mrs. Wenger's drug abuse education program is reaching communities all across America. The unselfish efforts of these two ladies are changing attitudes and saving lives.

D.C. Comics, a division of Warner Communications represented by William Sarnoff, and the Keebler Company, represented by Thomas Garvin, have worked together to produce and distribute 3 million drug awareness comic books. And the popularity of their comic book characters is helping to educate our young people about the dangers of drugs and the reasons for them to say no.

McNeil Pharmaceutical, represented by Jack O'Brien, is the driving force behind a drug abuse education program that establishes our nation's pharmacists as a local source of credible information and technical assistance on drug use and abuse. And today their program, Pharmacists Against Drug Abuse, is in 85 percent of our nation's retail pharmacies.

Each of you is demonstrating the unique American spirit of voluntarism. In your own way, you're helping resolve the drug abuse problem in a more effective manner than we could ever do with large Federal programs. We're grateful for the people you've helped and the people whose lives that you've touched and whose burdens you've lifted because you cared enough to extend a helping hand and a warm heart.

And now, I'm going to ask Nancy to help in the handing out of the awards.

[At this point, the certificates were passed out.]

With all due respect for Attorney General Smith and the Justice Department and all the others in our drug abuse program here in the attempt to intercept and keep drugs from crossing our borders and coming into the country, I think we all know that the real victory will only come not when we keep on trying—just trying to take the drug away from the customer—when we take the customers away from the drugs. And that's when we'll win this fight.

Now, before anyone leaves the room, there's one more piece of business. As part of our drug awareness campaign and our national strategy, I will now sign a proclamation designating the week of September 23d through the 29th as National Drug Abuse Education and Prevention Week. And I want to thank Senator Chiles, who sponsored the proclamation in the Senate, and Congressman Bennett, who sponsored it in the House. And would they please come up here and join us?

I know that both of you have a strong personal interest in this proclamation, and we're grateful to you for it. Now, it's time for me to stop talking and start writing. *[Laughter]*

[At this point, the President signed the proclamation.]

There is now a National Drug Abuse Week.

Representative Bennett. Thank you, sir.

The President. Thank you. And now the deed is done. *[Laughter]* I'll go back to work.

Note: The President spoke at 10:50 a.m. in the East Room at the White House.

Proclamation 5236—National Drug Abuse Education and Prevention Week, 1984
September 21, 1984

By the President of the United States of America

A Proclamation

During the past two decades, the use of illegal drugs in the United States spread at an unprecedented rate and reached into every segment of our society. The youth-oriented drug culture was foreign to most of our adult population. We lacked accurate information about the hazards of some of the most widely used drugs, and our efforts to combat the lies, misconceptions, and moral confusion surrounding drug abuse lacked credibility. There was a feeling of inevitability regarding widespread drug use and uncertainty over what was the right thing to do.

The early 1980s have brought a dramatic change. People no longer believe that drug abuse is inevitable. There is growing recognition that by working together to eliminate the abuse of drugs, we can make a real difference in the lives of our children and a better future for America.

One of the most effective weapons we have against drug abuse is our ability to communicate the truth about drugs to the user and the potential user. Research and the personal experience of families across the Nation are expanding our knowledge of drug abuse and how to stop it. This new knowledge is being used by parents, community volunteers, local officials, teachers, health care professionals, and young people themselves. These are the individuals who are closest to current potential drug users, and they can have the greatest influence in preventing the abuse of drugs.

Across America, all levels of government, businesses, educational institutions, civic groups, and individual citizens are organizing activities which will help persons of all ages to say "no" to drug abuse. These Americans are committed to raising the awareness of the dangers of drug abuse and creating a positive environment in which drug abuse is unacceptable behavior.

To call attention to these important efforts, the Congress, by House Joint Resolution 529, has designated the week beginning September 23, 1984, as "National Drug Abuse Education and Prevention Week" and has authorized and requested the President to issue a proclamation in observance of this week.

Now, Therefore, I, Ronald Reagan, President of the United States of America, do hereby proclaim the week beginning September 23, 1984, as National Drug Abuse Education and Prevention Week, and I call upon all Americans to observe this week with appropriate ceremonies and activities. Let all of us seek every opportunity to learn the truth about drug abuse and join in the national fight to create a drug-free America.

In Witness Whereof, I have hereunto set my hand this 21st day of September, in the year of our Lord nineteen hundred and eighty-four, and of the Independence of the United States of America the two hundred and ninth.

RONALD REAGAN

[*Filed with the Office of the Federal Register, 4:18 p.m., September 21, 1984*]

Nomination of Francis Stephen Ruddy To Be United States Ambassador to Equatorial Guinea
September 21, 1984

The President today announced his intention to nominate Francis Stephen Ruddy, of Texas, as Ambassador to the Republic of Equatorial Guinea. He would succeed Alan M. Hardy.

Mr. Ruddy was with the United States Information Agency as Assistant General Counsel (1969–1972) and Deputy General Counsel and Congressional Liaison (1973–1974). In 1972–1973 he was senior attorney of the Office of Telecommunications Policy, Executive Office of the President. He was counsel at Exxon in Houston, TX, in 1974–1981. Since 1981 he has been Assistant Administrator at the Agency for International Development, Washington, DC.

Mr. Ruddy graduated from Holy Cross College (A.B., 1959), New York University (M.A. 1962; LL.M., 1967), Loyola University Law School (LL.B., 1965), and Cambridge University (Ph.D., 1969). His foreign language is French. He was born September 15, 1937, in Jamaica, NY.

Nomination of the United States Representative and Alternate Representatives to the General Conference of the International Atomic Energy Agency
September 21, 1984

The President today announced his intention to nominate the following individuals as the Representative and the Alternate Representatives of the United States of America to the 28th Session of the General Conference of the International Atomic Energy Agency (Vienna, September 24–28):

Representative:

Richard T. Kennedy, Ambassador at Large and Representative of the United States to the International Atomic Energy Agency.

Alternate Representatives:

Helmut A. Merklein, an Assistant Secretary of Energy (International Affairs);

Nunzio J. Palladino, Chairman of the Nuclear Regulatory Commission; and

Richard Salisbury Williamson, Representative of the United States to the Vienna Office of the United Nations and Deputy Representative of the United States to the International Atomic Energy Agency.

Proclamation 5237—Columbus Day, 1984
September 21, 1984

By the President of the United States of America

A Proclamation

In October of each year, we are privileged to honor Christopher Columbus, the Italian explorer whose epic voyages to the New World still excite the imagination.

Columbus challenged the unknown when he sailed westward in 1492 with his tiny fleet of ships. Others had preceded him; some indeed may have visited the Western Hemisphere. Yet his discovery of the New World stands as a unique and momentous achievement. His voyages ushered in a new phase in history and enriched mankind with new opportunities. They revolutionized the way man thought of himself and his world. This New World that Columbus revealed to Europe soon came to symbolize hope, freedom, and opportunity for all. A stream of settlers arrived to build a new society out of their dreams of liberty, justice, and economic opportunity.

We Americans will always feel that we stand at the frontier. Today our voyage of discovery continues—to the vastness of outer space, to the depths of the sea, to the mysteries of life itself. The willingness to strike out in new directions and to take risks is still at work. This spirit has enriched our lives and expanded our horizons. Thus, it is appropriate that we, both as Americans and as Columbus' spiritual heirs, should take inspiration from his blend of daring, skill, enterprise, and imagination.

All Americans share in admiring Columbus' achievement. But those of Italian descent can take particular pride in honoring this bold son of Genoa who set forth in the service of Spain in search of the unknown. A host of other Italians have followed Columbus to this land, lending their talents and helping to create an unparalleled society of freedom and opportunity. This day is one of justifiable pride for Italy and Italians everywhere, and it symbolizes the respect we Americans have for our rich inheritance from the Old World.

In tribute to Columbus' achievement, the Congress of the United States, by joint resolution approved April 30, 1934 (48 Stat. 657), as modified by the Act of June 28, 1968 (82 Stat. 250), has requested the President to proclaim the second Monday in October of each year as Columbus Day.

Now, Therefore, I, Ronald Reagan, President of the United States of America, do hereby proclaim Monday, October 8, 1984, as Columbus Day. I invite the people of this Nation to observe that day in schools, churches, and other suitable places with appropriate ceremonies in honor of this great explorer. I also direct that the flag of the United States be displayed on all public buildings on the appointed day in memory of Christopher Columbus.

In Witness Whereof, I have hereunto set my hand this twenty-first day of September, in the year of our Lord nineteen hundred and eighty-four, and of the Independence of the United States of America the two hundred and ninth.

RONALD REAGAN

[*Filed with the Office of the Federal Register, 4:19 p.m., September 21, 1984*]

Proclamation 5238—Leif Erikson Day, 1984
September 21, 1984

By the President of the United States of America

A Proclamation

In the year 1000, Leif Erikson, charged by King Olav to convert the Nordic settlers in Greenland, set sail to the west. A terrible storm forced his vessel off course, and he came upon lands of which there was no previous knowledge. He found "fields of self-sown wheat" and a country rich with grapes and timber. His early explorations are a tribute to the indomitable and inquisitive spirit so characteristic of the Nordic peoples.

Leif Erikson could not have known at the time of his voyage how intermingled the fate and fortune of the Nordic peoples and the new land would become. During the nineteenth century and early part of the twentieth, millions of Erikson's descendants would join the great current of European migration to the United States. Brave pioneers from Norway, Sweden, Denmark, Finland and Iceland helped push the American frontier to the west, building communities and farms and enriching American life and culture. Others worked long and hard contributing to the great industries of the Northeast. Their accomplishments constitute a proud monument to the Nordic-

American heritage and to the development of our country. Democratic ideals, an abiding faith in the value of ingenuity and hard work, and a deep belief in the sanctity of the individual are among the many values and principles we share. Because of the extensive commerce and exchange of ideas and people between the United States and the Nordic region, we have enjoyed friendship, understanding, and appreciation for each other.

To commemorate the courage of Leif Erikson and in recognition of our long and fruitful relationship with the Nordic peoples, the Congress of the United States, by joint resolution approved September 2, 1964 (78 Stat. 849, 36 U.S.C. 169c), authorized the President to proclaim October 9 in each year as Leif Erikson Day.

Now, Therefore, I, Ronald Reagan, President of the United States of America, do hereby designate October 9, 1984, as Leif Erikson Day, and I direct the appropriate government officials to display the flag of the United States on all government buildings that day. I also invite the people of the United States to honor Leif Erikson by holding appropriate exercises and ceremonies in suitable places throughout the land.

In Witness Whereof, I have hereunto set my hand this twenty-first day of September, in the year of our Lord nineteen hundred and eighty-four, and of the Independence of the United States of America the two hundred and ninth.

RONALD REAGAN

[*Filed with the Office of the Federal Register, 4:20 p.m., September 21, 1984*]

Radio Address to the Nation on the Agricultural and Steel Industries
September 22, 1984

My fellow Americans:

When we took office in 1981, our goal was to help all of you build a new era of lasting economic growth without inflation. And we're getting closer. For the first time since the 1960's, America is enjoying strength in economic growth, business investment, productivity, and the creation of new jobs—6 million in the last 20 months— while at the same time, we're keeping inflation down.

Yesterday we learned that inflation for the last 12 months remains at 4.2 percent, only a third of 1980's 12.4 percent. We're enjoying an historic economic renewal. We can be proud of our accomplishments, but we can't and won't be satisfied until this expansion reaches every sector of our economy.

Two sectors in which millions seek their livelihood, steel and agriculture, have not shared fully in the recovery. This week we took additional action to help people in both steel and agriculture help themselves, so they can work their way out of difficulty and become full partners in our economic expansion, helping all of us build a stronger future.

The American steel industry, as you know, has been struggling through hard times in recent years. The steel companies and their workers have been trying hard to save their industry by cutting costs and modernizing their aging plants and equipment. And we've been trying to help. Our tax reduction, passed in 1981, encourages just such business investments to modernize smokestack America.

The industry is beginning to recover, but it's still climbing uphill on the international playing field. In some cases, new technology has simply reduced the need for steel products. But the industry has also been hurt by foreign subsidies and an overproduction of steel worldwide, with foreign imports biting into the U.S. steel industry's share of our domestic market, making the United States a kind of steel dump for the rest of the world.

Well, that simply isn't acceptable, so we've designed a comprehensive plan to cover the entire steel industry and enable us to take swift, effective action to keep the U.S. from being foreign countries' dumping ground.

I've instructed Ambassador Bill Brock, our international trade representative, to meet with representatives of those nations dumping steel and to seek their agreement to stop such practices. And I've made it clear that, as necessary, we'll initiate strong counteractions to defend American firms and workers from predatory practices of other nations.

Taken together, these actions can be expected to bring down the percentage of steel imports from its current 26 percent to about 18½ percent, excluding semifinished products. And they'll enable our steel producers to continue their modernization and compete on a level playing field again.

One thing I'm not doing, for it would damage our economy more than it would help, is imposing import quotas. That kind of protectionism is my opponent's policy and, just like his tax increase, it's the wrong policy. The lessons of history are clear. The costs of protectionism for one group would automatically be passed on to another. Inflation would be reignited, jobs would be destroyed, not saved, and foreign countries would retaliate against our exporters, like our farmers. And America doesn't need that kind of help.

I'm confident our plan will help steel producers rebuild and become stronger, more competitive, and profitable again. And that's how we're trying to help our farmers, as well. We've ended the last administra-tion's grain embargo, restored grain sales to the Soviet Union, and we've been able to bring down interest rates and sharply reduce inflation.

Unfortunately, our success against inflation, while helpful to farmers in most respects, has caused them some special problems. Many farmers took out loans in the late 1970's when inflation was soaring, and they assumed the value of the land they were pledging as collateral would keep rising with inflation. Well, now that inflation has plunged, those loans have become very difficult for some of those farmers to carry, so in the last 3 years the Farmers Home Administration has more than doubled its regular operating loans for farmers.

This week we announced another major initiative to assist farmers trying to cope with debt burdens. Farmers Home will permit a deferral for 5 years of up to 25 percent of principal and interest payments owed by farmers who need breathing room. The deferrals will be made on a case-by-case basis. For those not participating in FmHA, we're making available $630 million in guarantees of loans by private banks as part of rescheduling plans for troubled farmers.

The road back isn't easy. But by resisting quick fixes and helping those in steel and farming help themselves, we'll make sure all of us can, and will, go forward together.

Until next week, thanks for listening, and God bless you.

Note: The President spoke at 12:06 p.m. from the Oval Office at the White House.

Statement on the Observance of National Peace Through Strength Week
September 22, 1984

Sunday, September 23, 1984, marks the beginning of National Peace Through Strength Week. All Americans place great value on peace; it is part of our national character. Activities during Peace Through Strength Week will support a common-sense, reasonable approach to security, peace, and deterring war. Rallies in all 50 States on September 29th, organized by a bipartisan coalition of Americans, will be held under the auspices of the Coalition of Peace Through Strength and the American Security Council. These citizens will be expressing support for a strategy of peace based on a strong defense.

If history teaches us anything, it is that a strong defense is the prerequisite to a lasting peace, the only credible deterrent against aggression. And a strong defense will enable us to reach sound arms control agreements. Arms control, negotiated from strength, can significantly reduce the levels of weapons threatening mankind and enhance confidence between potential adversaries.

We Americans maintain our military strength with the fervent hope that it will never be used, and with the conviction that this is, indeed, the best way to preserve the peace. We maintain our defensive strength in concert with our allies and friends, whose freedom and independence is vital to our own security. Our national strength, of course, is not based only on the force of arms. The ideals of human liberty are them-

selves powerful weapons in the world competition between democracy and totalitarianism. Thus, it is fitting that Americans from all walks of life and many citizens of our fellow democracies are working to strengthen democratic institutions throughout the world. It is becoming clearer every day, especially to emerging countries in the Third World, that democracy is not only the best path to freedom but, also, the most effective way of achieving economic progress. Democracy is the way to a more peaceful world. The ultimate goal of Peace Through Strength Week is a world where the people of each nation are free to determine their own destiny and where no state threatens its neighbors.

Therefore, I commend the efforts of my fellow Americans who have organized this special week. Its purpose is consistent with America's continuing commitment to world peace, justice, and freedom.

Remarks at a Reception for the Heads of Delegations to the 39th Session of the United Nations General Assembly in New York, New York
September 23, 1984

Thank you all for being here. On behalf of my fellow citizens, it's a pleasure once again to welcome all of you to the United States.

As we gather for this, the 39th session of the United Nations General Assembly, we look forward to the upcoming 40th anniversary. It'll be commemorated by a series of events across the United States.

Much has been achieved in these last 39 years. Working together, through this institution, the governments of the world have made great efforts toward peace and improving the well-being of their peoples. But we also remain mindful of the failures we've witnessed of the world community to live up to the commitments in the charter. Some of the trends have been particularly discouraging in recent years.

The basic principles of the U.N., nonetheless, remain as worthy and as vital now as they were 39 years ago. Working together,

the family of nations can, and must, improve its efforts to combat international lawlessness and to promote freedom, humane values, and social and economic progress.

For our part, we in the United States still hold firm to the belief that within the structure of this institution we can improve the chances for peace on this planet. And whether we succeed in doing so is not dependent on luck or on any inevitable pattern of history. We have it within our power to make history; let's not be afraid to do so.

We should never fear to attempt to do that which the pessimists call impossible. Let us be optimistic about the potential for peace, and let us never, never be afraid to speak with one another.

In this era of electronic communications and high-tech wizardry, time and distance can no longer impede constructive dialog. Only people can do that. So, let us on the eve of a new U.N. General Assembly pledge again to one another, in the names of our peoples and for the good of all humankind, that we will continue to seek the kind of open and frank discussion which will help us to create a safer world.

This does not minimize the serious challenges and tangible differences that exist within our world body politic. Those differences are real and will require hard work and a large dose of good will to overcome. Yet there is reason for optimism. My country will not shirk the hard work or ration its good will in our effort to deal with differences peacefully. And we call upon other nations to make the same commitment.

For example, the United States wants nothing less than a realistic, constructive, long-term relationship with the Soviet Union, a relationship which would permit each of us to reduce, not increase, the number of our weapons, especially those nuclear weapons which threaten all humanity.

The ultimate goals of the United States are not so different now as 150 years ago when Andrew Jackson was President. Jackson said, "Peace and friendly intercourse with all nations are as much the desire of our government as they are the interest of the people." In a time of nuclear bombs and overwhelmingly expensive weapons, President Jackson's words ring even more true today.

The United States, as I will detail in my remarks tomorrow, is moving with renewed confidence and vigor in the arena of international affairs. We endeavor to further the prospects for peace, prosperity, and democracy—goals reflecting the desire and interest of our people.

I'll be stressing our commitment to these goals throughout this week, starting already in meetings with heads of state and government today, and in my speaking tomorrow to the General Assembly, and on Tuesday to the World Bank and International Monetary Fund, and with a number of other world leaders back in Washington.

This intense diplomatic activity complements your own diplomatic efforts. The United States will continue, through our much admired Ambassador, Jeane Kirkpatrick, and others, to be firm in advancing our interest and forceful in the advocacy of our democratic way of life. We will at the same time remain fair in approaching the interests of others. We expect nothing less of you. You should expect nothing less of us.

The United States will continue to work in the United Nations to promote peace and international security, reconciliation among nations, economic prosperity, human rights, and the rule of law. Our own commitment to the goals of the charter remain steadfast.

One of the advantages of having the United Nations in our country is an advantage for us in that it gives you a chance to better understand the American people. And when you return to your countries, I hope you'll convey to them our best wishes. I wish you all success in your upcoming session, appreciate, again, your joining us here tonight, and just thank you, and God bless you all.

Note: The President spoke at 7:09 p.m. at the Waldorf-Astoria Hotel. The reception was hosted by the United States for heads of state, foreign ministers, and heads of delegations to the United Nations session. Following the reception, the President returned to his suite at the hotel.

Address to the 39th Session of the United Nations General Assembly in New York, New York
September 24, 1984

Mr. President, Mr. Secretary-General, distinguished heads of state, Ministers, Representatives, and guests: First of all, I wish to congratulate President Lusaka on his election as President of the General Assembly. I wish you every success, Mr. President, in carrying out the responsibilities of this high international office.

It's an honor to be here, and I thank you for your gracious invitation. I would speak in support of the two great goals that led to the formation of this organization—the cause of peace and the cause of human dignity.

The responsibility of this assembly—the peaceful resolution of disputes between peoples and nations—can be discharged successfully only if we recognize the great common ground upon which we all stand: our fellowship as members of the human race, our oneness as inhabitants of this planet, our place as representatives of billions of our countrymen whose fondest hope remains the end to war and to the repression of the human spirit. These are the important central realities that bind us, that permit us to dream of a future without the antagonisms of the past. And just as shadows can be seen only where there is light, so, too, can we overcome what is wrong only if we remember how much is right. And we will resolve what divides us only if we remember how much more unites us.

This chamber has heard enough about the problems and dangers ahead. Today, let us dare to speak of a future that is bright and hopeful and can be ours only if we seek it. I believe that future is far nearer than most of us would dare to hope.

At the start of this decade, one scholar at the Hudson Institute noted that mankind also had undergone enormous changes for the better in the past two centuries—changes which aren't always readily noticed or written about.

"Up until 200 years ago, there were relatively few people in the world," he wrote.

"All human societies were poor. Disease and early death dominated most people's lives. People were ignorant, and largely at the mercy of the forces of nature."

"Now," he said, "we are somewhere near the middle of a process of economic development . . . At the end of that process, almost no one will live in a country as poor as the richest country of the past. There will be many more people . . . living long, healthy lives, with immense knowledge and more to learn than anybody has time for." They will be "able to cope with the forces of nature and almost indifferent to distance."

Well, we do live today, as the scholar suggested, in the middle of one of the most important and dramatic periods in human history—one in which all of us can serve as catalysts for an era of world peace and unimagined human freedom and dignity.

And today I would like to report to you, as distinguished and influential members of the world community, on what the United States has been attempting to do to help move the world closer to this era. On many fronts enormous progress has been made, and I think our efforts are complemented by the trend of history.

If we look closely enough, I believe we can see all the world moving toward a deeper appreciation of the value of human freedom in both its political and economic manifestations. This is partially motivated by a worldwide desire for economic growth and higher standards of living. And there's an increasing realization that economic freedom is a prelude to economic progress and growth and is intricately and inseparably linked to political freedom.

Everywhere, people and governments are beginning to recognize that the secret of a progressive new world is to take advantage of the creativity of the human spirit, to encourage innovation and individual enterprise, to reward hard work, and to reduce barriers to the free flow of trade and information.

Our opposition to economic restrictions and trade barriers is consistent with our view of economic freedom and human progress. We believe such barriers pose a particularly dangerous threat to the developing nations and their chance to share in world prosperity through expanded export markets. Tomorrow at the International Monetary Fund, I will address this question more fully, including America's desire for more open trading markets throughout the world.

This desire to cut down trade barriers and our open advocacy of freedom as the engine of human progress are two of the most important ways the United States and the American people hope to assist in bringing about a world where prosperity is commonplace, conflict an aberration, and human dignity and freedom a way of life.

Let me place these steps more in context by briefly outlining the major goals of American foreign policy and then exploring with you the practical ways we're attempting to further freedom and prevent war. By that I mean, first, how we have moved to strengthen ties with old allies and new friends; second, what we're doing to help avoid the regional conflicts that could contain the seeds of world conflagration; and third, the status of our efforts with the Soviet Union to reduce the level of arms.

Let me begin with a word about the objectives of American foreign policy, which have been consistent since the postwar era, and which fueled the formation of the United Nations and were incorporated into the U.N. Charter itself.

The U.N. Charter states two overriding goals: "to save succeeding generations from the scourge of war, which twice in our lifetime has brought untold sorrow to mankind," and "to reaffirm faith in fundamental human rights, in the dignity and worth of the human person, in the equal rights of men and women and of nations large and small."

The founders of the United Nations understood full well the relationship between these two goals. And I want you to know that the Government of the United States will continue to view this concern for human rights as the moral center of our foreign policy. We can never look at any-one's freedom as a bargaining chip in world politics. Our hope is for a time when all the people of the world can enjoy the blessings of personal liberty. But I would like also to emphasize that our concern for protecting human rights is part of our concern for protecting the peace.

The answer is for all nations to fulfill the obligations they freely assumed under the Universal Declaration of Human Rights. It states: "The will of the people shall be the basis of the authority of government; this will shall be expressed in periodic and genuine elections." The Declaration also includes these rights: "to form and to join trade unions," "to own property alone as well as in association with others," "to leave any country including his own and return to his country," and to enjoy "freedom of opinion and expression." Perhaps the most graphic example of the relationship between human rights and peace is the right of peace groups to exist and to promote their views. In fact, the treatment of peace groups may be a litmus test of government's true desire for peace.

In addition to emphasizing this tie between the advocacy of human rights and the prevention of war, the United States has taken important steps, as I mentioned earlier, to prevent world conflict. The starting point and cornerstone of our foreign policy is our alliance and partnership with our fellow democracies. For 35 years, the North Atlantic alliance has guaranteed the peace in Europe. In both Europe and Asia, our alliances have been the vehicle for a great reconciliation among nations that had fought bitter wars in decades and centuries past. And here in the Western Hemisphere, north and south are being lifted on the tide of freedom and are joined in a common effort to foster peaceful economic development.

We're proud of our association with all those countries that share our commitment to freedom, human rights, the rule of law, and international peace. Indeed, the bulwark of security that the democratic alliance provides is essential and remains essential to the maintenance of world peace. Every alliance involves burdens and obligations, but these are far less than the risks and sacrifices that will result if the peace-loving nations were divided and neglectful of their common security.

The people of the United States will remain faithful to their commitments. But the United States is also faithful to its alliances and friendships with scores of nations in the developed and developing worlds with differing political systems, cultures, and traditions. The development of ties between the United States and China, a significant global event of the last dozen years, shows our willingness to improve relations with countries ideologically very different from ours.

We're ready to be the friend of any country that is a friend to us and a friend of peace. And we respect genuine nonalignment. Our own nation was born in revolution. We helped promote the process of decolonization that brought about the independence of so many members of this body. And we're proud of that history.

We're proud, too, of our role in the formation of the United Nations and our support of this body over the years. And let me again emphasize our unwavering commitment to a central principle of the United Nations system—the principle of universality, both here and in the United Nations technical agencies around the world. If universality is ignored, if nations are expelled illegally, then the U.N. itself cannot be expected to succeed.

The United States welcomes diversity and peaceful competition. We do not fear the trends of history. We are not ideologically rigid. We do have principles, and we will stand by them, but we will also seek the friendship and good will of all, both old friends and new.

We've always sought to lend a hand to help others—from our relief efforts in Europe after World War I to the Marshall plan and massive foreign assistance programs after World War II. Since 1946 the United States has provided over $115 billion in economic aid to developing countries, and today provides about one-third of the nearly $90 billion in financial resources, public and private, that flows to the developing world. And the U.S. imports about one-third of the manufactured exports of the developing world.

But any economic progress as well as any movement in the direction of greater understanding between the nations of the world are, of course, endangered by the prospect of conflict at both the global and regional level. In a few minutes, I will turn to the menace of conflict on a worldwide scale and discuss the status of negotiations between the United States and the Soviet Union. But permit me first to address the critical problem of regional conflicts, for history displays tragic evidence that it is these conflicts which can set off the sparks leading to worldwide conflagration.

In a glass display case across the hall from the Oval Office at the White House there is a gold medal, the Nobel Peace Prize won by Theodore Roosevelt for his contribution in mediating the Russo-Japanese War in 1905. It was the first such prize won by an American, and it's part of a tradition of which the American people are very proud—a tradition that is being continued today in many regions of the globe.

We're engaged, for example, in diplomacy to resolve conflicts in southern Africa, working with the frontline states and our partners in the contact group. Mozambique and South Africa have reached an historic accord on nonaggression and cooperation. South Africa and Angola have agreed on a disengagement of forces from Angola, and the groundwork has been laid for the independence of Namibia, with virtually all aspects of Security Council Resolution 435 agreed upon.

Let me add that the United States considers it a moral imperative that South Africa's racial policies evolve peacefully but decisively toward a system compatible with basic norms of justice, liberty, and human dignity. I'm pleased that American companies in South Africa, by providing equal employment opportunities, are contributing to the economic advancement of the black population. But clearly, much more must be done.

In Central America, the United States has lent support to a diplomatic process to restore regional peace and security. We have committed substantial resources to promote economic development and social progress. The growing success of democracy in El

Salvador is the best proof that the key to peace lies in a political solution. Free elections brought into office a government dedicated to democracy, reform, economic progress, and regional peace. Regrettably, there are forces in the region eager to thwart democratic change, but these forces are now on the defensive. The tide is turning in the direction of freedom. We call upon Nicaragua, in particular, to abandon its policies of subversion and militarism and to carry out the promises it made to the Organization of American States to establish democracy at home.

The Middle East has known more than its share of tragedy and conflict for decades, and the United States has been actively involved in peace diplomacy for just as long. We consider ourselves a full partner in the quest for peace. The record of the 11 years since the October war shows that much can be achieved through negotiations; it also shows that the road is long and hard.

Two years ago, I proposed a fresh start toward a negotiated solution to the Arab-Israeli conflict. My initiative of September 1st, 1982, contains a set of positions that can serve as a basis for a just and lasting peace. That initiative remains a realistic and workable approach, and I am committed to it as firmly as on the day I announced it. And the foundation stone of this effort remains Security Council Resolution 242, which in turn was incorporated in all its parts in the Camp David accords.

The tragedy of Lebanon has not ended. Only last week, a despicable act of barbarism by some who are unfit to associate with humankind reminded us once again that Lebanon continues to suffer. In 1983 we helped Israel and Lebanon reach an agreement that, if implemented, could have led to the full withdrawal of Israeli forces in the context of the withdrawal of all foreign forces. This agreement was blocked, and the long agony of the Lebanese continues. Thousands of people are still kept from their homes by continued violence and are refugees in their own country. The once flourishing economy of Lebanon is near collapse. All of Lebanon's friends should work together to help end this nightmare.

In the Gulf, the United States has supported a series of Security Council resolutions that call for an end to the war between Iran and Iraq that has meant so much death and destruction and put the world's economic well-being at risk. Our hope is that hostilities will soon end, leaving each side with its political and territorial integrity intact, so that both may devote their energies to addressing the needs of their people and a return to relationships with other states.

The lesson of experience is that negotiations work. The peace treaty between Israel and Egypt brought about the peaceful return of the Sinai, clearly showing that the negotiating process brings results when the parties commit themselves to it. The time is bound to come when the same wisdom and courage will be applied with success to reach peace between Israel and all of its Arab neighbors in a manner that assures security for all in the region, the recognition of Israel, and a solution to the Palestinian problem.

In every part of the world, the United States is similarly engaged in peace diplomacy as an active player or a strong supporter.

In Southeast Asia, we have backed the efforts of ASEAN to mobilize international support for a peaceful resolution of the Cambodian problem, which must include the withdrawal of Vietnamese forces and the election of a representative government. ASEAN's success in promoting economic and political development has made a major contribution to the peace and stability of the region.

In Afghanistan, the dedicated efforts of the Secretary-General and his representatives to find a diplomatic settlement have our strong support. I assure you that the United States will continue to do everything possible to find a negotiated outcome which provides the Afghan people with the right to determine their own destiny, allows the Afghan refugees to return to their own country in dignity, and protects the legitimate security interests of all neighboring countries.

On the divided and tense Korean Peninsula, we have strongly backed the confidence-building measures proposed by the Republic of Korea and by the U.N. Command at Panmunjom. These are an important first step toward peaceful reunification in the long term.

We take heart from progress by others in lessening the tensions, notably the efforts by the Federal Republic to reduce barriers between the two German States.

And the United States strongly supports the Secretary-General's efforts to assist the Cypriot parties in achieving a peaceful and reunited Cyprus.

The United States has been and will always be a friend of peaceful solutions. This is no less true with respect to my country's relations with the Soviet Unon.

When I appeared before you last year, I noted that we cannot count on the instinct for survival alone to protect us against war. Deterrence is necessary but not sufficient. America has repaired its strength. We have invigorated our alliances and friendships. We are ready for constructive negotiations with the Soviet Union.

We recognize that there is no sane alternative to negotiations on arms control and other issues between our two nations which have the capacity to destroy civilization as we know it. I believe this is a view shared by virtually every country in the world and by the Soviet Union itself. And I want to speak to you today on what the United States and the Soviet Union can accomplish together in the coming years and the concrete steps that we need to take.

You know, as I stand here and look out from this podium, there in front of me I can see the seat of the Representative from the Soviet Union. And not far from that seat, just over to the side, is the seat of the Representative from the United States. In this historic assembly hall, it's clear there's not a great distance between us. Outside this room, while there will still be clear differences, there's every reason why we should do all that is possible to shorten that distance. And that's why we're here. Isn't that what this organization is all about?

Last January 16th, I set out three objectives for U.S.-Soviet relations that can provide an agenda for our work over the months ahead.

First, I said, we need to find ways to reduce—and eventually to eliminate—the threat and use of force in solving international disputes. Our concern over the potential for nuclear war cannot deflect us from the terrible human tragedies occurring every day in the regional conflicts I just discussed. Together, we have a particular responsibility to contribute to political solutions to these problems, rather than to exacerbate them through the provision of even more weapons.

I propose that our two countries agree to embark on periodic consultations at policy level about regional problems. We will be prepared, if the Soviets agree, to make senior experts available at regular intervals for indepth exchanges of views. I've asked Secretary Shultz to explore this with Foreign Minister Gromyko. Spheres of influence are a thing of the past; differences between American and Soviet interests are not. The objectives of this political dialog will be to help avoid miscalculation, reduce the potential risk of U.S.-Soviet confrontation, and help the people in areas of conflict to find peaceful solutions.

The United States and the Soviet Union have achieved agreements of historic importance on some regional issues. The Austrian State Treaty and the Berlin accords are notable and lasting examples. Let us resolve to achieve similar agreements in the future.

Our second task must be to find ways to reduce the vast stockpiles of armaments in the world. I am committed to redoubling our negotiating efforts to achieve real results: in Geneva, a complete ban on chemical weapons; in Vienna, real reductions to lower and equal levels in Soviet and American, Warsaw Pact and NATO conventional forces; in Stockholm, concrete practical measures to enhance mutual confidence, to reduce the risk of war, and to reaffirm commitments concerning nonuse of force; in the field of nuclear testing, improvements in verification essential to ensure compliance with the threshold test ban and peaceful nuclear explosions agreements; and in the field of nonproliferation, close cooperation to strengthen the international institutions and practices aimed at halting the spread of nuclear weapons, together with redoubled efforts to meet the legitimate expectations of all nations that the Soviet

Union and the United States will substantially reduce their own nuclear arsenals.

We and the Soviets have agreed to upgrade our hotline communications facility, and our discussions of nuclear nonproliferation in recent years have been useful to both sides. We think there are other possibilities for improving communications in this area that deserve serious exploration.

I believe the proposal of the Soviet Union for opening U.S.-Soviet talks in Vienna provided an important opportunity to advance these objectives. We've been prepared to discuss a wide range of issues of concern to both sides, such as the relationship between defensive and offensive forces and what has been called the militarization of space. During the talks, we would consider what measures of restraint both sides might take while negotiations proceed. However, any agreement must logically depend upon our ability to get the competition in offensive arms under control and to achieve genuine stability at substantially lower levels of nuclear arms.

Our approach in all these areas will be designed to take into account concerns the Soviet Union has voiced. It will attempt to provide a basis for an historic breakthrough in arms control. I'm disappointed that we were not able to open our meeting in Vienna earlier this month on the date originally proposed by the Soviet Union. I hope we can begin these talks by the end of the year or shortly thereafter.

The third task I set in January was to establish a better working relationship between the Soviet Union and the United States, one marked by greater cooperation and understanding. We've made some modest progress. We have reached agreements to improve our hotline, extend our 10-year economic agreement, enhance consular cooperation, and explore coordination of search and rescue efforts at sea.

We've also offered to increase significantly the amount of U.S. grain for purchase by the Soviets and to provide the Soviets a direct fishing allocation off U.S. coasts. But there's much more we could do together. I feel particularly strongly about breaking down the barriers between the peoples of the United States and the Soviet Union, and

between our political, military, and other leaders.

Now, all of these steps that I've mentioned—and especially the arms control negotiations—are extremely important to a step-by-step process toward peace. But let me also say that we need to extend the arms control process to build a bigger umbrella under which it can operate—a road map, if you will, showing where, during the next 20 years or so, these individual efforts can lead. This can greatly assist step-by-step negotiations and enable us to avoid having all our hopes or expectations ride on any single set or series of negotiations. If progress is temporarily halted at one set of talks, this newly established framework for arms control could help us take up the slack at other negotiations.

Today, to the great end of lifting the dread of nuclear war from the peoples of the Earth, I invite the leaders of the world to join in a new beginning. We need a fresh approach to reducing international tensions. History demonstrates beyond controversy that just as the arms competition has its root in political suspicions and anxieties, so it can be channeled in more stabilizing directions and eventually be eliminated if those political suspicions and anxieties are addressed as well.

Toward this end, I will suggest to the Soviet Union that we institutionalize regular ministerial or cabinet-level meetings between our two countries on the whole agenda of issues before us, including the problem of needless obstacles to understanding. To take but one idea for discussion: In such talks, we could consider the exchange of outlines of 5-year military plans for weapons development and our schedules of intended procurement. We would also welcome the exchange of observers at military exercises and locations. And I propose that we find a way for Soviet experts to come to the United States nuclear test site, and for ours to go to theirs, to measure directly the yields of tests of nuclear weapons. We should work toward having such arrangements in place by next spring. I hope that the Soviet Union will cooperate in this undertaking and reciprocate in a manner that will enable the two countries to establish the basis for verification for effective limits on underground nuclear testing.

I believe such talks could work rapidly toward developing a new climate of policy understanding, one that is essential if crises are to be avoided and real arms control is to be negotiated. Of course, summit meetings have a useful role to play. But they need to be carefully prepared, and the benefit here is that meetings at the ministerial level would provide the kind of progress that is the best preparation for higher level talks between ourselves and the Soviet leaders.

How much progress we will make and at what pace, I cannot say. But we have a moral obligation to try and try again.

Some may dismiss such proposals and my own optimism as simplistic American idealism, and they will point to the burdens of the modern world and to history. Well, yes, if we sit down and catalog year by year, generation by generation, the famines, the plagues, the wars, the invasions mankind has endured, the list will grow so long and the assault on humanity so terrific that it seems too much for the human spirit to bear.

But isn't this narrow and shortsighted and not at all how we think of history? Yes, the deeds of infamy or injustice are all recorded, but what shines out from the pages of history is the daring of the dreamers and the deeds of the builders and the doers. These things make up the stories we tell and pass on to our children. They comprise the most enduring and striking fact about human history—that through the heartbreak and tragedy man has always dared to perceive the outline of human progress, the steady growth in not just the material well-being, but the spiritual insight of mankind.

"There have been tyrants and murderers, and for a time they can seem invincible. But in the end, they always fail [fall]. [1] Think on it . . . always. All through history, the way of truth and love has always won." That was the belief and the vision of Mahatma Gandhi. He described that, and it remains today a vision that is good and true.

"All is gift," is said to have been the fa-

vorite expression of another great spiritualist, a Spanish soldier who gave up the ways of war for that of love and peace. And if we're to make realities of the two great goals of the United Nations Charter—the dreams of peace and human dignity—we must take to heart these words of Ignatius Loyola; we must pause long enough to contemplate the gifts received from Him who made us: the gift of life, the gift of this world, the gift of each other—and the gift of the present.

It is this present, this time that now we must seize. I leave you with a reflection from Mahatma Gandhi, spoken with those in mind who said that the disputes and conflicts of the modern world are too great to overcome. It was spoken shortly after Gandhi's quest for independence had taken him to Britain.

"I am not conscious of a single experience throughout my 3 months' stay in England and Europe," he said, "that made me feel that after all East is East and West is West. On the contrary, I have been convinced more than ever that human nature is much the same, no matter under what clime it flourishes, and that if you approached people with trust and affection, you would have ten-fold trust and thousand-fold affection returned to you."

For the sake of a peaceful world, a world where human dignity and freedom is respected and enshrined, let us approach each other with ten-fold trust and thousand-fold affection. A new future awaits us. The time is here, the moment is now.

One of the Founding Fathers of our nation, Thomas Paine, spoke words that apply to all of us gathered here today. They apply directly to all sitting here in this room. He said, "We have it in our power to begin the world over again."

Thank you. God bless you.

Note: The President spoke at 10:31 a.m. in the General Assembly Hall of the United Nations Headquarters Building. He was introduced by Paul Lusaka, President of the 39th Session of the General Assembly.

Upon arrival at the United Nations, the President was greeted by Secretary-General Javier Perez de Cuellar de la Guerra.

---

[1] *White House correction.*

Remarks on Signing the Drug Price Competition and Patent Term Restoration Act of 1984
September 24, 1984

Thank you all. I don't know why it is on some of these hot rallies out in the countryside the chairs are black instead of white, and they get very warm when you stand too long.

Members of the Congress who are here and distinguished guests and ladies and gentlemen, welcome to the Rose Garden. I know we've all had a busy day, but I'm happy we were able to arrange this ceremony.

I don't know whether you're aware or not, but I just returned from New York—literally minutes ago—where I addressed the United Nations on what the United States has been attempting to do—[applause]—well, thank you very much—what I was trying to do to help move the world closer to an era of lasting peace and freedom and human dignity. I'm certain you share my hope that the initiatives that were presented to the General Assembly will lead to a new beginning in the search for a safe and a proud future.

But now let me turn my attention to the real reason we're here this afternoon, signing into law the Drug Price Competition and Patent Term Restoration Act of 1984. And before I say anything else, I want to thank Senator Orrin Hatch, who sponsored this important legislation in the Senate, and Congressman Henry Waxman, who was the chief sponsor in the House. The legislation will speed up the process of Federal approval of inexpensive generic versions of many brand name drugs, make the generic versions more widely available to consumers, and grant pharmaceutical firms added incentives to develop new drugs.

Everyone wins, particularly our elderly Americans. Senior citizens require more medication than any other segment of our society. I speak with some authority on that. [Laughter] They use about 25 percent—we use about 25 percent of all the drugs sold. [Laughter] With this bill, elderly Americans will have access to safe and effective drugs at the lowest possible cost. Fact is, it's estimated that consumers will save more than a billion dollars over the next 10 years.

The bill will promote medical breakthroughs and drug innovation by granting drug companies up to 5 more years of patent protection for new drugs. And this extension will help compensate for the years of patent life lost due to the time-consuming, but essential, testing required by the Food and Drug Administration.

And I might add that the American people will benefit, because the Federal Government, the largest single consumer of drugs, will be able to purchase generic drugs at significantly lower cost. In 1983 alone, the Federal Government spent an estimated $2.4 billion for drugs through the Medicaid program and in veterans and military hospitals. And we're all for lowering government costs.

There's also a textile provision in the legislation which requires that clothing sold in the United States be conspicuously labeled to show country of origin and that mail-order and other catalogs indicate whether clothing was made in the U.S.A. or imported.

So, when you add it all up, this bill will provide regulatory relief, increased competition, economy in government, and best of all, the American people will save money, and yet receive the best medicine that pharmaceutical science can provide.

And now, on this warm day I think it's high time that I get over and sign the proclamation. I did just get off the helicopter—I'm signing the proclamation at 5 o'clock—I'm signing a bill. [Laughter]

Thank you all for being here.

Note: The President spoke at 3:30 p.m. in the Rose Garden at the White House.

As enacted, S. 1538 is Public Law 98–417, approved September 24.

Remarks at a White House Reception Marking the Beginning of National Historically Black Colleges Week
September 24, 1984

Good afternoon, and welcome to the White House. It's an honor to have each of you here as we mark the beginning of National Historically Black Colleges Week.

As educators, you know that education has always played a crucial role in the life of our nation, teaching the sons and daughters of parents from around the world a common language, English, and a common way of life, democracy. Our schools have uplifted our children, filled their hearts with hope, and given them the skills they need to make their way in the world with pride and self-reliance.

Like all our colleges and universities, your schools have performed these tasks. But your schools are special. For throughout our history, they did their work against a unique background of hardship and oppression. Just decades ago, almost 1 American in 10 lived a life that was separate and unequal because of the color of the skin. In parts of the country, black Americans were excluded from public life and from many of the professions, forced to eat in separate restaurants, to sleep in separate hotels, even to drink at separate fountains. And throughout those hard years, millions of black Americans saw education as a shining hope for advancement.

I remember how, during the war, I narrated a film about black pilots being trained at Tuskegee Institute—and one above all, Chappie James. And even though I was only a horse cavalryman, I can't tell you how proud I am that I'm now an honorary member of the Tuskegee Flyers. I'm not going to volunteer for a journey into space—*[laughter]*—but they were brave young men. And I remember how impressed I was by their esteem for Tuskegee and their love of learning. It was your colleges and universities—Tuskegee, Howard, Fisk, so many others—that turned their bright dream of education into a blazing reality.

I'm told that today your schools have awarded degrees to half of all the black business executives, 80 percent of all black Federal judges, and 85 percent of all black doctors. The place your schools hold in the history of our nation is unparalleled. It's one of courage and honor, and it's a place that makes historically black colleges worthy not only of our praise but of our loyalty and devotion.

For this reason, our administration has moved to strengthen historically black colleges across America. In September of '81, I signed Executive Order 12320, committing the Federal Government to increase its support of your schools. Indeed, in fiscal year '82, your schools received grants and other forms of assistance totaling some $564 million. And in fiscal year 1983, we increased the level to 606 million. In fact, even more significant, the order also called on the Federal Government to encourage the private sector to provide your schools with still more support.

And a year after we announced that Executive order, we issued a new Presidential directive that gave our commitment new strength and clarity. And this directive contained four important points. First, it told the Federal departments and agencies to look for ways to use Federal program funds to improve the administrative infrastructure of historically black colleges and universities.

And second, it directed the agencies to strive to increase the percentage of total available funds that black colleges and universities receive.

Third, it directed the agencies to step up efforts to eliminate regulations that are barriers to your full participation in Federal programs.

And last, the directive reviewed our emphasis on encouraging support from the private sector. This, once again, embodied our belief that there are vast, untapped sources throughout America, because for too long, too many have looked only to government.

Permit me to add that the self-reliance and opportunity that we want for your schools is just what we want for all black Americans, indeed, for all Americans.

We're working hard to create enterprise zones to help disadvantaged Americans, especially those in our inner cities, to get off welfare and onto the economic ladder. We're supporting a youth opportunity wage to help teenagers find jobs. And across the board, we're striving to create vigorous, long-term economic growth.

Opportunity builds prosperity, and prosperity means a better life for individuals, for families, and the institutions like historically black colleges and universities that Americans cherish.

Today many of your schools still have a long and difficult road ahead. But since we've begun to give you more support, success stories have been rolling in. When Meharry Medical College was threatened with its very survival, together we were able to give it a new life.

Meharry, you will remember, was in danger of losing its accreditation, because it lacked access to a sufficient number of patients and beds to provide its students with the proper clinical training. But we requested the Veterans Administration to expand an already existing affiliation with Meharry so that 200 additional teaching beds would become available. Today, Meharry, a school that over the last century has trained 40 percent of all black physicians, is going on with its important work.

Earlier this year, Fisk University ran into tough financial problems. And we helped put together a 19-member advisory task force made up of presidents of other historically black institutions, specialists from the Department of Education, and representatives of the private sector. And in July, the task force submitted to the Fisk board of trustees, a report outlining a number of sound financial strategies. The report also suggested that the university appoint a board of advisers, made up of distinguished individuals from the private sector, to assist Fisk in putting these strategies into practice.

Fisk accepted the recommendation and, with the help of the White House Office of Private Sector Initiatives and the Department of Education, selected a group of outstanding Americans to serve on that advisory board. I'm pleased to say that the members of the advisory board just met next door, and they're with us here now. And today, Fisk still has its work cut out for it, but it's back on its feet, and it's growing stronger.

Historically black colleges have enriched our nation in the past, and I just have to believe that your future will be even brighter. As we sign this proclamation designating the week beginning September 23d, 1984, as Historically Black Colleges Week, let us honor the brave men and women who dedicated themselves to the education of black Americans in decades gone by. But let's also look to the years ahead to the vital role that these colleges will play in training young Americans for full lives in traditional fields and in the new and limitless frontiers of science, technology, and space. So much of America's future lies in the dreams of your students. And together, we can all help make them come true.

Thank you, and God bless you. And now, I'm going to sign the proclamation. But I want you to know that it did begin the week on time, because I've already signed the bill before—[*laughter*]—before the date.

Thank you all. God bless you all.

Note: The President spoke at 5 p.m. in the East Room at the White House.

Proclamation 5239—National Historically Black Colleges Week, 1984
September 24, 1984

By the President of the United States of America

A Proclamation

The one hundred and three historically black colleges and universities in the United States have contributed substantially to the growth and enrichment of the Nation. These institutions have a rich heritage and tradition of providing the challenging higher education so essential to an individual's full participation in our complex technological society.

Historically black colleges and universities bestow forty percent of all degrees earned by black students. They have awarded degrees to eighty-five percent of the country's black lawyers and doctors and fifty percent of its black business executives. Throughout the years, these institutions have helped many underprivileged students to attain their full potential through higher education.

In recognition of the fact that the achievements and goals of these historically black colleges and universities deserve national attention, the Congress, by Senate Joint Resolution 340, has designated the week of September 23, 1984, as "National Historically Black Colleges Week" and authorized and requested the President to issue a proclamation in observance of this week.

Now, Therefore, I, Ronald Reagan, President of the United States of America, do hereby proclaim the week of September 23, 1984, as National Historically Black Colleges Week. I urge all Americans to observe this week with appropriate ceremonies and activities to express our respect and appreciation for the outstanding academic and social accomplishments of the Nation's black institutions of higher learning.

In Witness Whereof, I have hereunto set my hand this twenty-fourth day of September, in the year of our Lord nineteen hundred and eighty-four, and of the Independence of the United States of America the two hundred and ninth.

RONALD REAGAN

[*Filed with the Office of the Federal Register, 10:57 a.m., September 25, 1984*]

Remarks at the Annual Meeting of the Boards of Governors of the International Monetary Fund and World Bank Group
September 25, 1984

Mr. Chairman, Managing Director de Larosière, President Clausen, Governors of the International Monetary Fund, of the World Bank Group; and distinguished guests: On behalf of the American people, we are delighted to welcome you to the United States for your 39th annual meeting.

I'm honored once again to address the leaders of your institutions. Your quest to improve the condition of humankind, to offer opportunities for fulfillment in our individual lives and the life of our national and world communities places you in a position of responsibility and leadership second to none. You are true missionaries for a more prosperous world and a more peaceful world.

And we who are public servants in this international economic community know well the daily problems and pitfalls that obstruct our path to progress. Sometimes the immensity of these challenges and the attention they receive seem all but overwhelming to us.

But in these moments, let us remember and draw strength from the most powerful,

1365

enduring truth in human history: Free men and women are not destined to be powerless victims of some capricious historical tide; free men and women are themselves the driving force of history. And our future is never trapped in the hands of fate; our future will depend on our own freedom, courage, vision, and faith.

When I first spoke to you 3 years ago, I asked that we examine the terrible shocks inflicted upon the world economy during the 1970's; that all of us face up to the origins of those problems, and also recognize our ability to withstand and surmount them.

For our part, we said one conclusion seemed both undeniable and universally true. The societies whose economies had fared best during these tumultuous times were not the most tightly controlled, not necessarily the biggest in size, nor even the wealthiest in natural resources. What united the leaders for growth was a willingness to trust the people—to believe in rewarding hard work and legitimate risk.

So, the United States made a new beginning—one based on our conviction that we could only meet the challenge of contributing to world economic growth and of assuring that all countries, especially the poorest, participate fully in that growth by renouncing past policies of government regimentation and overspending and by taking decisive action to get our domestic house in order and restore incentives to liberate the genius and spirit of our free people.

And while we would not impose our ideas, our policies, on anyone, we felt obliged to point out that no nation can have prosperity and successful development without economic freedom. Nor can it preserve personal and political freedoms without economic freedom. Only when the human spirit can dream, create, and build; only when individuals are given a personal stake in deciding economic policies and benefiting from their own success—only then do societies become dynamic, prosperous, progressive, and free.

We invited all of you to join us and walk with us on this new path of hope and opportunity, and some of you have. We knew this endeavor would be neither short nor easy. We knew that it would require great effort and patience. But we were confident that once our people saw it through, the rewards would be far greater than anticipated.

I believe that confidence has been justified. As I said yesterday to the United Nations, we can speak again, and we should, of a future that is bright and hopeful—a future of prosperity that I believe is far nearer than most of us would ever dare to hope. By working together we can make it happen.

Our own economy is dramatically changed from only 3 years ago. Rewarding hard work and risk-taking has given birth to an American renaissance. Born in the safe harbor of freedom, economic growth gathered force and rolled out in a rising tide that has reached distant shores.

We are heartened that the strength of the U.S. economy is helping lead the world from recession toward a new period of lasting economic expansion, with lower rates of inflation in many countries. And we're convinced we can continue to offer this leadership in the future.

Permit me to elaborate. The United States has enjoyed 21 straight months of economic growth—the strongest growth since 1950. We've witnessed the creation of 6 million jobs and seen our expansion sustained by exceptionally low inflation. Consumer prices are rising by only around 4 percent now, compared with more than 12 percent in 1980.

And let me emphasize that we're determined to make another change from past policies. We intend to bring inflation down even more, and we're determined to keep it down by continuing to restrain the growth of our government spending. We have already cut the rate of that spending by more than half. And we're pushing hard for an amendment to our Constitution, placing mandatory limits on government's power to spend.

Fueling economic growth has been the record increase in venture capital and business investment, both results of new incentives in our tax structure. And innovation holds out the promise for continued strength in productivity growth and new breakthroughs in advanced technology.

We believe we have taken only the first small steps into the newest frontier, the technological revolution. By reaching for great gains in productivity, we can create a bounty of new jobs, technologies—in the quality of life surpassing anything that we have ever before dreamed or imagined. I tell you today from my heart: We in America want to share our knowledge and the blessings of progress with you and your citizens, because together, and only together, can we build a better world, a far better world.

So, just as we must do more to restrain public spending, we believe more can and must be done to increase personal incentives. We will not be satisfied until America challenges the limits of growth. We want to enact an historic simplification of our tax system that will enable us to significantly increase incentives by bringing personal income tax rates further down, not up.

We have noted the increased recognition that's given to the central role of incentives in promoting economic growth. The Wall Street Journal recently cited surveys that were published by the Organization for Economic Cooperation and Development as indicating that governments can best spark economic growth by spending less and cutting tax rates, not by planning an elaborate industrial policy. This is our strategy for growth, and it will allow us to keep America's deficit on its current downward path.

And as we continue moving forward, we're heartened to see that recovery abroad is gaining momentum. Growth of well over 3 percent is being projected for other industrial countries in 1984 and '85. And we're seeing a rise in developing country growth rates, led by those aggressively pursing outward-looking and market-oriented policies.

This broadening economic growth has had a significant impact on stimulating world trade. Your 1984 IMF annual report pointed out that "with the progress of economic recovery in the industrial countries, the volume of world trade began to expand quite strongly in 1983, and the prolonged deterioriation in the terms of trade of non-oil developing countries came to an end."

Expansion here in the world's largest single market has meant increased trading opportunities for other nations. Total U.S. imports rose 32 percent in the first half of this year. And for the full year, our imports are expected to exceed 1983 imports by over 25 percent. U.S. imports from the non-oil developing countries rose about 14 percent in 1983, and they're up by nearly 30 percent for the first half of 1984.

We sometimes hear complaints about U.S. interest rates, particularly by debtor nations, which are legitimately concerned about the additional debt-service costs that they must bear. But not enough mention is made of trade and the far greater benefits developing countries receive from renewed economic growth and open-market policies of the United States.

For the U.S. alone, imports from the non-OPEC LDC's during the first 7 months of this year increased by more than $12 billion over the same period last year. By comparison, a 1-percent increase in interest rates would increase net interest payments by the non-OPEC LDC's by only about $2½ billion. But we're not seeing an increase in interest rates. There's been a slight drop in the last several days, and I believe there will be more of that ahead.

So, we can be pleased at the improving outlook for the world's economy. But we can't be complacent. At the Williamsburg and London Economic Summits, my colleagues and I agreed that if we are to make the strength of the international economy stronger still, the sound domestic policies underlying current progress must be preserved.

I think we've all learned from bitter experience that quick fixes don't solve deep-seated problems. The more difficult path is to resist the temptation of politically expedient solutions or the pressure of powerful interest groups, and to instead make the hard choices necessary to advance the long-term good of all the people. But we must persevere.

Once the corner has been turned, once economic growth and financial health are built on a foundation of granite rather than playing cards, we will have opened the door of a new future of opportunity for our children and our children's children. For their sake as well as ours, we must not only go forward with domestic policies that encourage growth; we must staunchly resist policies that destroy it.

Let me underscore the special importance which the United States attaches to resisting protectionist pressures. All of us know how crucial world trade is to the health of our economies and how fiercely competitive trade is nowadays. Few of our industries are unaffected by the pressure on foreign goods and services, whether competing for sales at home or abroad. Our common challenge is to pursue policies permitting freer and fairer trade.

Now, I know there's been concern, especially among debtor countries, that pressures for trade protectionism in the United States could lead us to run up the flag, erecting new import barriers, and harming prospects for their export growth. Well, we believe our record should put those doubts to rest.

Requests for protection on tuna, stainless steel flatware, shoes, and copper have all been turned down. And only last week, I reaffirmed the U.S. commitment to an open world trading system by rejecting protectionist quota and tariff relief for the steel industry. I've decided instead to take vigorous action against unfair trade practices in steel that will prove to be in the best long-term interest of consuming and supplying nations alike.

But we're not just fighting protectionism; we want to go forward toward more open markets at the London summit. Well, we want to go forward—I should have put a period in there—because at the London summit, we pressed for new efforts to liberalize and expand international trade. Consultations are continuing among the GATT countries on the possible objectives, arrangements, and timing for a new negotiating round.

For the millions around the globe who look to us for help and hope, I urge all of you today: Join us. Support with us a new, expanded round of trade liberalization, and together, we can strengthen the global trading system and assure its benefits spread to people everywhere.

This is not just my challenge; this is our challenge. It can only happen if we make it happen. But if we do, if each of us is prepared to give a little, the people of the world will gain a lot.

Our sensible five-part debt strategy, endorsed at Williamsburg and strengthened in London, has shown itself to be sufficiently flexible and dynamic to meet the diverse needs of debtor nations. These nations in partnership with the IMF are charting a course of renewed prosperity and stability which can serve as a guidepost for others to follow. The international financial system is the ultimate beneficiary of these individual country success stories and is stronger today than when we met here last year.

Providing an environment to foster lasting, noninflationary growth requires financing from both internal and external sources. It has become clear that a variety of capital inflows in the developing countries will be necessary. Countries will have to rely less on external debt and more on direct private investment—both foreign and domestic.

Policies that attract foreign investors are identical with those policies that encourage domestic savings and investments and contribute to the efficient use of scarce capital resources: positive real interest rates, a realistic exchange rate, free convertibility of currency, and a respect for property rights—in short, an economic environment that allows investors to earn a fair deal and a fair, real after-tax rate of return.

At the last economic summit in London this June, we also urged our Finance Ministers to: "consider the scope for intensified discussion of international financial issues of particular concern to developing countries in the IBRD Development Committee, an appropriate and broadly representative forum for this purpose."

I welcome the decision by the members of the Interim Committee and the Development Committee to accept the United States proposal announced by Secretary Regan to sponsor an enhanced dialog on ways that the industrialized countries can better pursue our common goal of achieving sustained, noninflationary economic growth throughout the world. Your institutions represent the best means of cooperatively addressing the obstacles to realizing that goal.

As we go forward, we will support our

two great institutions, the IMF and World Bank, which have been the cornerstones of the international economic and monetary systems since World War II. The United States remains honored to be one of the "founding fathers" of both organizations. Besides their enormous contributions to individual freedom, prosperity, and initiative, these multilateral organizations are effectively handling even greater responsibilities as the technological revolution ushers in an increasing velocity of human transactions and greater global economic interdependence.

Last year the World Bank committed over $15 billion to supplement the efforts of developing member countries to strengthen their economies. In addition to its proven expertise as an investment project lender, we value highly the Bank's ability to provide helpful policy guidance and technical assistance and to act as a catalyst in encouraging private enterprise and investment capital.

We are committed to providing the agreed upon level of U.S. contributions to the IBRD selective capital increase, the seventh replenishment of IDA, and the capital increase of the IFC.

The IMF has always had a central role in assisting members facing serious balance-of-payments problems, and it has assumed leadership in helping debtor countries design economic adjustments which seek to restore economic and financial balance and creditworthiness. For our part, considerable effort went into negotiating and obtaining the necessary legislative concurrence for United States participation in the quota increase which provided resources for the Fund to deal with this difficult problem.

We don't want a world in which some nations go forward while others are left behind. We want a world in which all go forward together. And we can go forward together if our countries give up spending what need not be spent and leave more in the hands of all the people who work and earn. Let them plant the seeds of wealth, and we'll see the smallest dreams awaken and grow into golden dreams for all mankind.

Permit me to take a brief moment to speak about a subject of special interest and concern to our government—the particularly severe economic problems besetting sub-Saharan Africa. The Bank issued the third in a series of excellent reports on this subject, and we look forward to working with the Bank, the Fund, other donors, and African countries in developing a joint response.

Last January I submitted to the Congress legislation called the Economic Policy Initiative for Africa. And this initiative closely parallels the recommendations of the World Bank concentrating on flexible donor response to African economic policy reform initiatives. Our plans call for a U.S. contribution of $500 million over 5 years. And this would be in addition to ongoing U.S. economic assistance programs which are expected to run roughly at the billion-dollar level in the coming year, a 30-percent increase over such assistance levels a few years ago.

I look out at all of you this morning, people from so many different cultures and countries, speaking so many different languages, and I think, of course, how our nations spring from separate pasts, how many of us live at opposite ends of the Earth. But all of us, I'm convinced, have been brought together in this place by aspirations that bind us like friends and family. I'm talking about our determination to help people build a better life, to climb from the shadows of want into the sunlight of prosperity. That's what this job of ours is all about.

We're a little like climbers who begin their ascent from opposite ends of the mountain. The harder we try, the higher we climb, and the closer we come together—until that moment we reach the peak and we are as one.

What I'm describing actually did happen in real life. One American and two Japanese groups began climbing Mount Everest—the Japanese from the side of Nepal and the Americans from the side of Tibet. The conditions were so difficult and dangerous that before it ended, two climbers tragically lost their lives. But before that tragedy, these brave climbers all met and shook hands just under the summit. And then they climbed to the top together for their magnificent moment of triumph.

Distinguished colleagues and good friends, we are not asked to face the kind of perils those climbers did. Yet we do share the risks affecting the future economic well-being of our nations and of the world. But if those mountaineers could join hands at the top of the world, imagine how high our people can climb if all of us work together as powerful partners for the cause of good. Together, with faith in each other, with freedom as our guide, there is nothing that we cannot do.

Thank you very much. God bless you all.

Note: The President spoke at 10:11 a.m. in the International Ballroom at the Sheraton Washington Hotel at the meeting of the International Monetary Fund, the International Bank for Reconstruction and Development (World Bank), the International Development Association, and the International Finance Corporation.

Message on the Observance of the Jewish High Holy Days
September 25, 1984

The year 5745 of the Jewish calendar is about to be ushered in with the soul-stirring blast of the shofar. And while the ram's horn is traditionally meant to summon Jews to prayer and reflection, its message echoes beyond the walls of Jewish places of worship and affects others as well.

Nancy and I hear its call and are reminded by it that so much in our American heritage is drawn from the religious values enunciated during the Jewish High Holy Days. The liturgy of Rosh Hashanah and Yom Kippur emphasizes both the moral obligations men have to their Maker and the ethical responsibilities we owe to our fellows. Fundamentally, America stands for the same principles. Indeed, these values have been derived in large part from the Jewish tradition which is thereby inextrica-bly linked to our American spiritual heritage.

The ties between the Jewish and American traditions run deep and are related in no small way to the special relationship that exists between the United States and Israel—a relationship based on the common spiritual and ethical values encompassed in the shofar's call to prayer.

At this time of introspection and renewal, we extend our very best wishes that your prayers will be fulfilled. We share your hopes that during the coming year world understanding and peace will triumph over prejudice and violence so that we may say with the Prophet Isaiah, "Nation shall not lift up sword against nation, neither shall men learn war any more."

RONALD REAGAN

Remarks During a Meeting With Prime Minister Brian Mulroney of Canada and Space Shuttle Astronauts
September 25, 1984

The President. As part of Prime Minister Mulroney's visit to the United States, it's most appropriate to recognize our close and continuing cooperation in the pursuit of the many peaceful opportunities of space. Canada was our first international satellite partner during the early days of the space program, and that partnership has grown stronger ever since.

Most recently, we watched Canada's contribution to the space shuttle perform with perfection—the remote manipulator system, better known as the Canadarm. It's been used on almost every space shuttle mission.

And this past April, the Canadarm retrieved the crippled solar max satellite and then placed it safely back into orbit after repairing it on board.

And today I'm delighted to have the opportunity to introduce Canada's first astronaut, Dr. Marc Garneau. Early next month, Marc will be aboard space shuttle mission 41–G and will conduct about 10 experiments in space science and technology and life science. These important experiments will help build a better tomorrow in space and right here on Earth.

Marc is joined by two other members of next month's shuttle—Bob Crippen, the mission commander, and Kathy Sullivan. And Bob commanded the mission when the Canadarm was first used to deploy a satellite and was also aboard when solar max was retrieved and repaired. And Kathy will take the first spacewalk by an American woman, and I know how she's looking forward to that opportunity.

Astronaut Sullivan. Yes, sir, very much.

The President. The space shuttle has opened a new era to pursue the many scientific, educational, industrial, and commercial opportunities of space, and I'm proud that Canada is an important part of this adventure. And as we work to meet the next challenge, the development of a permanently manned space station, we want Canada and all of our friends to join us.

Our future can be shaped by our dreams and visions. And working together on the space shuttle and our space station we can push back the frontiers of space and open the doors to discovery, opportunity, and progress.

Mr. Prime Minister, let me close by presenting you with a photo album showing the Canadarm being used. I'm turning the wrong way, except I had to get this, didn't I? [*Laughter*] Also, it shows the Canadarm that was used on all the previous missions, also. And, also, we have a plaque, which I think we will just display and give to you without us—not that we're not both able-bodied—[*laughter*]—we are. But this contains the U.S. and Canadian flags that were flown on previous missions when the Canadarm was being used. So, please accept these as symbols of our strong friendship and our confidence in a bright future for both of our great nations.

The Prime Minister. Thank you, Mr. President.

Well, Mr. President, in a recent election campaign, my party and I campaigned on a program, in part, of refurbishing the relationship—historic relationship—of trust and friendship between the United States of America and Canada. And this implies no subservience. It invites merely a degree of maturity and understanding that our trade and our technological advances hinge upon an excellent relationship which my government and I will always work towards improving.

And I think, Mr. President, the indication of that in the past is the joint efforts that we have made in space in the peaceful pursuit of mutual objectives in that area, as we will continue to work in the peaceful pursuit of a durable peace for all mankind. And this, I think, symbolizes what two sovereign countries can do together.

[*At this point, the Prime Minister spoke in French. He then continued his remarks in English.*]

Our sincere thanks and congratulations to you, our astronauts, who are symbols of accomplishment and valor and courage and unity—symbols, hopeful symbols, for all mankind.

Mr. President, to you and to your colleagues, my thanks. And to the astronauts, our warm good wishes. Thank you.

[*At this point, the President, Prime Minister Mulroney, NASA Administrator James M. Beggs, and the astronauts viewed space program models.*]

The Prime Minister. Mr. President, just before you leave, although we're in a period of some austerity in Canada, we would like to make a presentation to you symbolizing Canada's contribution to our joint effort.

The President. Well, thank you very much.

The Prime Minister. And we would like to convey the good wishes and the pride of the people of Canada in our joint accomplishments.

The President. Well, thank you. Thank

you very much.

The Prime Minister. Thank you, Mr. President.

Note: The President spoke at 11:53 a.m. in *the Roosevelt Room at the White House.* *Prior to meeting with the astronauts, the* *President and the Prime Minister met in the* *Oval Office, together with their advisers.*

Remarks Following a Meeting With Prime Minister Brian Mulroney of Canada
September 25, 1984

The President. Well, it was with great pleasure that we welcomed Brian Mulroney back to the White House. He was here this past June and now returns as Prime Minister of Canada—America's neighbor, ally, and most important economic partner, and great friend.

I congratulated Prime Minister Mulroney on winning a decisive and historical electoral mandate from the people of Canada. As the other North American Irishman, I also wished him well in his new responsibilities.

The Prime Minister and I exchanged views on a broad range of global issues, reviewed our common search to advance our agenda for peace, particularly the search for real and equitable reductions in the levels of nuclear arms. I told him that in our efforts to build a lasting structure of peace and security, we shall continue to value the experience, the counsel, and the participation of our Canadian allies.

A healthy North American economic relationship is essential to the prosperity of our two countries. We discussed some potential ways of increasing trade and investment between us. The Prime Minister impressed upon me the importance his government attaches to environmental concerns, and we intend to pursue these issues together.

Frequent consultations are one of the hallmarks of the relationship between Canada and the United States, and I told the Prime Minister that I look forward to continuing the fruitful dialog that we had today. In addition, I've asked Secretary Shultz to continue the series of very productive regular meetings that he has had with his Canadian counterparts.

Even the closest of partners and allies may not always see things in exactly the same way. But we agree to keep each other's interests in mind, to keep one another informed, and to hear one another out on the issues which may arise between us. We, too, intend to give our neighbor the benefit of the doubt.

So, I thank you, Mr. Prime Minister, for coming here today. And, once again, congratulations on your decisive victory and *a la prochaine* [until the next time].

The Prime Minister. Thank you, Mr. President.

Mr. President, an hour ago you and I had the great pleasure of meeting Canadian and American astronauts soon to be launched into space. No endeavor better underscores our friendship or so dramatically indicates the potential for cooperation by our two countries in the service of mankind than the peaceful use of space. Such an effort, it seems to me, demonstrates to us all the tremendous potential for improved cooperation in joint development of our two countries.

Yesterday in the United Nations, you reached out to the Soviet Union with a message of peace, and you invited the leaders of the world to join in what we can accomplish together. We commend you, Mr. President, for this appeal and for your leadership in this vital area.

For our part, we intend to continue to seek opportunities for constructive dialog with the Soviet Union and with Eastern European countries. We will continue to contribute, as we have in the past, ideas which may help yield results in our common search for peace and security.

Our two countries have much to offer

each other and, I believe, together, to the world. President Kennedy once said that "Geography has made us neighbors, history has made us friends, economics has made us partners, and necessity has made us allies."

[*At this point, the Prime Minister spoke in French. He then continued his remarks in English.*]

The principal task, Mr. President, of our new government is economic renewal—to expand trade, to attract new investment, and to seek new markets. By establishing a climate for vigorous economic growth, we wish to create the new jobs that our people need and, we believe, deserve. We wish to mobilize our very best talents at home and to seek out new partners abroad. We feel a strong external voice is based on a vigorous domestic economy.

Our talks today have focused on strength-ening and, indeed, intensifying consultation between the executive arm of our two governments and also between the Congress and the Parliament of Canada. We want more coherence in the management of our relationship and more action in regard to our shared priorities.

And, so, Mr. President, we must deepen our understanding of what we share together and of the distinctive interests we have in international affairs. And I thank you, Mr. President, for your generous hospitality and for a most satisfying exchange of views. *Merci.*

Note: The President spoke at 1:08 p.m. at the South Portico of the White House. Earlier, the President and the Prime Minister held a working luncheon in the Family Dining Room.

Nomination of Jose Manuel Casanova To Be United States Executive Director of the Inter-American Development Bank
September 26, 1984

The President today announced his intention to nominate Jose Manuel Casanova to be United States Executive Director of the Inter-American Development Bank for a term of 3 years. This is a reappointment.

Since 1981 Mr. Casanova has been serving as Executive Director of the Inter-American Development Bank. Previously, he was president of Agro-Com Exports in Miami, FL (1979–1981), and a real estate broker with Presto Realty (1978–1981). He also served as a financial and management consultant (1977–1981). In 1976 he was senior vice president of the Flagship National Bank of Miami. In 1974–1976 he was president of Flagship National Bank of Westland in Hialeah, FL.

Mr. Casanova attended Babson Institute in Wellesley Hills, MA, Flagship College, and the University of Miami. He is married, has seven children, and resides in Miami, FL. He was born August 14, 1930, in Havana, Cuba.

Nomination of Robert Elsner To Be a Member of the Marine Mammal Commission
September 26, 1984

The President today announced his intention to nominate Robert Elsner to be a member of the Marine Mammal Commission for the term expiring May 13, 1987. He would succeed Robert Weeden.

Since 1973 Dr. Elsner has been serving as professor of marine science, Institute of Marine Science, at the University of Alaska.

Previously, he served as associate professor of physiology at Scripps Institution of Oceanography and in the department of pediatrics at the University of California at San Diego (1970–1973); visiting scientist, department of human physiology and pharmacology, University of Adelaide, South Australia (1969–1970); and associate research physiologist, physiological research laboratory, Scripps Institution of Oceanography (1963–1970). He also served as a distinguished lecturer at the University of Hawaii (1971) and was a member of the panel on biological and medical sciences, Committee on Polar Research, at the National Academy of Sciences (1971–1974).

He graduated from New York University (B.A., 1950) and the University of Washington (M.S., 1955; Ph.D., 1959). He is married, has three children, and resides in Ester, AK. He was born June 3, 1920, in Boston, MA.

Remarks and a Question-and-Answer Session at Bowling Green State University in Bowling Green, Ohio
September 26, 1984

The President. Thank you. My good friend, Del Latta, and fellow Congressmen who are here, Ralph Regula and Mike Oxley, the administration, the faculty, and you, the students of Bowling Green State:

It's an understatement for me to say at this moment that it's great to be here. I know I'm at the home of the Falcons, your NCAA championship hockey team, and your football team. And I've had greetings, personal greetings from the coach of your women's hockey team and your basketball coach, and I want to congratulate you again on beating the "Miami Whammy."

You know, your generation is really something. You've made love of country fashionable again. You've revived the American traditions of hard work and decency and a good-natured faith in the future. And I just thank you for helping turn our country around.

I want to talk to you about something that I know concerns all of you—peace—and the prospects for peace, our views on peace, and how we mean to achieve it. The wisest thing ever said about peace was also the simplest. It was when Pope Paul VI spoke before the United Nations in 1965, and he said, "No more war—war never again."

I have seen four wars in my lifetime. I've lost friends in those wars and the sons of friends. I've gone to school with the children of men who are still over there under those white crosses. We can't hear the words of Pope Paul VI without saying a heartfelt amen.

But how to achieve peace? Well, first we must define exactly what it is we want. In our case, we in the United States passionately desire peace with our neighbors, our allies, our adversaries.

With our neighbors and allies, we've made ourselves open to dialog and eager to be of assistance. When a NATO ally is having problems, we discuss it with them. We try to help them or make some compromise, if that's what's called for. When our Caribbean neighbors tell us that peace is threatened in that peaceful part of the world, we have helped by rooting out the warmakers, as we did in Grenada. And we try to be what Franklin Roosevelt declared us to be—a good neighbor.

To our adversaries, too, we must remain open. But there, an additional element is called for—firmness—so that our adversaries neither miscalculate our responses nor misjudge our resolve. So much woe has been caused by miscalculation, and so many wars. World War I, the war of my early boyhood, can be described as one long miscalculation. It's been called the war no one wanted.

Well, I believe that during the past few years we've once again shown our firmness and steadiness. And this has had a stabilizing effect on the world. Peace will not move forward unless effort is extended and ideas are put forth. And, so, we've made proposals for peace and put them on the table for all the world to see.

We have, to begin with, put forth one of the most extensive arms control programs in history. In Vienna, last spring, we put forward new proposals on reducing the conventional military forces in Europe. In Geneva, we put forward ideas for a worldwide ban on chemical weapons which have been used in Afghanistan and Kampuchea.

At the Conference on Disarmament in Stockholm—a series of proposals to help reduce the possibility of world conflict. Also, in arms reduction talks in Geneva, we proposed deep cuts in both U.S. and Soviet intercontinental nuclear forces and intermediate-range missiles. And during those START and INF talks—you know that START means the strategic nuclear missiles and the INF means the intermediate-range missiles that the Soviets have targeted on the countries of Europe—we proposed seven different initiatives, trying to meet their queries and their protests on some of the issues. None of them were offered on a take-it-or-leave-it basis. We were flexible. But the Soviets walked away from the bargaining table. We hope they'll return. We've told them this, and we'll tell them again. As a matter of fact, on Friday I'll be telling one of them again.

We're prepared to negotiate on nuclear arms reductions tomorrow if the Soviets so choose. I have had the privilege of appearing before the parliaments, the diets, the congresses of a number of countries in Europe and in Asia. And in every instance, I told them at one point or other in my address, a nuclear war cannot be won and must never be fought.

Now, we're ready to discuss a whole range of issues of concern to both sides, such as the relationship between offensive and defensive forces and space arms control. We've made new economic agreements with the Soviets. We've improved the communications instruments that link our Capital and theirs. In the meantime, we must consider what will make our defense, our ability to deter aggression, more stable and effective.

We work hard with our friends and allies to see that they feel safe and secure. And we work with scientists on the possibility of a nonnuclear defense system to see if it isn't possible to create a system that will neutralize the nuclear threat rather than rely on the threat of nuclear retaliation as our main option. And we continue to reach out to those with whom we have not been friends before.

Logic and experience might suggest that China would not be our friend, but China is. And our mutual friendship may be the most significant global achievement in the last decade. It shows our willingness to improve relations with countries that are ideologically very different from our own. And the impact of this friendship has a rippling effect. Here at Bowling Green, you have an exchange program with Fudan University in Shanghai, China. Well, I met the Fudan students a few months ago in Shanghai. And they desire peace every bit as much as we do. I did a question-and-answer session with them. You'd be surprised how much they wanted to know about you.

The world is a dangerous place. We try to be a good neighbor, but we must be strong enough and confident enough to be patient when provoked. But we must be equally clear that past a certain point, our adversaries push us at their peril. Uncle Sam is a friendly old man, but he has a spine of steel.

To give peace a chance to grow and settle in, we must remain strong. Our military strength is one part an illustration of our resolve and one part a means of deterring aggression. There is great talk these past few years of the lessons of this war or that and what we should have learned here or there. Well, we should remember the central lesson of World War II. Our allies tried very hard for peace, to the point of outright appeasement. If only they'd shown Germany early on that they would pay any price and bear any burden to ensure the survival of their liberties, then Britain might not have known the blitz and Dresden might not have known the flames.

From our earliest years, our Presidents have stressed the crucial role of strength in promoting stability. George Washington said, "There is nothing so likely to produce peace as to be well-prepared to meet a foe." He said we should remember that "timely disbursements to prepare for danger frequently prevent much greater disbursements to repel it."

Closer to our own times, John Kennedy said: "The primary purpose of our arms is peace, not war. Our preparation against danger is our hope of safety."

Well, we live in the age of nuclear arms, and the question of what to do about nuclear weapons is deeply frustrating for Americans. We're a nation of problem-solvers. And here we are faced with a problem that, so far, has resisted our best efforts.

Some propose unilateral disarmament: We disarm in the hope the other side will follow. Well, there are great saints and great sinners among us. Historically, unilateral disarmament has never worked; it has only encouraged aggressors.

It's frustrating, but here is the truth of the nuclear age: There are no cheap solutions, no easy answers. The only path to progress on this is the open door, the honest proposal, and such a path takes patience. But patience isn't inappropriate. Each day the world turns completely. Each day the world is reborn. Possibilities that yesterday didn't exist emerge and startle us.

We hold on. We remain prepared for peace. We know that we have an absolute moral obligation to try and try again. We know that in the quest for peace the work of man is the work of God. And He will bless us, and bless one of our efforts and make our prayer of peace come true.

I've heard there's a fellow going around the country that says that I don't answer questions. [Laughter] And I understand that now I'm going to have an opportunity to answer some questions, so fire away.

Student Moderator. [Inaudible]—earlier this morning, we randomly selected 14 students to participate in the question-and-answer session. And we simply passed out 3-by-5 cards and then drew 14 names. So, the first question will come from this side.

The President. All right.

Central America

Q. My name is Lisa Mecca, Mr. President. I'm a senior. I'd like to know if you feel that the current turmoil in Central America has

a possibility of turning into another Vietnam?

The President. No, I don't believe that. We have never had any thought in mind of armed aggression in there or of moving troops. As a matter of fact, with the memories of days gone by and gunboat diplomacy, our friends and neighbors in Latin America would be the first to say no to that. And they have—all of them—said to us, "We need your help; that is, in training and in supplies and so forth, but not your manpower. We'll provide that." And I have the greatest faith. We have seen after 400 years of mostly military dictatorships, now a democratic government in El Salvador. We, at the same time, have seen by outside interference—the Cubans and the Soviets—a totalitarian power on the mainland of the Americas: Nicaragua.

The revolutionary forces, the Sandinistas, were only a part of the revolution that overthrew the dictator, Somoza. All who wanted democracy joined together. And then the Sandinistas did what Castro did when he took Cuba. They, once they were in, they got rid of the other elements of the revolution. They exiled them, they jailed them. Many of them are now what we call the *contras*. And they gave their promises, however, during the revolution, to the Organization of American States that they wanted democracy, human rights, the right to vote, the right to join unions, freedom of the press, and so forth. But once in, they took over, and they have a totalitarian form of government. And they are also aiding the people who are trying to overthrow the democratic Government of El Salvador. And we have been trying to be helpful, but it is not at the risk of our intervening there with military force.

I better answer these shorter, or I won't get all 14.

Oh! [Laughter] You see how difficult it is for me to turn to the left. [Laughter]

U.S.-Soviet Relations

Q. Mr. President, Dave Biesiada. What do you hope to accomplish, or what is your specific goal that you hope to accomplish with Mr. Gromyko of the Soviet Union?

The President. It is my hope that while

we have met a number of times—I mean, our people—and have been in contact and all, that maybe we can open up a dialog about the suspicions that exist in both our countries: they charging that we intend war against them, we feel—and I think with better reason—that they really do have aggressive intent against us; but maybe a chance to open up a discussion and clear the air somewhat of those suspicions and then decide that here we are, the two superpowers in the world, the only two powers that can really bring about peace, or that if we don't, can bring about world destruction. And it's time for us to sit down together and recognize our joint responsibility.

Security at U.S. Embassies Abroad

Q. Hello, Mr. President. My name is Peggie Fitzpatrick, and I'd like to thank you for coming to Bowling Green State University and giving me this chance to present my question to you. I'd like to know if you think that you're going to have to beef up security in the Embassies around the world because of what happened in Lebanon?

The President. Yes, we're going to have to do everything we can to beef up security, and yet, let me call to your attention what the real choice comes down to. Is there any security that can make you 100-percent safe against a suicide who is intent on bringing in that destruction at the cost of his own life, as they have done in these bomb-type explosions? Remember, an Embassy is not a bunker. You can't build a fortress and hunker down. You are there to do business with the people of that country.

This last tragedy occurred at an Embassy building that is on a residential street. Now, we have put blocks up at the corners of that particular block there to try and slow down and check on vehicles coming through. But we can't close off the street. It isn't our country and there are, as I say, people living there.

The real protection, and where we're feeling the effects today of the near destruction of our intelligence capability in recent years—before we came here, the effort that somehow to say, well, spying is somehow dishonest and let's get rid of our

intelligence agents, and we did that to a large extent. Your biggest protection is to—and we're trying to—rebuild our intelligence to where you'll find out and know in advance what the target might be and be prepared for it.

But again, I have to say this for our Foreign Service personnel: they know their mission, they know they have to be there. Such courage. They're not in uniform, they're not fighting people, but their courage—because the other alternative would be to simply close down our Embassies worldwide and come back here to fortress America and have no representation there. And that, we cannot do. That would give the terrorists a victory that we're not going to give them, and I don't think anyone should.

Q. Hi, Mr. President. My name is Becky Holtzscher, and I'd just like to say you look great.

The President. Well, thank you.

U.S.-Soviet Relations

Q. Do you feel that the people of the United States and of the Soviet Union have a common goal in the meaning of the word peace?

The President. With regard to peace?

Q. Yes.

The President. Yes, with regard to the people. Unfortunately, the two societies are so different that the people of the Soviet Union only hear what their leaders want them to hear. We try, with Voice of America and a few things, and know that we have some listeners in those countries, although they have to probably go to the basement and pull all the blinds before they can listen to our radio. [*Laughter*] But the people of Russia, above all, want peace.

They lost 20 million people in World War II. Their country has been invaded time after time, even before the Soviet regime. And there is a real built-in desire on their part for peace. And we know that we want it. We want it because peace in America is such an attractive way to live—[*laughing*]—that a war is a terrible interruption.

One of the things we would like would be to have more of an exchange of people so that, person to person, Ivan could meet

Sam and Bill and Johnny over here, and vice versa. And we could learn more about each other as people.

The Nation's Economy

Q. Mr. President, I'm Dan McFarland, a junior here. I'd like to know if you foresee a continued growth in the economic recovery.

The President. Do I foresee growth, continued growth?

Q. Yes.

The President. Yes, as long as we can continue with the help of people like Del Latta, whose name was on there with Phil Gramm on the Gramm-Latta bill, which was our economic recovery.

We've had opposition to that in the Congress. My own degree was in economics, so I can speak harshly about economists—[*laughter*]—and their predictions that have been wrong. But back around the turn of the century, it was a classical economic belief that when we had business cycles and had what they called hard times in those days—no one had thought of the word recession or depression—the classic economists at that time said that it usually followed when the Government went beyond a certain level in the amount of money it took out of the private sector. Well, I believe that our problem today—the problem—we talk about the problem of the deficit, but the deficit is a result, not a cause. It is the result of the Government taking too much money from the private sector.

The philosophy of our program is a reduction in the cost of government. So far we have cut the increase in cost in government in half or more and, at the same time that through continued economic recovery—with a tax policy that offers stimulant to people, incentive to people to go out and produce, to business also—that then the growth in the economy will increase the revenues the Government gets without increasing the rate of tax on the individuals. And thus we will have continued growth, because we will bring government back down to size.

Q. Thank you.

Views on the Presidency

Q. Good morning, Mr. President. I'm Jeff

Frederick, and I'd like to know, when you're out of office, what do you want the American people to remember most about your Presidency?

The President. Hmm. [*Laughter*] You know if I could sum it up in one sentence—there could be very complicated answers to that. One sentence, though, that would sum it up is: If they'd just be able to say I gave the Government back to the people. [*Applause*]

Thank you.

Advice to Students

Q. Good morning, sir. Sir, my name's Robert McLaughlin. I'm a senior member of the U.S. Army National Guard. And my question isn't in regard to foreign policy, it's, what advice do you have for the college students gathered here today?

The President. What advice for the college students gathered here today?

Q. Yes, sir.

The President. Well, first of all, to believe in yourselves and believe in—well, you expressed your belief in the answer I just gave to that other question—but to recognize that system—the Founding Fathers were a unique group that came together in one period of history—and this system was built on the belief, for the first time in the history of mankind, that government derived its power from the people.

There are other constitutions that say a lot of the same things ours do, make the same promises ours do, except the difference is so great it's almost unobserved. Those other constitutions say we, the government, grant you these rights. Ours says we, the people, grant government the following rights.

Remember that over this last half century where we've gotten in the habit of turning more and more to government for help, every time you get help from government you must give up a certain element of freedom. Now, sometimes it's worth it. We give up the right to drive 90 miles down a crowded street—90-miles-an-hour—because we wanted safety for ourselves and others.

But always weigh government's offer, and remember that the system was built to be run on the level of government closest to the people: the local community for so much of what controls our lives, then the counties and the States, and finally, only those things should be done by the Federal Government that are the Federal Government's proper province. And when it does things it shouldn't do, it can't do any of them as well as the private sector can do them.

Lebanon

Q. Mr. President, my name is Scott Jacob, and my question is, what steps are the administration presently taking to help mediate a peaceful solution in Lebanon?

The President. We have been trying for a long time—and that was ·even part of our marines being there in the first place, part of the multinational force. Lebanon, as we know, for a number of years, more than a decade, has been torn in revolution. And it has factions in which the leaders have their own militias, their own military throughout the country. But then we've had the invasion by other countries. The Israelis felt justified in going in when they did because the Palestinian refugees were using their position in Lebanon to launch terrorist attacks across the Israeli border.

What we're trying to do is negotiate between Syria, between Libya—or, not Libya—between Lebanon and the Israelis, at the same time that we try to bring the influence of the other Arab States to bear in there. And we've made great progress with that.

Right now, our Ambassador Murphy is there. He is commuting between Beirut and Damascus and Tel Aviv. And we've had, before him, several other representatives. And they all want our presence there.

I proposed a plan in September of '82 that, basically, to get down to—if we can mediate and help bring about the kind of peace between Israel and the Arab States that was brought between Israel and Egypt, one of those states—in other words, have more Egypts—then we can bring peace to the Middle East. And that is the underlying problem, the reluctance of the Arab States to recognize the right of Israel to even exist as a nation. And this we're going to continue to try to do.

We brought our marines out after the ter-

rorist attacks actually because they had only been sent in, the multinational force, as a peacekeeping force while we helped Lebanon restore its government, which was non-existent—and they have a government now—help train their military. And we had the hope that then they could begin to take over those parts of the country now held by these militias that I spoke of, and the multinational force would be there behind the lines to maintain order.

Well, with the conflict that came up, that peacekeeping force, or chore, was no longer viable or practical. And that's why we came home.

Q. Thank you, Mr. President.

Student Moderator. Mr. President, there will be one final question.

The President. What?

Student Moderator. I said there will· be one final question.

The President. Is this the last one? All 14? I haven't been counting.

Steel Industry

Q. Mr. President, my name is Lori Smith, and I'm a senior. And I'm honored to be speaking to you right now. My question is: What was the basis for your recent decision not to impose barriers to foreign steel, and what do you feel will be the effect on the U.S. steel industry?

The President. Well, the U.S. steel industry is doing a job of rebuilding at the management level. Labor has contributed by taking some cuts in the previous standards that they had in pay and benefits and so forth. But the problem has been there is an overproduction of steel in the world. Everyone seems to want to be in that business. And a number of the countries have made us a dumping ground for steel. And they do this by subsidizing the cost, so that it can be sold at a competitive price here, against our own producers.

Now, those who advocated protectionism, quotas, shutting down, high tariffs, and so forth, that's a two-way street. And it is counterproductive. If we had established this on steel, then those other countries would have retaliated by, for example, shutting down on our agricultural products.

We were able to find out that we would

destroy more jobs in America than we would protect by the protectionist thing. But we haven't just said we're not going to do anything. We are now embarked on a program of dealing with our industrial partners and others in the world that are sending steel here, to make sure that it cannot be subsidized, it cannot be dumped on our market. And we're going to try to work out—we want free trade, but we want fair trade—so we have a program that is at work right now, and the steel industry is satisfied with it. They believe that this is giving them the breathing space they need to continue their modernization.

We were victims of some of our own generosity. After World War II, when we went out with the Marshall plan to help countries restore their industrial capacity, why, they built on the basis of the latest technology in the field. Well, we still had old-fashioned mills, and so forth, that had not come up and modernized, and then under the competition, they couldn't earn enough money to modernize. So, sometimes our opponents have our technology, modern means of production, and we haven't caught up.

Now, the steel industry is doing that and believes that they're—in fact, before I leave your State, I'm going to be visiting, at Canton, the Timken plant that is—[ap-

plause]. They have invested what amounts to a full third of their total capital capacity in this new plant and this new technology and, believe me, it won't have to worry about competition from anyone. It can hold its own.

So, this was the reason. Every time we've tried protectionism, it's a two-way street, and it ends up with us hurting ourselves and, in fact, hurting the whole world economy recovery. So, that isn't the answer.

I'm a veteran. I was looking for my first job back in the Great Depression, in 1932. And that worldwide depression really was prolonged and brought on by a thing called the Smoot-Hawley tariff, which thought that through a kind of general protectionism we could help ourselves, and we didn't. The only thing that finally ended the Great Depression was World War II, and I don't think that's a very good way of ending recessions or depressions.

Q. Thank you very much.

The President. Thank you.

Note: The President spoke at 11:10 a.m. in the university's Memorial Hall. Following his remarks, he attended separate receptions with students and faculty and also with local Republican leaders. He then traveled to Canton, OH.

Remarks at the Timken Faircrest Steel Plant in Canton, Ohio
September 26, 1984

Congressman Regula, State Representative Dave Johnson, who's here, and all of you ladies and gentlemen: Tim Timken, it's plain to see that you're following in the proud tradition of one of America's great men of commerce and industry, your great-grandfather, Henry Timken.

You know, being here in this particular place—and it's true—from some football I played myself, and then I became a sports announcer longer ago than I'm going to admit to—all the way over here, I found myself telling Jim Thorpe stories, and so forth, with regard to that Football Hall of Fame. But it is a thrill for me to see what's

happening here. I can now say with confidence, I've seen the future, and the future looks very good, indeed.

I'd just like to congratulate Tom Faught and his crew from the Dravo Corporation, the subcontractors on this project; all of the skilled craftsmen. From what I see, you're doing a quality job of which you can all be rightfully proud. With your energy and enthusiasm, with your dedication to efficiency and excellence, America is not just going to meet the competition; we're going to beat the competition.

Timken's courageous $500 million investment, representing about two-thirds of the total value of the company, is in the finest tradition of America's entrepreneurial spirit. The cooperation between everyone concerned—management, labor, Federal, State, and local government—is part of a new spirit that is emerging throughout this country. We're leaving the pessimists and the doom and gloomers behind.

The old ideas that spawned inflation, stagnation, and national self-doubt only a few years ago have given way to a new philosophy. Americans are rejecting the policies of something for nothing, rejecting politicians who try to divide us by exploiting envy and who offer programs with the claim, "We'll tax somebody else to pay for it." You know, that term about robbing Peter to pay Paul—it was some time ago that we began to realize, under their policy of robbing Peter to pay Paul, we were all named Peter. There weren't any Pauls left around. [*Laughter*]

But the American people, anymore, don't buy something-for-nothing schemes. We know that raising taxes, no matter what the big spenders say or try to make us believe, will mean a heavier burden for the working people of this country.

And let me ask what you think would be better for the future of America. Is it better to let them tax away your earnings because they'll know how to spend your pay better than you do? Or isn't it better for you to have more take-home pay and decide for yourself how that money will be spent? [*Applause*]

Well, I think it's better, too. And I think it's better, too, to have Timken and other companies like yours channeling their resources into job-creating investment rather than letting politicians tax it away. America doesn't need higher taxes and a heavier tax burden. America needs more high tech to modernize heavy industry. We need more take-home pay, more investment, more innovation, and more jobs.

My opponent made raising taxes his number one issue and the option that he would use first in solving our country's problems. My first option is expanding economic growth and increasing opportunity. I say, let's not focus on dividing the pie and everybody continually getting a smaller and smaller piece. Let's pull together and make a bigger pie so that everybody can have a bigger piece.

Standing here today and seeing this incredible new mill taking shape, I can't help but think of a telegram I received back in 1981. And I would have read it to you, except that Tim Timken has already done so. [*Laughter*] No, that's all right. [*Laughter*]

And I was very pleased to get it, and very pleased to have him remember, too, about that telegram. I've often wondered what kind of telegram I might have received had our policy been to increase taxes instead of reducing them.

This company didn't start out making steel. In fact, back in the 1890's, Timken was primarily a supplier to wagon and carriage builders. Mind you, I didn't see that for myself. I just heard about it. [*Laughter*]

But Timken has always been a vibrant and innovative company, never afraid of new challenges, never afraid to take advantage of new opportunities, and never afraid to compete. If America is to progress as a country, this is the kind of spirit our policies must promote.

There are those who call for protectionism and quotas which are shortsighted and temporary at best and which will make all of us a lot worse off in the long run. Certainly, we must ensure that other countries, our competitors, do not use unfair trade practices. I reaffirmed our determination to prevent this and charted a clear course of action to that effect last week. But a blunderbuss approach of quotas and trade barriers, encouraging stagnation by stifling competition, is not the way to a better future. It's a giant step back into the misery of a failed past.

America's heavy industries, like steel, will be just as much a part of our country's future as they are a part of our country's past. We're going to ensure this by hitting directly any country that attempts to dump its industrial products using unfair and illegal subsidies. But aggressive enforcement is only part of the answer. The kind of innovation that we underline here today at Timken is the most important part of the solution.

This mill is designed to produce the highest quality alloy steel at the lowest cost. While your workers in this mill will be paid comparable wages to any in the industry, their productivity will be substantially higher. It'll be energy efficient, using 22 percent less electricity, 27 percent less natural gas per ton of steel melted. It was designed to meet, and in many cases exceed, all of the EPA's clean air standards. It innovatively ties, as Tim Timken rightly points out, high tech and heavy industry.

And this type of commitment, commitment on the part of all of us, is the path to progress and an improved standard of living. I firmly believe that, if given the tools and the equipment we need, American workers can outproduce, outsell, and outcompete the pants off anyone in the world.

What you accomplish here will reap rewards throughout the system. Producing a higher quality product at a lower cost will help the auto and other heavy industries meet their competition, benefit your other customers. And eventually, in one way or another, everyone in this country will benefit. And that's what made America the great country it is, and that's what's going to make America even greater still.

There's been a lot said recently, with the lead story in a major magazine recently, about the new spirit spreading across America, something I've been calling the new patriotism. I couldn't help thinking about it when I was driving over here and we went past that Football Hall of Fame. Several years ago, there were those, even some of our own leaders, who seemed to be counting America out. Well, we aren't a nation of quitters. We're all on the same team—the American team. And it's good to see we're scoring touchdowns again.

Well, that's the way we are. And nobody should ever sell America short. During the dark days of World War II, Timken quickly adjusted its production line from steel tubes to gun barrels. By the end of the war, you did what the enemies of freedom thought was impossible, producing over a hundred thousand gun barrels used for antiaircraft guns, tanks, and the nose guns on the B–25 bomber.

Six thousand Timken employees marched off to fight for their country during that conflict. One of them was John Paul Moriarty. He was blinded when he was shot down over enemy territory in 1944. He suffered blindness and imprisonment, and when he finally got home, the city of Canton gave him a hero's welcome. His friends and neighbors pooled their money and provided this local boy—who gave his sight so they could remain free—enough money to build a home for his family.

And then, in March of 1946, John Paul Moriarty returned to the Timken Company. He was given a job operating special electronic gauges that had been specifically developed to enable the blind to inspect Timken bearings. John Paul Moriarty retired last year after 47 years of service to Timken, most of it as a blind employee.

Canton and Timken showed the world what America is all about. Thank you for letting me join you today. Thank you very much. [*Applause*] I—[*applause*]—all right. I'm willing. [*Applause*] Thank you all very much. Thank you.

If I could just make a personal note in here. If sometime again they happen to show the Knute Rockne film on television—[*laughter*]—when the Gipper scores that touchdown, if you'll look at the fellow in the dark sweater standing right over beside me before I start for that touchdown run, that was Jim Thorpe. He was playing an assistant coach in the picture. And it was a great thrill for me to get to meet the immortal Jim Thorpe. I just had to throw that in. I told you I was full of Jim Thorpe stories.

God bless you all.

Note: The President spoke at 2:53 p.m. in the steel plant's melt shop. Earlier, he was given a tour of the plant and was briefed by company officials on its operation.

Prior to his departure for Milwaukee, WI, the President met with local Republican leaders at the Akron/Canton Regional Airport.

Remarks at the Annual Family Oktoberfest in Milwaukee, Wisconsin
September 26, 1984

The President. Thank you.

Audience. 4 more years! 4 more years! 4 more years!

The President. All right. If that's the way you feel, I'm willing.

Well, thank you, Bob Kasten, for that very kind introduction. Thank you, and thank you all for a most heartwarming reception. I can only say to you in return, On Wisconsin!

It's great to be back in your proud city of Milwaukee and great to be with all of you here at Old Heidelberg Park. You know, Old Heidelberg Park—I can remember when they called it just plain Heidelberg Park. [*Laughter*] Of course, that was back when if somebody said, "Hey, kid," I answered. [*Laughter*]

But warm greetings to your outstanding Senator Bob Kasten. Believe me, we couldn't have accomplished all that we have without a Republican majority in the Senate, and Bob Kasten is in the front rank of that majority.

And a special thanks to one of Wisconsin's super Congressmen, Jim Sensenbrenner. Jim has worked long and hard in the House to put America back on its feet.

Jim and Bob, I can't tell you how much I'm looking forward to working with you in 1985 and in a few years to come.

Whenever I come to this beautiful State, your rolling hills and gentle valleys and lush pastures—and I have been here quite a bit, because for a large part of my life, I was a neighbor of yours just to the south in Illinois—I know I'm almost—well, I'm also going to see, in addition to all that beauty, some of the hardest working people in our country. And I know I'm looking at many of them right now.

All of you and your mothers and fathers and their parents stretching all the way back to the early 1800's, tens of thousands proud to trace their roots from Germany, thousands more from Serbia, Poland, Ireland, Norway, Sweden, Greece, and a dozen other nations. They came with few possessions, and they asked only the chance to live and work in freedom and peace.

Now, many went into the countryside and began to produce the best cheese and butter and milk in the world. And many stayed right here in Milwaukee. And together, they built a town of muscle, beauty, and pride. They manufactured machinery, produced metal products of all kinds, opened breweries, and made Milwaukee one of America's biggest ports. They gave this city a distinctive flavor, adapting the customs of the old country and the old world to the new. And as they stamped their character on Milwaukee, they enriched the cultural life of all Americans.

Today you've shown us that Milwaukee is just as proud as ever. You still have your ethnic pride. Your schools are better than ever. And you, the people of Milwaukee—hard-working, patriotic, and full of hope for our future—are what America is all about.

And now, if you don't mind, could I take a moment to give you a report on what we've been trying to do since we took office?

On the economic front, yes, we've been through some tough times. But Americans came through them together. We knew we had to work hard to correct the damage decades of government overspending and overtaxing had caused. And what do you know. The American people went to work, and we are getting the job done. Americans are working again, and America is working again.

Today inflation, as you were told, is down from more than 12 percent to an annual rate of about 4 percent. Interest rates, although still not as low as we want, are down substantially. Last year alone, America saw some 600,000 new business incorporations, and that is an all-time high in the history of our country. And during the past 20 months, America has created 6 million new jobs, by far the best performance of any country in the world.

And right here in Milwaukee, the economic expansion is beginning to take hold. In the last year, the unemployment rate in the Milwaukee area has fallen more than 3 percentage points. And in that same year, nearly 19,000 Americans have found work here in Milwaukee.

Now, we've been working to help Wisconsin farmers make the transition from the high inflation, high interest rates, and economic disasters of the past to stable growth, low inflation, and lower interest rates that all of us are bringing about.

We've eliminated the unfair, wrongheaded grain embargo. We've negotiated new agreements for grain with the Soviet Union. And last week, to help ease debt burdens, we announced that the Farmers Home Administration will defer for 5 years up to 25 percent of the principal and interest payments that farmers owe. And to help those who do not participate in the Farmers Home Administration programs, we will be making available $630 million in loan guarantees.

As the economic expansion continues, we're not going to rest until all Americans—and that means Wisconsin farmers and their families—share in the benefits.

My friends, our great nation has turned the corner. The shadows are behind us. Bright sunshine of hope and opportunity lies ahead. But I wouldn't take that for granted. So, let me just ask you: Do you feel better off than you did 4 years ago?

Audience. Yes!

The President. Is America better off than it was 4 years ago?

Audience. Yes!

The President. Well, good. You don't know how it warms my heart that you think that, too—[*laughter*]—because I think that way.

Now, despite the strength of this expansion, there's one sure way to ruin it. Now, you'd have to be something of an expert to find it. But when it comes to bringing economic growth to a grinding halt, our opponents are experts. They want to raise your taxes. And if you let them, they'll do it again and again and again.

You know, the people of Milwaukee are as well known for your love of good beer as the liberal Democrats are for their taxing and spending. The difference is you know when to stop. [*Laughter*]

The tax hike they've called for would be the equivalent of an additional tax burden of $1,800 for every household in Wisconsin and in America. Now, we all remember how Green Bay's beloved football coach, the great Vince Lombardi, used to say, "Winning isn't everything. It's the only thing." Well, it seems our opponents have adopted that philosophy, but with a new twist. They're saying, "Tax increases aren't everything. They're the only thing."

Audience. Boo-o-o!

The President. Well, come November, the American people will get to vote on their coaches—or on our coaches, and come November, I believe the American people will tell Coach Tax Hike to find another team.

Well, now, just so there isn't any doubt, I wonder if you'd help me conduct a little poll. Now, you can just answer yes or no.

Do you believe that the American people are undertaxed?

Audience. No!

The President. Will the working people of Milwaukee, the family farmers across this State, and America's economy all be stronger with a big tax increase?

Audience. No!

The President. Well, is his tax increase your idea of fairness and compassion?

Audience. No!

The President. Or do you share my belief that government in Washington might already be big enough?

Audience. Yes!

Audience member. Like the deficit is!

The President. So, rather than give more to Washington, DC, how about giving the American people more opportunities to work, to save, and to invest? [*Applause*]

Thank you very much. You've just confirmed my hunch.

Our pledge is for tax simplification, to make the system more fair, to make it easier to understand. Do you know that Einstein has admitted he cannot understand the Form 1040? [*Laughter*] And, so, you can bring everybody's income tax rates further down, and not up. That's what we believe is fair tax simplification and reform.

Now, tax simplification will provide powerful new incentives for economic growth. And it will help our economic expansion keep growing and spreading, from Maine to

Milwaukee to the California coast.

With your support, we'll fight for enterprise zones to help Americans in disadvantaged areas get off unemployment and welfare and start climbing the economic ladder. And we'll keep government under control by enacting a line-item veto and a constitutional amendment mandating that government stop spending more than government takes in.

Now, I know that there are many proud Democrats in Wisconsin, people who cherish the memories of F.D.R. and Harry Truman and John Kennedy. These men were leaders who believed in strength abroad and self-reliance at home. And to all those Democrats who might be here today—and I hope there are many—who feel that the present leadership of the Democratic Party is out of step with the rank-and-file Democratic membership of that party, the patriotic Democrats who so many times in the past were supporting the same things that we believe in; they who know that the leadership today of that party no longer stands behind America's role in the world, that it no longer represents working men and women, that it is abandoning the decent, patriotic Democrats of the J.F.K. and F.D.R. and Harry Truman tradition. And we say to you if you are here: Come on, walk with us down the path of hope and opportunity. It can be bipartisan.

Audience. 4 more years! 4 more years! 4 more years!

The President. All right.

Audience. 4 more years! 4 more years! 4 more years!

The President. Okay.

Audience. 4 more years! 4 more years! 4 more years!

The President. All right.

Audience. 4 more years! 4 more years! 4 more years!

The President. But add your strength to ours, and all of us can build something new for America, something far better than before.

You know, as our economy grows, we'll need to go forward with the bedrock values that sustained those first immigrants to Milwaukee and that nourish our families today—the values of faith; family; neighborhood; good, hard work. Together, we've already made an impressive start.

During the past 4 years, we've helped lead a grassroots revolution for excellence in our schools that will reach every child in our land. Just last week we learned that after nearly 2 years [decades] [1] of decline, scholastic aptitude test scores have gone up for the second year in a row. They increased a full 4 points. Now, that may not seem like very much, but it is the biggest increase in 21 years.

We must continue to crack down on crime. We say with no hesitation, yes, there are such things as right and wrong, and, yes, for hardened criminals preying on our society, punishment must be swift and certain. In 1980 our crime rate was rising. But last year, reported crime fell 7 percent, and that's the steepest drop since 1960.

In foreign affairs, today America is at peace. And since 1980 the tide of Soviet expansion has been turned.

Now, I know that many of you have relatives in Eastern Europe, in countries like East Germany, Hungary, and Poland. These brave people are never very far from my mind, and I know they aren't from yours. When we traveled to Europe in 1982, I visited the Berlin Wall, that grim line that divides the continent. And I saw those *polizei* looking at me very sternly with their guns, and I sneaked a foot across the line. [*Laughter*] Just wanted them to know I'd been there. [*Laughter*] But like all who visit that wall, I looked to the East. I saw the barbed wire and the guards, and understood, in a more powerful way, the value of human liberty. I pledge to you that in Europe we will do all in our power to defend the cause of freedom.

In Central America, we'll go on supporting the forces of democracy and economic growth. And I will tell Soviet Foreign Minister Gromyko, when I meet with him at the White House on Friday, the United States seeks no territorial expansion. We make no attempts to impose our will on anyone, but we remain unshakable in our commitment to freedom. And we will never again allow America to let down its guard.

---

[1] *White House correction.*

Well now, it's time for me to go——

Audience. No!

The President. Yes—oh—have to. But I see so many families here this afternoon, so many fine young people. May I just leave you with one last thought from my heart.

The American dream is a living thing, always growing, always presenting new vistas and challenges. In Old Heidelberg Park this afternoon—indeed, throughout Milwaukee and throughout Wisconsin—there are young couples saving to buy homes of their own; mothers and fathers who want to give their children a better education; men and women with dreams of making the good earth of this State still more fruitful, the good city of Milwaukee healthier and more prosperous, and America herself stronger and better still. My vision of America—and I know it's one you share—is of a land where all have the opportunity to work hard to make these dreams come true. My friends, together we can make America that shining land of opportunity and hope. And with you by our side, I know we will.

That wonderful song I mentioned earlier in my remarks has inspired tens of thousands. No other fight song has been adopted by so many high schools throughout the land—my own included—as "On Wisconsin." As a matter of fact, I was halfway through my high school football career before I knew that that was the real name of the song, that it wasn't "Onward Dixon." [*Laughter*]

Well, I think there's only one way we could top that song, and that's to put all our hopes and dreams for our country into one simple phrase: "On America."

Thank you all very much. God bless you all.

Note: The President spoke at 5:23 p.m. at the Old Heidelberg Park Fest Hall.

Following his remarks, the President returned to Washington, DC.

Appointment of Joseph Ben Trujillo as a Member of the National Advisory Council on Adult Education
September 26, 1984

The President today announced his intention to appoint Joseph Ben Trujillo to be a member of the National Advisory Council on Adult Education for a term expiring July 10, 1987. This is a reappointment.

He is president of JBT Financial Group in Denver, CO. He has been serving as vice president of Hicks Pension Services in Englewood, CO, since 1980. Previously he was president of Larimer Insurance Group, Inc., in Englewood. He was in insurance sales with Connecticut Mutual Life (1976–1978) and Connecticut General Life (1973–1976).

He graduated from Wichita State University (B.A., 1969) and New Mexico Highlands University (M.A., 1972). He is married and resides in Littleton, CO. He was born September 26, 1947, in Sante Fe, NM.

Message to the Congress Transmitting a Report on a National Strategy for the Prevention of Drug Abuse and Drug Trafficking
September 27, 1984

To the Congress of the United States:

In accordance with Title III, Section 305 of the Drug Abuse Prevention, Treatment, and Rehabilitation Act of 1972, as amended, I hereby transmit the 1984 National Strategy for the Prevention of Drug Abuse and

Drug Trafficking. The Strategy establishes a comprehensive national plan of action which includes prevention of drug abuse through awareness and action, drug law enforcement, international cooperation to eliminate the production and trafficking of illegal drugs, and health-related treatment and research activities.

I am pleased with the progress in raising public awareness of drug abuse problems and in strengthening our efforts to reduce the supply of illicit drugs, both domestic and international. Most important is the widespread recognition that the situation is not hopeless; that drug abuse can be conquered. Our citizens have begun numerous grassroots efforts which are likely to accomplish far more in preventing drug abuse than the Federal government, working alone, could hope to achieve.

I thank the Congress for its dedication and continuing support in the fight against drug abuse.

RONALD REAGAN

The White House,
September 27, 1984.

Note: The report is entitled "1984 National Strategy for Prevention of Drug Abuse and Drug Trafficking" (Government Printing Office, 124 pages).

Nomination of Cathryn C. Semerad To Be an Assistant Administrator of the Agency for International Development
September 27, 1984

The President today announced his intention to nominate Cathryn C. Semerad to be an Assistant Administrator of the Agency for International Development (External Affairs), U.S. International Development Cooperation Agency. She would succeed Jay F. Morris.

Mrs. Semerad is currently Associate Deputy Administrator for External Relations at the Agency for International Development. Previously, she was Executive Director, Advisory Committee on Voluntary Foreign Aid, AID (1981); and specialist, Office of Presidential Personnel, the White House (1979–1981).

Mrs. Semerad graduated from Skidmore College (B.S., 1965). She is married, has one child, and resides in Kensington, MD. She was born January 16, 1943, in Albany, NY.

Nomination of Mark L. Edelman To Be an Assistant Administrator of the Agency for International Development
September 27, 1984

The President today announced his intention to nominate Mark L. Edelman to be an Assistant Administrator of the Agency for International Development (Bureau for Africa), U.S. International Development Cooperation Agency. He would succeed Frank J. Donatelli.

Mr. Edelman is currently senior adviser to the Administrator and Executive Secretary at the Agency for International Development. Previously, he was Deputy Assistant Secretary, Bureau of International Organization Affairs, Department of State (1981–1983); program analyst, Agency for International Development (1981); legislative assistant to Senator John C. Danforth (1977–1981); and deputy commissioner of administration, office of administration, Jefferson City, MO (1975–1976).

Mr. Edelman graduated from Oberlin College (B.A., 1965). He is married and resides in Washington, DC. He was born June 27, 1943, in St. Louis, MO.

Message to the Congress Transmitting a Request for Supplemental Appropriations To Increase Security at United States Diplomatic Missions
September 27, 1984

To the Congress of the United States:

I am today forwarding to the Congress a request for Supplemental Appropriations for Fiscal Year 1985 totalling $110,200,000. These funds will be used solely to increase the security of United States diplomatic missions overseas.

This request represents another essential step in what will be a multi-year effort to counter the threats posed by a growing scourge against humanity—international terrorism. The Secretary of State is also forwarding separately a request for authorization of $366,278,000 for the next fiscal year. This first $110.2 million supplemental request is that portion of the total $366 million authorization that requires immediate appropriation. We would hope for prompt action on these proposals so that immediate steps can be taken and longer-term measures can be planned to better protect our diplomatic personnel and facilities abroad. In my FY–86 budget, we will forward to the Congress the next increment of a five-year program of security enhancements for our overseas missions. This program is now in the final stages of review.

The five-year program of improved protection is being prepared as part of the intense government-wide analysis I directed immediately after the terrorist attack against our Marines in Lebanon last October. When the final review is completed, this detailed action plan, reinforced by new legislation now pending in the Congress and separate measures being taken with our allies, will add considerably to our ability to counter this menace to all mankind. As the tragic events in Beirut have shown, we must do more to protect our citizens who serve our country overseas. This request continues our commitment to do just that

and complements actions already being implemented which are compatible with our longstanding policy:

—On July 23, 1983, I issued a public statement urging international cooperation against terrorism.

—In a message to the European Heads of State and Government on September 17, 1983, I made a similar direct appeal for their help in deterring terrorist attacks.

—In April 1984, the Administration submitted four bills to the Congress designed to strengthen our legal instruments for dealing with terrorists.

—In an effort to improve international cooperation in combatting terrorism, Western leaders at the London Economic Summit in June 1984 issued a seven point declaration on cooperative steps to be taken against terrorists.

—In April 1984, I also issued direction to:
• improve intelligence collection, analysis, and dissemination on terrorist groups and organizations;
• improve our response capabilities based on cogent analysis of what responses are most likely to deter future attacks; and
• better our security protection and awareness and take legal preventive action to thwart terrorist attacks before they occur.

The funds proposed in this request will help us move to implement this last step. Recent events underscore the urgency for proceeding rapidly with those measures which will improve security and protection.

International terrorism, by its very nature, is unpredictable and difficult to defend against—particularly when the attacker intends to give his life in the attempt to assassinate others. As long as rogue governments use the brutality of terrorism in attempts to achieve their ends, we must take measures such as these to reduce our vulnerability. No one can be certain that such attacks will not occur again in the future. We can be certain, however, that the enhancements made possible in the request for appropriations I have forwarded today and the authorization request, transmitted by the Secretary of State, will make such attacks much more difficult.

RONALD REAGAN

The White House,
September 27, 1984.

Executive Order 12488—Incentive Pay for Hazardous Duty
September 27, 1984

Amending Executive Order No. 11157 as it Relates to Incentive Pay for Hazardous Duty

By the authority vested in me as President of the United States of America by Public Law 98–94 and Section 301(a) of Title 37 of the United States Code, and in order to define the scope of one category of hazardous duty, it is hereby ordered as follows:

Section 1. Executive Order No. 11157 of June 22, 1964, as amended, is further amended by striking out subsection (g) of Section 109 of Part I and inserting in lieu thereof the following:

"(g) The term 'duty involving the servicing of aircraft or missiles with highly toxic fuels or propellants or the testing of aircraft or missile systems (or components of such systems) during which highly toxic fuels or propellants are used' shall be construed to mean duty performed by members as a primary duty that requires (1) removal, replacement, and servicing of the emergency power unit of an aircraft with H–70 propellant (30 percent water, 70 percent hydrazine); (2) participation by those personnel performing duties described in (g)(1) who must also participate in an emergency response force, spill containment, or spill cleanup involving H–70 propellant (30 percent water, 70 percent hydrazine); (3) handling and maintaining the liquid propellants (liquid oxidizer-nitrogen tetroxide; unsymmetrical dimethyl hydrazine) used in the Titan weapon system, if such duty requires qualification in the use of the Rocket Fuel Handler's Clothing Outfit and involves (A) launch duct operations, including flow, pressurization, on-load, set-up or tear down involving propellant transfer operations; (B) set-up, installation or tear down for fuel/oxidizer flow; (C) decontamination of equipment, including, but not limited to, the Rocket Fuel Handler's Clothing Outfit; (D) venting or pressurizing missile fuel or oxidizer tanks; (E) removing or replacing missile components while missile fuel and oxidizer tanks are loaded with such propellants; (F) transferring propellants between commercial and military holding trailers, or between holding trailers and fuel/oxidizer pump rooms; or normal preventive maintenance activities including, but not limited to, seal changes; (4) handling and maintaining the propellants, unsymmetrical dimethyl hydrazine and inhibited red-fuming nitric acid, used in the LANCE missile system; (5) handling, transporting or working with toxic fuels/propellants by members assigned to the Air Force Rocket Propulsion Lab (AFRPL) who (A) directly manage and inspect the activities of crew members conducting operations involving experimental rocket propulsion systems and components; (B) directly monitor and set up measurement instruments in operational areas where contamination is suspected or may be physically present; (C) install and remove instrumentation devices from propulsion systems and components; (D) perform final test preparation and immediate safety inspection duties around pressurized, active systems during prerun and postrun test periods; or, (E) install and repair electrical systems; (6) handling, loading/unloading and transporting toxic fuels and oxidizers at the precision sled track while working with the liquid rocket sled, which uses JP–X (a mixture of jet fuel (JP–4) and unsymmetrical dimethyl hydrazine) and red-fuming nitric acid and a propulsion; or (7) involvement with other toxic substances contained in missile or aircraft weapon system fuels or propellants as determined by the Secretary concerned. The entitlement to the pay provided for in this subsection is based upon the performance of such duty which has the potential for accidental or inadvertent exposure to highly toxic fuels or propellants or related substances and not upon actual quantifiable exposure to such substances. Therefore, neither this construction of the term nor the receipt of the pay provided

for in this subsection may be construed as indicating that any person entitled to such pay has been actually exposed to highly toxic fuels or propellants or related substances contrary to the provisions of any statute, Executive order, rule, or regulation relating to health or safety which is applicable to the uniformed services."

Sec. 2. This Executive Order shall be effective as of October 1, 1983.

RONALD REAGAN

The White House,
September 27, 1984.

[Filed with the Office of the Federal Register, 10:58 a.m., September 28, 1984]

Nomination of Two Members of the National Science Board
September 27, 1984

The President today announced his intention to nominate the following individuals to be members of the National Science Board, National Science Foundation, for terms expiring May 10, 1990.

Simon Ramo would succeed Eugene H. Cota-Robles. Mr. Ramo is currently director of TRW, Inc. He is married, has two children, and re-

sides in Redondo Beach, CA. He was born May 7, 1913, in Salt Lake City, UT.

Karen J. Lindstedt-Siva would succeed Charles Pence Slichter. She is currently an environmental scientist at Atlantic Richfield Corp. She is married and resides in Thousand Oaks, CA. She was born September 24, 1941, in Minneapolis, MN.

Appointment of Three Members of the National Advisory Council on Indian Education
September 28, 1984

The President today announced his intention to appoint the following individuals to be members of the National Advisory Council on Indian Education for terms expiring September 29, 1987. These are reappointments:

Fred Nicol, Jr., is currently an independent insurance life underwriter in Lander, WY. Additionally, since 1962 he has owned and operated a ranch. Mr. Nicol graduated from the University of Wyoming (B.A., 1970; M.Ed., 1973). He is married, has three children, and resides in Lander, WY. He was born October 4, 1945, in Riverton, WY.

Thomas E. Sawyer is currently vice president of WICAT Systems, Inc. He graduated from UCLA (B.S., 1959), Occidental College (M.A., 1969), and Florida State University (Ph.D., 1971). He is married, has four children, and resides in Orem, UT. He was born July 7, 1932, in Homer, LA.

Michael L. Stepetin is currently a committeeperson on the Urban Indian Council in Salem, OR. He attended the University of Oregon and Pacific Lutheran College. He is married, has five children, and resides in Portland, OR. He was born June 1, 1927, in Dutch Harbor, AK.

Statement on Signing the Longshore and Harbor Workers' Compensation Act Amendments of 1984
September 28, 1984

I have today signed S. 38, the Longshore and Harbor Workers' Compensation Act Amendments of 1984. The last amendments to this act in 1972 expanded worker coverage and provided relatively high benefits which resulted in excessive costs. Today's legislation addresses these issues and makes important reforms in workers compensation for injured workers, who contributed so much to our nation's vital maritime industry, and their families.

This legislation is the result of the hard work and cooperative spirit of employers, unions, and the insurance industry. It passed the Congress with strong bipartisan support and with the endorsement of this administration.

I want to congratulate all the parties to this consensus legislation. Their efforts strike a balance between continuing to provide fair and necessary benefits for injured workers and their families and, at the same time, giving employers, insurers, and the Labor Department the means to control program costs more effectively. The bill will accomplish this by clarifying the act's coverage to exempt certain categories of workers whose work activities are on land, putting reasonable limits on benefits and increasing the penalties for fraud and abuse.

Many Members of Congress joined in this bipartisan effort. I want to acknowledge, in particular, Senator Nickles, Representative Erlenborn, and Representative Miller of California who played significant roles in shaping this legislation, as did Senators Hatch, Kennedy, Nunn, Roth, and Rudman.

I would also like to take this opportunity to commend Congressman John Erlenborn who is retiring from the Congress this year after 20 years of outstanding and dedicated service. He has played a very significant role in shaping labor legislation during those 20 years, and it is fitting that he should be culminating his distinguished career in the Congress by playing a key role in the passage of this reform legislation.

Note: As enacted, S. 38 is Public Law 98–426, approved September 28.

Executive Order 12489—Continuance of Certain Federal Advisory Committees
September 28, 1984

By the authority vested in me as President of the United States of America, and in accordance with the provisions of the Federal Advisory Committee Act, as amended (5 U.S.C. App. I), it is hereby ordered as follows:

Section 1. Each advisory committee listed below is continued until September 30, 1985, unless terminated at a prior date by appropriate Executive order.

(a) Advisory Committee on Small and Mi-nority Business Ownership; Executive Order No. 12190 (Small Business Administration).

(b) Committee for the Preservation of the White House; Executive Order No. 11145, as amended (Department of the Interior).

(c) Federal Advisory Council on Occupational Safety and Health; Executive Order No. 12196 (Department of Labor).

(d) President's Commission on White

House Fellowships; Executive Order No. 11183, as amended (Office of Personnel Management).

(e) President's Committee on the Arts and the Humanities; Executive Order No. 12367 (National Endowment for the Arts).

(f) President's Committee on the International Labor Organization; Executive Order No. 12216 (Department of Labor).

(g) President's Committee on Mental Retardation; Executive Order No. 11776 (Department of Health and Human Services).

(h) President's Committee on the National Medal of Science; Executive Order No. 11287, as amended (National Science Foundation).

(i) President's Council on Physical Fitness and Sports; Executive Order No. 12345, as amended (Department of Health and Human Services).

(j) President's Economic Policy Advisory Board; Executive Order No. 12296 (Office of Policy Development).

(k) President's Export Council; Executive

Order No. 12131 (Department of Commerce).

Sec. 2. The following advisory committee is continued until December 31, 1984: International Private Enterprise Task Force; Executive Order No. 12395 (Agency for International Development).

Sec. 3. Notwithstanding the provisions of any other Executive order, the functions of the President under the Federal Advisory Committee Act that are applicable to the committees listed in Sections 1 and 2 of this Order, except that of reporting annually to the Congress, shall be performed by the head of the department or agency designated after each committee, in accordance with guidelines and procedures established by the Administrator of General Services.

RONALD REAGAN

The White House,
September 28, 1984.

[*Filed with the Office of the Federal Register, 11:19 a.m., October 1, 1984*]

Message to the Congress Transmitting a United States-Iceland Fishery Agreement
September 28, 1984

To the Congress of the United States:

In accordance with the Magnuson Fishery Conservation and Management Act of 1976 (Public Law 94–265; 16 U.S.C. 1801 *et seq.*), (the Act), I transmit herewith the text of a governing international fishery agreement between the United States and the Republic of Iceland, which was signed at Washington on September 21, 1984.

This agreement is one of a series negotiated in accordance with the Act. I hereby commend this agreement to the Congress and recommend early and favorable action to approve this agreement.

RONALD REAGAN

The White House,
September 28, 1984.

Statement by Principal Deputy Press Secretary Speakes on the Resumption of United States-Canada Negotiations on Pacific Salmon
September 28, 1984

The President is pleased to announce that negotiations with Canada on Pacific salmon

interception will resume in early December.

We have been urged to take this action by regional officials, including Governor Spellman of Washington and the U.S. congressional delegations of the States of Washington, Oregon, and Alaska.

It is our hope that an acceptable agreement would be reached quickly in view of the continuing conservation problems for Chinook salmon stocks.

Note: On September 26 the White House announced that the President had telephoned Gov. John Spellman to notify him of the resumption of negotiations.

Radio Address to the Nation on United States-Soviet Relations
September 29, 1984

My fellow Americans:

This has been a busy week of diplomatic activity for America. I've addressed the United Nations and the International Monetary Fund and World Bank meetings and met with a dozen world leaders. Among them were the new leader of our neighbor to the north, Canadian Prime Minister Brian Mulroney, and, as you know, Soviet Foreign Minister Gromyko.

To the delegates at the U.N., I emphasized America's dedication to world peace through confident and stronger alliances and a constructive dialog with our adversaries. I told them of the importance we attached to seeking peaceful solutions to regional conflicts plaguing many nations and the need for democratic principles and human freedom as the foundation for a more prosperous, peaceful world.

At the IMF and World Bank, I reported that an American economic renaissance is underway, leading the rest of the world from the darkness of recession toward brighter days of renewed hope and global prosperity.

World economic growth today is nearly twice what it was 4 years ago, and inflation in the industrial countries is half of what it was. The growing economic interdependence of our world is creating a riple effect of good news for those countries committed to sensible policies—policies which allow the magic of the marketplace to create opportunities for growth and progress, free from the dead weight of government interference and misguided protectionism.

But we can't build an enduring prosperity unless peace is secure. Our relations with the Soviet Union have been at the center of my attention, and yesterday I met with Foreign Minister Gromyko at the White House for a thorough exchange of views. I've said from the outset of my public life that a successful U.S. policy toward the Soviet Union must rest on realism, strength, and a willingness to negotiate.

Last January I spelled out clearly our goals for U.S.-Soviet relations: to reduce and eventually eliminate the threat and use of force in resolving disagreements; to reduce the vast stockpiles of armaments in the world, especially nuclear arms; and to establish a working relationship between our two countries marked by a greater understanding.

In our meeting yesterday, we covered all issues which separate us. And while I told Mr. Gromyko of our disappointment that his country walked out of the Geneva nuclear arms reduction talks last year, we remain ready to discuss the entire family of arms control issues as soon as they are. It's in both our interests that these talks commence promptly and that progress be made. Our two countries have no more solemn responsibility than to reduce the level of arms and to enhance understanding.

Mr. Gromyko and I also discussed major trouble spots in the world, and I told him that it's vital for us to exchange views and help find lasting solutions to these regional disputes. We didn't seek to gloss over the hard issues that divide our two countries. We were not looking to paper over these differences. Indeed, I made plain to Mr. Gromyko what it is about Soviet behavior that worries us and our allies.

But they were useful talks. I made it clear that we Americans have no hostile intentions toward his country and that we're not seeking military superiority over the U.S.S.R. I told him, "If your government wants peace, then there will be peace." And I said that the United States is committed to move forward with the Soviet Union toward genuine progress in resolving outstanding issues.

Pursuing peace, prosperity, and democracy are not new goals. They've been at the heart of an American foreign policy that down through the years has sought to promote individual freedom and human progress in the world.

I think one great change has taken place in the world over the last 4 years: The tide of freedom has begun to rise again. Four years ago, American influence and leadership were ebbing. Our defenses were neglected, our economy was collapsing, and other countries were being undermined by Communist-supported insurgencies. Today, our economy is vibrant, our strength is being restored, our alliances are solid, and peace is more secure.

Now the Soviets will return home to ponder our exchanges. And while they know they will not secure any advantages from inflexibility, they will get a fair deal if they seek the path of negotiation and peace.

Until next week, thanks for listening, and God bless you.

Note: The President spoke at 12:06 p.m. from Camp David, MD.

Remarks at Naturalization Ceremonies for New United States Citizens in Detroit, Michigan
October 1, 1984

Thank you all very much, and thank you very much, Judge Feikens. My fellow Americans—and I'm very proud to be the first to address you with those words—my fellow Americans, welcome to your country. Of all the things that a President does, nothing is as rewarding as events such as this. This is a ceremony of renewal. With you, today the American dream is reborn.

As you were saying the Pledge of Allegiance, it was clear to me, even from up here, that you weren't just reciting words that you'd memorized. You spoke with belief, and it was good to see, because the pledge not only contains the best definition of our country, it contains our greatest hope: to always remain "one nation under God, indivisible, with liberty and justice for all."

Today you've joined a people who are among the freest on the face of the Earth. We're a nation greatly blessed. We were founded by men and women who wanted it said of our country: Here the people rule. They created a philosophy of freedom that is expressed in the document by which our country was established, the preamble of which was read to you, the Constitution.

Now, I know that most Americans are immigrants from other countries, and most of those countries have constitutions. I haven't read all the constitutions of all the nations of the world, but of all that I have read, I've noticed a difference that is so subtle it almost escapes you, and yet it is so tremendous it describes the difference. Those other constitutions give the people, or grant the people, in most instances, many of the same rights that our Constitution says are yours. But those constitutions say that government grants you those rights. Our Constitution says we, the people, have those rights by grace of God by our birth, and we, the people, will grant to the government the following rights.

Our government—now your government—has no power or rights that we, the people, have not freely given to it. Now, this may seem a small distinction, but as I said, it is everything.

You've joined a country that has been called "The least exclusive club in the world—with the highest dues." America was founded by men and women who understood that freedom doesn't come free. It has a cost. But I don't suppose anyone would know the cost of freedom, the price of freedom better than you who have taken this oath today.

Some of you came from places that, sadly, have not known freedom and liberty. Some of you have come from places that don't offer opportunity. Some of you are probably here because you are, by nature, adventurous. And some of you have no doubt come here for a new start, to wipe the slate clean and begin your life anew.

These strike me as all good reasons. In fact, they're the very same reasons that our forefathers came here. And they did pretty well—so well, in fact, that two centuries after they invented this country it is still what they intended it to be: A place where the oppressed, the lost, the adventurous, can come for sanctuary and comfort and chance.

It's long been my belief that America is a chosen place, a rich and fertile continent placed by some Divine Providence here between the two great oceans, and only those who really wanted to get here would get here. Only those who most yearned for freedom would make the terrible trek that it took to get here. America has drawn the stoutest hearts from every corner of the world, from every nation of the world. And that was lucky for America, because if it was going to endure and grow and protect its freedoms for 200 years, it was going to need stout hearts.

Fifty million immigrants came to this country in the last 200 years. Some of the most recent have crawled over walls and under barbed wire and through mine fields, and some of them risked their lives in makeshift boats.

And I know that all of them felt as the immigrants of the early part of this century felt. So many of them steamed into New York, and as they would see the approaching skyline and the Statute of Liberty, they'd crowd to the side of the boat and say, "America! America!" And in that word they heard the sound of a New World. In that word they heard everything.

And all of them have added to the sum total of what your new country is. They gave us their traditions. They gave us their words. They enlivened the national life with new ideas and new blood. And I urge you—you probably don't need to be urged, but I'll urge you anyway, just for fun—urge you to remember, as they did, the land of your birth. Bring to us its culture and its heritage. We don't reject them. We need them. They enrich us.

You know, man can take unto himself a wife. A wife can take unto herself a husband. That doesn't mean that they abandon their mothers and fathers and forget them. So, you know, every now and then academics talk about assimilation and how our various ethnic groups have, with time, dropped their ethnicity and become more "American." Well, I don't know about that. It seems to me that America is constantly reinventing what "America" means. We adopt this country's phrases and that country's art, and I think it's really closer to the truth to say that America has assimilated as much as her immigrants have. It's made for a delightful diversity, and it's made us a stronger and a more vital nation.

But our diversity is not only ethnic. You'll find, if you haven't already, that this country is full of different and, sometimes, conflicting ideas and philosophies. Walk by a newspaper stand, and you'll see scores of magazines and newspapers arguing this point and that. Listen to television and radio, and you'll hear more than enough opinions with which to agree and disagree. In fact, if you don't over the next several years find one time, at least, when you feel like taking off your shoe and throwing it at a television screen, then you will have missed out on one of the great American moments. [*Laughter*]

Arguing is something of a tradition here. We like to disagree. But it's usually pretty good-natured arguing, and it doesn't tear us apart. I think you'll find that for all our disagreeing, Americans remain united around certain shared ideas and shared dreams—which takes me back to where I began. All of us want "one nation under God . . . with liberty and justice for all."

Most of the disagreeing just has to do with the best ways to secure liberty and justice and the best ways to protect them.

And so, today you join a happy country that is happier for your presence. You're adding your voices to the chorus, and in doing that you've become part of a great unending song.

And I want, as President, to thank you for something before I leave. There have been times in our recent history when some of our citizens have doubted if America is still all she was meant to be. They've wondered if our nation still has meaning. And then we see you today, and it's an affirmation. You, standing here, reveal we all must still stand for something. I know that the eldest among you is 92, and the youngest among you is 2. And we thank you all for the compliment of your new citizenship.

Thank you all, and God bless you.

Note: The President spoke at 11:27 a.m. in Hall B at Cobo Hall. Prior to the President's remarks, Federal District Judge John Feikens conducted the swearing-in ceremony for 1,548 new citizens.

Remarks and a Question-and-Answer Session at the Economic Club of Detroit in Detroit, Michigan
October 1, 1984

The President. Thank you very much, and thank you, Max, for taking me back to that other life of mine. I'd never heard that story before. I'm delighted to be with all of you distinguished ladies and gentlemen this afternoon, and I'm pleased to be back in the home of your winners, those great Detroit Tigers. You know, I can't help but feel a little kinship with Sparky Anderson: We both took over struggling teams, but now the future's looking bright again. [*Laughter*]

But it was here in Detroit that we embarked on a new beginning for America 4 years ago, and I'd like to speak with you today about what I consider the most important issue in the 1984 campaign—America's choice for the future.

This election offers the clearest choice in 50 years on the direction our country should take—a choice of whether we go forward together with the courage, common sense, and new spirit making America strong again, or whether we turn back to those policies that weakened our economy, reduced opportunities, and reversed America's tradition of progress.

I believe America works best when we trust our people—all our people. When we trust their vision, faith, judgment, and courage, when we give them opportunities to climb higher and reach for the stars, a million dreams can become the golden dream of America.

But we know that in the recent past, our government had stopped placing trust in the people, and too many dreams were allowed to die. Higher taxes, more government spending, and greater government intrusion—the same approach advocated today by my opponent—had dramatically changed the landscape of America.

We saw a once proud nation staggered by steady erosion of economic growth, punishing inflation and interest rates, a record peacetime tax burden, rising unemployment, and weakened defenses. We saw policies with devastating results—families encouraged to break up, bedrock values of work and strength of neighborhoods undermined, crime going up, our children's achievement in school going down. In retrospect, there was only one thing fair about those policies: They didn't discriminate; they made everybody miserable.

In short, America wasn't working very well. Now, I know the last administration didn't want these things to happen. I don't question my opponent's good intentions. He sincerely believes his philosophy of bigger government is in the best interest of America. Well, I would simply suggest that all of us remember, given the track record, that there is a well-known road paved with good intentions, but no one wants to go where it leads.

You know, I was once asked how I hoped, personally, to be remembered for my time as custodian of this office. I was appearing just a week or so ago before a college group when that question was asked by one of the students. Well, knowing that I believe that Americans do better by themselves, I said that with the courage of—millions of Americans are coming to grips with the problems that had built up for more than a decade—I said I would hope that I would be remembered as having given the government of this country back to the people.

Together we've made a new beginning, restoring America's economic and military strength, her sense of community and fidelity to shared values, and her spirit of national unity. We recognize that much remains to be done to help the people that were hurt most by past mistakes. But we believe our policies now in effect, with the initiatives we're supporting for the future, will continue to improve life and opportunity for all Americans. And with your support, we're going to get that job done and get it done right.

In 1980 history gave us a great challenge: to rescue a nation in crisis and to save America's future. We met that challenge. In 1984 America is being challenged again, this time to shape our future. We must make this nation so strong, so united that when today's young Americans become tomorrow's leaders, they will inherit an America that can remain the great shining light for progress and peace for generations to come.

And that's why I'm urging all of us in 1984 to join together. Let us go forward and build an American opportunity society, a society that ensures that every individual will have his or her chance to climb higher, to climb up to the ultimate in individual freedom, consistent with an orderly society, to achieve the fullness of creative human potential.

There's a true and tested path to a bright and hopeful future; but it's not the path of good intentions by bigger government. It's the path of greater responsibility in government and greater opportunity for every

man, woman, and child. And that's the America we've been working for, and that's the America we mean to keep working for.

Common sense and opportunity are essential to successful policies for economic growth. And economic growth is essential to a just and fair society.

Federal spending growth, which reached a 17-percent annual rate in 1980, contributed to back-to-back years of double-digit inflation and a 21½-percent prime interest rate, the highest since the Civil War.

Retirement savings were devastated. A family with the average amount of life insurance in 1976, $30,000, saw its value shrink to $20,725 in 1980. In 1979 and '80, working Americans' weekly earnings declined in real terms by 8.8 percent, the worst drop since World War II. Young families couldn't save to send their children to college; tuition costs has soared 41 percent in just 4 years. Soaring mortgage rates meant 10 million families could no longer afford to buy homes. The rates on car loans jumped from 10.9 percent in 1977 to 16½ percent in 1981. Grocery bills increased by 50 percent, and the price of a gallon of gas more than doubled.

The needy were hit hardest of all. A family on a fixed income of $8,000 in 1979 was about $600 above the poverty line, but in 1980 it was almost $400 below it, as double-digit inflation eroded purchasing power and pushed the poverty line up. Inflation reduced the real value of government benefits and especially hurt the poor who were forced to spend a larger share of their income on necessities. In the last administration, per person Aid to Families with Dependent Children fell 10 percent. The value of the maximum allotment of food stamps fell by almost 6 percent.

Now, these policies didn't just create unfair hardship, they were the very essence of unfairness. Despite the great torrents of rhetoric about compassion, the only people who benefited from those high inflation and interest rate policies were people wealthy enough to invest in expensive inflation hedges. Working Americans and the needy were left out in the cold.

Inflation and high interest rates are not caused by people living too well; inflation and high interest rates are caused by government living too well. So, we took action to bring runaway government spending under control. We cut its rate of growth by more than half. Experts warned it would take 10 years to bring inflation down to the level of the 1960's. Well, we did it in 2 years. And today the third-quarter gross national product deflater is estimated at 2.9 percent, and inflation stands at only 4.2 percent. Not only are we determined to keep inflation down, we'll not be satisfied until inflation is 0.0. Interest rates have fallen by more than one-third. That's still not enough, but the prime recently dropped, and I think we'll see more of that ahead.

What has this progress meant for Americans, especially families of average means? Well, in contrast to that 8.8 percent decline I just mentioned in real weekly earnings, in the last 2 years they have risen 3.2 percent. In December 1980 the weekly food bill for a family of four was $86.90. If inflation had continued at its double-digit rate, that family's food bill would be $127.57. But inflation, down dramatically, has kept that family's food bills down to $98.50, roughly one-fourth the rise that continued double-digit inflation would have meant.

While the value of the maximum allotment of food stamps fell by almost 6 percent in the last administration, the value of that same allotment has gone up by almost 8 percent during our administration.

We decontrolled the price of oil, and our critics claimed the cost of gas at the pump would skyrocket. Well, the price is down about 8 cents from where it was 3 years ago when we decontrolled.

The decline in interest rates, while not yet enough, has reduced the average cost of home mortgages by $143.00 a month, put home ownership within the reach of 5 million more Americans than before, and made car purchases more affordable, too.

Too many families are still not where they need to be, but our progress has made them more financially secure, they have more opportunities, and I happen to believe this is what fairness is all about.

In 1980 the misery index—you'll remember that; it was coined in that campaign to be used against Jerry Ford. It was the com-

bination, adding inflation rate and unemployment rate. Well, it was 12½ when they used it against Jerry Ford. They didn't mention it in 1980, because it was 20.5 by then. Today the misery index is down to 11.7.

We've made progess, but we can make more progress bringing inflation and interest rates down, if the United States Congress would make more progress bringing Federal spending down. [*Applause*] And some of the Congressmen here at the head table are applauding that, also, because they've been trying all they can.

I'm asking for your strongest support for two long-overdue reforms supported by the American people, but resisted by the Democratic leadership—a constitutional amendment mandating that government stop spending more than government takes in and a line-item veto giving a President authority to veto individual items on appropriation bills.

Now, just remember, you don't need to make them see the light, you just have to make them feel the heat. [*Laughter*] Forty-three State Governors have this authority, and when I was Governor of California I used the line-item veto more than 900 times. But legislation for a line-item veto is tied up in the Congress. Tell the Congress to give democracy a chance, and I promise you we'll get rid of the pork-barrel spending that slips through every year. Incidentally, none of those more than 900 vetoes in California were overridden.

Democrats in the House killed the balanced budget amendment in 1982, and their leadership still resists allowing a vote on that amendment. Now, I recognize that idea wouldn't be a cure-all; it wouldn't even go into effect right away. But I believe it would force the leadership of the Congress to work with the President on long-term budgets of real discipline—one that would not penalize those dependent on government for help—and it's high time that this be done.

If we'd received all the cuts that we've sent to Congress over the past 5 years, the deficit would be $40 billion less than it is right now. Having inherited the legacy of 42 unbalanced budgets in the last 50 years, I can tell you one thing with absolute certainty: We do not have a deficit problem in this country because the American people are not taxed enough. We have a deficit problem because the Federal Government has spent too much and taxed too much far too long.

Getting spending under control for good will keep the deficit on its downward path, help bring inflation and interest rates down more, provide greater security for all our people, and give investors and businesses the confidence they need to make long-term investments for our future.

But the other side of that equation is pursuing incentive policies for growth. And to meet our challenge—to build an American opportunity society—we must have tax policies that spur America to challenge the very limits of growth.

Now, I believe that the tax policies in place before we got to Washington were antigrowth, antipeople. Government always, under the guise of compassion, had penalized Americans with record taxes that reduced rewards for hard work, thrift, and risk-taking. They wanted us to substitute limits for the American dream, and for once they managed to do what they wanted.

Economic growth fell from 5.4 percent in 1976 to a minus three-tenths of 1 percent in 1980. Savings fell as inflation raised marginal tax rates so high it didn't pay to save. By 1979 and 1980, investment was declining, inflation had driven up the replacement cost of business equipment, but the tax laws mandated such slow writeoffs for the purchase of new equipment that many businesses were using up capital every year rather than replacing it. Little wonder that workers' productivity fell in '79 and '80— the first back-to-back years of decline in postwar history—and that housing, steel, autos, and our basic industries were in a slump.

In 1980 auto industry unemployment was over 20 percent, five times higher than in 1977. Between 1978 and 1980, steel workers' unemployment more than doubled; machine workers' unemployment nearly doubled. And between 1979 and 1980, unemployment among electrical equipment workers rose 57 percent and for construction workers, it rose 37 percent.

America was sinking, losing our can-do spirit and our stature as world economic leader. So, we began with a commonsense principle: Government must remove the burden of excessive taxes and restore opportunity to people.

We designed a program to take America in a new direction. And then we fought for and won: a 25-percent tax rate reduction for everyone who works and earns; tax indexing to keep government from using inflation to profit at your expense; a new capital cost recovery system, shortening depreciation schedules to encourage modernization of plants and equipment; estate tax reductions for family farms and small businesses; a reduction in the marriage tax penalty; an increase in the child care tax credit; deregulation of banking, allowing a higher rate of return for small savers; and new incentives for IRA's and Keogh contributions—the best collection of incentives for progress since the administration of John F. Kennedy. But even with this entire program in place, taxes average about 19 percent of gross national product. That is still marginally above historic levels.

As I said, the American people are not undertaxed. Over 90 million Americans will file personal income tax returns this year at rates about 25-percent lower than 4 years ago. A family with a 1984 income of $15,000 is paying $281 less in taxes than if our rate cuts hadn't passed. A family earning $30,000 is paying $914 less. And wealthy Americans are paying a higher share of the total tax burden than they were 4 years ago.

Our critics complained our tax cuts were unfair. This was after they fought the idea of any tax cut when we made it a major issue in the 1980 campaign. They also tried to do away with the third year of the tax cut and do away with indexing, which doesn't help those in the top tax brackets at all, but does help working families trying to keep from being pushed into those high brackets. Some people have labored so long at making government bigger, they've developed a knee-jerk addiction to tax increases. And every time their knee jerks, we get kicked. [*Laughter*]

Now, I majored in economics, but I never appreciated, until the great hue and cry over our program, how true it is that economics is the dismal science. When the shaky economy really started to falter in July of 1981, many blamed it on our program. Well, the trouble is our program hadn't even been adopted yet. We were still operating on the same budget we inherited. Our tax cuts and budget savings were not passed until August of 1981. The first tax cut didn't become effective until October of 1981, so that made it only one and a quarter percent for the year, and the full tax cut didn't go into effect until 1983.

Nevertheless, a sizable body of politicians and economists were ready to pronounce judgment on our program early on—in one case, very early on.

In August of 1980, before I was even elected, my current opponent said of our plan to reduce income tax rates across the board that: "It's . . . based on a 2-cent theory. Every leading economist rejects it . . . and for good reason . . . it is obviously, murderously inflationary." That's right, he said it was inflationary. I would have thought he should've known better how to recognize policies that are inflationary. [*Laughter*]

Lester Thurow, an economist often seen and quoted, said in October of 1982 just before recovery began that: "The engines of economic growth have shut down here and across the globe, and they are likely to stay that way for years to come . . ." That's right, he said years.

John Kenneth Galbraith, also in October of 1982 said, "We have . . . an unprecedented experiment in economic policy. It has failed." That's right, he said it failed.

And permit me to quote my opponent one more time. In December of 1982 he said, ". . . at most, I can only see a modest or anemic recovery coming as a result of the recent declines in interest rates and some pickup in consumer buying." And that's right, he said anemic. Well, again, I would have thought he should have known better how to recognize anemia.

What actually happened? From strength in autos and construction and renewed leadership in high technology, from a rebirth in productivity and surging investment to the creation of 6 million new jobs, America is in the midst of the best econom-

ic expansion in over 30 years. And, my friends, you ain't seen nothin' yet.

Now, also, 1 year ago we put into place a real job training program that substitutes the make-work policies of the past with training for real jobs in the marketplace. Over 700,000 people have been served by the Job Training Partnership Act, with a job placement rate in excess of 70 percent. Next year we'll do better; we'll serve a million people.

What we're seeing all across America, but what too many old guard economists still won't acknowledge, is the power of incentives beginning to create an American renaissance before our very eyes.

Commitments to the venture capital industry increased sixfold from 1980 to 1983. Business investment has risen almost 26 percent during this recovery, faster than any postwar recovery and more than double the rate of any recovery since 1958. The U.S. Patent Office records indicate that there have been, on average, about 6,000 more patent applications filed each year of this administration than during each year of the previous administration. New business incorporations set a record last year and will probably do so again this year. And private research is growing strongly, with the computer industry's 20-percent annual increase in research and development expenditures for 1983 to '85 leading the way.

Just as many failed to foresee when I was growing up how dramatically the invention of radio would transform our economy, so are many today ignoring how technological breakthroughs in computers, robotics, biotechnology, and information processing will revolutionize our economy with new jobs, products, and progress in the future. Our economy is no longer, as some believe, an old and quivering thing in the industrial age; it's being transformed into a strapping young adolescent, flexing its muscles in the increasingly advanced technological age.

Our secret weapon is the power of productivity. We've seen efforts to expand productivity pay off right here in Detroit for your automobile industry. New leadership by management, with aggressive, wise investments in new technology, together with strong, spirited cooperation by labor, have enabled Chrysler to expand productivity from 10.2 vehicles per employee per year in 1980, to nearly 20 vehicles per employee this year.

Other currents of progress are gathering momentum and will make our economy and society stronger and more successful. Three years ago, we established a National Commission on Excellence in Education, then went forth to lead a grassroots crusade to restore in our schools needed discipline, new emphasis on basics, merit pay for teachers, greater parental involvement, and standards of excellence that again sought the best for America.

Schools and communities all across America responded, and we're beginning to see the results. After 20 years of steady decline, scholastic aptitude test scores have risen 2 of the last 3 years, and this year's jump is the biggest in 21 years. And that's just a start. Young Americans are trying harder, they're doing better, and they can and will do better still. Their improvement should give us confidence that our work force will continue to grow more productive and more competitive in a fast-changing world.

And something else is invigorating America, giving us new hope for our future. Those guiding values of mind and heart and spirit—our faith, our love for family and neighborhood, our belief in peace through strength, and our commitment to protect the freedom which is our legacy as Americans—all have gained a new sense of worth in our lives, all are infusing America with the bounce of confidence and optimism that many thought we'd lost.

This new spirit is not only rewarding in its own right; it, too, helps our economy, helps our productivity, when men and women from labor and management come together in the workplace with renewed confidence in what they can do by pulling together as a team. In 1980, with Washington in charge, all they ever did was fumble. Well, in 1984 the people are back in charge, and America is scoring touchdowns again. And I think the world is about to learn that once we Americans put our minds to it and are provided the proper tools and equipment, we can outproduce, outsell, and outcompete anybody, anywhere in the world.

Now, all of us know our work is not yet done. We must help all those in agriculture and in the industries not back on their feet to participate fully in the expansion. And I pledge to you that I won't rest until every American who wants a job can find a job.

But my message to this nation is: We can meet this challenge together, and we will, because all of us are creating something new and very much better than before. Not only are Americans working again, America is working again.

We see what progress opportunity is bringing, and so we know that for our future nothing less than an American opportunity society will do. But we won't create those opportunities until we simplify our tax system to bring yours and everybody's income tax rates further down, not up; extend the full benefits of IRA's to spouses working in the home, as well as those working outside the home; pass enterprise zones legislation to restore distressed areas such as you have here in Detroit; couple enterprise zones with a youth opportunity wage to help teenagers learn skills and escape dependency and get on the economic ladder; go forward with initiatives to help public housing residents purchase their dwellings and take on the responsibility of home ownership; make America's educational system a great center of leadership for excellence; and summon all our skills and determination to push back the frontiers in space, technology, and science.

Everything that we've done, everything we mean to do, is to give the American people opportunities to make this great, free nation, greater and freer still. And that's why the choice in 1984 is so clear, because my opponent's policies would take us off the path toward an opportunity society and put us back on the path toward defeatism, decline, and despair.

My opponent, who opposed our tax program, said it would be murderously inflationary—before inflation went down; said there would be no recovery—before recovery began; and then said recovery would be only anemic—before the strongest economic expansion in 30 years; and now says there's no denying that the deficit must be reduced with tax increases. Well, forgive me, but judging from the record of those who are philosophically or constitutionally opposed to what we're doing, we might be better off if we consulted astrologers about what the deficit will be in 1989.

But there are two things we do know that are not a matter of prediction: First, my opponent is committed to large spending increases and a tax increase equivalent to $1,800 per household, and, second, those policies, which he has supported all his political life, gave America an economic hangover that we must never, ever suffer through again.

The differences and the choice for the future can be summed up this way: He put his faith in more power for the Government; we place ours in more opportunity for the people. He sees America wringing her hands; we see America using her hands. We see America—or he sees America divided by envy, each of us challenging our neighbor's success; we see an America inspired and uniting for opportunity, all of us challenging the best in ourselves. We believe in knowing when opportunity knocks, and he goes out of his way to knock opportunity.

I believe that we've all worked too hard, come too far to go back to those unhappy days of Washington controlling our destiny. But if we believe in ourselves, stick together, set our sights high for growth and, like our Olympic athletes, go for the gold, then nothing can hold us back. America will be a rocket of hope shooting to the stars.

Thank you for welcoming me back to Detroit, for giving me this chance to speak with you. And thank you for what you're doing to make America the source of all the dreams and opportunities she was placed on this good Earth to provide. God bless you all.

Mr. Johnson.[1] Thank you, Mr. President.

The President. Thank you.

Mr. Johnson. Now comes the hard part. We'll start the question-and-answer period with questions submitted from the audience. Mr. Fisher will be our moderator. Mr. Fisher?

---

[1] *Wesley R. Johnson, president of the Economic Club of Detroit.*

Mr. Fisher. Mr. President, the first question, of course, would be about the automobile industry, being in Detroit. The question is, 4 years ago when you successfully ran for the Presidency you said you wanted to help the auto industry. During an interview last month, you suggested the auto unions should show wage restraint and to aim at higher industry productivity. It appears the UAW and General Motors have achieved that goal. Now, what happens to the remainder of that equation, extension of voluntary restraints on Japanese autos until the yen-dollar misalignment and other problems with Japan are resolved?

The President. Now, the last part there—on the restraints?

Mr. Fisher. Yes, on voluntary restraints.

The President. Ah, I missed the last couple of words there.

Well, I think for one thing, and some figures—I know I threw a lot of statistics at you in there, but I think also when the auto industry's unemployment was up where I said it was, today it's down to 6.4 percent. And, yes, I guess I made a general statement when I knew the negotiations were going to begin. But with our fight against inflation, I just hope that everybody in the marketplace will keep inflation in mind and observe some restraint to make sure that we don't turn that tiger loose again.

Now, with regard to the voluntary restraints, they were put on by the Japanese industry itself and, believe me, totally voluntarily. Their Minister Abe had come here, and we met in the Oval Office and talked, and I told him our situation as frankly as I could, and what we were up against, and he went back, and very shortly they announced their willingness to have a voluntary restraint on imports. We never at any time asked for that. And we've since made great progress with Prime Minister Nakasone, who I believe is sincerely dedicated. He's got some political problems, I can understand that—[*laughter*]—with his legislature, and he is working hard.

We just had meetings recently in which we have probably increased the beef exports to Japan more than double over the next 4 years. And they again, without any urging from us, they modified somewhat, but held their voluntary restraint. And I'm hoping that they will continue. But I don't happen to believe in protectionism. There are times when necessarily, to let some industry that has been overwhelmed by some happening, let it get back on its feet, but for the most part I believe in free and fair trade because protectionism is a two-way street.

And again, I believe with what our industry is—the automobile industry is doing, and the product they have—I think parents out there ought to argue with their young people when their first car time comes along and they start looking at foreign brands, because I think we're making better than anybody's making.

Mr. Fisher. Thank you. Mr. President, what was it like to meet Mr. Gromyko? Were your talks constructive? Do you think you could become friends?

The President. I'm having an echo or something up here that gives me trouble, Max. I'm having awful trouble with this writing, too. [*Laughter*] Oh, what was it like to meet Mr. Gromyko, were my talks constructive, and do I think we could become friends?

I don't know whether we could become friends, or whether that's important, but I think the talk was very constructive. And all of us in Washington are very encouraged by the outcome of those talks. And we made it very plain: We don't like their system; they don't like ours. We're not out to change their system, and they better not try to change ours. But we are the two superpowers, and between us we could, if we got careless, we could destroy the world.

But by the same token, if we decide to stand together on some issues that should be of interest to both of us, namely, reduc-

tion and hopefully elimination of nuclear weapons, we can save the world. And I think that they've gone home with a recognition that we're looking at them realistically but, at the same time, we are ready to join with them in approaching this principal problem of runaway armaments in the world.

Mr. Fisher. I'm going to give you the last one personally.

The President. Up here I hear better.

Mr. Fisher. Yes. Who are you rooting for in the World Series? [*Laughter*]

The President. That's an unfair question. [*Laughter*] I'm supposed to be President of all the people. [*Laughter*]

I know why he's asking that. You see, years ago I was a sports announcer, and I was broadcasting, mainly, the Chicago Cubs games. And I was broadcasting them in 1935 when the Chicago Cubs set a record that still stands in all of baseball. The only mathematical chance they had to win the pennant was to win the last 21 games of the season, and they did it. But you can imagine that that buildup all that way, that there just had to be a psychological letdown after they had done that, and so Detroit beat them four games straight. [*Laughter*]

Well, thank you all very much for all of that, and I'm sorry—I think I talked too long. I was wanting to do more questions, but I guess we've run out of time. Thank you all very much.

Note: The President spoke at 12:45 p.m. in Hall C at Cobo Hall. He was introduced by Max Fisher, a member of the board of directors of the Economic Club of Detroit.

Following his remarks, the President attended a reception for members of the board of directors of the club.

Message to the Congress Reporting Budget Deferrals
October 1, 1984

To the Congress of the United States:

In accordance with the Impoundment Control Act of 1974, I herewith report two new deferrals of budget authority for 1984

totaling $299,000,000, and fourteen new deferrals of budget authority totaling $1,298,662,275 and one new deferral of outlays totaling $19,900,000 for 1985. The 1984 deferrals affect the Funds Appropriated to the President. The 1985 deferrals affect the Funds Appropriated to the President; the Departments of Agriculture, Defense, Health and Human Services, Interior, Transportation, and Treasury; the Pennsylvania Avenue Development Corporation, and the Railroad Retirement Board.

The details of these deferrals are contained in the attached report.

RONALD REAGAN

The White House,
October 1, 1984.

Note: The attachment detailing the deferrals is printed in the Federal Register of October 5.

Informal Exchange With Students From Bayou View Elementary School in Gulfport, Mississippi
October 1, 1984

The President. I am very proud that you'd come out this way, and, see, I think you even kind of came back early, didn't you, to be here? Well, and all those signs. Thank you very much. Tell me, I know I've only got a few seconds here, but sometimes some of the others, some of you must have said to yourself, "Boy, if I could ask him, I'd sure ask him." Would you like to throw a question at me, somebody?

Yes.

Q. [*Inaudible*]

The President. Do I support Federal aid for foreign countries? Yes, I think this is traditional with America. We've always tried to help our friends out and help developing countries. But I tell you, from the old days of just throwing money out there and not knowing where it went, we're trying to do it in a way now that will enable them to become self-sustaining and build their economy. And the biggest help we're being is buying from them the things that they have to sell that they make there.

Yeah. You.

Q. Are you going to put nuclear wastes——

The President. Am I going to what?

Q. Put nuclear wastes—[*inaudible*]?

The President. Am I going to put nuclear wastes in Mississippi? Well, our director of energy has said that we just were not going to do anything against the State's will, and having been a Governor myself of a State, I'm a great believer in States rights.

Q. Do you think you're better than Mondale?

The President. Do I think I what?

Q. Do you think you're better then Mondale?

The President. Do I think I'm better than Mondale? No, I don't think in this country anyone thinks that you're better than anyone else. I just think that I should keep on being President for 4 more years.

Here, you. You're going to have to come a little closer.

Q. Can you beat Mondale?

The President. Can I beat Mondale? Wait a minute until I turn to where the people of voting age are. [*Applause*] I think so. They just told me I can.

Well, thank you all again very much. I'm sorry to have to be so short. What was your question?

Q. [*Inaudible*]

The President. Oh, here's a question I have to answer. And I know the people behind me, after the signal they just gave, will be very happy. The young lady wants to know, am I going to raise taxes? No.

All right, thank you all very much. God bless you all. They tell me I have to get in the car and go.

Note: The President spoke at 4 p.m. to students who gathered at a point on the route of his motorcade from the Gulfport-Biloxi Regional Airport to the Broadwater Beach Hotel in Biloxi, MS.

Following the exchange, the President went to the hotel, where he remained overnight.

Remarks at a Reagan-Bush Rally in Gulfport, Mississippi
October 1, 1984

The President. Thank you very much, and thank you, Trent, for that introduction. I was having so much fun listening, I kind of hated to get up here. [*Laughter*] Thank all of you for a most heartwarming welcome.

It's great to be in Gulfport, and greetings to all of you who come from the delta, the home of the outstanding Congressman Webb Franklin. Webb can't be with us here tonight, because he's up there with my friend Billy Mounger, having a fundraiser up in Jackson—carry on so he can be back there again in the Congress.

And of course it's always a great pleasure to be here with Trent Lott, who, as minority whip in the House of Representatives, has worked with skill and devotion. And I know it's a great uphill battle and a very difficult one, but just as he remarked about a certain Speaker of the House of Representatives, wouldn't it be wonderful to be calling Trent Lott the majority whip? [*Applause*]

And we have with us here a candidate for the Congress who could add to our ranks up there, David Armstrong. Send him there. We need him.

Now, we couldn't have accomplished half of what we did without a Republican majority in the Senate, and Thad Cochran is in the first rank of that majority, and that's why he's there. He and some other stalwarts are battling against those who are still out for the old-fashioned idea of spending your money faster than you can send it in.

But it's great to be back in the South. You know, I'm always happy when I visit this part of the country, maybe because you make me feel so much at home. You in the South have always given our country more than its share of greatness and courage. Here are the traditions and values that shaped our land. Here is steadiness of purpose, fidelity to ideals, love of country. Our opponents may be ready to ignore this region, but Vice President Bush and I happen to consider that the South is worth respecting, worth listening to, and, yes, worth fighting for.

We've come here for one reason, and one reason only: to win. And we ain't just whistlin' Dixie.

The choice between us and our opponents is the cleanest [clearest] [1] our country has faced in more than 50 years. According to them, America's future is grim and getting grimmer. They say our people are despairing, that we have nothing to hope for but fear itself. Well, America has fallen on hard times, they claim, and they place the blame squarely on our administration. You know, sometimes I get the feeling that they don't like me very much. [*Laughter*]

But our opponents' rhetoric of gloom and doom is nothing but a nightmare. It's time for them to wake up and look at the facts.

Four years ago, the economy of the South and of all America was in a shambles. In just 5 years, taxes had nearly doubled. The average monthly mortgage payments more than doubled. And the real after-tax income of the average American actually began to decline. From 1979 through 1980, just 2 years, working Americans' weekly earnings declined in real terms by 8.8 percent. That was the worst drop since World War II.

Our defenses had grown so weak that many of our planes were too old to fly. And those that weren't too old couldn't fly for lack of spare parts or lack of pilots. Many of our ships couldn't leave port.

Today, just 4 years later, the United States of America is a very different place. It's stronger, more prosperous, and bursting with patriotism. Well, now, if, as our opponents insist, I have to take the blame, well, all right, if you'll share it with me. [*Applause*] This isn't a Reagan recovery, this is an American recovery.

---

[1] *White House correction.*

This great nation is moving forward again, and we're not going back to that unhappy past. We've knocked inflation down from 12.4 percent to 4.2. Productivity is up, consumer spending is up, and take-home pay is up. In contrast to that 8.8 percent decline in real weekly earnings that I mentioned, in the last 2 years they've risen 3.2 percent. You tell me whose policies are more fair to the working people of America. During the past 20 months, we've created 6 million new jobs. We've been creating more jobs every month than our allies in Europe have created over the last 10 years.

Your great success story has come as quite a shock to the professors and the economists. Back in October of 1982, one economist often seen and quoted claimed that "The engines of economic growth have shut down here and across the globe, and they're likely to stay that way for years to come."

That was just 2 months before the start of the best recovery in postwar history. That's why when I hear some of the projections they make for what it's going to be like in 1989, they're blowing smoke. They don't know what it's going to be like in 1989. It all adds up to a simple lesson: Don't trust the professional pessimists. [*Laughter*] Trust the American people.

My friends, I believe our great nation has turned the corner. The shadows are behind us, and the bright sunshine of hope and opportunity lies ahead. But I wouldn't want to take that for granted, so let me just ask you: Do you feel better off than you did 4 years ago?

Audience. Yes!

The President. Is America better off than it was 4 years ago?

Audience. Yes!

The President. Well, now, despite this strength of this expansion, there's one sure way to ruin it. You'd have to be something of an expert to do that, but when it comes to bringing economic growth to a grinding halt, our opponents are experts. After decades of a rising tax burden, they want to give the American people a massive new tax increase. They call it——

Audience. Boo-o-o!

The President. They call it bitter medi-

cine, but that's just because they think they can get us to swallow anything. [*Laughter*] I think the word shrimp means something different to our opponents than it does to Gulfport. To you, it's a livelihood; to them, it's your paycheck after they get their hands on it.

All told, their tax increase would be the equivalent of $1,800 in new taxes per household. Are we prepared to sit back and let them do that to America?

Audience. No!

The President. We all watched the Olympics this summer, and we cheered to see American athletes go for the gold. Well, making our economy bear the burden of their tax hike would be like having a coach tell an Olympic swimmer to do laps carrying an anvil or a runner to sprint with a ball and chain.

Come November, the American people will get to vote on our coaches, and come November, the American people are going to tell Coach Tax Hike to go find another team.

Our pledge is for tax simplification, to make the system more fair and easier to understand. Do you know that Albert Einstein has said he cannot understand the Form 1040? [*Laughter*] We want to make it simpler and easier, so that we can bring yours and everybody's income tax rates further down, not up. Tax simplification will provide powerful new incentives for economic growth.

We'll fight for enterprise zones, to help Americans in disadvantaged areas get off unemployment and welfare and start climbing the economic ladder. And we'll keep government under control by working for a line-item veto. I had it as a Governor, 43 Governors have it; the President needs it. And then a constitutional amendment mandating that government stop spending more than government takes in.

A southerner named Thomas Jefferson, back shortly after the Constitution was ratified and put into place, said it had one lack. It needed a clause to prevent the Federal Government from borrowing. Jefferson was right, and it's time we recognized it.

Now, you might have noticed that our opponents are trying to appeal to traditional Democrats by comparing themselves to Harry Truman. Well, President Truman kept a sign on his desk that said, "The buck stops here." But if our opponents are elected, their sign will say, "Your bucks stop here."

Forgive me, but Harry Truman believed, with F.D.R. before him and John Kennedy after him, in strength abroad and self-reliance at home. Now, to all those Democrats here today—and I hope there are many—there would have to be, in this place. [*Laughter*] And I hope that you feel that under its present leadership, the Democratic Party no longer stands behind America's role in the world, that it no longer represents the working men and women. So, we say to you—and I say this as one who, for most of my adult life, was also a Democrat: Come walk with us down the new path of hope and opportunity.

Add your strength to ours, and all of us can build something new for America, something far better than before. And it will be a true bipartisan achievement between millions of patriotic Democrats who know they can no longer follow the leadership of that party.

As our economy grows, we'll need to go forward with bedrock values that have always sustained the people of the South— the values of faith, family, neighborhood, and good, hard work. And together, we're already making an impressive start.

We've helped lead a grassroots revolution for excellence in education that will reach every child in this land. Recently, we learned that scholastic aptitude test scores have gone up a full 4 points. Now, that's the second improvement in the past 3 years and the biggest increase in those scores in 21 years.

We must continue to crack down on crime. We say with no hesitation, yes, there are such things as right and wrong, and, yes, for hardened criminals preying on our society, punishment must be swift and sure. In 1980 the crime rate was rising. Well, last year, reported crime dropped 7 percent, and that's the steepest decline since 1960.

No crime strikes harder at the heart of America than drug smuggling, for drugs tear families apart and turn healthy, productive Americans into sick people unable even to care for themselves—men and women who often turn to robbery to pay for their habit. We've established the National Narcotics Border Interdiction System, under the superb leadership of Vice President Bush, to wage war on drugs. And today drug seizures and arrests are at record levels. I know that Coast Guard men and women stationed here in Mississippi are playing a leading role in this vital effort.

In a case that just took place, days ago, the Coast Guard cutter *Acushnet*, right here in Gulfport, came across a fishing boat that flew no proper flag. The *Acushnet* pulled alongside, and five Coast Guard officers went aboard. Well, the Coast Guard officers knew for certain something was wrong when they saw that all the hatches had been nailed shut. In the end, they confiscated almost 4 tons of marijuana, towed the fishing boat into Gulfport, and made six arrests. I know that you'd like to join me in thanking the officers and crew of the *Acushnet* for a job well done.

In foreign affairs, America is at peace. Since 1980 not one nation has fallen to Communist aggression, while the people of one country, Grenada, have been set free.

And as I look south over the Gulf, I can't help thinking of one troubled part of the world—Central America. Some would have us take a position of weakness in Central America or withdraw from the region altogether. They want to hang a "Do Not Disturb" sign on our border and pretend there are no problems. But that would betray the brave people of Central America and ignore our own national interests, for if Central America falls, make no mistake about it, refugees will flood our borders. I pledge to you that we will give firm support to the forces of liberty, democracy, and economic progress and that we'll do so as long as I hold this office.

Audience. 4 more years! 4 more years! 4 more years!

The President. Well, I wasn't going to, but if you insist. [*Laughter*]

Now, I know that many of you have a special interest in the great effort to defend our freedom, whether you serve in our Armed Forces, help to build our ships, or are veterans that have served our nation with pride. Let me assure you, we're determined to give America defenses that are second to none.

Since we took office, we've built up our stocks of ammunition. We've replenished our military supplies, and we've begun work on new equipment, including important new aircraft. And today America is once again giving the men and women in our Armed Forces the pay, the training, and the respect they've always deserved.

One of our proudest accomplishments concerns the Navy. In the two decades before we took office, our total fleet had been cut nearly in half. Well, we've turned that around. In the past 4 years, we've added 44 ships to the fleet, bringing the total to 523, and that's well on our way to our goal of 600. Now, many of the new ships have been built right here in Mississippi. And when I look at the sleek ships around us, once again we can say with pride: Columbia is the gem of the ocean.

I told Soviet Foreign Minister Gromyko, when I met him at the White House on Friday, the United States seeks no territorial expansion. We make no attempts to impose our will on anyone; but we will never again allow America to let her guard down.

Well, now, I'm supposed to end my speech. But I——

Audience. No!

The President. Well, yeah, but I can't help but remark about something that I've seen more and more at rallies of this kind all over the country: so many bright, young faces here today, so many young people. Listen, I can remember a time when the only young people that ever came to one of our rallies looked like they couldn't join anything else. [*Laughter*] Listen, and I see enough short haircuts that I believe there are some people here that aren't in uniform, also. But they wear the uniform every day, men and women.

And may I stay just long enough to leave one message with you, one last thought from my heart: I have to tell you that nothing, and I mean nothing, has made me prouder these past 4 years than the young men and women who are serving our country in uniform. By any measure——

Audience. 4 more years! 4 more years! 4 more years!

The President. You know, by any measure, those young people I've mentioned are just the best. And I have to tell you something—and forgive me for using a word that you children should never use—well, none of us should—but it's been said that back in World War II—as a matter of fact, it is a fact that someone asked General George Marshall what was the secret of America's success, what was our secret weapon in World War II? And General Marshall said, "The best damned kids in the world." Well, the young men and women serving today are the grandsons and granddaughters of those heroes. And I'll tell you, he was right; they are still the best damned kids in the world.

Now and then on the news a commentator will be talking to one of our young people in uniform. And it's kind of struck me that so often you hear the—when the young man in uniform or woman in uniform answers, you so often the proud and lilting cadence of Charleston or Memphis or Jackson or Gulfport, Biloxi. The South was the home of patriots in 1776, when a southerner wrote our Declaration of Independence. And today, more than two centuries later, the South is the home of patriots still.

So, maybe when you see one of our young people in uniform walking along the street here in Gulfport or Biloxi or wherever, maybe, if you think of it, just nod and smile and say hello, and maybe let them know how all of us feel about them. It'll make you feel real good, and I know how good it'll make them feel.

Well, now I do have to go. And I——

Audience. No! 4 more years! 4 more years! 4 more years!

The President. All right. Four more years it'll be. And God bless you, and God bless America. Thank you very much. Thank you. Send us all back there.

Note: The President spoke at 6:25 p.m. at Joseph T. Jones Park. Following his remarks, the President returned to the Broadwater Beach Hotel, where he remained overnight. Earlier in the evening, the President attended a reception for local Republican leaders at the hotel.

The following day, the President traveled to Brownsville, TX.

Informal Exchange With Reporters on Arrival in Brownsville, Texas
October 2, 1984

Q. Mr. President, Walter Mondale says that you should look into these charges against Donovan; and if there's anything to them, he should resign. What's wrong with that?

Terrorism

The President. Well, first of all, let me make a statement.

Q. Please.

The President. You asked a question yesterday, and there was no time, and it was not the place to answer that. I thought that probably during the day, there would come an opportunity to answer. There didn't. So, let me just make a statement.

Your question had to do with Secretary Shultz.

Q. And who's responsible for Lebanon, sir.

The President. Who was responsible for Lebanon. Secretary Shultz had acknowledged a responsibility himself on the air on Sunday. That was typical of George, and I appreciate it very much. But the answer to the question is, I am responsible, as I said that I was on the previous tragedy. I was responsible—and no one else—for our policy and our people being there.

Q. But shouldn't——

Q. On that same subject, sir——

Q. ——the President be held accountable, sir?

Q. On that same subject, the old saying, you know, "You fool me once, my fault. Fool me twice. . . ." But the U.S. has——

The President. These terrorist activities——

Q. ——three times now.

The President. These terrorist activities have been going on worldwide and taken place against our allies. They've taken place against Arab States, the Greeks, the British, the French, ourselves. And obviously there is an international effort going to try and find a way to apprehend, to prevent these

things from happening. But how do you without knowledge beforehand of what a target is going to be or why someone, who with no regard to who they kill, is going to kill themselves in an effort to do this?

We're doing everything we can to finally try to get an international movement that can give us better protection——

Q. You were pretty tough on Mr. Carter in 1980, when the Iranian hostage situation happened. And now this has happened to us three times.

The President. No, Bill [Bill Plante, CBS News]. There, a government with whom we had relations, a government allowed this to happen. There was no war or anything else with regard to the hostages. And all I criticized the previous administration about was for our abandonment of the Shah and our allowing what happened to happen. I think it is a blot on our record.

Q. But you say you're responsible, sir. But are you to blame for lax security?

The President. We are doing our utmost to provide security——

Q. But it wasn't enough.

The President. ——at all of these places. No, it wasn't. And it wasn't because the threat had been while we were in a much less protected place, and we moved ahead of schedule into this place where the defenses were only about 75 percent complete.

Q. Mr. President, you say that you take responsibility, but shouldn't the people who actually made the decisions be held accountable?

The President. No, I'm not going to deliver somebody's head up on a platter, which seems to be the request of so many when things like this happen.

Q. So, there'll be no blame-finding here, sir?

The President. No, we've had an investigation. There was no evidence of any carelessness or anyone not performing their duty.

Q. Is the case closed, as far as you're concerned, sir?

The President. Yes——

Q. Can we ask you about Donovan, sir?

The President. Well, the case of terrorism will never be closed.

Secretary of Labor Raymond J. Donovan

Q. Walter Mondale says that you should immediately have someone investigate these charges, and if there's anything to them, Donovan should step down completely and resign. What's wrong with that?

The President. Well, he has already had a complete investigation of a great many charges—this through a grand jury—and he does not know, nor do any of us know, what is in the indictment or what he's being charged with. But I'm going to then—there isn't any point in taking a great many questions on this—I'm going to say one thing about this. There is a tradition in the law of our land that's as old as this country, that you are innocent until you're proven guilty. And Secretary Donovan took the step voluntarily of absenting himself and taking a leave of absence without pay while this issue is revolved—or resolved, and I accept that and I also——

Q. But how does it look having a Cabinet officer under indictment? There's hardly any precedent for that.

The President. I don't think there are many precedents for all the attacks and assaults that have been made on so many people of our administration, with allegations and charges that were without any foundation in fact and which were later revealed as having no foundation in fact; the people were cleared. There's a kind of a lynch atmosphere in that. Now, I can't say that about what has taken place here, and I can't comment. It is, again—it's before the courts. It is now a matter of law, and so I won't comment further on that——

Q. Well, Mr. President——

The President. ——except to say that he—

remind all of you—he is innocent unless proven guilty.

Q. Do you think it might be politics? He says it's politics.

Q. Do you believe this is political, if partisan politics are to blame?

The President. I'm not going to comment on that. That would be violating what I just said. It's before the courts. It's before the law and——

Q. Well, Secretary Donovan commented on it. He seemed to believe there's some kind of political vendetta here.

The President. He is the man who's charged, and I'm not going to comment.

Q. Why do you——

Q. Mr. President——

Q. Will this hurt you politically? I mean, the Democrats say this is part of the sleaze factor. Will this hurt you politically—the Donovan case?

The President. The only sleaze factor that I've seen in all of the things that have been going on in these 4 years, if there is one, is on the other side, with their baseless charges and accusations that have all been proven false.

Q. Mr. President, how long will Raymond Donovan remain as Labor Secretary?

Q. How can you say you still have confidence in his integrity when you don't know what's in the indictment, sir?

The President. I'm going to wait and see what the courts decide.

Q. How long will he remain your Labor Secretary, sir?

Q. Have you talked with Mr. Donovan, sir?

The President. I have not had a chance to talk to him.

Q. Why not?

The President. You know where I've been and what I've been doing.

Q. No telephone?

Note: The President spoke at 11:30 a.m. to reporters assembled alongside Air Force One, which had just landed at Brownsville-South Padre Island International Airport.

Remarks at a Reagan-Bush Rally in Brownsville, Texas
October 2, 1984

The President. Thank you very much, and thank you, Phil Gramm. And I hope the next time I'm here, I'll be able to say Senator Phil Gramm. But thank all of you for a most heartwarming welcome.

It's great to be in Brownsville, and it's a real pleasure to visit one of the most spirited campuses I've seen. All I can say, after touring your school, is *viva* Texas Southmost College.

Well, it's great to be in Texas again, and to be here with—as I said a little earlier in different words—one of Texas' greatest contributions to economic sense in Washington, Phil Gramm, and to see this Texas spirit in action here.

You know, when we were in Dallas in August, there were some of our people that were driving by the Texas Stadium, where the Cowboys play, and they were remarking about the stadium and how big it was and all, and then they noticed the interesting way in which the top sort of was scooped out to let in the sunlight. And they mentioned this to a Texan who was with them. And he said, "Sure, we do that so God can watch." Well, we can use more of that kind of spirit.

Now, there are so many things I want to talk with you about today, and just one of them is how the Texas spirit is spreading throughout the Nation. In the past 3½ years, as Phil was telling you, there's been a broad economic renewal in our country. The economy is expanding again, millions of jobs, as he told you, are being created; hundreds of thousands of new businesses are being incorporated. Inflation is down; interest rates are down, not down far enough, but at least they're moving in the right direction.

So, there's good news to report. And all of that good news is the direct result of the efforts of the American people, the efforts of all of you. It's your recovery. All we did was get the Government out of your way.

You know, the other day I was on a campus—a college up in Ohio, and I was taking some questions from the students.

And one of them said to me, "What do you want the American people to remember most about your Presidency?" Well, I hope they won't have to be remembering soon, but—[*laughter*]—I was taken aback. It's the kind of question you don't often hear—and you're a little surprised you hadn't thought about it—and then I said that I just felt if they'd remember that I gave the Government back to the people.

It's your government, after all, just as it's your country. And our guiding philosophy has been that you know best what's right for you. You don't need a big government in Washington to tell you what's right for you.

I look at all of you today, and I think of the people I met this morning as—just a little while ago here, in touring this campus. And it's just so clear that the people of Brownsville are a marvelous mixture of pride and enterprise, and you have a lot to be proud of here in your city.

Audience. We want Reagan! We want Reagan! We want Reagan!

The President. Thank you.

Audience. 4 more years! 4 more years! 4 more years!

The President. Thank you. Okay, I'm willing. [*Laughter*]

But we know that Brownsville and some other cities here in the Rio Grande Valley have had some special problems the past few years—economic problems and some bad turns in the weather. And I don't want you to think for a second that you're left out of the American renaissance.

Things are better in many cities in our country, but it's not enough, and we've got to do better. There are so many things left to do, so much of the future yet to be seized and shaped. But the first thing we've got to remember is that together we're on the right track.

John Kennedy once said that "A rising tide lifts all boats." Well, a rising tide of economic growth is going to lift the valley.

We must continue to keep forcing personal tax rates down, not up. We're going to

1411

fight for the working men and women of this country to keep a bigger share of what they earn. And as they spend it or save it, sales will go up, businesses will expand, the spirit of investment will continue to grow. Expanding businesses and new businesses will mean new jobs. And that'll mean new workers who join the work force and who pay their modest—and I underline modest—taxes. And the Government will get enough to operate. But the people—we, the people—will keep enough to flourish.

What I'm describing is a healthy spiral that is already growing and picking up speed like a whirlwind.

In contrast, there are those who say that to end poverty in America, we must go back to the old days of raising taxes again and again and again.

Audience. No!

The President. Oh, I don't doubt that they mean well in their own way. But their ideas are hopelessly old fashioned. They just don't understand that the American people are tired of the tax-and-tax and take-and-take mentality. And so, I know, are all of you. And I'm going to be ashamed of myself in a second for what I'm going to say. But I understand they did borrow their campaign song from your State. It's called, "Deep in the Heart of Taxes." [*Laughter*] Isn't that awful? [*Laughter*]

But our program doesn't rest only on growth. It rests on creative new ideas that'll make the future brighter for all of us—ideas like enterprise zones, in which the parts of a city that have known steady economic setbacks are revitalized by giving businesses tax incentives to go in and create jobs and opportunity. It's a great idea. And we're not going to stop fighting until enterprise zones flourish in those towns and cities that would benefit from them.

Incidentally, that's been before the Congress for 2 years now, and the leadership in the House of Representatives has refused to let it out of committee so they can vote on it.

There are ideas that we've already been able to implement. For instance, a year ago yesterday we started a real jobs program that works in partnership with private employers, determining in the local areas what are the jobs that are there available for the

trained workers. And, now, there used to be a costly Federal program called CETA, and lots of its jobs were just make-work, and the people who held them didn't receive any sound training. Well, in the first 6 months of our program, the Job Training Partnership helped train 500,000 people; and its placement in jobs, its rate is over 70 percent of those that go through the training, already placed in employment. Now, that's a program that works. And it's a success not just because it involves private employers who know the marketplace. It's a success because it operates on the principle that people don't want a handout; they want some help that will enable them to operate in the world as the independent souls they want to be.

You know, there's been a lot of confusion about this word "help." It's an election year, and maybe some people think it's in their interest to create a little confusion. But our philosophy has always been to help people achieve prosperity by giving them back their freedom, and to help those who truly need assistance, even if it's only for a while, as they try to get their share of the American dream.

Now, here at this school, for instance, there are a number of students who are receiving some sort of Federal financial aid for their tuition, and, believe me, they're students who really need that help. And their student loans haven't been cut. In fact, we recently asked the Congress to increase to $3,000 the grant aids for the truly needy.

But we've also made it our policy to help only those with a clear, demonstrable need. Those who can do it on their own shouldn't be taking the money we need to help those who couldn't receive a higher education without it. And, believe me, I know whereof I speak, because a long time ago I was on a campus getting a diploma, and I had to work my way through.

And I will say I've never regretted it for one minute. It was back in the Great Depression, so had to do it all. But I haven't regretted it. In fact, one of the better jobs I've ever had in my life was at that time—I was washing dishes in the girls dormitory. [*Laughter*]

Now, some of the people in this valley have really been hurt by the devaluation of the peso. And because of that, last year our administration became the first ever to set up a special southwest border initiative to give you the special attention that the border cities need. And after last winter's freeze, we directed the Farmers Home Administration to make more loans to local families without adequate housing. Now, this has encouraged new construction and employment in the valley.

We freed up more Federal funds for small business loans for farmers affected by the freeze. And the city of Brownsville, for example, was given funds to help build a supermarket in a deprived part of the city, and that construction is to create 43 permanent jobs and 30 construction jobs. We also provided financial assistance to help with bilingual programs in the schools of the valley.

Now, these are just three demonstrations of prudent Federal assistance in a case of clear and demonstrable need. In the past year alone, our administration has committed over a hundred million dollars to the valley.

And if I may make one more point on this: We believe passionately in public-private partnerships in this kind of assistance.

The money that we sent for the supermarket here in the valley was matched by $800,000 in private funds. And there's Project HOPE, another public-private partnership. Earlier I toured the labs where local students are being trained to work as health-care professionals here and in other border cities. And I know that program is going to be a great success and a great example of public and private cooperation.

Now, I've been talking on about the economy—something I tend to do because I think a healthy economy will truly transform the lives of the people of our country. But there's just one more thing I'd like to say about it. Sometimes it takes patience when you try something new. But I tell you, well, it's hard to hang on when times are tough. But I tell you with complete conviction, that if we stay on the right track nationally, then the people in the towns of the valley will make a comeback. It won't happen overnight, but it will happen in

Brownsville as it has happened in much of the rest of the Nation.

But let me say in closing that even though economic matters are important— well, the old, old saying is true: Man does not live by bread alone. Man lives by belief, by faith in things that are larger than himself. We really almost diminish all the things we are when we limit the debate to money and how it's distributed in our country. We lose a sense of the mystery in men's souls and the mystery of life.

I'm proud that we've tried the past few years to softly encourage respect for the traditional values of faith in God and respect for the family. The family, after all, is the main generator of the good things that people bring to the society at large. We're nothing without the family, and we've tried to reflect that knowledge in all that we've done in the past few years.

Now, just one more thing. I know that many of you know the word—and I hope I pronounce it correctly—*respeto.* Respect. Did I get it right?

Respect is an important thing. The United States never wants to be a bully or a braggart, but it's important to show the people of the world that we stand for something and we're proud of it. And though we're patient when provoked, well, Uncle Sam is a friendly old man, but he has a spine of steel.

And one of the things that I'm proudest of—do any of you have relatives in the Armed Forces—the Army, the Navy, the Marine Corps? Yes? Well, I'm glad to see that. One of the proudest things—or one of the things that I'm proudest of, is that we've helped the men and women of our Armed Forces receive the kind of respect they deserve.

Once again, they're being honored as the priceless professionals they are. They haven't had it easy. The men and women who protect this country never do. But we improved pay, improved their standard of living, and we started saluting them again. And morale is higher than it's ever been, and reenlistments are up. And I'll tell you, whenever you happen to see one of those young men and women in uniform on the street, if you just maybe give them a smile

1413

and a hello and indicate that you know how proud they make us, I think you'd feel just great after you did it, and I know they'd feel great.

Well, I've probably gone on too long here, but——

Audience. No!

The President. I like it——

Audience. 4 more years! 4 more years! 4 more years!

The President. Thank you. Okay, all right. Thank you. I don't get here often enough. I like it here. Can I come back? [*Applause*]

You know, you're reminding me of something that I saw yesterday. I went to a swearing-in ceremony for 1,548 new citizens, all being sworn in as new citizens of the United States. And it was wonderful, and it was a very moving experience. The oldest of them was 92, and the youngest was only 2. And as they took the Pledge of Allegiance for the first time, they spoke

with such a belief, and I thought that this is still—and will be hearing them always—". . . one nation, under God, with liberty and justice for all."

For that we must all be truly thankful, and I thank you so much for your wonderful hospitality. I go away from here feeling a little taller and, believe me, very proud, indeed. Thank you very much, and *vaya con Dios.* Thank you.

Note: The President spoke at 12:38 p.m. in Gorgas Hall at Texas Southernmost College.

Prior to his remarks, the President went to the college's Dr. Cortez Allied Health Building, where he received a briefing on Project HOPE by Albert A. Besteiro, president of Texas Southernmost College, and Pat Hobbs, dean of the vocational technical division. While at the building, he also toured a medical technology laboratory.

Following his remarks, the President traveled to Corpus Christi, TX.

Remarks at a Reagan-Bush Rally in Corpus Christi, Texas
October 2, 1984

The President. Thank you very much, and *muchas gracias.*

I'm very proud to have been introduced by your Congressman, but I hope soon to be, if you do what's right, your Senator, Phil Gramm.

Well, it's great to be back in Texas and——

Audience member. We love you, Ronnie!

The President. Thank you—and back in Corpus Christi visiting you again. I've campaigned here on more than one occasion, and I always notice how proudly the flag waves in the south Texas wind. It sort of says to visitors that the people here take patriotism seriously.

Well, together we're going to make certain that our country always stands for freedom and our flag continues to wave proudly. There is a new spirit in America, and I'm pleased to call it the new patriotism. All over the country, Americans are casting away the pessimism and self-doubt of the

last decade. We're coming together, people of every race, religion, and ethnic background, rejoicing in the freedom and the opportunity of this great land.

Four years ago when I was last here, I asked you for your support. I promised that if you so honored me, I would do my very best to help all of you to make America strong again, to rebuild her economy, strengthen her defenses, and to restore her confidence in the future. Well, it's been tough, but together we have, all of us and all of you, made a new beginning. We still have more to do, but I think we're headed in the right direction. And I think this election offers the clearest choice in 50 years—a choice of whether we go forward together to build on our own progress, or whether we go back to the defeatism and despair of the unhappy past.

Let me ask you. Does anyone want to go back to the days of high inflation?

Audience. No!

The President. Anyone want to go back to the days of economic stagnation and a heavier and heavier tax burden?

Audience. No!

The President. No, you don't want to go back, and the American people don't want to go back. They want to keep moving forward to jobs and opportunity, forward to stable prices and economic expansion, forward to a safer and a stronger America. I think the American people are proud of the recovery they built and confident about making tomorrow even better.

And I want you to know you did do this. I just told some people over in Brownsville a little while ago, as to this recovery, all we did was get the Government out of your way.

You know, those who are running down this comeback story, who are trying to make us fear our future, are running down the talent and the courage of the American people. And I just have a hunch that come election day, they're going to be sorry they did.

Unhappily, there are those who still believe they can divide us against ourselves by appealing to envy, promising something for nothing, and the American people aren't buying that anymore. And something else no one's buying is any scheme for raising Federal taxes based on promises from fast-talking politicians that somebody else will pay the bill.

My opponent has made an enormous tax increase his first option, the centerpiece of his campaign. Well, I think he's a little confused. Doesn't he know you don't want greater taxes, you want a greater Texas?

Raising taxes will not encourage people in Texas to work harder and be more productive; raising taxes will not stimulate investment; raising taxes will not give business the incentive to innovate and to make their companies more competitive. America doesn't need higher taxes. America doesn't need my opponent to rescue us from prosperity. America needs more growth.

Those who still need help will get help, and every American who wants a job will find a job as we keep on growing. The politicians and the economic gurus who gave us stagflation—stagflation, that took some doing, you know, to produce both economic

decline and inflation all at the same time. And those people claimed that our program wouldn't work. They said it wouldn't work before it had even been passed. And incidentally, when you meet somebody that maybe wonders why you're supporting Phil Gramm, you might remind him that one of the two names on the legislation that brought about the tax cuts and the economic progress and the reduction in government spending—the names were Del Latta and Phil Gramm. It was their bill.

Those same people warned us that cutting tax rates would lead to super inflation. Well, now that our economy is strong and growing, they're a little stuck, so they tell us now, it won't last. Well, I think it's about time we quit listening to politicians and so-called economic experts who keep selling America short. Of course, when one is so tied to the politics of the past and focusing on the negative, it's hard to have a vision of a better future.

But I don't know, I see America as a soaring eagle—strong, proud, and free. Now, I think there are those still around who secretly maybe agree with Ben Franklin's suggestion for our national bird. They'd rather have the symbol be a turkey. [*Laughter*]

Well, 4 years ago we were not only suffering terrible economic difficulties, our country was being counted out as a world leader. Our friends and adversaries alike looked at us as a nation in decline. Advocates of weakness—people who blamed the United States for all the troubles of the world—they claimed a weaker America would be a safer America because no one would have anything to fear from us. Well, no one has anything to fear from us if they mind their own business.

You know, those dedicated individuals in our Armed Forces, they were being treated as if they were at fault for world tensions. Well, we've turned that situation around, too. Today we're safer and more secure because America is rebuilding its defensive strength. It is strength, not weakness, that will ensure a peaceful future.

You know, President Eisenhower knew this when he wrote, "To be strong nationally is not a sin, it's a necessity." And a lot of our strength is based on the new pride in those who are serving in the Armed Forces. Morale's at a high point, and I'm told by their commanders that we've got the finest group of young people in the history of our country serving today. They're better educated. They're more dedicated than ever before. And as long as I'm President, they will never doubt that to the depth of our national soul, we appreciate the job they're doing, and we're proud of each and every one of them.

And something else: As long as I'm President, we're not going to quibble about supplying the weapons and the equipment that they need to do the job they're doing. We'll continue our strenuous efforts to cut waste and fraud and to get the very best deal we can, but we aren't going to play politics with the lives of those who are defending our country. As I said before, we don't want anyone to fear us, but——

[At this point, the President was briefly interrupted by the sound of an airplane.]

I thought he was campaigning in the South today. *[Laughter]*

But as I said, we don't——

Audience. 4 more years! 4 more years! 4 more years!

The President. Thank you.

Audience. 4 more years! 4 more years! 4 more years!

The President. Thank you.

Audience. 4 more years! 4 more years! 4 more years!

The President. Well, as I said before, we don't want anyone to fear us. But I said this in 1980, what our goal would be, and I think maybe we've reached it. And that is, we don't care if they even don't love us. We just expect them to repect us. And that's why we'll be strong.

You know, contrary to what the liberals would like us to believe, by restoring America's military strength, which the previous administration had permitted to erode, we're now in a better position to negotiate with any potential adversary. And just last week, I initiated a new effort to convince the Soviet Union to return to serious arms reduction negotiations.

I'm optimistic that if we remain firm, the Soviet Union will find it in its interest to join with us in reducing the number of weapons now threatening both our peoples. But we're not going to achieve this or anything else with self-doubt and unilateral concessions. I can assure you that we're trying our hardest to convince the Soviets to bargain realistically, to reach an agreement that is fair and verifiable.

And I think that Minister Gromyko has returned to the Soviet Union with a better understanding of what we are, who we are, and what we're looking forward to achieving in the way of peace in the world. It's incumbent for everyone to remember that it was not the United States that walked away from the negotiating table on arms reductions, it was the Soviet Union that walked away.

Now, in situations like this, we all stand together. A stronger America doesn't just mean better weapons; it means having the strength of character to meet our commitments. It means having the will and the political leadership to protect our national interests. And it means not shirking our responsibility to protect our children's future, even when it might be easier to ignore a potential threat.

When we got to Washington, the enemies of freedom were on the move. They were encouraged by what they saw as a lack of will in the previous administration. Central America was headed for a crisis. Well, I'm proud to say that we prevented a major catastrophe, something that might have endangered the security and the well-being of our country for many years to come. In the last 4 years, not 1 square inch of territory has been lost to Communist aggression. And, in one case, with quick and decisive action, we protected hundreds of American medical students from a potential hostile situation and restored freedom to the people of Grenada.

And it was so wonderful when some of those young men—well, all of them came back, all of the combat forces came back—and, before they left, said it was good to see "God bless America" written on the walls down there instead of "Yankee go home."

As was true in our efforts to turn around the economy, our struggle to protect Central America from Communist aggression—

that effort was hampered by obstacles thrown in our path by some liberals in the Democratic Party. And please note I said "some." They are out of step, and some of the leadership, out of step with the millions of patriotic Democrats in this land, the rank-and-file Democrats, and we're reaching out to all concerned Democrats and Independents, asking them to come walk with us down the new path of hope and opportunity and a secure America. I know they can no longer follow the advice of those who have taken this other course. I know, I think, because for a good part of my life I was a Democrat, too, and then found I could no longer follow the policies of what had developed in the leadership of that party.

Now, it's important that we elect right-thinking men and women to the Congress. And that's why it's also vital for you to send Phil Gramm to the United States Senate, so Texas can have the same high quality representation that Senator John Tower has been providing you. We couldn't have accomplished what we've accomplished if we had not had a majority in the Senate. I need Phil Gramm. America needs Phil Gramm.

We only have 1 month left. We have to work our hardest to get our message to every one of your friends and neighbors—Republicans, Democrats, and Independents alike. Every vote counts.

And I can't leave here without noticing something—here on either side of us these bands, these young people, these high school people, so many of you young people here in the crowd. For the rest of us who aren't that young anymore—[*laughter*]—

and my friends and fellow senior citizens down here from the Hill Haven Nursing Home, I'm delighted you're here—what we know is that all I've been talking about up here and all that this election is about is what kind of country we're going to turn over to those wonderful young people of ours. So many of us started out in a country where we knew no matter how beset we were with poverty or what seemed to be lack of opportunity or anything, we knew that anything was possible in this country of ours. And we have a sacred obligation to see that every succeeding generation sees that same kind of an America where there's no ceiling on where they can go and what they can do.

So, on election day, get everybody out to the polls. Don't let anyone—and listen, when I say polls, I mean those voting polls. [*Laughter*] Don't get get swept away with those public opinion polls. President Dewey told me not to look at the polls and get overconfident. [*Laughter*] So, just pretend we're one vote behind, and everyone has to get out there and vote.

All right. God bless you all. And I know I've got to get back on that airplane out there. But this has been wonderful of you to come out here, and I thank you all very much.

Audience. 4 more years! 4 more years! 4 more years!

The President. Thank you. Thanks very much.

Note: The President spoke at 2:40 p.m. at Corpus Christi International Airport.

Following his remarks, the President traveled to Houston, TX.

Remarks at a "Victory '84" Fundraising Dinner in Houston, Texas
October 2, 1984

The President. Thank you, Bill and Rita, thank you very much. You've made me very proud, indeed. Jack Rains, our dinner chairman; our other Governors—Governor Shivers, Governor Connally—Mr. Vice President and Barbara; Nancy; and Senator-

to-be very shortly, Phil Gramm; Mrs. Tower; you ladies and gentlemen:

I'm sorry, as you all are, that John had to be in Washington tonight—he's helping keep the Government running. [*Laughter*] Come to think of it, I may be doubly sorry.

[*Laughter*]

It's always wonderful to visit you folks, but I must admit, Texas has really been outdoing itself lately. A member of my staff told me that when he was in Dallas, he got in a cab and asked to be taken to the convention. And Dallas was kind of strange to him, and the cabdriver asked him, "Well, where's it being held?" Well, he didn't exactly know how to tell him where it was being held, so he said, "Well, it's a place, you know, there's a whole lot of people, and they're shouting and stomping and waving flags and having a heck of a time." And the cabdriver turned around and said, "Buddy, you're just describing the whole State of Texas." [*Laughter*]

I've covered a good deal of territory since we started this campaign year, and everywhere I go I see the same kind of spirit, confidence, and pride. America has left uncertainty behind, along with inflation, stagnation, and weakness. And on November 6th we're going to leave behind, once and for all, those politicians who gave us economic decline and national malaise.

In 1980 we promised the American people a new beginning. Our opponents and their economic gurus were saying that it couldn't be done even before we got started. And they were right. If we'd stuck to their policy, it couldn't have been done.

Instead, we set out on an entirely new path. Our goal was a fundamental change of direction. Instead of taxing away more and more of the working people's earnings, as was the case between 1976 and '81, we gave the people a 25-percent across-the-board cut in their tax rates.

Instead of throwing up our hands and claiming the growth in Federal spending was beyond control, we cut the growth rate in Federal spending by more than 50 percent.

Instead of centralizing more and more power in Washington, we've turned back programs to the States in the form of block grants. Sixty-two categorical Federal grants have been put into 10 block grants. And that reduced our own administrative overhead for managing them from 3,000 employees to 600. And it also reduced the number of pages of regulations for all of them from 885 pages to 30 pages. Instead of smothering our most productive citizens with redtape, we've trimmed away useless and counterproductive regulations, as you can see.

And, yes, instead of increasing the number of Federal employees, we've nearly 75,000 fewer nondefense Federal employees than there were 3 years ago.

Our aim has been to unleash the most productive power the world has ever known, the genius and energy of the American people. Our opponents, who had their chance to prove their stuff and failed miserably, placed their faith in Washington programs, high taxes, Federal bureaucracy, and government mandates. Well, we place our faith in the people. Our efforts are aimed not at harnessing the American people—leaving the politicians holding the reins—but, instead, on freeing them. And they haven't let us down.

There's a new spirit of teamwork alive in America. Management, labor, and State and local government have figured out that we're all on the same team, the American team. And isn't it good to see America, instead of punting on third down, scoring touchdowns again?

Those who are striving to divide America against itself by appealing to envy are finding out that Americans are too good to turn against each other. By working together, we're building a stronger and more vibrant America in which everyone will be better off.

After several years of decline, productivity is rising again. Real weekly earnings in the last 2 years have increased by 3.2 percent. But in 1979 and '80, in just those 2 years, they actually fell by 8.8 percent, the worst drop since World War II. You tell me whose policies are more fair to the working people of America.

Small business opportunities are exploding, and a whole new class of entrepreneurs, representing a cross section of our people, is emerging. In what Europe is calling the American miracle, almost 7 million new jobs have been created. Auto sales are up, interest rates are on the way down, and growth is robust and inflation is low.

The predictions of the so-called economic experts have been wrong, wrong, wrong.

The question we have to ask is: Does anyone really want to go back to the policies of the past?

Audience. No!

The President. Well, things are going so well, our opponents in this election don't seem to know what to talk about. So, they've decided to offer the voters a bold new idea. And what is this new proposal? Raise your taxes. [*Laughter*] Isn't that novel? [*Laughter*] Now, about the only difference between today and 12 years ago is that back then George McGovern's big idea was to give everybody a thousand dollars. [*Laughter*] Today they want to tax more than that away from you—and then some.

Raising taxes will accomplish nothing but cutting the legs out from under economic growth. Is there any wonder why increasing the tax load is about as popular with the American people as a skunk at a lawn party? [*Laughter*]

The difference between the two parties is as clear in this election—or more clear than at any time in the last 50 years. We Republicans offer more growth, lower tax rates, and a stronger America. Our opponents are still wed to the policies of lower expectations, bigger government, and higher taxes.

In foreign policy, the differences are just as great. Both the political parties want to reach arms control agreements with the Soviet Union. The difference lies in the fact that we believe it's best to negotiate with America's adversaries from a position of strength, as you've been told. And our opponents, as Vice President Bush has observed, keep mistaking weakness for peace.

And having mentioned George—and believe me, I am deeply grateful for what I've sat here and heard him say, but I'm grateful for more than that—let me just tell you that Texas couldn't have given a President a better Vice President than George Bush. He is in every sense of the word an invaluable part of our administration, and we thank you for lending him to us.

You know something? After a few years, George has been in more than 50 countries. He's been a part of every decision that we've made. I can't tell jokes about Vice Presidents anymore. [*Laughter*]

You've loaned me another great Texan: Jim Baker. This local boy keeps things running smoothly at the White House, and I rely on him as Chief of Staff and my right-hand man. And of course, this is nothing new. Americans have been relying on Texans since about 1845.

All of us, like you, believe that we must be firm in our commitments and firm in our resolve to protect American interests. Almost a year ago, I was faced with a tough decision. Communist thugs had just murdered Maurice Bishop and other leaders of the Government of Grenada. The lives of numbers of American medical students were in jeopardy. The governments of nearby island democracies, with little military protection of their own, asked for our help. We took action, and yet it took weeks for certain would-be American leaders to decide whether our action had been justified or not.

Even after seeing the overwhelming display of gratitude from the people of Grenada, there were those who cast aspersions on what we did there, suggesting that it was in some way akin to what the Soviet Union was doing in Afghanistan. Well, I've had some time to reflect on what happened in Grenada, and I can tell you we have no apologies. Our military personnel acted in the finest tradition of our country. They are, truly, heroes—every one of them.

Four years ago, our adversaries and even our friends were counting us out. Defeatism was the order of the day. Well, America is back, and we are rebuilding our defenses. And we have again assumed our role as the leading force for freedom in the world. We have a forceful and articulate individual, Jeane Kirkpatrick, representing us in the United Nations.

When we came to Washington, we faced a near crisis in Central America, a crisis that could, over time, have resulted in a direct threat to our southern border. Despite the roadblocks thrown in our way by some liberals in the House of Representatives, we've prevented what might have become or mushroomed into a major catastrophe in Central America. The danger isn't gone, but I'm proud to say not 1 square inch of territory has been lost to Communist aggression in the world in these last 3½ years.

It's vital that we make certain the voters

understand how important it is to elect a Congress which will support our efforts to keep America growing and building, to keep America strong and proud. Now, there's some fine people running for the House here in Texas, and I know you're putting out the maximum effort to get them elected. I understand that your voter registration efforts have been tremendous. Senator Tower and so many others of you are doing a fantastic job. And let's make certain that on election day the voters send Phil Gramm to the United States Senate.

Phil has proven himself a courageous representative of the values in which we so fervently believe. Never before, I believe, in our Governor's [government's] [1] history has someone decided, having just been elected to office, that he could no longer follow the dictates of the leadership of that party, and he changed. But he did more than that. He then resigned and returned to the voters who had sent him there as a member of one party and said, "Look, you can register your approval or disapproval of what I've done; you'll have to vote on me again in a special election." And they sent him back to Washington, as they should.

Winston Churchill once said, when he changed parties in his country, he said, "Some men change principle for party, and some men change party for principle." Phil has proven himself a courageous representative of—in all of this, as I say, in what we fervently believe.

Well, those values are attracting millions to our cause. We're reaching out to rank-and-file Democrats and Independents, asking them to come with us and walk down this new path of hope and opportunity. I know there are many here tonight. I'm very proud to know that you would come here. There was a certain sacrifice at the box office for you to do so. But to have you here—and I just want to say to all of you, having been a Democrat most of my life myself and found that there came a day when I could no longer follow the policies of the leadership of that party, I know that throughout this country there are millions of rank-and-file, patriotic Democrats who

love this country, who want the same things that we want for the country, and yet who find themselves unable to bless the decisions of the policymakers at the head of their own party today. Come with us on this particular march, and we'll truly have a bipartisan victory that will set this country to going forward again, with your help.

The great strength of our cause reflects our devotion to values that are so dear to the American people: respect for work; love of family, neighborhood, and country; and faith in God. And if all of us remain true to these values, nothing can hold America back.

Between now and November 6th, don't let up. I know that I can count on all of you.

I have to, though, say something a little nonpolitical in concluding here. I've been saying it all day throughout your State. And I've been saying it in other States, too. I don't know of anything in these 4 years that has made me more proud than the young men and women that are wearing our uniform today. You know, I've told them sometimes, and reminded them and——

Q. [*Inaudible*]—I want to give this to the President, please. This is my dream. [2]

The President. What?

Q. My dream for 10 years——

The President. Your dream for 10 years?

Q. Yes.

The President. To what?

Q. [*Inaudible*]—President Reagan, and this is for him.

The President. You what? Yes, take it and give it—yes. They will give it to me. They'll see that I get it. Ma'am, they'll see that I get it. Honest, they will. And thank you very much.

Q. Thank you, America.

The President. Thank you. And if you couldn't hear, she said, "Thank you, America."

---

[1] *White House correction.*

[2] *A woman later identified as Felicia Ughanze, of Nigeria, was attempting to hand the President a letter describing difficulties she and her husband were having with immigration procedures. A Secret Service agent accepted the letter, and the President later asked an assistant to look into the problem.*

And now—if I can, now, let me just go back to those young men and women that I was telling you about. I know sometimes you're going to see them on the street in the uniform and so forth. If you haven't thought about it before, maybe you kind of smile and say hello and even shake their hands. You'll feel real good after you've done it. And I know how good they'll feel. They're what George Marshall said of their grandfathers. Back in World War II, when somebody asked George Marshall what was the secret of our success, what was our secret weapon, and General George Marshall said, "The best damned kids in the world." And that's what we have again.

Now, about those polls, don't get carried away. President Dewey told me—[*laughter*]—that we should get out the vote. [*Laughter*] So, all of you, do what you're doing, and God bless you, and thank you for what you have done.

Note: The President spoke at 9:21 p.m. at the Albert Thomas Convention Center. He was introduced by former Gov. William Clements of Texas. Earlier in the evening, the President attended a reception for the dinner organizers at the Four Seasons Hotel, where he remained overnight.

The following day, the President returned to Washington, DC.

Nomination of John D. Ward To Be Director of the Office of Surface Mining Reclamation and Enforcement in the Department of the Interior
October 2, 1984

The President today announced his intention to nominate John D. Ward to be Director of the Office of Surface Mining Reclamation and Enforcement, Department of Interior. He would succeed James R. Harris.

Mr. Ward is currently director of the Colorado Division of Mines. Previously, he was manager, coal development, Rocky Mountain Energy Co. (1979–1982); manager, employee and government, Colowyo Coal Co.

(1975–1979); assistant to the director, western mining operations, W.R. Grace & Co. (1974–1975); and assistant to the president, Colowyo Coal Co. (1972–1974).

Mr. Ward graduated from Pennsylvania State University (B.S., 1955) and the University of Denver School of Law (J.D., 1962). He is married, has two chidren, and resides in Layfayette, CO. He was born May 22, 1928, in Wilkes-Barre, PA.

Proclamation 5240—National Community Leadership Week, 1984
October 3, 1984

By the President of the United States of America

A Proclamation

Local communities form the foundation of our Nation. Our Federal system of government is based on the determination of the people of the United States to govern themselves, to the extent possible, in small entities capable of responding quickly and

effectively to particular community values and needs.

Qualified and well-trained leadership at all levels of government, but particularly in our local communities, is essential to the maintenance and strengthening of our democratic institutions. Throughout the United States, many communities have established programs to help citizens identify and discharge the responsibilities involved in leadership positions assumed in their own communities. These programs have produced thousands of talented and well-trained local leaders who are aware of the unique problems confronting their communities and are well-prepared to devise innovative solutions for those problems.

The Congress of the United States, by House Joint Resolution 574, has designated the week beginning September 9, 1984, as "National Community Leadership Week" and has authorized and requested the President to issue a proclamation in observance of this week.

Now, Therefore, I, Ronald Reagan, President of the United States of America, do hereby proclaim the week beginning September 9, 1984, as National Community Leadership Week.

In Witness Whereof, I have hereunto set my hand this third day of October, in the year of our Lord nineteen hundred and eighty-four, and of the Independence of the United States of America the two hundred and ninth.

RONALD REAGAN

[*Filed with the Office of the Federal Register, 4:12 p.m., October 3, 1984*]

Proclamation 5241—Emergency Medicine Week, 1984
October 3, 1984

By the President of the United States of America

A Proclamation

Each year an estimated nine million people in this country sustain injuries which require immediate medical attention. Two groups of dedicated Americans provide this kind of medical care: emergency department personnel, who provide care in trauma centers, and emergency medical technicians and paramedics, most of them volunteers, who provide prehospital emergency care.

These emergency medical personnel throughout our Nation are specialists trained to handle illnesses and injuries which threaten life or limb. They must be available daily on a 24-hour basis to all patients who need medical aid. The efforts of these trained men and women have saved thousands of lives.

Vast improvements in emergency medicine have been made in the past fifteen years, and emergency department personnel have completed extensive training and continuing education to keep up with these improvements. The Departments of Transportation and Health and Human Services, together with State and local governments, have provided radio communications systems, equipment, and training courses for emergency medical personnel. These advances make it possible to respond quickly to the needs of the injured and to transport them to appropriate hospital emergency medical facilities within the "Gold Hour" after the injury. This is the time when emergency medical care is most effective in saving lives.

We salute the Nation's emergency medical services personnel: those who staff the ambulances, those who provide medical control, and those physicians and nurses in the trauma centers whose daily efforts are devoted to emergency medicine. We all depend upon their skills and dedication.

The Congress, by House Joint Resolution 545, has designated the week of September 16 through 22, 1984 as "Emergency Medicine Week" and has authorized and requested the President to issue a proclamation in honor of this observance.

Now, Therefore, I, Ronald Reagan, President of the United States of America, do hereby proclaim the week of September 16 through September 22, 1984 as Emergency Medicine Week.

In Witness Whereof, I have hereunto set my hand this third day of October, in the year of our Lord nineteen hundred and eighty-four, and of the Independence of the

United States of America the two hundred and ninth.

RONALD REAGAN

[*Filed with the Office of the Federal Register, 4:13 p.m., October 3, 1984*]

Proclamation 5242—World War I Aces and Aviators Day, 1984
October 3, 1984

By the President of the United States of America

A Proclamation

Ever since the Revolutionary War, Americans have heroically served their country in times of conflict. World War I, "the war to end all wars," began over seventy years ago in August 1914. The war spawned a new breed of warrior, the aviator, who engaged in single combat high above the conflict on the ground. The truly remarkable Americans who pioneered in this new form of military combat defended the skies of Europe with valor and distinction until the end of the war in 1918.

Some of these aviators achieved the title "Ace" by gaining at least five confirmed victories over opponents in the air. As aviators capable of great concentration and decisive action, they possessed what today we would call "the right stuff." Among America's greatest World War I Aces, Eddie Rickenbacker, Frank Luke, Raoul Lufbery and George Vaughn shot down a total of 78 enemy aircraft.

There are about sixty known surviving Aces of World War I. They meet periodically to share memories of a conflict familiar to many Americans only through history books. All Americans should express their gratitude and respect for these gallant air warriors for their extraordinary feats in defense of liberty.

The Congress, by Senate Joint Resolution 333, has designated September 21, 1984, as "World War I Aces and Aviators Day" and has authorized and requested the President to issue a proclamation in observance of this event.

Now, Therefore, I, Ronald Reagan, President of the United States of America, do hereby proclaim September 21, 1984 as World War I Aces and Aviators Day.

In Witness Whereof, I have hereunto set my hand this third day of October, in the year of our Lord nineteen hundred and eighty-four, and of the Independence of the United States of America the two hundred and ninth.

RONALD REAGAN

[*Filed with the Office of the Federal Register, 4:14 p.m., October 3, 1984*]

Proclamation 5243—National Adult Day Care Center Week, 1984
October 3, 1984

By the President of the United States of America

A Proclamation

Progress in medical science and the generally rising level of health care available from birth onwards have been among our Nation's greatest achievements in this century. As a result, more people are living to an old age than ever before.

The corollary to this achievement is an increase in the incidence of chronic illnesses affecting people as they age. Those who suffer these illnesses may require care over a long period of time, a fact which tests our Nation's ability to provide older Americans the kind of care that will allow them to continue to live independently in their communities.

The rapid growth of adult day care centers is a reflection of increasing community interest in developing long-term alternatives in community settings. Adult day care centers provide comprehensive personal, medical, and therapeutic help and also assist older people and the handicapped in achieving maximum levels of independence and social interaction. They provide much needed support for families as they care for their loved ones. Many adult day care centers throughout the country have recognized the vital needs of older people and the desire that many of them have to remain in their own homes as long as possible.

To increase public awareness of the importance of these centers, the Congress, by House Joint Resolution 505, has designated the week beginning September 23, 1984, as "National Adult Day Care Center Week" and has authorized and requested the President to issue a proclamation in observance of this event.

Now, Therefore, I, Ronald Reagan, President of the United States of America, do hereby proclaim the week beginning September 23, 1984, as National Adult Day Care Center Week.

In Witness Whereof, I have hereunto set my hand this third day of October, in the year of our Lord nineteen hundred and eighty-four, and of the Independence of the United States of America the two hundred and ninth.

RONALD REAGAN

[*Filed with the Office of the Federal Register, 4:16 p.m., October 3, 1984*]

Proclamation 5244—Child Health Day, 1984
October 3, 1984

By the President of the United States of America

A Proclamation

America as never before is the land of opportunity for all our children. But for some, that opportunity is denied by illness or disability. Although our health care system is the envy of the world, disease or accident can still deprive many of our children of this birthright of opportunity.

Today, we celebrate tremendous accomplishments in child health. The significant and steady decline in infant mortality, and the great strides in preventing such diseases as polio or measles, are proud examples of what can be accomplished by a free and vibrant medical care system.

On this Child Health Day, 1984, however, we must dedicate ourselves to increasing our efforts. Past achievements only suggest that greater things can be accomplished in the future. We must dedicate ourselves to making further progress in reducing infant mortality for our whole society, and we must also seek to reduce infant mortality in those areas where the level is higher than the national average.

There also are severely handicapped infants who require not only the love and support of their families but who also must have the help of many groups in their communities—doctors, hospitals, health departments, providers of health care, and others—if they are to thrive.

There are teenage mothers and teenagers who become involved with abuse of alcohol and other substances—all these young people need our help and attention. During the coming year, it is my hope that we can continue to demonstrate what a free, energetic, and enlightened society can do cooperatively to protect and improve the health status of our Nation's most vital asset, our children.

Now, Therefore, I, Ronald Reagan, President of the United States of America, pursuant to a joint resolution approved May 18, 1928, as amended (36 U.S.C. 143), do hereby proclaim Monday, October 1, 1984, as Child Health Day, 1984.

In Witness Whereof, I have hereunto set my hand this third day of October, in the year of our Lord nineteen hundred and eighty-four, and of the Independence of the United States of America the two hundred and ninth.

RONALD REAGAN

[*Filed with the Office of the Federal Register, 4:17 p.m., October 3, 1984*]

Proclamation 5245—National Birds of Prey Conservation Week, 1984

October 3, 1984

By the President of the United States of America

A Proclamation

This Nation has been blessed with a rich variety of wildlife, including more than fifty kinds of hawks, falcons, eagles, vultures, and owls. Known as birds of prey, these species possess extraordinary beauty, strength, and power of flight. Inhabiting virtually every territory, often coexisting with man, they are a vital part of many natural systems and contribute significantly to the quality of the human environment.

From time immemorial, the history of mankind has been intertwined with birds of prey. The silent flight of the owl, the breathtaking swoop of the falcon across a mountain cliff, the effortless soaring of vultures over the plains, and the often spectacular passage of hawks on migration have captured the imagination of Americans. Since 1782, the Bald Eagle has served as the National Emblem of the United States.

As our country continues to grow and develop, we must remember our natural heritage and the need to provide future generations with opportunities to experience the excitement of a majestic eagle, a plummeting falcon, or the haunting call of an owl at night. The prosperity of this Nation rests upon both our material wealth and those values that enrich the quality of life. The preservation and propagation of our magnificent birds of prey will mean that these noble creatures will continue to awe and inspire generations of Americans yet unborn.

To emphasize the efforts of the many Americans who share appreciation for birds of prey and the need for their continued welfare, the Congress, by Senate Joint Resolution 230 approved July 3, 1984, has designated the week of October 7 through October 13, 1984, as "National Birds of Prey Conservation Week" and authorized and requested the President to issue a proclamation for this observance.

Now, Therefore, I, Ronald Reagan, President of the United States of America, do hereby proclaim the week of October 7 through October 13, 1984, as National Birds of Prey Conservation Week. I encourage all Americans to observe this week by participating in appropriate ceremonies and activities planned by government agencies, individuals, and private associations and institutions throughout the country to promote the appreciation and conservation of birds of prey.

In Witness Whereof, I have hereunto set my hand this third day of October, in the year of our Lord nineteen hundred and eighty-four, and of the Independence of the United States of America the two hundred and ninth.

RONALD REAGAN

[*Filed with the Office of the Federal Register, 4:18 p.m., October 3, 1984*]

Proclamation 5246—National Neighborhood Housing Services Week, 1984
October 3, 1984

By the President of the United States of America

A Proclamation

America's neighborhoods, composed of individuals of diverse racial, ethnic, social, religious, and economic backgrounds, stand as a tribute to our Nation's democratic traditions and beliefs.

The preservation and improvement of the residential, commercial, and other facilities in neighborhoods throughout our country are essential to the strength of America's families and businesses. These have been and will continue to be the goals of the Neighborhood Housing Services programs.

Neighborhood Housing Services programs are partnerships of local residents, business leaders, and government officials. They have generated over two billion dollars in reinvestment funds to revitalize and preserve our country's neighborhoods. The success of these programs depends largely on the spirit of cooperation and voluntarism that is a hallmark of American life.

In recognition of those who have contributed their time, money, and energy to the preservation of our neighborhoods, the Congress, by House Joint Resolution 566, has designated the week beginning October 7, 1984, as "National Neighborhood Housing Services Week" and has authorized and requested the President to issue a proclamation in observance of this week.

Now, Therefore, I, Ronald Reagan, President of the United States of America, do hereby proclaim the week beginning October 7, 1984, as National Neighborhood Housing Services Week, and I call upon the people of the United States and interested groups and organizations to observe this week with appropriate activities and events.

In Witness Whereof, I have hereunto set my hand this third day of October, in the year of our Lord nineteen hundred and eighty-four, and of the Independence of the United States of America the two hundred and ninth.

RONALD REAGAN

[*Filed with the Office of the Federal Register, 10:18 a.m., October 4, 1984*]

Nomination of Richard H. Hughes To Be a Member of the Board of Directors of the Export-Import Bank of the United States
October 3, 1984

The President today announced his intention to nominate Richard H. Hughes to be a member of the Board of Directors of the Export-Import Bank of the United States for a term expiring January 20, 1985. He would succeed James Ernest Yonge.

Mr. Hughes is currently chairman of the board and chief executive officer of Hinderliter Industries, Inc., of Tulsa, OK. He is also affiliated with the Telex Corp.; Bray Lines, Inc.; Beverage Products Corp.; and Sierra Real Estate Equity Trust. He is a visiting professor in entrepreneurial management in the School of Business at Oral Roberts University.

He serves as a member of the American Business Conference and the Interstate Oil Compact Commission. He is also a member of the board of directors of the National Bar Foundation.

He graduated from Yale University (B.A., 1954) and Harvard Business School (M.B.A., 1959). He is married, has two children, and resides in Tulsa, OK. He was born October 9, 1932, in Tulsa.

Nomination of Frank H. Conway To Be a Member of the Foreign Claims Settlement Commission of the United States
October 3, 1984

The President today announced his intention to nominate Frank H. Conway to be a member of the Foreign Claims Settlement Commission of the United States, Department of Justice, for the term expiring September 30, 1987. This is a reappointment.

Since 1981 Mr. Conway has been a member of the Foreign Claims Settlement Commission of the United States. He has also been an attorney with the firm of Jameson, Locke and Fullerton, of Wellesley, MA since 1975. Previously he was associated with the New England Telephone and Telegraph Co., where he served as a management consultant, general labor relations supervisor, and division manager.

He graduated from Providence College (Ph.B., 1953) and Boston University School of Law (J.D., 1952). He is married, has four children, and resides in Wellesley, MA. He was born May 2, 1913, in Providence, RI.

Nomination of Annelise Graebner Anderson To Be a Member of the National Science Board
October 3, 1984

The President today announced his intention to nominate Annelise Graebner Anderson to be a member of the National Science Board, National Science Foundation, for a term expiring May 10, 1990. She would succeed Walter Eugene Massey.

Mrs. Anderson is a senior research fellow at the Hoover Institution in Stanford, CA. She served as Associate Director for Economics and Government in the Office of Management and Budget in 1981–1983. Previously, she was associate director for economic affairs with the Reagan-Bush transition in 1980 and senior policy adviser for the Reagan-Bush Presidential campaign; research fellow at the Hoover Institution, Stanford University in 1978–1980; associate professor of business administration (1979) and assistant professor of business administration (1975–1979) in the School of Business and Economics, California State University, Hayward; and project manager, organized crime, National Institute of Law Enforcement and Criminal Justice (1970–1971).

She graduated from Wellesley College (A.B., 1960) and Columbia University (M.A., 1965; Ph.D., 1974). She is married and resides in Portola Valley, CA. She was born November 19, 1938, in Oklahoma City, OK.

Nomination of Karen Pryor To Be a Member of the Marine Mammal Commission
October 3, 1984

The President today announced his intention to nominate Karen Pryor to be a member of the Marine Mammal Commission for the term expiring May 13, 1986. She would succeed Donald Kenneth MacCallum.

Ms. Pryor is a writer and biologist. She is the author of three books and numerous articles on marine mammals and learning and behavior. From 1976 to 1982, she was an independent New York-based consultant on marine mammals, and on animal behavior and training to both private and government agencies, including the United States Tuna Foundation, the National Science Foundation, the National Zoological Park, and the National Geographic Society.

She was cofounder and developer of Sea Life Park, HI, a commercial oceanarium, and of the Oceanic Institute, an adjoining private research facility, in 1960–1971.

She graduated from Cornell University (B.A., 1954). She is married, has three children, and resides in North Bend, WA. She was born May 14, 1932, in New York, NY.

Letter to the Speaker of the House and the President of the Senate Transmitting the Annual Report on Soil and Water Conservation Programs
October 3, 1984

Dear Mr. Speaker: (Dear Mr. President:)

Transmitted herewith is the annual report required by Sec. 7(c) of the Soil and Water Resources Conservation Act of 1977 (P.L. 95–192).

The Soil and Water Resources Conservation Act of 1977 (RCA) requires the Secretary of Agriculture to appraise the condition of the soil, water, and related resources on the nonfederal lands of the Nation and to develop a national soil and water conservation program for assisting landowners and land users in their future conservation activities on these lands.

The first appraisal, completed in 1980, was based primarily on the Department of Agriculture's 1977 National Resources Inventory. The 1977 Inventory provided a solid foundation for the appraisal and program.

The first program report, *A National Program for Soil and Water Conservation*, was completed in 1982. It set national conservation objectives and priorities, focused corrective action on areas of the country with the most critical problems, and strengthened the existing partnership among local and State agencies, organizations, and the Federal government for dealing with resource problems. Guided by this program, the Department of Agriculture has concentrated more technical and financial assistance than ever before in areas with the most serious problems of soil erosion and dwindling water supplies.

The Department of Agriculture has been reshaping its conservation programs using the 1980 appraisal and 1982 program as its blueprint. We look forward to steadily increasing gains in the fight against soil erosion and other resource problems in the years ahead.

Sincerely,

RONALD REAGAN

Note: This is the text of identical letters addressed to Thomas P. O'Neill, Jr., Speaker of the House of Representatives, and George Bush, President of the Senate.

The report is entitled "Annual RCA Progress Report, National Program for Soil and Water Conservation, Fiscal Year Ending September 30, 1983" (United States Department of Agriculture).

Nomination of Elizabeth Helms Adams To Be a Member of the National Advisory Council on Women's Educational Programs
October 3, 1984

The President today announced his intention to nominate Elizabeth Helms Adams to be a member of the National Advisory Council on Women's Educational Programs for a term expiring May 8, 1987. She would succeed Diana Powers Evans.

In 1976–1980 Mrs. Adams served as a trustee of the Thacher School in Los Angeles, CA, and as vice chairman of the development committee and a member of the education committee. In 1980 she also served as overseer of the Huntington Library and Art Gallery. She was a trustee of the Marlborough School (1969–1979) and on the executive council in 1980. She was vice president of the blue ribbon committee of the Los Angeles Music Center in 1979–1980.

She graduated from Finch Junior College in New York City. She is married, has five children, and resides in Valley Center, CA. She was born March 11, 1920, in Buffalo, NY.

Nomination of Tom C. Korologos To Be a Member of the United States Advisory Commission on Public Diplomacy
October 3, 1984

The President today announced his intention to nominate Tom C. Korologos to be a member of the United States Advisory Commission on Public Diplomacy for a term expiring July 1, 1987. This is a reappointment.

Since 1975 Mr. Korologos has been vice president and director of legislative affairs of Timmons and Co., Inc., a consulting firm representing corporate and association clients in the area of government relations. He has also been a member of the United States Advisory Commission on Public Diplomacy since 1981. He was director of congressional relations in the office of the President-elect in 1980–1981. He was Deputy Assistant to the President for Senate Relations for 4 years under Presidents Nixon and Ford. Previously he served as assistant to Senator Wallace Bennett (R–UT) for 8 years.

He graduated from the University of Utah (B.A., 1956) and Columbia University Graduate School of Journalism (M.A., 1958). He served in the United States Air Force in 1956–1957.

Mr. Korologos is married, has three children, and resides in Great Falls, VA. He was born April 6, 1933, in Salt Lake City, UT.

Nomination of Alfred Clinton Moran To Be an Assistant Secretary of Housing and Urban Development
October 4, 1984

The President today announced his intention to nominate Alfred Clinton Moran to be an Assistant Secretary of Housing and Urban Development (Community Planning and Development). He would succeed Stephen J. Bollinger.

Mr. Moran is currently Regional Administrator-Regional Housing Commissioner,

Region V, for the Department of Housing and Urban Development. Previously, he was legal counsel to the Governor of Illinois and director of the Governor's Office of Interagency Cooperation (GOIC) (1979–1982); Assistant United States Attorney (1976–1979); hearings referee, Bureau of Unemployment Insurance, State of Illinois (1975–1976); and assistant dean of students, University of Dubuque (1970–1973).

Mr. Moran graduated from the University of Dubuque (B.A., 1969) and Northwestern University School of Law (J.D., 1976). He is married, has one child, and resides in Chicago, IL. He was born June 20, 1948, in Chicago, IL.

Nomination of Ernest Eugene Pell To Be an Associate Director of the United States Information Agency
October 4, 1984

The President today announced his intention to nominate Ernest Eugene Pell to be an Associate Director of the United States Information Agency (Broadcasting). He would succeed Kenneth Y. Tomlinson.

Since 1983 Mr. Pell has been serving as Deputy Director, Voice of America, at the United States Information Agency. In 1982–1983 he was chief correspondent for WCVB–TV in Boston, MA, and Director of News and Current Affairs at the Voice of America. Previously, he was with NBC News as Pentagon correspondent (1980–1982); network correspondent (1978–1982); and Moscow correspondent and bureau chief (1978–1980). He was a television anchorman for WCVB–TV in 1977–1978 and with the Westinghouse Broadcasting Co. in 1963–1977.

Mr. Pell graduated from Harvard University (B.A., 1959) and Boston University (M.S., 1963). He is married, has two children, and resides in Bethesda, MD. He was born March 15, 1937, in Paducah, KY.

Nomination of Charles E. Courtney To Be an Associate Director of the United States Information Agency
October 4, 1984

The President today announced his intention to nominate Charles E. Courtney to be an Associate Director of the United States Information Agency (Programs). He would succeed W. Scott Thompson.

Since 1983 Mr. Courtney has served as Director of European Affairs for the United States Information Agency. He began with USIA as a junior officer trainee in 1962 and has served there most recently in the following positions: public affairs officer, Islamabad, Pakistan (1975–1976); public affairs officer, Ankara, Turkey (1977–1980); principal senior inspector, Washington, DC (1980–1981); Deputy Associate Director, Voice of America (1981–1982); Director, Office of North African, Near Eastern and South Asian Affairs (1982–1983); and Acting Counselor (1983). From 1976 to 1977, he served at the White House as the Director of Communication for the Vice President's Commission on Productivity and Quality of Working Life.

Mr. Courtney graduated from California State University (M.A., 1961). He is married, has three children, and resides in Arlington, VA. He was born June 11, 1936, in Modesto, CA.

Nomination of Barbara W. Schlicher To Be a Member of the Board of Directors of the National Corporation for Housing Partnerships
October 4, 1984

The President today announced his intention to nominate Barbara W. Schlicher to be a member of the Board of Directors of the National Corporation for Housing Partnerships for the term expiring October 27, 1987. She would succeed Frank J. Donatelli.

Since 1972 Mrs. Schlicher has been with Midlantic National Bank, serving as investment assistant (1972–1976); assistant trust officer (1974–1976); trust officer (1976–1979); and vice president and trust officer (1979–present).

Mrs. Schlicher graduated from Douglass College (B.A., 1972). She is married, has one child, and resides in Mountain Lakes, NJ. She was born September 19, 1949, in New York, NY.

Nomination of Two Members of the National Commission on Libraries and Information Science
October 4, 1984

The President today announced his intention to nominate the following individuals to be members of the National Commission on Libraries and Information Science for terms expiring July 19, 1989:

Daniel W. Casey would succeed Helmut A. Alpers. Mr. Casey has been a public library trustee since 1954 and was the first trustee appointed by the New York State Board of Regents to its Advisory Council on Libraries. He also serves on the council of the American Library Association. He is past president of the American Library Trustee Association. He is married, has two children, and resides in Syracuse, NY. He was born January 13, 1921, in Malone, NY.

Patricia Barbour would succeed Margaret S. Warden. She served as a social worker at the Wayne County Bureau of Social Aid in Detroit, MI. Since 1980 she has served on the National Advisory Council on Community Education and as a member of the executive board of the American Research Institute. She has three children and resides in Dearborn Heights, MI. She was born February 2, 1925, in Detroit, MI.

Nomination of Eugene B. Burroughs To Be a Member of the Federal Council on the Aging
October 4, 1984

The President today announced his intention to nominate Eugene B. Burroughs to be a member of the Federal Council on the Aging for a term expiring June 5, 1987. He would succeed Syd Captain.

Mr. Burroughs is director of the investment department at the International Brotherhood of Teamsters. He also serves as director of the Financial Analysts Federation and of the International Foundation of Employee Benefit Plans. He is a member of the editorial advisory board of Pension World and of the Institute of Chartered Analysts. He served as chairman of the Investment Policy Panel at the Pension Benefit Guaranty Corporation in 1975–1983.

Mr. Burroughs graduated from Benjamin Franklin University in 1955. He is married, has two children, and resides in McLean, VA. He was born August 22, 1931, in Washington, DC.

Remarks Following a Meeting With Republican Members of Congress and Congressional Candidates
October 4, 1984

The President. Thank you. I hope next year we have to build bigger stairs.

Well, I'm glad that our team is all here together today to remember an important commitment that we made to America's future. Four years ago our country faced the gravest economic crisis since the Great Depression, and many in this town were ready to throw in the towel and count America out. But not the Republican Party, not our team.

We said there's nothing wrong with America that our people can't and won't make right if government just will stand aside and get out of the way. So, we reached out to the people. We asked them to join with us to rescue our beloved nation, make a new beginning, and help America become strong and successful again.

Specifically, we pledged to work for cuts in growth of spending, to reduce waste, fraud, and abuse to a minimum, and dampen the fires of inflation while protecting those in need; for an across-the-board individual income tax cut and increased incentives for saving, investment, and capital recovery to put America back on the road to prosperity; for more private investment and permanent jobs, especially in our inner cities; and for strengthened defenses so America could have a credible foreign policy again and assure peace through strength here at home and greater stability in the world.

Well, with the support of the people, all of us have made some important changes. Federal spending growth, which reached a 17-percent annual rate in 1980, has been cut by nearly two-thirds. Tax rates have been cut for every working American, with new incentives for business to modernize and for entrepreneurs to start up new businesses. Next year, tax brackets will be indexed because we believe government must never again profit from inflation at the people's expense.

Unlike 4 years ago, today we're building a defensive strength. And today we're giving those brave young men and women who put their lives on the line for us the moral support, the weapons, and the equipment they need to get the job done.

We've also worked hard to strengthen the good and decent values of faith, family, work, neighborhood, and freedom. Those values have never failed America when we've lived up to them.

We've made a new beginning, and America today is a very different place than 4 years ago. It wasn't a coincidence in 1980 that the problems of inflation, interest rates, taxes, jobs, crime, and morale in the military were all getting worse, and our future looked bleak. And believe me, it's not a coincidence today that every one of those problems is being turned around, and our future looks bright again.

No army is as powerful as an idea whose time has come. In 1980 we said it's time to give this government back to the people. When Washington was calling the plays all we did was fumble. Today the people are back in charge, and we're scoring touchdowns again.

Now, the other side said it couldn't be done. But inflation, taxes, and interest rates are down. Jobs, investment, and growth are all up. The morale of our enlisted men and women is up, and their readiness and ability to protect freedom and preserve peace are better than ever before. Since 1980, not 1 square inch of territory has been lost to Communist aggression.

Today we're telling the people the Republican Party will not rest until every American who wants a job can find a job—from Brownsville to Buffalo to San Francisco Bay. And that's why the choice in '84 is so clear.

There comes a time when we must firmly choose the course we'll follow. On November 6th, the American people must decide whether we will go forward with the courage, the common sense, and new spirit that are making America strong again, giving us new opportunities and offering the best hope for all. Or will we turn back to the policies of high taxing and spending that weakened our economy, reduced opportunities, and brought hardship to so many?

I believe young Americans, Independents, and rank-and-file Democrats are making that choice. They're joining our team in larger and larger numbers because they can see that we offer the surest vehicle to progress, the one movement that's saying to every man and woman, without exception: America can only be great when each of you can reach for greatness, when you can reach for the stars and climb up to the ultimate in individual freedom to achieve your full God-given potential. So, we're urging all Americans: Come walk with us down this new path of hope and opportunity. Add your strength to ours, and together we'll become the most powerful force for progress that America has ever known.

All of us together can build on the progress we've made. We can lower everybody's tax rates further and create more jobs, rising take-home pay, and greater opportunities for all. We can extend the full benefits of IRA's to spouses working in the home, pass enterprise zones to restore distressed areas and give hope to those who are left out.

Could enterprise zones—couple those with a youth opportunity wage to help teenagers learn skills and escape dependency, start a new life, and go forward with initiatives to help public housing residents purchase their dwellings and assume responsibility for home ownership. We can push forward new frontiers in science, space, and technology. And we can strengthen the great grassroots movement we've helped lead to make America's educational system a great center of leadership for excellence.

Everything we've done, everything that we mean to do is to give every American the opportunity to make this great free nation greater and freer still.

Our opponent's policies would take us off the new path of an opportunity society, put us back on the old path of defeatism, decline, and despair. They propose a tax increase equivalent to more than $1,800 per household. That's more than $150 each and every month of the year. It's a ball and chain around the neck of America's families and America's future.

Their idea of compassion is bureaucratic compassion, which always begins with every family sending more to Washington, and ultimately leads to more suffering for those who need help the most.

We're building a new party, a grassroots opportunity party that seeks genuine compassion through new opportunities, new ideas, and new solutions that will mean a better life for all. And come November 6th, Americans will choose between two different teams. They can vote for the tax increase team that kicked off its campaign with a plan to take the equivalent of more than $150 a month, as I've said, from each household, a plan that will destroy growth, jobs, and bring back inflation, or they can vote for the team that wants to lower personal income tax rates, give every family more hope, so all of us can go forward together to build a better future for America.

We don't want to see the American people dragged back to that unhappy past. We're asking you to stick with us, and we're going to tell the world, "You ain't seen nothin' yet."

Thank you all. Thank you all, and God bless you all, and now, go get 'em. [*Laughter*] We'll see you out on the trail.

Audience. 4 more years! 4 more years! 4 more years!

The President. All right. All right. I'll sign. [*Laughter*]

Reporter. Mr. President, why have you shut down the Government, sir?

The President. What?

Q. Why have you shut down the Federal Government?

The President. Oh. Sam [Sam Donaldson, ABC News], normally I wouldn't take a question, but that is a challenge, not a question. [*Laughter*]

This has been typical of what has happened ever since we've been here. And you can lay this right on the majority party in the House of Representatives. Just once, just once it would be great to have a budget on time.

Audience member. Hear, hear!

Q. Mr. President——

The President. What did you say, Andrea [Andrea Mitchell, NBC News]?

Q. [*Inaudible*]—prepare for your debates with Mr. Mondale?

The President. What am I doing to——

Q. Prepare. To prepare for the debates.

The President. Just reminding myself of all that we've done and that he says we haven't done.

Note: The President spoke at 1:35 p.m. at the South Portico of the White House.

Proclamation 5247—National Employ the Handicapped Week, 1984
October 4, 1984

By the President of the United States of America

A Proclamation

Today we are at a benchmark in the employment of men and women with disabilities. We have made more progress than we would have dared dream of a century ago. But this very progress underlines the pressing needs which have not yet been met.

These are needs that will demand the utmost of all segments of our population—public and private, professional and volunteer, industry and labor, those who provide services and those who use them.

We have made great gains because of better training and job preparation, greater public understanding of disability, and the willingness of employers to accommodate jobs to disabled workers. We have actively encouraged this progress through programs such as equal employment opportunity and targeted tax credits. Disabled people have been given expanded opportunities for jobs with futures, but obstacles to the effective utilization of such opportunities remain, and technological advances are still beyond the reach of many who need them.

The Congress, by joint resolution ap-proved August 11, 1945, as amended (36 U.S.C. 155), has called for the designation of the first full week in October of each year as "National Employ the Handicapped Week." During this week, let us renew our commitment to increase opportunities for disabled citizens and to help them attain their personal goals.

Now, Therefore, I, Ronald Reagan, President of the United States of America, do hereby proclaim the week beginning October 7, 1984, as National Employ the Handicapped Week. I urge all governors, mayors, other public officials, leaders in business and labor, and private citizens to help meet the challenge of the future by ensuring that disabled people have the opportunity to participate fully in the economic life of the Nation.

In Witness Whereof, I have hereunto set my hand this fourth day of October, in the year of our Lord nineteen hundred and eighty-four, and of the Independence of the United States of America the two hundred and ninth.

RONALD REAGAN

[*Filed with the Office of the Federal Register, 10:24 a.m., October 5, 1984*]

Proclamation 5248—National Children's Week, 1984
October 4, 1984

By the President of the United States of America

A Proclamation

The future of our free society depends on our most important resource: our children. For ourselves as for every other society, our children are our future.

Over the course of human history, men and women in every time and place have chosen the family as the best institution for the raising and nurturing of children. Today, there is a renewed appreciation of the crucial role the family plays in producing healthy and self-confident children, who will mature into adults capable of forming the bonds of love and affection which sustain society.

Children grow best in families supported by the love of parents who pass on to them the rich moral heritage of our civilization and help develop their sense of responsibility to the larger community. Children who are confident of their own worth within a family will bring confidence and strength to our society.

National Children's Week provides an opportunity for us to reaffirm our commitment to ensuring our children a firm foundation for physical, mental, and spiritual growth. As we embrace the younger generation, let us remember that we hold the future in our hands.

The Congress, by House Joint Resolution 153, has designated the week of October 7 through October 13, 1984, as "National Children's Week" and has authorized and requested the President to issue a proclamation in observance of this event.

Now, Therefore, I, Ronald Reagan, President of the United States of America, do hereby proclaim the week of October 7 through October 13, 1984, as National Children's Week. I call upon government agencies and the people of the United States to observe this week with appropriate ceremonies and activities.

In Witness Whereof, I have hereunto set my hand this fourth day of October, in the year of our Lord nineteen hundred and eighty-four, and of the Independence of the United States of America the two hundred and ninth.

RONALD REAGAN

[*Filed with the Office of the Federal Register, 10:25 a.m., October 5, 1984*]

Proclamation 5249—National Quality Month, 1984
October 4, 1984

By the President of the United States of America

A Proclamation

A commitment to excellence in manufacturing and services is essential to our Nation's long-term economic welfare. Quality in manufacturing and services will contribute to increased productivity, reduced costs, and consumer satisfaction.

Historically, American craftsmen have shown great personal pride and interest in developing quality goods and services. Today, we must reinforce our pride of workmanship by renewing that commitment.

Improving the quality of American goods and services depends upon each of us. Individual workers, business managers, labor leaders, and government officials must all work to promote a standard of excellence in the public and private sectors.

To provide for a greater awareness of the need to ensure that American goods and services are of the highest quality, the Congress, by Senate Joint Resolution 304, has designated the month of October 1984 as

"National Quality Month" and authorized and requested the President to issue a proclamation in observance of this event.

Now, Therefore, I, Ronald Reagan, President of the United States of America, do hereby proclaim the month of October 1984 as National Quality Month, and I call upon the people of the United States to observe such month with appropriate ceremonies and activities.

In Witness Whereof, I have hereunto set my hand this fourth day of October, in the year of our Lord nineteen hundred and eighty-four, and of the Independence of the United States of America the two hundred and ninth.

RONALD REAGAN

[*Filed with the Office of the Federal Register, 10:26 a.m., October 5, 1984*]

Message to the Congress Transmitting a Report on Naval Petroleum Reserves
October 5, 1984

To the Congress of the United States:

In accordance with Section 201(3) of the Naval Petroleum Reserves Production Act of 1976 (10 U.S.C. 7422(c)), I wish to inform you of my decision to extend the period of maximum efficient rate production of the naval petroleum reserves for a period of three years from April 5, 1985, the expiration of the currently authorized period of production.

I am transmitting herewith a copy of the report investigating the necessity of continued production of the reserves as required by section 7422(c)(2)(B) of the Naval Petroleum Reserves Production Act of 1976. In light of the findings contained in that report, I hereby certify that continued production from the naval petroleum reserves is in the national interest.

RONALD REAGAN

The White House,
October 5, 1984.

Nomination of John W. Shannon To Be an Assistant Secretary of the Army
October 5, 1984

The President today announced his intention to nominate John W. Shannon to be Assistant Secretary of the Army (Installations and Logistics). This is a new position.

He is currently serving as Deputy Under Secretary of the Army. Previously, he was Special Assistant for Manpower, Reserve Affairs and Logistics in the Office of the Assistant Secretary of Defense (Legislative Affairs) in 1978–1981; Deputy Director for Manpower and Reserve Affairs in the Office of the Assistant Secretary of Defense (Legislative Affairs) in 1975–1978; and Congressional Liaison Officer (Manpower and Reserve Affairs) in the Office of the Secretary of the Army (Chief of Legislative Liaison) in 1972–1974.

He is a retired colonel in the U.S. Army and the recipient of numerous military awards, including the Legion of Merit, the Bronze Star, and the Combat Infantry Badge.

He graduated from Central State University (B.S., 1955) and Shippensburg College (M.S., 1975). He is married, has one child, and resides in Temple Hills, MD. He was born September 13, 1933, in Louisville, KY.

Proclamation 5250—National High-Tech Week, 1984
October 5, 1984

By the President of the United States of America

A Proclamation

Throughout this century, the United States has been the world's leader in high technology innovation and development. Because the economy of this Nation closely is tied to technological advances, maintenance of this leadership is a national priority. Americans must build on our unmatched body of technical knowledge and on our entrepreneurial spirit to bring new and competitive products to the market.

Our youth are the key to maintaining this leadership. Young Americans must receive the educational opportunities necessary to grow and develop in a high technology environment. By providing these opportunities, our national commitment to high technology development will be translated into real progress benefitting future generations.

To focus public attention on the importance of high technology development, the Congress by House Joint Resolution 453, has designated the week of September 30 through October 6, 1984, as "National High-Tech Week" and authorized and requested the President to issue a proclamation in observance of this week.

Now, Therefore, I, Ronald Reagan, President of the United States of America, do hereby proclaim the week of September 30 through October 6, 1984, as National High-Tech Week, and I call upon the people of the United States to celebrate this week with appropriate ceremonies and activities.

In Witness Whereof, I have hereunto set my hand this fifth day of October, in the year of our Lord nineteen hundred and eighty-four, and of the Independence of the United States of America the two hundred and ninth.

RONALD REAGAN

[*Filed with the Office of the Federal Register, 12:31 p.m., October 5, 1984*]

Remarks Following a Meeting With Defense Department Employees
October 5, 1984

Good afternoon. I'm glad to see all of you. Let me first assure our guests that we haven't gathered for a public hanging. [*Laughter*] We're here to recognize these outspoken and creative Defense Department employees who challenged the way that things were done in the past and who offer us a better, less expensive way of doing them in the future.

The 12 men and women here today didn't just complain about a problem; they did something about it. One challenged the price of an aircraft lighting kit, and that challenge resulted in the drop in price from $50 to $8 for every kit we buy. Another is an alert auditor who found some suspicious labor charges and kept looking until he gathered enough evidence to convict a dishonest contractor and obtain $450,000 in fines and recoveries.

But whether the savings was $200 or $2 million, each of these fine Defense employees standing here is proof of the energy, the competence, and the can-do spirit that we're finding throughout the ranks of the Pentagon today.

I think we should also take a minute to recognize their bosses, for if their supervisors had not provided an opportunity for creativity and innovation, then we would not be celebrating these savings and successes. I'm proud of the management reforms that Cap Weinberger has brought to the Pentagon. And I'm encouraged that he has a hotline that any employee—any American—can use to call in a complaint or suggestion. And, in fact, the toll-free number is 1–800–424–9098. [*Laughter*]

Now, there are two reasons why this ceremony here in the Rose Garden is so important: Four years ago, the American people gave us a mandate both to root out waste and fraud in the Federal Government and to rebuild our defenses which had suffered from a decade of neglect. We've been working hard to achieve both these objectives, and I think we can say that our hard work is paying off. We're tackling the tough problems that have plagued Defense management for so many years, and today we're safer, more secure than we were 4 years ago.

And this afternoon, we recognize that it's because of the dedication and achievement of the 12 people we honor here today and to the many other dedicated Defense employees they represent that America is once again able to fill its leadership role in the world.

We have ceremonies to honor the brave servicemen who fight in our wars. Today, we gather to honor the unsung heroes of peace. And so, to each of you, on behalf of the American people, thank you, keep up the good work, and God bless you.

Reporter. Mr. President, have you read the House—have you read——

The President. What?

Q. ——the House Intelligence Committee report on the bombing of Beirut? It said that we—you had adequate security, and there's no logical explanation for it being bombed.

The President. Helen [Helen Thomas, United Press International], I wouldn't take away from Mr. Mondale the opportunity to ask that question in the debate for anything in the world. [*Laughter*] Tune in. Listen in. [*Laughter*]

Q. Are you ready for the debate, Mr. President?

The President. What?

Q. Are you ready for the debate?

The President. Ready as I'm ever going to be.

Q. What's your strategy going to be?

Q. How important is it, sir?

Q. What is your strategy going to be?

The President. Just to tell the truth.

Q. Well, other than that? [*Laughter*]

The President. Well, I think in the world of politics that'd be so unusual that it ought to cause quite a standing ovation. [*Laughter*]

Note: The President spoke at 1:54 p.m. in the Rose Garden at the White House.

Proclamation 5251—National Spina Bifida Month, 1984
October 5, 1984

By the President of the United States of America

A Proclamation

Spina bifida is among the most common birth defects. Between one and two of every 1,000 babies in the United States are born with this problem. Infants with spina bifida may have incompletely developed spinal cords and suffer varying degrees of muscle paralysis and spine and limb deformities. Most develop hydrocephalus—a

potentially dangerous buildup of fluid and pressure within the brain.

Thirty years ago the majority of children with spina bifida died. Today, thanks to Federal and private programs of biomedical research, medical and surgical management of spina bifida has advanced to the point that nearly all children survive. But some of these survivors face various potential problems, including lack of mobility, incontinence, and learning difficulties. Once again, research has provided answers: early surgical closure of spinal defects to reduce the development of infection and hydrocephalus; improved neurosurgical techniques for relieving pressure on the brain; better antibiotics for treating life-threatening infections; lighter braces to aid in mobility; and new techniques to control bladder function.

Further improvements may be expected to result from research supported by the Federal government's National Institute of Neurological and Communicative Disorders and Stroke and the National Institute for Child Health and Human Development. Voluntary agencies including the Spina Bifida Association of America, the March of Dimes Birth Defects Foundation, and the National Easter Seal Society are also involved.

For the many investigators supported by these organizations, the greatest challenge is to find the cause of this crippling birth defect and develop ways to prevent it. Scientists working toward these goals are studying the formation of the spinal cord and factors that might influence its abnormal development.

In order to focus attention on the needs of spina bifida children for long-term care and on the emotional and financial difficulties faced by their parents, the Congress, by Senate Joint Resolution 275, has designated October 1984 as "National Spina Bifida Month" and authorized and requested the President to issue a proclamation in observance of the month.

Now, Therefore, I, Ronald Reagan, President of the United States of America, do hereby proclaim October 1984 as National Spina Bifida Month, and I call upon all government agencies, health organizations, and the people of the United States to observe this month with appropriate ceremonies and activities.

In Witness Whereof, I have hereunto set my hand this fifth day of October, in the year of our Lord nineteen hundred and eighty-four, and of the Indpendence of the United States of America the two hundred and ninth.

RONALD REAGAN

[*Filed with the Office of the Federal Register, 4:33 p.m., October 5, 1984*]

Nomination of James A. Lastowka To Be a Member of the Federal Mine Safety and Health Review Commission
October 5, 1984

The President today announced his intention to nominate James A. Lastowka to be a member of the Federal Mine Safety and Health Review Commission for a term of 6 years expiring August 30, 1990. He would succeed A.E. Lawson.

Since 1982 Mr. Lastowka has served as the General Counsel to the Federal Mine Safety and Health Review Commission. Previously, he was Acting General Counsel (1981–1982) and Deputy General Counsel (1980–1981) at FMSHRC; Assistant General Counsel to the Occupational Safety and Health Review Commission (1979–1980); supervisory attorney at FMSHRC (1978–1979); and attorney-adviser at OSHRC (1976–1978).

Mr. Lastowka graduated from Syracuse University (B.A., 1973) and Georgetown University Law Center (J.D., 1976). He is married and resides in Arlington, VA. He was born October 1, 1951, in Chester, PA.

Radio Address to the Nation on Drug Abuse
October 6, 1984

My fellow Americans:

This week my opponent unveiled with great fanfare his plan to combat dangerous drugs, a plan comprising what he called "four new initiatives." Well, forgive me, but his so-called new initiatives aren't new. Every one of them is by now an old initiative, begun by us more than 2½ years ago, when we first started the South Florida Task Force. Then, a year later, following the success of the task force, we extended these initiatives nationwide and set up the National Narcotics Border Interdiction System, known as NNBIS.

Consider my opponent's first new initiative: "Create a high-level drug coordinator." Well, perhaps he hasn't heard, but we already have drug interdiction coordination at the highest possible level of government. The Vice President has been in charge of the South Florida Task Force and NNBIS from the start. And under his direction, nearly two dozen Federal agencies have been brought into the war on drugs; many, including the Army, Navy, Air Force, and Marines, are more involved in fighting drugs than ever before. Working with the Coast Guard and civilian law enforcement agencies, the military has contributed directly to the interdiction and seizure of major quantities of marijuana and cocaine in the past 2 years.

The Vice President has worked closely with the Attorney General, who has created 13 new organized crime and drug enforcement task forces. And those task forces are bringing record numbers of indictments against the leaders of drug trafficking.

His second new initiative undertakes "broad international initiatives." Well, we're already working with other governments as no administration before has to stop the flow of drugs into our country. Bolivia and Peru recently began coca plant control programs. Pakistan has reduced its apium—or opium, I should say, poppy cultivation more than 90 percent. And Burma continues to expand its opium eradication effort. Colombia has begun spraying its marijuana crops and in the last year has located and destroyed major cocaine factories.

This past summer the Vice President met with the Presidents of five Latin American countries to discuss further efforts. And, as you saw this past week, expert cooperation between our Justice Department and the Italian Government led to arrests of Mafia leaders in the United States.

My opponent's third new initiative: "Step up American enforcement efforts." Well, someone should tell him that we've included $1.2 billion in the 1985 Federal budget for drug law enforcement—a 75-percent increase over the last budget of his administration.

During his administration, drug enforcement agencies and FBI agents were reduced by 10 percent. In our administration, the Department of Justice has added 1,200 new agents and prosecutors, and we've increased the special agents in customs from 600 to 1,000.

Apparently, he hasn't heard about the increase in radar balloons and Navy and Air Force surveillance flights to track planes attempting to slip across the Gulf of Mexico and the Mexican border, not to mention the Coast Guard, which is moving forward with its improved detection and surveillance program.

Finally, his fourth new initiative: "More State and local support." State and local officials are involved in the drug war as never before. Forty-seven States are now eradicating domestic marijuana. State and local law enforcement officials have expressed their satisfaction with the new high level of information sharing and cooperative efforts with the Federal Government.

At home and abroad we've seen record drug busts and convictions, and we've seen that in each of the last 2 years serious crime has dropped—the first time that's happened in consecutive years since the FBI began keeping statistics.

Let me mention something else, because for all the so-called new initiatives my opponent is proposing—that we've already begun—he did omit one very important one. We're not just increasing our efforts to limit the supply of drugs; we're also trying to limit the demand for drugs. And that's why Nancy's been joining with concerned parents and citizens all across our country to put out the word to young Americans: Stay away from drugs; they hurt and kill.

And we can all be proud of the way our young people have responded. In 1979 one in nine high school seniors used marijuana on a daily basis. By 1983 the number had dropped to 1 in 18—still too high, but a great improvement.

Just as Americans have pulled together to turn around so many other problems we inherited 4 years ago—inflation, record interest rates, taxes, no growth, falling test scores in school, and low morale in our military—so, too, we're coming together as a nation to tackle the drug problem.

So, the question I keep wondering about my opponent is, where's he been?

Until next week, thanks for listening, and God bless you.

Note: The President spoke at 12:06 p.m. from Camp David, MD.

Debate Between the President and Former Vice President Walter F. Mondale in Louisville, Kentucky
October 7, 1984

Ms. Ridings. Good evening from the Kentucky Center for the Arts in Louisville, Kentucky. I'm Dorothy Ridings, president of the League of Women Voters, the sponsor of tonight's first Presidential debate between Republican Ronald Reagan and Democrat Walter Mondale.

Tonight's debate marks the third consecutive Presidential election in which the League is presenting the candidates for the Nation's highest office in face-to-face debate.

Our panelists are James Wieghart, national political correspondent for Scripps-Howard News Service; Diane Sawyer, correspondent for the CBS program "60 Minutes;" and Fred Barnes, national political correspondent for the Baltimore Sun. Barbara Walters of ABC News, who is appearing in her fourth Presidential debate, is our moderator.

Barbara.

Ms. Walters. Thank you, Dorothy.

A few words as we begin tonight's debate about the format. The position of the candidates—that is, who answers questions first and who gives the last statement—was determined by a toss of a coin between the two candidates. Mr. Mondale won, and that

means that he chose to give the final closing statement. It means, too, that the President will answer the first question first. I hope that's clear. If it isn't, it will become clear as the debate goes on.

Further, the candidates will be addressed as they each wanted and will, therefore, be called "Mr. President" and "Mr. Mondale."

Since there will also be a second debate between the two Presidential candidates, tonight will focus primarily on the economy and other domestic issues. The debate, itself, is built around questions from the panel. In each of its segments, a reporter will ask the candidates the same general question. Then—and this is important—each candidate will have the chance to rebut what the other has said. And the final segment of the debate will be the closing segment, and the candidates will each have 4 minutes for their closing statements. And as I have said, Mr. Mondale will be the last person on the program to speak.

And now I would like to add a personal note if I may. As Dorothy Ridings pointed out, I have been involved now in four Presidential debates, either as a moderator or as a panelist. In the past, there was no problem in selecting panelists. Tonight, however, there were to have been four panelists participating in this debate.

The candidates were given a list of almost 100 qualified journalists from all the media and could agree on only these three fine journalists. As moderator, and on behalf of my fellow journalists, I very much regret, as does the League of Women Voters, that this situation has occurred.

And now let us begin the debate with the first question from James Wieghart.

Mr. Wieghart.

The Nation's Economy

Mr. Wieghart. Mr. President, in 1980 you promised the American people—in your campaign—a balanced budget by 1983. We've now had more and bigger deficits in the 4 years you've been in office. Mr. President, do you have a secret plan to balance the budget sometime in a second term, and if so, would you lay out that plan for us tonight?

The President. I have a plan—not a secret plan. As a matter of fact, it is the economic recovery program that we presented when I took office in 1981.

It is true that earlier, working with some very prominent economists, I had come up, during the campaign, with an economic program that I thought could rectify the great problems confronting us—the double-digit inflation, the high tax rates that I think were hurting the economy, the stagflation that we were undergoing. Before even the election day, something that none of those economists had even predicted had happened, that the economy was so worsened that I was openly saying that what we had thought on the basis of our plan could have brought a balanced budget—no, that was no longer possible.

So, the plan that we have had and that we are following is a plan that is based on growth in the economy, recovery without inflation, and reducing the share that the Government is taking from the gross national product, which has become a drag on the economy.

Already, we have a recovery that has been going on for about 21 months to the point that we can now call it an expansion. Under that, this year, we have seen a $21 billion reduction in the deficit from last year, based mainly on the increased revenues the Government is getting without raising tax rates.

Our tax cut, we think, was very instrumental in bringing about this economic recovery. We have reduced inflation to about a third of what it was. The interest rates have come down about 9 or 10 points and, we think, must come down further. In the last 21 months, more than 6 million people have gotten jobs—there have been created new jobs for those people to where there are now 105 million civilians working, where there were only 99 million before; 107, if you count the military.

So, we believe that as we continue to reduce the level of government spending—the increase, rate of increase in government spending, which has come down from 17 to 6 percent, and, at the same time, as the growth in the economy increases the revenues the Government gets, without raising taxes, those two lines will meet. And when they meet, that is a balanced budget.

Mr. Wieghart. Mr. President, the Congressional Budget Office has some bad news. The lines aren't about to meet, according to their projections. They project that the budget deficit will continue to climb. In the year 1989 they project a budget deficit of $273 billion.

In view of that, and in view of the economic recovery we are now enjoying, would it make sense to propose a tax increase or take some other fiscal measures to reduce that deficit now, when times are relatively good?

The President. The deficit is the result of excessive government spending. I do not, very frankly, take seriously the Congressional Budget Office projections, because they have been wrong on virtually all of them, including the fact that our recovery wasn't going to take place to begin with. But it has taken place.

But, as I said, we have the rate of increase in government spending down to 6 percent. If the rate of increase in government spending can be held at 5 percent— we're not far from there—by 1989 that would have reduced the budget deficits down to a $30 or $40 billion level. At the same time, if we can have a 4-percent recovery continue through that same period of time, that will mean—without an increase in tax rates—that will mean $400 billion more in government revenues. And so, I think that the lines can meet.

Actually, in constant dollars, in the domestic side of the budget, there has been no spending increase in the 4 years that we have been here.

Mr. Wieghart. Mr. Mondale, the Carter-Mondale administration didn't come close to balancing the budget in its 4 years in office either, despite the fact that President Carter did promise a balanced budget during his term.

You have proposed a plan combining tax increases and budgetary cuts and other changes in the administration of the Government that would reduce the projected budget deficit by two-thirds, to approximately $87 billion in 1989. That still is an enormous deficit that will be running for these 4 years. What other steps do you think should be taken to reduce this deficit and position the country for economic growth?

Mr. Mondale. One of the key tests of leadership is whether one sees clearly the nature of the problems confronted by our nation. And perhaps the dominant domestic issue of our times is what do we do about these enormous deficits.

I respect the President; I respect the Presidency, and I think he knows that. But the fact of it is, every estimate by this administration about the size of the deficit has been off by billions and billions of dollars. As a matter of fact, over 4 years, they've missed the mark by nearly $600 billion. We were told we would have a balanced budget in 1983. It was $200 billion deficit instead. And now we have a major question facing the American people as to whether we'll deal with this deficit and get it down for the sake of a healthy recovery.

Virtually every economic analysis that I've heard of, including the distinguished Congressional Budget Office, which is respected by, I think, almost everyone, says that even with historically high levels of economic growth, we will suffer a $263 billion deficit. In other words, it doesn't converge as the President suggests. It gets larger even with growth.

What that means is that we will continue to have devastating problems with foreign trade. This is the worst trade year in American history by far. Our rural and farm friends will have continued devastation. Real interest rates—the real cost of interest—will remain very, very high, and many economists are predicting that we're moving into a period of very slow growth because the economy is tapering off and may be a recession. I get it down to a level below 2 percent of gross national product with a policy that's fair. I've stood up and told the American people that I think it's a real problem, that it can destroy long-term economic growth, and I've told you what I think should be done.

I think this is a test of leadership, and I think the American people know the difference.

Mr. Wieghart. Mr. Mondale, one other way to attack the deficit is further reductions in spending. The President has submitted a number of proposals to Congress to do just that, and in many instances the House, controlled by the Democrats, has opposed them. Isn't it one aspect of leadership for prominent Democrats such as yourself to encourage responsible reductions in spending, and thereby reduce the deficit?

Mr. Mondale. Absolutely, and I proposed over a hundred billion dollars in cuts in Federal spending over 4 years, but I am not going to cut it out of Social Security and Medicare and student assistance and things—[*applause*]—that people need. These people depend upon all of us for the little security that they have, and I'm not going to do it that way.

The rate of defense spending increase can be slowed. Certainly we can find a coffeepot that costs something less than $7,000. And there are other ways of squeezing this budget without constantly picking on our senior citizens and the most vulnerable in American life. And that's why the Congress, including the Republicans, have not gone along with the President's recommendations.

Ms. Walters. I would like to ask the audience please to refrain from applauding either side; it just takes away from the time for your candidates.

And now it is time for the rebuttal. Mr. President, 1 minute for rebuttal.

The President. Yes. I don't believe that Mr. Mondale has a plan for balancing the budget; he has a plan for raising taxes. And, as a matter of fact, the biggest single tax increase in our nation's history took place 1977. And for the 5 years previous to our taking office, taxes doubled in the United States, and the budgets increased $318 billion. So, there is no ratio between taxing and balancing a budget. Whether you borrow the money or whether you simply tax it away from the people, you're taking the same amount of money out of the private sector, unless and until you bring down government's share of what it is taking.

With regard to Social Security, I hope there'll be more time than just this minute to mention that, but I will say this: A President should never say "never." But I'm going to violate that rule and say "never." I will never stand for a reduction of the Social Security benefits to the people that are now getting them.

Ms. Walters. Mr. Mondale?

Mr. Mondale. Well, that's exactly the commitment that was made to the American people in 1980: He would never reduce benefits. And of course, what happened right after the election is they proposed to cut Social Security benefits by 25 percent— reducing the adjustment for inflation, cutting out minimum benefits for the poorest on Social Security, removing educational benefits for dependents whose widows were trying—with widows trying to get them through college. Everybody remembers that; people know what happened.

There's a difference. I have fought for Social Security and Medicare and for things to help people who are vulnerable all my life, and I will do it as President of the United States.

Ms. Walters. Thank you very much. We'll now begin with segment number two with my colleague, Diane Sawyer.

Ms. Sawyer?

Leadership Qualities

Ms. Sawyer. Mr. President, Mr. Mondale, the public opinion polls do suggest that the American people are most concerned about the personal leadership characteristics of the two candidates, and each of you has questioned the other's leadership ability.

Mr. President, you have said that Mr. Mondale's leadership would take the country down the path of defeatism and despair, and Vice President Bush has called him whining and hoping for bad news. And, Mr. Mondale, you have said that President Reagan offers showmanship, not leadership, that he has not mastered what he must know to command his government.

I'd like to ask each of you to substantiate your claims—Mr. Mondale first. Give us specifics to support your claim that President Reagan is a showman, not a leader; has not mastered what he must know to be President after 4 years, and then, second, tell us what personal leadership characteristics you have that he does not.

Mr. Mondale. Well, first of all, I think the first answer this evening suggests exactly what I'm saying. There is no question that we face this massive deficit, and almost everybody agrees unless we get it down, the chances for long-term, healthy growth are nil. And it's also unfair to dump these tremendous bills on our children.

The President says it will disappear overnight because of some reason. No one else believes that's the case. I do, and I'm standing up to the issue with an answer that's fair. I think that's what leadership is all about. There's a difference between being a quarterback and a cheerleader, and when there's a real problem, a President must confront it.

What I was referring to, of course, in the comment that you referred to was the situation in Lebanon. Now, for three occasions, one after another, our Embassies were assaulted in the same way by a truck with demolitions. The first time—and I did not criticize the President, because these things can happen—once, and sometimes twice— the second time the barracks in Lebanon were assaulted, as we all remember. There was two or three commission reports, recommendations by the CIA, the State Department, and the others, and the third time there was even a warning from the terrorists themselves.

Now, I believe that a President must command that White House and those who work for him. It's the toughest job on Earth, and you must master the facts and insist that things that must be done are done. I believe that the way in which I will approach the Presidency is what's needed, because all my life that has been the way in which I have sought to lead. And that's why in this campaign I'm telling you exactly what I want to do. I am answering your questions. I am trying to provide leadership now, before the election, so that the American people can participate in that decision.

Ms. Sawyer. You have said, Mr. Mondale, that the polls have given you lower ratings on leadership than President Reagan because your message has failed to get through. Given that you have been in public office for so many years, what accounts for the failure of your message to get through?

Mr. Mondale. Well, I think we're getting better all the time. And I think tonight, as we contrast for the first time our differing approach to government, to values, to the leadership in this country, I think as this debate goes forward, the American people will have for the first time a chance to weigh the two of us against each other. And I think, as a part of that process, what I am trying to say will come across, and that is that we must lead, we must command, we must direct, and a President must see it like it is. He must stand for the values of decency that the American people stand for, and he must use the power of the White House to try to control these nuclear weapons and lead this world toward a safer world.

Ms. Sawyer. Mr. President, the issue is leadership in personal terms. First, do you think, as Vice President Bush said, that Mr. Mondale's campaign is one of whining and hoping for bad news? And second, what leadership characteristics do you possess that Mr. Mondale does not?

The President. Well, whether he does or not, let me suggest my own idea about the leadership factor, since you've asked it. And, incidentally, I might say that with regard to the 25-percent cut in Social Security—before I get to the answer to your question—the only 25-percent cut that I know of was accompanying that huge 1977 tax increase, was a cut of 25 percent in the benefits for every American who was born after 1916.

Now, leadership. First of all, I think you must have some principles you believe in. In mine, I happen to believe in the people and believe that the people are supposed to be dominant in our society—that they, not government, are to have control of their own affairs to the greatest extent possible, with an orderly society.

Now, having that, I think also that in leadership—well, I believe that you find people, positions such as I'm in who have the talent and ability to do the things that are needed in the various departments of government. I don't believe that a leader should be spending his time in the Oval Office deciding who's going to play tennis on the White House court. And you let those people go with the guidelines of overall policy, not looking over their shoulder and nitpicking the manner in which they go at the job. You are ultimately responsible, however, for that job.

But I also believe something else about that. I believe that—and when I became Governor of California, I started this, and I continue it in this office—that any issue that comes before me, I have instructed Cabinet members and staff they are not to bring up any of the political ramifications that might surround the issue. I don't want to hear them. I want to hear only arguments as to whether it is good or bad for the people—is it morally right? And on that basis and that basis alone, we make a decision on every issue.

Now, with regard to my feeling about why I thought that his record bespoke his possible taking us back to the same things that we knew under the previous administration, his record is that he spoke in praise of deficits several times, said they weren't to be abhorred—that, as a matter of fact, he at one time said he wished the deficit could be doubled, because they stimulate the economy and helped reduce unemployment.

Ms. Sawyer. As a followup, let me draw in another specific, if I could—a specific that the Democrats have claimed about your campaign—that it is essentially based on imagery. And one specific that they allege is that, for instance, recently you showed up at the opening ceremony of a Buffalo old-age housing project, when in fact, your policy was to cut Federal housing subsidies for the elderly. Yet you were there to have your picture taken with them.

The President. Our policy was not to cut subsidies. We have believed in partnership, and that was an example of a partnership between, not only local government and the Federal Government but also between the private sector that built that particular structure. And this is what we've been trying to do, is involve the Federal Government in such partnerships.

We are today subsidizing housing for more than 10 million people, and we're going to continue along that line. We have no thought of throwing people out into the snow, whether because of age or need. We have preserved the safety net for the people with true need in this country, and it has been pure demagoguery that we have in some way shut off all the charitable programs or many of them for the people who have real need. The safety net is there, and we're taking care of more people than has ever been taken care of before by any administration in this country.

Ms. Walters. Mr. Mondale, an opportunity for you to rebut.

Mr. Mondale. Well, I guess I'm reminded a little bit of what Will Rogers once said about Hoover. He said, "It's not what he doesn't know that bothers me; it's what he knows for sure that just ain't so." [*Laughter*] The fact of it is: The President's budget sought to cut Social Security by 25 percent. It's not an opinion; it's a fact. And when the President was asked the other day, "What do you want to cut in the budget?", he said, "Cut those things I asked for but didn't get." That's Social Security and Medicare.

The second fact is that the housing unit for senior citizens that the President dedicated in Buffalo was only made possible through a Federal assistance program for senior citizens that the President's budget sought to terminate. So, if he'd had his way, there wouldn't have been any housing project there at all. This administration has taken a meat cleaver out, in terms of Federal-assisted housing, and the record is there. We have to see the facts before we can draw conclusions.

Ms. Walters. Mr. President?

The President. Well, let me just respond with regard to Social Security. When we took office, we discovered that the program that the Carter-Mondale administration had said would solve the fiscal problems of Social Security for the next 50 years wouldn't solve them for 5. Social Security was due to go bankrupt before 1983.

Any proposals that I made at that time were at the request of the chairman, a Democrat, of one of the leading committees, who said we have to do something before the program goes broke and the checks bounce. And so, we made a proposal. And then in 1982, they used that proposal in a demagogic fashion for the 1982 campaign. And 3 days after the election in 1982, they came to us and said, Social Security, we know, is broke. Indeed, we had to borrow $17 billion to pay the checks. And then I asked for a bipartisan commission, which I'd asked for from the beginning, to sit down and work out a solution.

And so, the whole matter of what to do with Social Security has been resolved by bipartisan legislation, and it is on a sound basis now for as far as you can see into the next century.

Ms. Walters. Mr. President, we begin segment number three with Fred Barnes.

Religion

Mr. Barnes. Mr. President, would you describe your religious beliefs, noting particularly whether you consider yourself a born-again Christian, and explain how these beliefs affect your Presidential decisions?

The President. Well, I was raised to have a faith and a belief and have been a member of a church since I was a small boy. In our particular church, we did not use that term, "born again," so I don't know whether I would fit that—that particular term. But I have—thanks to my mother, God rest her soul—the firmest possible belief and faith in God. And I don't believe—I believe, I should say, as Lincoln once said, that I could not—I would be the most stupid man in the world if I thought I could confront the duties of the office I hold if I could not turn to someone who was stronger and greater than all others. And I do resort to prayer.

At the same time, however, I have not

believed that prayer should be introduced into an election or be a part of a political campaign—or religion a part of that campaign. As a matter of fact, I think religion became a part of this campaign when Mr. Mondale's running mate said I wasn't a good Christian.

So, it does play a part in my life. I have no hesitancy in saying so. And, as I say, I don't believe that I could carry on unless I had a belief in a higher authority and a belief that prayers are answered.

Mr. Barnes. Given those beliefs, Mr. President, why don't you attend services regularly, either by going to church or by inviting a minister to the White House, as President Nixon used to do, or someone to Camp David, as President Carter used to do?

The President. The answer to your question is very simple about why I don't go to church. I have gone to church regularly all my life, and I started to here in Washington. And now, in the position I hold and in the world in which we live, where Embassies do get blown up in Beirut—we're supposed to talk about that on the debate the 21st, I understand—but I pose a threat to several hundred people if I go to church.

I know the threats that are made against me. We all know the possibility of terrorism. We have seen the barricades that have had to be built around the White House. And, therefore, I don't feel—and my minister knows this and supports me in this position—I don't feel that I have a right to go to church, knowing that my being there could cause something of the kind that we have seen in other places, in Beirut, for example. And I miss going to church, but I think the Lord understands. [*Applause*]

Ms. Walters. May I ask you, please—[*applause*]—may I ask the audience please to refrain from applause.

Fred, your second question.

Mr. Barnes. Mr. Mondale, would you describe your religious beliefs and mention whether you consider yourself a born-again Christian, and explain how those beliefs would affect your decisions as President?

Mr. Mondale. First of all, I accept President Reagan's affirmation of faith. I'm sure that we all accept and admire his commitment to his faith, and we are strengthened,

all of us, by that fact.

I am a son of a Methodist minister. My wife is the daughter of a Presbyterian minister. And I don't know if I've been born again, but I know I was born into a Christian family. And I believe I have sung at more weddings and more funerals than anybody ever to seek the Presidency. Whether that helps or not, I don't know.

I have a deep religious faith. Our family does. It is fundamental. It's probably the reason that I'm in politics. I think our faith tells us, instructs us, about the moral life that we should lead. And I think we're all together on that.

What bothers me is this growing tendency to try to use one's own personal interpretation of faith politically, to question others' faith, and to try to use the instrumentalities of government to impose those views on others. All history tells us that that's a mistake.

When the Republican platform says that from here on out, we're going to have a religious test for judges before they're selected for the Federal court, and then Jerry Falwell announces that that means they get at least two Justices of the Supreme Court, I think that's an abuse of faith in our country.

This nation is the most religious nation on Earth—more people go to church and synagogues than any other nation on Earth—and it's because we kept the politicians and the state out of the personal exercise of our faith. That's why faith in the United States is pure and unpolluted by the intervention of politicians. And I think if we want to continue—as I do—to have a religious nation, lets keep that line and never cross it.

Ms. Walters. Thank you. Mr. Barnes, next question. We have time for rebuttal now.

Mr. Barnes. I think I have a followup.

Ms. Walters. Yes, I asked you if you did. I'm sorry——

Mr. Barnes. Yes, I do.

Ms. Walters. ——I thought you waived it.

Mr. Barnes. Yes, Mr. Mondale, you've complained, just now, about Jerry Falwell, and you've complained other times about other fundamentalists in politics. Correct me if I'm wrong, but I don't recall your ever complaining about ministers who are involved in the civil rights movement or in the anti-Vietnam war demonstrations or about black preachers who've been so involved in American politics. Is it only conservative ministers that you object to?

Mr. Mondale. No. What I object to—[*applause*]—what I object to—what I object to is someone seeking to use his faith to question the faith of another or to use that faith and seek to use the power of government to impose it on others.

A minister who is in civil rights or in the conservative movement, because he believes his faith instructs him to do that, I admire. The fact that the faith speaks to us and that we are moral people, hopefully, I accept and rejoice in. It's when you try to use that to undermine the integrity of private political—or private religious faith and the use of the state is where—for the most personal decisions in American life—that's where I draw the line.

Ms. Walters. Thank you. Now, Mr. President, rebuttal.

The President. Yes, it's very difficult to rebut, because I find myself in so much agreement with Mr. Mondale. I, too, want that wall that is in the Constitution of separation of church and state to remain there. The only attacks I have made are on people who apparently would break away at that wall from the government side, using the government, using the power of the courts and so forth to hinder that part of the Constitution that says the government shall not only not establish a religion, it shall not inhibit the practice of religion. And they have been using these things to have government, through court orders, inhibit the practice of religion. A child wants to say grace in a school cafeteria and a court rules that they can't do it because it's school property. These are they types of things that I think have been happening in a kind of a secular way that have been eroding that separation, and I am opposed to that.

With regard to a platform on the Supreme Court, I can only say one thing about that. I have appointed one member to the Supreme Court: Sandra Day O'Connor. I'll stand on my record on that. And if I have the opportunity to appoint any more, I'll do it in the same manner that I did in selecting her.

Ms. Walters. Mr. Mondale, your rebuttal, please.

Mr. Mondale. The platform to which the President refers, in fact, calls for a religious test in the selection of judges. And Jerry Falwell says that means we get two or three judges. And it would involve a religious test for the first time in American life.

Let's take the example that the President cites. I believe in prayer. My family prays. We've never had any difficulty finding time to pray. But do we want a constitutional amendment adopted of the kind proposed by the President that gets the local politicians into the business of selecting prayers that our children must either recite in school or be embarrassed and asked to excuse themselves? Who would write the prayer? What would it say? How would it be resolved when those disputes occur?

It seems to me that a moment's reflection tells you why the United States Senate turned that amendment down, because it will undermine the practice of honest faith in our country by politicizing it. We don't want that.

Ms. Walters. Thank you, Mr. Mondale. Our time is up for this round.

We go into the second round of our questioning, begin again with Jim Wieghart.

Jim?

Political Issues

Mr. Wieghart. After that discussion, this may be like going from the sublime to the ridiculous, but here goes. I have a political question for you, Mr. Mondale. [*Laughter*]

Polls indicate a massive change in the electorate, away from the coalition that has long made the Democratic Party a majority. Blue-collar workers, young professionals, their children, and much of the middle class now regard themselves as Independents or Republican instead of Democrats, and the gap—the edge the Democrats had in party registration seems to be narrowing.

I'd like to ask you, Mr. Mondale, what is causing this? Is the Democratic Party out of sync with the majority of Americans? And will it soon be replaced as the majority party by the Republicans? What do you think needs to be done about it, as a Democrat?

Mr. Mondale. My answer is that this campaign isn't over yet. And when people vote, I think you're going to see a very strong verdict by the American people that they favor the approach that I'm talking about.

The American people want arms control. They don't want this arms race. And they don't want this deadly new effort to bring weapons into the heavens. And they want an American foreign policy that leads toward a safer world.

The American people see this debt, and they know it's got to come down. And if it won't come down, the economy's going to slow down, maybe go into a recession. They see this tremendous influx and swamping of cheap foreign imports in this country that has cost over 3 million jobs, given farmers the worst year in American history. And they know this debt must come down as well, because it's unfair to our children.

The American people want this environment protected. They know that these toxic waste dumps should have been cleaned up a long time ago, and they know that people's lives and health are being risked, because we've had an administration that has been totally insensitive to the law and the demand for the protection of the environment.

The American people want their children educated. They want to get our edge back in science, and they want a policy headed by the President that helps close this gap that's widening between the United States and Europe and Japan.

The American people want to keep opening doors. They want those civil rights laws enforced. They want the equal rights amendment ratified. They want equal pay for comparable effort for women. And they want it because they've understood from the beginning that when we open doors, we're all stronger, just as we were at the Olympics.

I think as you make the case, the American people will increasingly come to our cause.

Mr. Wieghart. Mr. Mondale, isn't it possible that the American people have heard your message—and they are listening—but they are rejecting it?

Mr. Mondale. Well, tonight we had the first debate over the deficit. The President says it'll disappear automatically. I've said it's going to take some work. I think the American people will draw their own conclusions.

Secondly, I've said that I will not support the cuts in Social Security and Medicare and the rest that the President has proposed. The President answers that it didn't happen or, if it did, it was resolved later in a commission. As the record develops, I think it's going to become increasingly clear that what I am saying and where I want to take this country is exactly where the country wants to go, and the comparison of approaches is such that I think will lead to further strength.

Mr. Wieghart. Mr. President, you and your party are benefiting from what appears to be an erosion of the old Democratic coalition, but you have not laid out a specific agenda to take this shift beyond November 6th. What is your program for America for the next decade, with some specificity?

The President. Well, again, I'm running on the record. I think sometimes Mr. Mondale's running away from his. But I'm running on the record of what we have asked for. We'll continue to try to get things that we didn't get in a program that has already brought the rate of spending of government down from 17 percent to 6.1 percent, a program of returning authority and autonomy to the local and State governments that has been unjustly seized by the Federal Government. And you might find those words in a Democratic platform of some years ago—I know, because I was a Democrat at that time. And I left the party eventually, because I could no longer follow the turn in the Democratic leadership that took us down an entirely different path, a path of centralizing authority in the Federal Government, lacking trust in the American people.

I promised, when we took office, that we would reduce inflation. We have, to one-third of what it was. I promised that we would reduce taxes. We did, 25 percent across the board. That barely held even with—if it did that much—with the gigantic tax increase imposed in 1977. But at least it took that burden away from them.

I said that we would create jobs for our people, and we did—6 million in the last 20 or 21 months. I said that we would become respected in the world once again and that we would refurbish our national defense to the place that we could deal on the world scene and then seek disarmament, reduction of arms, and, hopefully, an elimination of nuclear weapons. We have done that.

All of the things that I said we would do, from inflation being down, interest rates being down, unemployment falling, all of those things we have done. And I think this is something the American people see.

I think they also know that we had a commission that came in a year ago with a recommendation on education—on excellence in education. And today, without the Federal Government being involved other than passing on to them, the school districts, the words from that commission, we find 35 States with task forces now dealing with their educational problems. We find that schools are extending the curriculum to now have forced teaching of mathematics and science and so forth. All of these things have brought an improvement in the college entrance exams for the first time in some 20 years.

So, I think that many Democrats are seeing the same thing this Democrat saw: The leadership isn't taking us where we want to go.

Mr. Wieghart. Mr. President, much of what you said affects the quality of life of many Americans—their income, the way they live, and so forth—but there's an aspect to quality of life that lies beyond the private sector which has to do with our neighborhoods, our cities, our streets, our parks, our environment. In those areas, I have difficulty seeing what your program is and what you feel the Federal responsibility is in these areas of the quality of life in the public sector that affects everybody, and even enormous wealth by one individual can't create the kind of environment that he might like.

The President. There are tasks that government legitimately should enforce and tasks that government performs well, and you've named some of them. Crime has come down the last 2 years, for the first time in many, many decades that it has

come down—or since we've kept records—2 consecutive years, and last year it came down the biggest drop in crime that we've had. I think that we've had something to do with that, just as we have with the drug problem nationwide.

The environment? Yes, I feel as strongly as anyone about the preservation of the environment. When we took office, we found that the national parks were so dirty and contained so many hazards, lack of safety features, that we stopped buying additional park land until we had rectified this with what was to be a 5-year program—but it's just about finished already—a billion dollars. And now we're going back to budgeting for additional lands for our parks. We have added millions of acres to the wilderness lands, to the game refuges. I think that we're out in front of most—and I see that the red light is blinking, so I can't continue. But I've got more.

Ms. Walters. Well, you'll have a chance when your rebuttal time comes up, perhaps, Mr. President. Mr. Mondale, now it's your turn for rebuttal.

Mr. Mondale. The President says that when the Democratic Party made its turn, he left it. The year that he decided we had lost our way was the year that John F. Kennedy was running against Richard Nixon. I was chairman of "Minnesotans for Kennedy;" President Reagan was chairman of a thing called "Democrats for Nixon." Now, maybe we made a wrong turn with Kennedy, but I'll be proud of supporting him all of my life. And I'm very happy that John Kennedy was elected, because John Kennedy looked at the future with courage, saw what needed to be done, and understood his own government.

The President just said that his government is shrinking. It's not. It's now the largest peacetime government ever in terms of the take from the total economy. And instead of retreating—instead of being strong where we should be strong, he wants to make it strong and intervene in the most private and personal questions in American life. That's where government should not be.

Ms. Walters. Mr. President?

The President. Before I campaigned as a

Democrat for a Republican candidate for President, I had already voted for Dwight Eisenhower to be President of the United States. And so, my change had come earlier than that. I hadn't gotten around to reregistering as yet. I found that was rather difficult to do. But I finally did it.

There are some other things that have been said here—back, and you said that I might be able to dredge them up. Mr. Mondale referred to the farmers' worst year. The farmers are not the victims of anything this administration has done. The farmers were the victims of the double-digit inflation and the 21½-percent interest rates of the Carter-Mondale administration and the grain embargo, which destroyed our reliability nationwide as a supplier. All of these things are presently being rectified, and I think that we are going to salvage the farmers. As a matter of fact, there has been less than one-quarter of 1 percent of foreclosures of the 270,000 loans from government that the farmers have.

Ms. Walters. Thank you, Mr. President. We'll now turn to Diane Sawyer for her round of questions.

Diane?

Abortion

Ms. Sawyer. I'd like to turn to an area that I think few people enjoy discussing, but that we probably should tonight because the positions of the two candidates are so clearly different and lead to very different policy consequences—and that is abortion and right to life. I'm exploring for your personal views of abortion and specifically how you would want them applied as public policy.

First, Mr. President. Do you consider abortion murder or a sin? And second, how hard would you work—what kind of priority would you give in your second term legislation to make abortion illegal? And specifically, would you make certain, as your party platform urges, that Federal justices that you appoint be prolife?

The President. I have believed that in the appointment of judges that all that was specified in the party platform was that they respect the sanctity of human life. Now, that I would want to see in any judge and with regard to any issue having to do

with human life. But with regard to abortion, and I have a feeling that this is—there's been some reference without naming it here in the remarks of Mr. Mondale tied to injecting religion into government. With me, abortion is not a problem of religion, it's a problem of the Constitution.

I believe that until and unless someone can establish that the unborn child is not a living human being, then that child is already protected by the Constitution, which guarantees life, liberty, and the pursuit of happiness to all of us. And I think that this is what we should concentrate on, is trying—I know there were weeks and weeks of testimony before a Senate committee, there were medical authorities, there were religious—there were clerics there—everyone talking about this matter of prolife. And at the end of all of that, not one shred of evidence was introduced that the unborn child was not alive. We have seen premature births that are now grown-up, happy people going around.

Also, there is a strange dichotomy in this whole position about our courts ruling that abortion is not the taking of a human life. In California, sometime ago, a man beat a woman so savagely that her unborn child was born dead with a fractured skull, and the California State Legislature unanimously passed a law that was signed by the then-Democratic Governor—signed a law that said that any man who so abuses a pregnant woman that he causes the death of her unborn child shall be charged with murder. Now, isn't it strange that that same woman could have taken the life of her unborn child, and it was abortion and not murder, but if somebody else does it, that's murder? And it used the term "death of the unborn child."

So, this has been my feeling about abortion, that we have a problem now to determine—and all the evidence so far comes down on the side of the unborn child being a living human being.

Ms. Sawyer. A two-part followup. Do I take it from what you've said about the platform, then, that you don't regard the language and don't regard in your own appointments, abortion position a test of any kind for justices—that it should be? And also, if abortion is made illegal, how would you want it enforced? Who would be the policing units that would investigate? And would you want the women who have abortions to be prosecuted?

The President. The laws regarding that always were State laws. It was only when the Supreme Court handed down a decision that the Federal Government intervened in what had always been a State policy. Our laws against murder are State laws. So, I would think that this would be the point of enforcement on this.

As I say, I feel that we have a problem here to resolve. And no one has approached it from that matter. It does not happen that the church that I belong to had that as part of its dogma. I know that some churches do.

Now, it is a sin if you're taking a human life. At the same time, in our Judeo-Christian tradition, we recognize the right of taking a human life in self-defense. And therefore, I've always believed that a mother, if medically it is determined that her life is at risk if she goes through with the pregnancy, she has a right then to take the life of even her own unborn child in defense of her own.

Ms. Sawyer. Mr. Mondale, to turn to you, do you consider abortion a murder or a sin? And bridging from what President Reagan said, he has written that if society doesn't know whether life does—human life, in fact, does begin at conception, as long as there is a doubt, that the unborn child should at least be given the benefit of the doubt and that there should be protection for that unborn child.

Mr. Mondale. This is one of the most emotional and difficult issues that could possibly be debated. I think your questions, however, underscore the fact there is probably no way that government should or could answer this question in every individual case and in the private lives of the American people.

The constitutional amendment proposed by President Reagan would make it a crime for a woman to have an abortion if she had been raped or suffered from incest. Is it really the view of the American people, however you feel on the question of abortion, that government ought to be reaching

into your livingrooms and making choices like this? I think it cannot work, won't work, and will lead to all kinds of cynical evasions of the law. Those who can afford to have them will continue to have them. The disadvantaged will go out in the back alley as they used to do.

I think these questions are inherently personal and moral, and every individual instance is different. Every American should be aware of the seriousness of the step. But there are some things that government can do and some things they cannot do.

Now, the example that the President cites has nothing to do with abortion. Somebody went to a woman and nearly killed her. That's always been a serious crime and always should be a serious crime. But how does that compare with the problem of a woman who is raped? Do we really want those decisions made by judges who've been picked because they will agree to find the person guilty? I don't think so, and I think it's going in exactly the wrong direction.

In America, on basic moral questions we have always let the people decide in their own personal lives. We haven't felt so insecure that we've reached for the club of state to have our point of view. It's been a good instinct. And we're the most religious people on Earth.

One final point: President Reagan, as Governor of California, signed a bill which is perhaps the most liberal proabortion bill of any State in the Union.

Ms. Sawyer. But if I can get you back for a moment on my point, which was the question of when human life begins—a two-part followup. First of all, at what point do you believe that human life begins in the growth of a fetus? And second of all, you said that government shouldn't be involved in the decisions. Yet there are those who would say that government is involved, and the consequence of the involvement was 1.5 million abortions in 1980. And how do you feel about that?

Mr. Mondale. The basic decision of the Supreme Court is that each person has to make this judgment in her own life, and that's the way it's been done. And it's a personal and private, moral judgment. I don't know the answer to when life begins. And it's not that simple, either. You've got another life involved. And if it's rape, how do you draw moral judgments on that? If it's incest, how do you draw moral judgments on that? Does every woman in America have to present herself before some judge picked by Jerry Falwell to clear her personal judgment? It won't work. [*Applause*]

Ms. Walters. I'm sorry to do this, but I really must talk to the audience.

You're all invited guests. I know I'm wasting time in talking to you, but it really is very unfair of you to applaud—sometimes louder, less loud—and I ask you, as people who were invited here, and polite people, to refrain.

We have our time now for rebuttal. Mr. President.

The President. Yes. Well, with regard to this being a personal choice, isn't that what a murderer is insisting on, his or her right to kill someone because of whatever fault they think justifies that?

Now, I'm not capable, and I don't think you are, any of us, to make this determination that must be made with regard to human life. I am simply saying that I believe that that's where the effort should be directed—to make that determination.

I don't think that any of us should be called upon here to stand and make a decision as to what other things might come under the self-defense tradition. That, too, would have to be worked out then, when you once recognize that we're talking about a life. But in this great society of ours, wouldn't it make a lot more sense, in this gentle and kind society, if we had a program that made it possible for when incidents come along in which someone feels they must do away with that unborn child, that instead we make it available for the adoption? There are a million and a half people out there standing in line waiting to adopt children who can't have them any other way.

Ms. Walters. Mr. Mondale.

Mr. Mondale. I agree with that, and that's why I was a principal sponsor of a liberal adoption law, so that more of these children could come to term, so that the young

mothers were educated, so we found an option, an alternative. I'm all for that. But the question is whether this other option proposed by the President should be pursued. And I don't agree with it.

Since I've got about 20 seconds, let me just say one thing. The question of agriculture came up a minute ago. Net farm income is off 50 percent in the last 3 years, and every farmer knows it. And the effect of these economic policies is like a massive grain embargo, which has caused farm exports to drop 20 percent. It's been a big failure. I opposed the grain embargo in my administration. I'm opposed to these policies as well.

Ms. Walters. I'm sitting here like the great schoolteacher, letting you both get away with things—because one did it, the other one did it. May I ask in the future that the rebuttal stick to what the rebuttal is. And also, foreign policy will be the next debate. Stop dragging it in by its ear into this one. [*Laughter*]

Now, having admonished you, I would like to say to the panel, you are allowed one question and one followup. Would you try, as best you could, not to ask two and three—I know it's something we all want to do—two and three questions as part one and two and three as part two.

Having said that, Fred, it's yours.

Federal Taxation

Mr. Barnes. Thank you. Mr. Mondale, let me ask you about middle-class Americans and the taxes they pay. Now, I'm talking not about the rich or the poor—I know your views on their taxes—but about families earning 25,000 to 45,000 a year. Do you think that those families are overtaxed or undertaxed by the Federal Government?

Mr. Mondale. In my opinion, as we deal with this deficit, people from about $70,000 a year on down have to be dealt with very, very carefully, because they are the ones who didn't get any relief the first time around.

Under the 1981 tax bill, people making $200,000 a year got $60,000 in tax relief over 3 years, while people making $30,000 a year, all taxes considered, got no relief at all or their taxes actually went up. That's why my proposal protects everybody from $25,000 a year or less against any tax increases, and treats those $70,000 and under in a way that is more beneficial than the way the President proposes with a sales tax or a flat tax.

What does this mean in real life? Well, the other day, Vice President Bush disclosed his tax returns to the American people. He's one of the wealthiest Americans, and he's our Vice President. In 1981 I think he paid about 40 percent in taxes. In 1983, as a result of these tax preferences, he paid a little over 12 percent, 12.8 percent in taxes. That meant that he paid a lower percent in taxes than the janitor who cleaned up his office or the chauffeur who drives him to work.

I believe we need some fairness. And that's why I've proposed what I think is a fair and a responsible proposal that helps protect these people who've already got no relief or actually got a tax increase.

Mr. Barnes. It sounds as if you are saying you think this group of taxpayers making 25,000 to 45,000 a year is already overtaxed, yet your tax proposal would increase their taxes. I think your aides have said those earning about 25,000 to 35,000, their tax rate would go up—their tax bill would go up a hundred dollars, and from 35,000 to 45,000, more than that, several hundred dollars. Wouldn't that stifle their incentive to work and invest and so on, and also hurt the recovery?

Mr. Mondale. The first thing is, everybody 25,000 and under would have no tax increase.

Mr. Reagan, after the election, is going to have to propose a tax increase, and you will have to compare what he proposes. And his Secretary of the Treasury said he's studying a sales tax or a value-added tax. They're the same thing. They hit middle- and moderate-income Americans and leave wealthy Americans largely untouched.

Up until about $70,000, as you go up the ladder, my proposals will be far more beneficial. As soon as we get the economy on a sound ground as well, I'd like to see the total repeal of indexing. I don't think we can do that for a few years. But at some point, we want to do that as well.

Mr. Barnes. Mr. President, let me try this

on you. Do you think middle-income Americans are overtaxed or undertaxed?

The President. You know, I wasn't going to say this at all, but I can't help it. There you go again. [*Laughter*] I don't have a plan to tax—or increase taxes. I'm not going to increase taxes. I can understand why you are, Mr. Mondale, because as a Senator you voted 16 times to increase taxes.

Now, I believe that our problem has not been that anybody in our country is undertaxed; it's that government is overfed. And I think that most of our people—this is why we had a 25-percent tax cut across the board which maintained the same progressivity of our tax structure in the brackets on up. And, as a matter of fact, it just so happens that in the quirks of administering these taxes, those above $50,000 actually did not get quite as big a tax cut percentage-wise as did those from 50,000 down. From 50,000 down, those people paid two-thirds of the taxes, and those people got two-thirds of the tax cut.

Now, the Social Security tax of '77—this indeed was a tax that hit people in the lower brackets the hardest. It had two features. It had several tax increases phased in over a period of time—there are two more yet to come between now and 1989. At the same time every year, it increased the amount of money—virtually every year, there may have been one or two that were skipped in there—that was subject to that tax. Today it is up to about $38,000 of earnings that is subject to the payroll tax for Social Security. And that tax, there are no deductions, so a person making anywhere from 10, 15, 20—they're paying that tax on the full gross earnings that they have after they have already paid an income tax on that same amount of money.

Now, I don't think that to try and say that we were taxing the rich, and not the other way around, it just doesn't work out that way. The system is still where it was with regard to the progressivity, as I've said, and that has not been changed. But if you take it in numbers of dollars instead of percentage, yes, you could say, well, that person got 10 times as much as this other person. Yes, but he paid 10 times as much, also. But if you take it in percentages, then you find out that it is fair and equitable across the board.

Mr. Barnes. I thought I caught, Mr. President, a glimmer of a stronger statement there in your answer than you've made before. I think the operative position you had before was that you would only raise taxes in a second term as a last resort, and I thought you said flatly that "I'm not going to raise taxes." Is that what you meant to say, that you will not—that you will flatly not raise taxes in your second term as President?

The President. Yes, I had used—"last resort" would always be with me. If you got the Government down to the lowest level, that you yourself could say it could not go any lower and still perform the services for the people, and if the recovery was so complete that you knew you were getting the ultimate amount of revenues that you could get through that growth, and there was still some slight difference there between those two lines, then I had said once that, yes, you would have to then look to see if taxes should not be adjusted.

I don't foresee those things happening, so I say with great confidence I'm not going to go for a tax.

With regard to assailing Mr. Bush about his tax problems and the difference from the tax he once paid and then the later tax he paid, I think if you looked at the deductions, there were great legal expenses in there—had to do, possibly, with the sale of his home, and they had to do with his setting up of a blind trust. All of those are legally deductions, deductible in computing your tax, and it was a 1-year thing with him.

Ms. Walters. Mr. Mondale, here we go again. It's time for rebuttal.

Mr. Mondale. Well, first of all, I gave him the benefit of the doubt on the house deal. I'm just talking about the 12.8 percent that he paid, and that's what's happening all over this country with wealthy Americans. They've got so many loopholes they don't have to pay much in taxes.

Now, Mr. President, you said, "There you go again," right?

The President. Yes.

Mr. Mondale. You remember the last time you said that?

The President. Mm-hmm.

Mr. Mondale. You said it when President Carter said that you were going to cut Medicare, and you said, "Oh, no, there you go again, Mr. President." And what did you do right after the election? You went out and tried to cut $20 billion out of Medicare. And so, when you say, "There you go again"—people remember this, you know. [*Laughter*] And people will remember that you signed the biggest tax increase in the history of California and the biggest tax increase in the history of the United States, and what are you going to do? You've got a $260 billion deficit. You can't wish it away. You won't slow defense spending; you refuse to do that——

Ms. Walters. Mr. Mondale, I'm afraid your time is up.

Mr. Mondale. Sorry.

Ms. Walters. Mr. President?

The President. Yes. With regard to Medicare, no, but it's time for us to say that Medicare is in pretty much the same condition that Social Security was, and something is going to have to be done in the next several years to make it fiscally sound. And, no, I never proposed any $20 billion should come out of Medicare; I have proposed that the program we must treat with that particular problem. And maybe part of that problem is because during the 4 years of the Carter-Mondale administration medical costs in this country went up 87 percent.

Ms. Walters. All right. Fine.

The President. I gave you back some of that time. [*Laughter*]

Ms. Walters. We can't keep going back for other rebuttals; there'll be time later.

We now go to our final round. The way things stand now, we have time for only two sets of questions, and by lot, it will be Jim and Diane. And we'll start with Jim Wieghart.

Social Welfare Programs

Mr. Wieghart. Mr. President, the economic recovery is real, but uneven. The Census Bureau, just a month ago, reported that there are more people living under poverty now, a million more people living under it, than when you took office.

There have been a number of studies,

including studies by the Urban Institute and other nonpolitical organizations, that say that the impact of the tax and budget cuts and your economic policies have impacted severely on certain classes of Americans—working mothers, head of households, minority groups, elderly poor. In fact, they're saying the rich are getting richer and the poor are getting poorer under your policies.

What relief can you offer to the working poor, to the minorities, and to the women head of households who have borne the brunt of these economic programs? What can you offer them in the future, in your next term?

The President. Well, some of those facts and figures just don't stand up. Yes, there has been an increase in poverty, but it is a lower rate of increase than it was in the preceding years before we got here. It has begun to decline, but it is still going up.

On the other hand, women heads of household—single women heads of household have—for the first time there's been a turndown in the rate of poverty for them. We have found also in our studies that in this increase in poverty, it all had to do with their private earnings. It had nothing to do with the transfer of payments from government by way of many programs.

We are spending now 37 percent more on food for the hungry in all the various types of programs than was spent in 1980. We're spending a third more on all of the—well, all of the programs of human service. We have more people receiving food stamps than were ever receiving them before—2,300,000 more are receiving them—even though we took 850,000 off the food stamp rolls because they were making an income that was above anything that warranted their fellow citizens having to support them. We found people making 185 percent of the poverty level were getting government benefits. We have set a line at 130 percent so that we can direct that aid down to the truly needy.

Some time ago, Mr. Mondale said something about education and college students and help of that kind. Half—one out of two of the full-time college students in the United States are receiving some form of Federal aid. But there, again, we found people that there under the previous ad-

ministration, families that had no limit to income were still eligible for low-interest college loans. We didn't think that was right. And so, we have set a standard that those loans and those grants are directed to the people who otherwise could not go to college, their family incomes were so low.

So, there are a host of other figures that reveal that the grant programs are greater than they have ever been, taking care of more people than they ever have. 7.7 million elderly citizens who were living in the lowest 20 percent of earnings—7.7 million have moved up into another bracket since our administration took over, leaving only 5 million of the elderly in that bracket when there had been more than 13 million.

Mr. Wieghart. Mr. President, in a visit to Texas—in Brownsville, I believe it was, in the Rio Grande Valley—you did observe that the economic recovery was uneven.

The President. Yes.

Mr. Wieghart. In that particular area of Texas, unemployment was over 14 percent, whereas statewide, it was the lowest in the country, I believe—5.6 percent. And you made the comment, however, that man does not live by bread alone. What did you mean by that comment? And if I interpret it correctly, it would be a comment more addressed to the affluent who obviously can look beyond just the bread they need to sustain them, with their wherewithal.

The President. That had nothing to do with the other thing of talking about their needs or anything. I remember distinctly, I was segueing into another subject. I was talking about the things that have been accomplished, and that was referring to the revival of patriotism and optimism, the new spirit that we're finding all over America. And it is a wonderful thing to see when you get out there among the people. So, that was the only place that that was used.

I did avoid, I'm afraid, in my previous answer, also, the idea of uneven, yes. There is no way that the recovery is even across the country, just as in the depths of the recession, there were some parts of the country that were worse off, but some that didn't even feel the pain of the recession.

We're not going to rest and not going to be happy until every person in this country who wants a job can have one, until the recovery is complete across the country.

Mr. Wieghart. Mr. Mondale, as you can gather from the question to the President, the celebrated War on Poverty obviously didn't end the problem of poverty, although it may have dented it. The poor and the homeless and the disadvantaged are still with us. What should the Federal Government's role be to turn back the growth in the number of people living below the poverty level, which is now 35 million in the United States, and to help deal with the structural unemployment problems that the President was referring to in an uneven recovery?

Mr. Mondale. Number one, we've got to get the debt down to get the interest rates down so the economy will grow and people will be employed.

Number two, we have to work with cities and others to help generate economic growth in those communities—through the Urban Development Action Grant Program. I don't mind those enterprise zones; let's try them, but not as a substitute for the others. Certainly education and training is crucial. If these young Americans don't have the skills that make them attractive to employees, they're not going to get jobs.

The next thing is to try to get more entrepreneurship in business within the reach of minorities so that these businesses are located in the communities in which they're found. The other thing is, we need the business community as well as government heavily involved in these communities to try to get economic growth.

There is no question that the poor are worse off. I think the President genuinely believes that they're better off. But the figures show that about 8 million more people are below the poverty line than 4 years ago. How you can cut school lunches, how you can cut student assistance, how you can cut housing, how you can cut disability benefits, how you can do all of these things and then the people receiving them—for example, the disabled, who have no alternative—how they're going to do better, I don't know. Now, we need a tight budget, but there's no question that this administration has singled out things that affect the most vulnerable in American life, and they're hurting.

One final point if I might. There's another part of the lopsided economy that we're in today, and that is that these heavy deficits have killed exports and are swamping the Nation with cheap imports. We are now $120 billion of imports, 3 million jobs lost, and farmers are having their worst year. That's another reason to get the deficit down.

Mr. Wieghart. Mr. Mondale, is it possible that the vast majority of Americans who appear to be prosperous have lost interest in the kinds of programs you're discussing to help those less privileged than they are?

Mr. Mondale. I think the American people want to make certain that that dollar is wisely spent. I think they stand for civil rights. I know they're all for education in science and training, which I strongly support. They want these young people to have a chance to get jobs and the rest. I think the business community wants to get involved. I think they're asking for new and creative ways to try to reach it with everyone involved. I think that's part of it. I think also that the American people want a balanced program that gives us long-term growth so that they're not having to take money that's desperate to themselves and their families and give it to someone else. I'm opposed to that, too.

Ms. Walters. And now it is time for our rebuttal for this period. Mr. President?

The President. Yes. The connection that's been made again between the deficit and the interest rates—there is no connection between them. There is a connection between interest rates and inflation, but I would call to your attention that in 1981 while we were operating still on the Carter-Mondale budget that we inherited—that the interest rates came down from 21½, down toward the 12 or 13 figure. And while they were coming down, the deficits had started their great increase. They were going up. Now, if there was a connection I think that there would be a different parallel between deficits getting larger and interest rates going down.

The interest rates are based on inflation. And right now I have to tell you I don't think there is any excuse for the interest rates being as high as they are because we have brought inflation down so low. I think it can only be that they're anticipating or hope—expecting, not hoping, that maybe we don't have a control of inflation and it's going to go back up again. Well, it isn't going to go back up. We're going to see that it doesn't.

And I haven't got time to answer with regard to the disabled.

Ms. Walters. Thank you, Mr. President. Mr. Mondale.

Mr. Mondale. Mr. President, if I heard you correctly, you said that these deficits don't have anything to do with interest rates. I will grant you that interest rates were too high in 1980, and we can have another debate as to why—energy prices and so on. There's no way of glossing around that. But when these huge deficits went in place in 1981, what's called the real interest rates—the spread between inflation and what a loan costs you doubled—and that's still the case today. And the result is interest costs that have never been seen before in terms of real charges, and it's attributable to the deficit.

Everybody—every economist, every businessman—believes that. Your own Council of Economic Advisers—Mr. Feldstein in his report told you that. Every chairman of the Finance and Ways and Means Committee, Republican leaders in the Senate and the House are telling you that. That deficit is ruining the long-term hopes for this economy. It's causing high interest rates. It's ruining us in trade. It's given us the highest small business failure in 50 years. The economy is starting downhill with housing failure——

Ms. Walters. Thank you, Mr. Mondale. You're both very obedient. I have to give you credit for that.

We now start our final round of questions. We do want to have time for your rebuttal.

We start with Diane—Diane Sawyer.

Presidential Campaign

Ms. Sawyer. Since we are reaching the end of the question period, and since in every Presidential campaign, the candidates tend to complain that the opposition candidate is not held accountable for what he or she says, let me give you the chance to do that.

Mr. Mondale, beginning with you. What do you think the most outrageous thing is your opponent said in this debate tonight? [*Laughter*]

Mr. Mondale. Do you want to give me some suggestions? [*Laughter*] I'm going to use my time a little differently. I'm going to give the President some credit. I think the President has done some things to raise the sense of spirit, morale, good feeling in this country, and he's entitled to credit for that. What I think we need, however, is not just that but to move forward, not just congratulating ourselves but challenging ourselves to get on with the business of dealing with America's problems.

I think in education, when he lectured the country about the importance of discipline, I didn't like it at first, but I think it helped a little bit. But now we need both that kind of discipline and the resources and the consistent leadership that allows this country to catch up in education and science and training.

I like President Reagan. And this is not personal—there are deep differences about our future, and that's the basis of my campaign.

Ms. Sawyer. Follow up in a similar vein, then. What remaining question would you most like to see your opponent forced to answer?

Mr. Mondale. Without any doubt, I have stood up and told the American people that that $263 billion deficit must come down. And I've done what no candidate for President has ever done, I told you before the election what I'd do.

Mr. Reagan, as you saw tonight—President Reagan takes the position it will disappear by magic. It was once called voodoo economics. I wish the President would say: Yes, the CBO is right. Yes, we have a $263 billion deficit. This is how I'm going to get it done. Don't talk about growth, because even though we need growth, that's not helping. It's going to go in the other direction, as they've estimated.

And give us a plan. What will you cut? Whose taxes will you raise? Will you finally touch that defense budget? Are you going to go after Social Security and Medicare and student assistance and the handicapped again as you did last time? If you'd just tell us what you're going to do, then the American people could compare my plan for the future with your plan. And that's the way it should be. The American people would be in charge.

Ms. Sawyer. Mr. President, the most outrageous thing your opponent has said in the debate tonight?

The President. Well, now, I have to start with a smile, since his kind words to me.

I'll tell you what I think has been the most outrageous thing in political dialog, both in this campaign and the one in '82. And that is the continued discussion and claim that somehow I am the villain who is going to pull the Social Security checks out from those people who are dependent on them.

And why I think it is outrageous—first of all, it isn't true. But why it is outrageous is because, for political advantage, every time they do that, they scare millions of senior citizens who are totally dependent on Social Security, have no place else to turn. And they have to live and go to bed at night thinking, "Is this true? Is someone going to take our check away from us and leave us destitute?" And I don't think that that should be a part of political dialog.

Now, to—I still—I just have a minute here?

Ms. Walters. You have more time.

The President. Oh, I——

Ms. Walters. You can keep going.

The President. Okay. All right.

Now, Social Security, let's lay it to rest once and for all. I told you never would I do such a thing. But I tell you also now, Social Security has nothing to do with the deficit. Social Security is totally funded by the payroll tax levied on employer and employee. If you reduce the out-go of Social Security, that money would not go into the general fund to reduce a deficit. It would go into the Social Security Trust Fund. So, Social Security has nothing to do with balancing a budget or erasing or lowering the deficit.

Now, again, to get to whether I am depending on magic, I think I have talked in straight economic terms about a program of recovery that I was told wouldn't work.

And then, after it worked, I was told that lowering taxes would increase inflation. And none of these things happened. It is working, and we're going to continue on that same line.

As to what we might do, and find in further savings cuts, no, we're not going to starve the hungry. But we have 2,478 specific recommendations from a commission of more than 2,000 business people in this country, through the Grace commission, that we're studying right now—and we've already implemented 17 percent of them—that are recommendations as to how to make government more efficient, more economic.

Ms. Sawyer. And to keep it even, what remaining question would you most like to see your opponent forced to answer?

The President. Why the deficits are so much of a problem for him now, but that in 1976, when the deficit was $52 billion and everyone was panicking about that, he said, no, that he thought it ought to be bigger, because a bigger deficit would stimulate the economy and would help do away with unemployment. In 1979 he made similar statements, the same effect, that the deficits— there was nothing wrong with having deficits.

Remember, there was a trillion dollars in debt before we got here. That's got to be paid by our children and grandchildren, too, if we don't do it. And I'm hoping we can start some payments on it before we get through here. That's why I want another 4 years.

Ms. Walters. Well, we have time now, if you'd like to answer the President's question, or whatever rebuttal.

Mr. Mondale. Well, we've just finished almost the whole debate. And the American people don't have the slightest clue about what President Reagan will do about these deficits. [*Laughter*] And yet, that's the most important single issue of our time.

I did support the '76 measure that he told about, because we were in a deep recession and we needed some stimulation. But I will say as a Democrat, I was a real piker, Mr. President. In 1979 we ran a $29 billion deficit all year. This administration seems to run that every morning. And the result is exactly what we see. This economy is starting to run downhill. Housing is off. Last report on new purchases, it's the lowest since 1982. Growth is a little over 3 percent now. Many people are predicting a recession. And the flow of imports into this country is swamping the American people.

We've got to deal with this problem, and those of us who want to be your President should tell you now what we're going to do, so you can make a judgment.

Ms. Walters. Thank you very much. We must stop now. I want to give you time for your closing statements. It's indeed time for that from each of you. We will begin with President Reagan.

Oh, I'm sorry, Mr. Reagan, you had your rebuttal, and I just cut you off because our time is going. You have a chance now for rebuttal before your closing statement. Is that correct?

The President. No, I might as well just go with——

Ms. Walters. Do you want to go with your——

The President. I don't think so. I'm all confused now.

Ms. Walters. Technically, you did. I have little voices that come in my ear. [*Laughter*] You don't get those same voices. I'm not hearing it from here—I'm hearing it from here.

The President. All right.

Ms. Walters. You have waived your rebuttal. You can go with your closing statement.

Closing Statements

The President. Well, we'll include it in that.

Ms. Walters. Okay.

The President. Four years ago, in similar circumstances to this, I asked you, the American people, a question. I asked: "Are you better off than you were 4 years before?" The answer to that obviously was no, and as the result, I was elected to this office and promised a new beginning.

Now, maybe I'm expected to ask that same question again. I'm not going to, because I think that all of you—or not everyone, those people that are in those pockets of poverty and haven't caught up, they couldn't answer the way I would want them to—but I think that most of the people in

this country would say, yes, they are better off than they were 4 years ago.

The question, I think, should be enlarged. Is America better off than it was 4 years ago? And I believe the answer to that has to also be "yes." I promised a new beginning. So far, it is only a beginning. If the job were finished, I might have thought twice about seeking reelection for this job.

But we now have an economy that, for the first time—well, let's put it this way: In the first half of 1980, gross national product was down a minus 3.7 percent. The first half of '84 it's up 8½ percent. Productivity in the first half of 1980 was down a minus 2 percent. Today it is up a plus 4 percent.

Personal earnings after taxes per capita have gone up almost $3,000 in these 4 years. In 1980—or 1979, a person with a fixed income of $8,000 was $500 above the poverty line, and this maybe explains why there are the numbers still in poverty. By 1980 that same person was $500 below the poverty line.

We have restored much of our economy. With regard to business investment, it is higher than it has been since 1949. So, there seems to be no shortage of investment capital. We have, as I said, cut the taxes, but we have reduced inflation, and for 2 years now it has stayed down there, not at double digit, but in the range of 4 or below. We believe that we had also promised that we would make our country more secure.

Yes, we have an increase in the defense budget. But back then we had planes that couldn't fly for lack of spare parts or pilots. We had navy vessels that couldn't leave harbor because of lack of crew or, again, lack of spare parts. Today we're well on our way to a 600-ship navy. We have 543 at present.

We have—our military, the morale is high. I think the people should understand that two-thirds of the defense budget pays for pay and salary, or pay and pension. And then you add to that food and wardrobe, and all the other things, and you only have a small portion going for weapons. But I am determined that if ever our men are called on, they should have the best that we can provide in the manner of tools and weapons. There has been reference to expensive spare parts, hammers costing $500. Well, we are the ones who found those.

I think we've given the American people back their spirit. I think there's an optimism in the land and a patriotism, and I think that we're in a position once again to heed the words of Thomas Paine, who said: "We have it in our power to begin the world over again."

Ms. Walters. Thank you, Mr. Reagan.

Mr. Mondale, the closing words are now yours.

Mr. Mondale. I want to thank the League of Women Voters and the city of Louisville for hosting this evening's debate. I want to thank President Reagan for agreeing to debate. He didn't have to, and he did, and we all appreciate it.

The President's favorite question is: Are you better off? Well, if you're wealthy, you're better off. If you're middle income, you're about where you were. And if you're modest income, you're worse off. That's what the economists tell us.

But is that really the question that should be asked? Isn't the real question is *will* we be better off? Will our children be better off? Are we building the future that this nation needs? I believe that if we ask those questions that bear on our future, not just congratulate ourselves but challenge us to solve those problems, you'll see that we need new leadership.

Are we better of with this arms race? Will we be better off if we start this star wars escalation into the heavens? Are we better off when we deemphasize our values in human rights? Are we better off when we load our children with this fantastic debt? Would fathers and mothers feel proud of themselves if they loaded their children with debts like this nation is now—over a trillion dollars on the shoulders of our children? Can we say, really say that we will be better off when we pull away from sort of that basic American instinct of decency and fairness?

I would rather lose a campaign about decency than win a campaign about self-interest. I don't think this nation is composed of people who care only for themselves. And when we sought to assault Social Security and Medicare, as the record shows we did, I think that was mean-spirited. When we terminated 400,000 desperate, hopeless, defenseless Americans who were on disability—confused and unable to defend themselves, and just laid them out on the street, as we did for 4 years, I don't think that's what America is all about.

America is a fair society, and it is not right that Vice President Bush pays less in taxes than the janitor who helps him. I believe there's fundamental fairness crying out that needs to be achieved in our tax system.

I believe that we will be better off if we protect this environment. And contrary to what the President says, I think their record on the environment is inexcusable and often shameful. These laws are not being enforced, have not been enforced, and the public health and the air and the water are paying the price. That's not fair for our future.

I think our future requires a President to lead us in an all-out search to advance our education, our learning, and our science and training, because this world is more complex and we're being pressed harder all the time.

I believe in opening doors. We won the Olympics, in part, because we've had civil rights laws and the laws that prohibit discrimination against women. I have been for those efforts all my life. The President's record is quite different.

The question is our future. President Kennedy once said in response to similar arguments, "We are great, but we can be greater." We can be better if we face our future, rejoice in our strengths, face our problems, and by solving them, build a better society for our children.

Thank you.

Ms. Walters. Thank you, Mr. Mondale. [*Applause*] Please, we have not finished quite yet.

Thank you, Mr. Mondale, and thank you, Mr. President. And our thanks to our panel members, as well.

And so we bring to a close this first of the League of Women Voters Presidential debates of 1984. You two can go at each again in the final League debate on October 21st, in Kansas City, Missouri. And this Thursday night, October 11th, at 9 p.m. eastern daylight time, the Vice President, George Bush, will debate Congresswoman Geraldine Ferraro in Philadelphia.

And I hope that you will all watch once again. No matter what the format is, these debates are very important. We all have an extremely vital decision to make.

Once more, gentlemen, our thanks. Once more, to you, our thanks.

Now, this is Barbara Walters wishing you a good evening.

Note: The debate began at 9 p.m. in the Robert S. Whitney Hall at the Kentucky Center for the Arts.

Remarks at a Reagan-Bush Rally in Louisville, Kentucky
October 7, 1984

The President. Thank you all very much. This certainly is a—[*applause*]. Every shelf is full.

Well, it's great to be back in Kentucky and back in the land of pioneer spirit and pride, and back here with Gene Snyder, and Hal Rogers, Larry Hopkins, and a man we need in the Senate—please send him there—Mitch O'Connell. McConnell. [*Applause*] McConnell. I must have been thinking of the Archbishop. I said O'Connell. McConnell. [*Laughter*]

But now, in the next few days, we'll probably see all kinds of polls and commentary saying this and that about the little argument that I've just finished—[*laughter*]—here tonight. [*Laughter*]

But I don't know. Let me ask you a question or two. In this debate, I really wanted to show that just maybe government is big enough already. I don't know whether I got that across. [*Applause*] And I know I said it, but I don't know whether it registered or not, that the American people aren't overtaxed, the Government's overfed. [*Applause*]

But let us all here—whether we said it before or not—agree that America must leave behind the failed policies of the past and go forward with opportunity and the bright promise of the future. I'll be happy if we come away with just those ideas.

We only have 4 weeks left, but the choice is as clear as any that America's faced in the last 50 years.

Audience. 4 more years!

The President. Will we go forward with the faith and courage to make America stronger, to offer hope and opportunity to all our people, including those who still are not back on their feet, as we heard so many times tonight? Or will we go back to the policies of soaring taxation and spending that weakened our economy, snuffed out so many opportunities, and threw so many millions into the cold embrace of genuine hardship?

Audience. No!

The President. Well, we've already seen what happens when we follow the policies that our opponents have so faithfully promised to restore—the failed policies of tax-and-tax and spend-and-spend. We saw this once proud nation of ours, a few years ago, staggered by a steady erosion of economic growth. And I don't care what was said tonight or out on the road in the campaign trail, this country was in an economic mess of enormous proportions in 1980.

They talk about fairness, but what could be more unfair than that punishing inflation that could take people down through the brackets of poverty simply by raising the prices of things and lowering the value of the money that they had?

We saw those interest rates, as I mentioned in the debate—21½ percent. And that closed down the housing industry, that closed down the automobile industry, both of which are dependent on credit buying, mortgage buying.

Then we saw the rising unemployment. And I don't care what they say, 107 million employed is a lot bigger than 99 million employed. And that's the difference between now and 1980.

Now, I didn't get a chance to reply tonight to all of those frequent references to an arms race. Well, you know, there was a cartoon back when we first started the rebuilding of the military that said it all for me. It was a picture of a couple of Russian generals talking to each other, and one of them said, "I liked it better when we were the only ones in the arms race." [*Laughter*] We're going to get them back to the table to talk disarmament. I don't mean arms limitations.

You know, some of the previous treaties that we've had I know were in good faith and all that, but all they did was set the rules for the continued arms race. When I got there, found out that SALT II, from the time that it was signed until I arrived in Washington—an expert in the field gave me the information that under the signing of SALT II, without breaking the treaty, the Soviet Union had added to their nuclear arsenal the equivalent of the bomb we dropped on Hiroshima. They had added that every 11 minutes in the years since the treaty had been signed.

Well, that isn't what we want. And I had the pleasure of telling Mr. Gromyko the other day that any time they're ready—[*applause*]. We're the only two that can destroy the world. Our two nations are the only two that can save it. And I told him that I'd like to start down the road with them, not to just arms limitation, but to the total elimination of all nuclear weapons in the world.

But I have a feeling, looking at all of you, that you agree with me about something else that's happened in these last few years, and that is that there's a whole different appreciation for the family in America—the bedrock values of our neighborhoods, the fact that our crime rates are coming down, the fact that now our schools in this last year have suddenly turned a corner and for the first time in 20 years we see the college entrance exams—the scores going up, instead of the steady decline that we knew. And it didn't come from any multibillion-dollar Federal program.

Yes, we appointed a commission, the best people we could find, and said, "Come back and tell us, what should we do about education in this country?" They did. And we passed it on to you, to the people in the communities, the people in the school districts, to the teachers and the parents and the students. And all over the United States it's happening. There are now the compulsory courses in math and science that have been abandoned in so many places—there are the added requirements for graduation. And the whole picture is looking up, to the place that the other day there was a poll taken about how people felt about their schools, and for the first time in about a decade the American people said they were very happy about their schools.

The things that were going on before we got here—and they talk about fairness. Well, I have to say, at least that I can say for the things that they were doing—they were fair. They didn't discriminate; they made everybody miserable. Now, since we're not going to raise the taxes, I didn't get a chance to give the figures tonight, but we have cost out what his proposed tax increase would do. It would raise the tax for every household in the United States by more than $1,800 a year, about $157 a month, and I just don't think we ought to let him do that to America.

Audience. No!

The President. So, we'll keep him reminded of that. We'll keep the people reminded of it. And you know, I can't help but think about this America here and what it's doing. We all watched the Olympics, and we saw our athletes go for the gold. Well, there are two teams in America today. There's the Washington tax increase team and the grassroots opportunity team. Now, making the economy bear the burden of our opponents tax hike would be like having some of those Olympic swimmers—their coach telling them that they had to swim while carrying an anvil—[*laughter*]— or a runner would sprint with a ball and chain. [*Laughter*] And that's what Coach Tax Hike and his tax increase team want to do—[*laughter*]—and they kicked off their campaign with that call this year. And they said it was a kickoff—I think it was a fumble. [*Laughter*]

We want to bring your tax rates further down, and not up. We want to create opportunities for all Americans, women and men, young and old, by controlling the size of government and giving you new incentives to work and invest and save.

And come November, the American people are going to decide which team is America's team and, come November, I just can't help but believe the American people are going to tell "Coach Tax Hike" and the whole tax increase team to head for the showers.

Audience. 4 more years! 4 more years! 4 more years!

The President. Thank you. All right. Well, I didn't really feel that way, but since you insist, okay. [*Laughter*]

Well, tonight I had a chance to talk a little bit about my past as a Democrat. And I can't help but believe that in this particular place, there must be many of you here who either were or still are, but you're here because you have found it difficult to follow the leadership of your party and the course that it's been taking since those days back there in the days of the Harry Trumans and so forth.

Well, to all of you, you who knew the part of F.D.R. and Harry Truman and J.F.K. and that tradition, let us say to you—and I do know how you feel, because I was there myself once—walk with us down this new path of opportunity, and we'll save this country in a bipartisan way.

Audience. 4 more years! 4 more years! 4 more years!

The President. You know, I'm so delighted to see you young people here, and it's true all over the country, because, you know, you're what this election is all about.

There are some of us here who are old enough to remember an America in which there was no ceiling. Any individual—you were free to fly as high and as far as your own ability and energy and determination would take you, without being penalized for the effort. And then we came to a period of years in which government started encroaching on everyone. And the last 4 years before we got here, they were telling us that we suffered from a malaise, that it was our fault, that we had to give up the idea of having some of the things we used to have, that there were eras of limits. Don't you believe it.

You young people, this is what it's all about. We're going to keep on going the path—he kept saying he didn't know what we were going to do. We're going to keep on doing what we've been doing for the last 4 years. And then you, you young people are going to start out life in the same kind of an America that we knew and that we started out life in. That's what it's all about.

So, I don't have anything else——

Audience. Nancy!

The President. I don't have anything else other than to say one last thing that I just— I like to mention once in awhile. And that is, that if there's one thing that I'm really proud of in these 4 years, it has been those young men and women of ours who wear our uniforms—our soldiers.

I'm going to quote someone, and I have to use a naughty word in doing it. But you'll forgive me for it. I think it belongs in the quote. Back in World War II, someone asked General George Marshall, the Commander in Chief of our Armed Forces, asked him what was our secret, what was our secret weapon. And General George Marshall said, "The best damn kids in the world." Well, today—[*applause*]. Those young people in uniform today are the grandsons and daughters of those World War II veterans. And I can say, after seeing them firsthand, after seeing what they did in Grenada—and it was so wonderful— when they pulled out, there weren't any signs written on the walls, "Yankee go home." The signs were, "God bless America."

And so, I just know once again I can say what George Marshall did: You bet, we've got the best damn kids in the world.

Thank you all very much. Thank you. Good night. God bless you all.

Note: The President spoke at 10:52 p.m. in the Atrium of the Hyatt Regency Hotel. Following his remarks, the President went to his suite at the hotel, where he remained overnight.

The following day, the President traveled to Charlotte, NC.

As printed above, the remarks follow the White House press release.

Remarks at a Reagan-Bush Rally in Charlotte, North Carolina
October 8, 1984

The President. Thank you all very much.

Audience. Reagan! Reagan! Reagan!

The President. Thank you very much, and, Jesse, thank you for that introduction. And, Eddie Knox, I am more proud than I can say of what you have just committed to here this morning. And I thank all of you very much. You have honored me greatly, and it's so great to be here.

You know, last night we had a little sparring in the political arena. But whether I won them or not, I know now that I have won the fruits of victory, because I get to be with all of you. And I can truthfully say, nothing could be finer than to be in Carolina in the morning.

Well, it's wonderful to see your enthusiasm. It's heartening, because this election is not a contest between Republicans and Democrats or between left and right; it's a contest between the future and the past. I have said on occasion that age is going to be an issue in this campaign—their ideas are just too darn old. [*Laughter*]

But this contest is being waged for the soul of our country and the will of its people. And it's good to know where you stand, and I'm proud to stand with you. I'm a great admirer of your State—not just because the sky is Carolina blue—I was a little worried that I might not be able to say that if the clouds didn't clear, but they did; the soil is fertile; your mountains are majestic; and it's not also because I feel a special affinity for one of your main industries— you cure tobacco and I'm trying to cure economics—[*laughter*]—but I admire your State because I admire your people. You were the first to vote for independence. And not too many years ago, when some people were burning our flag, you were waving it. Well, like the rest of the country, I'm impressed by your independence, and because of it, I truly treasure your support.

Now, we could begin today talking about how the economy is recovering and expanding, about how we've created 6 million new jobs, and 600,000 businesses were incorporated last year alone—that's a record in our

nation's history. But those are national statistics. Here in North Carolina, the unemployment rate 4 years ago was over 8 percent; it's now 6½. Now, that's not low enough, but it's a big improvement.

Here in Charlotte, construction is up; take-home pay is up; sales are up. In other words, I'm in a city that I would characterize as part of the national renewal. My opponents, of course, would say it's a pocket of despair. Well, I don't know about them. They go around insisting the economy is in a shambles and people are worse off than they ever were, and they've got to come back and raise our taxes to get things good again.

Audience. No!

The President. Well, now, I understand their attempts to convince you that things aren't better—that's what opponents do. And faced with the irrefutable fact of our national renewal, it hasn't been very easy for them. But let's stop for a moment and remember the mess they left us and what all of us have done—all of us—to turn our nation around.

In the past 3½ years we've cut the growth of government spending by nearly two-thirds. We have lowered personal tax rates by 25 percent for every taxpayer in the country. We cut inflation from 12.4 percent to 4.2, and we cut interest rates from 21½ to 12¾ and, in some banks, 12½.

Now, our opponents say the tax cuts were for millionaires. They say they weren't compassionate. But look at the record. Two-thirds of the income tax was being paid by two-thirds of the people, those under $50,000 a year. And two-thirds of the tax cut went to those same people. A typical family of four will have paid about $2,000 less in total income taxes during our administration. Our opponents would raise taxes the equivalent of almost $2,000—$1,890 per household, and that's a $157 more in taxes every month of the year. And they call that compassion.

Well, let's look at what their inflation did to us. When our opponents were in charge from 1976 to 1980—or through 1980—grocery bills increased by 50 percent. The price of a gallon of gas more than doubled. And in 1979 and '80, the weekly earnings of working Americans declined in real dollars, in real terms, by 8.8 percent, which was the first—or the worst drop since World War II. And the poor were hit hardest of all.

People on fixed incomes saw double-digit inflation kill their purchasing power. Families saw inflation make a joke out of their savings. And the truly needy who depend on government aid saw their benefits eroded by the destructive force of inflation. As a matter of fact, there were three increases during their time in the Aid for Dependent Children grant, and they still couldn't keep up. After the three increases, the people were worse off by several hundred dollars than they had been before.

And do you call that compassion?

Audience. No!

The President. Well, we cut inflation, and I'll tell you what it means: that 8.8 percent weekly—or decline in weekly earnings—within the last 2 years, weekly earnings have increased by 3.2 percent. Four years ago the weekly food bill for a family of four was almost $87. If my opponents' inflation rates had continued, that food bill would now be almost $128. Well, instead, we've kept the family's food bill down to $98.50, roughly one-fourth the rise that their inflation would have created.

Their interest rates were at 21½ percent the day they left office. Soaring mortgage rates meant 10 million families could no longer afford to buy homes. We cut those interest rates, and it helped reduce the average cost of home mortgages by $143 a month. It's brought home ownership within reach of 5 million more Americans, and it's made car purchases more affordable, too—but still not good enough, but far better than the mess that they left us.

And as we freed up the economy to grow, we created over 6 million new jobs in the last 21 months. More people are working this year than ever before in our history, and a job is the surest escape from poverty.

I want to stop for just a moment and say one of the things that makes us different from our opponents. We understand the need for jobs, real jobs, not make-work jobs.

We don't want to keep people on welfare, keep them in bondage as wards of the state. We know that people want to work. They want to contribute. They want to be a part of society. And we don't patronize them with handouts. We give them a chance through economic growth. And that's why I will fight his tax increase proposals, and I will fight to bring everybody's tax rates further down, not up. And I'll fight so that every American who wants a job can find a job, from the Carolina shore to San Francisco Bay.

They favor busing that takes innocent children out of the neighborhood school and makes them pawns in a social experiment that nobody wants. We've found out it failed. I don't call that compassion. My opponent helped impose a grain embargo that punished the American farmer for his administration's foreign policy defeats. And I don't call that compassion. The other side continued heavy estate taxes on the family farm. And that is not compassion. Well, we have practically eliminated that tax so that you can keep the farm in the family, and we have eliminated the inheritance tax for a surviving spouse. And that is compassion.

Now, they say they're going to bring their kind of compassion back. Should we let them?

Audience. No!

The President. You've answered already. Yes, we should keep giving a fair break to every citizen in our country.

The truth is, we're on the right track. But our national renewal isn't confined to the economy. More than prosperity, we have peace. I believe that we've made the world a more stable place. We're making quiet progress toward arms control, because we've not been mislead by empty talk and false promises. We've put America in a position of sufficient strength to achieve real and meaningful reductions in nuclear arms. And we did this knowing, as Teddy Roosevelt did, that the cry of the weakling counts for a little in the move toward peace, but the call of the just man, armed, is potent.

But there's another peace, the peace of the family, the peace that we're given through faith, through tradition, through fidelity to ideals. Our administration has tried these past few years to softly encourage the values by which our nation has flourished. And that's why we've tried to restore the right of voluntary prayer to our schoolchildren, to give tuition tax credits for parents who want to send their children to independent schools, and to foster legislation that recognizes that the family is the prime generator of the good things young people bring to this society as a whole.

We haven't always succeeded, but we'll never stop trying. And the truth is we have a philosophy and a spirit of renewal whose time has come. The columnists and pundits say that in 1980 the American voters took a turn to the right. Well, I think they missed the point. The fact is that quietly, unseen, and unheard, from Maine to California, a new understanding of the word "freedom" has swept this continent—freedom from heavy taxation, freedom from the Big Brother mentality that says that Big Brother knows best how to run your lives, that you're not bright enough to run your own lives.

America turned away from politicians who patronize, and it wasn't just a shift or a turn; it was a sea change. And we'll keep the new freedoms born of that change, and we will continue to make America stronger with them. The other day I was asked, "How do you want your administration to be remembered?" Well, the first thing I thought was, well, I'd rather that you not have to remember it anytime too soon— [*laughter*]—but I thought about it, and I said then—because I never thought about it before—I'd like my Presidency to be remembered as the one that gave the Government back to the people.

And because——

Audience. 4 more years! 4 more years! 4 more years!

The President. That's a good idea. I wish I'd thought of it. Oh, I don't fear the judgment of my fellow citizens on November 6th, but a fellow once told me that you can't count on victory until all the votes are counted. And I thanked President Dewey for that advice. [*Laughter*]

In 4 weeks we must all take part in the simplest but most essential of the democratic acts—we must make time and get to the polling place and vote. A vote is an expression of will, and the leaders of the opposition have got to start to understand the breadth and depth of the will of the people.

And so I say to all of you who see things as we do, don't take this election for granted. Don't pay any attention to the polls. Get out there and vote and see that your neighbor and your friend on either side votes.

And let me say to people of all political persuasions, from Independents to disenchanted Democrats, the welcome mat is out. I know that in a crowd, in this place, of this size, there have to be many Democrats who are here because they no longer can look with approval upon the way their leaders, the leaders of their party, have been taking them and this country. Well, I was one of you. I, too, was a Democrat for much of my adult life and, let me tell you, the welcome mat is out. We hope that you can join us this year because we need you, we want your help, and we know that we can do the things we're trying to do in a bipartisan way, together, as Americans, not just members of one party or the other.

Now, I hope to win reelection——

Audience. You will!

The President. [*Laughing*]—but if our great renewal is to take root, I'll need the help and support of good men and women in the Congress, and that's why we need people like Senator Jesse Helms. I wonder if you appreciate how hard he works for your State. He's one of my greatest supporters, too, and we need him back in Washington. What do you say? Will you send Jess back to help us? [*Applause*] All right. All right.

North Carolina couldn't have a more valuable export this year than Jesse Helms being sent to Washington. And let me say that we need Alex McMillen to join Jim Broyhill in Washington.

Now, I'm going to show you we're unselfish. Jim Martin—now Jim you can keep, but send him to Raleigh. We need him there, too.

Now, I know that I must go. You've been very patient. But can I come back?

Audience. Yes! Reagan! Reagan! Reagan!

The President. Thank you. You know, 30 years ago President Eisenhower came here to Charlotte. And he said that sometimes he found his job difficult, but what inspired him was the encouragement he got from the people in places like this. And he said, looking out at you, the people of Charlotte, ". . . the heart of America is always sound, and America's judgment . . . is always correct." And if a President knows that, he said, and hews to the wisdom of the people, then he can be certain that in the long run he will have done his job well.

Well, I look at all of you, and I feel the same way Ike did. And I thank you for continuing your traditions of inspiring Presidents, and thank you for your warmth and your kindness. And I particularly thank the young people of Matthews Elementary School who came here. They'd invited me to go there, and the schedule wouldn't permit that, so they came here. And I'm glad they did, and it's wonderful to see them.

But let me also say—and to those of you who back there can't be quite as conscious of it—down here in front are massed so many young people.

Audience. Reagan! Reagan! Reagan!

The President. All right.

Audience. Reagan! Reagan! Reagan!

The President. Thank you.

Audience. Reagan! Reagan! Reagan!

The President. They are what this elec-

tion is all about. Something happened in the years between when I was that age and where I am now. And some of what we had prided in—taken pride in having in America seemed to disappear, and that was the opportunity, the freedom, the belief that we the people are the most powerful element in our country, not any level of government. And there became in recent years a feeling that, well, there wasn't opportunity, that we had to resign ourselves to a lesser standard of life than we had known in the past.

Well, I want to say to all these young people, those who were saying that were blowing smoke. They didn't know what they were talking about. There is opportunity, unlimited opportunity. And that's what we're about to restore for all of you.

So, all of you, thank you again. You have really started my day right. And God bless you all. Thank you. Thank you very much.

Note: The President spoke at 12:26 p.m. at the Park. In his opening remarks, he referred to Senator Jesse Helms and Eddie Knox, the former Democratic mayor of Charlotte, who endorsed the President's bid for reelection.

Following his remarks, the President attended a reception for local Republican leaders. He then traveled to Baltimore, MD.

Remarks at a Dedication Ceremony for a Statue of Christopher Columbus in Baltimore, Maryland
October 8, 1984

Thank you. Thank you very much. And thank you, Mayor Schaefer, Commissioner Battaglia, members of the committee, and distinguished guests.

I'm pleased to be here in "Little Italy" with you to honor a man who reminds all Americans that we must always strive for the best, to push to the limits and beyond.

Americans of Italian descent have given a great deal to this country. Their contribution began 492 years ago when Christopher Columbus, the son of a Genoa weaver, set forth on a voyage of discovery that changed

the world. The ideals which many successive Italian immigrants brought with them are at the very heart of America. I'm speaking of hard work, love of family, patriotism, and respect for God. [*Applause*] Thank you.

Columbus challenged the unknown when he sailed westward in 1492. He was a man of vision who saw an opportunity, set down a plan, and then worked diligently to carry it forth. Contrary to what you may have heard in the last 24 hours, I do have a plan. I'd like to think that we're continuing on that initial course of discovery that he set for us so many years ago. We turned a vast wilderness, the most undeveloped land imaginable, into an economic dynamo, because we encouraged individuals with dreams to make those dreams come alive.

Looking out over the Inner Harbor, all that you've accomplished here in recent years, I know that's the kind of spirit that you have in Baltimore. You haven't been afraid to aim high, to chart a new course, and to change the future. You weren't satisfied to sit and wait or to be put off by those who kept discouraging you with all the reasons why you shouldn't go forward. With an eye for excellence, your architects and landscape designers, your contractors and working people have set out to create a place of commerce and beauty. Well, I think all of you can be proud of what you've accomplished.

The optimism I sense here, this optimism is something I've felt all over this country. America has quit listening to the gloom-and-doomers. We've left self-doubt and pessimism aside. We've reclaimed our heritage, personified by individuals like Christopher Columbus.

America has always been a vision of opportunity, a place where an individual could, with hard work, go as far as his own talents or her own talents would take them. And a few years ago, there were those who said that this vision of opportunity and freedom was dead, that we were a nation in decline, that we should lower our expectations. Murderous inflation and economic stagnation were the order of the day.

Well, last night I thought back to another night 4 years ago when I came to Baltimore for the first debate of the fall campaign. Well, as demonstrated in yesterday's debate, the central issue in this election is whether we're going to keep moving forward or go back.

Audience. 4 more years! 4 more years! 4 more years!

The President. All right. Thank you. Thank you very much.

America, like Baltimore, has made a new beginning, and we aren't going back. The American people are enjoying the fruits of economic expansion and low inflation. They put this country back together and have a right to feel good about what they've accomplished.

Baltimore's own H.L. Mencken had a description of Puritans which reminds me a bit of certain pessimists who can't bring themselves to admit America is back on the right track. Mencken said they have ". . . the haunting fear that someone, somewhere, may be happy." [*Laughter*]

Well, those who have never broken free from the mentality of tax and tax and spend and spend still think increasing taxes is the best way to solve America's problems.

Audience. No!

The President. We need a tax policy that offers incentives for people to work, save, and invest—all the things that will keep our economy growing and improve our well-being. We need a basic tax reform that will permit us to bring everybody's tax rates down.

And if we're to have progress, we must be willing to break from the past and use forward-looking, innovative ideas. One such idea is designating depressed areas of our country as enterprise zones—to encourage investment and to channel the strength of our free enterprise system to those areas and to those people who need it most.

Baltimore's Mayor Schaefer, who took me on a tour of your renewal areas 2 years ago, has been a strong supporter of this concept. For more than 2 years, we've been trying to get Federal enterprise zone legislation enacted, but the liberals who control the House of Representatives have bottled it up. Instead of focusing on raising taxes, I hope those who keep trying to impress us all with their use of the word "compassion" would help us free up the enterprise zone bill that is now tied up in the House.

Let's quit talking taxation and start providing jobs and opportunity to people who need new hope. The old welfare state didn't work; America needs new approaches. We don't need the failed Federal programs that create dependency and leave people in despair. Last year we replaced the old liberal CETA program with a Job Training Partnership Act. During its 9 years, CETA cost the taxpayers nearly $60 billion—$10 billion in 1979 alone. Only 18 cents out of every one of those dollars actually went to training, and only about one-third of the enrollees landed jobs.

Well, in our new program, overall costs have been reduced, and 70 percent of the money goes directly to training. And working with the private sector, we've provided tens of thousands of the hardcore unemployed with the skills they need to find and keep a job. And during the first 6 months of this program, which ended in March, 70 percent of those enrolled found jobs. The way to a better life for the less fortunate is not found in raising taxes and increasing spending. I say the best program to help those struggling to improve their lot is a meaningful, productive job.

And over 6 million new jobs have been created in the 21 months since the recovery started. In Europe they called it the "American miracle." Well, it's no miracle. It's not due to an uncontrollable cycle. It's due to our return to sensible and responsible Federal tax and spending policies, policies that encourage economic growth.

Our country needs leadership that can see beyond the demands of the special interest groups and prepare America for a better tomorrow.

I know there is an issue which the people of Baltimore are particularly concerned about, and it's a concern that I share. We've taken steps, with the strong support of your Senator Mac Mathias, to make certain that the new—or the next generation has a healthy and thriving Chesapeake Bay. It's a national treasure, and we're not going to lose it.

Helen Bentley, a former Chairman of the Federal Maritime Commission, has been very supportive of our efforts. She's also been in the forefront of the fight to see to it that Baltimore's Harbor is dredged. Well, Helen, thanks to you for all that you've done.

Representative Marjorie Holt is with us today. She is a strong voice for responsible government, and you can be proud of the job that she's doing in Washington.

What we're all working for is a strong, united, prosperous, and free America—the kind of country that God intended the United States to be.

When Columbus discovered America, he set in force a motion mightier than the world had ever known. People came here from every corner of the planet to be free and to improve their lot and that of their family. Well, we got off course a few years ago, but now we've set the good ship Columbia back sailing in the right direction. And I thank you for letting me be here to help you honor the man who started it all, Christopher Columbus.

Audience. Thank you!

The President. So, good luck, and God bless you, and God bless this precious land of ours found by Christopher Columbus. Thank you all very much. Thank you.

Audience. 4 more years! 4 more years! 4 more years!

The President. Thank you very much.

Note: The President spoke at 3:56 p.m. at President Street and Eastern Avenue, the gateway to "Little Italy," the heart of Baltimore's Italian-American community. The statue was dedicated to the city of Baltimore by the Italian American Organization United and the Italian-American community of Baltimore.

Following the ceremony, the President returned to Washington, DC.

Message to the House of Representatives Returning Without Approval a Bill for the Relief of Joseph Karel Hasek
October 8, 1984

To the House of Representatives:

I am returning herewith H.R. 1362, a bill for the relief of Joseph Karel Hasek.

I am sympathetic to the plight of hundreds of thousands of individuals who have fled the tyranny of communist rule imposed after World War II upon countries of eastern Europe and whose property has been confiscated by those governments. The United States government over the years has been successful in providing some measure of relief to some of these individuals by providing for the adjudication of these claims by the Foreign Claims Settlement Commission of the United States and by the negotiation of agreements with the offending governments to obtain funds for at least partial payment for such losses. The most recent example is the claims settlement agreement reached with the Government of Czechoslovakia by this Administration which has provided substantial although not full restitution for American citizens with valid claims against Czechoslovakia under international law. Such agreements have been possible only through adherence by the United States to the rule of international law that a government may only espouse such claims against a foreign government where American-owned property has been expropriated.

In 1958 the Foreign Claims Settlement Commission of the United States was authorized to determine the validity and amount of claims by United States citizens against the Government of Czechoslovakia caused by the confiscation of property owned at the time by United States nationals. Joseph Karel Hasek along with over 4,000 other claimants submitted claims to the Commission. After careful consideration the Commission was required to deny his claim due to the failure of Mr. Hasek to establish that any property owned by him was expropriated at a time when it was owned by a United States national. Mr. Hasek's claim was one of many denied on similar grounds. The Commission completed this program, and in 1962 all of its decisions became final and not subject to further review.

This bill would allow Mr. Hasek, but none of the others in like circumstances, to reopen his claim despite the termination of the program.

This bill directs that Mr. Hasek's claim be considered as valid despite the fact that it is not a valid claim for the United States to espouse under international law and the longstanding policy of the United States government. It seeks to provide special relief for one individual while ignoring the many thousands of United States citizens of Polish, Czechoslovakian, Yugoslavian, Bulgarian, Romanian, Hungarian, and German heritage who have suffered like losses but have been denied relief in a number of claim programs because their property was not expropriated at a time when it was owned by a United States national.

Finally, the bill would require payment to Mr. Hasek, who did not qualify for compensation, through the transfer to him of funds expressly obtained and set aside to compensate those American citizens who were claimants and did establish meritorious claims against Czechoslovakia for the confiscation of American-owned property. These claimants will therefore receive even less by way of restitution for their losses.

This result fails the elemental test of fairness and equity to thousands of American citizens who have suffered losses as egregious as those suffered by Mr. Hasek. I therefore have withheld my approval from H.R. 1362.

If relief is warranted in the case of Mr. Hasek, it centers on the beneficiary's claim that new evidence is available that was not available prior to the statutory expiration of the Czechoslovakian claims review in 1962. Accordingly, I would be willing to consider alternative relief legislation which would afford Mr. Hasek another review of the available evidence. I have directed my Administration to work with the Congress to consider such alternatives.

RONALD REAGAN

The White House,
October 8, 1984.

Note: The message was released by the Office of the Press Secretary on October 9.

Proclamation 5252—National Down's Syndrome Month, 1984
October 9, 1984

By the President of the United States
of America

A Proclamation

In the past decade, the United States has entered a new era of hope for its developmentally disabled citizens. This new age of enlightened understanding recognizes that developmentally disabled persons have a great potential for achieving and overcoming handicaps. Down's syndrome, a condition once thought to be without hope of positive change, is one of the best symbols of this changing attitude.

Progress is evident on several fronts. Research has uncovered the genetic basis for the condition and points the way to its ultimate prevention. Advances in medical treatment can minimize defects associated with the condition and have extended the life-span of those who have it. School doors have been unlocked to Down's syndrome children, and special education classes within mainstream school programs have been developed. Vocational training in preparation for gainful employment and independent living has become available.

These advances have not occurred by chance. They are the result of the collective effort of concerned physicians, scientific investigators, teachers and other professionals, parent groups such as the National Down's Syndrome Congress, and government. But the task remains unfinished. Public aware-ness and acceptance of the capabilities of persons who have Down's syndrome can greatly facilitate their being welcomed in all communities.

The Congress, by Senate Joint Resolution 254, has designated October 1984 as "National Down's Syndrome Month" and has authorized and requested the President to issue a proclamation in observance of this month.

Now, Therefore, I, Ronald Reagan, President of the United States of America, do hereby proclaim October 1984 as National Down's Syndrome Month, and I urge all Americans to join me in encouraging renewed efforts on behalf of the health and well-being of individuals with Down's syndrome. I invite all concerned citizens, agencies, and organizations to unite during October in support of appropriate observances and activities that will assist individuals with Down's syndrome and their families to a fuller and more rewarding life.

In Witness Whereof, I have hereunto set my hand this ninth day of October, in the year of our Lord nineteen hundred and eighty-four, and of the Independence of the United States of America the two hundred and ninth.

RONALD REAGAN

[Filed with the Office of the Federal Register, 2:38 p.m., October 9, 1984]

Proclamation 5253—Fire Prevention Week, 1984
October 9, 1984

By the President of the United States
of America

A Proclamation

Each year, fire strikes one out of ten homes in our country. Our Nation leads the world in technological achievements but, unfortunately, it also leads the world in per capita fire losses. Every hour one person dies, and every month $2 billion is lost as a result of fire. Between 2 percent and 3 percent of our gross national product is consumed in fires annually.

It is encouraging to note that, due to the increase in public fire education efforts and use of smoke detectors, there has been a leveling off of fire deaths in recent years.

Many homes, however, are still without these safety devices, and I urge community leaders to encourage their use and emphasize the need to keep them in good working order.

Removing the threat of fire from our families and businesses is a national priority. New initiatives are needed to educate the public concerning fire safety and to advise them how they may prevent or survive fire situations. More and more private sector and volunteer organizations are joining the efforts to reduce the Nation's fire loss and this is commendable.

Special recognition is due the efforts of over a million men and women, both volunteer and career, of our Nation's fire services who daily risk their lives to protect others. It is appropriate that we take time to thank them for their unselfish dedication to the principle of helping others in desperate need. Americans should also appreciate the work of all organizations concerned with fire prevention and control efforts—in particular those which are members of the Joint Council of National Fire Service Organizations.

Now, Therefore, I, Ronald Reagan, President of the United States of America, do hereby designate the week of October 7 through 13, 1984, as Fire Prevention Week. I call upon the people of the United States and interested groups, volunteer organizations, businesses, and governmental organizations to plan and to participate in fire prevention activities during this week.

In Witness Whereof, I have hereunto set my hand this 9th day of October, in the year of our Lord nineteen hundred and eighty-four, and of the Independence of the United States of America the two hundred and ninth.

RONALD REAGAN

[*Filed with the Office of the Federal Register, 2:39 p.m., October 9, 1984*]

Proclamation 5254—Mental Illness Awareness Week, 1984
October 9, 1984

By the President of the United States of America

A Proclamation

Mental illnesses are among the most misunderstood disorders. As a result, many of our citizens experience unnecessary pain. Stigma—a by-product of fear and misunderstanding—places an unwarranted burden on those with mental disorders and their families. It is of particular concern that the stigma associated with these problems often discourages people from seeking the help they need.

A recent National Institute of Mental Health research study found that one-fifth of adult Americans—over 24 million people—suffered a diagnosable mental disorder in the previous six months. In addition, an estimated 12 million children in this country have a mental disorder. Many will never reach full potential because their illnesses will go unrecognized and untreated.

The cost of mental illnesses to this Nation is in excess of $50 billion annually in health care and lost productivity. The cost in human suffering is beyond reckoning; however, the promise of relief is becoming a reality for many.

Research during recent decades has led to new and more effective drug, behavioral, and psychosocial treatments. For many, the pain of depression can be eased, suicide prevented, hallucinations and delusions assuaged, and crippling anxieties eliminated. Many children vulnerable to serious developmental and psychological problems can be protected by early diagnosis and intervention.

In recognition of the unparalleled growth in scientific knowledge about mental illnesses and the need to increase awareness of such knowledge, the Congress, by Senate

Joint Resolution 322, has designated the week beginning October 7, 1984 as "Mental Illness Awareness Week" and authorized and requested the President to issue a proclamation in observance of this week.

Now, Therefore, I, Ronald Reagan, President of the United States of America, do hereby proclaim the week beginning October 7, 1984, as Mental Illness Awareness Week. I call upon all health providers, educators, the media, public and private organizations, and the people of the United States to observe this week by participating in appropriate ceremonies and activities.

In Witness Whereof, I have hereunto set my hand this ninth day of October, in the year of our Lord nineteen hundred and eighty-four, and of the Independence of the United States of America the two hundred and ninth.

RONALD REAGAN

[*Filed with the Office of the Federal Register, 2:40 p.m., October 9, 1984*]

Remarks of the President and Prime Minister Shimon Peres of Israel Following Their Meetings
October 9, 1984

The President. We've just completed an intensive round of discussions with Prime Minister Peres and Foreign Minister Shamir. And may I say that our discussions reconfirm the close friendship, the mutual respect, and the shared values that bind our countries. Our ties remain unbreakable, continue to grow stronger.

It's been a particular pleasure for me to welcome Mr. Peres to the White House in his new capacity as Prime Minister. Mr. Shamir, of course, has been a frequent visitor to Washington, and I'm very pleased that we were able to meet with him again.

I want to pay special tribute to the leadership qualities of Prime Minister Peres and Foreign Minister Shamir. Both have shown courage and determination to put aside partisan politics and join together in a government of national unity in order to deal with Israel's most pressing problems. This demonstration of unity reminds us of democracy's great strength and the hope it offers for all the people of the world.

In our talks we focused on several issues. We discussed in some detail the plans of Prime Minister Peres and his partners in the new unity government for revitalizing the Israeli economy and putting it on the road to sustained recovery. And I'm impressed by the bold and wide-ranging steps the Prime Minister and his Cabinet colleagues are planning.

I know from our own experience how difficult the problem of economic readjustment is, yet how vitally important a strong economy is to national security. We've made clear our willingness to continue our dialog and to cooperate with Israel in the best way we can as Israel proceeds with its plans.

The new Government of Israel has already taken some steps to reduce inflation and increase economic growth and is working to develop additional steps. The economic support funds and other funds that the Congress has appropriated for Israel come at an opportune time, for they will enable Israel to develop its programs without having to divert undue attention to balance-of-payments problems. Should such problems arise, the U.S. Government will work closely with the Israeli Government to avert them.

Looking ahead, Prime Minister Peres has described a bright vision of Israel's economic future as a dynamic competitor in world markets. We have agreed to explore with Israel ways to enhance its growth and development prospects through structural adjustment, increased trade and investment, as well as American aid.

And Prime Minister Peres and I have decided to establish a joint economic development group of economic officials from our two governments and private economists to discuss Israel's economic recovery and development program. And this group will be an important forum for exchanging views on the full range of economic issues and examining ways to help support Israel's efforts.

The establishment of a free trade area between our two countries also offers great promise to Israel's economic future and to the United States. This will be the first such agreement that we've entered into with another nation. Prime Minister Peres and I have instructed our delegations to conclude negotiations within 30 days. I'm confident that this unprecedented agreement, by expanding Israel's export markets to the United States, will be important in helping Israel on the way to economic recovery, and it will also boost U.S. exports to Israel.

We also discussed the situation in Lebanon. The Prime Minister made clear the firm Israeli determination to withdraw fully from Lebanon as soon as security arrangements can be put in place to ensure the safety of Israel's northern border. I reassured him that the United States stands ready to help, provided the parties concerned want us to play this role and are committed to finding answers to the difficult issues involved. We agreed to stay in close touch on this subject in the days ahead.

And finally, I reaffirmed our fundamental commitment to Israel's national security. I'm pleased that we've agreed to consult in a systematic way on the U.S.-Israel security assistance program, a way that contributes most effectively to Israel's overall national security and the maintenance of its qualitative edge. Secretary Weinberger will be discussing this process and other security matters when he visits Israel next week.

I made clear to the Prime Minister and his colleagues our firm commitment to the goal of a just and lasting peace between Israel and all its Arab neighbors. Outstanding steps in that direction are United States Security Council Resolution 242, the Camp David accords on the historic Egyptian-Israeli peace treaty.

I reaffirmed today my initiative of September 1, 1982. At that time I set forth U.S. positions designed to bring the parties to the negotiating table, presumably with their own positions. The Prime Minister stressed that his government is also determined to move the peace process forward, and I join him in this great and common objective. In partnership, Israel and the United States will continue to work toward a common vision of peace, security, and economic well-being.

Prime Minister Peres, it's a great pleasure to have you here with us.

The Prime Minister. Thank you very much, Mr. President.

I want to thank the President of the United States for his understanding, his friendship, his hospitality, and may I say, Mr. President, that in our meetings the relations between the United States and America have reached a new level of harmony and understanding, which I am very grateful for.

I would like, from the outset, on behalf of all of the people of Israel, to thank the President, the Congress, and, first and foremost, the people of the United States, for the lasting friendship existing between our two people and countries.

Vice Premier Shamir and myself have had a series of most rewarding discussions with the President, Vice President, the Secretary of State, the Secretary of Defense, and their colleagues. I found in the White House a true friend of Israel and I understand—who understand our problems and dilemmas, aware of our difficulties, and closely follows our efforts to face them.

I'm grateful to the President for his warm and detailed statement and consider it an important contribution to the process of rebuilding the Israeli economy. Equally significant is my hope that the United States will continue to play an important role in reducing tension in our region and revitalizing the peace process.

I detailed to the President the position of our government of national unity on a wide range of issues in the political, security, and economic areas. The government of national unity was formed in the united city of Jerusalem in the spirit and the words of Prophet Ezekiel, who said, "And I shall give them an undivided heart and a new spirit."

Despite the differences between the policies of this government, we are all united in our thankfulness and confidence in the

United States of America. We are all united in our desire for peace. We are all united in the desire to bring our boys back from Lebanon, provided that the security of the northern part of Israel will be guaranteed. We are determined to tackle our economic difficulties head on.

Mr. President, our land is not a land for skeptics, but a cradle for believers, and this is more important than any passing economic difficulty. While we certainly build a primary responsibility for dealing with these problems and we have demonstrated our resolve with regard to each, nevertheless, the support of the President, the United States Government, and the American people is a source of strength and inspiration to all of us.

Again, Mr. President, I thank you from the depths of my heart for your understanding, friendship, and support in the long and short range of the destinies of Israel. Thank you very much.

Reporter. Mr. President, the Democrats say your age is now a legitimate issue in the campaign. Do you think it ought to be, sir?

The President. I'll challenge him to an arm wrestle anytime. [*Laughter*]

Q. Do you have a secret plan to cut Social Security? [*Laughter*]

Note: The President spoke at 1:32 p.m. in the Rose Garden at the White House.

Earlier, the President and the Prime Minister met in the Oval Office. They then held a working luncheon, together with U.S. and Israeli officials, in the Cabinet Room.

Remarks on Signing the Older Americans Act Amendments of 1984
October 9, 1984

The President. Thank you very much, and welcome to the White House.

I'm pleased that the Congress has completed action on a bill to reauthorize and improve the Older Americans Act—and it's not because I'm often reminded of what Francis Joseph Cardinal Spellman meant when he said there were three ages: youth, middle age, and "You're looking wonderful." [*Laughter*]

But now, before I say anything else, please let me thank all those in the Congress who worked so hard on behalf of this important legislation. Our senior citizens want and deserve to be full participants in American life. They want and deserve independence, quality health care, and economic security. The legislation that I'm about to sign will help older Americans achieve these worthy goals.

This legislation will continue a program which has provided essential services for older Americans since 1965—nutritious meals, information and referral services, transportation, and other types of assistance which make it easier to find self-fulfillment and rewarding involvement in community life. These important programs serve an es-

timated 13 million older Americans each year.

And I would also like to point out that the bill provides new help and hope for the victims of Alzheimer's disease and their families. As you know, Alzheimer's disease is the most common cause of intellectual impairment in older Americans. Until recently, this indiscriminate killer of mind and life had gone virtually undetected with the families of its victims virtually helpless. This legislation means more help is on the way.

All of us have much to do to make the lives of our senior citizens safe, rewarding, and enjoyable. This legislation will help to do that and do it in a way that provides greater flexibility in the management of the grants that finance these programs.

But in signing this important piece of legislation, I must note my strong constitutional reservations regarding the provisions that give the President pro tem of the Senate and Speaker of the House the power to appoint two-thirds of the members of the Federal Council on the Aging. Under this legislation, the Council clearly remains within the executive branch. Under the Constitution, therefore, members of the Council should not be appointed by officers of the Congress. And, accordingly, I strongly urge the Congress to enact legislation to repeal these new appointment provisions before June 5th, 1985.

And having gotten that message across, I'll sign the bill. And thank you, and God bless you all.

It is law.

Reporter. Mr. President, will you cut Social Security for future benefits?

Q. Mondale says you have a secret plan, Mr. President.

Q. Sir, will you extend your pledge not to cut Social Security benefits to future recipients, as well as present recipients?

The President. I think that—in a statement that I've released—has been made clear. That's exactly what I meant the other night.

Q. That's not what you said Sunday night, sir.

The President. Yes, it is, really.

Note: The President spoke at 3:37 p.m. in the Rose Garden at the White House.

In his remarks, the President referred to the fact that earlier in the day, Larry M. Speakes, Principal Deputy Press Secretary to the President, made the following statement to reporters during his daily press briefing:

"We note with chagrin that former Vice President Mondale finds himself in Cincinnati today talking about Social Security. I'm here to say that I have just spoken with the President, and Mondale ought to be ashamed. He's out to frighten the elderly. Mondale's statement is pure campaign rhetoric. The President will never stand for reduction of Social Security benefits for anybody, those now getting them or future recipients."

As enacted, S. 2603 is Public Law 98–459, approved October 9.

Statement on Signing the Social Security Disability Benefits Reform Act of 1984
October 9, 1984

I am pleased to sign into law H.R. 3755, the Social Security Disability Benefits Reform Act of 1984. This legislation, which has been formulated with the support of the administration and passed by unanimous vote in both Houses of Congress, should restore order, uniformity, and consensus in the disability program. It maintains our commitment to treat disabled American citizens fairly and humanely while fulfilling our obligation to the Congress and the American taxpayers to administer the disability program effectively.

When I took office on January 20, 1981, my administration inherited the task of implementing the continuing disability reviews required by the 1980 Disability Amendments which had been enacted and signed into law during the previous administration. Soon after the Department of Health and Human Services began the mandatory reviews, we found that trying to implement the new law's requirements

within the framework of the old, paper-oriented review process was causing hardships for beneficiaries. Accordingly, back in 1982, the Department began a long series of administrative reforms designed to make the disability review process more humane and people-oriented. These reforms included providing face-to-face meetings between beneficiaries and Social Security Administration (SSA) claims representatives at the very start of the review process.

These initial steps were followed by further important reforms announced by Secretary Heckler in June of 1983, including:
- classifying additional beneficiaries as permanently disabled, thus exempting them from the 3-year review;
- temporarily exempting from review two-thirds of cases of individuals with mental impairments while the decisionmaking standards were being revised; and
- accelerating a top-to-bottom review of

disability policies by SSA and appropriate outside experts.

While those June 1983 reforms went a long way towards humanizing the process, by the spring of 1984, it became apparent that legislation was needed to end the debate and confusion over what standard should be used in conducting continuing disability reviews. The administration worked with the Congress to develop this consensus legislation and, in the interim, took the additional step of suspending the periodic disability reviews pending implementation of new disability legislation.

One indication of the complexity of the issues involved is the fact that Congress held more than 40 hearings on the disability review process over a 3-year period before arriving at a consensus on this legislation.

One significant provision of H.R. 3755 is the so-called medical improvement standard that sets forth the criteria SSA must apply when deciding whether a disability beneficiary is still disabled. The standard this new legislation would establish for future determinations will restore the uniformity that is so essential to a nationwide program.

Another provision in H.R. 3755 would extend temporarily the ability of a Social Security disability beneficiary who has decided to appeal a decision that his disability has ended to have benefits continued up to the decision of an administrative law judge. This will prevent undue hardship to beneficiaries who are found on appeal to be still disabled while the new law is being put in place.

In addition, the legislation places a desirable moratorium on reviews to determine whether individuals with mental impairments are still disabled until revised criteria for evaluating these impairments are published. The Department of Health and Human Services has been working with mental health experts on these criteria.

Several other changes are written into this new law that will clarify and expedite the administration of the disability program.

I have asked Secretary Heckler to implement the provisions of this legislation as speedily and as fairly as possible. The Department of Health and Human Services will act promptly in reviewing individual cases so that no disabled beneficiary has to wait any longer than necessary for the proper decision on his or her case.

Note: As enacted, H.R. 3755 is Public Law 98–460, approved October 9.

Informal Exchange With Reporters on the Presidential Campaign
October 10, 1984

Q. Did Mondale take you up on arm wrestling?

The President. What?

Q. Did Mondale take you up on arm wrestling?

The President. He did?

Q. Did he? I don't know.

The President. No. No, I haven't heard from him.

Q. Do you think the age issue is important, the way they're building it up?

The President. No, I don't. I think it kind of shows again the same kind of desperate reaching for something that they did before.

Q. Mr. O'Neill said you looked tired the other night at the end of the debate. How did you feel then, sir? What do you think of the Speaker's characterization?

The President. I wasn't—no, I wasn't tired. And with regard to the age issue and everything, if I had as much makeup on as he did, I'd have looked younger, too.

Q. You didn't have any makeup on?

The President. No. I never did wear it. I didn't wear it when I was in pictures.

Q. And do you think you're going to win the next debate?

The President. Well, let's see what happens. I think the truth is on my side.

Q. And what about the Bush-Ferraro—how do you think that'll go?

The President. Well, we're going to wait and see that one. Looking forward to it.

Q. You're not picking a winner?

The President. No, no. Well, I know who's going to win.

Q. Do you think you lost Sunday night?

The President. What?

Q. Do you think you lost?

The President. I think if someone would go with the transcript and look at the fact that the figures and the facts that I gave were true, and were never rebutted in that debate, and that he kept repeating facts that I had rebutted because they were inaccurate, as a matter of fact, they had no basis in fact at all.

Q. But you did say Social Security—those on Social Security now, you did not speak of the future.

The President. Well, that was not on my mind, that I was separating that out. I guess that's just the way the answer came out, that I wouldn't. But, no, I meant that, that I've said over and over again. We're never going to take away from those people who are dependent on Social Security, now or in the future.

Q. Do you think the campaign has a new momentum? Do you think it's a new ballgame for Mondale? He seems to have a new spirit—patriotism.

The President. Well, I don't know. Our figures are holding up very well.

Q. Are we going to see a new Reagan campaign style now?

The President. You get what you see. That's me.

Q. Didn't you change your strategy, in that you did react to Mondale yesterday and previously you didn't? Isn't this a change of strategy?

The President. What's this?

Q. With the Social Security thing. Shortly after Mondale said it, you reacted.

The President. Well, because I am terribly concerned that this demogoguery about Social Security is frightening senior citizens. And there is just no fairness and no rightness at all in leaving these people uncertain as to what their situation is going to be when they have particularly no place else to turn but Social Security. And we're not going to let them down, and I've been saying that since before I was President.

Q. You really think that Mondale weakened the defenses of the country?

The President. What?

Q. You really think that Mondale weakened the defenses of this country?

The President. Well, he hasn't——

Q. You say so in a speech today.

The President. Let me say that from reports of many of the people that were part of that same administration, when President Carter in his last 2 years felt that he should start redressing the military imbalance, Mondale advised against it.

All right? I've got to run.

Q. Thank you.

Note: The exchange began at 8:55 a.m. at the South Portico of the White House as the President was preparing to leave for a trip to Michigan.

Remarks and a Question-and-Answer Session at St. Agatha High School in Detroit, Michigan
October 10, 1984

The President. Well, thank you all very much for a most heartwarming reception. I feel like I'm playing in theater of the round in here. [*Laughter*] It's good to be back in Michigan and great to be in Redford Township with the St. Agatha Aggies.

Now, I understand that you're in the midst of "Spirit Week," and I know you're looking forward to a great homecoming football victory. But I have an idea that your spirit isn't just for a week, but for always.

You know, really, in getting around the country as I have, your generation is really terrific, and I thank you for helping turn our country around in that regard. We've come here because you're what America is all about. You're America's future, and the future rests in the hopes and the dreams that you have inside your hearts. And helping you make those hopes and dreams come true is what this job of mine is all about.

Now, I've often been accused of being an optimist, and I hope so. All my life I've seen that when people have freedom and a vision, when they have the courage and opportunity to work hard, and when people believe in the power of faith and hope, they can accomplish great things. And today, right here in Michigan and all across America, in your factories and farms, and out at Tiger Stadium, we're meeting the challenge and accomplishing great things.

And I know how excited you are about the Tigers; they're a great team. And I can't take a side on the series now, what with a California team and with the Tigers— [*laughter*]. And having been a sports announcer and broadcasting major league baseball some years ago, I kept saying, well, maybe I could cheer for one and pray for the other. [*Laughter*] And then I realized that wouldn't work either, and I found myself being reminded of something—if you wouldn't mind a personal story—reminded of something that has to do with praying and athletics.

It was in a chalk talk in college. I was a freshman, and the lightest man on the line. And there that evening we were in a classroom, and the coach was diagramming plays on the board. And I don't know how it happened, but the coach evidently started it. It got around to prayer with regard to football. Well, I'd never gone in a game in my life in high school or college that I hadn't prayed before that game. But being a freshman, and all those big "hollegers" around me, I would have been the last person in the world to admit it. But as the talk went on, suddenly I was discovering that everybody on the team did the same thing—went into a game, but only after praying.

But the amazing thing is I'd worked out a prayer for myself. You can't pray to win.

We're all God's children, and how is He going to favor one side and not the other? So, knowing that was impossible, I'd figured out for myself that I would pray that I did my best, didn't make any mistakes, that no one would be injured on either side, and that the best team would win, and that we would all be content and satisfied, we wouldn't have any regrets of saying, "Oh, why did I do this or not do that?" when the game was over. And as the conversation went on, I discovered that every fellow in that room had worked that same thing out for himself.

So, that's why if I'm praying at all for the World Series games, I'll just be praying that the best team wins and that no one gets hurt and that we can all be happy when it's over. So, I hope you don't mind my sharing that with you.

You know, in the past few years there's been a grassroots revolution to recommit our schools to an agenda for excellence that will reach every child in this land. Teachers, school principals, school boards are joining with parents to bring back discipline and higher standings [standards], [1] proven values, and quality education. And what do you know? After 20 years of decline in the scholastic achievement tests for college entrance exams, the scores are going up.

I'm going to continue to get our—or in our efforts to get passed in the Congress the tuition tax credit bill. This bill would help hard-working parents who—like yours—who pay to send you to this school and to other independent schools throughout the country, and yet who are also paying their full share of taxes to support the public schools. And I think that only fairness dictates that there should be credit given taxwise for this double burden.

We've been working for excellence at all levels of our society, and the victories are those that all of us have achieved—our strong economy, our return to the values of faith, family, and neighborhood, and our determination to stay strong and be prepared for peace. These aren't just victories of an administration in Washington, they're victories of the people of this country. You made them possible.

---

[1] *White House correction.*

The wisest thing that's ever been said, I think, about peace was the simplest. It was when Pope Paul VI spoke before the United Nations in 1965. And he said, "No more war. War never again."

I have seen four wars in my lifetime. I've lost friends in those wars and the sons of friends. If we're prepared for peace, if we stay strong and we realize there are no cheap, easy solutions, no easy answers, a peace that brings liberty and human dignity will settle in and grow deeper.

I told Foreign Soviet Minister Gromyko just 12 days ago that we remain ready to reduce nuclear arms—hopefully to eliminate them altogether—ready to negotiate a fair deal, and ready to meet them halfway.

You know, each day the world turns completely, and so each day the world is reborn. Possibilities that yesterday didn't exist emerge to startle us. With your help and support we're going to keep on the path to a lasting peace. And with your help and support we're going to keep on getting victories for all the people. As long as we remember that the difference between having faith in people and faith in big government is the difference between success and failure, we're going to be able to reach for the stars. As long as we concentrate on hard work and high tech, not on hard times and high taxes, we can have the future of our dreams.

More than 208 years ago a small band of patriots began one of history's greatest adventures—something called America. These brave men and women laid everything on the line for freedom, independence, opportunity, and peace. And ever since, our country has been an inspiration to freedom-loving people everywhere and a magnet to millions of immigrants seeking the miracle that is America.

And let me tell you that I was very happy to be at the ceremony just 10 days ago when two of your classmates, those who led us in the Pledge of Allegiance—Sheila Della and Jennifer—became new American citizens.

That's proof that America's adventure isn't over yet; it never should be. Your generation will be ready to meet the challenges before you, so be confident, aim high, work hard, stick to your values, and you'll never

go wrong. The future is yours, and it's going to be terrific. And it's going to be better than anything that any of the rest of us ever knew because that's what America's been doing generation after generation.

To your principal, Mrs. Kolis, to Father Murphy, [2] to all your teachers, and especially to all of you, I can't tell you how much I appreciate your letting me join you here today. And I also have to thank especially my penpal, Carol, [3] who issued the invitation. You see, Presidents do get letters when you write. [*Laughter*]

Now, I know that that's all of the monolog. I know that we're going to have a dialog, and I've been looking forward to this, questions and answers for a limited period of time. So, when you're ready.

Mr. Sowden. Thank you, Mr. President.

Mr. President, Patrick Allgeyer has a question for you.

World Series

Q. Mr. President, do you think the Tigers have as good a chance of winning the World Series as you have of being reelected? [*Laughter*]

The President. I'm afraid to answer that question—[*laughter*]—because if I should guess wrong on that, just think, I'd have to spend the rest of the month worrying about what's going to happen. Just let me say I'll go back to that original prayer idea: May the best team win.

Q. Thank you, Mr. President.

The President. By the way, just taking wild shot here, what position do you play?

Q. Offensive tackle, sir. [*Laughter*]

The President. I thought so.

Q. Thank you, Mr. President.

The President. Thank you.

Mrs. Kolis. Mr. President, Dennis Shubitowski has a question for you.

Views on the Presidency

Q. Mr. President, is being the President

---

[2] *Father William Murphy, pastor of St. Agatha Parish.*

[3] *Carol Tumidanski, a junior, wrote to the President in August, inviting him to visit the school.*

of the United States really what you expected it to be?

The President. Yes. [*Laughter*] I had some experience. You know, I was Governor of California for 8 years, which is the most populous State in the Union. It's about 10 percent of the whole country in numbers of people. And, so, I found that there's a great similarity between that experience, being the chief executive officer of a State, and of the Federal Government. So, there weren't too many surprises.

At the same time, there were some. You see, the Presidency—you don't become President—the Presidency is an institution over which you have temporary custody. And I'll just tell you one little incident to illustrate what I mean. Every place I went—and those marines at the helicopter—they were throwing those salutes. Well, I was an officer in World War II, and I'm not in uniform, and so I knew I wasn't supposed to salute, or felt that I wasn't, and yet it bothered me. I'd try to nod and speak, and they'd still hold that salute.

So one day I was talking with the Marine Commandant, the head man, and I said to him—a marine had just saluted me—and I said, "You know, there ought to be some regulation," I said, "if I'm Commander in Chief, as I am now, of the Armed Forces, there ought to be a regulation that I can return salutes." And the general said, "Mr. President, I think if you did, no one would say anything." So, I learned that.

Q. Thank you, Mr. President.

Mr. Sowden. Mr. President, Glenn Williams has a question for you.

Nuclear Disarmament

Q. Mr. President, if you could do one thing to make the world a better place, what would it be?

The President. That one thing would be the total elimination of nuclear weapons and——

Mrs. Kolis. Mr. President, Janet McLarty has a question for you.

Women in the Space Program

Q. Mr. President, what do you think the first woman walking in space will do for women across the Nation?

The President. Oh, well, I think what's taken place in space already, with Sally Ride and her mission up there and now the two of them up on this present mission—I think it is just further proof and evidence that probably the last and worst era of discrimination that we've known has come to an end.

Mr. Sowden. Mr. President, Robert Iafrate has a question for you.

The President. All right.

High School Extracurricular Activities

Q. Mr. President, what clubs or activities were you involved with in your high school? [*Laughter*]

The President. I majored in extracurricular activities. [*Laughter*] In addition to athletics, I was in the drama club, and I wound up as president of the student body. And I'd been in the student senate before that. And it continued that way through college in which, then, I added a Greek letter fraternity to the list of things that I belonged to. I never dreamed when I was in the drama club that I might wind up making my living that way, but—[*laughter*]—I did.

But I believe—seriously, let me answer your question, Robert—that I believe that the extracurricular activities are just as important as every other part of education, that there is teaching and learning in all of those things. It brings more out of you. And I like the idea, however, that all of those things are based on retaining a level of grade for eligibility that shows that you are not neglecting studies in order to participate in them.

Q. Thank you, Mr. President.

Mrs. Kolis. Mr. President, Janet Sypniewski has a question for you.

Teenage Alcohol and Drug Abuse

Q. Mr. President, I know Mrs. Reagan spends much of her time working against alcohol abuse. How do you feel about this subject, especially among teenagers?

The President. I feel as strongly as she does, and that's really saying something because she is really wrapped up in this. Alcohol is just another form of drug, and all of them—there's just no place for them. You're growing up now, and you're laying, among other things, the physical foundation for the rest of your life. And it's just like buying a used car and then finding out the various places where it breaks down because somebody abused it in its younger days.

You only get this piece of machinery once. Take care of it. Really take care of it. And I'm prepared to tell you from personal experience that there'll come a place down the road when you'll really be happy that you did, because I've been 39 years old now for about 31-odd years. [*Laughter*]

Mr. Sowden. Mr. President, John Peltz has a question for you.

Medical Care

Q. Mr. President, do you favor a national health program? Why, or why not?

The President. When you say national health program, do you mean just encouragement of health or socialized medicine?

Q. Socialized medicine.

The President. Socialized medicine? No. Today, if you have to get sick any place in the world, get sick here in this country. We have the greatest medical care of any country in the world. And those countries that are practicing socialized medicine, the quality of the care has declined, the waiting list is forever, and the cost is far greater than it is here. In spite of the recent escalation in medical practice charges, the cost is greater.

I believe that—provide medicine and medical care for those people who cannot afford it for themselves, as we're doing. But the rest of it should be right out there in private enterprise, the same as we do everything else.

Q. Thank you, Mr. President.

Mrs. Kolis. Mr. President, James Kitchen has a question for you.

The President. All right.

Tuition Tax Credits

Q. Mr. President, do you think Congress will ever pass legislation for tuition tax credit?

The President. Yes, I do think that, if we will all remember that they work for us. We're going to continue pushing for this. But what we need to do—they need to hear from the people, and I have used this ex-

pression many times—they need to get letters; they need to be called when they're back in their districts and so forth, as to what it is we, the people, want. And the expression I've used is: It isn't necessary to educate them, it isn't necessary to make them see the light—make them feel the heat. [*Laughter*]

Q. Thank you, Mr. President.

Mr. Sowden. Mr. President, Dantes McSween has a question for you.

President's Legacy

Q. Mr. President, for future generations, do you want to be remembered as Ronald Reagan the actor, or Ronald Reagan, President of the United States? [*Laughter*]

The President. I'll take this one. [*Laughter*] Yes, I would like to be remembered for this. Oh, I made some pictures that I was proud of. I also made some that I hope will never show up on the late-late show. [*Laughter*] The studio didn't want 'em good, it wanted 'em Thursday. [*Laughter*] No, I would hope that I could accomplish something for which I would be remembered.

Q. Thank you, Mr. President.

Mrs. Kolis. Mr. President, Ken Craig has a question for you.

U.S. Relations With Other Countries

Q. Mr. President, when you become frustrated in your dealings with other countries, how do you deal with your frustrations? [*Laughter*]

The President. [*Laughing*] Well, I don't let them see it. [*Laughter*] I go home, and I talk it over with Nancy, and—[*laughter*]—she calms me down to a certain extent. But I have to say this: There have been less and less of those times as time has gone on in these last couple of years.

I believe that our relations now with other countries are better than they have been within my memory—our alliances with our friends and allies in NATO, the recent trip to China and what we accomplished there, and even with this recent visit with Mr. Gromyko. I think that he understands us a little better. I was rather frank with him, and I told him that we didn't like his system, but we weren't trying to change it for them, and they better not try to change ours.

And I think the frustrations are less. It is complicated. It is very touchy. The most frustrating thing today is the whole new thing in recent years of terrorism that's all over the world—these cowardly acts such as we've seen in the tragedies in Beirut, and all. That, and trying to establish whether there is some government, actual government that is inspiring this and supporting these terrorist movements, that is frustrating.

Q. Thank you, Mr. President.

Mr. Sowden. Mr. President, Mary Pittiglio has a question for you.

Q. Mr. President, how do you feel about traveling to different countries, especially those where there is political unrest?

The President. Well, it goes with the job, goes with the territory. And I have to tell you, I've had enough traveling by now in my life that I'm not crazy about it. But I must say, it does pay off, it does cement relationships: our recent trip to England for the summit conference—our allies there, the seven nations, the seven of us that are there together in dealing with our problems of trade, commerce, and so forth; our trip to Japan with Prime Minister Nakasone. He is, I think, an excellent man and dedicated to improving the relations with us. And so you come home, usually, with quite a feeling of accomplishment.

Q. Thank you.

Mrs. Kolis. Mr. President, Jennifer St. Croix has a question for you, sir.

Views on the Presidency

Q. Mr. President, being President and in the public eye, do you ever get any privacy?

The President. Yes. It isn't easy. You do know that you live in a fishbowl. But when you get up and through that gate at Camp David for weekends now and then, you certainly have a degree of privacy. We do, when we can, get to California to our ranch. And then there's a private life at home and within the walls of the White House. You don't always have a state dinner or things of that kind going on. So again, I think that I was probably more prepared for it by virtue of my experience as Governor than some people who, for the first time, find themselves in that fishbowl.

The understandable security precautions that have to be taken in the world the way it is today are frustrating, such as your friends and neighbors and parents and all who are outside here in crowds when we came in. And you'd love to be able to go over and say hello, and you can't do it.

Q. Thank you, Mr. President.

Mr. Sowden. Mr. President, thank you very much.

The President. All right. I want to thank you, but listen, I want to just—for you young ladies—I just want to give you one little experience, having mentioned summit conferences and so forth. The one before this one in England was held in Virginia, and held in that town that was the first British colony here and, really, the cradle of our nation. And the first meeting was to be held in what had been the British Governor's residence.

And we met that night for dinner, the first meeting, and I was all prepared for Margaret Thatcher, the Prime Minister of England. I was going to say to her, in that particular house, "Margaret, if one of your predecessors had been a little more clever, you would be hosting this gathering here in our country." [*Laughter*] And I started. I said, "Margaret, if one of your predecessors had been a little clever . . ." She quietly turned to me and said, "I know, I would have been hosting this gathering." [*Laughter*]

Well, thank you all, and God bless you.

Note: The President spoke at 11 a.m. in the gymnasium of the high school. He was introduced by Dian Kolis, principal, who moderated the question-and-answer session together with Robert Sowden, dean of students.

Following his visit, the President traveled to Warren, MI.

Remarks to the Heritage Council in Warren, Michigan
October 10, 1984

The President. Frank, I thank you very much. Reverend clergy, Mr. Mayor, Congressman Bill Broomfield, and all of you: I'll try something: *Dobry den* [Good day].

Well, I appreciate this chance to break bread with you. This center represents something special about America. We Americans came from many lands; we represent just about every race, religion, and ethnic group that's found on this planet. We take pride in our family heritage, passing it on to our children, just like you're doing here. Yet, what keeps us together, what cements our national unity, is our abiding love of freedom. And I think that's what America is all about.

And that's what this hall is all about, and I'm proud to be with you here today. I have always believed—and seeing these wonderful young people today and that entertainment, representing so many backgrounds—I just, I've always believed that somehow, Divine Providence put this continent here between the oceans to be found by people from every corner of the Earth, but who had that special love for freedom in their heart that would make them pick up, leave friends and family, and move to this at-one-time strange and completely undeveloped land. And we are so unique, there is no place on Earth quite like us.

If America is to remain the free and vibrant country that we want her to be, and if she's to be the great land of opportunity, we can't lose sight of those principles laid down by our Founding Fathers. And we must have the same courage and dedication as those brave souls who built America to do what is necessary to keep our country prosperous and to keep her secure from the threat of foreign tyrants and authoritarian ideologies.

A few years ago, we had great cause for concern. The economy was in a shambles. Murderous inflation, economic stagnation, oppressive taxation, and sky-high interest rates were all sapping the strength of our people. Instead of providing leadership, many elected officials joined a chorus of pessimists, bemoaning everything that was wrong with America.

Well, let me just say in the last 4 years we've made a new beginning. And I believe that on November 6th, the American people are going to tell the politicians of the past, "Forget it, we're not going back to that unhappy past."

Our people are enjoying the fruits of low inflation and high growth. Productivity is up. Real take-home pay is up. Business incorporations hit a record high last year—600,000 in that single year. Over 6 million new jobs have been created since the beginning of the recovery. Our European friends call it the American miracle.

Well, it isn't a miracle. It's just that the American people built this recovery. Our administration, with the help of good Congressmen like Bill Broomfield, just eliminated the roadblocks which took the form of irresponsible tax and spending policies, overregulation, and too much power centralized in Washington. Once we got the Government out of the way, the American people, just like they always have, got on with the job of making this a better country for all of us.

And that's especially true of you. When you needed a community center, you didn't go to the Government. Under Don Fedorak and Jerry Duzey's leadership, you got together, laid your plans, and went to work. And this center is a tribute to your enterprise. It serves the well-being of your entire community. It was completed back in 1978. But I can't help but think, had you gone to the Government with all its redtape and bureaucratic entanglements, this project probably would have cost, to begin with, twice as much, and you'd be paying for it through higher taxes. And, of course, we'd probably be meeting someplace else, because it wouldn't be finished yet. [*Laughter*] So, congratulations on a job well done.

And I know that you've done so much as individuals and as a community to help those newcomers to our shores build a new life, through organizations like the Ukrainian Congress Committee, the Ukrainian American Relief Committee, and the indigent fund of the Ukrainian National Women's League of America.

We need leaders who will encourage people to follow your example, to get involved personally, to strive on their own, to join with others to accomplish what they can before going to government. And that's what this election is all about. The choice this year is between two teams with two distinct philosophies. An opponent, unable to shake loose from the failed policies of the past, still trapped in the mentality of tax and tax and spend and spend, believes in bigger and bigger government. And that's why he made raising taxes the centerpiece of his campaign, his first option in dealing with the problems of America. His tax program would bring back inflation, would knock the legs out from under the recovery with a tax hike equal to $1,890 for every American household—that's more than $150 a month. He's got a knee-jerk reaction in favor of taxes. And every time his knee jerks, we get kicked. [*Laughter*]

Let me ask you, would you agree that raising taxes is the wrong way to make your family and your country strong?

Audience. Yes!

The President. All right. Well, I kind of expected that answer here in Michigan. [*Laughter*]

But instead of raising your taxes, we need to simplify the tax system, make it easier to understand, and make it easier for us to bring down your tax rates, not let them go up. Our opponents see an America in which every day is April 15th, tax day. [*Laughter*] Well, we see an America in which every day is the Fourth of July. Instead of raising your taxes, we'll promote policies that bring economic growth and increase opportunity. I think the best social program for the less fortunate who are trying to better their lot is a good job.

What we want is a strong and a prosperous America, an America that'll be entering the next century with confidence and optimism. Those wedded to the failed policies of the past, or tied too closely to special interest groups, may be unable to see the great potential that lies ahead.

How many of you watched on television as one of our magnificent space shuttles

blasted off into space or landed after a successful mission? I'm sure everyone has taken a look at that. I was proud to be there in the California desert to welcome back the *Columbia* and her gallant crew sometime ago. And I remember: Suddenly they rushed me up on the platform and they said, "Get ready, you know, it's coming," and was making its approach and would be landing in a few minutes, and I didn't see anything. And I said, "Well, where is it right now?" And they said, "It's just coming over Honolulu." [*Laughter*] And sure enough, in a matter of minutes, there it was and it was landing. [*Laughter*] When you stop and think that within a single lifetime of some of us, we've gone from the horse and buggy to that space shuttle—just in one lifetime.

If my opponent had his way, there never would have been a shuttle program. He led the fight against starting the shuttle program. He would have spent the money beefing up the bureaucracy in Washington, DC, and that wouldn't get you off the ground 1 inch. [*Laughter*]

But that program, by developing America's technological genius and by providing so many benefits, was an investment in the future. And it was worth every cent.

Today we're trying to make up for shortsighted decisions of the last decade. That's especially true in regard to our national security. Between 1970 and 1980, when the rest of the budget was skyrocketing out of sight, real spending for defense fell by over 20 percent. By the end of the decade, our Navy had dropped from over a thousand ships to under 500. Our Air Force was flying bombers that were, in some cases, older than the pilots.

Perhaps the policymakers—and this twisted logic is still around—they were making mistakes—or mistaking weakness, I should say, for peace. My opponent in this campaign has made a career out of weakening America's Armed Forces. He's always found one reason or another for opposing vital weapons systems and the modernization of our forces. As for me, I agree with President Dwight Eisenhower when he said, "To be strong nationally is not a sin. It is a necessity."

One of our top priorities since coming to

Washington has been rebuilding our defensive strength, and I make no apologies for that. I pledge to you that as long as I'm President, I will never shortchange the security needs of the United States of America.

We take our responsibilities very seriously. We are, for example, absolutely committed to root out waste and fraud and make certain that every defense dollar is used wisely. And those that you've heard lately talking about $500 hammers and $9,000 wrenches don't add, when they say that, that that's been going on for a long time. And when we got here, we started cleaning it up. We're the ones that brought those figures to light, made them public, and we are cleaning it up.

And there have been millions and millions of dollars in rebates returned to the Government as a result. And we, just a few days ago in the White House, the Rose Garden, recognized 12—some in uniform and some Defense Department civilian employees—who individually had tracked down and found some of these things that had resulted in millions of dollars of savings for us. There had been hundreds of indictments and convictions for fraud on the part of people, some people, that were doing these things.

But let's not kid ourselves. Even when we root out the waste, providing adequate defense is still an expensive proposition, especially when you're playing catchup. Now, those who are complaining the loudest about the cost are, for the most part, the same architects of a decade of neglecting America's security needs.

Well, I don't think America's listening to those voices anymore. New voices are being heard now, strong voices that advocate the cause of freedom, voices not ashamed to defend America's interests. There is one such advocate of whom I'm particularly proud. She's our Ambassador to the United Nations, Jeane Kirkpatrick. She represents a new realism in foreign policy. No longer do we apologize to tyrants about the American way of life, or apologize to those domestic critics who always blame America first.

She hadn't been in the United Nations very long until there was one of those days when about 27 countries on the floor blasted away at America for this or that. And the next afternoon, kind of abashed, they were calling on our Ambassador to apologize. They'd gotten 27 letters—each one of them had gotten a letter, 27 of them, the very next morning from Jeane Kirkpatrick. [*Laughter*]

We're building up the Voice of America so your message, our message, gets through to captive people everywhere. We seek no conflict with anyone. We've gone the extra mile and will continue to do so to reach arms reduction agreements. But from now on, when America negotiates, we'll negotiate from a position of strength.

Now, there's another group of Americans we should be thanking. During the previous administration, as preparedness sank, so did morale in our Armed Forces. And today, because they know how much we appreciate them, we've attracted the finest young men and women to the service who have ever served this country. But freedom, our freedom, is really in their hands. And their commanders tell me that we've got every reason to be confident and proud. And I hope if you see one of those young people now and then on the street in uniform somewhere, you'll tell him or her how grateful we are for the job they're doing.

There is a new spirit in America—well, it's not really new. We just recaptured some of that optimism and grit, that love of liberty and zest for life that have always been so much a part of America. And you represent the dream of America more than most. I know that many of you came here with little or no resources. With your hard work and the will to get ahead, you've built a good and decent life for your families, and that's what America is all about.

I hope I can count on your support, so that in the next 4 years we can make certain that we pass on a strong, free, secure, and opportunity-filled America to our children, to the next generation.

Audience. 4 more years! 4 more years! 4 more years!

The President. Thank you. Well, thank you very much. You've fed me well. Okay, I'll give in, I'll do it. [*Laughter*]

Your great poet, Taras Schevchenko, whose statue stands in our Nation's Capital, wrote words for all free people, and I'll conclude with those. He wrote:

". . . you shall overcome
God is with you
For strength and liberty and righteous truth
Are on your side."

Thank you. *Do pobatchenya* [Goodbye]. Goodbye. Thank you very much.

Note: The President spoke at 1:05 p.m. in the Banquet Room of the Ukrainian Cultural Center. He was introduced by Frank D. Stella.

Remarks at a Reagan-Bush Rally in Warren, Michigan
October 10, 1984

The President. It's great to be here at— [*applause*]—thank you. It's great to be here at Macomb Community College. We were looking for a good place to speak to the people of Warren, and I said Macomb was my first choice. It's wonderful to be back in Michigan, and I can say that because I was here just 10 days ago. I've been here four times since I've been President, and always for the same reason: I love your State.

Now, there are some cynics who think that I've come here because it's an election year.

Audience. No!

The President. This is such an obvious falsehood. I'm here on this lovely October afternoon to watch the leaves fall, to admire the way the crisp autumn sun hits the sparkling surface of Lake St. Clair. And now, of course, you know, if by chance we should pick up a few votes while we're here, well——

Audience. 4 more years! 4 more years! 4 more years!

The President. All right. Okay. All right.

I love your Michigan spirit. I'm inspired by it. And I am impressed by your Michigan football, and believe me, I speak from experience, because some years ago I was a sports announcer. I was broadcasting, as a matter of fact, an Iowa-Michigan game here in Michigan, and down on the field one of the fellows in the line for Michigan—his name was, I think, was Jerry Ford.

But I understand that you play a little baseball, too. Now, you know that because in this job I'm supposed to be President of all the people, I can't take sides on the Tigers-Padres issue. But just a little while ago, over at St. Agatha's High School, I promised the students there that—well, I told them I might try praying for one and cheering for the other, and, no, that wouldn't work, so I think my prayer'll just be, "Bless you, boys."

I expect an exciting contest, but then that's kind of what October's all about this year. But there are many things to talk about this October. On the way here, I was thinking of how to sum up 3½ years of effort by the American people to turn our economy and our nation around, how to sum up your success. And it seems to me that the past 3½ years have been an historic time in our country, a time of great renewal. Our nation has hope again, opportunity abounds, the American dream is reborn. And this is what I would call the overview. But would you like the facts to back it up? [*Applause*]

Well, we're enjoying the strongest economic expansion in 30 years. We've created more than 6 million new jobs in the last 22 months. And 600,000 new businesses were incorporated last year alone. And here in your State, in Michigan, brave technologies for men and women are putting forward advanced technologies, modernizing our world and our older industries, working to create new hopes, new jobs, and new dreams. And with labor and management pulling together with renewed confidence and spirit, our competitors are about to learn that once Americans put our minds to it, once we're provided the proper tools and equipment, we can outproduce, outcompete, and outsell anybody, anytime, anywhere in the world.

Now, none of this great national renewal happened by accident. It wasn't a matter of chance. Our renewal was the result of a policy aimed at lightening the tax burden on the American people. That's what helped get our economy moving again. And we intend to simplify the tax system so that we can push income tax rates further down, not up, and keep the expansion going.

Now, my opponent has another plan. He says he'll raise your taxes.

Audience. Boo-o-o!

The President. By 1989 he says that his tax would amount to $85 billion more per year.

Audience. Boo-o-o!

The President. Now, it's tempting to figure, when you hear that, that it's the other fellow's taxes that'll be raised. But let me tell you, they've been getting away with that for years. It's yours that will be raised.

We've already said that if my opponent is to keep all the promises that he's made, he would have to increase taxes by the equivalent of $1,890 per household.

Audience. Boo-o-o!

The President. Now, the red ink was barely dry on his massive $85 billion tax increase proposal before he revealed that part of his plan was for a second round of new tax increases. And these plans would leave a bottomless hole in the pockets of every working man and woman in this country.

On Sunday night, my opponent admitted that once his first huge tax hike was approved, that he would go for still more tax increases. And let me quote him. He said, "As soon as we get the economy on a sound ground as well, I would like to see the total repeal of indexing."

Audience. Boo-o-o!

The President. Now, I think you understand that indexing is the reform that we passed to protect you from the cruelest tax—the hidden tax caused by government using inflation to force you into higher and higher tax brackets. As you get a cost-of-living increase you move up. You're not any better off, you just kept pace with inflation. But suddenly you're in a higher percentage of tax bracket.

Now, that is scheduled by our tax program to go into effect on January 1st. That's when it begins. But Sunday, he said that he would repeal that protection. In fact, he said it before. But today, I gather that he says now, as of this morning, that he didn't mean that. Well, it's no wonder he thinks he goofed. The price of repealing index would be enormous. For a family earning $30,000, it would mean over $500 more in taxes per year by 1989. For a family earning 40,000, it'd be over $850 more.

And, now, you may not like the sound of that. But wait, it gets worse. The greatest hardship in his repeal of indexing would fall on those who can least afford it: everybody below the $25,000 earning line, everybody. The people that he claimed he would protect—the heaviest proportional burden falls on those least able to pay. In fact, it gets so bad as you go down the line that people earning $10,000 or less would have to pay about $200 a year more in taxes.

Well, it's nice that my opponent was willing to explain his two-part tax plan: raise taxes and raise them again. But it's the height of unfairness to make hard-working people pay even more taxes just to finance excessive campaign promises.

Now, believe me, this is one issue that affects every family in Michigan, every family in this country. One way or another my opponent's tax increases would not only stop the economy dead in its tracks; they would put a new and ever-increasing burden on you and your neighbors and your children. And he would turn us back to the old days where the politicians dance and you pay the piper.

The last thing we need now is a return to the policies of tax and tax and spend and spend. Those policies stifled creativity and growth. What we do need is a tax policy that offers incentives for people to work, save, and invest—all the things that'll keep the economy growing.

You know, it's hard sometimes to put recent events in historical perspective. We get caught up in everyday things. Sometimes we forget that we're part of a long continuum that stretches back two centuries to a little gathering in Philadelphia.

And those who gathered there envisioned

and created a totally new thing in history: a splendid union of States headed by a Federal Government whose members would be elected by the people and who would serve at the sufferance of the people. It was made clear from the beginning that the citizenry would allow the government certain rights—rights would not flow from the government to the people; it would be the other way around.

All over the world there are constitutions. And most of them promise a lot of the same things that ours guarantees. But there's one difference so fundamental that is tells the whole story. All those other constitutions say, "We, the government, allow you, the people, to do the following things." Ours says, "We, the people, allow you, the government, to do the following things."

Audience. 4 more years! 4 more years! 4 more years!

The President. All right.

Audience. 4 more years! 4 more years! 4 more years!

The President. All right. Thank you. That thing about we the people—that was changed a bit. And some decided that it was the state from which all blessings flow. So, we started some years ago to send more money and more power to the Federal Government in the hopes that it would give us better lives. But by the 1970's, it was clear that we had created chaos, disorder in the economy, wild inflation, government programs that tore up the fabric of the family and trampled on tradition.

Now, not all of what government has done has been bad. But in recent years, much of it was. And the worse things got, the more the Government took to blaming it on the people. Do you remember a few years ago, where they said the fault was ours? We had a malaise—that we were never going to have things as good again, and we might as well get used to it.

Well, in 1980 the American people declared their independence once again. We recognized, once and for all, that a government big enough to give you everything you want is big enough to take away everything you've got. And we recognize that after all this time, Henry David Thoreau was right: that government is best which governs least.

Now, we need government, of course. But when you go from government to big government—to government as the neighborhood bully—it's time for a change, and change we made. We started putting our house in order. When we cut tax rates 25 percent, we said, Washington, you've had enough. And when we cut inflation by two-thirds, we said, Economic chaos, your time is past. And we didn't do this for some of the people—we didn't do it especially for blacks or whites, or men and women, or old and young; we did it together, and we did it for everybody.

Now, the other side thinks of America as little more than a collection of special interest groups competing against each other, but they ought to wake up to what a united America accomplished while they were busy trying to manipulate this group and that.

I believe that we have returned to a proper understanding of who the American people are. We're the people who crossed the plains, scaled the mountains, won the West. We're the people who came up with the inventions that lit the world and filled it with sound and laughter. We're the people who twice in this century have fought in Europe and stood up for decency for all mankind. We're a people, in short, who don't need the supervision of government sophisticates to tell us what is right and good.

In the past few weeks, I've gone throughout this country, and I've talked to Americans, and I've taken questions from them. And one of the things that I've tried to talk about is how the revolution of 1980 is open to and eager for the help of the rank-and-file members of the Democratic Party. I hope that there are many present here today—I was one myself once. And whenever I talk about Franklin Delano Roosevelt or Harry Truman or John F. Kennedy, my opponents start tearing their hair out. They just can't stand it. Well, of course they can't, because it highlights how far they, the leadership today of the Democratic Party, has strayed from the strength of the democratic political tradition.

The good and decent Democrats of the rank and file, patriotic Democrats by the

Photographic
Portfolio

Overleaf: At a rally following debate with Walter F. Mondal[e] Louisville, KY, October 7. *Left* Broadcasting the Pepsi Firecra[cker] 400 auto race with Ned Jarret[t] of the Motor Racing Network in Daytona Beach, FL, July 4. *Below:* At a Spirit of America Festival in Decatur, AL, July 4 *Right:* Addressing the Republic[an] National Convention in Dallas August 23.

Left: Participating in a birthda celebration for Roy Acuff at th Grand Ole Opry in Nashville, September 13. *Below:* Campaig in Ottawa, OH, from the rear the "Heartland Special" during a whistlestop tour of Ohio, October 12. *Above right:* Greeti students at Bowling Green Stat University in Bowling Green, C September 26.

...e left: Lighting the National
...stmas Tree from the South
...co of the White House,
...mber 13. *Below:* Speaking at a
...gan-Bush rally in Millersville, PA,
...ber 29. *Above right:* At the
...iling of a commemorative
...p honoring Hispanic Americans
...e Rose Garden, October 31.
...v: Speaking at a Reagan-Bush
... in Chicago, IL, November 4.
...*leaf:* Helping to paint a mural
...ima, OH, during a whistlestop
... of Ohio, October 12.

millions, they haven't changed. Like their former leaders, they're clear-eyed about the world. They have few illusions, and they consider themselves to be Americans first, and not members of a special interest group.

When John Kennedy was President, he didn't push a program of dreary mediocrity with endless tax increases on those who dream of better days. He challenged Americans, just as we're challenging you today, to make America grow and to make America great by pushing for lower personal income tax rates for all the working people of America. And there was a great similarity between his tax cut program and the one that we implemented in 1981.

But the leaders of the present Democratic Party, as I've said, have gone so far left, they've left the mainstream. They no longer stand for what their great party always stood for. And that's a sad change; and I don't welcome it, because it's not good for this country. We see things as they are, and that's why I ask Democrats to listen to us, to give us a chance, to consider whether or not we don't, in fact, stand for the justice and decency that you've always cared about. We welcome you. You're not without a home. We're building a new grassroots opportunity party. We need your new blood, your ideas, your enthusiasm, and your energy.

Finally, I want to talk about the bright future I anticipate if we continue on the path that we've begun. We're going to continue to force personal income tax rates down, not up. We're going to continue curbing government's appetite. And that's going to keep the economy blooming. It is going to continue to grow. It's going to create millions of more jobs and new worlds of opportunity for all of us—all of us together. And with that new economic freedom, we'll have more time and more opportunity to explore the things of the soul. We'll be a nation even greater in art and learning and scientific inquiry; a nation great in observance and worship and love for the God who made us.

I'm talking about a future of flowering possibilities, a future that is safe, secure, and stable. That's the world that I envision. And I hope that you'll join me as we create that

future together. [*Applause*] I knew you would. You are, after all, the new revolution. And you're leading the way, as you always have.

And may I add something here?

Audience member. We love you, President Reagan!

The President. Thank you very much, but I'll tell you, if you do love me—[*applause*]—I can tell you right now—[*applause*]. Let me tell you——

Audience. 4 more years! 4 more years! 4 more years!

The President. All right. Let me tell you something right now. We couldn't have done the things that we've done if we hadn't had a majority in the United States Senate. And we need the help of Jack Lousma, who was a great astronaut, who will make a great U.S. Senator.

There you are. There he is.

Let me just add one thing here. One of the reasons that I wanted to be on a campus—because I figured that there might, as a result, be a lot of young people present, and there are. You're what this election and this campaign are all about.

Those people, a few years ago, were telling you to lower your expectations and hopes and be prepared for something that was kind of mundane and no longer like the America that you've heard about from your parents and grandparents in the past. Let me tell you something. No, our duty—when I say, "our," I mean people of my age and some younger—our duty is to make sure, and we're going to, that you have the same America of opportunity and hope and dreams and future that we had when we were your age.

So, thank you. Thank you.

Audience. 4 more years! 4 more years! 4 more years!

The President. Thank you very much. Thank you also for your time this afternoon, for your support, for your commitment, and for your faith that America's best days are still to come. And God bless you all.

Note: The President spoke at 2:25 p.m. in the fieldhouse at Macomb Community College. Following his remarks, the President returned to Washington, DC.

Statement on the Situation in El Salvador
October 10, 1984

I congratulate President Duarte for his great courage and foresight. His offer Monday to sit down next week with the guerrillas without preconditions and without arms to discuss their participation in the democratic system in El Salvador is an act of statesmanship. I applaud his leadership and support his decision. It appears as though the guerrillas have accepted President Duarte's offer. If only the commandantes in Nicaragua would make the same offer to the resistance forces there, we would all be much closer to true peace in Central America.

Nomination of Thomas Corcoran To Be a Member of the Board of Directors of the United States Synthetic Fuels Corporation
October 10, 1984

The President has nominated Thomas Corcoran to be a member of the Board of Directors of the United States Synthetic Fuels Corporation for the term expiring August 16, 1990. He will succeed Milton M. Masson, Jr.

Congressman Corcoran represents the 14th District of Illinois and has been serving in the U.S. House of Representatives since 1976. He serves on the House Energy and Commerce Committee, the Fossil and Synthetic Fuels Subcommittee, and the Post Office and Civil Service Committee.

In 1974–1976 he was vice president of the Chicago-North Western Transportation Co. Previously, he was the Washington lobbyist for Gov. Richard Ogilvie of Illinois (1969–1972), and in 1966–1969 he was an administrative assistant to the leadership in the State Senate of Illinois.

Congressman Corcoran graduated from the University of Notre Dame in 1961. He is married, has five children, and resides in McLean, VA. He was born May 23, 1939, in Ottawa, IL.

Nomination of Paul Webster MacAvoy To Be a Member of the Board of Directors of the United States Synthetic Fuels Corporation
October 10, 1984

The President has nominated Paul Webster MacAvoy to be a member of the Board of Directors of the United States Synthetic Fuels Corporation for the term expiring September 14, 1991. He will succeed A.G. Monks.

Mr. MacAvoy is dean of the graduate school of management at the University of Rochester in New York. He was a professor of economics and management at Yale University in 1976–1978 and a member of the President's Council of Economic Advisers in 1975–1976. Mr. MacAvoy was an associate professor for science management at the Massachusetts Institute of Technology (1963–1964). In 1961–1963 he was an associate professor at the University of Chicago. Mr. MacAvoy has authored numerous articles on economics and energy sources.

He graduated from Bates College (A.B., 1955) and Yale University (M.A., 1956; Ph.D., 1960; LL.D., 1976). Mr. MacAvoy is married, has two children, and resides in Rochester, NY. He was born April 21, 1934, in Haverhill, MA.

Letter to the Speaker of the House and the President of the Senate Transmitting a Report on Soviet Noncompliance With Arms Control Agreements
October 10, 1984

Dear Mr. Speaker: (Dear Mr. President:)

When I forwarded a report from my Administration to the Congress on Soviet Noncompliance with Arms Control Agreements on January 23, 1984, I said, "If the concept of arms control is to have meaning and credibility as a contribution to global or regional stability, it is essential that all parties to agreements comply with them." I continue to believe that compliance with arms control agreements is fundamental to the arms control process.

Congressional amendments to the FY 1985 Defense Authorization Bill calling for Administration reports on compliance issues, as well as for the transmittal of classified and unclassified versions of the report, *A Quarter Century of Soviet Compliance Practices Under Arms Control Commitments: 1958–1983* prepared by the bipartisan General Advisory Committee on Arms Control and Disarmament, demonstrate the priority that Congress places on compliance.

In response to the Congressional requirement, an unclassified version of the General Advisory Committee's report, a summation prepared by the Committee, is provided herewith. Because the Committee's full report contains extensive classified intelligence information, the classified version is being transmitted to the two Select Committees of the Congress on Intelligence.

The General Advisory Committee's report to me resulted from a year-long analysis, by this bipartisan independent body, of Soviet practices with regard to arms control treaties, other agreements, unilateral political commitments, and statements of policy. Neither the methodology of analysis nor the conclusions reached in this report have been formally reviewed or approved by any agencies of the U.S. Government. The report reflects the General Advisory Committee's attempt to assemble as complete as possible an historical record of Soviet behavior and to identify long-term patterns of Soviet compliance practices.

For its part, the Administration continues to be seriously concerned about Soviet behavior with regard to compliance with arms control obligations and commitments. We are actively pursuing several such issues in confidential discussions with the Soviet Union and are seeking explanations, clarifications, and corrective actions. Issues of concern continue to be intensively studied by appropriate agencies, and I intend to keep the Congress informed on this important matter in the future.

Increased understanding of compliance issues and a solid Congressional consensus on the importance of compliance to achieving effective arms control will strengthen our efforts to negotiate equitable and verifiable agreements and will assist as we seek the resolution of important unresolved compliance issues. I look forward to continued close consultation with the Congress as we seek to make progress in resolving compliance issues relating to existing arms control agreements and in negotiating sound arms control agreements.

Sincerely,

RONALD REAGAN

Note: This is the text of identical letters addressed to Thomas P. O'Neill, Jr., Speaker of the House of Representatives, and George Bush, President of the Senate.

Accordance of the Personal Rank of Ambassador to Charles R. Carlisle While Serving as Special Negotiator in the Office of the Assistant Secretary of State for Economic and Business Affairs
October 11, 1984

The President has accorded the personal rank of Ambassador to Charles R. Carlisle, of Vermont, in his capacity as Special Negotiator in the Office of the Assistant Secretary for Economic and Business Affairs, Department of State.

Mr. Carlisle entered the Foreign Service in 1956 as international economist in the Trade Agreements Division in the Bureau of Economic Affairs. He was political officer in Bogotá (1958–1960) and commercial officer in Melbourne (1960–1962). In 1962–1963 he attended advanced economic studies at Harvard University and was minerals officer in Santiago in 1963. In the Department he was economic planning officer of the Office of Cuban Affairs (1963–1966) and senior staff assistant to Assistant Secretary for Inter-American Affairs (1966–1967). In 1967 he was economic officer at the United States Mission to the North Atlantic Treaty Organization in Paris and Brussels. In the Department he was Chief of the Industrial and Strategic Materials Division in the Bureau of Economic and Business Affairs (1967–1968) and special assistant to the Under Secretary of State for Economic Affairs (1969–1970). He resigned from the Foreign Service in 1970.

In 1970–1971 he was Director of the International Action Branch of the United Nations Conference on Trade and Development and Chairman of the Lead-Zinc Producers Committee in 1971–1974. He was vice president of St. Joe Minerals Corp. in 1974–1983 and president of Man-Made Fibers Producers Association, Inc., in 1983–1984. In 1984 he became Special Negotiator in the Office of the Assistant Secretary for Economic and Business Affairs, Department of State.

Mr. Carlisle graduated from the University of Cincinnati (B.A., 1953) and Harvard University (M.P.A., 1963). His foreign languages are Spanish and French. He was born April 11, 1929, in Marietta, OH.

Nomination of Richard H. Jones To Be Deputy Administrator of the Federal Aviation Administration
October 11, 1984

The President has nominated Richard H. Jones to be Deputy Administrator of the Federal Aviation Administration, Department of Transportation. He would succeed Michael J. Fenello.

Since 1959 he has been a pilot for Eastern Airlines with the rank of captain. Since 1974 he has also been an attorney with the law firm of Lewis, Wilson, Lewis & Jones. He was in the private practice of law in 1964–1973. He has been serving as adjunct professor at the University of Southern California since 1980.

He has served as secretary of the Flight Safety Foundation since 1973. He was secretary and treasurer of the Airline Pilots Association, International (1969–1970); member (1970–1978) and chairman (1976–1978) of the Virginia Advisory Committee on Aviation; and president of the Bar Association of Air Carrier Pilots (1970–1972).

He graduated from Virginia Polytechnic Institute (B.S., 1958) and American University (LL.B., 1964).

Remarks at a White House Ceremony Honoring the Minority Small Business Persons of the Year
October 11, 1984

The President. I'm delighted to welcome you, the businessmen and women of the year, to the White House. And today, as part of Minority Development Week, we pay tribute to the minority business owners of our nation. And in a few minutes it'll be my great pleasure here to participate in the remainder of the ceremony with regard to them. I know they've—Mac has just presented them to you.

Not too long ago, I was asked to explain the difference between a small businessman and a big business man or woman. And my answer was, "Well, a big one is what a small one would be if the Government would get out of the way and leave him alone." [*Laughter*] Well, that's what we're trying hard to do—to help you all make it big. And the last thing you need is to climb aboard the economic train, and after a long, tough fight, to buy a ticket and then see the train come to a screeching, grinding halt.

Less than 4 years ago, the heavy freight of double-digit inflation, high taxes, record interest rates, and overregulation had stopped the economic train dead in its tracks. Well, that's all been changed. And today a strong and a vibrant America is settling in. Inflation has plummeted by nearly two-thirds, and it's staying down. Purchasing power is back in the hands of the consumers. And that's great news for America's business community. Productivity is rising, and economic growth is solid. And the best news of all is over 6 million more Americans have jobs than just 21 months ago, jobs that you are helping provide.

But we're far from finished. And there's much more that can and must be done. If the dream of America is to be strengthened, we mustn't waste the genius of one mind or the strength of one body or the spirit of one soul. We must use every capability we have. And the surest way to do that is to mobilize the power of private enterprise and let you work your magic.

I believe that when it comes to making sure that all Americans, from every walk of life, every color, creed, and religion have the chance to make it big, there's no better way than to keep the economy sparkling and the opportunities expanding for you and for all our citizens.

We know that given opportunities, minority firms can prevail in fair and open competition. You are a dynamic force in the marketplace. You're bringing hundreds of thousands of jobs to hard-working Americans, providing innovative products, needed services, and ideas and opportunities for the future. The only thing I want to see is your success grow and your numbers increase. And that's why we'll keep supporting, at every level of government, a broad range of programs to reach out to disadvantaged sectors of the community.

As you know, we'll soon enter the third year of our 10-year program to assist directly in forming 60,000 new minority businesses and to help expand at least 60,000 existing minority firms. The program is on schedule, and we're going to keep it that way.

We're seeing the same results in our objective to procure some $15 billion in minority business goods and services for the Federal Government through fiscal year 1985. And what this means is that your firms will receive nearly $3 billion more in Federal contracting in 3 years than was provided in all the 12 years during the last three administrations.

Now, we're determined to increase opportunities for minority businesses to participate in Federal procurement. And I might mention that these figures do not include procurement by recipients of Federal grants and cooperative agreements. And that adds an additional $6 billion to $7 billion to the total.

We want to see your business community continue to grow and grow. We're working hard to be sensitive to your concerns and to build on the beginning that we've made together. And I'm delighted to be able to take part in this celebration today. Minority

Enterprise Development Week provides an excellent opportunity to salute some of America's most successful entrepreneurs, the men and women who are the real heroes behind America's success.

God bless you for what you're doing, and we're going to continue to try and help in any way we can. The business men and women here today represent industries as diverse as steel, automobile, and computers. And they're all pioneers in America's continuing frontier of opportunity—the free market system.

And now for the most pleasant job that I've had all week, and I'm sure happy that it wasn't up to me to pick the winners. [*Laughter*] As far as I'm concerned, you're all winners, and we're very proud of what you're doing.

So, now I shall step back and we'll proceed with the ceremony for those who have already been named here today. And what a pleasure it is to honor them. Thank you.

Mr. Gonzales. Thank you very much, Mr. President.

First, I would like to take the privilege of announcing the winners from the Minority Business Development Agency, the awards that they're giving out.

First, Mr. President, is Peggy Shreve, who is president of the Frontier Engineering Company from Oklahoma.

Next, Mr. President, Herman Valentine, of Norfolk, Virginia's Systems Management American Corporation.

And now may I ask Jim Sanders, the head

of the Small Business Administration, for his awards, please.

Mr. Sanders. Mr. President, it's a great privilege for me to participate with you this morning in honoring these fine people.

First, I would like to present to you the Gamboa brothers, from El Paso—Frank, Albert. These are the winners, the small business minority winners of the year.

And our next small business minority winner of the year, Mr. President, is somebody you probably heard of a few years ago. He used to play a little basketball around Detroit. He turned into a steel all-star now—Dave Bing, Mr. President.

The President. Well, we have done it? [*Laughter*]

Mr. Gonzalez. We have done it.

The President. Well, all right. Well, again, thank you all for being here. And now, as the little girl in a letter told me one day, now get back to your office and go to work. [*Laughter*]

Note: The President spoke at 11:55 a.m. at the ceremony on the South Lawn of the White House. He presented the award recipients with certificates and plaques. Prior to the President's remarks, Secretary of Commerce Malcolm Baldrige introduced the award winners to the audience.

James H. Richardson Gonzalez is Director of the Minority Business Development Agency.

On June 19 the President signed Proclamation 5213, proclaiming the week of October 7 through 13 as Minority Enterprise Development Week.

Informal Exchange With Reporters on the Debate Between George Bush and Geraldine Ferraro
October 11, 1984

Q. Are you going to give the Vice President some advice?

The President. No, no. [*Laughter*]

The Vice President. I need it. I'll welcome it. [*Laughter*]

Q. You know that Senator Laxalt said that you were brutalized with facts and figures——

The President. Well——

Q. ——before, and that there's going to be a new Reagan with no facts and figures. [*Laughter*]

The President. No, I had told him that I had done a lot of homework myself, and probably too much of it without sitting back and relaxing.

Q. Are you going to sign the CR with the cutoff——

The President. Hmm.

Q. Are you going to sign the continuing resolution with the cutoff in Nicaraguan aid?

The President. I haven't seen it yet or what's coming over here, so I'll wait, Helen [Helen Thomas, United Press International].

Mr. Gray. Lights, please.

The President. Do you have any questions about the debate? [*Laughter*]

Q. Okay. What can you tell us? Do you think he's going to win?

The President. All I know is he's done a wonderful job for just about 4 years now, and I expect him to continue doing that tonight.

Q. Did you give him any advice on how to win?

The President. No. He understands how.

The Vice President. I learned the hard way on that one. [*Laughter*] Right from the master.

Q. Isn't it tougher to be against a woman?

The Vice President. That's what I keep reading. [*Laughter*] I don't think Barbara thinks so.

Q. Mr. President, Mr. Falwell is predicting that in your second term, he will be able to convince you to put on two conservative-leaning members on the Supreme Court. He's boasting to this effect.

The President. Well, I've made one appointment, and I give that as a pattern as to the criteria that will be employed.

Q. Sir, do you think in any way that your briefers are to blame for your performance last Sunday?

The President. No. No.

Q. You don't blame them at all?

The President. No. And I still say that if you read the transcript, you'll find that none of the facts that I presented were refuted. And my refuting of the misstatements of fact on the other side—there was no response to them.

Q. Do you feel as though you might want to do something a little differently to prepare for the next debate? Is there something you might do that you didn't do last time or cut out something that you did?

The President. No. I'm just going to be talking about foreign affairs instead of domestic affairs.

Mr. Gray. Lights, please.

Q. What do you think went wrong, then? What do you think really went wrong?

The President. Well, it doesn't seem to me as if an awful lot went wrong. [*Laughter*]

The Vice President. I know.

The President. I think the incumbent is— unless he drops a bomb on the other fellow—is going to automatically be tagged as not having done well because he didn't destroy somebody.

Q. So, you think that the incumbent is always at a disadvantage, sir?

The President. Sure, because he's under attack. I look back now at the times in debates when I wasn't the incumbent and never realized how easy it was to be on the other side.

Q. Are you a little anxious about the next debate, and are you anxious about Mr. Bush's performance tonight? [*Laughter*]

The President. No.

The Vice President. If he's not, I am. [*Laughter*]

Mr. Weinberg. Lights, please.

Q. Why are you anxious, Mr. Vice President?

The Vice President. I want to do well. We've got a great record; I've got a President to talk about. And we've got, you know, a lot going for us.

Note: The exchange began at 12:03 p.m. as the President and the Vice President were preparing to have lunch in the Vice President's office at the White House.

Robin Gray and Mark Weinberg are Assistant Press Secretaries to the President.

Proclamation 5255—Smokey Bear Week, 1984
October 11, 1984

By the President of the United States of America

A Proclamation

Our forests and grasslands constitute a major renewable natural resource of the Nation. As such, they must be carefully nurtured and protected if we are to pass on their precious legacy of use and enjoyment to future generations of Americans.

The importance of forests and grasslands to the stability of our environment in terms of air quality, water, wildlife, range, timber, and recreation is beyond calculation. Furthermore, the list of products from these lands that enhance our lives is extensive.

We are especially fortunate that as usage of our forests and rangelands has doubled over the past four decades, the number of acres damaged by wildfires has been reduced by half. This important development is due to increased public awareness of the dangers of fire, prompted in great measure by the untiring fire prevention efforts of Smokey Bear and his everpresent reminder, "Only you can prevent forest fires."

This year marks the fortieth anniversary of the introduction of Smokey Bear into the Cooperative Fire Protection Campaign conducted by the United States Department of Agriculture Forest Service, the Advertising Council, and the National Association of State Foresters. On this occasion, it is appropriate to acknowledge the success of this unique public service campaign to promote public concern for prevention of forest fires and wise stewardship of our forests.

The Congress, by Senate Joint Resolution 273, has designated the week of October 7, 1984, through October 13, 1984, as "Smokey Bear Week" and has authorized and requested the President to issue an appropriate proclamation.

Now, Therefore, I, Ronald Reagan, President of the United States of America, do hereby proclaim October 7, 1984, through October 13, 1984, as Smokey Bear Week, and I call upon all Americans to celebrate this week with appropriate ceremonies.

In Witness Whereof, I have hereunto set my hand this 11th day of October, in the year of our Lord nineteen hundred and eighty-four, and of the Independence of the United States of America the two hundred and ninth.

RONALD REAGAN

[*Filed with the Office of the Federal Register, 12:21 p.m., October 12, 1984*]

Proclamation 5256—General Pulaski Memorial Day, 1984
October 11, 1984

By the President of the United States of America

A Proclamation

General Casimir Pulaski fell at the Battle of Savannah 205 years ago, but his memory is still fresh among all those who prize freedom and value independence. General Pulaski was a patriot for two countries. The United States and Poland share the noble legacy of a hero who gave his life so that the torch of freedom would never be extinguished. In his native Poland, he struggled to oppose foreign occupation; in his adopted land, America, he fought to the death for the independence of the thirteen colonies.

In honoring General Pulaski, we also honor the generations of Polish Americans who, inspired by Pulaski's shining example and his spirit of self-sacrifice, have made great cultural, economic, and political contributions to American life. Without their achievements, the United States would be a very different and a far poorer country.

Polish Americans join with all of their fellow citizens in noting that the struggle for freedom and human rights continues. It is important to take this occasion to recommit ourselves to the support of the cause of genuine national reconciliation for Poland.

Now, Therefore, I, Ronald Reagan, President of the United States of America, do hereby designate Thursday, October 11, 1984, as General Pulaski Memorial Day, and I direct the appropriate Government officials to display the flag of the United States on all Government buildings on that day. In addition, I encourage the people of the United States to commemorate this occasion as appropriate throughout the land.

In Witness Whereof, I have hereunto set my hand this eleventh day of October, in the year of our Lord nineteen hundred and eighty-four, and of the Independence of the United States of America the two hundred and ninth.

RONALD REAGAN

[*Filed with the Office of the Federal Register, 12:22 p.m., October 12, 1984*]

Appointment of Four Members of the President's Committee on the National Medal of Science, and Designation of Chairman
October 11, 1984

The President today announced his intention to appoint the following individuals to be members of the President's Committee on the National Medal of Science:

Robert H. Cannon, Jr., to serve for the remainder of the term expiring December 31, 1984, succeeding William Louis Mills and for the term expiring December 31, 1987, reappointment. He is professor and chairman of the department of aeronautics and astronautics at Stanford University. He graduated from the University of Rochester (B.S., 1944) and Massachusetts Institute of Technology (Sc.D., 1950).

Roger D. Hartman, to serve for a term expiring December 31, 1986. He will succeed Herbert Brown. He is associate dean of research and grants at Oral Roberts University in Tulsa, OK. He graduated from William Jewell College (A.B., 1958), the University of Arkansas (M.S., 1960), and Oklahoma State University (Ph.D., 1967). He is married, has one child, and resides in Tulsa, OK. He was born November 4, 1935, in Kansas City, MO.

Laddie Hughes, to serve for a term expiring December 31, 1986. She will succeed Richard Atkinson. She is vice president of Hughes Distributing, Inc., in Mountain View, CA. She graduated from the University of San Francisco (B.S.). She is married, has five children, and resides in Palo Alto, CA. She was born January 25, 1925, in Trail, MN.

Rene F. Rodriguez, to serve for a term expiring December 31, 1986. He will succeed Roger Guillemin. He is an orthopedic surgeon in Jackson Heights, NY, and serves as assistant professor of orthopedic surgery at New York Medical College. He graduated from Salamanca University, Spain (M.D., 1963). He has one child and resides in Forrest Hills, NY. He was born September 30, 1937, in Remedios, Las Villas, Cuba.

The President also intends to designate Robert H. Cannon, Jr., as Chairman.

Remarks at the 40th Anniversary Dinner of the United Negro College Fund
October 11, 1984

Thank you, Christopher Edley, for that kind introduction, and thank you all for a heartwarming reception.

It's a pleasure to be here tonight with

Effi Barry, who chaired this dinner, and with so many friends and supporters of the UNCF. Nancy and I consider it a high privilege to serve as your honorary chairpersons, and I know that she would have been with me here tonight, except they've got her down in San Antonio, Texas. Politics may make strange bedfellows—they're kind of breaking some up now and then. [*Laughter*] Especially in campaign years.

But Vice President Bush has other things on his mind, as you can well imagine— [*laughter*]—but he asked me to give you his regards tonight. The United Negro College Fund has meant a great deal to George ever since he became an organizer for the Fund during his student days at Yale.

Education has always had a special place in the hearts of black Americans. Great figures like Frederick Douglass and Booker T. Washington grew up at a time when, in many parts of the country, it was actually against the law to teach black children to read and write. Yet, they overcame these injustices to become among the greatest educators our nation has ever seen.

In our own time, no less a figure than Dr. Martin Luther King, Jr., stressed the importance to black Americans of good education. Dr. King said, "We must forever conduct our struggle on the high plane of dignity and discipline." And he understood that no activity requires more discipline or confers greater dignity than the training of young minds.

Education has meant so much to black Americans because for so long, they had to fight for it. Just a few decades ago, almost 1 American in 10 lived a life that was separate and unequal because of the color of their skin—excluded from public life and from many of the professions. And throughout those hard years, millions of black Americans saw education as a shining hope for advancement. And it was the colleges you worked so hard to sustain—Tuskegee, Spelman, Fisk, and so many others—that turned that burning hope into a blazing reality.

I remember how, during the war, I narrated a film—I was in the Air Force myself, but they kept track of what my occupation had been before—I narrated a film about black pilots being trained at Tuskegee Insti-

tute. They were brave young men. And one of them would go on to become a great general, a great patriot, and a national hero—Chappie James.

I'll never forget how impressed I was by their esteem for Tuskegee and by their deep love of learning. And I slip in here a little bit and tell you that I'm extremely proud that just recently they made me an honorary member of the Tuskegee Flyers. Now, that's quite a step for a former lieutenant of horse cavalry.

But over the years, America's black colleges and universities have come to hold a unique place in history—a place that makes them worthy not only of our praise but of our loyalty and devotion. For many years, you in the United Negro College Fund have served these colleges and universities with just that, true loyalty and devotion. You've provided these schools and their students with millions of dollars in crucial funds. You've played a vital role in enabling their enrollment to grow by some 10 percent in the last 15 years. And each year there are 45,000 students on campus who are either receiving support directly from you or attending colleges that you help to maintain. Now, that's a record of which you can be mighty proud.

Our administration joins you in supporting our black colleges and universities. In September 1981, as you were told, I signed Executive Order 12320, committing the Federal Government to increase its support of historically black colleges and universities. In fiscal year 1982 these schools received Federal assistance totaling $564 million, and in fiscal year '83 we increased that level to $606 million.

Just as significant, my Executive order also called on the Federal Government to encourage the private sector to give these vitally important schools still more support. The self-reliance and opportunity that we want for America's black colleges and universities are just what we want for all our black citizens—indeed, for all Americans. We're working to create enterprise zones to help disadvantaged Americans, especially those in our inner cities, to get off welfare and onto the economic ladder. We're supporting the youth employment opportunity wage to help teenagers find jobs. And across the board, we're striving to create vigorous, long-term economic growth.

We believe that opportunity builds prosperity, and that prosperity means a better life for individuals, for families, and for the institutions, like black colleges and universities, that Americans cherish.

A genuine opportunity society—that's what we're trying to build, and that's what the United Negro College Fund is all about. Just think, the black colleges that you support have awarded degrees to half of all black business executives and 85 percent of all black physicians. And your support has been vital to nearly half of these institutions.

One of the most profound aspects of your work is to help black and white Americans come to realize that, in Dr. King's words, "their destiny is tied up with our destiny and their freedom is inextricably bound to our freedom. We cannot walk alone."

No, we can't walk alone. So much of our country's future lies in the dreams of students who depend on the United Negro College Fund. They're dreams of opportunity and prosperity; they're dreams of becoming doctors, lawyers, and statesmen; they're dreams of breaking new ground on the limitless frontiers of science, technology, and space. Together, let us walk into a bright future where all these precious dreams can and will come true.

Thank you, and God bless you all.

Note: The President spoke at 8:18 p.m. in the Washington Ballroom at the Sheraton Washington Hotel. He was introduced by Christopher Edley, president and chief executive director of the United Negro College Fund.

Informal Exchange With Reporters on the Presidential Campaign
October 12, 1984

Q. Mr. President, did Bush win?

Q. Did Bush win, sir?

The President. I don't think there was any question about it. I thought he was just great.

Q. [*Inaudible*]—by your briefers before your debate?

The President. Well, maybe I talked too much to him about how little time I spent on sitting and thinking and how much time I was, myself, woodshedding, to make sure that everything was fresh in my mind about all that we've done.

Q. Why did you say you were in the Air Force last night?

The President. What?

Q. Why did you say you were in the Air Force last night at that dinner?

The President. That I was——

Q. In the Air Force.

The President. I can't remember the context in which I said that. I was! I'm trying to remember what the context was in which I used that, but it was to get in a reference to the fact that I was there by way of the horse cavalry.

Q. Are you going to change your tactics for your next debate with Mr. Mondale?

The President. What's that?

Q. The way you're going to be briefed for your next debate with Mr. Mondale?

The President. I just personally will not find it necessary to keep reviewing the things that I already know, which is what I did the last time.

Q. Are you going to be yourself?

The President. What?

Q. Are you going to be yourself this time?

The President. Well, I thought I was myself the last time, except that I kind of flattened out.

All right? Thank you.

Note: The exchange began at 9:35 a.m. at the South Portico of the White House as the President was preparing to leave for a trip to Ohio.

Remarks at a Reagan-Bush Rally in Dayton, Ohio
October 12, 1984

The President. Thank you very much. And thank you, your good former Governor and my good friend, Jim Rhodes; the Members of the Congress that you have met already here—and please, send them back in this election, we need them in Washington—and all of you ladies and gentlemen.

It's great to be in Ohio again, and especially good to be in Dayton. I happen to like Ohio so much, that I decided to spend the day here. Now, as Jim told you and I'm sure you all know, we're about to embark on a train trip through your State. And of all the things we've done in this campaign, there's nothing I've looked forward to more.

We're taking the whistlestop tour of '84 to demonstrate that our government is once again on the right track, and our national renewal is not going to be derailed. I'll be traveling on the same train that Harry Truman used in the 1948 campaign. And all of us who remember what he said know that he spoke some very blunt truths, and that's what I hope to do today.

Sometime back I made a rather big statement. I said that this election is the most significant in half a century. And I said it because the issues of this campaign are so clear cut and the differences in philosophy and approach to government are so great, that this year America will either ratify the great turn that we made in 1980 or decide to go back to the old days and the old ways.

Well, in some ways I think we're like the pioneers who won the West—we can stick together, stand together, and move on together, or we can retreat in small groups from the challenges of a great new world. I think we'll decide as the pioneers did.

You know, like the pioneers, we might remember for a few minutes the desert we had to go through to get here. We've come a long way in less than 4 years. And together, we've put all of that old tired talk about malaise and the age of limits behind us. We have, together, disproved two major myths, fairy tales, about America: that her best days were behind her and that the people

were powerless to solve problems. Do you remember when they were telling us that and that we were going to have to get along with less? [*Applause*] Well, we have restored hope and confidence, faith and courage, and returned them as the birthright of every American.

In the economy, as you have been told, we reduced inflation by two-thirds, down to 4.2 percent for the last year. We got the prime interest rate—which by 1980 was the highest since the Civil War—we got that down by 40 percent. It's now down by 9 points. We cut unneeded Federal regulations, and this alone will save consumers and businesses about $150 billion over the next 10 years. Do you know that with a task force cutting back on regulations, we have eliminated your paperwork—government-required paperwork—by 300 million man-hours a year?

In education, we shifted the emphasis from how much government spends to how much students learn. And the result is a renewed commitment to excellence and scholastic aptitude test scores that are going up again for the first time in 20 years. In fact, this year they jumped 4 points, and that doesn't sound like much, but it is the biggest increase in 20 years.

Now, not everything is going up. We got tough on street crime and violent crime, and the crime rate has dropped for 2 years in a row. And it's the first time it's done that in a long time.

We've made America less dependent on foreign oil. We deregulated the oil prices. And, oh my, they said that gasoline would go to $2 a gallon. Well, gasoline prices are nearly a dime less than they were since we took office.

We saved the Social Security system from collapse while benefits continued to rise. And this is one—let me just pause and say here—this attack, so falsely based, that it's frightening so many senior citizens unnecessarily, I'm going to repeat what I said on a certain Sunday night recently. No one in our administration has any idea of pulling the rug out from under the people who are dependent on Social Security.

And there's one more item I'll mention. We cut tax rates by 25 percent for every taxpayer in the country. Now, I want to talk about that, about taxes, because taxation is an issue with profound economic consequences. We cut personal tax rates for every taxpayer in the country to stimulate economic growth and boost economic expansion. And to the surprise of some people, but not to us, it worked. With lower taxes, the economy created over 6 million jobs in the last 21 months alone. With lower taxes, nearly 900,000 businesses were incorporated in the 17-month period that ended in May of this year. Now, that's good for all of us. But it's especially good for those who, through no fault of their own, have been unemployed. You know, when you create just one job, when you release just one man or woman from the prison of unemployment, then you've changed their lives forever. And that's the moral element of taxation, letting the economy bloom so that the poor and the disadvantaged can have a chance.

Now, my opponent promises to raise your taxes. That's what he says. And believe me——

Audience. Boo-o-o!

The President. ——of all the promises he's made this year, that's the one he'd keep.

I believe that the American people will resoundingly reject his call for heavy new taxes, because, unlike him, they've learned from experience. They've learned that high tax rates discourage effort, investment, production, and enterprise. But low tax rates stimulate those things, and that creates jobs, and jobs are exactly what Ohio and every other State needs more of.

Now, let's talk about what the tax increases he'll need to pay for all his promises will do to you personally. If my opponent is to keep all the promises that he has made in this campaign—and we've priced them out—he would have to increase taxes by the equivalent of $1,890 per household. That's more than $150 a month for every household.

He started to expose more of his tax plans the other night. He said he would repeal indexing, which we passed to keep government from using inflation to force you into higher tax brackets. Now, that would mean an additional enormous tax increase. But now he's pulled back from that. He says he goofed the other night; he didn't mean to say that, according to him.

But even so, his increases wouldn't be just a hardship, they'd be like a second mortgage. But the Mondale mortgage is a mortgage on your future, to pay for his campaign promises. And let me tell you about that mortgage. The payments will get bigger and bigger and bigger. As he puts more heavy taxes on the people and on their businesses, the economy will slow down and slow down and slow down. And after that kills the recovery, he'll want to raise your taxes again and again to make up for it. Do you want to pay for his mistakes?

Audience. No!

The President. Well, my opponent says the deficit is the central issue; we say growth is the central issue. Now, he says higher taxes are the answer; we say higher taxes are the problem, because they kill growth, kill creativity, and kill productivity.

We want to simplify the entire tax system so we can bring yours and everybody's income tax rates further down, not up. And that's why this election is about the future, because it's about growth and opportunity for all Americans. We're talking about the kind of America we'll create for our children. And I think this is why—this, being able to imagine a better future for our young people and work toward it—that's why so many of the young people of the country support our philosophy, and I'm pleased to see so many of them here today.

Audience. 4 more years! 4 more years! 4 more years!

The President. Okay. All right. All right. All right, if anyone doubts the great renewal in this country, let them look at the bright and shining optimism of our young people—our high school students, college students, and our young working people. They are a new nation unto themselves. And it seems to me that they understand and support our philosophy, because they are idealists.

They believe in people. They believe that people deserve a chance, and that they can create miracles when given a chance. I'll tell you, there have been moving moments and heartening moments in this campaign, but nothing, nothing that I've seen has surpassed seeing the young people of our country give us their support.

Audience. Reagan! Reagan! Reagan!

The President. Thank you very much. Thank you. And Bush.

I know that you don't want to go back to the tired old past, that time of timidity and taxes, that moment of misfortune and malaise, that "Reign of Error." [*Laughter*]

Let's talk a little more about that reign, because our opponent's mistakes aren't limited to tax policy. Do you remember the grain embargo in which the American farmers paid for our opponent's foreign policy failures? [*Applause*] Now there's an example both of an unfair policy and of an artful attempt to get around it. My opponent says he always opposed it. Now that's funny, because in fact he supported it publicly, explicitly, and enthusiastically. He even questioned the patriotism of a Senator in his own party for calling it what it was—a dumb idea. But it's funny that he's having this little memory lapse. [*Laughter*] As you know, the symbol of our party is an elephant, and elephants have long memories.

Your State, Ohio, would be helped by Federal enterprise zones in which the run-down parts of a city get special help from tax incentives aimed at getting business men and women in there to open shops and run companies. Dayton, itself, has two State enterprise zones. They were created just more than a year ago, and they've already attracted more than a dozen new businesses into the area. Now that, too, would create jobs and growth and economic revitalization for troubled areas. But the Federal enterprise zone bill has been held hostage by the liberal Democratic leadership in the House of Representatives, the same people who want to work with my opponent to raise your taxes.

So tell me, are you, the good people of the Buckeye State, going to vote for them?

Audience. No!

The President. Well, I think you've already answered my next question, which was, are you going to lend your support to the American opportunity team so that all of us together can build a better future for our children and for America? [*Applause*]

Well, it is the choice, your choice, and it's the clearest, most important choice in 50 years.

I think now I hear the train whistle. [*Laughter*] You know, that train is the old U.S. One. And as I said, Harry Truman spoke from the back of that train, and Franklin Roosevelt and Dwight Eisenhower also spoke from it. Well, I speak from it because we mean to continue their tradition of a strong and vital America, and I speak from it because I think all of us this year will stay together and move forward with the force of a locomotive. We're on the right track, America's best days are ahead, and nothing can stop us because this train is bound for glory.

You know, there is a mother out there with a tiny baby on her shoulders. And I can't help but say, seeing that baby, that's really—there's another one!—[*laughter*]—that's what it's really all about, that those little babies when they begin to grow up will find the same golden-dream America that we found when we were babies and growing up in this country.

Thank you all. God bless you all. Thank you. Thank you all very much.

Note: The President spoke at 11:34 a.m. at the Old Montgomery Courthouse Mall. Following his remarks, the President went to Union Station, where he boarded the "Heartland Special" for a whistlestop tour of Ohio.

Remarks by Telephone to Crewmembers on Board the Space Shuttle *Challenger*
October 12, 1984

The President. Hello, Cripp? These phone calls between us seem to occur more and more frequently. We're going to start calling you the Nation's senior shuttle system—citizen, I should say—[*laughing*]. Now that you've spent nearly 400 hours on board the space shuttle, I think that could be your title.

Over.

Astronaut Crippen. Thank you very much, Mr. President. We appreciate your calling.

The President. Well, as you may know, today's call to you and the crew is a bit different. I happen to be on board a train right now in Dayton, Ohio. [*Applause*] And I hope you could hear that cheer from the crowd that's outside the train here.

And Dayton is where Wilbur and Orville Wright developed and built their early gliders and airplanes. I'm told that the Wrights spent about 7 years and a thousand dollars in development costs to build their early aircraft, the one that flew in 1903. Well, since the *Challenger* flies a little bit farther and maybe a little faster than the original Wright fliers, I suppose we can justify the slightly higher development costs that we have.

But your mission adds the most recent chapter to a story begun by the Wright brothers, and you are certainly providing your share of firsts.

Kathy, when we met at the White House, I know you were excited about walking in space. Was it what you expected?

Over.

Astronaut Sullivan. Yes, Mr. President. It was far more than I could have expected. I think it was the most fantastic experience of my life.

The President. Well, that's wonderful. And Sally, Sally Ride, it didn't take you long to get back into space. How is it the second time around?

Over.

Astronaut Ride. It's just as much fun the second time around.

The President. [*Laughing*]

Astronaut Ride. I think it will be more fun the third time.

The President. Okay, you're getting to be a veteran. I'd like to say hello to Canada's fine astronaut. Marc, a lot's happened since we talked last at the White House, and with all there is to do in this mission, I know that Cripp appreciates having three strong Canadian arms on board.

Marc, how have your projects been going?

Over.

Astronaut Garneau. Well, thank you, Mr. President. It's a great honor for me to be aboard this flight, and I'm having an incredible time, and it's just great to be here.

The President. Well, listen, to all of you, let me say congratulations and tell you how proud we are of what you're doing. I guess as you circle the Earth several more times, I'll be traveling by train across Ohio. So, you have a safe landing tomorrow, and God bless all of you.

Note: The President spoke at 12:27 p.m. from U.S. Car One of the "Heartland Special" in Dayton, OH.

Remarks During a Whistlestop Tour of Ohio
October 12, 1984

[1.] Dayton (12:30 p.m.)

This sounds a little old fashioned, I know, but we could say, from an earlier day of telephones here, that talking to the shuttle is kind of a party line. [*Laughter*]

But I'm glad that you could all listen in.

Those wonderful people that are up there, and what they're doing, and just to give you some idea of the miracle that's taken place in all this—and which if someone had his way several years ago, we wouldn't have had a shuttle program at all; he opposed it very much—but the time that I was present out at Edwards Air Force Base in California for the landing of the shuttle, they suddenly grabbed me and hustled me up on the platform. And they said, "It's, you know, getting close. It'll just be minutes now." And I got on the platform, and I couldn't see anything in the sky. And I said, "Well, where are they right now?" They said, "They're just over Honolulu." [Laughter] And believe me, they were on their glide path from Honolulu in. And in a matter of minutes, they landed there in California.

That's quite a miracle that we have going up there. But there are going to be a lot more miracles in the days ahead here in this country of ours, thanks to people like you.

So, God bless you all. And I think now they're ready to pull out, so we'll be on time at the next station. Thank you.

[2.] Sidney (2 p.m.)

The President. Well, ladies and gentlemen, thank you very much. It's wonderful to be here in Sidney, and great to be back in the Buckeye State.

How do you like our "Heartland Special" here? You know, Harry Truman rode this State in his whistlestop tour of 1948, and he spoke some very blunt truths. And that's what I'm going to do.

We're now 3½ weeks away from election day, and the American people are getting the full flavor of the clear choice that's facing them. It's a choice between two fundamentally different ways of governing and two different ways of looking at America. My opponent, Mr. Mondale, offers a future of pessimism, fear, and limits, compared to ours of hope, confidence, and growth.

Now, I don't fault his intentions. I know his intentions are good and that he means well. But we see things differently. He sees government as an end in itself, and we see government as something belonging to the people and only a junior partner in our lives.

They see people merely as members of groups—special interests—to be coddled and catered to. Well, we look at them as individuals to be fulfilled through their own freedom and creativity. My opponent and his allies live in the past. They are celebrating the old and failed policies of an era that has passed them by, as if history had skipped over those Carter-Mondale years.

On the other hand, millions of Americans join us in boldly charting a new course for the future. From the beginning their campaign has lived on promises. Indeed, Mr. Mondale has boasted that America is nothing if it is not promises. Well, the American people don't want promises, and they don't want to pay for his promises.

I think you want promise. You want opportunity and workable answers. It's fitting that we're campaigning today on Harry Truman's train, following the same route he took 36 years and 1 day ago. He was the last Democrat that I voted for; indeed, I campaigned for him in 1948.

Yes, I spent a great deal of my life as a Democrat. I respected Harry Truman's ability to stand for what he believes, his consistency of principles, and his determination to do the right thing. Mr. Truman could also make very plain the differences between himself and an opponent. And that's what I'm going to try to do today.

Let's start with the record, the record of the administration in which Mr. Mondale carried a full partnership. He—Mr. Carter, himself—said, "There wasn't a single decision I made during 4 years in the White House that Fritz Mondale wasn't involved in." Well, in those 4 years they took the strongest economy in the world, and they pushed it to the brink of collapse. They created a calamity of such proportions that we're still suffering the consequences of those economic time bombs.

That was no fresh-faced, well-fed baby they left on our doorstep in January of 1981. It was a snarling economic wolf with sharp teeth. The suffering of America, the deep and painful recession, and the outrageous and frightening inflation—these things didn't start by accidental ignition or spontaneous combustion. They came about through the concerted mismanagement of an administration of which Mr. Mondale was a part, and his liberal friends who controlled the Congress.

They gave us five—in little more than a year—five anti-inflation plans—five different economic plans. And with them they managed to give us the worst 4-year record of inflation in nearly 40 years. While it took them five plans to nearly triple inflation, it's only taken us one to cut it down by two-thirds.

Senior citizens were driven into panic by higher rents, exorbitant fuel costs, dramatically increasing food prices, and a Federal health care cost which went up, in those 4 years, 87 percent. And they called that fairness. They punished the poor and the young who struggled as prices of necessity shot up faster than others. Millions of Americans led a life of daily economic terror, fueled by these unrelenting costs.

Well, let's look at interest rates. My opponent has referred to something he calls real interest rates. Well, people don't pay interest rates based on some academic smokescreen or foggy economic theory. What they know is that when Jerry Ford left office the prime rate was 6¼ percent, and when Mr. Mondale left it was 21½ percent, the highest in 120 years.

Audience. 4 more years! 4 more years! 4 more years!

The President. All right. [*Laughing*] Okay, you talked me into it. [*Laughter*]

But in that time, the average monthly mortgage payments more than doubled. Young people couldn't buy homes, car loans were hard to get and expensive, the auto and the homebuilding industries were brought to their knees. It's little wonder that the American people were yearning for leadership back in 1980. After all this economic punishment, our opponents blamed you for living too well. They said that's what was at fault and that you had to sacrifice more.

Well, I found that it's not so much that our opponents have a poor memory of this ruinous past, they just have a darn good "forgetory." And one of the things they'd like most to forget is the misery index. Do you remember that?

That was where they added the unemployment rate and the inflation rate togeth-

er. And in 1976, in that campaign, the misery index was 12.6, and they declared that Jerry Ford had no right to seek reelection being responsible for that kind of a misery index, 12.6.

But now came the 1980 campaign, and they never mentioned the misery index. And I don't think my opponent will mention it in this campaign, possibly because when he left the Vice Presidency the misery index was more than 20 percent, and now it's only 11.6.

He's done a little slipping and sliding and ducking away from this record, but here in Ohio during the primaries, Senator Gary Hart got his message through by reminding the Ohio voters of the true record. And I quote. Senator Hart said, "Walter Mondale may pledge stable prices, but Carter-Mondale couldn't cut 12-percent inflation." "Walter Mondale," he added, "has come to Ohio to talk about jobs. But Carter-Mondale watched helpless as 180,000 Ohio jobs disappeared in the period between 1976 and 1980." Those are Gary Hart's words.

Well, those disastrous consequences didn't come about by accident. They came through the implementation of the very policies of out-of-control spending, unfair taxation, and worship of big government that my opponent still supports. His philosophy can be summed up in four sentences: If it's income, tax it. If it's revenue, spend it. If it's a budget, break it. And if it's a promise, make it. [*Laughter*]

All this year he has lavished his campaign with promises that staggered even his own Democratic opponents in the primary. Your own Senator Glenn was heard to say in frustration that Mr. Mondale, and I quote, "has just promised everything to everybody with no thought of how it's going to be paid for." And then he said, "Fritz, you cannot lead this country if you've promised everybody everything."

But of course there is a predictable answer by one who makes so many promises. His answer is higher taxes, and massive new tax increases are precisely what he proposes. A few weeks back he called his new plans "Pay as you go." What it is, of course, is nothing but the old plan: You pay, and he goes. [*Laughter*]

Those tax increases to pay for his promises add up to the equivalent of $1,890 per household. If Harry Truman had to apply a motto to this radical taxing scheme, he'd have to say not "your buck stops here"— "your buck never stops." [*Laughter*]

When the centerpiece of his economic program is backbreaking tax hikes, you can see why my opponent spends so much time using outrageous scare tactics.

Now, that's not my opponent's only tax extravaganza. He came up with still another one in our debate. He said, and I quote, "As soon as we get the economy on a sound ground as well, I would like to see the total repeal of indexing." Now, this tax is even worse, because it would be a dagger at the heart of every low- and middle-income taxpayer in America. It would mean bone-crushing new levies against those who can least afford them.

Indexing was a reform that we passed—it goes into effect on January 1st, this coming year—to protect you from the cruel, hidden tax, when government uses inflation to force you into higher tax brackets when you've maybe just gotten a cost-of-living pay raise trying to keep even.

Under his plan, here's what would happen to a family struggling on $10,000 per year: By 1989 they would be paying over 73-percent more in income taxes. For families making $30,000 a year, this tax would take over $500 more in '89, nearly $900 a year more for those making $40,000, and these assume modest inflation. If we had their higher double-digit inflation rates back, then all those tax collections would more than double. And we're told that he misspoke, that he actually meant to say just the opposite.

But on several occasions since 1982, he has expressly proposed the repeal of indexing. He's done this quite often. In politics they call this, sometimes, flip-flops. In this case—forgive me—I'm going to call it a Fritz-flop. [*Laughter*]

Indexing is one example, but there are many others. Yesterday he wanted to give a $200 tax break to every family dependent. Today he wants to raise taxes the equivalent of $1,890 per household. You know, he's done a lot of talk lately that there's a new and an older Reagan. And he doesn't mean my age when he's talking that. He

means that the old Reagan said things differently than the new Reagan is saying them.

Well, the old Mondale said that tightening the budget and reducing deficits would worsen a recession, and a new Mondale thinks higher taxes lead to a healthy economy. The old Mondale publicly supported Jimmy Carter's wrong-headed grain embargo, and a new Mondale claims he opposed it privately—awful privately; no one else ever heard him.

The old Mondale sponsored National Bible Week in the United States Senate. I think that's fine. The new Walter Mondale says there's too much religion in politics. And the old Mondale called the space shuttle a horrible waste, a space extravaganza, and led the fight to kill it in the Senate. And the new Mondale praises American technological achievement.

But just when you're beginning to lose faith, you find there is some constancy. The old Mondale increased your taxes, and the new Mondale will increase them again.

You know, in our debate I got a little angry all those times he distorted my record. And on one occasion I was about to say to him very sternly, "Mr. Mondale, you are taxing my patience." [*Laughter*] And then I caught myself. Why should I give him another idea? [*Laughter*] That's the only tax he hasn't thought about. [*Laughter*]

Well, from now until November 6th, we're going to make sure that the American people know about this choice on which their future depends. We have two roads to tomorrow: We have the road of fear and envy that he proposes. And on his road you frighten the elderly with false statements; you strive to divide Americans against each other, seeking to promote envy and portray greed. Franklin Roosevelt warned us that the only thing we had to fear was fear itself. Well, sadly and tragically, I think the only thing my opponent has to offer is fear itself.

When I said the elderly citizens—being frightened. Again, these repeated charges that somehow we're nursing a secret plan to undercut the people who are on Social Security and reduce or remove their benefits—I said it on Sunday night, and I will say it again: There is no one in this administration—and if there was, they wouldn't be here long—that has any intention of taking Social Security away from those people who have it and who deserve it.

We see things differently, as I said, because we see ourselves in a springtime of hope, ready to fire up our courage and determination to reach high and achieve all the best. We see a life where our children can enjoy—at last—prosperity without inflation. We see a life where they can enjoy the highest of creativity and go for the stars, not have their hopes and dreams crushed by politicians or taxed away by greedy governmentalists.

The American people are walking into tomorrow unashamed, unafraid. And again, I have to say something that I've been saying so often across this country, and I mean it with all my heart. One of the most thrilling things is to see so many young Americans present at these rallies.

Let me tell you, you are what this campaign and this election are all about. There's one thing that the rest of us and the people of my generation have to do before we leave the scene, and that is restore this country—as I think we've begun to do—so that one day you will find the same America of unlimited hope and opportunity that we were promised and found when we were young that had been left to us by our parents.

You know, I know you're ready for great opportunity, and I know this may gall our opponents, but—it's time for the train to move on—and I think maybe you'll all agree with me when I say just one more line: We think we've made a good beginning, but you ain't seen nothin' yet. [*Applause*]

All right. Thank you very much.

Audience. 4 more years! 4 more years! 4 more years!

The President. Thank you. Thank you. Let me just add a little postscript, and then I've got to get on that train. I know in a crowd this size there must be many of you who are Democrats, as I once was. And I must say this: You're not only welcome, but if you are here, I think you're here because— like happened to me once—you no longer can follow the policies of the leadership of

your party. It's true for millions of patriotic, right-thinking Democrats throughout this country. Well, I say to all of you, if you are here, don't be alone. Come on along with us, and between the two of us, between all of us, we'll get this whole thing straightened out—day after tomorrow.

Thank you very much. Thank you.

[*3.*] *Lima (3:48 p.m.)*

The President. Thank you very much.

Audience. 4 more years! 4 more years! 4 more years!

The President. Well, all right. I wasn't going to do it, but if you insist, okay. Four more—[*laughter*]. All right. Thank you all. It's great to be back in the Buckeye State and here in Allen County and the great city of Lima.

You know, in this job you get to meet some important people—heads of state, prime ministers, premiers, kings, and queens. But I've always said that the best part of this job is remembering that George Bush and I are working for you and nobody else. So, I just thought that I'd drop by today so you could hear a report from your two hired hands in Washington.

In 4 years here, the unemployment rate in Lima has fallen 4½ percentage points. And, you know, if you'll help me send a message to some Washington politicians this November, we'll get that rate down even further.

You've done a great job here in Lima. You've got agriculture; you've got basic industry. You've got some of the new industries that are opening up. You're helping keep our defenses strong by building the M–1 tank at the General Dynamics plant. You've got a refinery, a chemical company. The list keeps going. You're all the things a growing America is all about.

We're now 3½ weeks from election day, and the American people are getting the full flavor of the very clear choice that faces them. It's a choice between two fundamentally different ways of governing America and two distinct ways of looking at America. My opponent, Mr. Mondale, offers a future of pessimism, fear, and limits, compared to ours of hope, confidence, and growth.

Now, I don't fault his intentions. I know he sincerely means it and feels that way. He sees government—as some others do—as an end in itself. And we see government as something belonging to the people and only a junior partner in our lives. They see people merely as members of groups, special interests to be coddled and catered to. Well, we look at them as individuals to be fulfilled through their own freedom and creativity.

My opponent and his allies live in the past. They're celebrating the old and failed policies of an era that has passed them by, and if history had skipped over—as if history, I should say, had skipped over these Carter-Mondale years. On the other hand, millions of Americans join us in boldly charting a new course for the future.

From the beginning their campaign has lived on promises. Indeed, Mr. Mondale boasts that America is nothing if it isn't promises. Well, the American people don't want promises, I don't think. They don't want to pay for his promises. They want promise; they want opportunity and workable answers.

And it's fitting that we're campaigning today on Harry Truman's train—following the same route that he took 36 years and 1 day ago. He happened to be the last Democrat I voted for. [*Laughter*] And I campaigned for him in 1948. I respected his ability to stand for what he believes, his consistency of principles, and his determination to do the right thing.

Mr. Truman could also make very plain the differences between himself and his opponent. And my friends, that's just what we're going to do today.

Let's start with the record, the record of an administration in which Mr. Mondale carried a full partnership.

Mr. Carter, himself, said that ". . . there wasn't a single decision I made during 4 years in the White House that Fritz Mondale wasn't involved in." Well, in those 4 years, they took the strongest economy in the world and pushed it to the brink of collapse. They created a calamity of such proportions that we're still suffering the consequences of those economic time bombs.

There was no fresh-faced, well-fed baby lying on our doorstep on January 20 of 1981. It was a snarling economic wolf with sharp teeth. The suffering of America—the deep and painful recession, and the outrageous and frightening inflation—these things didn't start by accidental ignition or spontaneous combustion. They came about through the complete mismanagement of the administration of which Mr. Mondale was a part, and his liberal friends who controlled the Congress.

They gave us five—count them—just in a little more than a year—as everything was going to pot—they gave us five different anti-inflation plans and, at the same time with them, managed to give us the worst 4-year record of inflation in nearly 40 years. Now, while it took them five plans to nearly triple inflation, it's only taken us one to cut it by about two-thirds.

Senior citizens were driven into panic by higher rents, exorbitant fuel costs, dramatically increasing food costs, and Federal health care costs which went up a massive 87 percent in those 4 years. And they called that fairness.

They punished the poor and the young who struggled as prices of necessities shot up faster than others. Millions of Americans led a life of daily economic terror fueled by those unrelenting costs.

Let's look at interest rates. My opponent has referred to something that he calls now the real interest rates. Well, people don't pay interest rates on some academic smokescreen or foggy economic theory. What they know is that when Jerry Ford left office, the prime interest rate was 6¼ percent. And when Mr. Mondale left office, it was 21½ percent. That was the highest interest rate in 120 years.

Average monthly mortgage payments more than doubled. Young people couldn't buy homes; car loans were hard to get and expensive. The automobile and homebuilding industries were brought to their knees. It's little wonder that the American people yearned for leadership in 1980.

And after all this economic punishment, our opponents blamed you, because you lived too well. They told you you had to sacrifice more, that we were in an age of limits now. Well, I found out that it's not so much that our opponents have a poor memory of their ruinous past; it's just that they have an awfully good "forgetory." [*Laughter*] And one of the things they like most to forget is the misery index.

Now, some of you young people are too young to remember that, but in the 1976 campaign—8 years ago—they figured out a gimmick. They added up the rate of inflation and the rate of unemployment, and the total was the misery index. And at that time, in '76, it was 12.6. And they declared that the incumbent, Jerry Ford, had no right to seek reelection with that kind of a misery index.

Well, 4 years later, along came the 1980 campaign. They never mentioned the misery index. And I don't think my opponent will mention it in this campaign, possibly because it was over 20 when he left the Vice Presidency. And it's only 11.6 now.

My opponent has done a very good job of slipping, sliding, and ducking away from his record. But here in Ohio during the primaries, Senator Gary Hart got his message through by reminding you, the Ohio voters, of the true record. And I quote—he said, "Walter Mondale may pledge stable prices, but Carter-Mondale could not cure 12-percent inflation." "Walter Mondale," he added, "has come to Ohio to talk about jobs, but Carter-Mondale watched helpless as 180,000 Ohio jobs disappeared in the period between 1976 and 1980." Now, I didn't say that. Those are Gary Hart's words.

Those disastrous consequences didn't come about by accident. They came through the implementation of the very policies of out-of-control spending, unfair taxation, and worship of big government that my opponent still supports.

His philosophy can be summed up in four sentences: If it's income, tax it. If it's revenue, spend it. If it's a budget, break it. And if it's a promise, make it.

All this year—[*applause*]—all——

Audience. 4 more years!

The President. Thank you.

Audience. 4 more years! 4 more years! 4 more years!

The President. Okay.

Audience. 4 more years! 4 more years! 4 more years!

The President. All right.

Audience. 4 more years! 4 more years! 4 more years!

The President. Well, all this year, he has lavished his campaign with promises that staggered even his Democratic opponents. Ohio's own Senator Glenn was heard to say in frustration that Mr. Mondale, and I quote, "has just promised everything to everybody with no thought of how it's going to be paid for." And then again, Gary Hart responded and said, "Fritz, you cannot lead this country if you've promised everybody everything."

But, of course, there's a predictable answer by one who makes so many promises. That answer is higher taxes. And massive new tax increases are precisely what he proposes. A few weeks back, he called his new plan "pay as you go." But what it is, of course, is nothing but the old plan. You pay, and he goes. [*Laughter*]

Those tax increases to pay for his promises add up to the equivalent of $1,890 per household. If Harry Truman had to apply a motto to his radical taxing scheme, he would have to say that—you know that famous line, "The buck stops here." He would say this time, "Your buck never stops." When the centerpiece of his economic program is backbreaking tax hikes, you can see why he spends so much time using outrageous scare tactics.

Now, that's not my opponent's only tax extravaganza. He came up with still another one in our debate. He said, and I quote, "As soon as we get the economy on a sound ground as well, I would like to see the total repeal of indexing."

Now, this tax is even worse, because it would be a dagger at the heart of every low- and middle-income taxpayer in America. It would mean bonecrushing new levies against those who can least afford them. Indexing was a reform that we passed to protect you from the cruelest of taxes, the hidden tax when government uses inflation to force you into higher tax brackets just because you've gotten a cost-of-living pay raise.

And under the Mondale plan, here's what

would happen to a family struggling on $10,000 a year. By 1989 they would be paying over 73 percent more in income taxes if indexing, which begins on January 1st, is canceled. For families making 30,000 a year, the tax would take over $500 more in '89, nearly $900 a year more if someone was making 40,000. These assume modest inflation. If we had this higher, double-digit tax inflation rate back, the kind that they had, then all those tax collections would more than double what I've just told you.

Now, we're told since Sunday night that he misspoke, that he actually meant to just say the opposite. But on several occasions, on several occasions since 1982, he has expressly proposed the repeal of indexing. And he's done this quite often.

You know, in politics, they call that a flip-flop. In this case, you'll forgive me if I call it a Fritz-flop. [*Laughter*]

Yesterday, he wanted to give a $200 tax break to every family dependent, and today he wants to raise taxes the equivalent of $1,890 per household. You know, for some time, over the last several days at least, he was talking about a new Reagan and an old Reagan. Now, that had nothing to do with my age. The old Reagan was the first one. The new Reagan is now. And what he said that—well, he inspired me to do a little of that old and new business.

The old Mondale is on record as saying that the budget and reducing deficits could worsen a recession; the new Mondale thinks higher taxes lead to a healthy economy. The old Mondale publicly supported Jimmy Carter's wrong-headed grain embargo, and the new Mondale claims that he opposed it privately—very privately. [*Laughter*] The old Mondale sponsored National Bible Week in the U.S. Senate. I'm for that. The new Mondale says there's too much religion in politics.

The old Mondale called the space shuttle a horrible waste, a space extravaganza, and he personally led the fight in the United States Senate to kill the shuttle program. The new Mondale praises American technological achievement.

I had the privilege just a little while ago from the train of calling those people that are up there going around the Earth right now while I'm riding on the train, those

wonderful heroes of ours.

But just when you're beginning to lose faith, however, you find that there is some constancy. The old Mondale increased your taxes, and the new Mondale will do it again.

You know, in our debate, I got a little angry at all those times that he distorted my record. And on one occasion, I was about to say to him very sternly, "Mr. Mondale, you're taxing my patience." [*Laughter*] And then I caught myself. Why should I give him another idea? [*Laughter*] That's the only tax he hasn't thought of.

Well, from now until November 6th, we're going to make sure the American people know about this choice on which their future depends. Incidentally, when I was in school, I learned that "Thirty days hath September, April, June, and November." Now, I happen to realize that November only has 6 days. [*Laughter*]

But just when you're beginning to—well, let me just start again and say we have two roads to tomorrow. We have the road of fear and envy that he proposes. And on this road, you frighten the elderly with false statements. You strive to divide Americans against each other, seeking to promote envy and portray greed. Franklin Roosevelt warned us that the only thing we have to fear is fear itself. Well, sadly and tragically, the only thing my opponent has to offer is fear itself.

Well, that's the difference between us. We see America's best day ahead. We see ourselves in a springtime of hope, ready to fire up our courage and determination to reach high and achieve all the best. We see a life where our children can enjoy, at last, prosperity without inflation. And we see a life where they can enjoy the highest of creativity and go for the stars; not have their hopes and dreams crushed or taxed away by greedy governmentalists. The American people are walking into tomorrow unashamed and unafraid. They're ready for this great era of opportunity.

And I just have to say two more things here. Looking around—and when I see these young people in these band uniforms of their respective schools, I have to tell you that all over the country, in gatherings like this, I have been thrilled at seeing so many young people who are present here, because, you know, they're what this campaign and this election is all about.

Those of us—my generation and a few generations in between them and mine—all of us have a responsibility. All of us inherited an America that our parents and our grandparents had handed to us, in which the opportunity was unlimited. You knew, when you were growing up, that it was all dependent on you. You could do anything out there, fly as high and far as your own ability would take you, and you wouldn't be penalized for the effort. And our responsibility now, after some years of that having been taken away from us, is to be able to make that same promise to them—to all of you young people—that that's the kind of America we're going to turn over to you.

Audience. 4 more years! 4 more years! 4 more years!

The President. All right. And because of that, I'll give you a promise of something that'll take place in those 4 more years. Another thing that I think has been shameful in political campaigning—it was in the 1982 congressional campaigns; it is shameful in this campaign. And that is, for political advantage, to frighten so many of our senior citizens by telling them that we were somehow nursing a secret plan to reduce or take from them their Social Security benefits. Well, there is no one in our administration with such a plan, and if there was one there, he'd be gone.

I just want to set the record straight. We are not going to do anything to reduce or to take from the people now getting Social Security those benefits or to take them from the people that are anticipating them when they come to their nonearning years.

Now, I know this may gall our opponents, but I'll conclude by saying that I think all of you agree with us when we say: You ain't seen nothin' yet.

Thank you all very much. Thank you.

Audience. 4 more years! 4 more years! 4 more years!

The President. Thank you.

[4.] *Ottawa (5:11 p.m.)*

The President. Thank you all very much, and I thank your good Congressman Del Latta, who introduced me here today. And

I want you to know how much we need him back in Washington, DC. Remember that in that great program of cutting—or spending cuts and tax cuts that we put through in 1981 there were two authors' names on that bill. One was a Congressman from Texas, Phil Gramm, and the other one was your Del Latta.

But I thank all of you, too, for a heartwarming reception. It is great to be in Ottawa.

When President Harry Truman spoke to the people of Ottawa during his whistlestop tour in 1948 in this same car, he spoke these words: "We are in a campaign which will go down as one of the most important in the history of our country. And it's your campaign. It's your welfare that's at stake." Well, today we once again face an historic election. And once again, it's your welfare that's at stake.

We're now 3½ weeks from election day. And the American people are getting the full flavor of the very clear choice that is facing them. It's a choice between two fundamentally different ways of governing and two distinct ways of looking at America. My opponent, Mr. Mondale, offers a future of pessimism, fear, and limits, compared to ours of hope, confidence, and growth.

Now, I know that his intentions are good. I know that he's sincere in that and in what he believes. But he sees government as an end in itself, and we see government as something belonging to the people and only a junior partner in our lives.

My opponent and his allies live in the past, celebrating the old and failed policies of an era that has passed them by, as if history had skipped over those Carter-Mondale years. On the other hand, millions of Americans join us in boldly charting a new course for the future.

Now, it's fitting that we're campaigning today on Harry Truman's train, following the same route that he took 36 years and 1 day ago. He was the last Democrat I voted for. [*Laughter*] Indeed, in 1948 I campaigned for him.

Mr. Truman could make very plain the differences between himself and his opponent. And, my friends, that's just what I'm here to do today. Let us start with the record, the record of the administration in which Mr. Mondale carried a full partnership.

In those 4 years, they took the strongest economy in the world and pushed it to the brink of collapse. They created a calamity of such proportions that we're still suffering the consequences of those economic time bombs. That was no fresh-faced, well-fed baby that they left on our doorstep in January of 1981. It was a snarling economic wolf with sharp teeth.

The suffering of America—the deep and painful recession and the outrageous and frightening inflation—these things didn't start by accidental ignition or spontaneous combustion. They came about through the concerted mismanagement of the administration of which Mr. Mondale was a part, and his liberal friends who controlled the Congress.

They gave us five—in a little more than a year—they gave us five different anti-inflation programs, and then managed, with them, to give us the worst 4-year record of inflation in nearly 40 years. While it took them five plans to nearly triple in inflation, it's only taken us one to cut it by two-thirds.

Senior citizens were driven into panic by higher rents, exorbitant fuel costs, dramatically increasing food prices, and a Federal health care cost which went up a massive 87 percent in just those 4 years. And they called that fairness.

They punished the poor and the young who struggled as prices of necessities shot up faster than the others. Millions of Americans led a life of daily economic terror fueled by these unrelenting costs.

Let's look at interest rates. My opponent has referred to something now that he calls the real interest rate, and it concerns him greatly. Well, I don't think people pay interest rates on some abstract smokescreen or academic or foggy economic theory. What they know is that when Jerry Ford left office in 1976, the prime rate was 6¼ percent. When Mr. Mondale left office, it was 21½ percent, the highest in 120 years.

Average monthly mortgage payments more than doubled. Car loans were hard to get and expensive. The automobile and homebuilding industries were brought to their knees. And after all this economic punishment, our opponents blamed you, because you lived too well. They told you you'd have to learn to sacrifice more and live with less and within economic limits. Well, I found that it's not so much that our opponents have a poor memory of this ruinous past; they've just got a darn good "forgetory." [*Laughter*]

And one of the things they like most to forget is the misery index, where they added the unemployment rate and the inflation rates together. And then—they did this in 1976 in that election campaign, and the misery index then was 12.6. And they said that Jerry Ford, as the incumbent President, had no right to seek reelection with that kind of a misery index.

Well, then came the 1980 election. And they never mentioned the misery index. And I don't think my opponent will mention it in this campaign, possibly because it was over 20 when he left the Vice Presidency, and it's now down to 11.6.

You know, he's done a pretty good job of slipping, sliding, and ducking away from this record. But here in Ohio, during the primaries, Senator Gary Hart got his message through by reminding the Ohio voters of the true record. And I quote, "Walter Mondale," said Senator Hart, "may pledge stable prices, but Carter-Mondale could not cure 12-percent inflation." And then he added, "Walter Mondale has come to Ohio to talk about jobs. But Carter-Mondale watched helpless as 180,000 jobs disappeared in the period between 1976 and 1980." Now, those are Gary Hart's words.

And those disastrous consequences didn't come about by accident. They came through the implementation of the very policies of out-of-control spending, the very unfair taxation, and the worship of big government that my opponent still supports.

His philosophy can be summed up in four sentences: If it's income, tax it. If it's revenue, spend it. If it's a budget, break it. And if it's a promise, make it.

All this year, he has lavished his campaign with promises that staggered even his Democratic opponents. But, of course, there is a predictable answer by one who makes so many promises. And the answer to his promises is higher taxes. And massive new tax increases are precisely what he proposes. A few weeks back, he called his new plan "pay as you go." But what it is, of course, is nothing but the old plan. You pay, and he goes. [*Laughter*]

Those tax increases to pay for his promises add up to the equivalent of $1,890 per household in this country. If Harry Truman had to apply a motto to this radical taxing scheme, he would have to say that, "Your buck never stops." [*Laughter*] When the centerpiece of his economic program is backbreaking tax hikes, you can see why my opponent spends so much time using outrageous scare tactics.

Now, that's not my opponent's only tax extravaganza. He came up with still another one in our debate. He said—and I quote— "As soon as we get the economy on a sound ground as well, I would like to see the total repeal of indexing."

Now, this tax is even worse, because this would be a dagger at the heart of every low- and middle-income taxpayer in America. It would mean bonecrushing new levies against those who can least afford them. Indexing was a reform that we passed to protect you from the cruel hidden tax when government uses inflation to force you into higher tax brackets when you get a cost-of-living pay raise.

Under the Mondale plan, here's what would happen to a family struggling on $10,000 per year. By 1989 they would be paying over 73 percent more income taxes. Now, we're told since he said that on Sunday night that he misspoke and that he actually meant to say just the opposite. But on several occasions since 1982, he has expressly proposed the repeal of indexing. And he's done this quite often. In politics, you call this a flip-flop. But forgive me, I've decided to call it a Fritz-flop. [*Laughter*]

Indexing is one example, but there are many others. Yesterday, he wanted to give a $200 tax break to every family dependent. And today he wants to raise taxes the equivalent of $1,890 per household. Several days now out on the campaign trail, he's talked about me as a new Reagan and an old Reagan. Now, that has nothing to do with my age, because the old Reagan was when I was much younger and the new Reagan is now. [*Laughter*] But I decided to do some old and new Mondaleing.

The old Mondale said that tightening the budget, reducing government spending, and reducing deficits could worsen a recession and cause unemployment. The new Mondale thinks higher taxes lead to a healthy economy. The old Mondale publicly supported Jimmy Carter's wrong-headed grain embargo, and the new Mondale claims that he opposed it privately—very privately. [*Laughter*] The old Mondale sponsored National Bible Week in the U.S. Senate. I can go along with that. And the new Walter Mondale, though, says there's too much religion in politics.

The old Mondale called the space shuttle a horrible waste, a space extravaganza, and he personally led the fight in the United States Senate to try and kill the entire shuttle program before it even started. The new Mondale praises American technological achievement.

Well, I just thought that was appropriate today, when probaby right now—or possibly right now, I should say, I don't know where they are—but while we're riding across Ohio on this train, those young heroes of ours, male and female, are circling this Earth several times in that shuttle, which will land tomorrow. And God bless them, wherever they are.

Audience. Reagan! Reagan! Reagan!

The President. Well, now, with all this old and new Mondale, just when you're beginning to lose faith, finally you do find there is some constancy. The old Mondale increased your taxes. And the new Mondale will do it again.

You know, in our debate, I got a little angry all those times that he distorted my record. And on one occasion, I was about to say to him very sternly, "Mr. Mondale, you're taxing my patience." [*Laughter*] Then I caught myself. Why should I give him another idea? That's the only tax he hasn't thought of. [*Laughter*]

From now on until November 6th, we're going to make sure that the American people know about this choice on which their future depends. We have two roads to tomorrow. We have the road of fear and envy that Mr. Mondale proposes. On his road, you frighten the elderly with false statements.

And speaking of that, let me interrupt

myself for a moment and say one of the things that I think has been most shameful in the line of political demagoguery. We saw it in the congressional campaigns of 1982, and we're seeing it in this campaign, and that is when for purely political advantage, falsely, their candidates go around telling our senior citizens who are dependent on Social Security that we somehow have a secret plot in which we're either going to reduce their payments or take them away from them entirely. Well, I want you to know that if there was anyone in my administration that even had secretly such an idea, he'd be long gone.

We are not going to do anything to doublecross the people dependent on Social Security, or those anticipating Social Security when they come to their nonearning years. Their benefits are going to remain with them.

But he strives to divide Americans against each other, seeking to promote envy and portray greed. Franklin Delano Roosevelt warned that the only thing we have to fear in this country is fear itself. Sadly and tragically, the only thing my opponent has to offer is fear itself.

Well, that's the difference between us. We see America's best days ahead. We see ourselves in a springtime of hope, ready to fire up our courage and determination to reach high and achieve all the best. We see a life where our children can enjoy, at last, prosperity without inflation. We see a life where they can enjoy the highest of creativity and go for the stars, and not have their hopes and dreams crushed or taxed away by greedy governmentalists.

The American people are walking into tomorrow unashamed and unafraid. And, you know, I have to say—all over the country in meetings of this kind, I have been so thrilled and excited to see the turnout of young people at meetings of this kind, because——

Audience. 4 more years! 4 more years! 4 more years!

The President. Let me just say for all of you—or to all of you, you're what this campaign and what this election is all about. People of my generation and of several generations between mine and yours—[*laugh-*

ter]—we grew up in an America where, for the most part, we just grew up automatically knowing that there was no limit to what we could accomplish. There was no ceiling beyond which we couldn't go—that the hope, the opportunity, the golden dreams were there for all of us and dependent on us, and we could fly as high and far as our energy and our talent and ability would take us.

Then we've come to a period in recent years in which limits were placed; and that hope, we were told, was kind of shut off— that we were to expect something less.

Well, I'm glad you're here, all you young people, because I want to tell you the responsibility that the rest of us have and we're going to meet is to see that we turn over to you the same kind of America that our parents turned over to us, where there is hope and freedom for all.

Audience. 4 more years! 4 more years! 4 more years!

The President. All right. All right. I'm willing if you are.

But I know that you, the American people, young and old, are ready for this great new era of opportunity. And I know this may gall our opponents, but I think the people, all of you, agree with us when we tell you: You ain't seen nothin' yet.

Audience. U.S.A.! U.S.A.! U.S.A.!

The President. Thank you. Thank you very much. Now they tell me the train's going to whistle, and I'm going to have to leave and move on to the next stop——

Audience. No!

The President. Oh, I have to——

[*At this point, the President was presented with an Ottawa-Glansdorf High School T-shirt.*]

Thank you. Thank you all. God bless you.

[5.] *Deshler (6:12 p.m.)*

The President. Well, thank you very much. And I want you to know how proud I am when your Congressman, Del Latta, comes out here and introduces me. There were two names on that bill that cut the cost of government and that cut your taxes when we started our new program in '81.

And one of those two names was Congressman Del Latta.

Well, it's great to be in Deshler, home of the Deshler Flag and home of the Bavarian House. And it's great to see all of you here in this Buckeye State.

You know, in this job I have you get to meet some important people like kings and queens, and heads of state, and prime ministers, and so forth, but I've always said the best part of the job is remembering that George Bush and I are working for you and nobody else. So, I thought I'd just drop by today, and you could have a report from your two hired hands.

We're now 3½ weeks from election day, and the American people are getting the full flavor of the very clear choice that is facing them. It's a choice between two fundamentally different ways of governing and two distinct ways of looking at America. My opponent, Mr. Mondale, offers a future of pessimism, fear, and limits, compared to one—ours—of hope, confidence, and growth.

Now, I know that he's sincere, and I know that he is well intentioned, but——

Audience. We love you, Ronnie!

The President. Thank you.

——but he sees government as an end in itself, and we see government as something belonging to you, the people, and only a junior partner in your lives.

My opponent and his allies live in the past. They're celebrating the old and failed policies of an era that has passed them by, as if history had skipped over the Carter-Mondale years. On the other hand, millions of Americans join us in boldly charting a course, a new course for the future.

It's fitting that we're campaigning today on Harry Truman's train. And we're following the same route he took 36 years and 1 day ago. He was the last Democrat I voted for. [*Laughter*] And I campaigned for him in 1948. But Mr. Truman could make very plain the differences between himself and his opponent. My friends, that's just what we're going to do today.

Let's start with the record, the record of the administration that Mr. Mondale—in which he was carried as a full partner. In those 4 years they took the strongest economy in the world and pushed it to the brink

of collapse. They created a calamity of such proportions that we're still suffering the consequences of those economic hard times.

When we got there on January 20th, that was no fresh-faced, well-fed baby left on our doorstep. It was a snarling economic wolf with sharp teeth. And the suffering of America, the deep and painful recession, and the outrageous and frightening inflation—these things didn't start by accidental ignition or spontaneous combustion. They came about through the concerted mismanagement of the administration of which Mr. Mondale was a part, and his liberal friends who controlled the Congress.

They gave us five, in a little more than a year, five—you can count them—economic programs they said would curb inflation and wound up giving us the worst inflation in nearly 40 years. While it took them five plans to nearly triple inflation, it's only taken us one to cut it by about two-thirds.

Audience. 4 more years! 4 more years! 4 more years!

The President. Thank you. Thank you. I'm game.

You know, senior citizens were driven into panic by higher rents, exorbitant fuel costs, dramatically increasing food prices, and Federal health care costs which in those 4 years went up 87 percent. They called that fairness. They punished the poor and the young who struggled as prices of necessity shot up faster than others. Millions of Americans led a life of daily economic terror, fueled by those unrelenting costs.

Let's look at interest rates. My opponent has referred to something that he calls the real interest rate as being quite a punishment today. Well, people don't pay interest based on some academic smokescreen or foggy economic theory. What they know is that when Jerry Ford left the Presidency the interest rate, the prime rate was 6¼ percent, and when Mr. Mondale left office it was 21½ percent, the highest in 120 years.

Average monthly mortgage rates more than doubled. Car loans were hard to get and expensive. The automobile and home-building industries were brought to their knees. And after all this economic punishment, our opponents said the trouble was you live too well, and they told you you would have to sacrifice more, that we were now entering an era of limits, and things would never again be as good as they once were.

Well, I found out that it's not so much that our opponents have a poor memory of this ruinous past, they've just got a darn good "forgetory." [*Laughter*] And one of the things they like most to forget is the misery index.

Now, that was the thing—and some of you young people probably won't remember, but in 1976, in the campaign, they added the inflation rate to the unemployment rate, and it came to 12.6 percent. And they said that with that kind of a misery index, Jerry Ford had no right to run for reelection. It was so big.

Well, then came the 1980 campaign, and they never mentioned the misery index. And I don't think my opponent's going to mention it in this campaign, possibly because when he left the Vice Presidency it was over 20 percent and today it's only 11.6 percent.

Audience. We in Deshler think you're the best! 4 more years! 4 more years! 4 more years!

The President. He does a very good job of slipping and sliding and ducking away from his record. But here in Ohio, during the primaries, Senator Gary Hart got his message through by reminding the Ohio voters of the true record. And I quote. He, too, was a Democratic candidate. He said, "Walter Mondale may pledge stable prices, but Carter-Mondale could not cure 12-percent inflation." "Walter Mondale," he added, "has come to Ohio to talk about jobs, but Carter-Mondale watched helpless as 180,000 Ohio jobs disappeared in the period between 1976 and 1980."

Those disastrous consequences did not come about by accident. They came through the implementation of the very policies of out-of-control spending, unfair taxation, and worship of big government that my opponent still supports. His philosophy can be summed up in four sentences: If it's income, tax it. If it's revenue, spend it. If it's a budget, break it. And if it's a promise, make it.

All this year he has lavished his campaign

with promises that staggered even his Democratic opponents. But, of course, there is a predictable answer by one who makes so many promises, and his answer is very simple: higher taxes. And massive new tax increases are precisely what he proposes. A few weeks back he called his new plan "Pay as you go." Well, what it is, of course, is nothing but the old plan: You pay, and he goes. [*Laughter*]

Those tax increases, to pay for his promises, add up to the equivalent of $1,890 per household. If Harry Truman had to apply a motto to this radical taxing scheme—let me again say to the young people who perhaps don't remember, that Harry Truman was the one that sat in the Oval Office and said that "the buck stops here." I think today, with regard to my opponent's plans, he'd say, "Your buck never stops." [*Laughter*]

With the centerpiece of his economic program his backbreaking tax hikes, you can see why the opponent spends so much time using outrageous scare tactics.

Now, that's not my opponent's only tax extravaganza. He came up with still another one in our debate. He said, and I quote, "As soon as we get the economy on a sound ground as well, I would like to see the total repeal of indexing." Now, this tax is even worse, because it would be a dagger at the heart of every low- and middle-income taxpayer in this country. It would mean bone-crushing new levies against those who can least afford them.

Indexing was a reform that we passed to protect you from the cruel, hidden tax, when government uses inflation to force you into higher tax brackets. And they do that when you only get a cost-of-living pay raise that's supposed to keep you even with inflation, but you find yourself paying a higher percentage of tax.

Now, under the Mondale plan, here is what would happen to a family struggling on a $10,000 per year income: By 1989 they would be paying over 73 percent more in income taxes.

Now, we're told that he now says he misspoke the other night, that he actually meant to say just the opposite about indexing. But on several occasions since 1982, he has expressly proposed the repeal of indexing, and he's done this quite often. In politics they call this a flip-flop. But if you'll forgive me, I prefer to call it a Fritz-flop.

Well, indexing is just one example, but there are many others. Yesterday he wanted to give a $200 tax break to every family dependent, and today he wants to raise taxes the equivalent, as I've said, of $1,890 per household.

Now, lately in the campaign he's been talking about two Reagans. He said there was a new Reagan and an old Reagan. Now, that doesn't have anything to do with my age—[*laughter*]—because he said the old Reagan was the youngest. That was me some time ago. And then he was quoting the new Reagan, and he says I'm saying different things.

Audience member. You look good, Ronnie! [*Laughter*]

The President. Thank you. [*Laughter*] Thank you.

Well, I decided to copy him and do a little old and new Mondaleing myself. The old Mondale said that if you tightened the budget and reduced deficit spending, why you could worsen a recession and cause unemployment. And the new Mondale thinks that higher taxes will lead to a better economy. Now, the new Mondale thinks—or the old Mondale publicly supported Jimmy Carter's wrong-headed grain embargo, and a new Mondale claims he opposed it privately—very privately. [*Laughter*] The old Mondale sponsored National Bible Week in the U.S. Senate, and that's not bad. Now the new Mondale says there's too much religion in politics. Well——

Audience. Boo-o-o!

The President. Yes. [*Laughter*]

The old Mondale called the space shuttle a horrible waste, a space extravaganza, and he personally led the campaign in the Senate to kill it. Now the new Mondale praises American technological achievement. And while you and I are standing here, and I'm riding across your State in this train, we know that several young men and women of ours are riding several times around this Earth in the *Challenger*. And God bless those young heroes for what they're doing.

Audience. You're not getting older; you're just getting better.

The President. But you know, just when

you begin to lose faith in that old and new Mondale, why then you suddenly find there is some constancy. The old Mondale increased your taxes, and the new Mondale will do the same thing. [*Laughter*]

You know, in our debate I got a little angry some of those times when he was distorting my record. And on one occasion, I was about to say to him very sternly, "Mr. Mondale, you are taxing my patience." [*Laughter*] And then I caught myself. Why should I give him another idea? That's the only tax he hasn't thought of. [*Laughter*]

Well, from now until November 6th, we're going to make sure the American people know about this choice on which their future depends. And we have two roads to tomorrow. We have the road of fear and envy that he proposes. On his road you frighten the elderly with false statements.

And right now I'm going to interrupt myself. I think one of the things that has made me the most angry in this campaign and in the 1982 congressional campaign was when we heard the political demagoguery for personal, political advantage. We heard them frightening the people in this country who have to depend on Social Security, frightening them by telling them that we had some secret plan; that we were going to take their benefits away from them or reduce them drastically. And he's saying it again.

Well, if there's anyone in our administration that had any such idea, he wouldn't be there long. I want you to know I have no plan. And I will absolutely battle against any suggestion of reducing or taking the benefits these people on Social Security are getting or those who are anticipating going on Social Security and expecting to get. They're going to get those benefits the way they are.

But he strives to divide Americans against each other, seeking to promote envy and portray greed. Franklin Roosevelt warned that the only thing we have to fear in this country is fear itself. Well, sadly, tragically, the only thing my opponent has to offer is fear itself.

Well, that's the difference between us. We see America's best days ahead. We see ourselves in a springtime of hope, ready to fire up our courage and determination to reach high and achieve all the best. We see a life where our children can enjoy—at last—prosperity without inflation. We see a life where they can enjoy the highest of creativity and go for the stars, not have their hopes and dreams crushed by—or taxed away—by greedy politicans.

The American people are walking into the future unashamed and unafraid.

Audience. [*Singing*] We love you, Ronnie. Oh, yes, we do. We love you, Ronnie. We will be true. When you're not near us, we're blue. Oh, Ronnie, we love you.

The President. Thank you. Thank you very much. And now, let me say, it's mutual.

One of the most thrilling things in this whole campaign, wherever I've been, and in meetings like this, is to see the turnout of young people that come to these meetings. It's so wonderful, because I want to say to all of you young people that my generation—and several generations between yours and mine—grew up in an America in which you started out knowing that there was no limit to how high you could climb, how high you could fly, that is whatever your own ability and energy and effort would take you there would be no restriction or penalty for it. And we just took that for granted in this country.

And then we came to a time when people tried to tell us it wasn't that way, that there were penalties, and that there were limits and so forth, and to reconcile yourself to not doing that well.

Well, I think you are the very reason, and the most important reason for this election and this campaign, because——

Audience. 4 more years! 4 more years! 4 more years!

The President. Oh, wait. I just want to tell you—and I'm going to take the liberty, I think I speak for myself and those several other generations that I mentioned out here—what we're determined is that you're going to have the same kind of America that was turned over to us by our parents. That's what we're resolved to do and what we're going to do for all of you.

Audience. 4 more years! 4 more years! 4 more years!

The President. Well, all right. I know

you're all ready for this great new era of opportunity. And this may gall our opponents—the train's getting ready to whistle, and I have to move on to the next stop before darkness catches us——

Audience. No-o-o!

The President. I know. I wish I didn't, but I do. And, I say, it may gall our opponents, but I think that the people of this country agree with us when we say, "You ain't seen nothin' yet."

Thank you very much.

[*6.*] *Perrysburg (7:40 p.m.)*

The President. Thank you all. Thank you.

Audience. 4 more years! 4 more years! 4 more years!

The President. Thank you, Madame Mayor, for those kind words, and Del Latta for being here. And thank all of you. I must tell you, I've had a wonderful time visiting with the people of Ohio today. And I can't think of any finer way of ending my trip on the "Heartland Special" than visiting with you good people of Perrysburg.

I've got a great deal to be grateful to all of you for. You've sent to Washington a Representative who has been a tremendous force for responsible government—the Congressman I just mentioned—Del Latta. It's no coincidence that his name is on the bill that finally got control of Federal spending after decades of tax and tax and spend and spend. He is a true friend of the taxpayers and a great friend to those who depend on economic progress to give them a chance at a better life.

Well, now we're 3½ weeks from election day, and the American people are getting the full flavor of the very clear choice that is facing them. It's a choice between two fundamentally different ways of governing and two distinct ways of looking at America.

My opponent, Mr. Mondale, offers a future of pessimism, fear, and limits, compared to ours of hope, confidence, and growth. Now, I know that his intentions are good, and I know that he's sincere in what he believes. But he sees government as an end in itself, and we see government as belonging to you, the people, and only a junior partner in your lives.

My opponent and his allies live in the past. They're celebrating the old and failed policies of an era that has passed them by, as if history had skipped over the 4 Carter-Mondale years. On the other hand, millions of Americans join us in boldly charting a new course for the future.

Now, it's fitting that we're campaigning today on Harry Truman's train, following the same route that he took 36 years and 1 day ago. He was the last Democrat I voted for. I campaigned for him in 1948. Mr. Truman could make very plain the differences between himself and his opponent and, my friends, that's just what I'm going to do this evening.

Let us start with the record, the record of the administration in which Mr. Mondale carried a full partnership. In those 4 years, they took the strongest economy in the world and pushed it to the brink of collapse. They created a calamity of such proportions that we're still suffering the consequences of those economic time bombs.

You know, on that January 20th in 1981 that was no fresh-faced, well-fed baby that was left on our doorstep. It was a snarling economic wolf with sharp teeth. The suffering of America, the deep and painful recession, the outrageous and frightening inflation—these things didn't start by accidental ignition or spontaneous combustion. They came about through the concerted mismanagement of the administration of which he was a part, and his liberal friends who controlled the Congress. They gave us five— you can count them—in a little more than a year, five different anti-inflation plans, and then ended up giving us the worst 4-year record of inflation in nearly 40 years. While it took them five plans to nearly triple inflation, it's only taken us one to cut it by nearly two-thirds.

Senior citizens were driven into panic by higher rents, exorbitant fuel costs, dramatically increasing food prices, and Federal health care costs which went up a massive 87 percent. Some fairness. They punished the poor and the young who struggled as prices of necessity shot up faster than the other prices. Millions of Americans led a life of daily economic terror, fueled by those unrelenting costs.

Let's look at interest rates. Now, my opponent has referred to something that he calls real interest rates. Well, people don't pay interest rates on some academic smoke-screen or foggy economic theory. What they know is that when Jerry Ford left office—the end of 1976—the prime interest rate was 6¼ percent. When Mr. Mondale left the Vice Presidency it was 21½ percent, the highest in 120 years.

Audience. Boo-o-o!

The President. The average monthly mortgage payments more than doubled. Car loans were hard to get and expensive. The automobile and the homebuilding industries were brought to their knees. And after all this economic punishment, guess what? Our opponents blamed you as being the cause, because you lived too well.

Audience. Boo-o-o!

The President. You remember they told you you were going to have to sacrifice more. Well, I found out that it's not so much that our opponents have a poor memory for their ruinous past, they've just a got a darn good "forgetory." [*Laughter*]

And you know, one of the things they'd like to forget the most is the misery index. If you'll remember back in 1976, in that campaign, they put the inflation rate and the unemployment rate, added them together, and then called it the misery index. It came to 12.6 percent. And they said that Jerry Ford had no right to seek reelection with such a huge misery index.

Well, 1980 came along, and they didn't mention the misery index. And I don't think my opponent will mention it in this campaign, possibly because when he left office the misery index was more than 20 percent, and now it's down to 11.6.

My opponent's done a very good job of slipping, sliding, and ducking away from this record. But here in Ohio, during the primaries, a Democratic candidate for the nomination, Senator Gary Hart, got his message through by reminding the Ohio voters of the true record. And let me quote Senator Hart. "Walter Mondale may pledge stable prices, but Carter-Mondale could not cure 12-percent inflation. "Walter Mondale," he added, "has come to Ohio to talk about jobs, but Carter-Mondale watched helpless as 180,000 Ohio jobs disappeared in the period 1976 to 1980." Well, those were Gary Hart's words.

Those disastrous consequences did not come about by accident. They came through the implementation of the very policies of out-of-control spending, unfair taxation, and worship of big government that my opponent still supports. His philosophy can be summed up in four sentences: If it's income, tax it. If it's revenue, spend it. If it's budget, break it. And if it's a promise, make it.

All this year he's lavished his campaign with promises that staggered even his Democratic opponents. But, of course, there is a predictable answer by one who makes so many promises. The answer is higher taxes, and massive new tax increases are precisely what he proposes.

A few weeks back, he called for his new plan. He said it was "Pay as you go." Well, what it is, of course, is nothing but the old plan: You pay, and he goes. Those tax increases to pay for his promises add up to the equivalent of $1,890 per household, for every household in the United States.

Now, if Harry Truman had to apply a motto to his radical taxing scheme—I think recalling it for the younger people here who might not recall that it was Harry Truman who sat in the Oval Office and said, "The buck stops here." Well, I think with regard to my opponent's scheme he would say, "Your buck never stops."

When the centerpiece of his economic program is backbreaking tax hikes, you can see why my opponent spends so much time using outrageous scare tactics.

Now, that's not my opponent's only tax extravaganza. He came up with still another one in our debate. He said, and I quote, "As soon as we get the economy on a sound ground as well, I would like to see the total repeal of indexing." Well, this tax is even worse because it would be a dagger aimed at the heart of every low- and middle-income earner in America. It would mean new, crushing tax levies against those who can least afford them.

Indexing was a reform that we passed. It goes into effect on January 1st. And it's to protect you from the cruel, hidden tax, when government uses inflation to force you into higher tax brackets. You get a cost-of-living pay raise that's only meant to keep pace with inflation, but it pushes you into another, higher tax bracket, and you end up paying a higher percentage of tax.

Well, under his plan, what would happen to a family struggling on $10,000 per year? By 1989, they would be paying over 73 percent more in income taxes. Now we're told—and he has said in these last few days since the debate—that he misspoke, that he actually meant to say the opposite. But on several occasions since 1982, he's expressly proposed the repeal of indexing. He's done it quite often. In politics, they call that a flip-flop. You'll forgive me, I'm going to call it a Fritz-flop.

Indexing is one example, but there are many others. Yesterday he wanted to give a $200 tax break to every family dependent, and today he wants to raise taxes the equivalent of $1,890 per household.

Now, for the last couple of weeks in his campaign he's been talking about two Reagans. He says there's a new one and an old one. And he isn't, with that last term, referring to my age—[*laughter*]—because the old Reagan was younger. That was back there. And the new Reagan, now, is me at the present.

But he's been doing that so much that I decided to do some new and old Mondale-ing myself. The old Mondale said tightening the budget and reducing deficits could worsen a recession, increase unemployment. The new Mondale thinks higher taxes lead to a healthy economy. The old Mondale publicly supported Jimmy Carter's wrong-headed grain embargo. The new Mondale claims that he opposed it privately—very privately.

Audience member. Yeah!

Audience member. Give 'em hell, Ron!

The President. The old Mondale sponsored National Bible Week in the U.S. Senate, and that's fine. But the new Walter Mondale says there's too much religion in politics.

Audience. No way!

Audience. Boo-o-o!

The President. The old Mondale called the space shuttle a horrible waste, a space extravaganza, and in the United States Senate he personally led the fight to kill the space shuttle program.

Audience. Boo-o-o!

The President. Now the new Mondale praises American technological achievement. And well he should, because while I've been going across Ohio on this train, those brave young men and women, those heroes, have been up there going around the world several times in the *Challenger.* And God bless them for what they're doing.

But with all of those switches in the——

Audience. 4 more years! 4 more years! 4 more years!

The President. Thank you. Thank you very much. If you can take it, I can.

But now, with all that talk about his in-and-out, old-and-new style, there—and just when you could begin losing faith, still you find there is some constancy. The old Mondale increased your taxes. And you can count on him—the new Mondale will, too.

You know, in our debate I got a little angry at all those times he distorted my record. And on one occasion I was just about to say to him very sternly, "Mr. Mondale, you're taxing my patience." [*Laughter*] And then I caught myself. Why should I give him another idea? That's the only tax he hasn't thought of. [*Laughter*]

But from now until November 6th, we're going to make sure the American people know about this choice on which their future depends. We have two roads to tomorrow. We have the road of fear and envy that he proposes. On his road, you frighten the elderly with false statements.

And let me interrupt my thought right here to say something about that. Political demagoguery is unpleasant at best. But in the 1982 congressional elections, and now in this present election, there has been some cheap demagoguery, political expediency, when he has deliberately frightened, brought fear to elderly citizens who are dependent on Social Security for their livelihood, when he says that somehow we've got some secret plan that we're going to take those benefits away from you, or at least reduce them sizably.

Well, if there's anyone in my administration that has such an idea, he's gone tomorrow morning. There isn't anyone on our team that believes that. I tell you now, no, we will not tamper with the benefits of the people dependent on Social Security or those that you are expecting when you come to your nonearning years.

You know——

Audience. 4 more years! 4 more years! 4 more years!

The President. All right.

Audience. 4 more years! 4 more years! 4 more years!

The President. Thank you.

You know, they try to divide us with envy and greed. Franklin Roosevelt warned that the only thing Americans have to fear is fear itself. And sadly and tragically, the only thing my opponent has to offer is fear itself. Now, that's the difference between us. We see America's best days as still ahead. We see ourselves in a springtime of hope, ready to fire up our courage and determination to reach high and achieve all the best. We see a life where our children can enjoy—at last—prosperity without inflation. We see a life where they can enjoy the highest of creativity and go for the stars, not have their hopes and dreams crushed—or taxed away—by greedy politicians. The American people are walking into America unashamed and unafraid. They're ready for this great new era of opportunity.

And, you know, I have to interrupt myself again. I know it's almost time for the whistle to go and for me to leave, but——

Audience. No-o-o!

The President. Yes, yes, it is.

But one of the things that has just thrilled me more than anything in this campaign, all over the country in gatherings such as this, is to see the predominance of so many young people. Look at them. I'm so glad that you're all here, because this is what I want to say to you young people: My generation—and the several generations between mine and yours—[*laughter*]—this is for us an election in which you, you are the real meaning of this election.

There's been a period in recent years in our life here in America when we were told that opportunity wasn't the same as it used to be, that we couldn't have the dreams that we once had.

Well, I'm here to tell you, the meaning of

this election is that the people of my generation and those several other generations I mentioned are determined that you're going to have the same America when we turn it over to you that we had when our parents gave it to us.

Audience. 4 more years! 4 more years! 4 more years!

The President. All right.

Audience. 4 more years! 4 more years! 4 more years!

The President. You——

Audience. Reagan! Reagan! Reagan!

The President. God bless you.

Audience. Reagan! Reagan! Reagan!

The President. You are ready, I know, for this great new era of opportunity. And I know this may gall our opponents—I'm going to say it anyway.

Audience. Yes!

The President. With regard to the future, you ain't seen nothin' yet.

God bless you all. Thank you very much.

Note: The President spoke from the rear platform of U.S. Car One of the "Heartland Special" in Dayton, Ottawa, Deshler, and Perrysburg. In Sidney and Lima, he spoke near the train stations. Following the whistlestop tour, the President went to Camp David, MD, for the weekend.

U.S. Car One is the official designation given the Ferdinand Magellan when the car was purchased by the U.S. Government in 1946 for the exclusive use of the President of the United States.

Appointment of 12 Members of the Advisory Committee for Trade Negotiations
October 12, 1984

The President today announced his intention to appoint the following individuals to be members of the Advisory Committee for Trade Negotiations for terms of 2 years:

Jo Ann Doke Smith, of Micanopy, FL, is president of the National Cattlemen's Association. She was born May 9, 1939, in Gainesville, FL. She will succeed Samuel H. Washburn.

Warren S. Chase, of New York, NY, is vice president, Bank of Boston, and currently on assignment in Port-au-Prince, Haiti. He was born February 18, 1948, in Boston, MA. This is a reappointment.

Barbara Hackman Franklin, of Washington, DC, is senior fellow and director of the Wharton Public Policy Fellowship, the Wharton School, University of Pennsylvania. She was born March 19, 1940, in Lancaster, PA. This is a reappointment.

Francis P. Graves, Jr., of St. Paul, MN, is owner and president of Graves Aviation Co. He was born May 14, 1923, in Los Angeles, CA. This is a reappointment.

Richard Edwin Heckert, of Kennett Square, PA, is vice chairman of the DuPont Co. He was born January 13, 1924, in Oxford, OH. This is a reappointment.

Gerald E. Kremkow, of Honolulu, HI, is president of the Gerald Kremkow Co. He was born January 21, 1942, in Detroit, MI. This is a reappointment.

Lloyd I. Miller, of Cincinnati, OH, is president, chief executive officer, and director of American Controlled Industries, Inc. He was born May 1, 1924, in Cincinnati, OH. This is a reappointment.

Peter C. Murphy, Jr., of Eugene, OR, is president of the Murphy Co. He was born September 17, 1936, in Portland, OR. This is a reappointment.

John Roberts Opel, of Chappaqua, NY, is chief executive officer and president of the IBM Corp. He was born January 5, 1925, in Kansas City, MO. This is a reappointment.

Michael S. Robertson, of Falmouth, MA, is treasurer of Falmouth Marine, Inc. He was born July 20, 1935, in Boston, MA. This is a reappointment.

J. Gary Shansby, of San Francisco, CA, is president and chief executive officer of Shaklee Corp. He was born August 25, 1937, in Seattle, WA. This is a reappointment.

Thomas C. Theobald, of Darien, CT, is vice chairman of Citibank in New York City. He was born May 5, 1937, in Cincinnati, OH. This is a reappointment.

Appointment of Mae Sue Tally as a Member of the President's Export Council
October 12, 1984

The President today announced his intention to appoint Mae Sue Talley to be a member of the President's Export Council. She would succeed J. Paul Lyet.

Mrs. Talley most recently served as a consultant for Talley Industries (1976–1979). Previously, she was director of interior design and research at the Arizona Biltmore Hotel (1973–1976); president of Castle Hot Springs Corp. in Arizona (1971–1976); publisher and editor of the Arizonan (1965–1971); and executive vice president, Talco Engineering Co. (1949–1957).

Mrs. Talley attended the University of Pennsylvania and Indiana University. She is married, has two children, and resides in Washington, DC. She was born November 27, 1923, in Hampton, VA.

Proclamation 5257—National School Lunch Day, 1984
October 12, 1984

By the President of the United States of America

A Proclamation

Since 1946, the National School Lunch Program has made it possible for our Nation's children to enjoy nutritious, well-balanced, low-cost lunches. Now in its 38th year, the National School Lunch Program stands as an outstanding example of a successful partnership between Federal and State governments and local communities to make food and technical assistance available in an effort to provide a more nutritious diet for students.

The young people of our Nation are our greatest resource. The School Lunch Program demonstrates our commitment to the promotion of the health and well-being of our youth. Under its auspices, over 23 million lunches are served daily in nearly 90,000 schools throughout the country. The success of this effort is largely due to resourceful and creative food service managers and staff working in cooperation with government personnel, parents, teachers, and members of civic groups.

By joint resolution approved October 9, 1962, the Congress designated the week beginning on the second Sunday of October in each year as "National School Lunch Week" and authorized and requested the President to issue a proclamation of observance of that week.

Now, Therefore, I, Ronald Reagan, President of the United States of America, do hereby proclaim the week beginning October 14, 1984, as National School Lunch Week, and I call upon all Americans to give special and deserved recognition to those people at the State and local level who, through their dedicated and innovative efforts, have made it possible to have a successful school lunch program.

In Witness Whereof, I have hereunto set my hand this twelfth day of October, in the year of our Lord nineteen hundred and eighty-four, and of the Independence of the United States of America the two hundred and ninth.

RONALD REAGAN

[*Filed with the Office of the Federal Register, 12:23 p.m., October 12, 1984*]

Note: The proclamation was released by the Office of the Press Secretary on October 13.

Proclamation 5258—National Housing Week, 1984
October 12, 1984

*By the President of the United States
of America*

A Proclamation

The provision of a decent home and a suitable living environment for every American family continues to be a national housing goal. Homeownership and decent housing instill pride in our citizens and contribute to the vitality of communities throughout America. This year, a vibrant housing industry continues to provide jobs for thousands of our citizens and to play a major role in our Nation's economic recovery.

Housing comes in an almost infinite variety of forms from single-family detached dwellings to large urban skyscrapers. It is available for purchase or rent. It includes lovingly restored older buildings and prefabricated new ones. But whatever form it takes, good housing remains an essential part of the American Dream. The efficiency and success of free enterprise in responding to the great variety of market demands for housing deserve special notice and commendation.

In recognition of our Nation's commitment to housing and homeownership and the role that housing plays in our economic vitality, the Congress, by House Joint Resolution 606, has designated the week of October 14 through October 21, 1984, as "National Housing Week" and authorized and requested the President to issue a proclamation in observance of this week.

Now, Therefore, I, Ronald Reagan, President of the United States of America, do hereby proclaim the week beginning October 14, 1984, as National Housing Week, and I call upon the people of the United States and interested groups and organizations to observe this week with appropriate activities and events.

In Witness Whereof, I have hereunto set my hand this twelfth day of October, in the year of our Lord nineteen hundred and eighty-four, and of the Independence of the United States of America the two hundred and ninth.

RONALD REAGAN

[*Filed with the Office of the Federal Register, 12:24 p.m., October 12, 1984*]

Note: The proclamation was released by the Office of the Press Secretary on October 13.

Proclamation 5259—White Cane Safety Day, 1984
October 12, 1984

*By the President of the United States
of America*

A Proclamation

As increasing numbers of blind and visually handicapped people enter the American mainstream to live and work among sighted people, the public should be alerted to the significance of the white cane. The white cane is more than a guide for its users and a signal to others. Through the aid of a white cane and an informed and empathetic public, many blind and visually handicapped people can now enjoy the fullness of American life.

As we become sensitive to the needs of the blind and the visually handicapped, we remove shared burdens. As our visually handicapped citizens become more self-sufficient, the lives of those they touch are enriched by the example of their courage. Patronizing or pitying attitudes—barriers much worse than physical ones—will surely diminish as there is more interaction among us.

Sighted people should be aware that many white cane users lead independent lives and that others are well on their way to doing so. We should always provide them the kind of assistance that they need and appreciate.

In recognition of the significance of the white cane, the Congress, by a joint resolution approved October 6, 1964 (78 Stat. 1003), has authorized the President to proclaim October 15 of each year as White Cane Safety Day.

Now, Therefore, I, Ronald Reagan, President of the United States of America, do hereby proclaim October 15, 1984, as White Cane Safety Day. I urge all Americans to mark this occasion by acquainting themselves with the needs and accomplishments of blind and visually handicapped people, who want to make fuller use of their God-given potential, unhampered by misunderstanding on the part of sighted citizens.

In Witness Whereof, I have hereunto set my hand this twelfth day of October, in the year of our Lord nineteen hundred and eighty-four, and of the Independence of the United States of America the two hundred and ninth.

RONALD REAGAN

[*Filed with the Office of the Federal Register, 12:25 p.m., October 12, 1984*]

Note: The proclamation was released by the Office of the Press Secretary on October 13.

Executive Order 12490—National Commission on Space
October 12, 1984

By the authority vested in me as President by the Constitution and statutes of the United States of America, including Title II of the National Aeronautics and Space Administration Authorization Act, 1985 (Public Law 98–361) ("the Act"), and in order to establish a National Commission on Space, it is hereby ordered as follows:

Section 1. Establishment. (a) There is established the National Commission on Space. The Commission shall be composed of:

(1) fifteen members appointed or designated by the President (of whom no more than three shall be employees of the federal government) who by reason of their background, education, training, or experience possess expertise in scientific and technological pursuits, as well as the use and implications of the use of such pursuits, which allows them to contribute to the articulation of goals and rationale and the formulation of an agenda for the future direction of United States civilian space activity;

(2) not more than nine advisory, non-voting members designated by the President, representing the Federal departments and agencies set forth in Section 203(b)(1) of the Act, provided that no one of those departments and agencies shall have more than one employee appointed to the Commission; and

(3) two advisory, non-voting members appointed by the President of the Senate from among the Members of the Senate and two advisory, non-voting members appointed by the Speaker of the House of Representatives from among the Members of the House.

(b) The President shall designate a Chairman and a Vice Chairman from among the voting members of the Commission.

Sec. 2. Functions. (a) Pursuant to Section 204 of the Act, the Commission shall study existing and proposed United States space activities; formulate an agenda for the United States civilian space program; and identify long range goals, opportunities, and policy options for civilian space activity for the next twenty years.

(b) The Commission shall submit its plan and any recommendations for proposed legislation to the President and the Congress within 12 months of the date of this Order.

Sec. 3. Administration. (a) The heads of Executive departments, agencies and independent instrumentalities shall, to the extent permitted by law, provide the Commission, upon request, such information as it may require for purposes of carrying out its functions.

(b) Members of the Commission appointed by the President under Section 1(a)(1) from among private citizens of the United States may be paid at a rate not to exceed the daily equivalent of the annual rate of basic pay in effect under section 5332 of title 5, United States Code, for grade GS–18 of the General Schedule for each day, including traveltime, during which such members are engaged in the actual performance of the duties of the Commission. While engaged in the work of the Commission, both voting and non-voting members may be allowed travel expenses, including per diem in lieu of subsistence, to the extent permitted by law for persons serving intermittently in the government service (5 U.S.C. 5101–5107).

(c) To the extent permitted by law and subject to the availability of appropriations, the Administrator of the National Aeronautics and Space Administration shall provide the Commission with such administrative services, funds, facilities, staff and other support services as may be necessary for the performance of its functions.

Sec. 4. General Provisions. (a) Notwithstanding the provisions of any other Executive Order, the functions of the President under the Federal Advisory Committee Act which are applicable to the Council, except that of reporting annually to the Congress, shall be performed by the Administrator of the National Aeronautics and Space Administration, in accordance with guidelines and procedures established by the Administrator of General Services.

(b) The Commission shall terminate 60 days after submitting the report required by Section 2(b) of this Order.

RONALD REAGAN

The White House,
October 12, 1984.

[*Filed with the Office of the Federal Register, 11:02 a.m., October 15, 1984*]

Note: The Executive order was released by the Office of the Press Secretary on October 13.

Radio Address to the Nation on the Presidential Campaign
October 13, 1984

My fellow Americans:

The 1984 campaign is in full swing. And no matter who you are—student, construction worker, farmer, nurse, or high-tech entrepreneur—this election offers you the clearest choice for your future in many years.

The central economic issue in this campaign is growth. Will we have policies that give each of you opportunities to climb higher and push America to challenge the limits of growth, policies like those that in the 22 months have given this nation the strongest economic expansion in 30 years, or will we go back to those failed policies of the Carter-Mondale administration that inflicted unprecedented hardship on our people?

Our vision of strong economic growth is not a pipedream; it's a living accomplishment. And it can continue to get better, offering new hope for everyone, including all of you who have not yet recovered from the Carter-Mondale past.

We came to Washington with a pledge to make a new beginning by putting more power, earnings, and decisions back in your hands. That's why we passed the first tax rate reduction for everyone since President John Kennedy's program 20 years ago. And it's no coincidence that once those tax cuts took hold, the American economy woke up with a roar from years of economic slumber.

Think about this success, because you're the ones who made it happen and who can and must keep it going. Twenty-two straight months of economic expansion and yet inflation is only one-third what it was when my opponent was in office. Six hundred thousand new business incorporations last year—an all-time record. Over 6 million new jobs created; in fact, more jobs created on average each month than were created in all the Common Market countries combined during the last 10 years.

But we can't and won't be satisfied until every American who wants a job can find a job, until inflation is down to 0.0 and interest rates have been brought down more, until the farm community has fully recovered from the legacy of record interest rates, inflation, and the grain embargo—and until we modernize and make our older industries more competitive with new technologies. In other words, all of us have made great progress, but even greater challenges lie ahead.

We want to go forward with exciting new opportunities to help America challenge the limits of growth—for example, an historic simplification of our tax system, making the entire system more fair and easier to understand so we can bring yours and everybody's personal tax rates further down, not up.

My opponent has a very different vision— a gloomy vision of weakness that doesn't look to you with confidence or challenge you to dream great dreams and make America grow, but that places its trust in bigger government. We must ask ourselves one question: What has he ever done or said to suggest, let alone convince us, that his vision can do anything but fail?

The record is clear. In his administration, the only things that went up were inflation, interest rates, and taxes, while everything else—investment, productivity, earnings, savings, confidence, optimism, and growth—all fell apart.

Then, when we came along, he predicted our tax reduction would be, murderously inflationary. That was just before inflation dropped dramatically. He said there was no hope of recovery. Then economic recovery began. He said recovery would be anemic at best. That was before the strongest economic expansion in 30 years. Now he says the deficit cannot be brought down without new tax increases. And at this very moment, the deficit is coming down without new tax increases.

My opponent puts government first, which is why his policies fail and his predictions are wrong. We trust in you, and that spells success through economic growth. Nor has he learned from his mistakes. He has proposed to raise taxes by $85 billion. In fact, he would have to raise taxes the equivalent of $1,890 per household to pay for his promises.

And just this past week he began to reveal the rest of his plan. He said he would repeal indexing, the reform we passed to keep you from being taxed when inflation pushes you into higher and higher tax brackets. Now he says he goofed. Well— whatever. We do know he has a basic two-part plan: raise you taxes, and then raise them again.

Asking you to buy his failed policies is a little like someone expecting you to go to a used-car lot to buy back the lemon you got rid of 4 years ago. But you don't have to. You can stick with leadership that's working; leadership that trusts in you and offers growth and opportunity so all of us can go forward together to build a better American future.

Until next week, thanks for listening. God bless you.

Note: The President spoke at 12:06 p.m. from Camp David, MD.

Remarks and a Question-and-Answer Session at the University of Alabama in Tuscaloosa
October 15, 1984

The President. Thank you all very much. And, Senator Denton, I thank you very much.

You know, when I left the White House this morning, it was kind of good to say, "I'm Alabamie bound." But it is wonderful to be here at the University of Alabama, the home of the Crimson Tide. And, incidentally, I might say to the members of your football squad, and also to all of you who are such obvious supporters—I know you have a fine team and I know that you've been a little disappointed in part of the opening of the season. But then came last Saturday, and you became Lion tamers.

You'll never know how tempted I am to say you won one for the Gipper. [*Laughter*] You just stay with it, and I know you're going to win big this season.

Now, many States only have one great football team—and I know that this is going to shake the rafters, but—[*laughter*]—you have two powerhouses, the Auburn Tigers——

Audience. Boo-o-o! [*Laughter*]

The President. It isn't very often I asked to be booed. [*Laughter*]

Well, I know also that your campus is one of the most beautiful in the country. I know this because I've been reminded of it by a valued member of my staff, Margaret Tutwiler,[1] who hails from Alabama and who graduated from UA.

She told me of the discovery last month of the original foundation of the university rotunda that was built before the Civil War and how it was once the centerpiece of this campus. And now it's turned up and still solid. And I got to thinking about how after all this time that foundation is still there and standing strong. And I'm involved in a campaign for reelection—or didn't you know? [*Laughter*] I am seeking another term, because our work has begun, the foundation has been laid, and the building, though, is unfinished. There's much left to do.

The centerpiece of our administration is one word: freedom. The foundation has been a program aimed at lowering tax rates, revitalizing the economy, and creating opportunity so that every American gets a chance at a good life.

The present has benefited from our program, but it's the future that we're building. Inflation was over 12 percent when we

_____

[1] *Special Assistant to the President.*

came into office, and now it's down around 4. And that means the poor and the people on fixed incomes are finding it easier to get by.

Now, that's true, but it doesn't quite capture the larger point of what we're doing. When I came in here I started thinking about a phrase that you might be familiar with that expresses our philosophy of economic growth. It's "Roll tide, roll."

Audience. Roll tide, roll!

The President. Hey, that's great.

Over the past 3 years, we cut personal tax rates for all Americans by 25 percent. You know, when we spend our own money, businesses and entrepreneurs profit, expand, and create jobs. And it has the force of a rolling tide. When we put our tax savings in the bank, that capital is available for all kinds of expansion, which creates growth and opportunity and more jobs. And when you cut personal tax rates, you create an incentive that frees up all the boldness and creativity within us. And that too has the force of a rolling tide. Take away incentive and give up your dreams. All of us should be able to keep as much of the fruits of our labor as possible.

In 1980, when we took a new turn, we were declaring once again that the challenge of America begins with challenging its people—not challenging government to do more for them.

Now, the other night my opponent suggested that when I am reelected I intend to raise your taxes. Well, I agree with half of that statement—the part about being reelected. But as I said then—and I'll say again—my goal is to get personal tax rates further down, not up. And this is where he and I definitely differ. To pay for all the promises he's made, he would have to raise taxes the equivalent of $1,890 per household. That's more than $150 a month. I know that you and your parents have other things to do—or that you'd like to spend that money on—like tuition.

But we're talking about more than personal hardship here. If we go back to the old days of raising taxes and raising spending, we'll kill the prosperity that we're now enjoying. People will have less money, spend less money, save less money. No new jobs will be created, and many jobs will be lost. I don't think you want economic policies that will send you from the graduation line to the unemployment line.

Audience. No!

The President. You've been spending years receiving a fine education, and all of you have a great deal to contribute to make this world a better place. And you deserve wide open opportunities for your talents when you get out of school.

I think my opponent's economic policies and programs are about as bad as they can be. And when he comes down here and says his ideas are best for the South, he's handing you the ultimate Mason-Dixon Line. [*Laughter*] You know, buying his economic policies is like going to a used-car lot to buy back the lemon you sold them 4 years ago.

Now, prosperity at home is only part of what we're trying to achieve. We've been moving quickly these last 3½ years or so toward peace through strength. We know it's America's role in the world to stand for something.

We need to be a reliable friend to our allies and a good neighbor to our friends nearby, and you can't be any of those things without strength. We always want everyone in the world to understand that Uncle Sam is a friendly old man, but he has a spine of steel.

If I could just interject an aside here right now—today a momentous event will be taking place in the cause of peace in Central America, as President Duarte of El Salvador meets with the leaders of the Salvadoran guerrillas. President Duarte is participating at great personal risk, but it's a risk worth taking in the cause of peace, and the President has our prayers for success in this historic endeavor.

When we liberated Grenada from Communist thugs, we were being a good friend to our Caribbean neighbors who'd come to us and asked us to help restore peace to the island. We did it. And we liberated some American students in the process. And we can be proud of what we did that day, and proud of the young men and women in our Armed Forces who made that possible.

Now, my opponent by the way, seems to have that liberation confused with the Soviet invasion of Afghanistan. [*Laughter*] He said what we did in Grenada eroded our moral authority to criticize the Soviets. I've never had any problem criticizing them. [*Laughter*]

But my opponent seems confused about so many things. [*Laughter*] He said some years back that the old days of a Soviet strategy of suppression by force are over. And he said that just before the Soviet Union invaded Czechoslovakia. [*Laughter*] And then after they invaded Afghanistan, he said, "It just baffles me why the Soviets these last few years have behaved as they have." [*Laughter*] So much baffles him. [*Laughter*]

He said our administration's economic programs are obviously, murderously inflationary. And that was just before we lowered inflation from more than 12 percent to about 4. [*Laughter*] He said, "Sometimes we need a deficit to stimulate the economy." Now he says a deficit is dangerous. He says he cares about the middle class, and proudly declares, "I have consistently supported legislation, time after time, which increases taxes on our constituents." That makes you want to be one of his constituents again, doesn't it? [*Laughter*]

Well, he's for economic growth, but 4 years ago he said we needed an economic slowdown to bring down inflation. He promises Camelot, but he would give us a reign of error.

America is at peace, and the economy is in one piece. And I think if we all stick together, we'll move on together, and we'll recreate a country rich in opportunity and enterprise, growth, and creativity; a country even greater in areas of art and learning and scientific inquiry—even greater in worship and belief.

We need your help, and we can't do it without you. We need your idealism, your optimism, your faith. You're a very special generation, and I'm happy that the future is going to be in your hands.

Now, let me say that all of you have been well served by the efforts of your fine Members of Congress, Senator Jeremiah Denton, Congressman Jack Edwards, and Congressman Bill Dickinson.

Now, I have to leave soon, but I can't go without talking a minute about a great man that I was proud to call friend—Bear Bryant. He was sort of the essential American. And, you know, a few years back, I set a kind of a record here at the University of Alabama. I was here to go to a formal dinner where I was to be the after dinner speaker. And Bear invited me to come out and visit practice out here—football practice.

Well, the only way it could be worked out and the timing and all was that I had to put the tux on first. So, there I was out on the practice field throwing a ball around with about 65 fellows, and I was in black tie. [*Laughter*] Bear got quite a kick out of this. But he really started to laugh when it began to rain. [*Laughter*]

He was a leader, patriotic to the core, devoted to his players, and inspired by a winning spirit that wouldn't quit. And that's how he made legends out of ordinary people. He was a true American hero, and he was Alabama's own.

The greatness of America and the solution to her problems begins with the people—with all of you. You know that dreams, drive, courage, and creativity make all the difference. You know, better than anyone, that it's in the hearts of the people that the tide begins to roll.

I'm most grateful to you for asking me here. But now I'm going to quit having a monolog, because I understand we've got a little time that we can have a dialog, and some of you have some questions. Mondale says I don't do this.

Q. Good morning, Mr. President. My name is Chuck Kelley. I'm a senior——

The President. Did you see how I automatically turned to the right first instead of the left? [*Laughter*]

Go ahead.

Q. I'm a senior from Russellville, Alabama, and I'm currently serving as student government vice president.

Last week SGA President Ray Pate identified five student leaders on campus—from the Residence Hall Association, the Afro-American Association, IFC-Pan Hellenic, the CW, our campus newspaper, and the student government. He asked that each of us prepare a question for you that would be representative of our respective groups. In addition, Mr. President, before you arrived this morning, a number of other students were drawn—from a lottery drawing—to ask you another question.

Speaking for my fellow students, I think it is important to point out to the media present that these are our questions. They represent the thoughts and concerns of the students of the University of Alabama.

The President. All right.

Social Security

Q. Mr. President, many college students fear that the Social Security program will be defunct and no longer in existence 40 years from now when we are at the age to draw its benefits. Obviously, Mr. President, some structural changes must be made in the program to ensure its continued existence. I would like to know exactly what impact any changes that you plan to make in the program will have on college students as we begin our careers? And, also, what is the best piece of advice that you can give a graduating senior of this institution?

The President. All right. I think there's been a great deal of distortion about the whole subject of Social Security. I heard some of it on C-SPAN last night that was the same kind of distortion.

Let me just explain something. Social Security started out to be a plan—$3,000—or I mean 3 percent of $3,000 of earnings. That was back before inflation had started to take hold and come up to where it is. There were also some demographic errors—or projections that were made with regard to the ratio of worker to recipient so that under the previous administration—1977—they were faced with such a problem in Social Security, such imminent bankruptcy that they passed the biggest single tax increase in our nation's history—a Social Security tax that in several phases would be phased in between then and 1990. At the same time, they reduced by 25 percent the benefits for everyone born after 1916. And the first of those began to come onto Social Security in 1981.

They said that they had made Social Security safe for the next 50 years; they hadn't made it safe for the next 5. Incidentally, they were increasing the amount of money that was subject to the tax increases, too. It is now around $38,000 of earnings that are taxed, and it will go up to about 64,000.

When we came into office, we found out that the imminent bankruptcy was still there, and we set the time at about July of 1983. I tried to persuade the Democratic leadership of the Congress to join us in a bipartisan commission with the most expert advice, to sit down and find out how. But I said there must be one constraint: We must not pull the rug out from under people who are dependent on Social Security. They must be guaranteed they're going to get the checks that they're getting.

They refused. They refused to even discuss it. They would not talk to me about a commission. They would not in any way discuss it. So, we finally proposed a plan that made some changes with regard to fringe benefits and so forth, facing this imminent bankruptcy. They, then, in the 1982 congressional campaign went all over the country saying there was no threat, that there was no imminent bankruptcy, and that I just was an enemy and wanted to destroy Social Security.

Three days after the 1982 election we had to borrow $17 billion so the checks wouldn't bounce. And then they agreed that they would join us in a bipartisan commission. And we did put together a bipartisan commission. And I can tell you that I think for far more than 50 years, we can now look down to the future and see that for that long, at least, the program is on a sound financial basis, and you won't have to worry about it.

I hope I won't take that long on all the questions, or we'll run out of time here.

Prayer in Schools

Q. Hello, Mr. President. Glad to have you here. My name is Kim Kinsey. I'm from Monroeville, Alabama, and I'm a sophomore prelaw student in the school of arts and sciences here at the university. And I was wondering, considering the much-debated issue in the past about the school prayer to be fully reinstated—would you, if you were elected for a second term, strive to rekindle

the spark of interest, to make it your aim to turn this dream into a reality, thereby proclaiming this nation one nation under God? And if so, what steps would you take to do this?

The President. I am determined to do that. And I am going to try to explain to the people what it was we asked for.

We didn't ask, as my opponent says, for some planned prayer that politicians would write. I went to six different elementary schools—my father traveled around a lot when I was a kid—and in those times, as for 180 years, we had the right to pray in schools. I don't ever remember any organized prayer or anything of that kind.

All we asked for was to recognize that the Constitution, with that wall of separation between church and state, is interfering with the private individual's right to the practice of religion when it says you cannot pray if you want to, voluntarily, in a school. And we want that changed so that you can.

And I'll tell you how we're going to try to get it. It depends a lot on you and people like you, and you letting the representatives in Washington that have been sent there know how you feel. And it isn't necessary that you make them see the light; just make them feel the heat. We have some allies on our side.

Student Financial Aid

Q. Mr. President, my name is LeeAnne Parker, and I'm from Huntsville, Alabama, and I represent the Greek community by serving as Pan Hellenic president. And I would like to ask you what you feel the Federal Government's role should be in helping college students finance their education, and, as President, will you support more or less government financial aid for students? And I would also like to know why you chose to come to speak here at the university today.

The President. Well, they told me I was invited. [*Laughter*] But I will tell you also why I like it so much, and that is—all over this country, for a time—I grew up in a time when you didn't see young people attending political gatherings of any kind. But all over this country, I have seen your generation at rallies and at political gatherings and all, and I am so pleased with that, because you're what the election is all about. It's your America that we're feeling.

But now, I got so carried away, maybe I forgot about your question there—help me out. [*Laughter*]

Q. Okay. I wanted to know about the Federal Government's role in helping——

The President. Yes, helping students.

Q. Okay.

The President. Well, let me say also when we arrived and knew that we had to do something about the continued deficit spending of government, and started looking at a lot of programs, we found that some of the college loan programs—there was no limit on the income of the family that could also get these government-subsidized loans for their young people to go to college. We felt that the aid should be directed at those with real need. So, we've set a limit at about 130 percent of the poverty level.

We are actually—there is government help now for one out of every two students in the United States. And we have no intention of reducing that. We are also going to seek an increase in the Pell Grants, the outright grants. And we have a third program—the work-study program. I'm in favor of all of those, because I worked my way through school, and I had to borrow money to go to school. And one of the best jobs I ever had was one of those jobs in school. I washed dishes in the girls dormitory. [*Laughter*]

Legal Drinking Age

Q. Good morning, Mr. President. Welcome to the campus. I'm Ed Howard from Birmingham, and I'm representing the Crimson White—that's the campus newspaper. And so, our question for you is concerning the legislation that you signed into law that requires States to raise their legal drinking ages to 21. Why is this action not a contradiction of prior stances you've had against Federal intrusion in the State matters? And if it's a justifiable contradiction, does that now mean that the ends justify the means?

The President. I have to tell you that you're absolutely right, that my concern was over—having been a Governor for 8

years—this intrusion that I've been trying to eliminate since I've been President of the Federal Government. But in this particular instance, there was a tangled question with regard to State borders—and interstate type of thing where some States with one drinking law, and the others not—and then you had the traveling across the State line to where it was available, and then driving back, sometimes intoxicated—and the great loss of life that the accidents that we're having because of that.

And I had to say finally that in this instance and with the kind of gray area that was there, I had to say that the—when we saw the difference in areas where the drinking age had been increased and the difference in the accident rate, that I just thought that your lives were worth it.

Federalism

Q. Mr. President, my name is Simeon Spencer, and I'm a junior from Tuscaloosa, Alabama. And on behalf of the Residents Hall Association and the residential community of this campus, I'd like to extend to you our greeting and tell you that we're very glad to have you here. And as a resident of Tuscaloosa, my question is as follows: You are a strong believer in federalism and have made it clear that you'd like to see the bulk of programs from municipalities be implemented by the local governments. Studies have shown that they are unable at this present time to take this responsibility. If you were reelected, how do you plan to change this within the next 4 years?

The President. Well, we intend to help local and State governments in this transition. We're just not going to throw something at someone and say, "Here, it's all yours." And, certainly, there are standards that must be set as to what must be achieved in these programs.

But what we have found, and what I've found as a Governor, is that when the Federal Government lays a categorical grant out here, as it's called, and either provides it to the State or the local government, it is so surrounded with regulations and redtape that the Federal Government has the highest rate of overhead, of giving a dollar's worth of service to the people of any level of government or any private agency in the country. So, right now, we have taken 62 categorical grants, and we funneled them into what we call 10 block grants. And we've turned these 10 block grants over.

Now, let me just give you an example of what happens when you do that. When you recognize that at the local and State level—their priorities can't be determined by Washington. Washington doesn't know what is the priority in Tuscaloosa and can claim that it's the same as in Indianapolis. They vary, and local leaders should have some leeway, making these things work. What happened to the Federal Government in just these 62 grants? The administrative overhead—their personnel for manning the—supervising the 62 grants at the Federal level dropped from 3,000 employees to 600. At the local and State level, the regulations went from 885 pages down to 30. And we think that we can do a better job back here.

Now, let me add just one thing. If, however, any level of government—I don't anticipate trouble of this kind, but suppose at any level of government someone really violates the trust and starts pulling back and not doing what they're supposed to do with those block grants. If this is a violation of the constitutional rights of any citizen, then I contend that the Federal Government has a responsibility to go anywhere where even one citizen's constitutional rights are being violated, and to see that those rights are restored.

Coal

Q. Mr. President, my name is Frank Comenski, and I'm a junior in mining engineering, and I'm from here in Tuscaloosa. My question is: Mr. President, we in Alabama are concerned with the development of our most abundant resource, coal, as a leading energy source. What do you see for the future of coal as compared to other major energy sources such as oil, gas, and nuclear energy?

The President. I know that there are things we have to do with regard to the use of coal now. We've done a number of them regarding smokestack scrubbers and that sort of thing. There is no way that this country can ignore the great source of

energy—the greatest source of energy as to quantity that we have—and that is coal. It is a great export of ours also, and there must be use.

What we must continue doing also is research in finding out the best ways to utilize it at the lowest rate of pollution. And I believe in it very definitely, that we can't just turn that off and ignore it and say that we won't use it anymore.

Student Financial Aid

Q. Good morning, Mr. President. My name is Teleasa McLeod, and I'm a junior here at the university in the school of communications, and I'm from Luverne, Alabama. And I'm representing the Afro-American Association. And, unfortunately, this is your last question.

Going back to the issue of financial aid, we know that the income of middle-class families has increased, but now most middle-class families make too much money for their children to receive any substantial amount of financial aid. And yet their income is not enough to adequately meet the needs of the family and to educate their children. If reelected, what do you plan to do to help those who are being squeezed in the system at present?

The President. Well, I know right now that our Department of Education is looking at this problem to make sure that we do not penalize people who actually need and deserve help and cannot get it otherwise. On the other hand, we've also turned to the private sector and—with something we call the private initiative. And we have an office in the White House, but we had literally thousands of people from all over the country as volunteers in finding all the ways and the things that could be done. And education is one of those, also, in which private sources—when I said earlier that I had to borrow money—there weren't any such things as government loans; they were private foundations that you borrowed from, and paid back after you were out of school and back earning again.

So, between these two things, I hope that we can eliminate any hardship that we might have created for people that are close to that dividing line, and then just a little above it—it means no school. I think one of the things we should look at also is the work-study program, which I think could be probably expanded up to a higher level than we have. But we don't want to shut people out.

We did find—the thing we were trying to resolve is—I have to tell you, we found some people, with the interest rates so high, other than on those subsidized loans, that there were people that were borrowing the college loans—could well afford to send their sons and daughters to college—and borrowing the college loans and then buying government paper with them, investing in government paper to make a profit on the difference in interest from the same government that made the loan to them in the first place. And we didn't think that that was what the taxpayer wanted to work for.

Well, I know I have used up the time, and I hope my friends back there in the media were hearing what excellent questions can be asked—*[applause]*——

Q. [*Inaudible*]

The President. What? I don't——

Audience. Boo-o-o!

The President. I couldn't hear that question at all. I couldn't hear that, ma'am. So, listen, if you'll drop me a line with your question, believe me, I'll answer it.

Audience. 4 more years! 4 more years! 4 more years!

The President. Thank you. Thank you very much.

Audience. 4 more years! 4 more years! 4 more years!

The President. All right. Okay. You talked me into it.

Listen, thank you all, and God bless you.

Note: The President spoke at 10:33 a.m. in Memorial Coliseum.

Following his remarks, the President traveled to Macon, GA.

Remarks at a Reagan-Bush Rally in Macon, Georgia
October 15, 1984

The President. Thank you very much. And thank you, Mayor Israel, the great Gatlin Brothers Band, and my good friend, Congressman Jack Kemp, and all of you who are here today.

You remind me that only one thing can surpass the warmth of southern sunshine, and that's the warmth of a southern welcome. And now that I'm here, I don't mind letting you in on a little something—do you mind if I say, I got Georgia on my mind.

But every time I return here, I'm struck anew by the quiet beauty of this good land and the courage of her people. You who pledge your loyalty and stand by the eternal values, who, during those dark days when so many were burning our flag, you never stopped waving it. You make it so easy to say it's good to be back in the heart of Dixie.

The South is a never ending spring of America's spirit, a living devotion to those good things that bind us as a people— family, neighborhood, hard work, love of country, freedom, and, yes, faith in a just and merciful God.

It's a great privilege to celebrate with you the opening of the Georgia State Fair, to see again the Macon City Auditorium, which I'm told is the single largest copper-domed building in the world, and to be with your fine mayor, George Israel.

Speaking of celebrations, this isn't a giant matter that I'm going to suggest, but maybe just a little celebration. If you haven't heard the news, the mayor told you that the interest rates when we started were 21½ percent, and just recently they came down a little bit to 12¾—the prime rate. Well, just today—*[applause]*—wait a minute—just today, one of the major banks has started to slide again; it's down to 12¼.

Mayor Israel, a city where the local property tax has been cut by almost 25 percent; where crime rates have dropped dramatically; where, for decades, citizens have worked shoulder to shoulder with the fine personnel of Robins Air Force Base; where growth is strong and employment is up by 6,500; where graduation requirements in schools have been raised and students test scores are climbing—a town that accomplishes all this must have some pretty special people. And they must have a mayor who's one of America's best.

I'm so happy looking out today, and the first thing I saw when I came here was so many young people. I hope you're not too upset about having to miss some school.

Audience. No!

The President. But it's good to see you here and to be here with you. Your generation, you young people have really touched my heart. You're a very big part of the great renewal of spirit that's putting America back on top. And I just want you to know that working to create a future filled with hope and opportunity is what I happen to think this job of mine is all about.

I've come today to talk to all of you about a choice we'll be making for our future on November 6th. I think it's the clearest, most important choice we've faced in 50 years on the direction our country should take and, indeed, the kind of future we're trying to build together.

We've made a new beginning. We've said goodbye to that philosophy of government—or that philosophy, I should say, of government knows best that was dragging America down. And we've restored the one driving idea that made America great—here the people rule; here in America we're a government of, by, and for the people, and not the other way around.

I know you're proud of a long, excellent tradition in this State—Georgia football. And I hope you're as proud as I am of the change that we've been seeing across this nation. Four years ago, when Washington was calling the plays, all they did was fumble. Today, you're back in charge, and America's scoring touchdowns again.

In 1979 and 1980, when prices were out of control, my opponent said—and for once he was accurate—he said, "Inflation is killing everyone." But when he was asked what was the solution, he said, "There is no solution." Well, in 1981, while he was still wringing his hands, we were already

moving to get spending under control. We've reduced its growth, as you've been told by the mayor, by two-thirds, and today inflation is no longer 12.4 percent; it's down to 4.2.

But you young people must be confident that prices will be stable, and older Americans must never again live through the nightmare of seeing their savings wiped out. And that's why I support a constitutional amendment, mandating the Federal Government to stop spending more than it takes in. And that's why I support the line-item veto. Do you know that that was favored by a leader named Jefferson Davis, to permit a President to veto items of wasteful spending within an appropriations bill. When I had that as a Governor of California, I used it more than 900 times, and they never overrode the veto once. And that's why we'll continue to claw and struggle until we get inflation down to 0.0, and keep it there.

But what about my opponent? Do you think he's learned one thing from the terrible mistakes of the past?

Audience. No!

The President. You're right. Has he learned yet that frugality begins in Washington, DC, and not in the homes and neighborhoods of Georgia?

Audience. No!

The President. Do you think he supports the balanced budget amendment?

Audience. No!

The President. Or the line-item veto?

Audience. No!

The President. You're absolutely right. Only a few months ago, his principal primary opponent, Senator Hart, called Mr. Mondale's program, "A collection of old and tired ideas, held together by paralyzing commitments to special interests and constituent groups." Well, let me ask you who will do a better job of keeping prices down: the people who twiddled their thumbs while inflation soared and who would now take us back to the old and failed ways, or we who brought those towering inflation rates down and who will fight to bring them down more and keep them down for good? [*Applause*]

We'll keep inflation locked in its cage,

and we'll go forward with economic growth to create new technologies, new jobs, and new opportunities for your future.

We want to see America reach for the stars, not reach for excuses why we shouldn't. So, we passed the first tax rate reduction for everybody since John F. Kennedy's program. Today, one nation in the world can say that its jobs, investment, and productivity are up; that it's reaching new frontiers of science, technology in space, and that it's leading the world out of recession with the strongest economic expansion in 35 years. And you know the name of that nation. Its initials are U.S.A.!

And as you all might say, how 'bout them Dogs? But let me just add one thing. You ain't seen nothin' yet.

And we're doing this not only for some special groups—not for whites or blacks or men or women or old or young; we're doing it together, and we're doing it for everybody. And we won't rest until everybody who wants a job can find a job, from the coast of Georgia to San Francisco Bay.

Today, Americans are working again, and America is working again. And to make sure that good things keep leading to better things—investment, jobs, and growth all going up and the deficit continuing to come down—we want to simplify the entire tax structure so we can bring yours and everybody's personal income tax rate further down, not up.

Now, my opponent's been working for a much different philosophy—bigger government. And I must say, in doing this, he's been a real leader. No question about that. [*Laughter*] Sixteen times as a Senator he helped lead the way and voted for new tax increases. And as Vice President, he helped push through the biggest tax increase in our peacetime history in 1977. There are still two phases of that tax to go into effect between now and 1989.

And he got results. America suffered terrible inflation and interest rates, declining savings rates in investment, no growth, rising unemployment, back-to-back years of declining productivity, and the steepest drop in real weekly earnings in 35 years. And after we suffered all those horrors, he said, "I am ready to be President."

Audience. No!

The President. You know something? I think he's more ready to be our problem than our President.

But I must say, there was one thing that was fair about his policies of compassion. They didn't discriminate; they made everybody miserable. But I don't want to be unfair. Maybe he's learned from his mistakes.

Audience. No!

The President. Do you suppose that, given a second chance, he'd do anything differently than he's done all his political career?

Audience. No!

The President. No, I think you're right. He'd go right back to his knee-jerk yen for tax increases. And you know, every time his knee jerks, we get kicked. [*Laughter*]

Actually, to pay for all his campaign promises—and this isn't a guess—we cost this out on the computers—he'd have to raise taxes the equivalent of $1,890 per household. That's more than $150 each and every month. I call that the Mondale mortgage. [*Laughter*]

Now, he claims his tax increases would only hurt a certain group of people. Well, he's right about that. They would only hurt Americans who want to buy something or save something or invest in something. They wouldn't hurt anybody else. He wants to impose higher taxes on working people. But with his policies, there wouldn't be many of those. He would send students from the graduation line to the unemployment line.

Audience. Boo-o-o!

The President. You know, we deserve better than that. But hold on—hold on, he's got more. He started to expose more of his tax plans the other night. He said he would repeal indexing.

Now, that's the reform we passed to keep Washington politicians from using inflation to pull you into higher and higher tax brackets. And for the younger people who might not have thought about this at first—what it means is that when you get a cost-of-living pay raise, it's only supposed to make you keep even with inflation, so that you don't lose any purchasing power. They push you into a higher tax bracket, so you pay a higher percentage of tax, and you're worse off—not keeping even.

But then in the last few days, he said he goofed. He said that he didn't really mean to say that—that he was going to repeal indexing. Well, the only thing we know for sure is, he has a basic two-part plan: raise your taxes, and then raise them again. But I've got news for him. The American people don't want his tax increase.

Audience. No!

The President. And the rest of the news is he isn't going to get his tax increase.

There are many differences between us. He sees an America in which every day is April 15th, tax day. [*Laughter*] We see an America in which every day is the Fourth of July, Independence Day.

He sat by while scholastic aptitude tests went down and crime rates went up. But we've worked with you to strengthen our schools and neighborhoods, and now test scores are going back up, and crime rates are coming down.

And while he spent 4 years watching inflation get strong and our defenses grow weak, we've made inflation weaker and defenses stronger. And I am so proud to be able to say that during these last 4 years, not 1 inch of territory has been lost to Communist aggression.

The United States is more secure today than we were. And all of us are truly blessed to have the finest group of young men and women in military uniform that America has ever had. For the sake of all who risk their lives to keep us free, we must not fail to provide them the moral support, the weapons, and the equipment they need.

My opponent had one of the weakest records in the United States Congress for supporting a strong national defense. In 1968 he blissfully announced that the days of Soviet suppression by force were over. That was just before the Soviets invaded Czechoslovakia. Shortly after the invasion of Afghanistan, he said, "I can't understand—it just baffles me—why the Soviets these last few years have behaved as they have. . . . Why did they have to build up all those arms?" Well, probably because we were busy canceling ours.

But I'm afraid he's still baffled. Even Senator Fritz Hollings said, "Walter Mondale thinks the Soviet Union would never violate an arms control agreement. I think he's naive."

And you heard that I used to be a Democrat. You'll note that I'm quoting Democrats. Senator John Glenn said my opponent would "cut our Defense Establishment beyond all reality . . . cut the B–1, the Nimitz carrier, the Trident, the cruise missile, our foreign-based troops . . . would cut the M–1 tank, funds for the volunteer army, kill the shuttle, oppose procurement of the F–14, the Harrier, and the AWACS." Now, the only thing I—I don't know whether he would outlaw slingshots. [*Laughter*] But he would jeopardize the security of this nation, and we're not going to let him.

Audience. 4 more years!

The President. I believe——

Audience. 4 more years! 4 more years! 4 more years!

The President. All right.

Audience. 4 more years! 4 more years! 4 more years!

The President. Okay. I'll go for the 4 more years, but right now I'm trying to get 4 more minutes in before it really starts to rain. [*Laughter*] And if it does, I'll stay here if you will.

You know, I believe that the Democratic leadership today has abandoned the good and decent and responsible Democrats who believe in the principles that made our country great. I know there are many of you here who are Democrats or who were Democrats and did as I did. And I know that you're here—because I've met them all across this country—millions of patriotic Democrats who find they can no longer follow the leadership of their party down the path it's taking us.

Whenever I talk about F.D.R. or Harry Truman or John F. Kennedy, my opponents start tearing their hair out. They just can't stand it. And, of course, they can't, because it highlights how far they themselves have strayed from the strength of the Democratic political tradition. The good and decent Democrats of the rank and file haven't changed. Like their former leaders, they're clear eyed about the world. They have few illusions, and they consider themselves to be Americans first and not members of some special interest group.

When John F. Kennedy was President, he understood the Soviets. He understood Castro. He won passage of a law calling on the United States to prevent Cuba from extending its aggressive or subversive activities to any part of this hemisphere. Were he alive today, I believe he would be ashamed of those in the liberal Democratic leadership who would weaken our defenses, endanger our security, and sell out the cause of freedom in Latin America.

Nor would Kennedy support, as my opponent does today, a vision of such dreary mediocrity, endless tax increases on those who dream of better days. President Kennedy challenged Americans to make America grow, to make America great by pushing for lower personal tax rates for all the working people of this country. That's what we did before. And together, with people like you, that's what we want to do again. We want to reach a future where the American eagle soars. He would take us back to the day of the sore eagle. [*Laughter*]

The leaders of the Democratic Party today have gone so far left they've left the mainstream. But come November 6th, I believe they're going to get the shock of their lives. The South will rise again. And you will help lead this nation to a new, golden age of growth and opportunity.

We're not going back to a failed past; we're going forward to a glorious future. And we're going to build it together. And we're going to make it possible for you wonderful young people to reach for the stars. And when that day arrives, when you become tomorrow's leaders, we want to hand you a nation so strong, so united that your America will be a great shining light for progress and peace for generations to come.

Thank you all for always remembering what Faulkner called the old, living verities and truths of the heart—love and honor, pity and pride, and compassion and sacrifice. I thank you for remembering what America is and must always be—a willingness of the heart.

And, again, just one last word to these young people here and young people all over America. My generation and a few generations in between mine and yours, we knew an America and grew up in America, when we were your age, in which we just took it for granted that there was no ceiling on the opportunity for us, that it was up to us how far and how high we would fly, and we wouldn't be penalized for our effort. And then we went into a period in which some of that seemed to disappear, and people thought that we could regulate and regiment things and order society around.

Well, our job—those few other generations I mentioned and my own—our job is to see that we turn over to you the same kind of country that our parents turned over to us, in which the sky is the limit.

America's best days are yet to come. Thank you, and God bless all of you. And we beat the rain. Thank you.

Note: The President spoke at 3:49 p.m. at the front entrance of the Macon City Hall.

Following his remarks, the President traveled to Greenville, SC.

Statement on Signing the Central Intelligence Agency Information Act
October 15, 1984

I am pleased to sign into law H.R. 5164, the Central Intelligence Agency Information Act. It represents an initial effort toward needed reform of Freedom of Information Act requirements. Under its provisions, the Central Intelligence Agency will avoid timeconsuming review of certain operational files, which must in any case remain classified to protect intelligence sources and methods, and will devote its resources to expedited review of other information requests. Moreover, this law assures the public of continued access to information that is releasable.

This represents a small but important first step, accomplished in large part because of bipartisan cooperation in both houses. We are especially indebted to the leadership of Senators Goldwater and Moynihan and Representatives Boland and Robinson. I anticipate that in the future such relief will be expanded in scope. And I expect that it will become available to other agencies involved in intelligence, who also must protect their sources and methods and who likewise wish to avoid unnecessary and expensive paperwork.

Note: As enacted, H.R. 5164 is Public Law 98–477, approved October 15.

Statement on Signing a Bill Conferring United States Citizenship Posthumously on Wladyslaw Staniszewski
October 15, 1984

I am pleased to sign into law H.R. 960, which confers citizenship posthumously on Cpl. Wladyslaw Staniszewski, a national of Great Britain, who was killed in action on July 7, 1967, in the Republic of Vietnam while serving in the United States Marine Corps.

Corporal Staniszewski, who had immigrated to Brockton, MA, acted as an American when he willingly served the United States in a place of peril. He made the supreme sacrifice under our nation's colors and for our country. Today we simply confirm what Corporal Staniszewski earned on July 7, 1967.

Corporal Staniszewski has focused the Nation's attention on a matter we have overlooked far too long. At least 462 noncitizen servicemen from 64 countries sacrificed their lives in Vietnam. Among these was Lance Cpl. Jose Francisco Jimeniz of Mexico, who was awarded the Medal of Honor in upholding the highest traditions of the Armed Forces. Each was truly an American, and every one earned the right to be an American.

We cannot repay these men for their sacrifice, valor, or patriotism; but it is only right that we bestow upon each of them our nation's greatest honor: American citizenship.

It is my intention to submit to the 99th Congress legislation which will provide United States citizenship for all noncitizens killed in action in Vietnam while serving in the Armed Forces of the United States.

Note: As enacted, H.R. 960 is Private Law 98–33, approved October 15.

Question-and-Answer Session With Students at Greenville Technical College in Greenville, South Carolina
October 15, 1984

The President. Now, you've been informing me, and I understand that now—I don't know whether I can do as well in informing you—but they tell me that you have some questions.

Dr. Grastie. Yes, sir. Thank you, Mr. President. The students decided to draw numbers, and Todd Ingle has the first question for you.

Q. Hello, Mr. President. My name is Todd Ingle, and I'm a student here at Greenville Technical College. And my question is: What part do you think computer-age design and computer-integrated manufacturing plays in industry today, and what part do you think it will play in the near future?

The President. Oh, I think it's all important. I think what we're seeing here is the same type of thing that earlier in our time made us the great industrial power we were. We gave our workers the advantage of tools, and with their ability and the tools, we became the great industrial power and outcompeted most of the world.

Well, the world has moved on. And I think it's this—just what we've seen here—that, well, I will say again, as in my remarks out there: You give Americans the tools they need and the opportunity of this kind, and they'll outcompete anyone in the world. And I think we're going to see that.

Q. Thank you, Mr. President.

Q. Mr. President, my name is Tim Donald, and I would like to know why Congress cut $36.7 million from the appropriations bill you submitted for the Veterans Administration for the fiscal year of 1985?

The President. Well, all I can tell you is that they see things one way, and we see them another. They have certain targets that they think it's all right to cut and reduce, and yet they will turn right around and add to the spending that we have not asked for, because we believe that it wasn't as—or isn't as important. And this is about all that I can tell you.

Q. Thank you, sir.

Q. Mr. President, my name's John Sightler, and I was wondering what you thought the input of this high technology would be on the American industry on the world marketplace?

The President. Well, just what I've been seeing here, and what I've seen in some other plants—not schools, but plants where some of this is actually—or things of this kind are in operation—is, it's going to put us back in competition. When I see something here doing what it's doing, and I'm told how many times faster that is, and more accurate than the previous operation under older tools, and not computerized tools, then that—the per unit cost of the item—is going to put us back there in the marketplace and, as I say, outcompeting the others. And I have been in a few plants recently to see examples of what this is.

One, recently, was a steel plant. They are building it; it isn't finished yet. The investment that they're risking is equal to about two-thirds of the total capital assets of the company. But they know that with this, timewise and costwise, they will be able to be competitive with that particular steel from any part of the world.

Q. Thank you.

Q. Hello, Mr. President. My name is Hobie Taylor. And I'd like to know how you view the future of high technology in technical institutes such as Greenville Tech?

The President. Well, I think that it is changing and reshaping our whole industrial pattern and our society, for that matter. I know right now that because of an educational institution like this, industries are being attracted to your area because your graduates will be there as an available skilled force. I've seen this also happen in one of the cities in Texas which has become quite a competitor with places like Silicon Valley in California and because of the educational institutions in the area that have guaranteed that skilled labor force.

Q. Thank you, sir.

Q. Hello again. I'm Perry Talley, Mr. President. I want to see how you see technical development in the South for the future?

The President. Well, in these recent years the Sunbelt has presented an attraction that has drawn people to where the Sunbelt is the fastest growing, population-wise, area in the United States. And this was certainly not true for a time. So then, when you add to the salubrious climate and the other advantages that have made people in the past decide they'd like to live—*[laughing]*—here, you add to that the opportunity for jobs and technical training and so forth down here, I think you're going to see further population shifts, and you're going to see maybe a change that—with all due respect to some of the other Southern attributes, King Cotton, and so forth—I think you might find yourself with another attraction that changes the whole nature of your work, your opportunities, and your industry here.

Q. Thank you, Mr. President.

Dr. Grastie. Mr. President, we have time

for one more question. That will be from Mike Furillo.

Q. Mr. President, I work for Amco Lycoming Greer Division. And my question to you is, due to religious convictions and my responsibility to provide the best education possible, I've placed my children in a private Christian elementary school, and their tuition amounts to about 15 percent of my gross yearly income. And I'd like to know, will there be any legislation in the future that would give me a tax break on this tuition without it coming in the form of what the Federal Government would consider a subsidy, thereby giving the Government the right to regulate the school rules and school protocol?

The President. Well, you're looking at a representative of an administration that doesn't want the Federal Government being a senior partner. When, a little while ago in the briefing, we were talking about partnerships and participation, I almost wanted to add and say, "Yes, that's fine, we're very proud to be able to help in something of this kind; we don't want to be a senior partner." Now, that wasn't always true. There are other people who think government should be the senior partner.

But I have to say, with regard to what you were talking about and the tuition problem, I think the answer to that is very simple and it's very fair. We've tried to get it, and we've been unable to get it through the Congress, and that is that parents—education is compulsory in our country—and

parents are entitled to have a choice of whether they want to utilize the public school system or do as you're doing and use an independent school system for their education.

But you have to pay your full share in taxes for the support of public education without you using or benefiting from that education at all. And then, in addition, you, for wanting to put them in another kind of school, you're penalized in having to pay the double expense.

I think that we should have a program of tuition tax credits in which fairness is reinstituted for parents who choose not to utilize the pubic schools. It isn't going to hurt the public schools any. It is going to aid the independent schools because they are now more competitive. And what's wrong with education being competitive? What's wrong with having school systems in which they have to shape up and turn out educated graduates or they're not going to get the support? So, we're going to continue fighting for tuition tax credits for the people like yourself.

Q. Thank you very much, Mr. President.

The President. All right.

Note: The question-and-answer session began at 5:30 p.m. at the Advanced Machine Tool Resource Center, where the President had earlier received a briefing and a tour of the building.

Dr. Kay Grastie is vice president for education at the college.

Remarks at a Reagan-Bush Rally in Greenville, South Carolina
October 15, 1984

The President. Thank you very much.

Audience. 4 more years! 4 more years! 4 more years!

The President. All right. All right, you talked me into it.

Well, thank you, Carroll Campbell. I know how much you think about him down here, but would you mind kind of letting him live in Washington for a couple of more years? We'd like that very much. And

Dr. Thomas Barton, a Clemson Tiger; Mayor Bill Workman, and Senator Strom Thurmond.

I appreciate this chance to be with you today and to see firsthand your innovative and creative method of building a better future. I've just been in there and been treated to some of the wonders that are to be found in these buildings here.

President Dwight Eisenhower once

wrote, "The future will not belong—or will belong not to the faint-hearted, but to those who believe in it and prepare for it." And that's what this campus is all about.

All over America, people like you are making investments in new technology and precision training. And as Americans, working together as never before, we are seeing to it that the United States will not come in second.

I think our competitors in the world are in for an unpleasant surprise. Given the proper training, the tools and equipment, we can outproduce, outcompete, and outsell the pants off anyone, anytime, anywhere in the world.

I'm impressed with what I've seen here, especially the Advanced Machine Tool Resource Center. I'm aware of the extraordinary cooperation among the various levels of government and between the public and private sectors. What you're doing is part of the new spirit of enterprise that's sweeping this country. And it's in stark contrast to the pessimism and stagflation of just 4 years ago.

The American people rejected the politics of doom and gloom. In 1980 they voted for a fundamental change of direction, and that's exactly what we've given them. Instead of centralizing more and more power in Washington and taking an increasingly bigger tax bite out of working people's paychecks, we've returned to the people control of their own destinies. We've reversed the power flow.

And the difference between us and our opponents is a very basic one. When it comes down to a choice between expanding the power of government or keeping that power in the hands of the people, you side with government—or *they* side with government, but we will always side with you, the people.

And you haven't let us down. You built an economic recovery that's astounded the experts, especially those so-called experts quoted by my opponent. All we did was get the Government out of your way. They were wrong when they said it wouldn't work. We have high growth and low inflation now. Over 6 million new jobs have been created in the last 21 months. And even more important than the good economic news of today, we're laying the foundation of a happier and more prosperous tomorrow.

Productivity, after being in the doldrums for years, has come on strong for 2 years straight. Capital investment in new machinery and equipment has outpaced all expectations. These are omens for even brighter days ahead, for long-term economic expansion.

Now, my opponent wants to save us from prosperity. [*Laughter*] He'd do that by increasing your tax load the equivalent of $1,890 per household in the United States. We worked it out on a computer.

Audience. Boo-o-o!

The President. His insistence on higher tax rates is like playing Russian roulette with our economic security, only in the game the way he plays it, every chamber in the gun would be loaded. [*Laughter*] His program of high taxes sugarcoated with compassionate rhetoric is a disaster in disguise that will destroy our economic expansion, increase unemployment, and reignite inflation.

We don't need a policy of higher taxes; we need a policy of higher growth. And we don't need more power for government; we need more opportunity for people.

Now, he talked about me and taxes and what he says I'm going to do. Well, I'll tell you what we want to do. We want to simplify the tax system, make it more fair and easier to understand. When you hear that Albert Einstein said that he couldn't understand the Form 1040, you know our tax system is a little complicated. So, we want to do this to bring down yours and everybody's income tax rates further down, not up.

But my opponent even wants to eliminate indexing. That means that he wants you to be pushed by inflation into higher and higher tax brackets, to have less and less take-home pay. Now, we passed indexing—it goes into effect on January 1st—and the idea of it, of course, was to prevent a cost-of-living pay raise, in the days of inflation, that's supposed to make you keep even with inflation—to keep that from pushing you into a higher tax bracket where you pay a higher percentage of tax, and thus you're worse off, you haven't kept even at all. And it's a nice way, of course, in which the Congress can have a continuing tax increase without having to go through the unhappiness of introducing one for legislation and voting on it.

Supporters of economy-killing tax increases claim they're necessary to decrease the deficit. But at the same time, they're poised and ready to turn on the Federal spending spigot, which we've spent so much time turning off. With the strong support of individuals like your own Congressman Carroll Campbell, we have cut the rate of growth in Federal spending by over 60 percent. When we came here it was 17 percent a year. That was the increase. It's now down to 6.1 percent.

But Carroll is a strong voice for responsible government, and I hope you're doing everything you can to send him back to Washington. And while we're talking about responsible government, let's make certain that South Carolina reelects a man who's a giant in that cause—Senator Strom Thurmond. We need elected officials like Congressmen Campbell, Hartnett, and Spence, who have the vision and leadership to offer better options to the American people than simply raising taxes.

There are those so entangled in their promises to special interest groups they can't see a better future, much less plan for it. Well, this was never more clear than when my opponent strenuously opposed the space shuttle program. He led the opposition in the Senate in trying to kill us from having such a program. And then, just up until Saturday, we had those young people—men and women—those heroes, up there going around this country of ours. While I was going across Ohio on a train, they were going around the world about six or seven times. And the things that are coming out of that have made it worth every penny that it has cost—the additions, the improvements for our health, the medicines, the materials that are being developed.

Well, he opposed that when it was first proposed. He would have spent the money beefing up some bureaucratic programs in Washington, DC.

How many of you have seen one of those shuttles blast off into space or glide in for a smooth landing? I'm sure on television you've seen it, if not in reality. It is a magnificent sight, and it's a tribute to America's technological greatness. It's been worth, as I say, every cent.

Now, today there is a phenomenon that many of the pollsters can't understand, and I see it everywhere I go, and I see it here today. Young people from every background have rejected the politics of pessimism and are foursquare behind a strong, vibrant, and growing America.

And I want to thank all of you young people who are here with us today. We're working to see that when you get out of school, you have the same opportunity that Americans have always had in this country.

You know, a few years ago there were people around that were telling you, no, you know, we had to accept limits, that we weren't ever going to have things as good as they had been in the past. Well, they were blowing smoke. I have told, wherever I've gone—because all over the country today, at gatherings like this, I have seen so many young people. And I'm so proud and happy to see them there because I like telling you that my generation and a few generations between mine and yours—[*laughter*]—there were those of us that knew, just took for granted when we were your age that there was no limit to how high we could go, no limit on what we could do if we were willing to reach for it and go for it.

And what I'm determined this election is all about is to make sure that we hand you, when it comes your turn, the same kind of America that our parents handed us. We want you to have the same opportunity. We want you to have a real job when you finish your schooling, not just make-work or some temporary government job, but solid employment. We want to make certain that you have enough take-home pay and that prices and interest rates are reasonable enough so that someday, when you're ready, you'll be able to buy or build your own home.

Due to runaway inflation and the dramatic jump in interest rates under the last administration, millions of Americans found home ownership beyond their reach, and other millions found that the installment paying, the interest in buying a car was too high. And so, two great industries, housing and the automobile industry, ground to a halt.

Well, inflation is under control, and the record high 21½-percent prime rate that we inherited has come down. Until today, it had come down to 12¾ percent, and I don't know whether you've heard the news, but today one of the major banks in our country has just dropped it down another half point to 12¼ percent. And we expect even more progress on this front.

The average monthly mortgage rate payment has come down $143, putting 5 million more Americans in reach of buying their own homes. Now, I don't think it's selfish of you to want a good job or to own a home or to have a decent standard of living. You deserve that kind of future, and we aren't going to let our opponents tax it away.

Audience. 4 more years! 4 more years! 4 more years!

The President. Thank you. All right.

Audience. 4 more years! 4 more years! 4 more years!

The President. All right, thank you. Thank you very much. And while I'm doing that, let me just interject something here in this particular locale that I want to say.

I know the great importance of one particular industry to this area—textiles. And we have been working, and we are going to continue to work, with your elected Representatives, your Senator, your Members of the House in Washington. We've done some things; we'll continue to do more to see that we help you resolve the problems that have beset that industry.

I'm proud of the steps——

Audience. 4 more years, Reagan! 4 more years, Reagan! 4 more years, Reagan!

The President. All right. All right, I'll tell Nancy to unpack. [*Laughter*]

Well, I'm proud of the steps that we've taken to keep our country free and secure. During the last decade, and during the previous administration, our military strength was permitted to erode. But I think you here in South Carolina understand what too many in Washington have forgotten: Strength is the only true path to peace.

We've got an airbase out on the west coast there, and at the entrance to that airbase, above it, it tells the whole story. And it says, "Our profession is peace."

We've begun rebuilding America's defenses, and as long as I'm President, I will never shortchange the national security needs of the United States.

But now we're on a two-track course. And the other track is we've gone the extra mile to reach arms reduction agreements with the Soviet Union, and we'll continue to do so. But from now on, the United States will be negotiating from a position of strength.

The commanders of our military forces tell me that we have the finest and most dedicated group of young men and women serving in uniform in our Armed Forces than we've ever had in our history. You know, during the last administration, morale sank to a new low point. And many of those serving our country got the feeling that sacrifice, their sacrifice, was being taken for granted. I can promise you this: Those brave people in our Armed Forces will never doubt our unending gratitude for the job that they're doing.

And, you know, I like to suggest this: I hope if you, and especially you students, if you see your counterparts, those young people that are in uniform, down on the street sometime, that you'll maybe just go up and stick out your hand and tell them how proud we are and how thankful we are for their service to America. You'll feel real great after you've done it, and I know how they'll feel. They'll be walking about 3 or 4 inches taller than they were.

But looking out here today and thinking about all the young people I've met around the country, I think America has great days ahead. Charles Lindbergh wrote, "Short-time [short-term] survival may depend on the knowledge of nuclear physicists and the performance of supersonic aircraft, but long-term survival depends alone on the character of man."

As America heads into a new age of technology we have every reason to be confident that it will be an era of opportunity and freedom. The heart of America still burns bright with those values that made this a blessed land of liberty, the greatest and freest nation in our history. And with all of us together, we're going to keep it that way.

Today the United States is the leader of the world in so many ways. A great cleric, Pope Paul—or Pius XII, after World War II, made a statement when so much of the world was devastated and the future looked so bleak for everyone, and then he said a profound truth. He said, "The American people have a great genius for great and unselfish deeds. Into the hands of America God has placed an afflicted mankind." I

don't think there's anyone in America that would turn their backs on that challenge and that opportunity to serve mankind.

Well, I just want to thank you all very much and tell you that, if you don't mind, I'd like to stick around for 4 more years. God bless you. Thank you.

Note: The President spoke at 6 p.m. at the Allied Health Building on the Greenville Technical College campus.

Following his remarks, the President returned to Washington, DC.

Statement on the Death of Valeriy Marchenko
October 15, 1984

We have learned very recently of the death in a Leningrad prison hospital on October 7 of Valeriy Marchenko. Mr. Marchenko, who was only 37 years old, was one of the Soviet Union's most prominent human rights activists.

A journalist by profession, Mr. Marchenko had already served 8 years in prison—an ordeal which he barely survived. Nonetheless, this past March he was sentenced to an additional 10 years of imprisonment and 5 years of internal exile because he had written articles criticizing the harshness of

Soviet labor camps and the violations of human and national rights in the Ukraine. It is reported that an appeal by his family for amelioration of his conditions, based on his precarious health, was refused by the Soviet authorities.

We are deeply saddened and enraged by Mr. Marchenko's needless death. His brave struggle for individual liberties is an inspiration to all of us. And his death brings home the tragedy of the deteriorating human rights situation in the Soviet Union, a situation which all Americans deeply deplore.

Appointment of Five Members of the Board of Directors of the Federal National Mortgage Association
October 15, 1984

The President today announced his intention to appoint the following individuals to be members of the Board of Directors of the Federal National Mortgage Association for terms ending on the date of the annual meeting of the stockholders in 1985. These are reappointments.

Merrill Butler is president of Butler Housing Corp. in Irvine, CA, and Bullard Homes Corp. in Fresno, CA. He began his homebuilding career in 1956, when he founded the Butler-

Harbour Construction Co. in Anaheim, CA. He graduated from the University of Southern California in 1948. He is married, has three children, and resides in Newport Beach, CA. He was born February 18, 1925, in Los Angeles, CA.

James B. Coles has been owner and chairman of the board of James B. Coles, Inc., and the Coles Development Co., Inc., in San Diego, CA, since 1972. He is a member of the National Association of Home Builders. He graduated from San Diego State University (B.A., 1967). He is mar-

1547

ried, has two children, and resides in Del Mar, CA. He was born September 29, 1941, in Camden, NJ.

Bert A. Getz has been president and director of the Globe Corp., a holding company in Scottsdale, AZ, since 1959. He has also served as director of the Arizona Bank since 1970 and the First National Bank of Winnetka since 1968. He graduated from the University of Michigan (B.B.A., 1959). He is married, has three children, and resides in Scottsdale, AZ. He was born May 7, 1937, in Chicago, IL.

Dianne E. Ingels is a general partner in the York Co. in Denver, CO. She is also a real estate broker, investor, and consultant. She was president and broker, Ingels Co., Colorado Springs, CO, in 1976–1977. She was appointed to the Colorado Springs Urban Renewal Commission in 1972 and elected chairman of the commission in 1974. She graduated from the University of Colorado (B.S., 1963) and New York University (M.S., 1964). She was born August 8, 1941, in Denver, CO, and now resides in Colorado Springs.

James E. Lyon is chairman of the board and chief executive officer of the River Oaks Bank and Trust Co., the River Oaks Financial Corp., and Ruska Instruments Corp. He is a member of the World Business Council, American Institute of Banking, National Board of Banking, and the Houston Home Builders Association. He attended Rice University and the University of Houston. He has three children and resides in Houston, TX. He was born August 25, 1927, in Houston.

Proclamation 5261—Myasthenia Gravis Awareness Week, 1984
October 15, 1984

By the President of the United States of America

A Proclamation

For most of us, combing our hair or crossing the room to turn on the light are simple, routine tasks. But for more than 100,000 Americans who suffer from myasthenia gravis, these everyday activities are enough to exhaust them for hours.

Myasthenia gravis is a serious neuromuscular disease whose cause is not yet known. It can strike anyone at any time, draining people of their vitality, producing muscle weakness and abnormally rapid fatigue.

Though there is still much to be learned, scientists now know that myasthenia gravis depletes its victim of an essential chemical—without which nerve cells cannot tell muscles to work. Based on this knowledge, scientists have made important progress in managing this disorder. Today, several new forms of treatment are available, and myasthenia gravis patients can expect to lead nearly normal lives.

But because we still do not know how to prevent this disease, the quest for answers continues. Scientists supported by the Myasthenia Gravis Foundation and the Federal government's National Institute of Neuro-logical and Communicative Disorders and Stroke remain dedicated to this crucial research effort. These investigators are inspired by the courage and tenacity shown by myasthenia gravis patients and their families.

In order that the public be made aware of myasthenia gravis and the need to conquer this debilitating disorder, the Congress, by Senate Joint Resolution 295, has designated the week of October 14 through October 20, 1984, as "Myasthenia Gravis Awareness Week" and authorized and requested the President to issue a proclamation in observance of this week.

Now, Therefore, I, Ronald Reagan, President of the United States of America, do hereby proclaim the week beginning October 14, 1984, as Myasthenia Gravis Awareness Week. I call upon all government agencies, health organizations, communications media, and people of the United States to observe this week with appropriate ceremonies and activities.

In Witness Whereof, I have hereunto set my hand this fifteenth day of October, in the year of our Lord nineteen hundred and eighty-four, and of the Independence of the

United States of America the two hundred and ninth.

RONALD REAGAN

[*Filed with the Office of the Federal Register, 4:42 p.m., October 16, 1984*]

Note: The proclamation was released by the Office of the Press Secretary on October 16.

Remarks and a Question-and-Answer Session at the WILCO Area Career Center in Romeoville, Illinois
October 16, 1984

The President. Well, listen, I just want to tell you I think this is very exciting. And I know that you've come along in a world where maybe these things don't seem as astounding as they do to someone that's been around as long as I have. We are coming into a revolution that, I think, is every bit as great as the Industrial Revolution of the last century that shaped our world into the way we've known it. And there's just no limit to the heights that we can go and to the opportunities that are available to you. And this is so exciting to see, you having this opportunity.

I have been privileged recently to be in some industrial plants where already they are using some of what you, right here, are learning about the computerization of machinery, and former—just assembly lines as we once knew them, with human hands doing a number of things.

And it's truly unbelievable to see the progress that we're making, both with regard to productivity—the increase in it—the saving of time, and the fact that it's going to be able to be done much more economically. And I think that what you're learning here is what is going to see us—as we once did in that other Industrial Revolution—in this one, it's going to see us out there able to compete and probably outcompete most of the world with regard to industry and our productivity and all that's going on.

Now, I'm not going to go on any longer than this because they told me that—you see, I would be afraid to start asking you some questions because I'd reveal that I really don't know enough about this to ask the right questions—but it was suggested to me that maybe you might have a few questions for me. I know we don't have much time, but if you do, fire away.

Q. Mr. President, my name is Gary Scanlon. And my first question I'd like to ask you is, do you feel that your age would have any effect on you upholding another term in the office if you were reelected?

The President. Upholding——

Q. Another term in the office if you were reelected?

The President. This must be with regard to some of the things about my health and age and so forth. No, I feel fine; matter of fact, I've never felt better in my life. And, yes, I'm looking forward to 4 more years because we've just started, I think, what is necessary to complement the type of thing that's going on here with regard to our free enterprise system. And I want to see it come closer to being finished.

So, no, I feel fine. I got a little gym there in the White House. I work out every day, except when they put me out on the road this way. And I've made my physical test scores available to everyone and to the media and all. And the doctors all say—well, the way I put it is I'm not really this old—they mixed up the babies in the hospital. [*Laughter*]

Q. Thank you.

Q. Do we have another questioner?

Q. Mr. President, my name is Jim Kyle. And I was wondering, what do you think was your big accomplishment since you've been in office?

The President. Well, I could say the economy and the recovery that we've made, and I suppose that would sum it up entirely. And yet, there is another one that I'm awfully proud of, and that is the change of spirit in this land of ours. There was an era of pessimism and a feeling that things were never going to be as good again as they had been in the past. All of that's gone, and every place I go in the country I find the American people are gung ho and going forward.

But with the economy: the interest rates were 21½ and the inflation for 2 years had been double digit—13 and 12.4 for 2 years in a row. Unemployment, as we know, was tremendous. And the interest rates now—well, just the other day they took another little dip. The prime rate isn't 21½ anymore; it's now 13¼. I'm trying to think whether I want to go into the unemployment yet or talk about the taxes. As long as I'm talking interest rates, maybe I'd better talk about the taxes—the fact that we've been able to reduce the rate of increase of government spending from 17 percent a year down to around 6 percent a year.

And then we get to unemployment. We've created 6 million new jobs in the last 21 months. And there have been in the last 17 months 900,000 new business incorporations in America, which means they're going to be out looking for people to work. So, I think this kind of a turnaround—yes, I'm very proud of it.

Q. Mr. President, we do have a lot of classrooms to visit, so maybe we could have just one more question, and then we'll go on.

The President. All right.

Q. I'm Randy Kimmel. And, Mr. President, Mr. Mondale has mentioned that you're going to stop Social Security and Medicare. Is this true?

The President. Not at all. And if there's one thing that makes me angry in this campaign it is that pure political demagoguery for whatever advantage he thinks he can get out of saying those things. And he's not alone. Others have been saying them, too.

No, we were faced, when we came into office, with a Social Security system that in spite of the biggest tax increase in—single tax increase in history in the Social Security payroll tax—it was passed in '77 by the previous administration and the previous Congress—that Social Security was facing bankruptcy. And we started trying to talk to the opposition about—that we had to head it

off, as—by November of 1982, they wouldn't, they wouldn't discuss with us anything about it. And by 1982, we had to borrow $17 billion to keep Social Security checks from bouncing. Then when the '82 election was over, finally they agreed to sit down, join with us in bipartisan commission, and find a solution to the financial problems of Social Security. And we did.

And we can look, now, ahead into the future for another half a century, and as far as we can see Social Security is on a solid footing. But all through all of that discussion I made it plain that I would never hold still for any change in Social Security that pulled the rug out from the people that were depending on it or from those who are looking forward in the next several years to going on Social Security.

So, I can make that pledge. And I've said repeatedly that the President should never say never, but I will never hold still for, as I say, pulling the rug out from those people that are dependent on that progam.

Q. Thank you, Mr. President.

The President. All right.

Q. How about Medicare? The other half of the question: Will you ever stop Medicare?

The President. Helen [Helen Thomas, United Press International], I'm familiar with the problem, and as yet they have not—a problem similar, not quite as extreme yet, but similar to the Social Security problem. That fund, the Medicare fund, in the next several years, unless some adjustments are made, is going to—well, we're going to have to do something to correct it, because that fund is being drained as the Social Security fund had been drained.

But we are talking some proposals. But right now what we're talking is leaning on the medical field—doctors' fees, hospital costs, and so forth—as to having a fixed rate there for medicare patients. They've been a part of——

Q. Otherwise, would you have to cut?

The President. What?

Q. Would you have to cut, otherwise?

The President. Well, we're certainly not going to take that medical care away from the people that are getting it.

Q. Thank you, Mr. President.

[The President spoke at 10:40 a.m. in the electronics classroom following a briefing on the programs taught in that class. He then went to the auto mechanics classroom for another briefing. He spoke to students again at 11:03 a.m.]

The President. Thank you very much. I just thought I should point out to you today that I didn't come here alone. Standing over here is your Governor and your United States Senator and your Congressman from this area.

But I know that I only have a couple of minutes to go. And I also know that you're not enrolled here. *[The President was referring to 3- and 4-year-olds attending the WILCO Area Career Center preschool.]* *[Laughter]* They're visitors like I am, I'm sure, in the school.

Well, what I've seen here in the brief time that's been allowed—and I know I only have a minute or two now and we have to move on—but I've seen more than just a school. It is career training, and it is opportunity. And we are having a technological revolution that is every bit as great and probably even greater than the Industrial Revolution of more than a century ago that led to this great industrial power that we are.

It's a great promise here that you have of unlimited opportunities as you go forward with what you're learning here and what you're preparing to do at WILCO. You are looking ahead. You're getting sensible training that matches the needs of your community. And I'm very proud that our government could be, even in a limited way, a partner in what is going on here, because this is what America's all about. It is a partnership between the public sector and the private sector, and it has a record—I know that part of this is our own job-training program, the Federal Government—and you lead the Nation.

That program, nationwide, has an average rate of placement in jobs of 70 percent of the people that go through the training program. Well, you're topping that sizably; your job placement rate here is 85 percent. And I think you can all be proud that WILCO is a winner.

This career center proves something else,

I think, also. And that is what I mentioned a moment ago: That when we all work together—whether government, the private sector, the people themselves—we can really get things done. And that's been the secret of this nation of ours for these more than 200 years that we've been here.

And I want to thank you, and I want to thank the instructors and the staff for letting us visit here today. And I hope that we haven't interfered too much with the progress of—*[applause]*——

All right. Let me just say to you on behalf of these gentlemen that are with me here, and myself, today, it is such a thrill, certainly for me, to see you, of your generation, you young people, and the course that you have set yourselves on, because not too many years ago there were people in this country that were trying to tell us that, well, things would never again be as good as they once were.

Well, all I know is that—I think I probably top anyone in age in this room— *[laughter]*—but I want you to know that I was born into an America where as you grew up, you knew that there was no limit to what you could accomplish, that there was opportunity out there for anyone that wanted to go after it. And that's the kind of America we have again today, and that's the kind of America that we're determined that you're going to have—the same thing that we knew.

But it's up to you. The sky's the limit. There's every kind of opportunity out there for you.

And God bless all of you. And from what I've seen of you and other young people throughout this country, I'm pretty optimistic about the future of this country when it comes time for us to turn the leadership over to you. You're going to do darn well. So, aim high. *[Applause]*

Thank you very much. Thank you. I have to leave, but let me just say I shared some of your sorrow with regard to—well, first, the triumph of the Cubs getting as far as they did, but then—*[applause]*—the sorrow they didn't get farther.

Audience. Boo-o-o!

The President. No, I want to tell you something. My career started out as a sports announcer. And back in 1935, I was broadcasting the Cubs when the only way they could win the pennant was to win the last 21 games of the season—[*laughter*]—and they did it! So, I'm supposed to be nonpartisan now and on everybody's side, but I was kind of upset there in front of the TV set when they didn't go all the way. But it was a great accomplishment.

All right. Thank you.

Remarks and a Question-and-Answer Session at Bolingbrook High School in Bolingbrook, Illinois
October 16, 1984

The President. Thank you, Governor Jim Thompson, for that most gracious and—I'm very greatly honored by that introduction. And distinguished Members of the Congress, the officials of your school, and you, I thank you all for that heartwarming reception. It's great to be back in Illinois, and it's great to be back in the proud town of Bolingbrook.

I understand that this is your homecoming week. Well, since I'm back in my home State, this is homecoming for me, too. And I'll have to say, I've never felt more welcome than I do right now. So, may I express best wishes to a certain football team that's called the Raiders? I don't suppose you'd like to win one for the Gipper? [*Applause*]

But last year alone, on another score, 49 students from Bolingbrook High received Presidential Academic Fitness Awards.

I'd also like to congratulate everyone who helps make your school one of the best in the nation. Your outstanding principal, Everette Green, your dedicated faculty, your school board, and especially you, the students. Together, you can set a standard for all schools to follow.

And today, we have just 3 weeks before election day. And our choice is, as the Governor said, as clear as any has ever been before us. Should we go forward with new optimism, prosperity, and strength, or should we go back to the policies of soaring taxation and spending that weakened our economy, snuffed out so many opportunities and threw away so many—or threw so many, not away, but millions of people into hardship?

We've already seen what happens when we follow the policies that our opponents have so faithfully promised to restore, the failed policies of tax and tax and spend and spend.

We saw a once-proud nation staggered by a steady erosion of economic growth. We saw punishing inflation and interest rates, a record peacetime tax burden, rising unemployment, and weakened defenses. We saw families breaking up, bedrock values of work and neighborhood undermined, crime rates rising. You've probably noticed that our opponents talk a great deal about fairness. Well, in one sense their policies were fair: they didn't discriminate; they made everybody miserable. [*Laughter*]

Since the aim of education is to prepare America's youth for the future, it was only natural that when our leaders lost faith in that future many of our principals, teachers, and students felt robbed of their sense of purpose. Scholastic aptitude test scores underwent a virtually unbroken decline for 20 years, and science achievement scores showed a similar drop. School discipline began to break down, and we found out that many of our 17-year-olds were functionally illiterate.

When our administration came into office we put education at the top of the national agenda, and we worked to return States, local governments and, yes, your parents to their rightful place in education. And what do you know? We're seeing results. From Maine to Illinois to California, your parents, teachers, school administrators, and all of you have begun to make our schools stronger and better. Your achievement is up. And this year's scholastic aptitude test scores rose 4 points, and that was the largest increase in over 20 years.

Now, much as we'd like to, our administration would like to take credit, but we can't. It belongs to you. All we did was something that every President from Washington to Lincoln did: trust the people.

And when our opponents look at America—well, my opponent seems to only see big government and little people. And he has only one program to offer: raise our taxes, and then raise them again, so that government can be even bigger. His tax hike would be the equivalent of $1,890 per year per household in the United States. That's more than $150 each and every month. Do you think we should sit back and let that happen to America?

Audience. No!

The President. Well, I know you probably watched the Olympics this summer and cheered on our American athletes. Well, in our country today there are two teams—the Washington Tax Increase Team and the American Opportunity Team. And now, making the economy bear the burden of our opponent's tax hike would be like having a coach tell an Olympic swimmer that he had to swim down that pool carrying an anvil, or a runner to sprint with a ball and chain around his ankle. But that's just what Coach Tax Hike and his Tax Increase Team want to do.

And they kicked off their fall campaign with a call for $85 billion in new taxes. I said it was a kickoff. There are those who believe it was a punt—[*laughter*]—and we mean to turn it into a blocked kick.

We on the American Opportunity Team want to bring everybody's personal tax rates further down, not up. We want to create opportunity so that all Americans can go forward together with nobody left behind. And come November, the American people will decide which team is America's team.

When their Washington Tax Increase Team was in charge, all they did was fumble. Well, today the American Opportunity Team has the ball back, and all of us are scoring touchdowns again.

Inflation is down, while growth and jobs and investment are up. Crime is stopping—or dropping. Our defenses are stronger. Our people are united, and, yes, this beloved country of ours is at peace.

The great choice that our country must make in 3 weeks will decide not just who will occupy the White House or who will sit in the Congress, it'll determine the kind of America that we pass on to all of you, as the Governor said. And if our opponents have their way, too many of you students would have to go from the graduation line straight to the unemployment line, and that's not good enough for America.

If we win, we're going to build a future together that will enable every one of you to reach for the stars, and you'll know what it is to enter the work force or go to college in a land of prosperity, pride, and hope.

When I was a young man, you knew that if you dreamed big and worked hard there was no limit to how far you could go. We're determined to bring that kind of real opportunity back for you, our sons and daughters, and I guess in my case I'd better say, and our grandsons and granddaughters. [*Laughter*]

Well, we've already made a good beginning. But a big job awaits us to keep improving our schools, to lead the world toward new frontiers of science, technology, and space, and, yes, to bring the personal tax rates further down so we can create more jobs and more opportunity for a better future.

Together, we can and will make America a shining city on a hill where our young men and women can dream great dreams and make them come true.

Now, I'm going to stop with the monolog. I know that our time is limited, and we probably only have a few minutes left. But I understand that there are a few of you that could have some questions here, and I'd like to take those questions. I wish I could do more of that, but the time is limited. So, which microphone?

Q. Mr. President——

The President. Over here?

Arms Reductions

Q. My name is Biz Hanson, and as a young adult, I'm personally concerned about the possible threat of nuclear war in the future. What efforts are being made by your administration to negotiate with the Soviet Union?

The President. We're making every effort

we can to negotiate with the Soviet Union. What we inherited when we came here was an America that over the years had unilaterally disarmed. The administration before ours—they canceled the B–1 bomber. They said, "No, we won't build it." They didn't ask anything from the Soviet Union in terms of arms control or anything.

We felt that the only way we could really get real arms reduction—and this is what I campaigned on—we had a SALT II treaty signed with the Soviet Union. But all that was was legitimizing a continuation of the arms race. Since that treaty was signed, they've added 3,800 more warheads to their arsenal, nuclear warheads.

And incidentally, my opponent was the President of the United States Senate at the time, and a Democratic Senate under a Democratic administration refused to ratify that treaty for the reason that I just gave.

Now, we set out not only to restore our economy, as we have, but also to restore our defenses, because we believe that the only way we can persuade the Soviet Union to sit down and negotiate a limit on nuclear arms or a reduction of them is if they see that the United States is willing to go as far as it has to go to see that they don't stay ahead of us in weapons, that we're as strong as they are.

Q. Thank you, Mr. President.

The President. I had the pleasure of telling Mr. Gromyko just days ago that if they feel as we do and if they want peace as much as we do, then they'll join us in not just reducing the number of those nuclear weapons, but in eliminating them entirely from the world.

Social Security

Q. Mr. President, my name is Lori Rafter, and as a prospective recipient of Social Security, I'm concerned about my future. Exactly what benefits in your Social Security program are you planning on changing when you are reelected?

The President. I'm glad you asked that question—[*laughter*]—because my opponent's having a field day out there saying a lot of things that ain't so.

When we took office, Social Security was nearly bankrupt. There'd been—well, there had been inflation, for one thing. There had

been mistakes in projecting the ratio of workers paying into the fund to the people that are taking the benefits out. And I tried to persuade the leadership of the opposing party, the leadership of the Congress, to try, or to sit down with us and work out a plan that would put Social Security back on a sound footing at the same time it would not pull the rug out from under those people dependent on Social Security.

They refused to talk about it. In fact, they stood up publicly and denied that it was true when I said that Social Security could not, without a change, get past July of 1983; it would be bankrupt by then. And you know something? When they said that that wasn't true, they were right—it went broke in November of 1982. [*Laughter*] We had to borrow $17 billion to cover the checks we were sending out.

Well, then, with the 1982 congressional election over, then they agreed to sit down. And we put together a bipartisan commission, and we have fixed for as far as we can see into the future the fiscal situation of Social Security. And I can guarantee you, we're not going to pull the rug out from not only those who are getting it, but from those who are one day going to get it, and we are going to keep the program fiscally sound.

Environmental Issues

Q. Mr. President, my name is Brian Hastings. When you are reelected for your second term, do you plan to enforce or propose regulations to protect our environment?

The President. Thank you very much for asking that. [*Laughter*] Again, some misstatements—in fact, yes. And we have been doing a very fine job with regard to our environment. When we came here our national parks had been allowed to deteriorate to the point that they represented, through filth and dirt, actually a health hazard, and there were accident risks. In other words, there were safety risks to visitors going to the parks.

We decided to stop buying new land for the parks, temporarily, and we devoted $1 billion to a 5-year program of refurbishing our national parks before we added to them. We have just about completed that, ahead of schedule, and have now budgeted money for new additional parks. We've increased by millions of acres the wilderness areas, and air pollution and water pollution in America are the best that they've been since 1970. And we're continuing along that line.

We're continuing research with regard to acid rain, because what we've learned so far has just revealed to us how little we actually know about the cause of acid rain. So, we've doubled the money for researching on that.

And I can assure you that we are dedicated to environmental protection, because that, again—in addition to what the Governor told you—that, again, is something we want to turn over to you, and that is the beauty of this land of ours, the natural advantages that it has, and all of the pluses that it has with regard to fish, fowl, and mammals and woods and wilderness areas and recreational areas. And I'm very proud of our record.

Mr. Green. This will have to be the last question for the President for today.

Audience. Ooooh!

The President. Oh, I should have thrown the speech away and just gone to this to begin with.

Student Financial Aid

Q. Mr. President, my name is Riz Espinili. As a senior, I'm concerned about the forms of educational aid that are now available for middle-class students who plan on attending college. Exactly what are these forms and their benefits?

The President. Well, we have more money today going to student aid programs than was going to them when we came here 4 years ago. One out of two college students in the United States is receiving some form of Federal aid. It consists of three types: the low-interest college loans for students, the outright grants, and what's known as the work-study program, where we underwrite and make available on the campus jobs, so the students that are working their way through can have that help.

And as I say, there is more of that being done than has been done in the past. And we're not reducing it. As a matter of fact, we're discussing right now with the Educa-

tion Department increasing the amount—not the total amount—increasing the amount of each grant to keep pace with some of the rising costs of education. And believe me, I'm heart and soul in sympathy with that problem of a student, because I had to work my way through Eureka College right here in Illinois, and did work it through, and also had some loans before I got out.

And we have also—working with the private sector—we've done a thing that has turned on the private sector in this country as they haven't been turned on for years in doing things from the private sector: foundations put together; programs subscribed to by individual givers, like United Fund and so forth—doing more today than has been done in decades to help meet some of these same problems without having everything dependent on government.

But I can't resist telling you that in working my way through school, there were no government programs at that time. You had to get your loans from foundations, charitable groups and so forth, which I did. But also, if you have to work your way through school, I can tell you you won't regret it ever. And you might be as lucky as I was. One of the best jobs I've ever had was a job I had working my way through school—I was washing dishes in the girls' dormitory. [*Laughter*]

Thank you. All right. All right. I know I have to run for it now. We keep getting behind on these schedules. I don't know whether they don't—maybe I run over, or maybe they don't schedule enough time to get from one place to the other, but I have another group waiting for me at another place here.

And so, again, I wish we could have taken more of the questions here from you. And I have to tell you, you showed again the academic quality of this school—you asked darn good questions. Thank you very much. God bless you all.

Note: The President spoke at 11:34 a.m. in the gymnasium at the high school. He was introduced by Gov. James R. Thompson, Jr.

Following the question-and-answer session, the President traveled to Glen Ellyn, IL.

Remarks at a Reagan-Bush Rally in Glen Ellyn, Illinois
October 16, 1984

The President. Thank you all very much, and I thank Jim Thompson for that very wonderful and glowing introduction. And, Edna Duty, you and I know something that all of them must learn, and that is that age is what you'll have 15 years from where you are presently.

Well, it's wonderful to be here at the College of DuPage, and on such a modern-looking campus. Yesterday, I was down at the University of Alabama, and the architecture there is beautiful, with all the charm of the Old South. But here, in your buildings and sculpture, we see the sharp, clear lines of the future, and it's a very striking campus, indeed.

And it's great to be in Illinois. Your support has always been very important to me. And I want to express my admiration for your Governor, Big Jim Thompson, and all the fine members of your congressional delegation that are here today. And I'm pleased to be here with my friend Chuck Percy, whom we need back in the Senate.

You know, I think everyone should pay attention to the fact that true as the facts are that Governor Thompson gave you about how my opponent would increase taxes, I think you'd better pay attention to the fact that Chuck Percy's opponent has made it plain that if he was elected, he would strive for twice as much in increased taxes as Mr. Mondale is talking about. So, we don't need him in Washington. There's nothing I'd like more than to see all your fine candidates of our party in the Congress in Washington.

Illinois has a special significance for all of us. Abe Lincoln came to adulthood and practiced law here. The political party that lifted him to his greatness is the party that I represent, these others represent in the election of 1984. And, so, Illinois is a fitting place for my statement to you today.

Abe Lincoln said, we must disenthrall ourselves with the past—and then we will save our country. Well, 4 years ago, that's what we did. We made a great turn; we got out from under the thrall of a government which we'd hoped would make our lives better, but which wound up living our lives for us.

The power of the Federal Government had, over the decades, created great chaos—economic chaos, social chaos, international chaos. Our leaders were adrift, rudderless, and without a compass.

Four years ago, we began to navigate by certain fixed principles. Our North Star was freedom; common sense was our constellation. We knew that economic freedom meant paying less of the American family's earnings to the Government. And so, we cut personal income tax rates by 25 percent.

We knew that inflation, the quiet thief, was stealing our savings, and the highest interest rates since the Civil War were making it impossible for people to own a home or start a business or enterprise.

We knew that our national system of military defense had been weakened. So, we decided to rebuild and be strong again.

Audience. 4 more years! 4 more years! 4 more years!

The President. And this we knew——

Audience. 4 more years!

The President. This we knew would enhance the prospects for peace in the world. It was a second American revolution, and it's only just begun.

Audience. 4 more years! 4 more years! 4 more years!

The President. But what has already come of our efforts? A great renewal. America is back, a giant reemergent on the scene—powerful in its economy, powerful in the world economy, powerful in its ability to defend itself and secure the peace.

Audience members. Thank you!

The President. Thank you. But now——

Audience. Reagan! Reagan! Reagan!

The President. All right.

Audience. Reagan! Reagan! Reagan!

The President. All right.

Audience. Reagan! Reagan! Reagan!

The President. Thank you.

Audience. Reagan! Reagan! Reagan!

The President. Thank you. Thank you very much.

But, listen, 4 years after our efforts began, small voices in the night are scurrying about, sounding the call to go back, to go backward to the days of confusion and drift, the days of torpor, timidity, and taxes.

Audience. Boo-o-o!

The President. My opponent this year is known to you. But perhaps we can gain greater insight into his leadership abilities and his philosophy if we take a look at his record.

To begin with, his grasp of economics is well demonstrated by his economic predictions. Just before we took office, my opponent said that our economic program was obviously, murderously inflationary. And that was just before we lowered the inflation rates from 12.4 percent to 4.2 percent.

So, then we got our tax cuts. And right after we got those and started implementing them, he said the most that he could see was an anemic recovery. And that was right before the revitalized economy created more than 6 million jobs in 22 months. And it was right before 900,000 businesses were incorporated in a 17-month period—900,000 new businesses.

And then—but what I'm going to tell you now, I have to explain to some of you, I think, a little bit, because it was back in 1976, and some of you were very young in 1976, and our opponents created a thing called the misery index. They added the rate of inflation to the rate of unemployment. And, in the case of Jerry Ford, it came out at 12½ points. So, they said that no one had a right to even seek reelection with a misery index of 12½ percent.

Now, my opponent has said that our policies would deliver a misery index the likes of which we haven't seen in a long time. And you know, something? There was some truth in that, because we've got the misery index down to 11.6, and under them it was over 20.

You've noticed they aren't talking about the misery index anymore. And they didn't talk about it in 1980. But just before we took office, my opponent said that our economic program is obviously, murderously inflationary. Well, as I said, that, again, was before we had brought it down to where it is today.

But I'm not finished here. There's so much more to say about my opponent. His grasp of foreign affairs is demonstrated by his understanding of world events. Sometime back, he said, "The old days of a Soviet strategy of suppression by force are over." And that was just before the Soviet Union invaded Czechoslovakia. And after they invaded Afghanistan, he said, "It just baffles me why the Soviets, these last few years, have behaved as they have." [*Laughter*] Doesn't he know it's their nature? But then, there's so much that baffles him.

One year ago this month, we liberated Grenada from Communist thugs who had taken over their country in a coup. Now, my opponent called what we did a violation of international law that erodes our moral authority——

Audience. Boo-o-o!

The President. ——eliminates our moral authority to criticize the Soviet invasion of Afghanistan. Well, still I'll say this. His administration did mete out strong punishment after Afghanistan. Unfortunately, they didn't punish the Soviet Union; they punished the American farmers.

My opponent said that control of oil prices would cost American consumers more than $36 billion a year. Well, we decontrolled oil prices. It was one of the first things I did. And the price of gas went down 8 cents a gallon.

Now, you know, all of these things I just told you—I was thinking about all this the other day, and it just occurred to me that maybe all we need to do to get the economy in absolutely perfect shape is to get my opponent to predict absolute disaster.

He says he cares about the middle class, but he boasts—and I quote again—"I have consistently supported legislation, time after time, which increased taxes on my own constituents." Now, he's proud of that, no doubt; proud of the fact that he voted 16 times—he voted 16 times in the United States Senate to raise the taxes of all Americans. But this time he's outdone himself.

He's already promised, of course, as you've been told, to raise your taxes. But if, as the Governor said, he's to keep all the promises he's made to this group and that, he will have to raise taxes by the equivalent of $1,890 per household in the whole

United States. That's more than $150 a month.

Audience. Boo-o-o!

The President. You know, that's like having a second mortgage. And after the Mondale mortgage, we're sure to see more than a few foreclosures. [*Laughter*]

I think my opponent's tax plans will be a hardship for the American people, and I believe it will bring our recovery to a roaring stop. But I'll give it this. He gave me an idea for Halloween. [*Laughter*] If I could find a way to dress up as his tax program, I could just scare the devil out of all the neighbors.

Audience. 4 more years! 4 more years! 4 more years!

The President. Well, all right. If you young people can spend 4 years doing what you're doing, I guess I can spend 4 more years doing what I'm doing.

I think my opponent's tax plans would be a hardship for the American people, but I'll give it this—well, let me just stop instead and say, I want to do something much different than he would do. He wants to raise everyone's taxes so he'll have more money to spend on all his campaign promises. I want to lower yours and everybody's tax rates so your families will be stronger, our economy will be stronger, and America will be stronger.

Audience. Reagan! Reagan! Reagan!

The President. I also want to add, I'm going to really be glad to have Chuck Percy in Washington, because I know how hard he'll fight to protect your families' earnings than his opponent will.

You know, I look out at all you wonderful young people, and I want you to know nothing has warmed my heart like seeing so many of you at our rallies and our meetings like this. Believe me, working to give you a future filled with hope and opportunity is what this job of mine is all about.

My opponent supported the grain embargo, spoke out for it often. He even questioned the patriotism of a Senator from his own party when that Senator called the embargo unfair and unworkable. But, now, there's a new Mondale out there, and he seems to have changed his tune. He says that he privately opposed the embargo— very privately. [*Laughter*]

As a matter of fact, he was, in the last several months, or he has in the last several months claimed that he opposed a number of the administration policies when he was Vice President. Well, Jody Powell, who was also in that administration, says—and I quote—"I guess I was out of the room every time it happened." [*Laughter*]

After the Sandinista revolution in Nicaragua, my opponent said the "winds of democratic progress are stirring where they have long been stifled." And that was right before the Sandinistas slaughtered the Miskito Indians, abused and deported church leaders, slandered the Holy Father, and moved to kill freedom of speech.

After the hostages were taken in Iran, my opponent said it would be a temporary problem. Later, he called his administration's handling of the affair masterful.

Audience. Boo-o-o!

The President. Well, more recently, my opponent failed to repudiate the Reverend Jesse Jackson when he went to Havana, stood with Fidel Castro, and cried, "Long live Cuba! Long live Castro! Long live Che Guevara!"

Audience. Boo-o-o!

The President. And my opponent has never disassociated himself from that kind of talk.

I could say of his economic program that he will either "have to break his promises or break the bank." But I won't say it, because Senator John Glenn, Democrat of Ohio, has already said it.

Or I could call his economic program "a collection of old and tired ideas held together by paralyzing commitments to special interests and constituent groups." But Senator Gary Hart of Colorado, a Democrat, has already said that.

Well, I could predict that he will create deficits more than twice what they are now. But Senator Fritz Hollings of South Carolina, a Democrat, has also said that.

Now, if on political issues my opponent dares to be wrong, on domestic policy issues he has the courage to be cautious. A line-item veto to help control wild government spending? No, he says, that's not part of his liberal agenda.

I had that as a Governor of California—

line-item veto, to be able to veto out one of those porkbarrel items that had been smuggled into an otherwise good bill. I used that veto as Governor over 900 times, and it was never overridden once.

He opposed the idea of enterprise zones to help the most troubled neighborhoods in the inner city. But last Sunday night he said he's for them. Well, if he's for them, why didn't he ask Tip O'Neill to stop blocking the enterprise zone bill that he's had buried in the House committee ever since we introduced it?

Last week an American woman walked in space—Kathy Sullivan. Kathryn Sullivan made history, and she returned to a space shuttle in which some of the great scientific and medical advances of the future will be made and are being made. Cures for diabetes and heart disease may be possible up there. Advances in technology and communication. This is a tremendous challenge for us, and especially you young people who will be assuming leadership of our nation.

I don't see how anyone could fail to be supportive of that great achievement, the space shuttle. But my opponent led the fight against it as a horrible waste. When he was a Senator, he was the leader of the fight trying to prevent there from being a shuttle program.

Audience. Boo-o-o!

The President. The truth is, if my opponent's campaign were a television show, it could be named, "Let's Make a Deal." You'd get to trade your prosperity for the surprise behind the curtain. [*Laughter*] If his campaign were a Broadway show, it would be "Promises, Promises." [*Laughter*] And if his administration were a novel, it would only have a happy ending if you read it from the back end first. [*Laughter*]

Now, I've probably been going on too long here.

Audience. No!

The President. I was afraid you'd say that. But the point is, we were right when we made our great turn in 1980. We were right to disenthrall ourselves with the past. We were right when we rejected the old days of tax and tax and spend and spend. We were right to take command of the ship, stop its aimless drift, and get moving again. And we're not going back to the old

leadership and the old ideas that left us in so much trouble.

They can campaign on any issue they like. For us it's enough to say that we're part of a great revolution. It's only just begun, and we will never stop; we will never give up—never.

Audience. Reagan! Reagan! Reagan! 4 more years! 4 more years! 4 more years!

The President. All right.

Audience. 4 more years! 4 more years! 4 more years!

The President. Okay.

Audience. 4 more years! 4 more years! 4 more years!

The President. Listen, our best days are ahead of us. There are new worlds on the horizon. We're not going to stop until we all get there together. And I want to take up something that Governor Big Jim Thompson said up here just a little while ago. Seeing all you young people here in this crowd—seeing all of you is wonderful, but to see you young people especially. I just want to say the reason is that you're what this election and this campaign are all about.

What we're out to do is to restore something that has been missing for too long in this country. When my generation was back where you were, we just took it for granted that America was a place where whatever you wanted to do hard enough and bad enough and whatever you set out to do, you could do. And there was no limit, no penalizing of efficiency or ability in this country. This was the land for everyone. We could have an equal start—but not equal to the finish line—go wherever you could go— your energy and drive take you.

And then we went into a period where some people began telling us that it was an era of limits, that somehow we were never going to be able to go back to living at the same level that we had once before, that things had changed, gone down for all of us.

Well, that just wasn't true. And not only me but the people in those several generations between me and you that are here today—we, all of us, have one dream and one idea, and it's for you. We're determined that when it comes time for you to take over from us, you're going to take over the same kind of an America that we took over from our parents before us. And believe me——

Audience. Reagan! Reagan! Reagan!

The President. Believe me, you're a one-in-a-jillion generation, too. I've seen you from one end of this country to the other. We need your idealism. We need the zest that you have. [*Applause*] Thank you.

Well, I'll be more than proud to be walking for 4 more years with all of you. [*Applause*]

Thank you very much.

Audience. 4 more years!

The President. All right.

Audience. 4 more years! 4 more years! 4 more years!

The President. Thank you all.

Audience. 4 more years! 4 more years! 4 more years!

The President. All right.

Audience. 4 more years!

The President. And, now, God bless all of you. Thank you very much.

Note: The President spoke at 1:07 p.m. at the College of DuPage gymnasium. Prior to the President's remarks, Gov. James R. Thompson, Jr., introduced platform guest 96-year-old Edna Duty, who had registered to vote for the first time in 42 years, specifically to vote for the President's reelection.

Following his remarks, the President returned to Washington, DC.

Proclamation 5260—World Food Day, 1984
October 16, 1984

By the President of the United States of America

A Proclamation

The United States has a long tradition of sharing its rich agricultural abundance and technical expertise with those in need, and of leading the worldwide effort to eliminate hunger. All nations are not equally endowed with food potential, and the struggle against hunger continually presents us with challenges which sometimes appear overwhelming. However, we will not be diverted from our intention to achieve victory over world hunger.

The United States is dedicated to the proposition that real progress in eliminating hunger will be realized when more nations are able to produce or purchase enough food for their own people. It is heartening that the resurging economy of the United States is helping other nations toward new economic expansion, with lower rates of inflation and rising output in many countries.

This Nation—indeed, all nations—should move forward with domestic policies that encourage growth. At the same time we must vigorously resist policies which inhibit growth or discourage free and equitable international trade in food products.

Since the enactment of the Eisenhower Food for Peace Program in 1954, the American people have provided more than $33 billion in food aid to 164 nations. Thousands of technical experts have been sent to Africa, Asia, Latin America, and the Middle East to assist in the development of agricultural projects. We have trained tens of thousands of agriculturalists from developing nations to help them in building a sound economic foundation in their countries.

These efforts by other industrial countries and the United States have yielded promising results. Food production per person has increased 21 percent in the developing countries since 1954. Consumption of calories per capita has increased 7.5 percent since 1963. Unfortunately, Africa's progress in food production or the consumption of calories per capita have not shown equally encouraging results.

This year, the United States supports efforts by the Food and Agriculture Organization of the United Nations to recognize the role of women in agricultural development in the Third World. In some less developed countries, women and children constitute 80 percent or more of the agricultural work force—yet, rarely aided by modern agricultural technology, research or adequate training. We strongly support efforts to improve the efficiency of their agricultural techniques.

In recognition of the need to increase public awareness of world hunger, the Congress, by Senate Joint Resolution 332, has proclaimed October 16, 1984, as "World Food Day" and has authorized and requested the President to issue a proclamation in observance of that day.

Now, Therefore, I, Ronald Reagan, President of the United States of America, do hereby call upon the people of the United States to observe October 16, 1984, as World Food Day with appropriate activities to explore ways in which our Nation can further contribute to the elimination of hunger in the world.

In Witness Whereof, I have hereunto set my hand this sixteenth day of October, in the year of our Lord nineteen hundred and eighty-four, and of the Independence of the United States of America the two hundred and ninth.

RONALD REAGAN

[*Filed with the Office of the Federal Register, 10:45 a.m., October 16, 1984*]

Letter to President José Napoleón Duarte on the Situation in El Salvador
October 16, 1984

Dear President Duarte:

On behalf of all Americans, I wish to congratulate you for the bold step you have taken for peace in El Salvador. Despite great personal risk to yourself and your advisers, you went to La Palma armed only with the support of the Salvadoran people and your fervent desire for peace and democracy.

Your "offer of peace" for the armed left to rejoin El Salvador's political process, together with amnesty and an effort to assist those harmed by the war, is both historic and generous. I share your hope that the Salvadoran people will achieve their heartfelt desire for peace, pluralistic democracy and social justice. You have our hopes and prayers that this courageous initiative is the first step in a process that will bring a lasting peace through democracy to your nation.

Sincerely,

/s/ RONALD REAGAN

Statement on Signing the Federal Timber Contract Payment Modification Act
October 16, 1984

I have today signed into law H.R. 2838, which directs the Secretaries of Agriculture and the Interior to terminate certain contracts for the sale of timber from lands managed by the Forest Service and Bureau of Land Management upon payment of a buyout charge by the purchaser.

The legislation is intended to eliminate a problem that this administration and the Congress have acted upon forthrightly to resolve; namely, the severe economic distress that much of the forest products industry in the Pacific Northwest finds itself in as a result of high timber prices and inflation in 1979–1980. This legislation provides broader relief to purchasers of timber from these Federal lands than those measures already taken by the administration under the authority of existing law. Many holders of these contracts, most of which were bid in the period 1977–1980 and are now held at contract rates significantly higher than the current market, face the unavoidability of defaulting the contracts and perhaps being forced into bankruptcy if they are required to pay damages for the default. It was to avoid serious economic disruption to the industry and the resulting adverse impact to communities dependent upon a strong forest products industry that in July 1983 I authorized administrative relief in the form of 5-year extensions of those contracts with no interest payment requirement. We expected that under this program most purchasers would be able to work

their way out of financial difficulty. We viewed this program as the most equitable form of relief to all purchasers of Federal timber.

It now appears that our successful efforts to control inflation mean that market prices for wood products will not rise enough to prevent severe economic hardship to many forest-dependent communities unless the provisions of this new law are implemented. This legislation requires timber purchasers who will utilize its provisions to pay a charge in return for the relief provided.

Under all the circumstances, the legislation provides a balanced approach to resolving a many-faceted and difficult problem. Thus, I have signed the bill.

Note: As enacted, H.R. 2838 is Public Law 98–478, approved October 16.

Statement by Principal Deputy Press Secretary Speakes on United States-Soviet Relations
October 17, 1984

We agree with President Chernenko that there is no sound alternative to constructive development in relations between our two countries. We are pleased to see the emphasis he puts on positive possibilities for U.S.-Soviet relations. We will be studying his remarks carefully, and as was agreed during Deputy Prime Minister Gromyko's recent meeting with President Reagan, we will be pursuing our dialog with the Soviet Union and exploring the possibilities for progress through diplomatic channels.

President Reagan has repeatedly demonstrated that we are ready for cooperation with the Soviet Union. In April 1981, he sent a handwritten letter to President Brezhnev describing his feelings about the issue of war and peace, and to ask President Brezhnev to join him in removing the obstacles to peace. Since then, the United States has made practical proposals for forward movement in all areas of the relationship, including arms control.

Over the past year, for instance, the

United States and its allies have put forward new proposals for limits on strategic weapons, on intermediate-range nuclear weapons, on chemical weapons, and on conventional forces. On June 4 in Dublin, President Reagan stated our willingness to discuss the Soviet proposal for a mutual non-use-of-force commitment, if this would lead to serious negotiation on the Western proposals for practical steps to enhance confidence and reduce the risk of surprise attack in Europe. This summer we accepted a Soviet proposal to begin space arms control negotiations in Vienna without preconditions. At the United Nations last month President Reagan reiterated his desire to move forward in these fields and put forward a number of concrete new proposals for U.S.-Soviet cooperation. In his subsequent meeting with Deputy Prime Minister Gromyko, the President emphasized our strong desire to move to a more productive dialog across the board and put forward specific suggestions as to how we might do so.

We cannot agree with President Chernenko's version of recent history. It is the Soviet Union which has broken off negotiations on nuclear arms and backed away from its own proposal to begin space arms control talks. The United States stands ready to negotiate on these and other issues, but we cannot concur in the apparent Soviet view that it is incumbent upon the United States to pay a price so that the Soviet Union will come back to the nuclear negotiating table.

President Chernenko has stated that improvements in the U.S.-Soviet relationship depend on deeds, not words. We agree. When the Soviet Union is prepared to move from public exchanges to private negotiations and concrete agreements, they will find us ready.

Note: Larry M. Speakes read the statement to reporters assembled for the daily press briefing in the Briefing Room at the White House, which began at 12:35 p.m.

Remarks at a White House Ceremony Launching the Young Astronaut Program
October 17, 1984

Mike Collins, Jim Beggs, Jack Anderson, the men and women of NASA's astronaut class of 1984, and to you young people and to all of you who have worked so hard to make this ceremony possible, it's a great pleasure to welcome you to the White House. And I've been watching the clouds all day.

We're here today to launch the Young Astronauts Program, as you know, an exciting new project sure to inspire our young people, lift their spirit of adventure, and help prepare them for the challenges and opportunities ahead in space and on the ground.

But first, I want to congratulate the 17 members of NASA's astronaut class of 1984. I'm pleased that you're here today and able to take part in this ceremony. By accepting the challenge of space, you're carrying forward the same courage and spirit of all who have worn the NASA emblem, an emblem recognized the world over as a mark of unmatched professionalism, technology, and achievement.

I'm happy to see David Low here as a member of the class. And, David, we will never forget your father's life-long efforts as NASA Deputy Administrator, manager of the Apollo program, and a leader in planning the shuttle program. And Dr. George Low and the whole NASA team raised our sights and our hopes. And with the enthusiastic support of the American people, we touched the Moon and opportunity and progress.

Last Saturday we watched the perfect touchdown of the 13th shuttle mission. I couldn't help thinking that the *Challenger* crew was the same size as our original astronaut corps. Back then it was the *Mercury 7*, then the *Gemini 9*—all former test pilots and all men—and now, 90 astronauts, women and men, pilots, engineers, and scientists, and soon a teacher and representatives of other countries. And the opportunities will just keep on growing.

A few days ago I saw a cartoon showing two schoolchildren, and one asked the other, "I wonder why the President wants a teacher to be the first passenger on the shuttle?" And the answer was, "Probably to make sure no one has too much fun in outer space." [*Laughter*]

Well, that's not the reason. When the shuttle lifts off, all of America will be reminded of the crucial role teachers and education play in the life of our nation and of the importance of space to our future. I can't think of a better lesson for our children and our country.

Just recently I received a letter from a sixth-grader who lives here in Washington. He said he told his parents that one day he's going to be a pilot or an astronaut. And then he said, "Please accept me in the Young Astronauts Program if you can. This just might be the beginning of my future." Well, Damin, I, too, think this just might be the beginning of your future. Welcome to the program. I'm sure that you and your teachers are going to like it.

NASA, our Office of Private Sector Initiatives, the Department of Education, and the National Space Institute, with help from the National Science Teachers Association and other educational and aerospace groups, have designed an outstanding curriculum. You'll find incentives to pursue science and math and the chance to take part in exciting space-related activities. The end product will be knowledge, our greatest resource for meeting tomorrow's challenges with optimism and success.

And that's the driving force behind the Young Astronauts Program. This private sector program will be directed by the Young Astronauts Council here in Washington, under the leadership of Jack Anderson, Hugh Downs, and Harold Burson. And I want to thank Jack for his help in getting the program started. And I want to thank all of you for your support.

Just as our past achievements in space reassure us of our greatness, the Young Astronauts Program reassures us that we will keep dreaming new dreams and keep moving forward.

Let me say a word now to the young people who are here today. These grounds have seen some very proud moments, welcomed some very important people. But none have been more important than you, because you are America's future. In the years to come, it's going to be up to you to point the way and to keep America moving forward, and I believe you will succeed beyond what we can even imagine.

America's history has not been one of accepting what is, of knowing limits, but of striving and working to build what can be. And there's nothing we can't do if we set our minds to it. There's nothing we can't achieve. And that's the way it's always been in America. From the time that that first covered wagon with the pioneers headed west, to when our astronauts put the first American footprints on the Moon, we've proved that there is no problem so big that it can stop progress.

The sky's not the limit, because the opportunities of space are unlimited. Already, satellites let us communicate with each other at a moment's notice virtually anywhere on the globe. We can anticipate tomorrow's weather and prepare for it. We've used the technology developed for our space program to make our own lives safer and much better, from the computers in your classrooms to the cordless powertools in your Dad's workshop. Thanks to space technology doctors can now use sound waves to monitor babies before they're born, ensuring safer pregnancy and delivery for the mother and better health for the newborn. Firemen now have new lifesaving vests as a result of experiments conducted on the shuttle program. And sick people have new hope, with wonderful advances in medicine.

There's no doubt you're growing up in one of the most exciting times in our history, a time filled with extraordinary opportunity. There's a dazzling new world before us, and you have good reason to look forward to it.

The astronauts with us today work very hard to be ready for the future. And for them, the future is now. They'll guide the shuttle to even greater achievements, and they'll help build our space station. And maybe one day, one of you young astronauts can follow in their footsteps. But you must be ready. And that means mastering science, math, and computers—the wonderful world of high tech.

Someone once said that if you think education is expensive, try ignorance. I would add, if you think getting ready for the future is hard work, try not being ready.

Today we're well into a new era guided by technologies that were unknown just a generation ago. Many doors to discovery and progress are now opening. By choosing the Young Astronauts Program, you'll be able to walk through those doors.

Now, there's one final thought: The shuttle program gives us a glimpse of the incredible possibilities that await us. And they're all the result of commitments we've made over the past 25 years, commitments that we've honored.

Along the way, there've been the Doubting Thomases—there always are—like the shortsighted who never understood and who would have stopped the shuttle program before it ever had a chance. Well, I'd rather remember the wisdom of Carl Sandburg, a poet, who said: "Always the path of American destiny has been into the unknown. Always there arose enough of reserves of strength . . . to carry the nation through to a fresh start with ever-renewing vitality."

We'll rise to the challenge of those words. We won't be held back. We'll keep battling for the future, for new jobs and markets, for discovery, and for knowledge. We have a commitment to keep to our young people, our young astronauts, and we won't let them down.

So, from someone who can remember when they had their first ride in an automobile, thank you all, and God bless you.

Note: The President spoke at 1:38 p.m. on the South Lawn of the White House.

Letter to the Speaker of the House and the Chairman of the Senate Foreign Relations Committee on the Situation in Cyprus
October 17, 1984

Dear Mr. Speaker: (Dear Mr. Chairman:)

In accordance with Public Law 95–384, I am submitting herewith a bimonthly report on progress toward a negotiated settlement of the Cyprus question.

Since my previous report to you, United Nations Secretary General Perez de Cuellar met August 6 and 7 in Vienna with representatives of the two Cypriot communities to launch a new initiative in the search for a settlement to the Cyprus question. Those meetings resulted in the sides agreeing to enter into proximity talks in New York under the Secretary General's auspices. President Kyprianou and Mr. Denktash were in New York from September 10 through 20 for those meetings.

Upon the completion of that first round of proximity talks the parties agreed to return to New York for a second round beginning in mid-October. We understand the talks produced a clearer understanding of the respective positions of the parties and that in the second round the Secretary General will attempt to secure agreement to an outline of general points for eventual direct discussion between the parties.

High-ranking Administration officials have kept in close contact with both Cypriot sides, with United Nations officials, and with other interested parties throughout this period. Ambassador Jeane Kirkpatrick

met with United Nations Secretary General Perez de Cuellar on September 19, and Secretary Shultz saw President Kyprianou, as well as the Foreign Ministers of Greece and Turkey, on September 27. In addition, Special Cyprus Coordinator Richard Haass met September 25 with Mr. Rauf Denktash, leader of the Turkish Cypriot community, following the end of the first round of proximity talks in New York.

At these bilateral meetings we urged the Cypriot parties to use this important series of proximity talks to establish the basis for a fair and final settlement, and we reiterated our support for the Secretary General in his good offices role. I made this clear to the Secretary General when I met him on September 23 as well as in my address to the United Nations General Assembly on September 24 when I stated: "the United States supports the Secretary General's efforts to assist the Cypriot parties in achieving a peaceful and reunited Cyprus."

We have been pleased to see that both Cypriot parties have taken a serious approach to the Secretary General's initiative and have foregone actions that might damage the process. We will continue to strive for an environment conducive to serious discussions between the Cypriot parties and the Secretary General, away from the glare of publicity. We remain convinced that quiet diplomacy and a mutual spirit of compromise represent the best means of eventually achieving a reunited Cyprus in which all Cypriots can live in peace and security.

Sincerely,

RONALD REAGAN

Note: This is the text of identical letters addressed to Thomas P. O'Neill, Jr., Speaker of the House of Representatives, and Charles H. Percy, chairman of the Senate Foreign Relations Committee.

Statement on Signing the Housing and Community Development Technical Amendments Act of 1984
October 17, 1984

I am today signing S. 2819, the Housing and Community Development Technical Amendments Act of 1984. This legislation amends the Housing and Urban-Rural Recovery Act of 1983 to correct certain defects in the Department of Housing and Urban Development's community development block grant and assisted housing programs. It also contains provisions affecting the Department of Agriculture's rural housing programs and miscellaneous amendments to certain banking laws.

In signing this legislation, however, I must express my strong concerns regarding its provisions prohibiting the transfer of rural housing loan authority to other programs administered by the Farmers Home Administration. There have been several instances in recent years in which such a transfer has been used to provide vital and urgent funding to other, equally important sectors of the farm economy. I do not want this legislation to serve as a precedent for obstructing the interchange authority between Farmers Home Administration programs.

Note: As enacted, S. 2819 is Public Law 98–479, approved October 17.

Memorandum Returning Without Approval a Bill To Compensate Indian Tribes for Irrigation Construction Expenditures
October 17, 1984

I am withholding my approval from S. 1967, a bill "To compensate the Gros Ventre and Assiniboine Tribes of the Fort Belknap Indian Community for irrigation construction expenditures."

S. 1967 would reimburse the Gros Ventre and Assiniboine Tribes of the Fort Belknap Indian Community for $107,759.58 in tribal funds expended under applicable law for the construction of irrigation projects on the Fort Belknap Indian Reservation from 1895 to 1913. In addition, interest would be paid at 4 percent from the date of expenditure of the tribal funds until the date of payment of the principal pursuant to the bill.

On November 20, 1962, the Indian Claims Commission, after due deliberation, issued a detailed opinion carefully considering and dismissing (among other claims) a claim for the same reimbursement that would be provided by the bill. Fort Belknap Indian Community v. United States, 11 Ind. Cl. Comm. 479, 510–518, 543–549 (1962). The Commission found that construction of the irrigation system was "requested by the members of the Fort Belknap Community," that it has been of great and continuing benefit to the tribes, and "that its construction and maintenance have been consonant with the fair and honorable dealings clause within the meaning of the Indian Claims Commission Act." 11 Ind. Cl. Comm. 518–519. The tribes took no appeal from that decision.

The fair and impartial administration of justice and the protection of public resources from meritless special appropriations both require that those who have availed themselves of judicial remedies in asserting claims against the United States, and have had their claims fully and fairly adjudicated under our Constitution and laws, receive no more or less than that to which they have been adjudged to be entitled. Twenty-two years after the claims of these two tribes were dismissed by an impartial tribunal established by the Congress specifically to adjudicate such claims, this bill would authorize and appropriate to them all that they were previously found not to be entitled to.

Under the circumstances, the enactment of the bill would set aside established principles of justice and thereby encourage other and future efforts to obtain by legislation that which has been denied by a just adjudication.

For these reasons, I find the bill unacceptable.

RONALD REAGAN

The White House,
October 17, 1984.

Announcement of the Winners of the Presidential Awards for Excellence in Science and Mathematics Teaching
October 17, 1984

The President today announced the selection of 104 secondary school teachers to receive Presidential Awards for Excellence in Science and Mathematics Teaching. The first awards in the program were made in 1983 as a way of acknowledging the contribution of outstanding teachers and to provide models of excellence and encouragement to their colleagues and students.

The awards carry with them $5,000 grants from the National Science Foundation to the teachers' schools for use in science or mathematics instructional programs, and also stimulate additional support from participating private sector organizations. Teachers are selected by a group of professional teaching societies, coordinated by the National Council of Teachers of Mathematics and the National Science Teachers Association.

Note: A list of teachers receiving the awards accompanied the announcement.

Appointment of Ronald L. Alvarado as Special Assistant to the President for Intergovernmental Affairs
October 18, 1984

The President today announced his appointment of Ronald L. Alvarado to be Special Assistant to the President for Intergovernmental Affairs.

Mr. Alvarado has most recently served as chief of staff to Sacramento County Board of Supervisors Chairman Sandra R. Smoley.

In addition to his duties with the Sacramento County Board of Supervisors, Mr. Alvarado was Supervisor Smoley's principal liaison with the National Association of Counties during her tenure as president of that organization.

Mr. Alvarado served as a partner in the

management consulting firm of Patrick Patitucci and Associates from 1978 until 1982 in Sacramento, CA, where he advised local government clients on budget and finance issues. Previously he had been an originating partner of the Bristol Merchant Trading Co. where his responsibilities included international market development.

Mr. Alvarado graduated from Seattle University (B.A., 1972) and the Monterey Institute of Foreign Studies (M.A., 1977). He is single and resides in Washington, DC.

Statement by Principal Deputy Press Secretary Speakes on United States Policy Concerning Political Assassination
October 18, 1984

The United States Government has historically approved support to people and small countries resisting subversion or totalitarian oppression. Where such assistance is required, it is important that such support be consistent with American values and carried out so as to win and increase the loyalty and confidence of the civilian population. The administration has not advocated or condoned political assassination or any other attacks on civilians, nor will we. That is the clear policy of this administration as expressed in the President's Executive Order 12333 of December 4, 1981.

The President today asked the Director of Central Intelligence to direct the CIA Inspector General to investigate the possibility of improper conduct on the part of employees of the Central Intelligence Agency in regard to the publication of a manual for the Nicaraguan democratic resistance forces. This investigation will determine whether there were any violations of law or policy and whether there were any managerial deficiencies. All available information is being gathered, and the Director of Central Intelligence will be prepared to brief the congressional oversight committees promptly on the facts when they are determined.

The President has asked the Intelligence Oversight Board to investigate this matter, as well, and to report its findings directly to him as soon as possible.

Remarks at the Alfred E. Smith Memorial Dinner in New York, New York
October 18, 1984

Thank you very much. I have to catch the shuttle. [*Laughter*]

May it please Your Excellency, Archbishop O'Connor, and members of the reverend clergy, Governor Cuomo, Senators Moynihan and D'Amato, Mayor Koch, and Mr. Toastmaster, Sonny Werblin, and distinguished friends: I thank you for that welcome.

I must say, I have traveled the banquet circuit for many years. I've never quite understood the logistics of dinners like this, and how the absence of one individual could cause three of us to not have seats. [*Laughter*] But that's enough of that. [*Laughter*]

I'm grateful for your invitation and honored to be here. And I can't help but feel that four great Americans are with us here in spirit tonight: Al Smith, of course, the Happy Warrior, whom time and respect and affectionate memory have elevated beyond partisanship; the beloved Francis Cardinal Spellman, whose remarkable works of charity so notably include his establishment of this Al Smith Dinner 38 years ago; the great Jewish philanthropist,

Charles Silver. He was enlisted by Cardinal Spellman as chairman of these dinners and raised millions for hospitals serving all faiths; and finally, Terence Cardinal Cooke, that gentle soul whom I, for one, shall never forget.

All of them are gone now, gone to God— Cardinal Cooke and Charlie Silver within a year's passing, as you've been told. And all of them personify the great command-ment—to love our fellow man.

Here we are, then, at the height of a season marked by differences of opinion, and yet, all this striving and all these con-testing issues fade to insignificance in the clear light of example that these four men set for us, each one in his own unique way: Al Smith, in his lifelong struggles for the working man and woman; Cardinal Spell-man, as a prince and builder of the church; Charles Silver, as a friend and colleague in ecumenical service to humanity; and Cardi-nal Cooke, whom I knew best in circum-stances of dire spiritual need.

Nothing could have meant more to me and to Nancy than Cardinal Cooke's visit with us at the White House while I was recovering from young Mr. Hinckley's un-welcome attentions. His Eminence offered prayers and encouragement that main-tained us in a time of genuine personal need—a need far more serious, I know now, than we or almost anyone at the time real-ized.

And so it was only natural that Nancy and I should have been so profoundly grief-stricken upon learning in August of last year that the Cardinal was dying. Together, we telephoned our dear friend in New York to tell him of our heartfelt prayers for him and to thank him once again for all he had done to comfort and reassure us in our hour of need. Our prayerful concern for the Car-dinal, I assured him, was shared by millions of other Americans grateful for all that he had done on behalf of his country.

His letter of September 15th, which fol-lowed our call, said our prayers, good wishes, and loving concern "are a source of great comfort to me." But then he wrote, "I want you to know that I'm offering my prayers and my suffering for the gift of God's peace among all the members of His human family."

Nancy and I will always be grateful that we were able to visit him in New York and, as it turned out, only days before his death. We were told when we arrived that he had been in great pain for the previous 48 hours, so much so that they'd feared he wouldn't be able to receive us. But when we arrived, he was so much like his old self, it was hard to believe that he was desper-ately ill.

Being Terence Cooke, he couldn't resist doing a little lobbying in behalf of a cause that concerned him: "As a nation known for its compassion," he said, "the United States has accomplished so much through the years in advancing the cause of internation-al justice and peace through its programs of economic assistance to the less fortunate peoples of the world." And then he ac-knowledged the appropriation that I had approved for help to sub-Saharan African nations.

He also talked of my problems, and he said, "When I join the Lord I'll continue to pray for you." He paused, and then, with something of an abashed or self-deprecatory smile, very simply he added, "Maybe I'm being a little presumptuous in assuming I'll be with the Lord." Well, 11 days later he left us, and none of us have any doubt that he joined the Lord.

I have presumed to share this personal experience with you tonight because it says so much about our gentle friend, Terence Cooke. It says much also about Al Smith and Cardinal Spellman and Charlie Silver, for, linked in charity, linked in service, linked in humanity, they are linked by this occasion.

I think it should make us proud to have known these great Americans and their works of love for their fellow man. I think it should make us just a little bit prouder than ever to be Americans.

Archbishop O'Connor, I know that you're profoundly aware of the great tradition in which you now pursue God's work. And in this you have my every good wish and, I know, those also of a grateful nation. And if you wouldn't think that I was invading your field, could I just say, in addition to a heartfelt thank you to all of you, God bless you.

Note: The President spoke at 9:20 p.m. in the Grand Ballroom at the Waldorf-Astoria Hotel. He was introduced by Archbishop John J. O'Connor, Archbishop of New York and president of the Alfred E. Smith Memorial Foundation.

Prior to the dinner, the President attended a reception for dinner guests at the hotel. The President also greeted additional guests in the Empire Room and the Hilton Room before addressing the guests in the Grand Ballroom. Following the dinner, the President returned to Washington, DC.

Proclamation 5262—National Head Injury Awareness Month, 1984
October 18, 1984

By the President of the United States of America

A Proclamation

Head injury is a very serious national health problem. As many as 700,000 Americans are hospitalized every year for head injuries caused by motor vehicle accidents, sporting mishaps, and falls. Of these patients, roughly 100,000 die. Another 50,000—mostly under the age of 30—suffer permanent brain damage that prevents them from returning to schools, jobs, or normal lives.

Each of these grim statistics represents a person whose bright future was suddenly and tragically altered. Added to each victim's suffering is the emotional and financial burden the family must bear. The total cost to the Nation for special care and lost productivity is enormous.

Health care professionals and educators throughout our Nation are helping those with head injuries to live as normally as possible. Through rehabilitation therapy and vocational counseling, many head injury patients are learning to lead productive lives in our society. Such efforts have been promoted by two voluntary health agencies: the National Head Injury Foundation and the Family Survivial Project for Brain-Damaged Adults.

Biomedical research is also the source of increased hope. Investigators supported by the National Institute of Neurological and Communicative Disorders and Stroke are acquiring new information about what happens to the brain as a result of head injury. Leads from these studies will help scientists develop effective treatments to limit or prevent brain damage. With the combined support of voluntary health agencies and the Federal Government, the tragedy of head injury can be substantially reduced.

To encourage public recognition of and compassion for the complex problems caused by head injury, the Congress, by House Joint Resolution 638, has designated the month of October 1984 as "National Head Injury Awareness Month" and has authorized and requested the President to issue a proclamation in observance of this month.

Now, Therefore, I, Ronald Reagan, President of the United States of America, do hereby proclaim the month of October 1984 as National Head Injury Awareness Month. I call upon all government agencies, health organizations, communications media, and people of the United States to observe this month with appropriate ceremonies and activities.

In Witness Whereof, I have hereunto set my hand this eighteenth day of October, in the year of our Lord nineteen hundred and eighty-four, and of the Independence of the United States of America the two hundred and ninth.

RONALD REAGAN

[*Filed with the Office of the Federal Register, 11:09 a.m., October 19, 1984*]

Note: The proclamation was released by the Office of the Press Secretary on October 19.

Proclamation 5263—National Forest Products Week, 1984
October 18, 1984

By the President of the United States of America

A Proclamation

Aside from an industrious and imaginative people, no single natural resource has contributed more to the economic and social growth of this mighty Nation than its forests. Without forests to provide the renewable raw materials for our Nation, American history would have been written quite differently. Without the amazing power of forests to give birth to our great rivers and hold our soil in place, the United States would be much less productive. Without their great diversity as habitat and food source for wildlife, our rich array of fish, birds, and wildlife could not exist. These benefits from our vast forests have made this an abundant land.

The foresight we have shown in wise protection and use of forests ensures that they will continue to contribute to a bright future. Although a third of the United States—some 737 million acres—is forested, such continued abundance was in doubt at the beginning of this century. Forests were disappearing at an alarming rate, and timber famine was predicted. The forest conservation leadership of such people as President Theodore Roosevelt and the Nation's first trained forester, Gifford Pinchot, reversed that trend, leaving a legacy for which present and future generations can be deeply thankful.

The conservation legacy demonstrates that forests can be protected, while also being used for the economic and social benefit of mankind. Wood for our Nation's products is harvested from the vast forests but, like our food crops, new trees must be planted for the next generation. This simple, but critical, principle has proved its enduring worth beyond the dreams of the conservation pioneers. Each year we enjoy an abundance of harvest timber and, as a result, jobs for millions of workers in related industries.

To promote greater awareness and appreciation for the multiple benefits of our forest resources to the United States and world economy, the Congress, by Public Law 86-753 (36 U.S.C. 163), has designated the week beginning on the third Sunday in October as National Forest Products Week.

Now, Therefore, I, Ronald Reagan, President of the United States of America, do hereby proclaim the week beginning October 21, 1984, as National Forest Products Week and request that all Americans express their appreciation for the Nation's forests through suitable activities.

In Witness Whereof, I have hereunto set my hand this eighteenth day of October, in the year of our Lord nineteen hundred and eighty-four, and of the Independence of the United States of America the two hundred and ninth.

RONALD REAGAN

[*Filed with the Office of the Federal Register, 11:10 a.m., October 19, 1984*]

Note: The proclamation was released by the Office of the Press Secretary on October 19.

Proclamation 5264—Lupus Awareness Week, 1984
October 18, 1984

By the President of the United States of America

A Proclamation

Systemic lupus erythematosus (also known as lupus or SLE) is an inflammatory disease of connective tissue, which can produce changes in the structure and function of the skin, joints, and internal organs. Most often found in young women, lupus affects more than 500,000 victims. Ninety percent of these victims are women in the prime of life.

In recent years, the outlook for lupus patients has improved due to extensive and vigorous research. Positive results have emerged from studies uncovering several diverse defects of the immune system and from research on genetic and environmental factors influencing the disease. Studies on estrogen metabolism, data systems development and epidemiology have been fruitful. Evaluations of the course and treatment of the disease and its complications, and studies aimed at developing improved treatment, including new drugs and techniques, are all proving useful.

In order for us to take advantage of the knowledge already gained, public awareness of the characteristics and treatment of lupus—and of the need for continuing scientific research—remains essential. The Federal government and private voluntary organizations have developed a strong and enduring partnership committed to lupus research. I am confident that this concerted effort will ultimately uncover the cause and cure for this devastating disease.

In recognition of the need for greater public awareness of lupus, the Congress, by Senate Joint Resolution 239, has designated the week of October 21 through October 27, 1984, as "Lupus Awareness Week" and authorized and requested the President to issue a proclamation in observance of this week.

Now, Therefore, I, Ronald Reagan, President of the United States of America, do hereby proclaim the week of October 21 through October 27, 1984, as Lupus Awareness Week, and I call upon the people of the United States to observe this week with appropriate ceremonies and activities.

In Witness Whereof, I have hereunto set my hand this eighteenth day of October, in the year of our Lord nineteen hundred and eighty-four, and of the Independence of the United States of America the two hundred and ninth.

RONALD REAGAN

[*Filed with the Office of the Federal Register, 11:11 a.m., October 19, 1984*]

Note: The proclamation was released by the Office of the Press Secretary on October 19.

Proclamation 5265—National Women Veterans Recognition Week, 1984
October 18, 1984

By the President of the United States of America

A Proclamation

I am honored indeed to bring to the Nation's attention the remarkable contributions of women veterans. During World War I, the service of women on active duty as nurses, shipyard personnel, and battlefield telephone operators was indispensable. In World War II, women served in support and operational capacities around the world. Since World War II, women have been fully integrated into the military services. Today there are more than 1.2 million women veterans.

As active participants in America's defense, women serving in the Armed Forces have safeguarded our heritage. Their courage, selflessness, and dedication to duty deserve our deepest gratitude. Let us revere always the memory of those who gave their lives in military service; let us honor anew those who served valiantly on landing beaches, in field hospitals, and in prisoner-of-war camps.

Our laws grant equal rights, privileges, and benefits to women veterans; and my Administration will continue to ensure that women veterans are afforded the benefits and services to which they are entitled. I know that all Americans join me in saluting these patriotic and dedicated women and in expressing the Nation's appreciation for their service.

In order to show our appreciation for the contributions of women veterans, the Congress, by Senate Joint Resolution 227, has designated the week beginning November 11, 1984, as "National Women Veterans Recognition Week" and authorized and requested the President to issue a proclamation in observance of this week.

Now, Therefore, I, Ronald Reagan, President of the United States of America, do hereby proclaim the week beginning November 11, 1984, as National Women Vet-

erans Recognition Week.

In Witness Whereof, I have hereunto set my hand this eighteenth day of October, in the year of our Lord nineteen hundred and eighty-four, and of the Independence of the United States of America the two hundred and ninth.

RONALD REAGAN

[*Filed with the Office of the Federal Register, 12:05 p.m., October 19, 1984*]

Note: The proclamation was released by the Office of the Press Secretary on October 19.

Statement on Signing the 1984 Act To Combat International Terrorism
October 19, 1984

I have today signed into law H.R. 6311, the 1984 Act To Combat International Terrorism. This act will provide resources and authorities essential in countering the insidious threat terrorism poses to those who cherish freedom and democracy. International terrorism is a growing problem for all of us in the Western World—not just the United States. While we in the Western democracies are most often the targets, terrorist attacks are becoming increasingly violent and indiscriminate. Since the first of September, there have been 41 separate terrorist attacks by no fewer than 14 terrorist groups against the citizens and property of 21 nations. Sixteen of these were attacks against individual citizens and 18 of these were bombings or attempted bombings in which innocent third parties were victimized.

This nation bears global responsibilities that demand that we maintain a worldwide presence and not succumb to these cowardly attempts at intimidation. In several important ways, this act will enable us to improve our ability to protect those who serve

our country overseas:

—it authorizes payment of rewards for information concerning terrorist acts; and

—it provides for the authorization of $356 million of urgently needed security enhancements for United States missions abroad.

I am grateful that the Congress has responded swiftly to my request for these authorities and resources. This act is an important step in our multiyear effort to counter the pervasive threat international terrorism poses to our diplomatic personnel and facilities overseas. The act complements other actions now under review and separate measures taken with our allies aimed at significantly improving our ability to thwart this menace to mankind. While none of these steps guarantee that terrorist acts will not occur again, we can be certain that the measures made possible by this act will make such attacks more difficult in the future.

Note: As enacted, H.R. 6311 is Public Law 98–533, approved October 19.

Letter to Bishop Desmond M. Tutu of South Africa on Receiving the Nobel Peace Prize
October 19, 1984

Dear Bishop Tutu:

Please accept my congratulations and those of the American people on being named the 1984 recipient of the Nobel Peace Prize in recognition of your efforts on behalf of peaceful change in South Africa. All Americans join me in recognizing your labors in seeking to promote nonviolent change away from apartheid, toward a form of government based on consent of the governed and toward a society that offers equal rights and opportunities to all its citizens, without regard to race. The United States has heard the appeal for justice voiced by South Africans who suffer under apartheid rule. We continue to urge the South African Government to engage in a meaningful dialogue with all its citizens aimed at accomplishing a peaceful transition away from apartheid. We applaud you in being selected for this honor, and assure you that we share in these goals.

Sincerely,

/s/ RONALD REAGAN

Proclamation 5266—A Time of Remembrance for All Victims of Terrorism Throughout the World
October 19, 1984

By the President of the United States of America

A Proclamation

Terrorism poses an insidious challenge to the principles of freedom cherished by peace-loving peoples everywhere. Despicable acts such as the recent attack on Prime Minister Thatcher in England, the bombings of our Marine Amphibious Unit Headquarters, and of our Embassy facilities in Beirut, Lebanon, represent an attempt to strike at the very heart of Western democratic values. In the month of September, 37 attacks were carried out by 13 different terrorist groups affecting the people of 20 nations.

As a world power, the United States bears global responsibilities from which we must not shrink in the face of cowardly attempts at intimidation. Instead, we must strive to carry forward the heroic legacy of those brave people who, in the search for peace and justice, have lost their lives to international terrorism. Because terrorism poses such a pervasive and insidious threat to all free peoples and claims so many innocent victims in its indiscriminate brutality, we of the Western democracies have embarked on a course of improved cooperation to counter this scourge against humanity. To this end, it is appropriate that we reflect on the tragic loss of life that senseless terror leaves in its wake throughout the world. We do this not out of fear or trepidation, but to show our resolve that the free people of this world will not be deterred from our purpose by threats of terrorism.

The Congress, by Senate Joint Resolution 336, has designated October 23, 1984, as "A Time of Remembrance" for all victims of terrorism throughout the world and has authorized and requested the President to issue a proclamation in observance of this event.

Now, Therefore, I, Ronald Reagan, President of the United States of America, do hereby proclaim October 23, 1984, as a Time of Remembrance for all victims of terrorism throughout the world, and I urge all Americans to take time to reflect on the sacrifices that have been made in the pursuit of peace and freedom.

I further call upon and authorize all departments and agencies of the United States and interested organizations, groups, and individuals to fly United States flags at half-staff on October 23 in the hope that the desire for peace and freedom will take firm root in every person and every nation.

In Witness Whereof, I have hereunto set my hand this nineteenth day of October, in the year of our Lord nineteen hundred and eighty-four, and of the Independence of the United States of America the two hundred and ninth.

RONALD REAGAN

[*Filed with the Office of the Federal Register, 2:32 p.m., October 19, 1984*]

Proclamation 5267—United Nations Day, 1984
October 19, 1984

By the President of the United States of America

A Proclamation

The founding of the United Nations 39 years ago offered new hope that international political, economic, social and technical cooperation could be achieved in a more peaceful world. That hope remains, though we are aware of the difficulties in turning it into reality. The deeply rooted political conflicts that divide nations have at times prevented the proper use of the United Nations for the practical expression of the principles embodied in its Charter. We have been particularly disappointed with some of the actions taken at the United Nations in recent years, actions which fall far short of the high ideals on which that organization was founded.

The United States nonetheless continues to place considerable importance on the United Nations as the body designed to afford all nations opportunities for the peaceful settlement of disputes and for the promotion of technical cooperation in such areas as aviation, shipping, telecommunications, postal services and agriculture. It is the hope of the United States that the UN will live up to its founding principles and create the conditions which will encourage nations to cooperate for the furtherance of their common interests. It is vital that all member nations do their part in pursuit of this goal, that the principle of universality be upheld in UN actions, and that with respect to human rights all states be held to a single standard of justice.

The people and government of the United States feel a close identification with the mission of the United Nations and watch closely what happens there. We take seriously the content of the speeches made in the United Nations, and we take careful note of the votes cast by member countries. We are keenly conscious of the importance of the United Nations to the world community. With the experience gained from the past 39 years, we will work with other member nations to maintain international peace and security, to develop friendly relations among nations based on mutual respect, to find solutions to the problems that divide us, and to promote respect for the human rights of every individual.

Now, Therefore, I, Ronald Reagan, President of the United States of America, do hereby proclaim Wednesday, October 24, 1984, as United Nations Day and urge all Americans to acquaint themselves better with the activities and accomplishments of the United Nations. I have appointed Theodore A. Burtis to serve as 1984 United States Chairman for United Nations Day, and I welcome the role of the United Nations Association of the United States of America in working with him to celebrate this special day.

In Witness Whereof, I have hereunto set my hand this nineteenth day of October, in the year of our Lord nineteen hundred and eighty-four, and of the Independence of the United States of America the two hundred and ninth.

RONALD REAGAN

[*Filed with the Office of the Federal Register, 2:33 p.m., October 19, 1984*]

S–485132   0594(19)(30–DEC–86–13:36:39)   F1240i 02/03/83

Proclamation 5268—Veterans Day, 1984
October 19, 1984

By the President of the United States of America

A Proclamation

The eleventh hour is often used to mean "the last possible time." The First World War was ended on the eleventh hour—as well as the eleventh day in the eleventh month.

If the idealistic hope that World War I was "the war to end all wars" had been realized, November 11 might still be called Armistice Day. But World War II shattered that dream. And after the Korean War, Armistice Day became Veterans Day. Under that name, each November 11, our Nation shows its respect for those who have worn its uniform in defense of freedom.

Veterans Day has become a significant part of our national heritage as we recognize the important contributions of millions of our citizens whose military service has had a profound effect on history. More than 39 million in number, they fought and died from Bunker Hill to Bastogne, from the Marianas to the Mekong Valley in Vietnam. By preserving our freedom, they also made it possible for us to continue our search for a world at peace. That search remains the highest priority of my Administration. It is a debt we owe to the soldiers, sailors, and airmen who put their lives at risk so that their children and grandchildren would never need to know the horrors of war.

Veterans Day offers the Nation an opportunity to show our pride and say "thank you." Furthermore, it provides an important opportunity to rededicate ourselves to Lincoln's call to Congress and the American people "to care for him who shall have borne the battle, and for his widow and his orphan."

Eighty-five percent of the 28 million veterans alive today served during our country's wars. Just as they did not disappoint us in battle, they have not disappointed us in our present search for peace. Their service significantly influences America's role in world affairs, and they all deserve our gratitude.

I believe we should all seek ways to express our collective appreciation for their service and sacrifice. I invite all Americans to join me in observing Veterans Day—through appropriate ceremonies, activities and private thoughts on November 11.

In order that we may pay meaningful tribute to those men and women who proudly served in our Armed Forces, Congress has provided (5 U.S.C. 6103(a)) that November 11 shall be set aside each year as a legal public holiday to honor America's veterans.

Now, Therefore, I, Ronald Reagan, President of the United States of America, do hereby proclaim Sunday, November 11, 1984, as Veterans Day, and I invite all Americans to join with me in paying tribute to those patriots of all generations who have drawn upon their freedom for the will and the courage to fight for their country and the ideals for which it stands.

In Witness Whereof, I have hereunto set my hand this nineteenth day of October, in the year of our Lord nineteen hundred and eighty-four, and of the Independence of the United States of America the two hundred and ninth.

RONALD REAGAN

[Filed with the Office of the Federal Register, 2:34 p.m., October 19, 1984]

Proclamation 5269—Thanksgiving Day, 1984
October 19, 1984

By the President of the United States of America

A Proclamation

As we remember the faith and values that made America great, we should recall that our tradition of Thanksgiving is older than our Nation itself. Indeed, the native American Thanksgivings antedated those of the new Americans. In the words of the eloquent Seneca tradition of the Iroquois, ". . . give it your thought, that with one mind we may now give thanks to Him our Creator."

From the first Pilgrim observance in 1621, to the nine years before and during the American Revolution when the Continental Congress declared days of Fast and Prayer and days of Thanksgiving, we have turned to Almighty God to express our gratitude for the bounty and good fortune we enjoy as individuals and as a nation. America truly has been blessed.

This year we can be especially thankful that real gratitude to God is inscribed, not in proclamations of government, but in the hearts of all our people who come from every race, culture, and creed on the face of the Earth. And as we pause to give thanks for our many gifts, let us be tempered by humility and by compassion for those in need, and let us reaffirm through prayer and action our determination to share our bounty with those less fortunate.

Now, Therefore, I, Ronald Reagan, President of the United States of America, in the spirit and tradition of the Iroquois, the Pilgrims, the Continental Congress, and past Presidents, do hereby proclaim Thursday, November 22, 1984, as a day of National Thanksgiving. I call upon every citizen of this great Nation to gather together in homes and places of worship to celebrate, in the words of 1784, "with grateful hearts . . . the mercies and praises of their all Bountiful Creator. . . ."

In Witness Whereof, I have hereunto set my hand this nineteenth day of October, in the year of our Lord nineteen hundred and eighty-four, and of the Independence of the United States of America the two hundred and ninth.

RONALD REAGAN

[*Filed with the Office of the Federal Register, 2:35 p.m., October 19, 1984*]

Statement on Signing the National Archives and Records Administration Act of 1984
October 19, 1984

I am pleased to sign today S. 905, the National Archives and Records Administration Act of 1984.

This legislation establishes the National Archives and Records Administration—currently part of the General Services Administration—as an independent agency within the executive branch. The agency will be headed by the Archivist of the United States, who will be appointed by the President, with the advice and consent of the Senate.

The principal purpose of S. 905 is to extend independence to an agency that many believe has suffered as a result of its placement within the General Services Administration in 1949. I concur in this assessment, and my administration has supported independence for the Archives.

The public papers and other materials that the Archives safeguards are precious and irreplaceable national treasures, and the agency that looks after the historical records of the Federal Government should be accorded a status that is commensurate with its important responsibilities. Independence for the Archives this year, in which we are commemorating the 50th anniversary of its creation, is a particularly fitting step, both practical and symbolic, in achieving that important goal.

Note: As enacted, S. 905 is Public Law 98–497, approved October 19.

Statement on Signing a Bill Concerning Marine Sanctuaries and Maritime Safety
October 19, 1984

I have today signed S. 1102, which includes the Marine Sanctuaries Amendments of 1984 (Title I), the Maritime Safety Act of 1984 (Title II), and amendments to several other acts. The Maritime Safety Act adopts new safety regulations for vessels subject to its coverage. By adding new requirements to the Marine Protection, Research, and Sanctuaries Act of 1972, the Marine Sanctuaries Amendments set forth specific standards that the Secretary of Commerce must consider when designating a marine sanctuary.

Although I believe many of the amendments made by the Marine Sanctuaries Amendments will improve the procedures for designating marine sanctuaries, I have been advised by the Department of Justice that the method Congress has chosen in this title for preparing proposed regulations governing fishing within the United States Fishery Conservation Zone will raise fundamental constitutional questions unless the act is given a careful narrowing construction. Under the bill, these regulations are to be drafted initially by Regional Fishery Management Councils, which include members chosen by State governments. *See* 16 U.S.C. 1852. When a Council prepares a draft regulation, the Secretary of Commerce is directed to issue it as a proposed regulation "unless [he] finds the Council's action fails to fulfill the purposes and policies of this title and the goals and objectives of the proposed designation." *See* sec. 304(a)(5) of the Marine Protection, Research, and Sanctuaries Act of 1972, as enacted by the bill. The Department of Justice has advised me that the promulgation of regulations by persons, such as Council members, who are not appointed by the President, would violate the appointments clause, Art. II, sec. 2, cl. 2, of the Constitution. *See Buckley* v. *Valeo,* 424 U.S. 1, 126 (1976). For this reason, I am signing this legislation based on my understanding that the Councils will only make recommendations with respect to proposed regulations. It is the Secretary, not the Councils who must make the final decisions on the appropriate final action to be taken in response to recommendations transmitted by the Councils.

I fully support the important environmental goals that this legislation seeks to further. Nevertheless, this valid and worthy objective must be carried out consistent with the appointments clause.

Note: As enacted, S. 1102 is Public Law 98–498, approved October 19.

Statement on Signing the National Organ Transplant Act
October 19, 1984

Today I am signing into law S. 2048, the National Organ Transplant Act. This legislation covers an area in which I have been personally involved: promoting the donation of organs, especially liver transplants for children. I am pleased that the Congress worked with the administration to produce a bill that will enhance this effort.

This bipartisan legislation provides a framework that should help increase the overall supply of much needed organs and improve our ability to match donor organs with individuals in need of transplants. Over the last 3 years, I have urged the American people to remember that many lives could be saved through generous donations of life-saving organs. I have been encouraged by the response of the media and the public to this compassionate cause. This act will serve to support this ongoing work.

A 25-member task force is created by the act to examine and report on a wide range of important issues in the field of organ transplantation. The task force will also report on medical and economic issues related to immunosuppressive drugs, which are used to prevent organ rejection.

Also, the Government will provide support for the establishment of an Organ Procurement and Transplantation Network in the private sector to maintain a national registry that will be used to match available organs with people who need them.

I believe that this act strikes a proper balance between private and public sector efforts to promote organ transplantation, which should encourage families with loved ones who are awaiting a suitable organ. I am pleased to sign the National Organ Transplant Act that will support this humanitarian effort.

Note: As enacted, S. 2048 is Public Law 98–507, approved October 19.

Statement on Signing the Aviation Drug-Trafficking Control Act
October 19, 1984

I welcome the opportunity today to sign into law S. 1146, the Aviation Drug-Trafficking Control Act. This legislation represents an added step in our efforts to combat the illegal flow of drugs into this nation, recognizing and building on the Federal Aviation Administration's critical air safety role without prescribing a law enforcement role.

An individual whose pilot certificate is revoked by the Federal Aviation Administration (FAA) for carrying illegal drugs will now have to wait 5 years, rather than 1, before being able to appeal the denial of a new license by the FAA. For the first time, the FAA will also be able to revoke the registration certificate of an aircraft used in transporting illegal drugs. Other new provisions make it a crime for a person whose certificate has been revoked by the FAA, or who does not hold the proper certificate, to serve as an airman in connection with an aircraft transporting illegal drugs. The new criminal provisions further add to the possible sanctions against smuggling drugs by air, making the risks that much greater.

These provisions will not only provide an important deterrent to carrying illegal drugs by air but will also contribute to safer skies, since those who transport drugs by air typically show little regard for the safety of others whether in the air or on the ground.

Note: As enacted, S. 1146 is Public Law 98–499, approved October 19.

Statement on Signing a Bill Relating to Water Rights of the Ak-Chin Indians
October 19, 1984

I have signed today H.R. 6206, which reconfirms our commitment to the policy of Indian tribal self-determination and does so in a fiscally responsible manner.

Two years ago I announced a policy to pursue vigorously negotiations to settle outstanding Indian water rights. I am especially pleased to sign the Ak-Chin community water settlement, H.R. 6206, because it demonstrates the success of that approach.

H.R. 6206 ratifies a series of agreements negotiated by officials of the Department of the Interior with the affected parties over the past 2 years. It settles the outstanding water claims of the Ak-Chin Indian community, provides a permanent water supply to be delivered through the Central Arizona Project facilities, provides funds for water conservation, and provides that water not needed to satisfy the Ak-Chin entitlement will be available for allocation to other water users in central Arizona.

In 1978 the Congress and the previous administration enacted an Ak-Chin water settlement act which required the Federal Government to provide an interim supply of water beginning in 1984 and permanent water no later than 2003. H.R. 6206 more clearly fulfills the intent of the earlier act by providing a permanent water supply beginning in 1988 at less than half the cost of the previous temporary plan.

The Ak-Chin settlement embodies three policies of this administration: first, that Indian tribal governments can and should decide what is best for their people; second, that the complex issue of Indian water rights is better handled through negotiation rather than litigation; third, that we will fulfill our commitments in a fiscally responsible fashion. H.R. 6206 exemplifies how all parties can benefit from a negotiated settlement.

Finally, I would like to congratulate those people whose hard work and dedication to this process contributed greatly to the final enactment of this legislation. They include Senator Barry Goldwater, Congressmen Morris Udall and John McCain, the leadership of the Ak-Chin community, and Interior Secretary William Clark.

Note. As enacted, H.R. 6206 is Public Law 98–530, approved October 19.

Statement on Signing Amendments to the Bankruptcy Amendments and Federal Judgeship Act of 1984
October 19, 1984

I am pleased to sign today H.R. 6216, an act to amend the Bankruptcy Amendments and Federal Judgeship Act of 1984 to make technical corrections with respect to the retirement of certain bankruptcy judges. This legislation will allow all of the bankruptcy judges who otherwise are eligible to retire to receive the enhanced retirement benefits promised in the Bankruptcy Reform Act of 1978. These men and women continued to serve the Nation's bankruptcy system throughout the 2-year crisis between the Supreme Court's decision invalidating the bankruptcy courts' jurisdiction and the enactment of legislation creating a new, constitutional bankruptcy court structure.

When I signed that bankruptcy court legislation this past summer, however, I noted particular objection to two provisions that sought to continue the bankruptcy judges in office after Congress had allowed their terms to lapse. It is inconsistent with the Constitution for the Congress to make such appointments, and I urged that the Congress immediately repeal those provisions.

In this act, which provides retirement benefits for the bankruptcy judges, the Congress failed to address this continuing constitutional concern. Therefore, although I am approving H.R. 6216, I must express my disappointment that the Congress has left in place the one remaining uncertainty surrounding the operation of the new bankruptcy court system.

Note: As enacted, H.R. 6216 is Public Law 98–531, approved October 19.

Statement on Signing the Education Amendments of 1984
October 19, 1984

I am today signing S. 2496, the Education Amendments of 1984, which extends various education programs assisting groups such as students with limited English proficiency, Indian students, women, and adults in need of acquiring basic literacy skills.

My administration is committed to helping assure that educational opportunities are available to these groups and proposed to the Congress legislation to continue the Adult Education Act, the Bilingual Education Act, and the Indian Education Act. S. 2496 does reauthorize these laws.

I am especially pleased that the amendments to the Bilingual Education Act allow some flexibility for local school districts to use Federal funds for the many proven alternatives to the traditional methods in bilingual education that they believe are better suited to helping their limited English speaking students learn English. In the future I hope to work with the Congress to further expand this much needed flexibility.

I must note that this bill contains some undesirable provisions affecting the Department of the Interior's management responsibilities for education programs in the Bureau of Indian Affairs. These provisions would establish cumbersome and inflexible administrative procedures, initiate wasteful and duplicative practices, allow the Federal Government to intrude needlessly into tribal government processes, and undermine the management authority of the Secretary of the Interior. They are contrary to sound management principles and would not promote the delivery of quality education to Indian children. Fortunately, their implementation is being delayed by the Bureau of Indian Affairs 1985 appropriations language, and we will therefore have an opportunity to seek corrective amendments next year.

I greatly regret the bill would also revive, for 4 more years, Impact Aid "b" payments to school districts for children whose parents either work or live on Federal property, reversing the decision by the Congress in 1981 to end such payments after 1984. These children impose virtually no financial burden on most local school districts; yet the potential cost of the payments for them over the next 4 years would be nearly $2 billion. The congressional decision in 1981 to discontinue these payments was correct and should stand. If item veto authority were available to me, I would eliminate this portion of the bill. On the whole, however, I have determined that the bill's positive aspects warrant my approval.

Note: As enacted, S. 2496 is Public Law 98–511, approved October 19.

Statement on Signing the Department of Defense Authorization Act, 1985
October 19, 1984

The Department of Defense Authorization Act, 1985, that I am signing today, H.R. 5167, continues our previous efforts to rebuild America's defenses. Although the funding is substantially below my original request and even below my request submitted as part of our deficit reduction package last May, it is the most we could expect from the 98th Congress. And it allows us to continue our efforts, at a reduced pace, to preserve the peace and guarantee our freedom.

I am pleased that the major elements of our program continue to receive bipartisan congressional support. Our strategic deterrent posture is being strengthened, and the B–1B and ICBM modernization programs are right on schedule. Congress has provided the funds necessary to enable the Peacekeeper to become operational within 2 years, and we are working hard on a new small missile. This program is important to our national security and to the achievement of real arms control, and I am confident that the Congress will keep the program on track.

Since the dawn of the nuclear age, we have sought to reduce the risk of war by maintaining a strong deterrent and by seeking genuine arms control. Our dialog with the Soviets on arms control will also continue. We remain ready to reduce nuclear arms, ready to negotiate a fair deal, and ready to meet the Soviet Union halfway. With continued support from the American people and bipartisan support from the Congress, I am confident that we will see progress.

This bill also continues our efforts to improve the basic readiness and staying power of our conventional forces. Our men and women in uniform at last are getting the modern equipment and training they need to do their jobs. The job of rebuilding is not yet finished, but we have made a lot of progress in the past 3 years, and today our military forces are better equipped, better trained, and better led than ever before.

I am also pleased that this bill provides our service men and women a fair and honorable wage. Once again, young Americans wear their uniforms and serve their flag with pride. We must not return to the days when our military people suffered low morale and when they had to wonder from day to day if they could make ends meet. And the administration is committed to the supplemental funding necessary to carry out the education program contained in this bill.

The act establishes the United States Institute of Peace. I have been advised by the Attorney General that section 1706(f), relating to the President's power to remove members of the Board of Directors of the Institute, is neither intended to, nor has the effect of, restricting the President's constitutional power to remove those officers.

Much credit for passage of this bill goes to the congressional leadership. Howard Baker worked closely with Tip O'Neill on the broad outlines of the compromise, and leaders like Mel Price, Sam Nunn, and Bill Dickinson accomplished the tough bargaining to achieve the final result.

But as much as these fine legislators contributed to this bill and our security, there is one Senator whose contribution to our nation's defense over the years has been unique and enduring—that Senator is John Tower. The final passage of this Defense Authorization Act marks one of the last milestones in a legislative career spanning nearly 24 years in the Senate. His lasting contributions, and especially those during his outstanding service as chairman of the Committee on Armed Services, bear the mark of a true statesman and an extraordinary American. We can only hope that he will not consider his retirement from the Senate to be a retirement from public life. Thank you, John.

Note: As enacted, H.R. 5167 is Public Law 98–525, approved October 19.

Statement on Signing the Veterans' Health Care Act of 1984
October 19, 1984

I have signed H.R. 5618, the Veterans' Health Care Act of 1984. In signing the act, I must note my concern over sec. 101, which amends present law with respect to law enforcement powers of Veterans Administration personnel. This authority involves the most potentially intrusive of all government power, yet its utilization is critical to the preservation of ordered liberty. A responsible government must assure that it is granted cautiously and monitored closely. It is important that the Attorney General, as the Nation's chief law enforcement officer, play a key role in the coordination and use of such authority. Accordingly, I am instructing the Administrator of the Veterans Administration to coordinate and consult closely with the Attorney General on all aspects regarding law enforcement in this legislation, including any regulations promulgated thereunder.

I also note my concern over sec. 301, which will modify a reverter interest of the United States on some 35 acres of land in Los Angeles. In 1948, this land was transferred to UCLA on condition that UCLA would use the land for medical and research purposes only. This restriction was imposed because the property was originally part of a Veterans Hospital. Now, this section will direct the Veterans Administration to broaden the terms of the reverter. The value of the taxpayers' interest in this property has been placed at $100 million. I am concerned that this provision ignores both the justification for the original transfer in 1948 and the taxpayers' interest. This underscores the need for a better appreciation that Federal real property is an asset that deserves management in the interest of the taxpayer.

Note: As enacted, H.R. 5618 is Public Law 98–528, approved October 19.

Memorandum Returning Without Approval the Armed Career Criminal Act of 1984
October 19, 1984

I am withholding my approval from H.R. 6248, the "Armed Career Criminal Act of 1984."

This legislation would generally enhance the penalties under existing law applicable to a felon who has been convicted three times in a United States or State court of robbery or burglary and who receives, possesses, or transports firearms.

Although I certainly support the aims of H.R. 6248, I note that identical provisions were contained in the Administration's "Comprehensive Crime Control Act," which I approved on October 12, 1984, as part of P.L. 98–473. That legislation—marking the culmination of much hard work and effort on the part of members of my Administration and the Congress—is the most comprehensive revision of Federal criminal statutes to be enacted in many years.

Inasmuch as H.R. 6248 merely duplicates existing law, it is unnecessary. Accordingly, I decline to approve it.

RONALD REAGAN

The White House,
October 19, 1984.

Memorandum Returning Without Approval the National Oceanic and Atmospheric Administration's Atmospheric Oceanic Research and Services Act of 1984
October 19, 1984

I have withheld my approval from S. 1097, the "National Oceanic and Atmospheric Administration's Atmospheric and Oceanic Research and Services Act of 1984." S. 1097 would, among other things, authorize appropriations for various National Oceanic and Atmospheric Administration (NOAA) programs for fiscal year 1985, for which appropriations have already been enacted.

S. 1097 also contains, however, a number of undesirable provisions that would unduly effect the ability of the Department of Commerce to manage its programs responsibly and effectively. The provisions in title VI concerning the closings and consolidations of National Weather Service offices are particularly onerous and would have the effect of virtually precluding the consolidation or closing of such offices, even when such closings or consolidations are fully justified.

In addition, S. 1097 contains other highly objectionable provisions concerning the Department's activities. Section 205 of S. 1097 would result in excessive and unjustifiable delays in Department contracting-out activities, even when such contracting would be in the clear interest of the Nation's taxpayers. And, Section 202(b), which concerns the weather satellite program, is objectionable because it would lessen the Secretary of Commerce's discretion in managing that program, as well as require the inefficient use of a government asset.

This Act represents an unwarranted intrusion by Congress into matters normally and properly within the management discretion of the Executive branch. In the interest of efficient and economical conduct of government activities, therefore, I am constrained to withhold my approval of S. 1097.

RONALD REAGAN

The White House,
October 19, 1984.

Memorandum Returning Without Approval the Indian Health Care Amendments of 1984
October 19, 1984

I am withholding my approval of S. 2166, the "Indian Health Care Amendments of 1984," which would extend and amend the Indian Health Care Improvement Act.

Although I fully support the intent and objectives of the Indian Health Care Improvement Act, I believe this bill is seriously deficient in fulfilling those goals. My disapproval of the bill will in no way affect the continued delivery of health care services to our country's Indian population. Earlier this month I signed the Continuing Resolution Appropriations Act for fiscal year 1985, which includes $855 million for the Indian Health Service, an increase of $30 million over the prior year.

A number of serious flaws in S. 2166 compel my disapproval of this bill. Two provisions are especially troublesome.

First, a provision that I find totally unacceptable would actually reduce access to health services for Indians. That provision would have the effect of making Indians residing in Montana ineligible for certain benefits of State and locally supported health programs until and unless the availability of such benefits from the Indian Health Service has been exhausted. In my view, this provision for Indian citizens of Montana would set a precedent for potentially changing the fundamental relationship of the Indian Health Service to State and local entities, as well as depriving eligible Indians of benefits that should be due them by virtue of their citizenship in the State. As a matter of both principle and precedent, I cannot accept this provision.

Second, the mechanism established in section 602(d) of the bill for effecting the removal of the Indian Health Service from the Health Resources and Services Administration (HRSA) is unconstitutional and can have no legal effect. The Department of Justice has advised me that the Congress may not constitutionally delegate to a congressionally appointed body, such as the Commission on the Organizational Placement of the Indian Health Service established by this bill, the legislative authority to determine when legislation will take effect. Because section 602(d) does not comply with the clear requirements of the Constitution, I cannot give my approval to this bill.

Other serious flaws in S. 2166 that compel my disapproval would:

—duplicate existing authorities in most of its provisions;

—unnecessarily and wastefully change the organization of the Indian Health Service; and

—place increased emphasis on services that are not oriented toward the primary mission of the Indian Health Service.

The bill would allocate a significant portion of funding for various peripheral projects, such as unnecessary reports, interagency agreements, and regulations development. This would lead either to an unacceptable increase in total funding or to underfunding of the most critical area—provision of clinical health services to reservation Indians. The Administration has, on the other hand, proposed using most Indian health funds for this purpose, so that resources can be most effectively spent where

the need is the greatest.

For all these reasons, I find S. 2166 unacceptable.

As I indicated earlier, the action I am taking will have no adverse impact on the delivery of health services to Indians living on or near a reservation because the existing provisions of the Snyder Act provide all necessary authority for such services. Since 1955, utilizing the Snyder Act authorities:

—30 hospitals have been constructed;

—30 clinics and 58 field health stations have been constructed;

—Annual admissions to Indian Health Service and contract hospitals have more than doubled; outpatient visits have multiplied by approximately eight times; and the number of dental services provided has increased ten-fold.

Even more important are the achievements in terms of improved health status, which is, after all, the goal of the Indian Health Service;

—The infant mortality rate has decreased by 77 percent and the maternal death rate by 86 percent;

—The death rate resulting from pneumonia and influenza has decreased by 73 percent; and

—Death from tuberculosis has been reduced by 94 percent and the incidence of new active tuberculosis has been reduced by 84 percent.

Over the last decade, the Federal Government has supported the Indian Health Service with over $5 billion. The last budget that I submitted to the Congress projected spending an additional $4 billion through 1989.

My Administration's commitment to ensuring the continuing improvement of health services delivery to Indian people and Alaska natives is strong and clear.

RONALD REAGAN

The White House,
October 19, 1984.

Memorandum Returning Without Approval the Public Broadcasting Amendments Act of 1984
October 19, 1984

I have withheld my approval from S. 607, the "Public Broadcasting Amendments Act of 1984."

This bill would authorize appropriations of $200 million, $225 million, and $250 million, respectively, for fiscal years 1987, 1988, and 1989 for the Corporation for Public Broadcasting. It would also authorize appropriations of $25 million, $35 million, and $40 million for the Public Telecommunications Facilities Program administered by the Department of Commerce for fiscal years 1985, 1986, and 1987.

Public broadcasting has an important role to play in assuring that a wide variety of information and entertainment choices are made available to American viewers and listeners. Under S. 607, however, the authorizations for Federal subsidies to public broadcasting would increase dramatically. When all of the demands on the Federal budget are taken into account, I cannot endorse the levels of spending on public broadcasting contemplated by this legislation. They are incompatible with the clear and urgent need to reduce Federal spending.

It is important to note that current-year funding for these two programs totals only $174 million. The Oxley amendment would have resulted in a generous and barely affordable increase of 15 percent, to $200 million. S. 607 goes much further and raises first-year funding by 29 percent to $225 million for the two programs. By the third year under S. 607, combined funding would be $290 million, a 67 percent increase from the current budget year. Under present fiscal conditions, unrestrained increases of this magnitude—no matter how worthy the programs—are unacceptable.

Legislation that provides for Federal support of public broadcasting at realistic and reasonable levels and that provides public broadcasters with the means and incentives to explore alternative revenue sources would be both appropriate and welcome. If, however, we are to succeed in reducing Federal spending—as we must—the levels of spending contemplated by S. 607 cannot be justified.

In withholding my approval of S. 607, I want to emphasize that the continued operations of the Corporation for Public Broadcasting are not at risk. Funds for the Corporation have already been appropriated for 1985 and 1986, and funds for 1987 are contained in H.R. 6028, the Labor-Health and Human Services-Education 1985 appropriations bill, which recently passed both Houses of Congress.

I vetoed an earlier version of this legislation on August 29, 1984, for precisely the same reasons that I am withholding my approval of S. 607. I will continue to oppose and reject bills of this nature until and unless Congress presents me with a bill that is consistent with sound budget policy. This one is certainly not, and I decline to approve it.

RONALD REAGAN

The White House,
October 19, 1984.

Radio Address to the Nation on Foreign Policy
October 20, 1984

My fellow Americans:

Tomorrow, my opponent and I will debate foreign policy in Kansas City, so I'd like to talk to you about the foreign policy choices for our future as I see it.

In speaking about his economic policies, I've said my opponent is a man of the past whose administration's domestic policies failed and made America weak. Well, that goes for foreign policy as well. Mr. Mondale as a Senator, later as understudy to Jimmy Carter, and still today has seemed possessed with one simple but very wrong idea: American strength is a threat to world peace. And he's devoted a political career to opposing our strength, exposing us to dangerous, unnecessary risks.

As a Senator, he voted time and again against American strength, against techno- logical advances meant to better protect our security. He voted against the cruise missile, the B–1 bomber, the Trident sub- marine, and against salary increases for the military. Yes, he did vote for certain things. He voted for cutting U.S. troops in Europe, for cutting our military manpower, and for cutting our defense budgets.

How could a politician even face the young people who protect our freedom after he's voted to deny them the equip- ment and protection they need? My oppo- nent's Senate voting record on defense was so weak, he ranked right next to George McGovern.

The Carter-Mondale administration echoed this defeatist spirit. By the late 1970's, the policies of unilateral concession were giving the Soviet Union military ad- vantages over the United States and the West. The Soviets installed missiles that cre- ated new vulnerabilities in Europe and put new strains on the NATO alliance. During those years, the Soviet Union expanded its influence in Africa, Asia, the Middle East, and here in our own hemisphere. They overturned or took control of a new coun- try every year.

Meanwhile, the Carter-Mondale adminis- tration negotiated an arms agreement so weak they couldn't get it approved in a Senate controlled by their own party. My opponent talks about the Carter-Mondale years as a period of relaxed tension. Well, it's true they relaxed—but the Soviets didn't.

What troubles me most is how little he seems to have learned about the dangers of weakness and naive thinking. I don't ques- tion his patriotism; I do question his judg- ment. In 1968 he said that the days of Soviet suppression by force were over.

Then, the Soviets invaded Czechoslovakia. But he didn't learn. He voted against Amer- ican military strength during the 1970's, even as the Soviets were embarking upon the most massive military buildup in histo- ry.

After the Soviets invaded Afghanistan in 1979, Mr. Mondale still hadn't learned. He said, "I cannot understand. It just baffles me why the Soviets these last few years have behaved as they have. And why do they have to build up all those arms?" Well, today he still advocates unilateral cuts in important weapons systems, still argues for a freeze, which his own runningmate admits is not fully verifiable and Mr. Carter's former national security adviser de- scribes as a hoax.

Senator Glenn, a Democrat, has warned that "Walter Mondale's defense policies would emasculate America." Senator Hol- lings, a Democrat, said, "Walter Mondale thinks the Soviet Union would never violate an arms agreement. I think he's naive."

Well, to borrow Mr. Mondale's expression, he seems baffled by so much. He was con- fused about the rightness of freeing our stu- dents on the island of Grenada. He said that liberation took away our moral authority to criticize the Soviets about Afghanistan. Yet he could not bring himself to repudiate the Reverend Jesse Jackson after he had trav- eled to Cuba and said, "Long live Cuba! Long live Castro! Long live Che Guevara!"

Well, in the past 3½ years, our adminis- tration has demonstrated the true relation- ship between strength and confidence and democracy and peace. We've restored our economy and begun to restore our military strength. This is the true foundation for a future that is more peaceful and free.

We've made America and our alliances stronger and the world safer. We've dis- couraged Soviet expansion by helping coun- tries help themselves, and new democracies have emerged in El Salvador, Honduras, Grenada, Panama, and Argentina. We have maintained peace and begun a new dialog with the Soviets. We're ready to go back to the table to discuss arms control and other problems with the Soviet leaders.

Today we can talk and negotiate in confidence because we can negotiate from strength. Only my opponent thinks America can build a more peaceful future on the weakness of a failed past.

Until next week, thanks for listening, and God bless you.

Note: The President spoke at 12:06 p.m. from the Oval Office at the White House.

Remarks at a Reagan-Bush Rally in Kansas City, Missouri
October 21, 1984

The President. Thank you.

Audience. 4 more years! 4 more years! 4 more years!

The President. Thank you very much. Well, I wasn't going to, but you talked me into it.

Thank you all very much. It was good this afternoon to be able to say, "I'm going to Kansas City; Kansas City here I come."

The evening's festivities will soon begin, and I look forward to this debate. I relish the chance to talk about what divides our view of the world from my opponent's. We do see the world differently. He represents a school of thought that sees things in terms of limits and endless accommodation. He loves big government and trusts it more than he trusts the people. In his America, America is the victim, flinching under the blows of history. Well, that's his vision, and we'll leave him to it.

Audience. 4 more years! 4 more years! 4 more years!

The President. Thank you. All right. He has in his background some statements that he's made, showing his attitude with regard to the people, but we stand for the America of the people. And we have an honest faith in individuals. Our bias is toward the people and away from government. And we believe in encouraging growth and allowing the American people to unleash their daring.

We see an America of pride and power: powerful at home, powerful in the councils of the world, powerful in our ability to maintain the peace. Almost 4 years after we took office, our country is strong again.

Audience. U.S.A.! U.S.A.! U.S.A.!

The President. Yes, yes—our aircraft fly again, and our ships can leave port. We stand for something. And this is good for the world, it's good for the people, and it's good for the prospects of peace.

Now, my opponent says that he cares about arms control, and I share his concern. I share his concern, but what he may not know is that you can't treat an adversary like a special interest group. And you can't just give them everything they want, get a kiss, and call it peace. You have to be strong if you are to successfully negotiate mutually beneficial agreements.

Now, my opponent says he cares about freedom, and I believe him. But then, he should be rejoicing that under our administration, not one square inch of soil has fallen to the Communist control in these 4 years.

Audience. U.S.A.! U.S.A.! U.S.A.!

The President. All right. In fact, one nation, Grenada, was actually liberated from a band of Communist thugs. You know that exactly 1 year ago tonight, I directed our Armed Forces to proceed with planning to send our troops into Grenada. And they had 48 hours to put the plan together, and you know the result. I think that we are really ready. And so, we can celebrate tonight as—well, an evening for a celebration of freedom.

My opponent, in his hunger to succeed this evening, may try to deny some of the positions that he's long held on various questions. Well, he can change the tune, but he can't change the lyrics. As a matter of fact, we remember the whole record and may hum a few bars later on.

The American people believe in freedom and in the strength it takes to protect it. And so, we go to our work this evening knowing that all is not perfect in the world, but after almost 4 years of new leadership, much has improved.

Audience. 4 more years! 4 more years! 4 more years!

The President. Well, we don't claim to have remade the world, but we've made it better and safer—and safer than the world the Carter-Mondale administration left us. We have put America back on the map.

I'm going to do something I hadn't planned. I haven't told this story for a long time, but I want to. First of all, I want you to realize that our men and women in uniform—and God bless them, I think they're the best we've ever had—these young people, they are the peacekeepers. That's their mission—to keep peace, not to make war.

But I have to tell you about this one young fellow. He's over with our forces on the East German frontier in Europe. And one of our Ambassadors went up there on a trip visiting the troops and all. And as he

went back to his helicopter, this young trooper, 19 years old, followed him. And when he got there, the young trooper asked the Ambassador if he thought he could get a message to me. Well, the Ambassador allowed as how he could. That's what he's there for. [*Laughter*] But the young fellow then said—drew himself up and said, "Mr. Ambassador, will you tell the President we're proud to be here and we ain't scared of nothin'."

Audience. U.S.A.! U.S.A.! U.S.A.!

The President. U.S.A. forever, yes!

Thank you all. Thank you all for being here, and God bless you all. And I guess now I've got to go to work.

Note: The President spoke at 6:22 p.m. in the ballroom at the Westin Crown Center Hotel.

Debate Between the President and Former Vice President Walter F. Mondale in Kansas City, Missouri

October 21, 1984

Ms. Ridings. Good evening from the Municipal Auditorium in Kansas City. I am Dorothy Ridings, the president of the League of Women Voters, the sponsor of this final Presidential debate of the 1984 campaign between Republican Ronald Reagan and Democrat Walter Mondale.

Our panelists for tonight's debate on defense and foreign policy issues are Georgie Anne Geyer, syndicated columnist for Universal Press Syndicate; Marvin Kalb, chief diplomatic correspondent for NBC News; Morton Kondracke, executive editor of the New Republic magazine; and Henry Trewhitt, diplomatic correspondent for the Baltimore Sun. Edwin Newman, formerly of NBC News and now a syndicated columnist for King Features, is our moderator.

Ed.

Mr. Newman. Dorothy Ridings, thank you. A brief word about our procedure tonight. The first question will go to Mr. Mondale. He'll have 2½ minutes to reply. Then the panel member who put the question will ask a followup. The answer to that will

be limited to 1 minute. After that, the same question will be put to President Reagan. Again, there will be a followup. And then each man will have 1 minute for rebuttal. The second question will go to President Reagan first. After that, the alternating will continue. At the end there will be 4-minute summations, with President Reagan going last.

We have asked the questioners to be brief. Let's begin. Ms. Geyer, your question to Mr. Mondale.

Central America

Ms. Geyer. Mr. Mondale, two related questions on the crucial issue of Central America. You and the Democratic Party have said that the only policy toward the horrendous civil wars in Central America should be on the economic development and negotiations, with perhaps a quarantine of Marxist Nicaragua. Do you believe that these answers would in any way solve the bitter conflicts there? Do you really believe that there is no need to resort to force at all? Are not the solutions to Central America's gnawing problems simply, again, too weak and too late?

Mr. Mondale. I believe that the question oversimplifies the difficulties of what we must do in Central America. Our objectives ought to be to strengthen the democracies, to stop Communist and other extremist influences, and stabilize the community in that area. To do that we need a three-pronged attack: one is military assistance to our friends who are being pressured; secondly, a strong and sophisticated economic aid program and human rights program that offers a better life and a sharper alternative to the alternative offered by the totalitarians who oppose us; and finally, a strong diplomatic effort that pursues the possibilities of peace in the area.

That's one of the big disagreements that we have with the President—that they have not pursued the diplomatic opportunities either within El Salvador or as between the countries and have lost time during which we might have been able to achieve a peace

This brings up the whole question of what Presidential leadership is all about. I think the lesson in Central America, this recent embarrassment in Nicaragua where we are giving instructions for hired assassins, hiring criminals, and the rest—all of this has strengthened our opponents.

A President must not only assure that we're tough, but we must also be wise and smart in the exercise of that power. We saw the same thing in Lebanon, where we spent a good deal of America's assets. But because the leadership of this government did not pursue wise policies, we have been humiliated, and our opponents are stronger.

The bottom line of national strength is that the President must be in command, he must lead. And when a President doesn't know that submarine missiles are recallable, says that 70 percent of our strategic forces are conventional, discovers 3 years into his administration that our arms control efforts have failed because he didn't know that most Soviet missiles were on land—these are things a President must know to command.

A President is called the Commander in Chief. And he's called that because he's

supposed to be in charge of the facts and run our government and strengthen our nation.

Ms. Geyer. Mr. Mondale, if I could broaden the question just a little bit: Since World War II, every conflict that we as Americans have been involved with has been in nonconventional or irregular terms. And yet, we keep fighting in conventional or traditional military terms.

The Central American wars are very much in the same pattern as China, as Lebanon, as Iran, as Cuba, in their early days. Do you see any possibility that we are going to realize the change in warfare in our time, or react to it in those terms?

Mr. Mondale. We absolutely must, which is why I responded to your first question the way I did. It's much more complex. You must understand the region; you must understand the politics in the area; you must provide a strong alternative; and you must show strength—and all at the same time.

That's why I object to the covert action in Nicaragua. That's a classic example of a strategy that's embarrassed us, strengthened our opposition, and undermined the moral authority of our people and our country in the region. Strength requires knowledge, command. We've seen in the Nicaraguan example a policy that has actually hurt us, strengthened our opposition, and undermined the moral authority of our country in that region.

Ms. Geyer. Mr. President, in the last few months it has seemed more and more that your policies in Central America were beginning to work. Yet, just at this moment, we are confronted with the extraordinary story of a CIA guerrilla manual for the anti-Sandinista *contras* whom we are backing, which advocates not only assassinations of Sandinistas but the hiring of criminals to assassinate the guerrillas we are supporting in order to create martyrs. Is this not, in effect, our own state-supported terrorism?

The President. No, but I'm glad you asked that question, because I know it's on many peoples' minds. I have ordered an investigation. I know that the CIA is already going forward with one. We have a gentleman down in Nicaragua who is on contract to the CIA, advising—supposedly on military tactics—the *contras*. And he drew up this manual. It was turned over to the agency head of the CIA in Nicaragua to be printed. And a number of pages were excised by that agency head there, the man in charge, and he sent it on up here to CIA, where more pages were excised before it was printed. But some way or other, there were 12 of the original copies that got out down there and were not submitted for this printing process by the CIA.

Now, those are the details as we have them. And as soon as we have an investigation and find out where any blame lies for the few that did not get excised or changed, we certainly are going to do something about that. We'll take the proper action at the proper time.

I was very interested to hear about Central America and our process down there, and I thought for a moment that instead of a debate I was going to find Mr. Mondale in complete agreement with what we're doing, because the plan that he has outlined is the one we've been following for quite some time, including diplomatic processes throughout Central America and working closely with the Contadora group.

So, I can only tell you about the manual— that we're not in the habit of assigning guilt before there has been proper evidence produced and proof of that guilt. But if guilt is established, whoever is guilty we will treat with that situation then, and they will be removed.

Ms. Geyer. Well, Mr. President, you are implying then that the CIA in Nicaragua is directing the *contras* there. I'd also like to ask whether having the CIA investigate its own manual in such a sensitive area is not sort of like sending the fox into the chicken coop a second time?

The President. I'm afraid I misspoke when I said a CIA head in Nicaragua. There's not someone there directing all of this activity. There are, as you know, CIA men stationed in other countries in the world and, certainly, in Central America. And so it was a man down there in that area that this was delivered to, and he recognized that what was in that manual was in direct contravention of my own Executive order, in December of 1981, that we would have nothing to do with regard to political assassinations.

Mr. Newman. Mr. Mondale, your rebuttal.

Mr. Mondale. What is a President charged with doing when he takes his oath of office? He raises his right hand and takes an oath of office to take care to faithfully execute the laws of the land. A President can't know everything, but a President has to know those things that are essential to his leadership and the enforcement of our laws.

This manual—several thousands of which were produced—was distributed, ordering political assassinations, hiring of criminals, and other forms of terrorism. Some of it was excised, but the part dealing with political terrorism was continued. How can this happen? How can something this serious occur in an administration and have a President of the United States in a situation like this say he didn't know? A President must know these things. I don't know which is worse, not knowing or knowing and not stopping it.

And what about the mining of the harbors in Nicaragua which violated international law? This has hurt this country, and a President's supposed to command.

Mr. Newman. Mr. President, your rebuttal.

The President. Yes. I have so many things there to respond to, I'm going to pick out something you said earlier. You've been all over the country repeating something that, I will admit, the press has also been repeating—that I believed that nuclear missiles could be fired and then called back. I never, ever conceived of such a thing. I never said any such thing.

In a discussion of our strategic arms negotiations, I said that submarines carrying missiles and airplanes carrying missiles were more conventional-type weapons, not as destabilizing as the land-based missiles, and that they were also weapons that—or carriers—that if they were sent out and there was a change, you could call them back before they had launched their missiles.

But I hope that from here on you will no longer be saying that particular thing, which is absolutely false. How anyone could think that any sane person would believe you could call back a nuclear missile, I think is as ridiculous as the whole concept has been. So, thank you for giving me a chance to straighten the record. I'm sure that you appreciate that. [*Laughter*]

Mr. Newman. Mr. Kalb, your question to President Reagan.

Soviet Union

Mr. Kalb. Mr. President, you have often described the Soviet Union as a powerful, evil empire intent on world domination. But this year you have said, and I quote, "If they want to keep their Mickey Mouse system, that's okay with me." Which is it, Mr. President? Do you want to contain them within their present borders and perhaps try to reestablish détente—or what goes for détente—or do you really want to roll back their empire?

The President. I have said on a number of occasions exactly what I believe about the Soviet Union. I retract nothing that I have said. I believe that many of the things they have done are evil in any concept of morality that we have. But I also recognize that as the two great superpowers in the world, we have to live with each other. And I told Mr. Gromyko we don't like their system. They don't like ours. And we're not going to change their system, and they sure better not try to change ours. But between us, we can either destroy the world or we can save it. And I suggested that, certainly, it was to their common interest, along with ours, to avoid a conflict and to attempt to save the world and remove the nuclear weapons. And I think that perhaps we established a little better understanding.

I think that in dealing with the Soviet Union one has to be realistic. I know that Mr. Mondale, in the past, has made statements as if they were just people like ourselves, and if we were kind and good and did something nice, they would respond accordingly. And the result was unilateral disarmament. We canceled the B–1 under the previous administration. What did we get for it? Nothing.

The Soviet Union has been engaged in the biggest military buildup in the history of man at the same time that we tried the policy of unilateral disarmament, of weakness, if you will. And now we are putting up a defense of our own. And I've made it very plain to them, we seek no superiority.

We simply are going to provide a deterrent so that it will be too costly for them if they are nursing any ideas of aggression against us. Now, they claim they're not. And I made it plain to them, we're not. There's been no change in my attitude at all. I just thought when I came into office it was time that there was some realistic talk to and about the Soviet Union. And we did get their attention.

Regions Vital to U.S. Interests

Mr. Kalb. Mr. President, perhaps the other side of the coin, a related question, sir. Since World War II, the vital interests of the United States have always been defined by treaty commitments and by Presidential proclamations. Aside from what is obvious, such as NATO, for example, which countries, which regions in the world do you regard as vital national interests of this country, meaning that you would send American troops to fight there if they were in danger?

The President. Ah, well, now you've added a hypothetical there at the end, Mr. Kalb, about where we would send troops in to fight. I am not going to make the decision as to what the tactics could be, but obviously there are a number of areas in the world that are of importance to us. One is the Middle East, and that is of interest to the whole Western World and the industrialized nations, because of the great supply of energy upon which so many depend there. Our neighbors here in America are vital to us. We're working right now in trying to be of help in southern Africa with regard to the independence of Namibia and the removal of the Cuban surrogates, the thousands of them, from Angola.

So, I can say there are a great many interests. I believe that we have a great interest in the Pacific Basin. That is where I think the future of the world lies. But I am not going to pick out one and, in advance, hypothetically say, "Oh, yes, we would send troops there." I don't want to send troops any place.

Mr. Newman. I'm sorry, Mr. President. Sir, your time was up.

The President. All right.

Soviet Union

Mr. Kalb. Mr. Mondale, you have described the Soviet leaders as, and I'm quoting, ". . . cynical, ruthless, and dangerous," suggesting an almost total lack of trust in them. In that case, what makes you think that the annual summit meetings with them that you have proposed will result in agreements that would satisfy the interests of this country?

Mr. Mondale. Because the only type of agreements to reach with the Soviet Union are the types that are specifically defined, so we know exactly what they must do; subject to full verification, which means we know every day whether they're living up to it; and followups, wherever we find suggestions that they're violating it; and the strongest possible terms.

I have no illusions about the Soviet Union leadership or the nature of that state. They are a tough and a ruthless adversary, and we must be prepared to meet that challenge, and I would. Where I part with the President is that despite all of those differences we must, as past Presidents before this one have done, meet on the common ground of survival. And that's where the President has opposed practically every arms control agreement, by every President, of both political parties, since the bomb went off. And he now completes this term with no progress toward arms control at all, but with a very dangerous arms race underway instead. There are now over 2,000 more warheads pointed at us today than there were when he was sworn in, and that does not strengthen us.

We must be very, very realistic in the nature of that leadership, but we must grind away and talk to find ways of reducing these differences, particularly where arms races are concerned and other dangerous exercises of Soviet power.

There will be no unilateral disarmament under my administration. I will keep this nation strong. I understand exactly what the Soviets are up to, but that, too, is a part of national strength. To do that, a President must know what is essential to command and to leadership and to strength.

And that's where the President's failure to master, in my opinion, the essential elements of arms control has cost us dearly. He's 3 years into this administration. He said he just discovered that most Soviet missiles are on land, and that's why his proposal didn't work.

I invite the American people tomorrow—because I will issue the statement quoting President Reagan—he said exactly what I said he said. He said that these missiles were less dangerous than ballistic missiles because you could fire them, and you could recall them if you decided there'd been a miscalculation.

Mr. Newman. I'm sorry, sir——

Mr. Mondale. A President must know those things.

Eastern Europe

Mr. Kalb. A related question, Mr. Mondale, on Eastern Europe. Do you accept the conventional diplomatic wisdom that Eastern Europe is a Soviet sphere of influence? And if you do, what could a Mondale administration realistically do to help the people of Eastern Europe achieve the human rights that were guaranteed to them as a result of the Helsinki accords?

Mr. Mondale. I think the essential strategy of the United States ought not accept any Soviet control over Eastern Europe. We ought to deal with each of these countries separately. We ought to pursue strategies with each of them, economic and the rest, that help them pull away from their dependence upon the Soviet Union.

Where the Soviet Union has acted irresponsibly, as they have in many of those countries, especially, recently, in Poland, I believe we ought to insist that Western credits extended to the Soviet Union bear the market rate. Make the Soviets pay for their irresponsibility. That is a very important objective—to make certain that we continue to look forward to progress toward greater independence by these nations and work with each of them separately.

Mr. Newman. Mr. President, your rebuttal.

The President. Yes. I'm not going to continue trying to respond to these repetitions of the falsehoods that have already been stated here. But with regard to whether Mr. Mondale would be strong, as he said he would be, I know that he has a commercial out where he's appearing on the deck of the *Nimitz* and watching the F–14's take off. And that's an image of strength—except that if he had had his way when the *Nimitz* was being planned, he would have been deep in the water out there because there wouldn't have been any *Nimitz* to stand on—he was against it. [*Laughter*]

He was against the F–14 fighter, he was against the M–1 tank, he was against the B–1 bomber, he wanted to cut the salary of all of the military, he wanted to bring home half of the American forces in Europe. And he has a record of weakness with regard to our national defense that is second to none.

Audience member. Hear, hear!

The President. Indeed, he was on that side virtually throughout all his years in the Senate. And he opposed even President Carter, when toward the end of his term President Carter wanted to increase the defense budget.

Mr. Newman. Mr. Mondale, your rebuttal.

Mr. Mondale. Mr. President, I accept your commitment to peace, but I want you to accept my commitment to a strong national defense. [*Applause*] I propose a budget—I have proposed a budget which would increase our nation's strength, in real terms, by double that of the Soviet Union.

I'll tell you where we disagree. It is true over 10 years ago I voted to delay production of the F–14, and I'll tell you why. The plane wasn't flying the way it was supposed to be; it was a waste of money.

Your definition of national strength is to throw money at the Defense Department. My definition of national strength is to make certain that a dollar spent buys us a dollar's worth of defense. There's a big difference between the two of us. A President must manage that budget. I will keep us strong, but you'll not do that unless you command that budget and make certain we get the strength that we need. You pay $500 for a $5 hammer, you're not buying strength.

Mr. Newman. I would ask the audience not to applaud. All it does is take up time that we would like to devote to the debate.

Mr. Kondracke, your question to Mr. Mondale.

Use of Military Force

Mr. Kondracke. Mr. Mondale, in an address earlier this year you said that before this country resorts to military force, and I'm quoting, "American interests should be sharply defined, publicly supported, congressionally sanctioned, militarily feasible, internationally defensible, open to independent scrutiny, and alert to regional history." Now, aren't you setting up such a gauntlet of tests here that adversaries could easily suspect that as President you would never use force to protect American interests?

Mr. Mondale. No. As a matter of fact, I believe every one of those standards is essential to the exercise of power by this country. And we can see that in both Lebanon and in Central America.

In Lebanon, this President exercised American power, all right, but the management of it was such that our marines were killed, we had to leave in humiliation, the Soviet Union became stronger, terrorists became emboldened. And it was because they did not think through how power should be exercised, did not have the American public with them on a plan that worked, that we ended up the way we did.

Similarly, in Central America: What we're doing in Nicaragua with this covert war—which the Congress, including many Republicans, have tried to stop—is finally end up with a public definition of American power that hurts us, where we get associated with political assassins and the rest. We have to decline, for the first time in modern history, jurisdiction in the World Court because they'll find us guilty of illegal actions. And our enemies are strengthened from all of this.

We need to be strong, we need to be prepared to use that strength, but we must understand that we are a democracy. We are a government by the people, and when we move, it should be for very severe and extreme reasons that serve our national interests and end up with a stronger country behind us. It is only in that way that we can persevere.

Nicaragua

Mr. Kondracke. You've been quoted as

saying that you might quarantine Nicaragua. I'd like to know what that means. Would you stop Soviet ships, as President Kennedy did in 1962? And wouldn't that be more dangerous than President Reagan's covert war?

Mr. Mondale. What I'm referring to there is the mutual self-defense provisions that exist in the Inter-American treaty, the so-called Rio Pact, that permits the nations, our friends in that region, to combine to take steps—diplomatic and otherwise—to prevent Nicaragua, when she acts irresponsibly in asserting power in other parts outside of her border, to take those steps, whatever they might be, to stop it.

The Nicaraguans must know that it is the policy of our government that that leadership must stay behind the boundaries of their nation, not interfere in other nations. And by working with all of the nations in the region—unlike the policies of this administration and unlike the President said, they have not supported negotiations in that region—we will be much stronger, because we'll have the moral authority that goes with those efforts.

Lebanon

Mr. Kondracke. President Reagan, you introduced U.S. forces into Lebanon as neutral peacekeepers, but then you made them combatants on the side of the Lebanese Government. Eventually you were forced to withdraw them under fire, and now Syria, a Soviet ally, is dominant in the country. Doesn't Lebanon represent a major failure on the part of your administration and raise serious questions about your capacity as a foreign policy strategist and as Commander in Chief?

The President. No, Morton, I don't agree to all of those things. First of all, when we and our allies—the Italians, the French, and the United Kingdom—went into Lebanon, we went in there at the request of what was left of the Lebanese Government to be a stabilizing force while they tried to establish a government.

But the first—pardon me—the first time we went in, we went in at their request because the war was going on right in Beirut between Israel and the PLO terrorists. Israel could not be blamed for that.

Those terrorists had been violating their northern border consistently, and Israel chased them all the way to there.

Then we went in with the multinational force to help remove, and did remove, more than 13,000 of those terrorists from Lebanon. We departed. And then the Government of Lebanon asked us back in as a stabilizing force while they established a government and sought to get the foreign forces all the way out of Lebanon and that they could then take care of their own borders.

And we were succeeding. We were there for the better part of a year. Our position happened to be at the airport. Oh, there were occasional snipings and sometimes some artillery fire, but we did not engage in conflict that was out of line with our mission. I will never send troops anywhere on a mission of that kind without telling them that if somebody shoots at them, they can darn well shoot back. And this is what we did. We never initiated any kind of action; we defended ourselves there.

But we were succeeding to the point that the Lebanese Government had been organized—if you will remember, there were the meetings in Geneva in which they began to meet with the hostile factional forces and try to put together some kind of a peace plan. We were succeeding, and that was why the terrorist acts began. There are forces there—and that includes Syria, in my mind—who don't want us to succeed, who don't want that kind of a peace with a dominant Lebanon, dominant over its own territory. And so, the terrorist acts began and led to the one great tragedy when they were killed in that suicide bombing of the building. Then the multilateral force withdrew for only one reason: We withdrew because we were no longer able to carry out the mission for which we had been sent in. But we went in in the interest of peace and to keep Israel and Syria from getting into the sixth war between them. And I have no apologies for our going on a peace mission.

Mr. Kondracke. Mr. President, 4 years ago you criticized President Carter for ignoring ample warnings that our diplomats in Iran might be taken hostage. Haven't you done exactly the same thing in Lebanon, not once, but three times, with 300 Americans, not hostages, but dead? And you vowed swift retaliation against terrorists, but doesn't our lack of response suggest that you're just bluffing?

The President. Morton, no. I think there's a great difference between the Government of Iran threatening our diplomatic personnel, and there is a government that you can see and can put your hand on. In the terrorist situation, there are terrorist factions all over. In a recent 30-day period, 37 terrorist acts in 20 countries have been committed. The most recent has been the one in Brighton. In dealing with terrorists, yes, we want to retaliate, but only if we can put our finger on the people responsible and not endanger the lives of innocent civilians there in the various communities and in the city of Beirut where these terrorists are operating.

I have just signed legislation to add to our ability to deal, along with our allies, with this terrorist problem. And it's going to take all the nations together, just as when we banded together we pretty much resolved the whole problem of skyjackings sometime ago.

Well, the red light went on. I could have gone on forever.

Mr. Newman. Mr. Mondale, your rebuttal?

Mr. Mondale. Groucho Marx said, "Who do you believe?—me, or your own eyes?" And what we have in Lebanon is something that the American people have seen. The Joint Chiefs urged the President not to put our troops in that barracks because they were indefensible. They went to him 5 days before they were killed and said, "Please, take them out of there." The Secretary of State admitted that this morning. He did not do so. The report following the explosion of the barracks disclosed that we had not taken any of the steps that we should have taken. That was the second time.

Then the Embassy was blown up a few weeks ago, and once again none of the steps that should have been taken were taken. And we were warned 5 days before that explosives were on their way, and they weren't taken. The terrorists have won each time. The President told the terrorists he was going to retaliate. He didn't. They

called their bluff. And the bottom line is that the United States left in humiliation, and our enemies are stronger.

Mr. Newman. Mr. President, your rebuttal?

The President. Yes. First of all, Mr. Mondale should know that the President of the United States did not order the marines into that barracks. That was a command decision made by the commanders on the spot and based with what they thought was best for the men there. That is one.

On the other things that you've just said about the terrorists, I'm tempted to ask you what you would do. These are unidentified people, and after the bomb goes off, they're blown to bits because they are suicidal individuals who think they're going to go to paradise if they perpetrate such an act and lose their life in doing it. We are going to, as I say, we're busy trying to find the centers where these operations stem from, and retaliation will be taken. But we're not going to simply kill some people to say, "Oh, look, we got even." We want to know when we retaliate that we're retaliating with those who are responsible for the terrorist acts. And terrorist acts are such that our own United States Capitol in Washington has been bombed twice.

Mr. Newman. Mr. Trewhitt, your question to President Reagan?

The President's Age

Mr. Trewhitt. Mr. President, I want to raise an issue that I think has been lurking out there for 2 or 3 weeks and cast it specifically in national security terms. You already are the oldest President in history. And some of your staff say you were tired after your most recent encounter with Mr. Mondale. I recall yet that President Kennedy had to go for days on end with very little sleep during the Cuban missile crisis. Is there any doubt in your mind that you would be able to function in such circumstances?

The President. Not at all, Mr. Trewhitt, and I want you to know that also I will not make age an issue of this campaign. I am not going to exploit, for political purposes, my opponent's youth and inexperience. [*Laughter and applause*] If I still have time,

I might add, Mr. Trewhitt, I might add that it was Seneca or it was Cicero, I don't know which, that said, "If it was not for the elders correcting the mistakes of the young, there would be no state."

Strategic Missiles

Mr. Trewhitt. Mr. President, I'd like to head for the fence and try to catch that one before it goes over, but I'll go on to another question.

You and Mr. Mondale have already disagreed about what you had to say about recalling submarine-launched missiles. There's another, a similar issue out there that relates to your—it is said, at least, that you were unaware that the Soviet retaliatory power was based on land-based missiles. First, is that correct? Secondly, if it is correct, have you informed yourself in the meantime? And third, is it even necessary for the President to be so intimately involved in strategic details?

The President. Yes, this had to do with our disarmament talks. And the whole controversy about land missiles came up because we thought that the strategic nuclear weapons, the most destabilizing are the land-based. You put your thumb on a button and somebody blows up 20 minutes later. So, we thought that it would be simpler to negotiate first with those. And then we made it plain, a second phase, take up the submarine-launched or the airborne missiles.

The Soviet Union, to our surprise—and not just mine—made it plain when we brought this up that they placed, they thought, a greater reliance on the land-based missiles and, therefore, they wanted to take up all three. And we agreed. We said, "All right, if that's what you want to do." But it was a surprise to us, because they outnumbered us 64 to 36 in submarines and 20 percent more bombers capable of carrying nuclear missiles than we had. So, why should we believe that they had placed that much more reliance on land-based?

But even after we gave in and said, "All right, let's discuss it all," they walked away from the table. We didn't.

The President's Age

Mr. Trewhitt. Mr. Mondale, I'm going to hang in there. Should the President's age and stamina be an issue in the political campaign?

Mr. Mondale. No. And I have not made it an issue, nor should it be. What's at issue here is the President's application of his authority to understand what a President must know to lead this nation, secure our defense, and make the decisions and the judgments that are necessary.

A minute ago the President quoted Cicero, I believe. I want to quote somebody a little closer to home, Harry Truman. He said, "The buck stops here." We just heard the President's answer for the problems at the barracks in Lebanon, where 241 marines were killed. What happened? First, the Joint Chiefs of Staff went to the President, said, "Don't put those troops there." They did it. And then 5 days before the troops were killed, they went back to the President, through the Secretary of Defense, and said, "Please, Mr. President, take those troops out of there because we can't defend them." They didn't do it. And we know what happened.

After that, once again, our Embassy was exploded. This is the fourth time this has happened—an identical attack, in the same region, despite warnings—even public warnings—from the terrorists. Who's in charge? Who's handling this matter? That's my main point.

Now, on arms control, we're completing 4 years. This is the first administration since the bomb went off that made no progress. We have an arms race underway instead.

A President has to lead his government or it won't be done. Different people with different views fight with each other. For 3½ years, this administration avoided arms control, resisted tabling arms control proposals that had any hope of agreeing, rebuked their negotiator in 1981 when he came close to an agreement, at least in principle, on medium-range weapons. And we have this arms race underway. And a recent book that just came out by perhaps the Nation's most respected author in this field, Strobe Talbott, called "Deadly Gambits," concludes that this President has failed to master the essential details needed to command and lead us, both in terms of security and terms of arms control. That's why they call the President the Commander in Chief.

Good intentions, I grant. But it takes more than that. You must be tough and smart.

The President's Leadership

Mr. Trewhitt. This question of leadership keeps arising in different forms in this discussion already. And the President, Mr. Mondale, has called you whining and vacillating, among the more charitable phrases—weak, I believe. It is a question of leadership. And he has made the point that you have not repudiated some of the semidiplomatic activity of the Reverend Jackson, particularly in Central America. Did you approve of his diplomatic activity? And are you prepared to repudiate him now?

Mr. Mondale. I read his statement the other day. I don't admire Fidel Castro at all. And I've said that. Che Guevara was a contemptible figure in civilization's history. I know the Cuban state as a police state, and all my life I've worked in a way that demonstrates that. But Jesse Jackson is an independent person. I don't control him.

And let's talk about people we do control. In the last debate,[1] the Vice President of the United States said that I said the marines had died shamefully and died in shame in Lebanon. I demanded an apology from Vice President Bush because I had, instead, honored these young men, grieved for their families, and think they were wonderful Americans that honored us all. What does the President have to say about taking responsibility for a Vice President who won't apologize for something like that?

Mr. Newman. Mr. President, your rebuttal?

The President. Yes. I know it'll come as a surprise to Mr. Mondale, but I am in charge. And, as a matter of fact, we haven't avoided arms control talks with the Soviet Union. Very early in my administration I

---

[1] *Mr. Mondale was referring to an earlier debate between George Bush and Geraldine Ferarro, the Vice-Presidential candidates.*

proposed—and I think something that had never been proposed by any previous administration—I proposed a total elimination of intermediate-range missiles, where the Soviets had better than a 10—and still have—better than a 10-to-1 advantage over the allies in Europe. When they protested that and suggested a smaller number, perhaps, I went along with that.

The so-called negotiation that you said I walked out on was the so-called walk in the woods between one of our representatives and one of the Soviet Union, and it wasn't me that turned it down, the Soviet Union disavowed it.

Mr. Newman. Mr. Mondale, your rebuttal?

Mr. Mondale. There are two distinguished authors on arms control in this country—there are many others, but two that I want to cite tonight. One is Strobe Talbott in his classic book, "Deadly Gambits." The other is John Neuhaus, who's one of the most distinguished arms control specialists in our country. Both said that this administration turned down the "walk in the woods" agreement first, and that would have been a perfect agreement from the standpoint of the United States in Europe and our security.

When Mr. Nitze, a good negotiator, returned, he was rebuked, and his boss was fired. This is the kind of leadership that we've had in this administration on the most deadly issue of our times. Now we have a runaway arms race. All they've got to show for 4 years in U.S.-Soviet relations is one meeting in the last weeks of an administration, and nothing before.

They're tough negotiators, but all previous Presidents have made progress. This one has not.

Mr. Newman. Ms. Geyer, your question to Mr. Mondale.

Illegal Immigration

Ms. Geyer. Mr. Mondale, many analysts are now saying that actually our number one foreign policy problem today is one that remains almost totally unrecognized: massive illegal immigration from economically collapsing countries. They are saying that it is the only real territorial threat to the American nation-state. You, yourself, said in the 1970's that we had a "hemorrhage on our borders." Yet today you have backed off any immigration reform, such as the balanced and highly crafted Simpson-Mazzoli bill. Why? What would you do instead today, if anything?

Mr. Mondale. This is a very serious problem in our country, and it has to be dealt with. I object to that part of the Simpson-Mazzoli bill which I think is very unfair and would prove to be so. That is the part that requires employers to determine the citizenship of an employee before they're hired. I'm convinced that the result of this would be that people who are Hispanic, people who have different languages or speak with an accent, would find it difficult to be employed. I think that's wrong. We've never had citizenship tests in our country before, and I don't think we should have a citizenship card today. That is counterproductive.

I do support the other aspects of the Simpson-Mazzoli bill that strengthen enforcement at the border, strengthen other ways of dealing with undocumented workers in this difficult area and dealing with the problem of settling people who have lived here for many, many years and do not have an established status.

I have further strongly recommended that this administration do something it has not done, and that is to strengthen enforcement at the border, strengthen the officials in this government that deal with undocumented workers, and to do so in a way that's responsible and within the Constitution of the United States. We need an answer to this problem, but it must be an American answer that is consistent with justice and due process.

Everyone in this room, practically, here tonight, is an immigrant. We came here loving this nation, serving it, and it has served all of our most bountiful dreams. And one of those dreams is justice. And we need a measure—and I will support a measure—that brings about those objectives but avoids that one aspect that I think is very serious.

The second part is to maintain and improve relations with our friends to the south. We cannot solve this problem all on our own. And that's why the failure of this administration to deal in an effective and a good-faith way with Mexico, with Costa Rica, with the other nations in trying to find a peaceful settlement to the dispute in Central America has undermined our capacity to effectively deal diplomatically in this area as well.

Ms. Geyer. Sir, people as well-balanced and just as Father Theodore Hesburgh at Notre Dame, who headed the select commission on immigration, have pointed out repeatedly that there will be no immigration reform without employer sanctions, because it would be an unbalanced bill, and there would be simply no way to enforce it. However, putting that aside for the moment, your critics have also said repeatedly that you have not gone along with the bill or with any immigration reform because of the Hispanic groups—or Hispanic leadership groups—who actually do not represent what the Hispanic-Americans want, because polls show that they overwhelmingly want some kind of immigration reform. Can you say, or how can you justify your position on this? And how do you respond to the criticism that this is another, or that this is an example of your flip-flopping and giving in to special interest groups at the expense of the American nation?

Mr. Mondale. I think you're right that the polls show that the majority of Hispanics want that bill, so I'm not doing it for political reasons. I'm doing it because all my life I've fought for a system of justice in this country, a system in which every American has a chance to achieve the fullness in life without discrimination. This bill imposes upon employers the responsibility of determining whether somebody who applies for a job is an American or not. And just inevitably, they're going to be reluctant to hire Hispanics or people with a different accent.

If I were dealing with politics here, the polls show the American people want this. I am for reform in this area, for tough enforcement at the border, and for many other aspects of the Simpson-Mazzoli bill, but all my life I've fought for a fair nation. And despite the politics of it, I stand where I stand, and I think I'm right, and before this fight is over we're going to come up with a better bill, a more effective bill that does not undermine the liberties of our people.

Ms. Geyer. Mr. President, you, too, have said that our borders are out of control. Yet this fall you allowed the Simpson-Mazzoli bill—which would at least have minimally protected our borders and the rights of citizenship—because of a relatively unimportant issue of reimbursement to the States for legalized aliens. Given that, may I ask what priority can we expect you to give this forgotten national security element? How sincere are you in your efforts to control, in effect, the nation-state that is the United States?

The President. Georgie Anne, we, believe me, supported the Simpson-Mazzoli bill strongly—and the bill that came out of the Senate. However, there were things added in in the House side that we felt made it less of a good bill; as a matter of fact, made it a bad bill. And in conference—we stayed with them in conference all the way to where even Senator Simpson did not want the bill in the manner in which it would come out of the conference committee. There were a number of things in there that weakened that bill. I can't go into detail about them here.

But it is true our borders are out of control. It is also true that this has been a situation on our borders back through a number of administrations. And I supported this bill. I believe in the idea of amnesty for those who have put down roots and who have lived here even though sometime back they may have entered illegally. With regard to the employer sanctions, we must have that not only to ensure that we can identify the illegal aliens, but also, while some keep protesting about what it would do to employers, there is another employer that we shouldn't be so concerned about, and these are employers down through the years who have encouraged the illegal entry into this country because they then hire these individuals and hire them at starvation wages and with none of the benefits that we think are normal and natural for workers in our country, and the individuals can't complain because of their illegal status. We don't think that those people should be allowed to continue operating free.

And this was why the provisions that we had in with regard to sanctions, and so forth—and I'm going to do everything I can, and all of us in the administration are, to join in again when Congress is back at it to get an immigration bill that will give us, once again, control of our borders.

And with regard to friendship below the border and with the countries down there, yes, no administration that I know has established the relationship that we have with our Latin friends. But as long as they have an economy that leaves so many people in dire poverty and unemployment, they are going to seek that employment across our borders. And we work with those other countries.

Ms. Geyer. Mr. President, the experts also say that the situation today is terribly different quantitatively—qualitatively different from what it has been in the past because of the gigantic population growth. For instance, Mexico's population will go from about 60 million today to 120 million at the turn of the century. Many of these people will be coming into the United States not as citizens, but as illegal workers. You have repeatedly said recently that you believe that Armageddon, the destruction of the world, may be imminent in our times. Do you ever feel that we are in for an Armageddon or a situation, a time of anarchy, regarding the population explosion in the world?

The President. No. As a matter of fact, the population explosion, if you look at the actual figures, has been vastly exaggerated—over exaggerated. As a matter of fact, there are some pretty scientific and solid figures about how much space there still is in the world and how many more people we can have. It's almost like going back to the Malthusian theory, when even then they were saying that everyone would starve with the limited population they had then. But the problem of population growth is one, here, with regard to our immigration. And we have been the safety valve, whether we wanted to or not, with the illegal entry here, in Mexico, where their population is increasing and they don't have an economy that can absorb them and provide the jobs. And this is what we're trying to work out, not only to protect our own borders but to have some kind of fairness and recognition of that problem.

Mr. Newman. Mr. Mondale, your rebuttal?

Mr. Mondale. One of the biggest problems today is that the countries to our south are so desperately poor that these people who will almost lose their lives if they don't come north, come north despite all the risks. And if we're going to find a permanent, fundamental answer to this, it goes to American economic and trade policies that permit these nations to have a chance to get on their own two feet and to get prosperity, so that they can have jobs for themselves and their people. And that's why this enormous national debt, engineered by this administration, is harming these countries in fueling this immigration. These high interest rates—real rates that have doubled under this administration—have had the same effect on Mexico and so on, and the cost of repaying those debts is so enormous that it results in massive unemployment, hardship, and heartache. And that drives our friends to the south up into our region, and we need to end those deficits as well.

Mr. Newman. Mr. President, your rebuttal.

The President. Well, my rebuttal is I've heard the national debt blamed for a lot of things, but not for illegal immigration across our border—[*laughter*]—and it has nothing to do with it.

But with regard to these high interest rates, too, at least give us the recognition of the fact that when you left office, Mr. Mondale, they were 21½—the prime rate. It's now 12¼, and I predict it'll be coming down a little more shortly. So, we're trying to undo some of the things that your administration did. [*Applause*]

Mr. Newman. No applause, please.

Mr. Kalb, your question to President Reagan.

Armageddon

Mr. Kalb. Mr. President, I'd like to pick up this Armageddon theme. You've been quoted as saying that you do believe, deep down, that we are heading for some kind of biblical Armageddon. Your Pentagon and your Secretary of Defense have plans for

the United States to fight and prevail in a nuclear war. Do you feel that we are now heading perhaps, for some kind of nuclear Armageddon? And do you feel that this country and the world could survive that kind of calamity?

The President. Mr. Kalb, I think what has been hailed as something I'm supposedly, as President, discussing as principle is the recall of just some philosophical discussions with people who are interested in the same things; and that is the prophecies down through the years, the biblical prophecies of what would portend the coming of Armageddon, and so forth, and the fact that a number of theologians for the last decade or more have believed that this was true, that the prophecies are coming together that portend that. But no one knows whether Armageddon, those prophecies mean that Armageddon is a thousand years away or day after tomorrow. So, I have never seriously warned and said we must plan according to Armageddon.

Now, with regard to having to say whether we would try to survive in the event of a nuclear war, of course we would. But let me also point out that to several parliaments around the world, in Europe and in Asia, I have made a statement to each one of them, and I'll repeat it here: A nuclear war cannot be won and must never be fought. And that is why we are maintaining a deterrent and trying to achieve a deterrent capacity to where no one would believe that they could start such a war and escape with limited damage.

But the deterrent—and that's what it is for—is also what led me to propose what is now being called the Star Wars concept, but propose that we research to see if there isn't a defensive weapon that could defend against incoming missiles. And if such a defense could be found, wouldn't it be far more humanitarian to say that now we can defend against a nuclear war by destroying missiles instead of slaughtering millions of people?

Strategic Defense Initiative

Mr. Kalb. Mr. President, when you made that proposal, the so-called Star Wars proposal, you said, if I'm not mistaken, that you would share this very super-sophisticated technology with the Soviet Union. After all of the distrust over the years, sir, that you have expressed towards the Soviet Union, do you really expect anyone to take seriously that offer that you would share the best of America's technology in this weapons area with our principal adversary?

The President. Why not? What if we did—and I hope we can; we're still researching—what if we come up with a weapon that renders those missiles obsolete? There has never been a weapon invented in the history of man that has not led to a defensive, a counterweapon. But suppose we came up with that?

Now, some people have said, "Ah, that would make war imminent, because they would think that we could launch a first strike because we could defend against the enemy." But why not do what I have offered to do and asked the Soviet Union to do? Say, "Look, here's what we can do. We'll even give it to you. Now, will you sit down with us and once and for all get rid, all of us, of these nuclear weapons and free mankind from that threat?" I think that would be the greatest use of a defensive weapon.

Mr. Kalb. Mr. Mondale, you've been very sharply critical of the President's Strategic Defense Initiative. And yet, what is wrong with a major effort by this country to try to use its best technology to knock out as many incoming nuclear warheads as possible?

Mr. Mondale. First of all, let me sharply disagree with the President on sharing the most advanced, the most dangerous, the most important technology in America with the Soviet Union. We have had for many years, understandably, a system of restraints on high technology because the Soviets are behind us. And any research or development along the Star Wars schemes would inevitably involve our most advanced computers, our most advanced engineering. And the thought that we would share this with the Soviet Union is, in my opinion, a total non-STARTer. I would not let the Soviet Union get their hands on it at all.

Now, what's wrong with Star Wars? There's nothing wrong with the theory of it. If we could develop a principle that

would say both sides could fire all their missiles and no one would get hurt, I suppose it's a good idea. But the fact of it is we're so far away from research that even comes close to that, that the Director of Engineering Research at the Defense Department said to get there we would have to solve eight problems, each of which are more difficult than the atomic bomb and the Manhattan project. It would cost something like a trillion dollars to test and deploy weapons.

The second thing is this all assumes that the Soviets wouldn't respond in kind. And they always do. We don't get behind. They won't get behind. And that's been the tragic story of the arms race. We have more at stake in space satellites than they do. If we could stop, right now, the testing and the deployment of these space weapons—and the President's proposals go clear beyond research; if it was just research we wouldn't have any argument, because maybe someday, somebody will think of something—but to commit this nation to a buildup of antisatellite and space weapons at this time, in their crude state, would bring about an arms race that's very dangerous indeed.

One final point. The most dangerous aspect of this proposal is, for the first time, we would delegate to computers the decision as to whether to start a war. That's dead wrong. There wouldn't be time for a President to decide; it would be decided by these remote computers. It might be an oil fire, it might be a jet exhaust, the computer might decide it's a missile—and off we go.

Why don't we stop this madness now and draw a line and keep the heavens free from war? [*Applause*]

Nuclear Freeze

Mr. Kalb. Mr. Mondale, in this general area, sir, of arms control, President Carter's national security adviser, Zbigniew Brzezinski, said, "A nuclear freeze is a hoax." Yet the basis of your arms proposals, as I understand them, is a mutual and verifiable freeze on existing weapons systems. In your view, which specific weapons systems could be subject to a mutual and verifiable freeze, and which could not?

Mr. Mondale. Every system that is verifiable should be placed on the table for negotiations for an agreement. I would not agree to any negotiations or any agreement that involved conduct on the part of the Soviet Union that we couldn't verify every day. I would not agree to any agreement in which the United States security interest was not fully recognized and supported. That's why we say mutual and verifiable freezes.

Now, why do I support the freeze? Because this ever-rising arms race madness makes both nations less secure. It's more difficult to defend this nation. It's putting a hair-trigger on nuclear war. This administration, by going into the Star Wars system, is going to add a dangerous new escalation. We have to be tough on the Soviet Union, but I think the American people——

Mr. Newman. Your time is up, Mr. Mondale.

Mr. Mondale. ——and the people of the Soviet Union want it to stop.

Mr. Newman. President Reagan, your rebuttal?

The President. Yes, my rebuttal, once again, is that this invention that has just been created here of how I would go about rolling over for the Soviet Union—no, Mr. Mondale, my idea would be with that defensive weapon that we would sit down with them and then say, "Now, are you willing to join us? Here's what we"—give them a demonstration and then say— "Here's what we can do. Now, if you're willing to join us in getting rid of all the nuclear weapons in the world, then we'll give you this one, so that we would both know that no one can cheat; that we're both got something that if anyone tries to cheat . . . ."

But when you keep star-warring it—I never suggested where the weapons should be or what kind; I'm not a scientist. I said, and the Joint Chiefs of Staff agreed with me, that it was time for us to turn our research ability to seeing if we could not find this kind of defensive weapon. And suddenly somebody says, "Oh, it's got to be up there, and it's Star Wars," and so forth. I don't know what it would be, but if we can come up with one, I think the world will be better off.

Mr. Newman. Mr. Mondale, your rebuttal.

Mr. Mondale. Well, that's what a Presi-

dent's supposed to know—where those weapons are going to be. If they're space weapons, I assume they'll be in space. [*Laughter*] If they're antisatellite weapons, I assume they're going to be aimed against satellites.

Now, this is the most dangerous technology that we possess. The Soviets try to spy on us, steal this stuff. And to give them technology of this kind, I disagree with. You haven't just accepted research, Mr. President. You've set up a Strategic Defense Initiative, an agency, you're beginning to test, you're talking about deploying, you're asking for a budget of some $30 billion for this purpose. This is an arms escalation. And we will be better off, far better off, if we stop right now, because we have more to lose in space then they do. If someday, somebody comes along with an answer, that's something else. But that there would be an answer in our lifetime is unimaginable.

Why do we start things that we know the Soviets will match and make us all less secure? That's what a President's for.

Mr. Newman. Mr. Kondracke, your question to Mr. Mondale.

Strategic Weapons

Mr. Kondracke. Mr. Mondale, you say that with respect to the Soviet Union you want to negotiate a mutual nuclear freeze, yet you would unilaterally give up the MX missile and the B-1 bomber before the talks have even begun. And you have announced, in advance, that reaching an agreement with the Soviets is the most important thing in the world to you. Now, aren't you giving away half the store before you even sit down to talk?

Mr. Mondale. No. As a matter of fact, we have a vast range of technology and weaponry right now that provides all the bargaining chips that we need. And I support the air launch cruise missile, the ground launch cruise missile, the Pershing missile, the Trident submarine, the D-5 submarine, Stealth technology, the Midgetman—we have a whole range of technology. Why I disagree with the MX is that it's a sitting duck. It'll draw an attack. It puts a hair-trigger, and it is a dangerous, destabilizing weapon. And the B–1 is similarly to be opposed, because for 15 years the Soviet Union has been preparing to meet the B–1. The Secretary of Defense himself said it would be a suicide mission if it were built.

Instead, I want to build the Midgetman, which is mobile and thus less vulnerable, contributing to stability, and a weapon that will give us security and contribute to an incentive for arms control. That's why I'm for Stealth technology, to build a Stealth bomber—which I've supported for years—that can penetrate the Soviet air defense system without any hope that they can perceive where it is because their radar system is frustrated. In other words, a President has to make choices. This makes us stronger.

The final point is that we can use this money that we save on these weapons to spend on things that we really need. Our conventional strength in Europe is under strength. We need to strengthen that in order to assure our Western allies of our presence there, a strong defense, but also to diminish and reduce the likelihood of a commencement of a war and the use of nuclear weapons. It's in this way, by making wise choices, that we're stronger, we enhance the chances of arms control. Every President until this one has been able to do it, and this nation—or the world is more dangerous as a result.

Nuclear Freeze

Mr. Kondracke. I want to follow up on Mr. Kalb's question. It seems to me on the question of verifiability, that you do have some problems with the extent of the freeze. It seems to me, for example, that testing would be very difficult to verify because the Soviets encode their telemetry. Research would be impossible to verify. Numbers of warheads would be impossible to verify by satellite, except for with onsite inspection, and production of any weapon would be impossible to verify. Now, in view of that, what is going to be frozen?

Mr. Mondale. I will not agree to any arms control agreement, including a freeze, that's not verifiable. Let's take your warhead principle. The warhead principle— there have been counting rules for years. Whenever a weapon is tested we count the

number of warheads on it, and whenever that warhead is used we count that number of warheads, whether they have that number or less on it, or not. These are standard rules. I will not agree to any production restrictions—or agreements, unless we have the ability to verify those agreements. I don't trust the Russians. I believe that every agreement we reach must be verifiable, and I will not agree to anything that we cannot tell every day. In other words, we've got to be tough. But in order to stop this arms madness, we've got to push ahead with tough negotiations that are verifiable so that we know the Soviets are agreeing and living up to their agreement.

Support for U.S. Allies

Mr. Kondracke. Mr. President, I want to ask you a question about negotiating with friends. You severely criticized President Carter for helping to undermine two friendly dictators who got into trouble with their own people—the Shah of Iran and President Somoza of Nicaragua. Now there are other such leaders heading for trouble, including President Pinochet of Chile and President Marcos of the Philippines. What should you do, and what can you do to prevent the Philippines from becoming another Nicaragua?

The President. Morton, I did criticize the President because of our undercutting of what was a stalwart ally—the Shah of Iran. And I am not at all convinced that he was that far out of line with his people or that they wanted that to happen. The Shah had done our bidding and carried our load in the Middle East for quite some time, and I did think that it was a blot on our record that we let him down. Have things gotten better? The Shah, whatever he might have done, was building low-cost housing, had taken land away from the Mullahs and was distributing it to the peasants so they could be landowners—things of that kind. But we turned it over to a maniacal fanatic who has slaughtered thousands and thousands of people, calling it executions.

The matter of Somoza—no, I never defended Somoza. And, as a matter of fact, the previous administration stood by and so did I—not that I could have done anything in my position at that time—but for this revolution to take place. And the promise of the revolution was democracy, human rights, free labor unions, free press. And then, just as Castro had done in Cuba, the Sandinistas ousted the other parties to the revolution. Many of them are now the *contras*. They exiled some, they jailed some, they murdered some. And they installed a Marxist-Leninist totalitarian government.

And what I have to say about this is, many times—and this has to do with the Philippines, also, I know there are things there in the Philippines that do not look good to us from the standpoint right now of democratic rights, but what is the alternative? It is a large Communist movement to take over the Philippines. They have been our friend since their inception as a nation.

And I think that we've had enough of a record of letting—under the guise of revolution—someone that we thought was a little more right than we would be, letting that person go, and then winding up with totalitarianism, pure and simple, as the alternative. And I think that we're better off, for example with the Philippines, of trying to retain our friendship and help them right the wrongs we see, rather than throwing them to the wolves and then facing a Communist power in the Pacific.

Mr. Kondracke. Mr. President, since the United States has two strategically important bases in the Philippines, would the overthrow of President Marcos constitute a threat to vital American interests and, if so, what would you do about it?

The President. Well, as I say, we have to look at what an overthrow there would mean and what the government would be that would follow. And there is every evidence, every indication that that government would be hostile to the United States. And that would be a severe blow to our abilities there in the Pacific.

Mr. Kondracke. And what would you do about it?

Mr. Newman. Sorry. I'm sorry, you've asked the followup question. Mr. Mondale, your rebuttal?

Mr. Mondale. Perhaps in no area do we disagree more than this administration's policies on human rights.

I went to the Philippines as Vice President, pressed for human rights, called for the release of Aquino, and made progress that had been stalled on both the Subic and the Clark airfield bases. What explains this administration cozying up to the Argentine dictators after they took over? Fortunately, a democracy took over, but this nation was embarrassed by this current administration's adoption of their policies.

What happens in South Africa, where, for example, the Nobel Prize winner, 2 days ago, said this administration is seen as working with the oppressive government of South Africa. That hurts this nation. We need to stand for human rights. We need to make it clear we're for human liberty. National security and human rights must go together. But this administration time and time again has lost its way in this field.

Mr. Newman. President Reagan, your rebuttal.

The President. Well, the invasion of Afghanistan didn't take place on our watch. I have described what has happened in Iran, and we weren't here then either. I don't think that our record of human rights can be assailed. I think that we have observed, ourselves, and have done our best to see that human rights are extended throughout the world.

Mr. Mondale has recently announced a plan of his to get the democracies together and to work with the whole world to turn to democracy. And I was glad to hear him say that, because that's what we've been doing ever since I announced to the British Parliament that I thought we should do this.

Human rights are not advanced when, at the same time, you then stand back and say, "Whoops, we didn't know the gun was loaded," and you have another totalitarian power on your hands.

Mr. Newman. In this segment, because of the pressure of time, there will be no rebuttals, and there will be no followup questions. Mr. Trewhitt, your question to President Reagan.

Mr. Trewhitt. One question to each candidate?

Mr. Newman. One question to each candidate.

Nuclear Weapons

Mr. Trewhitt. Mr. President, could I take you back to something you said earlier, and if I'm misquoting you, please correct me. But I understood you to say that if the development of space military technology was successful, you might give the Soviets a demonstration and say, "Here it is," which sounds to me as if you might be trying to gain the sort of advantage that would enable you to dictate terms, and which I will then suggest to you might mean scrapping a generation of nuclear strategy called mutual deterrence in which we, in effect, hold each other hostage. Is that your intention?

The *President.* Well, I can't say that I have roundtabled that and sat down with the Chiefs of Staff, but I have said that it seems to me that this could be a logical step in what is my ultimate goal, my ultimate dream, and that is the elimination of nuclear weapons in the world. And it seems to me that this could be an adjunct, or certainly a great assisting agent in getting that done. I am not going to roll over, as Mr. Mondale suggests, and give them something that could turn around and be used against us. But I think it's a very interesting proposal, to see if we can find, first of all, something that renders those weapons obsolete, incapable of their mission.

But Mr. Mondale seems to approve MAD—MAD is mutual assured destruction—meaning, if you use nuclear weapons on us, the only thing we have to keep you from doing it is that we'll kill as many people of yours as you'll kill of ours.

I think that to do everything we can to find, as I say, something that would destroy weapons and not humans is a great step forward in human rights.

Mr. Trewhitt. Mr. Mondale, could I ask you to address the question of nuclear strategy then? The formal doctrine is very arcane, but I'm going to ask you to deal with it anyway. Do you believe in MAD, mutual assured destruction, mutual deterrence as it has been practiced for the last generation?

Mr. Mondale. I believe in a sensible arms control approach that brings down these weapons to manageable levels. I would like to see their elimination. And in the meantime, we have to be strong enough to make certain that the Soviet Union never tempts us.

Now, here we have to decide between generalized objectives and reality. The President says he wants to eliminate or reduce the number of nuclear weapons. But, in fact, these last 4 years have seen more weapons built, a wider and more vigorous arms race than in human history. He says he wants a system that will make nuclear wars safe, so nobody's going to get hurt. Well, maybe someday, somebody can dream of that.

But why start an arms race now? Why destabilize our relationship? Why threaten our space satellites upon which we depend? Why pursue a strategy that would delegate to computers the question of starting a war?

A President, to defend this country and to get arms control, must master what's going on. I accept his objective and his dream; we all do. But the hard reality is that we must know what we're doing and pursue those objectives that are possible in our time. He's opposed every effort of every President to do so, and in the 4 years of his administration he's failed to do so. And if you want a tough President who uses that strength to get arms control and draws the line in the heavens, vote for Walter Mondale. [*Applause*]

Mr. Newman. Please, I must again ask the audience not to applaud, not to cheer, not to demonstrate its feelings in any way.

We've arrived at the point in the debate now where we call for closing statements. You have the full 4 minutes, each of you. Mr. Mondale, will you go first?

Closing Statements

Mr. Mondale. I want to thank the League of Women Voters, the good citizens of Kansas City, and President Reagan for agreeing to debate this evening.

This evening we talked about national strength. I believe we need to be strong, and I will keep us strong. But I think strength must also require wisdom and smarts in its exercise. That's key to the strength of our nation.

A President must know the essential facts essential to command. But a President must also have a vision of where this nation should go. Tonight, as Americans, you have a choice. And you're entitled to know where we would take this country if you decide to elect us.

As President, I would press for long-term, vigorous economic growth. That's why I want to get these debts down and these interest rates down, restore America's exports, help rural America, which is suffering so much, and bring the jobs back here for our children.

I want this next generation to be the best educated in American history, to invest in the human mind and science again, so we're out front. I want this nation to protect its air, its water, its land, and its public health. America is not temporary; we're forever. And as Americans, our generation should protect this wonderful land for our children.

I want a nation of fairness, where no one is denied the fullness of life or discriminated against, and we deal compassionately with those in our midst who are in trouble.

And, above all, I want a nation that's strong. Since we debated 2 weeks ago, the United States and the Soviet Union have built a hundred more warheads, enough to kill millions of Americans and millions of Soviet citizens. This doesn't strengthen us. This weakens the chances of civilization to survive.

I remember the night before I became Vice President. I was given the briefing and told that any time, night or day, I might be called upon to make the most fateful decision on Earth—whether to fire these atomic weapons that could destroy the human species. That lesson tells us two things: One,

pick a President that you know will know if that tragic moment ever comes what he must know, because there'll be no time for staffing committees or advisers. A President must know right then. But above all, pick a President who will fight to avoid the day when that God-awful decision ever needs to be made.

And that's why this election is so terribly important. America and Americans decide not just what's happening in this country. We are the strongest and most powerful free society on Earth. When you make that judgment, you are deciding not only the future of our nation; in a very profound respect, you're deciding the future of the world.

We need to move on. It's time for America to find new leadership. Please, join me in this cause to move confidently and with a sense of assurance and command to build the blessed future of our nation.

Mr. Newman. President Reagan, your summation, please.

The President. Yes. My thanks to the League of Women Voters, to the panelists, the moderator, and to the people of Kansas City for their warm hospitality and greeting.

I think the American people tonight have much to be grateful for—an economic recovery that has become expansion, freedom and, most of all, we are at peace.

I am grateful for the chance to reaffirm my commitment to reduce nuclear weapons and, one day, to eliminate them entirely.

The question before you comes down to this: Do you want to see America return to the policies of weakness of the last 4 years? Or do we want to go forward, marching together, as a nation of strength and that's going to continue to be strong?

We shouldn't be dwelling on the past, or even the present. The meaning of this election is the future and whether we're going to grow and provide the jobs and the opportunities for all Americans and that they need.

Several years ago, I was given an assignment to write a letter. It was to go into a time capsule and would be read in 100 years when that time capsule was opened.

I remember driving down the California

coast one day. My mind was full of what I was going to put in that letter about the problems and the issues that confront us in our time and what we did about them. But I couldn't completely neglect the beauty around me—the Pacific out there on one side of the highway, shining in the sunlight, the mountains of the coast range rising on the other side. And I found myself wondering what it would be like for someone—wondering if someone 100 years from now would be driving down that highway, and if they would see the same thing. And with that thought, I realized what a job I had with that letter.

I would be writing a letter to people who know everything there is to know about us. We know nothing about them. They would know all about our problems. They would know how we solved them, and whether our solution was beneficial to them down through the years or whether it hurt them. They would also know that we lived in a world with terrible weapons, nuclear weapons of terrible destructive power, aimed at each other, capable of crossing the ocean in a matter of minutes and destroying civilization as we knew it. And then I thought to myself, what are they going to say about us, what are those people 100 years from now going to think? They will know whether we used those weapons or not.

Well, what they will say about us 100 years from now depends on how we keep our rendezvous with destiny. Will we do the things that we know must be done and know that one day, down in history 100 years or perhaps before, someone will say, "Thank God for those people back in the 1980's for preserving our freedom, for saving for us this blessed planet called Earth, with all its grandeur and its beauty."

You know, I am grateful to all of you for giving me the opportunity to serve you for these 4 years, and I seek reelection because I want more than anything else to try to complete the new beginning that we charted 4 years ago. George Bush, who I think is one of the finest Vice Presidents this country has ever had—George Bush and I have crisscrossed the country, and we've had, in these last few months, a wonderful experience. We have met young America. We have met your sons and daughters.

Mr. Newman. Mr. President, I'm obliged to cut you off there under the rules of the debate. I'm sorry.

The President. All right. I was just going to——

Mr. Newman. Perhaps I should point out that the rules under which I did that were agreed upon by the two campaigns——

The President. I know.

Mr. Newman. ——with the league, as you know, sir.

The President. I know, yes.

Mr. Newman. Thank you, Mr. President. Thank you, Mr. Mondale. Our thanks also to the panel, finally, to our audience. We thank you, and the League of Women Voters asks me to say to you, don't forget to vote on November 6th.

Note: The debate began at 7:01 p.m. in the Music Hall at the Kansas City Convention Center. Following the debate, the President attended a reception hosted by the League of Women Voters in the Little Theater. He then returned to the Westin Crown Center Hotel, where he remained overnight.

Informal Exchange With Reporters on the Presidential Campaign
October 22, 1984

The President. [*Inaudible*]—running across the country for the cause of cancer, across the United States.

Q. That's very courageous.

Mr. President, let me ask you a question: How did you do last night?

The President. What?

Q. How did you do last night?

The President. Why, I was waiting for all of you to tell me.

Q. Well, no, you're the——

Q. Did you win, Mr. President?

Q. What do you think?

Q. Wait, Mrs. Reagan——

Q. Wait. She just coached you.

Mrs. Reagan. He won.

Q. She just said you won. [*Laughter*]

Q. Is she coaching you again?

The President. She says I won.

Q. What do you say?

Q. What do you say?

The President. Well, it comes better from her than from me. [*Laughter*]

Q. Well, seriously, don't you think you did a little better than Louisville?

The President. Yes, I felt fine. I felt good about it. I was sorry there were so many things that there wasn't time to respond to that I think were misstatements of facts.

Q. Well, what would you have told us at the end of your summation had you finished it?

The President. I was talking about the wonderful young people that we've met on campuses and high schools and just out of school and going to work, and how wonderful they are, and the responsibility of my generation and the generations between mine and theirs——

Q. Why did you do better this time, sir?

The President. ——have to do to see that they have the same kind of country and hope and opportunity that we had growing up, and that was our responsibility.

Q. But that letter—you were reading a letter.

Q. Why did you do better this time, sir?

Q. You started to read a letter.

The President. I finished about that.

Q. You didn't tell us what was in the letter.

Q. You didn't say what was in the letter.

The President. Well, it was a letter that had to do with our times and so forth, but then aimed at the—[*inaudible*]—and I knew that I was writing to people that, as I say, already knew the outcome a hundred years from now, that we were just——

Q. If they were alive?

The President. ——just giving them personal observations and so forth in there, but hopefully something that might be interesting to the generations——

Q. Why did you do better this time, sir?

The President. What?

Q. Why'd you do better this time than in Louisville?

The President. Well, I think sometimes, sometimes you go kind of flat. And I didn't feel that good in Louisville. I felt kind of flat. But maybe I'd overcrammed and so forth.

Q. And last night, sir?

The President. Last night? I felt fine.

Q. But they didn't brutalize you with the process this time, right? [*Laughter*]

The President. I haven't felt brutalized since I've been here. Oh, once or twice, meeting with you people, maybe, but—[*laughter*]——

Q. Well, you're going to win the election now?

The President. What?

Q. You're going to win the election now?

The President. You know me. I never say that. I'm superstitious.

Q. Mrs. Reagan, tell us what you thought.

Q. Mrs. Reagan——

Q. He's going to win the election?

Q. Tell us what you thought, Mrs. Reagan. Let Mrs. Reagan tell us what she thought of the——

Mrs. Reagan. He won.

Q. He won?

Mrs. Reagan. He won.

Q. Is he going to win the election, Mrs. Reagan?

Q. Is he going to win the election, Mrs. Reagan?

Mrs. Reagan. And I loved it when he said the thing about the age.

Q. Mr. President, are you going to campaign for the Members of Congress now?

The President. What?

Q. Are you going to go out and campaign for Republican Members of Congress now?

The President. I've been doing as much of that as I can. I've been doing spot ads for them, things of that kind. And I'm going to continue doing all that I can, because, again, I think that—I think it's only fair that you ask the people—if you're asking the people to support the things that you advocate, then you ought to be asking them all to send you a team to help you do it.

Q. Mrs. Reagan, did he win the election?

Q. How did Mondale do last night?

The President. Oh, I thought he was his usual self.

Q. Now, you know we're all going to play that submarine thing. We're going to play that tape from that '82 press conference about recalling submarine missiles. And we're going to compare your words with what you say you said.

The President. All right. I was talking about the submarines and the airplanes, that *they* could be called back, in contrast to the inadvertent possibility of someone putting his thumb on the button and then finding out it was a mistake and no way to recall an attack—that you can call the submarines and the planes back before the launching point of a missile. And, also, the fact that those more conventional-type weapons, they're not as destabilizing in people's minds, because we know from previous wars they can be intercepted and knocked down or sunk. But never—how could anyone think that any reasonable—[*inaudible*]—would believe that you could turn a nuclear missile around and bring it home? I think that that shows a lack of intelligence on their part to believe that.

Q. Well, see, that's what you said. I know you say that's not what you meant——

The President. No, it was taken out of context. And I realize that all of you are on the record of having repeated this so often, but, now, try to to find your way back off the end of the limb. I won't cut it off on you.

Q. Why are you pulling out of Beirut——

The President. What?

Mrs. Reagan. And you're—[*inaudible*]—Sam [Sam Donaldson, ABC News].

Q. Absolutely, Mrs. Reagan.

The President. Why didn't I what?

Q. Why is the United States pulling out of Beirut?

The President. Why didn't we pull them out?

Q. Why are you pulling them out?

The President. We pulled out because the terrorist activities——

Q. No, I mean, why are we pulling out now?

Q. [*Inaudible*]

The President. No, we've reduced all over the world. Our Embassy staff is streamlined, because our Embassies are being pressed in every country in the world.

Q. Is that why you're—[*inaudible*]?

The President. But the thing is—I don't know what Mr. Mondale would do about this—but we're not going to hunker down and pull all of our representation of the world out in the face of terrorist acts. That's what they would like us to do.

Q. But you are reducing personnel—[*inaudible*].

The President. Yes, streamlining down so that there are as few people as possible, but maintaining our Embassy contacts.

Mrs. Reagan. We have to go now, Helen [Helen Thomas, United Press International]. I'll throw you an orange. [*Laughter*]

Q. Mrs. Reagan——

The President. This young man is an example of that generation I was talking about last night, also. And they're a wonderful generation.

Q. Mrs. Reagan, how do you feel as compared to after Louisville?

Mrs. Reagan. Better.

Q. Better? Why?

Mrs. Reagan. Because he won.

Q. They didn't do anything to him this time, huh?

Mrs. Reagan. No, sir.

Q. You're quoted as saying, "What have they done to Ronnie?" last time.

Mrs. Reagan. I didn't say that.

Q. You didn't say it?

Mrs. Reagan. No.

Q. Okay.

Mrs. Reagan. I'm quoted as saying lots of things I didn't say. [*Laughter*]

Q. I know.

Note: The exchange began at 9:55 a.m. near Air Force One as the President was preparing to leave the Kansas City Downtown Airport in Missouri for Palmdale, CA. Prior to the exchange, the President met at the airport with Jeff Keith, of Stamford, CT. Mr. Keith, who had lost a leg to bone cancer 10 years earlier, was running from Boston, MA, to Los Angeles, CA, to raise money for the American Cancer Society.

Remarks to Employees at a Rockwell International Facility in Palmdale, California
October 22, 1984

Governor Deukmejian, Senator Pete Wilson, our Congressmen here—and one who must be a Congressman and join them in Washington, Bob Dornan, along with Carlos Moorhead, Bill Thomas, and the members of your State legislature, your county government, and your local officials, and all of you ladies and gentlemen:

Being here among friends and with professionals of Rockwell, Lockheed, and Northrop, and feeling your home State pride, reminds us once again of America's renewed spirit.

We're entering the home stretch of the campaign—or didn't you know that? [*Laughter*] We've set our sights on victory. And I believe the election of 1984 will be a victory for us all—for the future over the past, for progress over failure, for hope over despair, and, yes, for strength over weakness.

And what an airplane! You know, I have no complaints about Air Force One, but I was wondering, does Rockwell take trade-ins? [*Laughter*]

Let me congratulate Sam Iacobellis, the men and women of Rockwell, the subcontractors around the country, and the whole aerospace industry. You are doing a magnificent job. And I know there could be no better group of people working together than you—the men and women of our aerospace team here in southern California.

The teamwork of the B-1B is something to behold—5,200 suppliers and subcontractors, 55,000 workers nationwide, with 17,000 workers right here in California—producing quality work ahead of schedule and under cost. Now, present company excepted, have you ever stopped to consider how quickly our problems would disappear if the Congress would give us quality work ahead of schedule and under cost? But as I say, I don't mean the Congressmen that are present here. They've been working on our side.

Yours is the work of peace. The B-1B strategic bomber—two-thirds the size of the aging B-52, with twice the payload—and I've learned since I've been here I was wrong about that; it's 2½ times the payload—with one one-hundredth of the radar cross section, and with the most advanced electronic defense system in the world—will keep America prepared for peace.

You know, those people who criticize and somehow think that in defending ourselves or having the weapons of defense that somehow that makes us warlike—I don't know whether you know this, but up at Fairchild airbase, where I'm going, up in the State of Washington, there's a sign over the gate that says, "Peace is our profession."

I'm delighted that just last week, the first production model successfully completed its initial flight. The readiness, the capability and resolve of our Armed Forces are the greatest guarantees we have that our young people will never again see the ugly face of war. There have been four wars in my lifetime. None of them started because America was too strong.

Earlier this year, on Memorial Day, America laid to rest the Unknown Soldier of Vietnam. A grateful nation opened its heart in gratitude for the sacrifices of those who have served. And a week later, on Omaha Beach, on the 40th anniversary of D-day, I spoke of Private First Class Robert Zanatta of the 37th Engineers, who was on the first assault wave to hit that beach. And on a nearby lonely, windswept point, we met the boys of Pointe du Hoc, the American Rangers, who more than 40 years ago took the cliffs and helped to end a war. And, you know, it gives me great joy to tell you that one of the men I met—one of those one-time boys of Pointe du Hoc—63 years old, on the day before I got there, with today's present Rangers, he climbed those cliffs again in 7 minutes just to see if he could do it.

But I made a pledge that day to always remember, to always be proud, and to always be prepared, so we may always be free. And I have no higher responsibility than to honor that pledge. No one, absolutely no one, should ever ask the sons and daughters of America to protect this land with less than the best equipment that we can provide.

If our sons and daughters can put their lives on the line to keep us free, then I believe it's immoral to give them anything less than all the tools, all the training and the equipment to do the job right. And it's up to us in this election to choose, and choose wisely, between a strong, safe America—an America at peace—or to slide back to the failed and dangerous policies of the past. There's no clearer issue in this campaign.

I don't question my opponent's patriotism and love of country. I only question his philosophy. He voted to delay or kill virtually every new strategic system—the B-1 bomber, the Trident submarine and Trident missile, the cruise missile, our ABM system, and the modernization of our ICBM force. And when it came to our conventional forces, the record was just as frightening, with votes to reduce U.S. ground forces overseas by 40 percent and to withdraw half of our military from Europe. When it came to aircraft, he voted to terminate the Navy's F-14 program, the Marines' Harrier, the A-7 for the Air National Guard, and to cut funds for the C-5 transport.

If it were up to my opponent, I'm afraid Rockwell might still be building the B-25—that is, if you were building anything at all. The truth is, if all his votes had prevailed, America would barely have any defense, any real means to protect the peace, any chance to preserve freedom. And we can't afford that kind of protection.

When my opponent joined the Carter-Mondale administration, he remained true to this record—$25 billion in defense budget cuts, naval shipbuilding programs slashed by half, Trident programs slowed down, military pay kept so low that our people couldn't wait to leave the service and, as you know all too well, the B-1 was cancelled.

Well, today candidate Mondale is promising more of the same. And when you add his promise of an $85 billion tax increase, you've got two promises that he's bound to keep.

Senator Glenn, a Democrat, summed it up pretty well: "The Mondale record goes far beyond a simple disagreement over specific weapons programs. I think it reveals a fundamental lack of support for an adequate national defense." I couldn't agree more. Mr. Mondale made a career out of weakening America's Armed Forces. Well, as long as I'm in this job, we will not shortchange the security needs of America.

This hostility to a strong, secure America—an America at the leading edge of technology—was also demonstrated in his opposition to the space shuttle. He called it a horrible waste, a space extravaganza. My opponent was the acknowledged leader of the fraternity of pessimists in the Senate, voting time and again to delete funds for the shuttle and to reduce overall NASA funding.

Well, I believe there's never a time when we should stop dreaming and striving and moving forward. The footprints on the Moon reawakened us to mankind's boundless horizon and showed us that America's future can be determined by our dreams and by our visions. Together, we've opened new doors to discovery, opportunity, and progress.

The era of Apollo spawned communications, weather, navigation, and Earth resource satellites, and many new industries. America built a technological base second to none, and all the while, served the down-to-Earth needs of our people. And today, thanks to the work that you're doing here with the shuttle, we're pushing the frontiers of space back even farther, and we're going to keep on pushing.

As long as it's my watch—if a horse cavalryman of the past can speak in naval terms—we'll accept the challenge of space and keep battling for the future, for discovery, for new jobs and markets, and for knowledge. We have a promise to keep—to ourselves and to our young. And let me say of our young people, they are a shining generation.

Traveling across the country and seeing our high school and college students has been a wonderful experience, as well as seeing those who have already taken their first steps out here into the working world.

They're bright. They're creative. They're idealistic. They have faith in themselves, faith in the future, and faith in America. And we must do all we can to see that the world they inherit from us is a world full of decency and daring as the world in which we were born.

You know, last night I got shut off because I ran out of time on my 4-minute finale. And I'm so delighted to see these young people who are here because what I wanted to say is that between my generation and theirs—there were a few of you in other generations in between—but all of us of those generations, our responsibility—we grew up in an America where we took it for granted that you could dream and make your dreams come true, if you set out to do that. And what we owe these young people—and they are very special—George Bush and I, as I said last night, have seen them all across this country—what we owe them is to see that we turn over to them the same kind of America of hope and opportunity that our parents turned over to us. And that's what we're going to do.

To give our future a chance, we must keep moving forward in new frontiers in science, technology, and space. And to give peace a chance to grow and settle in, we must remain strong. And those who have no vision of the future have no business leading America. And those who believe a weaker America is a safer America have no business guiding the destiny of our nation.

In 1981 we went to work repairing the damage caused by wrong-headed thinking. And besides working to restore the strategic balance, we started to rebuild our conventional forces. And today every major commander in the field agrees that America's military forces have better people, who are better armed, better trained, better motivated, with better support behind them.

If we were to stop now in midstream, we'd send a signal of decline, lessened will, and weakness to friends and adversaries alike. If we were to return to the time when we modernized our defenses in fits and starts, each time losing the security we gained earlier, then we would never be certain of our security. We'd never be able to convince the Soviet leadership that it is in their interest to sit down and negotiate equitable arms reductions. And the American people know it.

It's always easy to argue for reductions in defense spending, just as it's easy to pretend that one can call the Soviet leaders, as my opponent has proposed, and persuade them in a moment to alter the course they've followed for decades. It's also nonsense, and the American people know it.

There is no quick, easy way. The solution is firmness and patience. The only sensible and safe route is to make sure that we're prepared to defend freedom and prepared for peace. And the American people know that, too.

From our earliest years, our Presidents have stressed the crucial role of preparedness in promoting peace and stability. George Washington said, "There's nothing so likely to produce peace as to be well prepared to meet a foe." Harry Truman said, "The will for peace without the strength for peace is of no avail." And John Kennedy said, "The primary purpose of our arms is peace, not war. Our preparation against danger is our hope for safety."

Now, my opponents can't stand it when I start talking about Harry Truman or J.F.K.—I need to remind them that Harry Truman was the last Democrat I voted and campaigned for—but of course they can't, because it just shows them how far the leadership today of the Democratic Party has strayed from the great strengths of the Democratic political tradition. And nowhere is the drift more evident than in their unwillingness to keep us prepared for peace. And I think the American people know that.

Four years ago, our nation chose the road of peace through strength—a road built upon a realistic understanding of the world around us and the continuing faith in the American values. And 15 days from now, it will again be a time for choosing. We can be confident because we trust the American people.

And in view of some of the things that were said last night—to those of you that saw that—you hear about the bad relations that we now have between ourselves and the Soviet Union. Last year we sold them 23 million tons of grain, and our farmers benefited accordingly. And in the 4 years that we've been here, they haven't advanced by 1 square inch of territory anyplace in the world.

I know that I've been talking partisan politics, and I know that in a crowd like this there must be thousands of people who are Democrats. And I'm delighted, having been one for most of my life, because I know that all across this country there are millions of patriotic, dedicated Democrats who know they can no longer follow in the path of the leadership of their party, which has taken us down such strange paths, so foreign to what the leadership of the Democratic Party once believed.

Well, join us, and in a bipartisan way we'll make this country the way it should be. Thank you very much. God bless you. Thank you.

Note: The President spoke at 12:08 p.m. in Hangar 703 at the company's aircraft assembly complex. Prior to his remarks, the President was given a tour of the B–1B assembly area at the complex.

Following his remarks, the President traveled to San Diego, CA.

Remarks at a Reagan-Bush Rally in San Diego, California
October 22, 1984

The President. Thank you, Senator Pete Wilson, Governor Deukmejian, and it feels good to be back in California and with you here in San Diego.

I've come to San Diego asking for your support in every campaign that I've ever been in. And I'm here today to ask this last one time. [*Applause*] Well, I was going to ask if I could count on you, and you've already answered that. And thank you very much.

I see something here I've been noticing all over the country—the large number of young people. I know you're putting yourselves squarely on the side of a strong and a growing America. People of every age, race, and background are flocking to a banner of opportunity. And nowhere is that more clear than in California. Disadvantaged Americans are waking up to the failure of bureaucratic programs to bring them the economic opportunity they need to make real progress.

I'm especially pleased that Hispanic-Americans, who are so important to our California heritage, are joining us in increasing numbers. And here in California, we also see our coalition bolstered by Asian-Americans, many of them recent immigrants who have come here like our own forefathers and mothers for freedom and to improve their well-being.

Earlier this year, there was a candidate who claimed to be building a rainbow coalition. Well, we're building an American coalition, and that says it all.

I want to take this opportunity to thank you for sending to the Congress three Representatives who've been in the forefront of the battle for responsible government and a strong America—Congressmen Bill Lowery, Duncan Hunter, and Ron Packard. I've got a favor to ask: On election day make sure that you send them back to Washington; because if you're going to send me back there, I don't know what I'd do without them. You and all these fine candidates are part of a new spirit that's spreading across America.

You know—I assume that maybe some of you saw the debate last night. Well, the format for the debate is sometimes frustrating. When the other fellow's making a lot of misstatements, you don't have time always to challenge them. So, last night I told the people, for example, that Mr. Mondale had voted to kill the F–14 fighterplane. And he said he only voted to delay production. Well, that was one I didn't get to respond to. I'll do it here.

On September 29, 1971, he voted on an amendment by Senator Proxmire to kill the F–14. That was no vote to delay; that was a vote to delete. And fortunately, he failed.

The planes that did that job that the Senator was referring to, they were F–14's.

You know, as election day nears, the American people are getting the full flavor of the very clear choice facing them.

Is there an echo out here? [1]

It's a choice between two fundamentally different ways of governing and two distinct ways of looking at America. My opponent, Mr. Mondale, offers a government of pessimism, fear, and limits compared to ours of hope, confidence, and growth. He sees government as an end in itself. And we see government as something belonging to the people and only a junior partner in our lives. They see people merely as members of groups, special interests to be coddled and catered to. We look at them as individuals to be fulfilled through their own freedom and creativity.

My opponent and his allies live in the past, celebrating the old and failed policies of an era that has passed them by, as if history had skipped over those Carter-Mondale years. On the other hand, millions of Americans join us in boldly charting a new course for the future.

From the beginning, their campaign has lived on promises. Indeed, Mr. Mondale has boasted that America is nothing if it isn't promises. Well, the American people don't want promises, and they don't want to pay for his promises. They want promise. They want opportunity and workable answers. And that's why we're here—to talk about the record, the record of the administration in which Mr. Mondale carried a full partnership.

Mr. Carter himself said, "There wasn't a single decision I made during 4 years in the White House that Fritz Mondale wasn't involved in." In those years, they took the strongest economy in the world and pushed it to the brink of collapse. They created a calamity of such proportions that we're still suffering the consequences of those economic time bombs. What they left on our doorstep in January 1981 was a snarling economic wolf with sharp teeth.

---

[1] *The President was referring to a small crowd demonstrating nearby.*

The suffering of America, the deep and painful recession, and the outrageous and frightening inflation—these things didn't start by spontaneous combustion. They came about through the concerted mismanagement of which Mr. Mondale was a part, and his liberal friends who controlled the Congress.

They gave us five—count them—five different anti-inflation plans and managed to give us the worst 4-year record of inflation in nearly 40 years. While it took them five economic plans to nearly triple inflation, it's taken us only one to cut it by about two-thirds.

Senior citizens were driven into panic by higher rents, exhorbitant fuel costs, dramatically increasing food prices, and Federal health care costs, which went up a massive 87 percent. And they called that fairness.

They punished the poor and the young, who struggled as prices of necessities shot up faster than others. Millions of Americans led a life of daily economic terror, fueled by these unrelenting costs. And they called that compassion.

Well, let's look at interest rates. My opponent has referred to something he calls real interest rates. Well, people don't pay interest rates based on some academic smokescreen or foggy economic theory. What they know is that when Jerry Ford left office, the prime interest rate was 6¼ percent. When Mr. Mondale left office, it was 21½ percent, the highest in 120 years.

Average monthly mortgage payments more than doubled. Young people couldn't buy homes. Car loans were hard to get and expensive. The automobile and homebuilding industries were brought to their knees. It's little wonder that the American people yearned for leadership in 1980. And after all this economic punishment, our opponents blamed you, because you lived too well. And they told you you had to sacrifice more and that we were now in an age of limits.

Audience. Boo-o-o!

The President. Well, I found out that it's not so much that Mr. Mondale has a poor memory of his ruinous past; he's just got a darn good "forgetory." And now he says,

"I'm ready to be President." Well, forgive me, but——

I thought he was campaigning in someplace else.[2] [*Laughter*]

Forgive me, but I believe he's more ready to be our problem than our President.

Now, as Senator Wilson was telling you, on defense, too, he has a record of weakness, confusion, and failure. Before the invasion of Czechoslovakia, he announced that the days of Soviet suppression by force were over. And after the invasion of Afghanistan, he said just what you were told—that he was baffled. There's so much that seems to baffle him.

He was confused about the rightness of freeing our students on the island of Grenada. Senator John Glenn said that my opponent would "cut our Defense Establishment beyond all reality"—cut the B–1, the *Nimitz* carrier, the Trident, the cruise missile, the foreign troops; would cut the M–1 tank, funds for the volunteer army; kill the shuttle; oppose procurement of the F–14, the Harrier, and the AWACS. Now, I don't know if he'd outlaw slingshots—[*laughter*]—but he certainly would jeopardize our national security. And we're not going to let him do it.

Audience. 4 more years! 4 more years! 4 more years!

The President. Okay. All right. And, you know, if the Capital were in California, I'd agree to 40.

But, you know, something else that our opponents would like to forget is a gimmick from the 1976 campaign, where they added the unemployment and the inflation rates together, and the total—they called it the misery index. And at the end of 1976 it was 12.6, and they declared that the incumbent had no right to seek reelection with that kind of a misery index. Well, 4 years later we were in the 1980 campaign, and they never mentioned the misery index. And I don't think Mr. Mondale will mention it in this campaign, because by 1980 and when he left the Vice Presidency it was over 20. And it's now down around 11.

---

[2] *The President was referring to an airplane flying overhead.*

My opponent has done a very good job of trying to slip, slide, and duck away from this record. But we know now that those disastrous consequences didn't come about by accident; they came through the implementation of the very policies of out-of-control spending, unfair taxation, and worship of big government that my opponent still supports.

His philosophy can be summed up in four sentences: If it's income, tax it. If it's revenue, spend it. If it's a budget, break it. And if it's promise, make it.

All this year Mr. Mondale has lavished his campaign with promises that staggered even his Democratic opponents. Senator John Glenn was heard to say in frustration that Mr. Mondale, and I quote, "has just promised everything to everybody, with no thought of how it's going to be paid for." And Gary Hart said, "Fritz, you cannot lead this country if you've promised everybody everything."

But, of course, there is a predictable answer by one who makes so many promises. The answer is higher taxes. And massive new tax increases are precisely what he proposes.

Audience. Boo-o-o!

The President. A few weeks back, he called his new plan pay-as-you-go. But what it is, of course, is nothing but the old plan. You pay, and he goes. [*Laughter*]

Those tax increases to pay for his promises add up to the equivalent of $1,890 per household; that's more than $150 per month. I call it the Mondale mortgage. If Harry Truman had to apply a motto to this radical taxing scheme—and for the young people here who might not remember Harry Truman, he was the fellow that said about the desk that he sat at in the Oval Office, "The buck stops here"—I have a hunch that if he had to have a motto right now for this particular candidate that I've been talking about, he'd say, "Your buck never stops."

But hold on; he's got more. A couple of weeks ago, he said he would like to repeal indexing. Now, this tax is even worse, because it would be a dagger at the heart of every low- and middle-income taxpayer in America. It would mean bone-crushing, new levies against those who could least afford them. Indexing was a reform that we passed to protect you from the cruelest of taxes—the hidden tax that when government uses inflation to force you into higher tax brackets, just because you've gotten a cost-of-living pay raise—that's when your taxes go up.

And under the Mondale plan, here's what would happen to a family struggling on $10,000 per year. By 1989 they would be paying over 73 percent more in income taxes if indexing, which begins on this January 1st, is canceled.

And then Mr. Mondale reversed himself and said he'd made a mistake. Well, that's something he seems to do quite a lot. [*Laughter*] But the truth is, that several times between 1982 and now he has expressly proposed the repeal of indexing. In politics they call this a flip-flop. In this case, you'll forgive me if I call it a Fritz-flop.

Yesterday he wanted to give you a $200 tax break to every family dependent. And today he wants to raise taxes the equivalent of almost $2,000 a household. You know, for some time, over the last several weeks at least, he was talking about a new Reagan and an old Reagan. Now, that had nothing to do with my age. The old Reagan was the earlier one, the first one—the new Reagan is now. And when he said that, well, he inspired me to do a little of that old and new business.

The old Mondale is on record as saying that reducing deficits could worsen a recession. The new Mondale thinks higher taxes lead to a healthy economy. The old Mondale publicly supported Jimmy Carter's wrong-headed grain embargo. And the new Mondale claims that he opposed it—privately. Very privately. [*Laughter*]

The old Mondale sponsored National Bible Week. Well, old or new, I'm with him on that one. But this new Mondale says there's too much religion in politics. The old Mondale called the space shuttle a "horrible waste," a "space extravaganza." And he personally led the fight in the United States Senate to kill the shuttle program before it even started.

Audience. Boo-o-o!

The President. The new Mondale praises American technological achievement.

But just when you were beginning to lose faith you find that there is some constancy with him. The old Mondale increased your taxes, and the new Mondale will do it again.

You know, in our debates, I got a little angry all those times that he distorted my record. And on one occasion, I was about to say to him very sternly, "Mr. Mondale, you're taxing my patience." [*Laughter*] And then I caught myself. Why should I give him another idea? [*Laughter*]

Well, from now until November 6th, we're going to make sure the American people know about this choice on which their future depends. We have two roads to tomorrow. The road of fear and envy that he proposes—on his road, you frighten the elderly with false statements. You strive to divide Americans against each other, seeking to promote envy and promote greed. Franklin Roosevelt warned us, "The only thing we have to fear is fear itself." Well, sadly and tragically, the only thing that my opponent has to offer is fear itself. And that's the difference between us.

We see America's best days ahead of us. We see ourselves in a springtime of hope, ready to fire up our courage and determination to reach high and achieve all the best. We see a life where our children can enjoy at last prosperity without inflation. We see a life where they can enjoy the highest of creativity and go for the stars and not have their hopes and dreams crushed or taxed away by greedy governmentalists.

In 1980 the American people declared their independence all over again. We realized that when we went from good government to big government, it was time to put our house back in order.

Today we've returned to a proper understanding of who the American people are. We're the people who crossed the plains, scaled the mountains, won the West. We're the people who came up with the inventions that lit the world and filled it with sound and laughter. We're the people who twice in this century have fought in Europe and stood for decency for all mankind.

We're a people, in short, who don't need the supervision of government sophisticates to tell us what is right and good. And now the American people are walking into tomorrow unashamed and unafraid. They're ready for this great, new era of opportunity.

And, once again, I want to refer to these young people who are with us and these young people all over the country. I didn't get to finish last night what I was going to say. We ran out of time.

What I had already said is that all across this country in high schools, in schools on college and university campuses, and among younger people who have finished education and started out into life—seen them all across this country—and, believe me, to the rest of you, or of those other generations, these young people today are very special. Yes, you are. And you know what? The responsibility—and this is what I was going to say last night—the responsibility of my generation and those generations between mine and yours, our responsibility is to see that you grow up in the same kind of country that we grew up in, a country of hope and opportunity. And our job is to hand you an America that is free in a country—or a world that is at peace.

Audience. 4 more years! 4 more years! 4 more years!

The President. And now I——

Audience. 4 more years! 4 more years! 4 more years!

The President. All right.

Audience. 4 more years! 4 more years! 4 more years!

The President. All right.

Audience. 4 more years! 4 more years! 4 more years!

The President. And now——

Audience. 4 more years! 4 more years! 4 more years!

The President. All right. And now, I know this may gall our opponents, but I think the people agree with this when I say, you ain't seen nothin' yet.

Thank you very much. God bless you all.

Note: The President spoke at 2:39 p.m. at the San Diego County Administration Center.

Following his remarks, the President traveled to Medford, OR.

Remarks at a Reagan-Bush Rally in Medford, Oregon
October 22, 1984

The President. Thank you, Governor Atiyeh, ladies and gentlemen here on the dais, and all of you out there, thank you for a most heartwarming reception. It's great to be back in the beautiful State of Oregon, and it's great to be back in the proud town of Medford.

You know, there's something healthy about this part of the country where so many live so close to the land, growing fruit and farming, mining, lumbering. It's a life that produces qualities like character and self-reliance. Indeed, I can think of a few liberal Democrats that I wish, could come here to see it, and then stay. No, no—now wait a minute, you're right—that wouldn't be fair to the people of this good town.

But a special greeting to your outstanding Governor, Vic Atiyeh, your fine Senators, Mark Hatfield and Bob Packwood, and to your skilled and dedicated Members of the Congress, Bob Smith and Denny Smith. Believe me, we couldn't have accomplished all we have without the help of determined Republicans like Denny and Bob in the House, and a Republican majority—including Mark and Bob—in the Senate.

Recently, these fine Members of the Congress played a central role in passing a vital piece of legislation—the timber relief bill. The timber industry here in the Pacific Northwest has seen more than its share of hard times. And this legislation will enable the industry to gain the full benefits of our economic expansion. For thousands, this bill will mean more jobs, more opportunity, and renewed hope. And I'm happy to tell you that just a few days ago, last week, I signed that timber bill into law.

You know, Abe Lincoln said that we must disenthrall ourselves with the past, and then we'll save our country. Well, 4 years ago that's what we did. We made a great turn. We got out from under the thrall of a government which we'd hoped would make our lives better, but which wound up living our lives for us. The power of the Federal Government had, over the decades, created great chaos—economic chaos, social chaos, international chaos. Our leaders were adrift, rudderless, without a compass.

Four years ago we began to navigate by certain fixed principles. Our North Star was freedom, and common sense were our constellations. We knew that economic freedom meant paying less of the American family's earnings to the Government, and so we cut personal income tax rates by 25 percent. We knew that inflation, the quiet thief, was stealing our savings. And the highest interest rates since the Civil War were making it impossible for people to own a home or start an enterprise. We knew that our national military defense had been weakened, so we decided to rebuild and be strong again. And this, we knew, would enhance the prospects for peace in the world. It was a second American revolution—and it's only just begun.

But what already has come of our efforts? A great renewal. America is back—a giant, reemergent on the scene—powerful in its renewed spirits, powerful in its economy, powerful in the world economy, and powerful in its ability to defend itself and secure the peace.

But now, 4 years after our efforts began, small voices in the night are sounding the call to go back, go backward to the days of confusion and drift——

Audience. No!

The President. All right. And they would have us go back to the days of torpor, timidity, and taxes.

Audience. No!

The President. Now, my opponent this year is known to you——

Audience. Boo-o-o!

The President. ——but perhaps we can gain great insight into his leadership abilities and his philosophy if we take a look at his record.

To begin with, his grasp of economics is well demonstrated by his economic predictions. Just before we took office, my opponent said that our economic program is, ob-

viously, murderously inflationary. Now, that was just before we lowered inflation from above 12 percent to 4.

And just after our tax cuts, he said the most he could see was an anemic recovery. That was before our economy created more than 6 million new jobs in 21 months, and just before nearly 900,000 businesses were incorporated in less than a year and a half.

My opponent said that our policies would deliver a misery index the likes of which we haven't seen in a long time. And there was some truth in that. You know, you get the misery index by adding the rate of unemployment to the rate of inflation, and they invented that for the 1976 campaign. And they said that Jerry Ford had no right to seek reelection because his misery index was all of 12.6. Now, they didn't mention the misery index in the 1980 election because it had gone up to more than 20. And they aren't talking too much about it in this campaign, because it's down to 11.

My opponent said that decontrol of oil prices, which is one of the first things we did, would cost American consumers more than $36 billion a year. Well, we decontrolled oil prices, and the price of gas went down 8 cents a gallon. And they're still headed down.

Now, you know, it's just occurred to me that maybe all we have to do to get the economy in absolutely perfect shape is to get my opponent to predict absolute disaster. [*Laughter*]

He says he cares about the middle class, but he boasts, "I have consistently supported legislation, time after time, which increases taxes on my own constituents." Doesn't that make you want to be a constituent of his? [*Laughter*]

No, he's no doubt proud of the fact that he voted 16 times as a United States Senator to raise your taxes. And this year he's outdone himself. He's already promised, of course, to raise your taxes. But if he is to keep all the promises he's made to this group and that, we will have to raise taxes by the equivalent of $1,890 for every household. That's more than $150 a month. It's like having a second mortgage. And after the Mondale mortgage, we'd be sure to see more than a few foreclosures.

His economic plan has two basic parts: raise your taxes, and then raise them again. [*Laughter*] But I've got news for him: The American people don't want his tax increases, and he isn't going to get his tax increases.

His tax plan would bring recovery to a roaring halt. But I'll give it this: His plan did give me an idea for Halloween. If I could find a way to dress up as his tax program, I could scare the devil out of all my neighbors. [*Laughter*]

The difference between us is simply this: He sees an America in which every day is tax day, April 15th. We see an America in which every day is the Fourth of July, Independence Day. What we want is to lower your and everybody else's taxes, so that your families will be stronger, our economy will be stronger, and America will be stronger.

But I'm not finished here. I'm proud to say that during these last 4 years, not one square inch of territory has been lost to Communist aggression. And the United States is more secure than we were 4 years ago. I know they were complaining because they thought maybe I was speaking too harshly to the Russians, but on the other hand, maybe we got their attention.

But there's so much more to say about our opponent. His grasp of foreign affairs is demonstrated by the following: Sometime back, he said the old days of a Soviet strategy of suppression by force are over—and that was just before the Soviets invaded Czechoslovakia. And after they invaded Afghanistan, he said, "It just baffles me why the Soviets these last few years have behaved as they have." [*Laughter*] But then there's so much that baffles him. [*Laughter*]

One year ago we liberated Grenada from Communist thugs who had taken that country over in a coup. And my opponent called what we did a violation of international law that erodes our moral authority to criticize the Soviet invasion of Afghanistan.

Audience. Boo-o-o!

The President. Well, still, I'll say this: His administration did mete out strong punishment after Afghanistan. Unfortunately, they punished the American farmer, not the Soviet Union.

My opponent supported the grain embargo and spoke out for it often. He even questioned the patriotism of a Senator from his own party when that Senator called that embargo just what it was—unworkable and unfair. Now he seems to have changed his tune. He says he privately opposed the embargo—very privately. [*Laughter*] As a matter of fact, he has, in the last several months, claimed that he opposed a number of the administration's policies when he was Vice President. But as Jody Powell, who was also in that administration, said, "I guess I was out of the room every time it happened." [*Laughter*]

After the Sandinista revolution in Nicaragua, Mr. Mondale praised it, saying, "Winds of democratic progress are stirring where they have long been stifled." But we know that the Sandinistas immediately began to persecute the genuine believers in democracy and to export terror. They went on to slaughter the Miskito Indians, abuse and deport church leaders, slander the Pope, and move to kill free speech. So, why isn't my opponent speaking out now about those winds of democracy?

More recently, he failed to repudiate the Reverend Jesse Jackson, when he went to Havana, stood with Fidel Castro, and cried: "Long live Cuba! Long live President Fidel Castro! Long live Che Guevara!"

Audience. Boo-o-o!

The President. I could say of his economic program that he will either have to break his promises or break the bank. But I won't say it, because Senator John Glenn, a Democrat, already has said it. I could call his economic program a collection of old and tired ideas held together by paralyzing commitments to special interest groups. But I won't, because Senator Gary Hart, a Democrat, has already said that. I could predict that he will create deficits more than twice what they are now. But I won't, because Senator Fritz Hollings, a Democrat, has already said that.

Now, if on political issues my opponent dares to be wrong, on domestic policy issues he has the courage to be cautious. A line-item veto to help control wild government spending—no, he says, that's not part of the liberal agenda. Well, as Governor of California I had the line-item veto. Your Governor has a line-item veto. Forty-two other Governors in the United States have a line-item veto. And you know something? It works. And it would work at the Federal level if we can get them off the dime and get it.

He's long opposed enterprise zones to help the most economically troubled neighborhoods in the country. But then a few weeks ago, he said he's for them. Well, if he's for them, why doesn't he ask his friend, Tip O'Neill, to stop blocking the enterprise zone bill which is buried in a committee of the House of which he is the Speaker?

This month an American woman walked in space—the first to do so. Kathryn Sullivan made history. And she returned to a space shuttle in which some of the great scientific and medical advances of the future are being made and will be made. Cures for diabetes and heart disease may be possible up there; advances in technology and communication. And that's why I support the space shuttle. But my opponent personally led the fight against it and called it a horrible waste and tried to keep it from even being put into effect.

The truth is that my opponent's campaign, if it were a television show, it would be "Let's Make a Deal." [*Laughter*] You get to trade your prosperity for whatever is behind the curtain. If his campaign were a Broadway show, it would be "Promises, Promises." [*Laughter*] And if his administration were a novel, it would only have a happy ending if you read it from the back toward the front. [*Laughter*]

Now, I've probably been going on too long here, but——

Audience. No!

The President. ——but the point is, the point is we made a great turn in the road in 1980. And we were right to take command of the ship, stop its aimless drift, and get moving again. And we were right when we stopped sending out S.O.S. and started saying U.S.A. again.

Audience. 4 more years! 4 more years! 4 more years!

The President. All right.

Audience. 4 more years! 4 more years! 4 more years!

The President. Thank you. Well, you talked me into it.

And let me say here that the 1984 election isn't just a partisan contest. I was a Democrat once, for a great part of my life. And I always respected that party. But in those days, its leaders weren't in the "blame America first" crowd. Its leaders were men like Harry Truman, men who understood the challenges of the times. They didn't reserve all their indignation for America. They knew the difference between freedom and tyranny, and they stood up for the one and they damned the other.

To all the good Democrats who respect that tradition, I say, "You are not alone; you're not without a home." We're putting out our hands, and we're asking you—and I hope there are many in the crowd—come walk with us down this new path of hope and opportunity and, in a bipartisan way, we'll save this country.

Audience. 4 more years! 4 more years! 4 more years!

The President. Thank you. All right. Okay. All right.

And now, let me say something—I got interrupted trying to say this last night, ran out of time—[*laughter*]—to the young people of our country. [*Applause*] Look at that! Let me say that nothing, nothing has touched our hearts more than your wonderful support, all across this country. And you, you are what this election is all about. It's your future that we care so much about.

I didn't get a chance to say it last night, but my next line was going to be: Your generation is something special. You're truly something new on the scene. Your idealism and your love of country are unsurpassed. And I consider it our highest duty to make certain that you have an America that is every bit as full of opportunity, hope, confidence, and dreams as we had when we were your age.

All of us together are part of a great revolution, and it's only just begun. We'll never stop. America will never stop. We never give up. We'll never give up on our special mission.

There are new worlds on the horizon, and we're not going to stop until we all get there together. America's best days are yet to come. You ain't seen nothin' yet.

Audience. 4 more years! 4 more years! 4 more years!

The President. Thank you. Thank you all very much. Thank you for your wonderful hospitality and the warmth of your greeting. Thank you for your support. And God bless, God bless you. Thank you very much.

Note: The President spoke at 5:45 p.m. in the main terminal at the Medford-Jackson County Airport.

Following his remarks, the President traveled to Portland, OR, and the Westin Benson Hotel, where he remained overnight.

Remarks at a Reagan-Bush Rally in Portland, Oregon
October 23, 1984

The President. Thank you, thank you very much.

Audience. 4 more years! 4 more years! 4 more years!

The President. Thank you, thank you. I hadn't thought about it, but you've talked me into it.

Thank you very much. Governor, thank you for a very kind introduction——

Audience member. [*Inaudible*]

The President. ——and all of you for a warm welcome.

Audience member. [*Inaudible*]

The President. You know what? You know what? I may just let Mondale raise *his* taxes. [*Laughter*]

It's wonderful to be in Oregon, and it's wonderful to be in the City of Roses. And it's especially good to be at the University of Portland, home of the mighty Pilots. This unique, new center is a tribute to the great spirit of voluntarism that's exemplified by the Chiles Foundation.

I want to thank you right off for sending such fine representatives to Washington—Senators Mark Hatfield and Bob Packwood, Congressmen Bob Smith and Denny Smith, who is with us here. They've all helped us so much, and we're hoping that they'll stay in Washington for a long time. And they need company, so we hope that you will send your fine candidates there to be with them. And may I say, you have one of the best Governors in the country in Vic Atiyeh.

I feel very much at home here, partly because during the Republican convention, one of your State officials offered to change the name of your State to "Oreagan." But I'm told that your city has had an interest-

ing history with regard to names; that when the first settlers came here from the East, they saw its possibilities as a beautiful port. They cleared the area around here, cut down the trees, and made a tomahawk claim of the area. And then they chose to call it their own. And one of the main settlers insisted the city be called Boston. Another insisted it be called Portland, after Portland, Maine. And they settled it in a very gentlemanly manner. They flipped a coin. [*Laughter*] And so, Portland was born.

I'm involved, as you probably have heard, in kind of a contest now. It won't be settled by the toss of a coin—[*laughter*]—it'll be settled by the wisdom of good people like yourselves.

As your Governor told you—and I've been thinking, too, of what has been accomplished in these past 4 years, and what we had to overcome to get where we are. And it reminded me that in 1862 Abe Lincoln gave us some enduring advice. Abe Lincoln said, we must disenthrall ourselves with the past—and then we will save our country. Well, 4 years ago, that's what we did. We made a great turn. We got out from under the thrall of a government which we had hoped would make our lives better, but which wound up living our lives for us.

The power of the Federal Government had, over the decades, created great chaos—economic chaos, social chaos, international chaos.

Audience member. What about the deficit?

The President. Our leaders were adrift, rudderless, without a compass. And 4 years ago, we began to navigate by certain fixed principles. Our North Star was freedom, and common sense was our constellation.

We knew that economic freedom meant paying less of the American family's earnings to the Government. And so, we cut personal income tax rates by 25 percent.

We knew that inflation, the quiet thief, was stealing our savings, and the highest interest rates since the Civil War were making it impossible for people to own a home or start an enterprise.

We knew that our national military defense had been weakened, so we decided to rebuild and be strong again. And this we knew would enhance the prospects for peace in the world. It was a second American revolution, and it's only just begun.

But what already has come of our efforts? A great renewal. America is back, a giant reemergent on the scene—powerful in its renewed spirits, powerful in its economy, powerful in the world economy, and powerful in its ability to defend itself and secure the peace.

But now, 4 years after our efforts began, small voices in the night are sounding the call to go back, go backward to the days of confusion and drift, the days of torpor, timidity, and taxes.

My opponent this year is known to you, but perhaps we can gain a greater insight into his leadership abilities and his philosophy if we take a look at his record.

To begin with, his grasp of economics is well demonstrated by his economic predictions. Just before we took office, my opponent said our economic program is obviously, murderously inflationary. Now, that was just before we lowered inflation from above 12 percent to 4 percent.

Then, just after our tax cuts, he said the most that he could see was an anemic recovery; and that was right before our economy created more than 6 million new jobs in 21 months and just before a record nearly 900,000 businesses were incorporated in less than a year and a half.

Now, my opponent said that our policies would deliver a misery index the likes of which we haven't seen for a long time. Well, now, there was some truth in that. You know, you get the misery index by adding up the unemployment rate and the inflation rate. Now, they invented that for

the 1976 campaign. And they said that Jerry Ford had no right to seek reelection, because his misery index was 12.6. Now, they didn't mention the misery index in the 1980 campaign, because it had gone up to more than 20 percent. And they aren't talking too much about it in this campaign, because it's down around 11.

Now, my opponent said that decontrol of oil prices would cost American consumers more than $36 billion a year. Well, one of the first things we did was decontrol oil prices, and the price of gas went down 8 cents a gallon. And the prices are still headed down.

Now, you know, it's just occurred to me that maybe all we have to do to get the economy absolutely in perfect shape is to get my opponent to predict absolute disaster. I must say, though, he's learned some things. My opponent is concerned now about the deficit. But back during the Jerry Ford years, he proposed that the deficit should be doubled because a deficit would stimulate the economy.

Now, he says he cares about the middle class, but he boasts, "I have consistently supported legislation time after time which increases taxes on my own constituents." Now, doesn't that make you just want to be a constitutent of his? [*Laughter*] Now, he's no doubt proud of the fact that he voted 16 times as a United States Senator to increase taxes.

This year he's outdone himself. He's already promised, of course, to raise your taxes. But if he's to keep all the promises that he's made to this group and that, he will have to raise taxes by the equivalent of $1,890 for every household in the United States.

Audience. Boo-o-o!

The President. That's more than $150 a month. It's like having a second mortgage. [*Laughter*] And after the Mondale mortgage, we'd be sure to have more than a few foreclosures.

His economic plan——

Audience. [*Inaudible*]

The President. His economic—you know, I know I'm no concert baritone, so I know those can't be an echo of my voice. [*Laughter*] All right. Okay.

Audience. 4 more years! 4 more years! 4 more years!

The President. His economic plan has two basic parts: to raise your taxes and then raise them again. [*Laughter*] But I've got news for him. The American people don't' want his tax increases, and he isn't going to get his tax increases.

His tax plan would bring our recovery to a roaring stop. But I'll give it this: His——

Audience. [*Inaudible*]

The President. You know——

Audience. [*Shouts and applause*]

The President. Say—[*applause*]. Thank you.

Audience. [*Shouts and applause*]

The President. Say, you know, isn't that—now, there's a perfect example of where we solid citizens are—caught between the right and the left.

But I'll tell you, I got one idea from my opponent. If I could find a way to dress up in his tax program, I could go out on Halloween and scare the devil out of all the neighbors.

But he sees an America in which every day is tax day, April 15th. We see an America in which every day is Independence Day, the Fourth of July. What we want, and what we're trying to plan to do, is to lower yours and everybody's taxes so that your families will be stronger, our economy will be stronger, and America will be stronger.

But I'm not finished here. I'm proud to say that during these last 4 years, not 1 square inch of territory has been lost to the Communist nations. And the United States is more secure than we were 4 years ago.

Yet there's so much more to say about my opponent. His grasp of foreign affairs is demonstrated by the following: Sometime back, he said the old days of a Soviet strategy of suppression by force are over—that was just before the Soviets invaded Czechoslovakia. And after they invaded Afghanistan, he said, "It just baffles me why the Soviets these last few years have behaved as they have." But then there's so much that baffles him.

One year ago we liberated Grenada from Communist thugs, and my opponent called what we did a violation of international law that erodes our moral authority to criticize the Soviet invasion of Afghanistan. Well, I will say this: His administration did mete out some strong punishment after Afghanistan. Unfortunately, they didn't punish the Soviets; they punished the American farmers.

My opponent supported the grain embargo and spoke out for it often. He even questioned the patriotism of a Senator from his own party when that Senator called that embargo just what it was—unworkable and unfair. But now he seems to have changed his tune. He says he privately opposed the embargo—very privately. As a matter of fact, he has, in the last several months, claimed that he opposed a number of the administration policies when he was Vice President. He was a real thorn in their side. But as Jody Powell, who was also a member of that administration, said, "I guess I was out of the room every time it happened."

And after the Sandinista revolution in Nicaragua, he praised it, saying, "Winds of democratic progress are stirring where they have long been stifled." But we know that the Sandinistas immediately began to persecute the genuine believers in democracy and to export terror. They went on to slaughter the Miskito Indians, abuse and deport church leaders, slander the Pope, practice anti-Semitism, and move to kill free speech. So, why isn't my opponent speaking out now?

More recently, he failed to repudiate the Reverend Jesse Jackson when he went to Havana, stood with Fidel Castro, and cried: "Long live Cuba! Long live President Fidel Castro! Long live Che Guevara!"

I could say of his economic program that he will either have to break his promises or break the bank. But I won't say it, because Senator John Glenn, a Democrat, has already said that.

Now, I could call his economic program a collection of old and tired ideas held together by paralyzing commitments to special interest groups. But I won't say that, because Senator Gary Hart, a Democrat, has already said that. Now, I could predict that he will create deficits more than twice what they are now. But I won't say that, because Fritz Hollings, a Democrat, has already said that.

Now, if on political issues my opponent dares to be wrong, on domestic policy issues he has the courage to be cautious. A line-item veto would help control wild government spending and end some of the pork-barreling that goes on. I had a line-item veto as Governor of California. Your Governor has a line-item veto. Forty-two other Governors in this country have line-item vetoes. But my opponent says that's not part of the liberal agenda. So, a line-item veto will not be used to help that wild spending.

He has long opposed enterprise zones. This was a program we introduced to help the most economically troubled neighborhoods like some in our great inner cities. It was to use tax incentives and to stimulate the economy in those areas. And he's opposed that. But then a few weeks ago, he said that now he's for them. Well, if he's for them, why doesn't he ask Tip O'Neill to get out of the way and loosen the program that's been buried in a committee in the House for over a year?

Changed signals a little bit—this month an American woman walked in space—Kathryn Sullivan made history. And then she returned to a space shuttle in which some of the great scientific and medical advances of the future will be made. Already we're learning that it's possible—or it looks possible—that we're going to have cures for diabetes and heart disease—that are to be able to develop them up there in the shuttle—advances in technology and communication. That's why I support the space shuttle. But my opponent personally led the fight in the Senate against having the shuttle program at all. And he called it a horrible waste.

The truth is, my opponent's campaign, were it a television show, would be called, "Let's Make a Deal." [*Laughter*] You'd get to trade your prosperity for the surprise behind the curtain. [*Laughter*] Now, if his campaign were a Broadway show, it would be called "Promises, Promises." If the administration of which he has been a part were a novel, you'd have to read it from back to front to get a happy ending. [*Laughter*]

Now, I'll say something that a few here, at least, will agree with: I've probably been going on too long. But the point is—the point is we were right when we made our great turn in 1980. We were right to take command of the ship, to stop its aimless drift, and get moving again. And we were right when we stopped sending out S.O.S. and started saying U.S.A.!

Audience. U.S.A.! U.S.A.! U.S.A.!

The President. All right. Now, let me say here that the 1984 election isn't just a partisan contest. I was a Democrat once, for the better part of my life, for a long time. And I also respected that party. But in those days its leaders weren't the "blame America first" crowd. Its leaders were men like Harry Truman, men who understood the challenges of our times. They didn't reserve all their indignation for America. They knew the difference between freedom and tyranny, and they stood up for the one and damned the other.

To all the good Democrats, and I know—well, I hope, certainly, and I'm sure I know there are many among you—you are not alone and not without a hope. We're putting out our hands, and we're asking you to come walk with us down the new path of hope and opportunity.

We, together, in a bipartisan move can go forward with what has been started in this country. And to all of you young people, I want to tell you that all across this country, nothing has touched me more than your support, your enthusiasm, your patriotism. You are what this election is all about, and it's your future that we care so much about. And I've seen enough to know that your generation is really something special.

Audience. 4 more years! 4 more years! 4 more years!

The President. You're something pretty new on the scene. Your idealism and your love of country are unsurpassed——

Audience. [*Inaudible*]

The President. ——and I consider it——

Audience. [*Inaudible*]

The President. You know, I got interrupted on the debate when I was trying to talk about this same subject. I'm going to finish it this time.

I consider it our highest duty—and when I say that, I'm talking about my generation, my generation and a few generations in between mine and yours—it is our duty to make certain that you have an America that is every bit as full of opportunity, hope and confidence and dreams as we had when we were born into this America and when we grew up taking for granted that this country was a place of hope and opportunity, a place where you could dream and then make your dreams come true. And we must see, all of us together, that that is what America is going to continue to be, and that's the America we will turn over to you when it is your turn.

Audience. 4 more years! 4 more years! 4 more years!

The President. All right.

Audience. 4 more years! 4 more years! 4 more years!

The President. Thank you very much. Thank you. You know, I'll tell you a secret.

If the Capital was on the west coast, I'd go for 40.

America will never stop. It will never give up its mission, its special mission—never. There are new worlds on the horizon, and we're not going to stop until we get them all together.

And America's best days are yet to come. And I know it galls my opponents, but you ain't seen nothin' yet.

Thank you very much for your support. Thank you all, and God bless all of you.

Note: The President spoke at 9:30 a.m. at the Earl A. Chiles Center on the University of Portland campus.

Following his remarks, the President traveled to Seattle, WA.

Remarks at a Reagan-Bush Rally in Seattle, Washington
October 23, 1984

The President. Thank you very much.

Audience. 4 more years! 4 more years! 4 more years!

The President. All right.

Audience. 4 more years! 4 more years! 4 more years!

The President. Thank you very much. Thank you very much. I just told some people in Portland, you've talked me into that 4, and if the Capital were on the west coast, I'd go for 40.

But thank you, John, very much for that introduction. I'm thrilled to be here in Seattle, home of the Huskies. I'm glad to be here with Congressman Rod Chandler and your fine Republican candidates. Bill Ruckelshaus is here, as you've just—he's been introduced to you, but he didn't really need any introduction out here, and Governor John Spellman, who's brought this State through difficult times and will keep it going strong.

I have to tell you, John was most helpful with regard to that timber bill. He's worked with us on the creation of jobs, and he knows very well, and we all know, what Washington State's role is in creating a strong national defense. I know that one

western Governor knows a good Governor when he sees one, and John is another one, and I think he should be there for 4 more years.

I know that the Space Needle is a symbol of your city, and it stands for a city of pride and progress, a city and a country that is upward bound. And that Space Needle also symbolizes the great contest that's now going on in this crucial election, because it stands for the future. And my opponent seems to have a grudge against the future.

Abraham Lincoln said we must disenthrall ourselves with the past—and then we will save our country. And 4 years ago, that's what we did. We made a great turn. We got out from under the thrall of a government which we had hoped would make our lives better, but which wound up living our lives for us. The power of the Federal Government had, over the decades, created great chaos—economic chaos, social chaos, international chaos.

[At this point, the President was interrupted by hecklers in the audience.]

Our leaders were adrift, rudderless, and without a compass. Have you ever noticed in these big buildings there's an echo? [*Applause*]

Our leaders in the past have been adrift, rudderless, and without a compass. Four years ago we began to navigate by certain fixed principles. Our North Star was freedom; our constellation was common sense.

We knew that economic freedom meant paying less of the American family's earnings to the Government, and so we cut personal income taxes by 25 percent. We knew that inflation, the quiet thief, was stealing our savings. And we had the highest interest rates since the Civil War, and they were making it impossible for people to own a home or start an endeavor, an enterprise of any kind. We knew that our national military defense had been weakened, and we decided to rebuild and be strong again.

Audience. Reagan! Reagan! Reagan!

The President. Thank you. Thank you very much. And we knew this strength would enhance our prospects for peace in the world. It was a second American revolution, and it's only just begun.

But our efforts have brought about a great renewal. America is back, a giant reemergence on the scene. Our country is powerful in its renewed spirit, powerful in its economy, powerful in the world economy, and powerful in its ability to defend itself and secure the peace.

But now, 4 years after our efforts began, small voices in the night are sounding the call to go back, to go backward to the days of confusion and drift, the days of torpor, timidity, and taxes.

Audience. Boo-o-o!

The President. My opponent this year is known to you, but perhaps we can gain greater insight into his leadership abilities and his philosophy if we take a look at his record.

To begin with, his grasp of economics is well demonstrated by his economic predictions. Just before we took office, my opponent said our economic program is obviously, murderously inflationary. And that was just before we lowered inflation from about 12 percent to around 4. And just after our tax cuts, he said the most he could see was an anemic recovery. And that was right before our economy created more than 6 million new jobs in 21 months and just

before nearly—a record nearly 900,000 businesses were incorporated in less than a year and a half.

My opponent said that our policies would deliver a misery index the likes of which we hadn't seen in a long time. Well, now, there he was partially right. You get the misery index when you add up the rate of unemployment and the rate of inflation. Now, they invented that back in the 1976 campaign, and they said that Jerry Ford had no right to seek reelection because his misery index was 12.6. Now, you know, they didn't mention the misery index in the 1980 election—it had gone up to more than 20. And they aren't talking about it much in this campaign, because it's down around 11.

Now, my opponent said that decontrol of oil prices would cost American consumers more than $36 billion a year. Well, one of the first things we did was decontrol oil prices, and the price of gasoline went down 8 cents a gallon, and the prices are still headed down.

Now, you know, it's occurred to me that maybe all we have to do to get the economy in absolutely perfect shape is to get my opponent to predict absolute disaster. [*Laughter*]

He says he cares about the middle class, but he boasts, and I quote, he says, "I have consistently supported legislation, time after time, which increases taxes on my own constituents." Doesn't that make you want to be one of his constituents?

Audience. No!

The President. Now, he's no doubt proud of the fact that as a United States Senator he voted 16 times to increase taxes. But this year he's outdone himself. He's already promised, of course, to raise your taxes. But if he's to keep all the promises he's made to this group and that, he will have to raise taxes by the equivalent of $1,890 for every household in the United States.

Audience. Boo-o-o!

The President. Now, that's more than $150 a month. It's like having a second mortgage. And after the Mondale mortgage, there'd be a lot of foreclosures.

His economic plan has two basic parts: raise your taxes and raise them again. But I've got news for him: The American people don't want his tax increases, and the American people aren't going to get his tax increases.

Audience. 4 more years! 4 more years! 4 more years!

The President. All right. Okay, I'll go.

Audience. 4 more years! 4 more years! 4 more years!

The President. All right. I'll tell you, I have to give my opponent this, though. He's given me an idea for Halloween. [*Laughter*] If I can just figure out how to get a costume like his economic program, I'll wear it and scare the devil out of the neighbors. [*Laughter*]

He sees an America in which every day is tax day, April 15th. We see an America in which every day is Independence Day, the Fourth of July. What we want is to lower everybody's income tax rates so your families will be stronger, our economy will be stronger, and America will be stronger.

But I'm not finished here. I'm proud to say that during these last 4 years—on another subject—not 1 square inch of territory has been lost to Communist aggression, and the United States is more secure than we were 4 years ago.

Yet there's so much more to say about my opponent. His grasp of foreign affairs is demonstrated by the following: Some time back he said the old days of a Soviet strategy of suppression by force are over—and that was just before the Soviets invaded Czechoslovakia. And after they invaded Afghanistan he said, "It just baffles me why the Soviets these last few years have behaved as they have." But then, there's so much that baffles him.

One year ago we liberated Grenada from Communist thugs who had taken that country over in a coup. Do you know that my opponent called what we did a violation of international law that erodes our moral authority to criticize the Soviet invasion of Afghanistan?

Audience. Boo-o-o!

The President. But I will say this, though. The administration that he was a part of did mete out strong punishment—not to the Soviet Union, to the American farmers. The American farmers, they paid. Unfortunately, he supported the grain embargo, and he spoke out on it often. He even questioned the patriotism of a Senator from his own party when that Senator called that embargo just what it was—unworkable and unfair. But now he seems to have changed his tune. He says he privately opposed the embargo—very privately. As a matter of fact, in the last several months he's claimed that he opposed a number of the administration policies when he was Vice President. But as Jody Powell, who also was in that administration, said, and I quote, "I guess I was out of the room every time it happened." [*Laughter*]

And after the Sandinista revolution in Nicaragua, he praised it, saying, "Winds of democratic progress are stirring where they have long been stifled." But we know that the Sandinistas immediately began to persecute the genuine believers in democracy and to export terror. They went on to slaughter the Miskito Indians, abuse and deport church leaders, slander the Pope, practice anti-Semitism, and moved to kill free speech. So, why isn't my opponent speaking out about that fresh wind now?

More recently, he failed to repudiate the Reverend Jesse Jackson when he went to Havana, stood with Fidel Castro, and cried: Long live Cuba! Long live Castro! Long live Che Guevara!

Audience. Boo-o-o!

The President. You know, I could say of his economic program that he will either have to break his promises or break the bank. But I won't say it, because Senator John Glenn, a Democrat, has already said it. I could call his economic program a collection of old and tired ideas held together by paralyzing commitments to special interest groups. But I won't, because Senator Gary Hart, a Democrat, has already said that. I could predict that he will create deficits more than double what they are now. But I won't, because Senator Fritz Hollings, a Democrat, has already said that.

And now, if on political issues my opponent dares to be wrong, on domestic policy issues he has the courage to be cautious. A line-item veto to help control wild government spending—I had that when I was Governor of California. I don't know whether you're one of the 42 other States?—you have it. Your Governor has it. Forty-two other States have it here in the Union. But my opponent says that's not part of the liberal agenda.

He has long opposed, also, enterprise zones, to help the most economically troubled neighborhoods in the country to use tax incentives to go in to stimulate industry and business there to provide jobs for people. But then, a few weeks ago, he was a—deathbed confession—he said he's for them. Well, if he's for them, then why doesn't he ask Tip O'Neill to let our enterprise zone bill get out of the committee where it's buried in the House of Representatives?

This month an American woman walked in space—Kathryn Sullivan made history. And then she returned to that space shuttle in which some of the great scientific and medical advances of the future will be made, and are being made now. Cures for diabetes and heart disease may be possible up there; advances in technology and communications. That's why I support the space shuttle, as I know all of you do. But my opponent, as a Senator, led, personally, the fight in the Senate to try and kill the entire shuttle program. He called it a horrible waste.

Audience. Boo-o-o!

The President. The truth is, if my opponent's campaign were a television show, it would be "Let's Make a Deal." [*Laughter*] You get to trade our prosperity for the surprise hidden behind the curtain. [*Laughter*] If his campaign were a Broadway show, it would be "Promises, Promises." [*Laughter*] And if his administration had been a novel, if you read it, you'd have to read it from back to front for a happy ending. [*Laughter*]

I've probably been going on too long here, but——

Audience. No! 4 more years! 4 more years! 4 more years!

The President. You didn't mean with the "4 more years" that you wanted me to stay up here talking for 4 years?

The point is, the turn we made in 1980 was right. And we were right to take command of the ship, to stop its aimless drift, and to get moving again. And we were right when we stopped sending out S.O.S. and started saying U.S.A.!

Audience. U.S.A.! U.S.A.! U.S.A.!

The President. Thank you.

Let me say here that the 1984 election isn't just a partisan contest. I was a Democrat once—in fact, for a greater part of my life. And I always respected that party. But in these days, its leaders—or in those days—weren't the "blame America first" crowd. Its leaders were men like Harry Truman, men who understood the challenges of the times. They didn't reserve all of their indignation for America. They knew the difference between freedom and tyranny, and they stood up for one and damned the other.

To all the good Democrats who respect that tradition—and I hope there are many present here—I say, "You're not alone; you're not without a home. We're putting out our hands and we're asking you to come join us and walk down this new path of hope and opportunity with us."

But here in this State, we can't discuss those who have led the Democratic Party without talking about Washington's great son, the late Senator Henry "Scoop" Jackson. When we talk about Scoop Jackson we're reminded that, above all, politics is about principles, and Senator Jackson had among the strongest principles of anyone I've known. The first of those principles was that politics stopped at the water's edge. Time and again he provided the key leadership essential to preserving our nation's interests.

Not all of Scoop's colleagues took the same course. Indeed, my opponent almost always voted just the opposite when it came to maintaining the strength of the United States. In 1970, as measured by the national security index of the American Security Council, Senator Jackson had a rating of 80 on key issues, while Mr. Mondale had a zero. In 1972 Scoop again scored 80; Mr. Mondale again, zero. In 1974 and again in 1976, Henry Jackson scored 90, while Mr. Mondale scored zero and then managed to get an 11. [*Laughter*] Now, whether it's the old math or the new math, the bottom line is the same. On nearly every occasion the Senator, Henry Jackson, cast a vote for America's defense. You would not only find Walter Mondale voting against him, but in

37 or 38 times, you found him voting with George McGovern.

Audience. Boo-o-o!

The President. So, if you like George McGovern's defense policies, you'll love my opponent's. [*Laughter*] And today, we're not surprised to find that he would cancel the B–1 and the MX programs without requiring one single corresponding action by the Soviets.

By the way, wiping out the B–1 would also wipe out about 5,000 jobs in Washington State in 1986 and '87.

Audience. Boo-o-o!

The President. You know, in all the years that I negotiated union contracts—and I did; I was president of my union several times—I never heard of giving up your strongest negotiating leverage without getting something in return. Moreover, Mr. Mondale has never, to my knowledge, created—or criticized, I should say—his runningmate's support for a congressional proposal to slash our defense budget by more than $200 billion over the next 3 years, completely eliminating several new and essential systems and substantially reducing U.S. conventional presence abroad.

The very centerpiece of Mr. Mondale's policies has been his warm embrace of the so-called nuclear freeze. But he doesn't tell the American people that Brzezinski, Mr. Carter's and Mr. Mondale's own national security adviser, has called this a nuclear hoax that is not achievable and not verifiable.

Is it any wonder that my opponent's Democratic colleague, Senator Fritz Hollings, has said, "Walter Mondale thinks the Soviet Union would never violate an arms agreement. I think he's naive." And it can't come as any surprise that Senator John Glenn, who had been an astronaut and in the military himself, believes his opponent's would—or my opponent's policies "would leave this country emasculated."

My friends, Scoop Jackson left a legacy to America that rests on a timeless principle, the principle that's nurtured our beloved nation for two centuries: Peace and freedom flow from the same well, and that is the well of strength and preparedness.

America is the most generous and peaceful nation in the world. But our reserve must never be confused with our resolve. It's our resolve that will preserve the peace and keep our freedoms forever, and you have a sign in your State that exemplifies this. It's a sign which stands over the entrance to the Fairchild Air Force Base here in Washington, and it reads, Peace is our profession. And that says it all.

And now—I'm always so happy when I see an auditorium like this for a rally with so many young people. I started out to say something the other night in the debate and ran out of time. I'm going to finish it here.

To the young people of America, of our country, let me say, nothing, nothing has touched our hearts more than your wonderful support. You are what this election is all about. It is your future that we care so much about. Your generation is something special. You are truly something new on the scene. Your idealism and your love of country are unsurpassed. I consider it our highest duty to make certain that you have an America that is every bit as full of opportunity and hope and confidence and dreams as we had when we were your age.

My generation, and a few generations between mine and yours—[*laughter*]—we grew up in an America where we took it for granted that, yes, you could dream, and there was nothing to keep you from making your dreams come true except you and your own ability——

Audience member. [*Inaudible*]—war!

The President. ——and your hard work. And that's what our obligation is to you—those of us of those other generations—to make sure we hand you that kind of an America, an America that is free and in a world that is at peace.

All of us together are part of a great revolution, and it's only begun, and we'll never stop—never. This country must never give up its very special mission in the world. There are new worlds on the horizon, and we're not going to stop until we all get there together.

America's best days are yet to come. And I know it drives my opponents up the wall, but you ain't seen nothin' yet. Thank you very much. Thank you, and God bless you all.

Note: The President spoke at 12:12 p.m. at the Seattle Center.

Following his remarks, the President traveled to Columbus, OH, and the Hyatt on Capitol Square Hotel, where he remained overnight.

Remarks to the Ohio Association of Broadcasters in Columbus
October 24, 1984

Well, thank you, ladies and gentlemen. Thank you. As a former local broadcaster, let me tell you that it's good to be among the members of my former profession.

Coming in here, I couldn't help but reminisce and think about my first job at WOC, Davenport, Iowa. I don't know how—I'm not going to tell you how long ago that was. But it's not true that I was hired by Marconi. [*Laughter*] And it's similarly false that William Paley and David Sarnoff were my desk assistants. [*Laughter*]

But seriously, I look back on my years of local broadcasting as among the best in my life. Local is where you learn, and local is where you're introduced to the realities of the business.

And I was hired to broadcast some Big Ten football games at WOC. And that went well. I played football for 8 years. But when the season ended, then they put me on as a staff announcer which, as you know, meant long hours of playing records and reading commercials and cutting in and out of network programs.

But once a week, late at night, we would present a program of romantic organ music. [*Laughter*] And one night I was scheduled to be on duty for that particular program. Now, the music was provided by a local funeral home. [*Laughter*] And these shows were a kind of semicommercial. We got the music free, and the funeral home got a discreet plug at the end of the show.

Unfortunately, no one informed me of the direct financial relationship between the music and the sponsor in this, my first being on duty for that particular program. And my dramatic instinct just sort of rebelled at mentioning a mortuary after "Drink To Me Only With Thine Eyes."

[*Laughter*] So, I happily played the music and didn't do the plug.

The mortuary was not amused. [*Laughter*] And I was informed that I would be replaced. Well, I learned my lesson, and so things turned out that I stayed on. And I haven't had to face removal since—a record that I hope to continue this year.

Local radio and television stations are growing in influence, but they're still providing a valuable training ground for young journalists and broadcasters. This is where they learn how to do their jobs.

You see some of my friends over there— Sam Donaldson, Bill Plante, Chris Wallace. I believe it was on a network affiliate that Sam learned to yell. [*Laughter*]

But, of course, when I started there was no radio newscasting. That was declared unfair in the Fair Trade Practices Act. But it came later, and I did some of that— always limited to sports news.

But I'm happy to be here with all of you, anyway. I know that many of the facts of broadcasting are changing. This is a time of movement and change in your industry. The advent of cable has changed the realities, and deregulation is affecting your industry.

Beyond that, I think I sense this year something new on the scene. It seemed to me that local radio and TV stations covered this year's national political convention with an intensity beyond anything they've done in the past. Stations throughout the country were sending their own teams of reporters and producers and camera men and women. And they were competing with the networks for the story. And I see this as a good sign. It's not only an indication of the growing importance of local news coverage, it also, I think, promises greater variety in terms of what stories get covered and from what point of view. And it's my hope that this trend will turn out to be in the public interest.

We've lost an awful lot of daily newspapers in this country in the past few decades. And if it turns out with time that local TV and radio fill the gap in terms of offering alternative news outlets, well, then that'll be a very good thing, indeed.

We at the White House have noted, by the way, that local broadcasters are much more visible than they once were. In the last 5 years, Washington bureaus representing local stations have increased from about 15 to around 50. And we have at the White House a Media Relations Office to serve the needs of local stations and help them in whatever way we can, in various ways.

As your importance grows as disseminators of information, so the responsibility in all of you grows to be fair and balanced in your coverage. I know that all of you put a premium on fairness, and I urge you as you're bringing young people up through the ranks to be as stern with them about impartiality as you are with yourselves. The public—your ultimate clients—recognizes fairness and balance and respects it. I have great admiration for how local broadcasters do their jobs. I know you're in a very tough and demanding profession. I certainly found it so.

You know, it's just awful—I'll have to control myself because the urge to reminisce— I remember broadcasting a major league baseball game, a telegraphic report. Ninth inning, the Cubs and Cards, tied up nothing to nothing. And I saw the fellow on the other side of the window, my contact, with the earphones on, start to tap out the message he was getting. It came through to me, and I had Dizzy Dean on the mound and I had the ball on the way to the plate. And the message said—[laughter]—the wire's gone dead. [Laughter]

Well, ninth inning, and in those days with a half a dozen different stations broadcasting the same game, I decided I wasn't about to call for an interlude of transcribed music. [Laughter] I set an all-time record for a single batter standing at the plate and hitting successive foul balls. [Laughter] I don't know how long it took, but I was sweating. [Laughter] And I knew by that time that if I ever had to give in and say the wire'd—they'd know that I hadn't been broadcasting exactly the facts up till then. And finally I saw Curly start typing. So, I started another ball on the way to the plate, and then I got to giggling when the slip came through—I could hardly say—he said, "Jurges popped out on the first ball pitched." [Laughter]

Well, good luck to all of you, and God bless all of you. And thank you very much for letting me at least come in here and participate for a few minutes. And I'll promise not to reminisce anymore. Thank you.

Note: The President spoke at 10:10 a.m. in the Governor's Ballroom at the Hyatt on Capitol Square Hotel.

Remarks at a Reagan-Bush Rally in Columbus, Ohio
October 24, 1984

The President. Thank you. And you know—and you certainly made me feel right at home with Johnny Grant here, because all the way back to '66, running for Governor, Johnny Grant was always on hand. But I want to thank all of you for what you must know is a most heartwarming reception.

It's great to be back in the Buckeye State. And it's great to be in the proud capital of Columbus. And I want to give special greetings to Coach Woody Hayes, former Governor Rhodes, and Congressmen Chalmers Wylie and John Kasich, Clarence Miller and Michael DeWine.

Now, I hate to start off right away asking you for a favor.

Audience. [Inaudible]

The President. Okay. We need these fine representatives back in the Congress to keep the pressure on Tip O'Neill. Will you send them back?

Audience. Out with Tip! Out with Tip! Out with Tip!

The President. I'm with you. [*Laughter*] I wish I could say hello to your mayor, Buck Rinehart, but I know that he's away serving our country in the Naval Reserve.

You know, visiting you here makes me especially happy because it's very much like being at home. I'm from the Midwest, and I've always felt that the Midwest, States like this one, are kind of the heartland of America. Here there is steadiness of purpose, an appetite for good, honest work, and love of country. And Ohio is definitely a part of America's heartland.

Abe Lincoln said that we must disenthrall ourselves with the past—and then we will save our country. Well, 4 years ago, that's what we did. We made a great turn. We got out from under the thrall of a government which we had hoped would make our lives better, but which wound up living our lives for us. The——

Audience members. [*Inaudible*]

Audience. Boo-o-o! 4 more years! 4 more years! 4 more years!

The President. Thank you.

Audience. 4 more years! 4 more years! 4 more years!

The President. I knew that Mondale was here; I thought he'd gone home.

But let me just say, we got out from under the thrall of a government which we had hoped would make our lives better but which wound up living our lives for us. The power the Federal Government had over the decades created great chaos—economic, social, and international. Our leaders were adrift, rudderless without a compass.

Four years ago we began to navigate by some fixed principles. Our North Star was freedom, and common sense was our constellation. We knew that economic freedom meant paying less of the American family's earnings to the Government. And so, we cut personal income tax rates by 25 percent.

We knew that inflation, the quiet thief, was stealing our savings, and the highest interest rates since the Civil War were making it impossible for people to own a home or start an enterprise.

We knew that our national military defense had been weakened, so we decided to rebuild and be strong again. And this we knew would enhance the prospects for peace in the world. It was a second American revolution, and it's only just begun.

America is back. It's a giant, powerful in its renewed spirit, its economy, world economy, and powerful in its ability to defend itself and secure the peace.

But now, 4 years after out efforts began, small voices in the night are sounding the call to go back to the days of confusion——

Audience. Boo-o-o!

The President. ——the days of torpor.

Audience. Boo-o-o!

The President. Now, my opponent this year is known to you, but perhaps we can gain greater insight into his leadership abilities and philosophy if we take a look at the record.

Now, to begin with, his grasp of economics is well demonstrated by his economic predictions. Just before we took office, he said our economic program is obviously, murderously inflationary. And that was just before we lowered inflation rates from more than 12 down to 4.

And just after our tax cuts, he said the most he could see was an anemic recovery. That was right before the economy created more than 6 million new jobs in 21 months and just before a record nearly 900,000 businesses were incorporated in less than a year and a half.

Now, my opponent said that our policies would deliver a misery index the likes of which we hadn't seen in a long time. And there was some truth in that. You get the misery index by adding the rate of unemployment to the inflation rate. And they invented that in the 1976 campaign. They said that Jerry Ford had no right to seek reelection because his misery index was 12.6. Now, they didn't mention the misery index in the 1980 campaign, because it was more than 20. And they aren't talking about it too much in this campaign, because it's down around 11.

My opponent said decontrol of oil prices would cost American consumers more than $36 billion a year. Well, one of the first things we did was decontrol the oil prices, and the price of gasoline went down 8 cents a gallon.

Now, I think I have it all figured out. If we can get him—well, we can get the economy in absolutely perfect shape if we can get him to predict absolute disaster. He says he cares about the middle class. But he boasts, "I have consistently supported legislation, time after time, which increases taxes on my own constituents." Doesn't that make you just want to be one of his constituents? Now, he's no doubt proud of the fact that he voted 16 times as a United States Senator to raise your taxes.

Audience. Boo-o-o!

The President. But this year he's outdone himself. He's already promised, of course, that he's going to raise your taxes. But if he is to keep all the promises he's made to this group and that, he will have to raise taxes by the equivalent of $1,890 for every household in the United States.

Audience. Boo-o-o!

The President. Now, that's more than $150 a month. It's like having a second mortgage, the Mondale mortgage.

His economic plan has two basic parts: raise your taxes and raise them again. But I've got news for him. The American people don't want his tax increases, and you're not going to get his tax increases.

Audience. 4 more years! 4 more years! 4 more years!

The President. All right. He'd bring the economic recovery to a roaring halt. But I'll tell you, his ideas did give me an idea. If I could find a way to dress up in his tax program, I could scare the devil out of people on Halloween.

He sees an America in which every day is tax day, April 15th. We see an America in which every day is Independence Day, July 4th. We want to lower your taxes and everybody's taxes so your families will be stronger, our economy will be stronger, and America will be stronger.

Now, if I could switch the subject a little bit, I am proud also to say that during these last 4 years, not one square inch of territory in the world has been lost to Communist aggression.

Audience. Reagan! Reagan! Reagan!

The President. Yes. Right. Thank you.

The United States is more secure than we were 4 years ago.

But there's so much more to say about my opponent. His grasp of foreign affairs is demonstrated by the following: Sometime back, he said the old days of a Soviet strategy of suppression by force are over. That was just before the Soviets invaded Czechoslovakia. And after they invaded Afghanistan, he said, "It just baffles me why the Soviets these last few years have behaved as they have." But then there's so much that baffles him.

One year ago we liberated Grenada from Communist thugs who had taken over that country. My opponent called what we did a violation of international law that erodes our moral authority to criticize the Soviet invasion of Afghanistan. Well, I will say this: His administration did mete out strong punishment after Afghanistan. They punished the American farmer. My opponent supported the grain embargo.

Audience members. [*Inaudible*]

Audience. Boo-o-o!

The President. You know, I know it's going to break their hearts, but I can't understand a word they're saying.

Audience. 4 more years! 4 more years! 4 more years!

The President. Oh, bless you.

Audience. 4 more years! 4 more years! 4 more years!

The President. No, you know, I said that he supported the grain embargo. He even questioned the patriotism of a Senator from his own party when that Senator said the embargo was unworkable and unfair. But now, in this campaign, he seems to have changed his mind. He says he privately opposed the embargo—very privately.

As a matter of fact, he has, in the last several months, claimed that he opposed a number of the administration policies when he was Vice President. But as Jody Powell, who also was in that administration, said, "I guess I was out of the room every time it happened."

There's more about him. After the Sandinista revolution in Nicaragua, he praised it, saying "Winds of democratic progress are stirring where they have long been stifled." But we know that the Sandinistas immediately began to persecute the genuine believers in democracy and to export terror. They went on to slaughter the Miskito Indians, abuse and deport church leaders, slander the Pope, practice anti-Semitism, and move to kill free speech. So, why isn't he talking about them now?

More recently, he failed to repudiate the Reverend Jesse Jackson when he went to Havana, stood with Fidel Castro, and cried: Long live President Fidel Castro! Long live Che Guevara!

Audience. Boo-o-o!

The President. You know, I could say of his economic program that he will either "have to break his promises or break the bank." But I won't say it, because Senator John Glenn, a Democrat, has already said it. I could call his economic program "a collection of old and tired ideas, held together by paralyzing commitments to special interest groups." But I won't, because Gary Hart, a Democrat, has said that. I could predict that he will create deficits more than twice what they are now. But I won't, because Senator Fritz Hollings, a Democrat, said that.

Now, if on political issues my opponent dares to be wrong, on domestic policy issues he's got the courage to be cautious. A line-item veto to help control wild government spending? No, he says, that's not part of the liberal agenda. Well, as a Governor of California, I had line-item veto. I used it more than 900 times in those 8 years. Forty-two other Governors in this State—or 43 all told in the Nation have line-item veto.

He's long opposed enterprise zones. Now, this is a program that was to use tax incentives to develop industry and jobs in depressed zones, particularly in our inner cities throughout the country. He has long opposed that. But now, a few weeks ago he said he's for them. Well, if he is for them, why doesn't he ask Tip O'Neill to get out of the way and let the bill out of the committee where it's been buried for more than a year?

This month an American woman walked in space—Kathryn Sullivan made history. [*Applause*] They have to cheer for that, don't they?

And she returned to a space shuttle in which some of the great scientific and medical advances of the future will be made. Cures for diabetes and heart disease may be possible up there, we've learned already—advances in technology and communication. I support, as I'm sure all of you do, the space shuttle. But my opponent, in the United States Senate, led the fight against it all the way and called the whole program a horrible waste and tried to stop it.

Audience. Boo-o-o!

The President. You know——

Audience. Fritz is a wimp! Fritz is a wimp! Fritz is a wimp!

The President. You're tempting me beyond my strength.

But you know, if my opponent's campaign were a television show, it would be "Let's Make a Deal." You get to trade your prosperity for the surprise behind the curtain. If his campaign were a Broadway show, it would be "Promises, Promises." And if his administration had been a novel, you would have had to read it from the back to the front in order to have a happy ending.

Now, I've probably been going on too long here but——

Audience. No!

The President. All right. But the point is we were right when we made that turn. We were right to take command of the ship, to stop its endless drift, and to get moving again. And we were right when we stopped sending out S.O.S. and started saying U.S.A.!

Audience. U.S.A.! U.S.A.! U.S.A.!

The President. You know, my opponent's view of the mess in 1980 is not quite the same as yours and mine. That was apparent last Sunday when rhetoric collided with the record. Mr. Mondale claimed he would keep America strong. But for 6 straight years, the American Security Council gave him a flat zero in his support of a strong national defense. It was a tie for the worst record of the United States Senate. On 37 out of 38 issues, he voted down the line with George McGovern.

Audience. Boo-o-o!

The President. And that's the record, not rhetoric.

He said he supported the cruise missile, the Trident submarine, the Stealth bomber, and the Pershing missiles in Europe. But in the Senate, he opposed the cruise, the Trident, and the B-1 bomber. He opposed the M-1 tank, the *Nimitz* carrier, the C-5A transport plane, pay increases to support the all volunteer army, and he tried to kill the F-14 fighter. His so-called nuclear freeze proposal would stop the deployment of the Pershings and leave NATO at a more than 10-to-1 disadvantage in nuclear warheads in Europe. And that's the record, not rhetoric.

Audience. Boo-o-o!

The President. Now, Sunday night he said he would increase European conventional strength. But as Senator, he voted to cut U.S. troops in Europe by more than half, and twice again voted to reduce drastically U.S. forces overseas. He said he would offer no unilateral concessions to the Soviets, but he's already announced that he would end the B-1 and the MX programs without asking for anything in return.

Audience. Boo-o-o!

The President. And here in Ohio, ending the B-1 development could cost you 23,000 jobs in the next 2 to 3 years. And that's the record, and not rhetoric.

He said he would be tough on verifying arms agreements. But neither he nor his runningmate, when asked directly, were able to explain how their so-called nuclear freeze could be verified. Back in April, Mr. Mondale said every nuclear weapons system would be subject to a freeze, even though his runningmate now admits they couldn't verify Soviet violations in the form of stockpiling warheads. And that's the record, and not rhetoric.

But I—let me just say something.

Audience members. [*Inaudible*]

Audience. Boo-o-o!

The President. Let me just say something about the controversial nuclear freeze. I don't think there's any one of us that wouldn't like that. But the only sensible way to have a nuclear freeze is when we have persuaded the Soviets in joining us in the reduction of nuclear weapons down to an equal and verifiable level and then freeze.

Mr. Mondale said of a possible attack on this country, "Pick a President that you know will know, if that tragic moment ever comes, what he must know, because there'll be no time for staffing or committees or

advisers." Well, it took him 11 months to decide that rescuing our sons and daughters in Grenada was a good thing. And, believe me, that's the record, and not rhetoric.

And I will be seeing some of those young students in a few hours when I get back to the White House—they're coming in—and some of the men who helped rescue them.

Here in Ohio, just yesterday, he was telling your citizens that even though the steel industry suffered far too much under the Carter administration, he wanted you to forget the past. But he intends to take America back to the past of high taxes and high inflation, and his string of promises will send government spending out of control.

His approach to national defense is so like the previous administration that millions of Americans have decided we simply can't afford to go down that path again. So, when he asks us to forget the past, here with 2 weeks till election day, let's strike a bargain with him. We'll forget the past if he'll just quit trying to bring it back.

Audience. 4 more years! 4 more years! 4 more years!

The President. All right, as soon as I complete the 4 years undergraduate, I'll take the postgraduate course.

You know, this 1984 election isn't just a partisan contest. I was a Democrat for a good share of my life. And in those days, its leaders weren't the "blame America first" crowd. Its leaders were men like Harry Truman, men who understood the challenges of the times. They didn't reserve all their indignation for America. They knew the difference between freedom and tyranny, and they stood up for the one and they damned the other.

And to all the good Democrats who respect that tradition—and I hope there are many present, because, as I said, I was one myself—I would like to say, you're not alone. We're asking you to come walk with us down the new path of hope and opportunity.

Now, something that I couldn't quite finish on Sunday night. They shut me off. To the young people of our country, let me say that you are what this election is all about. I've been on a number of campuses, and I'm here now. And I want to tell you all, your generation is something special. Your idealism, your love of country are unsurpassed. And it's our highest duty to make sure that you have an America every bit as full of opportunity, hope, and confidence in dreams as we had when we were your age.

My generation, and a few generations between mine and yours—we were born into an America where we grew up just taking it for granted that you could dream and make your dreams come true, that there was nothing to stop you if you had the will and the desire to go after them. Now all of us together are part of a great revolution, and it's only just begun. America will never give up its special mission in the world.

There are new worlds on the horizon, and we're not going to stop until we all get there together. And those generations I told you about, mine and those others, our sacred responsibility is to see that we turn over to you an America that is free in a world that is at peace.

And America's best years are yet to come. And they're going to hate this, but you ain't seen nothin' yet.

Thank you all very much. God bless you all. Thank you.

Note: The President spoke at 12:03 p.m. at St. John's Arena on the Ohio State University campus.

Following his remarks, the President had lunch at the Tau Kappa Epsilon fraternity house and then returned to Washington, DC.

Remarks at a White House Ceremony Marking the First Anniversary of the Grenada Rescue Mission
October 24, 1984

The President. Well, good afternoon. I just flew in from Columbus. But I want to welcome to the White House this impressive delegation of American students who were on Grenada at the time of the rescue mission last year. I know many of you came to see us last year, also, and I am especially happy to have you here with us again. And I also want to welcome Ambassador Xavier of Grenada and our other distinguished guests.

Together we celebrate today, with joy, an anniversary of honor for America—your rescue and the liberation of our neighbor, Grenada, from the grip of oppression and tyranny. Just 1 year ago, Grenada's Governor General Paul Scoon and members of the Organization of Eastern Caribbean States called for our help.

Using military force is, I'm sure you realize, the most serious decision any President must make. It's an awesome responsibility. But the evidence to me was clear. At stake was the freedom of 110,000 Grenadians, the security of the democracies of the Eastern Caribbean and, most important, the safety and well-being of you American medical students trapped by events that were totally beyond your control. So, we approved a military operation to rescue you, to help the people of Grenada, and to prevent the spread of chaos and totalitarianism throughout the Caribbean.

Side by side, with forces from neighboring Caribbean democracies, the brave young soldiers, sailors, marines, and airmen accomplished their mission. They went to Grenada not to conquer, but to liberate, and they did. They saved the people, they captured tons of Soviet military equipment, and they averted a hostage crisis before it happened. And then those combat troops left the island so the Grenadian people could start a new life and give peace, freedom, and democracy, and self-determination a chance.

But today over 100,000 Soviet troops are still ravaging Afghanistan. There is a fundamental moral distinction between the Grenada rescue mission and the Soviet invasion of Afghanistan—a brutal and bloody conquest that aims to destroy freedom, democracy, and self-determination. It's the difference between totalitarianism and democracy, between tyranny and freedom. And it gives all of us hope for the future to know that you see the difference that others should have seen from the very beginning.

During the latter part of the 1970's, America passed through a period of self-doubt and national confusion. We talked and acted like a nation in decline, and the world believed us. Many questioned our will to continue as a leader of the Western alliance and to remain a force for good in the world. But I believe this period of self-doubt is over. History will record that one of the turning points came on a small island in the Caribbean where America went to take care of her own and to rescue a neighboring nation from a growing tyranny.

Our brave military personnel displayed the same love of liberty and personal courage which has made our nation great and kept her free. And this courage and love of country is also what we saw in Beirut at virtually the same time. And we will always honor those brave Americans. Let no one doubt that those brave men were heroes every bit as much in their peacekeeping mission as were our men in the rescue mission in Grenada.

And we continue to see this devotion and commitment every day. On the demilitarized zone in Korea, on the NATO lines in Europe, at bases from Diego Garcia to Guam, and on our ships at sea, young Americans are proudly wearing the uniform of our country and serving with the same distinction as those who came before.

Cicero once said, "Courage is that virtue which champions the cause of the right." Well, with us today is a small contingent of military personnel, a few of the heroes who took part in the rescue mission—two each, from the Army, Navy, Air Force, and Marines. And four of these brave young Americans are here with me on the podium, and the other four are sitting among the students that they rescued. So, I thank them for joining us today, and thank all of you. We're very grateful to all of you.

Also here on the podium is Miss Kathleen Major, who was a medical student and registered nurse 1 year ago. And when the fighting erupted, she immediately went to work treating the wounded. And, Miss Major, we thank you. It was good of you to come today.

Nineteen brave men died during the Grenada rescue, serving their country and the cause of freedom. One of them was Sean Luketina. He was a paratrooper seriously wounded by a rocket. He was evacuated to Puerto Rico, and there in the hospital slipped in and out of a coma. His father, Colonel Robin Luketina, a retired military officer who's here with us today, rushed to his bedside. And Colonel Luketina, I'm told that on one of those moments when your son regained consciousness, you asked him, "Sean, was it worth it?" And "Yes, Dad," he answered. And you asked again, "Would you do it again?" And he looked up at you and said, "Hell, yes, Dad." A few months ago, Sean died of his wounds. But he, Sean Luketina, gave his life in the cause of freedom. He did not die in vain. The young Americans he helped to rescue know that. The liberated people of Grenada know that. Grenada's neighbors know that. And Sean himself knows. So, let us honor him as he would have wished, by keeping faith with the policy of peace and deterrence that assures the survival of our freedom, keeps alive the hope of freedom for all the peoples of the world. This is the meaning of peace through strength. And let us always remember that America is the land of the free, because we're the home of the brave.

To Sean and all the men and women who served the cause of freedom, and to all of you, all of you students who are dedicating yourselves to saving human life: you are the hope of America. You are all America's future. Thank you for what you do, and God bless you.

Mr. Geller. President Reagan, distinguished members of the military, honored guests: It was a year ago that I stood at this podium and spoke about the Grenada evacuation. I spoke about how proud we were when the U.S. Army Rangers and other members of the military rescued us on the island of Grenada. I spoke about how happy we were to realize that America had not forgotten us and how proud we were to be Americans.

The decision to invade Grenada was a

tough one. It was a decision that called for quick and decisive action by a true leader. I want to thank you, Mr. President, once again for making that decision. Yes, it's been a year now since we left Grenada, and hardly a day goes by when I don't think about what went on there.

I think about our soldiers, the Navy Seals, the Air Force, the Marines, the Army Rangers, and the 82d Airborne. You know, all of the men who fought down there in Grenada are different. Some are tall, some are short, some are white, and some are black. They all have one thing in common, and that's conviction.

They all had the courage and conviction to stand up and fight for what they believe and for what America believes, as well. I want to tell America and all the students in America that the lessons we have learned in Grenada shall not be forgotten, that the Americans that died in Grenada did not die in vain. We, the students of St. George's University, have returned to become teachers for 2 days, to remind the citizens of America that we cannot forget that lesson, that freedom is just too precious, too valuable, to be taken for granted, and that we must stand up and protect that right whenever and wherever necessary.

President Reagan, you came to our aid when our freedom was in jeopardy. You made us proud to be Americans. On behalf of the students assembled here today, I'd like to thank you and all four branches of the Armed Forces for being there when we needed you. Thank you.

Ms. Major. President Reagan, members of the military, and honored guests: The events of Grenada are now a part of history, but our feelings will always remain alive inside of us. I can never forget the feeling of intense fear and the sense of relief when I first saw our Americans. I hope I never forget the feelings of pride and admiration for the finest military on the face of the Earth—the American military—and also my gratitude to their Commander in Chief, who made a most courageous decision. And, finally, I hope I never forget to say how proud I am to be an American.

President Reagan, it is with great honor I present this plaque, which reads, "October 25, 1984: In grateful appreciation to Presi-

dent Ronald Reagan for your decisive leadership which resulted in the liberation of Grenada and restored to us our freedom and our future. Presented on the first anniversary of the liberation of Grenada by the American students who were rescued that day."

Dr. Modica. Mr. President, as you know, I was probably the first person to voice reservations about your decision to go ahead with the rescue mission in Grenada last year. I know I certainly was the most publicized. During my State Department briefing the following day, I realized there were factors unknown to me which required that you make a tough and immediate decision. I then felt it my duty to publicly acknowledge the necessity of the mission, and I did so upon leaving the State Department that very day. I have realized over the past year that you have taken the greatest risk of your political career when you made the decision to act, rather than to ignore the plight of our students and the call for help from six Caribbean nations.

You had little to gain in taking military action, as the people of our nation have become increasingly unsupportive of such actions over the past decade. Had the mission failed in any way, you would have shouldered the entire blame. Recently we've been hearing a lot about leadership and strong leadership in recent weeks. The very definition of strong leadership is exemplified by your decisive action in Grenada. No wonder our renewed national pride has emerged from your ability to take action when necessary.

I know you will want to remember those brave men who gave their lives in the Grenada rescue mission. This replica of the memorial that will be unveiled on our Grenada campus October 29th bears the names of each of those fine young men who gave their lives. On behalf of its cosponsors, St. George's University, and the parents network of St. George's University, I am proud and honored to present it to you as our Commander in Chief.

The President. Thank you very much. But I came all the way back here from Columbus to honor all of *you.* [*Laughter*] And I'm deeply grateful. And you brought this on yourselves now. I know I've told this many times but, you know, when you get past 40, you have a tendency to tell the same story over and over again. [*Laughter*]

I just have to tell you a little story about Grenada here, and then I will get back to the office and go to work. This young lieutenant marine, flying a Cobra helicopter, was at Grenada and then went on to Beirut. And from Beirut he wrote back to the Pentagon to the Armed Forces Journal, and he said that there was one thing in all the news stories about Grenada that was so consistent and so repeated that he decided it was a code, and he was going to break the code.

That line was that Grenada produces more nutmeg than any other spot on Earth. [*Laughter*] So, he said, in breaking the code, number one, that is true—they produce more nutmeg than any other spot on Earth. He said, number two, the Soviets and the Cubans are trying to take Grenada. And number three, you can't have good eggnog without nutmeg. [*Laughter*] And number four, you can't have Christmas without eggnog. And number five, the Soviets and the Cubans were trying to steal Christmas. [*Laughter*] And number six, we stopped them. [*Laughter*]

Note: The President spoke at 3:30 p.m. in the East Room at the White House.

Albert Xavier is the Ambassador of Grenada to the Organization of American States, Charles R. Modica is the chancellor of St. George's University School of Medicine, and Jeffrey Geller is a medical student at the university who was rescued during the mission.

Statement on Signing a Bill To Restore Fish and Wildlife in the Trinity River Basin in California
October 24, 1984

I have signed today H.R. 1438, a bill that authorizes efforts to restore fish and wildlife in the Trinity River Basin in California. H.R. 1438 demonstrates that environmental programs can also be fiscally responsible.

The Trinity is a major river in northern California that has seen its fishery resources decline. H.R. 1438 is designed to restore the fishery in the river—which will benefit sportsmen, the Hoopa Valley Indian Tribe, and others interested in environmental quality. A fishery restoration program for the river has been an objective for over 10 years, and enactment of this bill is a major environmental achievement. Indeed, I first proposed a similar effort during my tenure as Governor of California, so I am especially pleased to see that early effort finally bear fruit.

The plan also demonstrates our continued commitment to fiscal responsibility. Where the prior administration unsuccessfully promoted a program of 100-percent Federal financing, H.R. 1438 incorporates a cost sharing arrangement under which local beneficiaries put up 50 percent, the Federal Government contributes 35 percent, and the State of California contributes 15 percent of the costs. Consequently, the bill ensures an improved environment at less cost to the Nation's taxpayers.

The legislation has enjoyed overwhelming support both in the House and the Senate. I would like to congratulate those responsible for this accord. I believe H.R. 1438 demonstrates this administration's commitment to the protection and enhancement of our natural resources in a fiscally responsible manner. In this way we are all winners.

Note: As enacted, H.R. 1438 is Public Law 98–541, approved October 24.

Statement on Signing the Veterans' Dioxin and Radiation Exposure Compensation Standards Act
October 24, 1984

I am pleased today to sign H.R. 1961, the Veterans' Dioxin and Radiation Exposure Compensation Standards Act. This bill represents the culmination of nearly 2 years of work between the administration and the Congress on the best way to handle the claims of veterans who believe they may have been injured by their exposure to Agent Orange in Vietnam or to low-level ionizing radiation from their participation in the atomic weapons atmospheric testing program in the 1950's and early 1960's or from the occupation of Hiroshima and Nagasaki. H.R. 1961 establishes a responsible and workable process for consideration by the Veterans Administration of these claims.

Over the past few years, questions have arisen regarding the long-term health effects resulting from Agent Orange exposure. We now know that the Agent Orange used in Vietnam was contaminated with trace amounts of dioxin. There is, however, substantial scientific uncertainty on whether this exposure to Agent Orange causes any long-term adverse health effects.

Two recent studies—the Ranch Hand morbidity and mortality study of the Air Force personnel who were involved in spraying Agent Orange, and the birth defects study by the Centers for Disease Control—concluded that there is no significant evidence of such adverse health effects. Nevertheless, the administration is firmly committed to continuing research on the health effects of Agent Orange exposure, and the Centers for Disease Control is now in the process of conducting a major epidemiological study to provide further information on this important question.

The bill also addresses the claims of those veterans who were exposed to low levels of ionizing radiation from the atomic weapons atmospheric testing program or from the occupation of Hiroshima and Nagasaki. While radiation indisputably has serious adverse health effects at high dose levels, there is scientific uncertainty about its adverse health effects at the very low levels underlying these claims.

This bill requires the Administrator of Veterans Affairs to publish regulations assuring the fair and consistent adjudication of these exposure claims. In doing so, the Administrator will have the assistance of a specially created advisory committee of scientists to evaluate the evidence and make appropriate recommendations. With the benefit of these recommendations, the Administrator will promulgate regulations grounded on the best available scientific and medical evidence.

Even though the available evidence does not suggest the existence of adverse long-term health effects from Agent Orange or low-level ionizing radiation exposure, because there is some uncertainty on this point, the Veterans Administration has for several years been providing free, comprehensive health care for any veteran who believes that he or she may have an illness traceable to either exposure. To date, there have been over 1 million instances of such care.

H.R. 1961 reaffirms the administration's strong commitment to the well-being of the men and women who have served this nation with honor and distinction. By giving the Veterans Administration the opportunity to conduct a careful, systematic review of the evidence underlying these claims, the bill accomplishes two important purposes:

—When veterans suffer from illnesses due to their exposure to Agent Orange or low-level radiation, it lays the groundwork for awarding the compensation to which they are rightfully entitled.

—But, as importantly, it will have the Veterans Administration provide assurance to those concerned about their health and the health of their children where past exposures have not triggered present dangers.

Veterans deserve to know the truth about the consequences of their exposure to Agent Orange or to low-level radiation, and they should not live in fear if that fear is unjustified. This bill will facilitate the search for that truth, and I am therefore pleased to sign it.

Note: As enacted, H.R. 1961 is Public Law 98–542, approved October 24.

Statement on Signing the Veterans' Benefits Improvement Act of 1984
October 24, 1984

I am pleased today to sign into law H.R. 5688, a bill that will increase certain benefits paid to veterans and make other improvements in veterans' programs.

Our nation provides compensation and other monetary benefits to service-disabled veterans and dependency and indemnity compensation (DIC) benefits to the survivors of those who died for our country. The administration has recommended increases in these monetary benefits each year so they will keep up with changes in the cost of living. The "Veterans' Benefits Improvement Act of 1984," which I am approving today, provides a 3.2-percent increase in compensation and DIC benefits effective December 1, 1984.

The bill before me also responds to the administration's recommendation for increases in GI bill educational benefits, which will help Vietnam-era veterans taking advantage of this opportunity, and other recommendations for needed increases in veterans' benefits.

Further, I am pleased to endorse the extension in the bill of the Federal Government's authority to make veterans' readjustment appointments (VRA's) to the civil service. The VRA authority helps service-disabled veterans obtain employment in the Federal Government.

This legislation requires the Veterans Administration to carry out two trial programs. Over a 4-year period the Veterans Administration will test whether vocational rehabilitation training and other techniques can be useful in expanding the employment prospects of certain disabled veterans considered to be unemployable. One trial program would cover certain service-disabled veterans and the other certain pensioners. The objectives of these programs are praiseworthy.

Programs for veterans are among the most important Federal responsibilities. I am therefore delighted to approve this bill.

Note: As enacted, H.R. 5688 is Public Law 98–543, approved October 24.

Statement on Signing the Local Government Antitrust Act of 1984
October 24, 1984

Today I am signing into law H.R. 6027, the Local Government Antitrust Act of 1984, which clarifies the application of the Federal antitrust laws to the official conduct of local governments. This bill provides much needed and timely relief for our cities, towns, school districts, sanitary districts, and other similar local governmental bodies from the threat of massive treble damages in the antitrust cases that are

being brought with increasing frequency against them. While the antitrust laws serve very important purposes, they were never intended to threaten public treasuries and the taxpayers' pocketbooks, or to disrupt the good faith functioning of local units of governments. The administration has been a strong supporter of this legislation, and I commend the efforts of the local officials and those in the Senate and House of Representatives who worked so hard for its enactment during the 98th Congress.

Note: As enacted, H.R. 6027 is Public Law 98–544, approved October 24.

Statement on Signing a Bill Amending the Volunteers in the Parks Act of 1969
October 24, 1984

I have signed today S. 864, an act to amend the Volunteers in the Parks Act of 1969, and for other purposes.

S. 864 would allow the expansion of the volunteer program in the National Park Service and permit such a program to be established in the Bureau of Land Management; require the National Park Service to implement a complex maintenance management system; and impose new requirements for congressional approval of contracts of the National Park Service, Bureau of Land Management, and Fish and Wildlife Service pursuant to Office of Management and Budget Circular A–76.

My administration proposed an expansion of the Volunteers in the Parks program of the National Park Service and creation of a similar volunteer program in the Bureau of Land Management of the Department of the Interior. The National Park Service program has been very successful, as highly motivated individuals have volunteered valuable services to the visitors to our national parks and to other National Park Service activities. By creating additional opportunities for Americans to provide volunteer services that advance the enjoyment and management of our parks and public lands, these precious resources that we all cherish can be fully utilized and protected. I am gratified that the Congress responded positively to the administration's proposals to enhance the preservation of our parks through the services of volunteers.

Although I have signed S. 864, I must note my reservations about it. Language was added to the bill that impairs the ability of the Department of the Interior to make sound management decisions on the most cost-effective way to provide support services. The Department is prohibited, in the National Park Service, Fish and Wildlife Service, and Bureau of Land Management, from cost-effective contracting for services, such as road maintenance, now performed by Government employees. For large activities, the Government is hampered from contracting even when productivity studies show clear and substantial savings can be made, without a loss of service, by relying on the private sector. This represents an unwarranted intrusion by the Congress into matters normally within the management discretion of the executive branch and shows a serious disregard for providing cost-effective services to the public and the taxpayer.

Notwithstanding the constraints and as otherwise permitted, I am directing the Department of the Interior to proceed with efficiency studies to effect productivity improvements in all areas. We will work with the Congress next year for their reconsideration of these and other intrusions into the efficient operations and management of the Federal Government.

Note: As enacted, S. 864 is Public Law 98–540, approved October 24.

Executive Order 12491—Establishment of Emergency Board No. 205 To Investigate a Railroad Labor Dispute
October 25, 1984

Establishing an Emergency Board To Investigate a Dispute Between The Long Island Rail Road and the Brotherhood of Locomotive Engineers

A dispute exists between The Long Island Rail Road and the Brotherhood of Locomotive Engineers representing employees of The Long Island Rail Road.

The dispute has not heretofore been adjusted under the provisions of the Railway Labor Act, as amended ("the Act").

A party empowered by the Act has requested that the President establish an emergency board pursuant to Section 9A of the Act.

Section 9A(e) of the Act provides that the President, upon such a request, shall appoint an emergency board to investigate and report on the dispute.

Now, Therefore, by the authority vested in me by Section 9A of the Act, as amended, (45 U.S.C. section 159a), it is hereby ordered as follows:

Section 1. Establishment of Board. There is hereby established a board of three members to be appointed by the President to investigate this dispute. No member shall be pecuniarily or otherwise interested in any organization of railroad employees or any carrier. The board shall perform its functions subject to the availability of funds.

Sec. 2. Report. (a) Within 30 days from the creation of the board, the parties to the dispute shall submit to the board final offers for settlement of the dispute.

(b) Within 30 days after submission of final offers for settlement of the dispute, the board shall submit a report to the President setting forth its selection of the most reasonable offer.

Sec. 3. Maintaining Conditions. As provided by Section 9A(h) of the Act, as amended, from the time a request to establish a board is made until 60 days after the board makes its report, no change, except by agreement, shall be made by the parties in the conditions out of which the dispute arose.

Sec. 4. Expiration. The board shall terminate upon the submission of the report provided for in Section 2 of this Order.

RONALD REAGAN

The White House,
October 25, 1984.

[Filed with the Office of the Federal Register, 4:33 p.m., October 25, 1984]

Executive Order 12492—Establishment of Emergency Board No. 206 To Investigate a Railroad Labor Dispute
October 25, 1984

Establishing an Emergency Board To Investigate a Dispute Between The Long Island Rail Road and the Brotherhood of Railway, Airline and Steamship Clerks, Freight Handlers, Express and Station Employes

A dispute exists between The Long Island Rail Road and the Brotherhood of Railway, Airline and Steamship Clerks, Freight Handlers, Express and Station Employes, representing employees of The Long Island Rail Road.

The dispute has not heretofore been adjusted under the provisions of the Railway Labor Act, as amended ("the Act").

A party empowered by the Act has requested that the President establish an emergency board pursuant to Section 9A of the Act.

Section 9A(e) of the Act provides that the President, upon such a request, shall appoint an emergency board to investigate and report on the dispute.

Now, Therefore, by authority vested in me by Section 9A of the Act, as amended, (45 U.S.C. section 159a), it is hereby ordered as follows:

Section 1. Establishment of Board. There is hereby established a board of three members to be appointed by the President to investigate this dispute. No member shall be pecuniarily or otherwise interested in any organization of railroad employees or any carrier. The board shall perform its functions subject to the availability of funds.

Sec. 2. Report. (a) Within 30 days from the creation of the board, the parties to the dispute shall submit to the board final offers for settlement of the dispute.

(b) Within 30 days after submission of final offers for settlement of the dispute, the board shall submit a report to the President setting forth its selection of the most reasonable offer.

Sec. 3. Maintaining Conditions. As provided by Section 9A(h) of the Act, as amended, from the time a request to establish a board is made until 60 days after the board makes its report, no change, except by agreement, shall be made by the parties in the conditions out of which the dispute arose.

Sec. 4. Expiration. The board shall terminate upon the submission of the report provided for in Section 2 of this Order.

RONALD REAGAN

The White House,
October 25, 1984.

[*Filed with the Office of the Federal Register, 4:34 p.m., October 25, 1984*]

Interview With Representatives of the Scripps-Howard News Service
October 25, 1984

Q. Mr. President, I'm Dan Thomasson, editor of Scripps-Howard News Service. I wish to say thank you in advance for your time in this busy schedule. We'll just go right from there.

Priorities in Second Term

Q. Mr. President, how are you today?

The President. Fine.

Q. Nice to see you again, sir. I'm Jim Wieghart with the Washington Bureau of Scripps-Howard.

I thought I'd like to ask you today, in a relaxed way, looking ahead to the next 4 years, what do you think will be your main priorities in your second term? And secondly, do you anticipate making any changes in the Cabinet in your second term?

The President. Well, first of all, the priorities are, in a sense, going to be a continuation. Economically, we're going to continue trying the same overall things that were part of our program to begin with, and that is to continue trying to reduce the share

that the government is taking from the private sector, from the gross national product, because I think that government can be, and was, a drag on the economy—still is.

This, we believe, will—if we proceed with this—will also take care of the deficit problem. Because the real, only real way to raise government's revenues are not through tax increases, which further increase the drag in the economy; they're from growth in the economy. And we're going to continue trying, also, to make government less of a burden on business and private individuals with excessive regulations.

To show you what can happen with just even a minor element in government: We lumped together 62 categorical grant programs into 10 block grants to local and State governments. That not only eliminated 3,000 people who had been administering the 62 grants at the Federal level, but it changed the regulations out there at the local and State level, which had taken 885 pages, reduced them down to 30. And it's this type of thing—much of this is what's contained in the recommendations of the commission that we had, and we're studying those 2,480 recommendations.

We're going to proceed, as I say, with all of that—with tax reform, hoping to simplify it and make it possible for rates to come down again at the same time we broaden the base and, hopefully, can get some of that $100 billion that is now not coming in because of the underground economy; and in the international scene, to continue our two-track policy. One of them is, of course, the building of our own defensive capability. But at the same time, the other track is to try and get the Soviet Union to join us in realistic arms reduction talks. The overall goal is peace, and this is what we'll continue.

Now, with regard to any Cabinet changes, I would be just satisfied if there were none at all. But I do know that while no one has said anything, other than the resignation we know about of the Attorney General who has to return, or feels he must return to his private practice, the—I know that when you ask, whenever I ask people to serve, whether on the staff or there, I made it plain that I'd take them for whatever time they could come. And if they then felt they had to leave, why I'd go out and find somebody else. No one has made any suggestions about that, but there possibly would be some that might want to get back to their own private lives. And if so, I would understand. But I have no intention of—in other words, I'm not unhappy with anyone.

Involvement of U.S. Citizens in Central America

Q. Mr. President, my name is David Brown, and I'm the executive editor of the Commercial Appeal in Memphis, Tennessee.

As you're aware, a group of private citizens—many of them from west Tennessee and from north Alabama—in the past year have been engaged in taking supplies to the rebels fighting the Sandinistas in Nicaragua. And not only have they taken supplies down there, but they have engaged in training. And two men were shot down and slain in the past few months. Since those

two men were killed, hundreds more citizens have joined this group known as the CMA. I'm wondering about your attitude, how you feel personally, about private citizens getting engaged in this way in what is happening in Central America.

And as I ask this question, there are 30 Memphians who are getting ready, who are prepared to fly to Honduras this weekend to work with groups, they say, are in that country who want to overthrow the Sandinistas. So, is there an ever-growing number of people in our country who want to do something on their own to, as they put it, stop communism before it gets to our borders, and how do you feel about it?

The President. Well, I have to say it's quite in line with what has been a pretty well established tradition in our country. Nothing was done legally about the formation of a brigade, a Communist brigade of Americans in the Spanish Civil War. In World War II, we had pilots being recruited to go to the Flying Tigers. I recall, if I'm correct, there were some people, even one very prominent actor from Hollywood who became an ambulance driver in the French Army in World War II.

So, I don't know. I'm not a lawyer, so I never asked about what is the actual legality of anything of that kind. But at the same time, as I say, it's been a tradition, and Americans have always done this. And I would be inclined to not want to interfere with them.

Q. Weren't the examples that you raised people who went to fight for governments who were fighting other governments' tyranny? In this case, we have Americans who are going to Central America to help rebels. They call them "freedom fighters." Do you see a difference there?

The President. Well, as I say, "I'm not so wise as those lawyer guys," as Mr. Service said in his poem. I haven't really gotten into that. I was giving you—my own personal reaction to it was it seemed to be a long and honorable tradition. And in a sense, our own interest in Nicaragua has to do with their overt support of guerrillas, themselves, who are trying to overthrow a duly elected government of a neighboring country—El Salvador. So, no one has raised the issue before of these individual Americans.

Q. If it would not be illegal, would there be anything wrong with it in your mind, in any other way? Morally? Or can they get in the way of our government in trying to do something about the problems in Central America?

The President. Well, if you get into the moral issue of it, we were certainly tested with regard to that Spanish Civil War I mentioned, because I would say that the individuals that went there were, in the opinion of most Americans, fighting on the wrong side.

Welfare Programs

Q. Mr. President, Angus McEachran from the Pittsburgh Press.

Mr. President, you took office 4 years ago, determined to drastically cut what you said were overly generous welfare programs. And in February of '81, just 1 month after taking office, you introduced 84 proposals to reduce or eliminate Federal programs that obviously took fat from the domestic side of the budget. Among those reductions was a 17.4-percent decrease in unemployment insurance, a 14.3-percent decrease in Aid to [Families with] Dependent Children, a 13.8-percent decrease in food stamps, a 28-percent reduction in child nutrition, a 6.8-percent decrease in Medicare, and a 2.8 in Medicaid.

Obviously, a great number of American people have agreed with you that some cuts were necessary. But the Urban Institute cites that the poverty level grew faster in the first 3 years of your Presidency than any other period since the fifties. The Congressional Budget Office in July reported that budget reductions alone—taking unemployment as an aside—but the budget reductions alone had pushed 560,000 people below the poverty line—325,000 of them children alone.

Mr. President, what further cuts in welfare spending will be necessary in the next Reagan administration? And secondly, how do you answer your opponents who say that you are practicing social Darwinism?

The President. Well, I answer them—first of all, I challenge the Urban Institute's figures. And I don't think that they can be substantiated at all, because we are spending more money today and helping more people than at any time in our nation's history. With regard to food, the increase in food programs is up 37 percent over what it was.

We made cuts in suggested increases. We have reduced—on the domestic side of the budget—we have reduced the rate of increase in spending from 17 percent down to 6 percent.

But in many of these figures, for example in food stamps, some of the so-called savings in food stamps—we're, incidentally, giving more food stamps to more people than we've ever done before in history. There are something like, oh, I think somewhere around 3 million more people are getting them than were getting them in 1980. But here we found, for example, that in food stamps, someone applied for food stamps, let's say it's 3 days before the end of the month, they were given the whole month's food stamps for the preceding month, for just those few days of the month left. Now, come the first of the month, they were due, again, a quota for the coming month. And we started giving them food stamps as of the day they asked for them, not retroactively for weeks before they'd put in the request. And that amounted to quite a percentage, in a reduction.

We also, in many of these programs, found that there were people who were above an income level as to where they should be eligible for these programs, and what we did was redirect the attention down. And we've set for ourselves a standard of 130 percent of poverty—that that was the limit. Above that, it would have to be an exceptional case. But if they're below 130 percent of poverty, they were helped. So, the result was, for example, in school lunches there was a big increase for those people that were truly below the poverty line.

What we did do was reduce somewhat the subsidy for the people up above that line. I think in one instance it prorated out—like the subsidy increased—these are people that pay something for the lunches, but not the full cost—I think one of those cuts meant that their personal payment was increased 3 cents per lunch.

But this is true of most of the figures. And I haven't really studied the ones I've seen—just sketchily—the Urban Institute's figures. But I don't see how they can claim those figures when we can show that in every instance and in every program we are spending more money and helping more people than ever before in our history.

So, we intend to preserve the safety net. There's never been any intention to do away with that or to eliminate it. But things, such as I suggested earlier in these 2,470 or 80 recommendations of that commission that we had of some 2,000 business people in this country, looking at areas where modern business practices could be put to work.

The Federal Government has a substantially higher overhead cost for delivering $1 of services to the people than any other level of government in this country. And I don't see why it should necessarily be higher for us than it is for them.

And so these are the areas where we think—when sometimes you see what looks like a reduction—well, maybe we've just been more efficient in getting the job done. But we haven't hurt the people that are dependent on the program.

Now, you mentioned Medicare. And I have to be frank and tell you, there is a problem with Medicare. It is not as bad as the problem we had with Social Security, in which it was slated to go bankrupt before July of 1983. Now, our opponents, and Tip O'Neill in the lead, they challenged us and said that wasn't true. And they were right; it wasn't true—the program went belly-up in November of 1982. It didn't get to July of 1983.

We borrowed $17 billion to keep the checks from bouncing. That was when we, then—after they had used it in the '82 campaign as demagogically as they had—that was when we went back and said, "Now—we've been asking you for 3 years—now will you sit down with us in a bipartisan commission and figure out an answer to this Social Security problem?" And they did. And we figured it out, and Social Security is as safe now as it can be, as far as we can see into the next century. And we didn't cut the benefits to the recipients in our bipartisan plan.

So, I think a lot of these figures to try and point out that we somehow have been trying to balance the budget on the backs of the needy is just not true. The needy are being cared for. And I'll have to get some of our people to go to work on that set of figures.

Environmental Issues

Q. Mr. President, what do you consider to be your administration's most important achievement in the field of conservation of natural resources?

The President. Well, they're very much more than anyone's giving us credit for.

Q. You've seen some criticism in Florida recently about that.

The President. Yes. Well, the one that they're presently saying the most about is the Superfund and the cleanup of the toxic waste dumps. Well, the Superfund was passed before we got here, and there had been very little time for this—for inventorying these dumps and where they may be in the country. And so, it's on our watch that we have found out, so far, that there are probably 1,400 or more such dumps that do represent the potential for being a toxic waste threat.

And so far, we have begun work on about 600 of them—completed work on a half a dozen. So, the campaign charges that we've only cleaned up six—well, we think we're doing pretty well.

What we had to do—now many of these, they take some study to find out if they truly are a threat—and what we're doing are rating them as to what are the most imminent threats, the most dangerous, and going at those as fast as we can. We're going to support, of course, the renewal of the Superfund next year when it's due, to continue on that.

But that's just one facet. We found that the parks were a threat healthwise, from a safety factor, and just simply from a point of pollution and cleanliness. The maintenance had been so poor over a number of years. So, we stopped for a time buying additional land for the parks and set aside a billion dollars for a 5-year cleanup plan of the national parks. That is just about completed now, a year ahead of schedule. And the parks are restored with regard to cleanliness and safety features that were being violated. And we now have budgeted for going back to purchasing land for parks.

We have added to the wetlands. We have added to the wildlife refuges. We have added millions and millions of acres to the national wilderness.

The pure air and pure water act, which were in place before we got here, are implemented to the point that we have the cleanest air and water that we've had since 1970—I mean it's been cleaned up since that time.

And the doubling of the research for acid rain was because we discovered that the more we had learned about acid rain, the more we found out we needed to know. And the truth of the matter is the cleanup would represent over $100 billion if you just simply said we must eliminate all the rest of sulfur dioxide from the air that industry is putting there. And yet we had to say—from the research that had been done so far—there was no assurance that that cleanup would solve the acid rain problem. We found, as we continued researching, a lot of things we'd never known before.

And so, we're going to continue as fast as we can with that research, and then we'll do whatever has to be done. We are experimenting with liming some lakes, which can restore those lakes.

But I don't know what other elements of it—you know, being the villain of the environmental piece is kind of strange for me, because we started the whole thing in California when I was Governor. And the Federal Government sent people out to see us because they said we were so far ahead of anything that they were doing.

Social Security

Q. Mr. President, Tom Tuley, from Evansville, Indiana—not far from Dixon, Illinois.

The President. Where?

Q. Not far from Dixon, Illinois.

The President. Oh, well.

Q. You mentioned Social Security. I asked our readers in advance of this trip what questions they would like to ask of the President, and my mail showed an overwhelming concern in our community for Social Security. There is a real fear that in a second term that you would cut benefits. How can you answer those people?

The President. This, of course, is the same demagoguery that they heard in 1982 and why, in all of 1981, we were never able to persuade our opponents to join us in what we asked for—the same bipartisan commission we eventually wound up with. And they were set on using that, and, of course, those people are frightened. And I think it's disgraceful—people that are dependent on Social Security, past their earning years, have no place else to turn, and someone comes around telling them that there are people that have got some secret plan to take this away from them.

Well, why hasn't anyone pointed out that the increase in taxes in 1977, in the previous administration, to try and straighten out Social Security—and they said that they had straightened it out till the year 2015, and they hadn't straightened it out—well, they said for 50 years—they hadn't straightened it out for 5.

And not only was it a massive tax increase, but everyone that was born after 1916 gets Social Security at a 25-percent less rate than the people that are presently on it. So, in 1981 the people who started going on Social Security, they're getting checks 25-percent lower than the others. That was part of that 1977 plan.

But, no, there would be no reason for us to change it. The program has been placed on a sound financial basis. And I just think if you ladies and gentlemen of the press would go out of the way a little bit to tell these frightened senior citizens that they're going to continue to get their payments, and no one is going to take anything away from them—in that regard, good Lord, I volunteered that if we got inflation below 3 percent, the law said we didn't have to give them a cost-of-living increase, and I said we would, anyway, because we had delayed them for 6 months during this new program of ours—that they'd gone without getting their raise for an extra 6 months before it was instituted. And I thought it was only fair that the first year that we did get this below the figure of the law, that we'd go ahead and give it to them anyway.

The point is—and you can, with a clear conscience, reassure them—Social Security is not a part of the deficit or the deficit problem. Social Security is entirely funded by a payroll tax. And if you reduced Social Security, that money wouldn't go into the general fund to pay back that; it would go back into the trust fund of Social Security.

So, when anyone starts saying, "What are you going to do about that, about reducing the deficit?"—it doesn't have anything to do with the deficit.

Nuclear Power

Q. Mr. President?

The President. Yes.

Q. Harry Moskos, Knoxville News-Sentinel. The antinuclear atmosphere intimidates private industry, making it skeptical about committing to long-term, long-scale energy demonstration projects. If the Government doesn't fund these projects, research vital to the Nation's energy future could be killed or hopelessly delayed. What is the administration's position?

The President. Well, I think there's an area in which you can say that you can't, just because someone is afraid to move forward on something, that the government, then, ought to finance that. I believe in nuclear power, and I think that the fear that's been generated of it is almost superstitious and unwarranted completely.

When you stop to think that here is a power source that we've had now in operation for quite some number of years, and there has never been a nuclear fatality in that industry, and then you compare that to coal mining and a few other things, you wonder why and how this fear is justified. I know that there's a thing that people think that a nuclear powerplant's something that can turn into a nuclear bomb and blow up. Well, that's impossible, and it can't.

But what we need is more education of the people that nuclear power is a safe source of energy. And there are other countries that have gone far beyond what we've done in that regard, and they've, most of them, had the same safety records that we've had in it.

I don't think it's a case of us funding this.

I think it's a case of, between all of us—one thing that government can do, and I've asked our people to do—and that is to see if we can't shortcut some of the requirements that we make. For example, when I was Governor of California, I discovered that someone that wanted to build a nuclear powerplant, they had to get 65 environmental clearances, and there was no one-window stop. They couldn't go to one place and get cleared.

Now, they could spend millions of dollars going down through this with the knowledge that when they got to the 65th, that one could cancel out all the progress that they'd made, and they still wouldn't be able to, even after they'd spent all those millions of dollars. It seems to me what we need is a kind of a, as I say, a one-window stop.

And, of course, this isn't all Federal Government. A lot of these requirements are at different levels of government. But this is one of the things that is—when you see a company that's spent billions of dollars and they still, then, can't get a clearance to operate—we've got to do something about that.

Medicare

Q. Mr. President—[*inaudible*]—granted what you say is true about Social Security, that it is now in a position where it can be funded adequately, what about Medicare? That's a problem coming up in your administration.

The President. Well, I did mention that earlier, but I didn't explain. It isn't as imminent; it's got several more years before it would find that. But it has a fund with its trust fund, the Medicare fund. And what we're suggesting right now, and are talking about, are some things, actually, rather than aiming them at the recipients, we're aiming at the providers.

And we have proposed to hospitals and doctors, but particularly the hospitals, that we have a set of fees for various ailments, and we're trying—we're doing that right now—in which the hospital accepts this. And if they can't provide the care within the fee, that's out of their pocket. But if they can provide it for less than the fee, they get that profit. They can——

Q. I doubt whether many will provide it for less. [*Laughter*]

The President. Well, no, because there's an incentive to provide it for less: that if they can provide the service less than our fee, they get to keep the difference.

Q. Oh, I see.

The President. Yes. But the other way then, the penalty is, if they spend more, that's out of their pocket.

Q. Sir, it doesn't just take a massive campaign with the hospital administrators, the whole medical profession?

The President. Well, we've had no great protest so far on this.

President's Closing Statement in Foreign Policy Debate

Q. Mr. President, before somebody else steps in and cuts us off after 4 minutes, can you finish the California time capsule letter that you were in the process of explaining? [*Laughter*]

The President. I had finished with the letter on the air and was simply getting to the point of what I was going to say. And I've been saying it on these college campuses the last few days that I've been out there, that I was going to say that we had the responsibility, all of us, as I put it, my generation and a few generations between mine and theirs, to see that they were turned over, by us—or we turned over to them—a nation that was free in a world that was at peace. And that was the gist of it.

But I have to tell you, I was telling the truth, and I ad-libbed that whole thing in the 1976 convention when Jerry Ford asked me to come down to the platform and say a few words. And that was the first—well, the only time up until now that I had ever voiced this. But what had happened, the idea was, what our people a hundred years from now are going to say about us, and did we do right by them or wrong by them?

But the thing was that I truly was riding down the coast—I said "driving." Actually, I was riding, and somebody else was driving, and I was trying to put down some notes. But when I was looking around and thinking, that is when it struck me, "Wait a minute, I'm talking about a letter as if I'm writing to some people that don't know

about us." And I realized that I had a much harder problem than I had thought, that that letter—how do you write to somebody that's read all about us in the history books, knows all our problems and what we did? And I wrote the letter then with that idea in mind: that what I could be telling them about they might not know was how we approached what we thought about in these things, and what were the controversies and so forth in the thinking.

Mr. Speakes.[1] Mr. President, you know that your time——

Q. Somebody is cutting you off.

Ms. Spaeth.[2] Mr. President, on that note I think we should close the session.

The President. Okay.

Ms. Spaeth. Thank these gentlemen, and my apology——

The President. Okay. Can't I take one more?

Q. I wanted to tell you I had lunch with Mel Laird yesterday, and he told me he sent a telegram to Edwin Newman, and he said: "Dear Ed, thank you for limiting the President's time. I was afraid he might take a left turn on Highway 101 and drive into the ocean." [*Laughter*]

The President. Well, you know, everyone had told me wrong. I was afraid that—I knew what I was going to say in that closing statement and had it all planned—but I was afraid it might be a little over 4 minutes. But our people gave me the wrong steer. They said because I was going last, that it didn't matter then anymore. I didn't know Mr. Newman was going to be so—[*laughter*]—gung ho, and he shut me off.

But I've told it to the kids, and I must tell you: 13,000 students at Ohio State University the other day, they just loved the finish. [*Laughter*]

Listen, I'm sorry that the questions kind of seemed to get me here on a filibuster on some of them. But they should have been yes-and-no questions.

Q. Mr. President?

---

[1] *Larry M. Speakes, Principal Deputy Press Secretary to the President.*

[2] *Merrie Spaeth, Special Assistant to the President and Director, Office of Media Relations.*

Ms. Spaeth. I have to close it now. Thank you.

The President. Well, I'll answer him while I'm walking out. Stay seated, please.

Q. This is a light question. Doonesbury's back in the papers in the country, and a lot of editors are getting a lot of heat from readers who think he's unfairly criticizing you. Some think it's a parody of your critics. Do you ever have occasion to read Doonesbury? And what do you think of it?

The President. I am a devoted comic strip reader. I read every comic strip in the paper. And so, when he came back I started reading him. I have to tell you that I think some of your readers are absolutely right. [*Laughter*]

Note: The interview began at 4:37 p.m. in the Cabinet Room at the White House.

The interview was released by the Office of the Press Secretary on October 26.

Remarks to Members of the Congregation of Temple Hillel and Jewish Community Leaders in Valley Stream, New York
October 26, 1984

Rabbi Friedman, Senator D'Amato, members of Temple Hillel, and to all of you, a very, very warm thank you for this wonderful greeting. It is a great honor for me to be here with you today.

I've covered a bit of territory since this campaign began. What's heartened me most is the new spirit that I have found around this country, a spirit of optimism and confidence, of pride and patriotism, that has been brought forth by a great American renewal.

America's greatest gift has always been freedom and equality of opportunity—the idea that no matter who you are, no matter where you came from, you can climb as high as your own God-given talents will take you. But a few years ago we were being told that this vision was no more, that America was in decline, and all of us had to lower our expectations.

I think you remember the disasters that defeatist spirit led to: the first back-to-back years of double-digit inflation since World War I, a 21½-percent prime interest rate, record taxation, declining growth, savings, investment, income, and confidence in our future—not to mention growing problems of crime and drugs and in education. Overseas, we had lost the respect of friends and foe alike. Our determination had grown weak, undermining commitments to even our closest friends like Israel. We talked and

acted like a nation in decline, and the world believed us.

Well, in 1981 the American people set out on an entirely new course. And working together, we have cast aside the pessimism, along with high inflation, stagnation, and weakness, in a wonderful rebirth of freedom, prosperity, and hope. And today we're seeing not humiliation and defeatism, but pride in ourselves, in our accomplishments, and in our country.

From New York Harbor to San Diego Bay, a strong economic expansion with low inflation is leading the rest of the world into recovery. America is back. America is on its feet. And America is back on the map. But we cannot and we will not rest until every American who wants a job can find a job.

A nation's greatness is measured not just by its gross national product or military power, but by the strength of its devotion to the principles and values that bind its people and define their character. Our civil rights: on that subject, we are enforcing the law with new determination. Since we took office, the Justice Department has filed more criminal charges on civil rights violations, brought more violators to trial, and achieved more civil rights convictions than any one before us. I've said this before, and I'll say it again: As President, I will continue to enforce civil rights to the fullest extent of the law.

That's why I have appointed to the Civil Rights Commission people like Commissioners Clarence Pendleton and Morris Abram and Staff Director Linda Chavez. They recognize that you cannot cure discrimination with more discrimination. I'm proud that they're serving on the Commission, and I intend to keep them there. And as long as I'm President, we'll have a Justice Department which argues for the rights of individuals to be treated as individuals, whether the case involves hiring, promotions, layoffs, or any other matter subject to the law.

And we're also remembering the guiding light of our Judeo-Christian tradition. All of us here today are descendants of Abraham, Isaac, and Jacob, sons and daughters of the same God. I believe we are bound by faith in our God, by our love for family and neighborhood, by our deep desire for a more peaceful world, and by our commitment to protect the freedom which is our legacy as Americans. These values have given a renewed sense of worth to our lives. They are infusing America with confidence and optimism that many thought we had lost.

You know, when you talk about human life, I think that means seeing that the immeasurable pain of the Holocaust is never dehumanized, seeing that its meaning is never lost on this generation or any future generation, and, yes, seeing that those who take our place understand: never again.

Now, perhaps that message should again be impressed on those who question why we went on a peacekeeping mission to Lebanon. Indeed, anyone who remembers the lesson of the Holocaust must understand that we have a fundamental moral obligation to assure: never again.

To help preserve that lesson for future generations, I'm satisfied that our General Services Administration has approved the use of the old Customs House by the New York City Holocaust Memorial Commission as a means of commemorating the Holocaust. And it will be a museum of the Jewish people in the Diaspora. It will serve to remind our children and our children's children the tragic consequences of bigotry and intolerance.

We in the United States, above all, must remember that lesson, for we were founded as a nation of openness to people of all beliefs. And so we must remain. Our very unity has been strengthened by our pluralism. We establish no religion in this country, we command no worship, we mandate no belief, nor will we ever. Church and state are, and must remain, separate. All are free to believe or not believe, all are free to practice a faith or not, and those who believe are free, and should be free, to speak of and act on their belief.

At the same time that our Constitution prohibits state establishment of religion, it protects the free exercise of all religions. And walking this fine line requires government to be strictly neutral. And government should not make it more difficult for Christians, Jews, Muslims, or other believing people to practice their faith. And that's why, when the Connecticut Supreme Court struck down a statute—and you may not have heard about this; it was a statute protecting employees who observed the Sabbath. Well, our administration is now urging the United States Supreme Court to overturn the Connecticut Court decision. This is what I mean by freedom of religion, and that's what we feel the Constitution intends.

And there's something else. The ideals of our country leave no room whatsoever for intolerance, for anti-Semitism, or for bigotry of any kind—none. In Dallas, we acted on this conviction. We passed a resolution concerning anti-Semitism and disassociating the Republic[an] Party from all people and groups who practice bigotry in any form. But in San Francisco this year, the Democratic Party couldn't find the moral courage or leadership to pass a similar resolution. And, forgive me, but I think they owe you an explanation. [*Applause*]

Thank you.

What has happened to them? Why, after the issue became so prominent during the primaries, did the Democratic leadership alk away from their convention without a resolution condemning this insidious cancer? Why didn't they turn their backs on special interests and stand shoulder to shoulder with us in support of tolerance and in unequivocal opposition to prejudice and bigotry?

We must never remain silent in the face of bigotry. We must condemn those who seek to divide us. In all quarters and at all times, we must teach tolerance and denounce racism, anti-Semitism, and all ethnic or religious bigotry wherever they exist as unacceptable evils. We have no place for haters in America—none, whatsoever.

And let's not kid ourselves, the so-called anti-Zionists that we hear in the United Nations is just another mask in some quarters for vicious anti-Semitism. And that's something the United States will not tolerate wherever it is, no matter how subtle it may be.

We have a tremendous watchdog on this, Jeane Kirkpatrick. She is one very forceful and determined woman. And she has defended Israel with persistence and courage, and America is very proud of Jeane Kirkpatrick. Contrast her performance with that sad moment on March 1st, 1980, when the American delegate to the United Nations actually voted in favor of a resolution that repeatedly condemned Israel. And why did my opponent remain silent? I ask you again, what has happened to the party of Harry Truman and Scoop Jackson?

I was once a member of that party, and for a great part of my life, myself. And I don't believe that what we've seen and what I've been talking about is true of the millions of rank-and-file, patriotic Americans; it is only true of an element of leadership that somehow seems to have lacked the courage to stand for what is right.

I'd like to remind you of an important, indeed, a key position of the United States. Ambassador Jeane Kirkpatrick has my explicit instructions that if Israel is ever forced to walk out of the United Nations, the United States and Israel will walk out together.

I think we've come quite a long way together, at home and abroad. Gone are the days when we abandoned principle and common sense. Gone are the days when we meekly tolerated obvious threats to peace and security. I can tell you today from my heart, America is prepared for peace. And because we're stronger than before, because we've regained our respect, and because our allies and friends know once again that we can be counted on, we're in a position to secure a future of peace—not peace at any price, but a true, meaningful, lasting peace supported by freedom and human dignity.

Now, make no mistake, if ever we were to heed those who would cripple America's defense-building program, we would undermine our own security and the security of our closest friends, like Israel. And as long as I'm President, that's not going to happen. Israel and the United States are bound together by the ties of family, friendship, shared ideals, and mutual interests. We're allies in the defense of freedom in the Middle East. And I'm proud to say, borrowing Prime Minister Peres' words of 2 weeks ago, relations between the United States and Israel "have reached a new level of harmony and understanding."

In partnership, Israel and the United States will continue to work toward a common vision of peace, security, and economic well-being. Our friendship is closer and stronger today, yes, than ever before. And we intend to keep it that way.

Let me leave you with one final thought. I know that many of you here today have your political roots in the Democratic Party. And I just want to say to all of you, to repeat what I said a moment ago, that I was a Democrat most of my life, and I know what it's like when you find yourself unable to support the decisions of the leadership of that party. But to you and to the millions of rank-and-file Democrats who love America and want a better life for your children, who share our determination to build a stronger America at home and abroad, I can only say: Come walk with us down this new path of hope and opportunity, and in a bipartisan way, we will keep this nation strong and free.

The spiritual values which the Jewish community represent are now being seen by the American public on a television series, "Heritage, Civilization, And The Jews." These are values we want and need in the Republican Party. We stand with you, working for an America that works for everyone, an America strong and successful, inspired and united for opportunity. We stand with you, committed and determined to help you protect the traditions and ethics that you hold dear. And we stand with you in your belief in the inviolability of the first amendment.

We stand with you in condemning any and all who preach or countenance bigotry, hatred, or anti-Semitism. And we stand with you in supporting the rights of Soviet Jewry and other believers. We will never be silent in the fight for human rights. We stand with you in support of our friend and democratic ally in the Middle East, the State of Israel. And together, we can build an even better future for our children and for America. And together, we will.

The other day I said something to a group of students in the White House that I will repeat to you: We are free. We are the land of the free, because we are the home of the brave.

Thank you, and God bless you all, and *lechayim.*

Note: The President spoke at 11:53 a.m. in the Main Sanctuary of Temple Hillel. He was introduced by Rabbi Morris Friedman.

Following the President's remarks, he went to Rabbi Friedman's residence for lunch. He then traveled to Fairfield, CT.

Remarks at a Reagan-Bush Rally in Fairfield, Connecticut
October 26, 1984

The President. Well, it's great to be here in Fairfield and back in Connecticut again. And I'm proud to be here today with your Congressman Stu McKinney. We need him back in Washington. And that goes for Congresswoman Nancy Johnson, too. She's had a first, great term, and we need her back in Washington.

Today I want to ask everyone in Connecticut to help out this administration by sending Larry Denardis back to the Congress from the third district, electing Herschel Klein in the first district, and Roberta Koontz in the second, and John Rowland in the fifth.

I am always glad to visit again with the good people who have given America some of its greatest Republicans—John Davis Lodge, Clare Boothe Luce, and, yes, a fellow named George Bush. He's a great friend, a strong right arm, and I think the finest Vice President this country's ever had.

I would also like to say hello to Donna and Bruce Keith, whose son, Jeff, is undertaking a courageous task to raise money for the American Cancer Society. Jeff, as you probably all know, is running from Boston to Los Angeles, and Nancy and I met him on Monday in Kansas City—where I'd gone for a little fracas of my own. Jeff's run is not only an inspiration, it's a challenge to all of us to go as far as our abilities will take us—

and a little bit farther. And I think that all of you probably are well aware of what he's doing and are proud of him, as we all are.

Now, you know that Nathan Hale was from Connecticut. Now, I'm not going to claim he was a Republican; that would be almost as bad as my opponent invoking the name of Harry Truman to defend his defense policies. I hope you've all noticed that my opponent, who back in the primaries sounded like he thought the world was "Mr. Rogers' Neighborhood"—[*laughter*]—has suddenly discovered that America has some dangerous adversaries out there. The man who, all his years in the Senate, voted against every weapons systems except slingshots—[*laughter*]—is now talking tough about our adversaries and the need for national security.

Audience member. He doesn't know what he's talking about!

The President. You're right. [*Laughter*] He doesn't. For those of you who are too far away to hear, a lady up here said, "He doesn't know what he's talking about." [*Laughter*] She's absolutely right.

And last minute conversions aren't going to hide the fact that these liberal Democrats don't represent traditional Democrats anymore. You know, national Democrats used to fight for the working families of America, and now all they seem to fight for are the special interests and their own left-wing ideology. We have a tremendous opportunity this year to join with a lot of disaffected Democrats and Independents to send a message back to Washington, a message that says the American people want a Congress that won't stalemate or obstruct our agenda for hope and new opportunity for the future.

Abe Lincoln said we must disenthrall ourselves with the past, and then we will save our country. Well, 4 years ago that's just what we did. We made a great turn. We got out from under the thrall of a government which we had hoped would make our lives better, but which wound up trying to live our lives for us. The power of the Federal Government, that it had over the decades, created great chaos—economic, social, and international. And our leaders were adrift, rudderless, without compass.

Four years ago we began to navigate by some certain, fixed principles. Our North Star was freedom, and common sense our constellations. We knew that economic freedom meant paying less of the American family's earnings to the government, and so we cut personal tax rates by 25 percent.

We knew that inflation, the quiet thief, was stealing our savings, and the highest interest rates since the Civil War were making it impossible for people to own a home or start an enterprise. And let me interject a news note, in case you've been busy this morning and haven't heard it: Led by Morgan, the bank, two other major banks joined them, and the prime rate came down to 12 percent as of this morning. And I'm sure that the other banks will soon follow.

Audience. 4 more years! 4 more years! 4 more years!

The President. All right. You'd better let me talk; it looks like it's going to rain.

We knew that our national military defense had been weakened, so we decided to rebuild and be strong again. And this we knew would enhance the chances for peace throughout the world.

It was a second American revolution, and it's only just begun. But America is back, a giant, powerful in its renewed spirit, its growing economy, powerful in its ability to defend itself and secure the peace, and powerful in its ability to build a new future.

And you know something? That's not debatable.

Yet 4 years after our efforts began small voices in the night are sounding the call to go back—back to the days of drift, the days of torpor, timidity, and taxes. My opponent this year is known to you, but perhaps we can gain greater insight into the world he would take us back to if we take a look at his record.

His understanding of economics is well demonstrated by his predictions. Just before we took office, he said our economic program is obviously, murderously, inflationary. That was just before we lowered inflation from 12.4 down to around 4 percent. And just after our tax cuts, he said the most he could see was an anemic recovery. And that was right before the United States economy created more than 6 million new jobs in 21 months.

My opponent said our policies would deliver a misery index the likes of which we haven't seen for a long time. Now, there he was partially right. You know you get the misery index by adding the rate of unemployment to the rate of inflation. They invented that in 1976, during the campaign that year. They said that Jerry Ford had no right to ask for reelection because his misery index was 12.6. Now, they didn't mention the misery index in the 1980 election, probably because it had gone up to more than 20. And they aren't talking too much about it in this campaign, because it's down around 11.

He said that decontrol of oil, the oil prices, would cost American consumers more than $36 billion a year. Well, we decontrolled oil prices. It was one of the first things we did. And the price of gas went down 8 cents a gallon.

Now, I have something figured out here—that maybe all we have to do to get the economy in absolutely perfect shape is to persuade my opponent to predict absolute disaster. [*Laughter*]

He says he cares about the middle class, but he boasts, "I have consistently supported legislation, time after time, which increases taxes on my own constituents." Doesn't that make you just want to be one of his constituents?

Audience. No!

The President. He's no doubt proud of the fact that as Senator he voted 16 times to increase taxes on the American people.

Audience. Boo-o-o!

The President. But this year he's outdone himself. He's already promised, of course, to raise your taxes. But if he's to keep all the promises that he's made in this campaign—we figured it out by computer—he will have to raise your taxes $1,890 for every household in this country.

Audience. Boo-o-o!

The President. That's better than $150 a month, that's the Mondale mortgage. But his economic plan has two basic parts: raise your taxes, and then raise them again. But I've got news for him: The American people don't want his tax increases, and he isn't going to get them.

If he got them, if he got those tax increases, it would stop the recovery. But I tell you, he did give me an idea: If I can figure out how to dress like his tax program, I'll go out on Halloween and scare the devil out of all the neighbors. [*Laughter*]

If his campaign were a television show, it would be "Let's Make a Deal." You give up your prosperity to see what surprise he has for you behind the curtain. [*Laughter*] If his plan were a Broadway show, it would be "Promises, Promises." [*Laughter*] And if the administration that he served in as Vice President was a book, you'd have to read it from the back end to the front to get a happy ending.

He sees an America in which every day is tax day, April 15th. But we see an America in which every day is Independence Day, July 4th. We want to lower your tax rates so that your families will be stronger, our economy will be stronger, and America will be stronger.

I'm proud to say that during these last 4 years, not 1 square inch of territory in the world has been lost to Communist aggression. And the United States is more secure than it was 4 years ago.

But my opponent sees a different world. Sometime back he said the old days of a Soviet strategy of suppression by force are over. That was just before the Soviets invaded Czechoslovakia. After they invaded Afghanistan, he said, "It just baffles me why the Soviets these last few years have be-

haved as they have." But then, there's so much that baffles him. [*Laughter*]

One year ago we liberated Grenada from Communist thugs who had taken over that country, and my opponent called what we did a violation of international law that erodes our moral authority to criticize the Soviets.

Audience. Boo-o-o!

The President. Well, there's nothing immoral about rescuing American students whose lives are in danger. But by the time my opponent decided that action was justified, the students were long since home.

After the Sandinista revolution in Nicaragua, he praised it. He said, "Winds of democratic progress are stirring where they have long been stifled." But we all know that the Sandinistas immediately began to persecute the genuine believers in democracy and export terror. They went on to slaughter the Miskito Indians, abuse and deport church leaders, practice anti-Semitism, slander the Pope, and move to kill free speech. Don't you think it's time my opponent stood up, spoke out, and condemned the Sandinista crimes? [*Applause*]

More recently, he refused, or failed to repudiate the Reverend Jesse Jackson, when he went to Havana and then stood with Fidel Castro and cried: "Long live President Fidel Castro! Long live Che Guevara!"

Audience. Boo-o-o!

The President. But let me try to put this in perspective. The 1984 election is not truly a partisan contest. I was a Democrat once myself, and for a long time, a large part of my life. But in those days, its leaders didn't belong to the "blame America first" crowd. Its leaders were men like Harry Truman, who understood the challenges of our times. They didn't reserve all their indignation for America. They knew the difference between freedom and tyranny and they stood up for one and damned the other.

To all the good Democrats who respect that tradition, I say—and I hope there are many present—you're not alone. We're asking you to come walk with us down the new path of hope and opportunity, and we'll make it a bipartisan salvation of our country.

This month an American woman walked in space—Kathryn Sullivan—and she made history. And she returned to a space shuttle in which some of the great scientific and medical advances of the future will be made. Cures for diabetes and heart disease may be possible up there; advances in technology and communications. But my opponent led the fight in the United States Senate against the entire shuttle program and called it a horrible waste.

Well, we support the space shuttle, and we've committed America to meet a great challenge—to build a permanently manned space station before this decade is out.

And now, I've probably been going on for too long up here——

Audience. No!

The President. ——but I just want to say the point is we were right when we made a great turn in 1980. Incidentally, I was mistaken when I said there, "before this decade is out." I should say within 10 years—a decade—we're hoping for that space station.

We were right to take command of the ship, stop its aimless drift, and get moving again. And we were right when we stopped sending out S.O.S. and started saying U.S.A.!

Audience. U.S.A.! U.S.A.! U.S.A.!

The President. You are right. The United States was never meant to be a second-best nation. And like our Olympic athletes, this nation should set its sights on the stars and go for the gold.

If America could bring down inflation from, as I said, 12.4 percent to 4, then we can bring inflation from 4 percent down to 0.0. If lowering your tax rates led to the best expansion in 30 years, then we can lower them again and keep America growing into the 21st century.

If we could create 6 million new jobs in 21 months, and some 9 million new businesses be incorporated in 18 months, then we can make it possible for every American—young, old, black, or white—who wants, to find a job.

If our States and municipalities can establish enterprise zones to create economic growth, then we can elect people to Congress who will free our enterprise zones bill from Tip O'Neill—it's been there for more than 2 years—so that we can provide hope and opportunity for the most distressed areas of America.

If we can lead a revolution in technology, push back the frontiers of space, then we can provide our workers—in industries old and new—all that they need. I say that American workers provided with the right tools can outproduce, outcompete, and outsell anyone in the world.

Audience member. Give 'em hell!

The President. Someone said, "Give 'em hell." Harry Truman—when they said that to Harry Truman, he said tell them the truth, and they'll think it's hell. Well, if our grassroots drive to restore excellence in education could reverse a 20-year decline in scholastic aptitude test scores—which it has—then we can keep raising those scores and restoring American academic excellence second to none.

If our crackdown on crime could produce the sharpest drop ever in the crime index, then we can keep cracking down until our families and friends can walk our streets again without being afraid.

And if we could reverse the decline in our military defenses and restore respect for America, then we can make sure this nation remains strong enough to protect freedom and peace for us, for our children, and for our children's children.

And if we make sure that America is strong and prepared for peace, then we can begin to reduce nuclear weapons and one day banish them entirely from the Earth. And that is our goal.

If we can strengthen our economy, strengthen our security, and strengthen the values that bind us, then America will become a nation ever greater in art and learning, greater in the love and worship of the God who made us and Who has blessed us as no other people on Earth have ever been blessed.

To the young people of our country—and I'm so happy to see so many of them here—let me, if I could, say to you young people: You are what this election is all about—you and your future.

Your generation is something special. Your love of country and idealism are unsurpassed. And it's our highest duty to make certain that you have an America every bit as full of opportunity, hope, confidence, and dreams as we had when we were your age.

You know, last Sunday night I didn't get to finish what I started to say, was going to finish with in that debate, so I can finish it now. I was talking about you young people. And I've seen you all across this country, and you are special. And what I was going to say was that my generation—and a few generations between mine and yours—that we grew up in an America where we took it for granted that you could fly as high and as far as your own strength and ability would take you. And it is our sacred responsibility—those several generations I've just mentioned—to make sure that we hand you an America that is free in a world that is at peace. And we're going to do it.

Audience. 4 more years! 4 more years! 4 more years!

The President. All right. Thank you. I really hadn't thought about it, but you've talked me into it. You know, if we can, all of us together—we're part of a great revolution, and it's only just begun. America is never going to give up its special mission on this Earth—never. There are new worlds on the horizon, and we're not going to stop until we all get there together.

America's best days are yet to come. And I know it may drive my opponents up the wall, but I'm going to say it anyway: You ain't seen nothin' yet.

Audience. Reagan! Reagan! Reagan!

The President. Thank you very much. Thank you, and God bless you all.

Note: The President spoke at 2:30 p.m. at the Fairfield Town Hall. Following his remarks, the President signed H.R. 5271 into law, an extension of the Wetlands Loan Act, which will establish a four-site national wildlife refuge in Fairfield County, CT. He then traveled to Hackensack, NJ.

Remarks at a Reagan-Bush Rally in Hackensack, New Jersey
October 26, 1984

The President. Thank you all very much for a most heartwarming welcome, and it's wonderful to be back in New Jersey. I was close by this past summer. I went to a church festival in Hoboken. And today it's good to be in Hackensack, the capital of Bergen County.

There are many things that are special about New Jersey. One of them is the caliber of the people that you send to the Congress. All of the successes we've had these past 4 years we owe to people like Congresswoman Marge Roukema, Congressman Jim Courter, and we need more people like Marge and Jim in Washington. And that's why I'm asking you to make Neil Romano a Congressman, and to make Mary Mochary a Senator, New Jersey's first woman Senator. We need them all in Washington.

And now, my friend and your great Governor, Tom Kean, has told us about the good news about Hackensack—that you're not only growing up; you're growing out.

You're rebuilding the inner city. You're attracting new businesses and new homeowners. So, you're very much a part of the great renewal that we've been trying to lead in Washington, but which has really been made possible by you, the people of this community, and you, the people of this State and this country.

That renewal began 4 years ago when America changed course, and we were guided in what we set out to do by the advice of a very great President. Abraham Lincoln said we must disenthrall ourselves with the past—and then we will save our country. Well, 4 years ago that's what we did. We made a great turn. We got out from under the thrall of a government which we had hoped would make our lives better, but which we found simply was trying to live our lives for us.

The power of the Federal Government, the power it had over the decades created great chaos—economic, social, and international. Our leaders were adrift. They were rudderless, without a compass. Four years ago, we began to navigate by certain fixed principles. And our North Star was freedom, and common sense were our constellations.

We knew that economic freedom meant paying less of the America's families earnings to the government. And so, we cut personal income tax rates by 25 percent.

We knew that inflation, the quiet thief, was stealing our savings, and the highest interest rates since the Civil War were making it impossible for people to own a home or start an enterprise.

And let me inject a little news item here. If you haven't heard the news, as of this morning, led by Morgan Guaranty and three other very great banks in the United States, the prime rate came down to 12 even.

Audience. 4 more years! 4 more years! 4 more years!

The President. All right.

Audience. 4 more years! 4 more years! 4 more years!

The President. All right. I wasn't going to, but okay, if you insist. [*Laughter*]

We knew a few years ago that our military defense had been weakened. So, we decided to rebuild and be strong again. And this, we knew, would enhance the chances for world peace. It was a second American revolution, and it's only just begun.

America is back, a giant, powerful in its renewed spirit, its growing economy, powerful in its ability to defend itself and secure the peace, and powerful in its ability to build a better future. And you know something? That's not debatable.

Yet 4 years after our efforts began, small voices in the night are sounding the call to go back—back to the days of drift, the days of torpor, timidity, and taxes.

My opponent this year is known to you, but perhaps we can gain a greater insight into the world that he would take us back to if we take a look at his record.

His understanding of economics is well demonstrated by his predictions. Just before we took office, he said our economic program is obviously, murderously inflationary. And that was just before we lowered inflation from above 12 percent down to 4.

And just after our tax cuts, he said that the most that he could see was an anemic recovery, and that was right before the United States economy created more than 6 million new jobs in 21 months, and 900,000 new businesses were incorporated in the last 18.

My opponent said that our policies would deliver a misery index the likes of which we haven't seen in a long time. Well, now, there was some truth in that. Now, you get the misery index from adding up the unemployment rate to the inflation rate. And they did that; they invented that back in 1976 in that campaign. And then they said that Jerry Ford had no right to seek reelection to the office of President, because his misery index was 12.6. Well, they didn't mention the misery index in the 1980 election, probably because it was over 20 by then. And they aren't talking about it too much in this campaign, because it's down around 11.

My opponent said that if we decontrolled oil prices, it would cost the American consumers more than $36 billion a year. Well, we did decontrol oil prices, one of the first things we did, and the price of gasoline went down by 8 cents a gallon.

Now, I've just been figuring that maybe, if we could get him—well, we could get the economy in absolutely perfect shape if we could only get my opponent to predict absolute disaster. [*Laughter*]

Now, he says that he cares about the middle class. And he boasts, "I have consistently supported legislation, time after time, which increases taxes on my own constituents." Doesn't that just make you want to be a constituent of his? [*Laughter*]

Audience. Boo-o-o!

The President. He's no doubt proud of the fact that as a United States Senator he voted 16 times to increase taxes. But this year, he's outdone himself. He's already promised to raise taxes. But if he's to keep all the other promises he made to this group and that, he will have to raise the taxes a prorated amount of about $1,890 for every household in the United States.

Audience. Boo-o-o!

The President. That prorates out to more than $150 a month. That's kind of like a second mortgage, a Mondale mortgage. [*Laughter*]

But his economic plan has two basic parts: One, to raise your taxes; and two, to do it again. [*Laughter*] But I've got news for him. The American people don't want his tax increases, and he's not going to get them.

His tax plan would bring this economic recovery to a roaring halt. But I'll give it this: It gave me an idea for Halloween. If I can figure out a costume that will look like his economic program, I could just scare the devil out of all the neighbors. [*Laughter*]

You know, if my opponent's economic program were a television show, it would be "Let's Make a Deal." [*Laughter*] You know, that's when you'd give up your prosperity in order for whatever surprise he had hidden behind the curtain. [*Laughter*] Now, if his campaign were a Broadway show, it would be "Promises, Promises." And if it were a book, the administration were a book that he served in, you'd have to read it from the back to the front to get a happy ending. [*Laughter*]

Audience. 4 more years! 4 more years! 4 more years!

The President. All right. All right. I will.

Audience. 4 more years! 4 more years! 4 more years!

The President. All right.

You know, he sees an America in which every day is tax day, April 15th. We see an America in which every day is Independence Day, the Fourth of July. Seriously, we want to lower your taxes, yours and everybody's in this country, so your families will be stronger, our economy will be stronger, and America will be stronger.

I'm proud to say that during these last 4 years, not 1 square inch of territory in the world was lost to Communist aggression. And the United States is more secure than it was 4 years ago. And yet my opponent sees a different world.

Sometime back he said the old days of a Soviet strategy of suppression by force are over. Now, he said that just before the Soviets invaded Czechoslovakia. And after they invaded Afghanistan, he said, "It just baffles me why the Soviets these last few years have behaved as they have." But then there's so much that baffles him. [*Laughter*]

One year ago we liberated Grenada from Communist thugs who had taken over that country. My opponent called what we did a violation of international law that erodes our moral authority to criticize the Soviets.

Audience. Boo-o-o!

The President. You're right. There is nothing immoral about rescuing American students whose lives are in danger. But by the time my opponent decided that action was justified, the students were long since home.

After the Sandinista revolution in Nicaragua, he praised that. He said, "Winds of democratic progress are stirring where they have long been stifled." But we know that those democratic winds he was talking about were the Sandinistas persecuting the genuine believers in democracy, exporting terror. They went on to slaughter the Miskito Indians, abuse and deport church leaders, slander the Pope, practice anti-Semitism, and move to kill free speech. Don't you think it's time that he stood up and spoke out and condemned the Sandinistas' crimes? [*Applause*]

But more recently, he failed to repudiate the Reverend Jesse Jackson when he went to Havana, stood beside Fidel Castro, and cried: "Long live President Castro! Long live Che Guevara!"

Audience. Boo-o-o!

The President. But let me try to put this in perspective. The 1984 election isn't just a partisan contest. I was a Democrat once. In fact, for the greater part of my life I was a Democrat. But in those days, the leaders of the Democratic Party weren't in the "blame America first" gang. Its leaders were men like Harry Truman, men who understood the challenges of the times. They didn't reserve all of their indignation for America. They knew the difference between freedom and tyranny, and they stood up for one and damned the other.

To all the good Democrats—and I hope there are many present here today—who respect that tradition of those previous leaders, I would like to tell you you're not alone. We're asking you to come and walk with us down this new path of hope and opportunity. We need you. And believe me, we can then say the salvation of this country is a bipartisan operation.

This month an American woman walked in space—Kathryn Sullivan made history. But after that walk in space, she went back to a space shuttle in which some of the great scientific and medical advances of the future will be made. Cures for diabetes and heart disease may be possible up there, advances in technology and communication. But my opponent as a Senator personally led the battle in the Senate against having the shuttle program at all. He called it a horrible waste.

Audience. Boo-o-o!

The President. You're right. We support the space shuttle, and we've committed America to meet a great challenge, because what we're going to do next is build a permanently manned space station, and we're going to do it within a decade.

Now, I've probably been going on too long here.

Audience. No!

The President. But the point is, we were right when we made our good turn in 1980. We were right to take command of the ship, stop its aimless drift, and get moving again. And we were right when we stopped sending out an S.O.S. and starting saying U.S.A.!

Audience. U.S.A.! U.S.A.! U.S.A.!

The President. All right. Thank you.

You know, the United States was never meant to be a second-best nation. Like our Olympic athletes, this nation should set its sights on the stars and go for the gold.

If America could bring down inflation from 12.4 percent to 4, then we can bring inflation now down from 4 to 0.0. And that's what we're going to do.

If lowering your tax rates led to the best expansion in 30 years, then we can lower them again and keep America growing into the 21st century.

If we could create 6 million new jobs in 21 months, and then we can make it possible for every American—young, old, black, and white—who wants a job to find a job.

If our States and municipalities can establish enterprise zones to create economic growth, then we can elect people to Congress who will free our enterprise zones bill from Tip O'Neill, who's had it buried in a committee for 2 years now, get it out on

the floor, and provide opportunity and hope for the most dispossessed areas of America.

If we can lead a revolution in technology and push back the frontiers of space, then we can provide our workers—in industries old and new—all that they need, because if you give American workers the tools they need, they'll outproduce, outcompete, and outsell anyone, anyplace in the world.

If our grassroots drive to restore excellence in education could reverse a 20-year decline in the scholastic aptitude test scores, then we can keep raising those scores and restore American academic excellence second to none.

If our crackdown on crime could produce the sharpest drop ever in the crime index—as it did last year—then we can keep cracking down until our families and friends can walk our streets again without being afraid.

If we could reverse the decline in our military defenses and restore respect for America, as we have, then we can make sure this nation remains strong, strong enough to protect freedom and peace for us, for our children, and for our children's children. And we're going to do that.

And if we make sure that America remains strong and prepared for peace, then we can begin to reduce nuclear weapons until we have eliminated them from the world entirely.

If we can strengthen our economy, strengthen our security, and strengthen the values that bind us, then America will become a nation even greater in art and learning, greater in the love and worship of the God who made us and who has blessed us as no other people have ever been blessed in history.

To the young people of our country—and I'm so pleased to see so many here as I've seen in meetings like this all around the country—let me say to you now—you young people—you are what this election is all about, you and your future. Your generation is something special. I've seen that from coast to coast.

You know, this is what I was starting to say at the end of the debate last Sunday night when I ran out of time, so I'm going to say it here. It is our highest duty to make certain that you have an America that is every bit as full of opportunity, hope, and confidence and dreams as we had when we were your age.

My generation—and then there were a few generations between mine and yours—those generations, we came into an America and grew up taking it for granted that you could dream and make your dreams come true, that there was no limit on what you could accomplish if you set out to do it and went after it. And I want to tell you that those generations I've just talked about that are above yours—our sacred responsibility is to hand you when it's your turn and you take over—we must hand you an America that is free in a world that is at peace.

All of us——

Audience. 4 more years! 4 more years! 4 more years!

The President. All right.

Audience. 4 more years! 4 more years! 4 more years!

The President. All right. We'll do it then.

Audience. 4 more years! 4 more years! 4 more years!

The President. All right. All of us together, all of us are part of a great revolution, and it's only just begun. America will never give up its special mission in the world, ever. There are new worlds on our horizon, and we're not going to stop until we all get there together. America's best years are yet to come.

And I know this is going to drive a few individuals crazy, but I'm going to say it: You ain't seen nothin' yet.

Thank you for your wonderful hospitality. Thank you, and God bless you all.

Note: The President spoke at 5:28 p.m. at the Hackensack City Hall complex.

Following his remarks, the President stopped at the Wellington Hall Nursing Home, where he greeted several of the residents. He then traveled to Camp David, MD, where he spent the weekend.

Radio Address to the Nation on the Presidential Campaign
October 27, 1984

My fellow Americans:

When I was asked recently what's been the greatest highlight of our campaign, I said the tremendous number of young people at our rallies and the tremendous outpouring of their spirit for America and our future.

To all of them, I just have to say: Your generation really sparkles. In my travels I have met you by the thousands, and I've seen enthusiasm and patriotism in your eyes that convince me you get high on America. Historians may look back at the strength of your spirit and common sense as key to the great American renewal in the 1980's.

Our generations are separated by more years than I care to admit; yet I feel a special bond of kinship with you. I think we share not only a great love for America but also an appreciation for the secret of America's success—opportunity.

America works best when we unite for opportunity, reaching for the stars and chal-lenging the limits of our potential. And America's greatest progress for everyone—whites, blacks, young, and old—begins not in Washington, but in our homes, neighborhoods, workplaces, and voluntary groups across this land.

We weren't meant to be a nation divided; we weren't meant to be a nation second-best. We were meant to be, as our Olympic athletes showed last summer, a people with faith in each other, courage to dream great dreams, opportunities to climb higher, and determination to go for the gold.

Providing opportunities for all of us to make this great, free nation greater and freer still is what we've been trying to do since we made a great sea change in 1981—a change to reverse the flow of power to Washington and begin restoring sovereignty to the people.

We knew that inflation and the highest interest rates since the Civil War were making it impossible for people to buy homes, start up businesses or, for that matter, even find jobs. So, we reduced spending growth and cut tax rates for everyone. We knew that our defenses had become dangerously weak. So, we started rebuilding to be strong again.

We've only begun to clear away the debris from decades of bad policies. Many people still need help. Nevertheless, America already has made a great comeback. Inflation, taxes, interest rates, and crime are down, but confidence, jobs, investment, growth, and achievement in our schools are up. And unlike 4 years ago when the Soviets were gaining influence and spreading instability throughout the world, since 1981 not 1 square inch of territory has been lost to Communist aggression. That's what makes the world a safer place.

Today our nation is at peace and our economy is in one piece. We're poised to meet great challenges for the future. We can reduce personal tax rates further, creating new jobs and opportunities for every American with nobody left behind. We can pass initiatives like enterprise zones to rebuild the distressed areas of our country and push on toward much greater progress in education, science, technology, and space.

This month an American woman, Kathryn Sullivan, made history walking in space, then returned to the space shuttle in which some of the great scientific and medical advances of the future will be made. That's why we support the space shuttle and why we've committed America to build a permanently manned space station within a decade.

And by keeping America strong and prepared for peace we'll have the best chance to begin reducing nuclear weapons and, one day, God willing, banish them entirely.

But before we do anything, you must choose: Will we keep moving forward on a new path toward a better future, or will we turn back to my opponent's philosophy—weaker defenses, inflationary spending, and huge tax increases?

The difference between us is that we look at a problem and see opportunity, and he looks at opportunity and sees a problem. We seek a tax system that rewards work and investment and stimulates growth. Mr. Mondale would bring back the very policies that destroy incentives, destroy opportunity, and destroy economic growth—policies that would cause enormous hardship and send many of you from the graduation line to the unemployment line.

We can do better, much better. We want you to have an America every bit as full of hope, confidence, and dreams as our parents left us. Come November 6th, I hope millions of you will make history by voting for your future—voting for opportunity, voting for leadership that trusts in you and the power of your dreams. If you do, we'll bring this nation together with new strength and unity. We'll make sure America's best days are yet to come.

Until next week, thanks for listening, and God bless you.

Note: The President spoke at 12:06 p.m. from Camp David, MD.

Remarks at a Reagan-Bush Rally in Millersville, Pennsylvania
October 29, 1984

Audience. 4 more years! 4 more years! 4 more years!

The President. Thank you very much. Thank you very much. I won't be a holdout. Let's make it unanimous. Well, thank you for a most heartwarming greeting. Every time I come up here, I get a chance to meet the wonderful people here. It reminds me of something that——

Audience. 4 more years! 4 more years! 4 more years!

The President. Now, if I say yes, does that make it eight? [*Applause*] Thank you.

But I've seen something on television, and then just from outside, I heard your response to a line about the saying, "You've got a friend in Pennsylvania." Well, I want you to know that as long as I'm President, Pennsylvania will have a friend in the White House.

As we approach this 1984 election—and it's just over the hill—it's more than fitting that we meet here in a cradle—one of the cradles of American democracy. You are a peace-loving people. But the citizens of Lancaster have always been in the front ranks of liberty. You were the arsenal of the colonies, and your men were some of the first volunteers to fill the ranks of Washington's army.

Now you've carried on that tradition by sending to Washington a representative who stands foursquare for a strong, free, and prosperous America—Congressman Bob Walker. So, I've come here bearing an important message and request. We need Bob Walker in the Congress to keep the pressure on Tip O'Neill. So, you send him back up there.

Now, I know that your Senators are not up for reelection this time around, but just let me thank you for giving us Senator Heinz and Senator Specter. They both reflect the kind of leadership one would expect from Pennsylvania. And considering the fine individuals I just mentioned, my good friend also, Drew Lewis, and your outstanding, and I truly mean nationally outstanding Governor, Dick Thornburgh. You folks are batting a thousand.

Abe Lincoln said that we must disenthrall ourselves with the past—and then we will save our country. Well, 4 years ago that's what we did. We made a great turn. We got out from under the thrall of a government which we had hoped would make our lives better, but which wound up living our lives for us.

The power of the Federal Government had over the decades, created great chaos—economic, social, and international. Our leaders were adrift, rudderless, without a compass. Four years ago we began to navigate by certain fixed principles. Our North Star was freedom, and common sense was our constellation.

We knew that economic freedom meant paying less of the family's earnings to the Government. So, we cut your personal income tax rates by 25 percent.

We knew that inflation, the quiet thief, was stealing our savings, and the highest interest rates since the Civil War were making it impossible for people to own a home or start an enterprise.

We knew that our national military defense had been weakened. So, we decided to rebuild and be strong again. And this, we knew, would enhance the prospects for peace in the world. It was a second American Revolution, but it's only just begun.

Still, America is back, a giant. It's powerful in its renewed spirit, its growing economy, powerful in its ability to defend itself and secure the peace, and powerful in its ability to build a better future. And you know something? What I said is not debatable.

Audience. U.S.A.! U.S.A.! U.S.A.!

The President. Thank you. Yet 4 years after our efforts began, small voices in the night are sounding the call to go back—back to the days of drift——

Audience. Boo-o-o!

The President. ——the days of torpor, timidity, and taxes.

Audience. Boo-o-o!

The President. Now, my opponent is known to you. But perhaps we can gain greater insight into the world he would have us taken back to if we take a look at his record.

His understanding of economics is well demonstrated by his predictions. Just before we took office, he said our economic program is obviously, murderously inflationary. Now, that was just before we lowered inflation from more than 12 percent down to around 4.

And just after our tax cuts, he said the most he could see was an anemic recovery. Now, that was right before the United States economy created more than 6 million new jobs in 21 months. And there have been 900,000 business incorporations in the last 18 months.

Now, then, my opponent said that our policies would deliver a misery index the likes of which we haven't seen for a long time. Now, there was some truth in that. Now, you know what the misery index was, they added up the rate of unemployment and the rate of inflation. And that was done; they invented that for the 1976 campaign. And then they said that Jerry Ford didn't have a right to seek reelection, because his misery index was 12.6. Now, they didn't mention the misery index in the 1980 campaign, probably because it was over 20. And they haven't been mentioning it in this campaign, because it's down around 11.

My opponent said that decontrol of oil prices would cost American consumers more than $36 billion a year. Well, we decontrolled oil prices—one of the first things we did—and the price of gas went down 8 cents a gallon.

Now, you know, maybe all we have to do to get the economy in absolutely perfect shape is to get my opponent to predict absolute disaster.

Now, he says he cares about the middle class, but he boasts—and I quote—"I have consistently supported legislation, time after time, which increases taxes on my own constituents." Doesn't that make you want to be one of his constituents?

Audience. No!

The President. He's no doubt proud of the fact that he voted 16 times as a United States Senator to raise your taxes.

Audience. Boo-o-o!

The President. But this year he's outdone himself. He's already promised, of course, to raise your taxes. But if he is to keep all the promises that he's made to this group and that, he will have to raise taxes by the equivalent of $1,890 for every household in the United States.

Audience. Boo-o-o!

The President. Now, that prorates out to more than $150 a month. It's like having a second mortgage, a Mondale mortgage. [*Laughter*]

His economic plan has two parts: raise your taxes, and then raise them again. But I've got news for him. The American people don't want his tax increases, and they're not going to get them.

Audience. We want Reagan! We want Reagan! We want Reagan!

The President. Thank you. You know, his tax increase, seriously, would bring this economic recovery to a halt, because the tax cut is one of the basic reasons for the recovery that we're having.

Now, I'm beginning to see more clearly—last week my opponents said to the voters, "Let's forget about the past." If I had his past, I'd want to forget about it, too. [*Laughter*]

You know, the killer inflation of the Carter-Mondale years was much more than a set of numbers on the misery index. With food prices going out of control, inflation was the unwanted chair at the dinner table. With gasoline prices moving up wildly, inflation was the unwanted passenger in every car. And with home prices and mortgages jumping to levels never seen before, inflation was the unwanted guest in every home. But it's not the past that worries us, it's the future. And I'm even more concerned now because——

Audience. We're number one! We're number one! We're number one!

The President. Did somebody just leave back there? I just took it for granted that was an echo. [*Laughter*] But, as I say, it's not the past that worries us—it's the future.

And I'm even more concerned now, because just last week my opponent used another familiar phrase from the past. "Trust me," he said. Well, the last time we trusted his administration, they took five—count 'em—five economic plans and nearly tripled inflation. Now, by contrast, we trusted the people, and with just one economic program, we cut inflation by two-thirds.

So, you can see that when we analyze what he has said in this campaign, our biggest concern is not whether he will forget the past, but whether he's going to bring it back. And when we see all the promises he's dangled before so many special interests, and recall that while in the Senate, he never once voted to sustain the veto of any spending bill, then we have much to worry about.

We're hoping the voters will deliver a message next week——

Audience member. We will!

The President. If you do, you'll be saying that you're simply not going to allow them to pick the American wallet again. High taxes, explosive inflation, and spending without limits might well have been the way out of the past. But if we do the right thing next week, we'll make sure they do not become the wave of the future.

If my opponent's campaign were a television show, it would be "Let's Make a Deal." [*Laughter*] You get to trade your prosperity for the surprise behind the curtain. If the campaign were a Broadway show, it would be "Promises, Promises." [*Laughter*] And if his administration had been a novel, a book, you would have had to read it from the back to the front to get a happy ending. [*Laughter*]

He sees an America in which every day is tax day, April 15th. We see an America in which every day is Independence Day, July 4th. We want to lower your and everybody's taxes, so your familes will be stronger, our economy will be stronger, and America will be stronger.

I'm proud to say that during those last 4 years, not 1 square inch of territory was lost to Communist aggression anyplace in the world.

Audience. U.S.A.! U.S.A.! U.S.A.!

The President. And the United States is more secure than we were 4 years ago. And yet my opponent sees a different world.

Sometime back my opponent said the old days of a Soviet strategy of suppression by force are over. That was just before the Soviets invaded Czechoslovakia. And after they invaded Afghanistan, he said, "It just baffles me why the Soviets these last few years have behaved as they have." [*Laughter*] But then there's so much that baffles him.

One year ago we liberated Grenada from Communist thugs that had taken over that country. Now, my opponent called what we did a violation of international law that erodes our moral authority to criticize the Soviets.

Audience. Boo-o-o!

The President. Well, there is nothing immoral about rescuing American students whose lives are in danger.

Audience. U.S.A.! U.S.A.! U.S.A.!

The President. Thank you. But you know, by the time my opponent decided that action in Grenada was justified, the students were long since home.

After the Sandinista revolution in Nicaragua, he praised it, saying, "Winds of democratic progress are stirring where they have

long been stifled." But we know that the Sandinistas immediately began to persecute the genuine believers in democracy, to export terror. They went on to slaughter the Miskito Indians, abuse and deport church leaders, practice anti-Semitism, slander the Pope, and move to kill free speech. Don't you think it's time my opponent stood up, spoke out, and condemned these Sandinista crimes? [*Applause*]

More recently, he failed to repudiate the Reverend Jesse Jackson when he went to Havana, stood with Fidel Castro, and cried, "Long live President Castro and Che Guevara!"

Audience. Boo-o-o!

The President. Let me put this in perspective. The 1980 election isn't just a partisan contest. I was a Democrat for the bigger half of my life. But in those days, its leaders weren't part of the "blame America first" gang. Its leaders were men like Harry Truman, men who understood the challenges of our times. They didn't deserve— or reserve all their indignation for the United States. They knew the difference between freedom and tyranny, and they stood up for one and damned the other.

To all the good Democrats who respect that tradition—and I hope there are many present—and I've been saying this all over the country—you are not alone. We're asking you to come and walk with us down that new path of hope and opportunity. And if you do, it will be that kind of bipartisan act for which this country is renowned and which will salvage and keep a great and powerful U.S.A.

This month, an American woman walked in space—Kathryn Sullivan made history. And she returned to a space shuttle, in which some of the great scientific and medical advances of the future will be made. Cures for diabetes and heart disease may be possible up there, advances in technology and communication. But my opponent, in the Senate, led the fight against the entire shuttle program and called it a horrible waste. Well, we support the space shuttle, and we've committed America to meet a great challenge—to build a permanently manned space station and to do so within a decade.

Now, I've probably been going on too long here.

Audience. No!

The President. Oh, that isn't what you meant by 4 more years, is it? [*Laughter*]

No, the point is, we were right when we made our great turn in 1980. We were right to take command of the ship, stop its aimless drift, and get moving again. And we were right when we stopped sending out S.O.S. and started saying U.S.A.!

Audience. U.S.A.! U.S.A.! U.S.A.!

The President. All right. The United States of America was never meant to be a second-best nation. Like our Olympic athletes, this nation should set its sight on the stars and go for the gold.

If America could bring down inflation from 12.4 to 4, then we can bring inflation down from 4 to 0.0. If lowering your tax rates led to the best expansion in 30 years, then we can lower them again and keep America growing into the 21st century. If we could create 6 million new jobs in 21 months, then we can make it possible for every American—young and old, black or white—who wants to find a job to find one.

If our States and municipalities can establish enterprise zones to create economic growth, then we can elect people to Congress who will free our enterprise zones bill from Tip O'Neill, where it's been buried in a committee in the Congress for 2 years, so that we can provide hope and opportunity for the most distressed areas of America.

If we can lead a revolution in technology, push back the frontiers of space, then we can provide our workers in industries old and new all that they need to out-produce—and I've said this many times—give the American workers the tools they need and they will outproduce, outcompete, and outsell anybody, anything, anywhere in the world.

If our grassroots drive to restore excellence in education could reverse a 20-year decline in the scholastic aptitude test scores, then we can keep raising those scores and restore American academic excellence second to none.

If our crackdown on crime could produce the sharpest drop ever in the crime index, then we can keep cracking down until our families and friends can walk our streets again without being afraid.

If we could restore the decline in our military defenses and restore America—or respect for America throughout the world—and we have—then we can make sure this nation remains strong enough to protect freedom and peace for us, for our children, and for our children's children.

And if we make sure that America remains prepared for peace, then we can begin to reduce nuclear weapons and, one day, banish them entirely from the world.

I've seen a sign in the back that says, "Nuclear War is No Joke." Well, that's a sign—I don't know whether it's meant hostilely or friendly—but I'll tell you something, I take it friendly for this reason: I've had the opportunity to tell parliaments in a number of countries around the world, a nuclear war cannot be won and must never be fought.

And if we can strengthen our economy, our security, strengthen the values that bind us, then America will become a nation even greater in art and learning, greater in the love and worship of the God who made us and who's blessed us as no other people on Earth have ever been blessed.

And now, a week ago Sunday I kind of got cut off in something that I was saying. I ran out of time on the debate. So, I'm going to say it here. To the young people of this country, let me say that you are what this election is all about, you and your future. Your generation is something special. Your idealism, your love of country are unsurpassed. I've seen you all across this country now in this campaign. And it's our highest duty to make certain that you have an America that is every bit as full of opportunity, hope, and confidence and dreams as we had when we were your age.

You know——

Audience. Let's go, Reagan! Let's go, Reagan! Let's go, Reagan!

The President. Thank you. I must tell you, speaking directly to you young people—my generation and a few other generations between mine and yours—[*laughter*]—we came into an America, we grew up in a land where we took it for granted that we could dream and make our dreams come true, and there was no limit to how high and far we could fly on the basis of our own ability and determination to do so. And what I was going to say on that Sunday night was—those other generations I've just mentioned, my own included, we have a sacred obligation to turn over to you when it is your time to take over—to turn over to you an America that is free in a world that is at peace.

All of us together are part of a great revolution, and it's only just begun. America will never give up its special mission, never. There are new worlds on the horizon, and we're not going to stop until we all get there together. And America's best days are yet to come.

But it depends—we're coming down to the wire, and I tell you, stop reading the polls. Don't let anything keep you, on November 6th, from getting out there and doing what we must do, and seeing that your neighbors get out there and get to the polls.

And when I mentioned your good Congressman, Bob Walker, and sending him back there—do you know that it has been

29 years, for 29 straight years, opponents of Republican Presidents and other Presidents—well, they weren't opponents of the Democratic Presidents—but for that many years, the Speaker of the House of Representatives in Washington, the chairman of every committee, they were all opponents of what we believe in and what we're trying to accomplish. And just once, send more back there like Bob Walker. Send them back so that one day, as a team together, we can get this job done.

And now I'll just finish by saying something that I know will drive our opponents up the wall, but I enjoy saying it: You ain't seen nothin' yet.

Thank you. Thank you all very much.

Audience. Ronald Reagan! Ronald Reagan! Ronald Reagan!

The President. Thank you.

Note: The President spoke at 10:23 a.m. at the Pucillo Gymnasium on the campus of Millersville University.

Following his remarks, the President traveled to Media, PA.

Remarks at a Reagan-Bush Rally in Media, Pennsylvania
October 29, 1984

The President. Well, I thank you. It's so wonderful to be in Pennsylvania. It's especially nice to be in Delaware County and here in Media.

I know that you're aware that one of my most important aides in the White House, Faith Whittlesey, was a county council member here, and worked in this courthouse. Well, we're keeping her working in the White House. And it's good to have your fine Governor and my good friend, Dick Thornburgh, here with us. He's a great Governor. And, another good friend of mine is here—Pennsylvania's Drew Lewis.

But I want all of you to know how much we appreciate your great representatives in Washington, led by Senators John Heinz and Arlen Specter. The Republican members of Pennsylvania's delegation to the

House and the Senate are, in my view, among the very best in the country.

Today I come bearing a special request. The voters of Delaware County have a fine, young Republican candidate. And if you agree with me that we've made progress, but our future can be even better, then please vote for Kurt Weldin on election day. [*Applause*] All right. Thank you. All right.

Now, we'll keep America, if you do what I just asked, on the new path of hope and opportunity. And to those in the neighborhood of northeast Philadelphia, vote for Flora Becker for Congress.

And, you know, just in case there might be some people across the State line—or that are listening across the State line—in a neighboring State, same name as the county—Delaware—there's a candidate we need in the United States Senate. He's John Burroughs. And there's another candidate we need in the House from Delaware, and that's Elise duPont.

You know, I hope to win a second term, but I just want to tell you something. I'll tell you quite frankly that if a gypsy looked into a crystal ball and said, "You can win this election with a lot of votes, or win by just a few votes, but get a sympathetic Congress"—I would choose the latter, the sympathetic Congress, because if we're to solidify the gains this country has made and continue to move onward with new opportunities for our future, we'll need a Congress that will help us do the job. So, please, help spread the word and get out the vote. And if you can, well, win those races for the Gipper.

But now I want to talk a little bit about the great renewal that's been taking place throughout our country these past few years. It's a renewal that was grounded in the wise advice of a wise old President.

Abe Lincoln said we must disenthrall ourselves with the past—and then we will save our country. Now, 4 years ago, that's what we did. We made a great turn. We got out from under the thrall of a government which we had hoped would make our lives better, but which wound up living our lives for us.

The power the Federal Government had over the decades created great chaos—economic, social, and international. Our leaders were adrift, rudderless, without a compass. Four years ago we began to navigate by certain fixed principles. Our North Star was freedom, common sense our constellations.

We knew that economic freedom meant paying less of the American family's income and earnings to the government. And so, we cut our personal income tax rates by 25 percent. And contrary to what my opponent says, that was across the board, from top to bottom, and not just for one section of the public.

We knew that inflation, the quiet thief, was stealing our savings, and the highest interest rates since the Civil War were making it impossible for people to own a home or start an enterprise.

We knew that our national military defense had been weakened. So, we decided to rebuild and be strong again. And this, we knew, would enhance the prospects for peace in the world. It was a second American revolution, and it's only just been begun.

But America is back, a giant, powerful in its renewed spirit, its growing economy, powerful in its ability to defend itself and secure the peace, and powerful in its ability to build a better future. And do you know something? You know something? What I just said is not debatable.

Yet 4 years after our efforts began, small voices in the night are sounding the call to go back, back to the days of drift, the days of torpor, timidity, and taxes.

Audience. Boo-o-o!

The President. Now, my opponent this year is known to you. But perhaps we can gain greater insight into the world he would take us back to, if we take a look at his record.

His understanding of economics is well demonstrated by his predictions. Just before we took office, he said that our economic program is obviously, murderously inflationary. That was just before we lowered inflation from more than 12 percent down to around 4.

And just after our tax cuts, he said the most he could see was an anemic recovery. Now, that was right before the United States economy created more than 6 million new jobs in 21 months, and incorporated 900,000 new businesses in the last 18 months.

My opponent said that our policies would deliver a misery index the likes of which we haven't seen in a long time. And there was some truth in that. You get the misery index, you know, by adding the rate of unemployment to the rate of inflation. And they invented that for the 1976 campaign. And they said that Jerry Ford had no right to seek reelection with a misery index of 12.6. Now, they didn't mention the misery index in the 1980 election, possibly because it was over 20. And they aren't talking too much about it in this campaign, because it's down around 11.

My opponent said decontrol of oil prices would cost American consumers more than $36 billion a year. Well, one of the first things we did was decontrol oil prices, and the price of gasoline went down 8 cents a gallon.

You know, I've got it figured out. All we have to do to get the economy in absolutely perfect shape is to get my opponent to predict absolute disaster.

He says he cares about the middle class, but he boasts, "I have consistently supported legislation, time after time, which increases taxes on my own constituents." Doesn't that make you just want to be one of his constituents? He's no doubt proud of the fact, as a United States Senator, he voted 16 times to increase the taxes on the American people.

Audience. Boo-o-o!

The President. But this year, he's undone—outdone himself. Well, he's maybe undone himself, too. [*Laughter*] He's already promised, of course, to raise your taxes. But if he is to keep all the promises that he made to this group and that, he will have to raise taxes by the equivalent of $1,890 for every household in the United States.

Audience. Boo-o-o!

The President. That's more than $150 a month. You know, it's like having a second mortgage, a Mondale mortgage.

But his economic plan has two basic parts: one, raise your taxes and two, raise them again. [*Laughter*] I've got news for him: The American people don't want his tax increases, and he isn't going to get his tax increases.

Audience. 4 more years! 4 more years! 4 more years!

The President. All right, all right. Okay, I'm game if you are.

You know, I'm now beginning to see more clearly why last week my opponent said to the voters, "Let's forget about the past." But it's not the past that worries us, it's the future.

And I'm even more concerned because now, last week, my opponent used another familiar phrase from the past. "Trust me," he said. [*Laughter*] Well, the last time we trusted his administration, they took five—count 'em—five economic plans and nearly tripled inflation. Well, by contrast, we trusted the people—you. And with just one economic program, we've cut inflation by two-thirds.

You know, if my opponent's campaign were a television show, it would be "Let's Make a Deal." [*Laughter*] You get to trade your prosperity for the surprise he has behind the curtain. Now, if his campaign was a Broadway show, it would be called "Promises, Promises." And if his administration were a novel, a book, you'd have to read it from the back end to the front in order to get a happy ending. [*Laughter*]

He sees an America in which every day is tax day, April 15th. And we see an America in which every day is Independence Day, the Fourth of July. We want to lower your taxes, and everybody's tax rates, so that your families will be stronger, our economy will be stronger, and America will be stronger.

I'm proud to say that during these last 4 years, on another subject, not 1 square inch of territory in the world has been lost to Communist aggression.

Audience. 4 more years! 4 more years! 4 more years!

The President. The United States is more secure than we were 4 years ago. And yet my opponent sees a different world.

Sometime back, he said the old days of a Soviet strategy of suppression by force are over. That was just before the Soviets invaded Czechoslovakia. And after they invaded Afghanistan he said, "It just baffles me why the Soviets, these last few years, have behaved as they have." But then, there's so much that baffles him.

One year ago we liberated Grenada from Communist thugs who had taken over that country. My opponent called what we did a violation of international law that erodes our moral authority to criticize the Soviets. Well, there is nothing immoral about rescuing American students whose lives are in danger. But by the time my opponent decided that action was justified, those students were long since safe at home.

After the Sandinista revolution down there in Nicaragua, he praised it by saying, "Winds of democratic progress are stirring where they have long been stifled." But we know that the Sandinistas immediately began to persecute the genuine believers in democracy and to export terror. They went on to slaughter the Miskito Indians by the thousands, abuse and deport church leaders, slander the Pope, and move to kill free speech, and practiced anti-Semitism. Don't you think it's time for my opponent to stand up, speak out, and condemn the Sandinista crimes? [*Applause*]

More recently, he failed to repudiate the Reverend Jesse Jackson when he went to Cuba, stood with Fidel Castro, and then said, "Long live President Fidel Castro and Che Guevara!"

Audience. Boo-o-o!

The President. And let me try to put this in perspective. The 1984 election isn't just a partisan contest. I was a Democrat once, and for a very long time, for a great share of my life. But in those days, Democratic leaders weren't the "blame America first" crowd. Its leaders were men like Harry Truman, men who understood the challenges of their times. They didn't reserve all their indignation for America. They knew the difference between tyranny and freedom, and they stood up for one and damned the other.

To all the good Democrats—and I hope there are many present—who respect that tradition, I say, you are not alone. We're asking you—those of you who have found out as I found out for myself, that I could no longer follow the leadership that had taken over that party—we're asking you, come walk with us down the new path of hope and opportunity. And in a truly bipartisan way, we will preserve the salvation of this country.

Now, Kathryn Sullivan made history. An American woman walked in space. She returned to a space shuttle in which some of the great scientific and medical advances of the future will be made. Cures for diabetes and heart disease may be possible up there, advances in technology and communication. But, again, my opponent in the Senate personally led the fight against the entire shuttle program and called it a horrible waste. Well, we support the space shuttle, and we've committed America to meet a great challenge, to build a permanently manned space station and to do it within a decade.

Now, I've probably been going on too long here. And I——

Audience. No!

The President. Well, this isn't what you meant about 4 more years. [*Laughter*]

No, the point is, we were right when we made our great turn in 1980. We were right to take command of the ship, stop its aimless drift, and get moving again. And we were right when we stopped sending out S.O.S. and starting saying U.S.A.!

Audience. U.S.A.! U.S.A.! U.S.A.!

The President. All right.

The United States of America was never meant to be a second-best nation. Like our Olympic athletes, this nation should set its sights on the stars and go for the gold.

Now, if America could bring down inflation from 12.4 to 4 percent, then we can bring inflation down from 4 to 0.0 percent.

If lowering your tax rates led to the best expansion in 30 years—and I think it was the key in that expansion—then we can lower them again and keep America growing into the 21st century.

If we could create 6 million new jobs in 21 months, then we can make it possible for every American—young and old, black or white—who wants a job to find one.

If our States and municipalities can establish enterprise zones to create economic growth, then we can elect people to Congress who will free our enterprise zones bill from where it is buried in committee by Tip O'Neill, and has been for 2 years, so that we can provide hope and opportunity for the most distressed areas of America.

If we can lead a revolution in technology and push back the frontiers of space, then we can provide our workers in industries old and new all that they need, because I believe with all my heart that if we give American workers the proper tools, they can outproduce, outcompete, and outsell anybody, anywhere in this world.

If our grassroots drive to restore excellence in education could reverse a 20-year decline in scholastic aptitude test scores—which it did—then we can keep raising those scores and restore American academic excellence second to none.

If our crackdown on crime could produce the sharpest drop ever in the crime index, as it did last year, then we can keep cracking down until our families and friends can walk our streets again without being afraid.

And if we could reverse the decline in our military defenses and restore respect for America—and we have—then we can make sure this nation remains strong enough to protect freedom and peace for us, for our children, and for our children's children.

And if we make sure that America remains strong and prepared for peace, then we can begin to reduce nuclear weapons and, one day, banish them from the Earth entirely.

Every once in a while in a crowd like this, I see some signs I assume are unfriendly that refer to nuclear weapons and so forth. Well, let me tell you something: I have said to a number of legislatures, to parliaments in countries around the world, in Asia and in Europe, I've spoken to them and every time I addressed them, I have said a nuclear war cannot be won and must never be fought.

And if we can strengthen our economy, strengthen our security, and strengthen the values that bind us, then America will become a nation even greater in arts and learning and greater in the love and worship of the God who made us and who has blessed us as no other people on this Earth have ever been blessed.

But right now, I want to tell you something I've seen all across the country, and I see it here again today. To the young people of our country, let me say that you are what this election is all about. It's about you—you and your future.

You know, I got cut off, ran out of time, in the debate a week ago Sunday. So, I'm going to say here what I was going to say there. And that is, to the young people here today, your generation is something special. Your idealism, your love of country are unsurpassed. It is our highest duty to make certain that you have an America every bit as full of opportunity and hope and confidence and dreams as we had when we were your age.

Let me just speak to some others here. My generation—and then there are a few other generations between mine and yours, you young people—well, we in those generations, we grew up in an America where we took it for granted that this was the

place where you could dream, and if you had the will and the desire and the energy, you could make your dreams come true. You could rise as high and far as your own strength would take you. And this is the responsibility of all those several generations I mentioned, other than yours, the younger generation. We have a sacred responsibility that when the time comes for us to turn the reins over to you, we hand you an America that is free in a world that is at peace.

All of us together are a part of a great revolution, and it's only just begun. America must never give up its special mission in the world, never. There are new worlds on the horizon, and we're not going to stop until we all get there together. America's best days are yet to come.

I mentioned all those other candidates, those Members of Congress that are seeking reelection in this election year, and urged you to see that they return to Washington, and send them some more company and make Tip O'Neill unhappy. But, also, I've been trying very hard not to read the polls. And don't you read them. President Dewey told me we must never become overconfident. [*Laughter*] So, get out the vote. Make sure your neighbors get there to vote. Don't anyone say, "Well, I'm not needed. I'm not necessary, stay home." I know of elections that were lost by less than one-half a vote per precinct in this country. So, turn out and vote.

But then I want to just ask you something else. You have honored me beyond anything I ever dreamed in my life, honored me by allowing me to serve you for these last 4 years. I ask you support. I ask for your votes and your help for 4 more years. [*Applause*] All right.

And one last thing, in addition to my thanks for your wonderfully warm welcome and your support, let me just say—and I know this will drive them up the wall: You ain't seen nothin' yet.

All right. Thank you.

Note: The President spoke at 1:04 p.m. at the Delaware County Courthouse.

Informal Exchange With Reporters on the Presidential Campaign
October 29, 1984

Q. Mr. President, Mondale said that the big themes of this last week are going to be that you don't care about the poor and the disadvantaged in this country and that you're going to get us nearer a nuclear war.

The President. He's been saying that—what's new about that? He and some of you have been saying that for so long, but I'm not going to believe it, because I know it isn't true.

Q. Are you headed for a 50-State sweep, sir?

The President. I don't know. I'm not going to comment on that. I'm just going to keep on campaigning and hope I win.

Q. How confident are you?

The President. I told you before: I am always only cautiously optimistic, and I run one vote behind.

Q. Could all these polls be wrong, Mr. President?

The President. I didn't say that. I just said that as far as I'm concerned, I'm not going to judge them.

Q. Aren't you beginning to think that maybe these polls are right, and you are headed for a landslide?

The President. I'd be scared if I thought that. I'd scare myself for even thinking that. I am happier when I think I'm—I've got to keep trying.

Q. You lost the Washington Post and the New York Times. There's a softball.

The President. Well, what's new about that?

Q. I don't know. [*Laughter*] We'll ask the questions here. [*Laughter*]

Q. Was there something you wanted to tell us?

The President. No. I just saw such a hungry look on both of your faces here—

[*laughter*]—that I couldn't walk by. If I walked by, it would confirm what Mr. Mondale says, that I'm heartless. See, I turned immediately, thinking I could—[*inaudible*].

Q. Mr. Mondale says you're so confident that you're sleeping at Camp David—[*inaudible*]—and you're not campaigning this weekend.

The President. Well, if I hadn't been overnight at Camp David, I would have been overnight in the White House, and either place is good sleeping.

Q. Can you retain the Senate? Can you retain the Senate and make gains in the House?

The President. All I can say is it is what we would like to do, and this is why I've been trying to help wherever I can.

Q. Thanks for coming over.

Q. You're right, that is nothing new.

Q. Have you all figured out—[*inaudible*]—terrorist attack—[*inaudible*]?

The President. Of course. And I would recommend to any of you that you read George Shultz's entire speech on the subject——

Q. Why did George Bush—[*inaudible*]?

The President. Well, you know, some people in your profession rushed up to him, quoted something that possibly—not correctly or out of context—and he responded to that, but not to what was in the speech.

Q. Thank you.

Note: The exchange began at 1:58 p.m. at Philadelphia International Airport in Pennsylvania as the President was preparing to board Air Force One for a trip to Parkersburg, WV.

Remarks at a Reagan-Bush Rally in Parkersburg, West Virginia
October 29, 1984

The President. It's great to be in West Virginia, and I'm delighted to visit your proud town of Parkersburg.

Two great American sports are taking

place this fall: politics and football. So, before I go any further, let me say hello to some great teams: the Williamstown High School Yellow Jackets, the Parkersburg South Patriots, and, yes, the Parkersburg Big Reds. And, yes, one more thing. How about them 'Eers? [*Applause*]

Well, a warm welcome to your mayor, Pat Pappas. Greetings to my good friend and your once and your future very great Governor, Arch Moore. I'd like nothing more than to work with Arch so we can see to it that West Virginia shares in the prosperity that is sweeping across America. We were Governors together, and I know that leadership means more—or he knows that leadership means more than just raising taxes.

And special regards to your outstanding candidates for the House of Representatives, Jim Altmeyer and Cleve Benedict. And you've got a candidate for Senate who as a member of the Republican opportunity team could do a lot for West Virginia. I ask you a favor for myself and for the people of West Virginia—on election day, vote against high taxes; vote for creative jobs programs. Vote for growth and opportunity by sending John Raese to the United States Senate.

You know, the Senate is one key to continuing what we've begun. West Virginia has a fine tradition for rising above partisanship when the national interest calls, a tradition that's well represented by your retiring Senator, Jennings Randolph. John Raese has the qualities of leadership necessary to continue that tradition and to do what's best and what's right for America. I need—and I think your State needs, if you'll permit me—John Raese in the United States Senate.

Jim, Cleve, and John are great candidates, and they'll make even better representatives in Washington, so please send them there.

You know, I'm always happy when I visit this part of the country because—maybe because you make me feel so much at home. You in West Virginia have always given our country more than your share of greatness and courage. Here is the steadiness of purpose, the fidelity to ideals, the love of country. And I want you to know that George Bush and I not only believe West Virginia is

worth visiting and worth listening to; we believe West Virginia is worth fighting for.

Abe Lincoln said we must disenthrall ourselves with the past—and then we will save our country. Well, 4 years ago, that's what we did. We made a great turn. We got out from under the thrall of a government which we had hoped would make our lives better, but which wound up trying to live our lives for us.

The power the Federal Government had over the decades created great chaos—economic, social, and international. Our leaders were adrift, rudderless, without a compass. Four years ago, we began to navigate by certain fixed principles. Our North Star was freedom, common sense was our constellations.

We knew that economic freedom meant paying less of a family's earning to government. So, we cut personal income tax rates by 25 percent. And contrary to what my opponent is saying, we cut them from top to bottom, evenly across the board, benefiting no—[*inaudible*]——

We knew that inflation, the quiet thief, was stealing our savings, and the highest interest rates since the Civil War were making it impossible for people to own a home or to start an enterprise.

We knew that our national military defense had been weakened, so we decided to rebuild and be strong again. And this, we knew, would enhance the prospects for peace in the world. It was a second American revolution, and it's only just begun.

But America is back. America is a giant once again, powerful in its renewed spirit, its growing economy, powerful in its ability to defend itself and secure the peace, and powerful in its ability to build a better future. And you know something? That's not debatable.

Yet 4 years after our efforts began, small voices in the night are sounding the call to go back. Go back to the days of drift, the days of torpor, timidity, and taxes. My opponent this year is known to you, but perhaps we can gain a greater insight into the world he would take us back to if we take a look at his record.

His understanding of economics is well demonstrated by his predictions. Just before we took office, he said our economic program is obviously, murderously inflationary. Now, that was just before we lowered inflation from above 12 percent down to around 4.

And just after our tax cuts, he said the most that he could see was an anemic recovery. Well, that was right before the United States economy created more than 6 million new jobs in 21 months. And there have been 900,000 new business incorporations in just the last 18 months.

My opponent said that our policies would deliver a misery index the likes of which we haven't seen in a long time. Now, there was some truth when he said that. You know, you get the misery index by adding the rate of unemployment and the rate of inflation. They invented that in the 1976 election. And they invented it so that they could say Jerry Ford had no right to run for reelection, because he had a misery index of 12.6. Well, now, they didn't mention the misery index in the election of 1980, probably because it was over 20. And they're not talking about it much in this campaign, because it's down around 11.

You know, my opponent said that decontrol of oil prices would cost American consumers more than $36 billion a year. Well, one of the first things we did was decontrol oil prices, and the price of gasoline went down 8 cents a gallon.

Now, I've figured out that maybe all we have to do to get the economy in absolutely perfect shape is to get my opponent to predict absolute disaster. [*Laughter*]

He says he cares about the middle class. But he boasts, "I have consistently supported legislation, time after time, which increases taxes on my own constituents." Doesn't that make you want to be one of his constituents? [*Laughter*] He's no doubt proud of the fact that as a United States Senator, he voted 16 times to increase your taxes.

Now, this year, he's outdone himself. He's already promised, of course, to raise your taxes. But if he is to keep all the promises that he has made during this campaign, he will have to raise taxes by the equivalent of $1,890 for every household in the United States.

Audience. Boo-o-o!

The President. Now, that's more than $150 a month. It's like having a second mortgage, a Mondale mortgage.

His basic plan has two parts: one, raise your taxes and the second, raise them again. But, you know, I've got news for him. The American people don't want his tax increases, and they're not going to get his tax increases.

His tax plan would bring this recovery of ours to a roaring halt, because one of the key, most significant things in the recovery we're having was the tax cut. I'm now beginning to see more clearly why last week my opponent said, "Let's forget about the past." It's not the past that worries me, it's the future. And I'm even more concerned because now, last week, my opponent used another familiar phrase from the past. "Trust me," he said. [*Laughter*]

Well, the last time we trusted the administration of which he was a part, they took five—you can count them—five different economic plans and nearly tripled inflation. And by contrast, we trusted the people— you. And with just one economic program, we've cut inflation by two-thirds.

If my opponent's television show were a television show, it would be "Let's Make a Deal." [*Laughter*] You know, you'd trade your prosperity for his surprise behind the curtain. [*Laughter*] And if his campaign were a Broadway show, it would be called, "Promises, Promises." [*Laughter*] And if his administration were a novel, a book, you'd have to read it from back to front to get a happy ending. [*Laughter*]

He sees an America in which every day is tax day, April 15th. We see an America in which every day is Independence Day, the Fourth of July. Seriously, we want to lower your taxes and everybody's taxes so your families will be stronger, our economy will be stronger, and America will be stronger.

And I'm proud to say—on another subject—that during these last 4 years, not 1 square inch of territory in the world has been lost to Communist aggression. And the United States is more secure than it was 4 years ago.

My opponent sees a different world. Sometime back, he said the old days of a Soviet strategy of suppression by force are over. That was just before the Soviets invaded Czechoslovakia. And after they invaded Afghanistan, he said, "It just baffles me why the Soviets these last few years have behaved as they have." But then, there's so much that baffles him. [*Laughter*]

Just 1 year ago we liberated Grenada from Communist thugs who had taken over that country. But my opponent called what we did a violation of international law that erodes our moral authority to criticize the Soviets. Well, there's nothing immoral about rescuing American students whose lives are in danger. By the time my opponent decided that action was justified, the students were home a long time.

After the Sandinista revolution in Nicaragua, he praised it, saying, "Winds of democratic progress are stirring where they have long been stifled." But we know that the Sandinistas immediately began to persecute the genuine believers in democracy and to export terror. They went on to slaughter the Miskito Indians in that country, abuse and deport church leaders, slander the Pope, practice anti-Semitism, and move to kill free speech. Don't you think it's about time that my opponent stood up and spoke out and condemned the Sandinistas crimes? [*Applause*]

More recently, he failed to repudiate the Reverend Jesse Jackson, when Jesse Jackson went to Havana, stood with Fidel Castro, and said, "Long live President Fidel Castro and Che Guevara!"

Audience. Boo-o-o!

The President. But let me try to put this in perspective. The 1984 election isn't just a partisan contest. I was a Democrat for a good share of my life—a majority share. But in those days, Democratic leaders weren't the members of the "blame America first" crowd. Its leaders were men like Harry Truman, men who understood the challenges of the times. They didn't reserve all their indignation for the United States. They knew the difference between freedom and tyranny, and they stood up for the one and damned the other.

To all the good Democrats—and I hope there are many present—who respect that tradition, I say, you are not alone. I know that across this country there are millions of good, patriotic Democrats who have found

in their hearts they can no longer follow the leadership of that party today. Well, we're asking you to come and walk with us down the path of hope and opportunity.

Believe me, together—and it can be a bipartisan task that we face—to make America strong and keep it strong once again. We need you, and you're certainly welcome.

Audience. 4 more years! 4 more years! 4 more years!

The President. All right. You talked me into it. [*Laughter*]

You know, this month an American woman walked in space—Kathryn Sullivan made history. And then she returned, after that walk, to the space shuttle in which some of the great scientific and medical advances of the future will be made. Cures for diabetes and heart disease may be possible up there—steps have already been taken to find that out—experiments in technology and communication. But my opponent led the fight in the United States Senate against the entire shuttle program—didn't want it even to begin, and called it a horrible waste. Well, we support the space shuttle, and we've committed America to meet a great challenge—to build a permanently manned space station, and to do it within a decade.

Now, I've been probably going on too long here, but——

Audience. No!

The President. That isn't what you meant by 4 more years, was it? [*Laughter*]

You know, the point is we were right when we made our big turn in 1980. We were right to take command of the ship, stop its aimless drift, and get moving again. And we were right when we stopped sending out S.O.S. and started saying U.S.A.!

Audience. U.S.A.! U.S.A.! U.S.A.!

The President. All right. You know, the United States was never meant to be a second-best nation. Like our Olympic athletes, this nation should set its sights on the stars and go for the gold.

Now, if America could bring down inflation from 12.4 percent to 4, then we can bring inflation down from 4 to 0.0, and we're going to do it.

If lowering your tax rates led to the best

expansion we've had in 30 years—and it was the key, as I said—then we can lower them again and keep America growing into the 21st century.

If we could create 6 million new jobs in 21 months and then make it possible for every American—young, old, black, or white—who wants a job to find a job; if our States and municipalities can establish enterprise zones to create economic growth, then we can elect people to Congress who will free our enterprise zones—the Federal bill that has been buried in a committee in the House of Representatives for 2 years—buried there by Speaker Tip O'Neill——

Audience. Boo-o-o!

The President. ——and bring it out to the floor for a vote so we can provide hope and opportunity for the most distressed areas of America, whether they be in the cities or rural.

If we can lead a revolution in technology and push back the frontiers of space, then we can provide our workers, in industries old and new, all that they need, which is mainly new and proper tools—because I believe with all my heart that the American worker, given the proper tools, can outsell anybody, can outcompete, can outproduce anybody, anywhere in the world, anytime.

If our grassroots drive to restore excellence in education could reverse a 20-year decline in scholastic aptitude test scores—and it has—then we can keep raising those scores and restore American academic excellence second to none.

If our crackdown on crime could produce the sharpest drop ever in the crime index—and it has—then we can keep cracking down until our families and friends can walk our streets again without being afraid.

If we could reverse the decline in our military defenses and restore respect for America—and we have—then we can make sure that this nation remains strong enough to protect freedom and peace for us, for our children, and for our children's children.

And if we make sure that America remains strong and prepared for peace, then we can begin to reduce nuclear weapons and, one day, banish them from the Earth entirely.

I've been interested in some of the scare tactics that my opponent has been using.

I've had the privilege in these 4 years of addressing the parliaments in several countries, both in Asia and in the United States. And in every instance, I took the opportunity to tell them that a nuclear war cannot be won and must never be fought. And, yes, a nuclear freeze makes strength if it follows negotiations that reduce the weapons in the world down to a verifiable and equal level on both sides.

And if we can strengthen our economy, strengthen our security, and strengthen the values that bind us together, then America will become a nation even greater in art and learning, and greater in the love and worship of the God who made us and who has blessed us here more than any other people on Earth have ever been blessed.

But now, a week ago Sunday—yesterday, a week ago yesterday, I didn't get to finish my closing remarks in the debate. [*Laughter*] I ran out of time. So, I'm going to say it here.

To you, the young people of this country, let me say that you—you and your future are what this election is all about. Your generation is something special. Your idealism and your love of country are unsurpassed. I have seen this in meetings of this kind all across the country in this campaign. It's our highest duty to make certain that you have an America every bit as full of opportunity, hope, confidence, and dreams as we had when we were your age.

You know, my generation—and then there are a few generations between mine and yours—[*laughter*]—but most of us grew up in a land where we took it for granted that we could dream the highest and finest of dreams, and if we were willing to try and work, we could make them come true, that there was no ceiling, no limit on what we could accomplish or how high we could fly by our own strength and ability. And then we came to a period when some people began telling us that, no, there was an era of limits, that things could never again be as good as they once were, and that you had to kind of give up some of your dreams for the future.

Well, I'll tell you, me and those—my generation, I should say, and those other generations I mentioned here—not yours—we have a sacred trust, and I think we're going to fulfill that trust. And that is, when the time comes to turn the reins over to you young people out there, we're going to turn over to you an America that is free in a world that is at peace. And your dreams can come true.

Audience. 4 more years! 4 more years! 4 more years!

The President. All right. Thank you. Thank you.

All of us together are part of a great revolution, and it's only just begun. America will never give up its special mission in the world, never. There are new worlds on our horizon, and we're not going to stop until we all get there together. America's best days are yet to come.

I spoke earlier about sending these won-derful candidates and officeholders back to their jobs. You know the job that Arch belongs in, and you know the jobs for these in Washington.

But I have been honored greatly by all of you in your allowing me to serve you for these past 4 years. And I ask for your vote. I ask for your support. I want to keep on with the job we started 4 years ago with that new beginning. I want it more than anything I've ever wanted.

Now, I know this sends my opponent up the wall, but—[*laughter*]—you ain't seen nothin' yet.

God bless you. Thank you all very much.

Note: The President spoke at 4:30 p.m. at the Parkersburg High School fieldhouse.

Following his remarks, the President returned to Washington, DC.

Appointment of Two Members of the Board of Directors of the Pennsylvania Avenue Development Corporation
October 29, 1984

The President today announced his intention to appoint the following individuals to be members of the Board of Directors of the Pennsylvania Avenue Development Corporation for terms expiring October 26, 1990:

Carl L. Shipley is currently a senior member of the law firm of Shipley, Smoak & Akerman in Washington, DC. He graduated from George-town University (B.S., 1942) and Harvard Law School (J.D., 1948). He is married, has two chil-dren, and resides in Washington, DC. He was born December 16, 1919, in Spokane, WA.

J. Upshur Moorhead would succeed Max N. Berry. He has most recently served as east coast liaison for the Los Angeles Organizing Committee (1983–1984) and as Special Assistant to the President for Private Sector Initiatives and Assistant to the Deputy Chief of Staff at the White House (1982–1983). He graduated from the University of Vermont (B.A., 1975). He was born May 1, 1952, in Washington, DC, where he now resides.

Remarks by Telephone to the Annual Convention of the United States League of Savings Institutions
October 30, 1984

The President. Greetings to all of you. And greetings to you, Chairman Paul Prior; greetings to your president, my good friend, Bill O'Connell, and to John Zellars, who'll become your chairman tomorrow.

You in our savings and loan industry, who do so much to help American families buy homes and cars, serve as pillars of your communities, and you certainly can all be very proud. And on behalf of the American people, I thank and commend you.

You know, just 4 years ago, we saw our nation staggered by a steady erosion of economic growth, punishing inflation and interest rates, a record peacetime tax burden, and rising unemployment. Retirement savings were devastated. In 1979 and '80 working Americans' weekly earnings declined in real terms by 8.8 percent. That was the worst drop since World War II. I know how hard your own savings and loan industry was hit with the housing market falling into disarray.

If I could inject a little news note—or maybe you've already heard—today the Commerce Department has announced the figures for the month of September in the sales of new, single-family homes. They increased in September by 21.9 percent over August. [*Applause*]

Mr. Prior. Did you hear that, Mr. President?

The President. I did. Thank you.

In 1980 the American people voted for a change, and when we took office, we made restoring our economy number one. Experts warned it would take 10 years to bring inflation down to the level of the 1960's. Well, we did it in just 2 years. It wasn't easy. And industries like your own faced hard times as we put a stop to economic chaos and laid the groundwork for a vigorous recovery. But today we've cut inflation by nearly two-thirds, all the way from 12.4 to 4.2 percent.

Interest rates have fallen by more than one-third. That's still not enough. A few months ago I went out on a limb with a prediction that we'd see interest rates drop again before the end of the warm weather. Well, we've had a beautiful Indian summer. And last Friday, the temperature here in town hit 75 degrees and the prime fell to 12 percent.

I don't want to make any more weather forecasts; but I do believe the financial markets are beginning to understand the depth of our commitment to the fight against inflation. This means interest rates should drop still further in the days ahead. And all those interest-rate sensitive activities like homebuilding and car buying will pick up and gather new strength.

From strength in autos and construction to renewed leadership in high technology, from a rebirth in productivity and surging investment to the creation of 6 million new jobs, America is in the midst of the best economic expansion in over 30 years. And your support has helped to make this possible. And I know that with your continued support during the next 4 years, we'll keep surging ahead.

Thank you for letting me join you in this way, and God bless you all.

Note: The President spoke at 10:53 a.m. from the Oval Office at the White House. The convention was held in Washington, DC.

Remarks at a Meeting With Reagan-Bush Campaign Leadership Groups
October 30, 1984

Audience. 4 more years! 4 more years! 4 more years!

The President. Thank you. You know what I've been saying out on the road at the rallies when they say that? You talked me into it. [*Laughter*]

Audience member. God bless you, President! God bless you, President!

The President. Thank you. Thank you very much. Thank you.

Well, Dixy Lee Ray, and Mike Sotirhos, Tirso del Junco, Legree Daniels, Dick Fox, and all of you ladies and gentlemen: Thank you, and welcome to the White House.

I think our meeting today reflects what could be the beginnings of a new phenomenon observers have been noticing—that is, if everything turns our right—an historic electoral realignment. And to the degree that's happening around the country, much of the credit goes to people of courage and leadership, like all of you.

For longer than any of us can remember, the Democratic Party has held the allegiance of a large number of Americans who were not well-served by the policies of that party. Yet voting habits are hard to change. I know; I was a Democrat myself for most of my adult life.

I've been all over the country in these last few months, and I'd like to make a little prediction for you today. I believe that next Tuesday we'll see a large number of voters joining our Republican ranks for the first time.

Now this is no mere political cycle, nor has it anything to do with the personalities of the candidates. We're attracting the support of people who have never voted with us before not because they're deserting the Democratic Party, but because the Democratic Party has deserted them.

For far too long now, the other party has taken for granted many of those who have faithfully given their support. Big city machines kept in power by organized voting groups were key to Democratic victories over the years; yet did these people find their lives improved by their unquestioned loyalty to the party? It's no mere coincidence that the most blighted areas of the country, places of desperation, are areas that have been political strongholds of the other party for many years.

Their policies are tax, tax, spend, spend, and no friend to those who want to improve their well-being. What the less fortunate need is not pity, but opportunity; not handouts, but jobs. That's the Republican program: more opportunity, more jobs, more take-home pay, a better future—with all of us going forward together.

The leadership of the other party gave us economic decline and high inflation. We've cut inflation by nearly two-thirds and have set in motion an economic expansion that will make everyone better off. Over 6 million new jobs have been created and nearly 900,000 new businesses have been incorporated—this latter figure in just the last 18 months.

And we offer innovative approaches to help the less fortunate. We've done our best to enact enterprise zone legislation which would channel resources and the creative energy of the private sector to those depressed areas that need it the most. The same politicians who so frequently use the word "compassion" have fought this idea and bottled it up in the House of Representatives.

I challenge my opponent to prove his leadership and convince the members of his party—Tip O'Neill, particularly—to give this idea a chance to help those in need.

Today we're part of a coalition of people who share some values that are traditional to America. Whether our forefathers and mothers came here from a Latin country, or from Africa, or from Asia, or from Europe—in my case, I guess it's Europe, Ireland and England—we hold dear those ideas that brought our forebears here. We're bound together by a love of family and neighborhood and a respect for God. We believe in hard work and peace through strength. And these are not Republican values, these are American.

Our opponents don't seem to see things this way. They view our country not as people of varied backgrounds who share common values and aspirations; instead, they see us as warring factions and interest groups. They try to divide us, using envy, and playing people off against each other by telling us we're competing for a piece of a pie that is ever getting smaller. Well, that's not our way. We don't see people as members of this group or that; we see them as Americans, with all the rights and opportunities that go with being American.

And about that pie—we also believe that we should work together to make a bigger pie, so everyone can have a bigger slice.

We still believe in the dream that brought people here from every corner of the Earth. Today we're reaching out as never before to people from every background to draw them into our coalition for progress. Our message to America is clear and direct: The Grand Old Party now stands for the Great Opportunity Party. And there's plenty of room for everyone. We aren't writing any group off or taking any group for granted. We're asking all of you to come walk with us down a path of hope and opportunity.

And I want to thank you all for being here today. I know Paul Laxalt and Margaret Hance, who've been doing a terrific job, will agree that the one thing that can defeat us is complacency. So, please, don't get over-confident. Let's remember the lesson that President Dewey taught us. [*Laughter*] On election day, make sure everyone gets out to vote. But I thank you again from the bottom of my heart for all you've done. And God bless you all.

Mr. Rollins. Mr. President——

Audience member. [*Inaudible*]

Mr. Rollins. Mr. President——

Audience member. [*Inaudible*]

Audience member. You deserve a noble praise, even though you are—[*inaudible*]—because all economists said that you were wrong. They must give you noble praise for making the economy look so better.

Audience member. Right!

Mr. Rollins. Mr. President, we have some great Americans who are former professional athletes—who've been part of the Athletes for Reagan-Bush and who've been traveling this country on your behalf—to present you a little award this morning.

We have Rosey Grier, Ernie Green, Don Newcombe, Floyd Patterson, and Willie Mays are here today with us.

Mr. Mays. Mr. President, do you mind stepping up, sir? [*Laughter*] I'm asking peacefully. [*Laughter*]

Well, anyway, when I first came to New York City they gave me a name. They called me the "Say-Hey Kid." And I'd like to present a shirt to you. It says, "Win One for the Gipper." And I think everybody—[*applause*]——

The President. Thank you very much. Thank you.

A moment ago, someone said something over here about the prognostications of some of the economists with regard to the recovery. And they didn't seem to be predicting it very enthusiastically. Well, having gotten a degree in economics myself, I'm the first that's able to say: There are too many economists in the world—[*laughter*]—that have got a Phi Beta Kappa key at one end of their watch chain and no watch on the other. [*Laughter*]

I've got to go back to work.

Note: The President spoke at 11:04 a.m. in the East Room at the White House to campaign workers and officials.

Edward J. Rollins, Jr., is Special Assistant to the President for Public Liaison.

Remarks on Signing the Trade and Tariff Act of 1984
October 30, 1984

Good morning, and welcome to the White House for the signing of this bill that Bill has been telling you about—the Trade and Tariff Act of 1984, a crucial piece of legislation and a triumph not just for freer and fairer trade, but for the legislative process itself.

I believe this bill represents the most important trade law approved by the Congress in a decade. In its first form, the bill was strongly protectionist and would have sharply limited our trade with other nations.

[*The President was interrupted by a loud noise from the public address system.*]

I'm not campaigning. [*Laughter*]

But I couldn't in good conscience have signed a bill containing those provisions, and I don't believe that many Members of the Congress could have supported it, either.

Then the bill went into a conference committee, and together, Senators, Representatives, and Bill Brock, our United States Trade Representative, rolled up their sleeves and went to work. In the words of an editorial in the Washington Post, "Most of the bad stuff in the bill got thrown out, and all of the good stuff stayed in." And the result is a fine piece of legislation that stands foursquare behind free and fair trade.

We know that if America wants more jobs, greater prosperity, and a dynamic, competitive economy, the answer is more world trade, not less. And this fine legislation builds on the Trade Act of 1974 that was signed into law by President Ford. That act promoted world trade by authorizing the President to liberalize trade with poorer nations, to engage in trade with negotiations, and to defend American interests in world markets.

The legislation before us today advances each of those efforts. To name some of the central provisions: This bill will extend the Generalized System of Preferences into a new decade. By encouraging 140 of the world's poorer countries to build their economies through trade, this program will give them a chance to help their people benefit from America's powerful economic expansion. In turn, it will help American industry by ensuring that less developed countries accept increased responsibility in areas like the protection of patents and trademarks in the international trading system.

While promoting free trade, this new act insists on something just as important—fair trade. A section of the bill originally known as Senator Danforth's reciprocity proposal gives the President new leverage to lower foreign barriers to trade, especially in the dynamic and rapidly growing areas of services, investment, and high technology.

With regard to our steel industry, this bill gives the President new authority to enforce agreements we may enter into with our trading partners as part of the steel policy that I announced on September 18th, 1984. This legislation will enable us to enforce steel export restraints, guard against unfair import surges into the American market, and help keep the United States from becoming the world's steel dump. And that means that we'll be better able to help our steelworkers get the fair shake they've always deserved.

I must add that while I support the act's emphasis on the need for reinvestment in our steel industry, it is the industry, not the government, that must make these investment decisions.

To strengthen relations with one of our closest allies, the bill contains a bold new initative authorizing the establishment of a free trade area agreement with Israel. When concluded, this agreement will completely eliminate the trade barriers between our two countries, allowing the duty-free entry of Israeli products into the United States while making the Israeli market wide open to American goods. Over the past 5 years, our trade with Israel has been growing at an average annual rate of some 10 percent. This bill will enable that vital economic partnership to grow even faster in years to come.

The act also opens the door to discussions with—or on mutual trade liberalization agreements with other countries. Fully consistent with our obligations on the general agreement on tariffs and trade, free trade agreements allow the free enterprise system to operate as it should—openly and vigorously. And these agreements will encourage American and foreign producers and workers to become as efficient and competitive as possible, and they will foster increased trade in services and greater investment both abroad and here at home.

The bill that I will be signing also makes refinements in our trade laws designed to help America's producers and workers deal with unfair trade practices. On balance, these refinements should go far to strengthen American trade laws and make them more effective and fair. We'll make certain that they're used not for protectionism, but for the promotion of free world trade.

Everyone who had a hand in passing this outstanding legislation deserves our thanks. Congratulations to the conferees, especially Congressman Dan Rostenkowski, chairman of the House Ways and Means Committee; Congressmen Barber Conable, Sam Gibbons, and Bill Frenzel; Senator Bob Dole, chairman of the Senate Finance Committee, and Senator Jack Danforth. And a special thanks to our United States Trade Representative Bill Brock. Bill worked tirelessly with great skill and dedication.

This Trade and Tariff Act of 1984 signals to the world that America does not fear free trade because the American people can produce and compete on a par with anybody in the world. The big winners today are dynamic new American industries, like telecommunications and high technology, American importers and manufacturers, and the American people themselves. Each of you has my heartfelt thanks and, more important, the gratitude of the Nation.

So, I thank you. And God bless you. And now, I'm going to stop talking and start writing.

Note: The President spoke at 11:49 a.m. in the Rose Garden at the White House.

As enacted, H.R. 3398 is Public Law 98–573, approved October 30.

Statement by Principal Deputy Press Secretary Speakes on Food Assistance to Ethiopia
October 30, 1984

As you know, the President has taken a personal interest in the famine situation in Africa, particularly the current crisis in Ethiopia.

Ethiopia's relief Commissioner Dawit Walde Giorgis will be in Washington Thursday, November 1, to meet with U.S. officials involved in the emergency food supply effort, including General Julian Becton, Director, Interagency Task Force on African Hunger, and U.S. Agency for International Development Administrator M. Peter McPherson.

The President discussed the situation in Ethiopia with Administrator McPherson by telephone Friday, and talked by telephone to Mother Teresa, who has requested U.S. assistance for projects she has undertaken there. The President asked Administrator McPherson to call Mother Teresa and offer additional assistance which he did.

In December 1983, the President asked for a high level interagency study of the worldwide hunger situation. This study was chaired by Ambassador Robert Keating, the President's envoy to Madagascar and Comoros. The President announced on July 10 of this year a major initiative to respond more quickly and effectively to the food needs of the people of Africa and the world suffering from hunger and malnutrition. His five-point program, announced then, includes:

1. The prepositioning of grain in selected Third World areas;
2. The creation of a special $50 million Presidential fund to allow a more flexible U.S. response to severe food emergencies;

3. The financing or payment of ocean and inland transportation costs associated with U.S. food aid in special emergency cases;
4. The creation of a government task force to provide better forecasts of food shortages and needs; and
5. The establishment of an advisory group of business leaders to share information on Third World hunger and food production.

In 1984 we have provided more food assistance to Africa than any administration in U.S. history. Our drought assistance for all of Africa last year totaled $173 million, which is twice the amount of 1983 assistance and three times the amount of 1982 assistance. For Ethiopia alone in this fiscal year, since October 1, 1984, we have obligated $45 million in drought assistance. This compares to $19 million last year to Ethiopia, which was the largest from any donor country.

With regard to the situation in Ethiopia, since October 2 aid to Ethiopia has included:

—$39 million for the shipment of 80,432 metric tons of food, one-fourth of which will be delivered to rebel-held areas of Eritria and Tigray through Sudan;
—$6.3 million in response to a Red Cross appeal for medicines and supplies;
—$100,000 for air transport of food to Makele, a central Ethiopian town cut off by frequent clashes along the road from the port.

The pressing short-term constraint is the distribution of food supplies now in country. Limiting factors include the shortage of trucks, poor roads, the insurgency, and the lack of support by the Ethiopian Government. To deal with some of these problems we have in recent days been providing gasoline for some Ethiopian Government planes to move food in country and are working with some private groups to augment that effort. In our meetings with Ethiopian officials this week, we will ask for more trucks to be made available, for priority access to port facilities, and for assurances that food can reach victims in rebel areas.

For the medium term, Western food aid commitments will keep the pipeline of emergency food full to capacity. Between now and the end of the year, approximately 200,000 metric tons will be arriving. For the longer term, we are developing with private agencies plans for the distribution of an additional 200,000 metric tons, along

with medicines, blankets, and other supplies. However, assessments of the need continue to rise, and the medium- and long-term requirements may increase substantially.

Basic to this whole effort is a more cooperative attitude from the Ethiopian Government and the dedication of more of their own resources. They reportedly spent a substantial amount for their Independence Day celebration, but have paid little attention to this problem. There are more than 6,000 trucks under government control for example, but only a few hundred are now available for emergency food shipments. However, we do sense some greater interest from them and we hope our negotiations this week with them will be productive.

The President will continue to monitor our relief efforts, and he has asked Administrator McPherson to report new developments to him.

Statement on Signing the Health Promotion and Disease Prevention Amendments of 1984
October 30, 1984

In signing S. 771, the Health Promotion and Disease Prevention Amendments of 1984, I must note my strong objection to section 8 of the bill, which would provide for a Council on Health Care Technology. In its initial stages, as well as finally constituted, the Council would perform significant governmental duties pursuant to a public law. Under the Constitution, the members of such a Council cannot be appointed by a congressional panel or by a body like the National Academy of Sciences, which is not an agency of the United States. (*Buckley* v. *Valeo*, 424 U.S. 1, 118– 141 (1976)) Moreover, the Council would intermingle governmental and nongovernmental, executive and legislative elements, in a manner which is inconsistent both with the Constitution and with sound government practices.

I have nevertheless approved S. 771 because section 8 does not constitute an integral element of it. I strongly urge Congress to amend section 8 in such a manner that the Council will be reconstituted either as a governmental agency, the members of which will be appointed in a manner which conforms with Art. II, section 2, cl. 2 of the Constitution, or as a private, nongovernmental organization whose members do not have significant duties pursuant to a public law. Pending the enactment of such remedial legislation, I shall, pursuant to section 684, title 2, United States Code, defer any budget authority that might provide for any grants to the Council.

Note: As enacted, S. 771 is Public Law 98– 551, approved October 30.

Statement on Signing a Nuclear Regulatory Commission Appropriations Bill
October 30, 1984

I have today signed into law S. 1291, an act to authorize appropriations to the Nuclear Regulatory Commission in accordance with section 261 of the Atomic Energy Act of 1954, and section 305 of the Energy Reorganization Act of 1974.

In signing this act, I note that one of its provisions, section 102(c)(2), purports to authorize congressional committees to waive all or part of a report-and-wait period otherwise required with respect to certain reallocations of funds by the Nuclear Regulatory Commission. The Attorney General has advised me that, under the Supreme Court's decision in *INS* v. *Chadha,* 103 S.Ct. 2764 (1983), the Congress, including committees of the Congress, may not be given power that has "the purpose of altering the legal rights, duties, and relations of persons, including . . . Executive Branch officials . . .," through procedures that bypass the constitutional requirements for valid legislative action. This important constitutional principle applies regardless whether the grant of such authority is intended to check or, as here, to facilitate, executive action. Because section 102(c)(2) of this act would authorize committees of the Congress, without participation by both Houses of the Congress and the President, to allow the Nuclear Regulatory Commission to implement proposed reallocations prior to expiration of the otherwise required waiting period, it does not conform to the requirements for legislative action articulated in *Chadha.* I strongly urge the Congress to discontinue the inclusion of such devices in legislation, because doing so serves no constructive purpose after *Chadha* beyond introducing confusion and ambiguity into the process by which the executive's obligations are discharged.

Note: As enacted, S. 1291 is Public Law 98–553, approved October 30.

Statement on Signing the Tandem Truck Safety Act of 1984
October 30, 1984

I am pleased to sign into law today S. 2217, the Tandem Truck Safety Act of 1984, which deals with commercial motor vehicle safety. My administration has consistently placed a high priority on safety in all forms of transportation. Since Secretary of Transportation Elizabeth Dole's first day on the job, she has forcefully and effectively espoused the cause of motor vehicle safety.

Far too many lives are needlessly sacrificed annually on our nation's highways. We have taken dramatic steps to lower this terrible toll. For example, I recently signed legislation to encourage the States to enact the age-21 drinking laws to address the serious national problem of drinking and driving among our young people.

Today we turn our attention to another area that can result in great safety benefits—the commercial motor vehicle industry. The continual changes the trucking industry makes to meet the Nation's diverse transportation needs present new challenges to maintain and enhance the industry's positive safety record. The trend toward larger commercial vehicles and smaller automobiles necessitates renewed attention to their operation on our highways. Two years ago we initiated the Motor Carrier Safety Assistance Program. This cooperative effort combines Federal and State resources to assist States to build and maintain strong and effective commercial motor vehicle safety programs.

The truck safety bill I sign today is an important piece of legislation that builds on this cooperative grant program. This bill will go a long way toward ensuring that our increasingly productive trucking and bus industries remain safe and become safer still. It also promotes uniform safety regulation of commercial motor vehicles by the States, thus reducing undesirable impediments to interstate commerce, and will assist in regulating the entry and ensuring the safety of foreign motor carriers. I believe this bill will give Secretary Dole and the Department of Transportation the tools needed to continue to improve safety on our nation's highways.

There is one provision in the bill that deserves clarification. I am signing S. 2217 with the understanding that section 209 of this bill does not purport to deny the Secretary of Transportation the ultimate responsibility for the selection and appointment of the members of the Commercial Motor Ve-

hicle Safety Regulatory Review Panel established by this bill. That ultimate responsibility must include the power to refuse to appoint any person submitted to the Secretary on a list by the Senate Committee on Commerce, Science, and Transportation or the House Committee on Public Works and Transportation, and to request the submission of additional lists if none of the persons appears suitable for appointment to the Secretary.

I express my appreciation to all the Members of the Congress, Secretary Dole, concerned representatives of the motor carrier industry, State officials, and all others whose cooperative efforts have led to enactment of this bill.

It is with great pleasure that I sign S. 2217.

Note: As enacted, S. 2217 is Public Law 98–554, approved October 30.

Statement on Signing a Bill Relating to Cooperative East-West Ventures in Space
October 30, 1984

I am today signing Senate Joint Resolution 236, relating to cooperative East-West ventures in space.

Space represents a challenging opportunity for the United States and for all of mankind—a challenge that, I am determined, we will meet. We stand today on the threshold of a great adventure. Beyond are vast opportunities—for the production of new materials, new medicines, and the expansion of our knowledge of the universe and of ourselves.

This must be a cooperative effort. We have worked with many other nations in our own space program, and this cooperation will strengthen and grow. Many countries have taken part in the successful Spacelab program, and I have invited other nations to take part in the development of a space station.

I find portions of the language contained in the preamble to the joint resolution very speculative. However, I have stated several times our desire to increase contacts with the Soviet Union, and we are prepared to work with the Soviets on cooperation in space in programs which are mutually beneficial and productive. As part of this effort, the United States has offered to carry out with the Soviet Union a joint simulated space rescue mission. We believe this and similar cooperative programs offer practical benefits for all mankind. It is in that spirit that I today sign this joint resolution.

Note: As enacted, S.J. Res. 236 is Public Law 98–562, approved October 30.

Statement on Signing the Commercial Space Launch Act
October 30, 1984

I am pleased to sign into law H.R. 3942, the Commercial Space Launch Act. One of the important objectives of my administration has been, and will continue to be, the encouragement of the private sector in commercial space endeavors. Fragmentation and shared authority had unnecessarily complicated the process of approving activities in space. Enactment of this legislation is a milestone in our efforts to address the need of private companies interested in launching payloads to have ready access to space.

This administration views facilitation of the commercial development of expendable launch vehicles as an important component of America's space transportation program. We expect that a healthy ELV industry, as a complement to the Government's space transportation system, will produce a stronger, more efficient launch capability for the United States that will contribute to continued American leadership in space.

In developing the administration's approach toward encouraging this emerging industry, I have been guided by the belief that the procedures a company must comply with before being permitted to launch a launch vehicle or a payload were duplicative and should be streamlined and otherwise made efficient. H.R. 3942 has translated this objective into a comprehensive licensing mechanism enabling launch operators to comply quickly and efficiently with existing Federal regulations. This in turn will act as a signal to private launch operators that this administration stands behind their efforts to open up this new area of space exploration.

I want to express my appreciation to the leadership of the Senate Commerce Committee, the House Science and Technology Committee, and their staffs for their dedication and hard work in this accomplishment. Additionally, I want to thank Secretary of Transportation Dole and Jennifer Dorn, Director of the Office of Commercial Space Transportation, for the enormous amount of work they have already done to prepare for the responsibilities they will have under this historic legislation.

Note: As enacted, H.R. 3942 is Public Law 98–575, approved October 30.

Memorandum Returning Without Approval the Health Research Extension Act of 1984
October 30, 1984

I am withholding my approval of S. 540, the "Health Research Extension Act of 1984," which would extend and amend the biomedical research authorities of the National Institutes of Health (NIH).

I have been assured by the Department of Health and Human Services that the Continuing Resolution gives adequate authority for current NIH activities in fiscal year 1985.

This Administration has a record of strong commitment to the support and conduct of biomedical research by the NIH. Each year since taking office, I have requested increases for biomedical research. In 1985, the NIH will receive its largest increase in appropriated funds in history. This increase will ensure the continued operation of the NIH for the coming year and will continue to assist in improving medical practice and the health of the American people.

Rather than improve our research efforts, however, the unfortunate result of S. 540 would be to impede the progress of this important health activity by:

• Creating unnecessary, expensive new organizational entities;

—two institutes would be created, an arthritis and a nursing institute. This reorganization of the NIH is premature in light of a study of the NIH organizational structure to be released in a few weeks by the Institute of Medicine/National Academy of Sciences.

—numerous bodies, such as a National Commission on Orphan Diseases, an Interagency Committee on Learning Disabilities, and a Lupus Erythematosus Coordinating Committee, would be created for which there are existing mechanisms that could or already perform such functions.

• Mandating overly specific requirements for the management of research that place undue constraints on Executive branch authorities and functions;

—new positions would be created and numerous reports required that would divert scarce resources away from the NIH central mission of basic biomedical research.

—the various NIH peer review groups would be exempted from the provisions of the Federal Advisory Committee Act and Office of Management and Budget oversight. This represents an unwarranted interference with internal Executive branch management over the largest number of advisory groups for any Federal agency.

• Going beyond the Administration's request to extend only expiring authorities by rewriting all the relevant statutes of the NIH;

—current law contains sufficient authority and flexibility to carry out the important research and training activities of NIH, to respond to public concerns, and to meet scientific needs and opportunities. Imposing a uniform set of authorities for each research institution disregards the more extensive mission of some institutes and overburdens smaller institutes which do not need these additional programmatic and advisory responsibilities.

—this attempt to recodify existing statutory language has resulted in some so-called technical revisions that will result in undesired operational changes in some of the institute programs.

I want to underscore my commitment to biomedical research and the National Institutes of Health. The NIH has stood as an example of excellence for 40 years. I do not believe that it is either necessary or wise to revise completely the laws under which it has so successfully operated.

I therefore find no reasonable justification for the extensive changes to the NIH mandated by S. 540. In order to better serve the promise and the future of our national biomedical research enterprise, I am withholding my approval of this bill.

RONALD REAGAN

The White House,
October 30, 1984.

Memorandum Returning Without Approval the Public Health Service Act Amendments of 1984
October 30, 1984

I am withholding my approval of S. 2574, the "Public Health Service Act Amendments of 1984," which would extend and amend various health professions and services authorities. I have been assured by the Department of Health and Human Services that the Continuing Resolution provides adequate authority for these programs for fiscal year 1985.

S. 2574 is a seriously flawed piece of legislation. The most serious of its many objectionable provisions include the following:

First, this bill contains authorization levels substantially in excess of my 1985 Budget. Full funding of all the programs in the bill through 1987 would total $2.4 billion, 41 percent more than the $1.7 billion contained in the Budget.

Moreover, S. 2574 would continue to increase obsolete Federal subsidies to health professions students and would maintain the static and rigid categorical framework to deliver such aid. The ability of medical schools to supply our society with health professionals has changed dramatically in the last 20 years. Today, our medical schools are producing nearly 16,000 new doctors each year. Although there may be some shortages of physicians and nurses in particular areas of the country, the Nation as a whole is facing a future surplus—not shortage—of physicians and nurses. Under these circumstances, S. 2574, a bill which continues excessive taxpayer subsidies to health professionals and maintains a rigid unworkable categorical framework, cannot be justified.

S. 2574 takes the wrong approach to health professions training. In contrast to the Administration's proposal for a single, omnibus reauthorization of all health professions authorities, which would permit maximum program flexibility to address current needs, the bill not only reauthorizes the existing plethora of narrow, categorical authorities, but also creates new programs. This approach to health professions training is outdated and fails to respond to the rapidly changing health care environment.

A more appropriate approach would recognize that the surplus of physicians has reduced the need for Federal financial assistance and would improve incentives for health professionals to locate in areas of the country where shortages exist. The Administration's health professions proposals would help meet these objectives.

S. 2574 would also repeal the Primary Care Block Grant authority—a key reform proposed by the Administration and enacted by the Congress in 1981 designed to restore State control, strengthen administrative efficiencies, and improve the delivery of health services. Thus, this bill would reverse a successful trend of increased State acceptance of health care responsibility that the Administration initiated. The block grant programs for preventive health and health services and alcohol and drug abuse have been successful. The primary care block grant was made optional by the Congress, and States have been hesitant to accept it. However, to close out the option at a time when States should be willing to consider another step toward greater autonomy is counterproductive and unacceptable.

This bill contains numerous other provisions that are either unnecessary or unacceptable, including authorization for new Federal National Health Service Corps scholarships that are not needed, since the number of scholarship recipients already bound to subsidized medical practice in rural areas is adequate.

For all these reasons, I find S. 2574 unacceptable.

RONALD REAGAN

The White House,
October 30, 1984.

Memorandum Returning Without Approval a Bill for the Relief of Jerome J. and Rita J. Hartmann
October 30, 1984

I am withholding my approval of H.R. 452, a bill "For the relief of Jerome J. Hartmann and Rita J. Hartmann."

The purpose of the bill is to allow the Hartmanns to file an action against the United States, notwithstanding any other provision of law or order of any court or administrative body, with respect to damage suffered by them due to the rise in the water level of Avon Lake, Iowa, allegedly caused by the negligent design, construction, and operation of the Red Rock Reservoir and related levees.

Jerome J. Hartmann and Rita J. Hartmann are the owners of property near the Red Rock Dam and Lake Red Rock project in Iowa, which was constructed by the United States Army Corps of Engineers and began operation in 1969. The Hartmanns' property includes Avon Lake, a former gravel quarry that the Hartmanns operated as a recreational lake.

In the spring of 1973, during a period of record rainfall and impoundment of record flood storage at Lake Red Rock, the level at Avon Lake and another nearby lake, Avondale Lake, rose to a record elevation. Operation of Avon Lake for recreation was suspended and approximately 100 homes in the area suffered some form of flood damage. By August of 1973, Lake Red Rock had returned to low levels but despite pumping of Avondale Lake by the Corps of Engineers, Avon and Avondale Lakes did not recede. In 1974, with no apparent influence whatever from Lake Red Rock, the levels at Avon and Avondale Lakes rose to new highs. The waters did not recede to normal levels until after 1974.

While I sympathize with the Hartmanns and all others who suffer losses from flood waters, I am compelled to withhold my approval of H.R. 452 on several grounds.

First, the Corps attempted to determine the cause of the rise in water levels at Avon and Avondale Lakes. The geology of the area was reexamined and water levels were monitored. A casual relationship between the Federal project and the fluctuations in water elevation levels at the private lakes has not been established.

Second, over fifty years ago, when it was embarking on a major program to build flood control projects, the Congress established Federal immunity (33 U.S.C. 702(c)) against claims for incidental or periodic flood damages that might be associated with such projects in recognition that these projects yield broad and substantial societal and economic benefits for the country.

Over the years, the Executive branch and the Congress have viewed this immunity as essential to continued Federal involvement in the area of flood control. Contrary to this long-standing national policy, H.R. 452 would establish an undesirable precedent and grant preferential treatment to the Hartmanns over residents of the area who may have similarly suffered flood damages. The circumstances of this case clearly do not warrant special treatment for the Hartmanns.

RONALD REAGAN

The White House,
October 30, 1984.

Memorandum Returning Without Approval a Bill for the Relief of Marsha D. Christopher
October 30, 1984

I am withholding my approval of H.R. 723, a private bill for the relief of Marsha D. Christopher, a Postal Service worker. I sympathize with Mrs. Christopher. The on-the-job injury to her resulting from an attack by a dog was severe, but I believe that enactment of this bill would set an undesirable and potentially costly precedent and would discriminate unfairly against the thousands of other postal workers and Federal employees who also incur job-related injuries.

Mrs. Christopher has received the benefits allowed to Federal workers injured on the job as provided by the Federal Employees' Compensation Act (FECA). The bill would waive the subrogation provisions of FECA, thus enabling Mrs. Christopher to receive and retain FECA benefits in addition to money recovered by her as the result of her private settlement with the owner of the dog. This would undermine the primary purpose of the subrogation provisions of the Act, which is to place the cost of compensation on the person or persons responsible for the injury and to relieve the taxpaying public of this expense.

RONALD REAGAN

The White House,
October 30, 1984.

Memorandum Returning Without Approval the American Conservation Corps Act of 1984
October 30, 1984

I am withholding my approval from H.R. 999, the "American Conservation Corps Act of 1984." This legislation would establish, within the Departments of Agriculture and the Interior, conservation-related employment programs for youths.

The programs that H.R. 999 would in effect reestablish—the Youth Conservation Corps (YCC) and the Young Adult Conservation Corps (YACC)—were terminated by Congress at my recommendation because they had proven to be costly and unnecessary. The American Conservation Corps (ACC) would duplicate other efforts for youth financed by the Job Training Partnership Act (JTPA), such as the Job Corps, JTPA State Block Grants, and the Summer Youth program. In fiscal year 1985, the Federal Government will spend nearly $2.2 billion on these programs, which will train about 1.5 million people. This training is done at a much lower per-capita cost than would be the case under the ACC, and is much more likely to result in permanent private sector jobs for their graduates because they involve the private sector in job training.

The ACC, however, would be based on the discredited approach to youth unemployment that relies on artificial public sector employment, just as did the Public Service Employment program operated under the Comprehensive Employment and Training Act until it was terminated by Congress in 1981.

Moreover, the ACC is not a necessary or effective way of managing Federal lands. The Federal Government currently spends over $4 billion annually on land management. This amount is adequate to fund all activities needed to ensure the preservation of these precious resources for this and future generations of Americans. Any conservation project that could be performed by the ACC could be done better and for less money under existing programs, because of less overhead for residential centers and the greater productivity of existing workers who are already well trained. In addition, I have recently signed S. 864, which would expand the National Park Service's volunteer program, and allow such a program to be established in the Bureau of Land Management. Under these worthwhile programs, including those administered by the Forest Service and the Fish and Wildlife Service, citizens offer valuable volunteer services to assist the Departments of Agriculture and the Interior in the management of Federal lands.

Finally, while the three year, $225 million ACC authorization is itself unwarranted, it would almost certainly grow. The Youth Conservation Corps began in 1971 as a $1 million pilot program, and was subsequently given a permanent authorization of $60 million annually, notwithstanding its inability to provide enduring, meaningful benefits for the trainees or the public. Moreover, the proponents of the ACC have already served notice that they intend to attempt in the next Congress to increase the ACC authorization to $300 million annually.

I believe that America's unemployed youth would be better served by reducing Federal spending so that more resources are available to the private sector of our economy to fuel a continuation of the current economic expansion that has added 6 million new jobs to the workforce over the last two years. If given the opportunity, the private sector is much more likely to offer young people promising career opportunities than temporary make-work Federal job programs such as the American Conservation Corps.

RONALD REAGAN

The White House,
October 30, 1984.

Memorandum Returning Without Approval a Bill Relating to Federal Expenditures for Manufacturing Technologies
October 30, 1984

I am withholding my approval of H.R. 5172, which includes the "National Bureau of Standards Authorization Act for Fiscal Year 1985" (Title I), clarifications of the role of the National Science Foundation in engineering research and education (Title II), and the "Manufacturing Sciences and Robotics Research and Development Act of 1984" (Title III). Title I would, among other things, authorize appropriations for certain Department of Commerce programs for fiscal year 1985, for which appropriations have already been enacted.

Title III of H.R. 5172 would establish a new program providing Federal financial support for a variety of research, development, education, and training activities, whose purported purpose would be to improve manufacturing technologies, including robotics and automation. These activities would total $250 million during fiscal years 1985–1988, and represent an unwarranted role for the Federal government. The decisions on how to allocate investments for research on manufacturing technologies are best left to American industry. It is highly doubtful that this Act and result-ing Federal expenditures would improve the competitiveness of U.S. manufacturing.

The new role for the Federal government contemplated by Title III could also serve as the basis for a Federal industrial policy to influence our Nation's technological development. This Administration has steadfastly opposed such a role for the Federal government.

My Administration has fostered the development of a robust and improving economy, which will do more than anything to improve the growth and productivity of the industrial sector. We will continue our efforts to improve the general economy, the regulatory environment, and tax policies that are essential if U.S. industry is to remain competitive. I cannot, however, approve legislation that would result in significant Federal expenditures with little or no assurance that there are any benefits to be gained.

I am, therefore, constrained to withhold my approval from H.R. 5172.

RONALD REAGAN

The White House,
October 30, 1984.

Memorandum Returning Without Approval a Bill Relating to Navajo Tribe Land Claims
October 30, 1984

I am withholding my approval of H.R. 5760, a bill "To declare that the United States holds certain lands in trust for the Cocopah Indian Tribe of Arizona, and for other purposes."

Title I of H.R. 5760 would declare that almost 4,000 acres of Federal land in Yuma County, Arizona, be held in trust by the United States for the benefit of the Cocopah Indian Tribe. I do not object to this provision.

Title II of H.R. 5760 would allow the Navajo Tribe to reassert against the United States, vague and uncertain claims originally brought in July 1950, but voluntarily and legally withdrawn by their counsel in October 1969. The propriety and finality of counsel's action were subsequently given exhaustive consideration. *Navajo Tribe* v. *United States*, 220 Ct. Cl. 350, 601 F.2d 536 (1979), *cert. denied*, 444 U.S. 1072 (1980). In the meantime, some claims which might be affected by H.R. 5760 have been settled or litigated, and others have been placed on a detailed trial schedule. Enactment of H.R. 5760 could compel protracted renegotiation, retrial or delay in the trial of these claims, based upon vague and speculative allegations.

Absent a compelling showing that a substantial injustice would result from adherence to procedural norms, the limitations of the Indian Claims Act and the procedures adopted for the adjudication of claims under the Act should not be frustrated by special legislation, such as that contained in title II of H.R. 5760. No such showing has been made here.

Title II would interfere with the fair and orderly adjudication of the claims of the Navajo Tribe and would constitute an affront to established rules, procedures, and principles for the resolution of Indian claims. It could serve to encourage other and future efforts to obtain by legislation that which has been unattainable through adjudication.

For these reasons, I find the bill unacceptable. If Title I were presented as a separate bill, I would have no objection to its enactment.

RONALD REAGAN

The White House,
October 30, 1984.

Interview With Editors of the Hearst Corporation
October 30, 1984

Q. We are very appreciative, as always, of this opportunity to be with you, and we know it's a very tight day, so were going to dispense with any formalities and get right with it.

We have here a representation of Hearst Washington personnel and a representation of our editors from around the country. Unfortunately, time and room would not accommodate all, but we appreciate the group that is here.

Priorities in Second Term

As a first question, Mr. President, I know that you are very carefully avoiding talking about a very major victory despite the fact that I'm sure you're confident of one. But my question has to do with, assuming that election and assuming it to be of significant proportions, what is your number one priority for a new administration?

The President. Well, it has a few parts to it. If there is a new administration—I mean, mine, for me. [*Laughter*]

Q. That's what I meant, too.

The President. If there is, I want to continue with what we called a new beginning back when we started this last 4 years—the economic recovery that we've had. And I want to continue on the road that we started in the international scene, which is aimed at peace. And that is the dual track.

Everyone seems to have overlooked in this campaign the fact that when we set out to rebuild our defenses, we said there was a second track of equal importance, and that was to engage the Soviet Union in legitimate talks to reduce weapons, particularly the strategic weapons. And while they've walked away from the table at this time, I can't believe they're going to stay away. I think its in their own interest to join us at that table again.

But the program that we started, which was based on the tax cuts to provide an incentive to get the economy growing again, the reducing of, first, the increase in Federal spending, which was at a rate of about 17 percent and is down around 6 percent now, to continue getting that down. And we have almost 2,500 recommendations by the Grace commission that we have a task force working on—we've implemented some already that we've been able to do administratively; others would require legislation—but to put those in place.

And I—you know, I have a memory of— we did that in California with the State and when the State was in a situation akin to what the present government of the United

States has been. And we found that the advice that we got and the program that was put forward by all those volunteers—leaders, business leaders throughout the State—well, the same thing has happened here, only we've had 10 times as many at the Federal level, which is fitting, because California is only about one-tenth the population of the Nation—recommendations that are simply based on putting modern business practices to work for government. And they worked. So, this is what we are going to do.

Q. Thank you.

The President. Bill?

Federal Budget Deficit

Q. Mr. President, we want to save your time, here. When you came into office, let's say you had 10 problems. I would say that you've certainly gone a way to solve them, if not solve at least half of them. Employment and lower taxes and—well, you know what they are, the things that you've done well. On a scale of one to five, of the remaining things, where would you put the deficit? They've put a lot of stress on it, and you hear some people stress it. What do you think about it?

The President. I think the deficit is important. I couldn't say it was unimportant, because for 30 years, out on the mashed-potato circuit, and long before I ever thought I'd be in public life, I'd been complaining about the deficit. [*Laughter*]

But for 50 years, the group and the philosophy that has dominated our government for most of that time has continued to tell us it doesn't mean anything and that—well, my opponent right now in the campaign, if you look at his past, he upheld the deficits when he was a part of government. He said they stimulated the economy; they worked against having too much unemployment. He even advocated once doubling the deficit.

Now, I don't feel that way. But I also am not going to panic in believing that the deficit right now—when you see the growth of the economy, when you see the way unemployment has gone down even while the deficits are going up. They talk about interest rates. Well, interest rates were coming down at their steepest drop at the same

time that the deficit was going up.

But I believe that you get at that deficit by bringing government, as I say, back into government's proper functions and running it in an efficient manner so that it isn't running away out there beyond your revenues, and at the same time, practicing things like the tax policies that have brought about the growth.

Now, the deficit this year is down about $20 billion less than it was last year. And we look at that and how did it happen. And it has come about partly, some, because we never did get all we wanted in cuts, but mainly in the growth of the economy, the improved receipts, even with the cut in the tax rate, the amount of revenues are up. And we just—we have to continue on that path and do more of it so it comes down faster than 20 billion a year.

Q. You have resisted repealing the indexing and the third year of the tax cut. Would you consider those as possible remedies if the deficit didn't come down as fast as you would like?

The President. I would have to say—and, of course, you know, I always get in trouble with this, because no matter how I try to hedge it and say I'm talking about if—a real hypothetical "if" and a thing that I don't believe is going to happen. It would have to be the last resort, entirely.

But I don't see anything where tax rates, increasing tax rates and the threat they are to economic growth—where that can be looked at as a legitimate solution. In the 5 years before we came here, taxes doubled in this country, and we had $318 billion worth of deficits.

So, I think that there were two things about the sudden increase in the level of deficits. Part was structural. It's been built-in over these 50 years in the Government, where the Congress would sit there and didn't have to increase the amount. It was already in law that it would increase. The second half of it was the recession that we went into.

Well, that had started in 1979. And when you hit bottom in that, you've got unemployed to take care of, and that increases government expenses. And you've lost the revenues that government was once getting from those people when they were employed.

Q. Inflation was going up.

The President. Inflation, yes.

Strategic Defense Initiative

Q. Mr. President, you have a vision of the future in which the American people could be defended against offensive nuclear weapons. Critics contend that if we develop an antimissile system, the Soviets will strive to catch up, and there'll be another costly arms race. To avoid that, to relieve the concern of our allies that the superpowers may control the skies, would you be willing to consider having all of the existing nuclear weapons powers—that is, our allies, China, and Russia—participate with us in joint research and development of a defense system that could conceivably save mankind from a nuclear holocaust?

The President. Well, I haven't suggested such a thing as that, but I know that it was my decision here and around this table with the Joint Chiefs of Staff—the nuclear missile is the only weapon in the history of man that has never automatically created a defensive weapon against it. And I said, certainly, there must be a better answer than a deterrent, which is all we have now—granted, it's worked for 40 years—in which we say, if you do it to us, our strike against you will be more than you can afford.

But it seems to me much more practical if you could find something that kills weapons instead of kills people. In other words, we're sitting here—if you really analyze it, we're saying that someday, if the Soviets attacked—and we always say that, because I don't think there's anyone in America or there's ever been an administration in this country that has ever contemplated that we would make war—start a war, make war on them.

We look—and I told this to Mr. Gromyko—that we look at them as the threat to us. And we think in terms of deterrence. But that deterrence is based on that someone would sit here where I'm now sitting and have to give the order that slaughtered millions of people on the other side. If they did, that's the only defense.

So, we were all in agreement that it was worth us starting out to find if we could

find a weapon that could intercept those missiles, and intercept them thoroughly enough, not just like having antiaircraft guns. Some of the bombers always get through. No, to really stop them.

And this was why on the debate the other night I said I could see—whether it's me here or someone else—I could see if we were successful and came up, with all of our technology—and there's no one in the world who can match it—with such a weapon, then I could see saying to the Soviet Union, telling them, and saying, "Now, will you sit down with us and do the practical thing, which is to get rid of those weapons? Because we can prove to you that they won't work anymore."

Q. We've got a Department of Defense without a defense.

The President. What?

Q. We've got a Department of Defense without a defense.

The President. Yes.

Latin America

Q. Mr. President, the Kissinger commission, as you know, on Central America, said there were two basic underpinnings of the permanent state of unrest in that part of the world and that the Communists are sure to exploit. And one of these was the high population growth rate, which it said—triple population in something like 30 years. And the other one was the decline in commodity prices and the continuing instability of commodity prices. Beyond trying to put into place such free-market elements as can be put into place in the region to address those questions, what specifically would your administration in the next 4 years do to address both problems; namely, the high growth of population in Central America, and the instability in commodity prices?

The President. Well now, we're talking Central America?

Q. Yes, sir.

The President. Yes. Well, here again, I believe that that bipartisan Kissinger commission gave us a very workable program. Three-fourths of that program was aimed at the social reforms and economic reforms that are needed in so many parts of Latin America, particularly now, in this instance in Central America; and one-fourth to help them with their security so that—such as El Salvador, where they're trying as desperately as they are to have a democracy, and to have an improved living for their people. You've got to protect them from the guerrilla forces, or provide them with the means of protecting themselves, is what we're doing, while they institute these reforms.

But it's akin to our Caribbean initiative. What we have to do is not just go there with aid—which has been too much of our practice in the past. What we have to do is restore their economies, or restore—I don't think they've ever had good ones—give them a basic economy in which they can become self-sustaining and where they can, by their own efforts, begin to improve the quality of living for their people.

Yes, the poverty down there is what makes them subject to subversion from outside—the kind that Cuba exports and the Soviet Union. And most of their revolutions in the past have simply exchanged one set of rulers for another set of rulers.

So, we're very serious about that plan, and we want to proceed with it. But it will be aimed at helping them. In the Caribbean plan, it grew out of a thing that we just started kind of, you might say, ad hoc, with the Caribbean, and that was—I called some people in New York who've always been willing to participate in public affairs, and people of means in industry and so-forth, about looking at the Caribbean for investment—to meet some of their problems by private investment in those areas. And they did a great deal of this. And from that we then came forth with the Caribbean initiative plan.

Now, this other is similar to that—but for Central America—and we want it implemented, we want to go forward. The difficulty that's holding you back is the violence that's going on.

But I think this is the answer—they've got to—and then, well, the other adjunct to that, the birth rate—we've been helping all over the world with information on family planning and so forth, trying to help other countries where they have this problem, which, once again, they can do it themselves.

The President's Age

Q. Mr. President, I have a question about your age. We've heard rumors about various problems that you have based on your age. We heard some very clever one-liners during the debate that I thought were some of the high points of the debate, as a matter of fact; but without resorting to one-liners, do you see age as an issue? Do you think age should be an issue? And are you willing, at any point in the next 4 years, to undergo any kind of competency testing or anything like that? How do you feel on that issue of age?

The President. Well——

Q. No one-liners. [*Laughter*]

The President. No, no one-liners. Let's put it this way: I think an issue of health is important. And I have been ready, and will continue to be ready anytime, to hand over any medical records. Having had a father-in-law who was a noted surgeon and a president of the American College of Surgeons—Loyal Davis—he was the one that started Nancy and myself on annual physical checkups. And we're going to continue those and make them available.

I'd be the first one—if my health were a factor—that I couldn't fulfill the requirements. But some of the things that have been bruted about are just not true. I haven't had any more tendency to drop off to sleep in a dull meeting—[*laughter*]— since I've been in this job than I used to have sometimes when I was in college listening to a dull lecture. [*Laughter*]

And I guess—well, I know I've been very blessed and very fortunate. Physiologically, all the doctors that examine me—even the strangers—tell me that physiologically I'm a lot younger than my years. Now, if that ever changes, then that would be, as I say, a matter of health. And I wouldn't want to be sitting in a rocking chair while things were going on around me that I couldn't participate in. [*Laughter*]

U.S.-Cuba Relations

Q. Mr. President, I'd like to pick up on Harry's question for a minute and get back to Central America. Even your harshest critics, at this date, going into the election, are conceding that your policy in Central

America is working. Mr. Duarte has turned out to be a courageous leader for pluralism. Even in Nicaragua, where Commandante Ortega will undoubtedly be reelected, there is a resurgence of interest on the part of the people that is notable, through the efforts of Arturo Cruz and others, toward pluralism. And the atmosphere seems to be shifting dramatically, in large, due to your efforts. Would you envision—or do you envision circumstances, therefore, in your second term, where it might be possible that you might open negotiations and seek for a renewal of friendship with Cuba? Might Cuba be to you what China was to Richard Nixon?

The President. I have to tell you that early in my administration we thought that we were hearing some signals from there—that that was wanted. And we did make a move, and nothing came of it.

Q. I recall that.

The President. Yes—they weren't ready——

Q. But circumstances are changed considerably.

The President. Now, circumstances change. yes. It would take them, or him—he is still in charge—it would take him being willing to divorce his marriage partner, the Soviet Union. And I have long dreamed of what it would be like to indicate to him that rejoining the family of the Americas could probably offer him far more, and his people far more, than he's getting in this partnership with the Soviet Union.

No, we won't close the door to that—just as in Central America now, with Nicaragua. We've had a man meeting the Nicaraguan Government representatives and talking what is needed—we're not—this whole thing—let's make it plain, and this involves the *contras*, too—it isn't overthrow of a government. It is getting that revolutionary government to return to the principles of revolution that it enunciated when it was fighting the revolution, which was democracy, human rights, free press, free labor unions, and so forth.

Now, the election isn't going to mean anything, because, as we all know, he's made it impossible—even if somebody in one of those splinter parties lets his name go on the ballot—we know that it is not a legitimate election. It reminds me of the little joke about the Kremlin. There was a break-in in the Kremlin one night, and someone stole next year's election results. [*Laughter*] That's what we're seeing down there.

But, yes, I don't know, when they're that indoctrinated and they don't change or give up very easily, I think that what we're seeing is a government very similar to that of the Soviet Union, where they're not about to make any changes that are going to eliminate their hold on all the power.

But you have to keep trying. And one thing out of this election—the very fact that men like Cruz will not run, I think, has brought out into the open how much dissatisfaction there is among the people of Nicaragua with the present regime.

But, yes, if there's—we'll keep watching for any hints or signs from Castro's Cuba, because that's one of the great tragedies of all time.

Food Assistance to Ethiopia

Q. Mr. President, the last couple of days Mr. Mondale has been advocating that something he would do would quickly move towards direct sea and airlift to relieve the starvation situation in northern Africa. Do you see any opportunity whereby the U.S. will be able to—despite the Marxist regime there—that we can do something about aiding more directly in that situation?

The President. We have been the single biggest contributor to Ethiopia—$19 billion [million] last year, but we've upped that to $45 billion [million] this year. We've—the total for Africa is about $173 billion [million] dollars. The problem I don't think has to do with—that they're Marxists so much, as just the inability of their bureaucracy to function. Much of the food that we've sent there is still sitting on the docks. And we are working all the time, and holding meetings—our people with theirs—on trying to get them to assign more vehicles for transportation of this food and to get it moving better.

We've done some of our help through some of the groups like Catholic Aid that do seem to be able to get to certain areas with this help. I talked on the phone the other day to Mother Theresa. She has four locations where her nuns are there—in Ethiopia—and talks of the people that are coming there, and they just can't get the food. And I have called our aid group here and put them in touch with her about the location of those, and where—how we can do this.

But we're working every minute trying to break this logjam. We've provided gasoline for their planes; we've done things of that kind. So, that is what has to be broken—is just—they don't have the infrastructure; they're not distributing what they're getting.

Geraldine Ferraro

Q. Mr. President, would you assess the impact of Geraldine Ferraro, first, in this election, and secondly, on the future of politics?

The President. Well now, I—first of all, from the standpoint of a woman being a candidate—high time. Fine. I wonder, though, if it can't be called a great breaking point, because if you look at—well, in our own administration, here, the positions, the gains that have been made in our country. I think it was inevitable that we're going to see, and see a Presidential candidate.

I think the problem was here that in the selection, it was someone who had not gone out and—well, for example, suppose there had been a woman candidate for the Presidency in their primaries and contesting, and then would be a logical choice, having presented herself before the whole electorate for the nominee as the Presidency—to say that's who I want to be my running mate. This kind of was reaching out, and I think it looked to too many people as if they were simply reaching just for that reason.

The other way it would be—say, here's a woman that came up to the place where she's accepted in the eyes of the people as being under consideration for the top spot. And sure, she's a logical choice. And I wish it had been that way. You can't look at a Margaret Thatcher and a Golda Meir and, for that matter, an Indira Gandhi and say, why should we be so different.

But we've made such gains. I think part of them—the Supreme Court now—I think

the Cabinet members that we have here. I think right now there are an awful lot of people in this country that would be ready to mark the ballot if Jeane Kirkpatrick ran for anything. She has become so respected and so popular throughout the country.

Q. But you don't think that Geraldine Ferraro had hit quite that mark.

The President. I don't think it hit quite that hard because of the factors that I just mentioned here. First of all, it wasn't that big a move. It was—to an extent, it was a logical thing that is going to happen and—whether this was the time or not. I guess what I'm saying is that that movement must be based not just purely on the sex of the candidate, but must be based, also, on the qualifications of the candidate.

Political Endorsements

Q. Mr. President, we've had a long tradition in this country of diplomats not getting involved in politics. And yet more than 20 Ambassadors appointed by you, including personal friends, have come out for Senator Helms, not for Senator Percy or not for other Republicans. Doesn't that bother you?

The President. Well, I'm not going to let myself be bothered by it. I was as surprised as anyone. I didn't know anything like that was going on or how it came about. Traditionally, I don't know whether—I've never looked it up to see whether there was any politically appointed Ambassador before that ever participated in a campaign or not. We know that traditionally the Secretary of State doesn't, and the Secretary of Defense and the Attorney General. Other Cabinet members have always been accepted as legitimate campaigners.

But, no, I was surprised, and as I say, I don't know how it came about. But there is no restriction, actually, or anything legally that binds them from doing such a thing.

Q. Well, I think the thing that I guess I'm getting at, the question that Mary Ann Dolan was raising about Central America and so Senator Helms——

Q. Bob, excuse me, no followups.

Q. Oh, all right.

Q. We don't have time.

The President. I'm sorry.

Ms. Spaeth. Mr. President, I believe you

have time for one more.

The President. Oh, how many more——

Q. I'll pass. I have a chance——

Press Coverage

Q. All right. If we're going to do one final, Mr. President, we've all been judging you and your opponent as the campaign has gone. Why don't you take a moment and judge us? What issues, if any, have not been articulated clearly to the American public during this campaign?

The President. I will tell you one. I said it in the debate the other night. I never said, and I never ever thought, and I would have thought anybody was crazy who did think that you could turn a nuclear missile around and call it back. I was talking about the submarines and the airplanes. And the funny thing is, since my opponent rushed forth with a quote from the press conference where that subject was discussed, I have had more people—and I've seen more letters to the editor in papers on campaigning around the country that are saying, well, it's perfectly apparent seeing that he was talking about the submarines and the airplanes, not the nuclear missiles.

And the thing I've also wondered—and maybe you want to ask some of your people about this—that took place at a press conference, the whole discussion and so forth, and what I was talking about as to why we wanted to begin the START talks on the ground-based missiles first. If anyone there had thought that I was talking about turning missiles around, why wasn't there a question? Why didn't they say, "Do you mean that you think you can recall the missiles?"

No, several days later, one fellow wrote a column and said I was so stupid that I believed that you can turn nuclear missiles around. And then it caught on. And I've heard them casually mention it on the air in talk shows over the weekend, members of the press saying the same thing. And, of course, Mr. Mondale picked it up and was off in full cry.

But that is one—and how, if it hadn't been for the debate—I didn't want to go out there and appear that he could tempt me into replying to his charges, so I kept waiting for somebody to ask me. And none of your colleagues ever did. So, in the debate I thought, "Here's my time to say it." And since then, there's never been any followup. No one's ever wanted to know what I was talking about.

Note: The interview began at 2:04 p.m. in the Cabinet Room at the White House. Among those meeting with the President were Hearst Corp. officers Frank Bennack, William Randolph Hearst, Jr., Robert Danzig, and Joseph Kingsbury-Smith; William Randolph Hearst III, publisher of the San Francisco Examiner; editors Stanley W. Cloud, James Rennie, Harry Rosenfeld, James Toedtman, and Ted Warmbold; and Robert Thompson, Victor Ostrowidzki, and Mary Ann Dolan.

Merrie Spaeth is Special Assistant to the President and Director, Office of Media Relations.

The interview was released by the Office of the Press Secretary on October 31.

Proclamation 5270—National Christmas Seal Month, 1984
October 30, 1984

By the President of the United States of America

A Proclamation

Chronic diseases of the lungs are responsible for large numbers of deaths and disabilities among Americans. More than 17 million people have chronic lung diseases, and an estimated 225,000 Americans will die this year from them. The cost to this Nation is nearly $30 billion in medical expenses and lost wages, and untold millions more in lost productivity.

Emphysema and chronic bronchitis afflict ten million Americans. Asthma affects another seven million people, two million of whom are children. Before the end of this decade, lung cancer will have surpassed breast cancer as the leading cause of cancer deaths among American women.

The American Lung Association (ALA), through its community lung associations, continues the tradition started in 1904 of leading the effort to control and prevent pulmonary diseases. The ALA is this Nation's first voluntary, nonprofit public health organization. Formed originally to combat tuberculosis, the ALA, together with its medical/scientific arm—the American Thoracic Society—now has widened its scope to include all forms of lung diseases and its causes, including smoking, air pollution, and occupational hazards.

To help pioneer and develop health education and research programs aimed at better treatment and prevention of lung diseases, the ALA relies on the sale of Christmas Seals. The Association has used Christmas Seals since 1907 to raise funds through private contributions to continue its research programs.

This year, 60 million homes will receive Christmas Seals. The funds raised through the sale of Christmas Seals have enabled the ALA to provide many millions of dollars for research programs on the prevention and control of lung diseases. Christmas Seals also have allowed the ALA to conduct vigorous public campaigns against air pollution and cigarette smoking. The use of Christmas Seals on holiday mail is a visible reminder that chronic lung diseases remain a serious public health problem, but one that can be in large part prevented through research and public education.

To increase public awareness of chronic lung diseases and the benefits realized by the sales of Christmas Seals, the Congress, by Senate Joint Resolution 324, has designated the month of November as "National Christmas Seal Month" and authorized and requested the President to issue a proclamation in observance of this month.

Now, Therefore, I, Ronald Reagan, President of the United States of America, do hereby proclaim the month of November 1984 as National Christmas Seal Month, and I call upon all government agencies and the people of the United States to observe this month with appropriate activities and by supporting the Christmas Seal program.

In Witness Whereof, I have hereunto set my hand this thirtieth day of October, in the year of our Lord nineteen hundred and eighty-four, and of the Independence of the United States of America the two hundred and ninth.

RONALD REAGAN

[*Filed with the Office of the Federal Register, 12:01 p.m., October 31, 1984*]

Note: The proclamation was released by the Office of the Press Secretary on October 31.

Proclamation 5271—National Diabetes Month, 1984
October 30, 1984

By the President of the United States of America

A Proclamation

Diabetes mellitus is one of the most serious medical and public health problems challenging this Nation today. Approximately 11 million Americans suffer from this disease. Although careful treatment can control many of the short-term metabolic effects of diabetes, the disease is also associated with serious long-term complications that affect the eyes, kidneys, nervous system, and blood vessels. Physical, emotional, and financial consequences of this disease impose an enormous burden on its sufferers, their families, and the Nation in general. Diabetes-related health care, disability, and premature mortality alone cost more than $14 billion annually. The nonmonetary costs are also staggering. Moreover, the prevalence of diabetes is increasing in the United States.

In recent years, there has been an enormous amount of progress in understanding, diagnosing, and treating diabetes. The National Diabetes Advisory Board, established by the Congress, has recently reported that "Not since the discovery of insulin over half a century ago has the outlook for clinical advances in the treatment and ultimate prevention and cure of diabetes been as promising as today." Researchers continue to discover clues to the causes of this disease and its complications. New and better forms of treatment are being developed and tested.

However, basic biomedical research and its translation into clinical practice still remain the bedrock of hope for discovering the ultimate answers to this complex disease and its myriad complications. The Federal government, in cooperation with the private sector, is deeply committed to supporting basic research on diabetes so that we can conquer this major public health problem for all present and future Americans.

To increase public awareness of diabetes and emphasize the need for continued research efforts, the Congress, by Senate Joint Resolution 299, has designated the month of November 1984 as "National Diabetes Month" and authorized and requested the President to issue a proclamation in observance of that month.

Now, Therefore, I, Ronald Reagan, President of the United States of America, do hereby proclaim the month of November 1984 as National Diabetes Month, and I call upon all government agencies and the people of the United States to observe this month with appropriate programs, ceremonies, and activities.

In Witness Whereof, I have hereunto set my hand this thirtieth day of October, in the year of our Lord nineteen hundred and eighty-four, and of the Independence of the United States of America the two hundred and ninth.

RONALD REAGAN

[*Filed with the Office of the Federal Register, 12:02 p.m., October 31, 1984*]

Note: The proclamation was released by the Office of the Press Secretary on October 31.

Proclamation 5272—National Hospice Month, 1984
October 30, 1984

By the President of the United States of America

A Proclamation

Hospice care is a humanitarian way for terminally ill patients to approach the end of their lives in relative comfort and dignity. Increasing numbers of patients have chosen to enter hospice programs in recent years because of the competent and compassionate care they provide outside of the hospital environment.

Hospices care for both patients and their families by attending to their physical, emotional, and spiritual needs. A team of physicians, nurses, social workers, pharmacists, counselors, and community volunteers work together to meet the needs of the terminally ill.

The importance of hospices as an integral part of our Nation's health care system is increasingly recognized. The growth of hospices was encouraged in November 1983 when the Federal government added hospice care to the benefits available to people under Medicare.

In order to encourage greater public recognition of hospice care, the Congress, by Senate Joint Resolution 334, has designated November 1984 as "National Hospice Month" and authorized and requested the President to issue a proclamation in observance of this month.

Now, Therefore, I, Ronald Reagan, President of the United States of America, do hereby proclaim November 1984 as National Hospice Month, and I call upon appropriate government officials, all citizens, and interested organizations and associations to observe this month with activities that recognize this important event.

In Witness Whereof, I have hereunto set my hand this thirtieth day of October, in the year of our Lord nineteen hundred and eighty-four, and of the Independence of the United States of America the two hundred and ninth.

RONALD REAGAN

[Filed with the Office of the Federal Register, 12:03 p.m., October 31, 1984]

Note: The proclamation was released by the Office of the Press Secretary on October 31.

Proclamation 5273—Commemoration of the Great Famine in the Ukraine
October 30, 1984

By the President of the United States of America

A Proclamation

The Ukrainian famine of 1932–1933 was a tragic chapter in the history of the Ukraine, all the more so because it was not the result of disasters of nature, but was artificially induced as a deliberate policy.

The leaders of the Soviet Union, although fully aware of the famine in the Ukraine and having complete control of food supplies within its borders, nevertheless failed to take relief measures to check the famine or to alleviate the catastrophic conditions resulting from it. In complete disregard of international opinion, they ignored the appeals of international organizations and other nations.

More than seven million Ukrainians, and millions of others, died as the consequence of this callous act, which was part of a deliberate policy aimed at crushing the political, cultural, and human rights of the Ukrainian and other peoples by whatever means possible. The devastation of these years continues to leave its mark on the Ukrainian people and has retarded their economic, social, and political development to an enormous extent.

In making this a special day to honor those who were victims of this famine, we Americans are afforded as well another opportunity to honor our own system of government and the freedoms we enjoy and our commitment to the right to self-determination and liberty for all the peoples of the world. In so doing, let us also reaffirm our faith in the spirit and resilience of the Ukrainian people and condemn the system that has caused them so much suffering over the years.

The Congress, by House Concurrent Resolution 111, has urged the President to issue a proclamation in mournful commemoration of the great famine in the Ukraine during 1933.

Now, Therefore, I, Ronald Reagan, President of the United States of America, do hereby designate Sunday, November 4, 1984, as a Day of Commemoration of the Great Famine in the Ukraine in 1933.

In Witness Whereof, I have hereunto set my hand this thirtieth day of October, in the year of our Lord nineteen hundred and eighty-four, and of the Independence of the United States of America the two hundred and ninth.

RONALD REAGAN

[Filed with the Office of the Federal Register, 12:04 p.m., October 31, 1984]

Note: The proclamation was released by the Office of the Press Secretary on October 31.

Proclamation 5274—National Drunk and Drugged Driving Awareness Week, 1984
October 30, 1984

By the President of the United States of America

A Proclamation

Driving impaired by alcohol or other drugs is one of our Nation's most serious public health and safety problems. Each year, drunk drivers account for tens of thousands of highway fatalities and hundreds of thousands of injuries.

This senseless carnage on our highways can be reduced through increased awareness of what can be done and a willingness to get involved in doing the right thing. We must not wait until personal tragedy strikes to become involved. It is too late for those who have already become the victims of the drunk drivers.

Strict law enforcement and just penalties are essential. Contrary to popular opinion, driving is not a right, but a privilege—which can and should be withdrawn when a drunken driver deliberately endangers others. We also need improved means of detecting intoxicated drivers before they cause an accident.

Statistics show that in many alcohol-related accidents, our young people are either the cause or the victim. In recognition of the considerable evidence that raising the legal drinking age reduces alcohol-related motor vehicle crash involvement among young drivers, the Federal government is encouraging each State to establish 21 as the minimum age at which individuals may purchase, possess, or consume alcoholic beverages. Many States have already raised the legal drinking age as a result of efforts of dedicated citizen volunteers and the growing awareness that motor vehicle accidents are the leading cause of death among young people.

We need informed, concerned citizens who are willing to get involved in generating awareness, education, and action to eliminate drunk and drugged drivers from our highways. With the continued involvement of private citizens working together, and action at all levels of government, we can begin to control the problem of drunken and drugged driving.

As the Presidential Commission on Drunk Driving recommended, we are seeking a long-term sustained effort that brings to bear the resources of our local, State and national levels of government. To that end, a National Commission on Drunk Driving has been formed to continue the work of the Presidential Commission.

In order to encourage citizen involvement in prevention efforts and to increase awareness of the seriousness of the threat to our lives and safety, the Congress, by Senate Joint Resolution 303, has designated the week of December 9 through 15, 1984, as "National Drunk and Drugged Driving Awareness Week."

Now, Therefore, I, Ronald Reagan, President of the United States of America, do hereby proclaim the week of December 9 through 15, 1984, as National Drunk and Drugged Driving Awareness Week. I call upon each American to help make the difference between the needless tragedy of alcohol-related accidents and the blessings of health and life. I ask all Americans to remember and to urge others not to drink or take drugs and drive.

In Witness Whereof, I have hereunto set my hand this thirtieth day of October, in the year of our Lord nineteen hundred and eighty-four, and of the Independence of the United States of America the two hundred and ninth.

RONALD REAGAN

[*Filed with the Office of the Federal Register, 12:05 p.m., October 31, 1984*]

Note: The proclamation was released by the Office of the Press Secretary on October 31.

Statement on the Assassination of Prime Minister Indira Gandhi of India
October 31, 1984

I want to express my shock, revulsion, and grief over the brutal assassination earlier today of Prime Minister Indira Gandhi of the Republic of India. The people of the United States join me in extending our deepest sympathy and condolences to the people of India and the Prime Minister's family as they mourn Mrs. Gandhi's death.

As Prime Minister of the world's largest democracy and Chairman of the Non-Aligned Movement, Mrs. Gandhi was a source of global leadership. Her determined efforts to promote peace, security, and economic development in South Asia and throughout the world will serve as a constant reminder of Mrs. Gandhi's commitment to protect the shared values of democratic nations.

The Prime Minister and I had personal correspondence recently regarding the scourge of terrorism. We agreed upon the necessity for freedom-loving states to strengthen our cooperation to stamp out this menace to humanity. Her senseless murder serves as a vivid reminder of the terrorist threat we all confront. We must therefore renew our determination to overcome this threat and ensure that Prime Minister Gandhi's accomplishments and memory will serve as an inspiration for humanity.

Note: Prime Minister Gandhi was shot outside her home by two members of her security guard and died a short time later in the All-India Institute of Medical Sciences. The shooting occurred at 10:40 p.m., e.s.t., on October 30.

On October 31 the President went to the Indian Embassy, where he signed the book of condolence and spoke with the Indian Ambassador to the United States, Kayatyani Shankar Bajpai. On the same day, the White House announced that Secretary of State George P. Shultz would represent the United States at the funeral services for Mrs. Gandhi.

Remarks at the National Headquarters of the Reagan-Bush Campaign
October 31, 1984

Audience. 4 more years! 4 more years! 4 more years!

The President. Well, as you can see, when I came in here I wasn't really on our side. And then, you can see that I've got buttons, and—*[laughter]*—you've all talked me into it. *[Laughter]*

But I welcome this chance, first of all, to say thank you to all of you. I know that some of you here, I have found out, were up all night and working. I know the long hours that many of you have put in. And I can only tell you that if I could manage it, I would schedule a Cabinet meeting so that we could all go over and take a nap together. *[Laughter]*

I know that all I should be doing is saying, over and over again, thank you, to all of you. I do know what you have been doing, and you young people, particularly. From someone who was a Governor back in the Vietnam days—*[laughter]*—I can't quite get used to this. *[Laughter]* But I am deeply moved by it.

And at the same time that I'm saying thank you, though, I have to tell you about one side of my nature; and that is I go to bed at night, and my last thought is what if everybody is reading the polls and isn't going to bother to vote? So, the last big chore is get out the vote. And don't get so busy that you don't vote yourselves. [*Laughter*]

But that's the one. I think of all those statistics of some past elections, like elections that were lost by less than a half a vote per precinct in the country, that that could have changed the balance and all. And I know I can't convince Wirthlin that we should hide the polls—[*laughter*]—but just don't take them seriously until Tuesday, and then be running around—if it works out all right—you can say, "I told you so." [*Laughter*]

But it's been a wonderful experience for me and an opportunity I welcome, to thank you all. I know how many of you are volunteers. And it's just a few more days, and I'm as nervous as you are tired. [*Laughter*] So, we'll sweat it out together.

But God bless you all, and thank you. [*Applause*]

I may do an encore. [*Laughter*]

Audience. 4 more years! 4 more years! 4 more years!

The President. All right, I'm game. I know this is my last campaign, so I'm going to—I know I'm accused, also, of telling anecdotes. But if you wonder why I should be nervous or anything in the face of all this, I'll tell you one little experience back from my sports announcing days.

I think a fellow out at Ohio State named "Show 'Em No Mercy" Schmidt was the coach. [*Laughter*] And he had a team that was said to be not only the greatest team in the country but one of the greatest teams of all time. And I was the only sportscaster in the country, I think, that predicted that on that Saturday afternoon Notre Dame would beat Ohio State.

And we were broadcasting another—a Big Ten game at the time. I happened to know that Notre Dame had lost their captain early in the season. And I mean lost him; he died of an injury. And they had dedicated the Ohio State game to him. And I believed enough in the Gipper that I went for Notre Dame, even though I hadn't played the Gipper yet. [*Laughter*]

But sitting in the press box, and the scores would come into us of other games, and they kept coming in. And it was Ohio State—13, Notre Dame—nothing, with 2 minutes to play. And, of course, the accompanying staff with me were having a lot of fun at my expense—silently, because the mikes were on and we were broadcasting the game.

Two minutes to play, and then the final came in: Notre Dame—18, Ohio State—13. [*Laughter*] Three touchdowns in 2 minutes. [*Laughter*]

So, I want to be on that Notre Dame side in this election. [*Laughter*]

All right. Thanks again very much.

Note: The President spoke at 11:07 a.m. to volunteers and staff at the headquarters in Washington, DC.

Remarks at a White House Ceremony To Unveil a Commemorative Stamp Honoring Hispanic Americans
October 31, 1984

Welcome to the White House.

Having spent so much of my life in California, I've always been aware of the many contributions that Americans of Hispanic descent have made to our country. And the pride, the dignity of the Hispanic community has been a source of strength, a deep well, of inspiration from which America has drawn in good times and bad, during peacetime and in times of danger and conflict.

Americans of Hispanic descent have added so much to our way of life, in government service, in the private sector, in the arts, and in every aspect of our culture. And today we gather to pay a special tribute to Americans of Hispanic descent who have placed their lives on the line in the defense of America.

The Postmaster General, at our suggestion, today is issuing a stamp commemorating this awe-inspiring record of courage and valor. And this stamp is the result of a concerted effort on behalf of the 10 surviving Hispanic Medal of Honor recipients, the United States Postal Service, and the Department of Defense. It's a fitting tribute to the men and women who have given such service to the cause of freedom.

It was 174 years ago when Father Miguel Hidalgo y Costilla rang the bells in his village. Like the sounding of our Liberty Bell, he was proclaiming to the world his people's resolve to live in freedom. That same love of freedom still rings in our hearts today, especially in the hearts of our fellow citizens of Hispanic descent that's been demonstrated time and again.

When danger threatened our Republic, Hispanics, as this stamp underscores, have been in the forefront of the defense of our freedom and independence. Thirty-seven of them, an incredible number, have received our highest military award, the Congressional Medal of Honor.

It was my honor to have presented the Medal of Honor, the last one awarded, to an Hispanic-American, to Master Sergeant Roy Benavidez. I've gotten to know Roy. He and the nine other Hispanic Medal of Honor recipients visited me here at the White House this spring. And when I met and spoke with them, I could clearly see that it was the values they were taught as children that gave them the strength to be the kind of men they grew up to be.

These values—devotion to family and respect for God, love of country and respect for honest work—these are the ingredients that have molded the character of Americans of Hispanic descent. This is the stuff of which heroes are made.

There's a place in Illinois that underscores what I'm saying. In the town of Silvis, in an Hispanic neighborhood, there's a street on which lived 22 very special American families. From these 22 families, 84 men served in World War II, Korea, and Vietnam. The two Sandoval families on that street sent 13 men, 6 from one family, 7 from the other. Three Sandoval sons never came back. They and five others who gave their lives for our freedom are honored by a special monument. Their street, once just plain Second Street, is now Hero Street, U.S.A.

There's an even bigger monument, and it's the one in the heart of every man, women, and child in this country who are thankful for the precious liberty we enjoy and grateful to those to whom we owe such a debt. The stamp that we issue today is our way of giving a heartfelt message to our wonderful Hispanic neighbors who have fought for their country, individuals to whom we owe so much. And the message is: You are truly American heroes.

I'd like to thank all of you for joining with us here today in this tribute. Thank you, and God bless you.

Note: The President spoke at 11:45 a.m. in the Rose Garden at the White House.

Accordance of the Personal Rank of Ambassador to John Douglas Scanlan While Serving at the Conference on Security and Cooperation in Europe Cultural Forum Preparatory Conference
October 31, 1984

The President today announced his intention to accord the personal rank of Ambassador to John Douglas Scanlan, of Hawaii, in his capacity as Chairman of the United States delegation to the Conference on Security and Cooperation in Europe (CSCE) Cultural Forum Preparatory Conference in Budapest, Hungary (November 21–December 5, 1984).

Mr. Scanlan served in the United States Navy in 1945–1946, and was an instructor at the University of Minnesota in 1955. In 1956 he entered the Foreign Service as he was general services officer in Moscow. He attended Polish language training at the Foreign Service Institute in 1960–1961. He was consular officer, then political officer in Warsaw (1961–1965), political officer in Montevideo (1965–1967), and principal officer in Poznan (1967–1969). In 1969–1971 he was Senior State Department Representative, NMCC, JCS at the Pentagon, and officer in charge of U.S.-U.S.S.R. Bilateral Affairs in the Department in 1971–1973. He was counselor for political affairs in Warsaw in 1973–1975, and was a member of the Executive Seminar in National and International Affairs at the Foreign Service Institute in 1975–1976. In the Department he was Special Assistant to the Director General of the Foreign Service in 1976–1977, and on detail to the United States Information Agency as Deputy Director for Europe in

1977–1979. In 1979–1981 he was deputy chief of mission in Belgrade. In 1981–1982 he was Deputy Assistant Secretary of State for European Affairs in the Department, and in 1983–1984 he was a Foreign Affairs fellow at the Fletcher School of Law and Diplomacy, Tufts University, in Medford, MA. In 1984 he became Chairman of the United States delegation to the Conference on Security and Cooperation in Europe (CSCE) Cultural Forum Preparatory Conference.

Mr. Scanlan graduated from the University of Minnesota (B.A., 1952; M.A., 1955). His foreign languages are Polish, Russian, Serbo-Croatian, Spanish, and French. He was born December 20, 1927, in Thief River Falls, MN.

Statement on the Death of Father Jerzy Popieluszko of Poland
October 31, 1984

All America shares the grief of the Polish people at the news of the tragic death of Father Jerzy Popieluszko. Father Popieluszko was a champion of Christian values and a courageous spokesman for the cause of liberty. His life exemplified the highest ideals of human dignity; his death strength-

ens the resolve of all freedom loving peoples to stand firm in their convictions. Father Popieluszko's spirit lives on. The world's conscience will not be at rest until the perpetrators of this heinous crime have been brought to justice.

Letter to the Speaker of the House and the President of the Senate Reporting on the Declaration of a National Emergency With Respect to Iran
October 31, 1984

Dear Mr. Speaker: (Dear Mr. President:)

Pursuant to Section 204(c) of the International Emergency Economic Powers Act (IEEPA), 50 U.S.C. Section 1703(c), I hereby report to the Congress with respect to developments since my last report of May 3, 1984, concerning the national emergency with respect to Iran declared in Executive Order No. 12170 of November 14, 1979.

1. The Iran-United States Claims Tribu-

nal, established at The Hague pursuant to the Claims Settlement Agreement of January 19, 1981, continues to make some progress in arbitrating the 3,848 claims which have been filed before it. In total, 330 claims have been resolved through award or withdrawal. Since my last report, the Tribunal has rendered 33 more decisions, for a total of 151 final decisions. Of these decisions, 111 have resulted in awards in favor of American claimants, of which 76 were awards on agreed terms, authorizing and approving payment of settlements negotiated by the parties, and 35 were adjudicated. Total payments to successful American claimants from the Security Account stood at just over $306 million as of September 30, 1984. Of the remaining 40 decisions, 19 dismissed claims for lack of jurisdiction, three partially dismissed claims for lack of jurisdiction, 13 dismissed claims on the merits, one approved withdrawal of a claim, three were awards in favor of the Government of Iran, and one was an award in favor of the United States Government.

2. In the past six months, the Tribunal has continued to make progress in arbitrating the claims of U.S. nationals for $250,000 or more. More than 33 percent of these claims have been disposed of through adjudication, settlement, or voluntary withdrawal, leaving 362 such claims on the docket. On August 6, 1984, the Tribunal rendered its largest non-bank award, almost $50 million, in favor of the R.J. Reynolds Co. In a significant development, Iran agreed to withdraw all of the cases that it had filed in the Dutch courts seeking to set aside certain Tribunal awards in favor of U.S. claimants. It also agreed to stay proceedings in Iranian courts against two U.S. claimants, as requested by the Tribunal, but has not yet complied with similar Tribunal requests in other cases.

3. The Tribunal has proceeded with its previously adopted test-case approach for arbitrating the claims of U.S. nationals against Iran for less than $250,000. The Department of State has submitted Supplemental Statements of Claim in 33 of these claims (including 14 of the 18 test cases selected by the Tribunal), and has filed major factual and legal memoranda in support of those claims. Supplemental Statements of Claim are being prepared for 91 additional claims. While Iran continues to resist efforts to resolve these claims expeditiously, we are pressing for early Tribunal action. A third senior legal officer has recently been hired by the Tribunal to work exclusively on these claims. Finally, the Tribunal recently issued three awards on agreed terms, reflecting settlements between U.S. claimants and Iran of these claims.

4. The Department of State continues to coordinate the efforts of concerned governmental agencies in presenting U.S. claims against Iran as well as U.S. responses to claims brought by Iran. Since my last report, the Tribunal has resolved three government-to-government claims based on contracts for the provision of goods and services. In one case, the United States received an award for costs incurred in providing instruction to Iranian students at the United States Coast Guard Academy. Of the other two claims (both brought by Iran), one (against the National Aeronautics and Space Administration) was dismissed on the merits, and the other (against the Atomic Energy Commission) resulted in an award to Iran. As in the past, these awards were rendered solely on the pleadings. The Tribunal has in addition set filing dates for pleadings in 10 government-to-government claims through the end of 1984. Although two hearings were scheduled in cases concerning the interpretation and implementation of the Algiers Accords, the Tribunal has postponed these hearings indefinitely. The United States, however, is fully prepared to proceed with these hearings and is also preparing rejoinders for submission to the Tribunal in two other cases.

5. In the last six months, there has also been a change in the composition of the Tribunal. On April 27, 1984, Gunnar Lagergren, the President of the Tribunal and Chairman of Chamber One, resigned effective October 1, 1984. Despite several rounds of discussion, the six party-appointed arbitrators were unable to agree on a successor. Accordingly, pursuant to the Tribunal's Rules of Procedure, the United States requested the independent Appointing Authority, M.J.A. Moons, the Chief Judge of the Netherlands Supreme Court, to designate a successor. On September 1, 1984, Judge Moons appointed Karl-Heinz Bockstiegel, a West German national, as a member of the Tribunal. On September 25, 1984, President Lagergren appointed Professor Bockstiegel as "acting President" pending a determination by the Tribunal (or, if necessary, the Appointing Authority) on whether he will serve as President. Professor Bockstiegel held the Chair of International Business Law and served as director

of the Institute of Air and Space Law at Cologne University.

6. The January 19, 1981, agreements with Iran also provided for direct negotiations between U.S. banks and Bank Markazi Iran concerning the payment of nonsyndicated debt claims of U.S. banks against Iran from the $1.418 billion escrow account presently held by the Bank of England. Since my last report, only one additional settlement has been reached. Mellon Bank of Pittsburgh received $12.4 million in settlement of its claim, of which $2.8 million was subsequently paid to Iran, primarily for interest on Iran's domestic deposits with the bank. Thus, as of September 30, 1984, there have been 26 bank settlements, totaling approximately $1.4 billion. Iran has received $619 million in settlement of its claims against the banks. About 20 bank claims remain outstanding.

7. On May 21, 1984, the Department of the Treasury amended Section 535.215 of the Iranian Assets Control Regulations to prohibit any transfer, except under license from the Office of Foreign Assets Control, of blocked tangible property in which, Iran has any interest whatsoever, the export of which requires the issuance of any specific license under U.S. law. This amendment was promulgated in order to help assure compliance with the export restrictions of U.S. law, particularly those with respect to properties having potential military application.

8. Significant developments have occurred at the Tribunal since my last report. On September 3, 1984, two Iranian arbitrators, Mahmoud M. Kashani and Shafei Shafeiei, assaulted Judge Nils Mangard, a third-country arbitrator, in an attempt to exclude him from the Tribunal. This unprovoked and unprecedented attack resulted in an indefinite suspension of Tribunal proceedings from September 5. In response to the attack, the United States filed a formal challenge seeking the removal of the two Iranian arbitrators in the event that the Government of Iran does not voluntarily remove them. A special chamber has been established to consider requests for withdrawals or terminations of claims and for awards on agreed terms until regular proceedings are reestablished.

9. Although the Tribunal made some progress in arbitrating the claims before it in the first few months of this reporting period, the attack on Judge Mangard in September has seriously disrupted and delayed proceedings. Significant American interests remain unresolved. Prehearing conferences and hearings scheduled for September and October have been postponed indefinitely. However, should the status of the two Iranian arbitrators who perpetrated the attack be resolved expeditiously, we believe that the Tribunal will be restored to its full functioning.

10. Financial and diplomatic aspects of the relationship with Iran continue to present an unusual challenge to the national security and foreign policy of the United States. I shall continue to exercise the powers at my disposal to deal with these problems and will continue to report periodically to the Congress on significant developments.

Sincerely,

RONALD REAGAN

Note: This is the text of identical letters addressed to Thomas P. O'Neill, Jr., Speaker of the House of Representatives, and George Bush, President of the Senate.

Message to the Congress Reporting Budget Deferrals
October 31, 1984

To the Congress of the United States:

In accordance with the Impoundment Control Act of 1974, I herewith report eight new deferrals of budget authority for 1985 totaling $107,881,834. The deferrals affect the Departments of Energy, Justice, and State, the Board for International Broadcasting, and the United States Information Agency.

The details of these deferrals are contained in the attached report.

RONALD REAGAN

The White House,
October 31, 1984.

Note: The attachment detailing the deferrals is printed in the Federal Register *of November 9.*

Informal Exchange With Reporters on Foreign and Domestic Issues
November 1, 1984

Q. How do you feel about setting out on this last campaign on your own behalf?

The President. Well, I'm delighted. No, I'm going to try everything I can do for all of the ticket. But the main thing is my message is going to be one very simple and clear: Get out the vote. Everyone vote. I think the tendency for some people to think that their votes aren't needed—we can't afford that.

Q. How confident are you of victory?

The President. You know me. I'm always just cautiously optimistic and one vote behind.

Q. Do you seriously think Walter Mondale could still overtake you at this point? Do you seriously believe that?

The President. I'm not going to comment on that. Allow a fellow a little superstition.

Q. How do you feel about this being your last campaign trip?

The President. Well, you could——

Q. A little nostalgic?

The President. ——you could have—no— well, you could have mixed emotions about that.

Q. What are yours?

The President. What?

Q. What are yours?

The President. Well, there's one of them that says enough's enough. [*Laughter*]

Q. Mr. President, did you really mean to suggest in your interview with the Hearst papers that Geraldine Ferraro is not competent to be Vice President?

The President. No. And I'm glad that the entire transcript has been released, because if you read it you will find we were talking about that whole subject of women in high office and so forth, in that sense. And, no, there was no criticism intended of her at all. It was a kind of a hypothetical discussion in answer to a hypothetical question.

Q. Mr. Reagan, what message is Secretary Shultz taking to India with him?

The President. Well, one of our deep sorrow and regret. We had good relations there. And this just is another one of those terribly needless tragedies. And I think we all feel it very deeply.

Q. Is Mr. Shultz going to try to meet with the Soviet envoy?

Q. Is there a danger, sir, that the Soviets would try to exploit that?

The President. I think that's always a danger with regard to the Soviets.

Q. How can we prevent it, sir?

The President. Just by being the good friend that we're trying to be to other nations.

Q. Is Mr. Shultz going to meet with the Soviet envoy in India?

The President. What?

Q. Is Mr. Shultz going to meet with the Soviet delegation?

The President. I don't know. There's been—I don't know whether their paths will cross or not.

Q. Mr. President, did you ever really expect to be this far ahead at this stage in the campaign?

The President. You're still trying to get me around to that question—[*laughing*]— that I've been avoiding. Frankly, the polls scare me because I still think that a lot of people could be tempted into going their own way and not bothering to vote.

Q. And your message to them?

The President. Vote. President Dewey told me to say that over and over again.

Q. When do you start looking at your second term?

The President. I've been looking at it for

the last year and a half, in case there is one. [*Laughter*]

Q. Are you going to miss all of this—the campaign?

The President. Why, how could anyone help but miss all of you? [*Laughter*]

All right. Thank you all very much.

Q. Thank you, Mr. President.

The President. You bet.

Note: The exchange began at 10:18 a.m. on the South Lawn of the White House as the President was leaving for a trip to Boston, MA.

Statement by Principal Deputy Press Secretary Speakes on Food Assistance to Africa
November 1, 1984

President Reagan today approved further measures the United States is taking in response to the growing food emergency in Africa.

The President approved food assistance to three more African countries: Kenya, 120,000 metric tons of food, valued at $25.5 million; Mozambique, 73,000 metric tons, valued at $12.7 million; Mali, 15,000 metric tons, valued at $6.9 million.

These new approvals total 208,000 metric tons valued at $45.1 million. This brings the total drought-related food assistance obligated to Africa in fiscal year 1985 (since October 1, 1984) to $131.0 million for 15 African countries. Niger and Chad are also under active consideration for food assistance.

M. Peter McPherson, Administrator of the Agency for International Development, will meet with Ethiopian Commissioner Dawit Walde Giorgis, Director, Ethiopian Relief Agency, today and tomorrow in Washington to discuss efforts of the Ethiopian and U.S. Governments to deal with the drought in that country. Subject to discussions with the Ethiopian Government, the President has authorized AID to contract with TransAmerica, a U.S. based airline, for two L–100 cargo planes to airlift emergency food supplies to drought victims within Ethiopia. The planes can arrive in Ethiopia on November 4th and 5th and remain for at least 60 days at a cost of approximately $2.4 million.

In fiscal year 1984 the United States provided more than 500,000 metric tons of emergency food to more than 25 African countries. The value of the food exceeded $173 million for fiscal year 1984.

The President is committed to addressing the drought emergency on an Africa-wide basis. In Ethiopia, the problem has largely been on the Ethiopian side, reflected in an inability or unwillingness to get the goods to the people in need. There are some signs of improvement now.

We note that the Soviet Union has announced that it will provide some limited transportation assistance to help deliver food in Ethiopia. We hope this means a basic change in Soviet policy. Their record has been one of overwhelmingly military-oriented programs in the Third World, with little assistance in terms of aid and development.

Proclamation 5275—National Alzheimer's Disease Month, 1984
November 1, 1984

By the President of the United States of America

A Proclamation

The month of November is traditionally a time for families to come together and give thanks for their blessings. It is fitting that November also be designated as National Alzheimer's Disease Month to express our compassion for those who suffer from this heartbreaking disorder and our appreciation for the many families who devote themselves to the care of afflicted loved ones who no longer can help themselves.

Alzheimer's disease is the major cause of serious confusion and forgetfulness in old age. The death of brain cells, a mark of this devastating disease, at first causes erratic behavior and unusual memory lapses and ultimately results in the "senility" once thought to be a normal part of old age.

Experts estimate that some two million Americans suffer from Alzheimer's disease, including between five and ten percent of our population over 65 and 20 percent of those over 80. If present trends continue, anticipated increases could double the number of victims in these age groups by the turn of the century.

In addition to the unhappy victims, untold numbers of others suffer the physical, emotional and financial burdens of caring for relatives who are ill with this disease. Families care for their ill relatives at home, if possible, and later in nursing homes. Between one-third and one-half of all patients in those institutions suffer from Alzheimer's disease or another serious irreversible form of dementia.

The medical research community is focusing special attention on this disease, and research is beginning to reveal many of its mysteries. Thus, research is providing the affected families with a great deal of hope. Until a cure is found, however, these families need our support and understanding. Public awareness of their problems is growing, due to the work of voluntary health associations—notably the Alzheimer's Disease and Related Disorders Association—but much remains to be done.

The Congress, by House Joint Resolution 451, has designated the month of November 1984 as "National Alzheimer's Disease Month" and authorized and requested the President to issue a proclamation in observance of this month.

Now, Therefore, I, Ronald Reagan, President of the United States of America, do hereby proclaim the month of November 1984 as National Alzheimer's Disease Month. Let us mark this month by striving to educate ourselves about Alzheimer's disease and by participating in appropriate activities and observances.

In Witness Whereof, I have hereunto set my hand this first day of November, in the year of our Lord nineteen hundred and eighty-four, and of the Independence of the United States of America the two hundred and ninth.

RONALD REAGAN

[*Filed with the Office of the Federal Register, 3:57 p.m., November 1, 1984*]

Proclamation 5276—National Blood Pressure Awareness Week, 1984
November 1, 1984

By the President of the United States of America

A Proclamation

High blood pressure is a disease that affects as many as 60 million Americans and is a major factor in the 1.25 million heart attacks and half-million strokes every year in the United States. Heart attacks annually kill 500,000 Americans, and the economic cost to the Nation in direct medical costs, lost work days and lost production will soar into the tens of billions of dollars.

Unfortunate as these statistics are, there are many encouraging signs that we are making progress in controlling this disease. Death rates from heart attacks and stroke have been declining dramatically for more than a decade. From 1972 to 1982, for example, the death rate for heart attack dropped by 27 percent, and for stroke by 42 percent.

Often called the silent killer because it usually exhibits no symptoms, high blood pressure is an insidious condition that may lead to heart attack, stroke or kidney damage. Along with cigarette smoking and elevated blood cholesterol, it is one of three major risk factors for cardiovascular diseases.

High blood pressure can be detected quickly and painlessly by use of an inflatable arm cuff and stethoscope. All Americans should take advantage of the high blood pressure screening activities in their communities, their work places and their public health facilities. Once detected, high blood pressure usually can be controlled very effectively. Weight loss, salt restrictions and exercise may be prescribed as possible remedies. When these do not work, a physician can select an appropriate treatment program from a wide range of drug therapies.

At least one of the factors responsible for the decline in death rates from heart attacks and strokes is enhanced awareness among the public and the medical profession of the dangers of high blood pressure and the steps that people can take to bring it under control. This growing awareness has been brought about largely through the efforts of the National High Blood Pressure Education Program, a coordinated program involving the Federal government, community volunteer organizations, medical associations, industry and labor, state and local public health agencies and many other groups. We must intensify our efforts to promote public understanding of the dangers of this prevalent condition and public knowledge that effective treatment methods are available.

To stimulate public awareness of the role high blood pressure plays in bringing about heart attacks and strokes and to encourage all Americans to check their blood pressure and obtain treatment if it is elevated, the Congress, by Senate Joint Resolution 260, has designated the week beginning November 11, 1984, as "National Blood Pressure Awareness Week" and authorized and requested the President to issue a proclamation in observance of this week.

Now, Therefore, I, Ronald Reagan, President of the United States of America, do hereby proclaim the week beginning November 11, 1984, as National Blood Pressure Awareness Week. I invite all interested government agencies and officials and the American people to observe this occasion with appropriate observances.

In Witness Whereof, I have hereunto set my hand this first day of November, in the year of our Lord nineteen hundred and eighty-four, and of the Independence of the United States of America the two hundred and ninth.

RONALD REAGAN

[Filed with the Office of the Federal Register, 3:58 p.m., November 1, 1984]

Proclamation 5277—National Reye's Syndrome Week, 1984
November 1, 1984

By the President of the United States of America

A Proclamation

Reye's Syndrome is a rare and often fatal illness that affects children under the age of 18 who are recovering from influenza or chicken pox. Reye's Syndrome can be deceptive, attacking just when it appears that the child is getting better. The symptoms—which include mental confusion, persistent or continuous vomiting, loss of energy, sleepiness and belligerent behavior—may develop quickly, sometimes within half a day. Immediate medical care is essential. If not treated promptly, a child suffering from Reye's Syndrome may go into coma and die.

The number of cases of Reye's Syndrome has dropped dramatically since continuous national surveillance was established by the Center for Disease Control in December 1976. This does not mean, however, that the public should become complacent about this illness. Although Reye's Syndrome is rare, it is life-threatening. About one-third of its victims do not survive.

Much remains to be learned about Reye's Syndrome, including what causes it and how it can be prevented. Voluntary organizations, such as the American Reye's Syndrome Association and the National Reye's Syndrome Foundation, have conducted educational campaigns to acquaint the public with this illness. Continued public education is essential so that parents and physicians can learn to recognize the symptoms of Reye's Syndrome and initiate treatment in its earliest stages.

To enhance public awareness of the gravity of Reye's Syndrome, the Congress, by Senate Joint Resolution 259, has designated the week of November 12, 1984, through November 18, 1984, as "National Reye's Syndrome Week" and authorized and requested the President to issue a proclamation in observance of that week.

Now, Therefore, I, Ronald Reagan, President of the United States of America, do hereby proclaim the week of November 12, 1984, through November 18, 1984, as National Reye's Syndrome Week, and I call upon the people of the United States to observe that week with appropriate ceremonies and activities.

In Witness Whereof, I have hereunto set my hand this first day of November, in the year of our Lord nineteen hundred and eighty-four, and of the Independence of the United States of America the two hundred and ninth.

RONALD REAGAN

[*Filed with the Office of the Federal Register, 3:59 p.m., November 1, 1984*]

Remarks at a Reagan-Bush Rally in Boston, Massachusetts
November 1, 1984

The President. Ladies and gentlemen, I thank all of you, and I thank Governor Volpe and Governor King. Governor Sununu, Senator Humphrey, Secretary Heckler, Mayor Collins, distinguished ladies and gentlemen:

It's wonderful to be in Massachusetts, the Bay State. And it's wonderful to be in Boston, the Hub. And do you know something? It's pretty darn good to be in the home of the world champion Boston Celtics.

You know, this last June I congratulated the Celtics in the Rose Garden. I couldn't do it in the Oval Office; the ceiling wasn't high enough. But there's someone else that I know you're very proud of, and that's your great All-American Heisman candidate from Boston College—Doug Flutie.

It's wonderful to see all of you and to stand up here with some of New England's great political leaders. I'm especially proud to stand today with your own Ed King and Ray Shamie—and that *is* Shamie. I said it once the other way. That's all right, because after January, we'll just call him Senator.

All of us need Ray Shamie in the Senate because he will work for growth and prosperity and jobs. And the people of Massachusetts know better than most that jobs are the key to opportunity. The immigrants who built this city certainly knew it. They worked hard to give their children a better chance to make sure they'd get ahead in America. The Italians did it; the Irish did it.

You know, up there on Beacon Hill there are cobblestone streets. And someone long ago once said, "Those aren't cobblestones, they're Irish heads." [*Laughter*] Well, as a hard-headed Irishman myself, I've always remembered that comment. And you know something? I don't object.

But the immigrants got ahead because they had jobs to help them get ahead. And we know, and Ray Shamie knows, that the key to more jobs is an expanding economy—or to an expanding economy, is low tax rates. And that's how we'll see to it that the young people of today and the poor people of our country get the chance they deserve.

Ray Shamie cares about the people of Massachusetts. He is the son of immigrants. He was not born to wealth and privilege. He became a high-tech pioneer. And he went into public service knowing that the odds were against him, but that the truth ultimately prevails. And he will prevail next Tuesday if you all help him. And I promise you that I will work closely with him in Washington to see that the sons and daughters of Massachusetts get the kind of future they deserve.

Now, I'm also honored today to stand with Senator Gordon Humphrey of New Hampshire, a great friend of ours and a man who has become a leader in the Senate. If the people of New Hampshire can hear us today, we're asking them to keep Gordon Humphrey in Washington. We need him there with Silvio Conte, one of the ablest men in the House of Repre-

sentatives. And we need the help of Ken Redding and Greg Hyatt and Lew Crampton. And New Hampshire needs the continued leadership of Governor Sununu.

Now, I come before you today as a candidate——

[*At this point, the President was briefly interrupted by hecklers in the audience.*]

There's an echo in here, isn't there? [*Applause*]

Audience. 4 more years! 4 more years! 4 more years!

The President. Thank you. All right. And it's fitting——

Audience. 50 States! 50 States! 50 States!

The President. Good enough. I'm with you. All right.

But as a candidate for the Presidency, it's fitting that I take my case to the city whose moral and intellectual fire ignited the American Revolution. For I speak today in this cradle of liberty of a second American revolution—one that was guided by some wise words by a wise old President.

Abe Lincoln said we must disenthrall ourselves with the past—and then we will save our country. And 4 years ago, that's what we did. We made a great turn. We got out from under the thrall of a government which we'd hoped would make our lives better, but which wound up trying to live our lives for us.

Four years ago we began to navigate by certain, fixed principles. Our North Star was freedom; common sense our constellations. We knew that economic freedom meant paying less of the American family's earnings to the Government, and so we cut taxes across the board by 25 percent. Yes, sir, we cut those——

Audience. Thank you! Thank you! Thank you!

The President. Thank you. All right.

We cut those taxes for everybody and not for any particular group. But there's one particular group here, that if they keep on yelling, I'm going to raise their taxes.

We knew that inflation, the quiet thief, and record interest rates were stealing our future. We knew that our national military defense had been weakened, so we decided to rebuild and be strong again, to be prepared for peace. It was a second American revolution. It has only just begun. But America is back, a giant on the scene.

Audience. U.S.A.! U.S.A.! U.S.A.!

The President. And that U.S.A. is powerful in its renewed spirit, powerful in its ability to defend itself and to keep the peace secure. And do you know something? That's not debatable.

But 4 years after our efforts began, small voices in the night are sounding the call to go back—back to the days of drift, the days of torpor, timidity, and taxes.

Audience. Boo-o-o!

The President. You know, my opponent's understanding of economics is well demonstrated by his predictions. Just before we took office, he said our economic program is obviously, murderously inflationary. And that was just before we lowered inflation from above 12 percent to down around 4. And just before we lowered inflation—or after our tax cuts, I should say—he said the most that he could see was an anemic recovery. And that was right before the United States economy created more than 6 million new jobs in 21 months. And in the last 18 months, there have been 900,000 new business incorporations in America. My opponent said that decontrol of oil, the prices, would cost the American taxpayers $36 billion a year. Well, we decontrolled oil prices—one of the first things we did—and the price of gasoline went down 8 cents a gallon.

You know, I have it all figured out. To get the economy in absolute perfect shape, we have to persuade our opponent to predict absolute disaster.

He says he cares about the middle class. But then he boasts, he boasts—and I will quote—he says, "I have consistently supported legislation, time after time, which increases taxes on my own constituents." Doesn't that make you want to be one of his constituents?

Audience. No!

The President. He's no doubt proud of the fact that as a United States Senator he voted 16 times to increase your taxes.

Audience. Boo-o-o!

The President. But this year he's outdone himself. He's already promised, of course, to raise your taxes. But if he is to keep all the other promises he made, he'll have to raise taxes by the equivalent of $1,890 for every household in the United States.

Audience. Boo-o-o!

The President. That figures out to about $150 a month. It's like having a second mortgage, a Mondale mortgage. Now, his economic plan has two parts: one, to raise your taxes, and the second, to raise them again. But I've got news for him: The American people don't want his tax cuts, and he's not going to get his tax cuts. Whoa, wait a minute. I was talking tax *increases.* He never asked for a tax cut in his entire career. I'm the tax-cutter. Let's keep that straight.

His tax plan would bring our recovery to a roaring stop. If my opponent's campaign were a TV program, it would be "Let's Make a Deal." [*Laughter*] You trade your prosperity for his surprise that's hidden behind a curtain. [*Laughter*] And if his campaign were a broadway show, it would be "Promises, Promises." [*Laughter*] And if it were a book, you'd have to read it from the back to the front to get a happy ending. [*Laughter*]

Audience. 4 more years! 4 more years! 4 more years!

The President. Thank you. Thank you very much. All right. All right.

You know, he sees an America in which every day is tax day, April 15th; we see an America in which every day is Independence Day, the Fourth of July. We want to lower yours and everybody's taxes, so your families will be stronger, our economy will be stronger, and America will be stronger.

And I'm proud to say that during these last 4 years, not 1 inch of territory has been lost to Communist aggression.

Audience. U.S.A.! U.S.A.! U.S.A.!

The President. Thank you. Thank you.

The United States is more secure than we were 4 years ago. And yet my opponent sees a different world. After the Soviets invaded Afghanistan, he said, "It just baffles me why the Soviets these last few years have behaved as they have." But then, there's so much that baffles him. [*Laughter*]

One year ago we liberated Grenada from Communist thugs who had taken over that country. And my opponent called what we did a violation of international law that erodes our moral authority to criticize the Soviets.

Audience. Boo-o-o!

The President. Well, I have news for him. There is nothing immoral about rescuing American students whose lives are in danger.

Audience. U.S.A.! U.S.A.! U.S.A.!

The President. Let me try to put this in perspective. The 1984 election isn't just a partisan contest. I was a Democrat once, for a large part of my life. But in those days, the Democratic leaders weren't in that "blame America first" crowd—[*referring to the hecklers*]—like we hear over here.

Its leaders were men like Harry Truman and, later, men like Scoop Jackson and John F. Kennedy—men who understood the challenges of the times. They didn't reserve all their indignation for America. They knew the difference between freedom and tyranny, and they stood up for the one and they damned the other.

Now, to all the good Democrats—and I hope there are many here—who respect that tradition, I say, "You're not alone." We're asking you to come walk with us down this path of hope and opportunity.

All across this country I know there are millions of good, patriotic Democrats who can no longer follow the leadership of that party. And I say to all of them, and all of you here today, come on, and let's, in a bipartisan tradition that is the glory of this country, keep this United States free and strong for all of us.

Last month——

[*At this point, the President was interrupted by hecklers.*]

Last month——

Audience. Long live the President! Long live the President! Long live the President!

The President. I'm not going to interrupt that. [*Laughter*]

Last month an American woman walked in space. Kathryn Sullivan made history. And she returned to a space shuttle in which some of the great scientific and medical advances of the future will be made. Cures for diabetes and heart disease may be possible up there—indeed, I have seen evidence already from experiments conducted

in the shuttle—advances, also, in technology and communications. But my opponent, as a Senator, personally led the fight against the shuttle program and called it a horrible waste.

Audience. Boo-o-o!

The President. Well, we support the shuttle program. And we've committed America to meet a great new challenge—to build a permanently manned space station and to do it within a decade. What America needs is high-tech, not high taxes.

Now, I've probably been going on too long up here, but——

Audience. No!

The President. [*Laughing and referring to the hecklers*] Oh? Well, I thought that's what they were saying over there. But the point is we made the right turn and a great turn in 1980. We were right to take command of the ship, to stop its aimless drift, and to get moving again. And we were right when we stopped sending out S.O.S. and started saying U.S.A.!

Audience. U.S.A.! U.S.A.! U.S.A.!

The President. You know, the United States of America was never meant to be a second-best nation. And like our Olympic athletes, this nation should set its sight on the stars and go for the gold.

If America could bring down inflation from 12.4 percent to 4 percent, then we can bring it down from 4 percent to 0.0. And we're going to do that. If lowering your tax rates led to the best expansion in 30 years, then we can lower them again and keep America growing right on into the 21st century. If we could create 6 million new jobs in 21 months, then we can make it possible for every American—young and old, black and white—who wants a job to find a job.

And if local governments can establish enterprise zones to create economic growth, as many of them have, then we can elect people to the Congress who will free our national enterprise zones program. We can pass that bill and provide hope for millions in the most distressed areas of America, and this we must do.

We're leading a revolution in technology, we're pushing back the frontiers of space, and if we give our workers the tools they need—in industries old and new—give American workers the proper tools, and they can outproduce, outcompete, and outsell anybody, anywhere in the world.

Our drive to restore excellence in education reversed a 20-year decline in the scholastic aptitude test scores. We're going to keep raising those scores and restore American academic excellence second to none.

Our crackdown on crime produced the sharpest drop ever in the crime index. And we're going to keep cracking down until your families and friends can walk your streets again without being afraid.

We have reversed the decline in our military defenses and restored respect for America throughout the world. And we're going to keep this nation strong to protect freedom and peace for us, for our children, and for our children's children. And if we make sure that America remains strong and prepared for peace, then we can begin to reduce nuclear weapons and one day banish them entirely from the face of the Earth.

I've seen a couple of signs about nuclear freeze. Well, nuclear freeze, yes—after we have reduced the numbers of those weapons down to where there is a fair and verifiable limit between us, yes, then we'll freeze.

And as we strengthen our economy, strengthen our security, and strengthen the values that bind us, America will become an ever greater nation—greater in art, greater in culture, and greater in love and worship of the God who made us and who has blessed us as no other nation on Earth has ever been blessed.

But if you don't mind now, I'm going to turn to something I didn't get to finish a week or so ago on that debate. I'll say it here. To the young people of our country who are with us today—and I can see you out there, and I'm so happy to see you—you young people are what this election is all about. It's you and your future.

All across this country, on many campuses, I've seen today's young people. And that generation, your generation, really sparkles. Your idealism, your love of country are unsurpassed. And I believe that my generation and those few generations between mine and yours, we have a sacred trust. And that is, when the time comes to

turn over the reins to you young people out there, that we turn over to you an America that is every bit as full of opportunity, hope, and confidence and dreams as we knew when we were your age in this country.

Audience. 4 more years! 4 more years! 4 more years!

The President. Well, I wasn't going to, but you talked me into it. All right.

Audience. Reagan! Reagan! Reagan!

The President. Thank you. And listen to me; I'm going to take the liberty of making a promise to you young people on behalf of my own and those other generations I mentioned: We're going to turn over to you an America that is free in a world that is at peace.

All of us together are part of a great revolution, and it's only just begun. America will never give up, never go back—never. We were born to be a special place between the two great oceans with a unique message to carry freedom's torch. To a tired and disillusioned world, we've always been a light of hope where all things are possible.

You know, throughout my life, I've seen America do the impossible. We survived a Great Depression that toppled many governments throughout the world. We came back from Pearl Harbor to win the greatest military victory in world history. In a single lifetime, my own, we have gone from horse and buggy to sending astronauts to the Moon.

We, as Americans, have fought harder, we've paid a higher price, done more to advance the freedom and dignity of man than any other people who ever lived on this Earth.

Ours is the land of the free because it is the home of the brave. And America's future will always be great because our nation will be strong. And our people will be free because we will be united—one people, under God, with liberty and justice for all.

Audience. U.S.A.! U.S.A.! U.S.A.!

The President. All right. As I——

Audience. Reagan! Reagan! Reagan!

The President. All right. As I leave here today——

Audience. No!

The President. As I leave the hub of the

universe, I understand how John Kennedy felt when he left to assume the Presidency. He stood one cold January day——

[*At this point, the President was briefly interrupted by hecklers in the audience.*]

I would think that even they would have the respect to listen to the words that I'm going to say in quoting John F. Kennedy.

He stood one cold January day before the members of your statehouse, and he said, "I carry with me from this State to that high and lonely office to which I now succeed more than fond memories and friendships. The enduring qualities of Massachusetts, the common threads of the Pilgrim and the Puritan, the fisherman and the farmer, the Yankee and the immigrant will not be and could not be forgotten in this Nation's Executive Mansion. They are part of my life, my conviction, my view of the past and my hopes in the future."

Well, you will not be forgotten. You could not be forgotten, nor could this day, not by me.

I am deeply honored that you have allowed me to serve you for these past 4 years. Much remains to be done. We must continue to build upon the new beginning that we started 4 years ago. So, I have come here to ask for you support and your vote.

America's best days are yet to come. And you know something? Some people over here are going to hate this, but you ain't seen nothin' yet.

Thank you. God bless you all. Thank you.

Note: The President spoke at 12:11 p.m. at the Boston City Hall.

Following his remarks, the President traveled to Rochester, NY.

Remarks at a Reagan-Bush Rally in Rochester, New York
November 1, 1984

The President. Thank you very much. I just want to say, I'm only trying to make it 2 and 0. What did you do for the Mercs last night when they made it 10 and 0?

Well, Senator Alfonse D'Amato, Congressman Horton, my good friend and your fine Republican committeeman, Dick Rosenbaum, all the others up here:

You know, the motto of the State of New York is "Excelsior"—ever upward. And I am pleased to be here with you today, asking for your support. Together we can keep not just the State of New York, but America headed ever upward.

Audience. U.S.A.! U.S.A.! U.S.A.!

The President. Thank you. All right. All right.

We've already made some progress in these last 4 years. And I want to thank New York for sending Senator D'Amato to Washington to help us get the job done. He's been an invaluable part of the team. And there's someone else that I think all America should thank—thank you, as a matter of fact, for lending to Washington—and that's Congressman Barber Conable. He fought

the good fight, and he laid the groundwork for so much of the progress that we've made in the last 4 years. He's been a force for responsible government and a champion of liberty, and he will be sorely missed.

The most important thing that all of you can do is make certain that come election day, you vote for Fred Eckert of this district so he can carry on the fight.

And please make sure that you vote for Anthony Murty of the 32d district to join Frank Horton, who's done a great job for you and for America.

Help spread the word. Get out the vote. And, if you can, just win some for the Gipper. But it's fitting with this election approaching that I'm here with you in Rochester—a town that is so synonymous with America's industrial might and our scientific and technological leadership in the world. Meeting with you in this building—a memorial to those many veterans from Rochester who fought for our freedom—reminds us of how much we have to be grateful for. And what this election is all about is preserving and building an even stronger, freer, and more prosperous America for our future.

Abe Lincoln said we must disentrall ourselves with the past—and then we will save our country. Four years ago, that's what we did. We made a great turn, we got out from under the thrall of a government which we had hoped would make our lives better, but which wound up trying to live our lives for us.

And 4 years ago, we began to navigate by some fixed principles. Our North Star was freedom; common sense our constellation. We knew that economic freedom meant paying less of the American family's earnings to the Government, and so we cut personal income tax rates by 25 percent. We knew that inflation, the quiet thief, and record interest rates were stealing our future. We knew that our national military defense had been weakened, so we decided to rebuild and be strong again to prepare for peace.

It was a second American revolution, and it's only just begun. But America is back, a giant on the scene, powerful in its renewed spirit, powerful in its growing economy, and powerful in its ability to defend itself and secure the peace. And do you know something? That's not debatable.

My opponent's understanding of economics is well demonstrated by his predictions. Just before we took office, he said our economic program is obviously, murderously inflationary. Now, that was just before we lowered inflation from above 12 percent down around 4. And just after we passed our tax cuts, he said the most he could see was an anemic recovery. And that was right before the United States economy created more than 6 million new jobs in 21 months. My opponent said that decontrol of oil prices would cost American consumers more than $36 billion a year. And we decontrolled oil prices—one of first things we did—and the price of gasoline went down 8 cents a gallon.

Now, I figured out that maybe all we have to do to get the economy in absolute perfect shape is if we can persuade my opponent to predict absolute disaster.

He says that he cares about the middle class, but he boasts, "I have consistently supported legislation, time after time, which increases taxes on my own constituents." Doesn't that make you just want to be one of his constituents?

Audience. No!

The President. He's no doubt proud of the fact that as a United States Senator he voted 16 times to increase your taxes.

Audience. Boo-o-o!

The President. But this year he's outdone himself. He's already promised, of course, to raise your taxes. But if he's to keep all the promises that he's made to this group and that, he will have to raise taxes by the equivalent of $1,890 for every household in the United States.

Audience. Boo-o-o!

The President. That's more than $150 a month. That's like having a second mortgage, a Mondale mortgage. Well, the American people don't want his tax increases, and he isn't going to get his tax increases.

You know, if my opponent's campaign were a television show, it would be "Let's Make a Deal." You get to trade your prosperity for whatever surprise he's got hidden behind the curtain. Now, if his campaign were a Broadway show, it would be "Promises, Promises." And if his administration were a novel, a book, you would have to read it from the back to the front to get a happy ending.

He sees an America in which every day is tax day, April 15th. And we see an America in which every day is Independence Day, the Fourth of July. We want to lower your taxes, yours and everyone's in this country, so that your families will be stronger, the economy will be stronger, and America will be stronger.

And on another subject, I am proud to say that during these last 4 years, not 1 inch of territory has been lost to Communist aggression.

Audience. U.S.A.! U.S.A.! U.S.A.!

The President. God bless you. Thank you. Thank you.

And the United States is more secure than it was 4 years ago. But my opponent sees a different world. After the Soviets invaded Afghanistan, he said, "It just baffles me why the Soviets these last few years have behaved as they have." But then, there's so much that baffles him. [*Laughter*]

One year ago we liberated Grenada from Communist thugs who had taken over that country.

Audience. U.S.A.! U.S.A.! U.S.A.!

The President. Now, my opponent called what we did a violation of international law that erodes our moral authority to criticize the Soviets.

Audience. Boo-o-o!

The President. Well, there is nothing immoral about rescuing American students whose lives were in danger.

But let me try to put this in perspective. The 1984 election isn't just a partisan contest. I was a Democrat myself for a good share of my life. And I feel there must be, in a gathering like this—as there have been all over the country—a great many Democrats who find they can no longer in clear conscience follow the leadership of the Democratic Party of today.

Back in those days, and when I was still a Democrat, the leadership of the party, they weren't the first—or they weren't the ones who joined that "blame America first" crowd. Its leaders were men like Harry Truman and, later, like Scoop Jackson and John F. Kennedy—men who understood the challenges of the times. They didn't reserve all their indignation and anger for America. They knew the difference between freedom and tyranny, and they stood firm for one and they damned the other.

To all the good Democrats who respect that tradition, I say, "You are not alone." We're asking you now, come walk with us on this new path of hope and opportunity and let us—in the tradition of this nation, which has been bipartisan—together make sure that we have a safe, a prosperous, and a free America.

You know, just——

Audience. 4 more years! 4 more years! 4 more years!

The President. All right. All right. If that's the way you feel about it, you've talked me into it.

You know, last month an American woman walked in space—Kathryn Sullivan made history. And then, having done that thing, she returned to the space shuttle in which some of the great scientific and medical advances of the times will be made.

Cures for diabetes and heart disease may be possible up there—I have seen evidence of that already from experiments already conducted—advances in technology and communication.

But my opponent led the fight against the entire shuttle program and called it a horrible waste.

Audience. Boo-o-o!

The President. Well, we support the shuttle program, and we've committed America to meet a great challenge—to build a permanently manned space station and to do it within a decade. What America needs is high tech, not high taxes.

The point is, we were right when we made our great turn in 1980. We were right to take command of the ship and not its aim—stop its aimless drift and get moving again.

[*At this point, there was a popping sound from somewhere in the audience.*]

You missed me. [*Laughter*] And we were right when we stopped sending out S.O.S. and started saying U.S.A.!

Audience. U.S.A.! U.S.A.! U.S.A.!

The President. Thank you. You know, the United States of America was never meant to be a second-best nation. And like our Olympic athletes, this nation should set its sights on the stars and go for the gold.

If America could bring down inflation from 12.4 percent to 4 percent, then we can bring it down further from 4 to 0.0, and we're going to do that. If lowering your tax rates led to the best expansion in 30 years, then we can lower them again and keep America growing right on into the 21st century. If we could create 6 million new jobs in 21 months, then we can make it possible for every American—young and old, black or white—who wants a job to find a job.

And if local governments can establish enterprise zones to create economic growth, as so many communities have, then we can elect people to the Congress who will free our national enterprise zones bill. We can pass that bill and provide hope for millions in the most distressed areas of America. And this, we must do. But it is going to take Congressmen there to help us break that legislation loose from where it has been buried for the last couple of years—in a committee in the House of Representatives under Tip O'Neill's control.

Audience. Boo-o-o!

The President. We're leading a revolution in technology, pushing back the frontiers of space. And I have always believed, and I believe now, if we give American workers the tools they need, those American workers can outproduce, outcompete, and outsell anybody, anywhere in the entire world.

Our drive to restore excellence in education—it resulted in the first time in 20 years—or it overcame, I should say, a 20-year record of decline in the scholastic aptitude test scores, and we've had the first increases in the last couple of years that we've had in 20. Well, we're going to keep raising those scores and restore American academic excellence second to none.

And our crackdown on crime produced the sharpest drop ever in the crime index. And we're going to keep cracking down until your families and friends can walk the streets of their neighborhoods and in these cities of ours without being afraid.

We have reversed the decline in our military defenses and restored respect for America throughout the world. And we're going to keep this nation strong to protect freedom and peace for us, for our children, and for our children's children. And if we make sure that America remains strong and prepared for peace, then we can begin to reduce nuclear weapons and one day banish them from the face of the Earth entirely.

And to those who have thought that possibly a nuclear freeze could be of help in that, let me tell you: Yes, when we can persuade the Soviets, in joining us, to reduce the numbers of nuclear weapons down to a fair and verifiable level between each other, then a nuclear freeze makes sense, and we'll have a nuclear freeze.

And as we strengthen our economy, as we strengthen our security, and strengthen the values that bind us, America will become a nation ever greater in art and learning, greater in love and worship of the God that made us and who has blessed us as no other people have ever been blessed on this Earth.

You know, I started to say something a couple of weeks ago in the debate and ran out of time. I'm going to say it now. And it is directed to the young people who are here with us today.

Audience. Youth are for Reagan! Youth are for Reagan! Youth are for Reagan!

The President. You young people, you are what this election is all about—you and your future. And I've seen you not only here but across the country—in city after city and small town after small town and on campuses, in schools—and your generation, I'm here to say, really sparkles!

Audience. U.S.A.! U.S.A.! U.S.A.!

The President. Your idealism and your love of country are unsurpassed. And my generation—and those several generations between mine and yours—[*laughter*]—we have a sacred trust, and that is, when the time comes to turn over the reins to you— you young people out there—we're going to turn over to you an America that is every bit as full of opportunity, hope, and confidence and dreams as we had when we were your age.

Audience. Youth are for Reagan! Youth are for Reagan! Youth are for Reagan! U.S.A.! U.S.A.! U.S.A.!

The President. All right. Here is our pledge—that of all these other generations I mentioned to you—we're going to turn over to you an America that is free, in a world that is at peace.

All of us together are part of a great revolution, and it's only just begun. America will never give up, never go back—never. We were born to a special place between these two great oceans with a unique mission to carry freedom's torch. To a tired and disillusioned world, we have always been a light of hope where all things are believed to be possible.

And throughout my life I've seen America do the impossible. In my younger days we survived a Great Depression, so worldwide and severe that it toppled governments in many places in the world. And we came back later from Pearl Harbor to win the greatest military victory in world history. And in a single lifetime—in a lifetime— we have gone from the horse and buggy to sending astronauts to the Moon.

But as a people, we Americans have fought harder, paid a higher price, done more to advance the freedom and dignity of man than any other people who ever lived on this Earth.

Ours is the land of the free because it is the home of the brave. America's future will always be great because our nation will be strong. Our nation will be strong because our people will be free. And our people will be free because we will be united, one people under God, with liberty and justice for all.

I am deeply honored that you've allowed me to serve you for these past 4 years. But much remains to be done. We must continue to build upon the new beginning that we started 4 years ago. So, yes, I am here to ask for your support and to ask for your vote. And I can say America's best days are yet to come.

I have a message that I want to deliver right now, in these last few days. The polls are scaring me to death, because I have a feeling that maybe some people are looking at them and saying, "Oh, we don't have to go and vote. It's all over." Well, President Dewey told me to tell you—[*laughter*]—that isn't true. Please, no matter what it takes, go to the polls and vote, and get others out to vote. Tell your neighbors to go and vote.

Audience. 4 more years! 4 more years! 4 more years!

The President. All right. And then, look, I don't want to spend those 4 more years alone. So make sure that these candidates and these Congressmen that I mentioned in my earlier remarks, make sure they're back there with me in Washington. We need them all.

And now, I know to any hecklers present, this will drive them up the wall. But I've got to close saying: You ain't seen nothin' yet.

Thank you, and God bless you all. Thank you very much.

Note: The President spoke at 3:02 p.m. at the Rochester War Memorial.

Following his remarks, the President traveled to Detroit, MI.

Remarks at a Reagan-Bush Rally in Detroit, Michigan
November 1, 1984

The President. Thank you very much. Thank you.

Audience. 4 more years! 4 more years! 4 more years!

The President. Okay. All right. Thank you very much. Thank you. I'm game if you are. All right.

Well, you know, I know how long you've been out here and I know what the weather has been like, and I tell you, I feel as if I should heed some advice I once got from a minister from out in Oklahoma. He told me a story about his first sermon. He had been ordained a minister, and then he was invited to preach at a little country church. And he worked for weeks on that first sermon. And he went out there, and he stood up in the pulpit and looked out at the church, and there was only one lone little fellow sitting out there in the otherwise empty pews. And he went down, and he said,

"Look, my friend, I'm just a young preacher getting started. You seem to be the only member of the congregation that showed up. Should I go through with it?" And the fellow said, "Well, I'll tell you, I'm a little old cowpoke out here in Oklahoma; I don't know about that sort of thing, but I do know this. If I loaded up a truckload of hay and took it out in the prairie, and only one cow showed up, I'd feed her." So, he got back up in the pulpit, took that as a cue, and an hour and a half later went down and said, "My friend, you seem to have stuck with me. What did you think?" And he said, "Well, like I told you, I don't know much about that sort of thing, but I do know this. If I loaded up a truckload of hay, took it out in the prairie, and only one cow showed up, I sure as hell wouldn't give her the whole load." [*Laughter*]

So, I think I'd better stop short of giving

you the whole load. But, it's a special thrill to be here in Michigan, weather or no. It's great to see autoworkers back on the job and your assembly lines rolling again.

You know, when we first proposed the steps that got our economy moving again, the professional politicians in Washington just laughed at us. And then one of them said to me, "You know, things just don't happen that fast." He said, "You're going to be surprised. You're in the 'big leagues' now." Well, I'll tell you, I decided they were due for a surprise. So, I went over their heads to you, the people. And your voices were heard in Washington for the first time in a long time. And you didn't exactly make them see the light, you made them feel the heat. [*Laughter*]

Well, we didn't get all that we asked for, but we got a lot of spending cuts. We cut the growth in government down from 17 percent a year to 6 percent a year. And we got that tax cut across the board. So, we're determined to keep that recovery strong so that all of us are working and going forward together again.

But I came here to tell you that those victories belong to you. You took your government back from the Washington establishment. There's a lot of politicians back here that haven't found out who they work for. They thought you worked for them. It's the other way around.

So, now I'd like to ask you to send them a message, another message, and that is: We need a man of courage and proven leadership for the United States Senate. Vote for Jack Lousma and send him back there.

I need Jack Lousma, Michigan needs Jack Lousma and, believe me, America needs Jack Lousma. He isn't afraid to vote against the special interests who want to spend more money and raise your taxes and regulate your lives. And while you're in the voting booth, a few days from now, voting for Jack Lousma, I hope you'll remember all of Michigan's Republican candidates, because they're all against higher taxes, for lower tax rates and a strong America.

And that goes especially for Tom Ritter who's coming on like a freight train in his race for the Congress. Vote for Jack and Tom and help us get a Congress that will vote and work for the people, not against

them, and we'll show 'em what "big leaguers" really are like.

For heaven's sakes, anybody that lives anyplace near Detroit knows what "big leaguers" are like.

Well, I want to get down to the meat of what I have to say here, so that we can all get in where it's warm. We knew that economic freedom meant paying less of the American family's earnings into the Government, and so we cut personal income tax rates, as I told you, by 25 percent. And contrary to what you're being told from the other side, that was 25 percent for everybody, not for any special segment of the society.

We knew that inflation was a thief that was stealing your earnings. We knew that our national military defense had been weakened, so we rebuilt that. And today we're better off than we were 4 years ago, we're more secure than we were 4 years ago, and we're respected throughout the world.

Now, some voices——

Audience. 4 more years! 4 more years! 4 more years!

The President. All right. All right. Okay. All right.

You know, we can understand a little bit about the economic theories of my opponent if we look at some of his predictions. Just before we took office, he said our economic program is obviously, murderously inflationary. He said that just before we reduced inflation from more than 12 percent down to 4. And then, after the tax cuts, he said all he could see was an anemic recovery. And that was just before the United States economy created a recovery that created 6 million more jobs in 21 months for the American people. He said that decontrol of oil prices would cost you $36 billion a year more. Well, we cut them—or we eliminated those controls, and gasoline went down 8 cents a gallon. I think all we have to do to get an absolutely perfect economy is to get him to predict absolute disaster.

As a United States Senator he voted 16 times for a tax increase on all of you. And he's proud of that. He boasts, "I have consistently supported legislation, time after time, which increases taxes on my own constituents." Doesn't that make you just want to be one of his constituents?

Audience. No!

The President. Well, of course, right now, to meet all his promises, in addition to his two-phase economic program—two phases: one, raise your taxes. He's already told you that. The second phase is, raise them again. Well, I don't think you want his tax increases, and I don't think he's going to get them. We're going to do our best to see if we can lower your tax rates so that we'll be even stronger than we are today.

I've got just one more here that I want to tell you—about his predictions. After the Soviets invaded Afghanistan, he said, "It just baffles me why the Soviets these last few years have behaved as they have." You know, there's so much that baffles him. [*Laughter*]

And then he was very upset and said that it was immoral of us to invade Grenada. Well, a year ago we went into Grenada, and I don't think there's anything immoral about sending in our forces to save the lives of American students when their lives are in danger.

Now, I just want to say two other things here real quickly, because this is getting pretty nasty for you.

Audience. No!

The President. Well, all right. Okay.

You know, I think 4 years ago, we turned things around in Washington to the extent that the Government stopped singing out S.O.S. and started saying U.S.A.! We were never meant to be a second-best nation. And so, like our Olympic athletes, we're going to go for the gold.

If we could bring inflation down from 12.4 to 4, we're going to bring it down from 4 to 0.0. Our tax cuts led to the greatest expansion that we've had in 30 years. In addition to those 6 million new jobs, in the last 18 months 900,000 new businesses were incorporated. Now, we've got some legislation bottled up there by Tip O'Neill's fellows in the Congress. That's why we have to have those Congressmen of yours back and have those other candidates back, also.

We're going to keep on the path that we're on. We're going to keep sustaining this economy of ours. You know, if my opponent's economic program were a television show, it would be "Let's Make a Deal." [*Laughter*] You know, you trade your prosperity for his surprise behind the curtain. [*Laughter*] And if it were a Broadway show, it would be "Promises, Promises." [*Laughter*] And if it were a book, you'd have to start at the back and read toward the front to get a happy ending. [*Laughter*]

But there's one other thing I want to finish here with. I didn't get to finish it a couple of weeks ago in the debate; I ran out of time. So, I want to say, all over this country I have seen our young people—your sons and daughters—and I see them here tonight. And I just want to tell you, this is a special generation. And if I could say to you young people, my generation—and a few generations between mine and yours—we lived in an America where you knew you could make your dreams come true if you just went for them. And me and those other few generations I just mentioned, we've got one sacred trust that we must keep with you young people. And that is to see, when the time comes that we turn the reins over to you, we turn over an America that is free in a world that is at peace. We're going to give to you an America where you can fly as high as your own ability will take you, and there will be no government holding you down.

Audience. 4 more years! 4 more years! 4 more years!

The President. All right. All right. All right.

Let me tell you something. I am more honored than I can say over the fact that you have allowed me to serve you for these last 4 years. And yes, I want to be there to finish the job that we started 4 years ago. And I came here to ask for your vote and your support.

And now, I just want to say one other thing. The polls just scare the life out of me. Don't believe those polls. President Dewey told me you should never be overconfident. [*Laughter*] So, I want to ask you this. On Tuesday, don't any of you think, well, they don't need my vote, everything looks good. Don't you believe it. Go to the polls and vote. And go there and vote for those candidates, for those Congressmen. Vote for

Jack Lousma. Send that team back there to help us.

And God bless you. I want to say one more thing. I know that there must be out here many of you who are Democrats, but who have found, as I found—because I was once a Democrat—you found that you cannot follow the course set by this present leadership. Well, then come walk with us down the path of hope and opportunity, and we'll have a bipartisan team that will keep America great and prosperous, strong and free. So, go to the polls, get your friends out there to the polls. And I'll say one last thing——

Audience. Give me an "R."

Audience. "R"

Audience. Give me an "E."

Audience. "E"

Audience. Give me an "A."

Audience. "A"

Audience. Give me a "G."

Audience. "G"

Audience. Give me an "A."

Audience. "A"

Audience. Give me an "N."

Audience. "N"

Audience. What does that spell?

Audience. Reagan!

The President. All right. My last message is intended to drive our opponents up the walls. It is: You ain't seen nothin' yet.

Okay. Thank you all. God bless you. Thank you.

Note: The President spoke at 5:55 p.m. at the Sears-Lincoln Park Shopping Center.

Following his remarks, the President went to the Westin Renaissance Center, where he remained overnight. The following day, the President traveled to Saginaw, MI.

Remarks at a Reagan-Bush Rally in Saginaw, Michigan
November 2, 1984

The President. Thank you all for that heartwarming reception—and heartwarming can be used on this particular day.

Well, it's good to be back in the great State of Michigan, and it's great to be in the Tri-City area. You know, being a native midwesterner, I'm always happy when I come to this part of the country—maybe because you make me feel at home.

But you in Michigan champion the bedrock values on which our country was built—belief in God, love of family, neighborhood, and good, hard work. Here are steadiness of purpose and strength of patriotism. My opponent may take a negative view of America, but he'd better not try to peddle his doom and gloom in Michigan.

Let me just ask you a question. Do you believe America is better off than it was 4 years ago? [*Applause*] Well, then I know what the answer would be if I asked the next question: Do you believe America's greatest days are yet to come? [*Applause*]

Well, let me tell you, you have some outstanding candidates for the Congress who feel just the same way. Jack Lousma served with distinction as a colonel in the Marine Corps and as an astronaut. He piloted the space shuttle *Columbia* on one of its first flights. And today he is a candidate for the United States Senate. And he believes in keeping your taxes down, and I can guarantee you, his opponent, the present incumbent, does not believe in keeping your taxes down.

But Jack knows that this will create opportunity for all Americans, and he believes in keeping America strong to keep America free and at peace. I need Jack Lousma, Michigan needs Jack Lousma, and so does America need Jack Lousma.

Bill Schuette is running for the Congress, and I have to tell you he's one of the finest candidates I've ever known. Bill believes, with me, that we can save you billions of dollars by cutting government waste and fraud, and that's what is the principal difference between him and his opponent, the present incumbent.

And Bill Schuette, Jack Lousma, and congressional candidate John Heussner are all determined to help us keep your taxes down. So, if you don't mind, I'm going to ask a favor. If you plan to vote for our ticket, please vote for our entire ticket. Help spread the word, get out the vote, and do you mind if I say, "Win 'em for the Gipper"?

You know, I remember that line that he spoke when he made that request, the Gipper, and he said, "Wherever I am, I'll know about it, and it'll make me happy." But if you do, we'll keep building our new future of opportunities for America.

You know, Abe Lincoln said that we must disenthrall ourselves with the past—and then we will save our country. And 4 years ago, that's what we did. We made a great turn, we got out from under the thrall of a government which we had hoped would make our lives better, but which wound up living our lives for us.

Four years ago we began to navigate by certain fixed principles. Freedom was our North Star, and common sense our constellations. We knew that economic freedom meant paying less of the American family's earnings to the Government, and so we cut personal tax rates by 25 percent across the board.

We knew that inflation, the quiet thief, that thief was stealing, along with record interest rates, stealing your future. We knew that our national military defense had been weakened, so we decided to rebuild and be strong again to be prepared for peace.

It was a second American revolution, and it's only just begun. But America is back, a giant on the scene, powerful in its renewed spirit, powerful in its growing economy, and powerful in its ability to defend itself and secure the peace. And do you know something? That's not debatable.

Yet 4 years after our efforts began, small voices in the night are sounding the call to go back, to go back to the days of drift, the days of torpor, timidity, and taxes.

My opponent's understanding of economics is well demonstrated by his predictions. Just before we took office, he said that our economic program was obviously, murderously inflationary. And just a short time later we brought inflation down from above 12 percent to around 4 percent. And just after our tax cuts, he said the most that he could see was an anemic recovery. And that was just before the United States' economy created 6 million new jobs in 21 months. My opponent said that decontrolling oil prices would cost you, the American consumers, $36 billion. Well, one of the first things we did was eliminate the control of oil prices, and the price of gasoline went down 8 cents a gallon.

I've got it figured out that all we have to do to get our economy in absolutely perfect shape is persuade him to predict absolute disaster. [*Laughter*]

He says he cares about the middle class, but he boasts, "I have consistently supported legislation, time after time, which increases taxes on my own constituents." Doesn't that make you want to be one of his constituents again?

Audience. No!

The President. He's no doubt proud of the fact that as a United States Senator he voted 16 times to raise your taxes.

Audience. Boo-o-o!

The President. But this year he's outdone himself. He's already promised, of course, to raise your taxes. But if he's to keep all the promises that he's made, he will have to raise taxes the equivalent of $1,890 for every household in the United States.

Audience. Boo-o-o!

The President. That's more than $150 a month. That's like having a second mortgage, a Mondale mortgage. [*Laughter*]

Now, he's got an economic plan, and it has two parts: one, raise taxes; two, raise them again. [*Laughter*] But I've got news for him: The American people don't want his tax increases, and he's not going to get his tax increases.

His tax plan would bring our recovery to a roaring stop. You know, if my opponent's campaign plan were a TV show, it would be "Let's Make a Deal." [*Laughter*] You trade your prosperity for his surprise that's hidden behind the curtain. And if his program were a Broadway show, it would be "Promises, Promises." [*Laughter*] And if it were a book, you'd have to read it from the back to the front to get a happy ending. [*Laughter*]

He sees a day in which every day is tax day, April 15th. Well, we see an America in which every day is Independence Day, the Fourth of July. We want to lower your taxes some more. We want to do it for everybody in this country so your families will be stronger, the economy will be stronger, and America will be stronger.

On another subject, I'm proud to say that during these last 4 years, not 1 inch of territory in the world has been lost to Communist aggression. And the United States is more secure than it was 4 years ago. But my opponent sees a different world. After the Soviets invaded Afghanistan, he said, "It just baffles me why the Soviets these last few years have behaved as they have." But then, there's so much that baffles him. [*Laughter*]

One year ago we liberated Grenada from Communist thugs who had taken over that country. And my opponent called what we did a violation of international law that erodes our moral authority to criticize the Soviets.

Audience. Boo-o-o!

The President. There is nothing immoral about rescuing American students whose lives were in danger.

But you know, let me try to put this all in perspective. The 1984 election isn't just a partisan contest. I was a Democrat once, and for a large part of my life. I'm sure there are many Democrats present; I hope so, because I know that all across this country are millions of patriotic Democrats who have found they can no longer follow the policies of the leadership of the Democratic Party today.

In those days when I was a Democrat, the leaders of the Democratic Party weren't members of that "blame America first" crowd. It's leaders were men like Harry Truman and, later, men like Senator Scoop Jackson and John F. Kennedy—men who understood the challenges of the times. They didn't reserve all their indignation for America. They knew the difference between freedom and tyranny, and they stood up for one and damned the other.

To all the good Democrats who respect that tradition of their party, I say, "You're not alone." We're asking you to come walk down the path of hope and opportunity

with the rest of us, and in a bipartisan way—a solid tradition of this country—we'll keep America prosperous and free and at peace.

Last month an American woman walked in space—Kathryn Sullivan made history. And then she returned to a shuttle, a space shuttle, in which some of the great scientific and medical advances of the future will be made. Cures for diabetes and heart disease may be possible up there—indeed, I've seen evidence of that from some of the experiments conducted already. There will be advances in technology and communications.

But my opponent led the fight against the whole shuttle system. He called it a horrible waste. Well, we support the space shuttle, and we've committed America to meet a great challenge—to build a permanently manned space station and to do it within a decade. What America needs is high tech, not high taxes.

Now, I've probably been going on too long here, but——

Audience. No!

The President. Thank you.

But the point is, we were right when we made that great turn in 1980. We were right to take command of the ship, to stop its aimless drift, and to get moving again. And we were right when we stopped sending out S.O.S. and started saying U.S.A.!

Audience. U.S.A.! U.S.A.! U.S.A.! Reagan! Reagan!

The President. All right.

The United States of America was never meant to be a second-best nation. Like our Olympic athletes, this nation should set its sights on the stars and go for the gold.

You know, if America could bring down inflation from 12.4 percent to 4, as we did, then we can bring it down from 4 to 0.0, and we're going to do that. If lowering your tax rates led to the best expansion in 30 years, then we can lower them again and keep America growing right into the 21st century. If we could create those 6 million new jobs in 21 months, then we can make it possible for every American—young and old, black or white—who wants a job to find a job.

And if local governments around this

country can establish enterprise zones to create economic growth, then we can elect people to the Congress who will free our national enterprise zones bill. This is a bill to go into the distressed areas of some of our rural areas and our major city areas and, through tax incentives, establish industry and work there that will give jobs to people that presently don't have them. Well, that bill has been buried in a committee of the Congress for more than 2 years now. And if we get the right people back there in the Congress, they will break it out, and we'll have this bill that will mean hope for millions in the most distressed areas of America.

We're leading a revolution in technology and pushing back the frontiers of space. And if we give American workers the tools they need in industries, old and new, then I think that American workers with the proper tools can outcompete, outsell, outproduce anyone, anytime, anywhere in the world.

Our drive in this last year and a half or so to restore excellence in education has reversed a 20-year decline in the scholastic aptitude test scores. And we're going to keep raising those scores and restore American academic excellence second to none.

Our crackdown on crime produced the sharpest drop ever in the crime index. And we're going to keep cracking down until your families and friends can walk on the streets at night without being afraid.

We've reversed the decline in our military defenses and restored respect for America. And we're going to keep this nation strong to protect freedom and peace for us, for our children, and for our children's children. And if we make sure that America remains strong and prepared for peace, then we can begin to reduce nuclear weapons and one day banish them entirely from the face of the Earth.

And as we strengthen our economy, strengthen our security, and strengthen the values that bind us, America will become a nation even greater in art and learning and greater in the love and worship of the God that made us and that has blessed us more than any other people on this Earth have ever been blessed.

Now, I ran out of time a couple of weeks ago on the debate, and I didn't get to finish something I started to say there. Well, I'm going to say it now. And it's to the young people of our country who are here with us today. You, you are what this election is all about—you and your future.

I have been seeing these young people all across the country—on campuses, in schools, in rallies of this kind. And I have to tell you, this generation of young people really sparkles. Your idealism, your love of country are unsurpassed. And I want to tell you that my generation and a few generations between mine and yours—[*laughter*]—we have a sacred trust. And that is, when the time comes to turn over the reins to you, you young people out there, we're going to turn over to you an America that is every bit as full of opportunity, hope, confidence, and dreams as it was when we were your age and growing up in America.

Audience. Reagan! Reagan! Reagan!

The President. All right. Thank you. Thank you.

And the line I was going to finish with 2 weeks ago on that debate was: We're going to turn over to you an America that is free in a world that is at peace.

Audience. 4 more years! 4 more years! 4 more years!

The President. Well, if you insist, okay. All right.

America will never go back, never. We were born to be a special place between the two great oceans with a unique mission to carry freedom's torch. To a tired, disillusioned world we've always been a light of hope where all things are possible. And throughout my life I've seen America do the impossible.

We survived a Great Depression that toppled governments in many parts of the world. We came back from Pearl Harbor to win the greatest military victory in world history. And in a single lifetime—in my lifetime—we have gone from the horse and buggy to landing astronauts on the Moon.

We Americans have fought harder, paid a higher price, done more to advance the freedom and dignity of man, than any other people who ever lived on this Earth.

Ours is the land of the free because it is the home of the brave. Our future will always be great because our nation will be strong. Our nation will be strong because we're free. And our people will be free because we're united—one people, under God, with liberty and justice for all.

I am deeply honored that you've let me serve you for these past 4 years. Much remains to be done. We must continue to build upon the new beginning that we started 4 years ago. So I've come here today to ask for your support and for your vote.

But now, I've gotten a little frightened reading the polls, and I'll tell you why. I have a terrible feeling that some may decide their votes aren't needed. Well, come Tuesday, every vote is needed. I have it directly from President Dewey: Go to the polls, vote. And I'll tell you, if you're going to vote for me, as you've just indicated, don't send me back there alone. Send these candidates back there with me to help do the job.

America's best days are yet to come. And I know it bothers my opponent very much, but I'm going to say it anyway: You ain't seen nothin' yet.

Thank you. God bless you all. Thank you very much.

Note: The President spoke at 10:23 a.m. in Hangar 5 at the Tri-City Airport.

Following his remarks, the President traveled to Cleveland, OH.

Remarks at a Reagan-Bush Rally in Cleveland, Ohio
November 2, 1984

The President. Thank you all very much. Thank you. Governor Rhodes, Senator Lausche, Mayor Voinovich, Mayor Perk, ladies and gentlemen, thank you all very much.

It's great to be in Ohio again and wonderful to be in Cleveland. When we were making our plans for this final campaign swing, there were so many places we wanted to visit, I said, "Just make sure that we get to the banks of Lake Erie, alongside the Cuyahoga. I love the Buckeye State, and I love Cleveland.

And, as you saw, a couple of people up here that I want to give special greetings to: Matt Hatchadorian of Ohio's 19th District and Robert Woodall of the 20th [21st]. They're determined Republicans, outstanding candidates, and they'll do a great job defending your interests. And I can tell you that the incumbents they seek to oust are not representing your interests, as far as I've been able to see. We need these two candidates in Washington to keep the pressure on Tip O'Neill. So, help spread the word, and get out the vote, and win 'em for the Gipper. And if you do, we can keep on building opportunities for America.

Your enthusiasm shows just how wrong our opponents are when they talk down America. I think it's about time they should give America a pat on the back.

You know, Abe Lincoln said we must disenthrall ourselves with the past—and then we will save our country. And 4 years ago, that's what we did. We made a great turn. We got out from under the thrall of a government which we had hoped would make our lives better, but which ended up trying to live our lives for us. Four years ago, we began to navigate by some fixed principles. Freedom was our North Star; common sense our constellations.

We knew that economic freedom meant paying less of the American family's earnings to the government, and so we cut personal income tax rates by 25 percent. And that was across the board; no special group of any kind got any special break. We knew that inflation, the quiet thief, and record interest rates were stealing our future. We knew that our national military defense had been weakened, so we decided to rebuild and be strong again to be prepared for peace.

It was a second American revolution, and it's only just begun. But America is back, a giant on the scene, powerful in its renewed spirit, powerful in its growing economy, and powerful in its ability to defend itself and secure the peace. And do you know something? That's not debatable.

Yet 4 years after our efforts began, small voices in the night are sounding the call to go back—back to the days of drift, the days of torpor, timidity, and taxes.

My opponent's understanding of economics is well demonstrated by his predictions. Just before we took office, he said that our economic program was obviously, murderously inflationary. So, right after he said that, we lowered inflation from above 12 percent down to around 4. And then just after we got our tax cuts, he said the most he could see was an anemic recovery. And that was right before the United States economy created more than 6 million new jobs in 21 months. He said that if we decontrolled oil prices it would cost you $36 billion. So, we decontrolled oil prices, and the price of gasoline dropped 8 cents a gallon.

I have it all figured out that the way we can get an absolutely perfect economy is if we persuade him to predict absolute disaster.

He says he cares about the middle class, but he boasts, "I have consistently supported legislation, time after time, which increases taxes on my own constituents." Doesn't that make you want to be one of his constituents?

Audience. No!

The President. He's no doubt proud of the fact that as a United States Senator, before he became Vice President, he voted 16 times to increase your taxes.

Audience. Boo-o-o!

The President. But this year he's outdone himself. He's already promised he's going to raise your taxes. But if he's to keep all the promises that he's made in this campaign— we've worked it out on the computer—it would raise your taxes about $1,890 for every household in the United States.

Audience. Boo-o-o!

The President. That's more than $150 a month. That's like having a second mortgage, a Mondale mortgage.

His economic plan has two parts. First, raise your taxes. The second part is, raise them again. [*Laughter*] But I've got news for him: The American people don't want his taxes, and they're not going to get them.

Audience. 4 more years! 4 more years! 4 more years!

The President. Okay. All right. That's what I came here to talk to you about.

You know, if my opponent's economic program were a television show, it would be "Let's Make a Deal." [*Laughter*] You trade your prosperity for whatever surprise he's got hidden behind the curtain. [*Laughter*] And if it was a Broadway show, it would be "Promises, Promises." [*Laughter*] And if it were a book, you'd have to start at the back and read it to the front in order to get a happy ending. [*Laughter*]

He sees an America in which every day is tax day, April 15th. We see an America in which everyday is Independence Day, the Fourth of July. We want to lower your taxes and those of everyone in the United States, so that our economy will be stronger and America will be stronger.

I'm proud to say that during these last 4 years—on another subject—not 1 square inch of territory in the world has been lost to Communist aggression. The United States is more secure than it was 4 years ago.

But my opponent sees a different world. After the Soviets invaded Afghanistan, he said, "It just baffles me why the Soviets these last few years have behaved as they have." Well, there's so much that baffles him. [*Laughter*]

One year ago we liberated Grenada from Communist thugs who had taken over that country. And my opponent called what we did a violation of international law that erodes our moral authority to criticize the Soviets.

Audience. Boo-o-o!

The President. There is nothing immoral about rescuing American students whose lives were in danger.

Now, let me try to put this in perspective. The 1984 election isn't just a partisan contest. I was a Democrat once, for a good share of my life. And I'm sure there must be Democrats here in this crowd. I hope so, because all over America, there are fine, patriotic Democrats who have found they can no longer follow the present leadership of that party.

The leaders, once, of the Democratic

Party weren't the kind that were in the "blame America first" crowd. Its leaders were men like Harry Truman and Senator Scoop Jackson, John F. Kennedy. They understood the challenges of our times. They didn't reserve all their indignation for America. They knew the difference between freedom and tyranny, and they stood for one and damned the other.

To all the good Democrats who respect that tradition, I say, "You are not alone." We're asking you to come walk with us down the path of hope and opportunity. We have a tradition of doing things in a bipartisan fashion in this country. And let's respect that tradition, and together we'll make an America that's strong and an America, prosperous and free.

Audience. U.S.A.! U.S.A.! U.S.A.!

The President. All right. All right. While we're talking about that country of ours, last month, an American woman walked in space. Kathryn Sullivan made history. And she returned to a space shuttle in which some of the great scientific and medical advances of the future will be made. Cures for diabetes and heart disease may be possible up there. I've seen the evidence already of experiments that have taken place already in the shuttles—advances in technology and communication.

But my opponent led the fight in the Senate against the whole shuttle program. He called it a horrible waste. Well, we support the space shuttle, and we've committed America to a great challenge, and that is to build a permanently manned space station and to do it in the next decade. What America needs is not high—it needs high tech, not high taxes.

But I think we were right in 1980 to make a turn. We were right to take command of the ship, to stop its aimless drift, and get moving again. And we were right when we stopped sending out S.O.S. and started saying U.S.A.!

Audience. U.S.A.! U.S.A.! U.S.A.!

The President. All right.

The United States of America was never meant to be a second-best nation. Like our Olympic athletes, this nation should set its sights on the stars and go for the gold.

And if America could bring down inflation from 12.4 percent to 4, then we can

bring it down from 4 percent to 0.0, and we're going to do that. If lowering your tax rates led to the best expansion in 30 years, then we can lower them again and keep America growing right into the 21st century. If we could create 6 million new jobs in 21 months, then we can make it possible for every American—young and old, black or white—to find a job, everyone that wants to find a job.

And if local governments can establish enterprise zones to create economic growth, then we can elect people to Congress who will free our national enterprise zones program, which has been buried in committee in the Congress for more than 2 years by Tip O'Neill. We can get it out there. We can provide hope for millions in the most distressed areas of America. And this we must do. And that means sending these two gentlemen on the platform with me up there to the Congress to help us do it.

We're leading a revolution in technology, pushing back the frontiers of space. And if we give our workers the tools they need, in industries old and new, well, I've always believed and I believe now—you give American workers the proper tools, and they will outproduce, outcompete, and outsell anybody, anytime, anywhere in the world.

Our drive to restore excellence in education reversed a 20-year decline in the scholastic aptitude test scores. We're going to keep raising those scores to restore American academic excellence to a place that it is second to none.

And while education scores are going up, we can be happy that one thing is going down. And that's crime. America was swept by an epidemic of crime in the years before we took office, with over 13 million reported crimes every year. With the help of the American people, we've begun to make real progress. Our national crackdown on crime has produced the sharpest decrease ever in the history of crime statistics and the first time that the serious crime index has shown a decline for 2 years in a row.

But this hasn't been very easy, especially with the strong obstacles that we faced in the House of Representatives. This is just one more illustration of how clear the choice is in this campaign. For 3 years, we had sitting in the House our comprehensive crime control act, including bail reform, tougher sentencing, and major reforms affecting drug trafficking. The bill had passed the U.S. Senate, where we have a majority, by a vote of 91 to 1. But a tiny handful of liberal Democrats decided they knew more than the people knew and smothered it for those 3 years. One on them even boasted that when the bill came to his committee, "It was dead on arrival."

Well, with a lot of effort we finally got this important legislation through the Congress, and now—in just a matter of weeks—it's law. It's this kind of thumbing their noses at our citizens that makes me believe that this year we'll find exactly what we found out in 1980: In the United States of America, the people are in charge, not the Democratic leadership of the House of Representatives. And next Tuesday, we hope the people will exercise their vote to make that message clear once again.

And one more thing. Our opponents don't seem to like the kind of judges we appoint. I'll tell you what I believe, and that is that we ought to appoint judges who restore respect for the laws and make criminals think twice before they commit a crime. And I'd be very pleased—if anybody wants an example of the judges I think we should appoint—I'd be very pleased to stand on the record of Sandra Day O'Connor in the Supreme Court.

We've reversed the decline in our military defenses and restored respect for America. And we're going to keep this nation strong to protect freedom and peace for us, for our children, and for our children's children. And if we make sure that America remains strong and prepared for peace, then we can begin to reduce nuclear weapons and, one day, banish them entirely from the face of the Earth.

My opponent talks of a nuclear freeze. Well, I'll talk of a nuclear freeze once we have reduced the number of weapons on both sides to an equal, verifiable limit. Then we can have a nuclear freeze.

And as we strengthen our economy, strengthen our security, and strengthen the values that bind us, America will become a nation even greater in its standard of living and in art and in learning, and greater in the love and worship of the God who made us and who has blessed us more than any people have ever been blessed here on this Earth.

Now, if you don't mind for a moment, I ran out of time a couple of weeks ago on the debate, and I would like to finish here what I didn't get to finish there. To the young people of our country who are here with us today, you young people are what this election is all about—you and your future.

Audience. Reagan! Reagan! Reagan!

The President. Yes, I've seen you all over this State and all over this nation as we've crisscrossed the country. Your generation really sparkles. Your idealism, your love of country—unsurpassed. And you know, my generation—and then there's several generations between mine and yours—well, those generations, when the time comes to turn over the reins to you young people out there, all of us are pledged to turn over to you an America that is every bit as full of opportunity, hope, confidence, and dreams as we had when we were your age.

And the last line I was going to say on the debate was: We are going to turn over to you an America that is free in a world that is at peace.

Audience. 4 more years! 4 more years! 4 more years!

The President. All right.

Audience. 4 more years! 4 more years! 4 more years!

The President. All right. I know it'll drive a few people back there in the corner out of their minds, but I'm game.

You know, all of us in this country—this country is a special place, born here between the two great oceans with a unique mission to carry freedom's torch. To a tired and a disillusioned world out there, we've always been a light of hope where all things are possible. And throughout my life, I've seen America do the impossible.

We survived a Great Depression when I was a young man that toppled foreign governments, many of them. We came back from Pearl Harbor to win the greatest military victory in all history. In a single lifetime, my lifetime, we have gone from the horse and buggy to putting astronauts on the Moon.

We Americans have fought harder, we paid a higher price, we have done more to advance the dignity and freedom of man than any other people that ever lived on this Earth.

Ours is the land of the free because it is the home of the brave. Our future will be great because our nation will be strong. And our nation will be strong because our people will be free. And our people will be free because we are united—one people, under God, with liberty and justice for all.

I'm deeply honored that you've allowed me to serve you for these past 4 years. But much remains to be done. We have to continue to build on the new beginning we

began 4 years ago. So, I came here to ask for your support and your vote. America's best days are yet to come. And—but if you're going to—and I thank you for that—don't send me back there alone. Send these gentlemen that I had up here beside me back there with me, so that we can get the job done.

And now, for that little group I mentioned back there—I know this will drive them up the wall, but you ain't seen nothin' yet.

God bless you, and thank you very much. Thank you.

Note: The President spoke at 12:46 p.m. at the Cuyahoga County Courthouse.

Following his remarks, the President traveled to Springfield, IL.

Remarks at a Reagan-Bush Rally in Springfield, Illinois
November 2, 1984

The President. Thank you, you all, for a heartwarming reception and what, in a way, is homecoming for me. Governor Thompson and ladies and gentlemen, it's great to be back in Illinois, and it's an honor to be back in the proud town of Springfield, your State capital and the home of Abraham Lincoln. Now, no matter what you may have heard, it isn't true that I knew him personally. [*Laughter*]

I might add that as we meet here in central Illinois, our Secretary of Agriculture is hard at work spreading the message in southern Illinois.

In 1861, just before beginning the long train journey east to become President, Abraham Lincoln stood near this spot and spoke to the people of this good town. He said, "A duty devolves upon me which is perhaps greater than that which is devolved upon any other man since the days of Washington." It was the duty of making certain, as Mr. Lincoln would later say at Gettysburg, that this nation under God shall have a new birth of freedom, and a government of the people, by the people, for the people, shall not perish from the Earth.

Well, ever since taking office, we've worked hard to restore government of the people, to give this blessed land a new birth of freedom and opportunity. Believe me, we couldn't have accomplished all that we have without the help of your outstanding Senator, Chuck Percy. Since 1967 Chuck has served in the United States Senate with dedication and skill. He has stood proudly for the people of Illinois, and he's worked tirelessly to help keep America strong, proud, and prosperous.

Now, you've got some other candidates around here, too, and I'll be talking about those in a minute. But during the past 4 years—let me continue with Chuck—he's worked to rebuild our nation's defenses, to bring your taxes down. And today, I'm running against an opponent who wants to raise your taxes, and so is Chuck running against that kind of an opponent. The difference is, while Mr. Mondale wants to hike your taxes, it seems that Mr. Simon wants to raise them even more than Mr. Mondale does. A vote for Mr. Mondale and Mr. Simon is a vote for failed policies of higher taxes, higher prices, and a weak defense.

But, you know, I believe and I think you'll agree, a vote for our team with Chuck Percy is a vote for America's future. So, if you plan to vote for me, please don't vote—[*applause*]. Well, but all right—[*applause*]—but please—all right——

Audience. 4 more years! 4 more years! 4 more years!

The President. That's what I came here to talk to you about. All right.

Audience. 4 more years! 4 more years! 4 more years!

The President. Well, all right. But in a way, you'd be voting against me if you voted for Chuck's opponent. So, don't do that. I need Chuck back in Washington, and so do the people of Illinois.

Your candidates, well, you've got a Congressman, Ed Madigan, and your candidates for the House, Ken McMillan and Randy Patchett and Dick Austin and my close friend and trusted adviser, Bob Michel—they're just as distinguished and just as committed to a future of low taxes, opportunity, and economic growth. So, please help spread the word. Get out the vote, and please win these votes—or these races for the Gipper. And if you do, we can keep building our new future of opportunities for America.

You know, Abe Lincoln said we must disenthrall ourselves with the past—and then we will save our country. Well, 4 years ago, that's what we did. We made a great turn. We got out from under the thrall of a government which we had hoped would make our lives better, but which wound up trying to live our lives for us. Four years ago, we began to navigate by certain fixed principles. Our North Star was freedom, and common sense our constellations.

We knew that economic freedom meant paying less of the American family's earnings to the government. And so, we cut personal income tax rates by 25 percent. And that was across the board. That wasn't any favor for some particular segment of our society. It was "even-Steven" all the way.

You know, my opponent's been talking a lot about business taxes, and he says that there's been thousands of businesses making profits that are not paying a single penny in taxes. Well, you know, that's true. There are provisions in the tax laws that allow for investment for increased production and things of that kind. But I'm surprised that he didn't mention that in the 4 years of Carter-Mondale, there was an average of 387,000 corporations a year that didn't pay any taxes, even though they'd made a profit. So, I don't know why he's just discovered that that goes on now.

But we knew then that inflation, the quiet thief, and record interest rates were stealing our future.

We knew that our national military defense had been weakened. So, we decided to rebuild and be strong again, to be prepared for peace. It was a second American revolution, and it's only just begun.

But America is back, a giant on the scene, powerful in its renewed spirit, powerful in its growing economy, and powerful in its ability to defend itself and secure the peace. And do you know something? That's not debatable.

Yet 4 years after our efforts began, small voices in the night are sounding the call to go back—to go back to the days of drift, back to the days of torpor, timidity, and taxes.

My opponent's understanding of economics is well demonstrated by his predictions. Just before we took office, he said our economic program is obviously, murderously inflationary. And right after he said that, we lowered inflation from above 12 percent to down around 4.

And then, just after our tax cuts were voted, and he said the most he could see was an anemic recovery. That was right before the United States economy created more than 6 million new jobs in 21 months.

My opponent said decontrol of oil prices would cost American consumers more than $36 billion. Well, one of the first things we did was decontrol the oil prices, and the price of gasoline went down 8 cents a gallon.

Maybe all we have to do to get the economy in absolutely perfect shape is persuade him to predict absolute disaster.

He says he cares about the middle class. But he boasts, "I have consistently supported legislation, time after time, which increases taxes on my own constituents."

Doesn't that make you just want to be one of his constituents? [*Laughter*] He's no doubt proud of the fact that as a United States Senator he voted to increase your taxes 16 times.

Audience member. [*Inaudible*]—like hell!

The President. You said it all. [*Laughter*] But this year he's outdone himself.

Audience. 4 more years! 4 more years! 4 more years!

The President. All right.

Audience. 4 more years! 4 more years! 4 more years!

The President. Okay. All right.

Audience. 4 more years! 4 more years! 4 more years!

The President. All right. I can take it if you can.

But now my opponent has promised, of course, to raise your taxes. But if he's to keep all the promises that he's made in this campaign, he'll have to raise taxes by the equivalent of $1,890 for every household in the United States.

Audience. Boo-o-o!

The President. Now, that comes down to more than $150 a month. That's like a second mortgage, a Mondale mortgage. [*Laughter*]

His economic plan has two basic parts, too: raise your taxes, and the second part is raise them again. [*Laughter*] But I've got news for him: The American people don't want his tax increases, and he isn't going to get his tax increases.

Audience. Reagan-Bush! Reagan-Bush! Reagan-Bush!

The President. All right. All right.

Audience. Reagan-Bush! Reagan-Bush! Reagan-Bush!

The President. All right. Reagan-Bush, we're a package.

His tax plan would bring our recovery to a roaring stop.

You know, if my opponent's campaign were a television show, it would be "Let's Make a Deal." [*Laughter*] You trade your prosperity for what he's got hidden behind the curtain. And if his administration were a play on Broadway, it would be "Promises, Promises." And if it were a book, a novel, you'd have to read it from the front to the back in order to get a happy ending.

I reversed that. You'd have to read it from the back to the front. [*Laughter*] Well, forgive me, I've been going since early this morning. I sabotaged myself right there. [*Laughter*]

He sees an America in which every day is tax day, April 15th. We see an America in which every day is Independence Day, the Fourth of July. We want to lower your taxes, yours and everyone's in this country, so that your families will be stronger, our economy will be stronger, and America will be stronger.

I'm proud to say that during these last 4 years—this is on a change of subject—not 1 square inch of territory anyplace in the world has been lost to Communist aggression. And the United States is more secure than it was 4 years ago.

But my opponent sees a different world. After the Soviets invaded Afghanistan, he said, "It just baffles me why the Soviets, these last few years, have behaved as they have." You know, there's so much that baffles him. [*Laughter*]

One year ago we liberated Grenada from Communist thugs who had taken over that country. My opponent called what we did a violation of international law that erodes our moral authority to criticize the Soviets. Well, there is nothing immoral about rescuing American students whose lives are in danger.

Let me put this in perspective. The 1984 election isn't just a partisan contest. I was a Democrat once myself, and for a great share of my life. But in those days—in those days, its leaders weren't the "blame America first" crowd. Its leaders were men like Harry Truman and, later, men like Senator Scoop Jackson, John F. Kennedy. They understood the challenge of their times. They didn't reserve all their indignation for America. They knew the difference between freedom and tyranny, and they stood up to the one and damned the other.

Now, to all the good Democrats—and I'm sure there must be many of you in this crowd, and I hope so—there have been in the rallies all across this country millions of patriotic Democrats who can no longer follow the policies of the leadership of that party. Well, you are not alone. Come and walk with us down this path of hope and opportunity. And in the finest tradition of America, we will have a bipartisan effort to keep this country free and prosperous and secure.

Last month, an American woman made history—Kathryn Sullivan walked in space. And then she returned to the shuttle in which some of the great scientific and medical advances of the future will be made. Cures for diabetes and heart disease may be possible up there, advances in technology and communication. I have seen some of the evidence already of the experiments in the shuttles with regard to those cures I mentioned. But my opponent led the fight in the United States Senate against the entire shuttle program and called it a horrible waste. Well, we support the space shuttle. And we've committed America to meet a great challenge—to build a permanently manned space station, and to do it within a decade.

Now, I've probably been going on too long here, but the point is——

Audience. No!

The President. Well, that's reassuring. [*Laughter*]

Audience. 4 more years! 4 more years! 4 more years!

The President. You don't mean talking up here? [*Laughter*]

Audience. 4 more years! 4 more years! 4 more years!

The President. All right. Thank you. But the point is, we made the right move when we made our great turn in 1980. We were right to take command of the ship, to stop its aimless drift, and to get moving again. And we were right when we stopped sending out S.O.S. and started saying U.S.A.!

Audience. U.S.A.! U.S.A.! U.S.A.!

The President. Yes. And the United States of America was never meant to be a second-best nation. Like our Olympic athletes, this nation should set its sights on the stars and go for the gold.

If America could bring down inflation—if America could bring down inflation from 12.4 percent to 4, then we can bring it down further, from 4 to 0.0. And that's what we're going to do.

If lowering your tax rates led to the best expansion in 30 years, then we can lower them again, and keep America growing right into the 21st century.

If we could create 6 million new jobs in 21 months, then we can make it possible for every American—young, old, black, or white—everyone who wants to find a job to find one.

And if local governments can establish enterprise zones, as you've done here in Illinois, to create economic growth, then we can elect people to Congress who will free our enterprise zones bill—the national bill—and we can pass that bill and provide hope for millions in the most distressed areas of America. This we must do. But it has been buried for more than 2 years in a committee in the House under the direction of Tip O'Neill.

Audience. Boo-o-o!

The President. We need these candidates here, all of them, back there in the Congress.

We're leading a revolution in technology, pushing back the frontiers of space. And if we give our workers the tools they need—and I have believed this always—you give American workers the proper tools, and they will outproduce, outcompete, and outsell anyone, anywhere in the world, anytime.

Audience. Reagan! Reagan! Reagan!

The President. All right. Our drive to restore excellence in education has reversed a 20-year decline in the scholastic aptitude test scores. And we're going to keep raising those scores and restore American academic excellence second to none.

Our crackdown on crime produced the sharpest drop ever in the crime index, and we're going to keep cracking down until your families and friends can walk your streets without being afraid.

We've reversed the decline in our military defenses and restored respect for America. And we're going to keep this nation strong to protect freedom and peace for us, for our children, and our children's children.

And if we make sure that America remains strong and prepared for peace, then we can begin to reduce nuclear weapons and, one day, vanish them entirely from the face of the Earth.

I know my opponent talks of a nuclear

freeze. Well, I'll talk of a nuclear freeze for just a split second. When we can have negotiations that reduce our weapons and the Soviet Union's weapons down to an equal, verifiable limit, yes, then we'll have a nuclear freeze, and not until.

And as we strengthen our economy, strengthen our security, and strengthen the values that bind us, America will become a nation even greater in its standard of living, in art and learning; and greater in the love and worship of the God who made us and who has blessed this people as no other people on Earth have ever been blessed before.

And now, a couple of weeks ago on the debate, I ran out of time, and I'm going to say now what I was going to say then. And it is addressed to the young people who are here today.

You young people are what this election is all about—you and your future. And, you know, I've seen you all over this country—on campuses, in schools, out here in rallies such as this one—as you're here today—and your generation really sparkles. Your idealism, your love of country are unsurpassed.

And, you know, my generation, and then, oh, a few generations between mine and yours—[*laughter*]—we grew up in an America where we just took it for granted that you could dream and make your dreams come true. But there was no limit to how high you could fly—just based on your own talent and ability.

Well, my generation and those several others in between that I mentioned, we have a very sacred trust. And that is to see that when the time comes to turn over the reins to you, that we turn over to you an America that is every bit as full of opportunity, hope, confidence, and dreams as we had when we were your age. We're going to turn over to you an America that is free in a world at peace.

All of us together are part of a great revolution, and it's only just begun. America will never go back—never. We were born to be a special place between these two great oceans, with a unique mission—to carry freedom's torch. And, to a tired, disillusioned world we've always been a light of hope, where all things are possible.

Throughout my life I've seen America do the impossible. When I was——

Audience members. [*Inaudible*]

Audience. 4 more years! 4 more years! 4 more years!

The President. Oh, thank you. Say, how about that, I thought for a minute there was an echo or something here, but you've made it go away.

But as I said, throughout my life I've seen America do the impossible. When I was a young man there was a Great Depression worldwide. It toppled governments throughout the world; here, we survived it. We came back from Pearl Harbor to win the greatest military victory that has ever been won in world history. And in a single lifetime—my own—we went from the horse and buggy to sending astronauts to the Moon.

We Americans have fought harder, paid a higher price, done more to advance the freedom and dignity of man than any other people who ever lived on this Earth. Ours is the land of the free because it is the home of the brave. America's future will be great because our nation will be strong. And our nation will be strong because our people will be free. And we're free because we're united. We're united—one people, under God, with liberty and justice for all.

I'm deeply honored that you have allowed me to serve you for these past 4 years. But much remains to be done. We must continue to build upon that new beginning we started 4 years ago. So, I ask for your vote——

Audience member. You got it!

The President. ——ask for your support. All right.

And there is one more thing, one more thing. Please, please be as scared of the polls as I am. Don't pay any attention to them, because it might tempt some of you to think your vote isn't needed. Well, let me tell you—all of you—go to the polls on Tuesday. Get your neighbors and your friends to go to the polls on Tuesday. Vote.

So, all right, America's best days are yet to come. And now, for a few unfriendly voices that I have heard—I just want to say something to send them up the wall. And that is—you ain't seen nothin' yet.

All right. Thank you all. God bless you all.

Note: The President spoke at 3:25 p.m. at the State Capitol Building.

Following his remarks, the President traveled to the Excelsior Hotel in Little Rock, AR, where he remained overnight.

Written Responses to Questions Submitted by France Soir Magazine
November 3, 1984

Description of United States

Q. How would you describe the U.S. to a young Frenchman?

The President. The United States is a nation of great size and many resources, but our richest resource is our people. They are fiercely independent, and—like the French—they cherish their liberty above all else.

It is a place where the cultures of many nations have blended to produce one culture, that which we call American. We saw a dramatic example of this during the summer Olympics in Los Angeles, when athletes from almost every nation in the world were met by host committees from the Los Angeles area, all of which were composed of people who had come from those countries and are now Americans.

Q. What is your most vivid memory?

The President. Frankly, I have so many outstanding memories that it would be impossible to select one as my most vivid. I'd like to answer that question the same way I'd answer one about what I consider the best day of my life—tomorrow. The best is always yet to come.

Favorite Childhood Book

Q. What was your favorite book as a young man?

The President. It was called "Northern Trails." I was quite young and impressionable when I read it, but it began for me a lifelong love of the outdoors. There was a magic world in those pages, and I was delighted to discover that such a world really does exist.

Value of Money

Q. What does money mean to you?

The President. I grew up in the Great Depression. That was a time when you learned that money could mean the difference between having or not having the basic necessities of life. Because God then blessed me with success, I have had the good fortune to also see that money can do more than provide necessities; it can make mankind's lot easier, afford leisure and recreation, and create opportunities for reflective and productive work.

Money can be an object of labor, but it serves its purpose best when it is not an object in itself, but an instrument of creativity, growth, and human progress. It has never had any meaning for me as an end in itself. Although I had very little money in my youth, I had a great deal of happiness. Therefore, I have never had to equate money with happiness, and I'll always be grateful to my parents for the very valuable lessons they taught me—entirely free of charge.

Physical Activities

Q. What kind of exercise do you get? How often?

The President. Before I became President, I spent a lot of time outdoors cutting brush, riding horses, and doing other work around my ranch. Now my time and opportunities for these activities are more limited—so I try to workout each day with exercise equipment. Horseback riding is still my favorite form of exercise, and I do it whenever possible.

Abortion

Q. Why are you against abortion? Is there any other choice if population growth becomes explosive?

The President. I am against abortion because it is the taking of an innocent life. While some argue that we cannot pinpoint at which moment life actually begins, I am firmly convinced that we must give the unborn child the benefit of the doubt. In my view, the unborn child has a right to life, and it is our moral obligation to protect and defend that right.

Too frequently I heard the argument that "imperfect life is too expensive to maintain and prolong." That worries me, because I believe that any society which concerns itself with the price of life rather than the intrinsic value of life itself has gone awry.

There are a wide variety of alternatives to abortion for dealing thoughtfully with population problems. We have only to look at the success of those nations which have enormous populations but which emphasize market-oriented economic policies to see that human freedom and dignity can be preserved, along with human life.

Movies

Q. Do you still take an interest in movies? Which two are favorites of yours? What American actor do you admire most?

The President. Movies are still one of my favorite forms of relaxation. However, I do find myself preferring the older films to much of what is produced today. Too many contemporary films today rely on nudity and profanity to attract an audience. I'd rather watch something that depends on good writing, a good script, and a first-class production. It wouldn't be fair of me to name favorite movies or actors.

Nancy Reagan

Q. Does Mrs. Reagan enjoy politics?

The President. Nancy has always had an active interest in politics. It's a good thing, because a large portion of our lives have been devoted to public life. I may be a bit prejudiced, but I think she is the perfect political wife as well as the perfect wife. She's always busy, and she takes an active role.

She has taken a keen interest in the problems of our youth, especially in the area of alcohol and drug abuse. And her work with the Foster Grandparents Program, too, is a special cause which brings the elderly and young people together.

Nancy has always understood the sacrifices we had to make, the hours apart, but she has always been at my side when I needed her, and I couldn't have a finer spokeswoman than she is.

President's Childrens' Occupations

Q. What are your children's occupations?

The President. As you know, Patti, who is an actress, has recently married, and she is now working on a novel. Ron has decided to leave his career in ballet to pursue journalism. Michael is in business and devotes much of his time to fundraising for charities through speedboat racing. Maureen is presently helping with my campaign, and she has been and is a successful businesswoman and radio personality.

All of my children are doing what they want to do, and they are doing it to the best of their ability. No parent could ask for more, and I am very proud of all of them.

Religion and Politics

Q. Is religion a guide for you?

The President. Yes, religion is a guide for me. To think that anyone could carry out the awesome responsibilities of this office without asking for God's help through prayer strikes me as absurd.

Q. Are politics and religion related?

The President. I believe that politics and religion are related, because I do not believe you can function in politics without some sense of morality. It is through our religious beliefs that our moral tradition in the West is descended. While a legislator or a President may not bring to his politics the specific tenets of his particular faith, each of us brings a code of morals to bear on our judgments.

There is much talk in my country now of religion interfering with politics. Actually, it is the other way around. Politics—legalization of abortion; attempts to fund abortion with taxpayers' money; prohibition of voluntary prayer in public schools; weakening of laws against pornography; failure to enforce civil rights legislation on behalf of helpless, severely ill infants—has moved across the barrier between church and state and has invaded the arena of religious beliefs.

Most of Western civilization is based on principles derived from the Judeo-Christian ethic. The wall of separation between church and state in America was erected by our forefathers to protect religion from the state, not the other way around.

Presidential Decisionmaking

Q. Do you think about individuals when you make decisions? Or must you think only of groups?

The President. In this nation, the rights of individuals are paramount. There are times when the rights of one individual—particularly when taken into consideration by our Supreme Court—can influence the rest of our population. Many decisions which I make, or are made by our legislative branch, are made on the basis of the good of the majority. Our civil rights laws were drawn up to protect the rights of individuals, regardless of race, sex, religion, or handicap.

Most Admired President

Q. What American President do you admire most? Why?

The President. I admire many of my predecessors in the Oval Office. However, I believe that Abraham Lincoln is my favorite. He stood at the helm of this nation during its most trying and tragic time. He functioned under the most difficult of circumstances, and I believe that he served with consummate dignity and humility.

Lincoln had a strong belief in the individual taking responsibility for himself. He was truly a "man of the people," and his love for all his countrymen—even those who stood across from him in the lines of battle—was all encompassing. We share many points of philosophy. Also, he had a wonderful facility with words and a delightful wit. This nation was well and honorably served by Abraham Lincoln.

Priorities in Second Term

Q. Why will you be reelected?

The President. I'm superstitious, so I'm not predicting the outcome. If I am reelected, it will be because Americans do not want a return to the policies of the past. They want to go forward, marching together as a nation with economic, military, and spiritual strength. They want to continue the resurgence that has made us a more reliable ally.

Q. What will be your top priorities in foreign affairs in a new term?

The President. My priorities will be to bring about a more constructive relationship between East and West, to strengthen our ties with our allies and friends around the world, to ensure peace and promote the growth of human freedom.

Now that the United States is restoring its military and economic strength and its national self-confidence, the conditions are better than ever for a more stable and mature relationship between the United States and the Soviet Union. It is time for the Soviets to return to the arms control negotiating table, because there is much work to be done to reduce the levels of weaponry, both nuclear and conventional. We are also prepared for a dialog on regional conflicts, both to avoid confrontations and to help bring about peaceful solutions.

Our relations with the industrial democracies in the Atlantic community and the countries of the Pacific Basin are the cornerstones of American foreign policy. We face many challenges together, and we can deal with them most effectively if we work together. There are many steps we allies can take to strengthen our common security, promote the expansion of the global economy, and work for world peace. In addition, the United States has many other friends around the world whose security, independence, well-being, and freedom are important to us.

We know that there are many regions of the world that have not yet shared in the economic recovery. We must ensure the continued openness and expansion of the world trading system and resist the protectionist pressures that could jeopardize the recovery. We must encourage sound economic policies in the developing world that will enable these countries to take better advantage of the spreading recovery.

Finally, the United States will continue its traditional role as peacemaker wherever the parties in a local conflict seek our help in promoting negotiated solutions. In Central America, southern Africa, the Middle East, and other regions, we will continue an active diplomacy for peace.

1742

Monetary Affairs

Q. Why is the dollar so strong? Will it get stronger if you are reelected?

The President. Fundamentally, the dollar is strong because the U.S. economy is strong. We are now completing the second year of our economic recovery, one of the strongest in our post-World War II experience. The recovery is being fueled by a vigorous expansion in business investment. The inflation rate remains low.

International investors appear confident that the policies which achieved these results will be continued. They have faith in the stability of our political and economic system and in our hospitality to free, market-determined capital flows. As a result of this confidence, net capital inflows into the United States have been very strong, with their positive effects on the exchange rate more than offsetting any negative effects of our current account deficit.

I don't want to get into predictions of the dollar exchange rate. Even the most learned economists don't do a good job in this kind of crystal-ball gazing, and Presidents shouldn't even try. But I will say this: In my second term we will ensure the long-term strength and vigor of the U.S. economy and seek to lead a world economic recovery.

Q. Do you believe a form of gold standard can still have a role to play in the monetary system?

The President. Early in my administration, I appointed a commission of 17 distinguished men and women—economists, public servants, and people in business—to study the question of the future role of gold in the monetary system. After careful deliberation, the majority of this commission, which was chaired by Treasury Secretary Regan, recommended that we should not return to a fixed gold standard. Some members felt that a gold standard would provide needed long-term discipline over monetary policies, but the majority view was that restoration of a gold standard would not be a fruitful way of achieving either domestic or international monetary stability.

Free Enterprise System

Q. Do you believe free enterprise is the best economic system?

The President. I firmly believe that the free enterprise system has proved itself the most effective in promoting economic growth and the welfare of the citizens of those countries where it is practiced. The free enterprise system is inherently linked to a democratic society. Just as people benefit from a free exchange of ideas in the political marketplace, so do they benefit from the freedom to "vote" by expressing their choices in a free market. A free market system ensures an efficient allocation of resources in response to the needs and wishes of the population and fosters creative energies in the productive sector.

U.S.-France Relations

Q. Is France's geographic position important for U.S. defense?

The President. Of course France's geography is important for Western defenses. But we value France as an ally for many reasons—our shared values, common adherence to democratic principles, and our mutual commitments to the prevention of Soviet attainment of military advantage. French forces in metropolitan France, as well as those in West Germany, play an important role in the defense of allied Europe. Although not integrated into NATO's military command structure, French forces can contribute effectively to the overall defense of the West and thus help deter any war in Europe.

Q. Can France count on the U.S. if it were attacked, even though the U.S. might be at risk?

The President. Frankly, I find the question puzzling. France is America's oldest ally. You fought by our side in our War of Independence. We fought by yours in this country's two most bloody world conflicts. We owe each other our very national existence. We are each pledged, through the North Atlantic Treaty, to treat an attack upon the other as an attack upon ourselves. I assure you America forgets neither our common history, nor our current commitments.

I know there are those who cast doubt upon the durability of America's commitment to Europe. Yet on my side of the Atlantic there is no doubt that America's security, its prosperity, and its freedom are inextricably linked to those of our European partners. Nearly a million American dough-boys arrived in France in World War I with the greeting, "Lafayette, we are here." A quarter of a million American soldiers, sailors, and airmen are in Europe today, as they have been for more than 30 years, the visible evidence of our continuing solidarity. Today America still says to Europe, "We are here, and we will stay as long as we are needed and wanted."

Q. How do you see the French when you think about them?

The President. I think of the French Revolution, the Rights of Man, and our common defense of democratic values for two centuries. Of course, no one who has ever visited France can forget the beauty of the country or the ingenuity and creativity of its people. But for me, France is, above all, the wellspring of Western culture and democratic ideas, and our ally, today as in the past, in their defense.

Significant U.S. Achievements

Q. What is the most significant American achievement of the last 20 years? Of the last 4 years?

The President. Certainly, our most significant achievement over the past 20 years—and it is one we share with others—must be the preservation and promotion of democracy. The solidarity of the Atlantic alliance has provided Europe the longest period of peace in its modern history, during which the West has achieved the greatest human

health, longevity, and prosperity in mankind's recorded experience. Other areas of the globe have been less fortunate. Yet everywhere the market economy system is increasingly seen as the most effective instrument for growth, and everywhere democracy is the inspiration and aspiration of mankind.

In the past 4 years, we have reinforced these achievements in many ways—by reinvigorating the American economy; by restoring America's faith in itself, in its institutions, and in its role in the world. We have begun, with our allies, to restore Western defenses and have set forward a comprehensive program for arms control.

Perhaps the most important specific step in this regard was the NATO alliance's implementation of the decision it took in December 1979 to restore the balance in intermediate-range nuclear missiles. Facing an unprecedented Soviet campaign of propaganda and intimidation, combined with a Soviet refusal to negotiate equitable limitations, the alliance stuck together and began the deployment of cruise and Pershing II missiles on time.

The resolute support of the French Government made an important contribution to Western solidarity on this crucial issue. As a result, the alliance is, I feel, stronger and more cohesive today than at any time in its recent history.

Note: As printed above, the questions and answers follow the White House press release.

Remarks at a Reagan-Bush Rally in Little Rock, Arkansas
November 3, 1984

The President. Thank you. Thank you very much.

Audience. 4 more years! 4 more years! 4 more years!

The President. That's what I came here to talk to you about. [*Laughter*]

Thank you very much. Thank you, ladies and gentlemen. It's wonderful to be in Arkansas. And if I have my history correct, it's

wonderful to be the first President since Harry Truman to stay overnight here in Little Rock.

Well, I must say, I admire your spirit. You know, back just a few years ago when other people were burning our flag, you were waving it. I don't know if a President ever thanked you for that, but I'm proud to thank you.

It's good to be in the home State of the University of Arkansas Razorbacks. Now, I understand the Razorbacks have a big game this evening. How do you think they're going to do?

Audience. Win!

The President. Well, then I have another question: How do you think we'll all do next week? [*Applause*]

Well—but let's not any of us be complacent. I'm telling you quite frankly that if a gypsy were to look into her crystal ball and say, "Mr. President, you can either win easily on Tuesday; or win with fewer votes, but with a Congress that will help you," I would choose the latter, because if we're to solidify our gains, the gains we've made in these past 4 years, we'll need a Congress that will allow us to move forward—a Congress that won't insist on going back to the bad old days and the bad old ways.

Arkansas is called "The Land of Opportunity." And you have some wonderful candidates for the Congress that will help our entire country continue to be a land of opportunity for everyone. I want to talk to you about Ed Bethune, who's going to be the first Republican Senator from Arkansas since Reconstruction.

Now, I know that many of the good people of this State are Democrats, and I respect that tradition. I was a Democrat, too, for most of my adult life. But I changed parties when the leadership of the Democratic Party changed course. Its current leaders have made that once great party into the plaything of the left, the hobby of the elite, and the home of the special pleaders. They don't represent America anymore, the way they once did.

But people like Ed Bethune do. He believes in a strong, a united country, an America of pride and power. And he's for a strong national defense. He's for prosperity. And he's for lower taxes. And I don't think his opponent could make those same statements.

Now, his opponent, the gentleman who said in 1980, "If Reagan is elected, it will be an unbelievable and unbearable experience."

Audience. Boo-o-o!

The President. Now, it hasn't really been that bad, has it?

Audience. No!

The President. Well, my friend Ed Bethune answered his opponent by saying, "If Ronald Reagan comes to Arkansas, it will be an unbelievable and unbearable experience for David Pryor."

And we need the can-do spirit of Judy Petty in the House of Representatives. She's for the policies that will create economic growth. And she's often said, "Young people don't want a welfare check. They want a paycheck." Well, we need more of that kind of thinking in the Congress. And we need Congressman Paul Hammerschmidt, too.

Will you send them all to Washington to help us?

Audience. Yes!

The President. And please send Woody Freeman to the statehouse.

We want Arkansas' entire congressional delegation to be a part of the great renewal that we began in 1980, a renewal that followed the wise advice of a wise old President.

Abe Lincoln said we must disenthrall ourselves with the past—and then we will save our country. Well, 4 years ago, that's what we did. We made a great turn. We got out from under the thrall of a government which we had thought would improve our lives, make them better; but which we found tried to live our lives for us.

Four years ago we began to navigate by certain fixed principles. Our North Star was freedom, and common sense were our constellations.

We knew that economic freedom meant paying less of the American family's earnings to the Government. And so, we cut personal income tax rates across the board 25 percent. And those in this campaign who are telling you that those taxes were unbalanced and benefited certain groups more than others; they're lying in their teeth. We cut them across the board for everyone.

We knew that inflation, the quiet thief, and record interest rates were stealing our future.

We knew that our national military defense had been weakened. So, we decided to rebuild and be strong again, and to be prepared for peace. You know, it really was a second American revolution, and it's only just begun.

But America is back; America is on the scene, powerful in its renewed spirit, powerful in its growing economy, and powerful in its ability to defend itself and preserve the peace. And do you know something? That's not debatable.

Yet 4 years after our efforts began, small voices in the night are sounding the call to go back—go back to the days of drift, the days of torpor, timidity, and taxes.

Audience. Boo-o-o!

The President. I'm with you. And any of those rumors suddenly that are being floated around desperately in these last couple of days about some suspected tax increases from our side—over my dead body. Don't you believe it.

My opponent's understanding of economics is well described by his predictions. Just before we took office, he said that our economic program was obviously, murderously inflationary. And it was just shortly after he said that that we reduced inflation from over 12 percent down to around 4.

And then, just after our tax cuts were adopted, he said the most he could see was an anemic recovery. And that was right before the United States economy created more than 6 million new jobs in 21 months.

And then he said that decontrolling oil prices would cost you $36 billion. Well, one of the first things we did was decontrol oil prices, and the price of gasoline went down 8 cents a gallon.

Now, I've got it figured out that all we have to do to get an absolutely perfect economy is to get him to predict an absolute disaster. [*Laughter*]

He says he cares about the middle class. But he boasts, "I have consistently supported legislation, time after time, which increases taxes on my own constituents." Doesn't that make you want to be one of his constituents? [*Laughter*] He's no doubt proud of the fact that as a United States Senator he voted 16 times in the Senate to increase your taxes.

Audience. Boo-o-o!

The President. But this year he's outdone himself. He's already promised, of course, to raise your taxes. But if he's to keep all the promises that he's made in this campaign,

he will have to raise taxes by the equivalent of $1,890 for every household in the United States.

Audience. Boo-o-o!

The President. That comes out to a little better than $150 a month. That's like having a second mortgage, a Mondale mortgage. [*Laughter*]

Now, his economic plan has two basic parts. One—missed me.[1] [*Laughter and applause*]

Thank you. Thank you. But as I was saying, his economic plan has two basic parts. One, raise your taxes, and two, do it again. [*Laughter*] But I've got news for him. The American people don't want his tax increases, and he's not going to get them.

You know, first of all, his tax plan would bring our recovery to a roaring stop. A tax cut is the principal reason for the recovery that we're having.

Now, if my opponent's campaign were a television show, it would be "Let's Make a Deal." [*Laughter*] You trade your prosperity for what he's got hidden behind the curtain. [*Laughter*] And if it was a Broadway show, it would be "Promises, Promises." [*Laughter*] And if it were a book, you would have to read it from the back to the front to get a happy ending. [*Laughter*]

He sees an America in which every day is tax day, April 15. Well, we see an America in which every day is Independence Day, the Fourth of July. We want to lower your tax rates, yours and everyone's in this country, so that our economy will be stronger, our families will be stronger, and America will be stronger.

And I'm proud to say—on another subject—that during these last 4 years, not 1 square inch of territory in the world has been lost to Communist aggression.

Audience. 4 more years! 4 more years! 4 more years!

The President. All right.

Audience. 4 more years! 4 more years! 4 more years!

The President. All right. All right.

You know, the United States is more secure than we were 4 years ago.

---

[1] *The President was referring to the noise of a balloon bursting.*

But my opponent sees a different America. After the Soviets invaded Afghanistan, he said, "It just baffles me why the Soviets these last few years have behaved as they have." [*Laughter*] Well, there's so much that baffles him. [*Laughter*]

One year ago we liberated Grenada from Communist thugs who had taken over that country. And my opponent called what we did a violation of international law that erodes our moral authority to criticize the Soviets.

Audience. Boo-o-o!

The President. There is nothing immoral about rescuing American students whose lives were in danger.

Let me try to put this in perspective apropos of something I said earlier. This 1984 election isn't just a partisan contest. I was a Democrat myself once, for a long time, bulk of my adult life.

Audience member. [*Inaudible*]

The President. And I was just going to say, I hope, though, that there are many out here who are still members of that party, but who are here because they've found they can no longer follow the policies of the leadership of that party.

Back in those days, when that gentleman and I were members of the party—[*laughter*]—its leaders weren't in the "blame America first" crowd. Its leaders were men like Harry Truman and Senator Scoop Jackson and John F. Kennedy, men who understood the challenges of our times. And they didn't reserve all their indignation for America. They knew the difference between freedom and tyranny, and they stood up for one and damned the other.

Now, all across this country, in rallies like this, I've been speaking to people that I knew many were Democrats. And those who respect that tradition that I just mentioned, I say you are not alone. We're asking you to come walk with us down that path of hope and opportunity and in the traditional bipartisan manner of this country. Together, we can keep this land prosperous, secure, and free.

You know, last month an American woman, Kathryn Sullivan, walked in space. And then she made her way back to the space shuttle in which some of the great scientific and medical advances of the future will be made. Cures for diabetes and heart disease may be possible up there. I've seen the evidence in experiments already conducted, advances in technology and communications.

My opponent led the fight in the Senate against the entire shuttle program—tried to shut it off, kill it before it was born. And he called it a horrible waste. And we've committed America to meet a great challenge— to build a manned space station, and to build it within a decade. And that's—and I think that you'll all agree, what America needs is high tech, not high taxes.

I've probably been going on too long here, but——

Audience. No!

The President. Bless you. That isn't what you meant by 4 years—up here. [*Laughter*] Well, the point is, we were right when we made the great turn in 1980, right to take command of the ship, to stop its aimless drift, and to get moving again. And we were right when we stopped sending out S.O.S. from Washington and started saying U.S.A.!

Audience. U.S.A.! U.S.A.! U.S.A.!

The President. Thank you. The United States of America was never meant to be a second-best nation. So, like our Olympic athletes, let's aim for the stars and go for the gold.

If America could bring down inflation from 12.4 percent to 4, then we can bring it down further, from 4 to 0.0, and that's what we've going to do.

If lowering your tax rates led to the best expansion in 30 years—and they did—then we can lower them again, and keep America growing right into the 21st century.

If we could create 6 million new jobs in 21 months, then we can make it possible for every American—young and old, black and white—every American who wants a job will be able to find one.

And if local governments can establish enterprise zones to create economic growth, then we can elect people to Congress who will free our enterprise zones bill. This is a bill to go into the distressed areas, rural and in our great inner cities, and, using tax incentives, bring industry in there to provide jobs and get people off welfare and to bring prosperity to those areas. And that bill, for more than 2 years, has been buried in a committee in the House of Representatives under the direction of Tip O'Neill.

Audience. Boo-o-o!

The President. And you know something? I think that Judy Petty and Bethune, and your other Congressman there, I think they can bust it out of there. That bill will provide jobs for millions in the most distressed areas of America. And this we must do.

We're leading a revolution in technology, pushing back the frontiers of space, and if we give our workers the tools they need—I have always believed this and I believe it more than ever—give American workers the right tools, and they will outproduce, outcompete, and outsell anyone, anyplace, anytime in the whole world.

Our drive to restore excellence in education has reversed a 20-year decline in the scholastic aptitude test scores, and we're going to keep raising those scores and restore American academic excellence second to none.

Our crackdown on crime produced the sharpest drop ever in the crime index, and we're going to keep cracking down until your families and friends can walk the streets and not be afraid.

We've reversed the decline in our military defenses and restored respect for America. And we're going to keep this nation strong to protect freedom and peace for us, for our children, and for our children's children. I have to tell you, of all the things I'm proud of in this job, nothing has made me more proud than those young men and women that are in the uniform of our military today. They're the best.

And if we make sure that America remains strong and prepared for peace, then we can reduce nuclear weapons and, one day, banish them entirely from the face of the Earth.

Every once in a while, I see along the street people with nuclear freeze signs, and I know that my opponent has adopted that and I know they're kind of trying to heckle me. But I'll tell them something, and I'll tell you: Yes to a nuclear freeze. After we have reduced nuclear weapons down to a verifiable and equal level on both sides, then we can have a nuclear freeze.

And as we strengthen our economy and strengthen our security—strengthen the values that bind us—America will become a nation even greater in its standard of living, in art, culture, and learning; greater in love and worship of the God who made us and who has blessed us more than any people on this Earth have even been blessed.

Now, I ran a little short of time a couple of weeks ago on the debate. [*Laughter*] And I'd like to finish what I didn't get to say there. And this is to the young people of our country who are here with us today.

To all of you I'd like to say: You are what this election is all about—you and your future. And I've seen our young people all across this country, on campuses, in schools, in rallies like this, and I can tell you, your generation really sparkles. Your idealism and your love of country are unsurpassed.

And, you know, my generation and—well, there are a few generations between mine and yours—[*laughter*]—we have a sacred trust. And that is, when the time comes to turn the reins of government and this country over to you, we're going to turn over to you an America that is every bit as full of opportunity, hope, confidence, and dreams as we had when we were your age.

And the last thing I was going to say in that debate was: We're going to turn over to you an America that is free in a world at peace.

All of us together are part of a great revolution, and it's only just begun. America will never give up, never go back. We were born to be a kind of special place—I've always believed that—that this great land was placed here between the two great oceans to be found by a special kind of people from every corner of the Earth—people with a love of freedom that made them pick up and leave home and friends to come here for the new opportunity that was present.

We have a unique mission—to carry freedom's torch. To a tired, disillusioned world we've always been a light of hope where all things are possible.

And throughout my life I've seen America do the impossible. When I was a much younger individual we survived a Great Depression that toppled governments in many countries of the world. We came back from Pearl Harbor to win the greatest military victory the world has ever known. And in a single lifetime, my own, we went from the horse and buggy to sending astronauts to the Moon.

But as a people, we Americans have fought harder, paid a higher price, done more to advance the freedom and dignity of man than any people who ever lived on this Earth. And America's future will always be great because our nation will always be strong. And our nation will be strong because our people are free. And our people will be free because we're united. "One people, under God, with liberty and justice for all." We're the home of the free because we're the land of the brave.

You have honored me greatly. I've been honored these past 4 years that you allowed me to serve you in that period of time. But much remains to be done, and we must continue to build upon the new beginning that we started 4 years ago. So, I have come here to ask for your support and to ask for your vote. [*Applause*]

All right. But now, let me ask one more thing. Don't send me back there alone. Send these people here, and send this one to the statehouse. I know what Governors mean in a National Government, having been one myself.

And let me tell you, stop looking at the polls—they scare me—because I think you might decide that—well, you've got something better to do, you don't need to vote on Tuesday.

Audience. No!

The President. President Dewey told me we should never get complacent or over-confident. [*Laughter*] So, go to vote, and get out the vote. America's best days are yet to come.

And now, one last line, that I know my opponent doesn't like at all—but you ain't seen nothin' yet.

Thank you. Thank you very much. God bless you all.

Note: The President spoke at 10:05 a.m. at the Statehouse Convention Center.

Following his remarks, the President traveled to Winterset, IA.

Radio Address to the Nation on the Presidential Campaign
November 3, 1984

My fellow Americans:

In 3 days this election campaign will be over, and America's future will be in your hands. As you discuss the election with family and friends in your homes and neighborhoods, I think there's one thing we can all agree on. We all want to vote for something, not against something. We want to vote for a better America, for a stronger country with our people pulling together; a future of peace, filled with hope and new opportunity, a future where our progress is limited only by our own dreams and determination and where Americans are working because America is working.

So, it seems to me the question to be asked is a straightforward one: Which team's record and proposals stand a better chance to enable you and your families to

enjoy a strong and successful future? Well, our opponents don't spend much time speaking about their record. And that's understandable. Their record speaks for itself.

After 4 years of controlling the White House and both Houses of Congress, they left America weaker, both at home and abroad. They would have us forget their legacy of an America second-best, double-digit inflation, record taxes and interest rates at home; growing instability and threats to peace abroad. I'd be willing to forget that record, too, if they weren't so bound and determined to give us more of that medicine that made us sick.

As for their new proposals, they differ from their old ones in only one respect: They've promised more. They will spend more, and they will raise your taxes much higher, the equivalent of $1,890 per household, more than $150 per month.

Now, my opponent wants very badly to make you believe his enormous tax increase proposal won't hurt your families. That's what his commercials say. And those commercials are every bit as believable as the ones he ran portraying himself as a person committed to a strong national defense, standing on the deck of a carrier, even though he voted against them, with F–14 fighters, which he also voted against, and beside American enlisted men, whose salary increases he opposed.

Our opponents are determined to bring back even more big taxing and spending than before. And if they regain control of this government, Americans may look back on our term as one brief oasis of prosperity in an endless desert of worsening inflation and recession.

Yes, their intentions are good. But good intentions aren't good enough. Their policies made America weak before. They would make us weak again today, and even weaker still in the future.

America can do better, much better. And the fact is, America is doing better. The principal difference is, our vision for America will let the eagle soar. Theirs will return us to the days of the sore eagle.

We still face great problems, but today our economy is stronger than 4 years ago because we've cut your tax rates, brought inflation and interest rates down, and created 6 million new jobs. And America is more secure, because we're rebuilding our defenses and our alliances to ensure peace through strength.

Today the United States expansion is leading the world into recovery, and that contributes to a safer, more prosperous world. Respect for America and confidence in America are rising again. And unlike 4 years ago, the United States is deterring, the Soviets aren't advancing, and all this, too, contributes to a safer world and a better future.

We've made a good start, but it's only a start. We want to lower your tax rates further to create more jobs and opportunities for every American with nobody left behind. And nobody left behind means we must continue our efforts to modernize our older industries and to rebuild our inner cities and distressed areas of America, so every American who wants a job can find a job.

We've sponsored enterprise zone legislation, to encourage business development and creation of jobs in distressed areas. But from day one, our enterprise zone proposal has been held hostage by the House leadership, the very people who act as if they expect black and Hispanic Americans to march in lockstep with the Democratic Party.

I can assure all of you who want the opportunity to begin climbing the economic ladder, to build a better life: If you give us your support, we will never take your votes for granted.

I believe Americans are coming together with new strength, confidence, spirit, and unity. From the bottom of my heart, I thank you for allowing me the honor of serving you these past 4 years. I urge you to vote on Tuesday, and I hope you'll cast your votes for our team, our entire team, so we can make even greater progress in building a strong, secure future of opportunity for all of you.

Until next week, thanks for listening. God bless you.

Note: The President's remarks were recorded at the White House on October 31 for broadcast at 12:06 p.m. on November 3.

Remarks at a Reagan-Bush Rally in Winterset, Iowa
November 3, 1984

Audience. 4 more years! 4 more years! 4 more years!

The President. Thank you all. Thank you all very much. Being out here in what's a rather cool, brisk day, I thank you for a heartwarming reception. If I didn't know better, I'd think maybe you were cheering for a certain football team—the Hawkeyes.

Well, you know, I leave here and go to Milwaukee, Wisconsin.

Audience. Awww!

The President. And I think its pretty convenient, and I hope it's an omen for the future—the score at the half is tied 10 and 10.

Well, special greetings to one of the finest Governors, also, in our nation, my friend, Terry Branstad. And to Debbie Deitering, Miss Iowa of 1984.

But it's great to be back in Iowa, and its great to be here in Madison County and in Winterset, the birthplace of a man who was a great patriot and a close friend, John Wayne. When I think of the Duke and all the other great Americans who've claimed this State as their home, I have to agree with the writer who said that "Iowa is top choice America, America cut thick and prime."

And a heartfelt welcome to the fourth graders of Winterset Elementary School. A few weeks ago, you all sent me letters, and I want to share one with you right now. It came from Tyson Bean of 609 West Short Street. And Tyson wrote, "Mr. President, my mom and dad watch you on television every night they can. I watch you, too. I think it's fun. But then a couple of minutes after it starts, I have to go to bed." [*Laughter*] Well, Tyson, today I think you're going to be able to stay up until the very end.

You know, just 4 years ago we saw this once proud nation saddled with a rising tax burden, devastated by soaring inflation and interest rates, and racked by a wrongheaded grain embargo. And since then, with the help of Roger Jepsen and Chuck Grassley in the Senate and with Tom Tauke and Jim Leach and Cooper Evans in the House, we've worked hard to turn America around. We've cut inflation by two-thirds, lifted that grain embargo, lowered interest rates, and helped to give our country a new spirit of self-confidence and pride. And I believe we've made real progress. And let me ask your view. Do you believe that America is better off than it was 4 years ago? [*Applause*] Well, then I don't suppose

I have to ask, because I'm sure you believe, then, America's best days are yet to come.

Well, you have outstanding candidates for the Congress who feel just the same way. For 6 years Roger Jepsen has served in the Senate with honor and skill. His opponent, Tom Harkin, is one of the most liberal leaders in the House. I'm sure he's sincere in that, but I do know that he has voted repeatedly against strong defenses and against our economic program of low taxes and high growth. But your senior citizen—Senator—has helped to—not a senior citizen yet—[*laughter*]—that's me. [*Laughter*] But your senior Senator has helped to rebuild our nation's defenses and bring your tax rates down, not up. And no one has worked harder to help farmers make the transition from the ruinous policies of the past to a stronger, more secure future.

Roger has told me about the concern that Iowa pork producers have with the growth of Canadian hog imports into our country. Well, I want you to know that I have directed Secretary Baldrige to make absolutely certain that our pork producers are getting the fair shake that they deserve. And if unfair subsidies are being used to undercut you, we'll take action.

Roger stands proudly for all of you in Iowa. And I'll need Roger back in Washington, especially when the debate on new farm legislation begins next year, and so will the people of Iowa need him back there. So, will you help send him there?

Audience. Yes!

The President. Jim Leach and Tom Tauke and Cooper Evans are outstanding Members of the House. It's time we gave them some company. And people like Bob Lockard, Darrel Rensink, and the outstanding candidate for Congress from your own Fifth District, Jim Ross Lightfoot—I have to tell you, Jim's one of the finest candidates I've ever known. No one could love our country more or be better informed about the concerns of this district. And he and I have a little something in common: We both got our start in radio. [*Laughter*]

Well, on behalf of Roger, Jim, and your other superb candidates, I must tell you that if we're to solidify the gains this country's made, we'll need a Congress that'll help us do the job. Spread the word, get out the vote and, if you can—well, win 'em for the Gipper.

Abe Lincoln——

Audience. 4 more years! 4 more years! 4 more years!

The President. All right. All right. That's what I came here to talk to you about. [*Laughter*]

Abe Lincoln said we must disenthrall ourselves with the past—and then we will save our country. And 4 years ago, that's what we did. We made a great turn. We got out from under the thrall of a government which we had thought would make our lives better, and then we found out it wound up trying to live our lives for us.

Four years ago we began to navigate by certain fixed principles. Our North Star was freedom, common sense our constellations. We knew that economic freedom meant paying less of your family's earnings to the Government, and so we cut personal income tax rates by 25 percent. And contrary to what some of our opponents say, that was 25 percent across the board. No one got any special treatment. It was "even-Steven."

We knew that inflation, the quiet thief, and record interest rates were stealing your future. We knew that our national military defense had been weakened, so we decided to rebuild and be strong again to be prepared for peace.

It was a second American revolution, and it's only just begun. America is back, a giant on the scene, powerful in its renewed spirit, powerful in its growing economy, and powerful in its ability to defend itself and secure the peace. And you know something? That's not debatable.

Yet 4 years after our efforts began, small voices in the night are sounding the call to go back—back to the days of drift, the days of torpor, timidity, and taxes.

My opponent's understanding of economics is pretty well demonstrated by his predictions. Just before we took office, he said our economic program is obviously, murderously inflationary. And that was just before we lowered inflation from more than 12 to down around 4 percent. And then, just after our tax cuts, he said that the most he could see was an anemic recovery. And

that was right before the United States economy created more than 6 million new jobs in 21 months. My opponent said that decontrol of oil prices would cost you $36 billion. Well, one of the first things we did was decontrol oil prices, and the price of gasoline went down 8 cents a gallon.

Now, I've got it figured out that all we have to do to get an absolutely perfect economy is persuade him to predict an absolute disaster. [*Laughter*]

He says he cares about the middle class, but he boasts, "I have consistently supported legislation, time after time, which increases taxes on my own constituents." Doesn't that make you just want to be one of his constituents?

Audience. No!

The President. He's no doubt proud of the fact that as a United States Senator he voted 16 times to increase your taxes.

Audience. Boo-o-o!

The President. But this year he's outdone himself. Of course, he's already promised to raise your taxes, but if he's to keep all the promises he's made to this group and that during this campaign, he'll have to raise taxes by the equivalent of $1,890 for every household in the United States.

Audience. Boo-o-o!

The President. That comes out to better than $150 a month. That's like having a second mortgage, a Mondale mortgage. [*Laughter*] Now, his economic plan has two basic parts: one, raise your taxes; second part, do it again. [*Laughter*] But I've got news for him: The American people don't want his tax increases, and he isn't going to get his tax increases.

His tax plan would bring our recovery to a roaring stop. You know, if my opponent's campaign were a television show, it would be "Let's Make a Deal." [*Laughter*] You give up your prosperity for the surprise he's got hidden behind the curtain. [*Laughter*] And if it were a show on Broadway, it would be "Promises, Promises." [*Laughter*] And if his administration were a novel, a book, you'd have to read it from the back to the front in order to get a happy ending. [*Laughter*]

He sees an America in which every day is tax day, April 15th; we see an America in which every day is Independence Day, the Fourth of July. Now, we want to lower your taxes, yours and everyone's in this country, so your families will be stronger, our economy will be stronger, and America will be stronger.

Audience member. Thank you, Mr. President!

The President. You're welcome. [*Laughter*]

And America is stronger because of the recovery. I wish I could take credit for it, but the credit really belongs to the American people who came through our economic distress with courage, commitment, and strength. But we're not going to rest until the recovery has reached all Americans, including those who feed and clothe our nation and the world.

As one who lived and worked in this great State for a number of years, I know the farmers here as friends and neighbors. The long road that you had to travel and still have to travel is something I care about personally. You've been patient and understanding during these last years of hardship.

But our job would be easier today if we hadn't had to overcome the killer inflation of 1979 and 1980. Our job would be easier without those outrageous interest rates— 21½ percent—that we inherited. And our job would be much easier if Mr. Carter and Mr. Mondale had not imposed that ineffective and totally wrong-headed grain embargo that I mentioned earlier.

Now, let me pause here for just a moment because former Agriculture Secretary Bob Bergland, a top farm adviser to my opponent and the man who implemented the grain embargo, said something this past week that I've got to answer. He said, and I quote, "The impact of the grain embargo is a fairy tale." Those were his words, "a fairy tale."

Well, if they think that embargo was a fairy tale, let them come to Iowa. Let them go to Illinois and Missouri and Ohio, Kansas, and the rest of America to see how farm families have had to struggle to recover from that fairy tale.

The only thing that embargo [did] was to fill up your bins and empty your wallets. We don't intend to hide behind their ex-

cuses. We're going to work to recapture those overseas markets they lost. We'll not rest until interest rates come down even farther. And we're going to fight to keep inflation down, so farmers and ranchers aren't buried again by out of control production costs.

On another subject a little farther away, I'm proud to say that during these last 4 years not 1 square inch of territory anyplace in the world has been lost to Communist aggression. And the United States is more secure than we were 4 years ago.

But my opponent sees a different world. After the Soviets invaded Afghanistan, he said, "It just baffles me why the Soviets these last few years behaved as they have." Well, there's so much that baffles him. [*Laughter*]

One year ago we liberated Grenada from Communist thugs who had taken over that country. And my opponent called what we did a violation of international law that erodes our moral authority to criticize the Soviets. Well, there is nothing immoral about rescuing American students whose lives were in danger.

Now, let me try to put this in perspective. The 1984 election isn't just a partisan contest. I was a Democrat once, back in those days when I was back here in Iowa. I was a Democrat for the greater part of my life. But in those days, the leaders of the Democrat Party weren't in the "blame America first" crowd. Its leaders were men like Harry Truman; later, men like Senator Scoop Jackson and John F. Kennedy—men who understood the challenges of the times. They didn't reserve all their indignation for our own country, for America. They knew the difference between freedom and tyranny, and they stood up for one and damned the other.

To all the good Democrats all over this country—I've said this, I know, and I hope that there are many of you here, just as I was one, and as you maybe still are—what I want to say to all of you: I know you respect that tradition of your party. But I say now, "You are not alone." We're asking you to come and walk with us down that path of hope and opportunity and in that tradition in this country of bipartisanship, between us, we can assure a prosperous, a secure, and a free America.

Last month an American woman, Kathryn Sullivan, made history. She walked in space. And she returned to a space shuttle in which some of the great scientific and medical advances of the future will be made. Cures for diabetes and heart disease may be possible up there, advances in technology and communication. On those health experiments, I've already seen enough evidence to know that progress is being made, and we may come up with some cures that are absolutely impossible anyplace but to make them up in space.

And yet my opponent, in the Senate, led the fight against the entire shuttle program, called it a horrible waste. Well, we support the space shuttle, and we've committed America to meet a great challenge—to build a permanently manned space station and to do it within a decade. What this country needs is high tech, not high taxes.

Now, if there's something that you've got to do yet this afternoon, I've probably been going on too long here. But the point is, we were right when we made our great turn in 1980, right to take command of the ship, to stop its aimless drift, and to get it moving again. And we were right when Washington stopped sending out S.O.S. and started saying U.S.A.!

Audience. U.S.A.! U.S.A.! U.S.A.!

The President. Yes. All right. The United States of America was never meant to be a second-best nation. Like our Olympic athletes, this nation should set its sights on the stars and go for the gold.

And if America could bring down inflation from 12.4 percent to 4, then we can bring it down further, from 4 to 0.0. And we're going to do that. If lowering your tax rates led to the best expansion in 30 years, then we can lower them again and keep America growing right into the 21st century. If we could create 6 million new jobs in 21 months, then we can make it possible for every American—young and old, black or white—who wants to find a job to find one in this country of ours.

And if local governments can establish enterprise zones to create economic growth, then we can elect people to Congress who will free our enterprise zones bill. We have a national program—it's been buried in a committee in the House for 2 years—to use tax incentives to set up businesses in distressed areas and put needy people to work. And that's why we need some of these gentlemen on the platform to move Tip O'Neill out of the way and get that bill out on the floor of the House.

We're leading a revolution in technology, pushing back the frontiers of space. And if we give American workers the tools they need—I've said this and I've believed it all my life, and I believe it more than ever now: Give American workers the right tools, and they will outproduce, outcompete, and outsell any other workers in the world, anyplace, at anytime.

Our drive to restore excellence in education reversed a 20-year decline in the scholastic aptitude test scores. Well, we're going to keep raising until we have academic excellence second to none.

Our crackdown on crime produced the sharpest drop in the history of the crime index last year, and we're going to keep cracking down until your families and friends can walk on the streets at night and feel safe.

We've reversed the decline in our military defenses and restored respect for America. And we're going to keep this nation strong to protect freedom and peace for us, for our children, and for our children's children. And if we make sure that America remains strong and prepared for peace, then we can begin to reduce nuclear weapons and one day banish them from the face of the Earth entirely.

Every once in a while I see some signs about nuclear freeze, and I know my opponent has talked of this—nuclear freeze. Yes, we can have a nuclear freeze, just as soon as we have negotiated nuclear weapons down to a verifiable, equal level on both sides—then we'll have a nuclear freeze.

And you know, Roger Jepsen's opponent seems to have been disturbed somewhat about what he calls expensive monkey wrenches and so forth that the Defense Department is buying that they could pick up for a few pennies here and there in a store. Well, let me just straighten him out on something. Who do they think has found out about those high-priced tools and is doing something about it?

That's been going on for a long time. You didn't hear about it 4 years ago. We're the ones that have dug it up. We're the ones that have gotten out hundreds of indictments and hundreds of millions of dollars in rebates because of that kind of flaw.

As we strengthen our economy, strengthen our security, strengthen the values that bind us, America will become a nation even greater in our standard of living, in art and learning, and greater in love and worship of the God who made us and who has blessed us more than any people have ever been blessed in the world.

Now, a couple of weeks ago in the debate, I ran out of time and didn't get to finish what I was going to say. I'm going to finish it here. It has to do with the young people of our country who are with us here today, because you are what this election is all about—you and your future. Your generation—and I've seen so many of this younger generation of ours across the country, in their schools, on the campuses, and in gatherings and rallies like this, just like those young people that are here—and I want to tell you, that generation really sparkles.

Your idealism and your love of country are unsurpassed. And I believe, you know, my generation—and there's a few between mine and yours—[*laughter*]—well, we grew up in an America where we took it for granted that we could dream and make our dreams come true; that we could fly as high and far as our own ability and determination would take us. Well, that's the responsibility of my generation and those few others I mentioned. To you young people today, let me tell you, we have a sacred trust, that when the time comes for us to turn the reins over to you, we're going to turn over to you an America that is free in a world at peace, that offers all the hope and opportunity that we knew when it was turned over to us.

Audience. 4 more years! 4 more years! 4 more years!

The President. All right. All right.

Audience. 4 more years! 4 more years! 4 more years!

The President. All right. I'm game. But don't send me there alone, send these helpers there with me.

We're all part of a great revolution, and it's just begun. America will never go back, never.

You know, this land of ours was placed here, I've always believed, between the two great oceans, with a unique mission to carry freedom's torch. To a tired, disillusioned world we've always been a light of hope where all things are possible. And throughout my life, I've seen America do the impossible.

When I was a young man, we survived a Great Depression that toppled governments all over the world. We came back from Pearl Harbor to win the greatest military victory in world history. In a single lifetime, my own, we have gone from horse and buggy to sending astronauts to walk on the Moon.

We Americans, as a people, have fought harder, paid a higher price, and done more to advance the freedom and dignity of man than any other people who ever lived on this Earth.

Ours is the land of the free because it's the home of the brave. And our future will be great because our nation will be strong. Our nation will be strong because our people will be free. And our people will be free because we're united—one people, under God, with liberty and justice for all.

I'm deeply honored that you've allowed me to serve you for these last 4 years. But, as I say, much remains to be done. We must continue to build on that new beginning that we started 4 years ago. So, I've come here today to ask for your support and for your vote.

I just want to say one other thing. I've stopped reading the polls. They frighten me. President Dewey told me we must never get complacent. [*Laughter*] So, don't look at them. Tuesday, don't think your vote isn't necessary. Go to the polls and get everyone else to get out and get the vote.

Much remains to be done, but we'll continue. And so, here we are, down to that decision. America's best days are yet to come. And then, there are some people back there who might be unhappy with what I'm going to say now, but I'm going to say it anyway: You ain't seen nothin' yet.

Well, now, I know that some of you have some important business to attend to, a very big football game. So, before I go, let me wish all the best to two of Iowa's outstanding teams, the Harlan Cyclones and, yes, the Winterset Huskies.

All right. Thank you all. God bless you. Thank you.

Note: The President spoke at 2 p.m. at the Madison County Courthouse.

Informal Exchange With Reporters in Winterset, Iowa
November 3, 1984

Q. Why did you want to visit John Wayne's home, his birthplace?

The President. Why did I want to visit that?

Q. Yes.

The President. Oh, my goodness. We were very good friends, and I was a great admirer and respected and loved Duke Wayne very much.

Q. Did you ever work together in a movie with him?

The President. No. And in fact, the last words I just said in there to his daughter—that was one of my great regrets, that we never happened to get together in a picture.

Q. What do you think that he would have to say about Walter Mondale? [*Laughter*]

The President. Pretty much what I've been saying.

Q. What about the tax plan?

Q. How well did you know him, Mr. President?

The President. What?

Q. How well did you know him?

The President. Oh, I knew him very well, yes. As a matter of fact, I'll give you one little insight on him. Back at the time when the actors had the first strike they had ever had to take in the motion picture business, and I was president of the guild, Nancy sometimes would—nightly, even—would go about the business of the meetings and everything that we were having, and she would be upset by the press and some of the things that were being said about us. And Duke Wayne—and this was before we knew him well—our friendship came out of this. The phone would ring every morning, and we knew it was particulary bad. And it would be Duke Wayne, who'd just talked to

Nancy and say, "I just thought you'd like to hear a friendly voice," and then would say things to buck her up and all——

Q. Do you think he'd take the Green Berets into Nicaragua? [*Laughter*]

The President. [*Laughing*] No, he'd just go in by himself. [*Laughter*]

Q. Do an imitation of John Wayne.

The President. What?

Q. Can you do a John Wayne imitation?

The President. No, I wouldn't try that. I'm a little better at Jimmy Stewart. [*Laughter*]

Q. Why did you come to Iowa? Why did you come to Iowa, really? Do you really think you have the election wrapped up, so you needed to campaign for Republicans here in Iowa, or——

The President. Oh, the people here that know me better will tell you that I never think I have anything wrapped up. I'm a pessimist about that.

Q. Do you think you can pull this out for Senator Jepsen?

The President. Of course.

Q. He's behind, according to the polls.

The President. Well, I don't believe those polls.

Q. Well, you're ahead, according to the polls.

The President. Well, I don't believe those either. [*Laughter*]

Q. Do you think you're going to lose?

The President. That's why I'm still campaigning. He's been a fine Senator. I'm sure the people of Iowa are going to see that he's back there.

Q. Mr. President, when you—[*inaudible*].

Q. [*Inaudible*]—making any predictions, now?

Q. Mr. President, when you said this

morning that taxes would be raised "over your dead body," did you mean to deny the Washington Post story that said that some people in the Treasury Department are preparing a plan to eliminate the deductions for State taxes?

The President. Well, Don Regan has already rejected that. The truth is, I have seen nothing of what they—they're looking at everything. I have seen what they were looking at, but I used that expression because it is an expression that means—as definitely as I can say it—that I am opposed to tax increases and will continue to be so. Right after I said it, I will admit, I hoped that no one took me literally. [*Laughter*]

Q. The Treasury Department is planning tax changes that would raise certain people's rates. The Treasury Department has these plans.

The President. Well, they may be things they're looking at, and we won't know until we're presented with the recommended plan. But we're not going to raise peoples' rates.

Q. Well, you're not for wiping out deductions though, are you?

The President. What?

Q. You're not for wiping—I mean, you're not against wiping out some of the deductions?

The President. Well, I haven't seen anything, Helen [Helen Thomas, United Press International], of what they're talking about. If they're talking about some compensating factor, remember, we want, also, simplification of the tax which has become so complex. And so, if they're looking at something of that kind where—it's got to be an even trade. We're not going to, under the guise of reform, turn around and have that reform mean that people are going to have their taxes raised.

Q. Mr. President, 3 days to go—you know you're ahead—a big victory?

The President. What?

Q. A big victory?

The President. I'd think it was big if it was only by one vote. [*Laughter*]

Q. Why are you suppressing the CIA manual findings until after the election?

The President. We're not. We turned them over to the—the oversight—the commission—the oversight commission of all intelligence. And Casey's been very forthcoming in his statements about it. And I think you're going to find that it was all a great big scare, and that there was nothing in that manual that had anything to do with assassinations or anything of that kind.

Q. Well, it told them how to proceed on assassinations.

The President. No.

Q. Well, you've read the manual now?

The President. What?

Q. You've read the manual now?

The President. No. But I know enough about the reports that have been made— some of the members in the intelligence committees in the Congress. And, no, there was nothing in that manual that talked assassination at all.

Q. Will you release that report when it gets to you, even if it's before the election?

The President. Sure, why not? Because I think it's going to clear the air——

Q. But, sir, it said "neutralize," didn't it? Isn't that the same thing?

The President. What?

Q. Didn't the manual say "neutralize?" And can't that be construed as meaning assassination?

The President. I suppose you could construe it any number of—several ways. But in the context in which it was recommended, actually, that was not the choice, the original choice of the word. The real word was "remove," meaning remove from office. If you came into a village or town, remove from office representatives of the Sandinista government. When they translated it into the Spanish, they translated it "neutralize" instead of "remove." But the meaning still remains the same.

Q. Well, how would you go about doing that without violence and force?

The President. No. You just say to the fellow that's sitting there in the office, "You're not in the office anymore." [*Laughter*]

Q. Mr. President, how did you feel when the Soviets implied that we had something to do with Indira Gandhi's assassination?

The President. I think it was probably the world's biggest cheap shot in a long, long time. They know better, of course. And I think to take advantage—I know that human life doesn't mean much to them—but to take advantage of a tragedy of this kind to try and gain some political advantage—it was a cheap shot.

Q. Is that why Shultz is not meeting with the Deputy Minister over there?

The President. I don't know that.

Q. Did you convey this word to the Soviets?

The President. They have been told that we don't like it.

Q. Thank you.

The President. Okay. All right.

Note: The exchange began at 3 p.m. as the President was completing a tour of the boyhood home of John Wayne.

Following the exchange, the President traveled to Milwaukee, WI.

Remarks at the Wesley Park Senior Center in Milwaukee, Wisconsin
November 3, 1984

Well, thank you, ladies and gentlemen, thank you very much. I'm a dessert man, myself, but—[*laughter*]—but I suppose it's really better for me that I didn't get to finish it, but it's delicious.

Well, it's very good to be in Milwaukee, and it's a joy to visit this Wesley—or Welsley Park retirement home. Nancy and I thank you for inviting us. And I would like to formally say hello to all of you octogenarians, nonagenarians, and, of course, the kids—my fellow septuagenarians. [*Laughter*] Did I get that right? I don't say those words very often—[*laughter*]—and I tend to mispronounce them, because I don't think in those terms.

I think I've just seen the things that you've made at the Christmas Bazaar, and I can see that your attitude toward life is similar to the fellow who said that—and this was pretty good advice—"old age is 15 years from where I am now." [*Laughter*] Do you remember the great baseball pitcher Satchel Paige? He once asked, "How old would you be if you didn't know how old you was?" [*Laughter*] Well, think about it—I did. That's why I've been 39 for the last 34 years. [*Laughter*]

But one of them—is something that I think has been the—some things I want to speak about just briefly, and one of them, I think, is the most disturbing part of the election campaign—the eagerness of some, for political purposes, to demagogue on the issue, actually, of Social Security. And it really leaves me steaming when they try to portray that some of us are having some plans in which secretly we're going to do something about depriving people who are dependent on that particular program.

When we came into office the problem was Social Security was facing bankruptcy. And we tried to get a bipartisan program together to salvage the program, and after the 1982 election, finally they agreed—when we had to borrow $17 billion to—so the checks wouldn't bounce. And I feel that the people in Social Security, who contributed all their lives in that program, invested, entrusted their money to the Government—and now, I want to make one thing plain, and I hope to be able to talk to my contemporaries about this, and say this, and that is: There is no secret plan to do anything about depriving people who are dependent on Social Security, and there never will be as far as I have anything to say about it.

Those who are dependent on this program are going to be able to depend on it. And we have now had that bipartisan get-together, and the program is sound fiscally for as far as we can see into the future, into the next century.

Now, there's another thing I want to talk about for just a second here. Most of us have had children and helped bring them up, one way or another, give them support and encouragement, teaching them. And now in traveling over the country in these past few months—and when I was Governor of California, there seemed to be a different era with the young people than there is now. I think you'd like to know if you had the opportunity to be on a campus or see them, today's young people are just the most wonderful young people that I can ever remember seeing. They're filled with patriotism and a love of country. They're serious about their lives and their wanting an opportunity and to get ahead. And it's just a magnificient thing to see. And you'd all be very proud.

Now, I mentioned that other time when I was Governor. I also would like to talk for just a moment about us and our generation. While I was Governor, that was in the era when I was being hung on a number of campuses in effigy, and they were burning flags and the school buildings down and so forth. But one day I got a demand from some student officers on the University of California nine campuses, a demand to see me. Well, if I went near the campus, I started a riot, so I was delighted.

Well, they came in in the uniform of the day, most of them barefoot, torn T-shirts, blue jeans, slouched into some chairs. And then one of them, as the spokesman, started in. And he said, "Governor, it's impossible for you to understand our generation." Well, I tried to pass it off, something that we all know. I said, "Well, we know more about being young than we do about being old." And he said, "No, I'm serious." He said, "You can't understand your own sons and daughters. You didn't grow up in an era in which there was instant electronic communications, computers figuring in seconds what it used to take people months and even years to figure, jet travel, space journeys out to the Moon, and so forth."

Well, he went on just long enough—usually, you know, the answer comes to you after you've gone home and you say, "I wish I'd said this." Well, he talked just long enough that the Lord blessed me with the answer. And when he paused for breath, I interrupted him, because I'd been thinking about something all the time he was saying these things. And I said, "You're absolutely right. We didn't have these things when we were your age. We invented them." It sure did change the subject in a hurry. [*Laughter*]

Now, I want to say one more thing just about us, and some of it came from that

particular dissertation on thinking of that answer. There have only been a few generations in all history in which a single generation presided over a great transition period. The young people of today are going to see things that we probably can't even imagine. They're going to see many marvels and wonders. They will never see, however, the transition that we saw, that in our single lifetime, we went from the horse and buggy to landing men on the Moon, to space travel, to all of this. And I can still remember the phones that you cranked to get the operator and say, "Number, please." And now they don't even have cords on them, if you want to get one of that kind, but any, whatever it's named.

And so, I think that we have nothing to apologize for. Those people who want to say, "Well, the people that went ahead of us, they didn't leave this or that for us." I think this generation of ours, we can sit back and smile easily, because—I've been saying to some people out on the road—I don't think anyone has ever done more to give dignity and freedom to our fellow man than we have in this, our single lifetime.

So, I think we have much to be proud of. And it's good to be here, and it's good to see all of you. And whatever happens on Tuesday, it's been a great honor to serve the past 4 years as your President. And it's something that I will treasure all my life. And I thank you for that.

So, I won't take any more of your time now, but thank you again for letting us be here with you.

And I'll tell you—and you'll all understand this, too—a dear friend of ours, George Burns—you know George—and he's still going, and he's making another movie in which, this time he's going to play God *and* the devil. [*Laughter*] But George has not only been a dear friend all my life, but he has become a great hero to me—he calls me "Kid." [*Laughter*]

Thank you all very much.

Note: The President spoke at 6:10 p.m. in the center's dining room. Prior to his remarks, the President was given a tour of the center's bazaar and had dinner with center members.

Remarks at a Reagan-Bush Rally in Milwaukee, Wisconsin
November 3, 1984

Audience. 4 more years! 4 more years! 4 more years!

The President. Thank you. That's what I came here to talk to you about.

Well, thank you all for a most heartwarming reception, and it's great to be back in Milwaukee, home of the Brewers and the Bucks and the best breweries in America. And it's great to be back in a State where your people vote in one voice—or unite in one voice, I should say—"On, Wisconsin." You know, that's the song, the fight song of the university—but when I was playing football many years ago in a high school down in Illinois, it was also our song. And all over the country I found more school bands that have made your song, their song. So, you have some universal music.

Well, yours is a beautiful State, of course. It's a wonderful, natural beauty of rivers and hills and valleys. But the best thing about Wisconsin is you, her people. I'm happy to be here with the sons and daughters of Wisconsin's immigrants, brave people who have followed their dreams to America, pushed back our frontiers, and built strong and thriving cities like this one.

Your church and the lovely mural here behind me remind us of our proud heritage, remind us how blessed we are to live in this land of hope and in a new world where all things are possible.

Audience member. Mr. President, I have a question for you.

Audience. Boo-o-o! 4 more years! 4 more years! 4 more years!

The President. Well, let me just suggest— let me just suggest that I go ahead, and maybe—maybe I'll answer your question in the remarks that I make here tonight.

Audience member. [*Inaudible*]

Audience. 4 more years! 4 more years! 4 more years!

The President. So, just listen, and see if it doesn't get answered and then—you know.

Audience member. One question——

The President. You know—shall I take the one question? All right.

Audience. No!

The President. What?

Audience member. [*Inaudible*]

The President. What? I don't know what you're—what? Don't?

Audience. No!

The President. All right. Okay. All right.

But we see this new hope of our country alive in the new patriotism and idealism of our young people, people like Kevin Hermening, who I know is down there. Yes, there he is. Kevin, as you know, was the youngest of our Americans taken hostage in Iran 5 years ago. He's traveled in 8 States speaking about his appreciation of America. And, Kevin, we appreciate what you're doing for America.

But I've come to ask for your support today for some of America's—or Wisconsin's finest, who are helping us build a better American future. And one of the bright stars in the United States Senate is not running this year. He's your own Bob Kasten. And I know that Bob agrees with me that we've got to keep America moving forward by reflecting all of Wisconsin's strong Republican Congressmen—electing them, I should say—Jim Sensenbrenner, Toby Roth, Tom Petri, and Steve Gunderson. And I wish I had time today to tell you how important each of them has been to our fight for the future. But please take it from me, America and Wisconsin need them back in Washington. Please see that they all get back there with us.

And then I can tell you also that we need—they need some company back there. So, what we need are more Republicans in the Congress to turn up the heat on Tip O'Neill. So, I'm hoping that come next January, thanks to your great efforts, we'll be seeing Peter Jansson, Dr. Albert Wiley, Dr. Robert Nolan, and Mark Michaelsen down in Washington, too.

And please help us by spreading the word to get out the votes. And if you can, win those races for the Gipper.

Audience. 4 more years! 4 more years! 4 more years!

The President. All right. And just like the Gipper said, "Wherever I am, I'll know about it, and I'll be happy." [*Laughter*]

Abe Lincoln said that we must disenthrall ourselves with the past—and then we will save our country. Four years ago, that's what we did. We made a great turn. We got out from under the thrall of a government which we had hoped would make our lives better, but we discovered that it was trying to live our lives for us.

Four years ago we began to navigate by certain fixed principles. Our North Star was freedom, common sense our constellations.

And we knew that economic freedom meant paying less of the American family's earnings to the Government, and so we cut personal income taxes by 25 percent. And contrary to what some are saying, that was across the board, "even-Steven" for everybody—no special groups favored.

We knew that inflation, the quiet thief, and record interest rates were stealing our future.

We knew that our national military defense had been weakened, so we decided to rebuild and be strong again—to be prepared for peace. It was a second American revolution, and it's only just begun.

But America is back, a giant on the scene, powerful in its renewed spirit, powerful in its growing economy, and powerful in its ability to defend itself and secure the peace. And do you know something? That's not debatable.

And yet, 4 years after our efforts began, small voices in the night are sounding the call to go back—back to the days of drift, the ways of torpor, timidity, and taxes.

My opponent's understanding of economics is well demonstrated by his predictions. Just before we took office, he said of our economic program, it is obviously, murderously inflationary. [*Laughter*] And that was just before we lowered inflation from above 12 down to around 4 percent.

And then, then just after we got our tax cuts, he said the most he could see was an anemic recovery. And that was right before the United States economy created more than 6 million new jobs in 21 months.

My opponent said that decontrol of oil prices would cost you $36 billion. Well, that was one of the first things we did—we decontrolled oil prices. And the price of gasoline went down 8 cents a gallon.

Now, I've got it all figured out that all we have to do to have an absolutely perfect economy is persuade him to predict absolute disaster. [*Laughter*]

He says he cares about the middle class, but he boasts, "I have consistently supported legislation, time after time, which increases taxes on my own constituents." Doesn't that make you just want to be one of his constituents? [*Laughter*] He's no doubt proud of the fact that as a United States Senator, he voted 16 times to raise your taxes.

Audience. Boo-o-o!

The President. But this year he's outdone himself. He's already promised, of course, to raise your taxes. But if he is to keep all the promises that he has made in this campaign, he will have to raise taxes the equivalent of $1,890 for every household in the United States.

Audience. Boo-o-o!

Audience member. But he won't have a chance! [*Inaudible*]—the election!

The President. Now, that prorates out to about, well, a little over $150 a month. That's like having a second mortgage, a Mondale mortgage. [*Laughter*]

His economic plan has two basic parts—two. First one, raise your taxes. Second part, do it again. [*Laughter*] But I've got news for him: The American people don't want his tax increases, and they're not going to get them. His tax plan would bring our recovery to a roaring stop.

If my opponent's campaign were a television show, it would be "Let's Make a Deal." [*Laughter*] You trade your prosperity for whatever he's got hidden behind the curtain. [*Laughter*] If it were a Broadway play, it would be "Promises, Promises." [*Laughter*] And if it were a book, you would have to read it from the back to the front to get a happy ending.

Audience. 4 more years! 4 more years! 4 more years!

The President. All right.

Audience. 4 more years! 4 more years! 4 more years!

The President. All right. You've talked me into it. All right. You know, he sees an America in which every day is tax day, April 15. And we see an America in which every day is Independence Day, the Fourth of July. We want to lower your taxes and everyone's taxes in this country so that your families will be stronger, our economy will be stronger, and America will be stronger.

And I'm proud to say that during these last 4 years—on another subject—not 1 square inch of territory anyplace in the world was lost to Communist aggression. And the United States is more secure than we were 4 years ago.

Yet my opponent sees a different world. After the Soviets invaded Afghanistan, he said, "It just baffles me why the Soviets these last few years have behaved as they have." But then, there's so much that baffles him. [*Laughter*]

One year ago we liberated Grenada from Communist thugs who had taken over that country. My opponent didn't cheer. He called what we did a violation of international law that erodes our moral authority to criticize the Soviets. Well, there is nothing immoral about rescuing American students whose lives are in danger.

And now if I can, let me try to put this in perspective. The 1984 election is not just a partisan contest. I was a Democrat once; in fact, for a good share of my life. But in those days, the leaders of the Democratic Party weren't in that "blame America first" crowd. Its leaders were men like Harry Truman, Senator Scoop Jackson, John F. Kennedy—men who understood the challenges of the times. They didn't reserve all their indignation for America. They knew the difference between freedom and tyranny, and they stood for one and damned the other.

Now, to all the good Democrats who respect that tradition I say—and I hope that there are some among you—I've said this all over this country when we have rallies of this kind. I know that in this country there are millions of patriotic Democrats who find they can no longer follow the policies of the present leadership of that party. Well, I say to you—if you are here—you are not alone. We're asking you to come and walk with us down that path of hope and opportunity, and in a bipartisan effort, which is a tradition of our country, between us, we will make sure that this is a prosperous, a free America.

Last month an American woman, Kathryn Sullivan, walked in space. And then she returned to a space shuttle in which some of the great scientific and medical advances of the future will be made. Cures for diabetes and heart disease may be possible up there, advances in technology and communications. I have seen evidence of those medical experiments that have been started already. And they're encouraging, and lead us to believe that we can—up there—find those cures, or make those cures, that we cannot make here on Earth. My opponent led the fight against the shuttle program in the United States Senate. He called it—that it was a horrible waste. Well, we support the space shuttle, and we've committed America to meet a great challenge—to build a permanently manned space station, and to do it within the next decade. What America needs is high tech, not high taxes.

I think I've been going on too long here, but the point is——

Audience. No!

The President. Well, that isn't what you meant by 4 more years, is it? [*Laughter*]

Well, the point is that we were right when we made that great turn in 1980. We were right to take command of the ship, to stop its aimless drift, and to get moving again. And we were right when we stopped sending out S.O.S. and started saying, U.S.A.!

Audience. U.S.A.! U.S.A.! U.S.A.!

The President. All right.

Audience. U.S.A.! U.S.A.! U.S.A.!

The President. All right.

The United States of America was never meant to be a second-best nation. Like our Olympic athletes, this nation should set its sight on the stars and go for the gold.

If America could bring down inflation from 12.4 percent to 4, then we can bring it down further from 4 to 0.0. And that's what we're going to do.

If lowering your tax rates led to the best expansion in 30 years, then we can lower them again, and keep America growing on into the 21st century.

If we could create 6 million new jobs in 21 months, then we can make it possible for every American—old and young, black or white—everyone who wants to find a job to find a job in this country of ours.

And if local governments can establish enterprize zones to create economic growth, then we can elect people to Congress who will free our enterprise zones bill, the national bill that is going to use tax incentives to go into distressed areas in the inner cities, and even in the rural areas, and bring in industry and jobs for those people who are presently wards of the Government, and bring them hope and opportunity. And it's been buried in a committee in the House of Representatives for more than 2 years, under the direction of Tip O'Neill. And that's why we want these candidates and these Congressmen of yours, returned to Washington, so that we can get that program out on the floor.

You know, I have thought that if we give our workers in this country the proper tools, the tools they need—and I believe this with all my heart—they can outproduce, outcompete, and outsell anyone, anywhere in the entire world, anytime.

Our drive to restore excellence in education reversed a 20-year decline in the scholastic aptitude test scores. Well, we're going to keep raising those scores and restore American academic excellence second to none.

Our crackdown on crime produced the sharpest drop in the history of the crime index. And we're going to keep cracking down until you and your families and your friends can walk on the streets of our cities at night without being afraid.

We've reversed the decline in our military defenses and restored respect for America. And I can tell you that of all the things in this job of which I might be proud, nothing am I more proud of than those young men and women of ours in the uniform of our military. They're special.

And we're going to keep this nation strong to protect freedom and peace for us, for our children, and for our children's children. And if we make sure that America remains strong and prepared for peace, then we can begin to reduce nuclear weapons and, one day, to banish them from the Earth entirely.

My opponent has talked of a nuclear freeze. And every once in awhile, I see people put posters up in front of me—Nu-

clear Freeze. Okay, a nuclear freeze—when we have reduced the nuclear weapons on both sides down to an equal, verifiable level, then we will have a nuclear freeze.

And as we strengthen our economy, strengthen our security, and strengthen the values that bind us, America will become a nation ever greater in its standard of living, in art and learning, and greater in the love and worship of the God who made us and who has blessed us as no other people have been blessed in this world.

And now, 2 weeks ago on the debate, I ran out of time. [*Laughter*] And I've decided to finish here what I didn't get to say there. And this is directed to the young people of our country who are here with us this evening.

You young people are what this election is all about—you and your future. I have seen them all across this country, on campuses, in schools, and in rallies like this. And I have to say, your generation really sparkles. Your idealism, your love of country are unsurpassed.

And I believe that, well, my generation—and there were a few other generations between mine and yours—[*laughter*]—our sacred trust is and what we must do for you. We grew up in an America where you could dream, you could make your dreams come true, you could fly as high and as far as your own ability and strength and talent would take you. And we—myself and those generations I mentioned—our sacred trust is, and we pledge to you—when it comes your turn, we're going to turn over the reins of an America that is free in a world that is at peace. And it will be an America in which you can dream and make your dreams come true and fly as high and far as your own strength can take you.

America will never give up and never go back—never. We were born to a special place, I think, this land of ours between the two great oceans, with a unique mission, and that was to carry freedom's torch. To a tired and disillusioned world, we have always been a light of hope where all things are possible.

And throughout my life, I've seen America do the impossible. We survived a Great Depression, when I was a young man—a

Great Depression that toppled foreign governments, many of them. Then we survived and came back from Pearl Harbor to win the greatest military victory in all the history of mankind's wars. In a single lifetime—my lifetime—we've gone from horse and buggy to sending astronauts to the Moon.

We Americans, as a people, have fought harder, paid a higher price, done more to advance freedom and the dignity of man, than any people who ever lived on this Earth. Ours is the land of the free because it is the home of the brave. And America's future will always be great because our nation will be strong. And our nation will be strong because our people will be free. And because we—we're free because we're united—one people, under God, with liberty and justice for all.

I'm deeply honored that you've allowed me to serve you for these past 4 years, but much remains to be done. We must continue to build upon the new beginning we started 4 years ago. So, I've come here tonight to ask for your support and ask for your vote. [*Applause*]

All right.

Audience. 4 more years! 4 more years! 4 more years!

The President. All right.

Audience. 4 more years! 4 more years! 4 more years!

The President. All right. But listen, don't send me back there alone. [*Laughter*] I want these people I've been talking about earlier here—I want your Congressmen that

are running, of course, for reelection now; and I want those candidates that are running for their first election here—I want them all back there with me, so that we can do those things that need to be done.

And the other thing that I would say to you is: I don't like looking at the polls any more. President Dewey told me not to get overconfident. [*Laughter*] So, please, don't get complacent; don't think your vote isn't necessary Tuesday. It's just that one simple thing: vote. And make sure your neighbors vote. Get everyone out to the polls. We need all those votes.

Audience. Landslide, U.S.A.! Landslide, U.S.A.! Landslide, U.S.A.!

The President. You taught them well. [*Laughter*]

Audience. Landslide, U.S.A.! Landslide, U.S.A.! Landslide, U.S.A.!

The President. All right.

Audience. Landslide, U.S.A.! Landslide, U.S.A.! Landslide, U.S.A.!

The President. America's best days are yet to come. And I know that my opponent doesn't like to hear me say this, but I'm going to say it: You ain't seen nothin' yet.

God bless you. Thank you very much. Thank you all.

Note: The President spoke at 6:36 p.m. at the St. Sava Serbian Orthodox Church Cultural Center. Following his remarks, the President went to the Milwaukee Hyatt Regency Hotel, where he remained overnight.

The following day, President traveled to Rochester, MN.

Remarks and a Question-and-Answer Session With Reporters in Rochester, Minnesota
November 4, 1984

The President. As you know, we just came from Milwaukee and, being that close, I just couldn't fly by Minnesota, particularly when I know our opponent's spending so much time in California. We're here to let the people of this great State know how much we care and that George Bush and I would be honored to have their vote on Tuesday.

From the very beginning we've been running a national campaign, taking our cause all over America. Everyone knows that we've never written off any State, nor taken any State for granted. And even more important, we'll never take the voters for granted. When people enter the voting booth, that's the most private and protected moment of them all.

I don't want this election to end without every American— and I sincerely mean all of them—knowing that we would like their support to continue the work that we're doing.

Now, I've seen some of these poll results, just as you have. The last time I looked up at Mount Rushmore, I didn't see President Dewey's face there. [*Laughter*] So today, once again, we want to urge our supporters to get out to the polls, to take their neighbors, to do all that's possible to see that our message gets to the people. And when they get to the polls, we would appreciate their support for the reelection of Minnesota's strong and effective Senator, Rudy Boschwitz. I need Rudy back in Washington again, as well as the two fine congressional candidates, Pat Trueman and Keith Spicer. And Keith is here with us today.

We need help to get tax rates down even lower, not up. We need help to keep America strong and always prepared for peace. We need help to keep control over the growth of government, so that we get back to the first principles in America: Here the people are in charge. And we need your help to get our initiatives passed into law— a balanced budget amendment, a line-item veto, enterprise zones, and tuition tax credits.

We need the help of every citizen to keep alive the fire of hope in America, to make opportunity our national watchword, so that we'll go into the next decade and the next century a strong, prosperous, and united nation, which will give the next generation the fullest of freedom in a world at peace.

End of statement.

Presidential Campaign

Q. Will the Gipper run up the score, Mr. President?

The President. What?

Q. Will the Gipper run up the score in the closing minutes?

The President. [*Laughing*] I don't think of it as running up the score. The Gipper would never quit before the final whistle.

Tax Reform

Q. Mr. President, you said yesterday that you would not use tax reform in any way as a guise for tax increases. In these closing days of the campaign, would you flatly, absolutely rule out, in a second term, supporting the idea of taxing unemployment or workmen's compensation benefits or changing the Federal deductions for State and local taxes?

The President. I just have to tell you that I have seen some of these reports and rumors about what is being considered. I have seen no report, as yet, directly from those who are working on the idea of tax reform. I know that the instructions to them are: we want a simplification; we want no increase in rates in the individual; if possible, to broaden the tax base to get some of that $100 billion that isn't presently being paid by people who owe it.

And I'm going to wait until I have the package in front of me and what the recommendations are. But again, as I say, one of the instructions is, this is not to become a guise for increasing taxes on the individuals more than——

Q. You are still holding out that possibility, then. Can you say, aside from what recommendations come to you, how you feel about the idea of taxing workmen's and unemployment compensation benefits, or changing those Federal deductions—[*inaudible*]——

The President. I have no idea that anything of that kind will be recommended to me. And I think that would have to—really, it would have to be proven to me that there was some excuse for doing such a thing. I don't believe that there is. I don't see——

Q. Mr. President——

The President. I don't see why the Government should be giving people money and then go through the expensive process of taking some of it away from them again.

Q. Mr. President, you have said—and you said again yesterday—that you would not raise taxes. You used the term "over my dead body." And at the same time, you back off a little bit, and you say, "Well, I'm talking about tax rates, not taxes." Is it still possible that people could have a tax increase, while having their rates reduced—[*inaudible*]——

The President. No, not the people presently paying taxes having their taxes increased. If there would be any increase in government's revenues, it would be in the broadening of the base to where we would then be getting some of the money that, as I say, is presently not being paid to the Government. And it's been estimated by many people that the amount is probably in the neighborhood of $100 billion of tax that is being avoided in the United States.

Now, those people who are honestly paying their taxes should not be penalized for that. And if there is a way that we can get some of that money that's not being paid, we're going to try to do it.

Latin America

Q. Mr. President, today's the day for elections in Nicaragua. Can you flatly rule out, if you're reelected, any kind of military intervention in Nicaragua?

The President. I've said many times, Bill [Bill Plante, CBS News], that there is no intention on our part whatsoever of troops going into Latin America anyplace, or any military help of that kind, nor has it been asked by anyone in Latin America. As a matter of fact, I think they would be very much opposed to it. They've expressed that feeling to us.

On the other hand——

Q. So, you're flatly ruling it out?

The President. On the other hand, should a President ever be in the position of, perhaps, encouraging more aggression down there by making such a statement? I'm just going to tell you that we have no plans whatsoever, nor any desire, to put forces into Latin America.

Q. What about increased aid, sir, for El Salvador and for the *contras* in Nicaragua?

The President. This would be in the manner of helping them, as we have been helping in the past. And we've proposed a plan—or had a plan proposed that we've adopted—and that is the plan from the bipartisan Kissinger-chaired commission that calls for a 5-year program of economic and social aid for about three-fourths of the amount, and about one-fourth to help them with their security by providing arms training and so forth. And we think that plan is what we want to follow.

Q. What about the *contras?* Are you going to continue to seek funding for them?

The President. Yes, because the Sandinista government is still supporting the guerrillas that are fighting against the duly elected government of El Salvador.

Press Coverage

Q. Mr. President, you never fully explained the joke you made last summer about bombing the Soviets. What prompted you to say something like that?

The President. I'm glad you asked that, because no one's ever bothered to ask. I was sitting in a room—granted, I should have been aware that there are no secrets. I was sitting in a small room, ready to do my radio broadcast, with a few of my own people around me, and actually I meant it as a kind of a satirical blast against those who were trying to paint me as a warmonger.

So, having to do a soundcheck, I simply said that for the soundman's benefit. I didn't know until later that a line had been opened, because one of you here complained—one of the TV networks or radio networks had complained that their line to the location was giving them some trouble.

I have to say that whatever my sin was in making a joke of that kind—even though it was intended in private for only a few people—I don't think that was any greater sin than the media, then, broadcasting it worldwide in such a way that it could create an incident.

Q. Well, you've spoken, sir, about the Russians losing 20 million people during World War II. Do you feel, in retrospect, that it was insensitive to make a joke like that?

The President. Whether it was right or wrong to make it, it was made in the privacy of a room and a few people close to me that I believed it would not go any further. And it was just on the spur of the moment I had to say something. And you get tired, sometimes, of counting to 10 as a voicecheck and so forth.

But, all right, I shouldn't have said it. But I will further emphasize, the media also shares in a responsibility for our national security. And I don't think they should have spread it. They weren't intended to hear it.

Black Voters

Q. Mr. President, do you think you've been fair to the American voter by not being specific on anything you're going to do after the election? I speak of taxes, I speak of possible adventurism abroad if you have a mandate. Also, you said that you don't want to write off any part of the electorate, but the blacks will not vote for you because they think that you have not been fair.

The President. And they think that because they do not know, nor have they been told, nor have we been able to get the message to them, of how much has been done. And I will charge right now that no administration previous to ours has done as much, has filed as many criminal charges for violation of the civil rights law, has done as much with regard to the helping of the historic black colleges and universities.

I could go on with more things that we've done. As a matter of fact, in our present employment training act, enterprise zones would be aimed very predominantly in a number of areas in the country at those people; the small business support, the fact that we have directed government contractors to use minority-owned firms—and that goes in the military, too, in the subcontractors in Defense—and we've vastly increased anything that has ever been done in the stimulation and development of minority-owned businesses.

Q. Mr. President, you said that many times——

Mr. Speakes.[1] We only have time for one more. It might be better to take it from the local press.

The President. Yes, you know, something——

Q. Mr. President, just one question on that, a followup on that. You've said that many times before, about the black situation, yet in all of your campaign appearances there are hardly ever any black people in your audiences. Why haven't you encouraged more appearances in black

---

[1] *Larry M. Speakes, Principal Deputy Press Secretary to the President.*

areas of the country to invite black people out to hear—personally from you—what your programs are?

The President. Well, in the areas where we've been, and in the cities that we've campaigned in, there's no block to anyone being present. But doesn't it indicate that, just what I've said, we're well aware that the overwhelming majority have been misled as to what our administration represents with regard to their interests. But we also know that all of those who do know of what we've done are highly supportive of us and are doing a lot to help try to get the message to the rest of the minority groups. But I will match our record against, as I've said, that of any other administration.

But listen, I think that what's just been suggested to me here is right. You people have at me other times, where is a chance for the local press?

Q. Mr. President, I'm a local press.

The President. Good.

Walter Mondale

Q. Perhaps we could get your explanation of the crowds that have been following former Vice President Mondale?

The President. What is my reaction to that?

Q. Yes. How do you account for his low standing in the polls, yet 100,000 people turn out? We've heard his explanation, what's yours?

The President. Well, I'm quite sure that—[*laughing*]—you know, this isn't going to be a scoreless game by the other side. And of course the supporters are coming out, and I would expect them to do that. And I'm not paying any attention to the polls. That's why I'm still campaigning right down to the wire as hard as I can.

Press Coverage

Q. Mr. President—[*inaudible*]—I understand that you haven't had a press conference since July. This will be one of the few that I understand that you've held. Is there a reason for that?

The President. Well, let me just say something else that no one's paid any attention to. If you add up the total time that I have done with regard to the press corps—standing under the airplane wing out there, meetings of that kind—that total time, since Labor Day, would amount to about 6 regular 30-minute press conferences. So the fact that we haven't called it a formal press conference and done it in the East Room of the White House, I think that that sort of belies the fact that I'm in a cocoon, and that I am not available to the media.

Vice President Bush

Q. Do you agree with Vice President Bush that your opponents are idiots for not agreeing with you?

The President. I was just going to cut this off, and I should have before that last question. [*Laughter*] No. I understand that he was referring to some hecklers in the crowd. And all I know is that the Vice President has been doing a yeoman job throughout the country in his campaigning, and I'm deeply indebted to him. And I believe him when he says that he was referring to hecklers in the crowd. And sometimes you do get a little impatient with some of them.

President's Trip to Minnesota

Q. Mr. President, sir, it's 2 days before the election, and you haven't been to Minnesota before in your Presidency. Do you think, perhaps, the Minnesota voters might look at this trip with a little bit of cynicism?

The President. It isn't cynicism. I just wasn't going to forgo the chance here. I haven't intervened much in the logistics; I have left it to those people who are planning campaigns as to where we go, and we can't go every place. But, as I say, we weren't going to miss this opportunity when we were this close.

But now, I've got to get going, because there are a lot of people down in St. Louis waiting.

Q. Why didn't you go to North Oaks, Mr. President?

The President. What?

Q. Why didn't you go to North Oaks, Minnesota, Mondale's home, instead of just coming to Rochester? [*Laughter*]

The President. Well, I didn't want to offend him.

Black Hispanics

Q. Mr. President, please, you know I feel discriminated against because people are talking here about blacks, and there are a million and a half black-Hispanic like me that have been shoulder to shoulder supporting your policy in Latin America. And the people say you have no support of the black. What about the black, naturalized American from Cuba, from Santo Domingo, from all Latin America who are people who—like others—who value and support your policies? Have they count or not?

The President. Well, they sure count with me. I'm glad that you made the statement here, and I hope that everyone recognized what you've just said. Thank you.

Q. What's the question? [*Laughter*]

The President. Thank you. God bless you. All right. Thank you.

[*The following segment of the question-and-answer session follows the White House press release.*]

Presidential Campaign

Q. Could you just take a minute to tell us how you feel about going into your last campaign, how it makes you feel to be heading home to California for the——

The President. A little bit mixed emotions. There's a certain amount of nostalgia with it, but it's sort of like you felt when coming up to your last football game of the season and knowing you weren't going to play football anymore.

Agricultural Policy

Q. I have a question for the local farmers, Mr. President. We're from Austin, Minnesota, a local station about 30 miles away from here. Farming is a big issue, obviously, here. What would another 4 years mean to farmers in southern Minnesota?

The President. I think that it would mean a great deal to the farmers, because I'm well aware of what their problems have been and the problems they're suffering right now. Those problems were the result of 21½-percent interest rates, of double-digit inflation for 2 years in a row, and of a very ill-advised grain embargo. And I don't think enough has been done in the past with regard to trade in other commodities. We have been working throughout the world now to stimulate markets. We canceled the grain embargo, as you know. Certainly, inflation has come down—and interest rates—and both must come down farther.

But all of this is aimed at—we're trying to develop world markets for our farm products. And the fact that we sold 23 million bushels—or metric tons, I should say, not bushels, metric tons—to the Soviet Union alone last year and have extended this to make another 10 million available right now—but then we've been dealing with Southeast Asia, and our trading partners—Japan.

I estimate that the sale of American beef to Japan will probably double over the next 4 years as a result of the things we've worked with them already. I think that the farmers should take a look at where they were under the previous administration, and how little was done for them and how much was done to them, and decide that, maybe, we're embarked on a different course.

Q. Will the grain embargo be emphatically ruled out in the next 4 years?

The President. What?

Q. The grain embargo—would that be——

The President. The only thing that I could ever see of the use of a grain embargo would be if this country were imposing a total boycott of everything, in which everybody in the country would participate. But to pick the farmers out as the hit, as the only people who are then going to participate in a boycott, that was decidedly unfair, and we're shooting ourselves in the foot.

Q. Thank you, Mr. President.

Note: The President spoke at 11:01 a.m. at the Rochester Municipal Airport.

Following his remarks, the President traveled to St. Louis, MO.

Remarks at a Reagan-Bush Rally in St. Louis, Missouri
November 4, 1984

Audience. 4 more years! 4 more years! 4 more years!

The President. Thank you very much. Four more years—that's what I came to talk to you about. [*Laughter*]

Well, I thank you, ladies and gentlemen.

Audience member. You're doing one hell of a job!

The President. Thank you. And I think you know how deeply grateful I am, not only to all of you for being out here but for a long-time and good friend, Bob Hope, to come here and interrupt his trip home to be here with us.

I'm proud to be here with you in St. Louis, a city of hope and expectations, the Gateway to the West. And I'd like to thank you for sending to Washington an individual who's been in the forefront of the battle to strengthen our economy and rebuild America's defenses, your fine Senator Jack Danforth.

You've also sent to the Congress three Representatives who are working hard to keep our economy growing and our country safe and secure. They're strong voices for responsible government, and come election day, please make sure you send back Gene Taylor, Tom Coleman, and Bill Emerson.

And I know you have other strong candidates. Carrie Francke is running in the Ninth Congressional District. Carrie is the kind of individual we can work with. It's a close race. We need your help, because we need Carrie in the Congress. And the same is true for Jack Buechner in the Second District. He's a former member of your general assembly. And Jack would be a major asset to our efforts to keep our taxes down and our economy growing. And here in this district, we have Eric Rathbone. We need Carrie, Jack, and Eric in Washington, and let's do our best to get them there.

Now—and if there's some people listening on the other side of the river, well, I hope they'll help us and do their best to keep Senator Chuck Percy in Washington.

You know, one of the accomplishments about which I'm most proud is that in these last 4 years we've reestablished the balance between Federal and State government. We tended for awhile to forget that this nation is unique in all the world. We are a federation of sovereign States, and we'd better keep it that way. And for that to work, we need to continue the strong leadership at the State level that's been provided to you by Kit Bond. And now we need John Ashcroft elected as Governor to continue that course. He's already done a fantastic job as attorney general, he can do even more as Governor. And to do that, he'll need the help and support of his fellow Republican statewide candidates—Mel Hancock, Roy Blunt, Wendel Bailey, and Bill Webster.

So, please help spread the word. Get out the vote, and if you can, well, win these races for the Gipper. And you know what the Gipper said. He said, "I'll know about it wherever I am, and I'll be happy." [*Laughter*]

We want a strong, a prosperous, and secure America. Abe Lincoln said that we must disenthrall ourselves with the past— and then we will save our country. Well, 4 years ago, that's what we did. We made a great turn, we got out from under the thrall of a government which we had hoped would make our lives better, but which wound up trying to live our lives for us.

Four years ago we began to navigate by certain fixed principles. Our North Star was freedom, and common sense our constellations.

We knew that economic freedom meant paying less of the American family's income to government, and that's why we cut personal tax rates by 25 percent across the board. I know there's been somebody out around saying that well, that tax wasn't fair. It benefited this group or that group. That tax was "even-Steven," across the board and benefited everyone equally.

Now, we knew that inflation, the quiet thief, and record interest rates were stealing our future. We knew that our national military defense had been weakened. So,

we decided to rebuild and be strong again to be prepared for peace. It was a second American revolution, and it's only just begun.

But America is back, a giant on the scene, powerful in its renewed spirit, powerful in its growing economy, and powerful in its ability to defend itself and secure the peace. And do you know something? That's not debatable.

And after—well, 4 years after our efforts began, there are small voices in the night, sounding the call to go back—to go back to the days of drift, the days of torpor, timidity, and taxes.

Audience. No!

The President. Well, you know, my opponent's understanding of economics is well demonstrated by his predictions. Just before we took office he said our economic program was obviously, murderously inflationary. And that was just before we lowered inflation from above 12 percent to down around 4.

And then, just after our tax cuts, he said the most he could see was an anemic recovery. And that was just before the United States economy created more than 6 million new jobs in 21 months.

My opponent said that decontrol of the oil prices—that government control of the oil prices, if we decontrolled it, it would cost you $36 billion. Well, one of the first things we did was decontrol oil prices, and the price of gasoline went down 8 cents a gallon.

Now, maybe all we have to do—I got it figured out here—to get the economy in absolutely perfect shape is persuade him to predict absolute disaster.

He says he cares about the middle class, but he boasts, "I have consistently supported legislation, time after time, which increases taxes on my own constituents." Doesn't that make you just want to be one of his constituents? [*Laughter*] He's no doubt proud of the fact that as a United States Senator he voted 16 times to raise your taxes.

Audience. Boo-o-o!

The President. But this year he's outdone himself. He's already promised, of course, to raise your taxes. But if he is to keep all the promises that he has made in this campaign, it would cost an amount equivalent to $1,890 for every household in the United States.

Audience. Boo-o-o!

The President. That's more than $150 a month. You know, that's like having a second mortgage, a Mondale mortgage. [*Laughter*]

Now, his economic plan has two basic parts: one, raise your taxes; the second, do it again. But I've got news for him: The American people don't want his tax increases, and he isn't going to get his tax increases.

Audience. 4 more years! 4 more years! 4 more years!

The President. All right. I wasn't going to, but you've talked me into it. [*Laughter*]

You know, if my opponent's campaign were a television show, it would be "Let's Make a Deal." [*Laughter*] You trade your prosperity for the surprise he's got hidden behind the curtain. [*Laughter*] And if his program were a Broadway show, it would be "Promises, Promises." And if it were a book, a novel, you would have to read it from the back to the front in order to get a happy ending. [*Laughter*]

He sees an America in which every day is tax day, April 15th. We see an America in which every day is Independence Day, July 4th. Now, we want to lower your taxes and everybody's taxes in this country, so your families will be stronger, the economy will be stronger, and America will be stronger.

And I'm proud to say that during these last 4 years—on another subject—not 1 square inch of territory in the world has fallen to Communist aggression. And the United States is more secure than it was 4 years ago.

But my opponent sees a different world. After the Soviets invaded Afghanistan, he said, "It just baffles me why the Soviets these last few years have behaved as they have." [*Laughter*] But then, there's so much that baffles him.

One year ago, we liberated Grenada from the Communists. And my opponent called what we did a violation of international law that erodes our moral authority to criticize the Soviets.

Audience. Boo-o-o!

The President. Well, there is nothing immoral about rescuing American students whose lives are being threatened.

You know, this 1984 election isn't just a partisan contest. I was a Democrat once; in fact, for the greater part of my life. And I have to believe—in this place, in a crowd like this—there must be many of you out there who are members of the Democratic Party. And I—back in—I know why you're here—because you know as well as I do, that back there aways, the leaders of the Democratic Party weren't members of the "blame America first" crowd. Its leaders were men like Harry Truman, Senator Scoop Jackson, John F. Kennedy—men who understood the challenges of our times. They didn't reserve all their indignation for America. They knew the difference between freedom and tyranny, and they stood up for one and damned the other.

Well, to all of you here who might be Democrats, who respect that tradition, I say: You're not alone. We're asking you to come and walk with us down that path of hope and opportunity.

We need——

Audience. 4 more years! 4 more years! 4 more years!

The President. All right.

Audience. 4 more years! 4 more years! 4 more years!

The President. All right. But to those Democrats that I've been addressing, let me just say—we need you. We need your help in what we're trying to do. And you and I together—all of us together in the best bipartisan tradition of this country, can keep an America that is secure, prosperous, and at peace.

Last month an American woman, Kathryn Sullivan, walked in space, and she made history. But then after she did that, she returned to the space shuttle in which some of the great scientific and medical advances of the future will be made. Cures for diabetes and heart disease—I have seen evidence already of the beginning experiments of medicines that can be produced up there that we can't produce here on Earth, advances in technology and communications. But, again, my opponent, as a United States Senator, personally led the fight against having a shuttle program. He called it a horrible waste.

Audience. Boo-o-o!

The President. Well, we support the shuttle program, and we've committed America to a great challenge. We're going to build a permanently manned space station and do it within the next decade. What America needs—America needs high tech, not high taxes.

Now, I've probably been going too long here.

Audience. No!

The President. That isn't what you meant by 4 more years, is it? [*Laughter*] Well, but the point is that we were right when we made our great turn in 1980. We were right to take command of the ship, stop it's aimless drift, and get moving again. And we were right when we stopped sending out S.O.S. and started saying U.S.A.!

You know——

Audience. U.S.A.! U.S.A.! U.S.A.!

The President. All right. You know, the United States was never meant to be a second-best nation. So, like our Olympic athletes, this nation should set its sight on the stars and go for the gold.

If we could bring inflation down from 12.4 percent to 4, then we can bring it down further from 4 to 0.0, and we're going to do that.

If lowering your tax rates led to the best expansion in 30 years, then we can lower them again and keep America growing right into the 21st century.

If we could create 6 million new jobs in 21 months, then we can make it possible for every American—old and young, black and white—everyone who wants to find a job, to find one in this country of ours.

If local governments and States can establish enterprise zones to create economic growth, then we can elect people like those I've mentioned earlier to Congress to help free our enterprise zones bill, a national bill, which has been buried in committee now in the House of Representatives by Tip O'Neill for more than 2 years.

Audience. Boo-o-o!

The President. We need that bill to provide hope for millions in the most distressed areas of America, and this we will do.

We're leading a revolution in technology in pushing back the frontiers of space. And if we give our workers the tools they need—I have always believed and I believe more than ever now—give American workers the proper tools, and they can outproduce, outcompete, and outsell anybody in the world, anytime, anywhere.

Our drive to restore excellence in education reversed a 20-year decline in scholastic aptitude test scores. And we're going to keep raising those scores and restore American academic excellence, second to none.

The crackdown on crime produced the sharpest drop ever in the crime index. And we're going to keep cracking down until your families and friends can walk on the streets at night without being afraid.

We have reversed the decline in our military defenses and restored respect throughout the world for America. And we're going to keep this nation strong to protect freedom and peace for us, for our children, and our children's children. And if we make sure that America remains strong and prepared for peace, then we can begin to reduce nuclear weapons and, one day, banish them entirely from the face of the Earth.

I know that my opponent has discussed nuclear freeze. And every once in awhile, I see a sign for it. Well, let me say this about nuclear freeze. When we have reduced nuclear weapons on both sides down to a verifiable, equal balance, then we will have a nuclear freeze.

And as we strengthen our economy, strengthen our security, and strengthen the values that bind us, America will become an even greater nation with a higher standard of living, with culture and art and learning, and greater in the love and worship of the God who made us and who has blessed us more than any people have ever been blessed on Earth.

And now, 2 weeks ago today, I didn't get to finish something I was saying in a debate. I'm going to finish now.

To the young people of our country who are with us today—you are what this election is all about, you and your future. Your generation really sparkles. Your idealism, your love of country are unsurpassed. I've seen you all across the United States, on campuses, in schools, and here in rallies, as you are here.

And I just want to tell you something. My generation and, well, a few generations between mine and yours, we have a sacred trust. We grew up in an America in which we just took it for granted that you could dream and make your dreams come true, if you are willing to go for them—that this was a land of opportunity, and it was denied to no one. Well, our sacred trust is, my generation and those of others I mentioned, to see that when it comes time to turn over to you young people the reins of this country, we're going to turn over to you an America that is free in a world at peace and in which you can dream and make your dreams come true.

All of us together are part of a great revolution, and it's only just begun. America will never give up, never go back. We will never be a second-best nation. This country was put here, this nation, between the two great oceans, so that people from every corner of the Earth, people who had a special love of freedom could find their way here. To a tired, disillusioned world, we've always been a light of hope where all things are possible.

And throughout my life, I've seen America do the impossible. When I was a young man, we survived a Great Depression worldwide that topped governments in many places in the world, but not here. We came back from Pearl Harbor and won the greatest military victory in world history. In a single lifetime, my own, we have gone from the horse and buggy to putting astronauts on the Moon.

And we, as a people, have fought harder, paid a higher price, and done more to advance the freedom and dignity of man than any people who ever lived on this Earth.

Ours is the land of the free because it's the home of the brave. [*Applause*]

All right. America's future will always be great because our nation will always be strong. Our nation will be strong because our people will be free. And our people will be free because we will be united—our people, one people, under God, with liberty and justice for all.

I'm deeply honored——

Audience. 50 States! 50 States! 50 States!

The President. All right. All right. I'm deeply honored that you have allowed me to serve you for these past 4 years, but much remains to be done. We must continue to build on that new beginning that we started 4 years ago. So, I have come here to ask for your support and for your vote.

But I just want to say—and with what you've just recently said about 50 States, I've been trying not to look at the polls because I looked up at Mount Rushmore, and I don't see President Dewey's face there. [*Laughter*] Don't be complacent. Day after tomorrow, don't think your vote isn't needed. Please, go to the polls. Vote. And if you're going to vote for me, don't send me back there alone. You send these other people that I've been talking about.

America's best days are yet to come. And I have something that I know my opponent doesn't like to hear—and I think there's a few people over here that aren't going to like to hear—but I'm going to say it anyway. I'm going to say it anyway. You ain't seen nothin' yet.

Thank you. God bless you all. Thank you.

Note: The President spoke at 2:12 p.m. at the Gateway Arch.

Following his remarks, the President traveled to Chicago, IL.

Remarks at a Reagan-Bush Rally in Chicago, Illinois
November 4, 1984

The President. Ladies and gentlemen— ladies and gentlemen——

Audience. 4 more years! 4 more years! 4 more years!

The President. All right.

Audience. 4 more years! 4 more years! 4 more years!

The President. That's what we came here to talk to you about. Thank you.

Ladies and gentlemen, there's no one in this hall that agrees more with what Governor Jim Thompson said about this Vice President than I do. And he's been working tirelessly in this campaign all over the country. But now, now, I have to explain so you'll understand that he and Barbara—I'm going to let them go now, because they've got a rally waiting for them down in Texas before this afternoon and evening is out. So, George and Barbara, God bless you and be on your way.

And now, while I'm also saying "thank you's," and it's a heartfelt thank you to Frankie—Frankie Avalon for what you've done—this change of schedule here. Bless you.

Governor Jim Thompson, Senator Charles Percy, Mayor Don Stevens, all our fine Republican Representatives—John Porter, Henry Hyde, and Lynn Martin—and outstanding candidates, thank you all very much.

It's wonderful to be back in my home State, Nancy's home State, back in the Land of Lincoln. And it's great to be in Rosemont and to be here in the house that Ray Meyer made famous, the home of the DePaul Blue Demons.

You know, there is a new winning spirit in Chicago led by Rick Sutcliff, Ryne Sandburg, and those wonderful Chicago Cubs. And Walter Payton and the Chicago Bears—it's good to see that the Bears are back and roaring.

But Nancy and I want to thank all of you for your heartwarming reception, and I want to thank you for your support—or help in—or support in helping us put America and our future back in the hands of the people. And, believe me, we couldn't have accomplished all we have without strong Republican leaders like Chuck Percy.

Chuck has defended the interests of your State with the same determination that he has protected the interests of our nation. And if we're going to build on the gains that we've made, we'll need Chuck Percy back there to help us do it. So, now, if by some chance you intend to vote for me, please don't vote against me by voting for Chuck's opponent. A vote for the Mondale-Simon ticket is a vote to go back to failed policies which gave us higher taxes, higher prices, and a weaker America.

Audience. Boo-o-o!

The President. And a vote for Chuck Percy, for our ticket, is a vote for America's future. So, please help, spread the word, get out the vote. And if you don't mind, win this one for the Gipper.

Abe Lincoln said we must disenthrall ourselves with the past—and then we will save our country. And 4 years ago, that's what we did. We made a great turn. We got out from under the thrall of a government which we had hoped would make our lives better, but which turned out to try to live our lives for us.

Four years ago, we began to navigate by certain fixed principles. Our North Star was freedom, common sense our constellations.

We knew that economic freedom meant paying less of the American families' earnings to the Government, and so we cut personal income taxes 25 percent across the board. And in spite of some of the loose talk on the other side in this campaign, that tax cut was "even-Steven" for everybody, and not for one particular group or the other.

We knew that inflation, the quiet thief, and record interest rates were stealing our future.

We knew that our national military defense had been weakened. So, we decided to rebuild and be strong again to be prepared for peace. It was a second American revolution, and it's only just begun.

But America is back—a giant on the scene, powerful in its renewed spirit, powerful in its growing economy, and powerful in its ability to defend itself and secure the peace. And you know something? That's not debatable.

Yet 4 years after our efforts began, small voices in the night are sounding the call to go back—back to the days of drift, the days of torpor, timidity, and taxes.

My opponent's understanding of economics is well demonstrated by his predictions. Just before we took office, he said our economic program is obviously, murderously inflationary. That was just before we lowered inflation from around 12 percent down to 4.

And just after we passed our tax cuts, he said the most he could see was an anemic recovery. Well, that was just before the United States economy created 6 million new jobs in 21 months.

My opponent said that decontrol of oil prices would cost you more than $36 billion a year. Well, one of the first things we did was decontrol oil prices, and the price of gasoline went down 8 cents a gallon.

Now, you know, I figured something out—if we can persuade—well, if we want an absolutely perfect economy, all we have to do is persuade him to predict absolute disaster. [*Laughter*]

He says he cares about the middle class.

Audience. Boo-o-o!

The President. Yes. But then, then he boasts, "I have consistently supported legislation, time after time, which increases taxes on my own constituents." Doesn't that make you want to be one of his constituents?

Audience. No!

The President. He's no doubt proud of the fact that as a United States Senator he voted 16 times to raise your taxes.

Audience. Boo-o-o!

The President. But this year he's outdone himself. He's already promised, of course, to raise your taxes. But if he's to keep all the promises that he has made in this campaign, he will have to raise taxes by the equivalent of $1,890 per household, every household in the United States.

Audience. Boo-o-o!

The President. Now, you know that's more than $150 a month. That's like having a second mortgage, a Mondale mortgage. [*Laughter*]

Now, his economic plan has two parts: the first, raise taxes; the second, do it again. [*Laughter*] But I've got news for him. The American people don't want his tax increases, and they're not going to get his tax increases.

Audience. 4 more years! 4 more years! 4 more years!

The President. All right.

Audience. 4 more years! 4 more years! 4 more years!

The President. Well, I hadn't thought about it, but you've talked me into it. [*Laughter*]

You know, if my opponent's campaign were a television show it would be, "Let's Make a Deal." [*Laughter*] You get to trade your prosperity for that surprise he's got hidden behind the curtain. Now, if his campaign were a Broadway show, it would be "Promises, Promises." And if that administration of which he was a part had been a book, you would have had to read it from the back to the front to get a happy ending.

He sees an America in which every day is tax day, April 15th. Well, we see an America in which every day is Independence Day, the Fourth of July. We want to lower your taxes and lower those for all the people in this country so that your families will be stronger, America will be stronger, this economy will be stronger.

I'm proud to say—on another subject— that during these last 4 years, not 1 square inch of territory in the world has been lost to Communist aggression. And the United States is more secure than we were 4 years ago.

Yet my opponent sees a different world. After the Soviets invaded Afghanistan, he said, "It just baffles me why the Soviets these last few years have behaved as they have." But then, there's so much that baffles him.

One year ago we liberated Grenada from the Communists who had taken over that country. My opponent called what we did a violation of international law that——

Audience. Boo-o-o!

The President. ——that erodes our moral authority to criticize the Soviets. Well, there is nothing immoral about rescuing American students whose lives were in danger.

But, you know, this 1984 election isn't just a partisan contest. I was a Democrat for a large part of my life, more than half of it. But in those days, the Democratic Party leaders weren't members of the "blame America first" crowd. Its leaders were men like Harry Truman, Senator Scoop Jackson, John F. Kennedy—men who understood the challenges of our times. They didn't reserve all their indignation for the United States. They knew the difference between freedom and tyranny, and they stood up for one and damned the other.

Now, to all the good Democrats who respect that tradition—and I hope there are many present, as there have been in meetings all over the country like this. I hope you are present, because I would like to tell you, you're not alone. We ask you to come and walk with us down the path of hope and opportunity. And in the bipartisan tradition of this country, between us and together, we can keep this nation prosperous, secure, and at peace. [*Applause*]

All right. Last month an American woman, Kathryn Sullivan, walked in space and made history. And then she returned to a space shuttle in which some of the great scientific and medical advances of the future will be made. Cures for diabetes and heart disease—and I have seen the evidence of some of the experiments already—to know that there is hope for that—that developments of cures up there that we cannot develop here on Earth. There will be, also, advances that we will make in technology and communication. But my opponent, as a United States Senator, led the fight personally against having a shuttle program. He said it was a horrible waste.

Audience. Boo-o-o!

The President. Well, we're for the shuttle program, and we're going to meet a great challenge. We're going to build a manned space station and do it within the decade. What America needs is high-tech, not high taxes.

Now, I've probably been going on too long here——

Audience. No!

The President. Well, all right. But the point is, we were right when we made our turn in 1980. We were right to take command of the ship, stop the drift, and get moving again. And we were right when we stopped sending out S.O.S. and started saying U.S.A.!

Audience. U.S.A.! U.S.A.! U.S.A.!

The President. All right. You know, the United States of America was never meant to be a second-best nation. Like our Olympic athletes, this nation sets its sight on the stars, and we go for the gold.

If America could bring down inflation from 12.4 percent to 4 percent, then we can bring it down from 4 to 0.0, and we're going to do that.

If lowering your tax rates could create those 6 million jobs, new jobs in 21 months, then we can make it possible for every American—or America to keep growing, right into the 21st century. We'll reduce them again.

You know, creating 6 million new jobs, as I said in the 21 months, can make it possible for every American—young and old, black and white—everyone who wants a job to find a job in this land of ours. And that is a goal that we will meet.

And if local and State governments can establish enterprise zones to create economic growth, then we can elect people to the Congress, those people I was talking about a little while ago, who will free our enterprise zone bill. We have a national bill to use tax incentives all over the country in distressed areas, to make it possible to have hope and jobs for millions of our people. And that bill has been buried for more than 2 years in a committee of the House of Representatives under the direction of Tip O'Neill.

Audience. Boo-o-o!

The President. We're leading a revolution in technology, pushing back the frontiers of space. And if we give our workers the tools they need—I've always believed this, and I believe it now more than ever—if you give American workers the tools they need, they will outproduce, outcompete, and outsell anyone, anywhere in the world, anytime.

Our drive to restore excellence in education reversed a 20-year decline in the scholastic aptitude test scores. Well, we're going to keep raising those scores and restore American academic excellence, second to none.

Our crackdown on crime has produced the sharpest drop ever in the crime index. And we're going to keep cracking down until your families and friends can walk the streets again without being afraid.

We've reversed the decline in our military defenses and restored respect all over the world for America. And we're going to keep this nation strong to protect freedom and peace for us, for our children, and for our children's children. And if we make sure that America remains strong and prepared for peace, then we can begin to reduce nuclear weapons and one day banish them entirely from the face of the Earth.

My opponent talks of a nuclear freeze. Every once in a while, I see banners thrust at me—"Nuclear Freeze." All right, yes—when we can reduce the nuclear weapons in the world on both sides down to an equal, verifiable limit, yes, we'll have a nuclear freeze.

And as we strengthen our economy, strengthen our security, strengthen the values that bind us, America will become a nation with a higher standard of living, even greater in art and learning, greater in the love and worship of the God who made us and who has blessed us as no other people on Earth have ever been blessed.

Now, 2 weeks ago, I didn't get to finish something I was saying on the debate. I'm going to finish it here.

To the young people of our country who are here with us today—you, you are what this election is all about, you and your future. Your generation—I've seen you all across this country, in schools, on campuses, in gatherings like this. And your generation really sparkles. [*Applause*]

All right. Your idealism and your love of country are unsurpassed.

And, you know, my generation—and there's a few between mine and yours—we grew up in an America where, for so long a time, we simply took it for granted, and it was true, that you could dream and make your dreams come true. It was up to you. Fly as high and as far as your own ability and talent and strength and determination would take you. But then we came into a time for a while there where there were people telling us that there was an era of limits and that things couldn't ever be again as they once were. Well, don't you believe it.

My generation and those other generations I mentioned, we have a sacred trust. And it is to turn over to you, when the time comes, an America that is free in a world that is at peace.

All of us together are part of a great revolution, and it's only just begun. America will never give up—will never go back. We were born to be a special place between these two great oceans with a unique mission to carry freedom's torch. To a tired

and disillusioned world we've always been a light of hope where all things are possible.

And throughout my life I have seen America do the impossible. When I was a young man we survived a great worldwide depression that made anything we've seen since look like a picnic. We survived that, although governments in many parts of the world were toppled simply by the force of that recession. We came back from Pearl Harbor and won the greatest military victory in world history.

And we as a people have fought harder, paid a higher price, done more to advance the freedom and dignity of man than any other people who ever lived on this Earth. Ours is the land of the free, because it is the home of the brave. America's future will always be great, because our nation will be strong. And our nation will be strong, because our people will be free. And our people will be free, because we're united—one people under God with liberty and justice for all.

I am deeply honored that you've allowed me to serve you for these past 4 years. But——

Audience. 4 more years! 4 more years! 4 more years!

The President. All right. All right. I will. All right.

Audience. 4 more years! 4 more years! 4 more years!

The President. All right. We must continue to build upon the new beginning we started 4 years ago. So, I have come here to ask for your vote and to ask for your support in doing that. And just as you were told earlier, I'll repeat: Don't read those polls anymore. Just don't get complacent. The last time I looked up at Mount Rushmore, President Dewey's face wasn't there.

Please get out and vote, and get your neighbors out to vote. And don't anyone decide your vote isn't needed and stay home. Every vote is needed.

And if you're going to vote for me, don't send me there alone. You send these other candidates and officeholders that I have already spoken of here today. And now——

Audience. Reagan! Reagan! Reagan!

The President. All right. America's best days are yet to come. And I'm going to say something—I know it drives my opponent up the wall, but I enjoy saying it—you ain't seen nothin' yet.

God bless you, and thank you all very much. Thank you.

Note: The President spoke at 5:12 p.m. at the Rosemont Horizon Arena.

Following his remarks, the President traveled to Sacramento, CA, and the Red Lion Motor Inn, where he remained overnight.

Informal Exchange With Governor George Deukmejian and Reporters in Sacramento, California
November 5, 1984

Governor Deukmejian. This is in honor of the fact that you are the first California Governor to become President of the United States. And so, I've declared this room, from now on, to be the President Ronald Reagan Cabinet Room.

Mrs. Reagan. Oh, George.

The President. Thank you very much, George. I can't tell you——

Governor Deukmejian. We're just very, very honored.

The President. ——how honored I am by that.

Mrs. Reagan. Very nice. That's very nice.

The President. Even the old friend in the corner.

Governor Deukmejian. Yes. Yes, we even have a friend. This was a gift that was given to me when I first came into office, and we've had that here in the Cabinet Room, as well.

Mrs. Reagan. Is this the same——

Q. Want to call a Cabinet meeting? [*Laughter*]

The President. With the original cast? [*Laughter*]

Governor Deukmejian. These desks are the same ones that were here when you were here.

Mrs. Reagan. Yes.

Governor Deukmejian. We've changed the chairs and kind of changed the carpet a little bit, but that's the same, yeah.

Q. Well, Mr. President, some of the polls are dropping a little bit today. You getting worried? [*Laughter*]

The President. I'll just wait for nightfall.

Q. Going to win?

The President. You know, Helen [Helen Thomas, United Press International], I'm

never going to say any answer to that.

Q. Even up to the last minute?

The President. Not up to the last—especially not up to the last minute.

Q. You mean, the last election, the last day, you're not going to—you're not going to break down and change your mind and tell us if you think you will?

The President. I'm not going to change now.

Q. Mr. President, how do you feel about it being the last day of your last campaign?

The President. Well, as I said yesterday in Minnesota, it's a little like coming up to that last football game and realizing that you've had all 4 years, and that's the last one you're going to play in.

Q. Mr. President, if you're reelected, will it make any difference to you knowing that you never have to worry about the realities of election politics again for your last 4 years? Will it make a difference in the way you handle the office.

The President. No, because I haven't let it make a difference in the way I've handled it up till now. I've had a standard rule sitting down at this table for 8 years and the one in Washington.

Q. You mean you won't be a lameduck on November 7th?

The President. Well, I've always felt that discussing the political ramifications of a measure as to whether it's good or bad for the people isn't the thing to do. You discuss it purely on whether it is right or wrong.

Q. What would be your priorities in a second term?

The President. Well, number one of all, of course, is peace—disarmament and the reduction in the world of nuclear weapons. But on the domestic scene, to continue with the policies that have led to the growth we now have, to make that an ongoing expansion so that we have a growing economy that'll provide jobs for the people that need them.

Q. Are you going to make a move toward the Russians so that there can be some kind of arms talks?

The President. Well now, Bill [Bill Plante, CBS News], I've always made the move toward it, and I've always wondered why so many people ask me, what are you going to do about it? What are they going to do about it?

Q. Well, do you have anything special in mind if you're reelected?

The President. Well, yes. We're going to pursue the fact that we submitted four different proposals to them—four different areas of arms reductions, not control—and they were the ones who walked away from the table. We're going to do everything we can to see if they'll come back.

Q. Well, that's what I mean, sir, if you'll forgive me. I mean, what will you do to get them back? Do you have something in mind?

The President. Well, we won't try to buy them back by increasing offers and so forth. We'll try to convince them that it is to their advantage as well as ours to have a settlement of this particular issue.

Q. You mean you're going to stick with your proposals that are on the table?

The President. Well, we've showed—we've told them we're flexible on that. When they objected to some things, we immediately said, well, come back and tell us what it is you object to. Let us discuss it. And they wouldn't take yes for an answer.

Q. Sir, do you think you'll concentrate on foreign policy in your second term as much as you've concentrated on domestic policy in your first term?

The President. Well, you have to concentrate on that. That's one of the prime responsibilities of the Federal Government—

maybe a little less attention to some things the Federal Government shouldn't have been doing in the first place.

Q. Are you still going to have trouble with O'Neill?

The President. Who ever has trouble with O'Neill? [*Laughter*]

Governor Deukmejian. If it isn't too presumptuous of me, Mr. President, I think if you invited the Russians to come to California, they would not refuse at all. They'd want to come here——

The President. Yes.

Governor Deukmejian. ——and they'd want to visit with you.

The President. Well, as I told a couple of other heads of state from Europe, too, if they'd only discovered America from this side, the Capital would be California. [*Laughter*]

Q. The arms talks in Sacramento, is that it? [*Laughter*]

The President. Why not?

Q. Do you like this room? Does it bring back memories?

The President. Of course it does, yes. A great deal done with it—we've left the subject that has me the most honored and impressed this morning, and I'm deeply grateful to you for this.

Governor Deukmejian. Well, we're very honored that you're here. And, from now on, anybody who comes into this room, whether they be visitors or legislators or anyone else, they will know that this is the President Ronald Reagan Cabinet Room.

The President. Well, I'm very proud.

Mrs. Reagan. That's nice.

The President. Very proud.

Mrs. Reagan. Thank you.

Q. John Wayne is going to preside. [*Laughter*]

The President. Yes.

Governor Deukmejian. Thank you.

Note: The President spoke at 9:45 a.m. at a dedication ceremony at the State Capitol Building.

Remarks at a Reagan-Bush Rally in Sacramento, California
November 5, 1984

The President. Thank you. And thank you, Governor Deukmejian, Senator Wilson, Congressmen Chappie and Shumway. It sure feels great to be home.

You know, there's a picture on the wall inside there that looks something like me. [*Laughter*] And I may just bathe all of you in warm nostalgia, now that I'm here where I have stood several times before. But I'm happy to be with old friends now as we reach the closing moments of this campaign.

I'd say many thanks, first, to Governor Deukmejian, who has been doing such a fantastic and wonderful job in leading this State. I think we all know that with "Duke" here, California is in good hands. And if I could, I'd like to ask you a favor. You've got two fantastic Congressmen from this area—Gene Chappie and Norm Shumway. They're solid members of the "opportunity team." And when you vote tomorrow, please send them back to Washington, too. You need them back there, and I can guarantee you, I need them.

We Californians came from every part of this country and, well, yes, from every part of the world. We came here for the golden opportunity that this State represents. And tomorrow the voters will determine if we're going to keep that dream alive. You know, this State is the only State I know, that if it were a nation, would be one of the top seven or eight economic powers of the world.

But I'm filled with so many memories of times before when I have stood here, including taking the oath of office to serve you as your Governor. The State I remember back in those days had some of the same economic problems that confront the Federal Government—and confronted it 4 years ago. And I remember saying, as I stood here and faced you, the people of California—I said that I believed that you—well, all of us together, the people of California, had an opportunity to start a prairie fire that would sweep across this country.

And do you know there were people in the East who said that California is a good place if you're an orange? They're not saying that anymore.

I think the prairie fire did reach there because now you hear them more and more saying, "Well, what happens in California is a forerunner of what is going to take place in the United States."

You know, when I got to Washington, someone, as a matter of fact it was Tip O'Neill, rather——

Audience. Boo-o-o!

The President. He rather condescendingly said to me, "You're in the big leagues now." And do you know something? I kind of thought here in California we were in the big leagues.

But Abe Lincoln said we must disenthrall ourselves with the past—and then we will save our country. And 4 years ago, that's what we did. We made a great turn. We got out from under the thrall of a government which we had hoped would make our lives better, but which we found wound up trying to live our lives for us.

Four years ago we began to navigate by certain fixed principles. Our North Star was freedom, and common sense our constellations.

We knew that economic freedom meant paying less of the American family's earnings to the Government, and so we cut personal income tax rates by 25 percent. And contrary to what some have been saying in this campaign, we did it across the board, without special favors for any particular group.

We knew that inflation, the quiet thief, and record interest rates were stealing our future. We knew that our national military defense had been weakened, so we decided to rebuild and be strong again to be prepared for peace. It was a second American revolution, and it's only just begun.

America is back, a giant on the scene, powerful in its renewed spirit, powerful in its growing economy, and powerful in its ability to defend itself and secure the peace. And do you know something? That is not debatable.

Yet 4 years after our efforts began, small voices in the night are sounding the call to go back—back to the days of drift, the days of torpor, timidity, and taxes. In fact, some of those small voices have come out here in the sunlight. [*Laughter*]

My opponent's understanding of economics is well demonstrated by his predictions. Just before we took office, he said our economic program is obviously, murderously inflationary. And that was just before we lowered inflation from above 12 percent to down around 4. And then just after our tax cuts, he said the most he could see was an anemic recovery. And that was right before the United States economy created more than 6 million new jobs in 21 months. He said that decontrol of oil would cost you $36 billion. Well, one of the first things we did was decontrol oil, and gasoline prices went down 8 cents a gallon.

Now, I have it all figured out that we can get the economy in absolute perfect condition if we can persuade my opponent to predict absolute disaster.

He says he cares about the middle class, but he boasts, and I quote, "I have consistently supported legislation, time after time, which increases taxes on my own constituents." Doesn't that make you want to be one of his constituents?

Audience. No!

The President. He's no doubt proud of the fact that he voted, as a United States Senator, 16 times to increase your taxes.

Audience. Boo-o-o!

The President. But this year he's outdone himself. He's already promised, of course, to raise your taxes. But if he's to keep all the promises that he's made in this campaign, he will have to raise taxes by the equivalent of $1,890 for every household in the United States.

Audience. No!

The President. That's more than $150 a month. That's like having a second mortgage, a Mondale mortgage. [*Laughter*]

His economic program has two parts: first, raise your taxes; second, do it again. [*Laughter*] But I've got news for him: The American people don't want his tax in-

creases, and they're not going to get his tax increases.

You know——

Audience. 4 more years! 4 more years! 4 more years!

The President. 4 more years? All right.

Audience. 4 more years! 4 more years! 4 more years!

The President. All right.

Audience. 4 more years! 4 more years! 4 more years!

The President. All right. You know, if the Capital were in California, I'd go for 40.

You know, if my opponent's—if his program was a television show, it would be "Let's Make a Deal." [*Laughter*] That is, you trade your prosperity for the surprise he's got hidden behind the curtain. [*Laughter*] And if his program were a Broadway play, it would be "Promises, Promises." [*Laughter*] And if it were a book, you would have to read it from the back to the front to get a happy ending. [*Laughter*]

He sees an America in which every day is tax day, April 15th; we see an America in which every day is Independence Day, the Fourth of July. We want to lower your taxes, and everybody's taxes in this country, so your families will be stronger, the economy will be stronger, and America will be stronger.

On another subject, I am proud to say that during these last 4 years, not 1 square inch of territory has been lost to Communist aggression. And the United States is more secure than we were 4 years ago.

Yet my opponent sees a different world. After the Soviets invaded Afghanistan, he said, "It just baffles me why the Soviets these last few years have behaved as they have." Well, there's so much that baffles him. [*Laughter*]

One year ago we liberated Grenada from the Communists who had taken over that country. And my opponent called what we did a violation of international law that erodes our moral authority to criticize the Soviets.

Audience. Boo-o-o!

The President. Well, there is nothing immoral about rescuing American students whose lives were in danger.

But now, let me, if I can, put this whole

thing in perspective. The 1984 election isn't just a partisan contest. I was a Democrat once, for the greater part of my life. But in those days, the leaders of that party weren't in the "blame America first" crowd. It's leaders were men like Harry Truman, Senator Scoop Jackson, and John F. Kennedy—men who understood the challenges of the times. They didn't reserve all their indignation for America. They knew the difference between freedom and tyranny, and they stood up for one and they damned the other.

Now, to all the good Americans who respect that tradition, all the good Democrats—and I have to believe that here in this crowd there must be many who have found they can no longer follow the leadership of their party, and yet they are loyal Democrats, they are patriotic Americans, I've seen them in meetings like this all over the country in this campaign—well, to all of you, I say, "You are not alone." We're asking you to come walk with us down the path of hope and opportunity and, in the best tradition of bipartisanship, join us in securing this country, making it prosperous, free, and making it safe and secure.

Last month an American woman, Kathryn Sullivan, made history. She walked in space. And then she returned to a space shuttle in which some of the great scientific and medical advances of the future will be made. Cures for diabetes and heart disease are possible up there, as they are not possible down here. I have seen evidence already of experiments that have begun that indicate there is hope, that we will find those cures—advances in technology and communication.

But my opponent, as a Senator, personally led the fight against having a shuttle program at all. He called it a horrible waste.

Audience. Boo-o-o!

The President. Well, we support the space shuttle, and we've committed America to meet a great challenge—to build a manned space center out in space and to do it within a decade. What this country needs is high tech, not high taxes.

I've probably been going on too long here.

Audience. No!

The President. [*Laughing*] That isn't what you meant by 4 more years, is it? Up here?

Well, the point is we were right when we made that great turn in 1980. We were right to take command of the ship, to stop its aimless drift, and to get moving again. And we were right when we stopped sending out S.O.S. from this country and started saying U.S.A.!

Audience. U.S.A.! U.S.A.! U.S.A.!

The President. That sounds real good.

The United States was never meant to be a second-best nation. And like our Olympic athletes, this nation should set its sights on the stars and go for the gold.

If we could bring inflation down from 12.4 percent to 4, then we can bring it down further, from 4 to 0.0. And we're going to do that. If lowering your tax rates led to the best expansion in 30 years, then we can lower them again and keep America growing into the 21st century. If we could create those 6 million new jobs in 21 months, then we can make it possible for every American—young and old, black or white—who wants a job to find a job.

And if local governments can establish enterprise zones to create economic growth, then we can elect people to the Congress who will free our enterprise zones bill, the national bill that we have in Washington that has been buried in a committee in the House of Representatives for more than 2 years under the direction of Tip O'Neill.

Audience. Boo-o-o!

The President. That bill can provide hope for millions in the most distressed areas of America. And so, you send these Congressmen back, and the other candidates back, who will help us blast that bill out of committee and get it to the floor and get it in action in this country.

You know, leading the revolution—as this country is—in technology, and pushing back the frontiers of space, I have always believed—and I believe it now more than ever—if we give American workers the tools they need, in industries old and new, they can outproduce, outcompete, and outsell anybody, anytime, anywhere in the world.

Our drive to restore excellence in education reversed a 20-year decline in the scholastic aptitude test scores. We're going to keep raising those scores and restore American academic excellence to where it is second to none.

Our crackdown on crime has produced the sharpest drop in the history of the crime index, and we're going to keep cracking down until your families and your friends can walk our streets without being afraid.

We've reversed the decline in our military defenses and restored respect for America all over the world. And we're going to keep this nation strong to protect freedom and peace for us, for our children, and for our children's children. And if we make sure that America remains strong and prepared for peace, then we can begin to reduce nuclear weapons and one day banish them from the face of the Earth entirely.

My opponent talks about a nuclear freeze, and every once in awhile some people, rather in an unfriendly way, shove a placard in my face that says, "Nuclear Freeze." Well, I can answer them and tell you something, too. Yes, when we have persuaded the Soviet Union to join us in reducing nuclear weapons to an equal and verifiable number, then we will have a nuclear freeze—but not until.

And as we strengthen our economy, strengthen our security, strengthen the values that bind us, America will become even greater—in its standard of living, and culture, in art and learning, and greater in the love and worship of the God who made us and who has blessed us more than any people have ever been blessed on this Earth.

Now, 2 weeks ago yesterday I didn't— well, I ran out of time on the debate, and I didn't get to finish something I was saying. I'm going to finish it now. And if you don't mind, I'd like to address it to the young people of our country who are with us here today.

Audience. 4 more years! 4 more years! 4 more years!

The President. All right. You young people, you're what this election is all about, you and your future. I've seen you all across this country on campuses, in schools, in rallies like this. And I can tell you, your generation really sparkles.

Your idealism and love of country are unsurpassed. And you know, my generation and—well, there's a few generations between mine and yours—[*laughter*]—well those generations that I'm talking about, we all grew up in an America where we simply took it for granted that we could dream and make our dreams come true. There was no limit to how high we could fly or how far we could go if we set out to do it.

And then we entered a brief period in which there were people telling us that now we were in a era of limits; that never again would anything be as good; that we'd have to reconcile ourselves to living with less. Well, may I speak on behalf of my generation and those several other generations I mentioned and say to you young people right now, we have a sacred trust, and we're going to keep that trust. And that is to turn over to you the reins, when it comes your turn, of an America that is free in a world that is at peace and where your dreams can come true.

Audience. 4 more years! 4 more years! 4 more years!

The President. All right.

All of us, all of us together are part of a great revolution, and it's only just begun. America will never give up, never go back—never. We were born to be a special place here between the two great oceans with a unique mission to carry freedom's torch throughout the world. To a tired, disillusioned world, we have always been a light of hope where they believe all things are possible.

And throughout my own life, I have seen America do the impossible. When I was a young man we survived a great worldwide depression that toppled governments throughout the world. We survived that. It made anything we've had since look like prosperity. We survived—well, we came back from Pearl Harbor and won the greatest military victory the world has ever seen. In a single lifetime we went from the horse and buggy to landing astronauts on the Moon.

And we as a people—and this is our heritage, all of us—we as a people have fought harder, paid a higher price, and done more to advance the dignity and freedom of man than any other people who ever lived on this Earth.

Ours is the land of the free because it is the home of the brave. America's future will always be great because our nation will be strong. And our nation will be strong because our people will be free. And we'll be free because we're united—one people, under God, with liberty and justice for all.

I was deeply honored to serve as your Governor. I have been deeply honored to serve in this office for these past 4 years. But much remains to be done. We must continue to build upon the new beginning that we started 4 years ago. I have come here today to ask for your support and for your vote.

And if I could, just one word of caution. Don't pay any attention to the polls. I looked up at Mount Rushmore, and President Dewey's face isn't there. [*Laughter*] Don't get complacent and think your vote isn't needed. Everyone, vote, get out the vote, get your neighbors to the polls.

Our best years are yet to come. And now, I'm going to say something with a certain little group in mind out there—I think it'll drive them up the wall. I enjoy saying it. And that is, you ain't seen nothin' yet.

God bless you all. Thank you very much. Thank you. Thank you very much.

Note: The President spoke at 10:26 a.m. at the State Capitol Building.

Following his remarks, the President traveled to Van Nuys, CA.

Remarks at a Reagan-Bush Rally in Van Nuys, California
November 5, 1984

The President. Governor Deukmejian, Senator Wilson, distinguished Members of the House of Representatives, former Senator George Murphy, Rosey Grier, and Frank Sinatra—my good friends—and my fellow Californians:

I can't tell you how great it feels to be back in southern California and among long-time friends. You know, I intend to come back here and live—about 4 years from now.

My special regards to Bobbi Fiedler. It's been a long time since she was organizing bus stops here in the valley. And she's doing a terrific job in the Congress. On election day, do me a favor: Send Bobbi back to Washington. And that goes for Congressmen Carlos Moorhead, Dan Lungren, Dave Dreier, and a candidate up here named, I hope, to be Congressman Dornan. And while you're at it, spread the word, also, and get out the vote for Richard Gomez and Claude Perry. And if you don't mind, try to win our California races for the Gipper.

But I am especially proud to be here with the students of Pierce College. Pierce is not only a fine college, but I understand you've got a football team with a 7–0 record this year.

Well, I hope our "opportunity team" does as well tomorrow as the Brahma's have been doing this season.

I've come to the people of the San Fernando Valley to ask for support many times before, and I'd like to ask you for this last time to be with us tomorrow.

Well, thank you——

Audience. 4 more years! 4 more years! 4 more years!

The President. All right.

Audience. 4 more years! 4 more years! 4 more years!

The President. Thank you very much. Thank you. I want you to know that just a little while ago up in Sacramento, I told them that if the Capital were in California, I'd try for 40.

But Abraham Lincoln said that we must disenthrall ourselves with the past—and then we will save our country. And 4 years ago, that's what we did. We made a great turn. We got out from under the thrall of a government which we'd hoped would make our lives better, but which wound up trying to live our lives for us.

Four years ago we began to navigate by certain fixed principles. Our North Star was freedom, and common sense our constellations.

We knew that economic freedom meant paying less of the American family's earnings to the Government, so we cut personal income taxes 25 percent across the board. Now, there have been some people around in this campaign that have been suggesting that maybe we did something for some special group. Our tax cut was across the board, "even-Steven" for everyone, no special group.

We knew that inflation, the quiet thief, and record interest rates were stealing our future. We knew that our national military defense had been weakened, so we decided to rebuild and be strong again to be prepared for peace.

It was a second American revolution, and it's only just begun. But America is back, a giant on the scene, powerful in its renewed spirit, powerful in its growing economy, and secure in the peace. And do you know something? What I just said is not debatable.

Yet 4 years after our efforts began, small voices in the night are sounding the call to go back—back to the days of drift, the days of torpor, timidity, and taxes.

Audience. Boo-o-o!

The President. You know, my opponent's understanding of economics is well demonstrated by his predictions. Just before we took office, he said of our economic program that it was obviously, murderously inflationary. And that was just before we lowered inflation from more than 12 down to around 4 percent. And just after our tax cuts, he said the most that he could see was an anemic recovery. And that was just before the United States economy created more than 6 million new jobs in 21 months. My opponent said decontrol of oil prices would cost American consumers more than $36 billion a year. Well, one of the first things we did was decontrol oil prices, and the price of gasoline went down 8 cents a gallon.

Now, I have it all figured out that all we have to do to get an absolutely perfect economy is persuade him to predict an absolute disaster.

He says he cares about the middle class——

Audience. Boo-o-o!

The President. ——but he boasts, and I quote, "I have consistently supported legislation, time after time, which increases taxes on my own constituents." Doesn't that make you just want to be one of his constituents?

Audience. No!

The President. He's no doubt proud of the fact that as a United States Senator he voted 16 times to raise your taxes.

Audience. Boo-o-o!

The President. But this year he's outdone himself. He's already promised, of course, to raise your taxes. But if he's to keep all the promises that he's made to this group and that in this campaign, he will have to raise taxes by the equivalent of $1,890 for every household in the United States.

Audience. Boo-o-o! Mondale—[*inaudible*].

The President. [*Laughing*] You're right. All right. Okay. All right.

You know, that figure that I just used prorates out to better than $150 a month. That's like having a second mortgage, a Mondale mortgage.

Audience. Boo-o-o!

The President. His economic plan has two parts, two: the first is, raise your taxes.

Audience. Boo-o-o!

The President. And the second is, raise them again.

Audience. Boo-o-o!

The President. But I've got news for him: The American people don't want his tax increases, and they're not going to get his tax increases.

Audience. 4 more years! 4 more years! 4 more years!

The President. All right. You talked me into it. All right.

You know, if my opponent's campaign were a television show, it would be "Let's Make a Deal." [*Laughter*] You give up your prosperity to get his surprise that's hidden behind the curtain. Now, if his campaign were a Broadway show, it would be "Promises, Promises." And if his administration were a novel, you would have to read it from the back to the front in order to get a happy ending.

He sees an America in which every day is tax day, April 15th. We see an America in which every day is Independence Day, the Fourth of July. We want to lower your taxes. We want to lower them for everyone in this country, lower the tax rates so your families can be stronger, our economy will be stronger, and America will be stronger.

I'm proud to say that during these last 4 years, on another subject, not 1 square inch of territory in the world was taken over by Communist aggression.

Audience. 4 more years! 4 more years! 4 more years! U.S.A.! U.S.A.! U.S.A.!

The President. All right, All right. And that U.S.A., the United States of America, is more secure than it was 4 years ago.

But my opponent sees a different world. After the Soviets invaded Afghanistan——

Audience. Boo-o-o!

The President. ——he said, "It just baffles me why the Soviets these last few years have behaved as they have." But then, there's so much that baffles him. [*Laughter*]

One year ago we liberated Grenada from Communists who had taken over that country. Now, my opponent called what we did a violation of international law that erodes our moral authority to criticize the Soviets.

Audience. Boo-o-o!

The President. Well, there is nothing immoral about rescuing American students whose lives are in danger.

But let me now, if I can, put something about this contest in perspective. The 1984 election isn't just a partisan contest. Now, I was a Democrat once, for a good share of my life. But in those days, its leaders weren't in the "blame America first" crowd. I hope that there are—and I'm sure there must be many Democrats in this audience, as there have been in so many appearances across the campuses——

Audience. No!

The President. But wait a minute. Wait a minute. I mean good, patriotic Democrats who have found, as I did, they can no longer follow the leadership of their party. These Democrats would be here because they remember when the party's leaders were men like Harry Truman, later men like Senator Scoop Jackson, John F. Kennedy—men who understood the challenges of the times. They knew the difference between freedom and tyranny, and they stood for one and damned the other.

But to those Democrats that I hope are here—because I know there are so many all over the country—and who believed in that tradition of the Democratic Party, I say, "You are not alone." We're asking you to come and walk with us down the path of hope and opportunity and, in the finest of bipartisan traditions, together we will make this country prosperous, secure, and free.

Now, last month an American woman walked in space—Kathryn Sullivan made history. And then she returned to the space shuttle in which some of the great scientific and medical advances of the future will be made. Cures for diabetes and heart disease may be possible up there; advances in technology and communications. I have seen some evidence of the medical advances I've just mentioned in the experiments that have already been conducted. But my opponent led the fight personally against having a shuttle program at all. He called it a horrible waste.

Audience. Boo-o-o!

The President. Well, we support the space shuttle, and we've committed America to meet a great challenge—to build a permanently manned space station and to do it within a decade. Now, what America needs is high tech, not high taxes.

Audience. We want you! We want you! We want you!

The President. All right.

Audience. We want you! We want you! We want you!

The President. Okay, you got me. All right. All right. All right.

I've probably been going on too long here——

Audience. No!

The President. All right. But——

Audience. 4 more years! 4 more years! 4 more years!

The President. [*Laughing*] You don't mean stay *here* 4 more years?

But you know, the point is that we were right when we made that great turn in 1980, right to take command of this ship, stop its aimless drift, and get moving again. And we were right when we stopped sending out S.O.S. and started saying U.S.A.!

Audience. U.S.A.! U.S.A.! U.S.A.!

The President. Thank you. All right.

You know, the United States of America was never meant to be a second-best nation.

Audience. No!

The President. Like our Olympic athletes, this nation should set its sights on the stars and go for the gold.

Now, if we could bring inflation down from 12.4 percent to 4, then we can bring it down further from 4 to 0.0. And we're going to do that. If lowering your tax rates led to the best expansion in 30 years, then we can lower them again and keep this country growing right into the 21st century. If we could create 6 million jobs in 21 months, then we can make it possible for every American—young and old, black or white—to find a job if they want to find a job.

And if local governments in our country can establish, as they have, enterprise zones to create economic growth, to use tax incentives to go into distressed areas and bring business and industry in there to provide jobs for the people that are without jobs now—well, we have such a bill at the national level to do that. And that bill has been buried for more than 2 years in a committee in the House of Representatives under the direction of Tip O'Neill.

Audience. Boo-o-o!

The President. Now that's why you send back to Washington those Congress people that I mentioned, and send back the candidates that I have mentioned so that we can get that bill out of committee onto the floor and start helping people that need our help.

Audience. No more Tip! No more Tip! No more Tip!

The President. I'll buy that. [*Laughter*]

You know, I've always believed, and I believe more than ever, if we give American workers the tools they need—in new industries and old—they can outcompete, outproduce, and outsell anybody, anywhere in the world, at anytime.

Our drive to restore excellence in education reversed a 20-year decline in scholastic aptitude test scores. We're going to keep raising those scores and restore American academic excellence, second to none.

Our crackdown on crime produced the sharpest drop in the history of the crime index, and we're going to keep cracking down until your families and your friends can walk the streets without being afraid.

We have reversed the decline in our military defenses and restored respect throughout the world for America. And we're going to keep this nation strong to protect freedom and peace for us, for our children, and for our children's children. And if we make sure that America remains strong and prepared for peace, then we can begin to reduce nuclear weapons and one day banish them entirely from the face of the Earth.

My opponent talks of a nuclear freeze——

Audience. No! No!

The President. ——stopping the building of nuclear weapons while we are at a disadvantage. Well, let me tell you, I'm for a nuclear freeze when we and the Soviet Union reduce the numbers of weapons down to an equal, verifiable level, and then we'll have a nuclear freeze.

And as we strengthen our economy, strengthen our security, and strengthen the values that bind us, America will become a nation even greater—in its standard of living, in art, in culture, and learning, and greater in the love and worship of the God who made us and who has blessed us as no people have ever been blessed.

Now, 2 weeks ago yesterday, I didn't get to finish something in that debate that I was starting to say. And I'm going to say it here. It is to the young people of our country that I want to direct myself right now.

You know, you are what this election is all about—you and your future. I have seen you all over this land, on campuses like this, in schools, and in rallies like this. And I want to tell you, your generation really sparkles.

Your idealism, your love of country are unsurpassed. Now, my generation—and then there were a few generations between mine and yours—well, we of those several generations, we grew up in an America where we just took it for granted that you could dream and make your dreams come true, fly as high and far as your own ability and effort would take you.

And then for a brief period we went into an era when voices were telling us that we were in an era of limits, and that never again would things be as good as they were, and that everyone should lower their sights and their ambitions.

Audience. No!

The President. Well, I want to tell you, my generation and those several others I mentioned, we have a sacred trust, and we're going to keep that trust. And it is that when the time comes to turn this nation over to you young people, we're going to turn over an America that is free in a world that is at peace.

Audience. Reagan! Reagan! Reagan!

The President. And it will be an America in which you can dream and make your dreams come true. All of us together, all of us are part of a great revolution that's only just begun. America will never give up and go back—never.

You know, I've always believed this land of ours was placed here between the two oceans to be found by a special kind of people, from every corner of the Earth, who would come here, and come here because of that special love of freedom that they had. And our unique mission is to carry freedom's torch. To a tired, disillusioned world, we've always been a light of hope where everything is possible.

And throughout my life, I have seen America do the impossible. We survived, when I was a young man, a great world-wide Depression that toppled governments in many parts of the world, but not here. We came back from Pearl Harbor to win the greatest military victory in all the history of war. In a single lifetime—my own—in that lifetime we have gone from the horse and buggy to landing astronauts on the Moon.

We, as a people, have fought harder, paid a higher price for victory and freedom, and done more to advance the freedom and the dignity of man than any people who ever lived on this Earth.

America's future—well, let me just say, ours is the land of the free because it is the home of the brave.

Audience. U.S.A.! U.S.A.! U.S.A.!

The President. America's future will always be great because our nation will always be strong. Our nation will be strong because our people will be free. And our people will be free because we will be united—one people, under God, with liberty and justice for all.

Now, I'm deeply honored that you've allowed me to serve you for these past 4 years, but much remains to be done. We must continue to build upon the new beginning that we started 4 years ago. So, I ask you for your support and your vote. I have come here to ask for that.

But also, I want to say I'm terrified by the polls. Please don't read them anymore. Don't get complacent. Tomorrow, don't think your vote isn't needed. Go and vote and take others with you to do that. And if you're voting for me, don't send me there alone. Send these other people that I've mentioned back there with me so we can get the job done.

America's best days are yet to come. And now, it may drive my opponent up the wall, but I just want to say one last thing: You ain't seen nothin' yet.

Thank you, and God bless you. Thank you. Thank you very much.

Note: The President spoke at 1:44 p.m. at Pierce Junior College.

Following his remarks, the President traveled to San Diego, CA.

Remarks at a Reagan-Bush Rally in San Diego, California
November 5, 1984

The President. Thank you, and thank you very much for that jersey. You know I played guard—right guard, that is. [*Laughter*]

Well, Governor Deukmejian, Senator Wilson, and all of you, thank you very much. It's great to be in San Diego, my good luck city.

Someone pointed out as we were coming over that this is the last rally of my election campaign. And 4 years ago, this particular day, it was also right here in this same place that we had that rally.

But there's so much to do and to plan for. These past few months have really been something. We took our campaign out to the country. We journeyed to the bright grid of the cities and the suburbs of the East, and we went to the broad avenues of the Sunbelt. We talked to farmers outside Des Moines and families in the shopping malls. On a whistlestop tour in Harry Truman's old train, I went across Ohio and saw the people of that State spill out, waving flags.

We've been to university and college campuses all across the country, yes. And we saw a dazzling new generation coming to life with an honest love for America—had a chance to talk to them about what our country is and can be, and through them, I think we touched the future.

It's been a wonderful journey. And one thing I know, the heart of America is bigger and stronger than ever. The people are together with the ties that bind. Faith and family and loyalty to a heritage—those are the ties that still bind.

We stand together, we Americans, and we're holding each other's hands, and we're walking into the future with pride in each other and a great faith. And I wanted to say so many times to so many of those crowds, to the people that would be just standing on the road as you drove by on your way, perhaps, to a rally or a meeting of this kind—and they'd be holding up signs, and they'd have flags—and I wanted many times to be able to stop and say, "Thank you for how easy you're making it for an old campaigner." But, now I have stopped, so I can say it to you, the people of my beloved California.

This is the most important election in this nation in 50 years. And if we're to win it, we must win more than the Presidency. We need a Congress that will tell Tip O'Neill that his days of obstructing the progressive legislation—[*applause*]. He's bottled up a great many bills that are necessary for the betterment of our country in the House of Representatives.

You know, just the other day Bob Hope was with us, and Bob said that I got my exercise by jogging three times around Tip O'Neill. [*Laughter*] Well, I can find something else to jog around. So, I won't miss him a bit.

We must solidify the gains that we've made in these past 4 years. And that's why I'm asking all of you to spread the word and get to the polls and reelect your fine Republican Congressmen.

We need Congressman Duncan Hunter in the House to keep—[*applause*]. This will make sure that our military, especially our Navy, is second to none. We need Congressman Bill Lowery. He fought hard to secure for San Diego a share of the high-tech jobs that are created in the last 4 years. And we need Congressman Ron Packard. He's a former school board member who sits on the Education and Labor Committee, and who knows education from the classroom up.

They're all fighting for excellence, for economic growth, and for an America of pride and power. And I don't want to go back there alone. Please, send them back there with us.

Audience member. We want Ronnie!

Audience member. You got it, Mr. Reagan!

The President. Thank you. Thank you.

You know, Abe Lincoln said we must disenthrall ourselves with the past—and then we will save our country. Well, 4 years ago, that's what we did. We made a great turn. We got out from under the thrall of a government which we had hoped would make our lives better, but which wound up trying to live our lives for us.

We learned to navigate on fixed principles. Freedom was our North Star, common sense our constellations.

We knew that economic freedom meant paying less of the American family's earnings to government. And so, we cut personal income tax rates 25 percent. And those people in this campaign who have been saying that we did it for particular and special groups, they don't know what they're talking about. We did it for everybody, "even-Steven," across the board.

We knew that inflation, the quiet thief,

was stealing our future. We knew that our national military defense had been weakened. So, we decided to rebuild and be strong again and be prepared for peace.

And now America is back, a giant on the scene, powerful in its renewed spirit, powerful in its growing economy, and powerful in its ability to defend itself and secure the peace. And do you know something? You know something? That's not debatable.

Yet 4 years after our efforts began, small voices in the night are sounding the call to go back—go back to the days of drift, the days of torpor, timidity, and taxes.

Audience. No!

Audience. Don't put us on the Fritz!

The President. [*Laughing*] A young man down in front here told me, "Don't put us on the Fritz." Not me. All right.

But, you know, my opponent's understanding of economics is well demonstrated by his predictions. Now, just before we took office, he said of our economic program, that it is obviously, murderously inflationary. And that was just before we lowered inflation from above 12 percent down to 4.

And just after our tax cuts, he said the most he could see was an anemic recovery. And that was right before the United States economy created more than 6 million new jobs in 21 months. In the last 18 months, 900,000 new businesses have been incorporated in America.

But my opponent said that decontrol of oil prices would cost you $36 billion. Well, one of the first things we did was decontrol oil prices, and the price of gasoline went down 8 cents a gallon.

Now, I finally figured it out that all we need to do to get an absolutely perfect economy is persuade him to predict absolute disaster.

He says he cares about the middle class, but he boasts, quote, "I have consistently supported legislation, time after time, which increases taxes on my own constituents." Doesn't that make you just want to be one of his constituents?

Audience. No!

The President. He's no doubt proud of the fact that as a United States Senator he voted 16 times to increase your taxes.

Audience. Boo-o-o!

The President. Yes. But this year he's out-done himself. We know, of course, that he's promised to raise your taxes. But if he's to keep all the promises that he's made in this campaign, he will have to raise taxes by the equivalent of $1,890 for every household in the United States.

Audience. Boo-o-o!

The President. That prorates out to more than $150 a month. That's like a second mortgage, a Mondale mortgage.

Now, his economic plan has two basic parts. First, the one is to raise your taxes, and the second part is to raise them again.

Audience. No!

The President. Well, I've got news for him. The American people don't want his tax increases, and they're not going to get his tax increases.

You know, if——

Audience. 4 more years! 4 more years! 4 more years!

The President. All right. All right. I just told some people just north of here who were saying that a little while ago, that if the Capital were in California I'd go for 40.

But if my opponent's campaign were a television show, it would be "Let's Make a Deal." You trade your prosperity for that surprise he's got hidden behind the curtain. [*Laughter*] And if his campaign were a Broadway show, it would be "Promises, Promises." And if it were a book, a novel, you would have to read it from the back to the front to get a happy ending.

He sees an America in which every day is tax day, April 15th. Well, we see an America in which every day is Independence Day, the Fourth of July. Now, we want to lower your taxes more. We want to bring them down for everyone in this country so that your families will be stronger, the economy will be stronger, and America will be stronger.

On another subject, I'm proud to say that in these last 4 years, not 1 square inch of territory anyplace in the world has been lost to Communist aggression.

Audience. U.S.A.! U.S.A.! U.S.A.!

The President. All right. Well, you know, the United States is more secure than we were 4 years ago.

But my opponent sees a different world. After the Soviets invaded Afghanistan, he said, "It just baffles me why the Soviets these last few years have behaved as they have." [*Laughter*] But then, there's so much that baffles him.

One year ago we liberated Grenada from Communists who had taken over that country. And my opponent called what we did a violation of international law that erodes our moral authority to criticize the Soviets.

Audience. Boo-o-o!

The President. There is nothing immoral about rescuing American students whose lives were in danger.

But let me try to put this in perspective. The 1984 election isn't just a partisan contest. I was a Democrat for a large part of my life. And its leaders in those days weren't members of the "blame America first" crowd. Its leaders were men like Harry Truman, the late Senator Scoop Jackson, John F. Kennedy—men who understood the challenges of the times. They didn't reserve all their indignation for America. They knew the difference between freedom and tyranny; and they stood up for one, and they damned the other.

I hope, and I feel sure, from other rallies like this across the country, there must be many of you out there who are Democrats—as there are all over America— Democrats who can no longer follow the policies of the leadership of that party. And I say to all of you, you are not alone. Come walk with us down the new path of hope and opportunity, and we can have a bipartisan effort in the finest tradition of this country that will keep this country secure and prosperous and free.

Audience. 50 States! 50 States! 50 States!

The President. I'm willing. All right.

Last month an American woman made history—Kathryn Sullivan walked in space. And then, having done that, she returned to a shuttle in which some of the great scientific and medical advances of the future will be made. Cures for diabetes and heart disease may be possible up there in space where we can't make them here on Earth. I have seen evidence of experiments already conducted that indicate that this is more than a possibility—advances in technology and communication. But my opponent, in the United States Senate, led the

fight against the entire shuttle program and called it a horrible waste.

Audience. Boo-o-o!

The President. Well, we support the space shuttle, and we've committed America to meet a great, new challenge. And that is to build a permanently manned space station and to do it within a decade. What America needs is high tech, not high taxes.

I've probably been going on too long here. It's beginning to——

Audience. No!

The President. It's twilight. All right. But the point is, we were right when we made our great turn in 1980. We were right to take command of the ship, to stop its aimless drift, and to get moving again. And we were right when we stopped sending out S.O.S. in every direction and started calling U.S.A.!

Audience. U.S.A.! U.S.A.! U.S.A.!

The President. All right. You know, the United States was never meant to be a second-best nation. And like our Olympic athletes, we set our sights on the stars, and we're going for the gold.

If America could bring down inflation from 12.4 percent to 4, then we can bring it down further, from 4 to 0.0. And we're going to do that.

If lowering your tax rates led to the best expansion in 30 years—and it did—then we can lower them again and keep America growing right into the 21st century.

If we can create 6 million new jobs in 21 months, then we can make it possible for every American—young and old, black or white—who wants a job, to find a job in this country.

Local governments, if they can establish enterprise zones to create economic growth—these are zones in which you use tax incentives and go into distressed areas, whether rural or inner city, and you bring in and stimulate business and investment and get jobs to the people there who haven't had them for a long time. Well, we've done that to a certain extent at many local levels. But we have a national bill to do that, a program nationwide. And for more than 2 years, it has been buried in a committee in the House of Representatives under the direction of Tip O'Neill, and we need that out on the floor to help our people.

We're leading a revolution in technology, pushing back the frontiers of space. I've always believed—and I believe now more than ever—if we give American workers the tools they need, they can outcompete, outsell, outproduce any other workers anyplace in the world, anytime.

Our drive to restore excellence in education reversed a 20-year decline in the scholastic aptitude test scores. Well, we're going to keep raising those scores and restore American academic excellence, second to none.

Our crackdown on crime produced the sharpest drop in the history of the crime index last year. We're going to keep cracking down until you and your families and your friends can walk our city streets without being afraid.

We've reversed the decline in our military defenses and restored respect for America. And we're going to keep this nation strong to protect freedom and peace for us, for our children, and for our children's children.

And in this city, where you so often see those in uniform and our military, I just have to tell you, of all the things I've been proud of in this job, nothing has made me more proud than the magnificent young men and women who are in the uniform of our military service.

And if we make sure that America remains strong and prepared for peace, then we can begin to reduce nuclear weapons and, one day, banish them from the Earth entirely.

My opponent has been talking about a nuclear freeze. And now and then, in a kind of an unfriendly way, some people shove signs in my face—"Nuclear Freeze." Well, when we can reduce Soviet and American weapons down to an equal and verifiable limit that there is no disadvantage to us, yes, then we'll have a nuclear freeze.

And as we strengthen our economy, strengthen our security, and strengthen the values that bind us, America will become a nation even greater in its standard of living, in its art, in its learning, and greater in the love and worship of the God who made us and who has blessed us as no other people

have ever been blessed.

Now, a couple of weeks ago I ran out of time on the debate. I didn't get to finish what I had set out to say. I'm going to say it here. And to many of you, if you'll forgive me, this is directed to our young people who are here with us today. [*Applause*]

All right. You are what this election is all about—you and your future. I've seen you all over this country, on campuses, as I said earlier, and universities and in high schools and out in rallies such as this. Your generation really sparkles. Your idealism and love of country are unsurpassed.

Now my generation—and there are several more between mine and yours—[*laughter*]—all of us, or most of us, grew up in an America where we took it for granted that we could dream and make our dreams come true, fly as high and far as our ability and effort would take us.

Then we came to a time not too long ago when people began telling us that those days were over, that we were in an era of limits, that there was a ceiling, and we never again could have things quite as good as they had been. Well, don't you believe it.

My generation, and those other generations I mentioned, we have a sacred trust—and we're going to fill that trust. And that is to see that when the time comes to turn the reins over to you, we're going to turn over to you a country that is free in a world that is at peace. And it will be a country in which you can dare to dream and know that you can make your dreams come true.

All of us together are just part of a great revolution, and it's a revolution that's only just begun. America will never go—give up, will never go back—never. We were born to be a special place between the two great oceans, with a unique mission to carry freedom's message. To a tired, disillusioned world, we have always been a light of hope where all things are possible.

Audience. We love Reagan!

The President. And throughout my life— thank you—I have seen——

Audience member. [*Inaudible*]

The President. I've seen in my lifetime America do the impossible—I do, too.

We survived, when I was a young man, a Great Depression, a worldwide depression that toppled governments in many parts of the world, but not ours. We came back from Pearl Harbor to win the greatest military victory in the history of the world. And in a single lifetime, my lifetime, we have gone from the horse and buggy to landing astronauts on the Moon.

As a people, we have fought harder, paid a higher price, done more to advance the freedom and dignity of man than any other people on Earth. Ours is the land of the free because it's the home of the brave. And our future will always be great because our nation will be strong. And our nation will be strong because our people are free. And our people will be free because we're united—one people, under God, with liberty and justice for all.

Here we're about to end the 1984 campaign. And I want to tell you, having stood here, as I said, 4 years ago, at this particular point—same point in that campaign—I'm deeply honored that you made the decision 4 years ago and allowed me to serve you for these past 4 years. Nancy and I will be forever grateful to all of you. But much remains to be done. We must continue to build on the new beginning that we started 4 years ago.

So, I've come here asking for your vote, asking for your support. But—[applause]. All right. But, also, I don't want to be sent back there alone. These other people I mentioned up here, the incumbent officeholders, Members of the House, the candidates. Send them back there with us, so that as a team we can carry on.

And now, just one last request—one last request. Don't read the polls. Don't get complacent. The last time I looked at Mount Rushmore, President Dewey's face wasn't up there. [Laughter] We need every vote, so make up your mind your vote is needed. Get out there and vote. Get your neighbors to vote. Go to the polls tomorrow.

Our best days are yet to come.

And now, for the last time in the campaign that I can say it—because I know it drives a certain candidate up the wall—I'm going to say it, and that is, you ain't seen nothin' yet.

Note: The President spoke at 4:30 p.m. at the Fashion Valley Shopping Center.

Following his remarks, the President went to Los Angeles, CA, and the Century Plaza Hotel, where he remained overnight.

Address to the Nation on the Eve of the Presidential Election
November 5, 1984

My fellow citizens:

The final hours of the campaign are upon us, and tomorrow America's future will be in your hands. I urge all of you, please, take time to vote. You are the guardians of this great democracy.

Tonight I want to share with you my views about the issues that directly concern our future, the future of our children, and the future of this dream we call America. This election offers us the clearest choice in many years: whether we go forward together with courage, confidence, and common sense, making America strong again; or turn back to policies that weakened our economy, diminished our leadership in the world, and reversed America's long-revered tradition of progress.

Four years ago tonight I asked you to join us in a great national effort to free America from leadership that said we suffered from a malaise, that told us we must learn to live with less, and that our children could no longer dream as we once had dreamed. And, yes, that inflation, taxes, no growth at home, and the steady loss of freedom and respect for America abroad were all beyond our control.

I told you what I'd believed all my life: The greatness of America doesn't begin in Washington; it begins with each of you—in the mighty spirit of free people under God, in the bedrock values you live by each day in your families, neighborhoods, and workplaces. Each of you is an individual worthy of respect, unique and important to the suc-

1793

cess of America. And only by trusting you, giving you opportunities to climb high and reach for the stars, can we preserve the golden dream of America as the champion of peace and freedom among the nations of the world.

Beginning the era of national renewal we promised on Inauguration Day hasn't always been easy. The professional politicians of Washington are set in their ways. As you worked harder to keep up with inflation, they had raised your taxes. When our industries staggered, they piled on more regulations. When educational quality slumped, they piled on more bureaucratic controls. They watched crime terrorize our citizens and responded with more lenient judges, sentencing, and parole. When the Soviets invaded Afghanistan, they punished our farmers with a grain embargo and neglected to rebuild our defenses. Those who spent a career doing these things made one thing plain: They didn't care how the American people had voted. They ridiculed our new ideas. House Speaker Tip O'Neill even warned us that things might not move as fast as we think they should because, "You're in the big leagues now."

But then we did something that shocked the old guard here in Washington—we took our case to you, the people. And you gave us your support. You told those "big leaguers" how double-digit inflation, high taxes, and outrageous interest rates had made it so difficult to buy homes, raise children, live on pensions, start businesses, or even find jobs. You said that our defenses had become dangerously weak, and you felt less secure. You made democracy work by sending one message to Washington loud and clear. The message was: We want a change, and we want it now.

You got their attention. Together we took command of a rudderless ship, adrift in a sea of confusion. We reduced the growth of spending from 17 percent to 6 percent, reduced regulations and paperwork, cut your income taxes by 25 percent, and indexed the rates so government can't profit by driving you into higher tax brackets when you get a cost-of-living pay raise. We provided incentives to modernize older industries and start up new ones, reduced estate taxes for family farms and small businesses, reduced the marriage tax penalty, and increased the child-care credit, the rate of return for small savers, and incentives for IRA's and Keogh contributions. We began to rebuild your defenses, which strengthened our alliances.

We still have much to do—to make our families more secure, to help many of you on our farms and in our inner cities, or working in older industries not yet back on their feet. There will be no final victory until we meet those challenges, until every American who wants a job can find a job, so that all of us are going forward together.

But we can and will, because one fact is not debatable: America has made an amazing comeback. Four years ago inflation, taxes, interest rates, and crime were all going up; tonight, they're coming down. Confidence, jobs, investment, growth, and achievement in our schools were all going down; now they're going up. The United States economy was dragging the world into recession, America was falling back, the Soviets were advancing—and all of that made peace less secure.

Tonight our expansion is leading the world into recovery, our alliances are stronger, we're deterring aggression, the Soviets are no longer advancing—and all of that makes peace more secure. As President Eisenhower once said, "Everything is booming but the guns."

On election eve 4 years ago I mentioned those who said America was in her fading years, that she had no more heroes, and I noted the news coverage about the death of my friend, John Wayne. One headline read, "The Last American Hero." I said then that no one would be angrier than Duke Wayne at the suggestion that he was America's last hero. Just before he died, he said in his unforgettable way, "Just give the American people a good cause, and there's nothing they can't lick." And you've proven he was right.

If anyone is looking for heroes, let them look at Main Street America—all of you who during these past 4 years proved that the big leagues aren't with the Washington establishment. The big leagues are out in the heartland with you—small business men and women, teachers, farmers, ranchers, blue-collar workers, homemakers, and high-tech entrepreneurs. You brought America back, and you're making us great again. All we did was get government out of your way.

But our opponents have a very different vision for your future. Where we look at a problem and see opportunity, they look at opportunity and see a problem. We believe in knowing when opportunity knocks; they seem determined to knock opportunity. We work to increase your take-home pay; they're working overtime to tax it away. Despite their good intentions, I don't believe they place enough faith in people.

Rather than encourage you to dream great dreams and provide opportunities to help America grow, they keep trying to make government grow. They do everything they can to save us from prosperity. And they keep right on giving us the same medicine that made us sick in the first place. They fought the idea of giving you a tax cut. If they'd had their way, average families would be paying over $900 more in taxes today. They've tried to repeal indexing, which protects working people from higher tax brackets. Indexing doesn't help the rich; they're already in the high brackets.

Well, we stopped them, but they kept predicting disaster. They said our tax reduction would be murderously inflationary. That was just before inflation was reduced from 12.4 to around 4 percent. They said there would be no recovery—just before recovery took off. Then they said it couldn't last—and now we have the best economic expansion in 30 years.

Their team has a plan that will raise taxes the equivalent of more than $150 per household every single month. They have a knee-jerk addiction to tax increases. And every time their knee jerks, we get kicked.

What has happened to the Democratic Party's concern for protecting the earnings of working people and promoting economic growth? Unlike today's Democratic leadership, President John F. Kennedy's program cut personal income taxes by 22 percent—just about what ours did. Then he coupled that with new incentives for industry,

which led to a surge in investment, productivity, jobs, real wages, and economic growth. Sounds like what's going on today, doesn't it? Well, sadly, our opponent's team is not in the tradition of President Kennedy and his predecessors, Truman and Roosevelt. Their policies never sent out an S.O.S. They proudly proclaimed U.S.A.!

Tomorrow we can vote to go forward with an America of momentum, or back to an America of malaise; go forward with an economy that's robust, or back to an economy that went bust; go forward with morale up, jobs up, and inflation and taxes down, or back to seeing things the other way around.

Why raise our taxes, when we can raise our sights? Why accept policies that ration our strength, when we can vote for policies that build our strength? Let's walk together on the new path of hope and opportunity and work in a new spirit of patriotism to improve our neighborhoods and communities and build a better America.

If the dream of America is to be preserved, we must not waste the genius of one mind, the strength of one body, or the spirit of one soul. Let us encourage all Americans—men and women, young and old, individuals of every race, creed, and color—to succeed and to be healthy, happy, and whole. Our goal is a society of unlimited opportunity which will reach out to lift the weak and nurture those who are less fortunate. And in spite of what you've heard in this campaign, we are giving more help to more people who need our help than ever in our history.

But the vision we outlined in 1980 does not come to an end simply because 4 years have passed. Our work is not finished. We must continue not only into the next 4 years, but into the next decade and beyond to meet our goal of sustained economic growth without inflation, a strong country prepared for peace.

We need your support for two long-overdue reforms resisted by the House leadership: a constitutional amendment to balance our budget and a line-item veto, giving a President authority to veto individual pork-barrel items within appropriations bills. Forty-three State Governors today have such authority. The President of the United States does not.

Lowering everybody's personal tax rates helped create the strongest economic expansion in 30 years. We shouldn't stop there. We can simplify our tax system, bring your tax rates down further, and keep the United States the undisputed leader for jobs, innovation, growth, and a better life for years to come.

A strong America will continue to push back frontiers of science and space, and discover wonders of the unknown, and achieve breakthroughs in medicine, technology, and communication that will enable the world to make great new leaps in human progress. We're going to maintain our leadership in space, go forward with our space shuttle program, and meet our challenge of building a permanently manned space station within a decade. We lead the world in advanced technology. We can use our knowledge and economic power to modernize our older industries. If we give our workers the tools they need, they can outproduce, outcompete, and outsell anybody, anytime, anywhere in the world.

Going forward together also means rebuilding the most distressed areas of our country, and that begins with getting your help to force that stubborn leadership in the House of Representatives to free our enterprise zone legislation it's had bottled up in committee for 3 years now. Then they should pass our youth opportunity wage to help teenagers learn skills and start climbing the economic ladder.

We'll keep moving forward with our grassroots drive to restore in our schools needed discipline, emphasis on basics, merit pay for teachers, greater involvement by parents, and standards of excellence that again seek the best for America. Young Americans are trying harder, and test scores show they are doing better for the first time in 20 years. Their improvement should give us confidence America will become more productive and competitive in this fast-changing world.

Our crackdown on crime, thanks to energetic support from citizens groups and local law enforcement agencies, has produced the sharpest drop ever in the history of the crime index. We intend to keep cracking down until your families and friends can walk your streets again without fear. And let's make a national commitment to save our children from the drug abuse that poisons their minds and bodies.

We have always followed two tracks in our defense and national security policies. One is to reverse the decline in our military defenses and restore respect for America. The other, equally important, is to search for peace through the negotiation of real arms reductions. We're proud to say that in the past 4 years, not 1 inch of soil has been lost to Communist aggression. By rebuilding our strength and making ourselves reliable again we can keep this nation strong enough to protect freedom and peace for us, for our children and our children's children. And one day, all nations can begin to reduce nuclear weapons and ultimately banish them from the face of the Earth.

This is our plan for the future. If you believe that America has made a new beginning, that we're moving forward again but could move much faster and farther by ending the obstruction in that Congress, will you support us by sending us a Congress we can work with?—one that believes in the same principles you do; a Congress that won't increase your taxes and spend our revenues uncontrollably.

We can strengthen our economy, our security, and the values that bind us. We can build an America even greater in science, literature, and the arts, and improve the quality of life for all our people. We can keep faith with the God who has made and blessed us as no other people have ever been blessed.

This is the world that can be for each child born November 6th, 1984: a world at peace and alive with freedom; a society of growth, opportunity, and progress.

In speaking tonight of America's traditional values and philosophy of government, we must remember the most distinctive mark of all in the American experience: To a tired and disillusioned world, we've always been a New World and, yes, a shining city on a hill where all things are possible.

Our alliances, the strength of our democratic system, the resolve of free people—all are beginning to hold sway in the world. We've helped nourish an enthusiasm that grows each day, a burning spirit that will not be denied: Mankind was born to be free. The tide of the future is a freedom tide.

This, then, is our historic task—it always has been—to present to the world an America that is not just strong and secure, but an America that has a cause and a vision of a future where all peoples can experience the warmth and hope of individual liberty.

Today America travels again the road of increased self-government and personal freedom. What a change from only those few years ago when patriotism seemed out of style.

I'm not sure anyone really knows when this new patriotism began or how it grew so quickly. Was its seed first planted that day our POW's, who had braved a horrendous captivity in North Vietnam, came home and said, "God bless America," and then actually thanked us for what we had done for them? Or maybe it was that unforgettable moment when after 444 days of captivity, our hostages came home from Iran to breathe American freedom again.

We've known great joy—as when we welcomed back our soldiers and those students from Grenada—but also enduring grief from the loss of brave men—on the Grenada rescue mission and on our peacekeeping mission in Beirut. Each gave his life for a noble cause. Each must be remembered and honored—forever.

I treasure a memory of a visit to Normandy, where I met the boys of Pointe du Hoc. And later, at Omaha Beach, I read from the letter of a loving daughter who had promised her father, a Normandy veteran, that someday she would go back there for him. She would see the beaches and visit the monuments and place flowers at the graves of his fallen comrades. "I'll never forget what you went through," she wrote. And, "Dad, I'll always be proud."

We should pray that as much as we honor those who died to make us free, we also fervently pray such sacrifice will never again be required; that there will be a day when new battlefields are never again created.

This and every election is what they sacrificed for. They gave everything to preserve and protect the vote you are free to exercise tomorrow. Regardless of how you choose, you must take the time to make that choice.

I'm profoundly thankful to all of you for giving me the privilege of serving you these last 4 years. I ask for your vote again for one purpose only—to complete the task we began together 4 years ago.

Along with George Bush—the strongest and finest Vice President in my memory—I've traveled all across our country this year. We've both seen our young people—your sons and daughters and grandchildren—tens of thousands of them. We've met them on college and university campuses, and younger ones in schoolrooms and playgrounds.

For me, a vivid recollection of them will be from a whistlestop train tour through Ohio in that historic car that once carried Franklin Roosevelt, Harry Truman, and Dwight Eisenhower across America. America had a smile in her heart that day. At each stop and through each community, whether gathered on their sidewalks, back lawns, or the plowed fields of their farms, again and again it was the young people I remembered—Cub Scouts in blue shirts and bright yellow kerchiefs, high school bands, college crowds, and little girls perched atop their dads' shoulders. Well, they and millions more like them are what this election is all about.

Watching the Olympic games last summer, Nancy and I were thrilled, as I'm sure you were, when we heard those repeated chants of U.S.A.! U.S.A.! Did it occur to you, as it did to us, that while each of those words—United States of America—is important, none is more so than the first. Yes, we are united. That is our rich heritage. There were moments in recent years when we wondered if we were still united, but not today. Crisscrossing this land these last few months, I have seen such proof of national unity I know our children will inherit an America that's united and coming together again.

There's more than the freshness of youth on those faces I've seen; there is the future and hope of all America. Tomorrow is theirs, a time when they can fly as high as their talents will take them. It's up to us to pass on to them a nation that's free in a world at peace.

If you honor George and me once again with your vote, we will do everything in our power to be worthy of it.

America is coming together again. We're building together. But what I'm really thankful for is that all across this shining land, we're hoping together. We can say to the world and pledge to our children: America's best days lie ahead. And you ain't seen nothin' yet.

Thank you, good night, and God bless you.

Note: The President's remarks were taped in the Oval Office at the White House on October 31 for broadcast on November 5. The broadcast was paid for by the Reagan-Bush '84 campaign.

Informal Exchange With Reporters While Viewing the Presidential Election Returns
November 6, 1984

Q. Mr. President, have you won the election?

The President. What?

Q. Helen [Helen Thomas, United Press International] wanted to know if you've won the election, sir.

The President. I'm not going to say anything until they tell me it's official. And I've never known a projection was official.

Q. Well, do you think you're likely to win?

The President. Well, let's say I'm cautiously optimistic.

Q. What do you think of that——

Mrs. Reagan. I'd go along with that.

Q. How are you feeling, Mrs. Reagan?

Mrs. Reagan. I'm glad it's over.

Q. How's your head?

Q. ——the bump?

Mrs. Reagan. My bump is gone.

Q. Are you feeling well?

Mrs. Reagan. Pardon me?

Q. Are you feeling well?

Mrs. Reagan. Yes, I just bumped into a chair.

Q. Is it making you dizzy at all, this particular bump?

Mrs. Reagan. No, it's tender, you know. I got out of bed to get a blanket. It was cold.

Q. Aha! He was cold, you say? [*Laughter*]

The President. I was?

Q. ——keep your eyes on the blanket, Mr. President? [*Laughter*]

Mr. Speakes.[1] We've got two waves to go, so you guys keep up a little bit——

The President. I helped her with the blanket, and then I helped her up. I caution all of you, in those fancy rooms where the bed is on a platform—with a step down after you——

Q. Are you happy?

Q. On a platform bed?

Mrs. Reagan. Yes, it was a platform bed. And those are dangerous, you know, when you're in a strange room and it's dark and you get up. And I just took a header.

Q. I hope you feel better soon.

Mrs. Reagan. Pardon me?

Q. We hope you feel better soon.

Mrs. Reagan. Thank you.

Mr. Speakes. Can we get all the bigger cameras in? Sam [Sam Donaldson, ABC News], do you want to come over here so we can get the cameras?

Television Announcer. ABC News now wishes to project the State of Maryland as the Presidential—[*inaudible*]. The State of Maryland for President Reagan.

Mrs. Reagan. Oh, isn't that nice?

Q. I thought that was a Democratic State, Mr. President.

Television Announcer. We now have a

----

[1] *Larry M. Speakes, Principal Deputy Press Secretary to the President.*

projection from West Virginia in the race for Governor, and our projection is that Senator Jay Rockefeller——

Q. Well, Governor, Senator.

Q. He was a Governor.

The President. A little while ago the projection was the other way.

Q. Mr. President, all three networks have projected you as the winner. What's your reaction, sir?

The President. Well, as I said, one of cautious optimism. I'm going to wait until I get it official.

Q. What does "official" mean, sir?

The President. Well, when they say that the count is definitely in—they've totaled and that's that.

Q. Mr. President, assuming you do have a very broad and deep mandate, what are you going to do with it in your second term?

The President. We're going to carry on the program that we started 4 years ago, accompanied with economic growth without inflation, a strong defense—every effort we can make to get arms reductions.

Q. Well, to what extent do you think you can do something new to get the Soviets to resume negotiations?

The President. Well, everybody keeps asking what are we going to do. They're the ones who walked away from the table. What are they going to do?

Q. Do you expect big shakeups, sir? Are you going to change the Cabinet—a lot of new faces?

The President. Well, no. I know that always there are people who have stayed as long as they can take away from their own careers and want to leave, although I haven't heard of any who have said that to me. But I would not be surprised by that. But I don't know of any——

Q. Let me ask Mrs. Reagan on camera how she feels—can we get the lights——

Q. Lights, please——

Q. Mr. President, what do you think the vote really means? Do you think that the country has gone conservative?

The President. I think that there has been a change, and the Government has seen a——

Q. Pardon me?

The President. I think the Government

has seen other policies that failed, and there's been a growing tendency to become more aware of the intrusiveness of the Federal Government and its continued expansion in power, and I think this is what's happened. And they see now that a different course is——

Q. Mrs. Reagan, how do you feel? You bumped your head yesterday——

Q. Tell us what happened last night.

Mrs. Reagan. Pardon me?

Q. You bumped your head. How do you feel?

Mrs. Reagan. I feel fine.

Q. You seemed a little wobbly, Mrs. Reagan. Are you a little dizzy?

Mrs. Reagan. Well, if you bumped your head, wouldn't you feel a little wobbly?

Q. Yes, but what happened?

Q. What happened?

Mrs. Reagan. I got out of bed to get a blanket, because I was cold. And the bed was on a platform, and I just misjudged, and I took a header and landed on a chair.

Q. Are you going to be downstairs for the celebration tonight?

Mrs. Reagan. Sure.

Q. What are your thoughts about being First Lady for the next 4 years?

Mrs. Reagan. Well, as long as I'm with my friend here. [*Laughter*]

Q. Are you happy he's won?

Mrs. Reagan. Of course I am.

Q. Are you going to say he's won, even if he doesn't?

Mrs. Reagan. Oh. [*Laughter*]

Q. I think you have.

Mrs. Reagan. Oh, Chris [Chris Wallace, NBC News], you tricked me. [*Laughter*]

Q. Mr. President, in your second term, do you think you'll get a chance to go to the Soviet Union? Would you like to?

The President. Well, whether the meeting is held there or someplace else, I have felt the need. Yes, it's time for us to get together and talk about a great many things and try to clear the air and the suspicions between us so we can get down to the business of reducing, particularly, nuclear weapons.

Q. Any new or different initiative on spending, Mr. President?

The President. To continue trying to

make the Government more efficient, eliminate extravagance and useless spending. That's why we're studying very carefully the Grace commission recommendations.

Q. Mr. President, are you planning to go to Asia in December?

Q. That's what we heard.

The President. I haven't made any——

Q. What?

The President. I haven't made any definite plans yet.

Q. How about tentative?

Mrs. Reagan. How could you go in December? That's Christmas.

Q. Australia. What about Australia?

Mrs. Reagan. That's Christmas. December's Christmas.

Q. I guess that means no, doesn't it?

Q. Italy's nice. [*Laughter*]

Q. If you are reelected, will you propose a summit with Chernenko?

The President. Well, we've been in constant touch with them, in communication, and they know that we're interested in carrying on discussions with them; and they profess to be eager to do the same thing. So, let's wait and see if they'll be more specific and definite once the campaign is over.

Q. What would you—you've never lost an election—you've lost some primaries—but what would you say to Walter Mondale? He must be feeling awful tonight.

The President. Well, I'm sure he does. I'm quite sure that there isn't anything I could say that would make him feel any better. I hope that we can close ranks for the good of the country, and—once the contest is over.

Q. Do you feel sorry for him?

The President. Well, yes, I think if you're in the race at all, you know how someone would—how you'd feel yourself. So, you can certainly sympathize with someone else.

Q. It's better winning than losing, though, isn't it? [*Laughter*]

Q. Thank you.

Q. Congratulations, Mr. President.

The President. Thank you.

Note: The exchange began at 5:30 p.m. as the President and Mrs. Reagan were watching the election returns on television in their suite at the Century Plaza Hotel in Los Angeles, CA.

Earlier in the day, the President and Mrs. Reagan left Los Angeles and went to the Veterans Memorial Building in Solvang, CA, where they delivered their absentee ballots. They then returned to Los Angeles and the Century Plaza Hotel, where they remained overnight.

Remarks at a Reelection Celebration in Los Angeles, California
November 6, 1984

Audience. 4 more years! 4 more years! 4 more years!

The President. Thank you. I think that's just been arranged.

Well, thank you all very much. It seems we did this 4 years ago, and let me just say, well, you know, good habits are hard to break.

Just a short time ago, Walter Mondale phoned me, and to——

Audience. Boo-o-o!

The President. No—to concede. He told me the people had made their decision and, therefore, we were all Americans, we'd go forward together.

But Nancy and I would like to express——

Audience. Nancy! Nancy! Nancy!

The President. They're yelling for you. They're yelling for you. Nancy, Nancy.

Audience. Nancy! Nancy! Nancy!

Mrs. Reagan. Thank you.

The President. Nancy thanks you.

You know, we could spend the rest of the next 4 years thanking all of those who have made this night possible. But there are a few I'd like to mention this evening. First, Nancy and I want to express our warmth and our deep gratitude to George and Barbara Bush.

Audience. Bush! Bush! Bush!

The President. And, George, if you're watching down there in Texas, thank you for campaigning so magnificently all across this country. And believe me, I'm very proud to have you as my partner for this next term. As far as I'm concerned, there has never been a finer Vice President.

And a thank you, too, to Paul Laxalt, our campaign chairman. Paul is in Washington, and I understand he's there watching in a room like this with people like yourself who are there for the same reason. And there is no better personal friend than I've ever had, and there's no better ally to have at your side when you're in a campaign.

And, Paul, we're grateful for all that you've done over the years. And all of you there in the Shoreham Hotel ballroom, a deep thanks for all that you have done.

And Paul would be the first to say how much help he had and what an outstanding job was done by Ed Rollins, our campaign director. And, Ed, please know how grateful I am for the way you put together the finest campaign organization, I think, in the history of American politics.

Our thanks, too, to Mayor Margaret Hance, our deputy campaign chairwoman. She gave of her time so generously.

Back in Washington, we owe so much to the great work of the Republican National Committee and its chairman, Frank Fahrenkopf. Frank and all those dedicated people who worked with him gave—well, they give politics a good name. We wouldn't have enjoyed this victory tonight without them.

And now, I have a special thank you for something that began here in this State almost 20 years ago. First by the dozens, and then by the hundreds, and finally by the thousands, we've seen our friends, all of you volunteers and workers who came to our side to help. From California, then across the United States, you have each given selflessly of yourselves. And I have no words to properly thank you for all that you've done.

We set out, I remember back those almost 20 years ago, and said that we could start a prairie fire here in California, one that would capture the intensity of our de-

votion to freedom and the strength of our commitment to American ideals.

Well, we began to carry a message to every corner of the Nation, a simple message. The message is: Here in America, the people are in charge. And that's really why we're here tonight. This electoral victory belongs to you and the principles that you cling to—principles struck by the brilliance and bravery of patriots more than 200 years ago. They set forth the course of liberty and hope that makes our country special in the world. To the extent that what has happened today reaffirms those principles, we are part of that prairie fire that we still think defines America—a fire of hope that will keep alive the promise of opportunity as we head into the next century.

Four years ago, when we celebrated victory in this same room, our country was faced by some deep and serious problems. But instead of complaining together, we rolled up our sleeves and began working together.

We said we would get inflation under control, and we did. We said we would get America working again, and we've created more than 6½ million new jobs. We said that we would work to restore traditional values in our society, and we have begun. And we said that we would slow down the growth of government and the rate of its spending increases, and we did. We said we'd get interest rates down, and we did. We said we would rebuild our defenses and make America prepared for peace, and we have.

Now, I wish I could take credit for this, but——

Audience. Yes!

The President. ——but the credit—no, the credit belongs to the American people, to each of you.

Our work isn't finished; there's much more to be done. We want to make every family more secure, to help those in our inner cities, on our farms, and in some of our older industries which are not yet back on their feet. And the recovery will not be complete until it's complete for everyone.

By rebuilding our strength, we can bring ourselves closer to the day when all nations can begin to reduce nuclear weapons and ultimately banish them from the Earth entirely.

You know, so many people act as if this election means the end of something——

Audience. No!

The President. The vision we outlined in 1980, indeed the passion of the fire that we kept burning for two decades, doesn't die just because 4 years have passed. To each one of you I say: Tonight is the end of nothing; it's the beginning of everything.

Audience. 4 more years! 4 more years! 4 more years!

The President. All right.

Audience. 4 more years! 4 more years! 4 more years!

The President. All right. Okay. All right.

What we've done only prepares us for what we're going to do. We must continue—not only into those next 4 years but into the next decade and the next century—to meet our goal of sustained economic growth without inflation and to keep America strong.

Our society is a society of unlimited opportunity which will reach out to every American and includes lifting the weak and nurturing the less fortunate.

We fought many years for our principles.

Now we'll work to keep those principles in practice. That's what we have to leave to our children, and to their children, and they are what this campaign was all about.

We've come together again. We're united again. And now, let's start building together and keep the prairie fire alive. And let's never stop shaping that society which lets each person's dreams unfold into a life of unending hope. America's best days lie ahead. And, you know, you'll forgive me, I'm going to do it just one more time: You ain't seen nothin' yet.

God bless you. Thank you all very much. Thank you.

Note: The President spoke at 9:31 p.m. in the Los Angeles Ballroom at the Century Plaza Hotel.

Earlier in the evening, the President received congratulatory telephone calls from the Vice President, Prime Minister Brian Mulroney of Canada, Crown Prince 'Abdallah of Saudi Arabia, and Prime Minister Yasuhiro Nakasone of Japan. Later that evening, he received a telephone call from Walter Mondale.

At the hotel, the President spent time with members of his family and attended receptions for administration and campaign officials.

Question-and-Answer Session With Reporters on Foreign and Domestic Issues
November 7, 1984

The President. Good morning. I don't have any opening statement, other than to say that, as you probably know already, we're going to take a couple of days now to wind down, and then we're looking forward to getting back to Washington at the beginning of the week.

Contents of Soviet Ship Docked in Nicaragua

Q. Mr. President, there are reports that a ship has docked in Nicaragua with perhaps Soviet Mig aircraft. Can you tell us, number one, if the ship does have the Soviet Mig's on it, and, if so, what the

United States intends to do about it?

The President. Well, I can't comment on any plan of what we might do. Right now, we have no—we, ourselves, have been alerted, and we've been surveilling that ship, but we cannot definitely identify that they have Mig's on there or planes of any kind. But we're keeping a careful watch. And then, as I say, I'm not going to comment on what might follow or what our procedure would be.

Q. If I may follow up without asking you to give specifics of your plans, several of your aides have said it would be a very serious matter.

The President. Yes.

Q. How would you view it?

The President. Well, I think it would be. We have informed them that for them to bring something that is absolutely unnecessary for them—these high performance craft, in here—indicates that they are contemplating being a threat to their neighbors here in the Americas.

Helen [Helen Thomas, United Press International]?

Tax Reform

Q. Mr. Mondale says that you'll be eating crow on your promises not to raise taxes. And since you have not revealed your plans on taxes during the campaign, do you think you can do so now?

The President. I have told you, the only thing that there is yet to be revealed is when the team that has been working on a tax reform proposal presents it to us, and we make a decision one way or the other on that, that would be the only thing. But there's nothing for me to reveal now, except that my position is solid. We're not going to try to deal with the deficit problem by raising taxes.

Q. But will you raise taxes at all, in terms of wiping out deductions?

The President. All I know is that in looking at everything, including the whole flat-tax idea and everything else, if that is done and means some changes in deductions, if we should decide that, then those would have to offset—or be offset with regard to the rates, so that it would not result in any individual having his taxes raised by way of a tax reform.

Report on the CIA Manual

Q. Mr. President, have you received the CIA report on the manual? When are you going to make it public? What did it say specifically? Did it recommend disciplinary action? And what are you going to do about it?

The President. I think you're going to find that—I haven't received it yet, but I'm expecting to, probably before I get back to Washington. But I have to say from whatever advance information I have, that there was much ado about nothing; that it is not a document that is teaching someone how to assassinate. There's nothing of that kind in it. It was actually a document trying to help leaders of the *contras* influence and win over the people, if they came into a community down there, and how they were to persuade the people that they were on the right side.

So, we're waiting to see what is in there. But I have had some information on it and have been assured that there's not one word in there that refers to assassination.

Q. Sir, if I could follow up, please. There, I think, have been reports that the report did recommend some disciplinary action. Are you pledged to follow the recommendations of the report, whatever it is?

The President. Well, I want to see the report first. I'm not going to commit in advance to anything.

Listen, with regard to the followups here, though, may I point out we've got a very limited time here. Now, Chris [Chris Wallace, NBC News], I said you, and then Andrea [Andrea Mitchell, NBC News].

Election Results

Q. Yes, sir. Clearly, you won a tremendous personal victory last night. But given the fact that the Republicans lost two seats in the Senate and that you didn't win as many seats in the House as you lost in the 1982 elections, how much of a mandate can the Republicans claim for next year?

The President. Well, I feel that the people of this country made it very plain that they approved what we've been doing. And we're going to continue what we've been doing and, if need be, we'll take our case to the people. But we have the same number of Senators that we had in 1981 when we got this program passed. And there's a possibility—I know that there are some seats still to be decided in the House—but there's a possibility of as many as 17, and that's more than have happened in elections of this kind—mid- or second-term elections—for Presidents in the past.

So, I'm satisfied with the way things turned out.

Q. Are you claiming a mandate then, sir?

The President. What?

Q. Are you claiming a mandate then?

The President. I'm claiming that I think

the people made it very plain that they approved of what we're doing and approved of the fact that things are better and the economy is expanding. And that's what we're going to continue to do.

Yes, Andrea.

Arms Control

Q. Mr. President, last night you said that it's time for you to get together and talk with the Soviets. What do you think the real chances are of a summit, and do you think that appointing an arms control envoy in your administration would help resolve the conflicts within the Cabinet over arms control policies?

The President. We don't have a conflict within the Cabinet. We're united on the idea of arms control, and I don't know where all this talk came from. And we're prepared to go forward with the arms control talks, and I have to believe that the Soviet Union is going to join us in trying to get together.

Q. Well, what about a summit?—a summit between you and your Soviet counterpart? And will you appoint an envoy?

The President. Well, the idea of an envoy is just some of the things that we've discussed with them. It's whether they would like to establish some separate, informal channel, so that we could keep in touch and then they would be able, on both sides, to recommend whether there was something that we should get together on and negotiate. We haven't decided on that—whether to do it or whether they would be willing to do it. But we've discussed that subject with them, and so it's under consideration.

Q. And the summit, sir?

The President. What?

Q. The summit?

The President. Well, a summit, as I say, yes. I proposed virtually that, with the idea of a kind of umbrella negotiations, when I spoke to the United Nations.

Budget Cuts

Q. Mr. President, if the defense budget can't be cut and Social Security can't be cut, as you've said, where do you make the spending cuts in the budget for the coming year?

The President. Well, as I say, we're look-ing at 2,478 recommendations submitted by the Grace commission. More than 2,000 of our leading citizens were together in making these recommendations. We have already implemented some 17 percent of them. And we know that we probably won't be able to do all of them, but we're studying them.

These are the things that have to do with not going along with the idea that the only way you can cut spending is to eliminate or reduce some program. What we're talking about is being able to do things government is supposed to do, but doing it more efficiently and economically. And there's evidence of that.

We've made a number of steps that have revealed that the Government is still larded with a lot of fat and still doing things in an old-fashioned way that business gave up a long time ago. So, we're going to do things of that kind.

With regard to Social Security, nothing but political demagoguery has ever been behind the bringing up of Social Security in the '82 election or in this election, because Social Security now is on a sound fiscal basis as the result of a bipartisan commission that I'd been asking for since 1981 and we finally got in 1983.

Besides, Social Security has nothing to do with the deficit. Social Security is fully funded by a payroll tax dedicated to Social Security, so it is not part of the deficit. If there was any change in the expenditures of Social Security, that would just mean the money would go back into the trust fund, or the payroll tax would be reduced accordingly.

Medicare

Q. What do you propose to do about Medicare?

The President. Let me just say about Medicare, we have a problem not as serious or not as imminent as the problem was with Social Security when we came here—that it was facing immediate bankruptcy.

Medicare—looking at the demographics and projecting ahead—we say several years from now could find itself in a problem of outgo exceeding the trust fund and the income in that fund. So we need to look at that as to how we can set it on the same kind of basis that will ensure into the future that the people are going to get the care they need.

We have already done some things—not in restricting the patient, but in putting some curbs on the expenditures out there capping out at the other end from the people who provide the services. And these are the type of things that we're looking at.

Now, Bill [Bill Plante, CBS News].

Poverty

Q. Mr. President, do you have anything to say this morning to the people who apparently feel they didn't participate in the Reagan revolution and who didn't vote for you yesterday?—specifically, the blacks, the poor, single mothers, those people whom studies show to be, in fact, somewhat worse off than they were?

The President. The truth is, Bill, they aren't worse off than they were. And that, again, has been some political demagoguery. We're going to make every effort to bring the truth and the facts to those people, but at the same time what we've called the safety net is still a top priority with us, and we're going to maintain that safety net.

Now, I heard as of this morning, one person on the air on one of the programs talking about the fact that there are more people living below the poverty line or at the poverty line than there were when we came here—absolutely true. But what they didn't add is that we have cut the rate of increase in poverty to just about half what it was under the previous administration. So, we have made gains. We have not been able to reverse that trend, and we hope that we can.

But that doesn't have anything to do with our programs. That has had to do with the outside income of those people, their own earnings and income, not—it is not the fault of any government program. If it were, we wouldn't have cut the rate of increase in poverty, as I say, almost in half, down from 9.1, I think it is, to 5 percent.

Presidential News Conferences

Q. Mr. President, this is your second press conference in less than a week. And before

that, there was a long time. Is this an indication that in your second term you're going to hold regular press conferences, say twice a week every month? [*Laughter*] Or will you commit yourself to a regular press conference schedule now that you're re-elected?

The President. Look, I won. I don't have to subject myself to—[*laughter*]——

No. And as I say, I don't think in just counting up the number of press conferences that it's been completely fair when you look at the other opportunities, such as this, a number of other things, and the fact that—as I was able to point out to some of you the other day—out there by the plane, since Labor Day, during the campaign I've actually spent the equivalent time with you of at least six press conferences.

Q. Well, sir, you can't consider that press conferences by the plane, when we're shouting questions at you, when they're not seen by the American public, the actual equivalent to when you have a televised news conference, when everyone can tune in and get the give-and-take unfiltered?

The President. Well—[*laughing*]—I think that it's pretty plain. I'm not talking about a shouted question as I get into the car. I'm talking about stopping, as I am here, and taking your questions.

Listen, I had recognized one, and then I know that our time is up—over, and I've got to go.

Korea

Q. Mr. President, during the last year, your successful campaign, you told the audience the past 4 years not 1 inch of soil has been lost to the Communist operation. There are still 40—the U.S. troops in Korea, the Korea still divided into two parts. How do you help the reunification of Korea Peninsula as a friend?

The President. If I understand correctly, you're asking about how do I envision, probably, the getting together of the two Koreas. Well, we certainly have been willing to encourage that and know that steps have been undertaken, some gestures by one side, and there have been gestures by the South Koreans or movements that way. I know that they have discussed with North

Korea having a single Olympic team, for example, representing all of Korea. We're hopeful that that can come about, and we have encouraged it, and we've discussed this with other countries that have an interest there—the People's Republic of China, Japan, and others.

But—oh, I can't do it, because I'm 5 minutes over now what the time was that we were supposed to have. So, we'll have to catch them on another time.

Q. Can we go one more?

The President. I can't do it. What?

Q. Can we go one more here?

The President. That was the one more, there. [*Laughter*]

Q. Oh, no.

The President. I can't do it. I just can't do it. We've gone over the time that was allotted.

Nancy Reagan

Q. How's Mrs. Reagan feeling, sir?

The President. That question I will take, how Mrs. Reagan is feeling. She's feeling much better. She had, as you know—I know there were some rumors started as to what could be wrong—she had a very nasty fall in the early morning, in Sacramento, in the bedroom there, and bumped her head quite severely. And it was affecting her for quite some time. But she's feeling much better—still has a pretty tender lump there on the side of her head. But that's what it was, and it's all going away now.

Q. Are you going to spend any time in Washington in the second term? [*Laughter*]

The President. I'm going to live there.

Q. Oh.

Q. What do you have to say to the State of Minnesota?

The President. Enjoyed my visit there. [*Laughter*]

Note: The exchange began at 9:46 a.m. in the Los Angeles Room at the Century Plaza Hotel in Los Angeles, CA.

Following the exchange, the President went to Rancho del Cielo, his ranch near Santa Barbara, CA, where he stayed for the remainder of the week.

Notice of the Continuation of the Iran Emergency
November 7, 1984

On November 14, 1979, by Executive Order No. 12170, the President declared a national emergency to deal with the threat to the national security, foreign policy, and economy of the United States constituted by the situation in Iran. Notices of the continuation of this national emergency were transmitted by the President to the Congress and the *Federal Register* on November 12, 1980, November 12, 1981, November 8, 1982, and November 4, 1983. Because our relations with Iran have not yet returned to normal and the process of implementing the January 19, 1981, agreements with Iran is still underway, the national emergency declared on November 14, 1979, must continue in effect beyond November 14, 1984. Therefore, in accordance with Section 202(d) of the National Emergencies Act (50 U.S.C. 1622(d)), I am continuing the national emergency with respect to Iran. This notice shall be published in the *Federal Register* and transmitted to the Congress.

RONALD REAGAN

The White House,
November 7, 1984.

[*Filed with the Office of the Federal Register, 2:07 p.m., November 7, 1984*]
Note: The notice was released by the Office of the Press Secretary on November 8.

Letter to the Speaker of the House and the President of the Senate on the Continuation of the Iran Emergency
November 7, 1984

Dear Mr. Speaker: (Dear Mr. President:)

Section 202(d) of the National Emergency Act (50 U.S.C. 1622(d)) provides for the automatic termination of a national emergency unless, prior to the anniversary date of its declaration, the President publishes in the *Federal Register* and transmits to the Congress a notice stating that the emergency is to continue in effect beyond the anniversary date. In accordance with this provision, I have sent the enclosed notice stating that the Iran emergency is to continue in effect beyond November 14, 1984, to the *Federal Register* for publication. Similar notices were sent to the Congress and the *Federal Register* on November 12, 1980, November 12, 1981, November 8, 1982, and November 4, 1983.

The crisis between the United States and Iran that began in 1979 has eased, but has not been fully resolved. Although the inter-national tribunal established to adjudicate claims of U.S. nationals against Iran and of Iranian nationals against the United States continues to function, full normalization of commercial and diplomatic relations between the United States and Iran will require more time. In these circumstances, I have determined that it is necessary to maintain in force the broad authorities that may be needed in the process of implementing the January 1981 agreements with Iran and in the eventual normalization of relations with that country.

Sincerely,

RONALD REAGAN

Note: This is the text of identical letters addressed to Thomas P. O'Neill, Jr., Speaker of the House of Representatives, and George Bush, President of the Senate.

The letters were released by the Office of the Press Secretary on November 8.

Letter Accepting the Resignation of T.H. Bell as Secretary of Education
November 8, 1984

Dear Ted:

It is with deep regret that I accept your resignation as Secretary of Education, effective December 31, 1984. Of course, I understand that you have made this decision for personal reasons, but I want you to know how greatly I will miss you as a member of my Cabinet.

When we entered office four years ago, there was a widespread feeling that American education was not meeting the high standard of excellence it had attained in the past. You gave voice to that feeling but, more than that, you provided leadership in developing solutions to the problems of our schools. As a result, there is a new dedica-tion in America to achieving educational excellence.

This dedication exists not only at the Federal level but also, and more importantly, at the grassroots level. In communities all across America, parents, students and teachers are devoting their time and energy to making their local schools as good as they can possibly be. You have provided these citizen activists with a clear and inspiring example of effective leadership in Washington, and you have made sure that the Federal government listens and responds to their concerns. This achievement is one that will continue to bear good fruit for many years to come, and I want to thank you personally for a job well done.

As you return to private life, it is with a great record of accomplishment. Nancy and I send you our best wishes for every future success and happiness.

RON

November 8, 1984

Dear Mr. President,

Because of personal circumstances that I have discussed with Jim Baker, I submit my resignation as U.S. Secretary of Education effective December 31, 1984.

The past four years have been the most challenging and exciting in my professional life. Serving the country as a member of your cabinet has been a signal honor.

I leave my position feeling that we are in the midst of a lasting and meaningful academic renewal that will benefit millions of learners in our nation's schools and colleges. It has been a pleasure to serve under your leadership in our quest for excellence in education.

Thank you for the privilege of serving in your cabinet, and may God bless you as you carry out your awesome responsibilities of providing leadership and direction for our great Republic.

Sincerely,

TED
T.H. Bell

Appointment of the General Chairman and Chairman of the 1985 Inaugural Committee
November 8, 1984

The President today announced the appointment of Michael K. Deaver, Assistant to the President and Deputy Chief of the White House Staff, to be General Chairman of the 1985 Inaugural Committee. In that capacity, he will have supervisory responsibility for all Inaugural activities and will report directly to the President.

Mr. Deaver is responsible for the Office of Presidential Scheduling and Appointments, the Office of Presidential Advance, the White House Military Office, the Office of the First Lady, and the Office of Public Affairs. He is a member of the National Productivity Advisory Council, Chairman of the White House Coordinating Committee on Private Sector Initiatives, and Chairman of the Outreach Working Group on Women. He has served as the Presidential liaison to the 1984 Olympic games, the U.S. Olympic Committee, and the International Olympic Committee. Mr. Deaver is also responsible for the communications planning, conceptualizing, and execution functions of the White House Office of Public Affairs.

The President also announced today the appointment of Ronald H. Walker to be Chairman of the 1985 Inaugural Committee. Mr. Walker will report to Mr. Deaver.

Mr. Walker is managing director/partner of the Washington, DC, office of Korn/Kerry International. He recently served as manager and chief executive officer of the 1984 Republican National Convention. Prior to joining Korn/Kerry, he was president of his own consulting firm in Dallas, TX. Mr. Walker was formerly associate director of World Championship Tennis and has served as Director of America's National Park Service. In addition, he served as a Special Assistant to President Richard Nixon, coordinating Presidential travel.

Appointment of 15 Members of the Presidential Advisory Council on the Peace Corps, and Designation of Chairman and Vice Chairman
November 8, 1984

The President today announced his intention to appoint the following individuals to be members of the Presidential Advisory Council on the Peace Corps. These are new positions. The President also intends to designate Colleen White as Chairman and Ed Young as Vice Chairman.

Colleen Toy White is a special assistant in the district attorney's office of Ventura County, CA. She was born June 19, 1944, in Wetumka, OK, and now resides in Camarillo, CA.

Ed Young is an agribusiness consultant and managing partner of Young Brothers, Inc., in Florence, SC. He was born September 7, 1920, in Florence, SC, where he now resides.

Katherine Milner Anderson is chairman of the board of Domino's Pizza of Washington, DC, Inc., and previously served as Associate Director of the Office of Cabinet Affairs at the White House. She was born December 16, 1947, in Gulfport, MS, and now resides in Alexandria, VA.

L. Francis Bouchey is a Washington, DC, based international and public affairs consultant who serves as the president of the Council for Inter-American Security, Inc. He was born October 3, 1942, in Yakima, WA, and now resides in Falls Church, VA.

Lucia del Carmen Lombana-Cadavid has served in financial and administrative positions with the Bank of America (Los Angeles); First National City Bank of New York (Medellin, Colombia) and the Sociedad Aeronautico de Medellin (Medellin, Colombia). She was born December 3, 1937, in Medellin, Colombia, and now resides in Alexandria, VA.

James G. Calhoun managed J.V. Calhoun Co., manufacturer representatives, for over 50 years. He was born October 8, 1926, in Philadelphia, PA, and now resides in Rosemont, PA.

Ben Kinchlow is cohost of the Christian Broadcasting Network program "The 700 Club" in Virginia Beach, VA. He was born December 27, 1936, in Uvalde, TX, and now resides in Virginia Beach.

Alicia Casanova is a part-time consultant to ACTION in Washington, DC. She was born March 2, 1937, in Havana, Cuba, and now resides in Bethesda, MD.

Pierre Manon is a management consultant and attorney in Palm Springs, CA. He was born April 21, 1914, in Bucharest, Romania, and now resides in Palm Springs.

Anthony T. Mercurio is a retired officer of the United States Army and a business consultant for National Dynamics. He was born April 18, 1934, in West Bend, WI, and now resides in El Paso, TX.

Alex Stiglitz has been self-employed as a real estate investor and small business adviser since coming to the United States in 1949. He is retired and is currently involved in community service as a volunteer crime prevention specialist in the Los Angeles County Sheriff's Department. He was born September 28, 1925, in Budapest, Hungary, and now resides in Los Angeles, CA.

James B. Taylor is executive director of the Young America's Foundation in Reston, VA. He was born June 23, 1943, in Philadelphia, PA, and now resides in Reston.

Jack M. Webb is head of the law firm of Jack M. Webb and Associates, which he founded in 1982. He was born February 23, 1936, in Monroe, LA, and now resides in Houston, TX.

Martha Barnes Weisend is involved in community service in Dallas, TX. She was born September 15, 1931, in Memphis, TN, and now resides in Dallas.

Sam H. Zakhem is vice president of corporate relations and economic affairs of Rocky Mountain Orthodontics. He was born November 25, 1935, in Lebanon and now resides in Denver, CO.

Appointment of Three Members of the Board of Foreign Scholarships
November 8, 1984

The President today announced his intention to appoint the following individuals to be members of the Board of Foreign Scholarships for terms expiring September 22, 1987:

Jeffrey B. Gayner is a reappointment. Since 1974 Mr. Gayner has been serving as director of foreign policy studies at the Heritage Foundation. He graduated from Washington & Lee University (B.A., 1967) and attended the University of North Carolina at Chapel Hill (1967–1969, 1971–1973). He was born February 27, 1945, in Cleveland, OH, and now resides in Washington, DC.

E. Victor Milione is a reappointment. He is president of the Intercollegiate Studies Institute,

Inc., in Bryn Mawr, PA, which he founded in 1953. He is also publisher of the Intercollegiate Review. He graduated from St. Joseph's University (B.S., 1950). He is married, has one child, and resides in Ardmore, PA. He was born May 12, 1924, in Havertown, PA.

John Willson would succeed Gerhart Niemeyer. He has served as professor of history in the department of history at Hillsdale College in Michigan. He was chairman of the honors program at Hillsdale College in 1976–1981. He graduated from Hobart College (B.A., 1962), the University of Wyoming (M.A., 1964), and Syracuse University (Ph.D.). He is married, has three children, and resides in Hillsdale, MI. He was born March 28, 1940, in Syracuse, NY.

Appointment of Patricia Jacobson as a Member of the National Voluntary Service Advisory Council
November 8, 1984

The President today announced his intention to appoint Patricia Jacobson to be a member of the National Voluntary Service Advisory Council. She would succeed James Webb.

Mrs. Jacobson is a Republican State committeewoman from Texas. She presently serves as a member of the Haltom-Richland

Chamber of Commerce. She was a member of the board of directors of the YMCA in Fort Worth, TX, in 1968–1976.

Mrs. Jacobson attended North Texas State University. She is married, has seven children, and resides in Fort Worth, TX. She was born December 23, 1926, in Houston, TX.

Appointment of Ginny Thornburgh as a Member of the President's Committee on Mental Retardation
November 8, 1984

The President today announced his intention to appoint Ginny Thornburgh to be a member of the President's Committee on Mental Retardation for a term expiring May 11, 1987. This is a reappointment.

Mrs. Thornburgh has been a member of the President's Committee on Mental Retardation since 1982. She is an active volun-

teer working with mentally retarded and physically handicapped persons. She served as a member of the boards of directors of the Home for Crippled Children in Pittsburgh (1968–1975, 1977–1978) and of the Allegheny County chapter of the Pennsylvania Association for Retarded Citizens (1969–1974, 1977–1978; president, 1974–

1975). She was honorary chairperson for the Pennsylvania Committee of the International Year of the Child.

She graduated from Wheaton College (B.A., 1961) and Harvard University (M.A., 1962). She is married, has four children, and resides in Harrisburg, PA. She was born January 7, 1940, in New York, NY.

Memorandum Returning Without Approval a Bill To Reauthorize the Equal Access to Justice Act
November 8, 1984

I am withholding my approval of H.R. 5479, a bill "to amend section 504 of title 5, United States Code, and section 2412 of title 28, United States Code, with respect to awards of expenses of certain agency and court proceedings, and for other purposes."

H.R. 5479 would permanently reauthorize and make a number of significant changes to the Equal Access to Justice Act. The Act allows the award of attorneys' fees to certain parties who successfully litigate against the government unless the government demonstrates that its position is substantially justified or that special circumstances exist that make a fee award unjust. Because the Equal Access to Justice Act expired on September 30, 1984, legislation is needed to reauthorize the Act.

I am firmly committed to the policies underlying the Equal Access to Justice Act and will make the permanent and retroactive reauthorization of the Act a high legislative priority of the Administration in the next Congress. Where the Federal government has taken a position in litigation that is not substantially justified, and thereby has caused a small business or individual to incur unnecessary attorneys' fees and legal costs, I believe it proper for the government to reimburse that small business or individual for those expenses. The Equal Access to Justice Act thus serves an important salutary purpose that should become a permanent part of our government. Unfortunately, H.R. 5479 makes certain changes to the Equal Access to Justice Act that do not further the Act's basic purposes and that are inconsistent with fundamental principles of good government. The most objectionable of these provisions is the change the bill would make in the definition of "position of the United States." Under this changed definition, the Act would no longer apply only to the government's position taken in the administrative or court litigation, but would extend to the underlying agency action. This would result in needless and wasteful litigation over what is supposed to be a subsidiary issue, the award of attorneys' fees, and would further burden the courts, which would have to hear the claims in each case not once, but twice. In addition, this change could also undermine the free exchange of ideas and positions within each agency that is essential for good government.

For example, this change would require courts in making fee determinations to examine the conduct of an agency even where that conduct is not at issue in the court's review of the merits of the case before it. This would mean that a fee proceeding could result in an entirely new and subsidiary inquiry in the circumstances that gave rise to the original lawsuit. This inquiry only could lead to far lengthier proceedings than required if the court is merely to examine arguments made in court, but also could lead to extensive discovery of how the underlying agency position was formulated, and who advocated what position and for what reasons at what time. In effect, every step of the agency decision-making process, at whatever level, could become the subject of litigation discovery. Such extensive discovery could inhibit free discussion within an agency prior to any final agency policy decision or action for fear that any internal disagreements or reservations would be the subject of discovery and judicial inquiry.

In addition, H.R. 5479 contains a provision that would require the United States to pay interest on any awarded attorneys' fees not paid within 60 days after the date of the award. As noted by the Comptroller General of the United States, this provision would give lawyers who have received awards under the Act more favorable treatment than any other group entitled to interest payments from the United States. I agree with the Comptroller General that to the extent any interest should be paid under the Act, it should be paid on the same basis as other interest payments made by the government on court judgments.

The Department of Justice, the Office of Management and Budget, and other concerned agencies have repeatedly expressed to the Congress their serious reservations about these and other provisions of H.R. 5479. I wholly support the prompt reauthorization of the Equal Access to Justice Act and believe that the reauthorization should be retroactively effective to October 1, 1984. In light of the permanent nature of a reauthorization, such a reauthorization should include modifications and improvements in the Act, which the Administration is willing to explore with the Congress.

Concurrently with this memorandum, I am issuing a memorandum to all agency heads concerning the Equal Access to Justice Act. This memorandum reaffirms my strong commitment to the policies underlying the Act and instructs agency heads to review the procedures of their agencies to ensure that agency positions continue to be substantially justified. Special attention is to be given to those agency positions that affect small businesses. In addition, each agency is to accept and assist in the preparation of fee applications which can be considered once the Act is reauthorized.

I look forward to approving an acceptable reauthorization of the Equal Access to Justice Act early next year. For the reasons indicated, however, I am compelled to withhold my approval of H.R. 5479.

RONALD REAGAN

The White House,
November 8, 1984.

Note: The memorandum was released by the Office of the Press Secretary on November 9.

Memorandum on Reauthorization of the Equal Access to Justice Act
November 8, 1984

Memorandum for the Heads of Executive Departments and Agencies

The authorities of the Equal Access to Justice Act (Title II of Public Law 96–481) expired on September 30, 1984, for all cases initiated after that date. While I strongly support the reauthorization of the Act and have worked closely with the Congress to that effect, I have today withheld my approval of the recently passed bill (H.R. 5479) reauthorizing the Act because certain of its amendments are unacceptable to the Administration. It is my hope and expectation that an acceptable reauthorization of the Act will be passed by the Congress early next year and that this reauthorization will apply retroactively to covered cases initiated on or after October 1, 1984.

Pending the reauthorization of the Equal Access to Justice Act next year, I am directing all agency heads to take the following actions.

First, agency heads shall ensure that the appropriate offices and personnel in their agencies understand that the Administration remains firmly committed to the policies underlying the Equal Access to Justice Act and that the failure to obtain an acceptable reauthorization of the Act this year should in no way be interpreted as a reduction in that commitment. In this regard, agency heads shall again review the procedures used by their agencies to ensure that agency positions are "substantially justified" within the meaning of the Act. Special attention shall be given to those agency positions that affect small businesses.

Second, agencies shall accept and retain on file any applications for awards of fees and expenses pursuant to section 203 of the Act (5 U.S.C. 504) and shall continue to provide an appropriate assistance in making such applications. Agencies will not, of course, be in a position to rule on these applications until the Act is reauthorized, but otherwise shall continue to accept such applications and provide necessary assistance as if the Act were in force.

Third, as for awards relating to judicial proceedings under section 204 of the Act, agencies shall continue to accept and retain on file any demands for settlement of claims for such awards even though such claims (for cases initiated on or after Octo-

ber 1, 1984) cannot be filed in court until the Act is reauthorized. Once the Act is reauthorized, such claims shall then be reviewed by the agency in accordance with the terms of the reauthorized Act.

The above measures will ensure that the policies underlying the Equal Access to Justice Act will continue in effect until the Act is reauthorized and that the protections afforded to litigants by the Act—particularly to small businesses—will not be denied during the period between the Act's expiration and its reauthorization.

RONALD REAGAN

Note: The memorandum was released by the Office of the Press Secretary on November 9.

Statement on Signing the Civil Service Retirement Spouse Equity Act of 1984
November 9, 1984

I am very pleased to sign H.R. 2300. Rewarding the Government's dedicated high-level executives, managers, and supervisors for sustained top-notch performance, as this bill will allow us to do, is a key element of management improvement in the executive branch.

Nearly 4 years ago, in my Inaugural Address, I promised the American people that we would "make government work." We are making some very important progress in keeping that promise with the enactment of the legislation I am signing.

The current merit pay system has been found seriously wanting by the Office of Personnel Management, the employing agencies, the Comptroller General, and, not least, the employees themselves. Further, the Grace commission report on the Government's personnel system found that we suffer from a "failure to properly recognize excellent performance with incentive awards and additional step increases" and that there is a "lack of credibility in the performance award (bonus) program for career executives."

This bill responds to criticisms of the

present system and strengthens and improves merit pay in a meaningful way. It is the product of a lot of hard work on the part of this administration and key members of both parties in the Congress with a strong interest in improving the system of paying and rewarding our managers and executives, including Senators Paul Trible and John Warner and Congressmen Frank Wolf and Bill Dannemeyer.

The changes this bill will make in our merit pay system for managers are very important indeed. These changes will ensure that we recognize our very best performers with meaningful financial rewards, both through the annual performance appraisal process and through special awards. In addition, this new system will help pave the way toward applying these important changes in the incentive and reward system to the rest of the Federal white-collar work force in the near future. Then, finally, performance will become the central feature of the Government's personnel system.

Senior executives will find much in this legislation to cheer about, too, not least of which is a change that will enable them to receive *all* of a bonus or Presidential rank award, and not just the amount permitted under the pay "cap." They will also have improved job security in case of reductions in force and will be given more notice than at present if they are to be reassigned to a different part of the country.

Finally, and very importantly, this measure contains significant changes that will improve equity for spouses under the Federal Government's employee retirement system. This set of changes embodies all of the major provisions of a bill that the administration submitted to the Congress. It permits former spouses of Federal employees to receive survivor benefits in accordance with orders from State courts. It also requires consent by a spouse before an employee can waive survivor benefits. These changes are similar to those enacted for private sector pension plans earlier this year with the active support of the administration.

I want to thank all of those who worked so hard to bring about passage of this bill this year and say to Federal employees: We want to give you all the encouragement we can to do your very best work, and we want to see that you are rewarded for it. This legislation should go a long way toward achieving that end and establishing an effective partnership for "making government work."

Note: As enacted, H.R. 2300 is Public Law 98–615, approved November 8.

Statement on Signing the Intelligence Authorization Act for Fiscal Year 1985
November 9, 1984

I am pleased to sign into law H.R. 5399, the Intelligence Authorization Act for fiscal year 1985. This act represents another step in my continuing effort to revitalize our Nation's intelligence capability. Given the ever-increasing difficulty of ensuring the security of this nation, it is essential that we have an Intelligence Community capable of meeting these diverse challenges. In authorizing sufficient appropriations and in providing new administrative authorities that enhance the ability of our intelligence agencies to perform their missions, Congress has, with this act, provided the basis for maintaining and building our intelligence capabilities. This act ensures that the Intelligence Community can continue to stay firmly on the path of progress that we and the Congress have charted together.

I sincerely regret the inability of the Congress to resolve the issue of continuing certain activities in Nicaragua that are important to achieving U.S. policy objectives. The necessity of U.S. support for this program is beyond question. I am signing this act with every expectation that shortly after the next Congress convenes it will provide adequate support for programs to assist the development of democracy in Central America.

Note: As enacted, H.R. 5399 is Public Law 98–618, approved November 8.

Statement on Signing the Federal District Court Organization Act of 1984
November 9, 1984

I am pleased to sign H.R. 6163, the Federal District Court Organization Act of 1984. This legislation accomplishes a number of key reforms that significantly improve the environment for technological innovation. By strengthening the rights of people who are willing to risk commercializing new ideas to reap their just rewards, this legislation encourages individuals to create and develop new technologies.

The most important provision in this act is the creation of a new form of intellectual property protection for semiconductor chip products. It is easy to copy chip designs. Innovators can invest tens of millions of dollars to create and market these semiconductors, while others can copy these designs at a tiny fraction of the cost. By creating penalties against copying, this legislation significantly enhances the incentives for firms to invest in new designs. Furthermore, the legislation includes a provision encouraging other countries to provide comparable protection for U.S. semiconductors sold abroad.

The stakes in this area are tremendous. Not only does the semiconductor industry annually ship about $14 billion of semiconductors, it also employs about 200,000 people. Perhaps most important, increasingly more powerful and cheaper semiconductors are at the heart of a wide range of technologies that have increased American productivity, competitiveness, and our standard of living.

The legislation also reaffirms certain basic principles of trademark law upon which all American businesses have traditionally relied to protect the marks enabling them to distinguish their products from others. Moreover, it extends the principle of contractor ownership of federally funded inventions to those made in government-owned, contractor-operated laboratories, which takes advantage of the private sector's ability to commercialize these inventions more effectively than the Government.

The Congress passed this legislation with strong bipartisan support. My administration strongly supported these provisions that strengthen intellectual property rights. This legislation takes a major step in spurring the creative genius of America's entrepreneurs.

Note: As enacted, H.R. 6163 is Public Law 98–620, approved November 8.

Statement on Signing the Saint Elizabeths Hospital and District of Columbia Mental Health Services Act
November 9, 1984

It is with great pleasure that I sign into law H.R. 6224, the Saint Elizabeths Hospital and District of Columbia Mental Health Services Act. This legislation, which has been developed with the participation of the administration and the District of Columbia government and was passed by unanimous vote in both Houses of the Congress, will make Saint Elizabeths Hospital an integral part of the District's mental health delivery system.

Since its establishment by the Congress in 1855, Saint Elizabeths Hospital has provided care to military personnel and to District of Columbia residents. The hospital has played an historic role in American psychiatry and continues to provide care, treatment, and rehabilitation services to approximately 1,700 inpatients. Located on more than 300 acres, it includes programs for adults, child and adolescent services, a forensic unit, an Hispanic unit, and an array of support programs necessary to ensure quality care.

The patient population of Saint Elizabeths has undergone significant shifts. For almost 100 years, most patients were Federal beneficiaries. Today, however, almost 90 percent of the inpatients and virtually all of the 2,800 outpatients are residents of the District of Columbia.

The hospital has maintained accreditation in all of its programs since 1978, receiving full accreditation by the Joint Commission on the Accreditation of Hospitals in 1980 as well as commendation by that body for the quality of care provided.

Enactment of the District of Columbia Self-Government and Governmental Reorganization Act provided impetus to the growing concern over the appropriateness of the Federal Government's operating Saint Elizabeths primarily for the benefit of the District of Columbia.

The transfer that H.R. 6224 makes possible means that the hospital will be controlled and supported at the local level. This will provide the people of the District of Columbia with an effective mental health services delivery system and will be in keeping with the modern practice of comprehensive programs for mental health care.

As provided by this legislation, the District of Columbia's plan for structuring and operating the new system will be developed in close consultation with officials of Saint Elizabeths Hospital, labor-management advisory groups, and professional and community groups in the District. In addition, public hearings will be held and plans submitted to the Congress for review. Thus, there are guarantees that the new unified system will provide a continuum of care with the full range of services that do not currently exist in the District. The groundwork for a comprehensive community-based system of mental health services is now in place.

Note: As enacted, H.R. 6224 is Public Law 98–621, approved November 8.

Statement on Signing the Patent Law Amendments Act of 1984
November 9, 1984

I have approved H.R. 6286, the Patent Law Amendments Act of 1984. The stimulation of American inventive genius requires a patent system that offers our inventors prompt and effective protection for their inventions. The Patent Law Amendments Act of 1984 effects a number of improvements in the patent system to achieve this goal.

The bill provides inventors with a new, efficient mechanism to protect their right to use their inventions without the need to expend scarce resources to obtain a patent. This procedure offers great cost savings potential to Federal agencies, which are the single largest filers of U.S. patents. It also closes a loophole in existing law which permitted copiers to export jobs and avoid liability by arranging for final assembly of patented machines to occur offshore. The act eliminates unwarranted technicalities in the patent law that threaten the validity of patents for inventions arising from corporate research teams.

Together with other provisions that enable the Patent and Trademark Office to streamline its operations, these provisions make our patent system more responsive to the needs of our inventors and industry. America must remain at the cutting edge of technology, and a strong and effective patent system is fundamental to this goal.

I am disappointed that the Congress chose to include in this bill a new National Commission on Innovation and Productivity. This Commission would be established to study the productivity of inventors employed by private companies and, more generally, to make recommendations for changes in U.S. laws to better foster innovation and productivity. I strongly believe that increased innovation is essential to our continued technological leadership. The White House Conference on Productivity and the President's Commission on Industrial Competitiveness have brought together experts from government, academia, and the private sector to evaluate the impact of Federal policy on innovation and productivity. Many of their recommendations have already been implemented. A new National Commission to address this issue would simply duplicate the work of these groups.

Employed inventors have contributed greatly to our country's competitiveness in high technology areas. Nevertheless, I believe that the private sector, rather than the Federal Government, is best able to decide on methods to stimulate increased productivity on the part of employed inventors. My administration will oppose any appropriation for the National Commission on Innovation and Productivity authorized by H.R. 6286.

I must also note my objection to the structure and composition of the National Commission on Innovation and Productivity. The Commission would be composed of three Senators appointed by the President of the Senate; three Members of the House of Representatives appointed by the Speaker; and three members appointed by the President, of whom one shall be an "appropriate" officer or employee of the United States, one shall be an employer who employs inventors, and one shall be an employed inventor. Such entities are severely destructive of the tripartite system of government established by the Constitution.

Although the Commission would appear to serve primarily legislative functions, this bill would place the Commission partly within the executive branch. I believe that creation of such a Commission, which is neither clearly within the executive branch, nor clearly within the legislative branch, tends to blur the functional distinction between the governmental branches that is fundamental to the concept of separation of powers. It would be more appropriate for the Commission to be composed either entirely of members selected by the legislative branch, if it is to serve primarily legislative functions, or entirely of members appointed by the President, if it is to serve the executive branch.

Note: As enacted, H.R. 6286 is Public Law 98–622, approved November 8.

Appointment of Marcia Israel as a Member of the Advisory Committee on Small and Minority Business Ownership
November 9, 1984

The President today announced his intention to appoint Marcia Israel to be a member of the Advisory Committee on Small and Minority Business Ownership. She would succeed Katherine D. Ortega.

Mrs. Israel is president and chief executive officer of Judy's, Inc., a group of specialty fashion stores located in five States. She is also creator and president of Golden Goose Electronics Corp., an electronic system used by retailers. She received the Merchandising Award of the Year given by the textile industry and the Los Angeles Times Woman of the Year Award in 1964 in the category of industry and finance, civic and philanthropic.

She is married, has two children, and resides in Los Angeles, CA. She was born in Cocheeton, NY.

Appointment of Two Members of the National Advisory Council on Adult Education
November 9, 1984

The President today announced his intention to appoint the following individuals to be members of the National Advisory Council on Adult Education for terms expiring July 10, 1986:

Daniel E. Brennan, Sr., will succeed Rawlein G. Soberano. Mr. Brennan has been a member of the law firm of Brennan, McNamara & Brennan in Bridgeport, CT, since 1981. Previously he was a member of the firm of Brennan, Daly, McNamara & Weihing in 1947–1981. He graduated from Notre Dame University (A.B., 1934) and Dickinson Law School (LL.B., 1938). He is married, has two children, and resides in Bridgeport, CT. He was born May 9, 1913, in Bridgeport.

Ronna Romney will succeed Patricia Smith. Mrs. Romney is a writer and lecturer and is active in church and community activities in Michigan. She serves as the honorary chairwoman for the American Cancer Society in the Detroit Metropolitan area for 1984 and was recently elected to serve as the national Republican committeewoman from Michigan. She is married, has five children, and resides in Bloomfield Hills, MI. She was born September 24, 1943, in Detroit, MI.

Appointment of David W. Belin as a Member of the President's Committee on the Arts and the Humanities
November 9, 1984

The President today announced his intention to appoint David W. Belin to be a member of the President's Committee on the Arts and the Humanities. This is a new position. Mr. Belin was designated by the majority leader of the Senate.

Mr. Belin is a senior partner of the Des Moines, IA, law firm of Belin, Harris, Helmick, Heartney & Tesdell. He has practiced law in Des Moines since 1954, except for two periods of government service: In 1963 he served as counsel to the Warren commission, and in 1975 he was executive director of the Rockefeller commission.

He serves on the board of directors of the Kemper Mutual Funds. He is a past member of the boards of the Des Moines Symphony, the Civic Music Association, and the Community Drama Association. In 1978 he received the National Conference of Christians and Jews Brotherhood Award.

Mr. Belin received undergraduate, master of business administration, and juris doctor degrees from the University of Michigan. He has five children and resides in Des Moines, IA. He was born June 20, 1928, in Washington, DC.

Appointment of Mitch Gaylord as a Member of the President's Council on Physical Fitness and Sports
November 9, 1984

The President today announced his intention to appoint Mitch Gaylord to be a member of the President's Council on Physical Fitness and Sports. He would succeed Leon J. Weil.

Mr. Gaylord was a member of the United States men's gymnastic team for the 1984 Summer Olympics. He received a gold medal in the men's overall title, a silver medal in the vault competition, and bronze medals for the rings and parallel bars. Mr. Gaylord has been in gymnastics for 11 years and is the originator of the "Gaylord Flip" on the high bar. He was a member of the American teams in the World Championships in 1981 and 1983. He won the all-around title in the NCAA Championships this past season.

He is a senior at the University of California at Los Angeles. He was born March 10, 1961, in Los Angeles, CA, and now resides in Van Nuys, CA.

Statement by Principal Deputy Press Secretary Speakes on the Central Intelligence Agency Psychological Warfare Manual
November 10, 1984

The President has reviewed the reports of the Intelligence Oversight Board (IOB) and the CIA Inspector General (IG) on the events surrounding the preparation of the Psychological Warfare Manual. Both reports were delivered to the President on November 8, 1984.

The CIA IG and the IOB both conducted detailed and extensive inquiries into the conceptual motives and administrative procedures surrounding the preparation of this manual. Both bodies noted that despite portions which could be misinterpreted, the manual had worthy purposes: instilling in Nicaraguan freedom fighters the knowledge of how to promote understanding of their goals among the people and counseling them on appropriate behavior in dealing with civilians.

Both reports found that there had been no violation by CIA personnel or contract employees of the Constitution or laws of the United States, Executive orders, or Presidential directives. The IG report identified instances of poor judgment and lapses in oversight at lower levels within the Agency. Recommendations for corrective measures to strengthen management and oversight within the CIA were approved, as well as disciplinary action where lapses in judgment or performance occurred. The President has directed that Director Casey brief the appropriate oversight committees of the Congress on the findings and recommendations contained in the IG report.

Appointment of the Membership of Emergency Boards Nos. 205 and 206 To Investigate Railroad Labor Disputes
November 10, 1984

The President has appointed the following-named persons to be members of Emergency Boards Nos. 205 and 206:

Eva Robins, of New York, NY, will serve as Chairman. She is an arbitrator and has served as assistant director of labor relations for the Borden Co. and as deputy chairman of the New York City Office of Collective Bargaining.

Thomas N. Rinaldo, of Williamsville, NY, is an attorney, arbitrator, and mediator.

Thomas F. Carey, of Jericho, NY, is an arbitrator with extensive experience in grievance, contract, and interest arbitration.

On October 25, 1984, the President created Emergency Boards Nos. 205 and 206 to investigate and make recommendations for settlement of current disputes between the Long Island Rail Road (LIRR) and employees represented by the Brotherhood of Locomotive Engineers and the Brotherhood of Railway, Airline and Steamship Clerks, Freight Handlers, Express and Station Employes.

The LIRR is the largest commuter railroad in the United States, transporting 283,000 passengers each weekday over a 330-mile system extending from Manhattan to the end of Long Island. In addition, the LIRR provides the only rail freight service on Long Island and connects with the Nation's rail system through New York City.

Earlier, on June 20, 1984, the President invoked the emergency board procedures of the Railway Labor Act applicable to commuter railroads and created Emergency Boards Nos. 202 and 203 to investigate and report on these same disputes. Emergency Boards Nos. 202 and 203 investigated the issues and prepared reports and recommendations for settlement of the disputes. The Boards' reports were submitted to the President on July 20, 1984.

Following the release of the reports and recommendations by Emergency Boards

Nos. 202 and 203, the parties unsuccessfully continued their attempts to resolve their differences. The statutory period allotted for this process expired at midnight, October 18, 1984.

Section 9A of the Railway Labor Act provides that a party to the dispute or the Governor of any State through which the service runs may request the President to establish a second emergency board if the dispute remains unresolved. Emergency Boards Nos. 205 and 206 were created in response to such a request made by Governor Cuomo. The parties will now submit their final offers to Emergency Boards Nos. 205 and 206 within 30 days, and the Boards will report their selection of the most reasonable offer within 30 days thereafter. During this 60-day period, and for 60 days after the submission of the report, the parties must maintain the status quo and refrain from engaging in self-help.

Remarks at Dedication Ceremonies for the Vietnam Veterans Memorial Statue
November 11, 1984

Senator Warner, thank you very much. And may I thank you, also, for the crucial personal support that you gave to the building of this memorial. I extend the thanks of the Nation, also, to all who have contributed so much to this fine cause.

Ladies and gentlemen, honored guests, my remarks today will be brief because so much has been said over the years and said so well about the loyalty and the valor of those who served us in Vietnam. It's occurred to me that only one very important thing has been left unsaid, and I will try to speak of it today.

It's almost 10 years now since U.S. military involvement in Vietnam came to a close. Two years ago, our government dedicated the memorial bearing the names of those who died or are still missing. Every day, the families and friends of those brave men and women come to the wall and search out a name and touch it.

The memorial reflects as a mirror re-

flects, so that when you find the name you're searching for you find it in your own reflection. And as you touch it, from certain angles, you're touching, too, the reflection of the Washington Monument or the chair in which great Abe Lincoln sits.

Those who fought in Vietnam are part of us, part of our history. They reflected the best in us. No number of wreaths, no amount of music and memorializing will ever do them justice but it is good for us that we honor them and their sacrifice. And it's good that we do it in the reflected glow of the enduring symbols of our Republic.

The fighting men depicted in the statue we dedicate today, the three young American servicemen, are individual only in terms of their battle dress; all are as one, with eyes fixed upon the memorial bearing the names of their brothers in arms. On their youthful faces, faces too young to have experienced war, we see expressions of loneliness and profound love and a fierce determination never to forget.

The men of Vietnam answered the call of their country. Some of them died in the arms of many of you here today, asking you to look after a newly born child or care for a loved one. They died uncomplaining. The tears staining their mud-caked faces were not for self-pity but for the sorrow they knew the news of their death would cause their families and friends.

As you knelt alongside his litter and held him one last time, you heard his silent message—he asked you not to forget.

Today we pay homage not only to those who gave their lives but to their comrades present today and all across the country. You didn't forget. You kept the faith. You walked from the litter, wiped away your tears, and returned to the battle. You fought on, sustained by one another and deaf to the voices of those who didn't comprehend. You performed with a steadfastness and valor that veterans of other wars salute, and you are forever in the ranks of that special number of Americans in every generation that the Nation records as true patriots.

Also among the service men and women honored here today is a unique group of Americans whose fate is still unknown to our nation and to their families. Nearly 2,500 of the names on this memorial are still missing in Southeast Asia, and some may still be serving. Their names are distinguished by a cross rather than the diamond; thus, this memorial is a symbol of both past and current sacrifice.

The war in Vietnam threatened to tear our society apart, and the political and philosophical disagreements that animated each side continue to some extent.

It's been said that these memorials reflect a hunger for healing. Well, I do not know if perfect healing ever occurs, but I know that sometimes when a bone is broken, if it's knit together well, it will in the end be stronger than if it had not been broken. I believe that in the decade since Vietnam the healing has begun, and I hope that before my days as Commander in Chief are over the process will be completed.

There were great moral and philosophical disagreements about the rightness of the war, and we cannot forget them because there is no wisdom to be gained in forgetting. But we can forgive each other and ourselves for those things that we now recognize may have been wrong, and I think it's time we did.

There's been much rethinking by those who did not serve and those who did. There's been much rethinking by those who held strong views on the war and by those who did not know which view was right. There's been rethinking on all sides, and this is good. And it's time we moved on in unity and with resolve—with the resolve to always stand for freedom, as those who fought did, and to always try to protect and preserve the peace.

And we must in unity work to account for those still missing and aid those returned who still suffer from the pain and memory of Vietnam. We must, as a society, take guidance from the fighting men memorialized by this statue. The three servicemen are watchful, ready, and challenged, but they are also standing forever together.

And let me say to the Vietnam veterans gathered here today: When you returned home, you brought solace to the loved ones of those who fell, but little solace was given to you. Some of your countrymen were unable to distinguish between our native distaste for war and the stainless patriotism of those who suffered its scars. But there's been a rethinking there, too. And now we can say to you, and say as a nation: Thank you for your courage. Thank you for being patient with your countrymen. Thank you. Thank you for continuing to stand with us together.

The men and women of Vietnam fought for freedom in a place where liberty was in danger. They put their lives in danger to help a people in a land far away from their own. Many sacrificed their lives in the name of duty, honor, and country. All were patriots who lit the world with their fidelity and courage.

They were both our children and our heroes. We will never ever forget them. We will never forget their devotion and their sacrifice. They stand before us, marching into time and into shared memory, forever. May God bless their souls.

And now I shall sign the document by

which this memorial has been gratefully received by our government.

And now it belongs to all of us, just as those men who have come back belong to all of us. Thank you.

Note: The President spoke at 4:30 p.m. at the Vietnam Veterans Memorial on the Mall. The "Three Fightingmen" statue by sculptor Frederick Hart was dedicated at the ceremony. Following his remarks, the President signed documents transferring the Vietnam Veterans Memorial to the Federal Government.

Remarks at the Welcoming Ceremony for the Grand Duke and Grand Duchess of Luxembourg
November 13, 1984

The President. Your Royal Highnesses, on behalf of the American people, Nancy and I welcome you to the United States.

America and Luxembourg are bound together by the golden cords of friendship and family. Beginning more than 100 years ago, thousands of Luxembourgers made the difficult journey across the Atlantic to the shores of the New World. And most traveled far inland, and they played a vital role in settling the plains and forests of Minnesota, Illinois, Iowa, and Wisconsin.

Today, in the hearty town of Rolling Stone, Minnesota, people still celebrate your national festivals and speak the language of your country.

It's literally true, Your Highness, that the people of America and Luxembourg are cousins; yet perhaps the strongest tie between us is the sturdy bond of common ideals and heritage, for Luxembourg and America share the glorious background of American—or of Western history, I should say—all the lessons that men learned during the centuries-long passage to civilization.

Both our nations cherish tolerance and rule of law. Both are guided by the will of the majority, while respecting the rights of the minority. Above all, both our peoples firmly believe that men and women can only achieve peace, prosperity, and self-fulfillment when they live in liberty. In the words of Pope John Paul II, "Freedom is given to man by God as a measure of His dignity."

In the past, the people of Luxembourg and America have stood together and fought together in the name of human liberty. Your Highness, you yourself fought side by side with American soldiers at Normandy just 40 years ago. The American Third Army, under General George Patton, played a central part in the liberation of Luxembourg. And in a graveyard outside Luxembourg City, General Patton and more than 5,000 American troops are laid to rest.

Today Luxembourg and America stand together still. Luxembourg offers stalwart support to the North Atlantic Treaty Organization, of which we're both members. Your nation works tirelessly to keep the Western alliance strong by keeping it vigorous and, in particular, by promoting a firmly united Europe. Luxembourg hosts the European Investment Bank, the Secretariat of the European Parliament, and the Court of Justice.

Just as we have shared the great challenges of the past, so Luxembourg and America share the bright hopes of the future.

Your Highness, our peoples are industrious and innovative. And despite the difficulties that often go with changing economic circumstances, we in America are seeing a sustained economic expansion, while you in Luxembourg are experiencing the growth of new industries and services.

In freedom, our peoples are conquering material need and making breakthroughs that will help millions to lead longer, fuller, and happier lives.

Your Highnesses, Luxembourg is a proud and beautiful land, a country of lush forests and dramatic valleys, of rolling farmland

and vigorous towns. It is our honor to welcome Luxembourg's beloved Grand Duke and Duchess to America. And it's our hope that while you're here, you will come to see some of our own nation's beauty and pride. May your time with us be joyful and rewarding.

The Grand Duke. Mr. President, ladies and gentlemen, the Grand Duchess and I are deeply moved by your so kind invitation, the warm welcome, and the numerous courtesies extended to us and to our party since our arrival in the United States.

Mr. President, this ceremony has for me a particular significance. How, indeed, could I forget that more than 40 years ago, in February 1941, I had the pleasure to accompany my mother, Grand Duchess Charlotte, and my late father as personal guests of President and Mrs. Roosevelt at the White House.

In bitter times, when the independence of our small country was at stake, we found comfort and guidance from a great President whose determination and leadership ultimately led to the final victory and recovery of democracy and freedom.

It was indeed a long and painful way to go before the United States and Allied forces hit the beachheads of Normandy on June 6th, 40 years ago. The marble crosses, thousands in number, reminded us both, and the other heads of Allied countries assembled at the Normandy memorials in June, of their sacrifice. We pledge never to forget their example. And I assure you that this promise is shared by all my fellow Luxembourgers, linked by a particularly strong bond to the men who gave their utmost during the Battle of the Bulge. More than 5,000 rest forever in our soil, with one of the great American soldiers, General George S. Patton.

Restoring peace and democracy was certainly not an easy venture. It appeared, however, that preserving them would be even harder and more challenging and would certainly have been impossible without the commitment of the United States.

The American engagement in Europe has provided the foundation for one of the longest periods of peace and prosperity our continent has ever enjoyed—to a large extent, our countries, to build the European Community.

And I recall in this respect, Mr. President, the declaration you made at Bonn in your speech on June 9th, 1982: "Europe's shores are our shores. Europe's borders are our borders. We will stand with [you] in defense of our heritage of liberty and dignity." We thank you for this statement and are pleased to assure that the fundamental values of the Atlantic alliance remain unchallenged on both sides of the Atlantic.

The links of my country with America are manifold. They go back to the times more than a century and a half ago when many of my countrymen immigrated to the north and northwestern regions. We are very proud of the fact that our blood keeps circulating in American veins and that your country has been, also, built up by the labor of my compatriots. Yet these ties have deepened since the last war. For some decades now, the ties of political life and of military defense have steadily strengthened. For about 20 years, economic realities of every kind provide us with an American presence in Luxembourg.

My countrymen and I are very proud of the links which thus unite the smallest country of the European Community to the great American nation. Such is the message I should like to transmit to you, Mr. President, with all my congratulations and best wishes for your new Presidency.

Thank you very much.

Note: The President spoke at 10:12 a.m. on the South Lawn of the White House, where Grand Duke Jean and Grand Duchess Josephine-Charlotte were accorded a formal welcome with full military honors.

Following the ceremony, the President and the Grand Duke met in the Oval Office.

Statement by Principal Deputy Press Secretary Speakes on the Visit of the Grand Duke of Luxembourg
November 13, 1984

Grand Duke Jean met with the President today. It was the first state visit from Luxembourg in over 20 years. This was of enormous significance to the Grand Duke, coming 1 day after the 20th anniversary of the Grand Duke's ascension to the throne.

Luxembourg has pursued a pro-U.S., pro-NATO foreign policy, and the President expressed to the Grand Duke his appreciation for Luxembourg's support in this effort. Luxembourg is an active member of the Atlantic alliance. It plays a pivotal role in our common security policies, particularly for logistics, reenforcement, and communications.

Luxembourgers, and the Grand Duke in particular, have a strong attachment to this country. The Grand Duke reiterated his family's great appreciation for our wartime assistance, beginning with the evacuation of the Royal Family in 1940. As you know, the Grand Duke lived in Washington during World War II.

The Grand Duke and the President had met previously at Normandy in June, and this was of special significance to the Grand Duke, who was then a lieutenant in the Irish Guards and participated in the Normandy invasion.

The Grand Duke recalled his experiences with the American Army that liberated Luxembourg 40 years ago. And he noted that he is especially pleased to be able to spend time this week with the U.S. Army's Fourth Infantry Division at Fort Carson, Colorado, and this is the unit that he accompanied on the liberation of Luxembourg.

The President, on his part, reviewed our efforts to reestablish a productive dialog with the Soviets on all issues, and in arms control, in particular. The President provided the Grand Duke an idea of where we hope to go in the second Reagan term. And in addition, the Grand Duke indicated that the strong vote of confidence the President received from the American electorate will enable this administration to deal with the Soviets from a position of great confidence.

The Grand Duke noted that Luxembourg will assume the Presidency of the European Community in the latter half of 1985. And he noted that he would want his government to work closely with the U.S. in managing the U.S. economic community relations.

President Reagan reviewed the latest developments in Central America, and of particular interest to the Grand Duke was the positive turn toward democracy in El Salvador under President Duarte.

Note: Larry M. Speakes read the statement to reporters assembled in the Briefing Room at the White House during his daily press briefing, which began at 12:34 p.m.

Appointment of Three Members of the Advisory Committee on the Arts of the John F. Kennedy Center for the Performing Arts
November 13, 1984

The President today announced his intention to appoint the following individuals to be members of the Advisory Committee on the Arts (John F. Kennedy Center for the Performing Arts). These are new appointments.

Ophelia De Vore Mitchell is chief executive officer of Ophelia De Vore Associates, Inc., in New York City. She is also publisher-editor of the Columbus Times newspaper in Columbus, GA. She is a member of the National Newspaper Publishers Association. She has five children and resides in New York, NY. She was born August 12, 1922, in Edgefield, SC.

Lillian Nicolosi Nall is first vice president of the Nevada Museum of Fine Art. She is a director of the Joseph Nicolosi Museum of Art in Los Angeles; founding member of the Art Museum Council of the Los Angeles County Museum of Art; director of the Beverly Hills Music Association; and president of the Nevada Art Gallery. She is married, has three children, and resides in Las Vegas, NV. She was born April 17, 1930, in Orange, NJ.

G. Robert Truex, Jr., is chairman and chief execu-tive officer of Rainier Bancorporation & Rainier National Bank in Seattle, WA. He was vice chairman of Small Business Enterprises Co. in 1968–1972. He served as a trustee of the California Institute of the Arts in 1968–1972 and was development committee chairman in 1968–1971. He is married, has two children, and resides in Seattle, WA. He was born May 29, 1924, in Red Bank, NJ.

Nomination of Six Members of the National Council on the Arts
November 13, 1984

The President today announced his intention to nominate the following individuals to be members of the National Council on the Arts for terms expiring September 3, 1990:

Joseph Epstein would succeed Thomas Patrick Bergin. He is a writer who has been editor of the American Scholar since 1975. He is past editor of Quadrangle-New York Times Books; past associate editor of the New Leader magazine; and past senior editor of Encyclopedia Brittanica. He is married, has two children, and resides in Evanston, IL. He was born January 9, 1937, in Chicago, IL.

Helen Frankenthaler would succeed James Rosenquist. She is an artist whose canvases hang in the Museum of Modern Art and other major museums throughout the world. In the past, she has taught at Yale, Princeton, and Hunter College. She was born December 12, 1928, in New York, NY, where she now resides.

Margaret Eleanor Hillis would succeed Robert Lawson Shaw. She is conductor of the Grammy Award winning Chicago Symphony Chorus. She is also conductor and music director of the Elgin Philharmonic Symphony and founder of the American Choral Foundation. She has re-ceived five Grammy Awards. She was born October 1, 1921, in Kokomo, IN, and now resides in Wilmette, IL.

M. Ray Kingston would succeed Bernard Blas Lopez. He has been an active supporter and participant in the arts in Utah for 30 years. He is vice president of FFKR Architects-Planners, Inc., in Salt Lake City. He is a recipient of the American Institute of Architects Silver Medal. He is married, has three children, and resides in Salt Lake City, UT. He was born October 7, 1934, in Ogden, UT.

Talbot Leland MacCarthy would succeed Rosalind W. Wyman. Mrs. MacCarthy is chairman of the Missouri Arts Council and treasurer of the Station List Publishing Co. She is also a trustee of the Arts & Education Council of Greater St. Louis. She is married, has two children, and resides in St. Louis, MO. She was born January 28, 1936, in St. Louis.

Carlos Moseley would succeed Jacob Lawrence. Mr. Moseley is chairman of the board of directors and past president of the Philharmonic-Symphony Society of New York. He has had a many-faceted career in music as a pianist, educator, government administrator, spokesman, counselor, and fundraiser. He was born September 21, 1914, in Laurens, SC, and now resides in Spartanburg, SC.

Nomination of Julius Belso To Be a Member of the Federal Council on the Aging
November 13, 1984

The President today announced his intention to nominate Julius Belso to be a member of the Federal Council on the Aging for a term expiring June 5, 1987. He would succeed Margaret Long Arnold.

Mr. Belso is a partner in the Biro-Belso

real estate firm in New Brunswick, NJ. He is vice chairman of the board of directors of the Magyar Savings & Loan Association and has been a member of the board of directors since 1965. He is former commissioner of the New Brunswick Human Rights Commission and former State-appointed commissioner to the New Brunswick Housing Authority.

He is married and resides in New Brunswick, NJ. He was born August 12, 1918, in Kerkakutas, Zala Megye, Hungary.

Proclamation 5278—Women in Agriculture Week, 1984
November 13, 1984

By the President of the United States of America

A Proclamation

Women have always played an equal role with men in the agriculture of the Nation. Early America was an agricultural society, and colonial women worked beside men to develop the new land. Together, they learned local agriculture from the Indians, erected log cabins, and cleared farmland. Pushing their clearings to the foothills of the Alleghenies, they passed through mountain gaps and crossed the prairies together in covered wagons.

Women were partners in American life from the founding of our first settlements. Men and women together in family enterprises began to process food, weave fabrics, and market food and fiber. As the settlements became towns and then cities, and as agricultural jobs became more specialized, women remained partners in the maturing of the agriculture of our Nation.

Today, agriculture employs 22 million people who work with food and fiber in growing, harvesting, processing, transporting, and retailing. Women are active in farm management, finances, and community life and in establishing agricultural policy. They are also active in all phases of agribusiness and in agricultural processing and marketing. It is appropriate, therefore, that we set aside a week to recognize the role of women in this most basic of all industries.

The Congress, by House Joint Resolution 554, has designated the week of November 11 through 17, 1984, as "Women in Agriculture Week" and authorized and requested the President to issue a proclamation in observance of this week.

Now, Therefore, I, Ronald Reagan, President of the United States of America, do hereby proclaim the week of November 11 through November 17, 1984, as Women in Agriculture Week. I call on all Americans to participate in appropriate events to pay tribute to women in agriculture whose talents, hard work, and dedication significantly contribute to the production and marketing of the Nation's food supplies.

In Witness Whereof, I have hereunto set my hand this thirteenth day of November, in the year of our Lord nineteen hundred and eighty-four, and of the Independence of the United States of America the two hundred and ninth.

RONALD REAGAN

[*Filed with the Office of the Federal Register, 11:03 a.m., November 14, 1984*]

Proclamation 5279—National Farm-City Week, 1984
November 13, 1984

By the President of the United States of America

A Proclamation

One of this Nation's greatest blessings is the abundant food supply on which we all depend each and every day of our lives. Our food stores, with row after row of wholesome, nutritious foods, display a sight so commonplace that Americans tend to forget the enormous effort involved in our complex system of food production, distribution, and marketing.

Our food supply depends upon the farmers who plant their crops and through hard work, faith, and patience, bring in a golden harvest. But it also depends on many people who live in towns and cities. It relies on those who provide farm equipment and production supplies for farmers, as well as on the processors who prepare the products for delivery throughout the Nation by a dependable network of transportation. Finally, we rely on the merchants who store and sell the agricultural products.

It is appropriate that we recognize the interdependence of all those involved in the system with a National Farm-City Week near Thanksgiving. As we give thanks for our food in this great land of freedom, let us also pause to salute the 23 million Americans who work directly in some essential task in agriculture, on farms, and in cities.

Now, Therefore, I, Ronald Reagan, President of the United States of America, do hereby proclaim the period November 16 through November 22, 1984, as National Farm-City Week. I call upon all Americans, in rural areas and in cities alike, to join in recognizing the accomplishments of our productive farm families and of our urban residents in working together in a spirit of cooperation.

In Witness Whereof, I have hereunto set my hand this thirteenth day of November, in the year of our Lord nineteen hundred and eighty-four, and of the Independence of the United States of America the two hundred and ninth.

RONALD REAGAN

[*Filed with the Office of the Federal Register, 12:04 p.m., November 14, 1984*]

Proclamation 5280—National Adoption Week, 1984
November 13, 1984

By the President of the United States of America

A Proclamation

Families have always stood at the center of our society, preserving good and worthy traditions from our past and entrusting those traditions to our children, our greatest hope for the future. At a time when many fear that the family is in decline, it is fitting that we give special recognition to those who are rebuilding families by promoting adoption.

More children with permanent homes mean fewer children with permanent problems. That is why we must encourage a national effort to promote the adoption of children, and particularly children with special needs. Through the Adoption Assistance and Child Welfare Act of 1980, some 6,000 children have been adopted who otherwise might not have been, and the number is growing. The recently enacted Child Abuse Prevention and Treatment Act will provide further assistance to couples who adopt children with special needs.

We must never forget those couples who know the anguish of prolonged waiting to welcome an adopted child into their home. One aspect of the tragedy of the 1.5 million abortions performed each year is that so many women who undergo abortions are unaware of the many couples who desperately want to share their loving homes with a baby. No woman need fear that the child she carries is unwanted. We must continue to promote constructive alternatives to abortion through the Adolescent Family Life program and by encouraging the efforts of private citizens who are helping women with crisis pregnancies.

National Adoption Week gives us an opportunity to reaffirm our commitment to give every child waiting to be adopted the chance to become part of a family. During this Thanksgiving season, let us work to encourage community acceptance and support for adoption and take time to recognize the efforts of the parent groups and agencies that assure adoptive placements for waiting children. Most importantly, let us pay tribute to those special couples who have opened their homes and hearts to adopted children, forming the bonds of love that we call the family.

The Congress, by Senate Joint Resolution 238, has designated the week of November 19 through November 25, 1984, as "National Adoption Week" and authorized and requested the President to issue a proclamation in observance of this week.

Now, Therefore, I, Ronald Reagan, President of the United States of America, do hereby proclaim the week of November 19 through November 25, 1984, as National Adoption Week, and I call on all Americans and governmental and private agencies to observe the week with appropriate activities.

In Witness Whereof, I have hereunto set my hand this thirteenth day of November, in the year of our Lord nineteen hundred and eighty-four, and of the Independence of the United States of America the two hundred and ninth.

RONALD REAGAN

[Filed with the Office of the Federal Register, 12:05 p.m., November 14, 1984]

Toasts of the President and the Grand Duke of Luxembourg at the State Dinner
November 13, 1984

The President. Your Royal Highnesses, Excellencies, and ladies and gentlemen:

Yesterday the people of Luxembourg marked a great day in the life of their nation, the 20th anniversary of the ascension to the throne of His Royal Highness Grand Duke Jean. Your Highness, on behalf of all Americans, permit me to give you and your people our heartfelt congratulations.

It's a deep honor to welcome you to the White House as you begin your visit to our country. Permit me to add that when you reach California, Nancy and I would like you to give that great State our love. *[Laughter]* You see, as the result of a certain political exercise that concluded a week ago, it looks as though we won't be living back there for—oh, maybe not till 1989. *[Laughter]*

Luxembourg possesses a thousand years and more of national history. It's a beautiful and a varied land, ranging from the forests and hills of the north to the fertile plains of the south. It's a prosperous country with a mighty steel industry and dozens of new industries and services gathering strength. And it's a nation of self-confidence and charm, with a gracious way of life based on an abiding love of family and freedom. Luxembourg is a proud and alluring country.

Yet Luxembourg acquires still greater strength and vitality as an active member of the family of nations. It was a founder of both the North Atlantic Treaty Organization and the European Community. In your free and fair world trade, Luxembourg has set an example for all nations to follow and shown the world that prosperity comes not with less but with more international trade.

Individual Luxembourgers have rendered outstanding diplomatic services. Robert

Schuman, one of the leading advocates of a united Europe, was a native of your country. Joseph Bech was instrumental in bringing the European coal and steel community to Luxembourg in 1951. And men like Gaston Thorn and Pierre Werner have played memorable roles in world diplomacy.

Over the years, relations between Luxembourg and the United States have been those of close and abiding friends. We view with the deepest respect your contributions to NATO, including the registration of AWAC's aircraft and your splendid efforts during the Enforcer exercises. And we look forward to consulting closely with your government when Luxembourg assumes the Presidency of the Council of the European Community during the latter half of next year.

Your Highness, we in the United States are convinced that the Western world faces a future of strength and prosperity. In recent years, the Western allies have stood together against the bluff and bluster of our adversaries and become more firmly united than ever. And although all of us have passed through difficult periods of economic adjustment, many of our basic industries are becoming more efficient, and breakthroughs in high technology and other new fields are leading our nations into a time of sustained growth. For Luxembourg, America, and so many other free nations, today our future promises not stagnation and decline, but opportunity and hope.

And tonight, as we look to the future, it's fitting to remain mindful of our past. Forty years ago, Your Highness, Americans and Luxembourgers fought side by side to liberate your nation. Throughout America today, there are thousands of men who can still recall the tear-streaked faces of your people when they realized that at long last they were free.

To me, the most memorable story is about a strapping young American named George Mergenthaler. For several weeks, George was stationed in the village of Eschweiler, in World War II. He had a winning personality, and before long, the good people of Eschweiler took him into their homes and hearts. They told him what life in the village had been like before the war

and then during the Nazi occupation. And George, in turn, opened his heart. He told the people that he was an only son, told them all his hopes for when the war was over. And in those few weeks, a deep bond formed between the people of that ancient village and the amiable young Yankee.

Some time afterward, the people of Eschweiler learned that George had taken part in a fierce battle on the plains between Luxembourg and Belgium. It was called the Battle of the Bulge. And it cost George his life.

Today, 40 years later, there is still a plaque honoring George Mergenthaler in the Eschweiler village church. It reads simply: "This only son died that others' sons might live in love and peace."

Well, Your Highness, today our sons and daughters know that peace. And the bond between our nations is truly a bond of love.

Now, ladies and gentlemen, if you would please join me in a toast to their Royal Highnesses, the Grand Duke and Duchess of Luxembourg, our friends.

The Grand Duke. Mr. President, Mrs. Reagan, the Grand Duchess and I would like to express our sincere gratitude for your invitation, your gracious hospitality, and your kind words regarding our country. May we express our great pleasure at this opportunity as the first head of state to congratulate you personally on the overwhelming result of your reelection to a second term as President of the United States. As a matter of fact, Mr. President, we had never any doubt about the outcome. [*Laughter*]

We are confident that this great nation, under your able leadership, will continue to give the necessary guidance to all the countries of the free world and encourage democracies in their endeavor to promote freedom.

There are no problems which separate the United States and Luxembourg. How could it be otherwise, when America, on two occasions, played a paramount role in the liberation of my country?

In 1918, as well as in 1944, young Americans gave their lives in order to free the Grand Duchy from foreign oppression. These sacrifices I recall at a particularly appropriate time: This year, 1984, marks the

40th anniversary of the liberation of occupied Europe, including Luxembourg, and the final victory of the Battle of the Ardennes.

The people of Luxembourg will never forget the generous help of their American friends, which twice preserved our freedom and our independence. Corresponding to our national motto, we wish to remain what we are. This is the reason why, after leaving Washington, I will visit Colorado Springs in order to pay tribute to the American Army and Air Force.

Mr. President, we all know relations between our two countries are excellent. I am convinced that we could improve them even more. As mutual understanding, upon which friendship is based, exists between us, there should be no difficulty to proceed successfully in this way.

Back home, my countrymen follow with interest and pride this visit of their head of state. They know it is a token of sympathy of a great nation to the Grand Duchy of Luxembourg.

I beg you to accept, Mr. President, along with all my thanks, my countrymen's best wishes of happiness and prosperity for your nation and yourself.

May I add a special thanks to you, Mr. President, for having mentioned my 20th anniversary which took place yesterday on the 12th of November when I took over from my dear mother. It was really awfully kind of you to mention it this evening. Thank you again.

May I ask you now to rise for a toast to the President of the United States of America, to the well-being and the prosperity of the American people, and to the friendship between Luxembourg and the United States.

Note: The President spoke at 9:49 p.m. in the State Dining Room at the White House.

Message to the Presidium of the Supreme Soviet of the Soviet Union on President Reagan's Reelection
November 14, 1984

Thank you for your message on the occasion of my reelection as President of the United States. I share your hope that the coming years will be marked by improved relations between our countries.

Despite our different political beliefs and perspectives on international problems, I am confident we can make progress on strengthening peace and resolving our differences through discussions and negotiations. We hope you will join us in the critical work needed to reduce international tensions and to create a safer world.

/S/RONALD REAGAN

Note: As printed above, the message follows the White House press release.

Recess Appointment of Peter Scott Bridge as United States Ambassador to Somalia
November 14, 1984

The President today recess appointed Peter Scott Bridges, of Louisiana, a career member of the Senior Foreign Service, class of Minister-Counselor, as Ambassador to the Somali Democratic Republic. He would succeed Robert Bigger Oakley.

Mr. Bridges served in the United States Army in 1955–1957. In 1957 he entered the Foreign Service on the Soviet desk in the Department. He was political officer in

Panama (1959–1961), attended Russian studies in Oberammergau (1961–1962), and was general services officer, then political officer, in Moscow (1962–1964). In 1964–1966 he was international relations officer at the United States Arms Control and Disarmament Agency. He was political officer in Rome (1966–1971) and chief of the political and economic section in Prague (1971–1974). In the Department (Bureau of Personnel) he was Chief of the Foreign Service Policy Studies Division (1974–1975) and Director of the Office of Performance Evaluation (1975–1976). In 1976–1977 he was Deputy Executive Secretary of the Department of State and Executive Secretary of the Department of Treasury in 1977–1978. In the Department of State he was Director of the Office of United Nations Political Affairs (1978–1980) and Director of the Office of Eastern European Affairs (1980–1981). Since 1981 he has been deputy chief of mission in Rome.

Mr. Bridges received his B.A. in 1953 from Dartmouth College and M.A. in 1955 from Columbia University. His foreign languages are Czech, French, Italian, Russian, and Spanish. He was born June 19, 1932, in New Orleans, LA. He is married and has four children.

Appointment of Holly H. Coors as a Member of the Board of Visitors of the United States Air Force Academy
November 14, 1984

The President today announced his intention to appoint Holly H. Coors to be a member of the Board of Visitors of the United States Air Force Academy for a term expiring December 30, 1986. She will succeed Sheila Evans Widnall.

Mrs. Coors presently serves as editor of the "people page" of the Saturday Evening Post. She is also a member of the American-Australian Bicentennial Commission for 1988. She is a member of the board of regents at CBN University in Virginia. In 1982 she was a member of the Peace Corps Advisory Council.

She is married, has five children, and resides in Golden, CO. She was born August 25, 1920, in Bangor, ME.

Remarks by Telephone to Crewmembers on Board the Space Shuttle *Discovery*
November 15, 1984

The President. Hello.

Commander Hauck. Good morning.

The President. Good morning. Is this Rick?

Commander Hauck. Yes, sir. How you doing, Mr. President?

The President. Well, just fine. And you? It's good to hear your voice. I'd like to say hello to all the crewmembers and just tell you how proud we are of you and what has been accomplished.

Commander Hauck. Well, thank you, sir. It was a difficult task, but one that was fun and involved a lot of hard effort on a lot of people's parts, both here and on the ground.

The President. Well, can I just say, Joe, you and Dale deserve a lot of credit for retrieving those satellites. You know, we've got a little gym here at the White House, and I pump a little iron whenever I get the chance. But I don't know about that satellite lifting; maybe that'll become a new high-tech Olympic sport.

Seriously, what's it like to hoist one and

hold a thousand-pound satellite?

Commander Hauck. A thousand-pound satellite up here weighs nothing at all.

The President. That should happen in my gym.

Rick, you and Dave and Anna were a great team keeping the *Discovery* right in position and working the Canadian arm during the retrieval operation. I guess you may have been a little busier than on previous flights, since you've been taking on some cargo.

Commander Hauck. Yes, sir, Mr. President, maybe a little bit. But, of course, all the missions are busy, and we all are always working hard.

The President. Well, Joe and Dale—how did the space backpack work for you? I guess—well, I'm sure it would have been hard to retrieve those satellites without it.

Astronaut Gardner. Mr. President, that man-maneuvering unit worked perfectly for both Joe on the first EVA and for myself on the second. The docking with the satellite and capture was exactly as we had trained to in simulators on the ground. It was a real pleasure doing it.

The President. Well, that's just great, and we were all keeping track, and everyone down here rooting and praying for you.

Anna, since this is your first flight, are there any surprises that you've encountered? And I couldn't help but wonder if you'd recommend a career as an astronaut to your daughter, Cristin?

Astronaut Fisher. Oh, that I would, Mr. President. The experience is just everything I expected, even more. Seeing the world below us, it makes you realize just how we're all just part of this world. It's a truly incredible experience, and I'm going to recommend it very highly.

The President. Well, that's wonderful.

Well, I just want you all to know how proud we are of what you've achieved on this mission. Our space program has reached another important milestone with your successful retrieval of those two satellites. You've demonstrated that by putting man in space, on board America's space shuttle, we can work in space in ways that we never imagined were possible. Bless you all.

Well, I have to go to work down here——

Commander Hauck. Thanks for your time, Mr. President. We have enjoyed your support in the past, and we look forward to your support in the future, sir.

The President. Well, you shall have it. I have to go to work down here on Earth. And I know you'll be finishing up to head back here tomorrow, so, have a safe return, and, I might add, a soft landing with those valuable satellites on board.

But just please know how proud all of us are of what you've done, and God bless you all.

Commander Hauck. Thank you, sir, very much.

The President. All right. Goodbye.

Commander Hauck. Bye-bye.

Note: The President spoke at 8:40 a.m. from the Residence at the White House.

The crewmembers included Frederick H. Hauck, Dale A. Gardiner, Anna L. Fisher, David M. Walker, and Joseph P. Allen.

Proclamation 5281—National Family Week, 1984
November 15, 1984

By the President of the United States of America

A Proclamation

Strong families are the foundation of society. Through them we pass on our traditions, rituals, and values. From them we receive the love, encouragement, and education needed to meet human challenges. Family life provides opportunities and time for the spiritual growth that fosters generosity of spirit and responsible citizenship.

Family experiences shape our response to the larger communities in which we live. The best American traditions echo family values that call on us to nurture and guide the young, to help enrich the lives of the handicapped, to assist less fortunate neighbors, and to cherish the elderly. Let us summon our individual and community resources to promote healthy families capable of carrying on these traditions and providing strength to our society.

National Family Week gives us a chance to honor families and to renew our commitment to the family strength that gives people the ability to withstand external influences and maintain their individual integrity. We should take this occasion to commend the loyalty family members show one another in facing the adversities as well as the joys of life together. And let us especially honor those Americans who, through adoption or foster care, have extended their families as centers of love and life to those in need of true family support.

The Congress, by Senate Joint Resolution 211, has designated the week of November 18 through November 24, 1984, as "National Family Week" and authorized and requested the President to issue a proclamation in observance of this week.

Now, Therefore, I, Ronald Reagan, President of the United States of America, do hereby proclaim the week of November 18 through November 24, 1984, as National Family Week. I invite the Governors of the several states, the chief officials of local governments, and all Americans to observe this week with appropriate ceremonies and activities. As we celebrate this Thanksgiving Week, I also invite all Americans to give thanks for the many blessings that they have derived from their family relationships and to reflect upon the importance of maintaining strong families.

In Witness Whereof, I have hereunto set my hand this fifteenth day of November, in the year of our Lord nineteen hundred and eighty-four, and of the Independence of the United States of America the two hundred and ninth.

RONALD REAGAN

[*Filed with the Office of the Federal Register, 11:41 a.m., November 15, 1984*]

Designation of Kathleen Wilson Lawrence as a Member of the Board of Directors of the Rural Telephone Bank
November 20, 1984

The President today announced his intention to designate Kathleen Wilson Lawrence to be a member of the Board of Directors of the Rural Telphone Bank, Department of Agriculture. She would succeed Ruth A. Reister.

Mrs. Lawrence has been serving as Deputy Under Secretary for Small Community and Rural Development at the Department of Agriculture since May of this year. In 1979 she formed the Lawrence Co., specializing in management consulting for political organizations and candidates. She served as campaign director for Governor Holton's 1978 Senate campaign and was northern Virginia director for the Obenshain and Warner Senate campaigns. Mrs. Lawrence was executive director of the National Federation of Republican Women in Washington, DC, in 1975. In 1968–1973 she was a staff assistant to the President in the White House Office of Public Liaison.

Mrs. Lawrence graduated from Queens College in 1960. She is married, has three children, and resides in Alexandria, VA. She was born December 7, 1940, in New York, NY.

Statement by Assistant to the President for National Security Affairs Robert C. McFarlane on United States-Soviet Nuclear and Space Arms Negotiations
November 22, 1984

The United States and the Soviet Union have agreed to enter into new negotiations with the objective of reaching mutually acceptable agreements on the whole range of questions concerning nuclear and outer space arms. In order to reach a common understanding as to the subject and objectives of such negotiations, Secretary of State George P. Shultz and Foreign Minister Andrey Gromyko will meet in Geneva on January 7–8.

Recess Appointment of 11 Members of the Board of Directors of the Legal Services Corporation
November 23, 1984

The President today recess appointed the following-named persons to be members of the Board of Directors of the Legal Services Corporation. These persons were nominated to the Senate on March 19, 1984, but were not confirmed prior to the Senate's adjournment on October 12, 1984.

Hortencia Benavides, of Texas. She will succeed Ronald B. Frankum.

LeaAnne Bernstein, of Maryland. She will succeed Albert Angrisani.

William Clark Durant III, of Michigan. He will succeed William J. Olson.

Paul B. Eaglin, of North Carolina. He will succeed Robert Sherwood Stubbs II.

Pepe J. Mendez, of Colorado. He will succeed Peter Joseph Ferrara.

Lorain Miller, of Michigan. She will succeed Milton M. Masson, Jr.

Thomas F. Smegal, Jr., of California. He will succeed David E. Satterfield III.

Claude Galbreath Swafford, of Tennessee. He will succeed Robert E. McCarthy.

Basile Joseph Uddo, of Louisiana. He will succeed Howard H. Dana, Jr.

Robert A. Valois, of North Carolina. He will succeed Donald Eugene Santarelli.

Michael B. Wallace, of Mississippi. He will succeed George E. Paras.

Statement by Principal Deputy Press Secretary Speakes on the Resumption of Diplomatic Relations With Iraq
November 26, 1984

The Governments of the United States and Iraq have agreed to resume diplomatic relations, effective today. This agreement was concluded today between President Reagan and Deputy Prime Minister and Foreign Minister of Iraq, Tariq M. 'Aziz. The two countries' diplomatic missions are upgraded as of this date from interest sections to Embassies, and their principal officers will hold the title of chargé d'affaires, pending the appointment of Ambassadors. Ambassadors will be appointed as promptly as possible under the nomination processes required within and between both countries.

Proclamation 5282—National Home Care Week, 1984
November 26, 1984

By the President of the United States of America

A Proclamation

Home care services, which are rapidly gaining acceptance throughout the Nation, allow the physically and mentally impaired who do not require skilled nursing home care to remain in their own homes, or to stay with their families, instead of being moved to an institution. Home care provides individualized support services to permit maximum independence for those in need of assistance.

Progress in medical science and the generally rising level of health care from birth are contributing to a greater number of people living longer. A corollary to this advance is an increase in chronic illnesses of the aged that require care over an extended period of time. Home care provides the assistance needed to help older Americans to maintain independence despite such illness. All Americans should commend those individuals who provide personal and health care in the home. Their skill and caring make the lives of those they serve fuller and more meaningful.

To give special recognition to the importance of home care services, the Congress, by Senate Joint Resolution 237, has designated the week of November 25, 1984, through December 1, 1984, as "National Home Care Week," and authorized and requested the President to issue a proclamation in observance of that week.

Now, Therefore, I, Ronald Reagan, President of the United States of America, do hereby proclaim the week of November 25 through December 1, 1984, as National Home Care Week, and I call upon all Government agencies, interested organizations, community groups, and the people of the United States to observe this week with appropriate programs, ceremonies, and activities.

In Witness Whereof, I have hereunto set my hand this twenty-sixth day of November, in the year of our Lord nineteen hundred and eighty-four, and of the Independence of the United States of America the two hundred and ninth.

RONALD REAGAN

[*Filed with the Office of the Federal Register, 2:26 p.m., November 26, 1984*]

Proclamation 5283—National Epidermolysis Bullosa Awareness Week, 1984
November 26, 1984

By the President of the United States of America

A Proclamation

Epidermolysis Bullosa, or "EB," is a group of hereditary disorders in which the skin forms blisters after minimal injury or even simple pressure. Symptoms of the disease can resemble severe burns and can be very painful and debilitating. Mucous membranes of the mouth, eye, and gastrointestinal tract may be affected and lead to scar-

ring, malnutrition, anemia, and even premature death.

As many as 25,000 to 50,000 Americans, mostly children, may suffer from EB. The disease can disable people physically because of the pain and anguish it causes, and it also places a severe financial burden on many families.

Basic research is just beginning to reveal the underlying causes of EB. New research findings and new approaches to diagnosis and treatment are needed to eliminate this affliction. The Federal government and private voluntary organizations have developed a strong and enduring partnership committed to EB research in order to reduce or eliminate the disease and its painful consequences.

The Congress, by Senate Joint Resolution 201, has designated the week of November 25 through December 1, 1984, as "National Epidermolysis Bullosa Awareness Week" and authorized and requested the President to issue a proclamation in observance of that week.

Now, Therefore, I, Ronald Reagan, President of the United States of America, do hereby proclaim the week of November 25 through December 1, 1984, as National Epidermolysis Bullosa Awareness Week. I urge the people of the United States and educational, philanthropic, scientific, medical and health care organizations and professionals to observe this week with appropriate programs, ceremonies, and activities.

In Witness Whereof, I have hereunto set my hand this twenty-sixth day of November, in the year of our Lord nineteen hundred and eighty-four, and of the Independence of the United States of America the two hundred and ninth.

RONALD REAGAN

[*Filed with the Office of the Federal Register, 2:27 p.m., November 26, 1984*]

Statement on a Treasury Department Study on Tax Reform
November 27, 1984

In my State of the Union Address last January, I asked the Secretary of the Treasury to develop a plan to make our tax system more fair and more simple, with greater incentives for economic growth and with a broader tax base so that personal tax rates could come down, not go up.

Today I have received the Treasury study. I want first to thank Secretary Regan. He and his staff have worked long and hard to come up with a most comprehensive study of the modern American tax system, along with recommendations for improving it.

The report is lengthy and complex. All of us will need time to study the entire document. We are willing to listen to the comments and suggestions of all Americans, and especially those from the Congress—its leaders and members of the tax writing committees. Secretary Regan has already briefed the Cabinet and some congressional leaders. Over the next several days he and his staff will be doing additional consultation.

At first glance, the Treasury study certainly proposes a simpler and fairer tax system, with lower rates for taxpayers and personal exemptions increased to $2,000. It is also something that I insisted upon: a tax simplification and not a tax increase in disguise.

I have asked Secretary Regan to make his study public at this time—prior to my own decisions on exactly what simplifying legislation to propose to the Congress—because I know that a task as difficult as overall simplification of our tax system will generate much debate, and I want all those interested in the subject to have the same information as we have.

Over the next few weeks, I intend personally to review the Treasury recommendations carefully, along with public and congressional reactions to them. I will present my tax simplification and reform plan to Congress early next year, when I hope we can move ahead in a bipartisan manner to benefit all Americans.

Statement by Principal Deputy Press Secretary Speakes on the Strategic Defense Initiative
November 27, 1984

Since the advent of nuclear weapons, we have largely depended upon the threat of prompt nuclear retaliation to deter aggression. This approach has worked, and we, along with our allies, have succeeded in protecting Western security for more than three decades. At the same time, we are constantly searching for better ways to strengthen peace and stability.

On March 23, 1983, the President announced a decision to take an important first step toward investigating the possibility of an alternative future which did not rely solely on nuclear retaliation for our security. This involves an intensified research program aimed at establishing how we might eliminate the threat posed by nuclear armed ballistic missiles.

The Strategic Defense Initiative (SDI) is a research program consistent with all our treaty commitments, including the 1972 ABM treaty. The United States is committed to the negotiation of equal and verifiable agreements which bring real reductions in the nuclear arsenals of both sides. To that end, the President has offered the Soviet Union the most comprehensive set of arms control proposals in history. We are working tirelessly for the success of these efforts, but we can and must be prepared to go further. It is intended that our research efforts under the SDI complement these arms reduction efforts and help to pave the way to a more stable and secure world.

In the near term, SDI research and development responds to the massive Soviet ABM effort, which includes actual deployments and thus provides a powerful deterrent to a Soviet breakout of the ABM treaty. In the long term, SDI may be the means by which both the United States and the Soviet Union can safely agree to very deep reductions and perhaps someday even the elimination of offensive nuclear arms.

In short, through the SDI research program the President has called on the best scientific minds in our country to turn their collective talents toward the cause of strengthening world peace by establishing the feasibility of rendering nuclear weapons impotent and obsolete. In doing so, the United States seeks neither military superiority or political advantage. Our single purpose with this initiative is to search for ways to make the world a safer place.

Remarks of the President and Prime Minister Kamisese Mara of Fiji Following Their Meetings
November 27, 1984

The President. It's been both an honor and a pleasure to have Prime Minister Ratu Mara of Fiji and his wife as our guests. And this is an historic occasion. The Prime Minister is the first head of state from the nine independent Pacific island nations to pay an official visit here at the White House. The Fijian nation he so ably represents is a model of democracy and freedom, a tremendous example for all the countries of the developing world.

Fijians can be proud, indeed, that in their country people from diverse religious, racial, and cultural backgrounds live and work together in peace and freedom. This accomplishment—and it is a great accomplishment—is a tribute to your democratic institutions and to the character of your people. Mr. Prime Minister, when you return to your country, I hope you will convey to your citizens the deep respect and admiration of the American people.

Fijians are our brothers and sisters in the

family of democratic nations. We share values that are at the heart of our societies, the most important of which is our abiding love of human liberty. That was underscored to many Americans who fought alongside Fijians in the Second World War during the Solomon Islands campaign, a turning point in the Pacific Theater. We stood together then in the cause of human freedom. That bravery is matched today by the magnificent commitment that your people have made to the cause of peace. Under your leadership, Mr. Prime Minister, Fiji has become a vital part of international peacekeeping missions in the Sinai and in Lebanon. And America knows all too well the price that peacekeepers sometimes pay. Your fallen heroes of peace have a place in our hearts.

Fijians have put themselves on the line and won the gratitude of peace-loving people everywhere. If more nations were as responsible in their international community as Fiji, it would be a far better world.

The Fijian peoples' sense of decency in the conduct of international affairs has been expressed on many occasions in recent years. And we, again, have found ourselves standing shoulder to shoulder in our condemnation of the brutal invasion of Afghanistan and the deliberate shooting down of a civilian Korean airliner. Americans also deeply appreciate your support of our efforts to rescue our students and restore democracy to the people of Grenada.

And I've enjoyed this opportunity to get to know Prime Minister Ratu Mara. He is a man to look up to in many ways. Oxford-educated and deeply religious, a man of conviction and wisdom, he has provided exemplary leadership for his people in the crucial beginning stages of democracy. His support of free enterprise and a market economy has enabled his people to enjoy stable economic progress. He has kept Fiji on a steady course and has always defended the principles on which his country was founded, principles that we Americans share. I'm particularly grateful for the sense of responsibility that he has demonstrated in the area of regional security. Having weighed his legitimate concern over nuclear issues against the defense needs of his country and the Oceania region, in 1983

Prime Minister Ratu Mara reopened Fiji's ports to all our American naval vessels. I know that such decisions are not easy and reflect a high degree of political courage. I applaud your statesmanship, Mr. Prime Minister.

I've thoroughly enjoyed our exchange of ideas today. The Prime Minister taught me the meaning of doing things the "Pacific way." He represents a vital and dynamic way. He represents an area of the world that is becoming increasingly important to the United States. We want to work more closely with the people of Fiji and Oceania to help their region continue on a course of stable economic progress and democratic government, free from international tensions and rivalries.

We seek cooperation and improved relations for the betterment of all our peoples. The Prime Minister's visit has been a significant step forward. For this visit, and for sharing your insights, I give you my heartfelt thanks: *vinaka*. I look forward to working closely with you in the future, and, Mr. Prime Minister, the people of the United States wish you and your wife a pleasant visit in the United States and a safe journey home. *Nisa moce.*

The Prime Minister. Well, Mr. President, I'm very pleased, indeed, that it has been possible for you to find time in your busy schedule to meet me on this occasion and soon after your reelection to the Presidency. This is an indication of the warm ties of friendship between our two countries.

Our meeting and discussions this morning has brought our relationship onto a new and exciting level. There is now much greater understanding and appreciation of each other's views and aspirations. Our two countries have stood together for those common principles of justice, freedom, and fairplay.

Fiji was used as a transit base for the American troops in the South Pacific during the Second World War. Our men fought side by side in the Pacific war in defense of our respective ways of life and shared values. Like your country, we stand for peace and appreciate determination to maintain peace and security everywhere.

We believe in peace, and we are ready to

play our part in order to demonstrate that belief. That is why we are involved in UNIFIL and the multinational force and observers in Sinai. But as a small island nation—and like others in the South Pacific and elsewhere—we look to you and your country for support and guidance in many of our endeavors.

This outlook is both sensible and logical in view of your vast size and what appears to us to be a country of unlimited resource. Moreover, there is a basic similarity and broadly common origin of many of our economic and political institutions. All these go to help our people feel at home in each other's company and make dialog and communication between our two countries meaningful and enjoyable.

Many young men and women from your country gave us loyal and devoted service through the Peace Corps. They worked with us at different levels of our administration and with our people in rural areas.

Your South Pacific AID program has been of considerable assistance to the development activities of the Fiji Government, voluntary organizations, and regional institutions in our country.

We are confident that your assistance will continue in the future, because we believe that you see it as part of your overall responsibility in our part of the world. And this is an effective guarantee for peace and stability in our islands.

Our meeting this morning gives us confidence that our relations will grow from strength to strength in the interests of both our countries and our peoples. Thank you, Mr. President.

Note: The President spoke at 1:17 p.m. at the South Portico of the White House.

Earlier, the President and the Prime Minister met in the Oval Office. They then joined their advisers for a working luncheon in the State Dining Room.

Message on the 25th Anniversary of the Antarctic Treaty
November 26, 1984

I am delighted to send greetings to all the scientists and station personnel of every nation in Antarctica as we mark the twenty-fifth anniversary of the Antarctic Treaty, sometimes called the Washington Treaty.

On December 1, 1959, in Washington, D.C., the twelve nations then active in Antarctica pledged themselves to an imaginative experiment in international cooperation and understanding. The Antarctic Treaty, signed that day, reserves a major region of our planet exclusively for scientific research and other peaceful endeavors. The Treaty bans all military activities, including the testing of weapons in Antarctica, and prohibits nuclear explosions and the disposal of radioactive wastes there. It guarantees the freedom of scientific research and establishes a consultative mechanism to allow the Treaty system to meet new challenges and adapt to new circumstances. To achieve these objectives, it embodies unique conflict-avoidance provisions per-

mitting countries which disagree over the legal status of Antarctica to work together harmoniously.

Now a quarter century later, we can all take pride in the accomplishments and vitality of this important treaty system. It has fully realized its objectives of maintaining Antarctica as an area free of conflict and devoted to peaceful international cooperation. Membership in the Treaty system has continued to expand and, within this system, effective steps are being taken to ensure that new activities in Antarctica are managed in a responsible fashion and do not threaten Antarctica's environment. The Antarctic Treaty represents an outstanding example of how countries with diverse political perspectives and interests—East and West, North and South—can work together for the benefit of all.

The Antarctic Treaty incorporates and extends to the realm of international relations the spirit of practical cooperation which scientists working in Antarctica have displayed from the earliest explorations onward. It is fitting, therefore, to commemorate the twenty-fifth anniversary of the Treaty by saluting the scientists and station personnel whose exciting and important work in Antarctica continue to reflect the universal ideals reflected in the Treaty. I commend your commitment to the search for knowledge and send my best wishes to all of you for a productive season.

/S/ RONALD REAGAN

The White House,
November 26, 1984.

Note: As printed above, the message follows the White House press release, which was released by the Office of the Press Secretary on November 28.

Interview With Representatives of the Washington Times
November 27, 1984

Q. Well, Mr. President, we know you're busy, so perhaps if we could just go ahead with a few questions.

The President. All right.

Priorities in Second Term

Q. It's been suggested you have only 6 to 18 months to accomplish your agenda before your postelection honeymoon with the Congress ends. What is your strategy to capitalize on your victory with an even more recalcitrant Congress, particularly after the 1986 congressional elections? Doesn't this threaten the completion of the Reagan revolution?

The President. Well, I've never thought that the completion of what we've been trying to accomplish is going to be easy, particularly as long as there is in the House a definite majority of the other side. On the other hand, we have accomplished, I think, a great deal. We'd be much further ahead if we'd gotten all that we'd asked for from the very beginning, but we're going to keep right on with those things and see what we can do.

First of all, I think we have to go after some budget reforms. You realize there hasn't been a budget since I've been here—and, I guess, even before I got here. The budgeting process is just a kind of a chaotic thing and, finally, you get a package of appropriation bills. Until we can have a budgeting process where you start out and set a figure as to what overall can be spent and, then, within that, negotiate out as to which program gets how much and arrive at a consensus on that, we're going to be in trouble.

We need to do that. We need the balanced budget amendment; we need the line-item veto if we're to do those things. We need economic growth for that. We've got to have the tax simplification program that we've been studying and working on. We've got to have such things as enterprise zones—everything that will help stimulate the growth of the economy, because that is the sure way back to sensible running of the Government.

And we've got the—it goes without saying—the defense and the security assistance measures and so forth. That we have to have. That's the top priority of government in the sense that that's the main constitutional requirement, is the security of the people.

And then there are social things that I think we want, having to do with abortion, school prayer, tuition tax credits, things of that kind.

And what we're going to do is try to work with the leadership of the Congress. And I'm not sure that it is even more hostile or inimical. If it is, and if it simply tries to throw roadblocks, then, yes, we take our case to the people.

Federal Budget Deficit

Q. Mr. President, the deficit has been described as a debt that the people, the American people, owe themselves. As such, does the deficit really matter, or has the slowdown in the economy forced you to reconsider whether growth can substantially reduce the deficit?

The President. Well, of course, we had this example this year in which some $20 billion came out of the deficit as it had been projected by ourselves for this present year, and that was almost entirely due to the economic growth. But when you say the deficit and does it really matter, well, for 50 years that's what the Democrats have been telling us, that it didn't, that we owed it to ourselves.

I think to look at just the deficit ignores the real problem. The deficit is a result. What you have to get at is the problem, and that is government is spending too much, and it's spending too big a share of the private sector—that's why my opposition to those who think that the only answer to deficit spending is higher taxes. Well, we've done that in the past, and all it did was take the burden off the backs of those who wanted to spend more, so they could just go ahead and spend more.

If you look at about the 5 years before we came here, taxes just about doubled, and the deficit came to over something like $318 billion. In fact, just a little while ago I was citing some figures. If you go back to '65—and in the years following '65 was when the Great Society got underway—'65 to '80, in those 15 years, the budget, the overall spending, increased about 4½ times. The deficit increased 38 times.

So, we go back to what the classical economists used to say at the turn of the century, that when we had, as they put it, business cycles and hard times, it was usually when government spending crept up to above—they never told you what the percentage was, but above a certain percentage of the gross national product, took that much more money out of the private sector. That's when you had hard times.

Well, I think that's what we've been seeing.

Tax Reform

Q. Mr. President, how far are you prepared to go to support the Treasury's modified flat-tax plan, and are you fully committed to pushing a comprehensive tax reform through Congress in this year? And if you

want a balanced budget, why don't you submit one? [*Laughter*]

The President. I haven't been able to get the budget I wanted as low as I wanted it without going that far.

I don't think there's anyone that would suggest that at this point you could suddenly come back and say, "Here, we're"—not without hurting an awful lot of people. What I think you have to do is look down the road and say, "Let's aim at a target here that we're going to get this budget on a declining pattern." And then maybe you can't exactly foretell the day at which it would happen, but if you can get the spending level, the share of private level coming—or even if it isn't coming down, if your budget continues to increase to meet needs and whatever inflation there is, but if it increases at a lower rate than it has been and if the growth of the economy you can bring up, those two lines are going to meet someday, and when they meet, you've balanced the budget. And as this one goes on past, you begin to get the surplus that you should use to reduce the national debt. And this is what we're trying to do.

Q. Excuse me, but the earlier part was, how far are you prepared to go to support the flat tax?

The President. Oh, that one, yes. Well, you kind of got me. There on my desk is the printed version of the whole study of the Treasury Department. And no decisions have been made. We've just had a briefing of the Cabinet on it; everyone is now studying it. I think it has come with a recognition that there are some options in there, that it is not a hard and fast plan. And so, I want to study this.

And then, when you say about Congress—we've got two tax proposals in Congress, and one from the Democratic side, one from the Republican side, not too far apart—as I don't think this one is too far apart.

Well, I think that it shows that the climate is there, that if we get going—and we want to take this up with the Democratic leadership; we also want to make it available to the public, to all the various groups out there, so that they understand what it is we're trying to do. And I think that with all of that pot there of three, you might say, proposals, I think we can come up with a plan that calls for simplification and lower tax rates in the areas that will make it more fair than the tax system is; certainly simplified.

And I know that there are some very interesting proposals the Treasury Department has come up with to do that with regard to easing the burden at the bottom, lowering the rates for everybody, and simplification, making it far more simple. For one thing, the going down to 3 tax brackets instead of 14 is a pretty good step.

Jeane J. Kirkpatrick

Q. Mr. President, even after the election there's still some muttering about the GOP gender gap. Now it looks like there isn't a senior foreign policy post in the White House for a woman who dazzled them in Dallas, Jeane Kirkpatrick. How can you let her leave the Cabinet, and what will you offer her to induce her to stick around?

The President. Well, she and I are scheduled for a talk this week. We've talked off and on, and I've known about her feelings now about the U.N. job. But I don't know when she talks whether she is determined that she wants to return to her previous profession in the academic world or whether she is still interested in government. And believe me, I want to find something for her in government if I can, because I count on her a great deal, and I value her abilities and her great intelligence too much to just sit there and let her go if there's a way to keep her.

So, I'm going to try to keep her. She's turned us around at the U.N., our position in the United Nations, and she did it.

Q. But there isn't any way she can function in the White House, is there?

The President. I don't see anything there that would be worthy of her. So, I'm going to—but it depends, first of all, on what are her desires—what is it, how strongly does she feel about whether she wants to leave entirely.

Q. But you would like her to stay on up at the U.N.?

The President. What's that?

Q. You would like her to stay on up at the U.N.?

The President. Well, except that I can't ask her to do that. That assignment has a way of kind of burning people out, and I think she's——

Q. So does yours. [*Laughter*]

The President. I think she's had about all of that that she wants.

Q. Are you above a little armtwisting to keep her?

The President. I did that to keep her there as long as she has. [*Laughter*] But I have to—no, it's difficult for me, when someone really has served and done the job and you know that they've kind of had it, it's very difficult for me to try to persuade them to do it.

Nuclear Arms Control

Q. Mr. President, why, after an overwhelming electoral victory, has arms control become such a high priority for you and that there's now a rush to the negotiating table? Isn't the "evil empire" evil any longer, or aren't you still concerned about the Soviet disdain for treaty obligations?

The President. I have been as critical as anyone of previous agreements in many instances where I thought somebody just made an agreement to have an agreement. I have all the quotes of Brezhnev and others with regard to détente and what they thought of it. I don't know whether you're aware that Mr. Brezhnev said that détente was serving their purpose and that by 1985, they would be able to get whatever they wanted by other means.

So, I have no illusions about them. But I do believe that the Soviets can be dealt with if you deal with them on the basis of what is practical for them and that you can point out is to their advantage as well as ours to do certain things.

Now, I think they have seen that if it's to be an arms race, if we are determined that we're not going to let them maintain or enlarge their superiority in weapons—and they know our industrial power and might—and they see that we're determined to not let them maintain or continue that lead, then, rather than an arms race, I think there's an advantage to them in saying, well, maybe we'd better find a different way. And believe me, I would not hold still for a deal that simply makes a deal.

Evil empire, the things of that kind, I thought—I wasn't just sounding off; I figured it was time to get their attention, to let them know that I was viewing them realistically. And I think it's worked. They— you know, everyone says about the horrible relations between the two of us, but they haven't gained an inch of territory in these 4 years. And in the 4 years before, there was Afghanistan and there was Ethiopia and South Yemen, and there they were, advancing down through Africa. So, I don't think the relations have been all that bad.

Q. Why do you think they've dropped the preconditions to the arms talks at this time?

The President. Dropped the——

Q. The preconditions to the arms talks.

The President. Well, I think they were kind of stalling until the election, also, and then decided, well, now they know who's going to be around for a while longer.

They've made a proposal, and we've said fine.

Nicaragua

Q. Mr. President, Congress has prohibited support for the *contra* forces fighting against the Government of Nicaragua. How can you live with this restriction? And doesn't it send a message to the world that it might be risky to be a friend of the United States, as it was when President Carter was here?

The President. Well, this is one of the things where I think the Congress, up till now, has been shortsighted and, in fact, irresponsible with regard to that situation down there. And we know that there was a kind of a consensus of feeling just recently among them, when they believed, as we all did, that possibly that ship was bearing high-performance planes, Mig's, to Nicaragua. We don't know for sure that it wasn't. We can't prove that it was; we can't prove that it wasn't, because of some maneuverings that went on. But there are six more Russian ships, as nearly as we can count, that are on their way to Nicaragua now with more arms. I think that maybe, if they remember that feeling that they had with regard to the possibility of high-performance planes, that they will see that there is value in our carrying on.

What we have are revolutionaries that only a short time ago they and the Sandinistas were all on the same side, fighting the same revolution—and fighting it ostensibly, and by their own claim, for democratic processes. Now, they got in and, a la Cuba under Castro, the one faction took over, has created a totalitarian Marxist state, and the others are still in the revolution, still trying for the democratic principles that they'd fought for in the beginning. And the very fact that the Sandinista element is continuing to support revolutionaries who are trying to overthrow a duly elected government, this is of itself of great interest to us.

Q. Sir, have you drawn a line that says if there are high-performance aircraft introduced into this theater, that there will be a reaction from us that——

The President. Well, we have let them and we've let the Soviet Union know that this is something we cannot sit back and just take, if they do that, because that is so obviously, then, a threat to the area. That's not—well, their whole military today isn't defensive. Their whole military is greater than all the combined countries of Central America put together, and it's so obviously offensive in nature that we can't ignore that. And that would be just the crowning thing to have those high-performance planes representing a threat to the area and to the hemisphere. And we've made it plain that we're not going to sit by quietly and accept that.

Q. Do you think, sir, that the Mig crate episode and the six ships that are believed on their way now is any way an attempt by the Soviet Union to test your resolve on this issue?

The President. I don't know whether it is or not. I know they——

Q. Sort of like the missile—Kennedy's Cuban crisis?

The President. Yeah. I know they do things like that. And so, we're keeping watch on what's there. We're not going to raise Cain over a purely domestic type cargo, or anything of that kind, but we are in contact with the Soviet Union.

Q. Do you know if weapons, or Mig's specifically, are on any of those six ships you mentioned?

The President. No. We do know that in several of the ports where those ships have touched down, there have been evidence of those aircraft and crates that could contain them. And we want to know that after the ships leave, those aircraft are still there.

Q. Was one of those places Libya, Mr. President?

The President. I would be guessing now, because my memory doesn't tell me. Of all the reports we've had, I don't know whether—I couldn't tell you specifically.

Q. Certainly that Black Sea port, though——

The President. Yes. I would think Libya would be a probability.

Terrorism

Q. Speaking of Libya, Mr. President, your administration's taken a strong rhetorical line against state terrorism. What are you going to do about Colonel Mu'ammar Qadhafi of Libya, the world's most prominent practitioner of terrorism?

The President. Well, again, it's one of those things that you can know and he can talk, but you couldn't go into court and prove that actually they were responsible for it, anymore than you could've a couple of other governments that we feel are apparently supporting terrorist movements.

So, what we do is try—intelligence is the most important thing with regard to terrorism: Can you, in some way, find or get access to information that would let you know where and when operations are planned. Can you get information that really ties a terrorist group to a certain force or a certain government. Among the things that we're trying to do is if—and we're having some reasonable success with getting together with the other nations to do what we did some years ago with regard to hijackings, so that we all pool our information; we all inform each other of everything that we know. And we take action so that there are no safe harbors for terrorists, that they can't cross a border and find that they won't be troubled.

Q. Excuse me, sir, I would have thought there was overwhelming evidence that Qadhafi was involved in terrorism everywhere, from Northern Ireland to Mindanao.

The President. Well, yes, except when the bomb goes off, can you establish——

Q. That particular bomb.

The President. Yes, sometimes you get those phone calls of somebody claiming credit. But when you get two or three different outfits claiming the credit, you say, "Well, which ones are just bragging?"

Q. Mm-hmm.

The President. The other thing is when it comes to if you can't intercept—punish, to retaliate, there again, you've got to be able to get some evidence as to where are the bases from whence come these terrorists that you could strike at. And at the same time, you have to recognize that you don't want to just carelessly go out and maybe kill innocent people. Then you're as bad as the terrorists.

Q. Well, if the terrorists are in a village living amongst people who are innocent, are they then safe from retaliation?

The President. Well, you know, that's a decision that I think you have to make on each particular case. I do know of one instance in which we thought we had pretty good evidence of the locale. But, again, to attempt to pick out the guilty would have been impossible. You would have wiped out a lot of innocent people who had nothing to do with it.

Q. Well, if you ever get a clearcut case, where you know exactly where the terrorists came from and that there's no question of their responsibility, what, then, is the nature of the retaliation?

The President. I think there what George Shultz said in his speech—that caused a little hoopla for a time—what he was saying to our people was that you must recognize that in this whole thing, if you're going to try to defend against terrorism, there are going to come some times when military action will be called for. And you need the public understanding of that and their awareness so that they will know it is necessary if you're to conquer this problem.

Namibia

Q. Mr. President, why is Assistant Secretary of State Chester Crocker negotiating with all sides in the Angola crisis to get the Cubans out and reach a settlement, except for Jonas Savimbi, who's one of the strongest anti-Communist leaders in the region there? And will you recognize Marxist Angola if the Cuban troops leave?

The President. What Secretary Crocker's been doing is actually having to do with Namibia—Namibia and its independence. And there is the 435 Resolution of the United Nations about Namibia's right to become a country. Well, right now, it's South Africa territory.

Now, South Africa is willing for Namibia to become independent, but not while on the northern border of Namibia sits Angola with the Cubans and the possibility remains of Namibia becoming another satellite of the Communist bloc. So, what he's back and forth negotiating is that—for to create Namibia, for Angola to agree to remove the Cuban troops, and South Africa has agreed that they will move out, and they will be helpful in making this a state. And he's made quite a bit of progress.

For the first time, Angola has made a declaration that they are prepared to bring about the withdrawal. It's a negotiating matter. They want to phase it, and they have some conditions on doing this. And so, he has come back just recently, but he'll be going back again.

But that's where it stands. And at least that's the first time in all the years that this has been going on that Angola has said, yes, they will remove Cuban troops.

Q. If the negotiations are successful, would you then recognize Angola, the Government of Angola, if the Cuban troops leave?

The President. I think that that would be a part of the negotiations that are going on.

Q. Doesn't that risk throwing someone like Jonas Savimbi to the wolves, in effect, though?

The President. Well, this is another problem, and I can't talk about that. No one wants to do that. But certainly that has to figure in the whole negotiations. No, we're not going to turn on him. But, somehow, there has to be a negotiation that involves that situation domestically in Angola.

The Middle East

Q. Mr. President, the Syrians seem now to have become the serious focus in the Middle East, and with your September 1982 peace plan at least grievously wounded, if not dying, do you think it can be revived, or, if not, do you have another initiative that you're going to pursue there?

The President. Well, no, I think that was the proper course to take, and I think that it is a little closer than it's been for some time. The very fact now that King Hussein has recognized Egypt, which kind of strengthens Egypt's position as being accepted back in the Arab community even though it has the peace treaty with Israel—the recognition the other day or the restoring of relations with Iraq is a step forward.

I think that there has been some trust built up by the moderate Arab States in the United States as an intermediary in trying to bring about—see, we're not trying to negotiate the peace. They have to negotiate the peace. Syria is, and still is, the stumbling block. But even so, now there is the negotiation going on with regard to the removal of Israel's troops from Lebanon.

So, I think that some things are coming together now which, if anything, including the fact that the PLO held its meeting in Amman instead of Damascus—I think these things are all leading toward the possibility again of getting the Arab States to agree to negotiate.

You see, they've been sitting there with the position that they refuse to recognize Israel's right to exist as a nation. Well, you can't negotiate with someone until that's removed. Well, Egypt did it. And now I think the attitude of Hussein shows that—Jordan can't be alone in doing that, but I think that what they're saying is that if the others can come together on this and enter into negotiations—the PLO; we now see them taking on the radical faction in their own midst that was pro-Syrian.

And we're going to do everything we can to hopefully encourage this.

Views on the Presidency

Q. A final question, Mr. President. And I want to thank you for being so generous with your time to us. As most Presidents go into their second term—and not many of them do nowadays, it seems——

The President. [*Referring to a tape recorder*]—somebody shut off there.

Q. That's all right. [*Inaudible*]

Many of them seem to start thinking about their place in history. What would you like to see be your legacy to this country from 8 years of Reagan Presidency?

The President. Peace and freedom and the Government back in the hands of the people.

Q. What will you settle for? [*Laughter*]

The President. What?

Q. What will you settle for?

The President. I'll only settle for that. I'm going to keep on trying. Why else would I be doing this? You know, I figure my future is in these next 4 years. That's one advantage in being my age.

Q. Well, thank you very much, Mr. Presi-dent, for your kindness today. We're grati-fied that, apparently, the Washington Times is amongst your morning reading. Is that true?

The President. Yes, oh, yes.

Q. My ambition is to get to be your age. [*Laughter*]

Note: The interview began at 4:33 p.m. in the Oval Office at the White House. Among those interviewing the President were Smith Hempstone, editor-in-chief, Woody West, managing editor, Wesley Pruden, deputy managing editor, Josette Sheeran, assistant managing editor, and Jeremiah O'Leary, White House correspondent.

The interview was released by the Office of the Press Secretary on November 28.

Proclamation 5284—Honorary United States Citizenship for William and Hannah Penn
November 28, 1984

Conferral of Honorary Citizenship of the United States Upon William Penn and Hannah Callowhill Penn

By the President of the United States of America

A Proclamation

In the history of this Nation, there has been a small number of men and women whose contributions to its traditions of free-dom, justice, and individual rights have ac-corded them a special place of honor in our hearts and minds, and to whom all Ameri-cans owe a lasting debt. Among them are the men and women who founded the thir-teen colonies that became the United States of America.

William Penn, as a British citizen, found-ed the Commonwealth of Pennsylvania in order to carry out an experiment based upon representative government; public education without regard to race, creed, sex, or ability to pay; and the substitution of workhouses for prisons. He had a Quaker's deep faith in divine guidance, and as the leader of the new colony, he worked to protect rights of personal conscience and freedom of religion. The principles of reli-gious freedom he espoused helped to lay the groundwork for the First Amendment of our Constitution.

As a man of peace, William Penn was conscientiously opposed to war as a means of settling international disputes and worked toward its elimination by proposing the establishment of a Parliament of Na-tions, not unlike the present-day United Na-tions.

Hannah Callowhill Penn, William Penn's wife, effectively administered the Province of Pennsylvania for six years and, like her husband, devoted her life to the pursuit of peace and justice.

To commemorate these lasting contribu-tions of William Penn and Hannah Callow-hill Penn to the founding of our Nation and the development of its principles, the Con-gress of the United States, by Senate Joint Resolution 80, approved October 19, 1984, authorized and requested the President to declare these persons honorary citizens of the United States of America.

Now, Therefore, I, Ronald Reagan, Presi-dent of the United States of America, do hereby proclaim William Penn and Hannah Callowhill Penn to be honorary citizens of the United States of America.

In Witness Whereof, I have hereunto set my hand this 28th day of Nov., in the year of our Lord nineteen hundred and eighty-four, and of the Independence of the United States of America the two hundred and ninth.

RONALD REAGAN

[*Filed with the Office of the Federal Register, 11:28 a.m., November 29, 1984*]

Memorandum on International Communications Satellite Systems
November 28, 1984

Presidential Determination No. 85–2

Memorandum for the Secretary of State, the Secretary of Commerce

By virtue of the authority vested in me by the Constitution and statutes of the United States, including Sections 102(d) and 201(a) of the Communications Satellite Act of 1962, as amended (47 U.S.C. 701(d), 721(a)), I hereby determine that separate international communications satellite systems are required in the national interest. The United States, in order to meet its obligations under the Agreement Establishing the International Telecommunications Satellite Organization (INTELSAT) (TIAS 7532), shall consult with INTELSAT regarding such separate systems as are authorized by the Federal Communications Commission. You are directed jointly to inform the Federal Communications Commission of criteria necessary to ensure the United States meets its international obligations and to further its telecommunications and foreign policy interests.

This determination shall be published in the *Federal Register.*

RONALD REAGAN

[*Filed with the Office of the Federal Register, 11:29 a.m., November 29, 1984*]

Note: The memorandum is printed in the Federal Register of November 30.

Letter Accepting the Resignation of William D. Ruckelshaus as Administrator of the Environmental Protection Agency
November 28, 1984

Dear Bill:

It is with great regret that I accept your resignation as Administrator of the Environmental Protection Agency.

There are very few men or women in public life more widely respected than you. Your reputation for leadership, thoughtfulness and personal integrity is based on a record of outstanding performance in every job you have held. So it wasn't hard for me to decide last year to ask you to serve once more as Administrator of the Environmental Protection Agency. Although my decision was an easy one, I know that your deci-sion to accept was very difficult, since it involved an extraordinary personal sacrifice in putting aside your career in the private sector and moving, with your family, across the continent from Washington State to Washington, D.C. In making your decision to accept, I know you did what you have consistently done: You looked first and foremost toward the public interest.

Since reassuming control of EPA, you have performed your duties in an exemplary manner and have justified fully the faith which I and so many Americans have in you. You have made absolutely clear our commitment to wise stewardship of the environment. In doing so, you have established the firm foundations on which your successor can continue to build—and in which Americans can have complete confidence.

I can understand your desire to return to private life at this time, but I want to express my personal and very warm thanks—as well as the appreciation of a grateful Nation—for the outstanding job you have done. Nancy and I send you and Jill our very best wishes for every future success and happiness.

Sincerely,

RONALD REAGAN

[The Honorable William D. Ruckelshaus, Administrator, Environmental Protection Agency, Washington, D.C. 20024]

Dear Mr. President,

It is with both regret and a sense of accomplishment that I submit my resignation as Administrator of the Environmental Protection Agency, effective January 5, 1985.

I regret that I will be leaving your administration. It has been an honor and a privilege to serve under your leadership and with your support.

My sense of accomplishment derives from the current state of E.P.A. Employee morale and competence is high; first-rate Presidential appointees are in place; a management system has been installed that is functioning well; and all of the programs have generated momentum.

In short, the ship called E.P.A. is righted and is now steering a steady course. I am convinced, Mr. President, that properly led, the dedicated people of E.P.A. will continue to serve well your administration and this country.

I have found again my association with our national government an enormously enriching experience. My thanks to you for having made that possible.

Like all Americans, I wish you the greatest success in your second term. In spite of my return to private life, you can call on me to help anytime, should the need arise.

My warmest personal regards.

Sincerely,

BILL
William D. Ruckelshaus

[President Ronald W. Reagan, The White House, Washington, D.C. 20500]

Note: The letters were made available by the Office of the Press Secretary.

Remarks at a Senate Republican Unity Dinner
November 28, 1984

Thank you, Howard. Ladies and gentlemen, Mr. Vice President and Mrs. Bush, Members of the Senate, members of the Cabinet, thank you all very much. This is a wonderful evening for all of us. The Grand Old Party became the majority party of the Senate in 1980, and it was reelected the majority party in 1982 and again in 1984. This is the first back-to-back-to-back Republican majority in the Senate in over 50 years. And we're going to stay the majority party.

Now I want to say a few words about Howard Baker. We had a sort of a roast for Howard a while back when he announced that he was leaving, and you can imagine

the sort of things that, at a roast, were said about him. Actually, it didn't go on very long because someone pointed out that if you can't say something nice about someone, you shouldn't say anything at all. So, we all put on our hats and went home. [*Laughter*]

But tonight it should be said formally by the leader of his party, who speaks, I know, for all of you, that Howard Baker has been one of the men who has kept the wheel of democracy turning. As a leader of the Senate, he has been endlessly patient and full of care and high purpose. He is a hero of the Republic. And I want to thank you,

Howard, and let you know you're going to be greatly missed.

I want to mention also John Tower of Texas, one of the giants of the modern Senate who has done great work for his nation. So, too, with Chuck Percy and Roger Jepsen, who served our party and our country extremely well. We'll miss them.

Our new majority leader in the Senate, Bob Dole, is a man of wit and wisdom. And we look forward to working closely with you, Bob, and with the new leadership slate.

Last week out at the ranch—and it's not true, by the way, that we had to get people to fly over and drop more brush for me to clear—[*laughter*]—last week out at the ranch, I was digging some irrigation ditches. And it occurred to me that digging ditches was precisely the kind of hard labor that I ought to be doing to prepare for the next 4 years, because our great victory now of 1984 is over and to the victor belong the toils. [*Laughter*] That is the saying, isn't it?

We live in historic times. The great change that we began 4 years ago has been called the Reagan Revolution. Well, let me correct something. You know as well as I do, it was really the Republican Revolution, and all of you are its leaders. I truly believe that we're now the majority party not only of the Senate but of the Nation. But if we're to keep our new status and hold it, indeed, if we're to continue to restore it—or deserve it, I should say, we must, all of us, join together and seize the challenges that history has seen fit to hand us.

We have an historic opportunity in the coming session to make our national tax system more just. We can make it fair and clear. And we can make sure that all those who take risks will be able to enjoy the rewards that those risks entail. We have the opportunity to create a tax system that will not punish all those who could and would be the most productive members of our society, and we must.

This is, as I said, an historic opportunity, and the time to seize it is now. Some of the most productive work of your political lives will be done over the next few years. And if all of us can do what we should about taxes, then history will recall us with kindness and

respect. The same holds true for our obligation to continue to cut Federal spending and get the budget monster back in its cage.

We have the continued opportunity to make it clear together in the wider theater of the world that we're absolutely committed to democracy and absolutely opposed to totalitarianism of whatever stripe. We have the responsibility to stand for freedom in a world lit by lightning, and together we must.

So many challenges before us, but together we can change the world. Here we are, all of us, together on this bright and brisk November evening. And I hope we remember this time together, remember the good feeling and the shared comitment in this room.

It's always a struggle for those of us in political life to take the long view and to brave decisions without regard to personal political cost. There are times when we fail in the struggle and times when we succeed. And I suspect the next few years will test us more than usual, but I know we're up to it. And I know that we Republicans will stick together, as united as the Union our party long ago fought to preserve. We'll have our battles ahead of us, but they're good battles, and they're worth fighting for.

My friends in the other party have been saying that our 49-State sweep was not a mandate and that I personally am a lame-duck. Well, if I'm so lame, I've decided to get a cast, and that'll be useful when I have to do some kicking. [*Laughter*] I won't finish that phrase. It's an old athletic saying. [*Laughter*]

I hope the loyal opposition realizes exactly how committed I am and you are to changing the status quo and improving our national life. We won't be resting on our laurels, even if we were so inclined, which we're not. History wouldn't allow it. We've been handed great opportunities and great challenges, and we intend to meet them together.

You know, I got into the habit during the campaign—understandable little political habit of milking the audience a little. I'd do the stump speech and then near the end I'd say, "I guess I've been going on too long here"—hoping that the audience would yell, "No!" And, of course, all fired up in partisan rallies, they usually would. And I found this most gratifying and allowed it to spill over to my private life until one day I said it to Nancy, and she said, "Yes, you are going on too long"—[*laughter*]—"and now it's time for you to rest your wonderful vocal cords." [*Laughter*] Now, that last part's my version of what she said. She said it in two words. [*Laughter*] So, that's what I'm going to do.

But let me say before I go that I've been very proud to work with you these past 4 years, and I'm very proud of the work that we've done. And now the next 4 years, let it continue.

Thanks so much to all of you. God bless you all.

Note: The President spoke at 10:36 p.m. in the Great Hall at the Library of Congress.

Message to the Congress Reporting Budget Deferrals
November 29, 1984

To the Congress of the United States:

In accordance with the Impoundment Control Act of 1974, I herewith report 14 new deferrals of budget authority for 1985 totaling $5,266,251,741 and three revised deferrals now totaling $6,114,100,232. The deferrals affect International Security Assistance, the Departments of Defense, Energy, Interior and Labor, the General Services Administration, and the Panama Canal Commission.

The details of these deferrals are contained in the attached report.

RONALD REAGAN

The White House,
November 29, 1984.

Note: The attachment detailing the deferrals is printed in the Federal Register of December 6.

Nomination of Lee M. Thomas To Be Administrator of the Environmental Protection Agency
November 29, 1984

The President today announced his intention to nominate Lee M. Thomas to be Administrator of the Environmental Protection Agency. He will succeed William D. Ruckelshaus, who has resigned.

Since July of 1983 Mr. Thomas has been serving as Assistant Administrator of EPA for Solid Waste and Emergency Response. For a time, from March until August 1983, he had served as Acting Deputy Administrator of EPA. Previously he served as Associate Director of the Federal Emergency Management Agency (State and Local Programs and Support), from 1981 to 1983. As such, Mr. Thomas managed all disaster

relief efforts at FEMA and was Chairman of the President's Task Force on Times Beach, Missouri. Prior to this, he was director, division of public safety programs, office of the Governor of South Carolina, from 1979 to 1981; an independent consultant from 1977 to 1979; and executive director, office of criminal justice programs, office of the Governor of South Carolina, from 1972 to 1977.

Mr. Thomas graduated from the University of the South (B.A.) and received a masters of education at the University of South Carolina. He is married with two children and lives in Woodbridge, VA. He was born June 13, 1944, in South Carolina.

Remarks of the President and Chancellor Helmut Kohl of the Federal Republic of Germany Following Their Meetings
November 30, 1984

The President. Chancellor Kohl and I met today to discuss a wide range of issues. Characteristic of our relationship, our talks were friendly, useful, and productive. There's a high level of cooperation and personal rapport between us. As always, I was glad to have such thorough consultations with the Chancellor and his government.

I call your attention to the joint statement issued as a result of today's discussions. It underlines our common commitment to improving East-West relations, improving NATO's conventional defenses, and intensifying our search for arms reductions.

We place special emphasis on overcoming the barriers that divide Europe, a division keenly felt by those living in Central Europe. I was pleased to reaffirm to Chancellor Kohl today our support for his efforts to lower the barriers between the two German states.

The close relationship between the United States and the Federal Republic is enhancing the opportunity for improved East-West relations. This is demonstrated by our successful efforts to carry out the NATO dual-track decision to seek genuine arms reductions agreements and modernize our defenses.

Today Chancellor Kohl and I firmly agreed that we will continue to place a high priority on the search for a responsible means of reducing the arsenals of nuclear weapons that now threaten humankind. And we call upon all men and women of good will to join us.

The solidity of the German-American partnership remains a crucial building block in the search for world peace. The people of our two countries, blessed with liberty and abundance, have a great desire for peace. Chancellor Kohl and I share that desire, and we'll continue to work diligently to bring about a more peaceful world.

The German-American relationship, now in its fourth century, must never be taken for granted. We launched a major initiative in 1982 to nurture an appreciation of ties between us to enhance German-American contacts at all levels. Chancellor Kohl and I noted today the enthusiastic public response in our respective countries, especially among our younger citizens, to the growing exchanges between our peoples.

In sum, our talks confirmed the closeness of our views and the commitment to work together. It was a pleasure to have Chancellor Kohl, Foreign Minister Genscher, and all of his party here. I wish them a smooth journey home, and I look forward to the next time that we can get together.

Thank you.

The Chancellor. Mr. President, ladies and gentlemen, my talk with President Reagan—with you, dear friend—today was, as always, intensive, close, and trustful.

My talk served to maintain the continuity of our very personal and friendly relationship. President Reagan and I made it a highly important moment in world affairs, and I sincerely hope that we were able to open up good and positive perspectives.

The fact that a new phase can be initiated in East-West relations is due, on the one hand, to the firm and united attitude of the Western alliance and, on the other, to our joint determination to continue to seek dialog and necessary negotiations with the East.

In our talk today, the President and I discussed the subject of East-West relations, arms control, and joint efforts in the alliance for improving its conventional defense capability.

The Government of the Federal Republic of Germany fully supports the development emerging in U.S.-Soviet relations, which are, in our view, the centerpiece of East-West relations in general. The President and I consider it important that the Western European allies be associated with this process, thus creating the conditions for the renewed bilateral U.S.-Soviet dialog being placed on a wider foundation in the medium and long term. The close, friendly, and trusting relationship with the United

States, as demonstrated in today's talks once again, is of great significance for the strengthening, cohesion, and solidarity of the alliance.

The President informed me of the American ideas for the exploratory talks to be started on 7th and 8th January 1985, between Secretary Shultz and Foreign Minister Gromyko. These talks, which are taking place on the basis of an umbrella concept developed by the United States, open up new perspectives and opportunities for arms control negotiations.

Mr. President, for very good reasons you referred in your remarks to the joint declaration which we have adopted. This declaration is intended to illustrate the link between improved East-West relations, concrete steps for arms control and disarmament, and the maintenance of our security through adequate defense.

One of the key elements of the joint declaration is the desire, particularly in view of the recent developments in East-West relations and in the field of arms control, to intensify and enhance the alliance's comprehensive, close consultations within this sphere.

Furthermore, we intend to ensure that the alliance strengthens further its conventional defense capability. To this end, we consider it necessary to coordinate the existing initiatives and proposals for better implementation of the valid NATO strategy, thus permitting the available resources to be used more effectively.

Our goal is to raise the nuclear threshold in this manner and to enhance the alliance's ability to defend itself against any kind of war, be it conventional or nuclear.

The joint declaration is of great importance in two respects. Firstly, it is being issued immediately after the overwhelming confirmation in office of the American President by the American people, and at the start of a new phase in East-West relations in which all nations, and not least the divided German nation, the two parts of Germany, place high hopes. We are thus affirming our desire to lay a new, a constructive and lasting foundation for stable East-West relations.

Secondly, ladies and gentlemen, by reflecting our full agreement on essential questions affecting our two countries, this statement constitutes a symbol and a future-oriented yardstick for close German-American cooperation. We are resolved to make our contributions towards further developing within the alliance our cooperation on this basis.

Though this was only a very brief working visit, ladies and gentlemen, I should like to express to you, Mr. President, my dear friend, our sincere thanks for the cordial hospitality extended to us and for the very friendly reception you have been giving to us.

It's good, in difficult times and at moments when you have to take difficult decisions, to know that you have a good friend in the White House, and we are appreciative and grateful for that.

Note: The President spoke at 1:25 p.m. at the South Portico of the White House. The Chancellor spoke in German, and his remarks were translated by an interpreter.

Earlier, the President and the Chancellor met in the Oval Office. They then held a working luncheon, together with U.S. and German officials, in the State Dining Room.

Joint Statement Issued at the Conclusion of Meetings With Chancellor Helmut Kohl of the Federal Republic of Germany
November 30, 1984

Commitment to Peace

The President of the United States and the Chancellor of the Federal Republic of Germany met today, at the President's invitation, to continue their regular exchanges on matters of common interest. Secretary

Shultz, Secretary Weinberger, and Foreign Minister Genscher took part in the talks.

The President and the Chancellor stressed the extraordinary importance of establishing a more lasting basis for peace in Europe and throughout the World. Noting the role of NATO in providing peace and security for Europe and North America in the more than thirty-five years since its founding, the President and the Chancellor are reassured by the clear determination which NATO has shown to safeguard its security and assert its unity.

President Reagan and Chancellor Kohl emphasized that the close relationship between the United States and the Federal Republic of Germany is fundamental to the maintenance of peace, and that continuing cooperation is essential to maintaining the common defense.

As democracies active in the Conference on Security and Cooperation in Europe (CSCE) process, our cooperation can be especially successful in demonstrating the human as well as political aspects of the search for peace. Committed to the Helsinki Final Act, and to the other pertinent multilateral and bilateral documents, we do not accept the division of Europe as permanent and shall work to lower the human costs of the tragic barrier which divides the continent, and in particular, the German people.

The President, and the Chancellor reaffirm the importance of continuing a balanced approach to East-West relations, as set out in the Harmel Report, ensuring the maintenance of necessary military strength and transatlantic political solidarity while pursuing a productive relationship between the countries of East and West through dialogue, cooperation and negotiation.

Such dialogue must be built on the recognition of mutual, legitimate security interests and be conducted on the basis of equal rights for all parties involved. Stable relations must be characterized by the renunciation of military force levels beyond legitimate defense needs and must be founded on strict observance of the ban on the threat or use of force, as enshrined in the United Nations Charter.

The Chancellor endorses the President's continued readiness to meet with the Soviet General Secretary at a carefully prepared meeting. The Chancellor also supports the U.S. proposal to hold regular, high-level talks and meetings which would demonstrate the will of both sides to cooperate on questions of peace, security and international stability. The President welcomes the continuing efforts of the Federal Republic of Germany to pursue dialogue and cooperation with the Soviet Union and with all the countries of Central and Eastern Europe. They urge the Soviet Union to join in a heightened effort to improve East-West relations, give fresh impetus to arms control, and fashion a constructive and stable relationship at the lowest possible level of armament.

The President and the Chancellor stressed that the Alliance's existing strategy of forward defense and flexible response has for many years played an indispensable role in preserving peace in Europe, and will continue to do so. The goal of this defensive strategy is and will remain to prevent any war. The President and the Chancellor reaffirmed the principle subscribed to by all NATO members that none of their weapons will ever be used, except in response to attack.

They are agreed that all requisite steps must be taken to maintain the effectiveness of the Alliance's military strategy and ensure continued deterrence. The expansion and modernization of Soviet and Warsaw Pact nuclear and conventional forces has intensified the need to strengthen the Alliance's force posture.

The United States and the Federal Republic of Germany regret that in contrast to NATO's agreed reductions, starting in 1980, of 2400 nuclear warheads, the Soviet Union has continued to build up its nuclear forces, while abandoning the bilateral Geneva arms control negotiations. The United States and the Federal Republic of Germany see it as imperative, both for eventual success in arms control negotiations and for the Alliance's security, that, in the absence of concrete results in the negotiations, NATO deployments proceed as envisaged under the 1979 decision. NATO has stated that it remains ready to halt, modify, or reverse deployments—including the removal and dismantling of missiles already deployed in Europe—in accordance with the terms of a balanced and verifiable agreement.

The President and the Chancellor consider it essential to redress the steadily growing conventional force imbalance favoring the Warsaw Pact. Therefore, an improved conventional defense posture would help ensure that the Alliance's capacity to act is fully preserved, that deterrence is strengthened, and that the nuclear threshold is raised. The President and the Chancellor, therefore, agreed on the need for a coherent Alliance approach to enhancing NATO's conventional capabilities, and are prepared to participate in Alliance efforts to make the necessary resources available.

The President and the Chancellor emphasized the importance of maintaining an equitable balance of effort and sacrifice among Alliance members. The Chancellor expressed his appreciation for the crucial contribution that the United States makes to Alliance security, in particular through the presence of American troops in Europe. The President expressed his appreciation for the German contribution to the common defense. In particular, he welcomed the Federal Government's recent decision toward sustaining the Bundeswehr's force structure. He also welcomed the recent initiatives of the Western European Union and the intensifying dialogue between the Independent European Program Group and their North American partners in identifying promising areas for resource cooperation. They also stressed the importance of making better use of available resources and technology through broader economic and arms cooperation among member nations.

Underscoring the basic policy of the North Atlantic Alliance, the President and the Chancellor reaffirm that deterrence and defense together with arms control and disarmament are integral parts of their security policy. They form necessary elements of a coherent strategy for securing a stable peace.

The President and the Chancellor reaffirm their commitment to achieve significant results in multilateral arms control negotiations, including Mutual and Balanced

Force Reductions (MBFR), the Conference on Security and Confidence-Building Measures and Disarmament in Europe (CDE), and the Conference on Disarmament (CD).

They stress the need for progress towards an MBFR agreement establishing parity in Central Europe and improving military stability. At the Stockholm Conference, they seek agreement on militarily significant confidence and security building measures (CSBMs) to be applied in the whole of Europe, thus allowing participants to reaffirm and make concrete the existing commitment to refrain from the threat or use of force.

They express their determination to work for progress on a verifiable, comprehensive, global ban on chemical weapons at Geneva.

The Chancellor takes special note of the President's readiness to discuss with the Soviet Union the full range of issues of concern to both sides: the reduction of intercontinental and intermediate range nuclear systems, the relationship between defensive and offensive forces, outer space arms control, improving the effectiveness of existing arms control arrangements, and agreeing to further measures to reduce the risks of conflict through accident, misunderstanding or miscalculation.

The President reiterates, and the Chancellor fully supports, the United States' continuing readiness to work with the Soviet Union in developing a conceptual framework for future negotiations leading to balanced and verifiable arms control agreements. The President and the Chancellor express their conviction that prompt and meaningful progress is possible. They stress the significance of the understanding reached between the U.S. and the Soviet Union to open a new phase of their arms control dialogue with the meeting between Secretary of State George Shultz and Foreign Minister Andrei Gromyko in Geneva.

The President and the Chancellor reaffirm the value and necessity of continued close and intensive consultations within the Alliance over the range of issues before it. In particular, the President and the Chancellor stress the importance of close consultations among the Allies on arms control matters and reiterate their resolve to continue to contribute actively to this process of consultation.

The President and the Chancellor pay tribute to the North Atlantic Alliance as the community of democratic states to which its members owe the preservation of peace and freedom. The President appreciates the vital contribution each ally makes to NATO defense and deterrence and reaffirms the United States' commitment to the common goal of maintaining peace and security in Europe. The President and the Chancellor are determined to strengthen further their efforts in the search for a stable and lasting peace in Europe and throughout the world.

Statement on the Performance of Republican Party Leaders
November 30, 1984

After a hard-fought and successful effort, it is customary to say that "you don't break up a winning team." I think this applies perfectly to our Republican Party leaders.

Senator Paul Laxalt has been a superb general chairman of the Republican Party. Similarly, Frank Fahrenkopf and Betty Heitman, as chairman and cochairman of the Republican National Committee, have been outstanding in their advancement of our party's candidates and ideas at all levels of government.

It is my hope that when the members of the Republican National Committee meet next month, they will vote to recognize Paul Laxalt, Frank Fahrenkopf, and Betty Heitman for a job well done by keeping them in their current party leadership posts.

Appointment of Two Members of the Board of Foreign Scholarships
November 30, 1984

The President today announced his intention to appoint the following individuals to be members of the Board of Foreign Scholarships:

M.E. Bradford, for a term expiring September 22, 1987. This is a reappointment. Dr. Bradford is professor of English at the University of Dallas. He graduated from the University of Oklahoma (B.A., 1955; M.A., 1956) and Vanderbilt University (Ph.D., 1968). He is married, has one child, and resides in Irving, TX. He was born May 8, 1943, in Fort Worth, TX.

Forrest McDonald, for the remainder of the term expiring September 22, 1985. He will succeed Lane Dwinell. Dr. McDonald is professor of history at the University of Alabama. He graduated from the University of Texas at Austin (B.A., M.A., 1949; Ph.D., 1955). He is married, has five children, and resides in Tuscaloosa County, AL. He was born January 7, 1927, in Orange, TX.

Remarks at a White House Reception for Kennedy Center Honorees
December 2, 1984

Good evening. Nancy and I are delighted to welcome you to the White House, a home that belongs to you and to all Americans.

You know, when this good old house was built our country was little more than a band of towns, a very thin band, running along the eastern seaboard—people clinging to the edge of a vast and untamed continent. And when it came to art, drama, and music, Americans looked back to the old country from where most had just come.

But as our nation grew and our people pushed West—plowing fields, felling forests, and building new cities and towns—a new and distinctive culture began to develop, a culture that was as fertile as this new land, as bold and confident as the American people. It took on the twang of the frontier fiddle, the joy of jazz, the excellence of the new American orchestras, and the sparkle of Hollywood movies. And today our nation has crowned her greatness with grace, and we gather this evening to honor five artists who have helped her to do so.

Lena Horne, when you started making movies a columnist wrote, "Lena Horne has put dignity into daring. She has given glamour manners. Hollywood has never before seen such a combination." And neither had the world.

And, Lena, you got your start at the age of 16 as a chorus girl at the legendary Cotton Club and then broke into the Big Band scene as a singer with Charlie Barnet. And during this period, one observer remarked that your voice could thaw the ice in a customer's drink. [*Laughter*] And in the 1940's you became the first black woman ever to be signed to a long-term Hollywood contract. And you've made unforgettable films like "Cabin in the Sky" and, an American classic, "Stormy Weather."

You often had to battle prejudice, but your work expanded the roles available to black performers. During the 1960's you became an ardent champion of civil rights, appearing in benefits, joining protests, and speaking out again and again. And through it all, you've played a direct and vital role in the cause of justice.

Today, Lena, your voice and style are as powerful and as renowned as ever. Your recent show, "Lena, the Lady and Her Music," was the longest running one-woman show in Broadway history. And you know something, Lena? After five decades, when you sing our spines still tingle and the ice still melts. [*Laughter*]

And Arthur Miller, you grew up in Harlem, graduated from high school, and decided to study drama at the University of Michigan. You worked for 2 years, including a job as a shipping clerk in a warehouse to save money for your tuition. After college you wrote radio dramas for the CBS Columbia Workshop and NBC's Cavalcade of America, supporting yourself by working as a truck driver and a steamfitter in the Brooklyn Navy Yard.

Your first Broadway effort, "The Man Who Had All the Luck," closed after four performances in November of 1944. [*Laughter*] Your disappointment would have made many young men give up. Not you. In 1947 you returned to Broadway with a play that no one who sees or reads will ever forget, "All My Sons." Two years later the Broadway curtain rose on a new Arthur Miller drama, one that many critics consider the greatest American play ever written, "Death of a Salesman." And that play ran on Broadway for 742 performances, was made into a motion picture, and today, more than three decades later, is still enjoying revivals around the world.

Since that brilliant work, you've continued to make rich contributions to American letters with plays like "The Crucible" and "A View From the Bridge." And today, Arthur Miller, you're one of America's most renowned living playwrights, and you're still writing strong.

Gian Carlo Menotti, you wrote your first opera back in Italy at the age of 11. When you were 13, your mother enrolled you in a conservatory in Milan. And in 1928, when you were 17, she took you to the Curtis Institute of Music in Philadelphia, armed with a letter from the wife of conductor Arturo Toscanini. Years later your teacher at the Curtis Institute would recall, and I quote, "Early on I told him, 'Gian Carlo, if I am to teach you we must come to an agreement, you and I. I promise you that I will be uncompromisingly severe. Do you promise to put in some very hard work?' "

Well, Gian Carlo promised, and he abided by his agreement. And today millions are grateful that you did. You've given a glorious medium new life with such operas as "The Consul," "The Saint of Bleecker Street," and, one of the best loved operas of all time, the Christmas classic, "Amahl and the Night Visitors."

Gian Carlo Menotti, you have always kept your Italian citizenship. But you've spent so many years among us and contributed so much to our national life, perhaps tonight you'll allow us to claim you as an honorary American.

And Isaac Stern, you were born in Russia and moved to San Francisco with your parents when you were 1. Your mother gave you piano lessons, but at 8 you were fascinated by the sound of a friend playing the violin. At 10 you began formal training in the violin at the San Francisco Conservatory. Your studies were paid for by a woman who recognized your promise. As you put it years later, "I got my break because of the faith and belief private people showed in my work."

At 11 you appeared with the San Francisco Symphony Orchestra. At 17 you debuted in New York. And by your midtwenties, you were performing some 90 concerts a year. Today your repertoire ranges from the classics to the moderns. And one critic has called you, "The only major violinist exclusively a product of American environment and training." And you've spent a lifetime showing how that American environment glitters with artistic excellence.

Danny Kaye, during one of your tours in England, Prime Minister Anthony Eden remarked, "Gad, sir, they treat him as if he were a nation." [*Laughter*]

Born in Brooklyn, you made your acting debut at age 5 in the role of a watermelon seed. [*Laughter*] At 13 you left home to become a clowning busboy on the Borscht Circuit in the Catskill Mountains. In your early twenties, you joined a troupe touring the Orient. Your resourcefulness on that tour became legendary. During a typhoon in Osaka, for instance, you sat on the edge of the stage, sang every song you knew, and spotlighted yourself by holding a flashlight in each hand. [*Laughter*]

When that tour was over, you played nightclubs in London and throughout the American East. At Camp Tamiment in Pennsylvania you met Sylvia Fine, a pianist and composer. And her witty, sophisticated satire was perfectly suited to your delivery and led to a great collaboration.

In 1940 your career soared when you stopped the Broadway show "Lady in the Dark" by performing a number in which you reeled off the names of 50 Russian composers in 38 seconds. [*Laughter*] Something else happened in 1940—Sylvia Fine became Mrs. Danny Kaye.

And signed by Sam Goldwyn, you starred in a succession of hit movies, including "Wonder Man," "The Kid From Brooklyn," "The Inspector General," "The Secret Life of Walter Mitty"—in which you played no fewer than seven roles—and the much-loved "Hans Christian Andersen." Forgive me, Danny, but I can't help wishing I'd had one or two of those roles. [*Laughter*]

In 1970 you returned to Broadway as Noah in Richard Rodger's musical, "Two by Two." And when you injured your leg, you decided that the show must go on, and for 10½ months you performed on crutches while wearing a plaster cast.

In the 1950's, Danny, you took on a new role, becoming ambassador at large for UNICEF, the United Nations children's organization. And since then, you've made scores of trips around the world on behalf of needy children and appeared at countless benefits as a guest symphony conductor.

Danny Kaye—comedian, actor, singer, and conductor—you've brought aid to thousands of children and helped millions of adults to feel young at heart.

Each of the artists we honor tonight overcame hardship and each suffered setbacks and failures. Indeed, Isaac Stern once said that after his New York debut, and I quote, "I was convinced that I didn't know my elbow from A flat." [*Laughter*] Yet they worked long and hard, following their dreams, and succeeded in bringing music, drama, and laughter into our lives. And tonight, as we appreciate their work, let us take comfort and inspiration from their lives.

Lena Horne, Arthur Miller, Gian Carlo Menotti, Isaac Stern, and Danny Kaye: On behalf of all Americans, thank you, God bless you.

Note: The President spoke at 6:17 p.m. in the East Room at the White House, where he and Mrs. Reagan hosted the reception honoring the recipients of the seventh annual Kennedy Center Honors for lifetime achievement.

Following the reception, the President and Mrs. Reagan attended the annual gala honoring the recipients at the John F. Kennedy Center for the Performing Arts.

Proclamation 5285—National Care and Share Day, 1984
December 3, 1984

By the President of the United States of America

A Proclamation

The spirit of neighbor helping neighbor flows like a deep and mighty river through the history of our Nation. We are proud of our strong and uniquely American tradition of voluntarism. Compassion, vision, and a fundamental sense of decency are the hallmarks of our national character and are reflected in the charitable works of our citizens.

During this holiday season, I call upon all Americans to reflect this spirit of generosity and cooperation by joining in partnership with others to provide food to those in need. I ask the agricultural and food industries to donate surpluses to food banks around the country and to complement government programs that are providing food assistance to low-income Americans. I look for the support of community groups, charitable organizations, and individuals in donating food items and in transporting and distributing them to those in need. Let the caring, sharing, and goodwill generated by private initiative spread across this great Nation of ours and bring joy to each and every individual.

Now, Therefore, I, Ronald Reagan, President of the United States of America, do hereby proclaim December 15, 1984, as National Care and Share Day and call upon the people of the United States to pay tribute to acts of charity and to promote community involvement in caring for the needs of our neighbors.

In Witness Whereof, I have hereunto set my hand this 3rd day of Dec., in the year of our Lord nineteen hundred and eighty-four, and of the Independence of the United States of America the two hundred and ninth.

RONALD REAGAN

[Filed with the Office of the Federal Register, 11:44 a.m., December 4, 1984]

Note: The proclamation was released by the Office of the Press Secretary on December 4.

Remarks at the Welcoming Ceremony for President Jaime Lusinchi of Venezuela
December 4, 1984

President Reagan. We welcome you to the United States, Mr. President.

President Lusinchi of Venezuela has been one of the finest of friends of our country. We have worked together in Central America to bring about the birth of democracy in many countries where that had not been known. And it's an honor today to welcome one of this hemisphere's shining examples of freedom and democracy, President Jaime Lusinchi of Venezuela.

President Lusinchi is a man dedicated to those principles of liberty that are held dear by the people of the United States. It's a pleasure for us to have as our guest an individual who played such an important role building freedom in his own country and who now, as a spokesman for his people, is such a force for good in this hemisphere.

Venezuelans do not take freedom for granted. It was just a generation ago when President Lusinchi and other brave Venezuelans, under the leadership of a great statesman and democrat, Romulo Betancourt, threw off dictatorship and began laying the foundation for a stable democratic society. Their struggle was not dissimilar to the one that's going on in Central America today. The fledgling Venezuelan democracy was immediately put to the test by Cuban-supported guerrillas and terrorists who would have turned Venezuela into a Marxist-Leninist dictatorship.

Mr. President, your triumph in this 10-year struggle, and the subsequent success of a freedom in your country, should serve as a model for today—the Venezuelan model, if you will. Granting amnesty to those guerrillas willing to put down their weapons and participate in the electoral process, Venezuela's leaders held firm to the principles of democratic government and individual freedom and never gave in to the armed Marxist-Leninist minority.

The peace, liberty, and seniority—or security, I should say, enjoyed in your country today is a result of that valor and determination. Nothing less should have been ex-

pected from the heirs of the Great Liberator, Simón Bolivar. He once said of Venezuela: "By establishing a democratic republic, she has declared for the rights of man and freedom of action, thought, speech and press. These eminently liberal acts will never cease to be admired."

Venezuelans who understand that democracy is a path to peace and progress can be proud that their government is standing shoulder to shoulder with the forces of democracy in Central America today. All freedom-loving people should rejoice that El Salvador and other countries in the region, like Venezuela before, are maintaining or establishing democratic governments, despite challenges of Soviet bloc-sponsored subversion.

The exception to this trend in Central America is Nicaragua, where a ruling clique of Sandinistas, allied with Cuban and Soviet dictators, have betrayed their citizens. Despite their assurances in 1979 to the people of Nicaragua, and to the Organization of American States, that they would hold genuinely democratic elections, they have, to the contrary, persecuted the democratic opposition parties, trade unions, and civic and religious organizations. Instead of free elections, they chose to hold a Communist-style sham election, orderly in form, but without the participation of the democratic opposition, because Sandinista-controlled gangs of thugs beat down freedom of speech and assembly, wiping out any chance for genuine political competition.

President Lusinchi, I hope you will work with me to ensure that the pledges of free elections and real democracy made to the OAS and to the Nicaraguan people are carried out.

Venezuela has been and continues to be a leading force in the Contadora process, which seeks peace in Central America, based on democratic principles, and we applaud your efforts. The United States places great importance on all 21 objectives of the Contadora process, which include truly democratic elections, as originally promised by the Sandinistas. The Contadora objectives, if put into practice simultaneously with effective verification, offer the best hope for peace in Central America. I can assure you that the diplomatic efforts of the United States are designed to attain these objectives.

Two decades ago the founder of modern Venezuelan democracy, President Romulo Betancourt, visited here and said, "If the United States and my country and Latin America can work together for democracy, we can increase and improve the conditions of life for all our people very rapidly." Well, his words rang true. In two decades, great things have been accomplished by the free people of Venezuela. The people of the United States are happy to have played a small role, offering a helping hand to people who have become close friends.

Venezuela, in turn, has assisted those working to better themselves in the Caribbean and Central America, making substantial contributions to the well-being of others through the San Jose Accord. Our relationship of trust and cooperation is good for our own peoples and benefits the entire hemisphere. It's something to be cherished, and we do not take it for granted.

I'm sure, Mr. President, that you're also pleased by the restoration of democracy in Grenada. Yesterday's election marked the first time a Marxist-Leninist dictatorship has been succeeded by a government that receives its authority from free elections. And congratulations are due to the people of Grenada.

Mr. President, we're keenly aware that Venezuela is now going through a period of economic adjustment. We support the responsible decisions that you are making to put your country back on the track to strong economic growth. We, too, have undertaken some fundamental reforms in recent years and more will be forthcoming.

We continue to believe that strong economic growth is the foundation of social justice, the key being greater incentives, opportunity, and freedom for every person. Each year in every corner of the globe, evidence continues to build. Today no objective observer can deny that individual freedom, not government control, is the strongest spark for economic development and human progress.

President Lusinchi, you have the confidence of your people and have our confidence as well. You also have our admiration. It's a pleasure to greet you on behalf of the people of the United States.

Welcome.

President Lusinchi. Mr. President, it is a great pleasure for me to be here in this beautiful city of Washington, responding to the kind invitation you have extended to me. Mr. President, I interpret this deference as a distinction marking my country and as an expression of good will of the Government of the United States.

I represent Venezuela, but also, in some way, I represent undoubtedly Latin America as a whole, in view of the identification of our populations, the community of our interests, and the coincidence of our aspirations. I thus come, Mr. Reagan, to hold with you and the senior officials of the Government of the United States a dialog that is to be frank, sincere, amicable, and thoughtful, as well.

I represent one of the soundest democracies of Latin America. I come from a country where pluralistic democracy constitutes an irreversible experience. Our history has been traumatic; you know it well. I am the sixth President of a process that, throughout the last 26 years, has shown Venezuelans that democracy enables them to progress in freedom. Our system rests on the free and secret practice of the universal right to vote.

The concept of alternativeness, of republican governments in an intrinsically democratic country such as ours, guarantees us a future of progress. We believe in the need for social reforms and embark on them in a frame of free expression of ideas. All this is inherent to our way of life and our way of understanding our political responsibility. For Venezuelans there is no valid alternative to democracy. Experience has shown it to be an indivisible truth.

We are a peaceful country and, therefore, believe in peaceful solutions to controversies. Our history has been one of friendship and solidarity. We do not interfere in the affairs of others and zealously watch over our own affairs. We have fought and shall continue to fight for the achievement of equity in international economic relations. We believe that the unprecedented advancement of science and technology enables all of mankind to reach rational levels of well-being if only the great statesmen of our times pursue in good will their mission in an ever more interdependent world.

Latin America is moving forward on the road to democracy, Mr. President. Countries of the South Cone, with their great tradition of intellect and historical achievement, tread again the path of liberty and democratic order they themselves had once opened up and pioneered. Let us encourage them at this time openly, unselfishly, and fearlessly in their process to freedom and enforcement of the fundamental values of the human spirit.

Simultaneously with this development in South America, contiguously to our countries in Central America, conflicts are raging, and their complexity, ever more apparent, are due to the summation of international factors to the already longstanding problems of the region traditionally ruled by inhuman dictatorships and insatiable oligarchies.

The conflict of Central America demands of all of us ponderation, equilibrium, and firmness if we are to cooperate in seeking solutions compatible with the essence and idiosyncracy of those depressed nations. We firmly believe that the solution to the existing crisis rests on an effective democratization of the region and the exclusion of external factors, be they continental or extra-continental.

We do not believe that the solution to this delicate and complex crisis of the Central American countries can be one of force or military involvement. Rather to the contrary, we believe that the only viable path and the only lasting solution rests on designing and implementing a policy of democratization, pluralism, social justice, and economic development for all the countries of the region to the exclusion of none, and without exerting any imposition.

As a member of the group of Contadora,

Venezuela has striven to seek a peaceful solution to Central America. And despite our own problems, we are continuing to implement a program of cooperation with the region in the field of energy, thus translating into facts our postulates of good will.

We are sincere in our practice of democracy, and thus none of us would feel—you, yourself, Mr. President—would not feel that we can meet our own expectations as long as in this continent, from the Canadian Arctic to the Tierra del Fuego, a democratic way of life has not become the practice and the resolve of all our countries.

Finally, I come, Mr. President of the United States, with an open mind and an open heart, free from all prejudices, and convinced of the soundness and fairness of our views to engage with you in a dialog—fruitful, I hope—for the consolidation of the relations traditionally friendly between Venezuela and the United States.

I thank you, Mr. President, in my own name, and on behalf of those who accompany me, for your kind words of welcome, which lead us to expect a positive exchange of ideas and mutual experiences. Your words correspond to the spirit of friendship and sympathy which, through the passing of time, has been characteristic of the relations between the United States and Venezuela.

Both nations, Mr. President, share the common ideas of Bolívar and Washington and those of the standard-bearers and shapers in the world of the Americas, of the principles of liberty, democracy, national independence, and respect for the dignity of man.

Thank you very much for your welcome.

Note: President Reagan spoke at 10:09 a.m. on the South Lawn of the White House, where President Lusinchi was accorded a formal welcome with full military honors. President Lusinchi spoke in Spanish, and his remarks were translated by an interpreter.

Following the ceremony, the two Presidents, together with U.S. and Venezuelan officials, met in the Oval Office.

Appointment of Margaret Noonan as Special Assistant to the President for Presidential Speechwriting
December 4, 1984

The President today announced the appointment of Margaret (Peggy) Noonan as Special Assistant to the President for Presidential Speechwriting.

Miss Noonan was appointed a speechwriter to the President in April 1984. For the previous 3 years Miss Noonan was a producer at CBS News in New York. From 1977 to 1981, she was a writer at the CBS radio network. Prior to that Miss Noonan was the director of editorial and public affairs for the CBS-owned radio station in Boston, MA. Her editorials and documentaries won numerous journalism awards, including the UPI-Tom Philips Award.

Miss Noonan graduated cum laude from Fairleigh Dickinson University in 1974. She was born in Brooklyn, NY.

Statement on Elections in Grenada
December 4, 1984

On Monday, December 3, the people of Grenada held their first democratic election since 1976. The election represents an achievement of historic importance, the first occasion in which a nation has returned to democracy after being freed from Marxist-Leninist rule.

The United States is proud to have played a part in the return of democracy to Grenada. On October 25, 1983, at the request of the Governor of Grenada and of the Organization of Eastern Caribbean States, the United States participated in the rescue mission which freed the Grenadian people from chaotic and brutal misrule. That action led to the creation on Grenada of an interim government, chaired by Mr. Nicholas Brathwaite, who deserves much of the credit for following through on the pledge to turn over the nation's administration through free and fair elections. The interim government also deserves admiration for the humaneness and respect for law which it has exercised in its treatment of those who served with the former Grenadian Government.

We applaud the Grenadian people for their peaceful, orderly, and genuinely democratic exercise of popular sovereignty on December 3. We look forward to working closely with the new Government of Grenada.

Proclamation 5286—National Pearl Harbor Remembrance Day, 1984
December 4, 1984

By the President of the United States of America

A Proclamation

On the morning of December 7, 1941, the Imperial Japanese Navy launched an unprovoked surprise attack on units of the Armed Forces of the United States stationed at Pearl Harbor, Hawaii. Over 2,400 United States citizens were killed and almost 1,200 were wounded in the attack. This battle marked our entry into World War II and galvanized the will of the American people to achieve ultimate victory.

Today, Japan is firmly united with us as

an ally in defense of the freedom we share. But the lesson of Pearl Harbor is as important today as it was over forty years ago. In an uncertain world, democracies should always seek peace but also be prepared to defeat aggression. Military strength can deter war and give diplomacy time to achieve its beneficial results.

The people of the United States owe a tremendous debt of gratitude to all members of our Armed Forces who served at Pearl Harbor and in the many battles that followed in all other theaters of action of World War II. Their selfless dedication and sacrifice will never be forgotten.

The Congress, by House Joint Resolution 392, has designated December 7, 1984, as "National Pearl Harbor Remembrance Day" and authorized and requested the President to issue a proclamation in observance of this event.

Now, Therefore, I, Ronald Reagan, President of the United States of America, do hereby proclaim December 7, 1984, as National Pearl Harbor Remembrance Day and call upon the people of the United States to observe this solemn occasion with appropriate ceremonies and activities and to pledge eternal vigilance and strong resolve to defend this Nation and its allies from all future aggression.

In Witness Whereof, I have hereunto set my hand this fourth day of December, in the year of our Lord nineteen hundred and eighty-four, and of the Independence of the United States of America the two hundred and ninth.

RONALD REAGAN

[*Filed with the Office of the Federal Register, 11:21 a.m., December 5, 1984*]

Toasts of President Reagan and President Jaime Lusinchi of Venezuela at the State Dinner
December 4, 1984

President Reagan. Good evening, and welcome to the White House.

This has been a special time for us. Today we've had the opportunity to exchange views and get to know President Lusinchi, an individual whose strength of conviction and personal bravery helped give birth to democracy in his country. Tonight we honor you, Mr. President, for what you've done, for what you're doing, and for the kind of man you are.

In this beautiful setting, the hard sacrifices of our own Founding Fathers seem so long ago, yet all of what we have has been built on the foundation they laid. President Lusinchi remembers well Venezuela's fight for political freedom. He was part of it. As a young man, he committed himself to the cause of democracy. He was arrested and tortured by the dictatorship. And, Mr. President, I'm told the beatings left welts on your back similar to the stripes of a tiger. Well, you had the spirit of a tiger, and you never gave up your ideals.

Venezuela is free today because it has people of such character. Last year you celebrated 25 years of continuous democratic government in Venezuela. Commemorating that, you said, "We have discovered that democracy and liberty go together inextricably together." It was fitting that last year was also the 200th anniversary of the birth of Simón Bolivar, a Venezuelan whose struggle gave independence to the hemisphere. Today you carry on the work of this truly all-American man. And when we say "American," we mean every one of us, from the North Slope of Alaska to the tip of Tierra del Fuego—all of us are Americans in this hemisphere.

I'd like to thank you, Mr. President, for what your country is doing for the cause of democracy in this hemisphere. Your support during the Grenada crisis was most appreciated. Your efforts in Central America and the Caribbean are of great importance to the future of freedom there. Your personal guidance to me in the years ahead will be as invaluable as it has been today.

We're proud to stand with you and to have you and your countrymen as our friends. Mr. President, you represent in so many ways, the deep ties between our two peoples. Today, instead of "Welcome," we should have said, "Welcome back," for you lived with us during your time of exile, studying medicine and working in Bellevue Hospital in New York.

As a political figure, you've been concerned about the freedom and progress of your people. As a physician, you understand human suffering. This understanding is reflected in the energetic commitment that you've made to battling the flow of narcotics through Venezuela and the Caribbean region. As you're aware, the drug abuse problem is something that your dinner partner, Nancy, and I feel strongly about. Nancy has spent many hours here trying to help the victims of drug addiction, especially young people.

For your efforts to stop illegal drugs before they reach our shore, you have our personal thanks.

Americans know there's a special spirit in Venezuela, and that spirit is hard to miss when you have Tony Armas hitting towering homeruns like they were the easiest thing to do. Well, the free people of Venezuela and the United States are on the same team, and we're up to bat. So, in keeping with the lessons Tony Armas has been teaching us, let's set our sights high, work as a team, and assure democracy and improving economic well-being for all the people of the Americas.

Now, will you all join me in a toast to President Lusinchi, the people of Venezuela, and the things that we can and will accomplish together.

President Lusinchi. Mr. President, Mrs. Reagan, I understand fully that this evening, this dinner, is a homage to my country, Venezuela, a country which, taking account the difference in dimensions, has much in common with the United States. For just as the United States, it is an integrator of races, religions, and ambitions. Your country and my country, Mr. President, are both lands of possibilities. I understand this fully, and this is why I believe that both the United States and Venezuela

have had a common history in the past and have for the future a common destiny.

This, in part, has made us very proud to be here and very happy to see that these Americans can organize things so well. They know so much and they understand so much that they were able even to make the climate work in favor of the beautiful reception we had this morning. And President Reagan has been very kind this evening to sit me beside your guardian angel on one side and a Venezuelan angel on the other side, Mrs. Cisnaros, who is highly representative of Venezuelan women.

I had thought to say a few words on this occasion, but your generosity and your warmth, Mr. President, have compelled me to use, before I say those words, all my old parliamentary resources. But one hesitates here on a visit of state such as mine—and I came here as head of government and President of the Republic of Venezuela—so I must say therefore, in this capacity, that we small countries seem to have cultivated somewhat the right to dissent; and discrepancy has often become the object of much worship, and disagreement with the strong has become the consolation often of the weak. At times, we disagree just to highlight the existing difference or simply to reaffirm our wish to exercise autonomous thought and action. There are many occasions to dissent, to express different views, or to celebrate coincidences. And this, also, is totally legitimate.

Even if the United States is the most powerful nation on Earth, besides holding diverging views, we also find with you many convergences and totally legitimate ones, as well. And I must say this very frankly, proudly, and candidly. In a ceremony such as the present one, I think it is much more intelligent, much more human, to highlight, rather, all that unites us, all that identifies us to each other and leave aside what might have been something that can separate this great world power from a country such as ours, cognizant of its dimensions and its possibilities.

Permit me to leave aside thoughts on important substance matters. I do not want to run the risk of appearing solemn when it would be out of place to do so. I am not a declared enemy of solemnity itself, but I do believe it must be exercised on appropriate occasions. Some people never depart from it and yearn to appear solemn every single hour and minute of their lives. I'm happy to say that this is neither your case, Mr. President, or mine. And, in part, this is because both of us are common men. In some way, must one become, after all, eligible for the benevolence of history, even if it is to be through the exercise of discretion.

I have come to the United States and to this mansion of Presidents as a spokesman and representative of a country and a people friendly to the United States. I have come to express our views on bilateral issues of two friendly nations—on issues of our hemisphere, we cannot and shall not be indifferent to and on world issues on which we Venezuelans do not exert much influence, but which affect us to a high degree.

The biggest pride of Venezuelans is perhaps to feel that we are a country that holds no prejudices, no dogmas, no intolerances. And I say this to you—I've said it to you, Mrs. Reagan, with great pride during this dinner—and I believe that this is what makes us firmly believe, in part, that in spite of our backwardness in some economic and social areas, we are a country the future will favor, perhaps because the future lies for those who, as ourselves, show an open mind and a willing heart.

I said before that all work today to make this a beautiful celebration for me, and even the fact that a year ago—it is just a year ago that I won elections, Mr. President, by as large a landslide as you did. [*Laughter*] And there is something even more important, because in our case, we even got all the votes of your Minnesota. [*Laughter*] So, today we have really given to us a great present—you have been so kind, you have shown to us so much graciousness. Your words have been so pleasant, you have given me the occasion to speak to your beautiful and distinguished wife, beautiful representative of American women we much admire.

And so, allow me also to take this occasion of having many common friends with us to congratulate you here, Mr. President, on your electoral victory and to wish you an

extraordinary second term. The Government, all the people of the United States, hope to get from you and as citizen of the world, all the contribution you and your country can make to peace, solidarity, a better living for all the people of this planet.

I know that you are an actor, but please allow me to be the first one to say something you told me this morning. Allow me the privilege of being your reporter tonight. You told me as we got down from the rostrum that when you started to speak—after both of us made the speeches this morning to your country, to my country, and to the world that had wanted, perhaps, to listen to us—you said that you had in the pocket of your overcoat the speech you had pronounced for the Duke of Luxembourg and that you had not used this overcoat until today. My speech, you had it in the pocket of your jacket. So, today I was almost called "Your Highness." I certainly do not have any special ambitions to be royalty, but I just wonder, the faces of the Venezuelans if they had heard this. [*Laughter*]

Mr. President, allow me again to thank you for this beautiful reception, for your kindness, and also for having invited distinguished friends of yours, people you love, and friends of mine—people who are of great value and precious to my own country, Venezuela. And allow me to exemplify and identify all of these fellow countrymen of mine with the name of Marisol Escobar, a famous sculptress who forged the image of the liberator, Simón Bolívar, and left this image at the United Nations forever in time.

Thank you again, Mr. President, Mrs. Reagan. You have in me, be assured of the fact, a loyal and sincere friend who admires you, esteems you; a friend good enough to dissent with you and to applaud at the same time all your kindness, your good will, and your good heart.

Thank you.

Note: President Reagan spoke at 9:55 p.m. in the State Dining Room at the White House. President Lusinchi spoke in Spanish, and his remarks were translated by an interpreter.

Statement on the Designation of Paul H. Nitze as Adviser to the Secretary of State at the Arms Control Talks in Geneva, Switzerland
December 5, 1984

At the recommendation of the Secretary of State, I have today asked Ambassador Paul Nitze to serve as adviser to the Secretary for the Geneva talks. Ambassador Nitze has a long history of distinguished service to his country, and I am very pleased that he has accepted.

Note: On the same day, the White House announced that the President and Secretary of State George P. Shultz discussed arms control and other issues during a luncheon meeting at the White House.

Following the luncheon, they met in the Oval Office with Ambassador Nitze for a discussion of the forthcoming Geneva talks. During the afternoon, the President held additional meetings with his advisers to discuss arms control issues.

Appointment of James Peter Covey as Senior Director of Near East and South Asian Affairs for the National Security Council and Special Assistant to the President for National Security Affairs
December 5, 1984

The President today announced the appointment of James Peter Covey as Senior Director of Near East and South Asian Affairs for the National Security Council and Special Assistant to the President for National Security Affairs.

Following service as interpreter/translator in the U.S. Army Security Agency in Berlin (1965–1969) and as a secondary school teacher in Kampala, Uganda (1970–1971), Mr. Covey entered the Foreign Service in 1971. Since then he has served as consular officer in Pretoria (1972–1974); watch officer in the State Department's Operations Center (1974–1975); special assistant to the Secretary of State (1975–1977); a fellow of the Center for Strategic and International Studies at Georgetown University (1977–1978); political officer for the State Department's Office of Israeli and Arab-Israeli Affairs (1978–1980); delegate to the Egyptian-Israeli-U.S. peace talks (1979–1980); deputy principal officer in Jerusalem (1980–1983); member of the Habib mission in Beirut (1982); and Deputy Executive Secretary of the Department of State (1983 to present).

Mr. Covey graduated from St. Lawrence University (B.A., 1965). He is married to Christine Ramsay Covey. They have two children and reside in Washington, DC. He was born March 7, 1944.

Remarks Announcing Additional United States Food Assistance to Africa
December 5, 1984

Jack, thank you very much.

I'm happy to announce that the United States is taking additional actions today to provide increased assistance to the victims of the terrible drought which affects major parts of Africa.

Three hundred thousand metric tons of wheat from our government reserve is being made immediately available for emergency food programs. In addition, $50 million from other accounts is being transferred for emergency food use. Finally, additional requirements are under review, and, if necessary, we will seek additional resources from the Congress.

These actions are in addition to unprecedented American efforts which have been underway for many months. During the last fiscal year, we provided 500,000 tons of emergency food to Africa. This $170-million grant was more than in any previous year. On July 10th of this year, I announced a five-point initiative to speed up U.S. delivery of emergency food aid. And in the past 2 months, we surpassed all of last year's levels—600,000 tons of food with a value of more than $250 million.

The people of Africa continue to be in desperate need and the cost in human lives, as Jack has told us, is horrible. The United States will continue to uphold our humanitarian tradition. While our emergency aid seeks to help remedy today's suffering, our regular programs of development and assistance will continue to work to eliminate the root cause of famine. These programs will help Africa grow more food in the years to come.

And beyond any governmental program, however, I want to pay tribute to the outpouring of support which the African crisis has produced in the private community. Organizations such as CARE, Catholic Relief, Lutheran World Service, AFRICARE, the Red Cross, the International Rescue Committee, Save the Children Fund, and many others have provided the manpower on the ground which has permitted programs to reach those most needing assistance. The contributions and support of millions of caring individuals have been absolutely stunning and are essential. And this is America at its very best.

We in the government and those in the private sector recognize that much more needs to be done. And in the weeks and months ahead, we'll do everything possible to assist in this important, life-saving work.

Thank you, and God bless you all. And I will now sign.

Note: The President spoke at 2:06 p.m. in the Roosevelt Room at the White House during a meeting with Members of Congress and administration officials. He was introduced by Secretary of Agriculture John R. Block, who also addressed the group.

Following his remarks, the President signed a statement concerning additional U.S. assistance. The statement is printed below.

Statement on Additional United States Food Assistance to Africa
December 5, 1984

A major disaster exists in the developing countries of Africa and South Asia. Therefore, today I am directing the Secretary of Agriculture to release up to 300,000 tons of wheat from the Food Security Wheat Reserve for use to provide urgent humanitarian relief to those suffering from widespread hunger and malnutrition. I am also directing the Food Aid Subcommittee of the Development Coordination Committee to determine and act upon the specific needs that can be met through release of this reserve.

I am taking this extraordinary action today because relief cannot be programmed for this purpose in a sufficiently timely manner under the normal means of obtaining commodities for food assistance due to the unanticipated and exceptional needs currently existing. This action will help maintain our generous response to the suffering of needy people and keep the pipeline supplied as we continue to assess needs and other possible responses.

This wheat will be provided under the auspices of the Public Law 480 title II donations program. This program distributes food to needy people through both private voluntary agencies and recipient governments.

RONALD REAGAN

Note: As printed above, the statement follows the White House press release.

Executive Order 12493—President's Commission on Executive Exchange
December 5, 1984

By the authority vested in me as President by the Constitution and statutes of the United States of America, and in order to amend the responsibilities of the President's Commission on Executive Exchange and to continue its work of benefiting both the Government and the private sector by enabling the most outstanding executives to work in the other sector, it is hereby ordered as follows:

Section 1. Establishment of the Commission. (a) The President's Commission on Executive Exchange is hereby continued.

(b) The Commission shall be composed of not more than thirty-six members who shall be appointed from time to time by the President from among leaders in the private sector and the Executive branch of the Government. The President shall seek, so far as he deems practicable or advisable, to appoint up to seventy-five percent of the Commission membership from the ranks of Chief Executive Officers, Chief Operating Officers, Chairmen, Senior Partners or other individuals of comparable rank and stature from the private sector. Executive branch members, to the extent the President deems practicable or advisable, may include Cabinet Secretaries, Agency Heads, and such other officials of comparable rank or position as deemed appropriate by the President.

The President shall designate a Chairman from among the members of the Commission. The Chairman and members shall serve at the pleasure of the President. Members of the Commission shall serve two-year terms or until a successor is appointed.

(c) Members of the Commission who are full-time officers or employees of the Federal government shall receive no additional compensation by reason of this Order, and members who are not such officers or employees shall serve without compensation, but each Commissioner shall be provided with travel expenses, including per diem in lieu of subsistence, as authorized by law.

Sec. 2. Functions of the Commission. (a) The Commission shall administer an Executive Exchange Program in which: (1) outstanding private sector executives, primarily those who have achieved senior level management positions, and also those exceptional managers who have unique qualifications and extremely high potential for policymaking positions, will be selected as Presidential Exchange Executives and assigned to positions in the Senior Executive Service or positions of comparable rank or stature, reporting, as appropriate, to Cabinet Officers, Ambassadors, Agency Heads, Under Secretaries, Assistant Secretaries or other high-ranking Government officials for not more than one year, with an extension of up to ninety days in extraordinary circumstances; and (2) career Federal Executives who are members of the Senior Executive Service, or equivalent level, will be selected as Presidential Exchange Executives and assigned for one year to positions in the private sector offering significant challenge, responsibility and regular and continuing contact with senior private sector officials.

(b) The Commission shall administer an Executive International Embassy Assignments Program in which exceptionally qualified private sector executives, primarily those who have achieved senior level management positions, and also exceptional managers who have unique qualifications and extremely high potential for policymaking positions, may be selected as Presidential Exchange Executives and, as appropriate, assigned for one year, with an extension of up to ninety days, to the Senior Foreign Service or other key positions in United States Embassies reporting to Ambassadors or other high-ranking Government officials.

(c) The Commission shall administer an education program which places the work experience of the Presidential Exchange Executives in the broader context of both Federal government and private sector operations and, to the extent desirable and appropriate, may include exposure to international economic and foreign affairs.

(d) The Commission shall supervise and review the operation of the Program, and may recommend to the President ways to promote and improve the Program.

(e) The Commission shall ensure that the Program operates in compliance with the merit principles set forth in Section 2301 of Title 5 of the United States Code.

Sec. 3. Responsibilities of Executive Agencies. Each Executive agency shall, to the extent permitted by law, provide the Commission with such assistance as may be necessary for the effective performance of its functions.

Sec. 4. Administrative Provisions. (a) The Office of Personnel Management shall provide the Commission with administrative services, staff support and travel expenses, as authorized by law. The Office of Administration, Executive Office of the President, may provide services to the Commission on a reimbursable basis pursuant to interagency agreement, as may be authorized by the Economy Act of 1932, as amended, 31 U.S.C. 1535 *et seq.*

(b) The Executive Director's responsibilities shall be to carry out the activities of the Commission.

(c) Executive Order No. 12136 of May 15, 1979 is revoked.

RONALD REAGAN

The White House,
December 5, 1984.

[*Filed with the Office of the Federal Register, 10:55 a.m., December 6, 1984*]

Note: The Executive order was released by the Office of the Press Secretary on December 6.

Remarks on Congratulating Doug Flutie, the 1984 Heisman Trophy Winner
December 6, 1984

The President. Fifty years ago Jay Berwanger, of the University of Chicago, was a powerful halfback and a hero to millions of football-loving Americans, including a certain sportscaster named Dutch Reagan. In 1935 he won a new award, the Heisman Trophy, and a great American tradition was born.

The list of Heisman Trophy winners reads like an honor roll. There was Nile Kinnick, of Iowa, who was a brilliant runningback and true patriot, who gave his life during World War II. There were the great young men of Notre Dame—Angelo Bertelli, John Lujack, and others who kept on going out there for the Gipper. In recent years we've seen players set new standards of excellence—champions like Earl Campbell, Her-

schel Walker; last year's trophy winner, Mike Rozier. And this year there's a young man who stands in a class by himself—Doug Flutie.

When Doug Flutie arrived on the Boston College campus in 1981, he was just a fourth-string quarterback. And since that time, he has put together the most prolific passing career any major college quarterback has ever had. He's given us fans a host of moments to remember, including a play during the final seconds of this year's Boston College-Miami game that will go down in football history.

With the score of Miami, 45, as you all well know, B.C., 41, and just seconds left on the clock, Doug took the snap, dropped back, and with the clock at zero, he fired a sky-high, 65-yard pass right—arched into the end zone and right into the hands of Boston College receiver Gerard Phelan.

B.C. won the game; Doug Flutie won our eternal admiration. And for 50 years the Heisman Trophy has stood for loyalty, courage, teamwork, and a ceaseless striving for excellence.

And, Doug Flutie, it's an award that you richly deserve. Congratulations, and God bless you.

Mr. Flutie. Thank you very much. It's indeed an honor for myself to be here in the presence and having the opportunity to meet the President. And thank you very much for your comments.

I'm excited to be here at the White House. And it is a great opportunity for my whole family, also.

I'd like to welcome the fellows from Gonzaga High School and wish you all the luck in the future. It's a once-in-a-lifetime opportunity for me. The Heisman Trophy is something that means a lot, and it's something that I never would have expected. And as for you guys, if you can dream it, it's possible. I never could have dreamed winning the Heisman or being here in this situation. And it's something I'll treasure for the rest of my life.

Thank you.

Mr. Reinauer. Mr. President, Mr. Vice President, it is an honor to be here today. And I'd like to inform everyone in honoring Heisman's 50th of the Downtown Athletic Club, for the first time in award history, we have made a reduced replica to bring to Washington today.

Mr. President, on behalf of the Downtown Athletic Club of New York and the Heisman Trophy Committee, it is a pleasure to make you an honorary Heisman winner.

The President. That's better than an Oscar. [*Laughter*]

Mr. Reinauer. Remember when we met you in New York and you came over with Archbishop O'Connor, you said, "Don't forget I played guard at Eureka." [*Laughter*]

The President. Yes. Well, thank you very much. I'm very pleased and proud to have this. I'm not even going to put it back down on the table. [*Laughter*]

Thank you all.

Note: The President spoke at 11:05 a.m. in Room 450 of the Old Executive Office Building.

Harold Reinauer is president of the Downtown Athletic Club.

Executive Order 12494—Hazardous Duty Pay
December 6, 1984

Amending Executive Order No. 11157 as it Relates to Pay for Hazardous Duty

By the authority vested in me as President of the United States of America by Section 301 (a) of Title 37 of the United States Code, and in order to define the scope of one category of hazardous duty, it is hereby ordered as follows:

Section 1. Executive Order No. 11157 of June 22, 1964, as amended, is further amended by striking out subsection (b) of Section 109 of Part I and inserting in lieu thereof the following:

"(b) The term 'duty involving the demolition of explosives' shall be construed to mean duty performed by members who, pursuant to competent orders and as a primary duty assignment (1) demolish by the use of explosives objects, obstacles, or explosives, or recover and render harmless, by disarming or demolition, explosives which have failed to function as intended or which have become a potential hazard; (2) participate as students or instructors in instructional training, including that in the field or fleet, for the duties described in clause (1) hereof, provided that live explosives are used in such training; (3) participate in proficiency training, including that in the field or fleet, for the maintenance of skill in the duties described in clause (1) hereof, provided that live explosives are used in such training; or (4) experiment with or develop tools, equipment, or procedures for the demolition and rendering harmless of explosives, provided that live explosives are used."

Sec. 2. This Order shall be effective immediately.

RONALD REAGAN

The White House,
December 6, 1984.

[*Filed with the Office of the Federal Register, 12:21 p.m., December 7, 1984*]

Note: *The Executive order was released by the Office of the Press Secretary on December 7.*

Remarks and a Question-and-Answer Session With Reporters on Foreign and Domestic Issues
December 7, 1984

1985 Federal Budget

The President. I have a brief statement here.

In the first few weeks attention has—or in the past few weeks, I should say, the attention has been focused heavily upon ways to control spending. And that's important, but let me try to put this in a broader perspective.

In the November elections, the people made clear that, first and foremost, they wanted to continue policies that would assure strong economic growth. So, the people voted against tax increases, and they were right. And they voted against wasteful government spending, and they were right. They voted for the expansion of opportunity for all, and that's what we mean to achieve with policies that will control spending, simplify the tax system, improve America's productivity and competitiveness, so that we can keep this great nation of ours moving forward.

End of statement.

Q. Mr. President——

The President. No, I'm going to start back a little ways here and move forward. I've done it the other way and never got back there.

Yeah, Lou [Lou Cannon, Washington Post].

U.S.-Soviet Negotiations

Q. Mr. President, since we've last seen you there's been a number of statements from the Soviets about arms control and desiring peaceful relations with this country. How do you assess the prospects now for a genuine arms control agreement? And are the Soviets just talking, or do you think they really want some kind of agreement?

The President. Well, Lou, there's no way for me to make a judgment on that until we get in conversation with them. I was very gratified when both Gromyko at the United Nations and Chairman Chernenko publicly made statements in which they expressed a desire to see the elimination of nuclear weapons—the same thing that I've been talking about for quite some time. So, we're willing to get into discussion with them on those subjects.

Tax Reform

Q. Mr. President, on Secretary Regan's tax package, why haven't you embraced that so far? And are you going to actually propose your own tax simplification package from the State of the Union address?

The President. No. That, like the present budget proposal that you've all been writing and talking about, is a working paper. And we have a Cabinet process, and we also have a process of consulting with our own leadership up on the Hill. And I think that it is probably the best and most complete study of the tax system and the best proposals for changing the tax system that has ever occurred within my lifetime. And it is presented, however, as a broad package in which, obviously, there are points that you want to look at. But we've been so busy with the immediate problem of the budget that we have just set aside for a bit the actual consideration of every phase of that tax proposal.

But I think that it is basically a fine proposal.

Kuwaiti Airline Hijacking

Q. Mr. President, the hostage and hijacking situation in Kuwait at the moment: What exactly is the United States Government doing about it, and do you think that the Iranian Government is at all collaborating with the hijackers?

The President. First of all, we are in touch with the heads of state of other countries, and we have, through other diplomats, been as much in contact as we can be. I have no evidence that I can lay out here that there is actual collaboration of the Iranians. I have to say, however, that they have not been as helpful as they could be in this situation or as I think they should have been.

Q. Will we do anything? Will we take any action? Will the United States take action?

The President. There isn't anything that I can discuss further about details in this whole tragic situation.

Tax Reform / Defense Spending

Q. Mr. President, you are saying this is a great tax plan—and no one expects you to know it, you know, detail for detail—but you have not come out for it. And until you take that kind of leadership, do you think you will get that kind of support? And I'd also like to tie in, how do you feel about defense cutting, since you have, you know, opened up with the budget situation?

The President. There are only two things in the whole budget discussion, Helen [Helen Thomas, United Press International], that actually can't be changed. One of them is social security and the other is the interest on the debt. Everything else we're discussing in the sense of—in the context of having a freeze on overall spending; in other words, no increase in spending over the 1945 [1985] [1] level. Now, that doesn't

---
[1] *White House correction.*

mean that, point by point, through all the government programs, there may be some increase, there may be some cut, there may be some eliminated, and a number that would actually be frozen at the same level. All of this, right now, is in the Cabinet process. We have made our first study on that.

With regard to the tax program, again, as I say, when you look—that's a voluminous document, and you don't just automatically look at the index and say, well, I'm for it or agin it.

I basically, from what I've known and the reports that I've had from the Secretary of the Treasury, I believe that this is the finest proposal that has ever been offered. This doesn't mean that there aren't certain options in there on specific items. But I think it is—it does simplify, it does reduce for most individuals, and it does broaden the base in the sense of getting some people or some businesses back to paying more of a fair share rather than leaving it to someone else.

Q. And how about the defense cuts?

The President. What? Oh.

Q. Are you going to go for any defense cuts?

The President. On defense. Well, as I said, that's included. But, again, I can't get into the specific details within that budget process because of the state that it is in right now. But I'd like to point out to you that without cutting back on our need to improve our defenses after years and years of neglect, the Defense Department itself, on its own, has found ability to cut its original request—its 5-year program of buildup that they launched in 1981—they have cut that by $116 billion to date.

And as soon as the Secretary is back from the NATO meetings, we'll be talking. Some of that has been made possible by the cut in inflation, but a lot of it has been done by improvements in management, things of that kind. So, we will discuss with him, then, as we're discussing with everyone else, each particular—we'll discuss his defense budget to see what he can contribute.

Meeting With Bishop Desmond Tutu

Q. Mr. President, Bishop Tutu has just come out and said that while you had a good meeting, that your policies have worsened the situation for blacks in South Africa. Would you, at this point, consider changing your policies and consider at least the idea of economic sanctions or of some harsher measures against the regime there?

The President. Well, Andrea [Andrea Mitchell, NBC News], we had a good meeting, and he made some suggestions and proposals. We had an opportunity to explain to him the things that we have been doing in what I like to call quiet diplomacy. I think many of them were a surprise to him. Some of the things that he suggested are things that we're already doing. But there were others that our State Department is taking heed of and we're going to look at very carefully.

I have to disagree with him on the fact that the situation has worsened. It has not. We have made sizable progress there in expressing our repugnance for apartheid and in persuading the South African Government to make changes. And we're going to continue with that policy.

Q. But the regime has become more repressive, and the arrests have increased. Would you consider any kind of economic sanctions? And do you feel that your policies have, at all, given credibility to that regime?

The President. I know that there has been a surge of violence here and there and that has resulted in violence from the other side. We regret this. But, as I say, I think that the policy we're following—and it wouldn't be quiet diplomacy anymore if I started talking about things openly—but we have made solid progress, and we want to continue doing that.

Q. Mr. President, it's not just the Bishop, as you know, who's been trying to put pressure on the United States Government to change its policies. There's been growing pressure from elsewhere in the international community. And I think a lot of people might be wondering how the United States can justify dealing with a nation that does not recognize something so basic as the concept of racial equality.

The President. Maybe some nations can't because, as I say, if you're practicing quiet diplomacy, you can't talk about it or it won't be quiet anymore. And I have always

believed that it is counterproductive for one country to splash itself all over the headlines, demanding that another government do something, because that other government then is put in an almost impossible political position. It can't appear to be rolling over at the demands of outsiders.

We are working—for example, many people are critical and some of the protests and the demonstrations here have voiced disapproval of American investment in South Africa, of American companies that are in business there. Well, this is based on ignorance when they say this. The simple truth is that most black tribal leaders there have openly expressed their support in American business investment there, because our American businesses go there and observe practices with regard to employees that are not observed by South African companies.

This is a source of employment where there is fairness where there is no discrimination in these American concerns; where they have jobs with opportunity. American business has spent over a hundred million dollars so far in education, in training, in management, in business, in things of that kind, in entrepreneurship. And for those who are criticizing, it's just that they're ignorant of that, and they don't know how much gain has been made for the blacks in South Africa that we're interested in helping.

1985 Federal Budget

Q. Sir, two questions of fairness on your prospective budget cuts. Republican leaders say they've told you that unless you include some defense scaleback, they can't sell it on the Hill, because it would not be perceived to be fair. And secondly, government workers complain that when you ask them to take a 5-percent pay cut—with a mean average working income of government workers of $24,000—you are asking them in a nonrecessionary time to do something that other Americans don't have to do.

The President. They're wrong about that other Americans don't have to do. We just thought in approaching this and making that suggestion about taking a pay cut—it starts with me—that we're doing something that has been done in a number of major industries in the United States. Coming out of the recession, labor renegotiated their contracts, and labor took cuts to help those industries in which they were employed get back on their feet, get back in business again. Is it fair for those who are employed by government, at a time when the deficit spending has become such a crisis that everyone is calling it the number one problem—the deficit—that government employees should be immune from the same thing that the other workers in America have done to try and help the economic situation?

The whole thing—our plan of the budget cuts, of what this request that we are talking about, the tax simplification program—is all aimed at ensuring continued economic growth, because we're not going to solve our problems, we're not going to solve the deficit problem without continued economic growth. And that's what all of our policies are aimed at doing.

Q. What about the other part, sir, that they will not—the Republican leaders—be able to sell your other cuts if you don't scale back defense?

The President. Well, we know that the image that's been created of the Defense Department—if all of you, hopefully, will headline the news that the Defense Department has already made $116 billion in cuts, maybe the people will change the image they have somewhat of an extravagant Defense Department. But we know that that's important. We know that it's important across the board, to see that everyone participates in trying to achieve this freeze. And so, we will be sitting down with Cap. But again, as I say, I'm not going to get into specifics on this, because it's still in the process.

Q. Senator Goldwater wants to kill the MX missile.

The President. I haven't had a chance to talk to him about that yet, but I wonder if what he isn't speaking is his resentment of the continued harrassment and niggling at that program that's been taking place in the Congress. That program is essential. It is the first modernized weapon in the strategic field that we have come up with after at least five such new systems by the Soviet Union.

Social Security

Q. Mr. President, you've said repeatedly "across the board," "fair," "everybody sharing in the burden of the spending cuts." How do you justify holding Social Security recipients harmless, other than the campaign pledge that you made under pressure from Mr. Mondale?

The President. Well, again, I have to point out, and none of you seem to pick up on it: Social Security does not contribute to the deficit. Social Security is totally funded by a payroll tax. If there was a reduction in Social Security outgo, only two things could be done: either you would reduce the Social Security payroll tax, or that money would revert to the Social Security trust fund. It would not, in any way, reduce the deficit.

Q. Could you not make a reduction in the rate of COLA's without that happening? There have already been adjustments in COLA's without cutting back on Social Security payroll tax.

The President. Yes, and much of this has been based on the levels of inflation. But again, as I've said, in 1983—after being victimized by political demagoguery unequaled in many years, regarding our supposed enmity towards Social Security, finally, having used it successfully in the campaign of '82—our opponents quieted their demagoguery and joined us in a bipartisan commission to put a bankrupt program, Social Security, on its feet. And we not only have done that, but contrary to what they said, we've improved Social Security so that the average married couple is getting $180 a month more than they were getting before we came here.

Q. Why are some of your own Republican chairmen in the Senate talking about taking some downward adjustments in Social Security?

The President. As I've said, the process is still going on. And now you're trying to trap me into discussing individual items in this. We'll came back at you when we know what the program is going to be.

Meeting With Bishop Desmond Tutu

Q. Mr. President, Bishop Tutu said that when he tried—when you had the discussion that you gave him no concrete proof of what constructive engagement has succeeded. And do you differ with that?

The President. Now, what?

Q. Bishop Tutu was asked if you had any policy—if any of your policies worked and specific examples of constructive engagement working in South Africa, and he said, no, that you had not given any specific examples.

The President. Well, we ran out of time, as a matter of fact, in our conversation, but he continued for another hour with the Vice President and the Secretary of State and others. So, I haven't had a report yet on this continued discussion.

But, no, I did tell him a number of the things and told him the very fact of our private investment and the things that I've told you and what it has meant to those who are employed by those companies over there. I told him also we have a government program we've been spending some millions of dollars over there in education and training—job training and so forth.

Q. Mr. President——

Federal Personnel Levels

Q. Sir, can you make cuts in the large, high-level Assistant Secretaries of Defense and other high-paying jobs like that, rather than cutting back the budget for women and children on nutrition and poor veterans and poorly paid civil servants?

The President. We're not destroying, in anything we're considering, the safety net. And, as I say, the cut in salaries, if this is one of the features that comes into the finished package, it will be across the board.

But I think I would like to point out also that if you compare the executive salary level in government, a great many people have to make a personal sacrifice in order to take those positions, because they are so far out of line with the comparable pay scales and benefits out in the private sector.

Q. But, sir, I mean we have more than we need in those Assistant Secretaryships——

The President. You mean more personnel?

Q. More Assistant Secretaries than we need. I think we could cut those back, because each one of them requires a staff.

The President. I have to tell you, we've had a task force on management that has been operating almost ever since we've been here that has recommended a great many changes and so forth. We're about 75,000 fewer employees than we once had in the Federal Government, and we're going to continue along that same line, up to and including the benefit of the Grace commission.

Federal Budget Deficit

Q. Mr. President, you made a point in the campaign of saying the deficit was going down because of economic growth. Since the election your own advisers have put out figures that the deficit went up by 30 billion. Were you wrong when you made that prediction? And do you still believe the deficit will go down because of growth?

The President. Growth improves revenues; tax increases, tax rates—high tax rates don't. They reduce government revenues, because they have an adverse effect on the economy. Yes, the fact that we came down about $20 billion between what had been predicted from '73 ['83] to '74 ['84]—in the '74 ['84] deficit, that was directly attributable to the improved economy, the improved revenues with the recovery, the fact there was a decline in spending for people who had been distressed before, and as they went back to work.

So, growth in the economy—look at what it can mean. There are 6 million more people working and paying an income tax, hopefully, than there were when we came here in 1980. There are 6 million, roughly 6 million more jobs than there have been in the past. We not only put some of the unemployed back to work—and you do know the change in the figures as of the month of November, that there has been a decline in unemployment—but we have also kept pace with the increasing number of people entering the job market. We now have more people employed than at any time in the history of the Nation.

Q. Why did the deficit go up 30 billion after the election, then? What accounts for the new estimates that it's over 200 billion, if it was only 170 in August?

The President. Well, some of the same things, including every year that you continue deficit spending you add that much more to the debt and that much more interest that has to be paid, a very sizable increase in that. So, that's just one of the factors.

But listen, I've used up twice as much time as I'm supposed to in here and——

Q. One question, Mr. President——

The President. All right, yours is the last question.

Federal Spending and Tax Reform

Q. During the campaign you said that taxes would be a last resort. You've spent the last several weeks looking over the budget and how to come to grips with the deficit. Are you any closer to going to that resort now than you were during the campaign?

The President. Not one bit. I believe that the two things we're looking at—that tax proposal and the budgeting proposal, when it's finally completed—are going to be consistent with what we've been seeking, and that is a policy that will stimulate growth at the same time that it will reduce unnecessary government spending. Let me leave you with just one figure: When you ask about puzzles, about deficits going up and so forth, between 1965 and 1980—or 1981,

includes 1980—the budgets of the Federal Government multiplied by 4½ times to what they were in 1965. The deficit multiplied by 38 times what it was in 1965. So, we think that there is a structural cause of much of the deficit spending, that unless we turn government policies around it's going to continue and is out of hand and will be out of hand.

All right.

Kuwaiti Airline Hijacking

Q. Mr. President, do you know of any Americans who were killed in this hijacking? I mean, do we have any definite information?

The President. Nothing more than you already have. We don't have actual facts as yet. We believe——

Michael Reagan

Q. Are you and Michael closer to resolving your differences, sir?

The President. What?

Q. Are you and your son Michael closer to resolving your differences?

The President. Sam [Sam Donaldson, ABC News], I think yesterday Nancy gave you a perfect answer: "Merry Christmas." [*Laughter*]

Q. Merry Christmas, Mr. President.

Note: The President spoke at 11:30 a.m. in the Briefing Room at the White House.

Informal Exchange With Reporters on the Release of Black Leaders by the Government of South Africa
December 7, 1984

Q. Mr. President, are there indications now that the Iranian Government is helping out these terrorists on the ground?

The President. So far, I don't know of any. There hadn't been up until the time that I left the office there. But I came over here not for some questions, but to add to our little meeting over there in the Press Room.

I did not know before, but since that meeting, I have received word that the South African Government has released the

11 prisoners, including a very prominent labor leader. And all of this—they were arrested 3 weeks ago; they were part of our discussion with Bishop Tutu. And this is the result of—since their arrest—3 weeks of work that we have put in in what I told you was quiet diplomacy. And today it bore fruit, and they're released.

Q. Is it the result of the demonstrations?

Q. Couldn't it be the result of the demonstrations, not of the quiet diplomacy?

The President. Well, I would have to think after 3 weeks of working with and talking with the Government over there that—I don't think that we're being too bold in taking credit for this.

Q. Did the demonstrations help your efforts in any way?

The President. I have no evidence of that, if they did.

Q. Mr. President, again, just on the terrorists, the terrorists now say they're going to kill all the Americans on the plane. Is there anything we can do about that? Can we do anything at all?

The President. Yes, we've been doing a number of things, and we've been working through channels that can communicate with the Iranian Government. It's a tragic situation and, as I said earlier, I don't think the Iranian Government—I can't charge that there's complicity, but I certainly don't think that there's been any effort or a proper effort to help.

Q. Where's the dog going to live? Is he going to stay at the White House?

The President. For a while. He'll probably wind up at the ranch.

Q. Is it housebroken?

The President. Not at that age, no. We still have that to undergo.

Mrs. Reagan. He's very well behaved.

The President. Nancy says he's very well behaved.

Q. Are you willing to divide your attention with the puppy?

The President. Don't you wish I was that anxious to stay with you? [*Laughter*]

Note: The exchange began at 3:09 p.m. at the South Portico of the White House as the President and Mrs. Reagan were leaving for a weekend stay at Camp David, MD.

The dog referred to in the questioning was the puppy presented to the President on December 6 by Kristen Ellis, the March of Dimes Poster Child.

Statement by Principal Deputy Press Secretary Speakes on the Release of Black Leaders by the Government of South Africa
December 7, 1984

The President and the American people welcome the news that 11 black South African leaders have been released by the South African Government today. This is an action that we have publicly and privately urged on the South African Government since the day these individuals were detained over 3 weeks ago. Among those released are key trade union officials, including Phiroshaw Camay and Chris Dlamini.

This action is evidence in our view that the South African Government is prepared to respond constructively to those, both within and outside the country, who support a meaningful dialog between the Government and representatives of all racial groups. As the President explained to Bishop Tutu today, we have long called for such a dialog which would encourage progress away from apartheid toward a system based on the consent of all South Africans. Similarly, we have long pointed to the importance of the healthy development of a genuine trade union movement in South Africa. Today's news lends hope to those prospects.

Note: Larry M. Speakes read the statement to reporters assembled in the Briefing Room at the White House at 3:30 p.m.

Remarks at a Ceremony Marking the Beginning of the President's Citation Program for Private Sector Initiatives
December 10, 1984

Thank you. And if you haven't been welcomed already—and I'm sure you have—welcome to the White House. We claim this building over across the street, too. [*Laughter*]

You know, when this grand building was built, volunteer effort was an everyday part of our national life. Farmers would travel miles to help out with a barnraising. Food was distributed to the needy by churches and volunteer groups. And when someone fell ill, he would more than likely be cared for by his neighbors. For decades this shining tradition of voluntarism helped to give life in America a sense of security and warmth.

Yet in recent years, I think we must admit that the focus on volunteer efforts began to fade somewhat. Too many began expecting big government to perform tasks that could have been done more efficiently and with greater humanity by the private sector. In many cases, billions of dollars were spent on government programs that failed to do any lasting good.

The American people saw what was happening, and when George Bush and I were elected they gave us a mandate which we interpreted as "end the waste and, wherever possible, shift the focus away from the slow-moving labors of the bureaucrats back to the caring and efficient efforts of the people themselves."

I treasure one story, an experience that happened before I came here. There was a gentleman whose social security payments stopped coming. And when he inquired, they said he was dead. [*Laughter*] He said he wasn't. [*Laughter*] You know, when a computer makes a mistake, it's a mistake. Finally he went in person and informed them that there he was, in the living flesh. And the computer said he was dead, and there wasn't anything that they could do. He'd been without the payments; he was destitute. And they—at least, thank heaven, there was someone there that turned to voluntarism in a way—they temporarily solved

his problem while they went to work to try and solve it permanently. They gave him the social security funeral allowance to tide him over. [*Laughter*]

Well, repeatedly I've tried to use this bully pulpit to stress the importance of volunteer efforts. And throughout government, we've urged the formation of partnerships between the public and private sectors. One of our most important steps was the establishment of our White House Office of Private Sector Initiatives, headed by our fine director, Jim Coyne, and the Private Sector Advisory Committee—or Council, a council that's made up of private citizens dedicated to encouraging volunteer efforts across the country.

The members of the Council and their Chairman, Bob Galvin, of Motorola, I know are with us today. And I want to thank you all for your outstanding work. Over the past 4 years, all these efforts have had a powerful effect.

Between 1980 and 1983, for example, total giving in our country rose by 35 percent to a record $64.9 billion. And that number happens to be greater than the gross national product of more than half of the nations of the world.

Last year alone, the United Way Campaign collected almost $2 billion, making 1983 the best year for that campaign in almost three decades. And last year was the third consecutive year that the increase in giving was higher than the inflation rate. And as Bob Galvin and his fellow members can tell us, the Private Sector Initiatives Advisory Council has found the American people are ready and eager to lend a hand.

The Council has been able to create outstanding programs—like partnerships in education, under which nearly 16,000 American schools have formed partnerships with businesses and professional organizations; the summer jobs program, which last summer provided hundreds of thousands of young people with their first employment; and a direct, dynamic initiative in Grenada, under which more than $1½ million has been committed, in Grenada, by private American concerns since the people of that island were set free.

Over the past 4 years the American people have gained new confidence in themselves and a new optimism about our nation's future. At the same time, we've rekindled an old ember of openness and generosity. And now we Americans are giving our time, money, and skills to good causes with renewed joy and dedication. And today it's our privilege to highlight two initiatives that will help to carry the spirit of American voluntarism even further.

First, National Care and Share Day, December 15th. On this date, Americans from Maine to California will contribute food to be shared with those in need. Groups ranging from the Salvation Army to the Grocery Manufacturers of America have generously agreed to take part. And I understand that in thousands of grocery stores across the country, collection centers will be set up for shoppers who want to make donations.

I signed the proclamation naming this date in the holiday season National Care and Share Day so that we could help to make this part of the year truly a time of good will toward all. And I urge every American to participate.

May I add one personal thought? In light of the tragedy in Ethiopia, last week I signed an order releasing 300,000 tons of wheat to the developing countries of Africa and South Asia. I know that private American efforts have already done much to help the needy around the world, especially in Ethiopia, and I would hope that on National Care and Share Day Americans would once again remember those nations that are less fortunate than our own.

Second, we're here to kick off a major new awards initiative called the President's Citation Program for Private Sector Initiatives. Businesses and associations on my Advisory Council will be able to fly the new "C Flag" and let the world know the program's motto, "We can, we care."

Now, everybody from Chicago knows that "C" stands for Cubs. [*Laughter*] But in this case it stands for something else—commitment. Often when we discuss voluntarism

we concentrate on the efforts of individuals. But each year, business and professional associations show just as much of that national quality—commitment—donating millions of dollars and thousands of hours.

The aerospace industry, for example, is assembling "Tech-net." That's a network of funding and personnel that helps to harness new technology on behalf of the disabled.

Safeway Stores, Incorporated, has long been involved in volunteer efforts, from support of Easter Seals to taking a major hand in promoting the National Care and Share Day and helping launch the Young Astronaut Program.

GTE has sponsored the Gift Program. That's Growth Initiative for Teachers, to help train math and science teachers.

And D.C. Comics, Incorporated, has produced comic books that teach children the dangers of drug abuse.

Permit me to give you one more example, and this one is a little close to my heart. Some months ago I devoted my Saturday radio talk to the problem of missing children. It so happened that Jim Kerrigan, chairman of the Trailways Bus Company, heard that talk and on the following Monday called the White House to say that Trailways would like to help. Working with the International Association of Chiefs of Police, Trailways put together a program where once a missing child was identified by local police, the youngster could ride home on a Trailways bus for free.

Perhaps you're wondering how much time passed between Jim's phone call and the first child's ride on a Trailways bus. It was 10 days. You know, I can't help thinking how long it would have taken and how many millions of taxpayers' dollars would have been spent if the program had been put together by a Federal agency. [*Laughter*]

Again and again, America's business and professional associations have shown this outstanding level of commitment. And the "C Flag," modeled on the famous "E Flag" of World War II, has been designed for them.

Across the country, businesses and associations with community involvement projects will be urged to register them with our Private Sector Initiatives [Partnership] DataNet, and when the projects are registered, the businesses and associations will be able to fly "C Flags" with pride. Of the companies that qualify for "C Flags" each year, 100 with outstanding programs will be selected for Presidential citations. And of these, each year 30 will receive a Presidential medal.

Now, these citations and medals we hope will become sought after, spurring businesses and professional associations on to even greater efforts. And as more and more "C Flags" snap in the breeze across our land, all Americans will be reminded of the vital role that our private sector plays in helping so many.

To those representatives of the first companies to receive "C Flags," my heartfelt congratulations. You're helping to show that Uncle Sam is back and standing tall, and he knows how to bend over and lend a helping hand.

And now I would like to unveil the first "C Flag" and present it to Peter Ueberroth for his leadership in the Olympics, a private sector initiative of unparalleled success, and on behalf of all the businesses which made the Olympics possible.

So, thank you, and God bless you all.

Note: The President spoke at 11:04 a.m. in Room 450 of the Old Executive Office Building. The ceremony marked the unveiling of the first major White House awards program recognizing the outstanding contributions made by businesses and associations to their communities.

In addition to Peter Ueberroth, commissioner of baseball and former chairman of the Olympics, who received the first "C Flag" from the President, 150 business and association executives also received "C Flags."

Remarks on Signing the International Human Rights Day Proclamation
December 10, 1984

Thank you very much. This ceremony marks more than another event on the White House calendar or another worthy cause for the national agenda, for in observing Human Rights Day, we rededicate ourselves to the cause of human dignity and freedom, a cause that goes to the heart of our national character and defines our national purpose.

So, today we dare to affirm again the commitment of the American people to the inalienable rights of all human beings. In reaffirming the moral beliefs that began our nation, we strive to make the United States what we pray to God it will always be—a beacon of hope to all the persecuted and oppressed of the world. And we resolve that as a people, we'll never rest until the blessings of liberty and self-government are extended to all the nations of the Earth.

Two years ago in London, when I called for a crusade for freedom and human rights, I noted that these ideals—embodied in the rule of law, under God, and in the institutions of democratic self-government—were on the march. Because these ideals represent the oldest and noblest aspirations of the human spirit, I said then that this power is irresistible when compared to totalitarian ideologies that seek to roll back mankind's march to freedom.

Today I want to take special note of evidence that this desire for self-determination, this recognition by the state of the inalienable rights of men and women everywhere, is nowhere stronger than close to our own borders in the lands of Latin America. In contrast to only a few years ago, today more than 90 percent of the people in Latin America and the Caribbean live in nations either democratically governed or moving in that direction.

While we're still doing all that we can to promote democratic change in nations such as Paraguay and Chile, we must not forget that over the last 5 years in Argentina, Bolivia, Ecuador, El Salvador, Honduras, Panama, Peru, and most recently, in Uruguay, military juntas have been replaced by elected civilian governments. And just last Monday, democratic values triumphed again as the people of Grenada freely elected a new civilian Prime Minister.

Today all who cherish human rights and individual freedom salute the people of the Americas for their great achievements. And we pledge to our neighbors the continued support and assistance of the United States as they transform our entire hemisphere into a haven for democracy, peace, and human rights.

In other nations farther from our shores, we've also seen progress toward reducing the repression of human rights and some strengthening of democratic institutions. In some of these nations, which have authoritarian governments but friendly ties to the United States and the community of democratic nations, quiet diplomacy has brought about humane and democratic change.

But we know there are occasions when quiet diplomacy is not enough, when we must remind the leaders of nations who are friendly to the United States that such friendship also carries responsibilities for them and for us. And that's why the United States calls for all governments to advance the democratic process and work toward a system of government based on the consent of the governed.

From our beginning, regard for human rights and the steady expansion of human freedom have defined the American experience. And they remain today the real, moral core of our foreign policy.

The United States has said on many occasions that we view racism with repugnance. We feel a moral responsibility to speak out on this matter, to emphasize our concerns and our grief over the human and spiritual costs of apartheid in South Africa, to call upon the Government of South Africa to reach out to its black majority by ending the forced removal of blacks from their communities and the detention, without trial, and lengthy imprisonment of black leaders. Such action can comfort only those whose vision of South Africa's future is one of polarization, violence, and the final extinction of any hope for peaceful, democrat-

ic government. At the same time, we note with satisfaction that the South African Government has released 11 black leaders, including the top leaders of two of that country's most important labor unions.

Because we care deeply about the people of South Africa and the future of that nation, we ask that the constructive changes of recent years be broadened to address the aspirations of all South Africans. Peaceful change in South Africa, and throughout southern Africa, can come only when blacks and whites find a durable basis to live together, when they establish an effective dialog, a dialog sustained by adherence to democratic values and a belief in governments based on the consent of the governed.

We urge both the Government and the people of South Africa to move toward a more just society. We pledge here today that if South Africans address the imperatives of constructive change, they will have the unswerving support of our government and people in this effort.

A few years ago, when I spoke of totalitarian ideologies as the greatest threat to personal freedom in the world today and the most persistent source of human suffering in our century, I also pointed out that the United States, too, has faced evils like racism, anti-Semitism, and other forms of intolerance and disregard for human freedom. So, while we work to see human rights extended throughout the world, this observance of Human Rights Day reminds us of our responsibility to assure against injustice and intolerance in our own land as well. And today I call on the American people to reaffirm, in our daily lives and in the workings of our private and governmental institutions, a commitment to brotherhood and equal justice under the law.

But we do a serious disservice to the cause of human rights if we forget that, however mistaken and wrong, however stumbling the actions of democracies in seeking to achieve the ideals of freedom and brotherhood, our philosophy of government permits us to acknowledge, debate, and then correct mistakes, injustices, and violations of human rights.

Let us always remember the critical

moral distinction of our time—the clear difference between a philosophy of government that acknowledges wrongdoing and injustice and one that refuses to admit to such injustices and even justifies its own assaults on individual liberty in the name of a chimeric utopian vision. Such brutal affronts to the human conscience as the systematic suppression of individual liberty in the Soviet Union and the denial of religious expression by Christians, Jews, and Muslims in that country, are tragic examples. Today, for example, the largest remaining Jewish community in Europe, Soviet Jewry, is again being exposed to a systematic anti-Semitic campaign. Ominously, teachers of the Hebrew language have been arrested and their efforts to preserve their culture and religion treated as a crime.

Soviet authorities are continuing to threaten many "refuseniks" with confinement in psychiatric hospitals, expulsion from their jobs, and internal exile. Yet thousands of Soviet Jews have applied for permission to emigrate. We have and shall continue to insist that those who wish to leave must be allowed to do so.

Our heart also goes out today to an individual who has worked so hard for human rights progress in the Soviet Union and suffered so much for his efforts—the Nobel Prize Laureate, Dr. Andrei Sakharov. Nothing more clearly illustrates the absence of what our Founding Fathers called a "decent respect to the opinions of mankind" than the cruel treatment of this great humanitarian. The Soviet Union, itself, would do much to regain respect within the international community if it would allow academician Sakharov and his wife, Yelena Bonner, to live the rest of their lives in dignity in a place of their own choosing. We're pleased to have the Sakharovs' son-in-law here with us today.

The Sakharovs are the best-known victims of human rights violations in the Soviet Union, but thousands of other Soviet citizens, such as Yuriy Orlov or Anatoly Shcharanskiy—whose wife, Avital, is here with us today—suffer in Soviet prisons and labor camps for the sole crimes of expressing a personal opinion, seeking to emigrate, or openly expressing their love of God.

We Americans recognize a special responsibility to speak for the oppressed, wherever they may be. We think here of special cases like the persecution of the Baha'i religious minority in Iran. But we also acknowledge a special obligation to speak for those who suffer the repression of totalitarian regimes, regimes that refuse to acknowledge and correct injustice and that justify absolute state power even as they seek to extend their cruel rule to other lands.

So, we call today for all free peoples of the world to unite in resisting and bringing to an end such intolerable practices as the suppression of free trade unionism, the campaign against the church and against political freedom in Nicaragua, the continuing Vietnamese occupation of Cambodia, and the barbaric war waged by Soviet troops in Afghanistan—a war which began 5 years ago this month with the Soviet invasion of that once nonaligned country.

As but one of the tragic consequences of Soviet actions in Afghanistan, more than one-third of the people of that country have fled from their homes and sought refuge in internal or external exile.

Finally, we welcome the recent steps taken by the Polish Government, but we urge that they are followed by lasting efforts for genuine, national reconciliation through effective dialog with the Polish people.

So, today we the people of the United States, in conjunction with other freedom-loving people everywhere in the world, rededicate ourselves to the cause of human rights, to the cause of democratic self-rule and human freedom. We reassert our belief that some day the repression of the human spirit and the special tragedy of totalitarian rule will be only a distant chapter in the human past. In doing so, we're deeply aware of our nation's long struggle toward achieving these goals and our own heritage of seeking to promote these ideals throughout the world.

Thomas Jefferson told us, "The mass of mankind has not been born with saddles on their backs." And the poet Archibald MacLeish once said: Some say the hope for "the liberation of humanity, the freedom of man and mind, is nothing but a dream. They are right. It is. It is the American dream."

Another great American literary figure, F. Scott Fitzgerald, suggested that America is "a willingness of the heart." We've recently read a great deal about the young people of this nation about whom, some say, this willingness of the heart no longer exists. Well, my own experiences with this generation suggest that the traditional idealism of the young, their hope to accomplish great things, their willingness to serve the cause of humanity, is not only intact but stronger than ever. And like every generation before it, this generation hungers for a cause, for a mission that will take it outside itself and let it help lift humanity beyond the material and the immediate to new heights of human and spiritual progress.

So, today let us challenge these young Americans to make our nation an even better example of what she was always meant to be—champion of the oppressed, defender of all who reach for freedom and to the right of self-determination. Let us challenge young Americans, excited by technological and material progress, to ensure that this progress enriches political freedom and human dignity as well. Here's a challenge that's worthy of our youth, of their vision, their energy, and their vigor. Let our younger generation lead young people throughout the world to join the democratic nations in promoting human rights and self-government and the cause of human freedom.

The other night at the Kennedy Center, they had a choir, a United Nations choir of 90 young people, children, in the costumes of their native countries from all over the world. And looking at them down there, singing together, I couldn't help but think, "Good Lord, if we turn it all over to them, they'd get along just fine together." And maybe the world should follow their lead.

There is in the Book of Genesis a story of great loss. It's a story of man alienated from his fellow man and turning to persecution and hatred for others. Well, I believe that history is slowly working itself back to the restoration of brotherhood and mutual respect among all the peoples of the Earth. So, today we rededicate ourselves to this vision and mission. We do so mindful that human might and will alone cannot achieve this goal, aware that our ultimate success will be determined by our faith in the power of prayer, in the promises of Him who made us and even now guides us in our quest for human dignity and freedom.

And now I shall quit talking and sign the proclamation.

[*At this point, the President signed the proclamation.*]

For the week beginning today, it is now recognized officially as Human Rights Week. And the 15th will be Human Rights Day.

Note: The President spoke at 1:09 p.m. in Room 450 of the Old Executive Office Building.

Proclamation 5287—Bill of Rights Day, Human Rights Day and Week, 1984
December 10, 1984

By the President of the United States of America

A Proclamation

On December 15, 1791, our Founding Fathers celebrated the ratification of the first ten amendments to the Constitution of

the United States—a Bill of Rights that has helped guarantee the freedoms that all Americans cherish.

For the first time in the history of nations, our Founding Fathers established a written Constitution with enumerated rights based on the principle that the rights to life and liberty come not from the prerogative of government, but inhere in each person as a fundamental human heritage. Americans believe that all persons are equal in their possession of these unalienable rights and are entitled to respect because of the immense dignity and value of each human being. With these great principles in mind, the Founding Fathers designed a system of government limited in its powers, based upon just laws, and resting upon the consent of the governed.

When Americans first proclaimed this noble experiment in self-government and human liberty, it seemed to some to be a utopian, unrealistic ideal. Today, virtually every nation in the world has adopted a written constitution expressing in varying degrees fundamental human rights. One hundred and fifty-seven years after the ratification of our Bill of Rights, on December 10, 1948, the United Nations adopted the Universal Declaration of Human Rights affirming an international consensus on behalf of the human rights and individual liberties that we value so highly.

Thirty-six years after the adoption of the Universal Declaration of Human Rights, however, it is clear that this consensus is often recognized more on paper than in practice. Throughout the world, many governments nominally adhere to the Universal Declaration of Human Rights while suppressing free elections, independent trade unions, due process of law, and freedom of religion and of the press.

The United States recognizes a special responsibility to advance the claims of the oppressed; to reaffirm the rights to life and liberty as fundamental rights upon which all others are based; and to safeguard the rights to freedom of thought, conscience, and religion. As we are free, we must speak up for those who are not.

As Americans, we strongly object to and seek to end such affronts to the human conscience as the incarceration in the Soviet Union of men and women who try to speak out freely or who seek to exercise the basic right to emigrate; the harsh treatment accorded one of the great humanitarians of our time, Andrei Sakharov, the denial of basic human rights and self-determination in Eastern Europe and the Baltic states; the failure of the Polish authorities to establish an effective dialogue with the free trade union movement in that country; the manifest injustices of the apartheid system of racial discrimination in South Africa; the persecution of the Baha'i religious minority in Iran; the lack of progress toward democratic government in Chile and Paraguay; the campaign against the Roman Catholic Church in Nicaragua; the suppression of freedom in Cuba and Vietnam; the brutal war waged by Soviet troops against the people of Afghanistan; and the continuing Vietnamese occupation of Kampuchea.

The American people recognize that it is the denial of human rights, not their advocacy, that is a source of world tension. We recall the sacrifices that generations of Americans have made to preserve and protect liberty around the world. In this century alone, tens of thousands of Americans have laid down their lives on distant battlefields to uphold the cause of human rights. We honor and cherish them all. Today, it is with an abiding sense of gratitude and reverence that we remember the great gift of freedom that they bequeathed to us.

As we give special thought to the blessings that we enjoy as a free people, let us not forget the victims of human rights abuses around the world.

Now, Therefore, I, Ronald Reagan, President of the United States of America, do hereby proclaim December 10, 1984, as Human Rights Day and December 15, 1984, as Bill of Rights Day, and call on all Americans to observe the week beginning December 10, 1984, as Human Rights Week.

In Witness Whereof, I have hereunto set my hand this 10th day of Dec., in the year of our Lord nineteen hundred and eighty-four, and of the Independence of the United States of America the two hundred and ninth.

RONALD REAGAN

[*Filed with the Office of the Federal Register, 10:46 a.m., December 11, 1984*]

Appointment of Two Members of the National Advisory Council on Indian Education
December 10, 1984

The President today announced his intention to appoint the following individuals to be members of the National Advisory Council on Indian Education for terms expiring September 29, 1987:

Gloria Ann Duus will succeed Terrance J. Brown. She is program director for the Office of Navajo Women in Window Rock, AZ. She graduated from the University of Utah (B.S.) and Northern Arizona University (M.S.). She is married, has three children, and resides in Yahtahey, NM. She was born March 6, 1951, in Brigham City, UT.

W.L. Martin will succeed Dennis Demmert. He is administrator of technical assistance for the Wisconsin Council on Criminal Justice in Madison, WI. He graduated from the University of Wisconsin (B.S.). He is married, has one child, and resides in Madison, WI. He was born August 25, 1946, in Shawano, WI.

Memorandum on the Delegation of Authority for Reports to Congress on Turkey and El Salvador
December 10, 1984

Memorandum for the Secretary of State, the Administrator, Agency for International Development

Subject: Delegation of Authority for Reports to Congress on Turkey and El Salvador

By virtue of the authority vested in me as President by the Constitution and the statutes of the United States of America, including Section 621 of the Foreign Assistance Act of 1961, as amended, and Section 301 of Title 3 of the United States Code, I hereby (1) delegate to the Secretary of State the functions vested in me by Title III of the Foreign Assistance and Related Programs Appropriations Act, 1985 (as enacted in P.L. 98–473) (the "Act"), under the un- numbered paragraph entitled "Military Assistance" insofar as they relate to Turkey; and (2) delegate to the Administrator of the Agency for International Development functions vested in me by Section 533 of the Act, to be exercised in consultation with the Secretary of State.

This memorandum shall be published in the *Federal Register.*

RONALD REAGAN

[*Filed with the Office of the Federal Register, 10:47 a.m., December 11, 1984*]

Note: The memorandum was released by the Office of the Press Secretary on December 11.

Nomination of Ronald Alan Pearlman To Be an Assistant Secretary of the Treasury
December 11, 1984

The President today announced his intention to nominate Ronald Alan Pearlman to be an Assistant Secretary of Treasury (Tax Policy). He would succeed John E. Chapoton.

Mr. Pearlman is currently Deputy Assistant Secretary for Tax Policy (Department of the Treasury). He has served as an adjunct professor of law, Washington University School of Law, since 1971. Previously, he was a partner (1971–1983) and associate (1969–1970) with the law firm of Thompson & Mitchell and attorney-adviser (tax), Office of the Chief Counsel, Interpretative Divi-

sion, Internal Revenue Service (1965–1969).

Mr. Pearlman graduated from Northwestern University (B.A., 1961; J.D., 1965) and Georgetown University Law Center (LL.M., 1967). He is married, has two children, and resides in Bethesda, MD. He was born July 10, 1940, in Hamilton, OH.

Statement by Principal Deputy Press Secretary Speakes on the Kuwaiti Airline Hijacking
December 11, 1984

We have received confirmation that the remains of the two murdered Americans departed Tehran for Frankfurt. The remains will be identified by U.S. military forensic specialists. After identification, tentative plans call for the bodies to be transported to Andrews AFB. I do not have an arrival time for you at this time.

Messrs. Kapar and Costa have been flown by a Kuwaiti aircraft to Kuwait, where they are being picked up by a USAF aircraft and will be transported to Frankfurt, West Germany. I understand they should be leaving Kuwait just about now, noon, December 11. A determination on their onward itinerary has not yet been made.

While we have not yet had a chance to fully debrief the survivors, many aspects of the Government of Iran's handling of this situation raise profound and disturbing questions to which we are seeking answers.

The fact of the matter is that two passengers were murdered by the hijackers, more were tortured, and many were brutalized for an extended period of time without any effective measures being taken by the Government of Iran. Granting selective media access, broadcasting statements and screams of tortured passengers, permitting photographers aboard the aircraft, clearly encouraged extreme behavior by the hijackers. The passengers, the families of the murdered passengers, and the world deserve answers from the Government of Iran.

Previous actions by the Government of

Iran have shown that it has the capability to act rapidly and effectively to end hijackings when it so wishes. On this occasion, when the lives of innocent American, Kuwaiti, and other citizens were at stake, it did otherwise. Two U.S. Government employees were murdered. We will probably never know what would have happened had the Iranian Government acted more firmly.

Now that the hijackers are in its custody, the Government of Iran has very clear obligations. Under the Hague Convention for Suppression of Unlawful Seizure of Aircraft, to which Iran is a party, the Government of Iran has an obligation to submit the hijackers' case to prosecutorial authorities or to extradite them to another country for trial.

Iran's failure to try or extradite several previous groups of hijackers is clear evidence that it has not met its obligations and reinforced the impression that it is sympathetic to and provides a safe haven for hijackers.

The American attitude and actions toward the Government of Iran in the aftermath of this tragedy will be conditioned by whether it meets its obligations and by our assessment of its role during this tragic incident. We have been and will continue to watch Iranian actions closely.

Note: Larry M. Speakes read the statement to reporters assembled in the Briefing Room at the White House during his daily briefing, which began at noon.

Remarks of President Reagan and President Seyni Kountché of Niger Following Their Meetings
December 11, 1984

President Reagan. It's been an honor and a pleasure to welcome President Kountché to Washington.

Our meeting takes place at a time when the world's attention is focused on the serious food crisis in Africa. Niger has not been spared the ravages of the drought. However, through the constructive efforts of President Kountché's government and the help of the international community, including the United States, the effects of the drought in Niger will be reduced.

Those who know President Kountché know that food self-sufficiency and the well-being of his people are his primary goals. He has gone about these objectives with pragmatic policies. President Kountché represents an impressive example of the kind of serious, concerned leadership that Africa will need to overcome its economic problems. His reputation as a dedicated and capable leader has been confirmed by his visit to Washington today.

In our conversations this morning, and at lunch, we covered many of the important international problems of the day, particularly those concerning Africa. We have benefited from President Kountché's views on the problems of drought and economic development in the Sahel, as well as the political problems of that region. We support Niger's efforts to maintain its independence and territorial integrity.

In many areas our views converge. On a few others, in a spirit of mutual respect, we've agreed to differ. We have an excellent bilateral relationship to which we both attach considerable importance.

Niger and the United States together are committed to the resolution of international problems through the pursuit of realistic dialog in international organizations and through the exercise of rational economic policies at home. And I have assured President Kountché of our support for him and his country, and I've expressed our admiration for his accomplishments at home and abroad.

President Kountché. Ladies and gentlemen, I have just had a very extensive discussion with President Ronald Reagan. We discussed bilateral cooperation, as well as African and international issues regarding the effects of world recession, the persistent drought and famine in Africa, and the flashpoints existing in almost all the continents. Our discussions were also especially focused on the role of the United States of America in the search for a better international political, economic. and military balance. And I can say that the views of our two countries were consistent with each other, and there were a good understanding on most of the issues discussed.

As far as Africa is concerned, you know that we are currently preoccupied by the harsh drought that is once again affecting extensive areas of our continent, the result of which is the reappearance of hunger in many countries, especially in extensive regions of the Sahel, in the whole of Africa, and eastern Africa.

I'm glad to note that both President Reagan and his administration are fully aware of this situation and that not only do they sympathize with us, but they are also seriously concerned by the great sufferings affecting several thousands of Africans that have been seriously hit. President Reagan and the American administration have already provided substantial food aid, and Niger is grateful to them for that. The President also assured me that the United States will continue to use significant means to decisively help in the crusade against hunger and death in Africa. And this is essentially in a humanitarian spirit.

We have also discussed the political issues that are currently haunting the African countries—Chad, western Sahara, but especially southern Africa, where the delays in the independence of Namibia and the persistence of apartheid in South Africa engender an untenable situation in the frontline states. President Ronald Reagan and I agree that more consultation between Africa and the United States of America will make it possible to remove the obstacles and solve these problems in serenity, in justice, and in the rule of law.

Besides, I would be right to say that through these discussions we were able to compare our common desire to see peace and security prevail throughout the world on the basis of the great ideals of the right of the peoples to self-determination and liberty, respect for all the countries' sovereignty and territorial integrity, respect for the countries' domestic political choice, and respect for the rules of good neighborliness and peaceful coexistence among the nations.

Naturally, we did not lose sight of the economic issues, because Niger and all Africa are severely hit by the economic crisis that unfortunately affects all the continents. In this regard, we both recognized that the United States have a top role to play in order to safeguard peace in the world and, mostly, to save the stability of small nations.

My conclusion, therefore, is that I am fully satisfied with these talks during which I congratulated President Ronald Reagan for all the efforts that he has been making and for the great vigilance that he has personally shown concerning Niger and regarding the problems of Africa. You know that in recent years, President Ronald Reagan

and his administration have launched a diversified, dynamic, and especially friendly and fruitful cooperation with my country. And I can say today that the United States of America are among our most active and most effective partners.

As for the President, he appeared as a man most devoted to his duties and to his nation. Moreover, I have been seriously impressed by the fact—by his awareness of the global problems, his worshiping of liberty and the fulfillment of man, his determination to build an American society ever stronger and more prosperous.

I wish him good health, a continuous clearmindedness, a growing clear sight to fulfill the well-deserved new term of office with which he has just been entrusted by the people, following his reelection, that in all aspects was a personal triumph and a general satisfaction expressed to him by the great American people.

I thank you.

Note: President Reagan spoke at 1:23 p.m. at the South Portico of the White House. President Kountché spoke in French, and his remarks were translated by an interpreter.

Earlier, the two Presidents met in the Oval Office. They then held a working luncheon, together with U.S. and Niger officials, in the State Dining Room.

Proclamation 5288—Wright Brothers Day, 1984
December 12, 1984

By the President of the United States of America

A Proclamation

This year marks the eighty-first anniversary of human flight in a powered, winged aircraft. The dedicated efforts of Orville and Wilbur Wright made this possible. In the years that have passed since that time, the world has undergone a revolution in transportation that has brought nations closer together and helped unite the global community in ways never before possible.

Though only 120 feet in length and 12 seconds in duration, the first successful flight of the Wright Brothers' aero-vehicle on December 17, 1903, was truly the "flight heard round the world." That flight—limited in immediate, practical application but infinite in conceptual progress—helped foster the Nation's spirit of innovation and dedication to technological advancement. This spirit has thrust the United States into world leadership in all facets of aviation, both civil and military. Aviation in the United States and throughout the world continues to build on the foundation provided by the Wright Brothers.

To commemorate the historic achievement of the Wright Brothers, the Congress, by joint resolution of December 17, 1963 (77 Stat. 402; 36 U.S.C. 169), has designated the seventeenth day of December of each year as Wright Brothers Day and requested the President to issue annually a proclamation inviting the people of the United States to observe that day with appropriate ceremonies and activities.

Now, Therefore, I, Ronald Reagan, President of the United States of America, do hereby proclaim December 17, 1984, as Wright Brothers Day, and I call upon the people of this Nation and local and national governmental officials to observe this day with appropriate ceremonies and activities, both to recall the accomplishments of the Wright Brothers and to provide a stimulus to aviation in this country and throughout the world.

In Witness Whereof, I have hereunto set my hand this twelfth day of December, in the year of our Lord nineteen hundred and eighty-four, and of the Independence of the United States of America the two hundred and ninth.

RONALD REAGAN

[*Filed with the Office of the Federal Register, 2:35 p.m., December 12, 1984*]

Statement by Principal Deputy Press Secretary Speakes on the Situation in Cyprus
December 13, 1984

The United States welcomes the announcement late yesterday by United Nations Secretary-General Perez de Cuellar that the two Cypriot communities have agreed to participate in a summit meeting in January. We view this as a very positive development, one that would create new opportunities to end the division of Cyprus and establish a reunited Cypriot Government.

Secretary-General Perez de Cuellar will have our full support as he works toward a settlement, and the United States Government extends its sincere appreciation for his efforts.

Note: Larry M. Speakes read the statement to reporters assembled in the Briefing Room at the White House during his daily press briefing, which began at 9:22 a.m.

Appointment of Nicholas F. Brady as a Member of the Commission on Executive, Legislative, and Judicial Salaries; and Designation as Chairman
December 13, 1984

The President today announced his intention to appoint Nicholas F. Brady to be a member of the Commission on Executive, Legislative, and Judicial Salaries for the period of the 1985 fiscal year of the Federal Government. He would succeed Thomas R. Donahue. The President also intends to designate him as Chairman.

Mr. Brady has been with the investment banking firm of Dillon Read & Co. since 1954 and currently serves as chairman and chief executive officer. He is also currently chairman of Purolator, Inc. In 1982 he was appointed to the United States Senate by New Jersey Gov. Thomas Kean to fill out the unexpired term of Senator Harrison

Williams.

Mr. Brady graduated from Yale University (B.A., 1952) and Harvard Business School (M.B.A., 1954). He is married, has four children, and resides in Far Hills, NJ. He was born April 11, 1930, in New York, NY.

Remarks on Lighting the National Christmas Tree
December 13, 1984

Thank all of you so much for being here. In just a moment I'm going to push the button that lights the National Christmas Tree. This is an old White House tradition I'm happy to continue.

I was in the White House a few moments ago looking out at all of you down there surrounding the tree, and I thought of how God gives us moments that lift us and that bring us together. For many of us, Christmas is a deeply holy day, the birthday of the promised Messiah, the Son of God who came to redeem our sins and teach us that most needed of all lessons, "Peace on Earth, good will among men." For others of us, Christmas marks the birth of a good, great man, a prophet whose teachings provide a pattern of living pertinent to all times and to all people. Either way, his message remains the guiding star of our endeavors.

I guess we all have our own favorite Christmas memories, for this is the time of year when most of us try to be better than our everyday selves.

For the past few years in this great house, I've thought of our first real Christmas as a nation. It was the dark and freezing Christmas of 1776, when General Washington and his troops crossed the Delaware. They and Providence gave our nation its first Christmas gift—a victory that brought us closer to liberty, the condition in which God meant man to flourish.

It always seems to me that Christmas is a time of magic. Each December we celebrate a Prince, the Prince of Peace, born in utter poverty. And the fact of his birth makes hearts turn warmest at the coldest time of the year.

Many of us do good at this time; most of us all mean to, but sometimes good intentions get lost in the hurry and bustle of the holiday season. Well, this is only the 13th day of December. We still have a dozen days to answer that letter of a child who wrote Santa Claus at the post office, or to buy an extra gift for a Toys for Tot program, or whatever. So, if you've forgotten to do it—well, do it, and do it tonight or tomorrow. One of the great messages of this season is that it's never too late to touch a life and maybe change the world forever for someone.

Over the next few weeks let us all remember those who serve our country abroad—the 800,000 men and women in uniform, the members of our Foreign Service, the people who work in our information agencies throughout the world, and the men and women in the Peace Corps. Even though they can't be at the table this Christmas, they must not be far from our hearts. And let me add, there is no one we hold in our hearts more closely than those MIA's—those missing in action in Southeast Asia, some of whom may be serving our country still. They, too, are absent at the table, and the gathering will never be complete until they return or are accounted for.

Now, I know you're all waiting, and in the immortal words of the astronaut Alan Shepard, "I'm going to stop talking and light the candle." Light it in a nation at peace, a nation united, for the ties that bind still bind. So, now I light the Nation's Christmas tree. May its thousand lights illuminate our best resolves and cast a great glow on our affection for each other, and our thanks for each other, and our love.

And do you know what? I've talked myself into the Christmas spirit. I'm going to give a gift right now. I'm not going to light the tree; I'm going to let Nancy do it.

Where's the button? Where do we go?

Note: The President spoke at 5:45 p.m. at

the South Portico of the White House during the annual Christmas Pageant of Peace.

Following his remarks, the President and Mrs. Reagan moved to a table surrounded by Washington-area children present for the ceremony, and Mrs. Reagan pushed the button which lit the National Christmas Tree, located on the Ellipse.

Interview With Tom Winter and Joseph Baldacchino, Jr., of Human Events
December 6, 1984

Q. Judging from the reports of the Cabinet meeting yesterday, the Reagan revolution seems to be right back on track.

The President. We've been spending hours and hours, item by item, on the budget.

Budget Deficit and Tax Reform

Q. And so right now you would say the budget has the higher priority than the tax reform?

The President. Well, they're both absolutely essential and have to do with the deficit in that the tax program is a part of our belief that growth in the economy is going to be a major contributor to the deficit going down. But the other track is the one that we have been dwelling on right now, which is the necessity for real budget reform.

Q. So, the $34 billion spending cuts we see in the paper, you're saying there may be more coming?

The President. Oh, well, we expect more. We've set our goal higher than that. What we're trying to project is a deficit reduction as a percentage of gross national product in three installments out there. The first one is the most important, because you're not going to get the others if you don't get the first one.

Q. Have you thought at all about saying, after all the individual cuts have been made and certain programs are abolished, that, "On top of this, I want a 5-percent cut from all of these programs because any manager worth his salt could cut 5 percent in waste alone?" If you recall, Frank Bow, the Ohio lawmaker, perennially used to ask for a 5-percent across-the-board cut.

The President. Yes, I know his theory, and I've said similar things without using the figure myself. But that ignores the cuts we've done so far, the cuts that we've already achieved, and the Grace commission recommendations that we have been aiming for.

I have always felt that it's wrong that every time you try to cut something, there are people who stand up and object and say, "What would you eliminate? Which program would you do away with?" And I've always said, "Wait a minute. Before you start doing away with a program, you find out what cuts you can make in the way the program is run." We've made great achievements in that we've reduced, first of all, by 75,000 the number of people in nondefense positions in Government. We've had a task force working on management practices, and these have been achieved in many of the cuts that we've made so far.

In the defense situation, the Pentagon has made dramatic reductions from its original 5-year program proposed in '81, and a great many of those can be attributed to management improvements, overhead elimination.

Let me give you a figure that will give you a glimpse of what can happen. We folded some 62 domestic categorical grants into 10 block grants to local and State government. In doing that, we found that that reduced the overhead of administering those programs by 3,000 employees at our end. Out at the local and State government end, 885 pages of regulations that had been imposed on them moved down to 30 pages.

So, this is very definitely a part of our procedure.

Q. Congress, including a lot of Republicans, seems to be saying that there's no way you can get these domestic savings unless you impose a freeze on military spending.

The President. Well, we're not going to make any cuts—I've spoken already of the reductions we've made—we're not going to make any cuts in defense spending that are going to drive us backward with regard to what we're trying to do in overcoming the years of neglect in guaranteeing our security. But we haven't dealt with defense simply because Secretary Weinberger has been over there at the NATO meetings. When he comes home, we'll be talking to him.

Q. You'll put Secretary Weinberger and Barry Goldwater in a room?

The President. Yes. But I think, though, that you've got to give Cap credit and give the Defense Department credit for what they've done already. The Defense Department has reduced by $116 billion the total of the 5-year projected program that they had called for in 1981. I sometimes used to chide Cap and say, "Look, Cap, why don't you leave this stuff in here to let the Congress find it and they'll be happy, because whatever you go up there with, they'll try to reduce it further."

But this gives me a chance, also, to say something else that hasn't been said anyplace that I know. All these figures about $500 hammers and wrenches and so forth, it's all true. But nobody has pointed out that *we're* providing those figures. This is what has been going on, and this Defense Department now is finding that and correcting it.

There have been millions of dollars in rebates. There have been hundreds of indictments for fraud. There have been a number of convictions. Some have gone to prison. There have been dismissals. But the whole picture that has been given to the people is that this is something that this Defense Department is responsible for.

Q. But aren't you really up against a general public perception that there's rampant waste in the Defense Department?

The President. I don't think there's any question——

Q. Has that been handled properly from a PR standpoint?

The President. I've said what I just said to you many times, but it doesn't get printed.

[*Laughter*] And it certainly doesn't make the evening news. But I think the people also have been treated to so many stories back over the years when things like that did happen that they're prepared to believe the worst.

The truth is we have made wonderful progress in the quality and quantity of manpower, weaponry, and everything else in our Defense Establishment. And as I say, we have also—we have definite programs going over there, providing incentives for people who find extravagances, even a hotline you can call anonymously.

Q. Is there any possibility that you could go along with Senator Goldwater's idea of scrapping the MX in order to cut the deficit?

The President. I have to wait and find out whether what Barry is talking about is impatience with all of the restrictions that have been put on the MX up there on the Hill and in Congress and the continued cutbacks.

We believe modernization of our strategic nuclear weaponry is essential. And MX is part of that. In the past 15 years, the Soviet Union has come up with development of more than five new systems, completely new, and we're still playing catchup. And if we're going to sit down with them in January and begin talking arms reduction, as they have agreed to talk, it would be a mistake to start unilaterally canceling out weapons systems before we do that. We've got to think at all times about how to keep our negotiating position as strong as possible.

So, we'll be talking with Barry. And as I say, I'm hopeful that he was talking about something else and not eliminating the system.

Q. Have you any reservations about the tax reform plan put out by the Treasury?

The President. There may be a couple of items in there that I want to look at very carefully. We want to make sure not to penalize someone or take away some necessary incentive. I've seen the Treasury report. I think they've done a fine job.

Q. What plans does the administration have now to try to get some aid going back to the *contras*?

The President. Oh, we're going to try. I

think that Congress, or that portion of it that's been blocking us, has been very irresponsible. The *contras* are veterans of the revolution that put the Sandinistas in power. And it was a total revolutionary effort aimed at democracy.

You only have to look at the promises the Sandinistas made to the Organization of American States, none of which have been kept. And what we're supporting are the people of Nicaragua who have now been subjected to a totalitarian, Marxist-Leninist state.

Q. But is there any realistic chance that such aid can get through Congress?

The President. We're going to do our best.

Q. Would you go to the people, go on television to make the case?

The President. Yes.

Q. Since covert aid seems to bother a lot of people, including the likely new head of the Senate Intelligence Committee, Senator Durenberger, one suggestion has been to recognize a government in exile which we could then aid overtly. Have you thought about that?

The President. Well, this would give us something that we would have to look at very closely, because right now we can honestly say that what we're trying to do is simply modify the existing situation and return to the principles that all of the parties and elements opposed to Somoza, including the Sandinistas, were fighting for, according to what they said.

Now, it's been revealed that they didn't mean it when they said it. Recognition of a government in exile would probably present some problems—very definite problems for us.

Angola

Q. On another foreign policy issue, but different continent, you've said that you wouldn't turn against Jonas Savimbi's people in Angola, but there are now reports that the U.S. is considering, along with South Africa, working with and recognizing the Angolan Government if the Cuban troops are removed. Is there anything to that? And what would happen to the UNITA forces?

The President. Yes. This is all part of the Namibian package that we've been negotiating. Now, the Savimbi forces are not a part of the negotiations; haven't been. But at the same time, Savimbi supports the removal of the Cubans from Angola and says there is no chance of reconciliation as long as they're there. So once the Cubans leave, UNITA and the Angolan Government would have a better chance of coming to a reconciliation.

If we were asked to in any way help in achieving a reconciliation between these two parties, we'd be very happy to do what we could.

Q. But are you saying that as part of the agreement to remove the Cubans the United States would not be weighing against Savimbi in any kind of internal struggle?

The President. No, that's an internal matter for them. And as I say, he himself says that he cannot achieve—or they cannot work for reconciliation until the Cubans are out.

Q. What about calling for elections within the country and making that part of our negotiating position?

The President. Again, I think the Savimbi forces and the Angolan Government recognize this is an internal problem. I say we won't turn them down if they believe that we, in any way, can be helpful in arriving at some kind of settlement.

Administration Personnel Changes

Q. So far there have been surprisingly few personnel changes in the administration since the election. Do you envision any?

The President. Here and there, there may be some. But right now, the only two we know of are the two that everyone else knows of. But you'll remember back when we were setting up the administration I said I would ask people to come that I thought were qualified, or best qualified, if they could only stay for a matter of a year or 2, however long they could stay, and then we'd try to find somebody equally good. I'm gratified by the fact that not only have they stayed through the first 4, but it seems that there's going to be quite a retention in this second 4-year period.

But I can't complain if some of them, during the second term, come to me and believe they have to return to their own private lives and careers. I'll sure hang on to them as long as I can, but I have no plans for making any changes.

Jeane J. Kirkpatrick

Q. Have you asked Jeane Kirkpatrick to stay on at the U.N.? If she doesn't, it seems that we'll lose her in government.

The President. She and I are scheduled to have a talk very shortly, and we had one scheduled which she had to cancel because of U.N. duties. I know how she feels about the United Nations. That place has a way of burning you out a little bit. And so I know how she feels in that.

Q. She has done very well.

The President. She's turned around what was a really tough situation for us in the U.N., where we were literally being picked on by about 140 other nations. And she's made all the difference in the world.

I don't know whether her desire is straight return to academia or whether there are other things that would appeal to her in government, but, believe me, if there's a way to keep her in the administration, I'll sure try.

Federal Budget

Q. If I could return to the first topic we were discussing—the budget and trying to reduce the deficit. I know that you pledged that you would not cut anyone's social security benefits. But in light of the reports that the administration is considering a 5-percent cut in pay for Federal workers, would it be a violation of your Social Security pledge if you were to forego the cost of living increase for 1 year? That wouldn't be a cut, would it?

The President. Well, I have to say my pledge during the campaign carried with it the clear implication that present Social Security beneficiaries would get their cost-of-living increases as well. I made that pledge and so, therefore, I feel bound by it.

This does not seem as serious to me as some people present it with regard to the deficit, because if you really analyze it, Social Security is not part of the deficit problem. Social Security is totally funded by a payroll tax. And if you made a reduction in some way of Social Security, you wouldn't do a thing for the deficit. That money would just go back into the Social Security trust fund.

And so, I don't feel that Social Security is really a part of fighting the deficit problem. I know that Congress incorporated it into the unified budget for reporting purposes. But as I say, if you look at it, there's no way that any savings at the Social Security end could go anyplace. You have one of two choices: reduce the Social Security payroll tax or leave it in the trust fund for the future.

And so, this doesn't strike me as a tough problem. And I'll tell you something else. I am not going to give some of those practicing demagogues who have made this a demagogic issue in the '82 election and who tried to do it again in the '84 election, I'm not going to give them a handle.

Q. No, but it looks as though some of the request for cuts in the Social Security COLA are now coming from Congress.

The President. I'll be glad to look at those requests.

Q. You could accede to their requests.

The President. I'll be glad to look at anything that they propose. [*Laughter*]

Q. In the face of the deficits, have you given up hope for achieving some of the new initiatives you've talked about in the past, such as tuition tax credits?

The President. Not at all.

Q. Enterprise zones?

The President. Not at all. Enterprise zones is very high on the list. I think that enterprise zones could probably be more effective in helping those people—unemployed, poverty-stricken who need help, who need opportunity—and improving the growth in the economy, which would further reduce the deficit, than almost any of the so-called social programs that have been a part of the Great Society.

No, we want that very definitely. And the tuition tax credit, I think, is just simple fairness. And we have not retreated from any of the social reforms that we asked for. We're going to try for them. But right now, we think that the two tracks aiming at the deficit and control of the budget and spending—we think that those have got to be the top priority.

Q. Now, you've said before that there would be two separate legislative packages: spending reduction and tax reform.

The President. Yes.

Q. And you still hold to that?

The President. Yes. I don't think we should put those into one package at all.

Q. Do you think the changes in the Senate leadership will have any effect on your getting your program through? Do you think it might be a little easier now?

The President. Well, I've gotten along very well with the leadership as it was, and I think I'll get along with the present leadership.

Q. There's just a little different style between Senator Dole and Senator Baker.

The President. Well, we've already had some meetings and gotten along just fine. And I think he's going to be very supportive of our efforts to reduce the deficit.

Q. And not too much pressure from him right now on taxes?

The President. No, no. As a matter of fact, he hasn't said a word about that.

Q. He must have heard you speak on that subject. Are you close to making any decision on the new Secretary of Education?

The President. No, we're delaying any appointment there because we've never given up our belief that the Department should be eliminated. Now, that doesn't mean we eliminate all the programs. We believe that they should be transferred back to other Departments where they had fit in before they created a Department of Education. But we don't believe that the Federal Government has that important a role to play that it should have a Cabinet agency at the Federal level.

Our Federal aid to education only amounts to about 8 percent of the total. Education, historically, has been a local and State function.

Q. One area of Federal support for education that many conservatives have questioned over the years, which exits now, is the expenditure of Federal funds for research and development of and promotion of new curriculum. Many conservatives feel

that that would be better left to the free market and to the local level, that they'll get more competition in that area. If an attempt is made to eliminate some Federal programs, would that area be one that might be dropped?

The President. I think they'd all be looked at, all of them, whether they were legitimately a Federal function and, thus, should be maintained, or whether that should be something left out there at different levels of government. But we haven't begun to look at that yet. We're still focusing on, hopefully, eliminating the Department.

Q. What about stopping all government grants to students and instead just give out nothing in the form of assistance but Federal loans?

The President. Again, as I say, we haven't really sat down and looked at some things of that kind. I do know that having worked my own way through school, I'm not adverse to seeing that there's help given to other students who have to do the same thing.

Congressional Election Results

Q. There's been a lot of talk since the election, pro and con, about whether or not the election results represent a mandate for you or not. And I wonder what you think about that?

The President. Well, whether I use that word or not, let me just say I think the people made it very plain that they approved of the course we've been on so far and what we've been trying to do. And I think they also indicated by their votes that they wanted us to continue on that course.

Q. In retrospect, do you think there's anything more that you could have done to help elect Republicans to the House and Senate?

The President. No. Actually, I was surprised that there was such a cry raised that we hadn't done that—maybe because people hadn't been out there in all the districts. First of all, I did an awful lot of TV ads and radio tapes and so forth for our candidates, letters—solicitation, fundraising letters, and so forth, for all of them. Granted, there was a limitation on how much personally I could do in actually campaigning with them, because when you're the incumbent you've got a job to do at the same time. But that was left to the congressional and Senate committees. And where they said they wanted me to go, I went.

Q. I guess people were talking about the possibility of a nationwide television program, maybe a half hour, in which you focused almost exclusively on the need to elect a Congress that would support you.

The President. Of course I said it every place I went——

Q. Well, you said it, and it was in——

Mr. Baker. It was in the 30-minute film the night of election eve.

Q. Oh, sure it was. And the Vice President made a pitch, also. I recognize that. But there have been people who said, well, there should have been a whole half hour devoted just to that since you were so far ahead in the polls.

The President. You know what our polls showed also, though. The problem with us in the House is the result of somebody else being in charge for the last 50 years in reapportionment, because the polls show that a majority of the people who voted for Members of Congress voted for Republican candidates. But we only elected a minority, about 40 percent of the total. They've got us all bunched up into as few districts as possible.

Cabinet Positions

Q. Have you considered naming Tom Sowell to the vacant chairmanship of the Council on Economic Advisers?

The President. Very frankly—well, I don't talk about anyone under consideration for an appointment until it comes time to say who it's going to be. I don't believe in embarrassing those then who might be considered or not. I have the highest respect for him, a fine man.

But also, I have to tell you that I'm considering whether or not I want even to fill that position.

Q. Why is that?

The President. Well, because in the Cabinet process we have, by way of the Treasury Department, Commerce, and others, I think I get some pretty capable economic advice.

Q. In other words, you might completely do away with the CEA?

The President. That's right. Yes.

Q. Then what about Energy, since we're talking about abolishing?

The President. Well, we still would like to achieve that. And the man who's doing the job would like to achieve it. But so far, we haven't been able to make a dent in that, or in the Education Department, up on the Hill.

Q. Well, but in the budget, do you call for Energy's abolition or breaking up its functions and then distributing them to other departments?

The President. No. First, the Department exists by legislation. We would have to get legislation to eliminate it as a Department.

Q. One last question. In the past, you have steadfastly refused to involve yourself in Republican primaries. Do you intend to hold to that position in the battle for the 1988 Republican nominations?

The President. Well, I've learned that making commitments this far in advance of anything is not the best idea. But I do have to say that I have always adhered to the idea that in this job you are the titular head of the party, and as such, you should let the party decide who the nominees would be. And so, as I say, I still believe in that as a policy.

Note: The interview took place in the Oval Office at the White House.

James A. Baker III is Assistant to the President and Chief of Staff.

As printed above, the interview follows the White House press release, which was released by the Office of the Press Secretary on December 14.

Informal Exchange With Reporters on the Defense Budget
December 14, 1984

Mr. Deaver. Mr. President, I'm very happy to give you the first Inaugural Plate for your second Inaugural.

The President. Well, all right. I'm very pleased to have this. I think there's nothing to do but to put it in action right now.

Q. Screw it on. Where's the screwdriver? [*Laughter*]

The President. High technology—it's all there. [*Laughter*] All right.

Q. Have you decided to cut the defense budget, Mr. President? And if so, by how much?

The President. Let me answer any questions you may have with just one statement on that. All of the things that I've been reading about this—which are obviously based on leaks—those leaks are without any solid foundation.

Q. Well, give us the story.

The President. We are still in the basis of negotiating—or not negotiating, that's the wrong term to use—of studying the whole package of what we're going to present to the Congress.

Q. [*Inaudible*]—says there's a paralysis, so that your entire budget process is bogged down with a paralysis because Weinberger won't give anything.

The President. They must have just caught me asleep at a Cabinet meeting. It wasn't paralysis. [*Laughter*]

Q. But isn't it true——

Q. Let him finish. Let him finish.

Q. Isn't it true that Weinberger hasn't agreed to give what the budget-cutters want him to give?

The President. I told you, we are, all of us—we haven't heard from all of the members of the Cabinet yet. We've been working at what is a very complicated task and a very large budget, and we're still working on that. And as soon as we're prepared to go to Congress with one, we'll go up there, but——

Q. Are you going to slow the rate of growth in defense, Mr. President? Are you going to slow the rate of growth in defense?

The President. There have been proposals with regard to the defense budget, also, and already there have been certain things that have been dropped from that budget.

Q. Well, is your goal still to cut the deficit by $100 billion; that is, in half, by 1989?

The President. Yes. To go the 4–3–2 percent of gross national product with regard to the deficit over the next—[*inaudible*].

Q. When will you make a final determination, Mr. President?

Q. Will you really get any more out of domestic spending, Mr. President?

The President. Again, I'm not prepared to answer on the figures, but, yes, we're making progress.

Q. When will you decide on defense?

The President. Oh, I wish I knew. You wait and you hear everybody's input. And so far, with the scheduling of the day, you come to the end of a meeting and you haven't resolved all of the issues yet.

Q. Apparently you didn't change Senator Goldwater's mind on the MX.

The President. No, but I'll keep working on that.

Mr. Deaver. Can we give the Vice President his plate now? Sam [Sam Donaldson, ABC News], I want to give the Vice President number 2, if you don't mind.

The Vice President. We've got it. Thank you all for all you're doing. Thank you.

Secretary Dole. Thank you very much.

The President. I'm sorry. I didn't know that I interrupted something.

Note: The exchange began at 10:55 a.m. on the South Grounds of the White House, where reporters had assembled for the presentation of the first set of commemorative Inaugural license plates to the President.

Assistant to the President Michael K. Deaver, general chairman of the Committee for the 50th American Presidential Inaugural, made the presentation to the President. The Vice President and Secretary of Transportation Elizabeth H. Dole also participated in the ceremony and received official Inaugural plates.

Recess Appointment of Bonnie Guiton as a Commissioner of the Postal Rate Commission
December 14, 1984

The President today recess appointed Bonnie Guiton to be a Commissioner of the Postal Rate Commission for the remainder of the term expiring November 22, 1988. She will succeed Simeon Miller Bright.

Since 1980 she has been vice president and general manager for Kaiser Center, Inc., and Kaiser Center Properties and chairman of the board of Merritt Park Corp. Previously, she was administrative manager of the planning and control divi-sion for Kaiser Aluminum & Chemical Corp. in 1979–1980; executive director for Marcus A. Foster Educational Institute in 1976–1979; and assistant dean of student services for Mills College in 1970–1976.

She graduated from Mills College (B.A.) and State University in Hayward, CA (M.S.). She has one child and resides in Oakland, CA. She was born October 30, 1941, in Springfield, IL.

Statement by Principal Deputy Press Secretary Speakes on an Agreement With Cuba Concerning Immigration and Refugee Matters
December 14, 1984

As the result of several years of efforts in a series of intensive discussions, the U.S. was able to reach agreement with Cuba today on the return to Cuba of approximately 2,700 who came to the United States in the Mariel boatlift of 1980. Representatives of the Department of State and the Immigration and Naturalization Service of the Department of Justice participated in these discussions.

Those persons to be returned to Cuba are ineligible to remain in the U.S. because they admitted to committing serious crimes in Cuba, have committed serious crimes in the United States, or suffer from severe mental disorders. It was agreed that these persons will be returned in a phased and orderly manner.

I would like to point out that those who will be returned represent only a very small percentage of the persons who came to the United States in the Mariel boatlift. The vast majority of these 129,000 persons have incorporated themselves into American life and are now being processed by INS under the Cuban Adjustment Act of 1966 for legal resident status.

Cuba's agreement to accept the return of those individuals removes an impediment under U.S. law and permits us to resume normal processing of visas for Cuban applicants, as had been the case in Havana prior to 1980. Processing of all immigrant visas, other than for immediate relatives of U.S. citizens, and processing of refugee applications have been suspended since 1980 because of Cuba's refusal to accept the return of persons whom the U.S. has declared excludable. Under the refugee program, ex-political prisoners in Cuba will be eligible to apply to come to the United States under established U.S. procedures. We cannot predict how many Cubans will apply for entry into the United States, but I would reemphasize that both those returning to Cuba and those applying to come to the U.S. will be handled in a phased and orderly process.

The talks were limited only to migration matters. Moreover, the conclusion of an agreement on this issue does not signal any change in U.S. policy toward Cuba. That policy reflects our serious concern about Cuba's international behavior. We see no evidence that Cuba is prepared to change that behavior.

Note: Larry M. Speakes read the statement to reporters assembled in the Briefing Room at the White House at 4:15 p.m.

Accordance of the Personal Rank of Ambassador to Donald S. Lowitz While Serving as United States Representative to the Conference on Disarmament
December 17, 1984

The President today announced his intention to accord the personal rank of Ambassador to Donald S. Lowitz, of Illinois, in his capacity as United States Representative to the Conference on Disarmament.

Mr. Lowitz has been engaged in the private practice of law in Chicago, IL, since 1952 and was a partner in his last firm of Aaron, Schimberg, Hess, and Gilbert in 1974–1984. He served as Assistant United States Attorney in the office of the United States Attorney for the Northern District of Illinois in Chicago in 1954–1959 and was General Counsel of the Office of Economic Opportunity in Washington, DC, in 1969–1971. In 1972–1978 he was a member and then Chairman of the Board of Foreign Scholarships and served as a consultant with the Executive Office of the President (1974–1975) and with the Department of Defense (1975). Since 1984 he has been United States Representative to the Conference on Disarmament, United States Arms Control and Disarmament Agency, in Washington, DC.

Mr. Lowitz received a bachelor of legal science in 1950 from the Northwestern University School of Commerce and his J.D. in 1952 from the Northwestern University School of Law. He was born April 16, 1929, in Chicago, IL.

Statement by Principal Deputy Press Secretary Speakes on the Defense Budget
December 18, 1984

The President has made his decision regarding the defense budget. The decision is based on his determination that all agencies and departments, including the Department of Defense, will be involved in the plan to reduce the deficit. Consistent with this directive, the budget originally submitted by Secretary Weinberger for fiscal year 1986 will be reduced by 11 [11.1] billion in budget authority and by 8.7 billion in outlays. These reductions will bring the President's fiscal year '86 request for defense to levels below the amounts previously approved in October in the congressional budget resolution for both budget authority and outlays.

These outlay reductions are larger than those originally recommended by the Office of Management and Budget and the budget core group. They are, therefore, consistent with the President's objective of achieving a freeze on total government spending for fiscal year '86. The President also emphasized his continued commitment to a strong national defense at adequate spending levels.

The President is also committed to a deficit reduction plan with the objective of shrinking the deficit at a percentage of gross national product from 4 percent in fiscal year '86 to 3 percent in fiscal '87 and 2 percent in fiscal '88.

Note: Larry M. Speakes read the statement to reporters assembled in the Briefing Room at the White House for his daily press briefing, which began at 9:32 a.m.

Statement by Principal Deputy Press Secretary Speakes on Steel Import Agreements
December 19, 1984

The President today is announcing agreements with seven countries—Japan, Korea, Brazil, Mexico, Spain, Australia, and South Africa—to establish limits on the importing of their steel to the United States.

On September 18, 1984, the President announced his decision to deal with unfair trade in steel by seeking negotiated agreements with major steel suppliers within a 90-day period. The 90 days ended yesterday. Today the President is very pleased with the successful conclusion of these negotiations, carried out by his United States Trade Representative. He considers these agreements to be a step in the right direction.

We believe that overall steel import penetration of the U.S. market will decline significantly as a result of these agreements and that the U.S. steel industry will be able to compete in the world markets.

Note: Larry M. Speakes read the statement to reporters assembled in the Briefing Room at the White House during his daily press briefing, which began at noon.

Message on the Observance of Christmas
December 21, 1984

Nancy and I are very pleased to send our warmest greetings to all those gathering with family, friends and neighbors to celebrate this Christmas season.

The first Christmas was a time of family joy for Joseph and Mary and the child Jesus. Although they had made a long journey to reach Bethlehem and were lodged in humble surroundings, they knew that the child Mary bore was a gift not to them alone, but to all mankind. The shepherds who gathered around the manger, and the wise men who traveled from the East to honor the King of Kings, knew that the star above Bethlehem was a guide not only for the pilgrims of that day, but for those in every age seeking the peace which passes understanding.

An early American hymn sang of the Christ-child that "this richest babe comes poor in being, more pearled within than to the seeing." More than any gift or toy, ornament or tree, let us resolve that this Christmas shall be, like that first Christmas, a celebration of interior treasures. And let us resolve to share our many blessings with others now and in the year to come—from the hungry or the helpless near at hand to those in trouble or turmoil in distant lands from Africa to Asia and beyond.

Today, as we gather with our family and friends to honor Christ, we can experience the same peace and joy as the shepherds and the Magi did almost two thousand years ago. If we make that peace and joy a part of our lives, our example will serve as a guide and an inspiration for everyone we meet. Nancy and I pray that the joy of this holiday season will remain with us all throughout the coming year. May God bless you.

RONALD REAGAN

Message on the Observance of Hanukkah
December 21, 1984

Geneva
Exchorgr'S

Nancy joins me in sending our warmest greetings to all those celebrating one of the most joyous times in the Jewish calendar, Hanukkah—The Festival of Lights.

This holiday commemorates the Maccabees victory over their oppressors and the valiant spirit of their battle. Two thousand years ago, God blessed their efforts to retain an independent Jewish commonwealth and to preserve the Jewish religion. Today, their descendants have been similarly blessed. Truly, Hanukkah is a festival whose celebration is meaningful in a contemporary as well as an historical context.

The candles of the Menorah attest to the victory of freedom and righteousness. May their light be a source of strength and inspiration to all of you and to all mankind.

Informal Exchange With Reporters on Foreign and Domestic Issues
December 21, 1984

Q. Mr. President, some conservatives are complaining that George Shultz is stacking the State Department with moderates and turning away from your policies.

The President. I have read all of that and, no, it is not true. And he and I have met and discussed all of the changes that are being made and most of those are just rotations. The individuals are going from one place to another. And it just isn't true.

Q. So, you approve of it, then?

Q. Are you satisfied with the way he's running the department?

The President. Yes, there's a limit to how long you prefer to leave, particularly, the career Ambassadors in one particular place. You give them a change of scenery.

Q. Did your advisers tell you you should get tough with Prime Minister Nakasone on trade?

The President. How can I get tough with a very good friend?

Q. Did they ask you to press him more on trade?

The President. No, he is being most cooperative, and he has some of the same problems I do. He has some people in government that don't always agree with what he's trying to do, but we have made great progress. But there's a long way to go yet, and he knows that, too.

Q. What do you think of Mr. Gorbachev and his criticism of "Star Wars"?

The President. Well, I know that in that great distance there's probably a reason why he doesn't know what he's talking about. He doesn't understand exactly what it is that we're researching, but we're going to be very pleased to let them know exactly what it is that we're talking about. And I think they'll see that maybe it's better if we have a world in which you've got some kind of a defense that maybe can destroy weapons without killing millions of people.

Q. But both Mitterrand and Thatcher are also concerned about it, sir.

The President. Well, I'll get them to understand what it is, too. Today the only defensive weapon we have is to threaten that if they kill millions of our people, we'll kill millions of theirs. I don't think there's any morality in that at all. We're trying to look for something that will make those weapons obsolete, and they can be eliminated once and for all. Mr. President, when you come back from Christmas and from New Year's, do you think you'll have a second honeymoon with the Congress?

The President. If I've had a honeymoon with the Congress, romance has been dead in Washington for 4 years.

Mr. Roussel. Thank you, Mr. President.

Note: The exchange began at 3:17 p.m. at the South Portico of the White House. The members of the press were assembled there to watch the President and Mrs. Reagan accept an 8-foot-square Christmas card from the citizens of Johnstown, PA. The card was presented to them by Mayor Herb Pfuhl.

Peter H. Roussel is Special Assistant to the President and Deputy Press Secretary.

Executive Order 12495—Establishment of Emergency Board No. 207 To Investigate a Railroad Labor Dispute
December 21, 1984

Establishing an Emergency Board To Investigate a Dispute Between Port Authority Trans-Hudson Corporation and the Brotherhood of Railroad Signalmen

A dispute exists between the Port Authority Trans-Hudson Corporation and the Brotherhood of Railroad Signalmen representing employees of the Port Authority Trans-Hudson Corporation.

The dispute has not heretofore been adjusted under the provisions of the Railway Labor Act, as amended ("the Act").

A party empowered by the Act has requested that the President establish an emergency board pursuant to Section 9A of the Act.

Section 9A(e) of the Act provides that the President, upon such a request, shall appoint an emergency board to investigate and report on the dispute.

Now, Therefore, by the authority vested in me by Section 9A of the Act, as amended (45 U.S.C. § 159a), it is hereby ordered as follows:

Section 1. Establishment of Board. There is hereby established a board of three members to be appointed by the President to investigate this dispute. No member shall be pecuniarily or otherwise interested in any organization of railroad employees or any carrier. The board shall perform its functions subject to the availability of funds.

Sec. 2. Report. (a) Within 30 days from the creation of the board, the parties to the dispute shall submit to the board final offers for settlement of the dispute.

(b) Within 30 days after submission of final offers for settlement of the dispute, the board shall submit a report to the President setting forth its selection of the most reasonable offer.

Sec. 3. Maintaining Conditions. As provided by Section 9A(h) of the Act, as amended, from the time a request to establish a board is made until 60 days after the board makes its report, no change, except by agreement, shall be made by the parties in the conditions out of which the dispute arose.

Sec. 4. Expiration. The board shall terminate upon the submission of the report provided for in Section 2 of this Order.

RONALD REAGAN

The White House,
December 21, 1984.

[Filed with the Office of the Federal Register, 10:53 a.m., December 24, 1984]

Announcement of the Establishment of Emergency Board No. 207 To Investigate a Railroad Labor Dispute
December 21, 1984

The President announced today the creation of Presidential Emergency Board No. 207 to investigate and make recommendations for settlement of a current dispute between the Port Authority Trans-Hudson Corporation and employees represented by the Brotherhood of Railroad Signalmen.

The Port Authority Trans-Hudson Corporation (PATH) is a wholly owned subsidiary of the Port Authority of New York and New Jersey. It is a rapid rail transit system connecting the cities of Newark, NJ, and Hoboken with Manhattan. Approximately 200,000 passengers are transported by PATH each weekday. About 55 million passengers were carried in 1983. PATH transports nearly 92 percent of rail passengers entering New York from New Jersey. PATH employs approximately 1,200 workers who help maintain and operate a fleet of about 300 passenger cars.

Earlier, on August 25, 1984, the President invoked the emergency board procedures of the Railway Labor Act applicable to commuter railroads and created Emergency Board No. 204 to investigate and report on this same dispute. Emergency Board No. 204 investigated the issues and prepared a report and recommendations for settlement. The board's report was submitted to the President on September 24, 1984.

Following the release of the report and recommendations by Emergency Board No. 204, the parties unsuccessfully continued their attempts to resolve their differences. The statutory period allotted for this process expires at midnight December 23, 1984.

Section 9A(e) of the Railway Labor Act provides that a party to the dispute or the Governor of any State through which the service runs may request the President to establish a second emergency board if the dispute remains unresolved. Emergency Board No. 207 was created in response to such a request made by the Port Authority Trans-Hudson Corporation. The parties will now submit their final offers to the board within 30 days, and the board will report its selection of the most reasonable offer within 30 days thereafter. From the time a request to establish a board is made until 60 days after the board makes its report, no change, except by agreement, shall be made by the parties in the conditions out of which the dispute arose.

Statement on the Fifth Anniversary of the Soviet Invasion of Afghanistan
December 26, 1984

Five years ago the army of the Soviet Union invaded Afghanistan, overthrew its government, and installed a puppet regime subservient to Moscow. This regime enjoys no popular support from the people of Afghanistan; it is propped up by the guns of 115,000 Soviet occupation troops.

For 5 years the Soviet Army has waged war on the proud and deeply religious people of Afghanistan, and there is still no end in sight. Nonetheless, for 5 years the people of Afghanistan, with legendary courage, have fought the occupying Soviet forces to a standstill.

This fifth anniversary of Afghan defiance stands in stark contrast to the joyful holidays we celebrate at this time of the year. Yet there is a message of inspiration in the cruel tale being written this winter in the mountain passes and valleys of Afghanistan.

The Afghan freedomfighters—the *mujahidin*—remind us daily that the human spirit is resilient and tenacious, and that liberty is not easily stolen from a people determined to defend it. The Afghan people are writing a new chapter in the history of freedom. We Americans salute their magnificent courage.

By overwhelming margins in the United Nations, the world community has repeatedly expressed its condemnation of the Soviet occupation of Afghanistan. For our part, the United States has made clear to Soviet leaders that the presence of Soviet occupying forces in Afghanistan constitutes a serious impediment to the improvement of our bilateral relations. We cannot and will not remain silent on Afghanistan. We join our voice with other members of the world community in calling for a prompt, negotiated end to this brutal conflict.

The way to end this tragic situation is based on the criteria advanced repeatedly by the United Nations: the withdrawal of Soviet forces from Afghanistan; the restoration of Afghanistan's independence and its nonaligned status; self-determination for the Afghan people; and the return of the millions of Afghan refugees to their homes with safety and honor. Until these goals are achieved, the Soviet Union will continue to pay a high price for its suppression of Afghanistan's freedom.

The history of independent Afghanistan goes back more than 2,000 years and is far from being finished. My deepest hope is to speak of freedom restored to Afghanistan by this time next year. In this season when people of good will everywhere turn their attention to the greatest blessing a nation can enjoy—peace at home and abroad—we will not forget the people of Afghanistan who are struggling to live once again among the free nations of the world. These brave people will continue to have the support of all Americans in their noble struggle.

Informal Exchange With Reporters on Foreign and Domestic Issues
December 27, 1984

Q. Mr. President, come on over and talk to us.

Q. Mr. President, how do you respond to the cuts in Medicare, the freeze?

The President. Well, it would be a continuation. It's something we're talking about as part of the whole budget process—the deficit process. It wouldn't be a further cut; it would be a continuation of the freeze.

Q. [*Inaudible*]—freeze?

The President. What?

Q. [*Inaudible*]—of the freeze—on payments——

The President. Yes. If that's what we need. We're still going over it and discussing all of those things.

Q. Why would it be necessary to freeze the doctors as well as at the hospital level?

The President. Well, for one thing medical care is the fastest increasing service that we have with regard to inflation.

Q. How do you feel about the Afghan anniversary today—the invasion of Afghanistan?

The President. A President once called a similar day a "day of infamy." I guess that's exactly what this is also, the anniversary of a day of infamy. There is no legitimate excuse for a great power like the Soviet Union that is doing what it is doing to the people of Afghanistan.

Q. How do you respond to criticism by certain people on Capitol Hill that we're not doing enough aidwise for the Afghan freedom fighters?

The President. Well, there's a line in the scriptures that says—that explains that: ". . . the assembly was confused, and they knew not wherefore they were gathered together."

Q. Senator Humphrey says a lot of the military aid for the Afghan resistance is getting lost in the pipeline.

The President. We do the best we can in anything of this kind, under very difficult circumstances. But, again, it's something that I don't think I'm going to comment on.

Q. Any New Year's resolution?

The President. What?

Q. New Year's resolution?

The President. New Year's resolution? Oh, yes—be nice to all of you, and then you'll reciprocate.

Well, Happy New Year!

Q. Happy New Year!

Note: The exchange began at 9:27 a.m. at the South Portico of the White House as the President and Mrs. Reagan were leaving for a trip to California.

Proclamation 5289—National Cerebral Palsy Month, 1985
December 27, 1984

*By the President of the United States
of America*

A Proclamation

For more than 700,000 Americans with cerebral palsy, life is a struggle to overcome the challenges posed by brain abnormalities present since very early life, often before birth. As cerebral palsy victims mature, they must confront lack of movement control and, possibly, seizures, loss of hearing, vision, or other senses, or mental or emotional impairment. This year, nearly 7,000 children will be born with cerebral palsy.

Health care professionals and educators throughout our Nation are making bold strides in helping those affected to deal with this disorder. Through physical rehabilitation and occupational therapy, many cerebral palsy patients are learning to lead happy, productive lives in the mainstream of society. These efforts have been spearheaded by two voluntary health agencies, the United Cerebral Palsy Associations, Inc. and the National Easter Seal Society.

Investigators supported by the National Institute of Neurological and Communicative Disorders and Stroke and by voluntary health agencies are developing new drugs and devices to alleviate the symptoms of cerebral palsy. Scientists also are learning how to prevent the disorder, particularly with closely monitored prenatal care to minimize risks to the developing child. With the combined efforts of concerned voluntary and public health agencies, the tragedy of cerebral palsy can be substantially reduced.

To encourage public recognition of and compassion for the complex problems caused by cerebral palsy, the Congress, by Senate Joint Resolution 309, has designated the month of January 1985 as "National Cerebral Palsy Month" and authorized and requested the President to issue a proclamation in observance of this month.

Now, Therefore, I, Ronald Reagan, President of the United States of America, do hereby proclaim the month of January 1985 as National Cerebral Palsy Month. I call upon all government agencies, health organizations, communications media, and the people of the United States to observe this month with appropriate ceremonies and activities.

In Witness Whereof, I have hereunto set my hand this twenty-seventh day of December, in the year of our Lord nineteen hundred and eighty-four, and of the Independence of the United States of America the two hundred and ninth.

RONALD REAGAN

[*Filed with the Office of the Federal Register, 11:28 a.m., December 28, 1984*]

Note: The proclamation was released by the Office of the Press Secretary on December 28.

Proclamation 5290—National Poison Prevention Week, 1985
December 27, 1984

*By the President of the United States
of America*

A Proclamation

Between 1962 and 1983, our Nation experienced an 80 percent reduction in childhood poisoning as a result of new, effective safety standards and greater consumer awareness. The number of accidental ingestions of household chemicals, cleaning products, and medicines among children under five years of age dropped from 500,000 to 100,000 during this period.

For the past 24 years, the Poison Prevention Week Council has coordinated a network of health, safety, business, and voluntary organizations to raise public awareness of the problem. In addition, the Consumer Product Safety Commission, which administers the Poison Prevention Packaging Act, requires child-resistant closures on many products that are potentially harmful to children.

While these efforts have been very successful, we must not be satisfied with the progress we have made. Because we believe that almost all such poisonings are preventable, we must continue working to reduce this annual toll by reminding parents and other family members of the steps they can take to avert these tragedies. We must remind them to keep household chemicals, cleaning products, and medicines out of the reach of children and to use re-securable, child-resistant closures on these products.

To encourage the American people to learn about the dangers of accidental poisonings and to take preventive measures, the Congress, by joint resolution approved September 26, 1961 (75 Stat. 681), author-

ized and requested the President to issue a proclamation designating the third week of March of each year as "National Poison Prevention Week."

Now, Therefore, I, Ronald Reagan, President of the United States of America, do hereby designate the week beginning March 17, 1985, as National Poison Prevention Week. I call upon all Americans to observe this week by participating in appropriate ceremonies and events.

In Witness Whereof, I have hereunto set my hand this twenty-seventh day of December, in the year of our Lord nineteen hundred and eighty-four, and of the Independence of the United States of America the two hundred and ninth.

RONALD REAGAN

[*Filed with the Office of the Federal Register, 12:20 p.m., December 28, 1984*]

Note: The proclamation was released by the Office of the Press Secretary on December 28.

Written Responses to Questions Submitted by Yomiuri Shimbun of Tokyo, Japan
December 28, 1984

U.S.-Japan Relations

Q. The year 1985 marks the 40th anniversary of the end of World War II. At this date, how do you perceive the present situation of the world, especially in regard to East-West relations?

The President. Those 40 years have seen some remarkable changes in the world. One of the most remarkable has been the reconciliation between former adversaries, including the United States and Japan. Today Japan and the United States are close partners and good friends. We share the common values of freedom and democracy. We are bound by a security treaty. Unfortunately, Japan, the United States, and other democracies continue to be confronted by a system that stands for different values.

U.S.-Soviet Relations

Q. Secretary of State Shultz will meet Soviet Foreign Minister Gromyko on January 7 and 8 in Geneva. Could you tell us something about your expectations of the meeting? What do you hope to agree to at this specific meeting? Six major items on the agenda of the U.S.-Soviet negotiations will be the status of space, strategic, intermediate-range, conventional, and chemical weaponry, as well as certain confidence-building measures. How could these items be interrelated with each other in the framework of an umbrella formula in the negotiations to follow up the Shultz-Gromyko meeting?

The President. I was encouraged that the Soviets agreed to resume a dialog on arms control issues and that we will have the meeting in Geneva to try to get the process moving again.

But we must temper our expectations with realism. A 2-day meeting cannot solve the complicated issues before us. We hope it will be a constructive beginning for further detailed negotiations, but it isn't an easy job. Only time will tell how rapidly the process moves, or in which specific framework.

Meaningful progress on arms control has a high priority in this administration. We have been working long hours to prepare for Secretary Shultz's meeting with Mr. Gromyko. The Secretary will enter those meetings with concrete suggestions on a full range of arms control issues. We hope the Soviets will show a similar constructive spirit.

The fundamental objective of our talks with the Soviets has to be kept in mind. We are not looking for an agreement for its own sake. We are striving to improve stability, reduce the risk of war, and to lower the levels of nuclear arms. That involves hard bargaining on issues of great mutual concern. The U.S. is committed to conduct that process seriously and creatively.

Q. Would you consider a summit meeting with General Secretary Chernenko before the completion of arms control talks? If so, what preconditions are necessary?

The President. As long ago as last June, I said that I was willing to meet at any time. Since then, I've met with Foreign Minister Gromyko, and our discussions were useful. The Soviets say they would want a very carefully prepared agenda for any summit meeting. That makes sense to me. In the past, meetings that there were not carefully prepared often led to great expectations and great disappointments, and I don't think we ought to go into something of that kind.

Q. In what way may the Western allies, including Japan, support successful U.S.-Soviet negotiations? Do you support independent action on the part of the allies for relaxation of tensions with the U.S.S.R. and the Eastern European nations?

The President. The United States is fully committed to reducing the threat of war. At the Williamsburg summit the Western leaders were united in their commitment to arms reductions and continued thorough and intensive consultations. Further, we noted that security is indivisible and must be approached on a global basis. Prime Minister Nakasone was a key participant in the discussions that led up to this united commitment.

Alliance solidarity behind NATO's 1979 dual track decision on INF modernization has prevented the Soviets from unilaterally dictating Western security policy. This solidarity stems from the extensive consultations which the U.S. conducts with its European and Japanese allies on arms control issues. These consultations have assured a consensus among the allies which is essential in dealing with the Soviets on these vital issues.

Q. How do you view the development of current Sino-Soviet relations? What will be the impact of the forthcoming U.S.-Soviet arms control talks on the tripartite relations between the U.S., U.S.S.R., and China?

The President. We welcome recent efforts by the Chinese and the Soviets to put their relations on a more normal footing. Differences between the Soviet Union and China run very deep, however, and center on three major problems: massive Soviet troop deployments along the Chinese border with the Soviet Union and Mongolia; Soviet support for the Vietnamese invasion of Cambodia; and the Soviet invasion of Afghanistan. These are serious impediments, it seems to me. The Chinese are very positive about our forthcoming arms talks with the Soviets. They want these discussions to bring a genuine reduction of nuclear weapons. They don't want the Soviets merely to redeploy their missiles, from west to east. We agree.

U.S.-Japan Relations

Q. As you prepare to receive Prime Minister Nakasone in Los Angeles in early January, we would like to ask about your fundamental assessment of U.S.-Japan relations today. For the promotion of friendly and constructive relations, what do you expect of Japanese policy in economic matters, defense, and foreign affairs?

The President. I'm looking forward to meeting again with my friend and your Prime Minister. We've had excellent meetings before. My visit to your country when he was my host was just wonderful. I think U.S.-Japanese relations are as good as they have ever been. When I meet with the Prime Minister on January 2, I know that we will begin our talks on the basis of our common desire to make the U.S.-Japan relationship even closer. I don't think there's any confusion about what it will take to succeed. Economically, we need to work hard to continue and enhance the progress made after our talks in Tokyo in November 1983. We have made progress in our security relationship, which will continue to develop to the benefit of both sides. But it is in foreign affairs that the real payoff of close U.S.-Japan relations can increasingly be found. As our ability to cooperate and coordinate our policies increases, so does the scope of what we can accomplish together. Our international cooperation will reflect our ability to handle problems in our bilateral relationship, including trade issues. It is my hope that as leading democracies and as the leading free world economies, Japan and America will be able to provide solutions by putting our heads—and our hearts—together in a partnership for the cause of good.

Q. Cooperation between the U.S. and Japan in a Pacific Basin initiative is said to be a leading topic of discussion in the upcoming Los Angeles meeting. Could you elaborate on your ideas about its realization?

The President. Although the United States has long been a two-ocean nation, in the past we focused most of our attention on our Atlantic coast because of our historic relationship with Europe. But during the past decade or so, the growth of democracy and the dynamic economic development of the Pacific region also have earned our admiration and our very close attention. As a result, while Europe certainly remains as vital as ever to us, a new perspective has emerged toward the Pacific. Japan, of course, plays a key role in this new American perspective. Both our countries are prepared to devote our resources and energies to seeking ways to cooperate with our neighbors in the Pacific. But it is important that we not be rushed in our eagerness to get started. Pacific Basin cooperation, in

whatever form it eventually emerges, will not be successful and will not last unless it has the full support of all our Pacific neighbors, and unless there is benefit for all. The Pacific Basin will be a topic of conversation between the Prime Minister and myself in Los Angeles, but it is too soon to talk about or expect any specific announcements or agreements.

Q. The United States trade deficit with Japan may reach $35 billion this year. Renewed calls for import surcharges are coming from Capitol Hill and industry circles. Will your present position on free trade change in response to calls for the protection of U.S. industries? And what are your expectations on Japan in light of the current deficit? For instance, as yet there are several unsettled matters concerning trade and the opening of the Japanese market: (1) the expansion of voluntary export restraints on '85 automobiles, (2) reduction of tariff rates on wood products and (3) total liberalization of agricultural products. We would appreciate any thoughts you might give us about specific approaches to settling these and other trade issues.

The President. I believe that free trade is a powerful force for progress and peace. The winds of commerce carry opportunities that help nations grow and bring citizens of the world closer together. Increased trade spells more jobs, higher earnings, better products, less inflation, and more cooperation. The freer the flow of world trade, the wider the benefits of economic progress.

Nowhere is free trade more important than in America's commercial ties with Japan—our largest overseas trading partner. And we are Japan's most important market. This year $85 billion in goods and services is flowing across the Pacific between our two nations. But the potential would be even greater if it were not for some trade barriers Japan still maintains which reduce competitive foreign imports.

We've worked hard to encourage Japan to open its domestic market fully to foreign products. We want American companies to have the same opportunity to sell their goods and services and to invest in Japan that your companies already enjoy in our market. You have responded by reducing some trade barriers and we appreciate these measures. The efforts by the Japanese Government to open capital markets for foreign participation and to liberalize the yen are also important steps in the right direction.

But many U.S. companies still cannot compete in Japan on an equal basis. High tariffs stymie our efforts to sell competitive U.S. exports like processed forest products. While there has been some liberalization of agricultural quotas, these should be eventually eliminated so that Japanese consumers have the chance to buy U.S., beef, citrus, and other farm products in quantities and at prices freely set in the marketplace. And I hope that the transformation of Japan's government telecommunications monopoly into a private company will allow U.S. suppliers of these products a fair shot at your market, just as Japanese companies already have here. Your question also refers to Japan's voluntary export restraints on automobiles which expires at the end of March. I think that it is premature for me to make any comment on this, and, in any case, this is a decision for the Japanese Government to make.

On the trade deficit with Japan—it will approach $35 billion by the end of the year—I realize there is no easy answer to this problem, but the sheer size of the deficit has generated growing protectionist sentiment in this country. Therefore, I urge the Japanese Government and people to move even more quickly to open Japan's market to competitive foreign products. If this is done, our trans-Pacific trade relations can continue to expand and flourish to the mutual benefit of our two countries.

Korean Peninsula

Q. With the Olympic games scheduled in Seoul in 1988, the Korean peninsula may become a focus of international attention. What is your evaluation of the current state of affairs on the peninsula as the date approaches? Do you have any initiatives in mind to maintain peace there? What role do you expect the neighboring nations of China, the U.S.S.R., and Japan to play in order to reduce tension on the peninsula?

The President. There has been considerable tension on the Korean peninsula since the North Korean invasion of the South in 1950. Such tension has at times grown even more serious, as, for example, after the North Korean bombing in Rangoon in October of 1983, which almost killed President Chun and did kill several of his key advisers. However, we have seen welcome signs of tension reduction between the two Korean states recently. Talks on economic cooperation and Red Cross talks on such matters as family unification have taken place, and representatives of both Korean Governments will meet again in January to discuss these topics. I think that peace initiatives or tension reduction measures, like the economic and Red Cross talks, must properly come from the two Korean Governments themselves. They must be the major interlocutors in any inter-Korean dialog, but Japan, China, the U.S.S.R., and the U.S. all have an interest in seeing that peace is preserved and that tension on the peninsula is reduced.

Regional Conflicts

Q. Are you planning any initiatives in your second term for the solution of problems in these specific areas of the world? What contribution do you expect from the allied nations, including Japan, to help solve regional conflicts?

The President. One way to solve regional conflicts is to convince the parties to the conflict that they have more to gain by seeking peace. The United States is committed to the peace process in the Middle East, Central America, southern Africa, and elsewhere.

Another way to deal with regional tensions is to create an environment of political stability and economic development that deals with the source of the problem. Japan has increasingly contributed to this process throughout the world through its growing aid programs. I hope Japan will continue to exercise a positive and increasingly visible diplomatic and economic role in the Asian region and throughout the world.

U.S. Economy

Q. Could you elaborate on your principal ideas about reducing the United States budgetary deficit and the high interest rates which are also matters of concern to your allies? Please comment on your position during the coming term.

The President. As a result of our economic policies, millions of jobs have been created, inflation has been cut sharply, interest rates reduced, and in general the U.S. economy has enjoyed a strong, sustained recovery. In turn, America's economic return has helped the economies of our trading partners, including Japan.

Let's look at the record. The U.S. should enjoy a 4-percent growth rate next year. Consumer incomes are rising at a steady pace and consumer confidence is strong. Robust business spending, spurred by our 1981 tax cuts, helped propel the current expansion, and prospects for continued strength in capital spending remain favorable. Inflation will remain low and under control in 1985. This news is good for the U.S. as well as its trading partners like Japan.

To ensure the strength and durability of economic expansion for the longer term, we need to get the Federal deficit and the growth in Federal outlays under better control. With the help of the Congress, we are determined to do so. My goal is to reduce the deficit to $100 billion by FY 1988.

There has been much criticism of the strength of the dollar by many of our allies. Critics have charged that the dollar is substantially overvalued because of high U.S. interest rates resulting from large budget deficits. They contend that the high dollar threatens the global recovery and the U.S. must "correct" its value.

These arguments are not supported by the facts. While the levels of interest rates have periodically played an important role in determining exchange rates, this has not been generally the case during this administration. The improved U.S. business climate and the sharp drop in our inflation are probably the key to the dollar's performance. I am sympathetic to the view that the value of the dollar is high, but I disagree that it is "overvalued." Such a view implies that we can calculate the "right" rate independent of market forces. I believe that we cannot do so.

Economic Summits

Q. The forthcoming Bonn summit marks the 40th anniversary of the end of World War II. What are your thoughts on the development of this organization as it convenes for the 11th time? What will be your basic position in the forthcoming talks?

The President. The annual economic summits are a very useful opportunity for the leaders of the seven main industrialized countries to explain to each other their perspectives and plans for their own economies and their participation in the world economy. In addition, it is an occasion to review the year ahead. Summits are not and cannot be meetings at which we draw up detailed blueprints for solving the world's problems. Whenever that was tried in the past, it failed. But a summit can and does give each participant a clearer understanding of how others see current problems and the tasks before us, so that we can better determine how we should be moving, both separately and together, to deal most effectively with our common agenda.

It is too early to say what will be the main themes of the Bonn summit. However, we have much unfinished business still before us. We need to reaffirm our determination to promote sustainable noninflationary growth in each of our economies. We need to move rapidly to begin a new round of trade negotiations as the best assurance against resurgent protectionist pressures. We need to continue the policies we outlined at the Williamsburg and London meetings to deal in the longer term with the debt problem and the need to integrate the developing countries more effectively into the open world trade and finance systems. As with previous economic summits, the Bonn summit will provide an opportunity for us to discuss informally the more important international political issues facing all our countries, of which the search for meaningful arms reduction is one of the most pressing. In this search, I'm proud to know that Japan is our ally and friend.

Note: As printed above, the questions and answers follow the White House press release.

Executive Order 12496—Adjustments of Certain Rates of Pay and Allowances
December 28, 1984

By the authority vested in me as President by the Constitution and laws of the United States of America, it is hereby ordered as follows:

Section 1. Statutory Pay Systems. Pursuant to the provisions of subchapter I of chapter 53 of title 5 of the United States Code, the rates of basic pay and salaries are adjusted, as set forth at the schedules attached hereto and made a part hereof, for the following statutory pay systems:

(a) The General Schedule (5 U.S.C. 5332(a) at Schedule 1;

(b) The Foreign Service Schedule (22 U.S.C. 3963) at Schedule 2; and

(c) The schedules for the Department of Medicine and Surgery, Veterans' Administration (38 U.S.C. 4107) at Schedule 3.

Sec. 2. Senior Executive Service. Pursuant to the provisions of section 5382 of title 5 of the United States Code, the rates of basic pay are adjusted, as set forth at Schedule 4 attached hereto and made a part hereof, for members of the Senior Executive Service.

Sec. 3. Executive Salaries. The Executive Salary Cost-of-Living Adjustment Act (Public Law 94–82; 89 Stat. 419) provides for adjustments in rates of pay and salaries as set forth at the schedules attached hereto and made a part hereof, for the following:

(a) The Vice President (3 U.S.C. 104) and the Executive Schedule (5 U.S.C. 5312–5316) at Schedule 5;

(b) Congressional Salaries (2 U.S.C. 31) at Schedule 6; and

(c) Judicial Salaries (28 U.S.C. 5, 44(d), 135, 153(a), 172(b), and 252) at Schedule 7.

Sec. 4. Pay and Allowances for Members of the Uniformed Services. Pursuant to the provisions of Section 601 of Public Law 98–525, the rates of monthly basic pay (37 U.S.C. 203(a)), the rates of basic allowances for subsistence (37 U.S.C. 402), and rates of basic allowances for quarters (37 U.S.C. 403(a)) are adjusted, as set forth at Schedule 8 attached hereto and made a part hereof, for members of the uniformed services.

Sec. 5. Effective Date. The adjustments in rates of monthly basic pay and allowances for subsistence and quarters for members of the uniformed services, and all other adjustments of salary or rates of basic pay provided for herein, shall be effective on the first day of the first applicable pay period beginning on or after January 1, 1985.

Sec. 6. Executive Order 12456 of December 30, 1983, as amended, is superseded.

RONALD REAGAN

The White House,
December 28, 1984.

[Filed with the Office of the Federal Register, 12:57 p.m., December 31, 1984]

Note: The schedules are printed in the Federal Register *of January 3, 1985.*

The Executive order was released by the Office of the Press Secretary on December 29.

Proclamation 5291—To Modify Duties on Certain Articles Used in Civil Aircraft and on Globes
December 28, 1984

By the President of the United States of America

A Proclamation

1. Pursuant to section 234 of the Trade and Tariff Act of 1984 (P.L. 98–573), I have determined that modifications in the Tariff Schedules of the United States (TSUS) (19 U.S.C. 1202), as set forth in the Annex to this proclamation, are appropriate in order

to provide duty-free coverage comparable to the expanded coverage provided by other signatories to the Agreement on Trade in Civil Aircraft (the Agreement; 31 UST (pt. 1) 619) as set forth in the Annex to the March 22, 1984, decision of the Committee on Civil Aircraft under the Agreement.

2. I authorize the United States Trade Representative, or his designee, on behalf of the United States of America, to implement the portion of the consolidated Annex to the Agreement which pertains to articles imported into the United States, recorded in the decision of March 22, 1984, upon his determination that the additional duty-free treatment to be accorded by the United States, as set forth in the Annex to this proclamation, is comparable to the expanded coverage provided by other signatories to the Agreement.

3. Pursuant to section 167(b) of the Educational, Scientific, and Cultural Materials Importation Act of 1982 (96 Stat. 2439, 19 U.S.C. 1202 note), I have determined that it is in the interest of the United States to implement, on a temporary basis, the duty-free treatment for such articles as are provided for in the amendment to section 163(c)(3) of that Act made by section 191(c)(2)(B) of the Trade and Tariff Act of 1984. These articles were omitted through technical error from the 1982 Act implementing the Nairobi Protocol (97th Congress, 1st Session, Senate Treaty Document 97–2, p. 9) to the Florence Agreement on the Importation of Educational, Scientific, and Cultural Materials, and from Proclamation 5021 of February 14, 1983 (48 F.R. 6883), providing temporary duty reductions to certain imported articles. I have also determined, pursuant to section 604 of the Trade Act of 1974 (19 U.S.C. 2483), to modify the TSUS to provide temporary duty reductions to such additional articles.

Now, Therefore, I, Ronald Reagan, President of the United States of America, acting under the authority vested in me by the Constitution and the statutes of the United States, including but not limited to sections 234 of the Trade and Tariff Act of 1984, section 167(b)(2) of the Educational, Scientific, and Cultural Materials Importation Act of 1982, and section 604 of the Trade Act of 1974, do proclaim that:

(1) Item 960.70 in part 4 of the Appendix to the TSUS is modified by inserting after "models)" the language ", globes,". This modification is effective with respect to articles entered, or withdrawn from warehouse for consumption, on or after November 14, 1984.

(2) The TSUS are further modified as provided in the Annex to this proclamation, attached hereto and made a part hereof.

(3) The modifications to the TSUS made by paragraph (2) shall be effective with respect to articles entered, or withdrawn from warehouse for consumption, on and after the date designated by the United States Trade Representative or his designee and published in the *Federal Register* along with his determination that the duty-free coverage provided by the United States is comparable to the expanded coverage provided by other signatories to the Agreement.

In Witness Whereof, I have hereunto set my hand this twenty-eighth day of December, in the year of our Lord nineteen hundred and eighty-four, and of the Independence of the United States of America the two hundred and ninth.

RONALD REAGAN

[*Filed with the Office of the Federal Register, 12:58 p.m., December 31, 1984*]

Note: The annexes are printed in the Federal Register *of January 3, 1985.*

The proclamation was released by the Office of the Press Secretary on December 29.

Executive Order 12497—President's Advisory Committee on Mediation and Conciliation
December 29, 1984

By the authority vested in me as President by the Constitution and laws of the United States of America, including the Federal Advisory Committee Act, as amended (5 U.S.C. App. I), and in order to extend the life of the President's Advisory Committee on Mediation and Conciliation, it is hereby ordered that Section 4(b) of Executive Order No. 12462 of February 17, 1984, is amended to read: "The Committee shall terminate on September 30, 1985, unless sooner extended."

RONALD REAGAN

The White House,
December 29, 1984.

[Filed with the Office of the Federal Register, 12:59 p.m., December 31, 1984]
Note: The Executive order was released by the Office of the Press Secretary on December 31.

Appendix A—Digest of Other White House Announcements

The following list includes the President's public schedule and other items of general interest announced by the Office of the Press Secretary and not included elsewhere in this book.

July 1

Following his return from Camp David, MD, the President hosted a barbecue for the diplomatic corps on the South Lawn of the White House.

July 2

The President met at the White House with members of the White House staff.

The President greeted members of the Herald Trumpeters, who are celebrating the 25th anniversary of the group's formation.

The President made the following recess appointments:

Erich Bloch, of New York, as Director of the National Science Foundation;

Robert N. Broadbent, of Nevada, as Assistant Secretary of the Interior;

Melvin A. Ensley, of Washington, as a member of the Federal Farm Credit Board, Farm Credit Administration;

Marianne Mele Hall, of New Jersey, as a Commissioner of the Copyright Royalty Tribunal;

Dodie Truman Livingston, of California, as Chief of the Children's Bureau, Department of Health and Human Services;

Martha R. Seger, of Michigan, as a member of the Board of Directors of the Federal Reserve System.

The President made the following recess appointments of members of the National Council on the Humanities:

William Barclay Allen, of California;

Mary Josephine Conrad Cresimore, of North Carolina;

Leon Richard Kass, of Illinois;

Kathleen S. Kilpatrick, of Connecticut;

Robert Laxalt, of Nevada;

James V. Schall, of California;

Helen Marie Taylor, of Virginia.

July 3

The President met at the White House with:

—members of the White House staff;

—Jay Hair, executive vice president, National Wildlife Federation; Russell Train, president, World Wildlife Fund; William Riley, president, Conservation Foundation; and Jack Lorenz, director, Izaak Walton League, for a luncheon meeting.

The President made the following recess appointments:

Donald Ian MacDonald, of Florida, as Administrator of the Alcohol, Drug Abuse, and Mental Health Administration;

Lando W. Zech, Jr., of Virginia, as a member of the Nuclear Regulatory Commission.

July 4

The President left the White House for a trip to Florida, Alabama, Michigan, and Texas.

The President declared a major disaster for the State of Nebraska as a result of tornadoes, severe storms, and flooding, beginning on June 11, which caused extensive property damage.

July 5

The President recess appointed Carol Gene Dawson, of Virginia, as a Commissioner of the Consumer Product Safety Commission.

July 6

Following his return to the Washington, DC, area from Texas, the President went to Camp David, MD, for the weekend.

July 8

The President returned to the White House from Camp David.

July 9

The President met at the White House with:

—members of the White House staff;

—the Cabinet Council on Natural Resources and the Environment;

—Weston Adams, U.S. Ambassador to Malawi, John W. Shirley, U.S. Ambassador to Tanzania, and Alberto Martinez Piedra, U.S. Ambassador to Guatemala, prior to their departure for their overseas posts;

—members of the American Coalition for Traditional Values.

In an Oval Office ceremony, the President presented the Presidential Citizens Medal posthumously to Dennis W. Keogh, a Foreign Service officer killed in a terrorist bombing in Namibia. Mrs. Keogh accepted the award on behalf of her husband.

July 10

The President met at the White House with members of the White House staff.

The White House announced that as an indication of the President's continuing interest in food aid and development aid for Africa, he has asked the Administrator of the Agency for International Development, M. Peter McPherson, to travel to African countries in the near future and report to him on actions the U.S. Government might take.

The President declared an emergency for the State of Wisconsin as a result of severe storms and tornadoes on April 27–28, which caused extensive property damage.

July 11

The President met at the White House with:
—members of the White House staff;
—the President's Foreign Intelligence Advisory Board;
—members of Citizens for America;
—the President's Economic Policy Advisory Board.

The White House announced that at the request of the President, the Vice President has accepted the invitation of President-elect León Febres-Cordero Ribadeneyra of Ecuador to visit Quito and will head the U.S. delegation to the inauguration of the President-elect on August 10. While in Quito, the Vice President is expected to meet with members of the Ecuadoran Government and other foreign delegations.

July 12

The President transmitted to the Congress the 20th annual report on the status of the National Wilderness Preservation System for calendar year 1983.

July 13

The President met at the White House with:
—members of the White House staff;
—Minister of Defense Manfred Wörner of the Federal Republic of Germany;
—State presidents of the American Farm Bureau Federation;
—members of the board of directors of the National Association of Security Dealers.

The President amended the major disaster declaration of June 27 for the State of Iowa. The President's action will permit the use of Federal funds in relief and recovery efforts in certain areas of the State which suffered damage from flooding during June.

The President transmitted to the Congress the ninth annual report of the Nuclear Regulatory Commission.

The President left the White House for a weekend stay at Camp David, MD.

July 15

The President returned to the White House from Camp David.

July 16

The President met at the White House with members of the White House staff.

The President spoke by telephone with Jim Mora, coach of the Philadelphia Stars, to congratulate him for his team's winning the U.S. Football League championship in Tampa, FL, on July 15.

July 17

The President met at the White House with:
—members of the White House staff;
—the Cabinet Council on Economic Affairs, to receive an economic update;
—the Cabinet Council on Commerce and Trade, to discuss the commercialization of space.

July 18

The President met at the White House with:
—members of the White House staff;
—the Vice President, for lunch;
—members of a trade mission to China.

July 19

The President met at the White House with Kenneth Bialkin, national chairman, David Brody, director, and Nathan Perlmutter, national director, Anti-Defamation League of B'nai B'rith.

July 20

The President met at the White House with:
—members of the White House staff;
—members of Girls Nation.

The White House announced that the President will meet with President José Napoleón Duarte of El Salvador at the White House on July 23.

The White House announced that the President has declared a major disaster for the State of Nebraska as a result of severe storms and tornadoes, beginning on or about April 25, which caused extensive property damage.

The White House announced that the President has declared a major disaster for the State of South Dakota as a result of severe storms and flooding, beginning on June 11, which caused extensive property damage.

The President recess appointed Robert A. Rowland, of Texas, as Assistant Secretary of Labor (Occupational Safety and Health).

The President left the White House for a weekend stay at Camp David, MD.

July 22

The President returned to the White House from Camp David.

July 23

The President met at the White House with:
—members of the White House staff;
—members of Boys Nation.

The President announced the members of the U.S. delegation to the second International Conference on Population, which will be held in Mexico City August 6–13:

Representatives:

James L. Buckley, Director of Radio Free Europe, will serve as Chairman;

Ambassador Alan Keyes, U.S. Representative on the Economic and Social Council of the United Nations; and

William H. Draper III, President of the Export-Import Bank of the United States.

Alternate Representatives:

Danny J. Boggs, Deputy Secretary of Energy;

Jacqueline Schafer, member of the Council on Environmental Quality;

Ben Wattenberg, author and a member of the Board for International Broadcasting.

Senior Government Advisers:

James L. Malone, Assistant Secretary of State for Oceans and International Environmental and Scientific Affairs;

Gregory J. Newell, Assistant Secretary of State for International Organization Affairs, or designee; and

M. Peter McPherson, Administrator of the Agency for International Development, or designee.

The President also accorded the personal rank of Ambassador to Mr. Buckley in his capacity as Chairman of the delegation.

July 24

The President met at the White House with:
—members of the White House staff;
—Manuel Fraga, leader of the Spanish opposition party;
—the Republican congressional leadership.

In a ceremony in the Roosevelt Room, the President received the first piece of the President's Signature Edition Character Jug. Sales of the 5,000 numbered pieces, made by Royal Doulton, are to benefit the James S. Brady Presidential Foundation. Present for the ceremony were Mr. Brady, Press Secretary to the President, who also received a jug from the President, Mrs. Brady, and representatives of the foundation, the Republican National Committee, and Royal Doulton.

July 27

The President met at the White House with:
—members of the White House staff;
—President-elect Nicholas Ardito Barletta of Panama;
—representatives of the Americas Society;
—Leonardo Neher, U.S. Ambassador to Upper Volta, Clint A. Lauderdale, U.S. Ambassador to Guyana, Alan W. Lukens, U.S. Ambassador

to the Congo, Paul H. Boeker, U.S. Ambassador to Jordan, and Larry C. Williamson, U.S. Ambassador to Gabon and Sao Tome and Principe, prior to their departure for their overseas posts.

The President transmitted to the Congress the 1983 annual reports on the activities under the Occupational Safety and Health Act of 1970 of the Departments of Labor and Health and Human Services, and of the Occupational Safety and Health Review Commission.

The President declared a major disaster for the State of Colorado as a result of severe storms, mudslides, landslides, and flooding, beginning on May 1, which caused extensive property damage.

The President announced his intention to designate A.C. Arterbery as Vice Chairperson of the Board of Directors of the African Development Foundation. He has served as a member of the Board since February 10.

The President requested the Congress to provide $407 million in fiscal year 1984 supplemental appropriations, including requests for the following:
—$392 million to fully fund the food stamp program for fiscal year 1984;
—$15 million for the Department of Education to provide grants to local educational agencies to repair school facilities damaged in declared official disasters.

The President also transmitted appropriations proposals for the Department of the Interior.

July 28

The President left the White House for a trip to California.

July 31

The President announced his intention to appoint the following individuals to be Governors of the Board of Governors of the American National Red Cross for terms of 3 years:

Secretary of Defense Caspar W. Weinberger is being reappointed;

Donald Ian MacDonald, Administrator of the Alcohol, Drug Abuse, and Mental Health Administration, Department of Health and Human Services, will succeed Edward Brandt;

Gilbert G. Pompa, Director of the Community Relations Service, Department of Justice, will succeed T.H. Bell; and

Samuel W. Speck, Jr., Associate Director of the Federal Emergency Management Agency, will succeed Louis O. Guiffrida.

August 1

The White House announced that the President would honor the request of Anne M. Burford to remove her name from consideration as

Chairman of the National Advisory Committee on Oceans and Atmosphere.

August 3

The President announced his intention to designate Elliot Ross Buckley as Chairman of the Occupational Safety and Health Review Commission. He will succeed Robert A. Rowland.

August 9

The President held a luncheon meeting at Rancho del Cielo, his ranch near Santa Barbara, CA, to discuss political issues with Stuart Spencer, consultant to the Reagan-Bush campaign, and James A. Baker III, Assistant to the President and Chief of Staff.

August 12

The President and Mrs. Reagan left Rancho del Cielo, their ranch near Santa Barbara, CA, and went to the Century Plaza Hotel in Los Angeles, CA, where they stayed during their 2-day visit to the city.

August 13

The President held a luncheon meeting with Secretary of State George P. Shultz at the Century Plaza Hotel in Los Angeles, CA. The President then met with Minister of Foreign Affairs Giulio Andreotti of Italy.

The President and Mrs. Reagan attended a wedding ceremony rehearsal for their daughter Patti Davis at the Hotel Bel-Air.

August 14

The President met at the Century Plaza Hotel in Los Angeles, CA, with members of the White House staff.

The President and Mrs. Reagan attended the wedding of their daughter Patti Davis to Paul Grilley at the Hotel Bel-Air.

The White House announced that the President has designated Harold Peter (H.P.) Goldfield, Assistant Secretary of Commerce for Trade Development, to serve as a member of the Board of Directors of the Overseas Private Investment Corporation. He will succeed Richard L. McElheny.

August 15

The President and Mrs. Reagan returned to Washington, DC, from California.

August 16

The President met at the White House with:
—members of the White House staff;
—the Cabinet, for a working luncheon;
—members of the President's Council on Integrity and Efficiency, to receive the Council's final report;

—Valerie Kurth, the 1984 Epilepsy Poster Child, Mr. and Mrs. Arthur R. Kurth, and Dr. Eli Goldesohn, chairman of the board of the Epilepsy Foundation.

The White House announced that in accordance with section 446 of the District of Columbia Self-Government and Governmental Reorganization Act of 1973, the President transmitted to the Congress the fiscal year 1984 District of Columbia budget supplemental, which provides for a net increase of $9.3 million for the General Fund and an increase of $15 million for the Capital Projects Fund. These requests are in District of Columbia funds and do not affect the Federal budget.

The President requested the Congress to provide the following for fiscal year 1984:
—$750,000 in offsetting amendments to supplemental requests now pending before the Congress for the Department of Agriculture to enable the Food Safety and Inspection Service to cover the cost of the recently enacted .5-percent increase to the January 1, 1984, Federal pay raise;
—$2 million in transfer authority for the Small Business Administration to enable the agency to process a greater-than-anticipated number of applications for disaster loans.

The President also transmitted 1984 and 1985 appropriations proposals for the legislative branch.

August 17

The President met at the White House with:
—members of the White House staff;
—members of the President's Council on Management Improvement.

The President declared a major disaster for the State of Utah as a result of severe storms, flooding, mudslides, and landslides, beginning on April 1, which caused extensive property damage.

August 20

On Air Force One from Washington, DC, enroute to Ohio and Illinois, the President telephoned Pete Rose to congratulate him and wish him luck in his new job as manager of the Cincinnati Reds baseball team.

Prior to his departure from Cincinnati, the President stopped briefly to greet construction workers on the highway near the David Carter Beard Bridge spanning the Ohio River. The President also telephoned 6-year-old Peter Ringen, of La Crescenta, CA, to commend him for his quick thinking and bravery in rescuing his mother from drowning in the family's swimming pool.

August 21

The President met throughout the day at the White House with members of the White House staff.

August 22

In the morning, the President left the White House for a trip to Texas and Illinois.

August 24

Following his return to the Washington, DC, area from Texas and Illinois, the President went to Camp David, MD, for the weekend.

August 26

The President returned to the White House from Camp David.

August 27

The President met at the White House with members of the White House staff.

The President declared a major disaster for the State of Pennsylvania as a result of severe storms and flooding, beginning on or about August 3, which caused extensive property damage.

August 28

The President met at the White House with:
—members of the White House staff;
—Anthony C.E. Quainton, U.S. Ambassador to Kuwait, Brandon H. Grove, Jr., U.S. Ambassador to Zaire, and Leon J. Weil, U.S. Ambassador to Nepal, prior to their departure for their overseas posts.

August 29

The President met at the White House with members of the White House staff.

In an Oval Office ceremony, the President received diplomatic credentials from Ambassadors Falilou Kane of Senegal, Gunther van Well of the Federal Republic of Germany, Joseph Edsal Edmunds of St. Lucia, Donald Aloysius McLeod of Suriname, Ignatious Chukuemeka Olisemeka of Nigeria, and Maati Jorio of Morocco.

The President hosted a reception for members of the Reagan-Bush headquarters staff on the State Floor of the White House.

August 30

The President met at the White House with:
—members of the White House staff;
—the Vice President, for lunch;
—the Cabinet Council on Legal Policy, to discuss administration efforts to reduce drug trafficking.

The President sent a letter of condolence to the widow of Tommie Douglas Benefield, a test pilot who was killed in the crash of a B–1 bomber test flight in California on August 29.

August 31

The President met at the White House with:
—members of the White House staff;
—Kathryn McDonald, widow of Representative Lawrence P. McDonald of Georgia, who was killed in the Soviet downing of Korean Air Lines flight 007 on September 1, 1983.

September 1

The White House announced that the President has designated Henry Bowen Frazier III as Acting Chairman of the Federal Labor Relations Authority.

September 2

While at the Irvine Marriott Hotel in Irvine, CA, the President telephoned the Muscular Dystrophy Association's 19th annual Labor Day telethon.

September 5

While in Chicago, IL, the President telephoned the winner of the Canadian national elections, Progressive Party candidate Brian Mulroney, who was at his home in Ottawa. In the 5-minute call, the President extended his congratulations and best wishes to Mr. Mulroney. During his campaign, Mr. Mulroney called for even closer ties to the United States. In the call the President reciprocated this wish and expressed his readiness to work closely with Mr. Mulroney to the mutual benefit of both Canada and the United States.

The President transmitted to the Congress the 1983 annual report of the Saint Lawrence Seaway Development Corporation.

September 6

The President met at the White House with:
—members of the White House staff;
—the Vice President, for a luncheon meeting;
—the Cabinet Council on Commerce and Trade, to discuss steel and copper cases before the International Trade Commission.

The President declared a major disaster for the State of New Mexico as a result of severe storms and flooding, beginning on or about August 8, which caused extensive property damage.

The President declared a major disaster for the State of Nevada as a result of severe storms and flooding, beginning on July 22, which caused extensive property damage.

September 7

The President met at the White House with:
—members of the White House staff;
—Emile Van Lennep, outgoing Secretary General of the Organization for Economic Cooperation and Development.

The President attended a White House briefing held in Room 450 of the Old Executive Office

Building for members of the media who cover space, science, and education issues.

The President met in the Indian Treaty Room of the Old Executive Office Building with a group of women executives of major corporations and financial institutions.

In the afternoon, the President left the White House for a weekend stay at Camp David, MD.

September 9

Following his visit to Doylestown, PA, the President returned to Washington, DC.

The President telephoned Alf Landon to express his best wishes on the occasion of Mr. Landon's 97th birthday. Mr. Landon, who was a Republican candidate for President in 1936 and a 2-term Governor of Kansas, was at his home in Topeka when the President placed the call.

September 10

The President met at the White House with:
—members of the White House staff;
—Rev. T.J. Jemison, president, and other leaders of the National Baptist Convention, USA;
—Secretary of Agriculture John R. Block, Chairman, and other representatives of the Combined Federal Campaign.

September 11

The President met at the White House with:
—members of the White House staff;
—the Republican congressional leadership;
—Lord Carrington, Secretary General of NATO;
—a group of Members of Congress, to discuss farm issues;
—a group of Republican Members of Congress, to discuss steel issues.

September 12

The President requested the Congress to provide additional fiscal year 1985 appropriations for the following purposes:
—$319.6 million for multilateral development banks to provide for the U.S. contribution to these institutions that was due in 1984. Congress deleted these funds from the 1984 supplemental appropriations bill. These funds are needed to honor the U.S. commitment to these institutions;
—$8.4 million to enable the Coast Guard to remove a railroad bridge that obstructs navigation on Newark Bay, NJ. This bridge is owned by the bankrupt Central Railroad Company of New Jersey, and the Federal Government is filing a claim with the trustee of the railroad for reimbursement for the expenses of removing the bridge.
Appropriation language also is requested to provide a $300 million limitation on the contingent

liability for a trade credit insurance program for Central America.

September 14

The President met at the White House with members of the White House staff.

In the morning, the President sent a message to Prime Minister Shimon Peres of Israel in which he reaffirmed the strong, enduring ties that bind the United States and Israel.

September 17

The President met at the White House with:
—members of the White House staff;
—the steering committee for Democrats for Reagan-Bush.

September 18

The President met at the White House with:
—members of the White House staff;
—Senator Jesse Helms of North Carolina and several agricultural leaders;
—the Cabinet Council on Commerce and Trade;
—a group of steel industry executives.

The White House announced that the President has invited Prime Minister Brian Mulroney of Canada to meet with him in the United States. Prime Minister Mulroney has accepted the invitation and will meet with the President at the White House on September 25.

The White House announced that the President has invited Prime Minister Shimon Peres of Israel to make an official working visit to the United States. The Prime Minister has accepted the invitation and will meet with the President at the White House on October 9.

September 19

The White House announced that the President has nominated Paul A. Volcker to be United States Alternate Governor of the International Monetary Fund for a term of 5 years. This is a reappointment.

Prior to leaving the White House for visits to Connecticut and New Jersey, the President met with chapter presidents of the U.S. Jaycees.

September 21

The President met at the White House with:
—members of the White House staff;
—Noboro Takeshita, Finance Minister of Japan and Chairman of the International Monetary Fund-World Bank joint annual meeting which will be held in Washington September 24–28;
—Arthur A. Hartman, U.S. Ambassador to the Soviet Union, to discuss U.S.-Soviet relations;
—a group of outstanding airmen in the U.S. Air Force.

The President transmitted to the Congress the sixth biennial report under the National Manufactured Housing Construction and Safety Standards Act of 1974.

The President declared a major disaster for the State of North Carolina as a result of Hurricane Diana, beginning on or about September 12, which caused extensive property damage.

The President and Mrs. Reagan went to the Southeast Washington home of 7-year-old Rudolph Hines, where they had dinner with him and his parents, Stephanie Lee and Chett Hines. Rudolph was selected as the President's pen pal after the White House adopted his school, the Martin Luther King, Jr. Elementary School, as part of the National Partnerships in Education Program.

September 23

In the morning, the President went to New York to attend the 39th Session of the United Nations General Assembly. While in New York, the President stayed at the Waldorf-Astoria Hotel. Later in the day, the President hosted a working luncheon at the hotel for U.N. Secretary-General Javier Perez de Cuellar de la Guerra. He then held a series of separate meetings with President Raúl Alfonsin of Argentina, President Mobutu Sese Seko of Zaire, Prime Minister Kåre Willoch of Norway, and Jaime Cardinal Sin of the Philippines.

September 24

In the morning, the President addressed the 39th Session of the United Nations General Assembly in New York. Following his address, the President returned to the Waldorf-Astoria Hotel, his residence while in New York, where he met with Prince Norodom Sihanouk and Son Sann of Kampuchea. Before returning to Washington, DC, the President also met with Senator Howard H. Baker, Jr.

The President transmitted to the Congress the fourth annual report on activities undertaken by the United States Synthetic Fuels Corporation to implement the development of synthetic fuels under the Defense Production Act of 1950, as amended. The report covers the period from July 1, 1983, through June 30, 1984.

September 25

The President met at the White House with:
—members of the White House staff;
—Dr. Henry A. Kissinger, former Secretary of State;
—Joe Kittinger, transatlantic balloonist.

The President hosted a reception in the State Dining Room at the White House for the Justices of the Supreme Court of the United States.

The President declared a major disaster for the State of New York as a result of severe storms and flooding during the period August 11 through 14, which caused extensive property damage.

September 26

The White House announced that the President sent messages to President Mohammed Hosni Mubarak of Egypt and King Hussein I of Jordan congratulating them on the resumption of diplomatic relations between their countries.

In the morning, the President left the White House for a trip to Ohio and Wisconsin. While Air Force One was on the ground at Canton, OH, the President spoke by telephone with Secretary of State George P. Shultz, who was in New York. Secretary Shultz called the President following his meeting in New York with Soviet Foreign Minister Andrey A. Gromyko.

September 27

The President met at the White House with:
—members of the White House staff;
—President Fernando Belaúnde Terry of Peru;
—Ambassador Robert Oakley, Director and Coordinator for Security Policies and Programs at the State Department, who reported on his preliminary inquiry into security measures at the U.S. Embassy annex in Beirut;
—Secretary of State George P. Shultz, who reported on his meeting in New York with Soviet Foreign Minister Andrey A. Gromyko;
—Foreign Minister Abdel Meguid, of Egypt.

The President transmitted to the Congress a report of the activities of the United States Government in the United Nations and its affiliated agencies during the calendar year 1983.

The President requested the Congress to provide $306.6 million in additional fiscal year 1985 appropriations for the Veterans Administration to enable the agency to continue to acquire properties upon foreclosure of VA guaranteed housing loans.

The White House announced that the President has invited Prime Minister Kamisese Mara of Fiji to make an official working visit to the United States. Prime Minister Mara has accepted the invitation and will meet with the President at the White House on November 27.

September 28

The President met at the White House with members of the White House staff.

In the morning, the President, Soviet Foreign Minister Andrey A. Gromyko, and U.S. and Soviet officials met in the Oval Office. The President and the Foreign Minister then met privately. The meeting was followed by a luncheon in the State Dining Room which was attended by the President, the Foreign Minister, and an expanded group of U.S. and Soviet officials and advisers.

The President spoke by telephone with former President Jimmy Carter to discuss remarks the President made about the intelligence community during a question-and-answer session with students at Bowling Green State University on September 26.

Prior to leaving the White House for a weekend stay at Camp David, MD, the President signed several pieces of legislation in the Oval Office. The signing ceremonies were attended by congressional sponsors and cosponsors of the bills.

September 30

The President returned to the White House from a weekend stay at Camp David, MD.

October 1

The President left the White House for a trip to Michigan, Mississippi, and Texas.

October 2

The President declared a major disaster for the State of Texas as a result of severe storms and flooding, beginning on or about September 6, which caused extensive property damage.

The President announced his intention to designate the following individuals as members of the National Commission on Agricultural Trade and Export Policy. These are new positions:

Deputy Secretary of Agriculture Richard E. Lyng;

Under Secretary of Agriculture for International Affairs and Commodity Programs Daniel G. Amstutz;

Assistant Secretary of Agriculture for Economics William G. Lesher.

October 3

The President returned to the White House from a trip to Michigan, Mississippi, and Texas.

The President met at the White House with leaders of the Veterans of Foreign Wars.

October 4

The President met at the White House with:
—members of the White House staff;
—the Vice President, for lunch.

October 5

The President met at the White House with members of the White House staff.

The President transmitted to the Congress the 14th annual report on hazardous materials transportation for calendar year 1983.

The President left the White House for a weekend stay at Camp David, MD.

October 7

The White House announced that en route to Louisville, KY, on Air Force One, the President telephoned Walter Payton of the Chicago Bears to congratulate him on breaking the National

Football League career rushing record previously held by Jim Brown of the Cleveland Browns.

October 9

The President met at the White House with:
—members of the White House staff;
—the Cabinet Council on Economic Affairs.

In Oval Office ceremonies, the President signed a proclamation proclaiming the week beginning October 7 as Fire Prevention Week; and H.R. 1904, which extends and amends the authorities for the Department of Health and Human Services child abuse prevention and treatment and adoption opportunities programs and authorizes a new demonstration program for family violence prevention and services.

In the afternoon, the President attended a reception for leaders of the National Fraternal Congress of Americans in the State Dining Room at the White House.

The President designated the delegation, led by Secretary of State George P. Shultz, to represent the United States at the inauguration of His Excellency Dr. Nicolas Ardito Barletta as President of the Republic of Panama in Panama City on October 11. The members of the delegation are:

George P. Shultz, Secretary of State, Personal Representative of the President with the rank of Special Ambassador, head of the United States delegation

Representatives of the President with the rank of Special Ambassador:

Everett Ellis Briggs, American Ambassador to Panama

Paula Hawkins, U.S. Senator from the State of Florida

Carroll Hubbard, Jr., U.S. Representative from the State of Kentucky

Robert L. Livingston, U.S. Representative from the State of Louisiana

Harry Walter Shlaudeman, Ambassador at Large

J. William Middendorf II, Permanent Representative to the Organization of American States with the rank of Ambassador

Langhorne A. Motley, Assistant Secretary of State for Inter-American Affairs

Arnold C. Harberger, Ph.D., professor of economics, University of Chicago

October 11

The President met at the White House with members of the White House staff.

In a ceremony in the Roosevelt Room, the President signed into law the National Cooperative Research Act of 1984. As enacted, S. 1841 is Public Law 98–462.

The President telephoned the Vice President, who was in Philadelphia, PA, following the conclusion of the Vice President's debate with Geraldine A. Ferraro.

The President announced his intention to appoint the following individuals as members of the Martin Luther King, Jr. Federal Holiday Commission. These are new positions:

Clarence M. Pendleton, Chairman of the Commission on Civil Rights

Lawrence F. Davenport, Assistant Secretary for Elementary and Secondary Education, Department of Education

Rosslee Green Douglas, Director of the Office of Minority Economic Impact, Department of Energy

George Walter Armstrong, Associate Director, Office of Presidential Personnel, the White House

October 12

The White House announced that prior to leaving Lima, OH, the President spoke by telephone with Prime Minister Margaret Thatcher of Great Britain. The President extended condolences to the families of victims of the bombing incident that morning in Brighton and expressed hope that the nations of the world would stand together in an effort to rid the world of terrorism.

Following the whistlestop tour of Ohio, the President went to Camp David, MD, for a weekend stay.

October 14

The President returned to the White House from Camp David.

October 16

The President recess appointed Rosemary M. Collyer as General Counsel of the National Labor Relations Board. She is currently serving as Chairman of the Federal Mine Safety and Health Review Commission.

October 17

The President met at the White House with:
—members of the White House staff;
—Archbishop Roman Arietta of San José, president of the Secretariat of Catholic Bishops of Central America.

In an Oval Office ceremony, the President signed the Toy Safety Act of 1984. As enacted, H.R. 5818 is Public Law 98–491.

The White House announced that the President has withheld his approval from H.R. 2859, a bill for the relief of John Brima Charles.

October 18

The President met at the White House with members of the White House staff.

October 19

The President met at the White House with members of the White House staff.

October 25

The President met at the White House with:
—members of the White House staff;
—Judge Irving R. Kaufman, Chairman of the President's Commission on Organized Crime, who presented an interim report on the Commission's findings.

In separate Oval Office ceremonies, the President received the American Sportscasters Association Award and the Hero of Young America Award.

The White House announced that President Reagan has invited President Seyni Kountché of Niger to make an official working visit to the United States. President Kountché has accepted the invitation and will meet with President Reagan at the White House on December 11.

October 26

The President designated Richard V. Backley as Acting Chairman of the Federal Mine Safety and Health Review Commission.

The President recess appointed James A. Lastowka as a member of the Federal Mine Safety and Health Review Commission for a term of 6 years expiring August 30, 1990.

The President left the White House for a trip to New York, Connecticut, and New Jersey. Following his remarks in Hackensack, NJ, the President went to Camp David, MD, for a weekend stay.

October 28

The President returned to the White House from Camp David.

October 30

The President met at the White House with:
—members of the White House staff;
—the National Security Council.

The President declared a major disaster for the State of Texas as a result of severe storms, high winds, and flooding, beginning on October 19, which caused extensive property damage.

October 31

The President met at the White House with members of the White House staff.

On the occasion of the 30th anniversary of Algeria's independence, the President asked Secretary of Energy Donald P. Hodel to lead the delegation to Algiers to represent the United States at ceremonies there on November 1. Included in the delegation to accompany Secretary Hodel are Sanford McCormack, president and chairman of the board of McCormack Oil and Gas Partnership, Carlos Perez, president of Banana Services, Inc., Charles Tyson, vice president of Upbrook International, and U.S. Ambassador to Algeria Michael H. Newlin.

The President declared a major disaster for the State of Louisiana as a result of severe storms and flooding, beginning on October 18, which caused extensive property damage.

November 1

The White House announced that the President has asked Secretary of State George P. Shultz to head the U.S. delegation to the funeral of Prime Minister Indira Gandhi of India. The other members of the delegation will be:

Senator Howard H. Baker, Jr., of Tennessee

Senator Daniel P. Moynihan of New York

Representative Stephen J. Solarz of New York

John Sherman Cooper, former Senator from Kentucky and former U.S. Ambassador to India

John Kenneth Galbraith, economist and former U.S. Ambassador to India

Robert F. Goheen, former U.S. Ambassador to India

Mary M. McDonald, member, board of commissioners of Cook County, IL, and trustee, Association of Indians in America

Ronald H. Walker, managing director, Korn Ferry International

S. Dillon Ripley, former Secretary of the Smithsonian Institution and chairman of the American Committee for Indian Cultural Programs in the United States

In the morning, the President left the White House for a trip to Massachusetts, New York, Michigan, Ohio, Illinois, Arkansas, Iowa, Wisconsin, Minnesota, Missouri, and California.

November 4

The White House announced that the President asked James A. Baker III, Assistant to the President and Chief of Staff, to call Secretary of Health and Human Services Margaret M. Heckler about coordinating with the Office of Management and Budget to have the Federal Government upgrade the shelter for the homeless, run by the Community for Creative Non-Violence, in Washington, DC.

The White House announced that the President has directed M. Peter McPherson, Administrator of the Agency for International Development, to go to Ethiopia to assess the drought and hunger situation and for discussions with Ethiopian officials.

November 7

President Reagan received congratulatory telephone calls after his reelection from President Miguel De la Madrid Hurtado of Mexico, President Mohammad Zia-ul-Haq of Pakistan, and former President Gerald R. Ford.

November 8

The President spoke by telephone with Representative Guy Vander Jagt of Michigan, who called to express his appreciation for the President's efforts on behalf of Republican congressional candidates.

The President telephoned Mitch McConnell to congratulate him on his election as U.S. Senator from Kentucky.

November 9

The President announced his intention to designate Peter H. Raven as Chairman of the National Museum Services Board. He would succeed Douglas Dillon.

November 11

The President returned to Washington, DC, from Santa Barbara, CA.

November 13

The President met at the White House with:
—members of the White House staff;
—the Cabinet, to discuss goals and policy objectives for the second term and the current status of the fiscal year 1985 Federal budget.

The White House announced that President Reagan has invited President Jaime Lusinchi of Venezuela to make a state visit to the United States. President Lusinchi has accepted the invitation and will meet with President Reagan at the White House on December 4.

November 14

The President met at the White House with:
—members of the White House staff;
—Richard Leaky and members of the board of directors of the National Geographic Society, for lunch;
—Secretary of State George P. Shultz and Assistant to the President for National Security Affairs Robert C. McFarlane, to discuss the global agenda and foreign policy for the President's second term;
—the President's Task Force on Legal Equity for Women, to receive a report on the Task Force's activities.

The White House announced that the President has asked the Vice President to represent the administration at the funeral of the Rev. Martin Luther King, Sr., at the Ebenezer Baptist Church in Atlanta, GA, on November 15. In addition, it was announced that the President sent a letter of condolence to Coretta Scott King on the death of her father-in-law.

November 15

The President met at the White House with:
—members of the White House staff;
—the Cabinet, to discuss the Nation's economy and the fiscal year 1985 Federal budget;
—Clarence Bacon, newly elected commander of the American Legion;
—members of the Presidential Advisory Committee on Small and Minority Business Ownership, who presented their annual report.

The President attended a reception for the American Security Council's Coalition for Peace Through Strength in the State Dining Room at the White House.

The White House announced that the President has invited Chancellor Helmut Kohl of the Federal Republic of Germany to make an official working visit to the United States. Chancellor Kohl has accepted the invitation and will meet with the President at the White House on November 30.

November 16

The President met at the White House with:

—members of the White House staff;

—the Vice President, Assistant to the President for National Security Affairs Robert C. McFarlane, and M. Peter McPherson, Administrator of the Agency for International Development, who reported on his recent trip to Ethiopia to assess the drought and hunger situation in that country;

—the Vice President and Minister of Foreign Affairs Sahabzada Yaqub Khan of Pakistan.

In a Rose Garden ceremony, the President received the 37th annual Thanksgiving turkey from representatives of the National Turkey Federation.

The White House announced that the President will meet with Tariq Mikhayl 'Aziz, Deputy Prime Minister and Minister of Foreign Affairs of Iraq, at the White House on November 26.

The White House announced that the President has invited Prime Minister Wilfried Martens of Belgium to make an official working visit to the United States. Prime Minister Martens has accepted the invitation and will meet with the President at the White House on January 14, 1985.

November 19

The White House announced that the President was saddened to learn of the death of former Senator George D. Aiken of Vermont and that he expressed his and Mrs. Reagan's sympathy privately to Mrs. Aiken.

The President participated in the signing up of Rancho del Cielo, his ranch near Santa Barbara, CA, in the Santa Barbara County Sheriff's Department's Operation ID Program. Representatives of the sheriff's department and the California Farm Bureau visited the ranch to give the President an ID number and to help mark the farm and ranch equipment.

November 21

The White House announced that the President will meet with Prime Minister Yasuhiro Nakasone of Japan in Los Angeles, CA, on January 2, 1985.

November 25

The President returned to the White House from California.

November 26

The President met at the White House with:

—members of the White House staff;

—Tariq Aziz, Deputy Prime Minister and Foreign Minister of Iraq;

—a group of Cabinet-level and White House staff advisers, to receive an overview of the Treasury Department's tax reform study.

In an Oval Office ceremony, the President received diplomatic credentials from Ambassadors Tommy T.B. Koh of Singapore, Carlos Tunnermann Bernheim of Nicaragua, U Maung Maung Gyi of Burma, Kjell Eliassen of Norway, Mohamed Sahnoun of Algeria, and Mario Ribadeneira of Ecuador.

November 27

The President met at the White House with:

—members of the White House staff;

—the Cabinet;

—Howard H. Baker, Jr., outgoing Senate majority leader.

The President recess appointed the following individuals:

—Rosalie Gaull Silberman as a member of the Equal Employment Opportunity Commission for the remainder of the term expiring July 1, 1985. She would succeed Cathie A. Shattuck.

—Pauline Crowe Naftzger as a member of the National Museum Services Board for a term expiring December 6, 1988. She would succeed Neil Harris.

—Mary L. Azcuenaga as a Federal Trade Commissioner for the term of 7 years from September 26, 1984. She would succeed Michael Pertschuk.

The President recess appointed the following individuals as members of the National Advisory Council on Women's Educational Programs:

—Elizabeth Helms Adams, for a term expiring May 8, 1987. She would succeed Diana Powers Evans.

—Peter Douglas Keisler, for a term expiring May 8, 1987. He would succeed Maria Pornady Shuhi.

November 28

The President met at the White House with:

—members of the White House staff;

—a group of Cabinet-level and White House staff advisers, to review a list of domestic and military programs that could be reduced or eliminated to reduce the deficit to target levels;

—representatives of the Alzheimer's Disease Foundation.

The White House announced that the President has invited Prime Minister Margaret Thatcher of Great Britain to make an official working visit to the United States. Prime Minister Thatcher has accepted the invitation and will meet with the President at Camp David on December 22.

The President recess appointed the following individuals:

—Barbara W. Schlicher as a member of the Board of Directors of the National Corporation for Housing Partnerships for the term expiring October 27, 1987. She will succeed Frank J. Donatelli.

—Edward J. Philbin as a Federal Maritime Commissioner for the term expiring June 30, 1989. He will succeed James V. Day.

The President recess appointed the following individuals as members of the Board of Directors of the United States Synthetic Fuels Corporation:

—Tom Corcoran, for the term expiring August 16, 1990. He will succeed Milton M. Masson, Jr.

—Paul Webster MacAvoy, for the term expiring September 14, 1991. He will succeed Robert A.G. Monks.

—Eric Reichl, for the remainder of the term expiring September 14, 1986. He will succeed C. Howard Wilkins.

The White House announced that the Aggregate Report on Personnel, prepared pursuant to title 3, United States Code, section 113, for the fiscal year 1984, is being transmitted to the Speaker of the House and the President of the Senate.

November 29

The President met at the White House with:
—members of the White House staff;
—the Republican congressional leadership;
—the Vice President, for a luncheon meeting;
—a group of Cabinet-level and White House staff advisers, to discuss budget issues.

In an Oval Office ceremony, the President presented the Congressional Gold Medal posthumously to Leo Ryan, U.S. Representative from California, who was killed in Guyana in 1978 by followers of Jim Jones, the leader of the Peoples Temple. The ceremony was attended by members of the late Congressman's family.

The President met in the Oval Office with Capt. Lewis Hiller, Jeff Kass, and Gregg Turay, the American winners of the 1984 Nansen Medal, the highest international honor for those who aid refugees. The captain and two crewmembers of the merchant ship *Rose City* lead in the rescue of 85 Vietnamese refugees whose boat was foundering in the South China Sea on September 21, 1983.

The President recess appointed Neal Peden as Assistant Administrator of the Agency for International Development. He will succeed Elise R.W. duPont.

November 30

The President met at the White House with:
—members of the White House staff;
—a group of Cabinet-level and White House staff advisers, to discuss budget issues.

The President recess appointed John D. Ward as Director of the Office of Surface Mining Reclamation and Enforcement. He will succeed James R. Harris.

In the afternoon, the President left the White House for a weekend stay at Camp David, MD.

December 2

The President returned to the White House from Camp David.

December 3

The President met at the White House with:
—members of the White House staff;
—Assistant Secretary of State for African Affairs Chester A. Crocker, who reported on developments in southern Africa;
—a group of Cabinet-level and White House staff advisers, to discuss nondefense budget issues;
—Lou Rawls, to express appreciation and congratulate him for his fundraising efforts on behalf of the United Negro College Fund;
—a group of Cabinet-level and White House staff advisers, to continue the discussion of nondefense budget issues;
—Members of Congress, to discuss their recent trip to Ethiopia to assess the drought and hunger situation.

December 4

The President met at the White House with:
—members of the White House staff;
—a group of Cabinet-level and White House staff advisers, for an up-to-date summary of nondefense spending decisions.

In an Oval Office ceremony, the President received the official 1984 Christmas Seals of the American Lung Association from entertainer Pearl Bailey, the 1984 Christmas Seal chairman.

The President went to Walter Reed Army Medical Center to visit Senator John C. Stennis of Mississippi, whose left leg had been amputated on November 30. The President presented Senator Stennis with a jar of jellybeans.

December 5

The President met at the White House with:

—members of the White House staff;
—33 new Republican Members of the 99th Congress;
—the Cabinet, heads of major Agencies, and members of the White House staff, for an outline of the general strategy for budget spending reductions.

The President attended a briefing for corporate executives in Washington for 2 days of activities dealing with world hunger. The meeting was held in Room 450 of the Old Executive Office Building.

December 6

The President met at the White House with:
—the Republican congressional leadership, to discuss budget issues;
—a group of sponsors of the Young Astronaut Program.

In a White House ceremony, the President met with 6-year-old Kristen Ellis, of Hebron, KY, the March of Dimes Poster Child. The President presented Kristen with a jar of jellybeans, and Kristen presented the President and Mrs. Reagan with a black 12-pound puppy, a sheep dog.

December 7

The President met at the White House with:
—members of the White House staff;
—Bishop Desmond M. Tutu of South Africa;
—the Vice President, for a luncheon meeting.

The President participated in an Oval Office ceremony for the presentation of the Lloyds of London Silver Medal to the crew of the space shuttle *Discovery,* whose mission resulted in the return of two space satellites.

The President recess appointed John W. Shannon as an Assistant Secretary of the Army (Installations and Logistics).

The President left the White House for a weekend stay at Camp David, MD.

December 9

Following their return from Camp David, the President and Mrs. Reagan participated in the taping of the NBC television program "Christmas in Washington" at the National Building Museum.

December 10

The President met at the White House with:
—members of the White House staff;
—a group of Cabinet-level officials and White House staff members, to discuss defense spending budget issues;
—a Red Cross delegation, including Richard Schubert, president of the American National Red Cross, Senator John C. Danforth of Missouri, actor Charlton Heston, and a number of businessmen, who reported on their trip to Ethiopia to review famine relief efforts;

—Secretary of Defense Caspar W. Weinberger.

The White House announced that on the evening of December 9, the President sent a message to Jabir al-Ahmad al-Jabir Al Sabah, Amir of Kuwait, in which he praised Kuwait's refusal to give in to the demands of the hijackers of the Kuwaiti airliner in Tehran, Iran.

In an Oval Office ceremony, the President received diplomatic credentials from Ambassadors Adrien Raymond of Haiti, Asterius Magnus Hyera of Tanzania, Pablo Mauricio Alvergue of El Salvador, Mohsin Ahmed Alaini of Yemen, A.Z.M. Obaidullah Khan of Bangladesh, Ghazi Muhammad Al Gosaibi of Bahrain, and El Sayed Abdel Raouf El Reedy of Eygpt.

The President declared a major disaster for the U.S. Virgin Islands as a result of Tropical Storm Klaus and flooding, beginning on or about November 5, which caused extensive property damage.

December 11

The President met at the White House with:
—members of the White House staff;
—Jeane J. Kirkpatrick, U.S. Representative to the United Nations.

The White House announced that the President has accepted Prime Minister Brian Mulroney's invitation to visit Canada in March 1986, with the exact date to be worked out later. This visit reciprocates the Canadian Prime Minister's September 25 trip to Washington and reflects the excellent state of relations between the two countries.

The President recess appointed Ralph E. Kennickell, Jr., as Public Printer. He would succeed Danford L. Sawyer, Jr.

The President and Mrs. Reagan hosted a Christmas party for Members of Congress on the State Floor of the White House.

December 12

The President met at the White House with:
—members of the White House staff;
—representatives of Gannett newspapers and television stations;
—members of the International Private Enterprise Task Force;
—Senator Barry Goldwater of Arizona;
—a group of Cabinet-level officials and White House staff members, for a working luncheon to discuss defense spending budget issues;
—members of the 1984 and 1985 U.S. Savings Bonds Volunteer Committees.

The President participated in the planting of a sugar maple tree on the North Grounds of the White House.

The President telephoned William J. Schroeder, the second recipient of an artificial heart, at Humana Heart Institute in Louisville, KY.

The President recess appointed the following individuals to be members of the Marine Mammal Commission:

Karen Pryor, for the term expiring May 13, 1986, and *Robert Elsner,* for the term expiring May 13, 1987.

The President recess appointed John N. Griesemer to be Governor of the U.S. Postal Service for the remainder of the term expiring December 8, 1986. He will succeed John R. McKean.

The President and Mrs. Reagan hosted a Christmas party for members of the press on the State Floor of the White House.

December 13

The President met at the White House with:
—members of the White House staff;
—the Vice President, for lunch;
—representatives of the Future Farmers of America;
—Jeana Jo Alessio, 1984 West Virginia Strawberry Festival Queen, and Senator Robert C. Byrd of West Virginia;
—participants in the World Games for Deaf Athletes.

The President recess appointed Richard H. Jones as Deputy Administrator of the Federal Aviation Administration. He will succeed Michael J. Fenello.

The President and Mrs. Reagan hosted a Christmas party for members of the press on the State Floor of the White House.

December 14

The President met at the White House with:
—members of the White House staff;
—a group of intergovernmental leaders, including Gov. John Carlin of Kansas, chairman, and Gov. Lamar Alexander of Tennessee, vice chairman, National Governors' Association; Mayor Hernan Padilla of San Juan, PR, of the U.S. Conference of Mayors; Mayor George Voinovich of Cleveland, OH, president, National League of Cities; Speaker John Martin of Maine, chairman, State-Federal Assembly; Commissioner Earl Baker of Chester, PA, chairman, Finance and Taxation Committee, National Association of Counties; George Miller, president, National Association of Towns and Townships; and Representative Jane Monroney of Delaware, chairman, State-Federal Affairs Committee, Council of State Governments.

The President met in the Roosevelt Room with Michael K. Deaver, Assistant to the President and Deputy Chief of Staff, who is serving as general chairman of the Committee for the 50th American Presidential Inaugural. Other officials of the committee were also present for the meeting. The President then participated in a ceremony on the South Grounds of the White House, where he was presented with the first set of commemorative Inaugural license plates produced by the committee.

The President recess appointed William J. McGinnis, Jr., as a member of the Federal Labor Relations Authority for a term of 5 years expiring July 1, 1989. He would succeed Ronald W. Haughton.

December 15

The President and Mrs. Reagan hosted an open house Christmas reception at the White House for White House military and United States Secret Service personnel.

December 16

The President and Mrs. Reagan hosted an open house Christmas reception at the White House for White House and Executive Office Building staff.

December 17

The President met at the White House with:
—members of the White House staff;
—a group of incoming White House fellows.

The President went to the Old Executive Office Building for the presentation of Rank Awards, including the Distinguished Executive Award and the Meritorious Executive Award, to senior Government executives.

The President and Mrs. Reagan hosted a Christmas reception at the White House for the United States Secret Service.

December 18

The President met at the White House with:
—members of the White House staff;
—Ciriaco de Mita, leader of the Italian Christian Democratic Party, to discuss U.S.-Italy relations.
—the Joint Chiefs of Staff.

In the afternoon, the President attended a farewell reception for Secretary of Education Terrel H. Bell in the Roosevelt Room at the White House.

The White House announced that the President has invited Prime Minister Bettino Craxi of Italy, who is also President of the European Community, to make an official working visit to the United States. Prime Minister Craxi has accepted the invitation and will meet with the President at the White House on March 15, 1985.

December 19

The President met at the White House with:
—members of the White House staff;

—Ambassador Edward L. Rowny, Special Representative for Negotiations, U.S. Arms Control and Disarmament Agency, to discuss preparations for the upcoming arms control talks in Geneva, Switzerland;

—the Cabinet, to discuss management initiatives underway throughout the administration.

December 20

The President met at the White House with:

—members of the White House staff;

—Senator John Tower of Texas, for a farewell visit;

—the Vice President, for a luncheon meeting;

—representatives from the private sector, including Harris D. Machus of the National Restaurant Association, J. Alexander McMahon of the American Hospital Association, Michael D. Mooslin of Naugles, Inc., and T. Kent Titze of the National Council on Rehabilitation and Therapy Through Horticulture, whose organizations have supported the administration's initiative to expand private sector employment opportunities for the handicapped.

The President and Mrs. Reagan hosted a Christmas reception at the White House for members of the White House senior staff.

The White House announced that the President has authorized the award of a $1 million grant to the U.S.-ASEAN Center for Technology Exchange by the Agency for International Development.

December 21

The President met at the White House with members of the White House staff.

The White House announced that the President recess appointed Richard H. Hughes as a member of the Board of Directors of the Export-Import Bank of the United States for a term expiring January 20, 1985. He will succeed James Ernest Yonge.

In the afternoon, the President left the White House for a weekend stay at Camp David, MD.

December 22

Prime Minister Margaret Thatcher of the United Kingdom traveled to Camp David, MD, to meet with the President. Following her arrival, the Prime Minister and the President called on Mrs. Reagan and met privately at Aspen Lodge. They then went to Laurel Lodge for an expanded meeting and working luncheon with U.S. and British officials. The Prime Minister was then flown to Andrews Air Force Base, MD, for the return trip to England.

December 23

The President and Mrs. Reagan returned to the White House from Camp David, MD.

December 24

The President met at the White House with members of the White House staff.

December 25

The President and Mrs. Reagan spent Christmas at the White House with members of their family and friends.

December 26

The President met at the White House with members of the White House staff.

The White House announced that the President has invited Prime Minister Robert Hawke of Australia to make an official working visit to the United States. The Prime Minister has accepted the invitation and will meet with the President at the White House on February 7, 1985.

December 27

The President and Mrs. Reagan left the White House for a trip to California. In the afternoon, they arrived in Los Angeles and went to the Century Plaza Hotel, where they remained overnight. The President and Mrs. Reagan had dinner in their suite at the hotel with their son Ron and his wife Doria.

December 28

While in Los Angeles, CA, the President visited Dr. John William House at the doctor's office and had a routine ear examination.

The President recess appointed Terrence M. Scanlon as Chairman of the Consumer Product Safety Commission. He will succeed Nancy Harvey Steorts. Mr. Scanlon has been serving as a Commissioner since March 24, 1983.

December 29

While at the Century Plaza Hotel in Los Angeles, CA, the President and Mrs. Reagan visited with the President's son Michael, his wife Colleen, and their children, Cameron and Ashley Marie.

The President and Mrs. Reagan left Los Angeles and traveled to the home of Walter and Leonore Annenberg in Palm Springs, CA, where they stayed through New Year's Day.

December 31

While at the residence of Walter and Leonore Annenberg in Palm Springs, CA, the President met with Robert C. McFarlane, Assistant to the

President for National Security Affairs, to discuss the upcoming arms control talks in Geneva and the Strategic Defense Initiative.

The White House announced that the President sent a message to Rajiv Gandhi, following his election as Prime Minister of India. The message, dispatched on December 29 and delivered over the weekend, extended the President's "warm congratulations" on the Prime Minister's party's impressive election victory.

The President recess appointed Helmut A. Merklein as Administrator of the Energy Information Administration. He will succeed J. Erich Evered.

Appendix B—Nominations Submitted to the Senate

The following list does not include members of the Uniformed Services, nominations to the Service Academies, or nominations of Foreign Service officers.

Submitted July 23

Leon Jerome Weil,
of New York, to be Ambassador Extraordinary and Plenipotentiary of the United States of America to the Kingdom of Nepal.

Robert W. Helm,
of Virginia, to be an Assistant Secretary of Defense, vice Vincent Puritano, resigned.

The following-named persons to be Associate Judges of the Superior Court of the District of Columbia for terms of 15 years (new positions—Public Law 98–235 of March 19, 1984):

Susan Rebecca Holmes, of the District of Columbia.
Rufus Gunn King III, of the District of Columbia.
Colleen Kollar-Kotelly, of the District of Columbia.
A. Noel Anketell Kramer, of the District of Columbia.
Robert Isaac Richter, of the District of Columbia.
Emmet G. Sullivan, of the District of Columbia.
Robert Samuel Tignor, of the District of Columbia.

Andrew John Strenio, Jr.,
of Maryland, to be a member of the Interstate Commerce Commission for a term expiring December 31, 1985, vice Reginald E. Gilliam, Jr., resigned.

Walter C. Wallace,
of New York, to be a member of the National Mediation Board for the term expiring July 1, 1987 (reappointment).

Submitted July 24

Crete B. Harvey,
of Illinois, to be a member of the Federal Farm Credit Board, Farm Credit Administration, for a term expiring March 31, 1990, vice John D. Naill, Jr., term expired.

Submitted July 24—Continued

John B. Waters,
of Tennessee, to be a member of the Board of Directors of the Tennessee Valley Authority for the term expiring May 18, 1993, vice Simon David Freeman, term expired.

Andrew Lewis Frey,
of the District of Columbia, to be an Associate Judge of the District of Columbia Court of Appeals for the term of 15 years, vice John W. Kern III, retired.

Submitted July 25

Larry C. Williamson,
of California, a career member of the Senior Foreign Service, Class of Counselor, to be Ambassador Extraordinary and Plenipotentiary of the United States of America to the Gabonese Republic and to serve concurrently and without additional compensation as Ambassador Extraordinary and Plenipotentiary of the United States of America to the Democractic Republic of Sao Tome and Principe.

The following-named persons to the positions indicated, to which positions they were appointed during the last recess of the Senate:

Robert N. Broadbent,
of Nevada, to be an Assistant Secretary of the Interior, vice Daniel N. Miller, Jr., resigned.

Donald Ian Macdonald,
of Florida, to be Administrator of the Alcohol, Drug Abuse, and Mental Health Administration, vice William E. Mayer.

Dodie Truman Livingston,
of California, to be Chief of the Children's Bureau, Department of Health and Human Services, vice Clarence Eugene Hodges.

Carol Gene Dawson,
of Virginia, to be a Commissioner of the Consumer Product Safety Commission for the remainder of the term expiring October 26, 1985, vice Samuel D. Zagoria, resigned.

Marianne Mele Hall,
of New Jersey, to be a Commissioner of the Copyright Royalty Tribunal for the unexpired

Submitted July 25—Continued
term of 7 years from September 27, 1982, vice Katherine D. Ortega, resigned.

Melvin A. Ensley,
of Washington, to be a member of the Federal Farm Credit Board, Farm Credit Administration, for a term expiring March 31, 1990, vice George Warrent Lacey, term expired.

Martha R. Seger,
of Michigan, to be a member of the Board of Governors of the Federal Reserve System for a term of 14 years from February 1, 1984, vice Nancy Hays Teeters, term expired.

The following-named persons to be members of the National Council on the Humanities for terms expiring January 26, 1990:

William Barclay Allen, of California, vice Charles V. Hamilton, term expired.
Mary Joseph Conrad Cresimore, of North Carolina, vice Louis J. Hector, term expired.
Leon Richard Kass, of Illinois, vice M. Carl Holman, term expired.
Kathleen S. Kilpatrick, of Connecticut, vice Harriett Morse Zimmerman, term expired.
Robert Laxalt, of Nevada, vice Sister Joel Read, term expired.
James V. Schall, of California, vice Leon Stein, term expired.
Helen Marie Taylor, of Virginia, vice Mary Beth Norton, term expired.

Erich Bloch,
of New York, to be Director of the National Science Foundation for a term of 6 years, vice Edward A. Knapp, resigned.

Lando W. Zech, Jr.,
of Virginia, to be a member of the Nuclear Regulatory Commission for the term of 5 years expiring June 30, 1989, vice Victor Gilinsky, term expired.

Robert A. Rowland,
of Texas, to be an Assistant Secretary of Labor, vice Thorne G. Auchter, resigned.

Submitted July 27

Anthony Cecil Eden Quainton,
of Washington, a career member of the Senior Foreign Service, Class of Minister-Counselor, to be Ambassador Extraordinary and Plenipotentiary of the United States of America to the State of Kuwait.

Robert E. Barbour,
of Tennessee, a career member of the Senior Foreign Service, Class of Minister-Counselor, to

Submitted July 27—Continued
be Ambassador Extraordinary and Plenipotentiary of the United States of America to the Republic of Suriname.

Brandon Hambright Grove, Jr.,
of the District of Columbia, a career member of the Senior Foreign Service, Class of Minister-Counselor, to be Ambassador Extraordinary and Plenipotentiary of the United States of America to the Republic of Zaire.

Helen J. Valerio,
of Massachusetts, to be a member of the National Advisory Council on Women's Educational Programs for a term expiring May 8, 1987 (reappointment).

William Lee Hanley, Jr.,
of Connecticut, to be a member of the Board of Directors of the Corporation for Public Broadcasting for the remainder of the term expiring March 26, 1987, vice Karl Eller, resigned.

Clifford J. Murino,
of Colorado, to be a member of the National Science Board, National Science Foundation, for a term expiring May 10, 1990, vice Edwin Ernest Salpeter, term expired.

Helen M. Eversberg,
of Texas, to be United States Attorney for the Western District of Texas for the term of 4 years, vice Edward C. Prado, resigned.

Submitted July 30

Charles D. Baker,
of Massachusetts, to be Under Secretary of Health and Human Services, vice John A. Svahn, resigned.

Edward J. Streator,
of New York, a career member of the Senior Foreign Service, Class of Career Minister, to be the Representative of the United States of America to the Organization for Economic Cooperation and Development, with the rank of Ambassador.

Submitted August 1

Paul M. Bator,
of Massachusetts, to be United States Circuit Judge for the District of Columbia Circuit, vice a new position created by P.L. 98–353, approved July 10, 1984.

Submitted August 1—Continued
Juan R. Torruella del Valle,
of Puerto Rico, to be United States Circuit Judge for the First Circuit, vice a new position created by P.L. 98–353, approved July 10, 1984.

Emory M. Sneeden,
of South Carolina, to be United States Circuit Judge for the Fourth Circuit, vice a new position created by P.L. 98–353, approved July 10, 1984.

Frank H. Easterbrook,
of Illinois, to be United States Circuit Judge for the Seventh Circuit, vice a new position created by P.L. 98–353, approved July 10, 1984.

Cynthia Holcomb Hall,
of California, to be United States Circuit Judge for the Ninth Circuit, vice a new position created by P.L. 98–353, approved July 10, 1984.

Charles E. Wiggins,
of Virginia, to be United States Circuit Judge for the Ninth Circuit, vice a new position created by P.L. 98–353, approved July 10, 1984.

Thomas J. Aquilino, Jr.,
of New York, to be a Judge of the United States Court of International Trade, vice Frederick Landis, retired.

Submitted August 2

Robert R. Davis,
of Illinois, to be a Commissioner of the Commodity Futures Trading Commission for the term expiring April 13, 1989, vice Philip M. Johnson, resigned.

Submitted August 10

Robert D. Stuart,
of Illinois, to be Ambassador Extraordinary and Plenipotentiary of the United States of America to Norway.

Mario F. Aguero,
of New York, to be a Commissioner of the Copyright Royalty Tribunal for the term of 7 years from September 27, 1984 (reappointment).

Lloyd Kaiser,
of Pennsylvania, to be a member of the Board of Directors of the Corporation for Public Broadcasting for a term expiring March 1, 1989, vice James T. Hackett, term expired.

Rosalie Gaull Silberman,
of California, to be a member of the Equal Employment Opportunity Commission for the remainder of the term expiring July 1, 1985, vice Cathie A. Shattuck, resigned.

Submitted August 10—Continued
Richard E. Carver,
of Illinois, to be an Assistant Secretary of the Air Force, vice Russell D. Hale, resigned.

Submitted September 5

Harvey J. Feldman,
of Florida, a career member of the Senior Foreign Service, Class of Minister-Counselor, to be the Alternate Representative of the United States of America for Special Political Affairs in the United Nations, with the rank of Ambassador.

William L. Eagleton, Jr.,
of Washington, a career member of the Senior Foreign Service, Class of Minister-Counselor, to be Ambassador Extraordinary and Plenipotentiary of the United States of America to the Syrian Arab Republic.

Melvyn Levitsky,
of Maryland, a career member of the Senior Foreign Service, Class of Counselor, to be Ambassador Extraordinary and Plenipotentiary of the United States of America to the People's Republic of Bulgaria.

Pauline Crowe Naftzger,
of California, to be a member of the National Museum Services Board for a term expiring December 6, 1988, vice Neil Harris, term expired.

Nam Pyo Suh,
of Massachusetts, to be an Assistant Director of the National Science Foundation, vice Francis Severin Johnson, resigned.

Rita R. Colwell,
of Maryland, to be a member of the National Science Board, National Science Foundation, for a term expiring May 10, 1990, vice Ernestine Friedl, term expired.

Submitted September 6

H. Ted Milburn,
of Tennessee, to be United States Circuit Judge for the Sixth Circuit, vice a new position created by P.L. 98–353, approved July 10, 1984.

James F. Holderman, Jr.,
of Illinois, to be United States District Judge for the Northern District of Illinois, vice a new position created by P.L. 98–353, approved July 10, 1984.

Richard F. Suhrheinrich,
of Michigan, to be United States District Judge for the Eastern District of Michigan, vice Russell James Harvey, retired.

Submitted September 6—Continued

James H. Jarvis II,

of Tennessee, to be United States District Judge for the Eastern District of Tennessee, vice a new position created by P.L. 98–353, approved July 10, 1984.

Thomas A. Higgins,

of Tennessee, to be United States District Judge for the Middle District of Tennessee, vice L. Clure Morton, retired.

James R. Laffoon,

of California, to be United States Marshal for the Southern District of California for the term of 4 years (reappointment).

Withdrawn September 6

Paul M. Bator,

of Massachusetts, to be United States Circuit Judge for the District of Columbia Circuit, vice a new position created by P.L. 98–353, approved July 10, 1984, which was sent to the Senate on July 31, 1984.

Submitted September 10

Jon R. Thomas,

of Tennessee, to be Assistant Secretary of State for International Narcotics Matters, vice Dominick L. DiCarlo, resigned.

J. Stapleton Roy,

of Pennsylvania, a career member of the Senior Foreign Service, Class of Minister-Counselor, to be Ambassador Extraordinary and Plenipotentiary of the United States of America to the Republic of Singapore.

William Arthur Rugh,

of Maryland, a career member of the Senior Foreign Service, Class of Minister-Counselor, to be Ambassador Extraordinary and Plenipotentiary of the United States of America to the Yemen Arab Republic.

Carl Edward Dillery,

of Washington, a career member of the Senior Foreign Service, Class of Counselor, to be Ambassador Extraordinary and Plenipotentiary of the United States of America to Fiji, and to serve concurrently and without additional compensation as Ambassador Extraordinary and Plenipotentiary of the United States of America to the Kingdom of Tonga, Ambassador Extraordinary and Plenipotentiary of the United States of America to Tuvalu, and Ambassador Extraordinary and Plenipotentiary of the United States of America to the Republic of Kiribati.

Submitted September 10—Continued

Charles R. Norgle, Sr.,

of Illinois, to be United States District Judge for the Northern District of Illinois, vice a new position created by P.L. 98–353, approved July 10, 1984.

Howell Cobb,

of Texas, to be United States District Judge for the Eastern District of Texas, vice Joe J. Fisher, retired.

Vilma Rosso Taracido,

of New York, to be Assayer of the United States Assay Office at New York, New York, vice Saul Silverman.

Linda M. Combs,

of North Carolina, to be Deputy Under Secretary for Management, Department of Education, vice Charles L. Heatherly, resigned.

Joe O'Neal Rogers,

of Virginia, to be United States Director of the Asian Development Bank, with the rank of Ambassador, vice John Augustus Bohn, Jr.

Howard D. Gutin,

of Texas, to be a member of the Board of Directors of the Corporation for Public Broadcasting for a term expiring March 1, 1989, vice William Lee Hanley, Jr.

Mary L. Azcuenaga,

of the District of Columbia, to be a Federal Trade Commissioner for the term of 7 years from September 26, 1984, vice Michael Pertschuk, term expiring.

Submitted September 11

William D. Keller,

of California, to be United States District Judge for the Central District of California, vice a new position created by P.L. 98–353, approved July 10, 1984.

Ronald E. Meredith,

of Kentucky, to be United States District Judge for the Western District of Kentucky, vice a new position created by P.L. 98–353, approved July 10, 1984.

F.A. Little, Jr.,

of Louisiana, to be United States District Judge for the Western District of Louisiana, vice Nauman S. Scott, retiring.

William G. Young,

of Massachusetts, to be United States District Judge for the District of Massachusetts, vice a

Submitted September 11—Continued
new position created by P.L. 98–353, approved July 10, 1984.

George La Plata,
of Michigan, to be United States District Judge for the Eastern District of Michigan, vice a new position created by P.L. 98–353, approved July 10, 1984.

R. Allan Edgar,
of Tennessee, to be United States District Judge for the Eastern District of Tennessee, vice H. Ted Milburn, elevated.

Walter S. Smith, Jr.,
of Texas, to be United States District Judge for the Western District of Texas, vice a new position created by P.L. 98–353, approved July 10, 1984.

Submitted September 12

The following-named persons to be Representatives and Alternate Representatives of the United States of America to the 39th Session of the General Assembly of the United Nations:

Representatives:

Jeane J. Kirkpatrick, of Maryland.
Jose S. Sorzano, of Virginia.
Charles McC. Mathias, Jr., United States Senator from the State of Maryland.
John H. Glenn, Jr., United States Senator from the State of Ohio.
Robert D. Ray, of Iowa.

Alternate Representatives:

Richard Schifter, of Maryland.
Alan Lee Keyes, of California.
Harvey J. Feldman, of Florida.
Preston H. Long, of New York.
Guadalupe Quintanilla, of Texas.

Submitted September 13

Edward J. Philbin,
of California, to be a Federal Maritime Commissioner for the term expiring June 30, 1989, vice James V. Day, term expired.

John N. Griesemer,
of Missouri, to be a Governor of the United States Postal Service for the remainder of the term expiring December 8, 1986, vice John R. McKean.

The following-named persons to be members of the Boards of Trustees of the Federal Hospital Insurance Trust Fund; the Federal Old-Age and Survivors Insurance Trust Fund and the Federal Disabilty Insurance Trust Fund; and the Federal Supplementary Medical Insurance Trust Fund for

Submitted September 13—Continued
terms of 4 years (new positions—P.L. 98–21 of April 20, 1983):

Mary Falvey Fuller, of California.
Suzanne Denbo Jaffe, of New York.

Submitted September 17

Edith H. Jones,
of Texas, to be United States Circuit Judge for the Fifth Circuit, vice a new position created by P.L. 98–353, approved July 10, 1984.

Joseph H. Rodriguez,
of New Jersey, to be United States District Judge for the District of New Jersey, vice a new position created by P.L. 98–353, approved July 10, 1984.

Herman J. Weber,
of Ohio, to be United States District Judge for the Southern District of Ohio, vice a new position created by P.L. 98–353, approved July 10, 1984.

Submitted September 18

Charles H. Dallara,
of Virginia, to be United States Executive Director of the International Monetary Fund for a term of 2 years, vice Richard D. Erb, resigned.

Jasper R. Clay, Jr.,
of Maryland, to be a Commissioner of the United States Parole Commission for a term of 6 years, vice Oliver James Keller, Jr., term expired.

Paul A. Volcker,
of New Jersey, to be United States Alternate Governor of the International Monetary Fund for a term of 5 years (reappointment).

Submitted September 19

John C. Lawn,
of Virginia, to be Deputy Administrator of Drug Enforcement, vice Frederick A. Rody, Jr.

William J. McGinnis, Jr.,
of New Jersey, to be a member of the Federal Labor Relations Authority for a term of five years expiring July 1, 1989, vice Ronald W. Haughton, term expired.

Reese H. Taylor, Jr.,
of Nevada, to be a member of the Interstate Commerce Commission for a term expiring December 31, 1985 (reappointment).

The following-named persons to be members of the National Museum Services Board for the terms indicated:

Submitted September 19—Continued
For the remainder of the term expiring December 6, 1986:

Faye Barrett Howell, of Georgia, vice Dorothy J. Tyson, resigned.

For a term expiring December 6, 1988:

Richard J. Herczog, of California, vice Emily Rauh Pulitzer, term expired.

Lawrence A. Wright,
of Vermont, to be a Judge of the United States Tax Court for a term expiring 15 years after he takes office, vice Darrell D. Wiles, retired.

Submitted September 21

Michael Huffington,
of Texas, to be an Assistant Secretary of Commerce, vice Lawrence J. Brady, resigned.

P.A. Mack, Jr.,
of the District of Columbia, to be a member of the National Credit Union Administration Board for the term of 6 years expiring August 2, 1989 (reappointment).

Francis Stephen Ruddy,
of Texas, to be Ambassador Extraordinary and Plenipotentiary of the United States of America to the Republic of Equatorial Guinea.

The following-named persons to be the Representative and Alternate Representatives of the United States of America to the 28th Session of the General Conference of the International Atomic Energy Agency:

Representative:

Richard T. Kennedy, of the District of Columbia.

Alternate Representatives:

Helmut A. Merklein, of Texas.
Nunzio J. Palladino, of Pennsylvania.
Richard Salisbury Williamson, of Virginia.

Submitted September 27

Mark L. Edelman,
of Missouri, to be an Assistant Administrator of the Agency for International Development, vice Frank J. Donatelli.

Cathryn C. Semerad,
of Maryland, to be an Assistant Administrator of the Agency for International Development, vice Jay F. Morris.

Submitted September 28

Howard D. McKibben,
of Nevada, to be United States District Judge for the District of Nevada, vice a new position created by P.L. 98–353, approved July 10, 1984.

Submitted October 3

Jose Manuel Casanova,
of Florida, to be United States Executive Director of the Inter-American Development Bank for a term of 3 years (reappointment).

Frank H. Conway,
of Massachusetts, to be a member of the Foreign Claims Settlement Commission of the United States for the term expiring September 30, 1987 (reappointment).

John D. Ward,
of Colorado, to be Director of the Office of Surface Mining Reclamation and Enforcement, vice James R. Harris.

Elizabeth Helms Adams,
of California, to be a member of the National Advisory Council on Women's Educational Programs for a term expiring May 8, 1987, vice Diana Powers Evans, term expired.

Richard H. Hughes,
of Oklahoma, to be a member of the Board of Directors of the Export-Import Bank of the United States for a term expiring January 20, 1985, vice James Ernest Yonge, resigned.

Karen Pryor,
of Washington, to be a member of the Marine Mammal Commission for the term expiring May 13, 1986, Vice Donald Kenneth MacCallum, term expired.

Robert Elsner,
of Alaska, to be a member of the Marine Mammal Commission for the term expiring May 13, 1987, vice Robert B. Weeden, term expired.

Annelise Graebner Anderson,
of California, to be a member of the National Science Board, National Science Foundation, for a term expiring May 10, 1990, vice Walter Eugene Massey, term expired.

Simon Ramo,
of California, to be a member of the National Science Board, National Science Foundation, for a term expiring May 10, 1990, vice Eugene H. Cota-Robles, term expired.

Karen J. Lindstedt-Siva,
of California, to be a member of the National Science Board, National Science Foundation, for a term expiring May 10, 1990, vice Charles Pence Slichter, term expired.

Submitted October 3—Continued

Tom C. Korologos,
of Virginia, to be a member of the United States Advisory Commission on Public Diplomacy for a term expiring July 1, 1987 (reappointment).

Submitted October 5

Alfred Clinton Moran,
of Illinois, to be an Assistant Secretary of Housing and Urban Development, vice Stephen J. Bollinger, deceased.

Eugene B. Burroughs,
of Virginia, to be a member of the Federal Council on the Aging for a term expiring June 5, 1987, vice Syd Captain, term expired.

The following-named persons to be members of the National Commission on Libraries and Information Science for terms expiring July 19, 1989:

   Patricia Barbour, of Michigan, vice Carlos A. Cuadra, term expired.
   Daniel W. Casey, of New York, vice Helmut A. Alpers, term expired.

Barbara W. Schlicher,
of New Jersey, to be a member of the Board of Directors of the National Corporation for Housing Partnerships for the remainder of the term expiring October 27, 1984, vice Frank J. Donatelli, resigned.

Barbara W. Schlicher,
of New Jersey, to be a member of the Board of Directors of the National Corporation for Housing Partnerships for the term expiring October 27, 1987 (reappointment).

Charles E. Courtney,
of California, to be an Associate Director of the United States Information Agency, vice W. Scott Thompson.

Ernest Eugene Pell,
of Maryland, to be an Associate Director of the United States Information Agency, vice Kenneth Y. Tomlinson.

John W. Shannon,
of Maryland, to be an Assistant Secretary of the Army (new position—P.L. 98–94 of September 24, 1983).

James A. Lastowka,
of Virginia, to be a member of the Federal Mine Safety and Health Review Commission for a term

Submitted October 5—Continued
of 6 years expiring August 30, 1990, vice A. E. Lawson, term expired.

Melvin T. Brunetti,
of Nevada, to be United States Circuit Judge for the Ninth Circuit, vice Herbert Y. C. Choy, retired.

Ann C. Williams,
of Illinois, to be United States District Judge for the Northern District of Illinois, vice a new position created by P.L. 98–353, approved July 10, 1984.

Donald E. Walter,
of Louisiana, to be United States District Judge for the Western District of Louisiana, vice a new position created by P.L. 98–353, approved July 10, 1984.

Mark L. Wolf,
of Massachusetts, to be United States District Judge for the District of Massachusetts, vice a new position created by P.L. 98–353, approved July 10, 1984.

Alice M. Batchelder,
of Ohio, to be United States District Judge for the Northern District of Ohio, vice a new position created by P.L. 98–353, approved July 10, 1984.

Submitted October 10

Richard H. Jones,
of Virginia, to be Deputy Administrator of the Federal Aviation Administration, vice Michael J. Fenello, resigned.

The following-named persons to be members of the Board of Directors of the United States Synthetic Fuels Corporation for the terms indicated:

For the term expiring August 16, 1990:

   Tom Corcoran, of Illinois, vice Milton M. Masson, Jr.

For the term expiring September 14, 1991:

   Paul Webster MacAvoy, of New York, vice Robert A.G. Monks, resigned.

Submitted October 11

Eric Reichl,
of Connecticut, to be a member of the Board of Directors of the United States Synthetic Fuels Corporation for the remainder of the term expiring September 14, 1986.

Appendix C—Checklist of White House Press Releases

The following list contains releases of the Office of the Press Secretary which are not included in this book.

Released July 4

Statement:
Guatemala's July 1 Constituent Assembly elections—by the U.S. delegation to observe the elections

Advance text:
Remarks at the Spirit of America Festival in Decatur, AL

Released July 5

Advance text:
Remarks at dedication ceremonies for the General Motors Assembly Plant in Orion Township, MI

Released July 6

Advance texts:
Remarks at the 102d annual convention of the Texas State Bar Association in San Antonio (2 releases)

Released July 9

Text:
Citation of the Presidential Citizens Medal awarded posthumously to Dennis W. Keogh

Released July 10

Advance text:
Remarks on signing Proclamation 5220, Food for Peace Day, 1984

Fact sheet:
Food aid initiative

Released July 11

Advance text:
Remarks on signing the 14th annual report of the Council on Environmental Quality

Released July 12

Transcript:
Exchange with a reporter on the 1984 Presidential campaign

Released July 12—Continued
Advance text:
Remarks at the annual "campvention" of the National Campers and Hikers Association in Bowling Green, KY

Released July 13

Advance text:
Remarks at a White House luncheon for elected Republican women officials and candidates

Released July 17

Fact sheet:
United States-Soviet Union direct communications link

Announcement:
Nomination of Susan Rebecca Holmes, Rufus Gunn King III, Colleen Kollar-Kotelly, A. Noel Anketell Kramer, Robert Isaac Richter, Emmet G. Sullivan, and Robert Samuel Tignor to be Associate Judges of the Superior Court of the District of Columbia

Released July 18

Statement:
President's meeting with aerospace industry executives and government trade officials who will visit China from July 21 to July 28—by Larry M. Speakes, Principal Deputy Press Secretary to the President

Fact sheet:
H.R. 4170, the Deficit Reduction Act of 1984

Announcement:
Seizure of illegal narcotics under the National Narcotics Border Interdiction System

Released July 19

Advance text:
Remarks at the summit conference of Caribbean heads of state at the University of South Carolina in Columbia

Released July 20

Advance text:
Remarks at a White House ceremony marking the observance of the 15th anniversary of the Apollo II lunar landing

Released July 20—Continued

Fact sheet:
15th anniversary of the Apollo II lunar landing

Fact sheet:
National policy on the commercial use of space

Released July 24

Statement:
Consumer Price Index for June—by Larry M. Speakes, Principal Deputy Press Secretary to the President

Announcement:
Nomination of Andrew Lewis Frey to be an Associate Judge of the District of Columbia Court of Appeals

Announcement:
Submission to the President of the reports of Emergency Boards Nos. 202 and 203 to investigate labor disputes between the Long Island Rail Road and the Brotherhood of Locomotive Engineers, the Brotherhood of Railway, Airline and Steamship Clerks, Freight Handlers, Express and Station Employees, and the American Railway Supervisors Association

Fact sheet:
Legislative priorities listed in the opening statement to the President's 26th news conference

Released July 25

Advance text:
Remarks at a Reagan-Bush rally in Austin, TX

Transcript:
Remarks of the Vice President at a Reagan-Bush rally in Austin, TX

Released July 26

Advance text:
Remarks at a Reagan-Bush rally in Atlanta, GA

Advance text:
Remarks at a Reagan-Bush rally in Elizabeth, NJ

Advance text:
Remarks at the St. Ann's Festival in Hoboken, NJ

Released July 27

Announcement:
Nomination of Helen M. Eversberg to be United States Attorney for the Eastern District of Texas

Released July 28

Advance text:
Remarks to members of the U.S. Olympic team in Los Angeles, CA

Released August 1

Announcement:
Nomination of Paul M. Bator to be a United States Circuit Judge for the District of Columbia Circuit, Frank H. Easterbrook to be a United States Circuit Judge for the Seventh Circuit, Cynthia Holcomb Hall to be a United States Circuit Judge for the Ninth Circuit, Emory M. Sneeden to be a United States Circuit Judge for the Fourth Circuit, Charles E. Wiggins to be a United States Circuit Judge for the Ninth Circuit, and Juan R. Torruella del Valle to be a United States Circuit Judge for the First Circuit

Announcement:
Nomination of Thomas J. Aquilino, Jr., to be a Judge of the United States Court of International Trade

Statement:
President's meeting with Archbishop Pio Laghi, Apostolic Delegate to the United States—by Larry M. Speakes, Principal Deputy Press Secretary to the President

Released August 6

Transcript:
Press briefing following his meeting with the President at Rancho del Cielo, the President's ranch near Santa Barbara, CA—by the Vice President

Released August 13

Advance text:
Remarks to United States medalists of the summer Olympic games in Los Angeles, CA

Released August 16

Advance text:
Remarks on signing H.R. 4325, the Child Support Enforcement Amendments of 1984

Released August 17

Advance text:
Remarks at a White House luncheon marking the 40th anniversary of the Warsaw uprising

Fact sheet:
40th anniversary of the Warsaw uprising

Transcript:
Press briefing on the Vice President's financial situation—by Dean Burch and Peter Teeley

Released August 19

Advance text:
Remarks at the Missouri State fair in Sedalia

Released August 20

Advance text:
Remarks at a Reagan-Bush rally in Cincinnati, OH

Advance text:
Remarks at a Reagan-Bush rally in Decatur, IL

Advance text:
Remarks at an agricultural forum in Decatur, IL

Released August 22

Advance text:
Remarks at a Reagan-Bush rally in Dallas, TX

Released August 23

Advance text:
Remarks at an ecumenical prayer breakfast in Dallas, TX

Advance text:
Remarks to the Republican National Hispanic Assembly in Dallas, TX

Advance text:
Remarks at a fundraising luncheon of the Republican National Committee in Dallas, TX

Advance text:
Remarks accepting the Presidential nomination at the Republican National Convention in Dallas, TX

Released August 24

Advance text:
Remarks to members of the Republican National Committee and the Reagan-Bush campaign staff in Dallas, TX

Advance text:
Remarks at the 85th national convention of the Veterans of Foreign Wars in Chicago, IL

Statement:
Response to former Vice President Walter F. Mondale's request for six debates during the 1984 Presidential campaign—by James A. Baker III, Assistant to the President and Chief of Staff

Released August 27

Statement:
Productivity and costs in the business sector for the second quarter—by Larry M. Speakes, Principal Deputy Press Secretary to the President

Released August 27—Continued

Advance text:
Remarks during a visit to Jefferson Junior High School

Advance text:
Remarks to winners of the Secondary School Recognition Program Awards

Released August 28

Advance text:
Remarks on presenting the 1983 Young American Medals for Bravery

Released August 29

Statement:
Index of leading economic indicators for July—by Larry M. Speakes, Principal Deputy Press Secretary to the President

Released August 30

Advance text:
Remarks during a visit to the Goddard Space Flight Center in Greenbelt, MD

Transcript:
Press briefing on administration efforts to reduce drug trafficking—by Attorney General William French Smith

Released August 31

Advance text:
Remarks to chapter presidents of the Catholic Golden Age Association

Released September 3

Advance text:
Remarks at a Reagan-Bush rally in Fountain Valley, CA

Advance text:
Remarks at a Reagan-Bush rally in Cupertino, CA

Released September 4

Advance text:
Remarks at the 66th annual convention of the American Legion in Salt Lake City, UT

Released September 5

Advance text:
Remarks at the "Choosing a Future" conference in Chicago, IL

Released September 6

Advance text:
Remarks at the international convention of B'nai B'rith

Announcement:
Nomination of H. Ted Milburn to be United States Circuit Judge for the Sixth Circuit

Announcement:
Nomination of James F. Holderman, Jr., to be United States District Judge for the Northern District of Illinois, Richard F. Suhrheinrich to be United States District Judge for the Eastern District of Michigan, and James H. Jarvis II to be United States District Judge for the Eastern District of Tennessee

Announcement:
Nomination of Thomas A. Higgins to be United States District Judge for the Middle District of Tennessee

Announcement:
Nomination of James Robert Laffoon to be United States Marshal for the Southern District of California

Released September 7

Announcement:
Nomination of Howell Cobb to be United States District Judge for the Eastern District of Texas

Announcement:
Nomination of Charles R. Norgle, Sr., to be United States District Judge for the Northern District of Illinois

Released September 9

Advance text:
Remarks at a Polish festival in Doylestown, PA

Released September 11

Announcement:
Nomination of William D. Keller to be United States District Judge for the Central District of California

Announcement:
Nomination of Ronald E. Meredith to be United States District Judge for the Western District of Kentucky

Announcement:
Nomination of F.A. Little, Jr., to be United States District Judge for the Western District of Louisiana

Released September 11—Continued
Announcement:
Nomination of William G. Young to be United States District Judge for the District of Massachusetts

Announcement:
Nomination of George La Plata to be United States District Judge for the Eastern District of Michigan

Announcement:
Nomination of R. Allan Edgar to be United States District Judge for the Eastern District of Tennessee

Announcement:
Nomination of Walter S. Smith, Jr., to be United States District Judge for the Western District of Texas

Fact sheet:
U.S.-Soviet long-term grain agreement

Released September 12

Advance text:
Remarks at dedication ceremonies for the Santa Maria Towers in Buffalo, NY

Advance text:
Remarks at a luncheon with community leaders in Buffalo, NY

Advance text:
Remarks at a Reagan-Bush rally in Endicott, NY

Fact sheet:
U.S. Army's new light infantry divisions

Released September 13

Advance text:
Remarks at the High Technological Corridor Board meeting in Nashville, TN

Advance text:
Remarks at a birthday celebration for Roy Acuff in Nashville, TN

Released September 14

Announcement:
Nomination of Edith H. Jones to be United States Circuit Judge for the Fifth Circuit

Announcement:
Nomination of Joseph H. Rodriguez to be United States District Judge for the District of New Jersey and Herman J. Weber to be United States District Judge for the Southern District of Ohio

Released September 15

Advance text:
Remarks at the annual dinner of the National Italian American Foundation

Released September 18

Transcript:
Press briefing and statement on the President's steel import relief determination—by Ambassador William E. Brock, U.S. Trade Representative

Released September 19

Advance text:
Remarks at a Reagan-Bush rally in Waterbury, CT

Advance text:
Remarks at a Reagan-Bush rally in Hammonton, NJ

Announcement:
Nomination of Lawrence A. Wright to be a Judge of the United States Tax Court

Released September 20

Advance text:
Remarks at a Reagan-Bush rally in Cedar Rapids, IA

Advance text:
Remarks to farmers in Norway, IA

Advance text:
Remarks at a community picnic in Fairfax, IA

Statements:
On the report of the Independent Counsel investigating his financial affairs—by Edwin Meese III, Counsellor to the President (2 releases)

Advance text:
Remarks to employees of Westinghouse Furniture Systems in Grand Rapids, MI

Advance text:
Remarks at a Reagan-Bush rally in Grand Rapids, MI

Released September 21

Statement:
Consumer Price Index for August—by Larry M. Speakes, Principal Deputy Press Secretary to the President

Released September 23

Transcript:
Press briefing on the President's meetings and activities while in New York City to address the

Released September 23—Continued
39th Session of the United Nations General Assembly—by Secretary of State George P. Shultz

Fact sheet:
U.S.-Soviet relations

Advance text:
Remarks at a reception for heads of state and delegations to the 39th Session of the United Nations General Assembly in New York, New York

Released September 24

Advance text:
Address before the 39th Session of the United Nations General Assembly in New York, New York

Fact sheet:
U.S. nuclear testing

Transcript:
Press briefing on the President's meetings and activities while in New York to address the 39th Session of the United Nations General Assembly—by Secretary of State George P. Shultz

Fact sheet:
S. 1538, Drug Price Competition and Patent Term Restoration Act of 1984

Released September 25

Advance text:
Remarks at the annual meeting of the Boards of Governors of the International Monetary Fund and the World Bank Group

Announcement:
Submission by Presidential Emergency Board No. 204 of its report to the President concerning a dispute between the Port Authority Trans-Hudson Corporation (PATH) and the Brotherhood of Railroad Signalmen

Released September 26

Advance text:
Remarks at Bowling Green State University in Bowling Green, OH

Advance text:
Remarks at the Timken Faircrest Steel Plant in Canton, OH

Advance text:
Remarks at the annual Family Oktoberfest in Milwaukee, WI

Released September 28

Announcement:
Nomination of Howard D. McKibben to be United States District Judge for the District of Nevada

Transcript:
Press briefing on the President's meeting with Soviet Foreign Minister Andrey A. Gromyko—by Secretary of State George P. Shultz

Released October 1

Advance text:
Remarks at naturalization ceremonies for new U.S. citizens in Detroit, MI

Advance text:
Remarks to the Economic Club of Detroit in Detroit, MI

Advance text:
Remarks at a Reagan-Bush rally in Gulfport, MS

Released October 2

Advance text:
Remarks at a Reagan-Bush rally in Brownsville, TX

Advance text:
Remarks at a Reagan-Bush rally in Corpus Christi, TX

Advance text:
Remarks at a "Victory '84" fundraising dinner in Houston, TX

Released October 5

Statement:
Unemployment rate for September—by Larry M. Speakes, Principal Deputy Press Secretary to the President

Transcript:
Press briefing on methods for reducing waste, fraud, and abuse in the Department of Defense—by Deputy Secretary of Defense William Howard Taft IV and Joseph H. Sherick, Inspector General, Department of Defense

Announcement:
Nomination of Melvin T. Brunetti to be United States Circuit Judge for the Ninth Circuit

Announcement:
Nomination of Alice M. Batchelder to be United States District Judge for the Northern District of Ohio, Donald E. Walter to be United States District Judge for the Western District of Louisiana, Ann C. Williams to be United States District

Released October 5—Continued
Judge for the Northern District of Illinois, and Mark L. Wolf to be United States District Judge for the District of Massachusetts

Released October 8

Advance text:
Remarks at a Reagan-Bush rally in Charlotte, NC

Advance text:
Remarks at dedication ceremonies for a statue of Christopher Columbus in Baltimore, MD

Released October 10

Advance text:
Remarks at St. Agatha High School in Detroit, MI

Advance text:
Remarks to the Heritage Council in Warren, MI

Advance text:
Remarks at a Reagan-Bush rally in Warren, MI

Statement:
Regarding the President's May 18 medical examination and report—by Dr. Daniel Ruge, Physician to the President

Released October 11

Advance text:
Remarks at the 40th anniversary dinner of the United Negro College Fund

Released October 12

Advance text:
Remarks at a Reagan-Bush rally in Dayton, OH

Released October 15

Advance text:
Remarks at the University of Alabama-Tuscaloosa in Tuscaloosa

Advance text:
Remarks at a Reagan-Bush rally in Macon, GA

Advance text:
Remarks at a Reagan-Bush rally in Greenville, SC

Released October 16

Advance text:
Remarks at Bolingbrook High School in Bolingbrook, IL

Advance text:
Remarks at a Reagan-Bush rally in Glen Ellyn, IL

Released October 18

Advance text:
Remarks at the Alfred E. Smith Memorial Dinner in New York, New York

Released October 22

Transcript:
Interview of Senator Paul Laxalt, chairman of the Reagan-Bush Reelection Committee, by ABC's "Good Morning America"

Transcript:
Question-and-answer session with reporters on the Presidential debate and the campaign—by Mrs. Reagan

Advance text:
Remarks at a Rockwell International facility in Palmdale, CA

Transcript:
Interview of Senator Paul Laxalt, chairman of the Reagan-Bush Reelection Committee, by NBC News "Today"

Transcript:
Interview of Edward J. Rollins, Jr., director of the Reagan-Bush Reelection Committee, by "CBS Morning News"

Released October 23

Advance text:
Excerpts of remarks at a Reagan-Bush rally in Seattle, WA

Released October 24

Advance text:
Excerpts of remarks at a Reagan-Bush rally in Columbus, OH

Statement:
Consumer Price Index for September—by Larry M. Speakes, Principal Deputy Press Secretary to the President

Advance text:
Remarks at a ceremony marking the first anniversary of the rescue mission in Grenada

Released October 26

Advance text:
Remarks to members of the congregation of Temple Hillel and Jewish community leaders in Valley Stream, NY

Advance text:
Remarks at a Reagan-Bush rally in Fairfield, CT

Released October 29

Advance text:
Excerpt of remarks at Reagan-Bush rallies in Pennsylvania and West Virginia

Released October 31

Statement:
Index of leading economic indicators for September—by Larry M. Speakes, Principal Deputy Press Secretary to the President

Released November 1

Advance text:
Remarks at Reagan-Bush rallies

Released November 2

Advance text:
Excerpt of remarks at a Reagan-Bush rally in Cleveland, OH

Statement:
Unemployment statistics for October—by Larry M. Speakes, Principal Deputy Press Secretary to the President

Released November 3

Advance text:
Excerpt of remarks at a Reagan-Bush rally in Winterset, IA

Released November 4

Advance text:
Remarks in Rochester, MN, prior to a question-and-answer session with reporters

Transcript:
Remarks at a Reagan-Bush rally in Chicago, IL—by the Vice President

Released November 6

Transcript:
Question-and-answer session with reporters on Mrs. Reagan's condition following a fall at the Red Lion Inn in Sacramento, CA—by Larry M. Speakes, Principal Deputy Press Secretary to the President

Released November 7

Transcript:
Question-and-answer session with reporters on the election results—by James A. Baker III, Assistant to the President and Chief of Staff

Released November 7—Continued

Transcript:
Press briefing on the election results—by Edward J. Rollins, Jr., director of the Reagan-Bush Reelection Committee

Released November 16

Transcript:
Press briefing on U.S. food assistance to Ethiopia and other African nations affected by the drought—by M. Peter McPherson, Administrator of the Agency for International Development

Released November 22

Transcript:
Press briefing on the resumption of U.S.-Soviet negotiations—by Robert C. McFarlane, Assistant to the President for National Security Affairs

Released November 29

Transcript:
Press briefing following the President's meeting with the Republican congressional leadership—by Senate Majority Leader Robert Dole and House Minority Leader Robert H. Michel

Fact sheet:
President's meeting with the American winners of the Nansen Medal, the highest international honor for those who aid refugees

Released December 3

Transcript:
Press briefing following his meeting with the President to discuss developments in southern Africa—by Assistant Secretary of State for African Affairs Chester A. Crocker

Released December 4

Advance text:
Toast at the state dinner honoring President Jaime Lusinchi of Venezuela

Released December 5

Transcript:
Press briefing on the President's announcement concerning additional U.S. food assistance to Africa—by Secretary of Agriculture John R. Block

Released December 5—Continued
and M. Peter McPherson, Administrator of the Agency for International Development

Released December 6

Statement:
On the President's meeting with the Republican congressional leadership to discuss budget issues—by Larry M. Speakes, Principal Deputy Press Secretary to the President

Transcript:
Press briefing on the President's meeting with the Republican congressional leadership to discuss budget issues—by Larry M. Speakes, Principal Deputy Press Secretary to the President, Senate Majority Leader Robert Dole, and House Minority Leader Robert H. Michel

Released December 10

Advance text:
Remarks at a ceremony marking the observance of International Human Rights Day

Released December 11

Transcript:
Press briefing following her meeting with the President to report on the situation in the United Nations General Assembly—by Jeane J. Kirkpatrick, U.S. Representative to the United Nations

Released December 13

Advance text:
Remarks on lighting the National Christmas Tree at the Christmas Pageant of Peace

Released December 14

Statement:
Producer Price Index for November—by Larry M. Speakes, Principal Deputy Press Secretary to the President

Fact sheet:
Resumption of U.S. immigration and refugee programs in Cuba

Appendix D—Acts Approved by the President

Approved June 30

S.J. Res. 297 / Public Law 98–330
A joint resolution to designate the month of June 1984 as "Veterans' Preference Month".

Approved July 2

S.J. Res. 257 / Public Law 98–331
A joint resolution to designate the period July 1, 1984, through July 1, 1985, as the "Year of the Ocean".

H.J. Res. 492 / Public Law 98–332
A joint resolution making an urgent supplemental appropriation for the fiscal year ending September 30, 1984, for the Department of Agriculture.

S.J. Res. 298 / Public Law 98–333
A joint resolution to proclaim the month of July 1984 as "National Ice Cream Month" and July 15, 1984, as "National Ice Cream Day".

S. 1135 / Public Law 98–334
An act to consent to the Goose Lake Basin Compact between the States of California and Oregon.

Approved July 3

S.J. Res. 59 / Public Law 98–335
A joint resolution to authorize and request the President to designate February 27, 1986, as "Hugo LaFayette Black Day".

S.J. Res. 150 / Public Law 98–336
A joint resolution to designate August 4, 1984, as "Coast Guard Day".

S.J. Res. 230 / Public Law 98–337
A joint resolution to designate the week of October 7, 1984 through October 13, 1984 as "National Birds of Prey Conservation Week".

S.J. Res. 303 / Public Law 98–338
A joint resolution to designate the week of December 9, 1984, through December 15, 1984, as "National Drunk and Drugged Driving Awareness Week".

S. 837 / Public Law 98–339
Washington State Wilderness Act of 1984.

Approved July 3—Continued
H.R. 5565 / Public Law 98–340
An act to direct the Architect of the Capitol and the District of Columbia to enter into an agreement for the conveyance of certain real property, to direct the Secretary of the Interior to permit the District of Columbia and the Washington Metropolitan Area Transit Authority to construct, maintain, and operate certain transportation improvements on Federal property, and to direct the Architect of the Capitol to provide the Washington Metropolitan Area Transit Authority access to certain real property.

S.J. Res. 270 / Public Law 98–341
A joint resolution designating the week of July 1 through July 8, 1984, as "National Duck Stamp Week" and 1984 as the "Golden Anniversary Year of the Duck Stamp".

Approved July 6

H.R. 5953 / Public Law 98–342
An act to increase the statutory limit on the public debt.

Approved July 9

S.J. Res. 238 / Public Law 98–343
A joint resolution to designate the week beginning November 19, 1984, as "National Adoption Week".

S. 2403 / Public Law 98–344
An act to declare that the United States holds certain lands in trust for the Pueblo de Cochiti.

H.J. Res. 555 / Public Law 98–345
A joint resolution to designate July 20, 1984, as "Space Exploration Day".

H.J. Res. 544 / Public Law 98–346
A joint resolution to designate the week beginning September 2, 1984, as "National School-Age Child Care Awareness Week".

H.R. 4921 / Public Law 98–347
An act to provide for the selection of additional lands for inclusion within the Bon Secour National Wildlife Refuge, and for other purposes.

Approved July 9—Continued

S.J. Res. 278 / Public Law 98–348
A joint resolution to commemorate the one hundredth anniversary of the Bureau of Labor Statistics.

S.J. Res. 306 / Public Law 98–349
A joint resolution to proclaim July 10, 1984, as "Food for Peace Day".

H.J. Res. 566 / Public Law 98–350
A joint resolution to designate the week beginning on October 7, 1984, as "National Neighborhood Housing Services Week".

H.J. Res. 604 / Public Law 98–351
A joint resolution to designate July 9, 1984, as "African Refugees Relief Day".

Approved July 10

S. 2375 / Public Law 98–352
Small Business Secondary Market Improvements Act of 1984.

H.R. 5174 / Public Law 98–353
Bankruptcy Amendments and Federal Judgeship Act of 1984.

H.R. 5404 / Public Law 98–354
An act allowing William R. Gianelli to continue to serve as a member of the Board of the Panama Canal Commission after his retirement as an officer of the Department of Defense.

S. 2729 / Private Law 98–15
An act for the relief of Jean Willhelm Willrich.

Approved July. 11

H.R. 5950 / Public Law 98–355
An act to increase the Federal contribution for the Quadrennial Political Party Presidential National Nominating Conventions.

H.J. Res. 567 / Public Law 98–356
A joint resolution to designate 1984 as the "Year of the St. Lawrence Seaway" and June 27, 1984, as "St. Lawrence Seaway Day".

Approved July 13

H.R. 3825 / Public Law 98–357
An act to establish a boundary for the Black Canyon of the Gunnison National Monument, and for other purposes.

H.R. 4308 / Public Law 98–358
An act granting the consent of the Congress to an interstate compact for the preparation of a feasibility study for the development of a system of high-speed intercity rail passenger service.

Approved July 13—Continued

H.R. 3922 / Public Law 98–359
Postal Savings System Statute of Limitatons Act.

H.R. 3927 / Private Law 98–16
An act for the relief of Kenneth L. Perrin.

Approved July 16

H.R. 5653 / Public Law 98–360
An act making appropriations for energy and water development for the fiscal year ending September 30, 1985, and for other purposes.

H.R. 5154 / Public Law 98–361
National Aeronautics and Space Administration Authorization Act, 1985.

H.R. 3075 / Public Law 98–362
Small Business Computer Security and Education Act of 1984.

Approved July 17

H.R. 4616 / Public Law 98–363
An act to amend the Surface Transportation Assistance Act of 1982 to require States to use at least 8 per centum of their highway safety apportionments for developing and implementing comprehensive programs concerning the use of child restraint systems in motor vehicles, and for other purposes.

H.R. 4997 / Public Law 98–364
An act to authorize appropriations to carry out the Marine Mammal Protection Act of 1972, for fiscal years 1985 through 1988, and for other purposes.

H.R. 5155 / Public Law 98–365
Land Remote-Sensing Commercialization Act of 1984.

H.R. 5740 / Public Law 98–366
Barrow Gas Field Transfer Act of 1984.

H.R. 5753 / Public Law 98–367
Legislative Branch Appropriations Act, 1985.

H.J. Res. 548 / Public Law 98–368
A joint resolution authorizing the President's Commission on Organized Crime to compel the attendance and testimony of witnesses and the production of information, and for other purposes.

Approved July 18

H.R. 4170 / Public Law 98–369
Deficit Reduction Act of 1984.

Approved July 18—Continued

H.R. 3169 / Public Law 98–370
Renewable Energy Industry Development Act of 1983.

H.R. 5713 / Public Law 98–371
Department of Housing and Urban Development—Independent Agencies Appropriation Act, 1985.

Approved July 23

H.R. 29 / Public Law 98–372
An act to recognize the organization known as the Polish Legion of American Veterans, U.S.A.

Approved July 31

S. 373 / Public Law 98–373
An act to provide for a comprehensive national policy dealing with national research needs and objectives in the Arctic, for a National Critical Materials Council, for development of a continuing and comprehensive national materials policy, for programs necessary to carry out that policy, including Federal programs of advanced materials research and technology, and for innovation in basic materials industries, and for other purposes.

Approved August 7

H.J. Res. 577 / Public Law 98–374
A joint resolution designating August 1984 as "Polish American Heritage Month".

H.R. 1492 / Public Law 98–375
Christopher Columbus Quincentenary Jubilee Act.

Approved August 10

H.R. 559 / Public Law 98–376
Insider Trading Sanctions Act of 1984.

Approved August 11

H.R. 1310 / Public Law 98–377
Education for Economic Security Act.

Approved August 16

H.R. 4325 / Public Law 98–378
Child Support Enforcement Amendments of 1984.

H.R. 4952 / Public Law 98–379
An act to authorize the Secretary of Defense to provide assistance to certain Indian tribes for expenses incurred for community impact planning activities relating to the planned deployment of the MX missile system in Nevada and Utah in the

Approved August 16—Continued
same manner that State and local governments were provided assistance for such expenses.

Approved August 17

S.J. Res. 302 / Public Law 98–380
A joint resolution to designate the month of September 1984 as "National Sewing Month".

S. 268 / Public Law 98–381
Hoover Power Plant Act of 1984.

S. 1145 / Public Law 98–382
An act to recognize the organization known as the Catholic War Veterans of the United States of America, Incorporated.

S.J. Res. 248 / Public Law 98–383
A joint resolution designating August 21, 1984, as "Hawaii Statehood Silver Jubilee Day".

S.J. Res. 272 / Public Law 98–384
A joint resolution recognizing the anniversaries of the Warsaw uprising and the Polish resistance to invasion of Poland during World War II.

Approved August 21

H.J. Res. 529 / Public Law 98–385
A joint resolution to designate the week of September 23, 1984, through September 29, 1984, as "National Drug Abuse Education and Prevention Week".

H.J. Res. 574 / Public Law 98–386
A joint resolution to designate the week beginning on September 9, 1984, as "National Community Leadership Week".

H.J. Res. 583 / Public Law 98–387
A joint resolution to designate January 27, 1985, as "National Jerome Kern Day".

H.J. Res. 587 / Public Law 98–388
A joint resolution designating the month of August 1984 as "Ostomy Awareness Month".

H.J. Res. 597 / Public Law 98–389
A joint resolution to designate the week beginning September 2, 1984, as "Youth of America Week".

S. 1224 / Public Law 98–390
An act to provide for the disposition of certain undistributed judgment funds awarded the Creek Nation.

S. 1806 / Public Law 98–391
An act to recognize the organization known as the Jewish War Veterans of the United States of America, Incorporated.

Approved August 21—Continued

S. 2556 / Public Law 98–392
An act to authorize appropriations for the American Folklife Center for fiscal years 1985 and 1986, and for other purposes.

S. 2820 / Public Law 98–393
An act to name the Federal Building in McAlester, Oklahoma, the "Carl Albert Federal Building".

S.J. Res. 338 / Public Law 98–394
A joint resolution to congratulate the athletes of the United States Olympic team for their performance and achievements in the 1984 winter Olympic games in Sarajevo, Yugoslavia and the 1984 summer Olympic games in Los Angeles, California.

S. 1429 / Public Law 98–395
Small Business Development Center Improvement Act of 1984.

Approved August 22

H.R. 6040 / Public Law 98–396
Second Supplemental Appropriations Act, 1984.

Approved August 23

H.R. 4280 / Public Law 98–397
Retirement Equity Act of 1984.

Approved August 24

S. 746 / Public Law 98–398
An act to establish the Illinois and Michigan Canal National Heritage Corridor in the State of Illinois, and for other purposes.

Approved August 27

H.R. 5890 / Public Law 98–399
An act to establish a commission to assist in the first observance of the Federal legal holiday honoring Martin Luther King, Jr.

S. 1547 / Public Law 98–400
An act to amend the conditions of a grant of certain lands to the town of Olathe, Colorado, and for other purposes.

S. 2036 / Public Law 98–401
An act to require the Secretary of the Interior to convey to the city of Brigham City, Utah, certain land and improvements in Box Elder County, Utah.

Approved August 28

H.R. 4596 / Public Law 98–402
An act to amend section 1601(d) of Public Law 96–607 to permit the Secretary of the Interior to

Approved August 28—Continued
acquire title in fee simple to McClintock House at 16 East Williams Street, Waterloo, New York.

S. 2085 / Public Law 98–403
An act to provide continuing authority to the Secretary of Agriculture for recovering costs associated with cotton classing services to producers and to authorize the Secretary of Agriculture to invest funds derived from fees for certain voluntary grading and inspection services.

H.R. 1652 / Public Law 98–404
The Reclamation Safety of Dams Act Amendments of 1984.

H.R. 3787 / Public Law 98–405
An act to amend the National Trails System Act by adding the California Trail to the study list, and for other purposes.

H.R. 4707 / Public Law 98–406
Arizona Wilderness Act of 1984.

H.R. 5604 / Public Law 98–407
Military Construction Authorization Act, 1985.

S. 2201 / Public Law 98–408
An act to convey certain lands to the Zuni Indian Tribe for religious purposes.

Approved August 29

H.R. 4214 / Public Law 98–409
An act to establish a State Mining and Mineral Resources Research Institute program, and for other purposes.

H.J. Res. 452 / Public Law 98–410
A joint resolution recognizing the important contributions of the arts to a complete education.

Approved August 30

H.R. 5712 / Public Law 98–411
Departments of Commerce, Justice, and State, the Judiciary, and Related Agencies Appropriation Act, 1985

H.J. Res. 600 / Public Law 98–412
An act to amend the Agriculture and Food Act of 1981 to provide for the establishment of a commission to study and make recommendations concerning agriculture-related trade and export policies, programs, and practices of the United States.

Approved September 21

H.J. Res. 505 / Public Law 98–413
A joint resolution designating the week beginning September 23, 1984, as "National Adult Day Care Center Week".

Approved September 24

H.J. Res. 545 / Public Law 98–414
A joint resolution designating the week of September 16 through 22, 1984 as "Emergency Medicine Week".

S.J. Res. 333 / Public Law 98–415
A joint resolution to designate September 21, 1984, as "World War I Aces and Aviators Day".

S.J. Res. 340 / Public Law 98–416
A joint resolution to designate the week of September 23, 1984 as "National Historically Black Colleges Week".

S. 1538 / Public Law 98–417
Drug Price Competition and Patent Term Restoration Act of 1984.

Approved September 25

S.J. Res. 275 / Public Law 98–418
A joint resolution to designate the month of October 1984 as "National Spina Bifida Month".

S. 1546 / Public Law 98–419
Deepwater Port Act Amendments of 1984.

H.R. 5177 / Public Law 98–420
An act granting the consent of Congress to an amendment to the Wheeling Creek Watershed Protection and Flood Prevention District Compact entered into by the States of West Virginia and Pennsylvania.

S. 806 / Public Law 98–421
An act to provide for a plan to reimburse the Okefenoke Rural Electric Membership Corporation for the costs incurred in installing electric service to the Cumberland Island National Seashore.

S.J. Res. 25 / Public Law 98–422
A joint resolution redesignating the Saint Croix Island National Monument in the State of Maine as the "Saint Croix Island International Historic Site".

S.J. Res. 334 / Public Law 98–423
A joint resolution to provide for the designation of the month of November 1984, as "National Hospice Month".

Approved September 25—Continued
S.J. Res. 335 / Public Law 98–424
A joint resolution to designate the week beginning on May 19, 1985, as "National Tourism Week".

Approved September 28

H.R. 1437 / Public Law 98–425
California Wilderness Act of 1984.

S. 38 / Public Law 98–426
Longshore and Harbor Workers' Compensation Act Amendments of 1984.

S. 2418 / Public Law 98–427
An act to authorize and direct the Librarian of Congress, subject to the supervision and authority of a Federal, civilian, or military agency, to proceed with the construction of the Library of Congress Mass Book Deacidification Facility, and for other purposes.

S. 2155 / Public Law 98–428
Utah Wilderness Act of 1984.

S. J. Res. 336 / Public Law 98–429
A joint resolution to proclaim October 23, 1984, as "A Time of Remembrance" for all victims of terrorism throughout the world.

H.R. 9 / Public Law 98–430
Florida Wilderness Act of 1983.

H.J. Res. 453 / Public Law 98–431
A joint resolution designating the week of September 30 through October 6, 1984, as "National High-Tech Week".

S. 1735 / Public Law 98–432
Shoalwater Bay Indian Tribe—Dexter-by-the-Sea Claim Settlement Act.

H.J. Res. 153 / Public Law 98–433
A joint resolution to designate the week beginning October 7, 1984, as "National Children's Week".

H.R. 71 / Public Law 98–434
High Plains States Groundwater Demonstration Program Act of 1983.

H.R. 1250 / Public Law 98–435
Voting Accessibility for the Elderly and Handicapped Act.

S.J. Res. 304 / Public Law 98–436
A joint resolution to designate the month of October 1984 as "National Quality Month".

Approved September 28—Continued

S.J. Res. 254 / Public Law 98–437
A joint resolution to designate the month of October 1984 as "National Down's Syndrome Month".

S.J. Res. 227 / Public Law 98–438
A joint resolution designating the week beginning November 11, 1984, as "National Women Veterans Recognition Week".

S. 598 / Public Law 98–439
An act to authorize a land conveyance from the Department of Agriculture to Payson, Arizona.

H.R.743 / Private Law 98–17
An act for the relief of Theda June Davis.

H.R. 2387 / Private Law 98–18
An act for the relief of Benjamin B. Doeh.

S. 277 / Private Law 98–19
An act for the relief of Marlon Dolon Opelt.

S. 301 / Private Law 98–20
An act for the relief of Kim Hae Ok Heimberger.

S. 435 / Private Law 98–21
An act for the relief of Joseph Antonio Francis.

S. 514 / Private Law 98–22
An act for the relief of Seela Jeremiah Piula.

S. 692 / Private Law 98–23
An act for the relief of Charles Gaudencio Beeman, Paul Amado Beeman, Elizabeth Beeman, and Joshua Valente Beeman.

S. 798 / Private Law 98–24
An act for the relief of Grietje Rhea Pietens Beumer, Johan Christian Beumer, Cindy Larissa Beumer, and Cedric Grant Beumer.

S. 1060 / Private Law 98–25
An act for the relief of Samuel Joseph Edgar.

S. 1140 / Private Law 98–26
An act for the relief of Patrick P.W. Tso, Ph.D.

Approved October 3

S. 2040 / Public Law 98–440
Secondary Mortgage Market Enhancement Act of 1984.

H.J. Res. 653 / Public Law 98–441
A joint resolution making continuing appropriations for the fiscal year 1985, and for other purposes.

H.J. Res. 392 / Public Law 98–442
A joint resolution to designate December 7, 1984 as "National Pearl Harbor Remembrance Day"

Approved October 3—Continued
on the occasion of the anniversary of the attack on Pearl Harbor.

H.R. 1150 / Private Law 98–27
An act for the relief of Teodoro N. Salanga, Junior.

H.R. 1236 / Private Law 98–28
An act for the relief of Andrew and Julia Lui.

H.R. 5343 / Private Law 98–29
An act for the relief of Narciso Archila Navarrete.

S. 1989 / Private Law 98–30
An act for the relief of Vladimir Victorovich Yakimetz.

Approved October 4

H.R. 5297 / Public Law 98–443
Civil Aeronautics Board Sunset Act of 1984.

S. 2732 / Public Law 98–444
An act to amend the Wild and Scenic Rivers Act to permit the control of the lamprey eel in the Pere Marquette River and to designate a portion of the Au Sable River, Michigan, as a component of the National Wild and Scenic Rivers System.

H.R. 5147 / Public Law 98–445
Eastern Pacific Tuna Licensing Act of 1984.

H.J. Res. 554 / Public Law 98–446
A joint resolution to designate the week of November 11, 1984, through November 17, 1984, as "Women in Agriculture Week".

H.J. Res. 605 / Public Law 98–447
A joint resolution regarding the implementation of the policy of the United States Government in opposition to the practice of torture by any foreign government.

H.J. Res. 606 / Public Law 98–448
A joint resolution to designate the week of October 14, 1984, through October 21, 1984, as "National Housing Week".

S. 2614 / Public Law 98–449
Indian Financing Act Amendments of 1984.

S. 32 / Public Law 98–450
Record Rental Amendment of 1984.

S. 2000 / Public Law 98–451
An act to allow variable interest rates for Indian funds held in trust by the United States.

S. 1770 / Public Law 98–452
An act to extend the lease terms of Federal oil and gas lease numbered U–39711.

Approved October 4—Continued
H.R. 718 / Private Law 98–31
An act for the relief of Samuel C. Willet.

Approved October 5

H.J. Res. 656 / Public Law 98–453
A joint resolution making further continuing appropriations for fiscal year 1985.

H.R. 5561 / Public Law 98–454
An act to enhance the economic development of Guam, the Virgin Islands, American Samoa, the Northern Mariana Islands, and for other purposes.

Approved October 6

H.J. Res. 659 / Public Law 98–455
A joint resolution making further continuing appropriations for fiscal year 1985.

Approved October 9

H.J. Res. 649 / Public Law 98–456
A joint resolution changing the date for the counting of the electoral votes in 1985.

H.R. 1904 / Public Law 98–457
Child Abuse Amendments of 1984.

S.J. Res. 322 / Public Law 98–458
A joint resolution designating the week beginning on October 7, 1984, as "Mental Illness Awareness Week".

S. 2603 / Public Law 98–459
Older Americans Act Amendments of 1984.

H.R. 3755 / Public Law 98–460
Social Security Disability Benefits Reform Act of 1984.

Approved October 10

H.J. Res. 663 / Public Law 98–461
A joint resolution making further continuing appropriations for fiscal year 1985.

Approved October 11

S. 1841 / Public Law 98–462
National Cooperative Research Act of 1984.

S.J. Res. 201 / Public Law 98–463
A joint resolution to provide for the designation of the week of November 25 through December 1, 1984, as "National Epidermolysis Bullosa Awareness Week".

S. 2688 / Public Law 98–464
An act to authorize appropriations for fiscal year 1985 to carry out the Natural Gas Pipeline Safety

Approved October 11—Continued
Act of 1968 and the Hazardous Liquid Pipeline Safety Act of 1979, and for other purposes.

S.J. Res. 237 / Public Law 98–465
A joint resolution to designate the week of November 25, 1984, through December 1, 1984, as "National Home Care Week".

S. 197 / Public Law 98–466
An act to direct the Secretary of the Department of Transportation to conduct an independent study to determine the adequacy of certain industry practices and Federal Aviation Administration rules and regulations, and for other purposes.

S.J. Res. 273 / Public Law 98–467
A joint resolution to designate the week of October 7, 1984, through October 13, 1984, as "Smokey Bear Week".

S.J. Res. 324 / Public Law 98–468
A joint resolution designating the month of November 1984 as "National Christmas Seal Month".

H.R. 5221 / Public Law 98–469
An act to extend through September 30, 1988, the period during which amendments to the United States Grain Standards Act contained in section 155 of the Omnibus Budget Reconciliation Act of 1981 remain effective, and for other purposes.

H.R. 3130 / Public Law 98–470
An act to authorize amendments to a certain repayment and water service contract for the Frenchman Unit of the Pick-Sloan Missouri River Basin Program.

S.J. Res. 260 / Public Law 98–471
A joint resolution designating the week beginning on November 11, 1984, as "National Blood Pressure Awareness Week".

S.J. Res. 295 / Public Law 98–472
A joint resolution to provide for the designation of the week of October 14 through October 20, 1984, as "Myasthenia Gravis Awareness Week".

H.R. 4968 / Private Law 98–32
An act to provide for the conveyance by the Secretary of Energy of surface rights to certain parcels of land located on Naval Petroleum Reserve Numbered 2 in the State of California on which private residences are located.

Approved October 12

H.J. Res. 648 / Public Law 98–473
A joint resolution making continuing appropriations for the fiscal year 1985, and for other purposes.

H.R. 3979 / Public Law 98–474
Comprehensive Smoking Education Act.

Approved October 13

H.J. Res. 654 / Public Law 98–475
A joint resolution increasing the statutory limit on the public debt.

Approved October 15

S.J. Res. 332 / Public Law 98–476
A joint resolution to proclaim October 16, 1984, as "World Food Day".

H.R. 5164 / Public Law 98–477
Central Intelligence Agency Information Act.

H.R. 960 / Private Law 98–33
An act to confer citizenship posthumously on Corporal Wladyslaw Staniszewski.

Approved October 16

H.R. 2838 / Public Law 98–478
Federal Timber Contract Payment Modification Act.

Approved October 17

S. 2819 / Public Law 98–479
Housing and Community Development Technical Amendments Act of 1984.

H.R. 2878 / Public Law 98–480
An act to amend and extend the Library Services and Construction Act.

H.R. 5540 / Public Law 98–481
Coos, Lower Umpqua, and Siuslaw Restoration Act.

H.R. 3697 / Public Law 98–482
Fire Island National Seashore Amendments Act of 1984.

H.R. 2889 / Public Law 98–483
An act to amend the National Historic Preservation Act, and for other purposes.

H.R. 3601 / Public Law 98–484
An act to modify the boundary of the Pike National Forest in the State of Colorado, and for other purposes.

Approved October 17—Continued
H.R. 4932 / Public Law 98–485
An act to withdraw certain public lands in Lincoln County, Nevada, and for other purposes.

H.R. 4994 / Public Law 98–486
An act to exempt from taxation by the District of Columbia certain property of the Jewish War Veterans, U.S.A. National Memorial, Incorporated.

H.R. 5223 / Public Law 98–487
An act to amend the Federal Meat Inspection Act and the Poultry Products Inspection Act to exempt restaurant central kitchens under certain conditions from Federal inspection requirements.

H.R. 5513 / Public Law 98–488
An act to designate the Delta States Research Center in Stoneville, Mississippi, as the "Jamie Whitten Delta States Research Center".

H.R. 5631 / Public Law 98–489
An act to provide for the acquisition of a visitor contact and administrative site for the Big Thicket National Preserve in the State of Texas.

H.R. 5782 / Public Law 98–490
An act granting the consent of Congress to an amendment to the Delaware River Basin Compact.

H.R. 5818 / Public Law 98–491
Toy Safety Act of 1984.

H.R. 5997 / Public Law 98–492
An act to designate the United States Post Office and Courthouse in Pendleton, Oregon, as the "John F. Kilkenny United States Post Office and Courthouse".

H.R. 6623 / Public Law 98–493
An act to amend the Act providing for the incorporation of certain persons as Group Hospitalization, Inc.

Approved October 19

S. 416 / Public Law 98–494
An act to amend the Wild and Scenic Rivers Act by designating a segment of the Illinois River in Oregon and the Owyhee River in Oregon as components of the National Wild and Scenic Rivers System, and for other purposes.

S. 566 / Public Law 98–495
An act to direct the Secretary of Agriculture to release on behalf of the United States a reversionary interest in certain tracts of land conveyed to the South Carolina State Commission of Forestry, and to direct the Secretary of the Interior

Approved October 19—Continued
to convey certain mineral interests of the United States in such land to such Commission, and for other purposes.

S. 648 / Public Law 98–496
An act to facilitate the exchange of certain lands in South Carolina.

S. 905 / Public Law 98–497
National Archives and Records Administration Act of 1984.

S. 1102 / Public Law 98–498
An act to provide authorization of appropriations for title III of the Marine Protection, Research, and Sanctuaries Act of 1972, and for other purposes.

S. 1146 / Public Law 98–499
Aviation Drug-Trafficking Control Act.

S. 1151 / Public Law 98–500
Old Age Assistance Claims Settlement Act.

S. 1330 / Public Law 98–501
An act to establish a National Council on Public Works Improvement to prepare three annual reports on the state of the Nation's infrastructure, to amend the provisions of title 31, United States Code, relating to the President's budget to require it to separately identify and summarize the capital investment expenditures of the United States, and for other purposes.

S. 1510 / Public Law 98–502
Single Audit Act of 1984.

S. 1688 / Public Law 98–503
An act to amend the Act of October 18, 1972, to authorize additional authorization of appropriations for Sitka National Historical Park, Alaska.

S. 1790 / Public Law 98–504
An act to authorize the Secretary of the Interior to enter into contracts or cooperative agreements with the Art Barn Association to assist in the preservation and interpretation of the Art Barn in Rock Creek Park in the District of Columbia, and for other purposes.

S. 1868 / Public Law 98–505
An act to add $2,000,000 to the budget ceiling for new acquisitions at Sleeping Bear Dunes National Lakeshore.

S. 1889 / Public Law 98–506
An act to amend the act authorizing the establishment of the Congaree Swamp National Monument to provide that at such time as the principal visitor center is established, such center shall

Approved October 19—Continued
be designated as the "Harry R. E. Hampton Visitor Center", and for other purposes.

S. 2048 / Public Law 98–507
National Organ Transplant Act.

S. 2125 / Public Law 98–508
Arkansas Wilderness Act of 1984.

S. 2303 / Public Law 98–509
Alcohol Abuse, Drug Abuse, and Mental Health Amendments of 1984.

S. 2483 / Public Law 98–510
An act to rename Dulles International Airport in Virginia as the "Washington Dulles International Airport".

S. 2496 / Public Law 98–511
Education Amendments of 1984.

S. 2616 / Public Law 98–512
An act to revise and extend the programs of assistance under titles X and XX of the Public Health Service Act.

S. 2663 / Public Law 98–513
An act pertaining to the inheritance of trust or restricted land on the Lake Traverse Indian Reservation, North Dakota and South Dakota, and for other purposes.

S. 2773 / Public Law 98–514
Georgia Wilderness Act of 1984.

S. 2808 / Public Law 98–515
Mississippi National Forest Wilderness Act of 1984.

S.J. Res. 80 / Public Law 98–516
A joint resolution to grant posthumously full rights of citizenship to William Penn and to Hannah Callowhill Penn.

S.J. Res. 259 / Public Law 98–517
A joint resolution to designate the week of November 12, 1984, through November 18, 1984, as "National Reye's Syndrome Week".

S.J. Res. 299 / Public Law 98–518
A joint resolution to designate November 1984, as National Diabetes Month.

S.J. Res. 309 / Public Law 98–519
A joint resolution authorizing and requesting the President to designate January 1985, as "National Cerebral Palsy Month.

H.R. 2372 / Public Law 98–520
An act to recognize the organization known as the Navy Wives Clubs of America.

H.R. 3401 / Public Law 98–521
An act to designate the United States Post Office and Courthouse located at 245 East Capital Street in Jackson, Mississippi, as the "James O. Eastland United States Courthouse".

H.R. 3402 / Public Law 98–522
An act to designate that hereafter the Federal building at 100 West Capital Street in Jackson, Mississippi, will be known as the Doctor A.H. McCoy Federal Building.

H.R. 4025 / Public Law 98–523
An act to authorize the Administrator of General Services to transfer to the Smithsonian Institution without reimbursement the General Post Office Building and the site thereof located in the District of Columbia, and for other purposes.

H.R. 4164 / Public Law 98–524
Carl D. Perkins Vocational Education Act.

H.R. 5167 / Public Law 98–525
Department of Defense Authorization Act, 1985.

H.R. 5183 / Public Law 98–526
An act to direct the Secretary of Agriculture to convey certain National Forest System lands to Craig County, Virginia.

H.R. 5603 / Public Law 98–527
Developmental Disabilities Act of 1984.

H.R. 5618 / Public Law 98–528
Veterans' Health Care Act of 1984.

H.R. 5787 / Public Law 98–529
An act to remove an impediment to oil and gas leasing of certain Federal lands in Corpus Christi, Texas, and Port Hueneme, California, and for other purposes.

H.R. 6206 / Public Law 98–530
An act relating to the water rights of the Ak-Chin Indian Community.

H.R. 6216 / Public Law 98–531
An act to amend the Bankruptcy Amendments and Federal Judgeship Act of 1984 to make technical corrections with respect to the retirement of certain bankruptcy judges, and for other purposes.

H.R. 6225 / Public Law 98–532
An act to prevent disruption of the structure and functioning of the Government by ratifying all reorganization plans as a matter of law.

H.R. 6311 / Public Law 98–533
1984 Act to Combat International Terrorism.

H.J. Res. 482 / Public Law 98–534
A joint resolution authorizing the Law Enforcement Officers Memorial Fund to establish a memorial in the District of Columbia or its environs.

H.J. Res. 551 / Public Law 98–535
A joint resolution providing for reappointment of Anne Legendre Armstrong as a citizen regent of the Smithsonian Institution.

H.J. Res. 552 / Public Law 98–536
A joint resolution providing for reappointment of A. Leon Higginbotham, Junior, as a citizen regent of the Smithsonian Institution.

H.J Res. 580 / Public Law 98–537
A joint resolution authorizing the Kahlil Gibran Centennial Foundation to establish a memorial in the District of Columbia or its environs.

H.J. Res. 638 / Public Law 98–538
A joint resolution designating October 1984 as "National Head Injury Awareness Month".

H.J. Res. 655 / Public Law 98–539
A joint resolution designating February 16, 1985, as "Lithuanian Independence Day".

S. 1711 / Private Law 98–34
An act providing for a fifteen-year extension of patent numbered 3,376,198.

H.R. 437 / Private Law 98–35
An act for the relief of Patrick Starkie.

H.R. 932 / Private Law 98–36
An act for the relief of Harry Chen Tak Wong.

H.R. 1072 / Private Law 98–37
An act for the relief of Margot Hogan.

H.R. 1152 / Private Law 98–38
An act for the relief of Tomoko Jessica Kyan.

H.R. 1426 / Private Law 98–39
An act for the relief of Phillip Harper.

H.R. 1713 / Private Law 98–40
An act for the relief of Elizaveta Fankukhina.

H.R. 1865 / Private Law 98–41
An act for the relief of Nery De Maio.

H.R. 1932 / Private Law 98–42
An act for the relief of Mireille Laffite.

H.R. 2418 / Private Law 98–43
An act for the relief of Anis Ur Rahmaan.

H.R. 3382 / Private Law 98–44
An act for the relief of Dennis L. Dalton.

Approved October 19—Continued
H.R. 5691 / Private Law 98–45
An act for the relief of Sutu Bungani William Beck.

H.R. 6228 / Private Law 98–46
An act providing for an extension until April 21, 1992, of five patents relating to oral hypoglycemic drugs of the sulfonylurea class.

Approved October 24

S. 864 / Public Law 98–540
An act to amend the Volunteers in the Parks Act of 1969, and for other purposes.

H.R. 1438 / Public Law 98–541
An act to provide for the restoration of the fish and wildlife in the Trinity River Basin, California, and for other purposes.

H.R. 1961 / Public Law 98–542
Veterans' Dioxin and Radiation Exposure Compensation Standards Act.

H.R. 5688 / Public Law 98–543
Veterans' Benefits Improvement Act of 1984.

H.R. 6027 / Public Law 98–544
Local Government Antitrust Act of 1984.

Approved October 25

S. 2583 / Public Law 98–545
An act to authorize United States participation in the Office International de la Vigne et du Vin (the International Office of the Vine and Wine).

S. 2947 / Public Law 98–546
An act to designate the lock and dam on the Warrior River in Hale County, Alabama, as the "Armistead I. Selden Lock and Dam".

H.R. 6257 / Public Law 98–547
Motor Vehicle Theft Law Enforcement Act of 1984.

Approved October 26

H.R. 5271 / Public Law 98–548
An act to extend the Wetlands Loan Act.

Approved October 30

S. 66 / Public Law 98–549
Cable Communications Policy Act of 1984.

S. 543 / Public Law 98–550
The Wyoming Wilderness Act of 1984.

S. 771 / Public Law 98–551
Health Promotion and Disease Prevention Amendments of 1984.

Approved October 30—Continued
S. 1160 / Public Law 98–552
An act to authorize Douglas County of the State of Nevada to transfer certain land to a private owner.

S. 1291 / Public Law 98–553
An act to authorize appropriations to the Nuclear Regulatory Commission in accordance with section 261 of the Atomic Energy Act of 1954, and section 305 of the Energy Reorganization Act of 1974.

S. 2217 / Public Law 98–554
An act to provide for exemptions, based on safety concerns, from certain length and width limitations for commercial motor vehicles, and for other purposes.

S. 2301 / Public Law 98–555
Preventive Health Amendments of 1984.

S. 2499 / Public Law 98–556
Maritime Appropriation Authorization Act for Fiscal Year 1985.

S. 2526 / Public Law 98–557
Coast Guard Authorization Act of 1984.

S. 2565 / Public Law 98–558
Human Services Reauthorization Act.

S. 2706 / Public Law 98–559
An act to amend the Hazardous Materials Transportation Act to authorize appropriations for fiscal years 1985 and 1986, and for other purposes.

S. 3021 / Public Law 98–560
An act to name the Federal Building in Elkins, West Virginia, the "Jennings Randolph Federal Center".

S. 3034 / Public Law 98–561
An act to grant a Federal charter to the National Society, Daughters of the American Colonists.

S.J. Res. 236 / Public Law 98–562
A joint resolution relating to cooperative East-West ventures in space.

H.R. 89 / Public Law 98–563
An act to permit the transportation of passengers between Puerto Rico and other United States ports on foreign-flag vessels when United States flag service for such transportation is not available.

H.R. 597 / Public Law 98–564
An act to amend sections 2733, 2734, and 2736 of title 10, United States Code, and section 715 of title 32, United States Code, to increase the maxi-

mum amount of a claim against the United States that may be paid administratively under those sections and to allow increased delegation of authority to settle and pay certain of those claims, and for other purposes.

H.R. 1095 / Public Law 98–565
An act to grant a Federal charter to the 369th Veterans' Association.

H.R. 1870 / Public Law 98–566
Vietnam Veterans National Medal Act.

H.R. 1880 / Public Law 98–567
Cigarette Safety Act of 1984.

H.R. 2645 / Public Law 98–568
An act to amend the Act of August 15, 1978, regarding the Chattahoochee River National Recreation Area in the State of Georgia.

H.R. 2790 / Public Law 98–569
An act to amend the Colorado River Basin Salinity Control Act to authorize certain additional measures to assure accomplishment of the objectives of title II of such Act, and for other purposes.

H.R. 2823 / Public Law 98–570
An act to amend title I of the Reclamation Project Authorization Act of 1972 in order to provide for the establishment of the Russell Lakes Waterfowl Management Area as a replacement for the authorized Mishak National Wildlife Refuge, and for other purposes.

H.R. 3150 / Public Law 98–571
An act to direct the Secretary of Agriculture to convey, for certain specified consideration, to the Sabine River Authority approximately thirty-one thousand acres of land within the Sabine National Forest to be used for the purposes of the Toledo Bend project, Louisiana and Texas, and for other purposes.

H.R. 3331 / Public Law 98–572
An act to authorize the exchange of certain lands between the Bureau of Land Management and the city of Los Angeles for purposes of the Santa Monica Mountains National Recreation Area.

H.R. 3398 / Public Law 98–573
Trade and Tariff Act of 1984.

H.R. 3788 / Public Law 98–574
Texas Wilderness Act of 1984.

H.R. 3942 / Public Law 98–575
Commercial Space Launch Act.

H.R. 3971 / Public Law 98–576
An act to provide that any Osage headright or restricted real estate or funds which is part of the estate of a deceased Osage Indian who did not possess a certificate of competency at the time of death shall be exempt from any estate or inheritance tax imposed by the State of Oklahoma.

H.R. 4209 / Public Law 98–577
Small Business and Federal Procurement Competition Enhancement Act of 1984.

H.R. 4263 / Public Law 98–578
Tennessee Wilderness Act of 1984.

H.R. 4354 / Public Law 98–579
An act to designate the Federal Building and United States Courthouse in Ocala, Florida, as the "Golden-Collum Memorial Federal Building and United States Courthouse".

H.R. 4473 / Public Law 98–580
An act to designate the Federal Archives and Records Center in San Bruno, California, as the "Leo J. Ryan Memorial Federal Archives and Records Center".

H.R. 4585 / Public Law 98–581
An act to authorize appropriations for the Office of Environmental Quality and the Council on Environmental Quality for fiscal years 1985 and 1986, and for other purposes.

H.R. 4700 / Public Law 98–582
An act to designate the Federal Building and United States Courthouse at 1961 Stout Street, Denver, Colorado, as the "Byron G. Rogers Federal Building and United States Courthouse".

H.R. 4717 / Public Law 98–583
An act to designate the Federal Building and United States Courthouse in Las Vegas, Nevada, as the "Foley Federal Building and United States Courthouse".

H.R. 4966 / Public Law 98–584
An act to recognize the organization known as the Women's Army Corps Veterans' Association.

H.R. 5076 / Public Law 98–585
Pennsylvania Wilderness Act of 1984.

H.R. 5121 / Public Law 98–586
Virginia Wilderness Act of 1984.

H.R. 5189 / Public Law 98–587
An act to amend section 3056 of title 18, United States Code, to update the authorities of the United States Secret Service, and for other purposes.

H.R. 5252 / Public Law 98–588
An act to redesignate the Veterans' Administration Medical Center located in Poplar Bluff, Missouri, as the "John J. Pershing Veterans' Administration Medical Center".

H.R. 5323 / Public Law 98–589
An act to designate the United States Courthouse Building in Hato Rey, Puerto Rico, as the "Clemente Ruiz Nazario United States Courthouse".

H.R. 5358 / Public Law 98–590
Honey Research, Promotion, and Consumer Information Act.

H.R. 5402 / Public Law 98–591
An act to designate the United States Post Office and Courthouse in Utica, New York, as the "Alexander Pirnie Federal Building".

H.R. 5716 / Public Law 98–592
An act providing for the conveyance of public lands, Seneca County, Ohio.

H.R. 5747 / Public Law 98–593
An act to designate the Federal building in Oak Ridge, Tennessee, as the "Joe L. Evins Federal Building".

H.R. 5832 / Public Law 98–594
An act to authorize two additional Assistant Secretaries for the Department of the Treasury.

H.R. 5833 / Public Law 98–595
An act to improve certain maritime programs of the Department of Transportation and the Department of Commerce.

H.R. 5846 / Public Law 98–596
Criminal Fine Enforcement Act of 1984.

H.R. 6000 / Public Law 98–597
An act to designate the Table Rock Lake Visitors Center building in the vicinity of Branson, Missouri, as the "Dewey J. Short Table Rock Lake Visitors Center".

H.R. 6007 / Public Law 98–598
District of Columbia Retired Judge Service Act.

H.R. 6100 / Public Law 98–599
An act to clarify the intent of Congress with respect to the families eligible for a commemorative medal authorized for the families of Americans missing or otherwise unaccounted for in Southeast Asia.

H.R. 6101 / Public Law 98–600
An act to amend the Panama Canal Act of 1979 to authorize quarters allowances for certain em-

ployees of the Department of Defense serving in the area formerly known as the Canal Zone.

H.R. 6112 / Public Law 98–601
An act to amend the Tax Equity and Fiscal Responsibility Act of 1982 with respect to the effect of the 1985 increase in the Federal unemployment tax rate on certain small business provisions contained in State unemployment compensation laws.

H.R. 6221 / Public Law 98–602
An act to provide for the use and distribution of certain funds awarded the Wyandotte Tribe of Oklahoma and to restore certain mineral rights to the Three Affiliated Tribes of the Fort Berthold Reservation.

H.R. 6296 / Public Law 98–603
The San Juan Basin Wilderness Protection Act of 1984.

H.R. 6299 / Public Law 98–604
An act to ensure the payment in 1985 of cost-of-living increases under the OASDI program in title II of the Social Security Act, and to provide for a study of certain changes which might be made in the provisions authorizing cost-of-living adjustments under that program.

H.R. 6303 / Public Law 98–605
Osage Tribe of Indians Technical Corrections Act of 1984.

H.R. 6430 / Public Law 98–606
An act to amend the River and Harbor Act of 1946.

H.R. 6441 / Public Law 98–607
An act to eliminate restrictions with respect to the imposition and collection of tolls on the Richmond-Petersburg Turnpike upon repayment by the Commonwealth of Virginia of certain Federal-aid highway funds used on such turnpike.

H.J. Res. 158 / Public Law 98–608
A joint resolution to make technical corrections in the Act of January 12, 1983 (Public Law 97–459).

H.J. Res. 332 / Public Law 98–609
A joint resolution to designate the week beginning May 20, 1985, as "National Medical Transcriptionist Week".

H.J. Res. 594 / Public Law 98–610
A joint resolution designating the week beginning February 17, 1985, as a time to recognize volunteers who give their time to become Big

Approved October 30—Continued
Brothers and Big Sisters to youths in need of adult companionship.

S. 149 / Private Law 98–47
An act for the relief of Adel Shervin.

S. 2449 / Private Law 98–48
An act for the relief of the Sisters of Mercy of the Union, Province of Saint Louis, Missouri.

H.R. 440 / Private Law 98–49
An act for the relief of Fredrick Francisco Akers.

H.R. 2087 / Private Law 98–50
An act for the relief of Hans Robert Beisch.

H.R. 2671 / Private Law 98–51
An act for the relief of Edgar Gildardo Herrera.

H.R. 4401 / Private Law 98–52
An act for the relief of Shu-Ah-tsai Wei, her husband, Yen Wei, and their sons, Teh-fu Wei and Teh-huei Wei.

H.R. 5728 / Private Law 98–53
An act to permit aliens lawfully admitted for permanent residence who are employed by the American University of Beirut to return to the United States as special immigrants after completion of such employment.

H.R. 6438 / Private Law 98–54
An act for the relief of Joseph Karel Hasek.

Approved October 31

H.R. 2568 / Public Law 98–611
An act to amend the Internal Revenue Code of 1954 to extend for 2 years the exclusion from gross income with respect to educational assistance programs, and for other purposes.

H.R. 5361 / Public Law 98–612
An act to amend the Internal Revenue Code of 1954 to extend for one year the exclusion from gross income with respect to group legal services plans, and for other purposes.

H.R. 5492 / Public Law 98–613
Atlantic Striped Bass Conservation Act.

Approved November 8

H.R. 1314 / Public Law 98–614
Reorganization Act Amendments of 1984.

H.R. 2300 / Public Law 98–615
Civil Service Retirement Spouse Equity Act of 1984.

H.R. 2867 / Public Law 98–616
The Hazardous and Solid Waste Amendments of 1984.

H.R. 5386 / Public Law 98–617
An act to amend part A of title XVIII of the Social Security Act with respect to the payment rates for routine home care and other services included in hospice care.

H.R. 5399 / Public Law 98–618
Intelligence Authorization Act for fiscal year 1985.

H.R. 6028 / Public Law 98–619
Departments of Labor, Health and Human Services, and Education and Related Agencies Appropriation Act, 1985.

H.R. 6163 / Public Law 98–620
An Act to amend title 28, United States Code, with respect to the places where court shall be held in certain judicial districts, and for other purposes.

H.R. 6224 / Public Law 98–621
Saint Elizabeths Hospital and District of Columbia Mental Health Services Act.

H.R. 6286 / Public Law 98–622
Patent Law Amendments Act of 1984.

H.R. 6342 / Public Law 98–623
An act to approve governing international fishery agreements with Iceland and the EEC; to establish national standards for artificial reefs; to implement the Convention on the Conservation of Antarctic Marine Living Resources; and for the other purposes.

Subject Index

Name Index